THE CORRESPONDENCE OF
Washington Allston

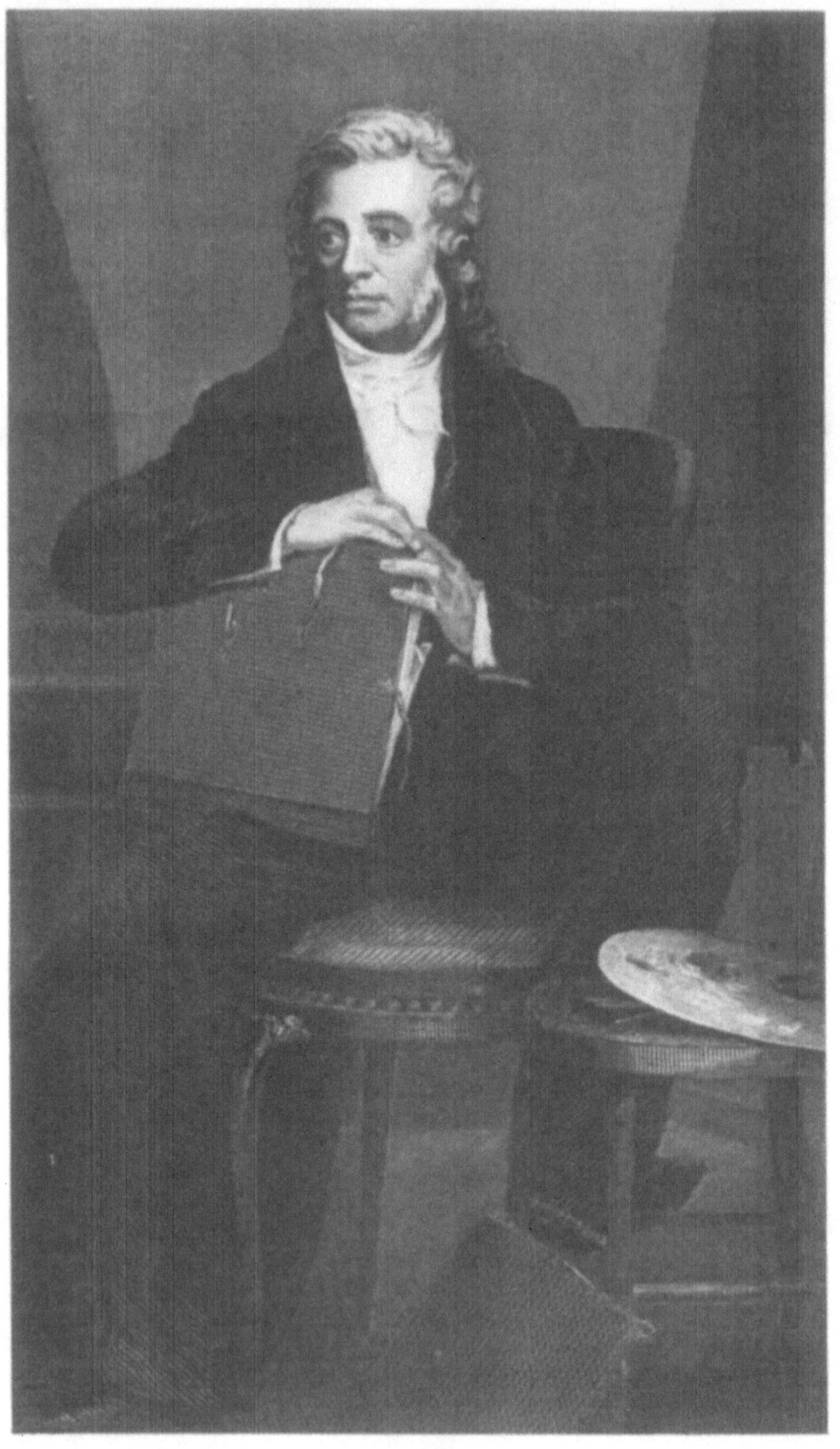

THE CORRESPONDENCE OF
Washington Allston

NATHALIA WRIGHT,
Editor

THE UNIVERSITY PRESS OF KENTUCKY

Publication of this book has been assisted by a grant from the University of Tennessee Better English Fund, established by John C. Hodges.

Frontispiece: *Washington Allston*. Engraving of the portrait by Alonzo Chappel, in *National Portrait Gallery of Eminent Americans*, ed. Evert A. Duyckinck (New York, 1862), vol. 1, facing page 458.

Scholarly publisher for the Commonwealth, serving Bellarmine College, Berea College, Centre College of Kentucky, Eastern Kentucky University, The Filson Club, Georgetown College, Kentucky Historical Society, Kentucky State University, Morehead State University, Murray State University, Northern Kentucky University, Transylvania University, University of Kentucky, University of Louisville, and Western Kentucky University.

Editorial and Sales Offices: Lexington, Kentucky 40508-4008

Library of Congress Cataloging-in-Publication Data

Allston, Washington, 1779-1843
[Correspondence]
The correspondence of Washington Allston / Nathalia Wright, editor.
p. cm.
Includes bibliographical references and index.
ISBN: 978-0-8131-5545-6
1. Allston, Washington, 1779-1843—Correspondence. 2. Artists—United States—Correspondence. I. Wright, Nathalia. II. Title.
NX512.A513A3 1992
759.13—dc20 91-13823
[B]

This book is printed on recycled acid-free paper meeting the requirements of the American National Standard for Permanence of Paper for Printed Library Materials.

To the Memory of
Ralph Henry Gabriel, American Historian

"And he dreamed, and behold a ladder set up on the earth, and the top of it reached to heaven: and behold the angels of God ascending and descending on it."

Genesis 28:12

"Gabriel blew a sour note here."

Yale undergraduate marginalia
in a copy of *The Course of American Democratic Thought*

CONTENTS

List of Illustrations viii
Acknowledgments ix
Texts and Editorial Policy xii
Abbreviations, Short Titles, and Sources xvi
Chronology xviii
Introduction 1
THE CORRESPONDENCE, WITH EDITORIAL LINKS
Letters 1-10 (Before 22 March 1795-23 October 1800) 7
Juvenilia 21
Letters 11-15 (25 August 1801-3 October 1803) 25
France, Switzerland, and Italy, 1804-1808 38
Letters 16-20 (29 December 1804-7 May 1809) 49
Boston, 1808-1811 58
Letters 21-26 (18 February 1812-2 January 1814) 60
The Dead Man Restored 66
Letters 27-31 (12 January-5 July 1814) 69
The Bristol Exhibition, 1814 74
Letters 32-48 (22 October 1814-9 May 1817) 76
Belshazzar's Feast 102
Letter 49 (21 May 1817) 108
Paris, 1817 110
Letters 50-145 (October or November 1817-21 June 1827) 111
The Boston Athenaeum Exhibitions 238
Letters 146-268 (12 August 1827-14 July 1839) 243
The Exhibition of 1839 421
Letters 269-353 (21 August 1839-4 July 1843) 431
Undated Letters (Letters 354-361) 520
Death and Funeral 523
Outlines and Sketches 527

Appendices

1. Biographical Notes 530
2. Artistic Masters 584
3. Writings 593
4. Reading 612
5. Technique in Painting 619
6. Religious Beliefs 625
7. Politics 629
8. Interest in Drama 631
9. Interest in Music 632
10. Influence and Reputation 634
11. Recipients and Correspondents 638
12. Catalogue of Allston Paintings and Drawings Referred to in the Correspondence 640

Selected Bibliography 647

Index 649

ILLUSTRATIONS

Engraving of the Portrait of Allston by Alonzo Chappel Frontispiece
First Page of First Extant Manuscript Letter xiii
First Page of Draft Letter to Gulian C. Verplanck 287
Two Pages of Letter to Samuel Webber 484
First Page of Last Extant Manuscript Letter 515
Paintings of Washington Allston [*follow page 44*]
Self-Portrait, 1805
Ann (Channing) Allston
Samuel Taylor Coleridge, 1814
The Dead Man Restored to Life by Touching the Bones of the Prophet Elisha
Jacob's Dream
Belshazzar's Feast
Uriel in the Sun
Rosalie
Italian Landscape, ca. 1828-1830
Heliodorus Driven from the Temple
Ship in a Squall

ACKNOWLEDGMENTS

I wish to thank those in charge of the following collections for allowing copies of letters by Washington Allston to be made and for granting permission within their jurisdiction to publish those letters: The Boston Athenaeum; the Trustees of the Boston Public Library; the City of Bristol (England) Record Office; the Chicago Historical Society; the Rare Book and Manuscript Library of Columbia University, New York; the Connecticut Historical Society, New Haven; Dartmouth College Library, Hanover, New Hampshire; the Georgia Historical Society, Savannah; Haverford College, Haverford, Pennsylvania; Houghton Library, Harvard University, Cambridge, Massachusetts; the Manuscript Division of the Library of Congress, Washington, D.C.; Longfellow National Historic Site, Cambridge, Massachusetts; the Massachusetts Historical Society, Boston; the William L. Clements Library of the University of Michigan, Ann Arbor; the New-York Historical Society; the Rare Books and Manuscripts Division of the New York Public Library; the Historical Society of Pennsylvania, Philadelphia; the Van Pelt Library of the University of Pennsylvania, Philadelphia; the Pierpont Morgan Library, New York; the collection of David Richardson of Washington, D.C.; the South Caroliniana Library of the University of South Carolina, Columbia; the Special Collections Department of the University of Virginia Library, Charlottesville; Wellesley College Library, Wellesley, Massachusetts; the Wordsworth Trust of Dove Cottage, Grasmere, England; and Manuscripts and Archives and The Beinecke Rare Book and Manuscript Library of Yale University, New Haven, Connecticut. For permission to quote letters from Horatio Greenough to Allston printed in *Letters of Horatio Greenough, American Sculptor* (1972) I thank the University of Wisconsin Press, Madison.

Quotations from *The Letters of Washington Irving*, vol. 1, 1802-1823, edited by Ralph M. Aderman, Herbert L. Kleinfield, and Jennifer S. Banks, copyright © 1982 by G.K. Hall & Co., and *The Journals and Notebooks of Washington Irving*, vol. 1, 1803-1806, edited by Nathalia Wright, are reprinted by permission of Twayne Publishers, an imprint of Macmillan Publishing Co. Quotations from *Collected Letters of Samuel Taylor Coleridge*, 1956, 1959, edited by Earl Leslie Griggs; *The Letters of William and Dorothy Wordsworth*, 2nd edition, 1970, edited by Ernest de Selincourt; and *The Letters of Charles Dickens*, 1974, edited by House, Storey, and Tillotson, are reprinted by permission of Oxford University Press. *The Letters of Elizabeth Palmer Peabody*, edited by Bruce A. Ronda, copyright © 1984 by Bruce A. Rhonda, published by Wesleyan University Press, are quoted with the permission of the University Press of New England. *The*

Letters of Ralph Waldo Emerson, edited by Ralph Rusk, copyright © 1939 by Columbia University Press, New York, are quoted by permission of the publisher.

I also wish to thank the following people in several of these repositories for their kind and patient assistance in obtaining other information there, especially Peter Drummey of the Massachusetts Historical Society; Jonathan Harding, formerly of the Boston Athenaeum; Robin M. Carlaw, Barbara Meloni, and Sarah A. Polirer of the Harvard Archives; and Jennie Rathbun of the Houghton Library. I am further grateful to a number of librarians in special collections for similar assistance, particularly Jean Ashton of the New-York Historical Society; Karie Diethorn of the Longfellow Historic Site; Martha Forrester of the Cambridge Public Library, Cambridge, Massachusetts; Eugenia A. Fountain of the Essex Institute, Salem, Massachusetts; Jack Robertson of the University of Virginia Library; Holly K. Shaw of the Charleston, New Hampshire, Public Library; Nadia S. Smith of the University of Vermont Library, Burlington; and Lois H. Ward of the Ohio Wesleyan University Library, Delaware, Ohio.

For identification of several persons or paintings I am indebted to the following: Guiseppe Bisaccia, Charles S. Longley, Alice L. Roberts, and Henry F. Scannel, Boston Public Library; Courtney Braun, Department of European Paintings, the Metropolitan Museum of Art, New York; Kathleen Catalano, Longfellow Historic Site; Greg Eghigian, the Joseph Regenstein Library, University of Chicago; Daniel Feller, the Papers of Andrew Jackson, Hermitage, Tennessee; Francis W. Greenacre of the Bristol (England) Museum and Art Gallery; Ann S. Hainhart, the New England Historic and Genealogical Society, Boston, Massachusetts; Eilene E. Moeri, Hobart and William Smith Colleges Archives, Geneva, New York; Phoebe Peebles, Fogg Art Museum, Cambridge, Massachusetts; Katherine Powers and Elizabeth M. Furdon, the Episcopal Diocese of Massachusetts Library and Archives, Boston, Massachusetts; Ruth Quattlebaum, Phillips Academy, Andover, Massachusetts; Karen L. Ranney, New Haven and New York; Susan Ravdin, Bowdoin College Library, Brunswick, Maine; Joyce Ann Tracy, American Antiquarian Society, Boston, Massachusetts; and Richard B. Trask, Danvers Archival Center, Danvers, Massachusetts.

For guidance to certain letters otherwise undiscovered I am indebted to Beth Darlington of Vassar College, Poughkeepsie, New York, and Mary Jo Viola of Baruch College, CUNY, New York. For South Carolina material I thank Mrs. Harold A. Moore of Charleston; for material in Boston, Frank P. Bruno of Boston; and for material in England, Sue Beach of Bristol, R.A. Bowden of the Marylebone Library of the City of Westminster in London, the assistants to the Head of the Reading Room in the British Library, London, and William C. Pickering of Cambridge. For enabling me to see paintings by Allston in England I am grateful to Ronald W. McLaren of Oxshott, England, and for photography to Donald W. Spears of Maryville, Tennessee.

I also wish to thank Flossie E. Wise and Margaret S. Humphreys of the

Interlibrary Loan Department of the John C. Hodges Library of the University of Tennessee, Knoxville, for their long-standing helpfulness in obtaining material from other repositories, and Biddanda Ponnappa in the Non-Print Department of the library for his knowledgeable and patient assistance there. I thank too the staff of the Maryville College Library, Maryville, Tennessee, for guidance in that collection.

For reading the manuscript I am most grateful to the readers for the University Press of Kentucky, who corrected several errors and made many valuable suggestions about its organization. For revisions in the notes and appendices I am grateful to Joanne S. Ainsworth. For typing the manuscript carefully, patiently, and with corrections of errors that might otherwise have gone unnoticed, I wish to thank Bertha Kinsinger. I have benefited extensively from the study of Allston's aesthetic philosophy by Professor Regina Soria of Rome, the preeminent authority on the subject and on the general subject of American artists in Italy, generously shared over many years.

No one interested in Allston can proceed very far without depending on the comprehensive and illuminating study of him by William H. Gerdts and Theodore E. Stebbins, Jr., *"A Man of Genius": The Art of Washington Allston.* Professor Gerdts has also been most kindly helpful in answering questions I have posed to him in correspondence and in reading the manuscript. Certainly this book would not have been possible without him. Nor would it have been possible without the pioneering study by Edgar P. Richardson. *Washington Allston: A Study of the Romantic Artist in America;* he was most generous in the few letters I had from him in the last years of his life.

For having copies of the manuscript made and especially for financially aiding in its publication I am grateful to the English Department of the University of Tennessee, administrator of the John C. Hodges Better English Fund.

TEXTS AND EDITORIAL POLICY

The present edition of Washington Allston's correspondence consists of all the letters by him and all those to him which have been located. The only prior collection of his correspondence is represented by Jared Flagg's *Life and Letters of Washington Allston,* in which 76 letters by him and 26 to him are printed, though hardly any in their entirety. Of the 280 letters written by him, original manuscripts have been found for 214. Of the remainder, 42 are in printed versions, 20 are manuscript copies by others, and 4 are typed copies. Of the 80 written to him, original manuscripts have been found for 50. Of the remainder, 26 are in printed versions, 1 is a manuscript copy, 1 is a typed copy, and 2 are summarized.

Allston wrote plainly and with care, without flourishes, and fairly small, though he did not always form letters definitely. He inclined lines slightly to the right, generally preserved margins and paragraphing, and punctuated according to standard practice, though it is sometimes difficult to distinguish his colons from his semicolons, both of which he used rarely, and to be sure of his capitals, though he customarily, it is significant to note, capitalized Art and Artist. He used the dash chiefly to mark a shift of subject within a paragraph rather than indenting on a new line, thereby saving space. His surviving drafts indicate that he revised extensively, certainly in letters of importance, such as those regarding commissions, but also in ordinary ones, such as those to Thomas Brown, Jr., and even to his close friend Samuel F.B. Morse, most of the revisions being of sentence structure and word order. He frequently substituted another word for the one originally written, however, reflecting a desire for both precision and connotation. He often added to his paragraphs by interrupting them with passages written in the margins of the page and by writing postscripts at the end, sometimes on all the pages.

The letters are here reproduced with a minimum of editorial alteration. Superscript letters have been brought down to the line, but the omissions of periods after the abbreviations of titles such as Mr., Mrs., and Esqur. and of months of the year have been observed. Words inadvertently repeated and false starts have not been retained. Canceled words and phrases are enclosed in angle brackets. Editorial additions and doubtful readings are enclosed in square brackets. Annotations have been reproduced when they contain pertinent information, such as the date a letter was received or answered, but marks made by collectors, repositories, editors, and postal officials identifying the writer, addressee, date, and general content have been omitted, together with postmarks. In copies the punctuation is exactly as in the originals and the ampersand (&) is used in place of "and," a

Allston's earliest extant manuscript letter (No. 10), sent to John Knapp from Newport, Rhode Island, dated October 23rd 1800. Manuscript in Massachusetts Historical Society, Boston.

practice which Allston occasionally followed. Misspellings, which are few, have been silently corrected except in proper names, but old spellings, such as "shew" for "show" have been preserved. These practices have also been observed in reproducing the letters to Allston, except that cancellations have not been noted.

The letters have been numbered consecutively and arranged chronologically. If a letter undated by Allston has been assigned a date, an explanation is given in a note. The seven undated letters for which no date seems possible to assign are placed at the end of the sequence in alphabetical order according to the names of the addressees. Biographical sketches of the correspondents and of others mentioned in the correspondence but identified only by name in the notes or not otherwise identified there are given in Appendix 1.

Identification of each painting by name and date is given after the first reference to it in the text or in a note. The catalog number and the present location or eventual disposition of each, if known, are given in the Index. General facts about the composition and reception of each are given in a note after the first reference to it. Of the drawings only what seem to be the most important are noted; the catalog number for each is given in the Index.

The chief repository of Allston mauscripts is the Massachusetts Historical Society. It contains in various collections 115 letters by Allston, 30 letters to him, 3 of his sketchbooks, his "Color Book," fragments of unpublished writings by him, copies by him of some of his published poems and those of others, the "Notes" of Richard Henry Dana made for a biography of him, the reminiscenses of Leonard Jarvis prepared for Dana's use, and many letters containing references to him. Unless otherwise noted, all manuscript letters by and to him and all copies by Dana, as well as other manuscript items cited without a location being given, are here. Twenty-seven other repositories, including two in England, have letters by him.

The Longfellow National Historic Site contains the next largest collection of Allston material. It consists chiefly of notes assembled by Henry Wadsworth Longfellow Dana, Jr., Richard Henry Dana's grandson, for the purpose of writing a biography of Allston, including copies or typescripts of a few letters by and to Allston, several drawings and caricatures by him, his first portrait of Edmund T. Dana, and a number of books which he owned. All references to this material are to the Allston Papers in this repository.

Allston's correspondents in these letters number ninety-five, over half of them, fifty-nine, being represented by only one letter. The greatest number to one person are those to John S. Cogdell, thirty-three, followed by eighteen to Charles R. Leslie, fifteen to Morse, fourteen to James McMurtrie, nine to William Dunlap, and nine to William Wordsworth. The identity of only one seems unrecoverable. Probably these were very nearly all, if not all, that were written to these persons. The largest group that would seem to have been lost were those to his mother, to which he often referred in his letters to John S. Cogdell. Very few letters to William

Ellery Channing and Richard Henry Dana are extant, and none to Edmund T. Dana (he saw these friends almost daily except during his years abroad) and only two to Samuel Taylor Coleridge, to whom he was closest in England but with whom he apparently had little communication afterward. Most of his commissions were for Bostonians, with whom he was in communication personally. Many of those to whom he did write complained repeatedly that he seldom did so, and some who wrote to him accused him of never writing to them at all. It is probable that this collection represents the bulk of the letters he wrote, excepting perfunctory notes.

Those persons who wrote to Allston number a few more than twenty-nine, those collaborating with Jacob Bigelow in one letter being unknown. Of this number, eight are not represented in extant letters written by him. The greatest number to him by one person are thirteen from James McMurtrie, followed by ten each from Horatio Greenough and Charles R. Leslie, then six from Gulian C. Verplanck, and five each from Sir George H. Beaumont and Morse. The most conspicious group of letters written to him that seem to have been lost were those from Cogdell, though it seems likely that there were a number of others from Morse if not other correspondents and that his mother and perhaps other members of his family wrote a substantial number that apparently have not been preserved. There were, without doubt, yet other letters that because of their ephemeral nature he did not preserve.

ABBREVIATIONS, SHORT TITLES, AND SOURCES

For full bibliographic information not given here, see the Selected Bibliography, pages 638-39.

B: Kenyon Castle Bolton III's catalog of Allston's drawings in "The Drawings of Washington Allston (A Catalog Raisonné)."

BA: Boston Athenaeum, Boston, Mass.

BI: British Institution, London.

Channing: William Ellery Channing.

Dana: *The Journal of Richard Henry Dana, Jr.*

Dunlap: William Dunlap. *History of the Rise and Progress of the Arts of Design in the United States.*

Flagg: Jared B. Flagg. *The Life and Letters of Washington Allston.*

Fogg: Fogg Art Museum, Harvard University, Cambridge, Mass.

G: William H. Gerdts's catalog of Allston's paintings, in Gerdts and Stebbins, *"A Man of Genius": The Art of Washington Allston (1779-1843).*

HA: Harvard University Archives, Cambridge, Mass.

Houghton: Houghton Library, Harvard University, Cambridge, Mass.

LA: Washington Allston. *Lectures on Art, and Poems,* ed. Richard Henry Dana, Jr. New York: Baker and Scribner, 1850.

LC: The Library of Congress, Washington, D.C.

Leslie: Charles Robert Leslie. *Autobiographical Recollections.*

MFA: Museum of Fine Arts, Boston.

MHS: Massachusetts Historical Society, Boston.

NAD: National Academy of Design, New York.

NEGHR: New England Genealogical and Historical Register.

O&S: Outlines & Sketches by Washington Allston. Boston: n.p., 1850.

PAFA: Pennsylvania Academy of Fine Arts, Philadelphia.

R: Edgar P. Richardson's catalog of Allston's paintings in Richardson, *Washington Allston: A Study of the Romantic Artist in America.*

RA: Royal Academy, London.

RHD: Richard Henry Dana, Sr. A page number afterward refers to his manuscript "Notes" on Allston in the Dana Papers, Massachusetts Historical Society.

SCHGM: South Carolina Historical and Genealogical Magazine.

SS: Washington Allston. *The Sylphs of the Seasons, with Other Poems.* London: W. Pople; Boston: Cummings and Hilliard; Cambridge: Hilliard and Metcalf, 1813.

Sweetser: Moses Sweetser. *Allston.*

WA: Washington Allston.

Unfootnoted facts about Allston's life and works come from Flagg, from Richardson, and from Gerdts and Stebbins. If there is a discrepancy between the last two accounts, that of

Gerdts is taken. The notable material from Flagg that is unfootnoted comes from the recollections of Richard Henry Dana, Jr., the conversations between Henry Greenough and Allston about Allston's technique, and letters from various persons to Richard Henry Dana, Jr., after Allston's death. Page numbers are supplied, however, for all quoted passages from them. Material from Sweetser is so acknowledged, but only quoted passages are footnoted. Facts about Allston's drawings come from Bolton. Citations to books owned by Allston come from Eliza Johns, "Washington Allston's Library."

Unfootnoted information about other persons comes from general encyclopedias and biographical dictionaries. Those most often employed without credit are the following:

Allgemeines Lexikon der Bildenden Kunstler, ed. Ulrich Thieme and Felix Becker. Leipzig: Wilhelm Engelmann, 1907-50.

Biographical Directory of the American Congress, 1774-1971. Washington, D.C.: GPO, 1971.

Dictionary of American Biography. 1928-37; rept., 1943.

Dictionary of National Biography. 1908-09.

Enciclopedia Italiani di Scienze, Lettere ed Arti. Rome: Instituto della Enciclopedia Italiani Foundata da Giovanni Treccani, 1929-37.

The Encyclopedia Britannica. 11th ed., 1911; 14th ed., 1929.

The New-York Historical Society's Dictionary of Artists in America, 1564-1860, ed. George C. Groce and David H. Wallace. New Haven: Yale Univ. Press, 1957.

Facts about persons holding U.S. government positions, which are unfootnoted, come from the National Archives, Washington, D.C.

All printed poems by Allston are in his *Lectures on Art, and Poems,* which incorporates these in *The Sylphs of the Seasons, with other Poems,* but if quotations are given, a distinction is made between these two publications.

CHRONOLOGY OF WASHINGTON ALLSTON'S LIFE

1779 *5 November,* Washington Allston born at Brook Green Domain, All Saints' Parish, District of Georgetown, South Carolina.

1781 Father, William Allston, Jr., died.

1784 Mother, Rachel (Moore) Allston, married Henry Collins Flagg.

1784 or 1785 Sent to Mrs. Melescent Calcott's school in Charleston, South Carolina.

1787 *Spring.* Sent to Newport, Rhode Island, to Robert Rogers' school.

1796-1800 Attended Harvard.

1800 *August-November.* In Newport.

November. Went to Charleston.

1 April. Henry Collins Flagg died.

May. Sailed to London.

1803 *October-November.* Left England for the Continent. Arrived in Paris 20 November.

1804 Late *November* or early *December.* Left Paris and traveled through Switzerland and Italy.

1805 Early *January.* Arrived in Rome.

1807 In Florence.

1807 or 1808 In Naples.

1808 *March.* Left Rome.

24 April. Sailed from Leghorn to America, arriving in Boston in the summer.

1809 *19 June.* Married Ann Channing.

1811 *Summer.* Sailed to England on 11 July, arriving in London in August.

1811-13 *The Dead Man Restored to Life by Touching the Bones of the Prophet Elisha.*

1812 Received commission from Sir George Beaumont for *The Angel Releasing St. Peter from Prison.*

1813 Early *Summer.* Went to Clifton because of illness.

July. The Sylphs of the Seasons, and Other Poems published.

20 November. Moved to Bristol.

1814 *25 July–24 September.* Exhibition of paintings in Bristol.

1815 *2 February.* Wife died. Moved to 8 Buckingham Place, Fitzroy Square.

1817 *Spring.* Began *Belshazzar's Feast.*

October and November. In Paris.

1818 *20 January.* Elected honorary member of the American Academy of the Fine Arts.

Last week of *August–12 October.* Sailed to Boston,

18 November. Elected an honorary associate of the Royal Academy.

1819 *9 February.* Elected honorary member of the New York Historical Society.

Summer. In Cambridge and Cambridgeport.

1820 First Tripartite Agreement for the purchase of *Belshazzar's Feast*. Altered its perspective.

1821 *April*. Confirmed in St. Paul's Church, Boston. "The Hypochondriac" and "Written in Spring" published in *The Idle Man*.

1825 Member of Board of Artists of Bunker Hill Monument Association.

1827 First annual exhibition of the Boston Athenaeum, in which twelve paintings shown. Elected honorary member of the National Academy of Design.

1828 *9 July*. Gilbert Stuart died.
December. John Prince's barn sold.

1830 *1 June*. Married Martha Remington Dana and moved to Cambridgeport.
Late *Summer*. Occupied new painting room.

1830-33 Negotiated regarding commission to paint one of the panels in the rotunda of the Capitol.

1834 *25 July*. Coleridge died.

1838 "The Doolittle Fragments" published in the *Boston Daily Advertiser*, 14 June, 25 July, 28 August.

1839 Elected honorary member of Georgia Historical Society.
February. Beginning of failing health.
25 April–10 July. Exhibition of paintings at Harding's Gallery.
25 December. Mother died.

1841 Elected president of the Boston Artists' Association.
Fall. *Monaldi* published in Boston.
10 November. Sister Mary (Allston) Alston died.

1842 *Fall*. Moved into new house.

1842-43 *Winter*. Read lectures on art to Henry Wadsworth Longfellow and Cornelius Conway Felton.

1843 *9 July*. Died.

1847 Exhibition of eleven paintings at Boston Athenaeum.

1850 Exhibition of thirty-one paintings at Boston Athenaeum.
Lectures on Art, and Poems and *Outlines & Sketches* published.

INTRODUCTION

Allston's Place in American Cultural History

In the history of American culture Washington Allston occupies a unique position as both artist and writer. Many other artists—Thomas Cole, Rembrandt Peale, Horatio Greenough, William Page, and William Wetmore Story, for example—wrote for publication, and several writers—among them Washington Irving, E.E. Cummings, John Dos Passos, William Carlos Williams, and Sherwood Anderson—drew or painted. Allston's achievement in both areas, however, is without parallel. Literature and art are, moreover, intimately interwoven in both his paintings and his writing.

Allston was the first American to rely solely on his art for his livelihood. As the first important painter to emerge after the Revolution he went beyond portraiture, to which most of his predecessors were limited, into landscape and dramatic narrative. He is, in fact, the only American artist to have realized the full scope of the visual arts, exploring not only genre and humor in painting but sculpture and modeling and architectural forms. He is also the only American to have formulated a comprehensive philosophy of art, which was, indeed, the only one written in English during the nineteenth century. He was a child of late-eighteenth and early-nineteenth-century romanticism, with its subjectivity and paradoxical concept of nature, and he attached himself strongly to the artistic traditions of the Renaissance; but he was essentially independent of both European and American currents in art and thought. Both his portraits and his landscapes, untypical of those of the day, go beyond representation, and his aesthetic theory was far in advance of his time. He was, significantly in these respects, the first American artist or writer to win recognition on the international scene.

Allston was, however, in one sense not a great artist. He was not prolific and he left many unfinished paintings. His most original works are evocations of a happy or serene mood—in landscapes early in his career and in feminine images later—accompanying a state of reverie or dreams. It is a serenity arising from transcendence rather than from a resolution of conflict, the hallmark of the greatest art. The subjects of his historical paintings are drawn from dramatic episodes in literature, not from American history, which at the time consisted chiefly of military action, and his treatment of conflict, such as it is, in the depiction of scenes like the dead man restored to life, Jeremiah prophesying, Saul and the Witch of Endor, Miriam singing, the angel pouring out the vial of wrath, and Heliodorus has a forced histrionic air. His failure to finish *Belshazzar's Feast,* is fundamentally the result of a profound antagonism between inner impulses and outward or public pressures;

and whatever else motivated his final return to America in 1818, it was a deep-seated necessity that impelled him to retire into a private life. His poems, most of them inconsiderable in themselves, are further testimony of his disposition to dream or reverie. His philosophy of art is also transcendent rather than cognizant of a struggle between opposing forces. His inability to face a threat to unity or harmony is sadly evident in his letters regarding the disposition of the slaves he inherited at his mother's death and was probably at a deeply subconscious level as much responsible as were his artistic needs and his sedentary and passive nature for his failure to return to South Carolina after his youth. It is significant that the religious doctrine to which he was increasingly committed was sacramental rather than naturalistic or rationalistic. In his personal life this inclination to transcendence was manifest in the characteristics of solitary independence and even a certain unworldliness, which, for all his sociality and mild Epicureanism, his contemporaries generally noted in him and which they tended to describe in religious terms. Both his work and his life could in one sense be called escapist.

Allston's paintings have nevertheless the distinguishing feature of all great works of art. In terms of the history of the arts in America they anticipate the brooding, often dreamlike quality of much of the painting and the prominent element in both painting and literature that are distinctively American. In a broader context, all his paintings are explorations of an interior realm of the mind and spirit of man and not merely depictions of external scenes and historical events. In this venture he was most successful in certain portraits and ideal heads, but it may be seen also in his landscapes and even his historical pieces. His term for this interior realm was the Ideal, which he found represented chiefly by the Italian painters of the Renaissance. He often contrasted them with the Dutch realists, whom he regarded as lesser artists, though he found in their best paintings the mind of the artist at work. The preeminence he gave to color in his paintings, less circumscriptive as it is than line or form, and his ultimate dematerializing of it into light make up the chief technical evidence of his commitment to the Ideal. That he admired the Italian school chiefly for its Ideality and its coloring attests doubly to the inward nature of both his art and his life. His lectures on art, unfinished though they were in conclusion, predicated the primacy of ideas with respect to perceptions of the senses, in both artist and spectator, both man and nature. His most successful expressions of his vision, both in painting and in writing, were significantly, moreover, achieved in America.

In a final sense, indeed, Allston must be called a great artist, virtually without comparison in the history of American culture. His best work projects an image of unalloyed human happiness. In this sense it achieves what other painters did not: Thomas Eakins with his melancholy, Winslow Homer with his stoicism, John Singer Sargent with his brilliance. Such a vision is hardly to be found not only in American painting but in American literature as well. Unresolved conflict dominates much of the fiction and the poetry, and the serenity of the transcendentalists is essentially intellectual. Allston produced, in fact, a unique version of the American dream, in other than the political and social terms in which it has almost altogether been described. It may be called a fit illustration for the declaration that among the inalienable rights of all men is "the pursuit of Happiness."

Allston was not a great letter writer. He wrote few letters, most of them short and purposeful, habitually apologized for what he wrote and for his aversion to and procrastination in writing to all, and expressed his deepest concerns to only a few correspondents. Those of his letters that have survived nevertheless constitute a remarkably continuous index of his activities from his earliest years to his last weeks of life, the chief lacunae being for his Italian sojourn and his years in America from 1808 to 1811. They document the composition of almost every one of his major works and many minor ones as well. They are also a record, if largely by implication, of the major influences on his art and thought. A few are important for the germs they contain of his philosophy of art as finally developed. Though their diction is generally formal, the appearance of proverbs, aphorisms, colloquialisms, anecdotes, quotations, and literary allusions often gives them an oral tone which reveals him in his role as a memorably engaging conversationalist. They reveal, finally, his most distinctive personal characteristics, from his wit and playfulness with intimates through his generosity to his lofty moral ideals. The letters written to him are, on the whole, evidence that both his achievement and his charm were widely recognized. The greatest impression he made and the greatest influence he exerted on his contemporaries were, in fact, personal, not professional, and though he enjoyed an unusual amount of appreciation and patronage during his lifetime he founded no school and had slight influence on the work of the painters who followed him, who generally espoused the realistic tradition. He evoked a deep and lasting image, however, in the consciousness of those who knew him and even of those who never saw him or his work as one totally devoted to the pursuit of art, refusing submission to all other insistent and potentially overpowering demands, by which so many creative Americans have been frustrated or defeated. Altogether, his letters are an invaluable part of the total picture of his life, thought, and creative achievement, for which he occupies a secure position in the cultural history not only of America but of the Western world.

THE CORRESPONDENCE
With Editorial Links

1. To William Ellery Channing Newport[1]
[1795 before 22 March][2]

Give my love to Ned,[3] and tell him that I have at last finished "Mount Vesuvius."[4]

[RHD said this sentence was the close of this letter and that in it Allston related a dream he had of "walking slowly on the hill in Newport, and seeing a spacious mansion, overshadowed by a lofty elm—nature and art in rivalry set all off with bowers and woodbine—a fair lady in a bower, who blushes at seeing him, then comes forward, and he falls upon his knees before her, while she confesses to having perceived an attachment."][5]

ANNOTATION: Sophomore. SOURCE: Flagg, p. 10. Apparently Flagg's sources for this and the next three letters were copies by RHD.

1. WA was sent from Charleston, S.C., to Newport, R.I., accompanied by his mother's brother John E. Moore, in the spring of 1787, at the age of twelve, partly because of frail health but mainly to be prepared for college. Several members of the family of his stepfather Henry C. Flagg lived in Newport, and Flagg made the arrangements. WA attended the classical school there operated by Robert Rogers and lived with the Rogers family. A portrait of him was painted by a French artist about this time (Henry Wadsworth Longfellow Dana, "Allston at Harvard—1796 to 1800," *Cambridge Historical Society Publications* 19 [1943]: foll. p. 16). In Newport he met Channing and his sister Ann. 2. Flagg said the annotation referred to Channing's sophomore year in Harvard, which was 1795-96. 3. Edmund T. Dana (1779-1859). Unless otherwise noted, references in the notes are to him rather than to his nephew of the same name. 4. According to his brother William, this was a copy of an old painting and was WA's first painting in oil (RHD, p. 21). He saw Vesuvius himself sometime between 1805 and 1808 and referred to it in *Monaldi* and his lectures on art. 5. This dream, in essence repeated in one he had in Florence in later years, is the earliest recorded manifestation of WA's lifelong attachment to the feminine ideal.

2. To William Ellery Channing Newport [22 March 1795]

My temper is naturally quick and resentful for a few mintues, but, believe me, in the cooler time of reflection I repine in secret if I have offended.[1] I wish to make reparation, but a foolish pride, which too many think honorable, stops me and obliges me to do a thing which I inwardly abhor.

SOURCE: Flagg, p. 10.

1. WA was noted for his animation and excitability, but never for resentment.

3. To William Ellery Channing [Newport, June 1795]

I am sorry to tell you that I am disappointed of my expectation of seeing you at Cambridge as a fellow-student, as my father-in-law[1] has fixed on Providence College.[2] Mr. Taylor, contrary to our expectation at his entrance, as usher, is generally esteemed, and resembles Mr. Hawes more than any tutor we have had since the departure of that grave-comic-foolish-wise man.[3] Apropos, I think it my duty to warn you to guard your heart against the fatal shaft of Cupid,[4] which has so often left dreadful monuments of its triumph by the temptation of minds which,— "O, horribile dictu, mihi frigidus horror membra quatit, gelidusque coit formidine sanguis."[5] Shall I proceed, or shall I forbear? Well, now my emotion has subsided, I will proceed, and without keeping you in further suspense; you must know that Eben Richardson,[6] that wonderful luminary of Newport City, has fought a terrible battle with that little devil Cupid, who has vanquished him (though not past recovery) with a dose of ratsbane. But poor Eben, repenting after the battle, declared his defeat, and begged assistance of the doctor.

SOURCE: Flagg, pp. 10-11.

1. WA's stepfather, Henry Collins Flagg. 2. Rhode Island College, founded in 1764 at Warren, R.I., which was moved to Providence in 1770. In 1804 its name was changed to Brown University (Walter C. Bronson, *The History of Brown University, 1764-1814* [Providence, R.I.: The University, 1914], pp. 34-36, 155-56). Flagg changed his mind. 3. Presumably Taylor and Hawes were attached to the school in Newport operated by Robert Rogers that both WA and Channing attended. 4. Subsequently WA copied the figure of this mythical personage in a painting by Rubens and painted it, together with that of Psyche, twice. 5. From the fourth word to the end, the quotation is from Virgil's *Aeneid* 3. 29-30, being Aeneas's description of his feelings when the myrtle he attempted to pull up in order to make a sacrifice to Venus and other deities oozed blood ("A cold shudder shakes my limbs, and my chilled blood freezes with terror"). 6. Unidentified.

4. To William Ellery Channing [Newport, 19 December 1795]

I would not willingly hurt any human being, much less one whom I had called my friend.[1]

I thank you for the satisfaction you express at my intention of entering Cambridge. . . . and what parts of the Greek Testament[2] [I should study]. [He also asked, in Flagg's words, for a "particular account of the examination".]

SOURCE: Flagg, p. 11.

1. At this point Flagg interjected the comment: "I remember his once telling me that when at Newport he was fond of shooting, but that having once wounded a bird, and being obliged to wring its neck to put it out of pain, he never fired at another." 2. He owned a New Testament in Greek and Latin, *HKAINH ΔIAΘH'KH. Novum Testamentum, cum Versione Latina Ariãe Montani*, ed. Jan Leusden (Lyons and London, 1772).

5. To William Ellery Channing [Newport, 14 February 1796]

Last week's paper favoured us with one of the greatest poetical productions (entitled "Georgiana")[1] I may venture to say that this century has produced; & I am sure, were I not credibly informed to the contrary, I should have fancied it the work of *Shakespeare or some other celebrated English Poet*. But I will not attempt a preface, as the piece which I send you will speak sufficiently for itself, without the assistance of a school boy's scrawl: & likewise send you one of my own, addressed to it, not that I put myself on an equality with the *noble Poet;* but relying on this maxim, "that a compliment is always acceptable to a poet, tho' from a fool,"[2] Therefore I assumed sufficient presumption to offer it to Mr. Barber.[3] But whether from negligence or design of some I trusted it with, the author's name was circulated about, before it came out; & I thought it high time to prevent its publication. Therefore to fill up my paper I will give it for the criticism of a leisure hour—a hem! a hem!

"An Address to the Great Georgiana

Hail! band celestial of this happy land,
Whose genius soars beyond the reach of man;
Cease not to lend thy Heavenly-favour'd muse
For "Mercy's" grace (which sure you can't refuse)
Nor let dark silence hide thy fire divine,
But in Columbia's land a *Homer shine!*
  Thus much to thee, Georgiana's noble bard,
My humble prayer is offer'd (sure not hard.)
  And now, O Muses all, ye heav'nly Nine!
Once more O, grant my pen thy aid divine.
T'address Georgiana's muse my pen inspire
And lend for once a more than mortal fire!
Advice to thee, *most mighty work,* I'd fain
Bestow (if ere I can) in humble strain.
But, O direful task! I fear I'll find to paint
Praises which Shakespeare's colours show'd too faint;
Much less t'advise an eighth terrestrial Wonder,
Whose muse bids fair to *Poets*—mortal thunder.
But my presumption thou, O noble muse,
In pitying condescension will excuse.
  In short, now ceremonious preface left,
T'advise again I'll strive, of fear bereft.
In rich Albion's[4] land as fame records,
Great *Grub-Street*[5] was, surpassing words;
Whose favour'd soil the friendly Nine had crown'd
With favours rare immortal Fame renown'd,
And e'en* Corduba's[6] bards, though once so fam'd
Could equal ne'er the mighty *grubs* I've nam'd!
And, O, had I but thy descriptive pen;

Born thus to soar above the power of men!
Had I but thy divine, immortal fire,
My Muse would charm Apollo's tuneful lyre:[7]
Not that I'd equal thee, for (thanks to God)
My humble pen's forbid a Poet's blood.
Now here, great GEORGIANA, bend thy way;
Admission I'll insure thy Heav'nly lay.
In Grub-street College great, whose fame renown'd,
With diffidence my humble pen did sound;
Here but repeat that all-enchanting line
Which thy muse sung—"To social man—a rich mine"—
Or Georgia's description—full of—"cotton"—;
The rhyming line—"Beef, pork, & excellent mutton."[8]
And take my word (as Spain's great knight) they'll dub
Georgiana's muse, a noble Grub-Street-Grub!"

"*A town in Spain Baetica"[9]

ANNOTATION: Copied by / Father RCD [Ruth Charlotte Dana]. SOURCE: Manuscript copy by RHD.

1. This poem, signed "Rhode Island, February 1, 1796," appeared in the *Newport Mercury*, 9 February 1796, as a sequel to a poem entitled "Guillotina," which was printed in the *Connecticut Courant* on 4 January 1796, and subsequently in the *Newport Mercury*. It recounted the Spanish attempts to invade the territory that became the colony of Georgia and concluded with a description of the rich natural resources, crops, and produce of the region, all in crude rimed couplets. 2. If WA is quoting, the source has not been identified. A similar sentiment is expressed in Jonathan Swift's "Cadenus and Vanese," lines 769-72: "'Tis an old maxim in the schools, / That flattery's the food of facts; / Yet now and then your men of wit / Will condescend to take a bit." 3. Henry Barber (d. 1800), publisher and editor of the *Newport Mercury* from 1780 intermittently until his death (Clarence S. Brigham, *History and Bibliography of American Newspapers, 1690-1820* [Worcester, Mass., American Antiquarian Society, 1947], 2:9981).
4. The oldest name of the island occupied by England, Scotland, and Wales, often, as here, used to refer to England alone. 5. A London street (now Milton Street) famed for being the habitation of literary hacks. 6. The Latin name of Cordova (Span. Córdoba), capital of the province of Cordova in Spain. It was the birthplace of M. Anneus Seneca the rhetorician, his son L. Anneus Seneca the philosopher and dramatist, and his grandson Lucan the poet, as well as other men of letters in later times. 7. As patron of music, in addition to other activities of men, Apollo is commonly depicted with a lyre. 8. The quotations are of line 4, the last word of line 66, and all of line 67 of "Georgiana." 9. The name in Roman times of the province in which Cordova was located.

6. To Henry Collins Flagg [Cambridge, 21 October 1796][1]

Honored Sir: Your kind letter I received a few weeks since, by the way of Rhode Island, added to the the pleasure I received from Mr. Avery's[2] letter that you were all well, in hearing from you myself. Perhaps you may think that my long neglect did not deserve even that; but when you consider our retired situation, and the difficulty of knowing opportunities, your goodness cannot hesitate to excuse my silence. Mr. Avery has been so kind as to give me a general invitation to spend the vacation at his house, but the bustle of Boston suits my disposition as much less than I expected, as my situation at Cambridge exceeds it.

The gratitude which I feel toward you for your paternal solitude, I hope the future conduct of my life will evince. The Doctor[3] with whom I live has shown a friendship for me that I wish may never be forgotten; tho' the great distance I live from college[4] makes my exercises rather disagreeable, the reflection of my situation makes me forget to complain. In short, I want nothing but your company in Carolina to make a wish vacant.

Give my sincere love to mama,[5] and likewise to my sisters,[6] with a kiss for Henry and Toby.[7] I subscribe myself,

Your grateful and affectionate, / Washington Allston.

SOURCE: Flagg, pp. 15-16.

1. WA was in Cambridge, Mass., by August 1796, and shortly afterward entered Harvard. According to Flagg this was the first letter he wrote from there. He was the first American artist and one of the very few ever to receive a formal education. Though undistinguished as a student, he was in maturity, partly through his independent reading, the best educated one of his time. Like many of his college mates, he was dealt mild punishment for tardiness; for absence at prayers, at recitations, and from college; and for neglect of collegiate duties. He was active in extracurricular activities, but most of his leisure was spent in drawing, painting, reading, and writing. The deep personal impression he made then, as described by his classmate Leonard Jarvis, was much the same as he made all his life: a pale complexion, expressive eyes, wavy black hair (later white and flowing), graceful movements, melodious voice, modest manner, fashionable dress, love of conversation and of late hours, dilatoriness, and the taste of an epicure—he once went without breakfast in anticipation of dining with old Major Thomas Brattle. He was generally popular and had a certain worldly charm and wit and a combination of reticence and assurance that Jarvis thought in the style of young Marlow in Oliver Goldsmith's *She Stoops to Conquer.* A portrait of him about this time was painted by Frederick Walker (H.W.L. Dana, "Allston at Harvard—1796 to 1800," foll. p. 16). In Cambridge,if not earlier in Newport, he met RHD and Edmund T. Dana. 2. John Avery, Boston merchant. He was prominent in various political activities during the American Revolution and served as the first secretary of state of Massachusetts from 1780 until his death (Clifford K. Shipton, ed. *Sibley's Harvard Graduate Graduates, 1765-1760* [Boston: MHS, 1968], pp. 384-89). 3. Benjamin Waterhouse. At this time he lived on the north side of the Common in Cambridge. WA roomed and boarded there, sharing a room with his classmate from Charleston Robert D. Wainright, during his first and part of his second year in college. Their room was the southwest one up one flight to the left from the front door. (H.W.L. Dana, "Allston at Harvard," p. 16; a picture of the house is reproduced following p. 48.)
4. After moving from Waterhouse's, WA had a room alone nearer the college, in the house on the north side of the Boston Road of the retired classicist Stephen Sewall, and boarded with the eccentric lawyer Joseph Bartlett on the same street. He lived in the room above Sewall's, on the western side. At the back were two closets, in one of which he kept his painting materials, in the other a supply of fuel. In college accounts his bill for fuel was one of the largest in his class, and Jarvis remembered that he would pile bed clothes and even a chair or two on top of himself for

warmth. His sensitivity to cold was lifelong. His college mate John Codman roomed in the same house with him, presumably this one, for two years (Dana 1:188; a picture of it is reproduced in H.W.L. Dana, "Allston at Harvard," following p. 48; see also p. 24). In the interim he apparently had a room in the house of tutor Levi Hedge (Walter Channing, "Reminiscences of Washington Allston," *Christian World* [Boston], 22 July 1843. 5. Rachel (Moore) Allston Flagg.
6. WA's sister Mary Allston and his half-sisters Elizabeth Allston and Eliza Moore Flagg.
7. WA's half-brothers Henry Collins Flagg, Jr., and Ebenezer Flagg.

7. To Robert Rogers

[of Newport, Rhode Island] [Cambridge, 28 October 1797]

My Worthy Sir: Impressed with emotions of the sincerest gratitude, I sit down to acknowledge my obligations to you for the kind letter I have just this moment received from you. Never before have I felt such cruel sensations as I do now from reading those reproaches which are so justly merited by my unpardonable neglect.[1]

That any of my friends should suppose me capable of one ungrateful or indifferent feeling toward them is an arrow which could not be inflicted more poignantly in my breast. But I do not, cannot blame anyone for entertaining such an idea of me; my conduct in that particular has given grounds too specious hardly to admit a doubt in the judgment of the most unsuspicious; but, as God is my witness, no one has a truer affection for his friends and relatives than I pride myself in possessing. Were it possible that my mother could see and know the inward feelings of my heart, I could wish no other testimony to convince her that the want of affection for her is the last sin which could obtain a residence in my heart. But, however I may deserve any of these reproaches, I cannot omit thanking you for the solicitious advice your kind attention has honored me with.

It is my greatest misfortune to be too lazy, and by the few mortifications I have already set with on that account I predict many evils in my future life. I have always the inclination to do what I ought; but by continually procrastinating[2] for tomorrow the business of today, I insensibly delay, until at the end of one month I find myself in the same place as when I began it. You, no doubt, will allow all this to be very candid, and that I speak as I should do, but is it not more probable, you will observe, that these professions are good as far as they are professions, but how am I to know you will act up to them unless you practice them? I know it is very easy to promise one thing and do another. We seldom find anyone who is unwilling to acknowledge his faults and promise to reform; but there are very few who will resist the slightest obstacle or temptation to make good his professions. The most abandoned profligate at particular times will not hesitate to accuse himself of the greatest atrocities, and very frequently resolve to reform; yet no sooner is he under similar circumstances than we see him plunge as heedlessly into the same vices as if no such resolutions were ever made. But, sir, I assure this is not, nor, I trust, will be, the case with me. I began to practise before I attempted these. Three weeks since I wrote to mama, the Doctor,[3] and my sister,[4] some of which letters for length may serve for two or three each. And more, I have made a resolution which I flatter myself I shall be able to maintain, to write to Carolina every month, and, as opportunity offers, send them on. So much, sir, I have troubled you about myself. . . .

SOURCE: Flagg, pp. 16-18.

1. Rogers had remonstrated with WA for the infrequency of his letters to his mother during his second year in college. 2. He was notorious for procrastination and protracted deliberation all his life. 3. Henry C. Flagg. 4. Mary Allston.

8. To Henry Collins Flagg [Cambridge, 23 June 1800]

My Honored Sir: Yours of May 19th I have just received. Agreeable to your wish, tho' I have nothing material to add at present, I seize the present opportunity once more to acknowledge the receipt of three separate remittances of one hundred and twenty dollars each. With regard to my expenses at Commencement I cannot make any accurate calculation. It is unusual on that day for those who have exercises to perform, generally to give an entertainment, and that entertainment seldom comes short of two or three hundred dollars, indeed some exceed six. But as I have no ambition to shine beyond my abilities, I have thought proper to limit my magnificence to fifty. That sum I hope will enable me to entertain a small party with some degree of elegance; accordingly I propose to invite about twenty gentlemen. As I make no pretenses to gallantry, and am besides intimate with families who are totally unacquainted with each other, whom I should necessarily be obliged to invite, I have thought proper to dispense with the company of ladies. The exercise assigned me for Commencement is a poem; the subject which I have selected is "Energy of Character."[1]

I look now for Mr. and Mrs. Young,[2] and anticipate much pleasure in returning with them to Carolina.[3] As you are more acquainted with the expense of travelling, I have submitted to you the regulation of that article. Be assured, sir, if I prove extravagant, I shall be more so from ignorance than wilfulness. I am not wholly insensible to the pleasures of the world, therefore shall not be governed entirely by necessity; but I flatter myself, at least, in being able to restrain their gratification within due bonds. I wait your intended remittance with some degree of anxiety, since the last has not emancipated me entirely from debt, the sums owing, however, are small. My duty to mamma, and remembering me to all, believe me still,

Yours grateful and affectionate / Washington Allston.

SOURCE: Flagg, pp. 18-19.

1. The exercises took place on 16 June 1800. (A copy of the program is in the South Caroliniana Library, University of South Carolina.) A fragment, in WA's early handwriting, may have been the conclusion of the poem, all that seems to have been preserved. In it he was probably influenced by James Thomson's *The Castle of Indolence* 2:lii, 7-8, with its mention of Milton and Shakespeare, and lxiv-lxv, which contained the phrase "such energy was ours." It consists of twelve lines of

heroic couplets, upbraiding one "Whose lukewarm soul like stagnant lake serene / Can calmly rot unenvied and unseen," and urging him, "content," to "some polar region find, / Cold as his heart, and barren as his mind, / Unruffled there, without, or smile, or groan, / Sneak thro' the world unknowing and unknown," and offering others "the task, inspired with nobler flame, / To climb the rocks that rough the road to fame." He cited Milton, "godlike Newton," and "whirlwind Shakespeare" as having done so and concluded "Be ours to rise with genius conscious pride / And view creation but a hall to stride." WA was placed seventh in the program of twelve participants because, Jarvis remembered, his recital of his poem on the death of Washington the preceding year had drawn so much applause in contrast to the cold reception of the oration by the president which preceded it that he was placed far from the president on this occasion so as not to detract from his performance. Allston had a particularly high regard for Sir Isaac Newton. In "The Hypochondriac" the narrator says that "Newton probably pined for the sight of those distant stars whose light has not yet reached us" (*LA*, p. 182), and in the "Introductory Discourse" of his lectures on art the idea of the infinite is illustrated in a variation of that sentence. In a passage among his manuscripts, possibly meant to be included in this essay, he wrote: "It was an ancient saying that the highest wisdom was to be sensible of our ignorance. Nor is it indeed a small matter to know how much there is around us which we *cannot* know. This was the source of the sublime humility of Newton, when he compared himself to a little child on the seashore who had been all his life sporting with pebbles. For he had stood thus upon the shore of the mighty deep of human ignorance; whose unfathomable darkness no one knew better, since no one had sounded it at greater depth. . . . Newton the last man therefore to exclaim with the Roman Poet 'Exegi monumentum, aere perennius [I have reared a monument more durable that brass]'" (Horace, *Ode* 3.30). In the margin: "N.B. Not decided whether I shall use this or not. *Decided to reject.*"
2. Probably Thomas and his mother Martha (Allston) Young, who was WA's great-aunt, of Youngville Plantation on the Waccamaw River near the Allston plantation in Georgetown County, S.C. WA's sister Mary married Thomas Young (Joseph A. Groves, *The Alstons and Allstons of North and South Carolina* [Atlanta: Franklin Printing and Publishing Co., 1901], pp. 26-28; Emma B. Richardson, comp., "Dr. Anthony Cordes and Some of His Descendants," *SCHGM* 43 [1942]: 142; Barbara K. Nord, *The Flagg Family in South Carolina: The Nineteenth Century* [Austin, Tex.: Peripatetic Press, 1984], p. 90). 3. WA did not go to South Carolina until December 1800.

9. To Rachel (Moore) Allston Flagg

Newport,[1]
August 12, 1800

My Dear Mother: Yours, dated July 19th, was handed me a few days ago. I should have answered it immediately by post, but hearing of an opportunity by water I have waited till now for that.

It is needless to express my feelings on account of the Doctor's illness.[2] You know my heart and its numerous obligations to that honored man, and can easily conceive its sufferings. I know not, my dear mother, how it will be in my power to return his services. In all respects and at all times has he acted toward me with the affection of a father; I cannot therefore repay him but with the affection of a son.

I am now at Newport. The town is crowded with strangers, and gayer than I ever knew it; but I feel so little relish for its amusements that I fancy it will be no great self-denial to comply with your wishes on my return. Be assured, dear mother, your request shall not necessarily be repeated. I will live as "snug" as you can desire. I feel no curiosity now to visit Charleston, and flatter myself 'twill be no difficult task to keep out of it when in Carolina. I have become so habituated to a country life (for Cambridge is but a rural village) that I shall think myself full happy enough in Waccamaw or St. Thomas.[3]

It is so long since I have mentioned anything about my painting that I suppose you have concluded I had given it up. But my thoughts are far enough from that, I assure you. I am more attached to it than ever; and am determined, if resolution and perseverance will effect it, to be the first painter, at least, from America. Do not think me vain, for my boasting is only conditional; yet I am inclined to think from my own experience that the difficulty to eminence lies not in the road, but in the timidity of the traveller. Few minds capable of conceiving that are not adeqate to the accomplishing of great designs; and if there have been some failures, less blame, perhaps, is to be ascribed to the partiality of fortune than to their own want of confidence.

In a word, my dear mother, I already feel a fortune in my fingers. With what little skill I possess at present, I am persuaded, did my pride permit, I could support myself with ease and respectability; but I am content to remain poor as I am until painting shall have been formally established as my profession. I have a few pieces by me, which I intend sending on soon by water.[4]

I write by this to sister Polly,[5] and perhaps a few lines to the Doctor. Eliza, I hear, is quite a belle. As I am a beau, tell her I shall give her a few lessons in the art of heart-catching.[6]

Remember me to all, and believe me still your dutiful, affectionate son,

Washington Allston.[7]

Source: Flagg, pp. 19-21.

1. WA remained in Cambridge a few weeks after his graduation from Harvard and then went to Newport. 2. Henry C. Flagg died on 1 April 1801. 3. By "Waccamaw" WA refers to the neck of land between the Waccamaw River and the Atlantic Ocean in South Carolina, where several members of his parents' families had plantations. He was born, according to most accounts, on his father's rice plantation on the Waccamaw River in All Saint's Parish. His mother's family was from St. Thomas's Parish at the southern end of the neck. According to another tradition he was born there, at Mooreland, her father's plantation on the Cooper River (Mabel L. Webber, "Moore of St. Thomas' Parish," *SCHGM* 27 [1926]: 166). 4. He sent at least *Landscape with Banditti (Landscape with a Bridge and a File of Horsemen)* (1798) and, according to his brother William, the heads of Judas Iscariot (1800-1801), *St. Peter When He Heard the Cock Crow* (1800-1801), and *Christ Looking at Peter* (RDH, p. 6) and several watercolors, all of which he took to England in 1801, and probably *A Rocky Coast with Banditti* (1800), which he probably also took to England. 5. Mary Allston. 6. Jarvis said that WA had made known his affection for Ann Channing before he was a junior in college. 7. According to Flagg, this is the "last" of WA's "early letters" (p. 19).

10. To John Knapp Newport, October 23rd 1800.

To you sir, this may appear strange; it may appear impertinent; it may appear astonishing; but to me, sir, who am as uncorrupted, as unprotected by power, it is a duty which every honest man out of office should observe towards every rogue in.

Did I address myself to a man of principle, misled by the enthusiasm of some favorite hypothesis, I would appear in the character of a counsellor, of an honest citizen, who, in pity for the errors of his judgment, would now offer his correction, as a tribute due to the well-meaning, tho' miscalculating, goodness of his heart. But when we see great talents, a sound judgement, and every requisite necessary to the preservation of order, to the support of government; when, I say sir, we see these rare endowments prostituted to the vilest purpose, when we see them meanly stoop to become the tools of a mob, I know not whether we should more pity the cowardice, than execrate the wilful wickedness of their debaser. You have no doubt done me the justice to acknowledge the truth of this portrait. You should, likewise, with me, recoil with abhorrence from the original. But all view not one picture with the same emotions. Every parent can discover beauties ever in the deformities of their children. You, doubtless, have derived no little satisfaction from the contemplation of yours.

You laugh at my idle indignation. The horse flounces at the biting of a fly; but he cannot shake him off. I am, it is true, little more than an insect; but, with the body of an emmet, will I pursue you with the sting of <the> a scorpion; with the constancy of a shadow, will I follow you to your den, and fright the monster with his deformity. You shall tremble if I breathe. You shall foam with anger; but your attacks will I repell, as the porcupine resists the idle arrows of the hunter. Mean, weak, and impotent designer! did you <but> only labour for yourself, at least some degree of merit had been yours. But when, with the pusilanimous good nature of a coward, you are content to sin for others; who does not detest you, as the weak, and woodenhearted assassin, who lets himself for hire, as a mere *machine* to digest the crimes of others—Had you rather come forward with the noble spirit of a robber; had you, like him, professed the trade of murder for subsistance, we would have met you on your <own> ground, and, while we sought for your destruction as the unruly madman of society, we would have yielded you, as an individual, the noble gratulations of a hero.—Hey! what the devil have I been about?—Excuse me, Jack, I thought I was writing to Mr. Jefferson.[1]—Your being a man *"in Office"* [Mr. Davis's!!!][2] was the occasion of my mistake.

Rome.[3] October 1800.

I have not been three days at Rome. How charming are the italian women! Nature seems here to have concentred all her beauties. In other countries she has bestow'd only one feature; but in Rome the countenance is perfect. *There* she has given souls without bodies; *here* they both exist in the same being; each, serving as a foil to other, contributes mutually to the advantage of both. You well know what are my ideas on beauty. Were you in Rome you need only behold Signiora P——to be convinced of their truth. *You* are likewise an admirer of beauty? Have you never seen the morning sun ascend from the blushing bosom of the ocean? You have not then beheld her eyes opening to diffuse "celestial rose red" over the downy surface of her cheeks. You admire music? When she opens her mouth you no longer behold a mortal; her lips appear to be those of an angel's pronouncing pardon to the damn'd. You are fond of sentiment? It is impossible to think meanly in her presence; you become abstracted from mortality, and hear the sacred oracle of Delphos[4] dispensing wisdom to the universe. Oh, Jack, I would have *you* here as the only man in the world capable of enjoying the conversation of such a woman. "Is she pedantic," I hear you ask, "for that, of all things <things> follies in a woman I abhor." Precisely the reverse. Are you a shepherd? In her conversation you recline on banks of violet. Are you a philosopher? The world becomes a cabinet; you fill each vacant draw[er], and disencumber others of their burthen. Are you a divine? The image of Magdalene[5] is before you, and every tear, like dews from heaven, becomes a brilliant for her Saviour's crown. Are you a painter? You behold the grace of Guido in her form; the frown of Angelo is on her brow[6]; her gait assumes the majesty of Raphael. Are you a musician? You are transported to the spheres;

> You hear the harps of thousand angels breathe,
> And meet in harmony voluptuous death.[7]

In short, you behold in her, not *one* colour only; but, like a prism, from the rays of genius she collects, combines, and separates their <proper> hues. Could she talk but on one subject with the same skill as she now converses on all, then perhaps she might with you be a pedant. But, how different is Signiora P. With such talents, as I have just described, she possesses that insuperable modesty, which makes her apparently the listener on every subject. She commands to a degree the wonderful art of saying fine things without appearing to be conscious of it. She can teach, tho' a pupil; she can be an angel, tho' on earth. In a word, Jack she is that very woman, who, of all the world besides, appears to have been created to live in a—*garret* with you! In a *garret*—!—"only think of that master Brook!"[8]—Climax, by the Lord!

Need I add your letter gave me pleasure? If you have known what it is after two hours rhyme-hunting to run down one new idea, you can have some conception of what I felt. Your good letter arrived as a seasonable remedy against one of those damn'd easterly winds, of which you complain; and I can truly assure you, I received more real pleasure in its perusal, than I could any way have expected, tho' I had travelled thro' the country it describes. By the by, Jack, I think travelling in this country a devilish stupid thing, unless one meets with some queer quiz or other. Our country is at present so young that few of our towns bear an[y] traits of originality. The same taste (or rather no-taste) the same architecture, and the same sentiments are to be found in all parts of the United States. If one meets with a curiosity it is either a bear, a dancing dog, or a learned pig. Sometime, to be sure, we may light on a connoisseur, or something of that kind to laugh at; but for your buildings, your paintings, your music, give me old England *"for my money!"* [9] To be sure this country of ours is *"in the main"* a very good one; in no other place <it> must it be confessed, are there better citizens, or better *men,* but I am still of opinion that the best coat of arms for America would be a pudding for her body, a bag of cotton for her head, and a bag of dollars for her heart.

I am proud to acknowledge that my sentiments correspond with yours, concerning what you call *"living in the world."* Your ideas, like your cloaths are there subjected to the shears of fashion. Some mental tailor is the rage, he cabbages for lack of cloath himself, and in a short time, the whole *piece* of your understanding is reduced to a short, insignificant, sparrow-tail'd coatee. And what is still worse this damnd fashion is but the shadow of that hideous monster, called *Equality.* The fool and the sage, the diggers of Parnassus and Peru,[10] are, by her, all reduced to a level. The tall man and the short man must walk alike; the fat one and the lean one wear the same cloaths; and all, but the parson and the beggar, assume the face of cheerfulness—they poor devils, having to court affliction for their subsistence.

Yours, dear Jack, to the third heaven under Mahommet's whig.[11]

Washington Allston[12]

Pray give my love to your dear little cow-babies.

I saw Judge Paul here.[13] He told me the Club[14] met the evening before exhibition; and you were obliged to grease his belly after supper. I hope the cow-pox will be merciful to your *calves*.

I heard that Tudor[15] lately won a race at a quarter stretch with the English racer, Wells.[16] I have got into a cursed hole where I am daily entertained with various duets and triets. Viz scolding swearing, and child crying. I only want the fiddle you used to play on to make the cer [rest of word blotted out] complete

Day is night.
Black is white.
Bad is good.
Water's blood.

I heard you have lately become a child of Thespis, and made your debut in Alexander.[17] I should like to have seen that pretty little humming bird, Mr. Hosmare,[18] on your helmet by way of crest.

I hope the little Aaronet[19]
Still plays on his flageolet;

[line of drawings of a coffin, cross-bones, a skull, scales, a shovel, a dagger, a candle, and an eye]

That Forster[20] still to recitation goes,
And Jarvis[21] nourishes his infant nose.
Too precious nose, it sure deserves to share
The largest portion of its owner's care.
For think, O Jacky, what to *it* would hap
Should but his mouth in grizly horror gape!
The tender snout does oer the chasm bend—
Think, Jacky, think how easy 'twould descend.

Tell Jarvis I am like to meet with a case for his nose. I have bought a pair of stilts for Baldwin.[22]

Miss [word blotted out] the celebrated [drawing of a bell] is here. She is now Mrs. Derby.[23] Miss B [rest of word blotted out] left this place before I came. Tell Putnam to cast a Sheep's eye at miss [drawing resembling a tree] for me. How does Doctor [drawing of a pitcher pouring liquid and two houses][24] cowpox come on? Tell [drawing of two wells][25] he is a sad fellow for not answering my letter. I told him [drawing of a well] I might probably pay you a visit before I go.[26] I hear that your friend [word blotted out] is studying law. I should like to see him and Mac [word blotted out][27] engaged on opposite sides of the same causes.

Pray Jack do you shave as often as ever? Pitty you did not own a share in a shoe-brush manufactory, what a vast saving would there be of your bristles!

I shall leave Newport about the middle of November, so I beg you would not forget to answer this before that time.

Remember me to Marquis Sumner.[28] Tell him I have once a <day> week a levee of ladies at my room. Nothing is new heard of but *Allston's Gallery.* It has become quite a lounge for the beau mond. [This page contains six caricatures, four of which are labelled: "Counsellor Knapp," "The Apollo Belvidere,"[29] "The Venus de Medici copied from the celebrated statue at Florence,"[30] and "Bartlet[31] of Newbury Port."]

ADDRESSED: Mr. John Knapp / At Mr. Davis's Office / Boston / Massachusetts. ANNOTATED IN ANOTHER HAND: Newport 22 June Paid 20. SOURCE: Manuscript.

1. Thomas Jefferson (1743-1826) was elected president of the United States a few weeks after the date of this letter. WA's satirical reference reflects the Federalist criticism of him prevalent in New England and his own political sympathies. 2. WA's brackets. John Davis (1761-1847), jurist, was at this time U.S. attorney for the district of Massachusetts. Knapp was studying law in his office. These quotation marks and the next set of them appear to have been used to satirize the two phrases. 3. WA is being facetious; he did not leave America until 1801. His college theme "Procrastination is the Thief of Time" concerns a young artist who goes to Rome. 4. The oracle of Apollo at Delphi. 5. Mary Magdalene, the woman from whom Jesus cast seven devils and who was present at the crucifixion and the resurrection, is traditionally identified with the unnamed sinful woman who annointed the feet of Jesus at the house of a Pharisee, weeping as she did so, as described in Luke 7:37ff. 6. Guido Reni and Michelangelo. 7. If WA is quoting, the source has not been identified. It seems likely that the lines are his own, echoing

language of Thompson, particularly *The Seasons,* "Summer," line 558: "Angelic harps are in full concert heard," and *The Castle of Indolence* 1:xiv, 6-7: "Than these same guilful angel-seeming sprights / Who thus in dreams, voluptuous, soft and bland." 8. No explanation for this nickname has been found. The quotation is presumably a phrase used by Knapp and one of his friends in conversation. 9. The special punctuation of this and the phrase in the next sentence reflects WA's consciousness of colloquialisms, of which he was fond. 10. Parnassus was the mountain in Greece sacred to Apollo and the muses. Peru is noted for its mineral mines, especially of silver. 11. According to the Koran there are seven heavens, one above the other. 12. The remainder of the page contains several groups of words, together with drawings, separated by lines drawn around them, written upside down and sidewise, which are here treated as eight paragraphs. 13. Unidentified. 14. Presumably the coffee club instituted in WA's senior year in college. Each member had a nickname and he put them in a song sung at the meetings. Jarvis said that the rules were that they had no rules but to meet every Thursday evening and had no potation stronger than coffee. WA was also an honorary member of the Porcellian club, another social organization at Harvard. 15. John Henry Tudor (1782-1802), a college classmate of WA's. 16. Presumably Benjamin Welles, a college classmate of WA's. 17. Probably "The Rival Queens, or The Death of Alexander" by Nathaniel Lee. 18. Rufus Hosmer (1778-1839), a college classmate of WA's. He became a lawyer. About 1810 WA wrote a poem about him, "An Elegy in Exile," consisting of five stanzas of sixteen lines each and one line of rimed couplets, together with a two-line refrain referring to his hometown of Stowe, Mass., satirizing his acting in Shakespearean roles in college and an apocryphal visit to Haiti, where his talent was unknown and where the king, speaking pidgin English, would have killed him but for the intervention of his daughter. 19. Aaron Fall Putnam (1782-1809), a college classmate of WA's. 20. Andrew Foster (d. 1831), a college classmate of WA's. He became a doctor. 21. Leonard Jarvis. 22. Loammi Baldwin, a college classmate of WA's. 23. Unidentified. 24. Benjamin Waterhouse. He was an early experimenter with cowpox to vaccinate against smallpox. 25. Benjamin Welles. 26. To South Carolina. 27. Probably Charles Macomber (d. 1835), of the Harvard class of 1799. 28. Probably William Hyslop Sumner (1780-1861), of the Harvard class of 1799, who became a lawyer. He owned WA's *Landscape* (1798; G Fig. 3). 29. *The Apollo Belvedere* is in the Vatican Museum in Rome. The caption is written below and "Counsellor Knapp" above a drawing of a bespectacled man wearing a judge's wig. WA saw the statue in Paris in 1804 and described it in his lecture "Art" and also in *Monaldi.* He could have seen engravings of this work and the *Venus dei Medici* in Thomas Dobson's *Encyclopedia,* 18 vols. (Philadelphia, 1798), which he borrowed from the Harvard Library. 30. The *Venus dei Medici* is in the Uffizi Gallery in Florence. The caption is written below a drawing of an ugly woman flirting with an ugly man. WA saw the statue presumably in 1804 and referred to it in *Monaldi.* 31. William Bartlett (b. 1782) of Newburyport, Mass., of the Harvard class of 1801, became a merchant. The caption is written across a drawing of a man with an enormous stomach.

JUVENILIA

Allston drew and painted from an early age. Besides his painting of Vesuvius, to which he referred in his letter to Channing before 22 March 1795, his compositions at that time included several drawings: three of log huts and blockhouses, probably copied from a book on architecture; *Santo Domingo Black Boy,* which depicted a house servant refugee from a revolt, who was wearing a liberty cap with a tricolor tassel and cockade and carrying a book in one hand and a shoe brush in the other, which he took from Newport to Cambridge; a caricature of his French class, showing the class seated except for one boy reading and Ducio, the master, holding a pig and directing the class to pronounce *oui* like the pig; a scene from John Brown's tragedy *Barbarossa,* depicting the "splendidly robed tyrant" and the slave Selim "surrounded by black mutes"; several scenes from Ann Radcliffe's *The Mysteries of Udolpho,* in which the castle formed the background; and Octavian from George Colman's play *The Mountaineers,* all remembered by his brother William.[1] Probably in Newport before he went to college he also drew a scene in ink from the romance *Count Roderick's Castle* and painted several watercolors, including one of *The Siege of Toulon by Napoleon.* Either in Newport or early in his Harvard years he drew a copy of a portrait of Rubens. None of these pieces seems to have been preserved except the drawings of log huts and blockhouses.

In college he painted several compositions from literary works, at least five landscapes, nine portraits, three comic pieces, and two grotesques and produced a considerable number of miscellaneous drawings and caricatures. From Thomson's "Summer," he painted Damon and the nude Musidora, shocking his landlord "Don" Clark, Jarvis remembered, who nevertheless said, "It was as natural as life!" and he was "quite a genio." From Schiller's *Robbers* he painted the scene in which Charles de Moore meditates suicide; possibly about this time he acquired his copy of Schiller's *Don Carlos,* translated by G.H. Noehden and J. Stoddard (London, 1798). From Robert Southey's description of cruelty in his verse drama *Joan of Arc* 2.172-73, he drew a maniac crushing a dove. None of these pieces seems to have survived except some of the pen-and-ink caricatures.

The landscapes were *Landscape with Rustic Festival* (1798); *Landscape* (1798; G Fig. 3), painted on one of his shirts; *Landscape with Banditti (Landscape with a Bridge and a File of Horsemen); A Rocky Coast with Banditti;* and *Landscape* (*Aeneas and Achates Come Ashore* [?]) (ca. 1800), from the *Aeneid,* lines 173-76. He may have painted three more (ca. 1798, 1799, and ca. 1799), but they are not further identified.

The portraits were of his classmate John Harris, a miniature in watercolor (1796); Benjamin Waterhouse's son Andrew (1796-97), then about seven, which Waterhouse thought was his first use of oil; Waterhouse's mother Hannah (Proud) Waterhouse (1796-97), of whom he also made a full-length seated drawing; himself, unfinished (1796-1800); Edmund T. Dana, in pastel (ca. 1797); Harvard president Joseph Willard, on the back of *Landscape* (1798; G Fig. 3); Robert Rogers, in the fall of 1800;[2] according to Sweetser, the Newport painter and instrument maker Samuel King (1800?); and according to Jarvis, Ann Channing, a miniature done from memory. He later said he could paint from memory the portraits of all those in college with him. He also copied John Smibert's copy of Van Dyck's portrait of Cardinal Bentivoglio.

The three comic pieces, done in his freshman year, were the watercolors entitled *The Buck's Progress,* signed and dated 10 November 1796; *The Introduction of a Country Lad to a Club of Town Bucks; A Beau in His Dressing Room;* and *A Midnight Fray.* Each had a rhymed couplet beneath the subtitle, which was subsequently cut off, and several of the figures represented some of his college friends, including Channing, as well as himself. He was imitating Hogarth's series *The Rake's Progress,* but he was also satirizing the current outbreak of "buckism" among Harvard students, called "high fellows" by Jarvis, who were rebelling against the authorities by breaking rules, dressing flamboyantly, and espousing atheistic opinions such as those expressed in Thomas Paine's *Age of Reason.* That work, the second volume of which appeared the year before Allston's painting, was shown on top of a pile of other books in the last sketch.

He also painted in college two grotesques: *The Tippler* (1799), based on an engraving in Horace Walpole's *Anecdotes of Painting,* which he borrowed from the library, and *Tragic Figure in Chains* (1800), possibly derived from *Scene in a Madhouse* in *The Rake's Progress* or the Philadelphia painter Robert E. Pine's *Mad Woman in Chains.* The latter is related to a drawing on the flyleaf of his copy of Charles Churchill's *Poems* (London, 1765).

In college he produced also a number of miscellaneous drawings and a great many caricatures, mostly in pen and ink, some in pencil, most of which have not been preserved. He often drew a small head or figure while writing a sentence, Jarvis said, and remembered that he covered the walls of one of his rooms with fanciful or grotesque watercolor sketches, including one of a countryman walking rapidly, entitled *Walking with a Good Stick.* More seriously he made drawings to illustrate an essay by Waterhouse for a foreign correspondent. Of those which have survived one depicts a hunter with a long rifle in a wooded landscape, a rail fence and a mansion in the distance, and another is *Old Man Resting against a Rock* (ca. 1799-1800). On the verso of the first is a poem which has been crossed out and on that of the second there are ten lines of verse beginning, "Steal, soft enchantress, open my soul, / Mould every thought to my control." He drew caricature figures on his mathematics manuscripts which illustrate problems in mensuration and which, Jarvis said, elicited laughter from the examiners. Others include two of Napoleon, one showing him at Toulon and the other bearing the inscription "Behold the Conqueror of Egypt" and having on the same sheet the figure of President Willard, an old woman seated in a chair, and two heads. He also made drawings in the books, besides that by Churchill, which he owned. One of his projects involved not only painting but modeling. For a masquerade in his junior year in which he and Jarvis took the roles, respectively, of Don Quixote and Sancho Panza, he carved heads in wood and made paper masks and for himself a pasteboard suit of armor painted the color of steel.

One of the surviving drawings is of particular note. It depicts a river landscape with a tree in the background similar to his landscapes of the period. It is of interest otherwise, however, for being on the verso of a sheet beginning, "My Dear Mother," the only known evidence of a letter written to her while he was in college.

A few weeks after his graduation he returned to the satiric mode of his *Buck's Progress* and in Newport painted two such pieces: *The Squinting Fiddler,* which began as a portrait of Dr. Armand Auboyneau and was altered when Auboyneau temporarily left town, and *The French National Convention as a Rasher of Frogs*. In Newport at this time he also painted the head of Judas Iscariot and the heads in *St. Peter when He Heard the Cock Crow* and *Christ Looking at Peter.*

In Charleston in 1800 and 1801 he painted *Robbers Fighting with Each Other for the Spoils over a Murdered Traveller* and *Satan at the Gates of Hell Guarded by Sin and Death,* from Milton's *Paradise Lost* 2.648ff., which his brother William said he first sketched on the bare floor of his room and then on paper. Charles Fraser said he took the painting of Satan to England and later destroyed it. In 1801 he supposedly also painted a portrait of his half-brother Ebenezer Flagg, then six. His own portrait was painted by the Philadelphia miniaturist Jeremiah Paul.

Allston also wrote from an early age. His first known composition is the poem "An Address to the Great Georgiana," sent in his letter of 14 February 1796 to Channing. The numerous allusions in it reflect his literary bent, manifest in his painting and writing, and the satire represents his inclination to this mode, chiefly in his early years.

His literary compositions in college were also predominantly satiric, but they included lyrics and were in prose as well as poetry. Among them were a half-burlesque allegory on the death of the college barber, John Gally, which Jarvis said were his first lines to be made public; descriptions of the Visigoth king Roderigo and of Frederick I, called Barbarossa; a satire on the current Illuminati and other secret societies; several poems and a bombastic political prose piece written when a poem was rejected, which were printed in *The Massachusetts Centinel;* and several poems inspired by Ann Channing.

Only two of these pieces seem to have been preserved or identified as published. The untitled pastoral poem beginning "Ah, where is my Phillida gone?" consists of seven stanzas, each having two quatrains in rhymed trimeter, spoken by Phillida's lover Corydon, the name of a shepherd in Virgil's *Eclogues*. It has as an epigraph lines 861 and 862 of Thomson's "Spring." For the last stanza he drew a sketch of a wooden bridge over a stream with trees at the side, which is signed and dated 10 July 1799. The other poem, "Modern Sublimity Cooked to the Most Fashionable Palates," is not altogether finished, the manuscript containing several unincorporated revisions. It consists of some thirty-six lines of blank verse satirizing the United States in relation to European nations and is illustrated on the verso by a drawing of a male figure in costume, dated 1799 in another hand.

As the poet as well as the secretary and vice-president of the Hasty Pudding Club, to which he was elected in 1798 in his junior year, he established the tradition of keeping the records in rhyme. One of his poems written in this capacity, dated 7 March 1799 and signed as secretary, recounts the time when a large pot of hasty pudding was eaten after mealtime, as was customary, in the room of his classmate Moody Noyes. He illustrated it with a drawing of a person thus engaged. At the request of the club he wrote a poem in celebration of Washington's birthday in 1799, for which occasion he was asked to construct a wooden stage for the speakers. In consequence, at the request of the faculty, he wrote an "Elegaic Poem" for the commemoration on 21 February 1800 of Washington's death. Jarvis remembered that it was so movingly delivered the audience repeatedly applauded though they had been cautioned not to do so because of the solemnity of the occasion. He refused, however, to give a copy to be included in the official publication of the proceedings on that occasion, out of modesty, the president said. At the commencement exercises of his class later that year he delivered another poem of his own.

The most noteworthy of his literary compositions in college was the narrative sketch "Procrastination is the Thief of Time," the title containing a mispelling of the word "Thief," which was not repeated in the sketch itself. It was written for the senior class in English composition and differed significantly from most of the other pieces written for that class in being a narrative rather than an essay on some moral saying much like the title it bore. It was also more than twice as long as any other. Though another piece of satire, it is also a serious depiction of the ideal artist as Allston conceived of him all his life and of which he himself became an example. Bernardo, the central character, is a young Italian painter having Allston's tendency to daydream; admiring, like Allston, Michelangelo, Raphael, Correggio, Claude, and Salvator Rosa, whose soul he feels is "in unison with his own"; and having, like Allston, a low opinion of the realism of Dutch painters, in particular his teacher, the Dutch Mynheer Van Hoofsniken. He goes to Rome to study and is on his way to success when he falls in love with the maiden Rosalia, forsakes his art, and dies untimely. The conclusion is precipitous and his ludicrous epitaph reads, "Behold Death came, and shov'd him in the grave."

This sketch contains, moreover, several echoes of Allston's reading in college. The title is from Edward Young's *The Complaint; or, Night Thoughts on Life, Death, and Immortality* 1.393, and Bernardo is like the speaker in that poem in having a "melancholy" disposition and in meditating during night rambles on the ephemeral nature of man and his achievements. As he dedicates himself to fame, his feelings are described in the lines from Shakespeare's *Julius Caesar,* "There is a tide in the affairs of men / Which, taken at the flood, leads on to fortune." Allston borrowed a copy of Shakespeare's works from the college library, and in a letter written at a later date quoted these lines again. The allusion to a "celebrated crucifixion" by Michelangelo in Saint Peter's, presumably *The Crucifixion of St. Peter* in the Pauline Chapel, was taken from William Duff's *Essay on Original Genius . . . in Philosophy and the Fine Arts* (London, 1767), which he also borrowed from the library.

Altogether, Allston's juvenilia, both painting and writing, are remarkable for their variety and their prefiguration of later works, in subject as well as technique. They reflect his disposition toward both the gay and the tragic, his sensibility of both the historic and the personal, and his management of several genres and of both satiric and lyric modes.

The portraits have a spare or no background and a timeless air, like all those he painted. All are in marked contrast to the realism of John Singleton Copley and the idealizations of Gilbert Stuart and to the courtly English tradition.

The landscapes, for all the influence of Salvator Rosa, are typical of all his landscapes in being less representational than projections of mood. The subsequent ones are distinctively introspective, drawn from the mind and from memory, generally with pastoral figures and frequently with architectural details. All are in marked contrast to the later wilderness paintings of the Hudson River school and the grandiose works of the painters of the West, both of which exploited the primitive character of nature which distinguished the American scene from the European. As a landscapist he was chiefly affiliated with the seventeenth-century school represented most notably by Claude and Nicolas Poussin.

Above all, these early pieces testify to the close connection which Allston saw and exemplified in all his works between painting and writing, especially poetry and drama. He illustrated works of literature, including his own compositions, made drawings on pages of books which he owned, and incorporated details from literary works by others in what he wrote. Two early works—*Tragic Figure in Chains* and the drawing of a maniac crushing a dove—treat the same subject as his poem "Will the Maniac," written at an equally early age, and thus anticipate his later practice of composing poems to accompany his paintings.

1. RHD, p. 12. 2. Ibid., pp. 2, 13.

11. To Charles Fraser London. August 25 [1801][1]

Were it in my power, I would certainly make an excuse for having so long delayed writing you; but, as I have none to make, I shall throw myself on that candor, which my short acquaintance with you has encouraged me to expect.—You have no doubt anticipated much, & will, I apprehend, be not a little disappointed at the account of what I have seen. <As you perhaps surmised[?]> I landed in this country big with the anticipation of every species of grandeur. No city thought I then to be compared with London; no people with its inhabitants. But I have found London but a city, and its inhabitants like the rest of the world: much in them to admire, more to despise, and still more to abhor. As to the country it is beyond my expectation beautiful and picturesque; and the appearance of the people that of <happiness> health and contentment; in short every leaf seemed to embody a sentiment, and every cottage to contain a venus. But when I arrived in London, what a contrast! Figure to yourself the extremes of misery and splendor & you will have a better idea of it than I can give: Scarcely a luxury but you may command here; and scarcely a scene of wretchedness but you may witness at the corner of every street. Indeed the whole city appears to be composed of princes and beggars. I had no idea before of pride unaccompanied by some kind of merit. But here no one has pride without fortune. Indeed the most respectable among the middle ranks appear to have no <pride> consequence but in boasting of the acquaintance of some one in rank; and among the greater part, so shameful is their venality they will condescend to flatter the most infamous for a penny. It is said in their defence that every man must live, and in so populous a country one must not be scrupulous about the means. But I can conceive of no necessity that should induce a man to degrade himself before those with whom he cannot but feel an equality, and whom he has too frequently occasion to despise.—But it is time to conclude with this, for I know you must be impatient to read something about the arts.

You will no doubt be surprised that among the many painters in London I should rank Mr. West[2] as the first. I must own I myself was not a little surprised to find him such. I left America strongly prejudiced against him; and indeed I even *now* think with good reason, for those pictures from which I had seen prints would do no credit to a very inferior artist, much less to one of his reputation. But when I saw his gallery[3] and the innumerable excellences which <they> it contained, I pronounced him one of the greatest men in [the] world. I had looked upon his understanding with indifference, and his imagination with contempt. But I have now reason to suppose them both vigorous in the highest degree. No fancy could have better conceived and no pencil more happily embodied the visions of sublimity, than he has in his inimitable picture from Revelation.[4] Its subject is the opening of the seven seals; and a more sublime and awful picture I never beheld. It is impossible to conceive any thing more terrible than death on the white horse; and I am certain no painter has exceeded Mr. West in <the expression of> fury horror and despair which he has represented in the surrounding figures. I could mention many others of similar merit; but were I particular on each, I should not only tire you, but write myself asleep.

Of Fuseli[5] I shall speak here after. I have seen but a few of his pictures, therefore cannot so well judge at present. They are however sufficient to entitle him to immortality. Indeed his Hamlet[6] alone, were it not for the picture I have just mentioned, would undoubtedly place him in the first seat among the english artists. Another picture also of his that I admire much represents Sin separating Death and Satan.[7] The attitude of Satan is beyond improvement sublime; and the others are such, as none but Fuseli could have painted. In short it is the only picture I ever saw, that was worthy of being joined with the name of Milton. The following are some extemporaneous lines I made on it.

Artist sublime, I own thy powerful spell
I feel thy fire, and hear the blasts of Hell;
I see thy monster from the canvas stride,
While chilly tremors o'er my senses glide;
Thro' heaving throttle vainly gasp for breath
And feel the tortures of approaching death.
I hear thy Satan's rebel thunders roll
While awful tempests gather round my soul.
Convulsive now I lift the admiring eye,
And now with horror from his presence fly;

Still in suspense, as laboring fancy burns,
I hate, admire, admire, and hate by turns.

Opie[8] comes next in rank. As a bold and determinate delineator of character he has not a superior. He is surpassed however by Northcote[9] in effect. But that is a subordinate excellence. Indeed were it not the english artists might well stand in competition with many of the ancient masters. You have seen a print fom Northcote's Arthur.[10] The original I must own is[11] a beautiful thing. But Opie has painted from the same subject,[12] and I assure you the two pictures will not bear a comparison. You may think I exaggerate when I say that his head of Arthur is the divinest thing I ever beheld. But I assure you it is no less. His Hubert I do not like. It is not equal to Northcote's. But his two villains, are such, as the devil nourishes in the cradle. They have murder written on every feature; and I cannot but think that Opie, like Salvator Rosa, must have lived among banditti, to have so admirably portrayed them.

"Are these all" you will ask. All indeed, I assure you, that are worth mentioning. I had forgot however the portrait painters. The two first are Lawrance[13] and Sir William Beechey. But even Lawrance cannot paint so well as Stuart.[14] And as for the rest they are the damndest stupid wretches that ever disgraced a profession. But I include not the miniature painters. That is a line I am but little acquainted with; therefore am not able to judge. As far however as my judgment extends, I can pronounce Mr. Malbone[15] not inferior to the best of them. He shewed a likeness he painted of me to Mr. West, who complimented him very highly. "I have seldom," said he, "seen a miniature that pleased me more." I could mention also some compliments, which he paid me; but I should blush to repeat, what I cannot think I deserve.

Your friend White[16] I like much. He has a spice of literature about him, which makes him not the less agreeable to me, who am about (mirabile dictu!) to publish a book.[17]—By the by how long do you suppose Trumbull was about his Gibraltar?[18] It is truly a charming picture; but he was a whole year about it; therefore it ought to have been better. I have no idea of a painter's *labouring* up to fame. When he <can not> ceases to attain reputation without it he becomes a mechanic. Trumbull is no portrait painter. By this picture alone he has gained credit. But it is indeed *credit* purchased at a most exorbitant interest.

I have lately painted several pictures. But am now about one that will far surpass anything I have done before. The subject is from this passage of scripture; "and Christ looked upon Peter." [19] It contains twenty figures, which are about two feet in height; on the whole making the best composition I ever attempted. The two principal groups are Christ between two soldiers, who are about to bear him away, the high priests <and> &c. and Peter surrounded by his accusers. The other groups are composed of spectators variously affected; men, women, & children.—I shall not write to Mr. Bowman[20] until I know where to direct my letters. I suppose in about two months he will have returned from the Northward; when I shall avail myself of the first opportunity to acknowledge the very great attention he has shewn me. I look upon that man as a father. He has one of the best hearts, and I am sure his understanding is equal to his goodness. Indeed I shall never be able to make a suitable return for his kindness.

Next week I shall apply for admission into the Academy.[21] The very first figure that I drew from plaister, Mr. West said would admit me. It is from the Gladiator.[22] He was astonished when I told him it was my first, and paid a compliment (too pretty to be repeated!!!) to the correctness of my eye. He also observed that I not only preserved the form, but what few artists think of, the expression of my subject.—You see by this account that I am not very modest. Indeed I despise the affectation of it. But my principal motive in being thus particular is to encourage you by proving that much greater men, than either you or I, were once no better than ourselves. And could I convince you, by flattering myself, of the dignity of *your* powers, I would boast as much again. Believe me, sir, it is no proof of vanity that a man should suppose himself adequate to more than he has already peformed. Confidence is the soul of genius. Great talents to a timid mind are of as little value to the owner as the gold of a miser, who is afraid to use it. Great men rise but by their own exertions. It is the fool and child of pusillanimity alone that are *boosted* up to fame. How are we to learn our own powers without a trial? Accident will indeed sometimes discover them. But are we all to wait for accident? No sir, the principle of self love was implanted in us to excite emulation; and he violates a law of nature, who yields to despair, without a previous trial of his powers. A little seasonable vanity is the best friend we can have. Not that silly conceit, generally founded on adventitious advantages, which exalts us but in our own imagination. But I mean the confidence which arises from a determination to excel, and is nourished by a hope of future greatness. The great Buffon[23] thought there were but three geniuses in the world; two besides himself. And what was the consequence? His application was indefatigable. He was a genius and ought to surpass other men. He did surpass them. Caesar, giving an account of his conquest, said, "veni, vidi, vici."[24] No man perhaps had so great an opinion of his own strength, and no man was capable of more. When a man is thus confident he is not to be discouraged by difficulties; but his exertions rather strengthen as they increase. It was a saying of Alcibiades, and I believe a very <true> just one, that "when souls of a certain order did not perform all they wished, it was because they had not courage to attempt all they could."[25]

Why then, my friend, should you despair? You have talents. Cultivate them; and it is not impossible that the name of Fraser may one day be as celebrated as those [of] Raphael or Michael Angelo. Resolve to shine, and believe me, the little wishes of *to day* will soon vanish before the more substantial joys of *tomorrow*. In the mean time let me advise you to beware of *love*. Love and painting are two opposite elements; you cannot live in both at the same time. Be wise in time, and let it not be said, when future biographers shall record your life that,—"*Mr. Fraser promised much.—His genius gave symptoms of expansion beyond mortality—But love, alas, untimely love, had set a seal upon his fame. His soul, which was just before about to grasp a world, is now imprisoned within the bosom of a girl. Where now are those mighty schemes, which were to elevate him to the summit of fame? Where are those characters which were to inscribe the name of "Fraser" on the front of Time? Alas! a woman's tears have washed them from his memory. No longer is he anxious to be distinguished from the crowd; no longer does the spirit of Michael Angelo point the way to heaven; is he blessed with a smile from his mistress, his ambition is contented; he seeks no other heaven than the bed of roses on her bosom.*—No, Fraser, let not this be said of you. Love in its place <is not> I revere; but it is not at all times to be indulged. <[undecipherable word] in beautiful girls [two words undecipherable]> There are many very beautiful [girls ?] in Charleston. But Raphael and Michael Angelo are still more beautiful than they.

Believe me with sincereity / your friend / Washington Allston

Remember me to all who enquire after me.

ADDRESSED: Mr. Charles Fraser / King Street / Charleston / South Carolina / North Carolina—Wade Hampton[26] / Capt. Flagg.[27] SOURCE: Manuscript. Printed in Flagg, pp. 42-48.

1. Shortly after 18 May 1801 WA sailed from Charleston to England, with Edward G. Malbone. They arrived in London about the middle of May and took rooms together. After Malbone left in November 1801, WA moved to Buckingham Street off Fitzroy Square, a neighborhood popular with artists. By May 1802, when he was listed in the catalog of the RA exhibition, he was living at 37 Brewer Street nearby. 2. Benjamin West. 3. West's gallery contained paintings by other artists besides himself. 4. West's first painting entitled *Death on the Pale Horse*, from Rev. 6:8, executed as one of a series of paintings for the Chapel of Revealed Religion at Windsor Castle. 5. Henry Fuseli. 6. Fuseli's *Hamlet Breaking from His Attendants to Follow the Ghost*, in Boydell's Shakespeare Gallery. 7. From Milton's *Paradise Lost* 2.724-26. 8. John Opie (1761-1807), English portrait painter. 9. James Northcote. 10. Hubert and Arthur, from Shakespeare's *The Life and Death of King John*. 11. Beginning with the next page of the manuscript the pages are numbered by WA 7 through 14. 12. *Arthur Supplicating Hubert*. 13. Sir Thomas Lawrence. 14. Gilbert Stuart. 15. Edward Greene Malbone. 16. John Blake White (1781-1859), South Carolina artist, lawyer, and dramatist. At this time he was in London studying with West and living on Fitzroy Square. Fraser gave WA and Malbone letters of introduction to him. During WA's stay in London, until White left in October 1803, they were often together, going to Bristol and staying in Bath for three weeks in November 1802 until their money ran out, going with three others, including Edmund T. Dana, in April 1803 to Windsor, where they saw the royal family parade on the terrace, visiting Hampstead and Hampton Court Palace, joining those calling themselves the "Midnight Crew" at convivial gatherings, balls, and masquerades, and probably frequenting the "Carolina Coffee House" ("The Journal of John Blake White," ed. Paul R. Weidner, *SCHGM* 42 [1941]: 55-71, 99-117, 169-86; 43 [1942]: 35-46, 103-17). In his journal at this time White described WA as displaying more than Malbone "a fine and inventive genius, of a mind for 'exhausting worlds, and then inventing new.' A man possessed of an elevated fanciful and poetic mind, destined one day to honor and adorn the

profession of his choice" (42:62). On his way home he visited the Danas in Boston and met WA's mother and sisters in Newport.

Among the other American companions of WA and Blake at this time were WA's college mates Sidney Willard and Arthur M. Walter, who went with them to Windsor and, with Dana, often attended the theater and Parliament, and William Austin, also on the excursion to Windsor. Austin, later celebrated for his story "Peter Rugg, the Missing Man," was writing *Letters from London, Written During the Years 1802 & 1803* (1804), which he read to WA, Dana, and Walter and which they liked. WA owned a copy. (*Literary Papers of William Austin With a Biographical Sketch by his son James Walker Austin* [Boston, 1890], pp. viii, ix; Dana, 2:472; Willard, *Memories of Youth and Manhood* [Cambridge, Mass., 1855], 2:165; Joseph B. Felt, *Memorials of William Smith Shaw* [Boston, 1852], p. 170). 17. Probably WA was planning to publish a book of poems, possibly to include some of those he wrote in college. 18. John Trumbull (1756-1843), history and portrait painter. He and WA knew each other in London, when he lived there from 1793 to 1804 and from December 1808 to August 1815. He painted three versions of *The Sortie Made by the Garrison of Gibralter,* depicting the victory of the English over the Spanish in 1781, the first begun in 1787 and the third finished in 1789 (*The Autobiography of Colonel John Trumbull, Patriot-Artist, 1756-1843,* ed. Theodore Sizer [New Haven: Yale University Press, 1953], pp. 114, 148-50). 19. *And Christ Looked at Peter* (1801), from Luke 22:61: "And the Lord turned and looked upon Peter," when the cock crowed three times after Peter had three times denied knowing Jesus. The other paintings referred to probably included the portrait of Mathias Spalding (1801), a physician colleague of Benjamin Waterhouse at Harvard; *A Sea Coast with Banditti;* and two comic pieces in the style of Hogarth: *A French Soldier Telling a Story* (1801-1802) and *The Poet's Ordinary* (1802-1803), the first bought and the second commissioned by South Carolinan John Wilson of the European Museum in London. About November 1801, when WA was apprehensive of the cost of moving into quarters by himself, he submitted several watercolor sketches to a publisher, who said he would accept all he could supply. One was *Trees in a Landscape* (ca. 1801-1804). During his stay in London at this time he also painted *A Man of the Theatre* (1803); *Caius Marius in the Dungeon,* or *Marius at Minturnae,* which apparently depicted the captive Roman general and consul so impressing the soldier who was to slay him that the soldier dropped his sword, a subject also treated by Fuseli; and possibly a portrait of John Kemble after Lawrence. About that time he also painted *Romantic Landscape* (ca. 1803), made a partial copy of James Barry's *Crowning the Victors at Olympia,* and drew one of the sons in the antique group *Laocoön.* 20. John Bowman (1754-1807), a native of Scotland, emigrated to the colony of Georgia about 1765 and eventually settled in Charleston. He was well educated, widely traveled, and noted for his philanthropies (Elizabeth Heyward Jervey, copier, "Marriage and Death Notices from the City Gazette," *SCHGM* 30 [1930]: 159-60). 21. WA was given permission on 3 October 1801 to draw as a probationer, then after two drawings, one of the *Apollo Belvedere,* as a registered student; and on 23 October, on the recommendation of West, fully admitted to the schools of the RA. The size of the average class at this time was about twenty-five, and the emphasis was on drawing, first from casts and then from life, for a period of two years. WA produced a few drapery studies but did not complete the full course. He exhibited paintings there in 1802 (*French Soldier Telling a Story; Landscape, Banditti on Horseback* [*Landscape with Banditti* (?)], and *A Seacoast with Banditti*), in 1803 (*Landscape* [possibly *Romantic Landscape*]), and during his later residence in England in 1814, 1815, 1816, and 1818, and in 1819. Another art institution with which he was associated shortly after arriving in London was "the British school," which was opened on 28 October 1802 in its gallery on Berners Street, under the sponsorship of the Prince of Wales, the only other place besides the RA for exhibitions by artists. WA and Trumbull were among those who showed there. It failed to support itself, however, and was closed after a little more than eighteen months (William T. Whitley, *Art in England, 1800-1820* [New York: Hacker Art Brooks, 1928], 1:45-48). 22. A cast of the antique statue called *The Fighting Gladiator* or *Borghese Warrior* in the Louvre. WA probably also submitted a drawing of a skeleton, as was customary; one of the subject is among his surviving drawings. 23. George Louis Leclerc, Comte de Buffon (1707-88), French naturalist, whose great work was the forty-four volume *Histoire naturelle*. WA borrowed a copy of the translation, *Natural History*, from the Harvard library when he was a student. 24. Suetonius, *Divus Julius* 27.2. The statement refers to the success of Julius Caesar in the Pontiac Campaign. 25. The source of the quotation has not been identified, but it is probable that WA was paraphrasing. Plutarch in his life of the Athenian Alcibiades (450?-404 B.C.) recorded that his contemporaries believed that if he failed in any endeavor it was because of his neglect. 26. The name of a ship. 27. Probably a relative of Henry C. Flagg.

12. To John Knapp

51 Upper Titchfield Street Marylebone
London February 27, 1803

Dear Knapp

I know not what returns to make for your admirable letter. It is now very late and this must go in the morning; but I should not forgive myself to let this opportunity pass without writing you. You must however be satisfied with little more than my good intentions for this time. But rest assured I shall avail myself of the next opportunity to write you [leng ?] [manuscript torn] thily; I have many things to say to you, and many you might like to hear.

Believe me sincerely your friend / Washington Allston

P.S. I have written Welles,[1] and mentioned in my letter a likeness which I have drawn from memory of poor Tudor.[2] I will send by the first private conveyance three copies of it; one for yourself, one for Welles, and the third (if you & Welles approve the likeness) to his mother. N.B. Direct your letters in future to the care of Mr. John Paterson[3] No 68 Old broad Street near the Royal Exchange.

ADDRESSED: Mr. John Knapp / Boston / Massachusetts / *pr the Galen* / North America. ANNOTATED: W.A. has written B. Welles by the Minerva A.M.W. / [Arthur Maynard Walter]. SOURCE: Manuscript.

1. Benjamin Welles. In a letter to John H. Tudor from Boston dated 27 [?] October 1801 Welles said he had received a letter from WA and summarized part of its contents as follows: "he [WA] is much interested in yr welfare and his remembrance is breathed sweetly to you—He is rapidly becoming the great man we all so pleasantly and strongly [?] we [?] pictured—Fuseli and West have [word undecipherable] him, and flattered him—or rather convinced him of his excellencies in his profession—" (Welles Family Papers, MHS). 2. John H. Tudor. He suffered from poor health and died in 1802 (HA). 3. John Paterson was head of the firm of Paterson and Company, wholesale hosiers in London (*Holden's* [London] *Triennial Directory* for 1805-1807).

13. To John Knapp

London, July 28, 1803.

Dear Knapp: The relief of confession is always so great that I know not whether we do not frequently what is wrong for the pleasure of acknowledging it, as an epicure will often go without food for the increasing gratification of his appetite. At least so I am willing you should account for my neglect. Besides, I may also lay claim to another motive—the pleasure of undeceiving a friend where circumstances may have induced him to doubt our attachment. But, however agreeable the last may be, I cannot assign it here as a serious motive, for in that case I should suppose you (which I am far from thinking) both ignorant and suspicious of my character. My silence, I dare say, you will attribute to laziness, and you know me too well to expect that I shall deny it; you will therefore excuse me if I do not attempt a thorough vindication.

Your letter, by Wyre,[1] I have received. You complain much of stagnation, but the activity of thought you display in describing your situation goes very little toward convincing me that your complaint is serious; and unless I should consider you as one of those unfortunate gentlemen who fancy themselves oysters, while they are reasoning like philosophers, I must still hold to the opinion that you were possessed of the same feelings, that you are the same acute observer, and the same poet,[2] as when I left you. Your observation about critics may not be confined to America. I have found it applicable more particularly in London. There are indeed a few daring spirits who judge for themselves; but of the few who dare, there are still fewer those whose judgment is sanctioned by their candor or their taste. It is sufficient, however, to be received that an opinion is pronounced with boldness, as every one is willing, when done, to reverence what he had the courage to attempt.

Neither do I think it should be confined to London. For when we reflect that to judge with propriety the critic should be enabled to incorporate his mind with his author, it is not so wonderful that so few should be fond of, as that so many should be capable of, judging anywhere. I hope, however, you were not led to the observation alluded to under any apprehension for yourself. If you were, I take the liberty to say you were wrong; for an original genius will command attention at least, if not admiration, among any people; and that such is yours you will not think it flattery if I declare. This critical timidity I apprehend, will continue to increase in every society where the literary candidates are themselves afraid. When a man undertakes a great design, and expresses a doubt whether he shall be successful, we are always ready to commend his modesty; but we lose that admiration of his powers which a proper confidence will never fail to inspire. Let modesty be considered in an agreeable light, but only as a buoy on the ocean of literature, to warn each adventurer of the wreck beneath it. By you, my friend, it always has been, and I hope always will be, considered as the most graceful ornament of private life. I only request that you would lay it aside in the literary world.

I have made these observations under a persuasion that you will aspire to salute the great toe of the holy Pope Apollo,[3] or, in other words, that you had either begun or intended to begin a poem. You will do right not to neglect your profession. But you should never forget what you owe to the future fame of your country; you should never forget that the muses who nursed you and watched round your cradle are now mystically anticipating the future reputation of their favorite, and though they behold the scythe of Death level him in his course, still hoping to enjoy the never-dying glory of his labors.

You were so good as to give me some advice in your last, for which I thank you. This you may consider only as a return. But I offer it with sincerity; and would urge it with effect, if it should be necessary. Your powers, my friend, are such as heaven has bestowed on few; and you have already given no little promise that they were not given in vain; let not that promise be forgotten, or ever hereafter remembered with regret. What think you of a poem in the manner of Spenser?[4] It is not a popular mode of versification, and the simplicity of his style (at least as much as Beattie[5] had adopted) is admirably suited to the wildness of Indian story. Not that I would have you imitate him in preference to writing from yourself, for your own style has a decided character, and one that I should be sorry you should change; but I mean only that you should write in the same stanzas and adopt some of his words. However, in whatever metre, in whatever words, I beg you will write. I have not forgotten your "Wacoon chanting from some viewless cliff." By the by, I never answered your poetical letter which I received last winter. My reason is my hearing afterward you had sailed for Europe.[6]

Mr. Derby,[7] who will take charge of this letter, goes sooner than I expected, so I will break off here and write in a few days in continuation. I go to France in about two months.[8]

SOURCE: Flagg, pp. 49-51.

1. Probably Flagg's misreading of the manuscript for Wyer. Edward Wyer (1781-1839), a classmate of WA's at Harvard, left college at the end of his sophomore year and joined the navy. He was on duty in the Mediterranean at this time and during the hostilities between France and England became the bearer of letters from Englishmen in France to their families and friends in England. In later years he held various political positions in Europe and the United States (HA; Edward William Callahan, ed., *List of Officers of the Navy of the United States and of the Marine Corps, from 1775 to 1900* [New York: L.R. Hamersly, 1901], p. 606; 26th Cong., 1st sess., 1839, Senate Doc. 24). 2. Knapp, like WA, delivered a poem, "Distinction," at the commencement exercises of their college class. He had seven poems published in the periodical the *Monthly Anthology* (1:1-6 [1803-1804] and another, on the Bunker Hill Monument, in the *Boston Courier.* One was on Arthur M. Walter and one on the Court Street elm tree near the jail in Boston. Among his other poems was an ode for the anniversary of the Washington Benevolent Society in 1815, which was sung on that occasion (HA). 3. An allusion to the practice by the faithful of kissing the toe of the bronze statue of St. Peter in St. Peter's Basilica in Rome. 4. Edmund Spenser. WA borrowed a copy of *The Faërie Queene* from the Harvard library when he was a student.
5. James Beattie (1735-1803), Scottish poet and essayist best known for *The Minstrel,* a long, unfinished poem in the manner of Spenser. 6. Knapp went to Europe to improve his health shortly after the Peace of Amiens ended in April 1803 (HA). 7. Probably Richard Crowninshield Derby (1777-1854), Boston merchant, brother of the celebrated Salem merchant Elias Haskins Derby (*Boston City Directorys,* 1805 and later; "Genealogy of the Derby Family," comp. Perley Derby, *Historical Collections of the Essex Institute* 3 [1861], 203, 287). 8. WA left London for the Continent in November 1803.

14. To John Knapp London, August 24, 1803

Dear Knapp: As I promised you a letter in continuation of my last, I will resume a subject in which I feel no little interest. The high opinion I entertain of your talents may be an excuse (if you should deem one necessary) for my boring you to exert them. Do not suppose I think you wanting in confidence or enthusiasm, as a man of genius I know you possess them both; but you may, probably, weigh too scrupulously the effect of your labor in America. It is, therefore, that I would urge the exertion of your powers—of powers capable of the sublimest flights in the regions of fancy. If you will not write for yourself, at least write for your country; and should the critics attack you, answer them in the language of Euripides, when the Athenians criticised him, "I do not compose my works in order to be corrected by you, but to instruct you." [1]

I do not see why every author is not adequate to the judging of his own peformance. Surely the mind which is capable of conceiving a great plan may also possess an equal power to analyze its principles. The affection which parents feel for their offspring I know is opposed to it; but without the severity of Virgil,[2] a father may obtain a temporary ignorance of his child by sending him away. Then it may be urged a return would naturally increase his affection. True; but the same novelty that displays the accomplishments will discover the defects of his offspring. Strong memories stand likewise in the way of this; but Pope says men of genius have short memories.[3] Whether true or false, I will not undertake to determine. I am satisfied to answer that very retentive memories have been rare, and many geniuses have been remarkable for their absence; besides, a man of great memory can never be alone; he is always in company with the thoughts of other men.

In reply to all this, you will naturally ask what I have done. I cannot answer that I have done anything, but I mean to do something. My profession will always be painting, but I have not serenaded the Muses so many cold wintry nights for nothing;[4] they shall grant me a favor before I die. The "notable plot for a tragedy," you allude to, I have with many alterations completed.[5] The dialogue, however, is still unfinished. But I resumed it not long since, and have advanced in it considerably, so that I hope, ere many moons, the voice of Melpomene[6] will decide its fate. I will quote from it an address to the moon, by the principal female character. She is destined to move in a conspicuous sphere, and I intend her to represent the combination of a masculine mind and an ambitious spirit with vehement passions, nor yet destitute of feminine delicacy. Ambition, however, is her predominate feature. How far the address is in character, I leave you to judge.

"To the Moon."

"Olympia,[7] pale queen of mystery, I hail thy beams.
Now all is dark save here and there to view,
Where mid thy dim and solemn empire rise
Vast rocks and woods and towers and gorgeous towns.

So o'er the shadowy regions of my soul
Hope's mystic rays reveal the dusky forms
Of Fancy's wild creation. To thy power,
O potent sorceress, I yield my soul.
Watch o'er my thoughts and round my glowing brain,
While darkness veils in dread sublimity,
Pour thy majestic visions; for to thee,
Alone to thee, belongs the mighty charm
That swells the heart in towering confidence,
Scorning the coward prudence of the world
To meet the vast conceptions of the mind."

I believe it has been the case with many who have conceived great plans, which have been rendered abortive by the opposite opinions of those they live with, that they only wanted the confidence which solitude inspires to carry them to perfection. I speak of all plans, whether good or bad. A man in society and a man alone are two different beings. It is unfortunate, however, for the world that so many have not felt the want of this solitary confidence. It would be a curious speculation to calculate the mischief that many villains would make were they not restrained by the fears awakened by virtuous examples. I will quote one more passage by the same character, simply as expressive of the same energy.

She replies to the Prince, who is her lover and hints at making her his mistress. Her indignation is not more inspired by love than ambition, for her principal object is his throne.

. . ."to purchase love?
Oh, blasphemy to love. As soon, mean reptile,
Mayst thou purchase life and bribe the worms
That revel in thy grave their feasts forego,
And weave their volumes into flesh again."

The second line, you will perceive, is defective in measure, but it will be corrected in due time. I have not time to add another line. You will excuse my abrupt conclusion, and, believe me, your friend,

Washington Allston.

SOURCE: Flagg, pp. 51-54.

1. The quotation is from Discourse 5 of Sir Joshua Reynolds's *Discourses,* in which he cautions the young artist against pandering to popular taste. Euripides (480-406, B.C.), Athenian tragic dramatist, was frequently criticized by contemporary comic dramatists. 2. Virgil left directions that after his death all his writings which had not been published be destroyed and in his last illness intended to burn the manuscripts of the *Aeneid,* which he had not finally corrected. 3. Alexander Pope. The allusion is to *The Dunciad* 4.619-20: "O Muse! relate (for you can tell alone, / Wits have short memories and Dunces none." 4. Apparently WA continued to write poetry during his first few years after college. 5. Nothing further seems to be known of this

work, which apparently was related to the genre of heroic drama, as popularized by Nathaniel Lee, with whom WA was familiar, among other poets. The quotation is presumably from a letter from Knapp to WA. 6. The muse of tragedy in Greek mythology. 7. A female proper name designating an inhabitant of Olympus.

15. To Elias Vanderhorst

51 Upper Titchfield Street
London October 3, 1803

Dear Sir: I am unwilling to leave England without assuring you that I still hold yourself and family in remembrance.[1]

It was my intention to have paid you my respects in person; but the same necessity which prolonged my stay in England has prevented my visiting Bristol.[2]

I have heard of my cousin Eliza's marriage,[3] and wish her every happiness. Remember me also to Mr. and Mrs. Taylor.[4]

Believe me, sir / Your affectionate nephew / Washington Allston

P.S. The enclosed to Colonel Trumbull I will thank you to forward immediately. I shall leave London on Saturday.[5]

ANNOTATED: "Washington Allston's letter to his Uncle (great) Van De Horst." SOURCE: Typescript, Dana Papers, of a letter in the possession of Arnuldus Vanderhorst of Bristol, England.

1. WA spent a day in Bristol in November 1802 in the company of John B. White, at which time he presumably met Vanderhorst and his family. He and White put up at the Bush Tavern, which White called "one of the most elegant and best attended" of any in England, and visited the celebrated hot wells and a basket factory ("The Journal of John Blake White," 43:184-85). Apparently WA's brother William visited Vanderhorst the year before with a letter from their mother to him. She also gave WA a letter to him, dated 15 May 1801, in which she described WA as "amiable and diffident to a degree. his pursuits are very different from his Brother. he goes to Europe for the purpose of Improving his tallants in the art of painting. His fort is historical painting: and his genius is very great. he carries with him a Number of [page torn] know will say a fond Mother can see no foible, but be you assured, you will find him all that is amiable and Clever, his greatest fault is rather too much diffidence but he is very Young. tell your Girls he is particularly so before the Ladies. they must make him sociable. he improves much upon acquaintance—and promises himself a great deal of pleasure in visiting you and your Charming family. I flatter myself he will find himself as [*sic*] home in your house. his visits to Bristol will be to [*sic*] as he has no letter to that place—he is not obliged to go abroad for a livelyhood. his fortune tho not great is independent,[6] but his love for painting is so great [page torn] ever visiting England. [When WA came of age in November 1800 he was entitled to receive the estate left him by his father's will of 1781, which consisted of a plantation of three tracts of land (one on the Waccamaw River, called Springfield, and two on the seaside), totaling 978 acres, and his share of the remainder of the estate after all bequests had been fulfilled. The executorship was turned over a few years later by Francis Allston, a newphew of his father, to his mother and Henry C. Flagg. On 15 and 18 May 1801 WA gave power of attorney to the lawyer Hugh Paterson, William Hassell Gibbes, who was the husband of his half-sister Elizabeth, and John E. Moore. According to Sweetser, one of the executors offered him less than its value for part of the estate, which he took before going to England and deposited with a London banker, drawing on the capital until it was exhausted. The

bulk of his inheritance was sold in 1804, the bill of sale being dated 30 January of that year for Springfield and one seaside tract, totaling about 340 acres, twenty-four Negroes, several head of oxen and cattle, and a cypress flat, all for £4,343, to a Benjamin Allston, probably WA's half-brother. £1,000 was to be paid on 10 February 1804 and the remainder in five equal installments to be finished by 1 January 1809, including interest (Joseph A. Groves, *The Alstons and Allstons of North and South Carolina* [Atlanta: Franklin Printing and Publishing Co., 1901], pp. 34-37; Nord, pp. 4-7). John Vanderlyn was probably referring to the first installment when he said at the time they were together in Italy that WA's patrimony was $1,000 (Louise Hunt Averill, "John Vanderlyn, American Painter [1775-1852]" [Ph.D. Diss., Yale University, 1949], p. 335.)]" (typescript, Dana Papers). In connection with his trip to Bristol, WA may have visited Wales. His sketch "The Doolittle Fragments.—No. 3. A Night Adventure in Wales," in the *Boston Daily Advertiser,* 28 Aug. 1838, is based on an experience he had there during his first stay in England, and he referred to the mountains of Wales in his "Color Book." 2. Presumably WA refers to his increasing activity in painting and in the RA. 3. Eliza Cooper Vanderhorst (d. 1844), daughter of Elias Vanderhorst. She never married (City of Bristol Record Office). Probably WA confused her with her sister Harriot Cooper Vanderhorst, the third daughter of Vanderhorst, who was married on 7 February 1804 to Henry Thomas Shewen, a lieutenant in the royal navy (Jeannie Hayward Register, copier, "Marriage and Death Notices from the City Gazette," *SCHGM* 27 [1926]: 22). 4. John Duncombe Taylor and Mary Cooper (Vanderhorst) Taylor. 5. 8 October. He was departing for the Continent. The ship was delayed over a week at Gravesend and did not sail until early in November (Averill, p. 55).

France, Switzerland, and Italy, 1803-1808

In the fall of 1803 Allston left England on his way to Paris and Rome and did not return to America until the early summer of 1808. Only three letters written by him during this period seem to have been preserved, and almost certainly he wrote few others, probably only to his mother or other members of his family. His activities are known chiefly from the accounts of others with whom he was then associated but also from subsequent references to them in his letters, in his autobiographical romance *Monaldi*, and in his lectures on art. A few of his associates became some of his closest frends as well as most important correspondents. These years are also memorialized in his painting, in both practice and theory, as the most formative years of his life.

He traveled from London to Paris in the company of John Vanderlyn; Colonel John Mercer, then secretary to James Monroe in the settlement of United States claims under the Louisiana Purchase; and a third person, possibly Dr. Joseph William Maxwell. En route they were detained over a week on the Thames by bad weather. They remained several days at Rotterdam and at Antwerp, where both Allston and Vanderlyn were ill. After passing through Brussels, they arrived in Paris on 20 November.[1]

In Paris Allston's address was no. 1, Place Vendôme. Among other Americans in the city whom they met were Sidney Willard and, the following spring, Joseph C. Cabell, later prominent in the founding of the University of Virginia. Cabbell's taste for the fine arts was so stimulated by Allston that he made detours in his travels to see galleries and in Rome purchased many engravings of works by old masters.[2] They also met William Hazlitt, at that time an art student. In later years Allston enjoyed describing the dinners he had had in Paris at this time and on his later visit. He also remembered the German tailor he had employed on his first visit, who, when Vanderlyn's remittance was once delayed, had advanced him 1,000 francs, and whom Allston had recommended to Jarvis in 1811. Probably soon after he arrived on his first visit he acquired his copies of Thomas Nugent's *Pocket Dictionary of French and English* (London, 1793), François Alberti's *Dictionnaire François-Italien* (Venice, 1793), and possibly C.M. Gattel's *Nuevo Diccionario Portatil, Español e Ingles* (Paris, 1803), and Mouffle d'Angerville's *The Private Life of Louis XV*, translated by John O. Justamond (Dublin, 1781).

While in Paris Allston painted *Rising of a Thunderstorm at Sea* (1804) and *Cupid Playing with the Helmet of Mars* (1804), a detail from Rubens's *Henry IV Receiving the Portrait of Maria de' Medici* in the Louvre, and exhibited one and possibly two paintings at the 1804 Salon, held in the Musée Napoléon, the one being listed as *Paysage—Site Sauvage* (possibly *Romantic Landscape*). They were apparently badly shown, according to Vanderlyn. Dunlap said he painted four "original pictures" there (2:165), but no other record of a fourth seems to exist. He later recalled in conversation with Henry Greenough that certain young French artists ridiculed to Vanderlyn the dullness of his copy from Rubens before the glazing had been done but that a Roman cardinal passing by complimented him as understanding what he was about. His "Sonnet on the Luxembourg Gallery," which also commemorated his visit to Paris at this time, chiefly praised Rubens, whose paintings he presumably also saw in Antwerp.

Most of Allston's time in Paris was spent in the Louvre and Luxembourg galleries, where he most admired the Venetian painters of the Renaissance. With few exceptions, he was not impressed by French art, committed as it was during his time to neoclassicism. Richard Henry Dana, Jr., recollected his once saying that he never found in it a sense of the sublime or anything that reached his higher nature, and calling the cemetery of Père-Lachaise in Paris "the most finical baby-house that you can imagine," Mount Auburn Cemetery in Cambridge being much more beautiful. Two other collections in the Louvre, one certainly, must have drawn his attention: the landscapes of Nicolas Poussin, in which there was currently a great revival of interest and which subsequently influenced his own, and the pieces of antique sculpture recently brought from Italy. The work in Paris that most impressed him was the *Apollo Belvedere,* recently brought from Italy by Napoléon, on exhibit in the Musée Napoléon, which he later called "the place of its glory." In the figures in several of his paintings he was influenced by its pose. He described it at length in his lecture "Art," calling it "a vision . . . of another world," which impressed him as "a sudden intellectual flash, filling the whole mind with light,—and light in motion," and comparing its effect on the mind to that on the senses of the first sight of the sun emerging from the ocean.[3] In *Monaldi,* the title character laments the matter-of-fact age that quarrels with it because the skin wants suppleness and speaks of its "exquisite proportions" and "his celestial lightness, his preternatural majesty" (p. 84).

Allston's visit to Paris at this time marked his single greatest development as an artist: his commitment to the Venetian school, with its introduction of light, color, and space into Western painting, abandoned in the neoclassical movement. Though he became familiar with this school in London, through the theory and practice of Reynolds, West, and others, it was in the great works of Titian, Veronese, and other Venetians in the Louvre that it was first fully presented to him. The two chief technical practices of theirs that he adopted were the use of light, transparent colors, laid on in different pigments in layers rather than side by side and even mixed with each other, and the subsequent application of colored glazes. For mixing colors he used a brush rather than a palette knife as the Italians did, which, he said, made "mud" of the tints; he took up the practice, he told Henry Greenough, after hearing Hazlitt, while copying a painting by Titian in Paris, describe it as looking as though the colors had been "twiddled."[4] Glazing was a departure in particular from Italian practice at the time. In Greenough's novel *Ernest Carroll* the title character says that Italian painters consider a painting finished when the impasto is dry, is angered at "the stupidity of the modern Italian academies" who hold a painter estimable when he paints without glazing, and concludes, "I should as soon think of saying that the *improvisatore* was your only true poet."[5] Both techniques are first definitely seen in Allston's work in *Rising of a Thunderstorm at Sea* and the paintings done shortly afterward in Italy.

Rising of a Thunderstorm at Sea, his first masterwork, was also the first expression of his response to the sea, which together with the Italian landscape was one of the two great natural scenes that captivated his imagination. It inspired only three more of his works of art, but he repeatedly referred to it in his poems and his lectures on art, nearly always also as in a state of storm. In *Rising of a Thunderstorm at Sea* he was probably influenced by some of the paintings of Turner, but both it and his only other surviving marine piece are unlike most of the contemporary paintings in this category in having little or no narrative detail and in depicting the sea as vast, powerful, and inhuman. In this respect they are in accord with the typically American vision of it, not only in such paintings as those of Winslow Homer but in the fiction of Melville and Stephen Crane. In his lectures on art he used a storm at sea to exemplify, citing his own experience, the element of danger in the sublime, the idea of the infinite, and the relation of parts to mass, when a single breaking wave was intersected by many lines yet a "terrible unity" prevailed; described dramatically one of Vernet's paintings of the subject; compared the *Farnese Hercules* to the ocean in repose "in its awful sleep" but "unfathomed swell"; and in a generally romantic vein characterized childhood as the careless time when "the heart and the fancy" seem "to launch again into this morning world, as on a sunny sea." In "The Sylphs of the Seasons" he referred to the "dreadful calm" of the ocean after a storm, yet heaving in air its "mountain-billows. . . . As if a living thing it were, / That strove in vain for rest"; in "The Angel and the Nightingale" compared the gathering of the nightingale's admirers to an ocean tempest; in "To My Sister" called memory of the past "A shadowy mass of shapes at random cast / Wide on a broken sea"; and in "The Calycanthus" described the soul as living in all that lives "E'en as the ever-changing Ocean, / Whether in calmed rest or motion / Its own transforming image gives."[6] In his sonnets on Samuel Taylor Coleridge and Rubens he employed sea imagery to describe both men.

Allston left Paris for Italy in August or September 1804 in the company of Benjamin Welles and presumably Maxwell. With them was a Belgian servant, John Josse Vandermoere.[7] They traveled by way of Switzerland, passing through Geneva and entering Italy by the St. Gotthard Pass. Three letters written by him in Italy survive, but by far the greatest part of his stay in that country is represented by his painting and his nonepistolary writing.

The Alps made a great impression on him. He made a note of "Voltaire's residence" at Ferney and drew pencil sketches of Mont Pilat and Mont Blanc as well as other mountains, trees, and ferns presumably in that region, which served as studies for the landscapes he painted in Italy and several subsequent ones. It was in studying Mont Pilat, he told Henry Greenough, that he first conceived the process he developed for painting mountains. In "The Sylphs of the Seasons" he referred to the Alps as having "many a mountain pine" and in "To the Author of 'The Diary of an Ennuyée'" called them "mountain kings."[8]

Mount Blanc particularly impressed him, as reflected in both his painting and his theory of art. *Landscape with a Lake* (1804), *Diana and her Nymphs in the Chase* (1805) and both *Italian Landscapes* of about 1805 depict its central peak, and the first two include the water at the base from the five torrents flowing down its sides to form the rivers Arne and Arvliron; in the last two the water is at a distance. In his sketch he modified the shape of the peak by reversing that of Mont Pilat, but he was faithful to the sheer elevation of the higher mountain in his painting. Though sometimes not so clearly identifiable, it or a stylization of it reappears in nearly all his later Italian landscapes and in several other paintings, including portraits and figures. Several of his landscapes painted in America before his first visit to Europe depict mountains beside bodies of water, but in the general style of Salvator Rosa rather than as the result of personal observation. In the "Introductory Discourse" of his lectures on art he devoted a paragraph to a description of Mont Blanc as an example of the theory of the sublime evoking the emotion of fear or terror. He called it "that mighty pyramid of ice, in whose shadow might repose all the tombs of the Pharaohs," which a traveler perhaps looks upon as his own yet "cannot away from it," and continued in an imaginative description of ascending it, a feat that had been accomplished by only a few climbers at the time he saw it: "A terrible charm hurries him over frightful chasms, whose blue depths seem like those of the ocean; he cuts his way up a polished precipice, shining like steel,—as elusive to the touch; he creeps slowly and warily around and beneath huge cliffs of snow; now he looks up, and sees their brows fretted by the percolating waters like a Gothic ceiling, and he fears even to whisper, lest an audible breath should awaken the avalanche: and thus he climbs and climbs, till the dizzy summit fills up his measure of fearful ecstasy"[9].

He passed through Bellinzona,[10], spent a night at Lake Maggiore, and apparently stopped in Milan, where he copied a detail from Titian's *Adoration of the Magi* (ca. 1804-11). He certainly stopped in Florence and either then or later in Bologna. His "Sonnet on Seeing the Picture of Aeolus by Pellegrino Tibaldi, in the Institute at Bologna," in which the "kindred mind" of Tibaldi is said to acknowledge the "mighty spell" of Michelangelo, commemorates his visit there,[11] where the Bologna Institute of Science and Art housed the collection of Count Luigi Ferdinando Marsoli, as does the meeting of Monaldi and Maldura in the Bologna seminary. He spent about two months in Siena in order to learn Italian and went to Rome early in 1805. His familiarity with the route between Siena and Rome is reflected in *Monaldi* in the travels of Maldura and Fialtro. From then until March 1808, when he left to return to America, he was in Rome most of the time. Leslie remembered his saying that on the evening of his arrival he was called on by an Italian poet who presented him with an ode of congratulation, addressing him as *"A young English nobleman from America, descended from the celebrated Washington"* and calling him *"our valourous antipode"*.[12]

Allston lived most of the time in Rome on the Pincian Hill, as did most of the artists and foreigners. From the spring of 1805 to 1807 he apparently rented rooms in the Villa Malta at the foot of the Via Sistina, adjacent to the Villa Borghese. Presumably during this period he painted *The Garden of the Villa Malta* and also made a drawing of the subject. He was out of the city from about 15 February to 10 March 1806, at the nearby hill town of Olevano, where he rented a house. It was at that time a popular resort of German landscape painters, among them Joseph Koch, Gottleib Schick, and Johan C. Reinhart. The Scot George A. Wallis and Koch were there at the same time, and Coleridge, who arrived in Rome a few weeks after him, shared his house. He was apparently out of the city again a few months later, possibly, like other residents, seeking to avoid the threat of malaria in the summer, during which time he received his mail at the Caffè Greco, a favorite gathering place of the artists, a short distance away. By 1807 he was at no. 26, Via Gregoriana, adjacent to the church of Trinità dei Monti.[13] His residence in the city is commemorated by his later *A Roman Lady Reading* (ca. 1831); by *Evening Hymn* (1835), in which the partially shown building with Doric columns in the background resembles the facade of the Tempietto, the famous temple built by Bramante with columns of that order in the Piazza dei Trinità dei Monti; and by his sonnets on a group from the *Last Judgment* by Michelangelo in the Sistine Chapel and on the painting of Abraham and the three angels in the Loggia of Raphael in the Vatican.

His chief companions in Rome were Washington Irving, who was there from March 1805 to the spring of 1806, and Coleridge, who was there from December 1805 to May 1806. Both left vivid descriptions of him at that time. A number of other Americans passed through the city, including Nicholas Biddle of Philadelphia, Colonel George Gibbs of Newport, Rhode Island, William Carter of Virginia, and Richard and George Sullivan of Boston, but no other artists.

For the most part he associated with more than fifty young German artists, almost that many from France, and others from Spain and Russia, as well as Italians. He was closest to the Germans, among them Franz and Johann Riepenhausen, Koch, whom he remembered in a note about "Koch's landscapes" in a memorandum, and most notably Schick, who learned the technique of underpainting and glazing from him and named him on 10 December 1807 godfather of his second son. It may have been in recollection of Schick's painting of Noah's sacrifice as well as of Koch's that Monaldi paints the subject, though West had also done so. The Germans long remembered Allston for his coloring and as late as 1844 still had one of his works.[14] He later recalled that a German professor of painting in Rome had asked what colors he used to so much resemble the old masters and when showed his method of glazing said he had often heard of *velatura* (a thin wash of color over a painting already dry) but had never known before what it meant. Others whom he knew there, besides those referred to in letters by or to him, included several Italian artists—the painters Filippo Benucci, Bernardo Castelli, and Gaspare Landi, and the sculptor Antonio Canova—the Italian mathematician and politician Gioacchino Pessuti, and the Italian art historian Giuseppe Antonio Guattani, all of whom he named in *Monaldi;* the French painter Paulin-Jean-Baptiste Guérin; the Spanish sculptor José Alvarez de Pereira y Cubero; the German art historian Baron Karl Friedrich Rumohr; and the Prussian consul Wilhelm von Humboldt and his brother the naturalist Alexander von Humbolt. He later recalled a conversation he had with one of the French artists, who, talking vaguely on the subject, defined the sublime as "Le plus beau," as he recorded in the "Introductory Discourse" of his lectures on art, or "Trés bien," as Richard Henry Dana, Jr., recollected, a definition with which Allston disagreed.[15]

While in Rome, Allston chiefly visited museums, galleries, and churches, on one occasion, as Dana, Jr., recollected, seeing Mme de Staël at an illumination of Saint Peter's, whom he described as waving a wreath with a beautiful hand and arm but having "a face like a figurehead—coarse features and a vulgar mouth."[16] Presumably he went once a week to Saint Luke's Academy, as Monaldi did. He also went to the French Academy, drew from life, and learned to model in clay. In later years he said it was good for an artist to keep a tub of clay at hand wet and ready for use.[17] Canova admired his sculptures, but in his opinion Canova had no genius. They probably met in London when Canova visited there in 1816.

Among the older atists whose work he saw and referred to in his lectures on art were Michelangelo and Raphael, whom he now studied more fully, Annibale Carracci, Antony Raphael Mengs, and, if not earlier, Nicolas and Caspar Poussin. In January 1807 he and Vanderlyn visited a collection of paintings for sale and he bought a copy of a Veronese, which he thought an original, for little more than a hundred dollars; Vanderlyn regretted he had not the means to buy one for himself, but eventually did so.[18] He was said to have declared about this time, according to Sweetser, that he would rather see a picture he could not equal than one he could surpass and, in later years, thinking of the old masters, that he would rather be the second painter in the world than the first, because then he would have someone to look up to.

Monaldi contains numerous references to Roman edifices and neighborhoods: the Campo Viccino, which Maldura's apartment overlooks; the Corso; the Coliseum; the Ponte Malle; the papal palace on Monte Cavallo, for which Monaldi paints a series of pictures; the Arch of Titus, which Monaldi describes as "that proud pile . . . so dark and desolate within" but which speaks from without in the sun to his heart; the Baths of Caracalla, whose ruins console him in his misfortune; the church of Sant' Andrea della Valle, with its painting by Giovanni Lanfranco; the *Apollo Belvedere* and the *Antinuous Belvedere* or *Hermes* in the Vatican; Genazzano, where Monaldi has family estates; and Viturbo, north of the city. The atmosphere in the vicinity of the Campo Viccino is vividly described:

> The air was hot and close, and there was a thin yellow haze over the distance like that which precedes the scirocco, but the nearer objects were clear and distinct, and so bright that the eye could hardly rest on them without quivering, especially on the modern buildings, with their huge sweep of whited walls, and their red-tiled roofs, that lay burning in the sun, while the sharp, black shadows, which here and there seemed to indent the dazzling masses, might almost have been fancied the cinder-tracks of his fire. The streets of Rome, at no time very noisy, are for nothing more remarkable than, during the summer months, for their noontide stillness, the meridian heat being frequently so intense as to stop all business, driving everything within doors, with the proverbial exception of dogs and strangers. . . . It was now high noon, and the few straggling vine-dressers that were wont to stir in this secluded quarter had already been driven under shelter; not a vestige of life was to be seen, not a bird on the wing, and so deep was the stillness that a solitary foot-fall might have filled the whole air.[19]

Allston painted some seventeen pieces while he was in Italy, apparently only two of which were done outside Rome. Six were landscapes: *Landscape with a Lake, Diana and Her Nymphs in the Chase,* two *Italian Landscapes* (ca. 1805), *Morning in Italy* (ca. 1805-1808) and *Landscape Study* (ca. 1805).

Landscape with a Lake, his first painting done in Italy, was a virtual study for *Diana and Her Nymphs.* Both are departures from the tradition of Rosa and were based on sketches made in Switzerland. Both exhibit not only his new coloristic procedure but the recessed background and the monumentality and balance of forms, both natural and human, which characterize his later landscapes and history paintings. Both have a cool coloring, which soon gave way in his painting to warmer tones, especially in portraits and figures.

Diana and Her Nymphs was his first heroic composition and the largest thus far to be completed. Early though it is, it is one of his great achievements. He was probably influenced by Koch's *Heroic Landscape with Rainbow* and possibly by Zampieri Domenichino's treatment of the same subject. He made several studies for it and based the background on scenery not only in Switzerland but around Olevano. Though classical in subject and though some critics wished to rank it as a historical work so as to have it displayed in the Pantheon, it has an essentially timeless character. It was exhibited in a studio in the Orte di Napoli section of the city.[20] It was widely praised in Rome by his fellow artists, including foreigners; by critics, notably Guattani in *Memorie Enciclopediche romanesulle belle art;* and by others, including Coleridge. In particular Allston's ability in sculptural modeling and his talents as a poet were acknowledged. Of all his paintings it proved to be the most admired in his day. When it was cleaned and repaired after being brought to Boston sometime after 1818, however, it was so injured by the cleaner Haworth that he said he no longer acknowledged it as his work, and Asher B. Durand, who saw it in 1835, said that in part it was like Allston's work but that he would not believe other parts to be by him.[21]

Beginning with *Italian Landscape* (G12), all Allston's landscapes, with the exception of the one of American scenery, contain most of the same essential compositional elements: a mountain peak in the background, usually near the center; water in the middle; a conspicuous tree or group of trees in the foreground, the single tree usually to the left and bent; architectural forms, frequently to the right; and a bridge. The first three appear in the earlier *Landscape with a Lake,* the architecture being added in Italy. Even *Landscape: Time, after Sunset* (ca. 1819), which lacks a mountain, has the suggestion of an Italian hill town in the background. The figures in these paintings are classical or pastoral, in contrast to the peasantry treated by later American painters in Italy; only *Romantic Landscape* and one drawing by him depicting Italian peasants are known. *Italian Landscape* is also notable for representing several ages in the figures in what are apparently family groups, from childhood through maturity in a mother, to old age, which altogether allegorize the span of human life against a background of nature as a human habitation. Similar groups appear in later landscapes and all seem to anticipate the series of paintings of a mother and child that he did later.

Two or three other paintings, two of them the only portraits, were inspired by his association with Coleridge. That of Coleridge (1806) was not finished, since he left Rome beforehand. Allston may have intended it partly as a companion piece to a second one of himself already done (1805), since in size, general pose of the figure, setting, and tone they are similar. Both exhibit his first utilization of his new coloristic procedure in the category of portraiture and are his first portraits after becoming familiar with those done by Titian. The self-portrait is one of his most distinguished.

Coleridge also inspired Allston's *Jason Returning to Demand His Father's*

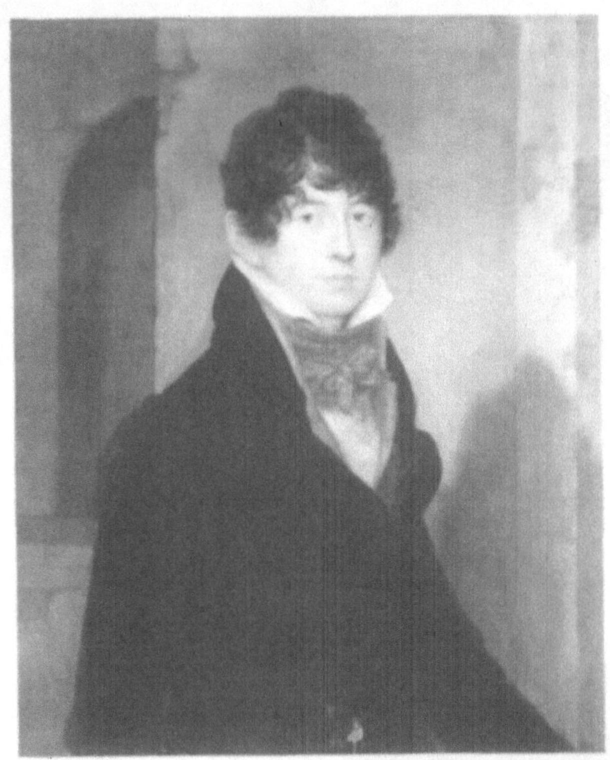

Self-Portrait, 1805. Oil on canvas, 31½ × 26½ in. Museum of Fine Arts, Boston, Bequest of Miss Alice Hooper.

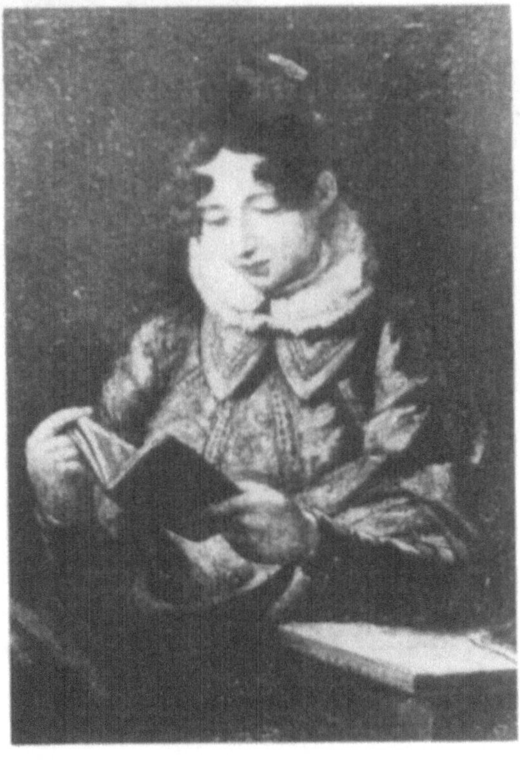

Ann (Channing) Allston, 1809-1811. Oil on canvas, 17½ × 15¾ in. Henry Channing Rivers.

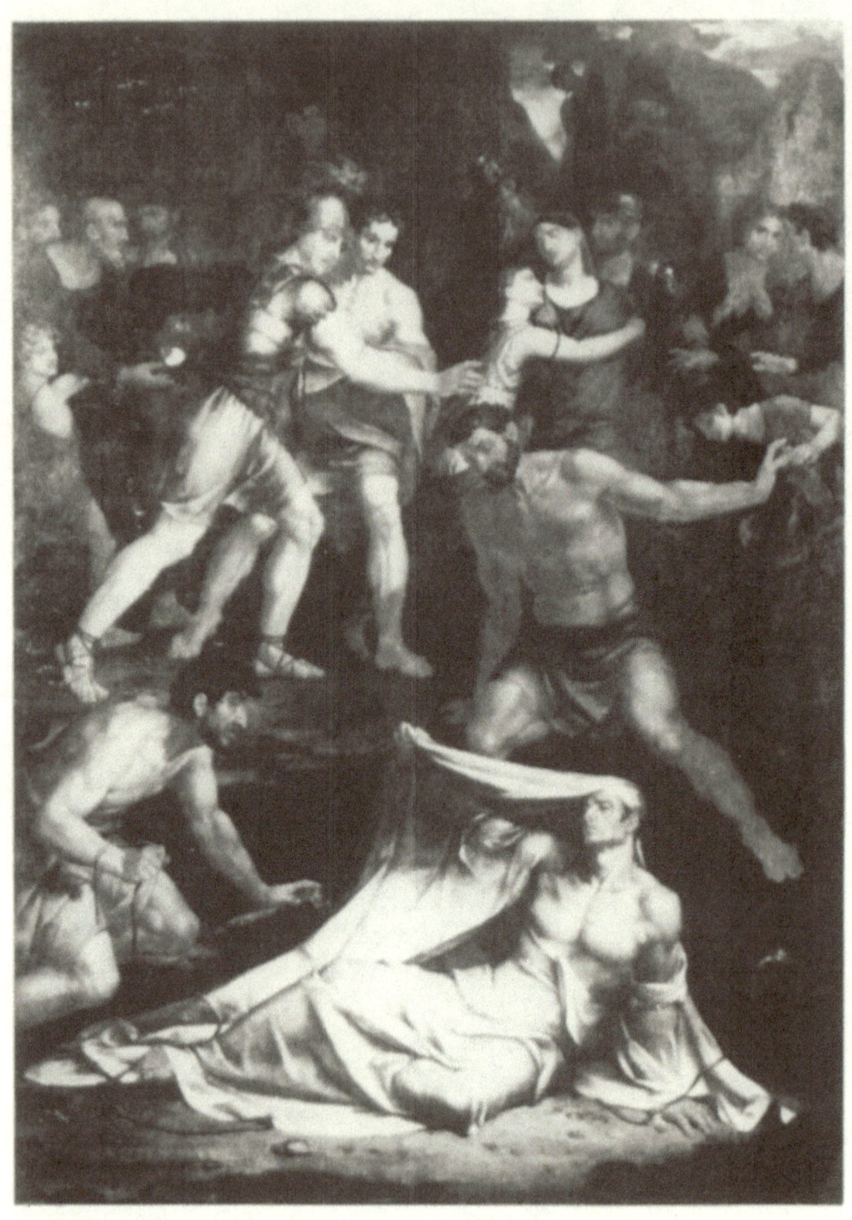

The Dead Man Restored to Life by Touching the Bones of the Prophet Elisha, 1811-1814. Oil on canvas, 156 × 120 in. Pennsylvania Academy of the Fine Arts, Philadelphia.

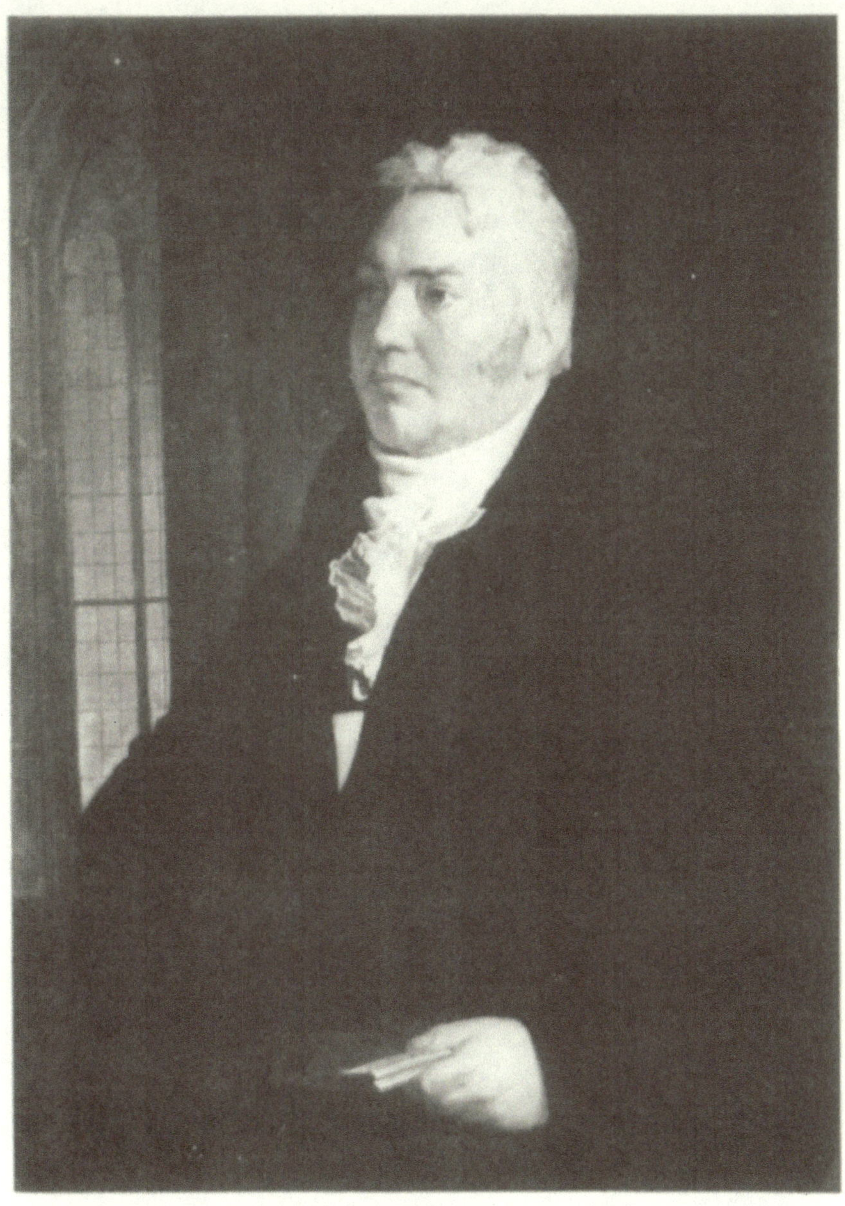

Samuel Taylor Coleridge, 1814. Oil on canvas, 44 × 33½ in. National Portrait Gallery, London.

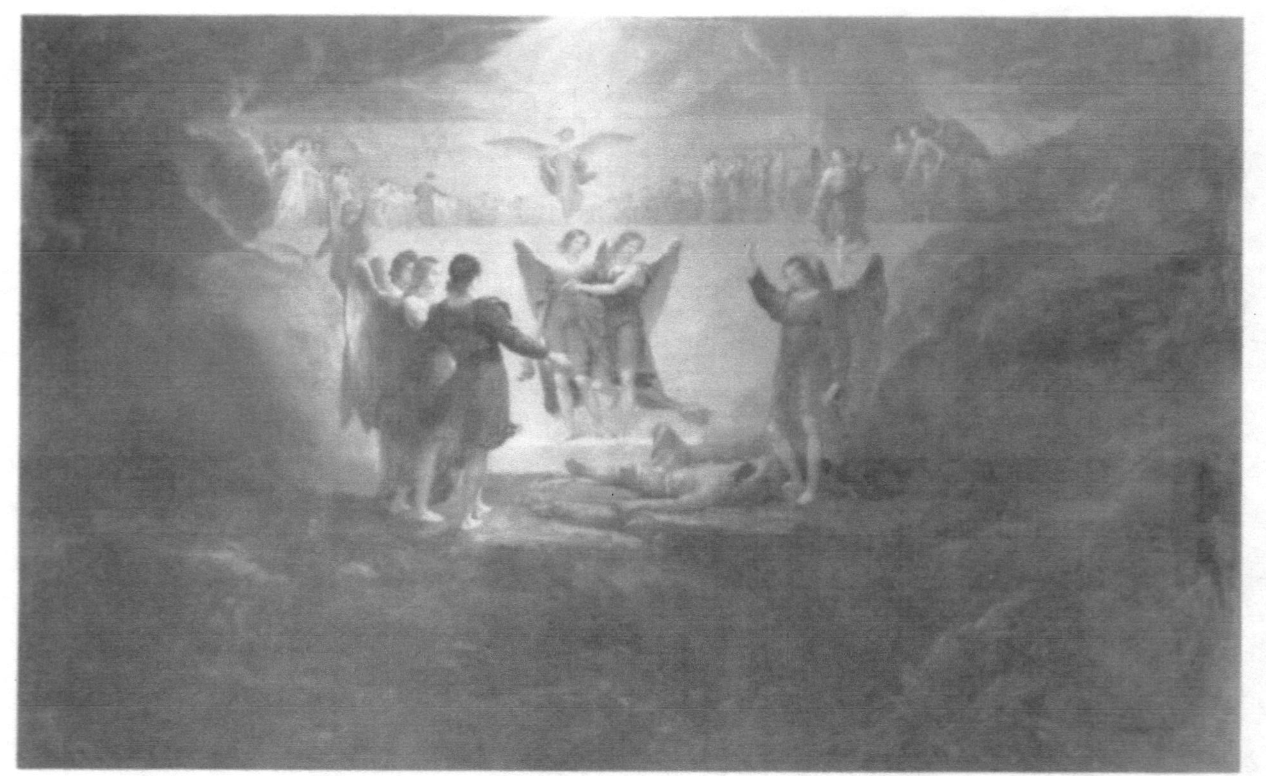

Jacob's Dream, 1817. Oil on canvas, 62 × 94 in. National Trust, England.

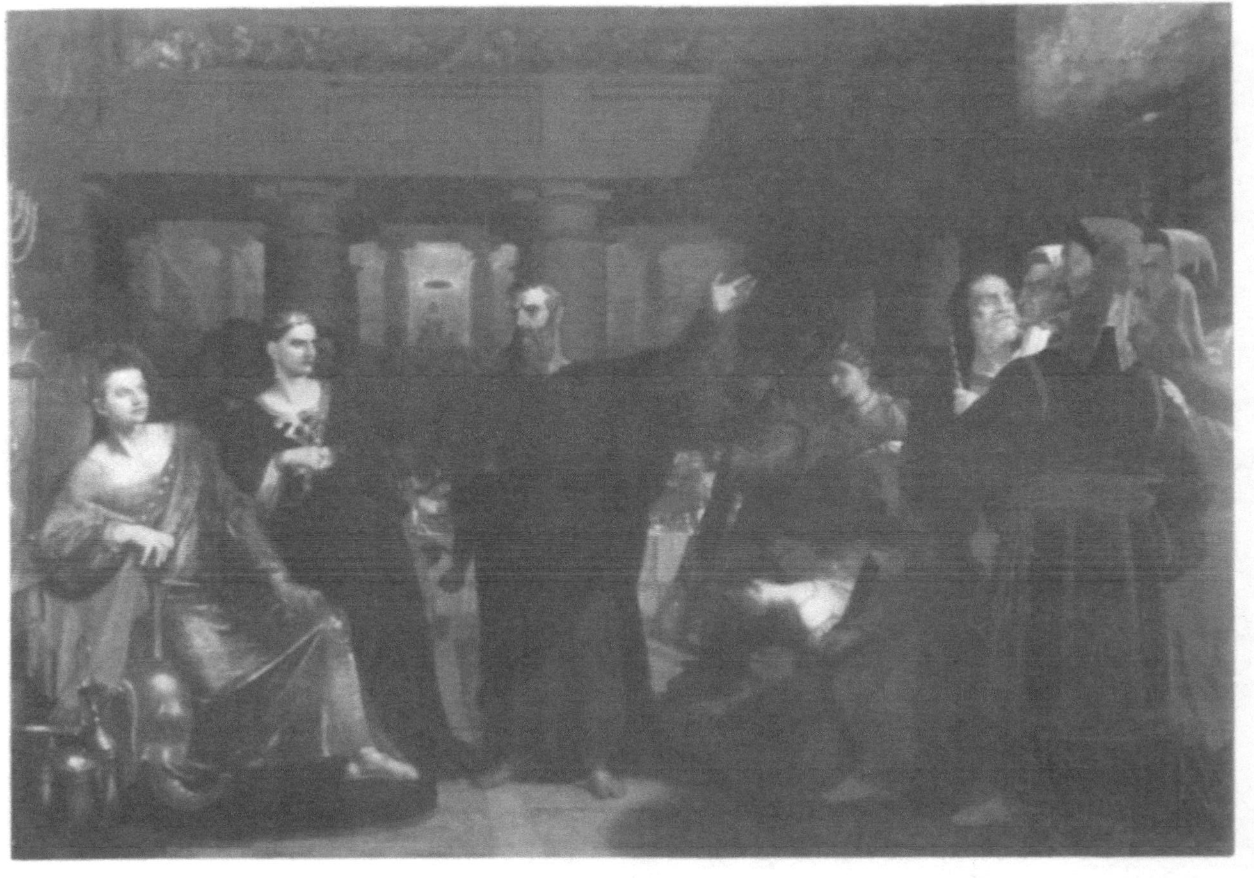

Belshazzar's Feast, 1817-1843. Oil on canvas, 144⅛ × 192⅛ in. Detroit Institute of Arts.

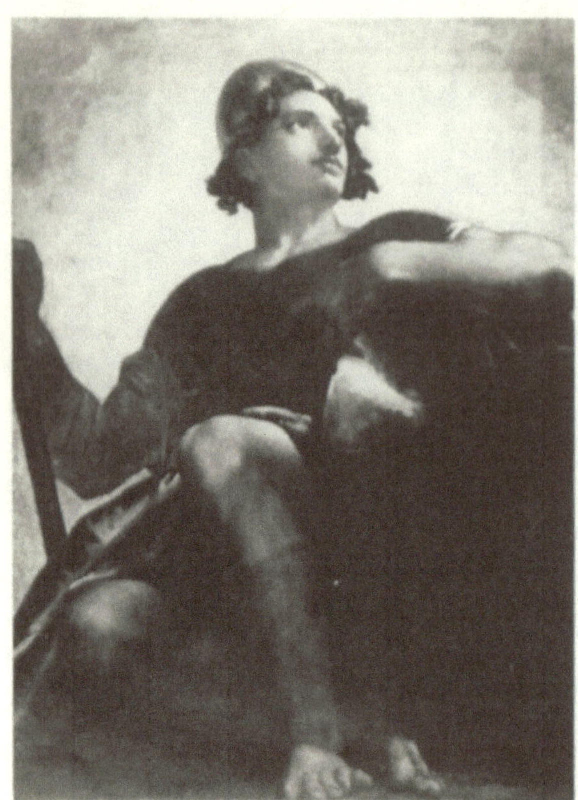

Uriel in the Sun, 1817. Oil on canvas, 97⅝ × 78 in. Mugar Memorial Library, Boston University.

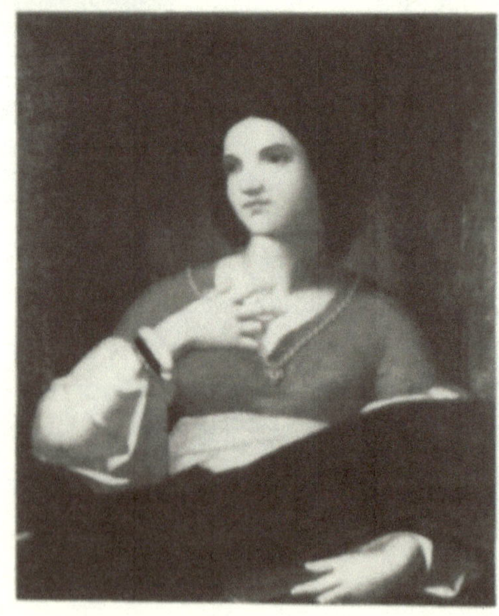

Rosalie, 1835. Oil on canvas, 38½ × 28⅝ in. Society for the Preservation of New England Antiquities, Boston.

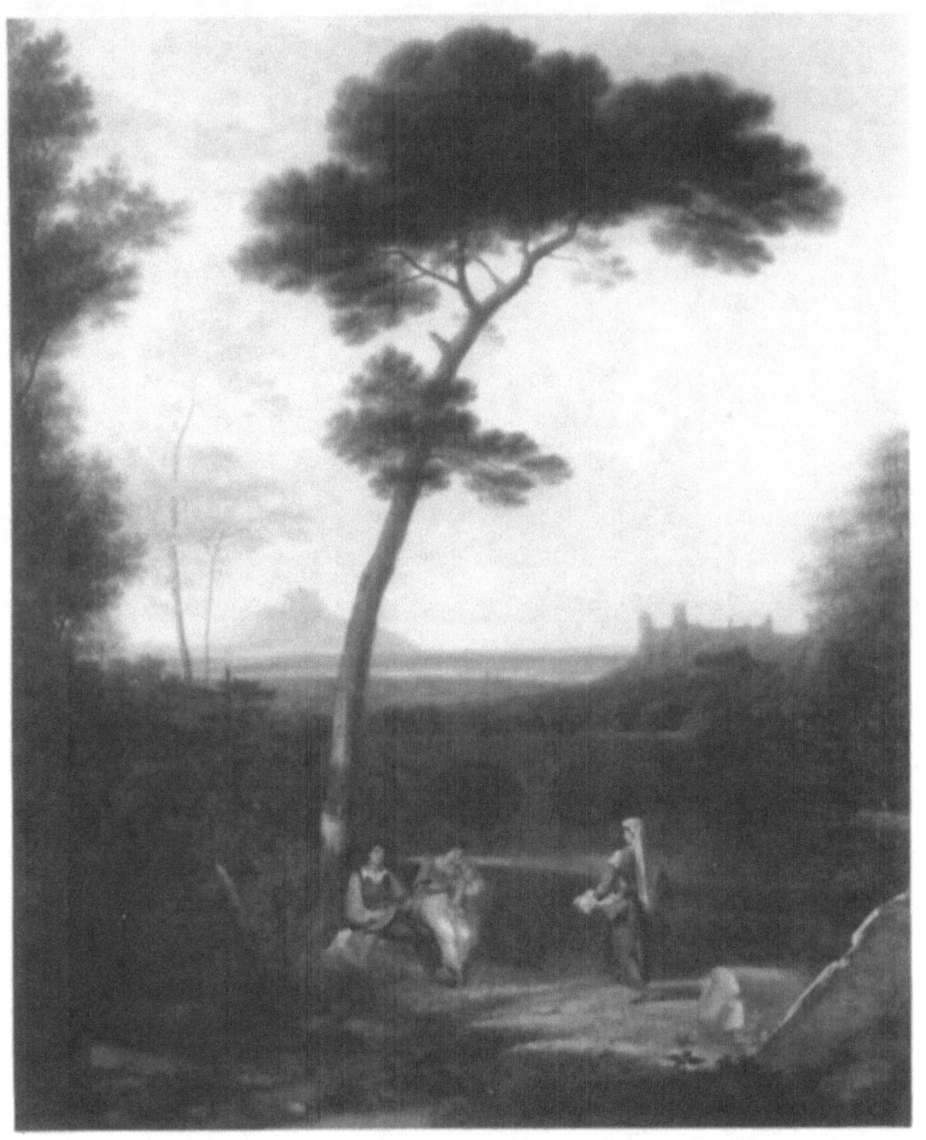

Italian Landscape, ca. 1828-1830. Oil on canvas, 30¼ × 25¼ in. © Detroit Institute of Arts, Founders Society Purchase, D.M. Ferry, Jr. Fund.

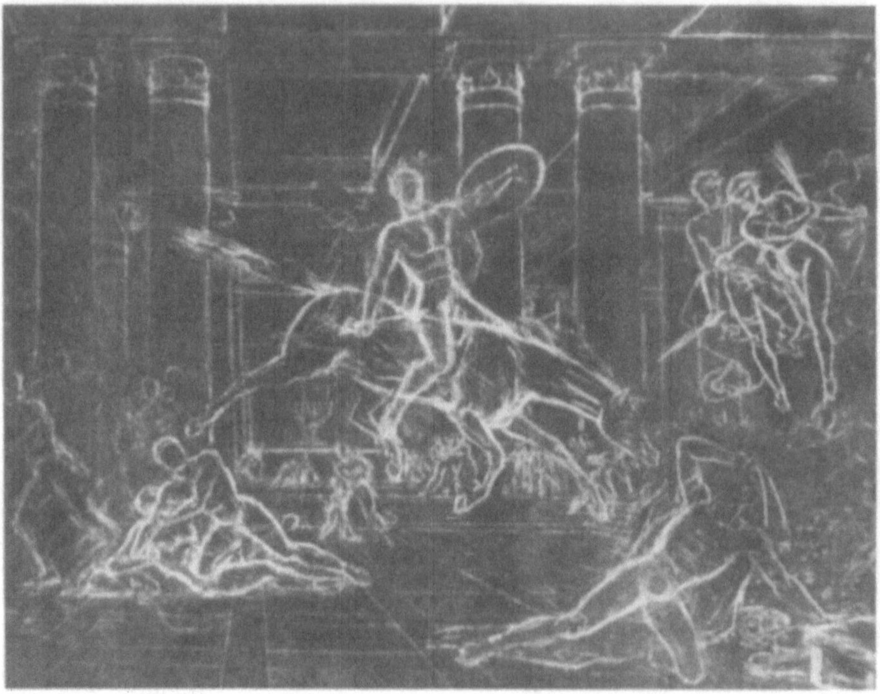

Above, *Heliodorus Driven from the Temple,* ca. 1830s. Chalk on canvas, 44¾ × 56¾ in. Lowe Art Museum, University of Miami, Florida.

Below, *Ship in a Squall,* before 1837. Chalk on canvas, 48⅛ × 60 in. Fogg Art Museum, Harvard University, The Washington Allston Trust.

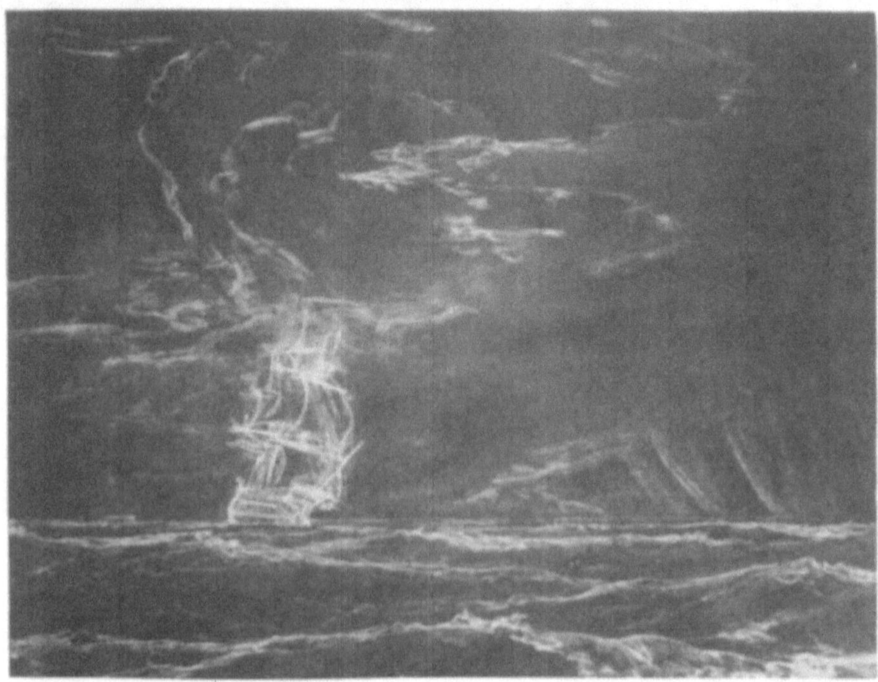

Kingdom (ca. 1807?-1808) from the story of the Argonauts, best known in the *Argonautia* by Apollonius Rhodius. He apparently began it before Coleridge left Rome. Coleridge told Southey on his return to England that it was "almost finished" then and that Allston had employed on it "18 months without Intermission."[22] He himself was later quoted as saying, "the remaines of Coleridge [*sic*] enthusiasm excited" him to commence it, that he made models for all the figures, worked on it for two years, when the political situation made him decide to leave Rome, and boxed all his materials and the picture for shipment to England, but that the captain of the ship was unwilling to receive the boxes, thinking they would cause his ship to be seized, and that "a friend took the trouble" to send them to him in England nine years later.[23] It was his first dramatic narrative and his largest conception, in which he was possibly influenced by the German Asmus Carstens's *Jason at Iolcos* and the Italian Vincenzo Camuccini's *Death of Caesar.* Leslie said it was admired by some but by others thought too imitative of Raphael and Nicolas Poussin. The subject obliquely reflected Allston's own journeying to the country that most represented the great works of art of the past which he claimed as his heritage. He continued, moreover, to be interested in the character of Jason. In his poem "A Fragment" ("O, who hath lived the ills to know") he described the form of Monaldi there as being such as "if ancient Greece had seen, / Like Jason's had been deified" and went on to picture an altar to Apollo being decked with flowers by "virgin hands," presumably in reference to an episode involving Jason and the maids of Medea as recounted by Apollonius.[24]

In Italy Allston also painted three scenes from Shakespeare, drawing for the first time on this source. The first was *Falstaff Enlisting His Ragged Regiment* (1803-1808) from *King Henry IV, Part 2,* 3.2. When it was exhibited at the Boston Athenaeum in 1827 the sentence from that scene, "Prick me Bullcalf till he roar again," was printed with the entry in the catalog. A second painting featured the same character: *Falstaff Playing the Part of the King* (1806-1808) from *King Henry IV, Part 1*,2.4. Leslie said it had figures the size of life.[25] According to Sweetser it was about four feet long and contained a dozen figures, most of which were portraits of actors then on the English stage. A third scene from Shakespeare was painted, according to his cousin John Ashe Alston, who owned it, in Florence in 1807: *Casket Scene from "The Merchant of Venice"* (1807) from 3.2.1-138. He also made a drawing from that play, which Thomas Sully later admired.[26]

Allston also apparently painted biblical scenes in Italy: *David Playing before Saul* (ca. 1805) from 1 Sam. 16:23; and *Moses and the Serpent* (ca. 1805), from Exod. 4:2-4. The subject of the second was also painted by West. Both are, however, in decided contrast to the works he is known to have produced at this period and apparently are preliminary sketches.

Perhaps the most noteworthy completed painting which Allston did in Italy was *Cupid and Psyche* (1805-1808). Richard Henry Dana, who saw it in America on Allston's return from Italy, called it "small," but he was apparently not remembering it accurately.[27] Wordsworth described it in detail to his wife, having seen it in London in 1812. It was, he said, the size of "good large folio" and depicted in the center the two figures, "about a span long," naked, "human in everything but their wings . . . fronting you but their faces inclined with an expression of enthusiastic love towards each," but resting against each other, standing "upon the edge of a bluish brook, that plainly reflects their forms, and in the arbor of a dark green grove, whither they are supposed to have retired after a shower, the ground being yet moistened & freshened with the rain drops." Unlike common representations of him, Cupid was represented not "like a boy, but a tall young man" and Psyche "as tall for a female," he with wings "tipped with purple like those of an angel" and she with "short wings something like those of a butterfly." The flesh he thought "beautiful painted white and almost luminous & shaded off on the outline of the form." Altogether it took him by surprise, largely because the coloring was not like that in any other painting he had seen.[28] Allston took it with him to England in 1811, where it was much admired, by Coleridge as well as Wordsworth, particularly for the coloring, which Coleridge compared to Titian's, and by the painter Charles Dawe for the modeling.[29] Leslie described the figures as being the size of life but mistakenly said it was the second painting done by Allston after coming to England in 1811; probably he was remembering that it was the first of those in his studio at that time which attracted attention.

Many of the drawings Allston made in Rome were of nude models of young women and youths in chalk, some of which he used in late paintings in America. Baron Rumohr said he limited himself to drawing from the antique and the nude during all of 1806, to correct a vagueness in his design. One landscape with trees and a tempietto with a statue may be of a scene in Rome or in Versailles. He apparently produced other compositions in Rome, probably sketches only, of classical subjects, among them stories of Homer and of the apples of the Hesperides and the work of Protogenes, the fourth century B.C. Greek painter.[30] A drawing of three apples and a branch, later acquired by his college classmate Charles Lowell, was probably one of them.

Allston often spoke of his years in Rome, one of the two highlights in his life along with his association a few years later in London with the leading artists and writers of England. He apparently learned in Rome more than he had in London about his art. Horatio Greenough recalled his saying, "When I first went abroad I groped for five years in the dark."[31]

It was during this period of his Italian sojourn, too, that the Italian landscape made its deep and lasting impression on him. He remembered particularly the scenery around Olevano. Many years later, after comparing "Italian distance" with that of other countries, he was glad that he had "lived three weeks in the country & on the very spot where Gaspar & Nicolo Poussin lived & studied. And I had new landscapes like theirs every hour in the day as the time and the light and the weather changed. The changes were so fast that I could only make memoranda and write down the colors. That was about forty miles from Rome."[32]

He owned several books on Rome: *Nuova Roccolta delle pire belle vedute di Roma dissergnate, e intagliate da celebri autori* (Rome, 1771), Angelo Dalmazzoni, *The Antiquarian or the Guide for Foreigners of Rome to go the rounds of the antiquities of Rome* (Rome, 1803), and Charles Knapp Dillaway, *Roman Antiquities and Ancient Mythology* (Boston and New York, 1831).

Allston's visit to Florence in 1807 was probably somewhat longer than the one he made in 1804, though not as long as the year recorded by Flagg. At that time, if not before, he saw the statues by Michelangelo in the Medici Chapel, the *Venus dei Medici,* and paintings by Leonardo and Fra Bartolomeo, all of which he referred to in his lectures on art; he also probably visited the Academy of the Fine Arts, whose president Pietro Benvenuti he knew, and the Della Crusca Academy, of which Maldura in *Monaldi* is a member. His opinion of the *Venus dei Medici* was not very high, to judge from its being one of the statues of antiquity to which Maldura's poem is compared. He may have met the Dutch landscape painter Jakob Phillip Hackert, who died that year in Florence and of whom he spoke disparagingly to Elizabeth Peabody. He later described, Richard Henry Dana, Sr., recollected, a dream he had there of a beautiful woman, which affected him for days. It not only bore a resemblance to the dream of which he wrote to Channing in 1795 but reflected his lifelong idealization of young women in both his painting and his writing. The figure of Portia in *Casket Scene* was the first of them to appear in his painting. His much later *Tuscan Girl* (1831), with its accompanying poem, and *Lorenzo and Jessica* (1832), with the dome of the Duomo, the Campanile, and the façade of a building resembling the Pitti Palace in Florence in the background, more obviously commemorate his visits in the city. It would seem that it was associated in his imagination particularly with *The Merchant of Venice.* According to Flagg he also visited Venice, which would have been about this time, but there seems to be no other evidence that he did so.

Allston's travels south of Rome are not represented in any of his paintings, but his acquaintance with Naples and its environs, like his visit to Bologna, is well documented in his writing. In *Monaldi,* Maldura's arrival in Naples is described as if by an eyewitness: "The day had begun sultry, but was now closing, after a refreshing shower, with one of those delicious atmospheres known only in the south; so sweet! so bright!—as if the common air had suddenly given place to the humid sighs of answering orange groves and the intermingled breath of enamored flowers—as if the dripping trees and fields had actually been flooded by liquid gold from the sun; then the hum of insects, the twittering of birds, and the ceaseless darting of innumerable lizards, so filling the ear and eye with sound and motion, as if the very ground and air were exulting in life!" The Bay of Naples is said to be one which could not be painted by words, with its colors of sapphire and amethyst, harmony of lines, light and shadow, "dazzling expanse," and above all "the living, conscious joy with which they seemed to send up their shouts of praise to the immeasurable depths above."[33] His lectures on art also reflect his visit to Naples, in the citation of Vesuvius as an example of the sublime and the extended description of the *Farnese Hercules* in the National Museum, which through "a piece of marble, cold, immovable, lifeless," is called the "immortal offspring" of Glycon, "this *visible image of Truth,"* giving form and substance to "a pure Idea" as never before so perfectly, "this tremendous personification of strength" even in repose, comparable to the ocean in this respect, possessing "more than mortal powers," having *"essential life,"* affecting the spectator as being "in the stirring presence of a superior being" and appealing to "that in man, which the senses cannot reach, nor the plumb of the understanding sound."[34] In *Monaldi,* Vesuvius, with its outward gaiety and peace and inner restlessness and fire, is recognized by Maldura to be "the very type of himself," and Monaldi in his madness is confined in a hut on its slope. Probably

Allston heard the celebrated mezzo-soprano Girolamo Crescentini sing in Naples, as Monaldi does.

Though several American artists from the colonies preceded him, Allston was the first to go to Italy from the nation. He stayed longer than any before him and was the first to paint a substantial number of works there. His experience constituted the most profound and lasting impression on him, not only because of the great works of art he saw but because of the landscape. At least ten of his landscapes are recognizably Italian, although only five were painted in Italy, and at least four paintings with figures, together with the poem accompanying one, have Italian titles or recognizable Italian backgrounds. In his later writings especially he drew repeatedly on his Italian memories. His lectures on art rely extensively for examples of theoretical points on his responses to art he saw in Italy. In the poem "The Angel and the Nightingale," the "Soul-dissolving Stir" among the birds gathered to hear the nightingale is said to be such as was not known "in soft Italia's courts."[35] *Monaldi* is laid in Italy, has an Italian cast of characters, and contains much local color: numerous allusions to specific localities; passing references to Saints Francis of Assisi, Rosalia of Palermo, and Januarius, or Gennaro, of Naples; and references to Montepulciano and Orvieto wines, to a *Sbirro,* or police officer, to the coins, sequins, and baicci, to Catholic orders and convents, to the notorious eighteenth-century Count Alessandro di Cagliostro, and to Vittorio Alfieri, who died the year before Allston went to Italy, as well as to Crescentini and to several Italians whom he knew in Rome. The narrator, in a mood of reverie typical of Allston's imagination, speaks of there being "sometimes so striking a resemblance between the autumnal sky of Italy and that of New England at the same season, that when the peculiar features of the scenery are obscured by twilight it needs but little aid of the imagination in an American traveller to fancy himself in his own country."[36] His greatest tribute to Italy in words was his poem, "To the Author of 'The Diary of an Ennuyée,' One of the Truest and Most Beautiful Books Ever Written on Italy."

Three Italian authors inspired Allston in both painting and writing. Dante furnished the subject of *Beatrice* (ca. 1816-19), and Rosalia in *Monaldi* reads from the *Inferno.* Three of Metastastio's poems are cited in his writings: Rosalia sings from *Cino Riconosciato* 3.12, 31, 32, 35, 36; the epigraph for the poem "Myrtilla" is from *Zenobia* 1. 1. 83-84; and *Semiramide* 1.10.23 ff., as sung by his niece Charlotte Dana, prompted the composition of the poem "Rosalie." Two paintings and possibly a third reflect his acquaintance with Tasso's *Jerusalem Delivered.* Two of his paintings from Shakespeare are from *The Merchant of Venice,* and the original title of his poem "Rosalie" was "Rosalia." So closely was he associated with Italy by others that upon hearing of his death, Ralph Waldo Emerson described him to Margaret Fuller as "the solitary link as it seemed between America & Italy."[37]

He owned works by or about several Italian authors: Francisco Berni's *Orlando Innamorato,* 4 vols. (London, 1781); Boccaccio's *Il Decamerone* (London, 1802); a copy of Dante's *Divine Comedy* (Venice, 1790); Charles Marguerite Jean Baptiste Mercier Dupaty, *Travels through Italy . . . Translated from the French by an English Gentleman* (London, 1788); Giovan Battista Guarini's *Il Pastor Fido* (London, 1778); a volume of Metastasio (Lucca, 1804); Tasso's *La Gerusalemme* (Basel, 1743) and

La Gerusalemme Liberata, 2 vols. (London, 1778); Georgio Vasari's *Vite de' piu Eccelenti pittori scultori e architetti*, 8 vols. (Florence, 1770); Richard Henry Wilde's *Conjectures and Researches Concerning the Love, Madness, and Imprisonment of Tasso* (New York, 1842); and volume 5 of *Parnaso e gli Italiani Viventi* (Pisa, 1798-1824), with illustrations by Angelica Kauffman. He also owned *Rudiments of Ancient Architecture*, 4th ed. (London, 1810), which he inscribed; *Della Pittura Veneziana* (Venice, 1797); M. Guelfi Borzacchini's *The Tuscan Master; or, A New and Easy Method of Mastering the Italian Language* . . . (Bath, 1791); and a number of Italian dictionaries: M.A. Baretti's *Dizionario delle lingue Italiana ed Inglese* (London, 1798); F. Bottarelli's *Italiano, Inglese, e Francese Dizionario* (Nice, 1791), and *English, French, and Italian Dictionary* (Nice, 1792); as well as Alberti's French-Italian dictionary.

1. Averil, pp. 55-56; Washington Irving, *Journals and Notebooks*, vol. 1, ed. Nathalia Wright (Madison: Univ. of Wisconsin Press, 1969), 262, 296. 2. Carol Minor Tanner, *Joseph C. Cabell, 1778-1856* (Ph.D. diss., University of Virginia, 1948), p. 36; Philip Alexander Bruce, *History of the University of Virginia* (New York: Macmillan, 1920), 1:148-49. 3. *LA*, pp. 100-101. 4. Flagg, pp. 185, 186. 5. *Ernest Carroll; or, Artist Life in Italy* (Boston, 1858), pp. 58-59. 6. *LA*, pp. 60, 161-62, 98-99, 322, 330; *SS*, p. 33. 7. Irving, *Journals and Notebooks* 1:296. 8. Unnumbered sheet, Dana Papers; *SS*, p. 41; *LA*, 378. 9. *LA*, p. 580. 10. Dunlap, 2:165. 11. *SS*, p. 151. 12. Leslie to RHD, 7 Sept. 1843, 28 Jan. 1844 (Dana Papers). 13. Diana J. Strazdes, *Washington Allston's Early Years, 1796-1811* (Ph.D. diss., Yale University, 1982), p. 106. 14. Unnumbered sheet (Dana Papers); Ernest Platner, "Die Kunst in Rom von ihrer Wiederstellung bis auf unsere Zeit," in Platner, C. Bunson, E. Gerhard, and W. Röstal, *Beschreibung der Stadt Rom*, vol. 1 (Stuttgart, 1827), 486-87. 15. *LA*, p. 64; Flagg, p. 366. 16. Flagg, p. 365. 17. Elizabeth P. Peabody, *Last Evening with Allston, and Other Papers* (Boston: D. Lothrop and Co., 1886), p. 3. Unless otherwise noted, all further references to Peabody are to this work. 18. Averill, p. 208. 19. *Monaldi*, pp. 65, 64. 20. Strazdes, p. 116. 21. RHD, p. 30, Addition. 22. *Collected Letters of Samuel Taylor Coleridge*, vol. 3, ed. Earl Leslie Griggs (Oxford: Clarendon Press, 1969), 43. 23. "Color Book," pp. 64-66. 24. *LA*, p. 373. 25. RHD, p 22, Addition. 26. Walter Channing. 27. RHD, p. 220. 28. *The Love Letters of William and Mary Wordsworth*, ed. Beth Darlington (Ithaca: Cornell Univ. Press, 1981), pp. 220, 136-37. 29. *Collected Letters* 3:352. 30. RHD, p. 43. 31. *Letters of Horatio Greenough, American Sculptor*, ed. Nathalia Wright (Madison: Univ. of Wisconsin Press, 1972), p. 344. 32. "Color Book," pp. 44-46. 33. *Monaldi*, p. 208-10. 34. *LA*, pp. 58, 99-100. 35. *LA*, p. 302. 36. *Monaldi*, p. 190, 197, 216, 211, 114, 179, 7. 37. *The Letters of Ralph Waldo Emerson*, ed. Ralph L. Rusk (New York: Columbia Univ. Press, 1939), 4:408.

16. To Benjamin Welles

Siena. December 29th 1804

Dear Welles: I was sorry for your disappointment on account of the shortness of my letter, but, I assure you, it was short from necessity, not from choice. It should not have surprised you after the horrible vacuity of our journey. For my own part, I am somewhat astonished that I was able to collect, much less to join even two ideas.

I am happy to know that your opinion of women is not so bad as you once intimated at Florence. I say *know,* because I was never certain what you thought of them; though I greatly doubted, at the time of your railing whether you were in earnest. But it gives me pleasure to be assured by yourself, that, what I have always delighted to consider as the surest basis of earthly happiness has not been seriously disapproved by you. Whether my hopes be founded on truth, or are merely the offspring of an ardent imagination, still, I must confess, I should be very unwilling to relinquish at last, what have so long been the cause of <my> the purest emotions, and my most agreeable moments. Nay, so far am I willing to obey their influence, that I should find no difficulty in persuading myself of the impossibility of experiencing a rational pleasure without them. Without being poetical, I think the source of every thing refined, benevolent, and pure, may be traced in woman. From them we learn the holy pleasure of gratitude; from them we receive the first impressions of religion; and imbibe from their tenderness the gentle principles of benevolence, and "all the charities of father, son, and brother." [1] Were a man to marry for nothing more, than for the purpose of avoiding the miseries and vices of celibacy, his motive would be sufficient. But I am unwilling to think that the only inducement. There is, in my opinion <another,> a much stronger one; I mean the real prospect of positive enjoyment in the certain reflection of being beloved by, at least, one object in the world. Nor do I consider as nothing the <comforting> mysterious hope of extending our existence in the persons of our children. If, in opposition to this, we place before us the insulated barrenness of a single life; its unregarded miseries in sickness, and comfortless solitude in old age; we shall scarcely hesitate to consider matrimony as the greatest blessing on earth. I shall never forget the pathetic advice of an old man, whom a mistaken notion of liberty had kept aloof from the sex, untill it was too late to <change> alter his situation. "By all means," said he, "get a wife. I, who am now old, and have passed those days, when the attempt to please was received with pleasure; and when the flatteries of youth were reflected back on their author; I, who have survived these times; who have outlived my friends, and can no longer be gay with a good grace, am left, as you see, the <martyr to> victim of old age, without a companion to talk to of my youth, and, in the case of sickness, with at best, but the miserable consolation of being able to hire a nurse, <and> or to pay for a physician. If you marry a scold, I advise you to be married. It is better to have even such an object, attached to you from long habit, than to bury yourself in the solitude of a comfortless independence." However powerful these arguments may be to those who are in want of better motives, I thank heaven, it has not fallen to my lot to acknowledge their influence. I shall marry, because I have found a woman[2] with every quality that may insure me an agreeable existence; a woman, in whose affection I place no less dependence for the improvement of my virtue, than for the promotion of my happiness.

My heart palpitated when I came to that part of your second letter where you began to speak of the Boston news—but, alas, <what was> how shall I express my sorrow, and mortification too when I learned the unexpected fate of Knapp.[3] I had long pleased myself with the triumph he would obtain in the public acknowledgement of his abilities. Nay, so extraordinary is the intelligence, contained in your correspondent's letter, that I am unwilling still to believe such to be the public opinion. They cannot be so wholly blind to merit, so wholly void of taste, but that some one must have discerned, and admired his genius. There are men in Boston who are both able to discover, and willing to appreciate talents; and, depend upon it, we shall hear of things totally different from <your> the opinion of your correspondent. If we do not, most heartily will I join with you. "Odi profanum vulgus et arceo."[4] I think Knapp the truest Poet our country has produced, and incapable of <producing> writing any thing "flimzy."[5] Such, too, is your opinion. Now, I have charity enough to believe there are others in Boston, who have sufficient taste to agree with us. I would not arrogate to ourselves a presumptuous superiority. I only mean to say, that we are not wholly blind to uncommon merit. If Knapp publishes his poem, I will stake my pretensions to taste that he acquires more reputation, than any poet of our country; if not in Boston, at least in some place equally capable of judging.

I little thought in my last, when joking about the earthquake that happened here some years ago, that I should have to tell you in my next of one that I had felt. Such, however, is the case. We experienced two shocks very sensibly. The first of which was the most violent, and shook the house so much that the Dr.[6] & I appeared to be bowing to each other. He desires to be remembered. Your friend Washington Allston.

SOURCE: Manuscript, Welles Family Papers, MHS.

1. Possibly WA is quoting from Welles's first letter referred to. 2. Ann Channing. 3. WA apparently refers to the report that the poem which Knapp delivered at the meeting of the Phi Beta Kappa Society at Harvard in August 1804 was unfavorably criticized (HA). 4. Horace's *Ode* 3.1.1, where he begins to comment on contemporary Roman life. ("I hate the uninitiate crowd and keep them far away.") 5. Probably a quotation from Welles's correspondent. 6. Probably Joseph William Maxwell, an American physician who graduated from the University of Edinburgh in 1803 (Samuel Lewis, "List of the American Graduates in Medicine in the University of Edinburgh, from 1705 to 1866, with their Theses," *NEGHR* 15 [1861]: 90).

17. To Hugh Paterson

Rome 10 April 180[5][1]

Mr. Hugh Paterson / of Charleston

Sir: I herewith transmit you a Credit, together with a letter of advice of the same, in favour of Mr. <[undecipherable word] Benjamin Welles>[2] Levi Hedge[3] of Boston, for forty eight pounds, nineteen shillings & sixpence sterling—the said sum being advanced me by him at Rome, and which Credit I rely on your honouring, and placing to my account,[4] on his delivering up my note of hand, dated 10 April, 1805, for that sum—

I remain with respect / Dr. Sir yrs sincerely / Washington Allston

SOURCE: Manuscript, Houghton.

1. Page torn. 2. WA wrote "Benjamin Welles." The words have been canceled, an undecipherable word written above them and canceled, and "Levi Hedge" written above that word in another hand. About this time Welles and Maxwell left Rome for Naples and subsequently traveled to Paris (Irving, *Journals and Notebooks* 1:420). 3. Levi Hedge (1766-1844), philosopher, was a tutor in philosophy at Harvard from 1795 to 1810, and from 1810 to 1832 was professor of logic and metaphysics there. 4. Presumably that which Paterson was in charge of as holding power of attorney for WA for the sale of his property inherited from his father.

18. From Samuel Taylor Coleridge

[Florence.][1]
Tuesday, June 17th, 1806

My dear Alston: No want of affection has occasioned my silence.—Day after day I expected Mr Wallis[2]—Benvenuti[3] received me with almost insulting coldness, not even asking me to sit down / neither could I by any enquiry find that he ever returned my call / and even in answer to a very polite note enquiring for Letters sent a verbal message, that there was one and I might call for it.—However, within the last 7 or 8 days he has called and made this amende honorable / he says, he forgot the name of my Inn, & called at two or three *in vain / whoo!* I did not tell him, that within 5 days I sent him a note, in which the Inn was mentioned, & that he sent me a message in consequence / & yet never called for 10 days afterwards. However, yesterevening the Truth came out / he had been bored by Letters of recommendation, & till he received a Letter from Mr Migliorini[4] looked upon me as a *Bore* / which however he might & ought to have got rid of in a more gentlemanly manner / Nothing more was necessary than the day after my arrival to have sent his Card by his Servant. But I forgive him from my Heart / It should however be a Lesson to Mr Wallis, to whom & for whom he gives Letters of *Rec.* / —

I have been dangerously ill[5]—for the last fortnight / & unwell enough, Heavens knows, previously—but about 10 days ago on rising from my bed I had a manifest stroke of Palsy along my right side, and right arm / My Head felt like another man's Head—so dead was it, that I seemed to know it only by my left hand, and a strange sense of Numbness—violent attempts to vomit, each effort accompanied by involuntary & terrific Screams—Enough of it / continual vexations & preyings upon the Spirit / I gave Life to my Children[6] / and they have repeatedly given it to me / for by the Maker of all things, but for them I would try my chance. But they pluck out the wing-feathers from the mind—I have not entirely recovered the *sense* of my side or hand / but have recovered the use. I am harrassed by local & partial Fevers.

This day at Noon we set off for Leghorn / all passage thro' the Italian States &

Germany is little other than impossible for an Englishman / & Heaven knows, whether Leghorn may not be blockaded / However we go thither & shall go to England in an American Ship[7] / Inform Mr Wallis of this & urge him to make his way—assure him of my anxious thoughts & fervent wishes respecting him / and of my Love for Trajan[8] & his Family—Tell Mr Migliorini that I should have written him long ago but for my ill-health; but will not fail to do it on my arrival at Pisa[9] / from thence too I will write a Letter to you / for this I do not consider as a Letter.—Nothing can surpass Mr Russell's[10] Kindness & tenderheartedness to me: and his understanding is far superior to what it appears on first acquaintance / I will write likewise to Mr Wallis / O *conjure* him not to leave Amelia[11] behind!—

I have heard in Leghorn a sad sad character of one of those, whom you call acquaintance—but who call you their dear Friend / —

My dear Alston! somewhat from increasing age, but much more from calamity & intense pre-affections my heart is not open to more than kind good wishes in general; to you & to you alone since I have left England,[12] I have felt more / and had I not known the Wordsworths[13] should have loved & esteemed you *first* and *most* / and as [it] is, next to them I love & honor you / Heaven knows, a part of such a Wreck as my Head & Heart is scarcely worth your acceptance—

S.T. Coleridge

Direct to me, at Mr Degen's,[14] Leghorn / God bless you!—

ADDRESSED: Al Signre / Sigre Allston / Pittore / Americano / Caffe Greco[15] / Strada de' / Condotti / Roma. SOURCE: Coleridge, *Collected Letters* 2:619-20.

1. Coleridge left Rome for England on 18 May, in consequence of Napoleon's demand for the expulsion of all British subjects from papal territory and the imminent arrival of French troops in Rome, but he also had some fears for his personal safety on account of his public criticism of Napoleon. He intended to go to Germany but finding that impossible because of the political situation took ship from Leghorn instead. He was in Florence en route there briefly at the end of May and also from about 10 to 17 June (Donald Sultana, *Samuel Taylor Coleridge in Malta and Italy* [Oxford: Blackwell, 1969, pp. 294-99). 2. George Augustus Wallis. He returned to England with Coleridge. 3. Pietro Benvenuti (1769-1844), the chief Tuscan painter of the day, professor of painting at the Academy of Fine Arts in Florence. WA probably met him there on the way to Rome in the autumn of 1804 and seems to have given Coleridge a letter to him.

4. Unidentified. 5. Coleridge's health and use of opiates worsened about 1800 and continued to give him wretched spells both physically and mentally until he went to live with Dr. James Gillman in 1816. 6. Coleridge had three children who lived to adulthood, all of whom achieved prominence in letters: Derwent (1800-83), Hartley (1796-1849), and Sara (1802-52). 7. The *Gosport*, which sailed from Leghorn on 23 June. En route it was boarded by a Spanish privateer and Coleridge was forced to throw overboard all his papers, including all but two notebooks and presumably some of what he had written about WA (Sultana, pp. 38-99).

8. Trajan Wallis (b. ca. 1796), Wallis's son. He became a painter. 9. Coleridge arrived in Pisa on 22 June but apparently did not write WA from there (Sultana, p. 397). 10. Thomas Russell, a young artist from Exeter whom Coleridge met in Rome and who traveled with him from there (Sultana, p. 293). 11. Emilie was a daughter of Wallis. 12. Coleridge left England in April 1804 for Malta, where he acted as secretary to the governor for ten months. From there he went to Italy, spending nearly eight months in Naples and Rome. 13. William Wordsworth

and his sister Dorothy (1771-1855). Coleridge met them in the summer of 1795. 14. Probably Frederick Degan, who was U.S. consul in Naples from 1805 to 1809 (Irving, *Journals and Notebooks* 1:224). 15. The Caffè Greco, a short distance from the Piazza di Spagna, was a favorite resort of artists and foreigners in Rome.

19. To John Vanderlyn Leghorn, 23rd April, 1808[1]

My dear Sir: Your letter from Paris[2] reached me in this place a few days ago, having been forwarded hither by the Marquis Torlonia.[3] That spirit of procrastination by which I, as well as yourself, am persecuted, prevented my replying to it before; by consequence [I] put it entirely out of my power to send you the answer to which it is entitled; for, I must candidly acknowledge that it afforded me more pleasure than I expect you to receive from the perusal of this. Your observations on the famous picture[4] which made such a noise, in report, at Rome, are exactly such as I expected from you. If you think it any compliment, I give them my approbation; which I conceive may readily be hazarded, from my little knowledge of art, & greater knowledge of man; both of them convincing me of the impossibility of effecting at will a total change of style, no less than of manners. Depend upon it (to use a dogmatical phrase) no man who possessed from nature a true feeling for *colour,* could ever have prevailed on himself to live to the age of forty in a total neglect of it.

I have often thought, that, if I pleased, I could become a famous general; but as I never either felt, or discovered to others any signs of a military genius, I have great reason to suspect, in my *modest moments,* that were I to assume the character I should make as ridiculous a figure in the camp, as the gentleman above mentioned in his Venetian masquerade.

Art will do a great deal; but nature *has done* more. The first may teach a man to draw a correct outline; I mean after a model: may teach him to put figures together, so that they appear neither awkward nor embarrassed; to dispose of light & shadow, so as to correspond with common reason: But to the last alone is reserved the province of feeling & expressing the beauty of form; of painting the soul, of giving life & motion to a group; & expression, & harmony, & magic to the mystery of the chiaro'scuro.[5]

Perhaps you will be surprised to find me so soon on my way home. You will be more so when I tell you I have been here six weeks. The truth is the situation of my country as it now respects Europe, may [makes] me apprehend a loss of our neutrality.[6] Perhaps I looked too far. But a man who is expected home by his bride, is not likely to risk so much, as one who is so occupied by the whole sex together, as to think of no woman in particular. I therefore thought it prudent (though six months before it may be necessary) to cross the Atlantic while I was permitted. But I am afraid, if I run on at this rate, I shall write more nonsense than either you may wish to read, or will be conducive to my health;—I say, my health; for 'tis past midnight, & I sail to-morrow for New York.

By the by, some of your prints (I believe about a dozen) are arrived. They are still in the counting-house of Filippo & Antonio Filichi[7] of this place, who will keep them until they hear from you in what manner they shall be forwarded. I myself would have sent them; but as I heard of no private opportunity, & knew the courier to be very expensive, I thought it better to let them remain where they are.

Adieu, my dear sir, & believe me, with unfeigned esteem,

Yours sincerely, / W. Allston.

P.S. My address in America is to the care of Messrs. John & Samuel Welles,[8] Boston, Massachusetts. N.B. You ([blank space]) write to Messrs. Filichi in French or ([blank space]. My respects to Mr. Skipwith.[9]—I hope your Marius[10] is safe arrived. My cases[11] are all here; but they will not accompany me. I shall only take Cupid & Psyche & the little Falstaff.[12]

What queer times for a painter! By the by, if you should ever get so rich as to *wallow in wealth*, I pray you to send me a manikin from Paris!

ADDRESSED: Monsieur Jean Vanderlyn / Peintre Americain / aux soins de Monsieur Fulwar Skipwith, Consul Gen / eral des Etats Unis, Paris. ANNOTATED: Copy of Allston's Letters to / Vanderlyn, from originals lent me by Robt / Gosman,[13] of Rondout, New York, Jan'y 5th / [RHD's line] 53. SOURCE: Manuscript copy by RHD. A copy in another hand, with omissions and a slightly variant endorsement, is in the Dana Papers; it is endorsed in still another hand: *Allston* 1808 to / *Vanderlyn* / Copy by Gosman / to RHD 1843. Printed, except for the first sentence, in Flagg, pp. 78-79.

1. WA left Rome about 9 March 1808 and sailed to Leghorn. His *Coast Scene on the Mediterranean* (1811) would seem to be a recollection of that experience. 2. Vanderlyn was in Paris from December 1807 to the fall of 1815 (Averill, p. 74). 3. Giovanni Torlonia (1785-1829), founder of the family title and fortune, was the Marchese di Romavecchi and Torlonia.
4. Presumably Camuccini's *Death of Caesar.* It made a great stir in Rome when it was exhibited. 5. This paragraph contains the earliest known written expression by WA of two fundamental tenets of his philosophy of art: the importance to the artist of a study of works of art by others and of nature. In the later development of this philosophy he placed increasing importance on the great works by artists of the past but found the source of supreme artistic expression in the mind of the artist rather than in either art or nature. 6. At this time the Napoleonic Wars were approaching their climax and American neutrality was growing more precarious. The Embargo Act was passed in December 1807 and the French army entered Rome on 2 February 1808. The rumor reached WA, he later said, that there would be war between America and France, in which case he would have been taken prisoner and detained until its end ("Color Book," p. 63). By 9 February he had his belongings boxed for shipping. 7. Not otherwise identified. 8. John and Samuel Welles, to whom Benjamin Welles was related, were merchants in Boston who had a counting room there for several years (*Boston City Directory*, 1803-13; Albert Welles, *History of the Welles Family in England and Normandy* . . . [New York, 1876], pp. 121, 124). 9. Fulwer Skipwith was U.S. consul general to France from 1795 to 1799 and commercial agent in Paris from 1801 to 1815, when he was appointed consul there. He was host to many Americans at his house in Paris and villa at Neuilly (Averill, p. 21).
10. *Marius on the Ruins of Carthage* was painted by Vanderlyn in Rome in 1806-1807, partly inspired by WA's *Caius Marius in the Dungeon*, or *Marius at Minturnae*. Vanderlyn introduced the fox in his painting after seeing one on a visit to the ruins of Roma Vecchia outside Rome in the company of WA and two other artists (Averill, p. 71). 11. There is some uncertainty about the

contents of WA's cases prepared for shipment from Leghorn at this time. Certainly they contained casts, prints, and copies of two paintings by Veronese. Coleridge, who said there were "two or three valuable works of the Venetian School," said they also contained a portrait of himself, and *Jason* (*Collected Letters* 3:43). Apparently there were also four drawings of *Jason*, "Una Marina," "Amore e Psiche," "un retratto," "due comedie" (presumably *Landscape with a Lake*, *Cupid and Psyche*, the portrait of Coleridge, and the two paintings of Falstaff, a head of Christ on the Cross by Jacopo Bassano, and "La virtù ed il vizio" and "Amore trionfante sopra la faza" (the copies of the Veronese paintings). These items were listed for export by WA with the government in Rome on 16 February 1808. (A. Bertolotti, "Esportazione di oggetti di Belle Arti da Roma, per l'Inghilterra," *Archivio Storico . . . della Città e Provincia di Roma*, [1880], 4:90). These cases did not reach England until the summer of 1815. Presumably he had sent earlier the paintings done in England and Paris, certainly *Rising of a Thunderstorm at Sea*, *Casket Scene*, and *Diana and Her Nymphs*, the latter being sent early in 1806 (*The Notebooks of Samuel Taylor Coleridge*, ed. Kathleen Coburn [New York: Pantheon Books, 1961], N II 2813 [6 Mar.-3 Apr. 1806]); all three were exhibited at Bristol in the summer of 1814. It is probable, however, that other cases contained some if not all of the other paintings done in Italy and a number of drawings. Apparently he sent them all to the care of Thomas Brown, Sr., in London. 12. *Falstaff Enlisting His Ragged Regiment*. 13. Gosman wrote a life of Vanderlyn, "Biographical Sketch of John Vanderlyn, Artist," but it was never printed. Two manuscript versions are in the New-York Historical Society.

20. From John Vanderlyn Paris May 7, 1809

Mr. Allston / My dear Sir: Though naturally I am as backward or averse to writing as anyone can be, still am I unwilling to let escape the present opportunity as they are now so seldom without troubling you with some lines were it only to say that I am still in being & ever mindful of my acquaintances and at least the worthiest of them—

Your letter from Leghorn came safe, I was at first a little surprised to learn of your sudden departure from Rome, but your apprehension of being detained probably longer than you wished by the communication being cut off (as eventually has happened) was motive sufficient I think for determining you to make the sacrifice you did in breaking off from your studies & the work you had in hand—I trust you arrived safe after a pleasant passage & that followed by a happy meeting of all your friends; although I have not yet had the satisfaction to hear in any way of you since you left Leghorn—I wish I could flatter myself with a letter from you by the Vessel now expected here—informing me of your health & that in spite of the times you meet with sufficient encouragement in the exercise of your profession, yealding you both pleasure & profit—I take it for granted that you are now out of the possibility of becoming an old Batchelor and that I may venture to felicitate you on the occasion & there certainly is no one whom I more sincerely wish all the bliss & enjoyment that a happy union can afford than yourself.

I believe you have Mr. Stuart now in Boston,[1] pray how do you like his portraits now? Your candid opinion whether pro or con, you may rely upon my descretion, for it is only to satisfy my own curiosity.

Oh in your letter you never mentioned what you did with my Paul Veronese[2] on leaving Rome, I am still ignorant whether you left it there or if you took it with you. I have written about it to Mons Descamp,[3] but have never rec'd his answer—I intend writing again in a few days both to Descamp & Mr. Day[4]—I wished to have it cleaned as you know—& on that account I imagine you left it behind you & probably with Mr. Day—though my pecuniary means are still skanty—I will endeavor to have it cleaned & conveyed to me here—that is if I find that I can remain here some time yet, which becomes uncertain considering the turbulent times. It would seem that by the accounts though indirect rec'd here that our country is on the eve of engaging in war, but I hope it may still be avoided, we few Americans here are anxiously waiting the arrival of the Vessel from our Government, & to know what measures have been adopted, we expect they will be somewhat decisive.

As to myself I am, Perhaps you may wish to know that [what] I am about—in answer I can't say much to my satisfaction, I came here with the expectation of finding some employment from Americans here in the Portraits & also to have an opportunity of studying from this way pictures in the Louvre but have been a good deal disappointed in both I have not without difficulty found some employment in Portrait and then but poorly but it has been attended with more trouble than profit & I have not been able to see & as to my intention & wish for the Louvre Gallery I have not been able to indulge myself much with the sight of its pictures as their greater part were taken down before I got here & since they have been all taken down & the Gallery is shut & will remain so until they have completed making the sky lights etc., which may not be done under a year or more.

I am desirous to make a copy of some good picture there (probably Raffiel St. Cecilia[5] if I can get the permission) & to make another historical picture as a pendant to my Marius something in the female to make it more engaging to the American spirit—all with a view that on my return I may make a small exhibition & derive some pecuniary advantage therefrom—from what I have been able to learn I am encouraged to expect some success & if so it will enable me to discharge my debt & get a little ahead which I have so long [end of source]

SOURCE: Averill, pp. 217-18.

1. Gilbert Stuart moved to Boston from Washington in the summer of 1805. 2. Paolo Cagliani, known as Paolo Veronese. The painting by him of which Vanderlyn bought a copy in Rome was presumably *L'Infedelta (La Contessa d' Amore),* one of four paintings originally in the imperial collection at Prague (Guido Piovene, *L'Opera completa del Veronese* [Milan, 1968], pp. 107-108). 3. Guillaume Descamps (1779-1858), French etcher and engraver. He spent several years in Rome. 4. Alexander Day (1773-1841), English painter and art dealer. He spent most of his early years in Italy. 5. Raphael's *Saint Cecilia,* in the Academy of Fine Arts in Bologna, one of the works of art brought from Italy to Paris by Napoleon, was at this time in the Louvre.

BOSTON 1808-1811

Allston arrived in Boston from Leghorn in late May or early June 1808 and spent the next three years there. At this time he had few correspondents in America or abroad and no letters by or to him seem to have been preserved. His activities, however, both personal and professional, were numerous and of great importance in relation to his subsequent career and to his correspondence.

He first resided in a house at the corner of Magazine and Auburn Streets[1] and had his studio on Court Street, on the south side between Brattle and Cornhill streets, in a building famous for having been occupied by a succession of artists, including Smibert, Copley, Trumbull, Samuel King, and John Johnston. By 1810 his studio was on Devonshire near State Street.

On 19 June 1809 he married Ann Channing, and they soon took up residence at 7 Federal Street. The morning after the wedding Jarvis found him at work painting as usual. Reporting the event to her grandfather, William Ellery, Channing said he was sure Allston would make her happy but feared there was too little taste for the arts in America to encourage him. When West heard the news he commented that Allston should never have considered such a step since he was married to his art (Walter Channing). Immediately afterward he visited his half-brother Henry C. Flagg, Jr., then a student at Yale, in New Haven, whom their mother was also visiting.

During his stay in Boston Allston painted at least eight portraits, the largest group of his paintings in that category. He was listed in *Boston City Directory* for 1810 as "portrait painter." All but two of the subjects were members of his family: Francis Dana Channing, his brother-in-law (1808-1809); Edmund T. Dana (1809); Henry C. Flagg, Jr. (1809); his mother (1809); his wife (1809-11); Lucy (Ellery) Channing, his mother-in-law (1811); Channing (1811); and, according to Walter Channing, Joseph Stevens Buckminster, his college classmate. He owned a copy of *Buckminster's Sermons by the late Rev. J.S. Buckminster, with a Sketch of his Life* (Boston, 1814). The portraits of his mother, mother-in-law, and Channing, for all their spareness, are some of his most evocative, and that of Francis D. Channing is particularly distinguished.

He also painted *Coast Scene on the Mediterranean*, which had a group of figures in the foreground; *Catherine and Petruchio, Grumio and the Tailor* (1809), from *The Taming of the Shrew* 4.3.119-69, for which he made a study; *The Valentine* (1809-11); and the comic *The Poor Author and the Rich Bookseller* (1811), the last three in Court Street.[2] The last may have had particular reference to some of his literary friends who were having difficulty in making their enterprises succeed, among them Richard Henry Dana, William Tudor, who graduated from Harvard the year Allston entered, and others contributing to short-lived periodicals such as the *Monthly Anthology*. *The Valentine* is one of his most appealing female heads. It has the general pose of the figure in the portrait of his wife and may have been inspired by her, though according to Sweetser her sister Lucy was the model. It was engraved by James Longacre for *The Common-Place Book of Romantic Tales* (1831). Jarvis said that he also painted, on Devonshire Street, an American landscape, otherwise unidentified, and a sunrise, which was presumably *Coast Scene on the Mediterranean.* Of the latter, Jarvis commented that it was proof that he had never seen a sunrise, since he put the reflection of the sun in the water widening as it approached the foreground. Sarah Clarke called it "Sunrise on the Mediterranean."[3] Like Jarvis, his brother William was referring to his habit of late rising when he said, apparently of this painting, that Allston must have genius to paint what he had never seen. It was probably during this time that he also painted *Italian Landscape* (1810) and *Alpine Landscape* (1810), though the former may have been erroneously dated. When Edmund S. Quincy, Josiah Quincy's son, asked him if he needed a rest after such activity, he replied that he required only a change, painting portraits and landscapes alternately.[4]

During these years in Boston Allston also composed most of the poems published in *The Sylphs of the Seasons, with Other Poems*. Probably it was about this time, possibly in connection with the writing he was doing, that he acquired a copy of John Walker, *A Critical Pronouncing Dictionary and Exposition of the English Language*, 3d American ed. (New York, 1807). In the summer of 1810 Anna Cabot Lowell, Charles Lowell's sister, described him as "a poet as well as a painter," going on to say that "His manners are polished; his mind improved and his morals pure" but that he was going to England soon because of the lack of art patrons in America.[6]

In his portraits at this time Allston introduced a figure withdrawn from the outside world, which he depicted increasingly as a dreamer or contemplative. That of Francis D. Channing is a profile, and in both his portrait of his wife and *The Valentine* the subject is reading. He also began, with *Coast Scene on the Mediterranean,* to depict his landscapes in a half-light, of early morning or late afternoon or evening, giving them a hazy or dreamlike atmosphere, unlike the clarity of *Landscape with a Lake* and *Diana and Her Nymphs* or the partly dark *Rising of a Thunderstorm at Sea.* A dream consciousness is also evident in some of his poems written then, particularly "The Sylphs of the Seasons: A Poet's Dream" and "Sonnet on Rembrandt: Occasioned by His Picture of Jacob's Dream."

It is significant that these paintings and poems were produced in America, as were his later figures in reverie, twilit landscapes and seascapes, and all his later writings. Most of his later poems are about dreams or visionary experiences, the painter Monaldi is characterized as a dreamer, and in his lectures on art he described the artist as a daydreamer and a work of art as inducing a trancelike state in the spectator. The nature of Allston's imagination was, indeed, meditative, and it was most dominantly expressed during his years in America, where he was isolated from large social and especially artistic centers. Two of his close friends emphasized this aspect of his character, C.C. Felton saying that he "lived in a world of his creation," and William Ware, though noting his socialities, calling him "essentially a solitary."[5]

In the summer of 1810 Anna Cabot Lowell, Charles Lowell's sister, described him as "a poet as well as a painter," going on to say that "His manners are polished; his mind improved and his morals pure" but that he was going to England soon because of the lack of art patrons in America.[6]

On 11 July 1811, Allston sailed with his wife and Samuel F. B. Morse, then an art student, from New York to Liverpool on the *Lydia,* taking with him only a few paintings, including *Cupid and Psyche* and the portrait of his mother. They reached Liverpool in twenty-six days, where they stayed at the Liverpool Arms Hotel, but because of the war between England and America, which was declared on 18 June, were granted by the mayor only a ten-day permit to remain; his name was Drinkwater, but Morse, with uncharacteristic humor, declared that from the appearance of his face it might be "Drinkbrandy." After a week they went on to London.

1. Arthur Dexter, "The Fine Arts in Boston," in *The Memorial History of Boston, Including Suffolk County, Massachusetts, 1630-1880,* vol. 4, ed. Justin Winsor (Boston, 1881), p. 393. 2. RHD, pp. 1, 15. 3. "Our First Great American Painter," *Atlantic Monthly* 15 (1865): 131. 4. Quincy to Samuel Gardner Drake, 3 Dec. 1872, Wellesley College Library. 5. Felton, review of Athanasius Raczynski, *Histoire de l'Art Modern en Allemagne, North American Review* 47 [1843]: 397; Ware, *Lectures on the Work and Genius of Washington Allston* (Boston, 1852), p. 117. 6. "Letter of July 23, 1810 from Anna Cabot Lowell to Mrs. Anna Grant of Leggan, Scotland," *Proceedings of the MHS,* 2d ser., 18 (1904): 314-15. 7. Samuel Irenaeus Prime, *The Life of Samuel F. B. Morse, LL.D.* (New York, 1875), pp. 30-31.

21. To Samuel Finley Breese Morse

[London,[1]
18 February 1812][2]

My dear Sir: I forgot to tell you how to use the Asphaltum.[3] If you mix it with *oil* it will never dry. You must thin it with *spirits of Turpentine* to the consistency that you wish—and, when so thinned, put it into a small gallipot. When thus prepared, you may use it freely with any other colours on your pallette, their being ground in oil notwithstanding. The Asphaltum was prepared by Rowny,[4] and dries well without sugar of lead.

Yrs sincerely / W. Allston

Tuesday Evening / 18 Feby.

SOURCE: Manuscript, Morse Papers, LC.

1. In London the Allstons lived first at 49 London Street, near Fitzroy Square, and for most of Allston's residence in the city during the next few years his painting room was at 22 Charlotte Street, off Fitzroy Square. Their friends the Nathaniel Amorys lived nearby and in the fall of 1811 derived, Mrs. Amory said, "great pleasure" from their society. They were together every day after devoting an hour or two to music and as much time to reading (Mary P. Amory to Mrs. Jonathan Amory, 3 Sept. 1811, Amory Papers, MHS). 2. Presumably this letter was written to Morse in 1812, when he was beginning his study of painting with WA in London. In February 1813 and 1814 he was in Bristol and by February 1815 such advice as that given in this letter would seem to have been too late. 3. In his "Color Book," in the section entitled "To Prepare Drying-Oil," WA gave the proportions for combining several ingredients in which most pigments were to be mixed (pp. 7-8). He habitually used asphaltum in glazing, in order, he told Henry Greenough, to "deepen the tone" (Flagg, p. 187), but it damaged both his own work and that of several artists who followed his advice, having the result of darkening the painting and necessitating cleaning. First used by Rembrandt, the practice was revived by eighteenth-century British artists, notably Reynolds. 4. T. Rowney, color preparer, at 30 Bartlett's Building in London (*Post-Office London Directory* for 1812).

22. From George Howland Beaumont Coleorton Hall,
Ashby-de-la-Zouch,[1] August 21, 1812.

My Dear Sir: Your picture[2] gave me so much satisfaction and so fully answered all the expectations which had been raised in my mind respecting your power, that I cannot refrain from troubling you with a line or two of congratulation; if you accomplish the work with the same happiness with which it is conceived (and I have no doubt upon the subject), I think I may venture to promise you the approbation of all those whose judgments are deserving of your consideration. I could not well judge the effect of light and shadow in the state in which I saw it; but I take it for granted you intend to make it very powerful, having Rembrandt more in your mind than S. del Piombo,[3] with regard to that part of the arrangement. I think large portions of shadow, "deep, yet clear," blank almost at a sudden glance, yet broken with nameless tints and mysterious approaches to shape, have a wonderful effect upon the mind in subjects of this elevated description. In this particular Rembrandt is so happy that the little picture of "The Crucifixion" now before me, makes my very blood run cold, and I have frequently thought, in spite of his Dutch virgins and occasional vulgarities, there is as much of the true sublime in the light and shadow of Rembrandt as in the lines of Michael Angelo. At any rate, it would be well to endeavor to unite excellencies which if brought together would, according to my feelings, delight and astonish the world. With regard to color, I should wish you by all means to avoid a large portion of cold tint, but I am taking liberties which I hope you will excuse for the sake of my zeal, and I will now come to the business of my letter.

I have a great desire to place a work of yours in this church; there is a place which I think would afford a good light to a picture of small dimensions, a whole length, perhaps something larger.[4] I will now be very open with you. My expenses in building, etc., have been, and continue to be, so very heavy that I cannot afford more than two hundred pounds for this indulgence, and if that sum appears inadequate, I trust you will tell me so with the same friendly spirit which I take the liberty to use.

If this offer meets with your approbation, perhaps in the course of a month or two you may find time to leave your work for a little relaxation and look at the spot, the more time you can afford us the better. We shall be here till the end of October. We may hope for a fine autumn. I have now taken up much of your time, and will only add Lady Beaumont's[5] best wishes to those of,

Your faithful and devoted friend, / Geo. Beaumont.

SOURCE: Flagg, pp. 90-91.

1. Beaumont's family estate in Leicestershire. 2. The study for *The Dead Man Restored* (1811). 3. Sebastiano del Piombo (1435-1547), Italian painter. 4. *The Angel Releasing St. Peter from Prison* is 124½ by 108½ inches. 5. Lady Beaumont, who married Beaumont in 1778, was the former Margaret Willes, member of a prominent family. She was very enthusiastic about painting and poetry, especially Wordsworth's poetry.

23. To John Vanderlyn London, 28 June, 1813

My dear Sir: This will be handed you by our countryman, Dr. Cushing;[1] for whom I take the liberty to solicit some of those friendly attentions, without which even novelty in a foreign country has but few charms; & whom I am persuaded you will find on acquaintance to be possessed of those agreeable qualities for which he would wish *all* of our countrymen to be distinguished.

I avail myself also of this opportunity to assure you that I have not forgotten those for which *you* first demanded my esteem; nor do I think the time will soon come when the recollection of the many pleasant hours we have passed together will cease to give pleasure.

Pray, when you write, be particular in letting me know what you have done, & are doing. I shall hardly welcome your letter if you omit it. As to what I am about[2] I shall leave Dr. Cushing to inform you. Believe me, my dear sir, most sincerely yours,

W. Allston.

Can you send me any news of any of our Roman friends—Paulin[3] Granet[4] Odevarre[5] & Stockoff,[6] &c? If they are in Paris give them my best regards. My address is to the care of Samuel Williams, Esqre.,[7] No. 13, Finsbury Square, London.

ADDRESSED: John Vanderlyn, Esqre. Paris. Fav/oured by Dr. Cushing. ANNOTATED: Letter 2nd. [The second letter of WA to Vanderlyn lent to RHD by Robert Gosman.] SOURCE: Copy by RHD.

1. Ezekiel Dodge Cushing (1790-1828), physician. He graduated from Harvard in 1808 and received the degree of M.B. from Dartmouth in 1811, studied medicine in London and Paris, and subsequently practiced in Boston and in Hanover, Mass. (HA). 2. WA was unusually busy during the years 1811-13 in London. In December 1811 he intended to exhibit two or three pictures, all "poetical or history paintings," the number being kept small partly on the advice of Coleridge, who thought it "impolitic to appear to be *trying* in half a dozen ways, as if his mind had not yet discovered its main current" (*Collected Letters* 3:352). He was engaged principally on *The Dead Man Restored,* the first painting he undertook on returning to London. After that came *Diana Bathing* (1812), which prompted West to extended comment. He called his son Raphael and exclaimed that no one was doing anything like it; he said the color was Titian's and advised WA to follow it up, pointing out that many people would give two hundred guineas for a picture of that size who had not room in their houses for larger ones. When WA mentioned the subject of West's paintings of Venus and Adonis, West suggested that he paint it but not have the figures the size of life (Prime, pp. 73-74). When it was exhibited at the BI in 1814, Hazlitt in the *Morning Chronicle* for 5 February praised it for its drawing, and the *Examiner* for 6 March for its "air of reality" and a delicacy not surpassed by Guido. It was followed by *Christ Healing the Sick* (1813), a subject also painted by West, for which he made two studies but which he did not complete. He was dependent in it on Raphael's *Death of Ananias* and *Christ's Charge to St. Peter.* He also worked on *Dido and Anna* (1813-15), from the *Aeneid* 4.20, which he did not complete. *Study from Life* (1813-15), begun in the last of these years, may have been a study for the figure of Anna. During this period he obtained permission to join the class at the RA to draw from the nude and drew, Benjamin Haydon reported, from the recently arrived Elgin Marbles. He also prepared for an engraving of a scene in his poem "The Paint-King," presumably to be included in *SS,* and

superintended the publication of the volume. His drawings included two of the head of his wife, one in pencil and one in chalk, and one in chalk of one of her ears. Possibly it was about this time that he became acquainted with the art critic and dilettante Richard Payne Knight, of whose *An Analytical Inquiry into the Principles of Taste* he owned a copy (2d ed.; London, 1805); and with the engravers James Storer and John Greig, of whose *The Antiquarian and Topographical Cabinet: Containing a Series of Elegant Views of the Most Interesting Objects of Curiosity in Great Britain* (London, 1808, 1811) he owned volumes 2, 4, and 10. 3. Maximo Paulino dos Reis (1781-after 1846), Portugese history and portait painter, studied in Rome from 1802 to 1813. 4. François Marius Granet (1777-1849), French architectural and history painter, was in Rome from 1802 to 1819. He was famous for his *Choir of the Capuchin Monastery in the Piazza Barbarini at Rome,* of which he painted fourteen or fifteen versions. One was purchased by Benjamin Wiggin of Boston and exhibited there in 1820, at which time WA expressed admiration of it (*Boston Daily Advertiser,* 22 Feb. 1820). 5. Joseph Dionysius Odevarre (1778-1830), Belgian history and portrait painter, spent eight years in Rome. 6. Joseph Otto Stockard von Bernkopf (1766-1833), Austrian officer and amateur watercolor painter, served in the Austrian army in Sardinia in 1799 and 1800 against Napoleon's forces. 7. Samuel Williams, banker. He graduated from Harvard in 1790 and was for several years a merchant in Boston. In 1796 he went to London and eventually became a partner in the banking firm of Welles and Williams, with a branch in Paris. He was a friend of Trumbull and a small art collector. During WA's second stay in England he acted as his banker and financial agent. In 1825 he failed in business and at last returned to America (HA; Irving, *Letters,* ed. Ralph M. Aderman, Herbert L. Kleinfield, and Jennifer S. Banks [Boston: Twayne, 1978], 1:575-76, 607-609, 2:145-47 and passim, 3:393; Irving, *Journals and Notebooks,* vol. 2, ed. Walter A. Reichert and Lilian Schlissel [Boston: Twayne Publishers, 1981], p. 90; Swan, p. 157; Lawrence Park, *Gilbert Stuart: An Illustrated Descriptive List of his Works* [New York: William Edwin Rudge, 1926], 2:854). He was a brother of Charles and Timothy Williams.

24. To Samuel Finley Breese Morse[1]

[Clifton,[2]
13 November 1813]

I will thank you to tell your Landlady that I shall take possession of the room[3] <on> a week from next Monday, at the terms <of> on which you agreed (12 pr week): the next beginning from that day, to be paid weekly.

You had better I think engage the Colourman to do the room on monday so as to give it a week to dry. The colour of course as you like.

Saturday, Novbr. 13 1813
yrs sincerely / W Allston

SOURCE: Manuscript, Morse Papers, LC.

1. Morse was in Bristol during the early months of 1813, for five months from October 1813, and for the last six months of 1814 (*Samuel F. B. Morse: His Letters and Journals,* ed. Edward Lind Morse (Boston: Houghton Mifflin, 1914), 1:119, 163, 169). 2. In the spring or early summer of 1813 WA became ill after working unceasingly on *The Dead Man Restored.* In April he and his wife, Morse, and Charles R. Leslie made a ten-day excursion to Hampton Court, Windsor, Oxford, and Blenheim, perhaps in an effort to give him rest (Leslie, pp. 190, 193). Presumably about this time, according to Sweetser, accompanied by Morse, he was treated, without success, for a pain in his thigh by the noted surgeon Dr. John Abernethy, whose Scots accent he afterward imitated. In the early summer, at the invitation of Elias Vanderhorst, he went with his wife to

Bristol, accompanied by Morse, Leslie, and for part of the way by Coleridge, who brought from London the eminent physician Dr. George Leman Tuthill. On the recommendation of Vanderhorst the Allstons moved to Clifton, a suburb noted for its medicinal waters, where Leslie stayed with them for two weeks (Leslie, pp. 23-24). Their address was 5 Richmond Place. By 5 September WA was back in London at work on *The Dead Man Restored,* when Coleridge and Southey visited him and Southey reported that he looked like a ghost but was improving. Shortly afterward he returned to Clifton, with a letter by Southey dated 17 September introducing him to Dr. John King there and saying he was suffering from the effects of lead poisoning (*New Letters of Robert Southey,* ed. Kenneth Curry [New York: Columbia Univ. Press, 1961], 2:68, 73). 3. Presumably 18 Pritchard Street, Portland Square, in Bristol, to which the Allston's moved on 22 November (Coleridge, *Collected Letters* 3:459). They did not take a whole house until their return to London later in the year.

25. To Samuel Taylor Coleridge

[Clifton, November 1813, between 17 and 20][1]

From your letter I conclude Mrs Morgan is better—*WELL,* I hope. Bless her bright Eyes! I wish, they were the illumined Windows of a *Heart* of Sunshine!—& the inexpressible archness, yet timidity, shrewdness yet meekness, in her Sister's![2]—I doubt, whether the Sun's Beams ever did or will visit any of better Hearts than theirs!—As to my own Health, Mr King[3] told me a few days since, that if no accident occurred to obstruct my present progress, I should in short time be a *well man:* and indeed I *seem* such even *now* in all but strength.

[Coleridge summarized the rest of this letter, from which he quoted this passage in his letter to Mrs. John Morgan of 20 November 1813, by saying "Mrs A. is but poorly—bashfulness alone has prevented her (A. says) from writing to you; but she loves you dearly. They remove on Monday from Clifton to No. 18, Pritchard Street, Portland Square, Bristol."]

Source: Coleridge, *Collected Letters* 3:459.

1. The date at which the Allstons moved from Clifton to Bristol. 2. Mary Morgan was the wife of John J. Morgan, and her sister was Charlotte Brent, who lived with them. Coleridge's poem "The Two Sisters" was addressed to them and at his suggestion WA gave the second painting he did of two sisters, after *Dido and Anna,* the title of *The Sisters* (ca. 1816-17). 3. John King. He began treating WA probably in late September, visiting him twice a week, and by late October had successfully performed several operations on him for stricture or thickening of the colon (Coleridge, *Collected Letters,* 3:444; Leslie, pp. 24-25). WA credited him with saving his life, though he never fully recovered his health.

26. To Samuel Finley Breese Morse

London,[1]
January 2, 1814

My Dear Sir: In the first place, I wish you and all of Mr. Visscher's[2] family a happy New-Year. Last week I wrote you a letter that must have been vastly *entertaining*—

as how? because it was altogether about my *own affairs*. Now, for the sake of symmetry, I send you another of the same kind.

Since my return I have had the courage to examine the state of my finances at my banker's, and found the balance in my favor to have been reduced to so small a sum as makes me think 'tis time to look about me;[3] and to endeavor, as soon as possible, after the proper *ways and means* for increasing it. On considering the subject, I was naturally led to the landscape[4] in Bristol, when it occurred to me that *perhaps* the price I had fixed for it (viz., six hundred guineas) might be too high for that market; and that I should stand a better chance of selling it by reducing it to five hundred. I would thank you to consult with Mr. Visscher on this point; for I depend so much on his judgment, that I should not hesitate a moment to put it at five hundred guineas, provided he should think *that* a more salable price. Will you write me immediately and let me know his opinion?

I gave the finishing touch to my picture[5] yesterday and shall send it to the gallery[6] to-morrow. Leslie's picture[7] will do him great honor; he has improved it very much since his return.[8] As to my "*own beautiful self,*" Mrs. A. says I am a *picture* of health. At any rate I find my health every day improving, and promise myself the pleasure of sending Mr. King a very favorable bulletin. Pray be particular in letting us know how his two patients in Mr. Visscher's family bear this cold fog. We have had it so thick and brown here, that it might well have passed for Shakespeare's "*blanket of the dark*" that Macbeth speaks of.[9] Mrs. A. unites with me in best regards to our friends in Portland Square,[10] and yourself.

Sincerely yours, / W. Allston

SOURCE: Prime, p. 72.

1. WA and his wife returned to London from Bristol at the end of November 1812 or the beginning of December 1813. 2. Harman Visger. 3. Coleridge said in September 1814 that WA's little property had been lost by a London bankruptcy (*Collected Letters* 3:354), presumably of the firm with which he deposited the sum paid him for the sale of his patrimony. It has not been identified. 4. *Diana and Her Nymphs*. 5. *The Dead Man Restored*. 6. The British Institution for Promotion of the Fine Arts was commonly called the British Gallery or the Gallery. WA also exhibited *Diana and Her Nymphs* there in 1814 and other paintings in 1816, 1817, and 1818. 7. *Saul and the Witch of Endor*. 8. Leslie had recently returned to London from Clifton, where he had accompanied the Allstons. 9. *Macbeth* 1.5.54. The phrase is spoken by Lady Macbeth after hearing that Duncan is coming to Macbeth's palace. 10. Visger lived at Portland Square in Bristol and Morse lived nearby.

THE DEAD MAN RESTORED

The Dead Man Restored to Life by Touching the Bones of the Prophet Elisha, from 2 Kings 13:20-21, was Allston's most famous painting during his lifetime and the one that most established his prominence in England and America. The subject was a rare one in art, though West had recently painted it. It was his first dramatic composition after the unfinished *Jason* and his largest completed painting. The sum paid for it by the Pennsylvania Academy of Fine Arts, $3,500, was by far the largest he received for any painting.

He began work on it soon after he arrived in London in the fall of 1811 and continued so constantly, without even stopping for a midday meal, until he was forced by the illness thus brought on to leave the city for several weeks in the summer of 1813. He worked on it briefly in the fall, and on 1 January 1814 he gave it what he called finishing touches. As he was doing so, he was visited by an impecunious stranger, who offered to write, for a fee, a favorable notice for a newspaper, saying he was following West's example in painting scriptural subjects. Allston refused, objecting that such a notice would seem like a puff, to which the man replied that since it would not be written by him it would not be a "Puff Direct" but that it might indeed be called a "Puff Oblique." In the end Allston gave him half a crown.[1]

He had intended to show it privately, he hoped in 1813, in the exhibition room in Spring Gardens in Charing Cross, but when John Young, keeper of the British Institution at the time, offered to allow him three weeks to work on it there, he sent it there. It was exhibited there in 1814, at which time it received a prize of two hundred guineas as one of the finest historical paintings in the exhibition. In June it was sent to Bristol for the exhibition of Allston's paintings in that city, and for two weeks before the opening there he worked on it again, chiefly on the coloring. At that time Coleridge said he had "restored it to his original conception," with a "truly Michael Angelesque figure."[2]

In preparation for it he made a small study and, Leslie said, a sculpture of the central figure and one of the head in clay. According to Coleridge, he modeled all the figures in clay.[3] In the composition he may have been influenced by the Ilissos figure from the Parthenon pediment, which was among the Elgin Marbles; the figures of Raphael's Heliodorus in the *Stanza of of Heliodorus* in the Vatican and Ananias in *The Death of Ananias;* and Sebastiano del Piombo's *Raising of Lazarus* in the collection of John J. Angerstein in London. For the first time he demonstrated, with success, his first style of monumental color, distinguished by the repetition of primary colors in different parts of the composition. As in *The Angel Releasing St. Peter from Prison* (1814-16), *Jacob's Dream* (1817), *Uriel in the Sun* (1817), and *Belshazzar's Feast* (1817-43), divine power is represented by a luminosity in contrast to deep shadows.

It received almost universal praise, while it was still in his studio, in both exhibitions in England, and subsequently in America. When West saw it in August 1812, he exclaimed that it reminded him of the fifteenth century, took the clay head at first for an antique and said that there was not a sculptor in England who could do anything like it, and suggested only the addition of another figure. For the next two or three days, Leslie said, Allston was in high spirits and the picture "advanced amazingly rapid."[4] Lawrence and Beechey also admired it. Hazlitt wrote a notice in the *Morning Chronicle* for 5 February 1814 in which he praised the "choice and originality of the subject," composition, drawing, knowledge of the human figure, recognized some affinity with the work of Raphael but some dependence on the school of Charles Le Brun, and concluded that though it demonstrated "genius," Allston had been too attentive to "the instrumental and theoretical part of his art." The critic in the *Examiner* for 13 February was more favorable, saying that Allston's study of the old masters and the antique had resulted in a "rich, ocular, and intellectual treat." The notice was reprinted in the *Analectic Magazine* for August 1815.

Coleridge, who praised it on more than one occasion, reported that the marquis of Stafford wished to buy it and that he, Beaumont, and the collector William Howell Carr wanted to acquire it for the British Institution but were dissuaded partly because of growing anti-American sentiment and partly because of West's "bad mouthing."[5] When Mrs. Frances Trollope saw it at the Pennsylvania Academy of the Fine Arts in June 1830 she was sufficiently impressed to mention it in her *Domestic Manners of the Americans* (1832), where she said that Allston was spoken of as "an artist of great merit" and whose manner, she was told, was "much improved" since.

Allston wrote an extended description of it in which he meticulously distinguished between the various emotions represented by the figures, much as Le Brum had in his celebrated *Expressions des passions:* the "gradual recoiling of life upon death" in the dead man, the "astonishment and fear, modified by doubt" of the figure at the feet, the unqualified immoveable terror" of the figure at the head, the "violent and terrified action" of the soldier rushing from the scene to illustrate a contrast to the firmness supposed to belong to the military character and to show his emotion to proceed "from no *mortal* cause," the "terror overcome by curiosity" of the figure grasping the soldier's arm, and the unconscious participation of the boy too young to comprehend the nature of the miracle, the "episode" formed by the wife and daughter of the dead man, in which the wife is "unable to withstand the conflicting emotions of the past and the present" and the daughter's possible "joy and astonishment" at the revival of her father is "wholly absorbed in distress and solitude" for the mother, the contrasting impulsive behavior and "mild and devotional character" of the two young men, and the "alarm" of the sentinels in the distance, who also "mark the depth of the Picture." It was printed, preceded by the passage from Kings, in the catalogs of the exhibitions of his paintings in Bristol in 1814, in Philadelphia in 1816, and in Boston in 1839.

The Dead Man Restored brings together three of the major elements in Allston's painting: biblical subject matter, the miraculous, and ideal figures after the example of Michelangelo. As his first completed history painting, it is typical of them all in being drawn from a biblical or literary source. All represent an oblique response to the paucity of history in the American experience as well as a positive one to European tradition, rejecting as he repeatedly did subjects drawn from American history such as were treated by Trumbull and others. It is also the first surviving painting after *Jason* in which he introduced a large number of figures, which are, as in most of the other paintings in which he did so, disposed in a generally pyramidal pattern, with the focal figure at or near the center foreground and depicted in violent movement. Most significant of all, the work is his first treatment in painting of the supernatural, of which he was keenly conscious from early childhood. The fascination it had for him is manifest in all his paintings of biblical subjects, which depict miracles, visions, signs, witchcraft, angels, and prophets; of Shakespeare's witches, fairies, and other nonhuman characters; of scenes from Ann Radcliffe's Gothic romances; and of angelic and allegorical characters from *Paradise Lost.* All convey a sense of mystery and most depict astonishment and terror in the features and attitudes of the main figures.

His writings also reflect this fascination. In many of his poems—"The Sylphs of the Seasons," "The Paint-King," "The Angel and the Nightingale," "The Night-Mare," "The Calycanthus," and "The Magic Slippers"—he referred to nonhuman creatures, among them fiends, ogres, angels, conjurors, fairies, and spirits, and in a few described such creatures represented by Michelangelo, Raphael, and Reynolds. The narrator of "The Hypochondriac" occasionally dips into ghost stories. Jarvis remembered that in college Allston would be so terrified by reading tales of horror that he was almost afraid to go to bed until he made sure there was no goblin under it or in the closet, and in later years he was noted for being a good teller of ghost stories, by Coleridge, Irving, John Howard Payne, and C.C. Felton among others. The Gothic romances of which he was fond contained a large element of the supernatural. On a more philosophical level, in the "Introductory Discourse" of his lectures on art and in a few poems, he placed both man and nature in a context of the supernatural or the infinite, saying that the mind was able to go beyond the known or finite into the otherwise unknown, that man and nature were related in a mysterious correspondence, and that the apprehension by man of the idea of the infinite from material senses and events was "the sole mystery," that idea being "*out* of his nature," and was reflected from the "Maker of his mind."[6]

It is nonetheless true, however, that *The Dead Man Restored,* like all his paintings of biblical and literary subjects, with their heroic scale, monumental forms, and violent action, does not express Allston's distinctive imaginative vision as do his smaller and quieter portraits, landscapes, and solitary figures. The former reflects the European influences most strong during his years in England and Italy, the latter being done mostly in America. Only a few of his finished later American paintings are in any way similar to the major works of his European years. Possibly he himself was acknowledging this fact about *The Dead Man Restored* when in speaking to John Neagle in later years he seemed to be not proud of it except for the central figure[7] and when he regretted the introduction in it of the wife and daughter.

1. Flagg, p. 101. 2. *Collected Letters* 3:517. 3. Ibid. 3:307. 4. Leslie, p. 179. 5. *Collected Letters* 3:510, 534. 6. *LA,* pp. 59-60. 7. Anna Wells Rutledge, "Dunlap Notes," *Art in America* 39 (Feb. 1951): 41.

27. To Samuel Finley Breese Morse 49 London Street
Fitzroy Square. Wednesday 12 Jany. 1814

My dear Sir: Having a great deal of business to attend to this morning, I can spare but a moment for writing. I must however avail myself of that to thank you for the agreeable intelligence contained in your letter to Leslie: but in a particular manner to request, (or rather to advise) you not to take a share in the intended raffle.[1] For this I can offer two reasons: first, that the price of a share is too much for you to risk upon an uncertainty; second, that I much fear, should you win, that the world <will> may suspect (on account of our connexion) that I was in some way interested in it.—I think upon the whole you had better not take one; but wait until you can paint <an> a Landscape equal to it yourself; which, I make no doubt, you will ere long be able to do if you are industrious. <However>

I shall follow your advice in not being too sanguine respecting its success. But hope is pleasant, and I shall therefore indulge it until I hear from you again. I am quite satisfied that it should go at five hundred; and as soon as it is sold I shall, according to my promise, bespeak an elegant frame for it.[2]

I have at least the satisfaction to inform you that my large Picture is in the British Gallery, and, moreover, hung in the place where Mr. West's was.[3]

You have added much to the above agreeable intelligence by your favourable account of the invalids at Mr. Visgers. Give our love to them all.

Yours with as much sincerity as haste, / W Allston.

P.S. In your letter to me (received a week since) you omitted *the "Fitzroy Square"* in the superscription. You must recollect it in future; as some of my letters have been lost in consequence of that omission; there being several London Streets in London.

<N.B. You observe that I have nothing to do with>
I wrote to my good Mr. King the other day.

ADDRESSED: S.F.B. Morse Esqure. / Care of Herman Visger Esqre. / Portland Square / Bristol. SOURCE: Manuscript, Morse Papers, LC. Printed in part in Prime, p. 85.

1. There were plans in Bristol to raffle WA's *Diana and Her Nymphs* (Prime, p. 85).
2. Presumably it would have cost somewhat less than the frame for the larger *Dead Man Restored,* for which WA paid sixty guineas (Prime, p. 58). 3. West's *Christ Healing the Sick in the Temple,* which made a great stir when it was exhibited at the BI, which paid an enormous price for it. The spot WA referred to was at the end of one of the rooms, an advantageous one (Prime, p. 73).

28. From George Howland Beaumont Dun[m]ow,
January 16, 1814.

My Dear Sir: I am truly sorry to hear your health has been in such a bad state. I hope, however, you will feel the benefit of the air you have inhaled at Clifton more in London than whilst you were upon the spot. This I know is not infrequently the case. I assure you I have been very anxious on your account, and have been prevented from writing only by having some accident mislaid your letter and not being able to recollect the address. I am sincerely sorry for your sufferings and heartily wish it were in my power to relieve them. I am very glad to hear you have completed your picture,[1] which I have no doubt will do you great credit. I should have been happy to have been in town at the time the arrangement of the British Gallery took place, but I am at present attending Lady Beaumont, my mother,[2] in an illness which has every appearance of ending fatally, altho' she is now somewhat better; this I hope will excuse me for writing in haste. In such an anxious state it is difficult to confine one's thoughts to other subjects. I will therefore only add at present, that I like the subject you mention extremely;[3] it is simple, well known, and capable of a pungent effect, which I would wish you to push to the utmost bounds of propriety.

I remain, my dear sir, with every good wish, most faithfully yours,

George Beaumont.

I shall be happy to hear of the progress of your health, and when you can with prudence attend to a sketch, I should be glad to have it sent here, for my stay at this place may probably be long.

SOURCE: Flagg, p. 103.

1. *The Dead Man Restored.* 2. Rachel (Howland) Beaumont, of Dunmow, Essex. 3. WA suggested the subject of *The Angel Releasing St. Peter from Prison* for the painting Beaumont commissioned. Beaumont had suggested the subject of the Resurrection.

29. To John Howard Payne [London February 1814]

My dear sir: I herewith return you Sargent's Poems,[1] a number of the Portfolio,[2] & Eustaphieve's Play,[3] with the 2 volume of Knickerbocker.[4] The first vol of the last was lent to Mr. Coat,[5] an american who is now dead. I <pro> cannot possibly get it this week as he died at Brompton,[6] but you shall have it, if it can anyway be procured, in the course of the next.

These are, I think, all the books I have of yours. If you have lent me more they must be among Morse's.

We shall be glad to see you. Thanks for the books.

Yrs sincerely W. Allston

ADDRESSED: J.H. Payne Esqre / 32 Southampton Street / Covent Garden. ANNOTATED, presumably by Payne: Washington Allston / London Feb 1814. SOURCE: Manuscript, John Howard Payne Papers, Rare Book and Manuscript Library, Columbia University Library.

1. Probably *Hubert and Ellen, with Other Poems* (Boston, 1812; 2d ed., 1813) by Lucius Manlius Sargent (1786-1867), Boston author, antiquary, and temperance advocate. He was a brother of the painter Henry Sargent. 2. *The Port Folio* (1801-27), Philadelphia literary magazine.

3. Akxiei Grigor'evich Eustaphieve (1783-1837), Russian author. From 1813 to 1821 he was Russian consul in Boston *(Boston City Directory).* His play, *Alexis the Czarewitz: A Tragedy in five acts,* was published in his *Reflections, Notes, and Original Anecdotes, Illustrating the Character of Peter the Great* (Boston, 1812; 2d ed., 1814). 4. Irving's *History of New York.* It was first published in New York in 1809 in two volumes. The second edition, also in two volumes, was published in New York and Philadelphia in 1812 and contained the first of several major revisions. It is probably this edition to which WA refers. 5. Mr. Coate, originally from Philadelphia, later of Montreal and England. In America he was a clergyman and traveled among the Indians as a missionary, but a tendency to consumption forced him to give up preaching. In England he brought out a number of specimens of ornamental penmanship in the form of letters to members of the nobility, for which Beechey sought to obtain him subscribers. He was also befriended by West and at one time obtained permission for Morse and Leslie to look at a collection of paintings by old masters about to be sold. He lived on Warren Street, near WA in London (Leslie, p. 185). 6. A village in Yorkshire.

30. To Jedidiah Morse London, 15 March, 1814.

My dear Sir: Though your son[1] has informed me that you mention having written me twice, I have not had the pleasure of receiving more than one letter from you. In reply to your inquiries respecting the necessity of his continuing longer abroad, I have no hesitation in saying that his return home at present would be of the greatest disadvantage to him; having arrived just at that stage of his Art, when, as he is most capable of appreciating their excellence, his studying the works of the Old Masters is the most necessary. And here, perhaps, it may be well to observe that of the time required to complete the education of an Artist no calculation can be made from what is usually allotted to the study of the learned professions. Three years is, I think, generally considered sufficient for the Law and Physick; if not sufficient to make able professors, at least, enough to qualify, and entitle students to the privilege of practice. This, however, is very far from being the case with respect to the higher departments of the Art. In the first place, the rudiments are to be mastered; then materials must be collected; and, lastly, a taste is to be <acquired> superadded, which is to regulate the knowledge thus acquired, or in other words, to animate the mechanick with the intellectual. As the term required for the attainment of these must in a great measure depend on the degree of ability in the student, it is impossible to affix to it any precise limits. <To show,> If we would learn, however, how little of the art a student is allowed by Nature to carry to his first lesson, it might, perhaps, be estimated, when we know that there are few artists, who are capable, after three years of study, even of *perceiving* the higher excellences of the Great Masters.

With regard to the progress which your son has made, I have the pleasure to say that it is *unusually* great for the time he has been studying: and indeed such as to make me proud of him as a pupil, and to give every promise of future eminence. He has arrived, as I before observed, at a stage in his art that enables him to converse with the Old Masters: at the time to profit by the experience of ages: in short, to become acquainted with his own powers, or rather, to learn how to use them. Should he be obliged to return *now* to America, I much fear that all which he has acquired would be rendered abortive. It is true he could there paint very good portraits; but I should grieve to hear at any future period that on the foundation now laid, he shall have been able to raise no higher superstructure than the fame of a portrait painter.[2] I do not intend here any disrespect to portrait painting: I know it requires no common talent to excel in it.—His model of the dying Hercules,[3] which I suppose you have already received, will make any thing more that I can *say in favour of your* son's genius appear superfluous.

In addition to this *professional report*, I have the sincere satisfaction to give my testimony to his conduct as a man; which is such as to render him still worthy of being affectionately remembered by his moral and religious friends in America. This is saying a great deal for a young man of two & twenty in London; but it is not more than justice requires me to say of him—Mrs. Allston unites with me in best respects to yourself & Mrs. Morse.[4] I am, dear sir, with respect,

Your obedient servt / W. Allston

ADDRESSED Revd. Jedediah Morse, D. D. / Charleston, near / Boston / Massachusetts, / North America. / Favd by / Barney Smith Esqr.[5] SOURCE: Manuscript, Morse Papers, LC. Printed in part in Morse, 1:131-32.

1. Samuel Finley Breese Morse. In his letter to his parents of 10 and 26 August 1813 he said that WA would write them on the subject of his returning to America (Morse, 1:114). 2. In his letters to his parents of 2 May 1814 and 3 May 1815 Morse said he could not be happy painting portraits only (Morse, 1:132, 176). 3. As WA had done for his *Dead Man Restored*, Morse modeled in the fall of 1812 a clay figure for his painting *The Dying Hercules*, depicting Hercules struggling with the poisoned shirt of Nessus. WA thought it better than all he had done in England put together, urged him to send a cast home, and said he would write friends in Boston to call on Morse's father to see it there. Six casts were made (Morse, 1:85-86, 102-104, 107, 119, 134, 185; Prime, pp. 46, 64, 79-80, 454). 4. Elizabeth Ann (Breese) Morse, from New Jersey. 5. A merchant, originally a shopkeeper, in business with George A. Otis in Boston (*Boston City Directory* for 1800-13).

31. To Samuel Finley Breese Morse[1] [Bristol[2] 5 July 1814]

My Dear Sir,—I received your last on Saturday and should have answered your first letter but for two reasons.

First, that I had nothing to say; which, I think, metaphysicians allow to be the most natural as well as the most powerful cause of silence.

Second, that, if I had anything to say, the daily expectation which I entertained of seeing you allowed no confidence in the hope that you would hear what I had to say should I have said it.

I thank you for your solicitude, and can assure you that both Mrs. Allston and myself are in every respect better than when we left London. Mr. King received me, as I wished, with undiminished kindness, and was greatly pleased with the pictures.[3] He has not, however, seen the large one, which, to my agreeable surprise, I have been solicited from various quarters to exhibit,[4] and that, too, without my having given the least intimation of such a design. I have taken Merchant Tailors' Hall (a very large room) for this purpose, and shall probably open it in the course of next week.

Perhaps you will be surprised to hear that I have been retouching it. I have just concluded a fortnight's hard work upon it, and have the satisfaction to add that I have been seldom better satisfied than with my present labor. I have repainted the greater part of the draperies—indeed, those of all the principal figures, excepting the Dead Man—with powerful and positive colors, and added double strength to the shadows of every figure, so that for force and distinctness you would hardly know it for the same picture. The "Morning Chronicle" would have no reason now to complain of its "wan red."[5]. . .

I am sorry that Parliament has been so unpolite to you in procrastinating the fireworks. But they are an unpolished set and will still be in the dark age of incivility notwithstanding their late illuminations. However I am in great hopes that the good people of England will derive no small degree of moral embellishment from their pure admiration of the illustrious General B——,[6] who, it is said, for drinking and gaming has no equal.

SOURCE: Morse, 1:147-48.

1. Morse was in London at this time. 2. WA and his wife were apparently in Bristol by May, at Visger's. By the time of the Bristol exhibition of his paintings his address was at Michael Humphry's, 16 Paul Street, off Portland Square. 3. Those brought from London for the Bristol exhibition. 4. *The Dead Man Restored.* 5. The *Morning Chronicle* (1769-1862) was a London journal. The quotation is from Hazlitt's review of *The Dead Man Restored.*
6. Gebhard Leberecht von Blücher (1742-1819), Prussian field marshal, who led the victory of the allies over Napoleon in the spring of 1814. He visited England in the summer and was everywhere received with great enthusiasm. Morse described some of the festivities in London in his letter to his parents of 15 June (Morse, 1:142-47).

THE BRISTOL EXHIBITION 1814

The exhibition of Allston's paintings in Bristol was the first of his two one-man shows and one of the earliest such shows of a living artist held in England. It opened on 25 July and closed on 24 September 1814. The hours were from twelve to seven each day except Sunday; Admission was one shilling or a permanent ticket for three shillings. Altogether there were eleven paintings. Eight were listed in the catalog,[1] all for sale, in the following order: *The Dead Man Restored, A Scene in an Eating House* (1813), *Hebe* (before 1814), *Rising of a Thunderstorm at Sea, Casket Scene, Rain at Sea* (before 1814), *Diana Bathing*, and *Diana and Her Nymphs*. The catalogue also contained Allston's descriptions of *The Dead Man Restored* and of *A Scene in an Eating House*. The latter, like the former, focused on the psychological states depicted, describing it as "The different and characteristic expressions produced by the same accident on men of different countries, exemplified in the affected condolence, conscious indifference, and good-natured mirth, of a Frenchman, a Dutchman and an Englishman: the Sufferer an intinerant Fidler." Possibly the pencil *Tavern Scene* was a study for it. About a month afterward he added three pieces: *Italian Landscape*, or *Italian Scenery* (1814), which was exhibited at the Royal Academy earlier that year, at which time it was compared in the *Examiner* to Turner's *Dido and Aeneas* and said to show that Allston had studied the great Italian painters and the Poussins; and two portraits, presumably that of John King (1814) and a second one of Coleridge (1814), painted for Coleridge's friend Josiah Wade of Bristol, both done in late July and August.

Italian Landscape, or *Italian Scenery*, was apparently the first landscape in which Allston used the method of painting foliage he followed thereafter. He told Henry Greenough that he had developed it by accident when he was painting a landscape in which a large tree was the most prominent feature. Finding when it was finished that it was "flat and opaque," that "the air did not circulate through the leaves and branches," and that he had to *"either make a spoon or spoil a horn"*[2] he resolved on "a bold experiment." As Greenough said he put it, "I took pure yellow ochre and dotted leaves all over it wherever I wished the branches to come forward. This gave my tree the appearance of having had a shower of yellow ochre from a dredging-box. When it was dry I gave it a thin glaze of megilp and gold-size, just tinged with asphaltum, and found to my surprise that these last touches were, by the glazing, so assimilated to the former painting that no one could have discovered that they were not painted at one and the same time." He afterward glazed the masses with asphaltum and blue. The result, he said, was that the tree was better than any he had previously painted, and from that time he reduced the process to "a regular system" in painting trees and even plants in the foreground, stating, "I paint in the forms of my plants with yellow ochre, Naples yellow, and ultra-marine, and then glaze and touch into my glaze. This gives form, light, shade, and the color of plants; everything but texture; to give this, I finally give them a thin glaze of yellow ochre, which adds the texture also."[3] Apparently the landscape to which he referred was this one. In it the foremost tree in its solitary state is more eye-catching than any in earlier landscapes and has predominantly yellow foliage.

During the exhibition, Coleridge, who suffered a serious indisposition at the time but was determined nothing should interfere with his part in it, delivered six lectures in Bristol on the fine arts illustrated by the paintings, which appeared with the title "On the Principles of Genial Criticism concerning the Fine Arts" in *Felix Farley's Bristol Journal* for 13, 20, 27 August and 10, 24 September. He thought them the best things he had ever written and proposed to extend their number to sixteen or twenty for publication in the *London Courier* but never did; a few months before his death he was still regretting their "loss," but they were reprinted by Joseph Cottle in 1837. They contained his first statement of several of the aesthetic principles he set forth shortly afterward in *Biographia Literaria,* notably that characterizing art as affording pleasure in contrast to the truth of science or moral philosophy, in which he followed Kant, and that describing the connection between the objective and the subjective realms being brought about by a third faculty or agency. Some passages were echoed not only in his letter to Allston of 25 October 1815 about the importance of nature to the artist but in that to John J. Morgan of late July 1815 referring to Raphael's *Galatea,* which they saw together in Rome. He gave *The Dead Man Restored,* which he called Allston's "great" and "grand" picture, as the chief example of his definition of beauty as multiplicity in unity and *Galatea* as a second example. He pronounced the paintings in general "admirable," cited *The Dead Man Restored, Hebe, Diana and Her Nymphs,* and *Rising of a Thunderstorm at Sea* as elucidating the "fundamental doctrines of color, ideal, form, and grouping," said he looked with a stronger and more pleasurable emotion at *Diana and Her Nymphs,* since it had been the occasion of his first acquaintances with Allston in Rome, and noted that a woman had told him she never stood before that painting without seeming to feel the breeze blow out of it upon her.[4]

The reviews, however, were not altogether favorable. The *Bristol Gazette* for 4 August called it a "very exquisite treat" and commented approvingly at length on *A Scene in an Eating House,* but the *Bristol Mercury* for 29 August expressed anti-American sentiments, and the *London Sun* spoke of the premium given *The Dead Man Restored* by the British Institution as due to "an attempt rather than merit." The only purchaser was Visger. Morse attributed the fact and his own failure to gain patronage in Bristol to anti-Americanism.[5]

Coleridge thought Allston unfairly treated by the press, notably by Thomas Taylor, editor of the *Sun,* and by professed admirers and patrons, including West and Beaumont, and felt that he had not learned of "the excessive meanness of Patrons, of the Malignant Envy & Brutality of the Race of Painters," chiefly "from vulgar Birth & want of the Discipline of classical & gentlemanly education," a subject on which he often lectured Allston.[6] Allston expressed the same sentiment in a footnote to his poem "The Two Painters," saying that the exceptions to generosity in artists were due to "narrowness of circumstances, and poverty of intellect."[7]

Though they were not exhibited, Allston also painted in 1814 a portrait of Emmeline (Edgeworth) King, wife of John King and sister of Maria Edgeworth, the novelist; one of Southey, according to Sweetser; and, in Bristol, *The Agony of Judas,* from Matthew 27:3-4. Richard Henry Dana, Jr., recollected that he thought the last the finest he had ever painted, but after showing it to a few friends, who agreed with him that it was too dreadful to be attached to his name, he destroyed it. He also began, in London, a portrait of West intended to be three-quarters or full length, but lacking both spirit and time finished only the head. The body and drapery were added in 1837. He planned to present it to Harvard but being pressed for money sold it to the Boston Anthenaeum through subscription in that year.[8]

1. *Catalogue of W. Allston's Pictures, Exhibited at Merchant Tailor's Hall, Broad Street, Bristol. July 25th, 1814* (J.M. Cutch, Printers). 2. WA was found of proverbial expressions, which were often remembered by those who knew him. 3. Flagg, pp. 195-96. 4. *Biographia Literaria, with his Aesthetical Essays,* ed. John Shawcross (Oxford: Clarendon Press, 1907), 2:305. 5. Morse, 1:153. 6. *Collected Letters* 3:510. 7. *SS,* p. 58. 8. RHD, p. 32, Addition.

32. To Mary Cooper (Vanderhorst) Taylor

At Mr. Humphrys'[1]
Paul Street, Portland Square. Oct. 22d, 1814

My dear Cousin: Mrs. Allston informed me yesterday that my Uncle was desirous of possessing three of my pictures viz: the Italian Landscape, the Comic-Piece & one of the Sea-Pieces,[2] for which he offered two hundred guineas. The Comic-Piece has cost me so much time and labour that I do not feel I could afford to part with it for less than a hundred guineas, the original price. I would, however, dispose of the Italian Landscape, together with the Casket Scene from Shakespear [*sic*] & the largest Sea-Piece for two hundred gs. Should my Uncle approve of these three last, it would make me most happy to have him possess them.[3]

Upon enquiring this morning I find that my Pictures are still at the Canal Office, and that they will not leave Bristol until Wednesday next. Could you favour me with an answer before that time?

Mrs. Allston joins me in best regards to Mr. Taylor & yourself.[4]

I am sincerely yours / W. Allston

P.S. I believe I forgot to mention that I should not require another sitting before friday.[5]

ADDRESSED: Mrs. Taylor—/ Care of E. Vanderhorst Esqr. / Park Street. SOURCE: Manuscript, City of Bristol Record Office, Reference 8032 (75).

1. Michael Humphreys was apparently a gentleman, with no trade (*Bristol City Directory* for 1814). 2. *Italian Landscape,* or *Italian Scenery; A Scene in an Eating House;* and *Rising of a Thunderstorm at Sea,* and *Rain at Sea.* 3. Vanderhorst bought *Italian Landscape,* or *Italian Scenery; A Scene in an Eating House;* and *Rain at Sea.* His daughter Mary inherited them all.
4. In February 1815 the Taylors invited WA and Samuel Williams to visit them but WA declined, probably on account of the recent death of his wife. 5. For WA's portrait of her. It was commissioned by her father, from whom she inherited it. It or the portrait of Mrs. King may have been the one described by RHD as being of "a lady who was dressed out in the richest colours & bedizened with Jewels," who added that WA used to tell him how he "revelled in Jewelry & Velvets at the sitting" (p. 7).

33. From John Vanderlyn Paris 24th Novemr 1814—

Dear Sir: This I hope you will receive by the hands of Mr. Miller,[1] a countryman of ours, who visits London previous to making his tour to Italy. Mr. M. has spent some years in Paris, and has during that time independent of other studies paid considerable attention to Painting and he naturally on that account will bestow the more value on a friendly introduction to your acquaintance which I take the liberty to ask for him. Mr. M. is perfectly conversant with the state of the fine arts here & will I am persuaded be able to give you as satisfactory information as you can wish for. He only proposes to spend a few weeks in London, during which time I hope you may have it in your power to procure him the pleasure, or point out the way of seeing what is most interesting in the circle of Art & Artists. I envy Mr. M. the pleasure & gratification he will have in seeing the state of the fine arts in England. I however hope to receive thro' him a more detailed satisfactory account of your large picture[2] & also Mr. West's last works[3] both of which I have heard the highest praises given to lastly by Mr. Wallis (who is a near neighbour of mine) yet tho' Mr. W. is an Artist I confess he has not given me a clear distinct idea as to the distinguishments of either of your works—Mr. Wallis by the way has meet [met] with nearly the same luck as your two pictures had, which you, when here sent to the Exhibition,[4] he sent them four Landscapes one of which was not put up & (that I took to be the best) the other three were placed in bad and indifferent lights, he was much provoked, & with just reason for there are a number of others exhibited in good lights, and certainly inferior to his on merit, he has taken his pictures from the Exhibition. It is almost inconceivable how differently mankind see in works of art particularly, and to what extent mode & fashion or prejudice regulates the public taste, that this should be the case with respect to the capricious forms of a bonnet or hat &c one can easily conceive, but that in the production of the pencil which have nearly the same objects or appearances of nature as Mode, they should differ so widely in the imitation of her whether it be a Tree or Rock; but it proves that Mankind do not love & respect truth equally. It is hard perhaps to say if the bulk of Mankind were different in this point during the ages of the old Schools, but certainly the old painters were not such impudent liars & sinners against nature (as their works prove) as the present school. By the by I hope you are not the only exception to this imputation & that I may also rank as one, but to quit this tone of levity and to talk more seriously as I am also more so disposed—I shall endeavor to give you some account of myself which I am very sorry to say is not so favourable as I could wish nor as (I flatter myself, you could desire to hear). It has all along been my intention to write you a long letter previous to my leaving Paris for the U. States, but it appears as tho' that period, should never arrive. It has been my serious wish & intention for these two years back to return home, but [I] have been disappointed in every good occasion that has offered. Last fall I had the most promising hope of going in the John Adams from Holland, but I received the permission from the British Admty too late & did not leave me time to reach the

Vessel before she was to sail, and I have [do] not choose to embark in a Vessel liable to capture & therefore I find myself as it were a Prisoner in Paris, and my interest and wishes most sincerely call me hence so urgently that I become daily more & more disinterested and fretful on the subject. I now look forward again to the Spring as the period of my delivery from captivity to those whose purse is better furnished. The obstacles are less, but that is and has been a serious difficulty with me. As to my occupations here I have little to do, & that little I am, or have been all along so poorly compensated, as does not even suffice to pay current expenses, moderate as they are. I have never received a sol[5] for any historical picture, save the small one I painted for Mr. Barlow[6] at the time you was here, for which I rec'd 25 Louis. 'Tis true I have not painted many, but enough however to run myself in debt and to discourage me, who have but a small share of confidence and as little persiverance & yet I have as much affection and love for my Art as I believe any one. I begin however to believe that I have acquired some more confidence in my Art of late from further insight perhaps in it & partly also from a stronger persuasion that some dashing and daring is necessary and not to be too uneasy as to the result. And one would suppose that when a man's mind has been so far cultivated and improved by study & reflection & after having seen all the first examples in Art, he can't fail of producing something worthy of being looked at. Whether I am persuaded by the former or latter of these reasons or both I don't pretend to say, but had I [a] small sum of money before me I would greatly prefer to occupy myself this winter with some historical picture or landscape in preference to paint portraits to keep from starving. I hope however to find time to do something that way.

I have requested of Mr. Miller to consult you with respect to a Panorama[7] speculation, that is to ascertain if possible on what terms I could make an arrangement with the London Proprietor of the Panoramas. I have this last autumn made drawings by the Camera oscuro & painted some sketches of the same spot taken from the upper terrass of the garden of Versailles, which shews the whole of the facade of the Palace, and the most general & comprehensive view of the garden. The celebrity of this Garden or park which is allowed to be perhaps the first of the regular kind in the world made me think that it might excite as much curiosity as any place whatever. I have been rather confirmed in this opinion by the strangers that I have seen there whilst engaged with my sketches particularly the English. It will be much sooner painted than a view of a town or city and will be less tedious. My project at first was to carry the sketches with me to America to execute there if it promised success, but since that it has struck me that I might perhaps previously draw some profit from it in London. This is what I have begged Mr. Miller to endeavour to learn, and I must you to second him with your advice so far as you can. I would willingly say something about the exhibition here, but it is really too indifferent and uninteresting to be able to say any thing worth hearing, & I besides Mr. Miller [*sic*] will be better able to satisfy your curiosity on this score. There is a large picture of Monsieur Granet, a small landscape or two of Chauvin,[8] both of which authors you knew in Rome. Monsieur Descamps formerly of the Strada fratina Casa Batoni[9] but now here has had his large picture there of the young women of Sparta encouraging their fellow citizens to defend their town &c Mr. Paulin has lately left Rome (during the last revolution) and returned to his estate near Marseilles. Odevare & Stockoff are in their native country (Bruges). So time alas! disposes us. I could have wished & indeed I entertained some hope of seeing you here on a visit, your old acquaintance Mr. L. Jarvis hopes so too. He talked of writing you, to induce you to come. Mr. J. is at present absent on a voyage to the North (Norway). I have experienced a great deal of friendship from Mr. Jarvis & must attribute it somewhat to you & to the art, for both of which I know he has the greatest regard.

Want of time obliges me to close this letter which I believe is long enough. Hoping soon to have the pleasure of hearing more circumstantially from you, & wishing you an amelioration of health—I remain

Dear Sir— / Sincerely your friend and humble Servt / Jno. Vanderlyn
Washington Allston Esqr

ADDRESSED: Washington Allston Esqr / London / Mr. Miller. SOURCE: Manuscript, Historical Society of Pennsylvania.

1. J.M. Miller, New York portrait painter. 2. *The Dead Man Restored.* 3. West's chief work of this period was his enormous *Christ Rejected,* which was exhibited for four months from June 1814 to great crowds and received extravagant praise (Robert C. Alberts, *Benjamin West: A Biography* [Boston: Houghton Mifflin 1978], pp. 367-68). 4. The annual Paris Salon of works of art held in the Musée Napoleon in the Louvre. 5. A French coin equal to the twentieth part of a livre. 6. Joel Barlow (1754-1812), American poet and statesman, lived abroad for many years. He was in Paris from 1797 to 1805. 7. Panoramas, pictorial representations of an extensive scene visible from one point of view, were popular especially in England for several years after the first was executed there in 1788. 8. Pierre Athanase Chauvin (1744-1832), French landscape painter. He went to Italy in 1802. 9. The house in the Via Frattina of Pompeo Batoni (1708-87), Tuscan painter, who spent most of his life in Rome.

34. To Jedidiah Morse

London,[1] 4 August, 1815

My dear sir: I cannot suffer my young friend to leave me[2] without some testimonial, which, however unnecessary for his welcome reception by the friends who so well know him, <I> may yet shew my esteem for his character, and the interest I take in his welfare. It is a subject of no slight gratification to me that I can with sincerity congratulate you on, what religious parents must above all others appreciate—the return of a son from one of the most dangerous cities in the world, with unsullied morals.

This should indeed be a cause of lasting satisfaction to you, that the foundation you had laid in his mind was too strong to be shaken even by the assaults of those who have been trained to, and grown formidable in, vice: for this may be said with truth of multitudes who dwell in this metropolis. With respect to the progress made by him in his art, I trust that the specimen which he takes with him (Appollo Marpessa & Idas)[3] will justify the expectations of his friends. This picture was intended to be offered <at> next winter at the Royal Academy for the prize. But that he could not be allowed to do unless he should remain here until November, to make a sketch at that particular time, which should entitle him to stand as a candidate: a piece of mere formality which they might & ought to have dispensed with. But they resist all kinds of improvement from too great a dread of innovation. I regret much his disappointment, as I have every reason to think he would be successful: his picture being much superior to any I have seen offered on many occasions. If he meets with encouragement he will be a great painter. I cannot conclude this without expressing the deep sense I have felt of his kindness to me in my affliction.[4] From him and my young friend Leslie I have received every attention which distress could receive from kind and compassionate natures. They were kind to me when kindness was indeed needed. Pray present my respects to Mrs. Morse, and believe [me] respectfully

Yrs / W. Allston

ADDRESSED: Revnd. J. Morse DD. / Charlestown / Massachusetts. SOURCE: Manuscript: Gratz Collection, Historical Society of Pennsylvania.

1. WA and his wife returned to London from Bristol in the fall of 1814 and took a house at 11 Tinney Street. The day after her death he moved to 8 Buckingham Place, Fitzroy Square, where Morse and Leslie lived. 2. Morse left London on 5 August and sailed from Liverpool for America on 21 August (Prime, p. 89; Morse, 1:186). 3. Morse's *The Judgment of Jupiter*, which depicted the choice required of the mortal Marpessa between her lovers, the mortal Idas and Apollo, was praised by West as well as WA. Eventually Morse presented it to John Ashe Alston. 4. The death of Mrs. Allston, suddenly, on 2 February 1815. Allston was deeply affected by it and, though with difficulty, Leslie and Morse dissuaded him from attending the funeral for fear the pain would be more than he could bear. Only Leslie, Morse, and John Howard Payne were there. She was interred in the burial ground of St. Pancras's Chapel in London. Dunlap's statement that he suffered "a temporary derangement or prostration of . . . intellect" was vigorously denied by Leslie, and Irving went so far as to say that he thought "a dash of melancholy had increased the amiable and winning graces of his character" (Leslie to RHD, 28 Jan. 1944; Dunlap, 2:172-74; Irving, "Washington Allston," in Evert A. Duyckinck and George L. Duyckinck, eds., *Cyclopaedia of American Literature*, vol. 2, pt. 1 [New York, 1866]). He continued for some time, however, to be disturbed. Jarvis remembered his reading aloud in the summer of 1815 lines he had written about his feelings at the time. He was so concerned about the "diabolical" imprecations forcing themselves into his mind, which distressed "a man so sincerely religious," as Leslie put it, that he wished to consult Coleridge about them but asked Leslie to do so instead. In response Coleridge told Leslie, "Allston should say to himself, *'Nothing is me but my will'* " and predicted that then they would cease or cease to trouble him (Leslie, pp. 34-35). Probably soon afterward he wrote a poem apparently about a portrait of Ann, either his or Malbone's in which he said that "serene and silent Art, / By Heaven's own light" could impart "A milder solace to the heart" than song which was known to both the departed and the bereaved

(Gulian C. Verplanck, *An Address delivered at the opening of the tenth Exhibition of the American Academy of the Fine Arts, May, 1824* [New York, 1824], pp. 32-33).

35. To John Vanderlyn London, 17th August, 1815

My dear Sir: I have the pleasure to inform you that my Casts & Pictures, together with your Paul Veronese, which were left packed up in the same case, seven years ago at Leghorn, are at last arrived, & [are] now in the London Custom-House. Having been formerly a student of the Royal Academy, I am entitled to free admission for my own works, prints, casts, & all that may be considered as the tools & materials for an artist's study; & by means of Mr. West & another Inspector of the Royal Academy, who have signed a declaration, certifying that such are the contents upon examination of my Cases, I am exempted from paying duty upon anything but the pictures of Paul Veronese; these being *old pictures* upon which the duties are *invariably* exacted.

I have therefore been obliged to pay a duty of eight pounds sterling upon my Paulo.[1] I should have been glad to have escaped this enormous tax, but there was no honourable mode of avoiding it. Yours is still deposited, & now in a separate case, at the Custom-House, where it will remain until I have your directions what to do with it. If you wish to have it in France, & you have any correspondent to receive it in Havre or any other port open to the English, it shall be forwarded immediately; or if you prefer sending it to New York, let me know to whom I shall direct it there, & it shall be shipped for America as soon as I receive the necessary information.

My own works have suffered very much from their long *imprisonment;* but the old Pictures, both yours & mine, are in as good order as when first packed. Yet I own I was very much disappointed to find how much I had overrated their excellence: for upon examining them with my present eyes, which have acquired perhaps some acuteness from experience, I was convinced they were not originals. However I would not rely only on my own opinion, I therefore asked the opinion of Mr. West, who did not hesitate in pronouncing them both copies, for he had seen the originals, which he said were formerly in the Orleans Collection;[2] & moreover had had the original[3] of *mine* for several weeks formerly in his own house. He however said they were not only very admirable copies, but they were old Venetian copies.—I should not have much felt this disappointment, were I not just now rather straitened for cash; & I had hoped, when I heard of their arrival, to have sold mine for a good sum; but nobody buys copies here, knowing them to be such; & as I am neither knave nor picture-dealer, I would sooner burn it than palm it on any one for an original.—I am now about a large picture of St. Peter released from Prison by the Angel:[4] When that is finished I shall begin another still larger.[5]—If I can possibly contrive to afford it, I will endeavour to pay you a visit in Paris for two or three weeks in the autumn.—[6]

Pray favour me with an immediate answer, & tell me all about yourself, what you are doing & are about yourself, what you have been doing & are now doing. Believe me, dear sir, with sincere esteem, very truly yours—

W. Allston

N.B. Direct me to the care of Samuel Williams, Esqre. N. 13, Finsbury Square, London. This letter will be handed you by Mr. Wm. Gibbs,[7] whom you already know. The duty on your Paul Veronese is the same with mine, eight pounds; but you will not have to pay that or any other duty if it be sent either to France or America. You must however write me immediately on this subject, as they will not allow anything to remain after a certain time at the Custom-House, when, if it be not removed, they sell it to pay the duties. Are any of our Roman acquaintances now in Paris, Odevarre, Paulin, Stockhove? Remember me to them.

ADDRESSED: A Monsieur Jean Vanderlyn, Paris. ANNOTATED: Letter 3rd. The Originals of the above Letters were rec'd by me today from Mr. Gosman, that I might copy them. He acts as Lit. Executor, I believe, of the late Mr. Vanderlyn. [Jany 25th / 53 (RHD's line).] SOURCE: Manuscript copy by RHD.

1. The painting by Veronese of which WA bought a copy was *Il Disinganno (Le Pere d'Amore)*, another, like that of which Vanderlin bought a copy, originally in the imperial collection at Prague, which Leslie described as depicting Hercules, Cupid, and two female figures (Piovene, pp. 107-108; RHD, p. 22, Addition). Both Veronese copies were exhibited at the BI in 1816. Many years later WA lent his to the New York painter Paul Oakley to copy; in 1838 his nephew George W. Flagg wrote Asher B. Durand expressing his eagerness for its return. 2. The collection of the dukes of Orleans at the Palais Royal in Paris, formed by Philippe II and dispersed by Louis Philippe Joseph, called Philippe Egalite, during the French Revolution. It was exhibited for sale in London on 26 December 1798 and following days. 3. RHD wrote "originals," probably by mistake. 4. *The Angel Releasing St. Peter from Prison,* from Acts 12:7-8. The subject was painted also by Raphael and West. By mid-November Leslie reported WA half through and by 30 January 1816 finished (Prime, pp. 92, 97). It was his first large commission, for which he made an unusually large number of studies (ca. 1813-15). In the figure of the angel he was influenced by Raphael's painting and in the figure of St. Peter possibly by the *Laocöon* and the *Apollo Belvedere*. Many years later it was reported that Morse sat for the head of St. Peter. The features of the angel may have been those of his wife. He painted the background over in strong color, contrary to West's theory that backgrounds should not be repainted, and told Henry Greenough that it was as perfect as anything he had painted or ever would paint, though calling it a "happy accident" (Flagg, p. 190). When the English painter John Martin, noted for his architectural compositions, visited his studio while he was painting the stairway he asked Martin to make a drawing putting the stairs in perspective, but when Martin delayed he painted them himself. Beaumont wanted somewhat of a smile given the angel instead of the original perfect calm and WA yielded, though against his better judgment (RHD, p. 8, Addition). The central figure is Allston's first treatment in painting of angels, of which he had already taken notice in his sonnet on Raphael's painting of those before the tent of Abraham, and which he treated in half a dozen other paintings from the Bible and from *Paradise Lost* and in writing. The English painter Thomas R. Hofland thought his angels "certainly the most *angelic* that ever the mind's eye beheld, the only ones that fully embody the MILTONIC idea" ("Outlines and Sketches by Washington Allston:

Allston's Lectures on Art and Poems," *Knickerbocker* 35 [1850]: 537). WA also treated angels in his sonnet on a statue of an angel by Luigi Bienamé, in the poem about Horatio Greenough's group of angel and child and in the "Introductory Discourse" of his lectures on art. There he gave as the "brightest example" of the Infinite "the Angelic Nature," illustrated it by references to the witches in *Macbeth,* the ghost in *Hamlet,* and archangels in *Paradise Lost,* and the angels appearing to Lot, Abraham, and the soldiers at the sepulchre of Jesus, and characterized it at length (*LA*, pp. 61-64). 5. The next large painting that WA undertook was *Belshazzar's Feast.* 6. WA did not go to Paris until 1817. 7. Probably William Gibbs (1757-1829), who was an eminent genealogist in Lexington (Josiah Willard Gibbs, *Memoir of the Gibbs Family of Warwickshire, England, and the United States of America* [Philadelphia, 1879], p. 14; "Graduates of Harvard University Originating from Salem," NEGHR 5 [1851]: 520.

36. To James McMurtrie London 6th Septr. 1815

Dear Sir: In pursuance of your request that I would fix the price of my picture of *The Dead Man Revived,* which you have kindly and generously undertaken, in conjunction with Mr. Sully,[1] to dispose of for me, I beg you to consider this as full authority to sell it, in any way you may judge best, for the sum of Seven hundred Pounds sterling. Two hundred and fifty guineas is the price of the Landscape;[2] the disposal of which I also leave to your own and Mr. Sully's judgment.

I have only now to add a request that you will present my grateful acknowledgements to Mr. Sully for the interest he has been so good as to express in my behalf, and once more to beg your acceptance of my warmest thanks.

Believe me dear Sir

Your obliged and faithful humble servant / Washington Allston

James McMurtrie Esq.

SOURCE: Manuscript copy. All the copies of WA's letters to McMurtrie are in the same hand, which is not McMurtrie's.

1. Thomas Sully. He and McMurtrie proposed to exhibit or sell WA's *Dead Man Restored* in Philadelphia. 2. Presumably *Diana and Her Nymphs.* WA, until December 1818, and McMurtrie referred to it as "landscape."

37. From Samuel Taylor Coleridge 25 Octr 1815 Calne—[1]

My dear Allston: I could have wished to have learnt more particulars from you respecting Yourself. I have, perhaps, felt too great an awe for the sacredness of Grief.[2] But those of our Household know, with how deep and recurrent a sympathy I have followed you: and *I* know, what consolation it has been to *me,* that YOU have in every sense the consolations & the undoubting Hopes, of a Christian. Blessed indeed is that Gift from above, the characteristic operation of which is to transmute the profoundest sources of our Sorrow into the most inexhaustible sources of our Comfort. The very Virtues, that enforce the Tear of earthly regret, fill that Tear with a Light not earthly. There is a capaciousness in every *living* Heart, which retains an aching Vacuum, what, and how so ever numerous, it's present Freight of worldly Blessings may be—: and as God only can *fill* it, so must it needs be a sweet and gracious incarnation of the Heavenly that what we deeply loved, but with fear & trembling, we must now love with a love of Faith that excludeth fear! love it in God & God in it!—

From such Thoughts none but an abrupt Transition is possible.—I pass therefore at once, by an effort, to the sphere, in which you are *appointed,* because highly *gifted,* to act—and in this I can but pour forth two earnest wishes. First, that *equal* to the Best in Composition, & I most firmly believe, *superior* in the charm of coloring, you would *commend* your Genius to the universally intelligible of your παμγλοσσου τεχυηs, EXPRESSION![3] Second, that you never for any length of time absent yourself from Nature, and the communion with Nature: for to you alone of all contemporary Artists does it seem to have been given, to know what Nature is—not the dead Shapes, the outward *Letter*—but the Life of Nature revealing itself in the Phaenomenon, or rather attempting to reveal itself—Now the power of producing the true Ideal is no other, in my belief, than to learn the Will from the Deed, and then to take the Will for the Deed. The great Artist does what Nature would do, if only the disturbing Forces were abstracted.—[4]

With regard to my MSS, I had no other wish and had formed no higher expectation than this:—that a Copy-right, as exclusive [as] the American Law permits, should be vested in some one Book-seller, who should have the Copy time enough to get it printed in America two months before the work could arrive from England—that is to say—to have it published in Boston or Philadelphia at the time of it's first publication in England—and that the Bookseller in return for the Copy & Copy-Right should secure to me some portion, say one third, of his net profits. If this can be done, I shall think it worth while to continue the Transcription: tho' the ultimate profits should be but from 20£- to L0||S0||D0||. One volume of 500 pages Octavo contains the History of my Life and opinions, the second my Poems, composed since 1795[5]—i.e. those not in my Volume of 'POEMS,' already printed.[6]

In the Ode on the Death of General Ross,[7] if I ever finished it, I shall utter a voice of lamentation on the *moral* War between the Child & the Parent Country,[8] a War laden with curses for unborn generations in both Countries! You may well believe, therefore, that I shall not make myself an accomplice directly or indirectly, by flattery—or by Abuse, in what I regard as a crime of no ordinary guilt, the feeding or palliating the vindictive antipathy of the one party, or the senseless, groundless, wicked Contempt and Insolence of the other.—Even now it would not be too late, if the Spirit of Philosophy could be called down on Ministers and Governments. The true Policy is palpable and simple—A child wearied out by undue exercise of parental Authority elopes, marries with an independent fortune, and sets up for himself—The matter is irrevocable—a reconciliation takes place, and the Parent himself is convinced that he had acted tyranically & under false notions of the extent of his Authority, & that in the same proportion his Child had acted justifiably.—What then would a good Parent do?—Evidently, treat the Child with the kindness of a Parent, but with additional respect and Etiquette, as now a Householder, and himself the Master of a Family—& this he will shew in the character of his Messengers, in the style of his Letters, &c—But if in addition to the duties of family love, their two Trades or Estates played into each other's Hands, so that the one could not really prosper without increasing his Dealings [wi]th the other, (suppose the Father a Shoe-maker, for instance, and the Son a Tanner & Currier) then Common Self-love would dictate the abandonment of every act & impulse of Jealousy.—Were I Dictator, I would not only send to America men of the highest Rank and Talent, with more than usual Splendor, as Ambassadors, Ministers, &c; but would throw open not only the West India, but the whole Colonial Trade to the Americans, confident that every new City, that should thence arise in the United States, would add a new Street to some Town in G. Britain.—Alas! that the Dictates of Wisdom should be but the Dreams of Benevolence, to be interpreted by Contraries! The malignant Witchcraft of evil Passions reads good men's Prayers backward!—And I cannot help dreading, that the Hot Heads of both Countries will go on to make folly beget folly, both the more wrong in proportion as each is Right! How little then ought we to value Wealth & Power, seeing that every nation carries it's only formidable Enemy in it's Bosom—and the Vices that make it enemies elsewhere are but the Systole to it's Diastole.

Morgan (my saying concerning whose apprehensions you took more seriously than I meant),[9] Mrs. M. and Charlotte Brent send their Love to you—. I have received a most flattering Letter from Lord Byron.[10] Should my Tragedy[11] be accepted (of which I have little doubt) I shall, God willing, see you about Xtmas!

Mean time may God bless you / & / S.T. Coleridge.—

Let me hear from you soon.—

Friday last (20th) my 44th Birth-day:[12] and in *all* but the Brain I am an *old* man! Such ravages do anxiety & mismanagement make.

ADDRESSED: W. Allston, Esqre / 8. Buckingham Place / Fitzroy Square / London.
SOURCE: Coleridge, *Collected Letters*, vol. 4 (1959), pp. 606-609. The manuscript is in the MHS.

1. Coleridge was staying with the John J. Morgans at Calne in Wiltshire. 2. Coleridge refers to the death of Mrs. Allston. 3. Coleridge used many of the words in the sentence in his letter to Morgan of late July 1814, written during the exhibition of WA's paintings in Bristol. WA, he wrote there, "has but *one* thing to do—Having arrived at perfection, *comparative* perfection certainly, in colouring, drawing, and composition, to be as equal to these three in his *Expression*, (not of a particular Passion but of the living, ever-individualizing *Soul*, whose chief & best meaning is *itself*) as even in *this* he is superior to other artists," adding "He will remember the Galatea of Raphael in the Farnesini which we saw—& understand" (*Collected Letters* 3:520-21). 4. Coleridge expressed the ideas and used many of the words in the last three sentences in his essay "On Poesy or Art," which may have been one of the lectures he delivered in 1818: the artist "merely absents himself for a season from her [Nature], that his own spirit, which

has the same ground with nature, may learn her unspoken language in its main radicals. . . . not to acquire cold notions—lifeless technical rules—but living and life-producing ideas. . . . The artist must imitate . . . the *Natur-geist* of nature. . . . Each thing that lives has its moment of self-exposition, and so has each period of each thing, if we remove the disturbing forces of accident." In this passage in the essay he also declared that the essence of what the artist thus produced was "the universal in the individual, or the individuality itself" (*Biographia Litaria* 2:258, 259). In one of his aphorisms WA seemed to echo these words in defining originality in art as "the individualizing the Universal; in other words, the impregnating some general truth with the individual mind," and in *Monaldi*, he referred to "the individualizing power by which we recognize genius, or the originating faculty" (*LA*, p. 172; *Monaldi*, p. 76). 5. Coleridge's project to have a two-volume work such as he described was not carried out, but *Biographia Literaria* carried the subtitle *Biographical Sketches of My Literary Life and Opinions*. 6. *Poems on Various Subjects* (1796). 7. Major General Robert Ross (1766-1814), commander of the British expeditionary force against the coasts of the United States in the War of 1812, was fatally wounded in the destruction of Washington in 1814. Coleridge never finished the poem. 8. Coleridge had a great interest in America and American-English relations, early manifest in his and Southey's plan to establish a pantisocracy. 9. John J. Morgan. 10. George Gordon, Lord Byron (1788-1824) wrote Coleridge on 31 March 1815 in answer to Coleridge's request for aid in securing a publisher for his works much as described in this letter to WA, encouraging Coleridge particularly to remember the success of his play *Remorse*, which he had helped get produced (*The Works of Lord Byron*, vol. 3, *Letters and Journals*, ed. Rowland E. Prothero [London, 1898], pp. 190-92. 11. Coleridge's play *Zapolya* (1816) was rejected for production by the committee of the Drury Lane Theatre. WA owned a copy. 12. 21 October 1815 was Coleridge's forty-third birthday.

38. From Samuel Finley Breese Morse Boston,[1] April 10, 1816

My Dear Sir: I have but one moment to write you by a vessel which sails to-morrow morning: I wrote Leslie by New Packet some months since, and am hourly expecting an answer. I congratulate you, my dear sir, on the sale of your picture of the "*Dead Man.*" I suppose you will have received notice before this reaches you, that the Philadelphia Academy of Arts have purchased it for the sum of thirty-five hundred dollars. Bravo for our country![2] I am sincerely rejoiced for you, and for the disposition which it shows of future encouragement. I really think the time is not far distant when we shall all be able to settle in our native land with profit as well as pleasure. . . . I long to spend my evenings again with you and Leslie; I shall certainly visit Italy (should I live and no unforeseen event take place) in the course of a year or eighteen months. Could there not be some arrangement made to meet you and Leslie there? You will now be in funds, and perhaps would not dislike to visit again the scenes of your early studies. Do write me, if it is but a line, and say if it cannot be so arranged. . . . My conscience accuses me, and hardly too, of many instances of pettishness and ill-humor toward you, which make me almost hate myself, that I could offend a temper like yours; I need not ask you to forgive it, I know you cannot harbor anger a minute, and perhaps have forgotten the instances; but I cannot forget them. If you had failings of the same kind, and I could recollect any instances where you had spoken pettishly or ill-natured to me, our accounts would have then been balanced, they would have called for mutual forgetfulness and forgiveness; but when on reflection I find nothing of the kind to charge you with, my conscience severely upbraids me with ingratitude to you, to whom (under Heaven) I owe all the little knowledge of my art which I possess; but I hope still I shall prove grateful to you; at any rate, I feel my errors and must mend them.

I was at a large party at William Walter Channing's[3] a few evenings since; I there saw your *"Katherine and Petruchio."* It reminded me of old times.

I have just completed a Kitcat[4] landscape, a sea-piece on a common half-length upright, a ship in distress on the top of a small piece of a single wave which occupies the whole foreground; she comes out against a bright bank of clouds, *such as you like,* is scudding directly toward you under a close-reefed foresail. I bought a famous model of a seventy-four a week or two since, seven feet long and five feet high, completely rigged and perfect in every part; all the blocks traverse, so that I can brace or square the yards at pleasure, or place that in what state of dishabille I please. I gave twenty dollars for it, and it was sold a few weeks before for one hundred. I shall keep it to paint from always. Please write me soon and tell me all about yourself and Leslie. Remember me most particularly to Leslie, Collard,[5] Lonsdale,[6] Collins,[7] Haydon,[8] Mr. and Mrs. Hewlings,[9] Cregan,[10] Martin,[11] Lane[12] (if in London), and *the Bridges* [Bridgens][13]

Yours most sincerely, / Samuel F.B. Morse.

SOURCE: Prime, pp. 94-95.

1. Morse lived with his parents in Charlestown, Mass., and in Boston from his return to America in 1815 to the summer of 1816 (Prime, p. 90). 2. The sale was made on 28 March 1816 (President and Directors of the PAFA to McMurtrie, 28 Mar. 1816, Cadwalader Collection, Historical Society of Pennsylvania.) 3. He does not seem to be called William elsewhere.
4. A canvas somewhat less than half-length in size, so-called because it was used by Sir Geoffrey Kneller for portraits of members of the Kit-Cat club in London (named for the tavern of Christopher Cat, where it met), the room in which they were to be hung being too low for full-length canvases. 5. Frederick William Collard. 6. James Lonsdale. 7. William Collins, English painter. 8. Benjamin Robert Haydon. 9. Unidentified. It is possible the manuscript was misread. 10. Martin Cregan (1788-1870), Irish portrait painter, who lived for several years in London. 11. John Martin. 12. John Bryant Lane (1788-1868), English history and portrait painter. In 1817 he went to Rome, where he stayed ten years. 13. Mr. and Mrs. Bridgen. Prime probably misread the manuscript.

39. From James McMurtrie

April 15th [1816]

Since writing the foregoing[1] (original pr W.T. Johnson[2] via Liverpool) I have made sale of the picture of the "Dead Man Raised" to the Pennsylvania Academy of fine Arts for the sum of three thousand five hundred dollars payable in 3 installments say 4.8. & 12 months.[3] I consider this a great sale for *This Country* particularly as it is now placed under a *permanent roof,* which I well know you will prefer to its travelling about from place to place. I had very nearly sold it to R. Peale[4] for $3000. *Conditionally.* Subject to yr future decision, and I actually offered it at $3250. His answer to my letter not being definitive I conceived myself quite at liberty to receive any other offer which might be made. As fast as the payments come round you shall receive the remittances. The charges will be rather heavier than I at first supposed—it was valued at 600 Dollars. The duty will therefore be about 200.—the freight 25 & a trifle of shippg charges at Liverpool—say in all $235 to 240. The nett amt will be about $3260. Were it not for the rate of Exchg being so much against remitting you wd receive something more than £700. I hope it will grow better. You will most probably receive the first remittance of $1000. before I receive any advice from you. With respect to the balance if you wish any other disposition made of it you will please direct me, as your orders shall be punctually fulfilled. I hope you will approve of what has been done in selling &c. I will send you out some papers in which yr picture is mentioned. It is needless for me to recapitulate the enconiums it receives from every one. I have a much better opinion of the taste of my countrymen than I ever had. The exhibition opens at the Academy this day.[5] Yr picture has an entire side of the wall to itself, fronting the entrance light from above. I have not seen it in its place but can readily imagine the effect it will produce. I am sorry yr landscape has not arrived—I think I might have disposed of it. Your 2 small paintings of "Silence"[6] & "Diana"[7] wd have been purchased immediately.

In my letter to Mr. Leslie of 16 ulto I requested he wd make me a Copy of Mr. West's "head of Christ" by Guido.[8] If he can do it on a pannel I shd prefer it. Shd however Mr. Leslie be better employed, which I most sincerely pray may be the case, tell him to think no more on the business.

Referring to my former letters I remain with great regard

Dear Sir / Yours very sincerely / James McMurtrie

ADDRESSED: W. Allston Esquire / No. 8 Buckingham Place / Fitzroy Square / London.
SOURCE: Manuscript copy. All McMurtrie's letters to Allston are in the same hand, which is not that of the copies of Allston's letters to him, and is presumably his own. He employed numerous abbreviations, which have been allowed to stand, and capitals, which have been reduced to lowercase letters in most instances, since their use is highly inconsistent.

1. McMurtrie's letters to WA of 16 and 18 March 1816. They do not seem to have been preserved. In one or both he apparently reported negotiations with Rubens Peale for the purchase of *The Dead Man Restored,* proposed that WA produce a painting from his sketch of *Christ Healing the Sick,* and asked him to help identify the artists of certain drawings. 2. Unidentified. Probably a Philadelphian traveling to Liverpool. 3. Part of the sum was raised by subscriptions of $20 each, but the larger part was obtained by the mortgaging of the PAFA building in 1817.
4. Rubens Peale (1784-1865), still-life and animal painter, whose chief activity was museum management. He and WA probably met in London when he was there in 1802 and 1803, assisting his brother Rembrandt in the exhibition of a skeleton of a mammoth or mastedon which their father, Charles W. Peale, had assembled (Charles Coleman Sellers, *Charles Willson Peale* [New York: Scribner's, 1969], p. 301). At this time he was in charge of Peale's Museum in Philadelphia, established by his father for the exhibition of specimens of natural history as well as paintings.

5. Paintings by WA were exhibited more often at the PAFA than anywhere else except the BA: in 1816, 1817, 1818, 1822, 1826, 1831, 1842, and 1843. 6. (Before 1816) Unidentified, unless it was *Contemplation* (ca. 1817-18; G38, Lord Egremont, Petworth House, Sussex, England). 7. *Diana Bathing*. 8. In December 1816 Leslie wrote his sister that he was going to do so. The painting was in the painting school of the RA (Leslie, p. 202).

40. To James McMurtrie London 13th June 1816[1]

To / James McMurtrie Esqre.

Dear Sir: Your several favours of the 16th and 18th March; on the subject of Mr. Peale's offer, arrived at the same time; and, agreeably to your request, I should have replied to them immediately on their receipt: but hearing the day after, thro' a Boston correspondent,[2] that the Picture of "The Dead Man" was already sold to the Pennsylvania Academy for the sum of three thousand five hundred dollars, I thought it better to delay writing until I should receive confirmation of this account from yourself: which I had no doubt the next arrival from Philadelphia would bring. I have now the pleasure of acknowledging your subsequent kind favour of April 15th, containing the expected particulars of the sale. When you first made me the generous offer of taking out my picture, you may remember with what implicit confidence I submitted the entire management and disposal of it to yourself and Mr. Sully. I would not have done this, if I had not been fully assured that, whatever might be the event, I should have every reason to be gratefull: For, even if it had wholly failed of profit, I should still have felt myself indebted for every exertion that kindness and liberality could make. If such would have been my feelings in the event of a total failure [an event too, which I suffered myself almost to anticipate], you may well judge what I now feel at the account of this most agreable result. I beg you both to accept my warmest and most grateful acknowledgement. The sale is in every respect highly gratifying, both as affording me a very seasonable [pecuniary] supply, and on account of the flattering circumstances attending it. As necessary and acceptable as the money is to me, I assure you I think more of the honour conferred by the Academy in becoming the purchasers of my work. Will you express to them my sense of the honour done me?

If I am constrained from various circumstances to disappoint you as to the [your] proposal respecting a picture from my sketch of "Christ Healing," I trust you will believe me as sensible of your kindness in making it, as it it had been in my power to comply with it [not insensible to the kindness that dictated it; and also hope that the proposal which I in my turn will make will be as agreeable to you as if it had been in my power to comply with the first]. Upon reconsidering the sketch some months since (though still pleased with the general arrangement) I found the principal incident so *faulty* and *inefficient*, and myself at the same time so unable to suggest any one better that I was forced to come to the resolution of relinquishing it [the subject] altogether; or at least to lay it by for some future and more propitious period, in the hope that my imagination might then supply a more suitable incident.*[3] It is of the first importance to a large work, that the principal incident should be obvious and striking, leaving no doubt on any one of its meaning. Now in the incident I allude to I have attempted to express the *miracle of restored health* to a sick man, and that I have failed in this is certain; because not one who has seen it (and I have shewn it to several) has been able to guess my intention. I could easily express *disease;* in any stage of languor or emaciation. But there would then be *no incident;* merely a sick man waiting to be healed; which is but repeating what Mr. West has already so admirably done. My object was not to treat the subject thus, but in a very different way; that is, to shew both the *operation* and the *effect* of a *miracle*. The blind boy or rather the boy that *was* blind (which you may recollect in the sketch) is I think a very happy incident; for the miracle there is obvious, and clearly explains itself; but as it is a miracle which has been *already* wrought, it becomes necessarily subordinate. Had I been equally successful in the principal object, who is supposed to be under the *immediate influence* of the Saviour's *word,* I should not only be satisfied, but have reason to think I had achieved something great . . . I still like all the rest of the sketch; but this great and radical defect in it has long compelled me to give it up. But were I even perfectly satisfied with it, I am afraid it would not be in my power to paint it on a large scale for less than nine hundred or a thousand guineas, without a *loss;* as it would employ me full 18 months or two years, and in addition to my present expenses, I should be obliged to hire another large room.

But, though it is not in my power, for the reasons above stated, to engage in a <very> large picture from this sketch, I should be most happy to undertake another subject [for you] of five or six figures, size of life; which would make a picture about the size of the St. Peter in Prison:†[4] and this I could do for the sum you mentioned, say five hundred guineas. Such a picture I could paint in my present room, and could finish, I should hope, in somewhat less than a year. Should this be agreeable to you, you will [please to] say what kind of subject you would prefer. I think Scripture subjects, as being most known and interesting to the world, are the best.—Perhaps some splendid subject—uniting brilliancy of colour with strong character and expression. Should the preceding meet your views, you have every reason to depend on my very *best* efforts.

Whenever you send the Portfolio of Drawings I will with pleasure attend to your request respecting them. Mr. West, who is, I believe one of the most learned in Europe in these things will be happy, I am sure, to assist me in assigning to them the names of their proper authors. [I know that he has a great esteem for you.]

Since you still encourage me with the hope of selling the Landscape, I will send it out in the course of the summer. I think I gave you a memorandum of the price. I do not recollect whether it was 150 or two hundred guineas. If it is worth anything, it is worth two; having cost me four months hard labour. However I should be content with 150 gs. provided I get that sum without loss by exchange. At the same time I shall send the [little] picture of the Virgin and Child,[5] which, as I know it to be a great favourite with you, I beg you to accept as a small testimony of my esteem. I have lately improved it very much.‡—I have sold the Gil Blas[6] to our countryman Col. Drayton.[7] A nobleman wished to have bought it, but he was too late. Before you get this, it will <shipped> have arrived, I suppose, in Philadelphia; having been sent there to the care of Mr. John Vaughan.[8] Should you see it, I think you will find it improved. I have retouched it since you saw it here.

I do not remember whether Mr. Leslie had begun his "Murder of Rutland by Clifford,"[9] before you left London. It is now in the Exhibition at Somerset House,[10] and does him great *honour.* It is very finely conceived and painted with a powerful hand. The figure of Rutland alone is sufficient to confirm his just pretensions to *genius:* a word but too often misapplied. He possesses the rare merit of combining the excess of imploring terror with uncommon beauty. Clifford is also a fine though opposite character; and the background is managed with great spirit.

Mr. West has begun on a grand scale the subject of Death on the Pale Horse.[11] You must well remember his admirable sketch.

Begging you once again to accept my best thanks, I remain, dear Sir,

With great esteem / Yrs sincerely and obliged / Wa. Allston

In a letter to Mr. Leslie, Mr. Delaplaine[12] has done me the honour to inquire my terms for a large picture, 15 feet, figures size of life. I have requested Mr. Leslie to rely that I could not undertake it without loss for less than a thousand guineas, which I fear will be a disappointment to him.

My address is "to the care of Samuel Williams, Esq. No. 13 Finsbury Square."
James McMurtrie Esq. / Philadelphia / North America

*I may here observe that the universal failure of all painters ancient and modern in their attempts to give even a tolerable idea of the Saviour, has now determined me never to attempt it. Besides, I think his character too holy and sacred to be attempted by the pencil.—October 25. This note does not occur in the original letter of 13 June, but is here added in the copy (all in Mr. Allston's writing) of October 25.
†By the bye the St. Peter employed me more than six months after you left London, instead of *two,* as I had calculated.
‡Having repainted the Mother's head and the whole of the Infant, as well as retouched the back-ground.

SOURCE: Manuscript copy. Printed in part in Dunlap, 2:175-176.

1. WA sent McMurtrie a copy of the original of this letter, together with his letter of 25 October 1816, which copy differed in several respects from the original. Neither the original nor WA's copy seems to have been preserved. The most significant differences between them apparently were three additional passages in WA's copy, which were given in footnotes in the copy of the original which was made at the instance of McMurtrie. Other differences between the original and WA's copy appear in Dunlap, where the quotations seem to be from WA's copy; the major ones are

indicated within brackets, but the others, which are mostly omissions of short phrases and variations in word order or sense, are not noted. 2. Morse, in his letter of 10 April 1816. 3. WA expressed the same sentiment on several other occasions. When he copied Veronese's *Marriage at Cana* the next year he altered the figure of Christ in such a way that it was not the central point in the painting, as it was in the original. 4. It is 124½ by 108½ inches. 5. *A Mother Watching her Sleeping Child* (1814). He later painted a larger picture of the same subject, *Mother and Child* (1829), for which he made an unfinished study, and the similar unfinished *Mother with Child in her Lap.* His *Family Group* (ca. 1835), also unfinished, is related to these pieces. 6. *Donna Mencia in the Robbers' Cavern* (1815), from Alaine-René Lesage's *Gil Blas,* book 1, chap. 10, It depicts the scene in which the heroine, just recovered from the shock of her husband's murder, finds herself with Gil Blas captive of the bandit Rolando. Opie painted the same scene, of which Sully made a copy. It was the first painting WA did after his wife's death, and he said he was constantly in tears as he worked on it. It was exhibited at the RA in 1815, where it was disadvantageously hung but received a favorable review in the *Examiner* for 14 May, in which the character and the execution were praised and the contrast between the emotions aroused by Donna Mencia and those aroused by her captors was noted. It was exhibited at the BI in 1816, the PAFA in 1816 and 1817, and in Charleston, S.C., in 1823. RHD, Jr., recollected that WA later said, referring to another death in the family, that it was a blessing to have work in time of trouble. Asked by George W. Flagg, who admired it more than any other in the 1839 exhibition of his paintings in Boston, how he could have painted at such a time, he replied that nothing except want of money could prevent his painting. 7. William Drayton. He saw the painting when it was exhibited at the RA in Pall Mall in 1815 and liked it well enough to buy it without knowing who the artist was. He had done so by the end of January (Prime, p. 98). WA wrote him one letter about it, which does not seem to have survived. Drayton later made a watercolor copy of it. 8. John Vaughan (1756-1841), merchant and cultural promoter, was born in Jamaica of English parents but spent most of his life in Philadelphia. His portrait was painted by both Stuart and Sully (Edward Biddle and Mantle Fielding, *The Life and Works of Thomas Sully* [Philadelphia: Kennedy Graphics, 1921], p. 303; William H. Furness, "John Vaughan," in Henry Simpson, *The Lives of Eminent Philadelphians now Deceased* [Philadelphia, 1859], p. 921; Park, 2:778). 9. Leslie's *Murder of Rutland by Lord Clifford* was from Shakespeare's *King Henry VI,* Part 3 2.1. 10. The RA and other learned societies occupied one end of this building until 1838. 11. West's second painting with this title was much more elaborate than his first. 12. Joseph Delaphine (1777-1824) of Philadelphia published *Delaplaine's Repository of the Lives and Portraits of Distinguished American Characters* in 1816; it went through several editions and involved him in controversy. WA was evidently in correspondence with him earlier. In November 1814 Leslie sent a message through Morse to WA that if he mentioned Leslie in his letter to Delaplaine he would consider it a great honor to be called his pupil (Prime, p. 73). Presumably for his *Repository* he asked Morse in 1816 to paint a portrait of John Adams for half price (Morse, 1:132).

41. To Samuel Finley Breese Morse

[London, Summer, after 16 June 1816][1]

My dear Sir: I will not apologize for having so long delayed answering your kind letter,[2] being, as you well know, privileged by my friends to be a lazy correspondent. I was sorry to find that you should have suffered the recollection of any hasty expressions you might have uttered to give you uneasiness. Be assured that they never were remembered by me a moment after; nor did they ever in the slightest degree diminish my regard or weaken my confidence in the sincerity of your friendship or the goodness of your heart. Besides, the consciousness of warmth in my own temper would have made me inexcusable had I suffered myself to dwell on an inadvertent word from another. I therefore beg you will no longer suffer any such recollections to disturb your mind; but that you will rest assured of my unaltered and sincere esteem.

Your letter, and one I had about the same time from my sister Mary, brought the first intelligence of the sale of my picture, it being near three weeks later when I received the account from Philadelphia. When you recollect that I considered the "Dead Man" (from the untoward fate he had hitherto experienced) almost literally as a *caput mortuum,* you may easily believe that I was most agreeably surprised to hear of the sale. But, pleased as I was, on account of the very seasonable pecuniary supply it would soon afford me, I must say that I was still more gratified at the encouragement it seemed to hold out for my return to America—not that I expect as ready a sale for every large picture I might paint; but from the growing interest in the arts, which the present purchase appears to indicate among our countrymen, I think I may reasonably reckon a *quantum sufficit* of taste in them to calculate on at least a decent support from future exhibitions. The "St. Peter" has been long finished, exhibited,[3] and sent home to Sir G. I worked on it for three weeks after it came out of the Gallery; repainted the angel's head, and made other alterations. Sir G. and Lady Beaumont expressed themselves highly pleased with it. The Gil Blas was bought by Lieutenant Drayton, of South Carolina. 'Tis now, I believe, at Philadelphia. In Somerset House I exhibited a landscape.[4] You saw the dead color of it last summer. I inclose a short notice of it from the *Examiner.*[5] I don't remember whether Leslie had begun his "Death of Rutland" before you left London. He has made a fine picture of it. The head of Rutland is very beautiful, and yet full of expression. Indeed, the whole picture is firmly and well painted. By-the-by, I have given up the subject of *"Christ Healing the Sick,"* and have made a sketch of another much finer, which I think by all odds my best composition; it is both picturesque and *highly* impassioned.[6] When I have begun it *in large* (which will be as soon as I shall have found a good painting-room) I will tell you what it is, and more about it. You find I have not been sparing about my own concerns; so, if you don't tell me *more* about yourself and your pursuits in your next than you have done in your first letter, I shall become modest, and write more in future about *matters and things in general. . . .*

Very truly yours, / W. Allston

SOURCE: Prime, pp. 94-95.

1. By the time he wrote this letter WA had received the notice of his *Morning in Italy* in the *Examiner* for 16 June 1816. 2. That of 10 April 1816. 3. It was exhibited at the BI in 1816, at which time it was favorably reviewed. In *Annals of the Fine Arts,* possibly by Haydon, he was called one of the principal history painters in England. In the *Examiner* for 11 February it was pronounced "interestingly energetic" and WA a proper representation of his native

land, though the figure of the angel was judged too substantial. Beaumont first told Wordsworth he thought the figure was too materially dressed. Possibly some of the changes WA made after its exhibition took into account this and similar criticisms. What seemed to please him most, Leslie reported, was the "very high opinion" which Haydon had of it (Prime, p. 97). 4. *Morning in Italy* was exhibited at the RA in 1816 and at the BI in 1817. 5. *The Examiner* (1808-80), a London weekly periodical devoted to literature and politics, was founded by Leigh Hunt, who was the editor until 1821, and his brother John. It regularly reviewed WA's paintings, almost always favorably. The notice of *Morning in Italy* appeared in the issue of 16 June 1816, which commented that in it "art elegantly mixes with and sets off Nature" and called the colors in general "well mingled into a dun and natural hue" in contrast to which the yellow touches gave "a delicate sprightliness" looking "like a smile on a dejected face." 6. Presumably *Belshazzar's Feast*.

42. To Samuel Taylor Coleridge [5 October 1816]

Pray tell Mr. and Mrs. Gillman[1] how grateful I feel for their kindness.[2] Mrs. G. has a gentleness and delicacy of feeling, which so tempers her inflexible love of *right* that is impossible not to love virtue in her. And in Mr. G. I have found strength of mind and manly integrity which command both my respect and esteem. You who know me know how I *must* appreciate them.

SOURCE: Alexander W. Gillman, *The Gillmans of Highgate, with Letters from Samuel Taylor Coleridge &c., Illustrated with Views and Portraits, Being a Chapter from the History of the Gillman Family,* (London, n.d.), p. 20.

1. James Gillman (1782-1839) was an English surgeon who lived in Highgate, a suburb of London. In April 1816 Coleridge went to live with him and his wife Anne (Harding) Gillman, and with his help overcame his addiction to opium. WA owned a copy of his *A Dissertation on the bite of a Rabid Animal, being the substance of an essay which received a prize from the Royal College of Surgeons in 1811* (London, 1812). 2. Probably WA had recently stayed with the Gillmans.

43. To James McMurtrie London 25 Octbr. 1816

My Dear Sir: I have at length the pleasure to inform you that, availing myself of your continued kindness, I have shipped and addressed to you the two Pictures mentioned in my letter to you of June last, viz. the Landscape and the Mother and Child. I wish you not to consider it now as the *"Virgin and Child,"* but simply as a Mother watching her sleeping offspring. A "Madonna" should be *youthfull;* but my mother is a matron. Besides there are other reasons, which I have not room to state,[1] that would fix the propriety of the change now made in the title.—The first, the landscape, to be exhibited and disposed of in any way that shall seem best to you; Of the other I beg your acceptance, as a small testimony of my esteem and gratitude. I have a double pleasure in offering this little present, inasmuch as since the retouching, I think it one of my best works, and as I know it will be possessed by one who can *truly* appreciate whatever merit it may have. It does not always happen that the possessors of pictures are also possessed of taste; and therefore is it a source of no small gratification to an artist to know that his works are cherished by those who will neither mistake, nor overlook their excellences, however few or subordinate.

In my letter of June, alluded to just before, I had fixed the price of the Landscape at from two hundred to 150 guineas. Upon reconsidering this last price, I think it so low as to be tantamount to a complete sacrifice; I must therefore request you not to part with it by any means for less than two hundred guineas. Though I am very much in want of money I should prefer keeping it all my life to disposing of it at so much below it's value. But I commit it to such good hands that I feel <persuaded> perfectly easy as to the event.

I am much chagrined that the ship Severn, which sails immediately for Philadelphia (not taking freight) would not receive the pictures. She is the only ship here for Philadelphia, and I am told there is no probability for another offering from this port before the spring. I have therefore shipped them in the Victory which goes to New York. I have done this by the advice of my friends in the City, who tell me that you will get this advice of their arrival before the ship can be completely unloaded, and will therefore have time to write to your correspondent in New York in ad[vice?] to their entry, and transmission to Philadelphia.—I enclose an Invoice (also by their advice) in order to facilitate their entry. But would it not be possible to obtain an exemption from the duties by means of the Penna. Academy? for I find that all pictures, casts, prints etc intended for their use, are now free by law.—I think the duties on pictures in America are unconscionable. Here, where they are considered very severe, the highest duty on the very largest picture (even of 30 feet) never exceeds eight pounds sterling; for after four feet square the duty does not increase whatever may be the size.

The first instalment, if I understand you right, of the purchase money of my Picture of the "Dead Man," was due about the middle of August last. If not already on the way hither, I would thank you to remit it as soon as you receive this. Probably you might think of waiting for a more favourable exchange, but I am now so exceedingly pressed for money, that I must beg you to remit it, howsoever unfavourable the exchange. My address is "to the care of Samuel Williams Esqure., 13 Finsbury Square, London."

My paper will not admit of any notice of the present world of art here.—Leslie's picture of Clifford is, I suppose, arrived. I think you will agree with me that it does him great honour. He desires his best regards to you. Pray present mine to Mr. Sully, and believed me with a true sense of your kindness

Sincerely Yours / Washington Allston

N.B. Together with this you will receive a copy of my answer (written June 13th last and forwarded) to your several favours of 16 & 18th March and 15th April; the original of which I trust you have long ago duly received.

Leslie has just painted two fine portraits of our Ambassador Mr. Adams[2] and his Lady.[3]

SOURCE: Manuscript copy. Printed in Flagg, pp. 123-25.

1. Possibly the change was related to the death of WA's wife. 2. John Qunicy Adams (1767-1848) was minister to the Court of St. James from 1815 to 1817. During that time he visited and dined with WA frequently and entered the occasions in his diary. He admired WA's *Beatrice, Italian Landscape* (presumably *Italian Landscape,* or *Italian Scenery*), *Mother Watching Her Sleeping Child,* and *Rebecca at the Well* (1816), but thought the staircase in *Jacob's Dream* too great a departure from the ladder in the scriptural account. He saw *Beatrice* in September 1816, as did Leslie, who reported that it had been recently done (Prime, p. 99). At that time WA also showed Adams several sculptures he had made, presumably those for *The Dead Man Restored.* 3. Louisa Catherine (Johnson) Adams (1775-1852).

44. To Myndert Van Schaick 8 Buckingham Place,

Fitzroy Square London, Novbr. 13th, 1816.

My dear Sir: Together with this you will receive your long-expected Picture:[1] which is now shipped on board the Traveller, Captn. John Loyd,[2] for New York. The subject of it is Rebekah at the Well, on her first meeting with the head Servant, or Steward, of Abraham. See the 24th Chap. of Genesis.—It is considered by my friends here as one of the best of my smaller pictures; and I hope it will please you—I painted it "con amore" for two reasons: first, because it was to be possessed by one for whom I have a real esteem, & secondly because the subject, partaking of a pastoral, yet elegant simplicity is one of a kind that I most delight in. The camels in it are done from drawings which I made from a living one now at Exeter 'Change.[3]—But the less an Artist says about his own works the better. Besides, pictures are supposed to speak a universal language and consequently have no need of an interpreter.—Before I quit the subject, however, I would request a favour, which is, that <you> if it should be perfectly convenient, & agreeable to yourself and friends (not otherwise) <that> you would allow it to be exhibited at the next Exhibition of the Academy in Philadelphia.[4] It may possibly be of some service to my reputation there, being of a different class from my other works in that city.—By the advice of Mr. Hone (he taking the responsibility on himself)[5] I have sent it in a frame, <It is far> which is so much cheaper, and more elegant than any I ever saw made in America, that I doubt not you will approve of what I have done.—To return again to the picture (which I thought to have just now dismissed) I must observe that, being so recently finished, I was afraid to varnish it before it went; but by the time it reaches you <it> the colours will be quite hard enough to bear varnishing; and my friend Vanderlyne,[6] who is I understand now in New York, will I dare say do it at my request with pleasure. I hope, however, that he will have some varnish that he can depend on, and that will not *chill.*—The picture requires it very much.—So you see the picture has left me no room to say any thing else. I can therefore only add, that I wish Mrs. Vanschaick[7] & yourself every happiness that you can enjoy in our highly favoured Country.—They would make us believe here in the Ministerial Papers[8] that the United States are more distressed than Great

Britain! But I know better things. Heaven grant that our countrymen may not abuse their blessings.

Believe me, dear sir, truly / Washington Allston

I wrote you some months since by Captain Stewart,[9] of New York.

ADDRESSED: M. Van Schaick Esqre. / New York / Pr Ship / Traveller / North America.
SOURCE: Manuscript, Houghton.

1. *Rebecca at the Well,* from Gen. 24:17-27. WA was still working on it in early September (Prime, p. 98). Possibly the subject of the search for a wife was related to the recent death of his wife. The features may have been hers. It contained also an oblique reference to angels, since in the biblical account Abraham promised his servant that one would go before him to help him find a wife for Isaac. It was exhibited at the American Academy of Fine Arts in 1817. Early in 1829 efforts were made by William Cullen Bryant and Gulian C. Verplanck, editors of the literary annual *The Talisman,* to have it engraved by John J. Heilson, lecturer on anatomy at the NAD and amateur artist for that publication, but nothing came of the matter (*The Letters of William Cullen Bryant,* ed. William Cullen Bryant II and Thomas G. Vose [New York: Fordham Univ. Press, 1975] 1:275). 2. No such name appears in the *New York City Directory* for this or adjacent years. A John Lloyd is listed in 1812, but without occupation. 3. The east end of the Exeter Exchange, located in the Strand, was used at this time for the exhibition of living subjects of natural history (Thomas H. Shepherd, *London and its Environs in the 19th Century. Illustrated by a series of Views From Original Drawings . . .* [London, 1829], p. 65). 4. It was exhibited there, with the title *Jacob and Rebecca,* in 1818. 5. Philip Hone (1780-1851) was a wealthy New Yorker best known for the secret diary he kept from 1828 to 1851. He was active in social and political circles and had a large library and art collection. Apparently he visited London about this time. He went abroad again in 1821. At the time of WA's death he wrote an account of him in his diary. 6. John Vanderlyn. 7. Not further identified. 8. Presumably WA refers to the London newspapers giving special attention to English ministerial politics. The leading ones were the *Morning Post* and the evening *Courier,* both owned by Daniel Stuart, a friend of Coleridge, who wrote for both (H.R. Fox Bourne, *English Newspapers* [London, 1887], 1:292-372). 9. William A. Stewart, shipmaster (*New York City Directory,* 1812-17).

45. From George Howland Beaumont [Autumn 1816]

My Dear Sir: I am just returned from the church, where your picture[1] hangs in full view, and I must say it appears to such advantage that I hope sooner or later you will see it in this light. Some time or other you will perhaps be induced to visit Mr. Wordsworth and your friends in the north, and then you will recollect this place is hardly out of your way.

Time has mellowed the colors, and the general tone is much improved. Did you not take the idea of the angel's wings from those of the dove? It appears so to me, and I think them most appropriate. The bluish gray suits the picture admirably, and the downy softness of the inside of the wing is excellently described. As to the background of the picture, it is, I think, perfect, the gloom and depth set off the figures to the best advantage.[2]

To you who have been accustomed to the extended lakes of America, our comparatively small pools would appear trifling; still, however, I think you would be much gratified with the sight of them, for the mountains are high enough to induce the clouds to repose upon their bosoms, and that is the criticism by which I judge what is the proper height of a mountain. Those upon the Wye, although well formed, are not high enough to produce the most sublime of all landscape effects—the union of the earth with the heavens. A foggy cloud, shapeless and forlorn, will sometimes drizzle upon them; but I like to see fair, floating summer clouds arrested in their course, unable to resist the strong attraction of the mountain.

I hope your head has not been affected by this last dreary weather, and equally unpleasant autumn winds; but in spite of them we were often favored by many magnificient cloud effects, and as I had a pretty good view from my window, with pen and pencil I set the weather at defiance.

Lady Beaumont desires me to thank you for the great pleasure your picture has given her.

I am, dear sir, your most faithful servant,

G. Beaumont.

Have you seen Coleridge lately?

SOURCE: Flagg, pp. 92-93.

1. *The Angel Releasing St. Peter from Prison.* 2. Probably Beaumont knew of the experiment which WA had made with this part of the painting. WA quoted part of this sentence in his conversations with Henry Greenough (Flagg, p. 191).

46. From James McMurtrie Philadelphia Feby 5th 1817

Dear Sir: I have already written you by this opportunity—but I cannot refrain from saying something of your pictures which I have opened since I wrote you.[1] The large landscape is at Mr. Sully's[2] & I can scarcely say I have seen it. That pleasure is yet to come—but I perfectly remember it having seen it in your painting room. Mr. Sully is delighted with it, and has he says already reaped great advantage from having it near him. But how shall I speak of your charming picture of the "Mother & Child." I have numbers calling on me daily to see it. Mr. Sully says it combines the excellence of Raphael & Guido—and is taken altogether the most precious picture he ever saw. Mr. Volozan[3] a french artist decidedly the most learned of his profession in this City & withal a most severe critic is of the same opinion: and what I think of still more importance is that people who never admired a picture before have been enthusiastic in their praise—so much dignity in the mother tempered with such sweetness of expression. The profound repose of the Child. The exquisite finish of every part. In short my Dear Sir I am so delighted in having such a treasure that all my old favourites have lost their value entirely—I am wholly engrossed with it. It is a *subject* I most delight in. Mrs. McMurtrie[4] is as warm an admirer of it as myself and is most desirous of a personal knowledge of the author. At present it is in my parlour, but I shall shortly remove it to Mr. Sully's exhibition room, where both it & the landscape will be exhibited. Can you my Dear Sir paint another picture for me of the same size as the "Mother & Child"?[5] The subject I leave entirely to yourself—merely suggesting that a Landscape with *one or two* figures wd be most desirable—an "Ariadne"[6] for instance—at the moment of waking & finding herself deserted. Some subject which wd allow the female figure to be introduced without indelicacy, and a fine landscape. Mr. Sully says leave the subject to Mr. Allston. So I do leave it, only requesting you will have the goodness to inform me the terms for such a picture, which I shall immediately forward. Please also add the prices of those of several figures of that size, and whether it wd be agreable to you to paint a few for some of my friends from whom I cd receive orders at once. I am very desirous of at least having yr works amongst us if we cannot have yourself.

Again permit me to offer you my warmest thanks for your splendid present & believe me to say very sincerely—

Your obliged friend / J. M. McMurtrie

Tender & pathetic subjects are better calculated for the taste of this country at present than any others—

Washington Allston Es

ADDRESSED: Washington Allston Esqe / 8 Buckingham Place / *Fitzroy Sqr. London.*
SOURCE: Manuscript.

1. *Diana and Her Nymphs* and *A Mother Watching Her Sleeping Child.* They were exhibited, the second with the title "Lady and Sleeping Child—A Fancy Picture," at the PAFA in May 1818. Two months later *Diana and Her Nymphs,* together with works by other artists, was again exhibited there, with the description "Landscape and Figures—Morning Scene in Italy. 1805." 2. Sully's room was in Philosophical Hall for many years (*Philadelphia City Directory,* 1813-23). 3. Denis Volozan, French landscape artist, who worked in Philadelphia from 1811 to 1820. 4. She was a half-sister of the painter Henry Benbridge (*The Diary of William Dunlap,* Collections of the New-York Historical Society 64 [New York, 1931], 3:914). 5. *A Mother Watching Her Sleeping Child* is 23½ by 18 inches. 6. Ariadne, daughter of Minos and Pesiphae, gave Theseus the clue of thread by which he found his way out of the Labyrinth, where he killed the Minotaur, but he failed to keep his promise of marriage and, according to the general version of her fate, deserted her on the island of Naxos. Vanderlyn's painting of her, nude, done in 1812, made a great sensation. There seems to be no evidence that WA took this suggestion of McMurtrie's, but according to Sweetser he painted another classical female figure in 1817, *Clytie,* in Greek mythology a sea nymph beloved but deserted by the sun god, who was changed into the heliotrope, a flower which is supposed always to turn its head in the direction of the sun.

47. To Washington Irving

8 Buckingham Place,
Fitzroy Square London, April 15, 1817[1]

I have made a design for your Knickerbocker,[2] but I shall say nothing about it, as I hope you will soon be here to see it.

[I have] added four new incidents to the first three acts of the play.[3]
[P.S.] I have completed a sketch, and am making other preparations for a large picture;[4] but more of this when I see you. I promise myself much advantage as well as pleasure from your society the ensuing summer.

SOURCE: Pierre M. Irving, *The Life and Letters of Washington Irving* (New York, 1862), 1:361.

1. Irving was in Liverpool at this time, where he was helping his brother Peter in the branch of the family business there (Stanley T. Williams, *The Life of Washington Irving* [New York; Oxford Univ. Press, 1935], 1:150-51). 2. The drawing, *Wouter von Twiller's Decision in the Case of Wandle Schoonhoven and Barent Bleecker* (1817; G fig. 37), for an engraving for a scene in Irving's *A History of New York from the Beginning of the World to the End of the Dutch Dynasty . . . by Diedrich Knickerbocker,* book 3, chap. 1. It was intended to be used in the third edition but appeared finally in volume 2 of the two-volume edition published by John Murray in London in 1824, with engravings of his and Leslie's designs by Charles Rolls, John Romney, William Finden, and A.W. Warren. 3. Pierre M. Irving added here, "he was intending to offer to the theatres." Presumably this was a play being written by WA, but nothing further about it seems to be known. A few years later Irving, who was also a devotee of the theater, tried his hand at play writing (Williams, 1:265-72). 4. *Belshazzar's Feast.*

48. To Washington Irving London, 9th May, 1817,
8 Buckingham Place, Fitzroy Sq.

Dear Irving: Your sudden resolution of embarking for America[1] has quite thrown me, to use a sea-phrase, all a-back; I have so many things to tell you of—to consult you about, &c., and am such a sad correspondent, that before I can bring my pen to do its office 'tis a hundred to one but the occasions for which your advice would be wished, will have passed and gone. One of these subjects (and the most important) is the large picture I talked of soon beginning: The prophet Daniel interpreting the *handwriting on the wall* before Belshazzar.[2] I have made a highly finished sketch of it, and I wished much to have your remarks on it. But as your sudden departure will deprive me of this advantage, I must beg, should any hints of the subject occur to you during your voyage, that you will favor me with them, at the same time you let me know that you are again safe in our good country. I think the composition the best I ever made. It contains a multitude of figures, and (if I may be allowed to say it) they are without confusion. Don't you think it a fine subject? I know not any that so happily unites the magnificent and the awful: a mighty sovereign, surrounded by his whole court, intoxicated with his own state—in the midst of his revellings, palsied in a moment under the spell of a preternatural hand suddenly tracing his doom on the wall before him; his powerless limbs, like a wounded spider's shrunk up to his body, while his heart, *compressed to a point,* is only kept from vanishing by the terrific suspense that animates it during the interpretation of his mysterious sentence: his less guilty, but scarcely less agitated queen, the panic-struck courtiers and concubines, the splendid and deserted banquet table, the half-arrogant, half astounded magicians, the holy vessels of the Temple, (shining, as it were, in triumph through the gloom,) and the calm, solemn contrast of the Prophet, standing like an animated pillar in the midst, breathing forth the oracular destruction of the empire! [3] The picture will be twelve feet high by seventeen feet long.[4] Should I succeed in it even to my wishes I know not what may be its fate. But I leave the future to Providence. Perhaps I may send it to America. Agreeably to your request I send, by the coach, the design for Knickerbocker. The subject is Wouter Van Twiller's decision in the case of Wandle Schoonhoven and Barent Bleecker. I think the astonished constable the best figure. Indeed, that relating to him appeared to me the driest part of the joke. Let me know how you like it. If you don't like it—mind—I sha'n't be offended. 'Tis a sad bore to be obliged to laugh through complaisance; so I won't take it amiss even though you should be grave upon it. By-the-bye, I should like to know whether that lawsuit satirizes any *living* persons. If so, I should be sorry, for though they may cheerfully join in the laugh themselves at a ridiculous description, they would not so well bear a pictured personal caricature. Do let me know, and I will make a design from another part of the book that shall hurt nobody. Now, don't laugh at me. I would only be a harmless creature. I send at the same time a design by Leslie.[5] The subject is the Dutch courtship. It is really a very beautiful drawing. If you mean to have them engraved, I think they had better be done here. They could not engrave them well in America. Here they would be well done, and much cheaper. If you think so too, and will leave them with your brother to be sent to me, I will see that they are properly done. You will probably see in New York a little picture of Rebecca at the Well, which I painted last summer for my friend Van Schaick. My friends here thought it one of my best pictures. I hope he likes it. I have not heard. I shall not regret that I have written so much about myself if it induce you, in return, to favor me with some of your plans and projects.

Wishing you a prosperous voyage, and happy meeting with your friends, I remain truly your friend,

Washington Allston.

SOURCE: Pierre M. Irving, 1:362-64.

1. Irving, who was still in Liverpool, did not return to American until 1832. He thought of going at this time in order to see his aged mother. 2. *Belshazzar's Feast*. Sometime in 1817 and possibly in connection with this work WA painted four portraits of Jews which testified particularly to his affiliation with Rembrandt: two entitled *Head of a Jew* and *Isaac of York*. All but one *Head of a Jew* were unfinished. The other *Head of a Jew* and *Sketch of a Polish Jew* were painted at one sitting, according to Sarah Clarke (p. 136). 3. WA's description of it in this paragraph, like those he wrote for *The Dead Man Restored* and *A Scene in an Eating House*, emphasized the various contrasting emotions exhibited by the figures. 4. The painting is 144⅛ by 192⅛ inches. 5. Leslie's design was for Irving's *History*, book 3, chap. 4, in the third edition.

BELSHAZZAR'S FEAST

Allston's most ambitious and largest painting, which occupied him from 1817 to his death and was never finished, was *Belshazzar's Feast,* from Daniel 5:24-28. His work on it became increasingly traumatic, and criticism of it was more extensive and controversial than about any other of his paintings. The subject had been treated by many painters of the past, among them Rembrandt, as well as contemporaries of Allston's, including West, and by several writers of the day, notably Byron, and by the composer Georg Friedrich Handel. He made two full studies for it in 1817, one in sepia, in which two serving boys in the lower left corner are among the dismayed audience, and one in color, in which the boys have been replaced by the golden vessel seized by the Babylonians, but did not begin painting until the beginning of 1818. He also made numerous drawings of parts, in pencil, ink, and chalk, including Belshazzar's figure and left hand, heads of the magicians, and columns of the temple. In place of the handwriting on the wall he introduced a large refulgent area in the upper-right-hand corner.

When he took it to America in 1818 he expected it to be finished in a few months. It was not unrolled until September 1820, however, because of his occupation with painting several small pictures for income. Shortly afterward, on the advice of Stuart, whose opinion he asked, he changed the perspective. At Stuart's suggestion he also painted the right hand of the king clenched, to express more intensity of feeling, instead of open, by which he intended to contrast Daniel's calmness with the excitement around him, but subsequently he restored it to his first conception.[1] The change of perspective necessitated larger figures and a lower lamp; in repainting it he was said to have drawn fully 20,000 lines and circles, taking him six weeks.[2] It was probably in the early stage that, according to Sweetser, some of his friends stood for models, and later that it was predicted Daniel's face would represent Webster.

In 1820 a form of advance purchase, a Tripartite Agreement subscribed to by twelve individuals, most of them his patrons, in the amount of $10,000 was drawn up, entrusted to three others for him to draw upon when in need. The subscribers were Warren Dutton, Patrick T. Jackson, Isaac P. Davis, Nathaniel Amory, Thomas H. Perkins, Loammi Baldwin, David Sears, William S. Rogers, Samuel A. Eliot, Benjamin Welles, the merchant James Perkins, Thomas H. Perkins, Jr., the merchant Samuel Appleton, George Ticknor, Timothy Williams, all of Boston, and John S. Cogdell of Charleston, South Carolina. Shares were $500 each; all but Amory, who held six shares, held one. Dutton, Jackson, and Davis as trustees held the document, for which $1 was given. It stipulated that Allston would not publicly exhibit the painting without the permission of the subscribers, that they would not unnecessarily come to see it, that he alone would determine when it was finished, at which time the trustees would convey it to the subscribers, and that the unpaid balance would be turned over to him within ten days thereafter.

From the time it was unrolled in 1820 he worked on it with repeated reports that it was nearly finished until 1828, when he moved to a smaller studio and it was rolled up again until 1839. After giving Leslie in May 1821 an estimated time of six weeks for its completion, he told Joshua H. Hayward, who was to report to Leslie and Gilbert Stuart Newton in London, that it was finished except for the glazing and retouching and would be out by October. Late that month Sully said it was two-thirds finished, with Belshazzar completed but not Daniel, and in the summer of 1823 Chester Harding, who saw it with Jonathan Mason, said all but Daniel was done. In January 1825, he hired, at the sum of $600 a year, the Columbian Museum to put the last touches on it in anticipation of exhibiting it there and held the place for nine months, hurrying the picture framer John Doggett to get the frame done so that it could be shown during the visit of Lafayette to Boston in June for the laying of the cornerstone of the Bunker Hill Monument. In that month the Exhibition Room of Ethan Allen Greenwood's New England Museum was cleared for his use instead.[3] In 1826, about December, Sully noted that he seemed "dissatisfied with *one* particular head" and would not call it finished until he had satisfied himself altogether; Sully was confident nevertheless that it would be finished and said Jonathan Mason agreed with him.[4] Early in 1827 Doggett, who went to measure it for inclusion in the first exhibition of the Boston Athenaeum Gallery in May, said all the principal figures were done, the king being dressed in a cloth of gold;[5] the trustees gave him the use of the upper floor until 1 April for its completion. When it did not appear Trumbull inquired in a letter to the committee in charge of the exhibition, "Will Allston's picture ever be finished?" The English Mrs. Basil Hall, who met Allston in October at the house of George Ticknor, reported that he was to be married when it was finished.[6]

By 1827 he had drawn $5,000 of the sum allotted him by the Tripartite Agreement and on 9 May a second agreement was drawn up, without Williams, enabling him to draw $1,500 more. He became increasingly unwilling to have his work seen by anyone and told Jarvis that if it were, he believed he would never finish it. When the property on which his studio stood was sold in 1828 he was so anxious lest the representatives of the new owner, L.M. Sargent, see it that he proposed they enter the room with their backs to it. Harding gave him his studio while he was in Washington in the winter of 1828, but found on returning that no progress had been made on it and that he had told Loammi Baldwin he had blotted out four years' work.[7] He also became increasingly sensitive about public questionings as to when it would be done. Richard Henry Dana, Jr., recollected that about three weeks before his death he told his wife that he would have to stop and finish a small painting to sell and on her asking why he did not finish it instead and get the money for it, replied, "Don't you think of me as all the rest of the world does."[8]

Meanwhile in England John Martin painted the subject and Henry Hart Milman published *Belshazzar: A Dramatic Poem,* of which Allston owned a copy (Boston, 1822). In America several artists, including Thomas Cole, Joseph Steward, and Hugh Reinagle, also treated the subject, probably influenced by him. In his untitled poem beginning "Of mind, and its mysterious agencies, / And most of all, its high creative power," delivered before the Phi Beta Kappa Society of Yale in 1825, James Gates Percival referred to Allston's painting as his "mighty task" and deplored the necessity of his producing lesser works.[9]

In 1839 it was unrolled for the fifth time, and from then until his death he worked on it more or less continually. It would have been unrolled before that time, Richard Henry Dana said, had he not agreed to sit for his bust to Shobal Vail Clevenger during three weeks in the late summer of that year.[10]

About 1841 he began to make several changes in the composition besides those described to Collins in his letter of 21 May 1821, which last ones seem to have been chiefly of accessory parts. The principal figural addition to his final conception was that of the kneeling girl among the Chaldeans. He told John Greenough, who returned in the spring of 1841 from Europe, that there were five pictures under the one he was then painting.[11] When Greenough saw part of it through a crack in the door, he said the king was finished, corresponding to the figure in the colored sketch. Edmund T. Dana said Allston told him, presumably about this time, that he had finished the king and was satisfied with it. Ticknor, however, said he had known "as a secret" from Allston in 1841 that the king had been painted over but that Allston told him within the last year of his life that he had at last fixed upon his final design, with which he was satisfied, and that he would never change it. Morse also saw it about that year and said the king's right hand was finished and open but the figure was painted over.[12]

Three days after Allston's death the painting was examined by a group consisting of Richard Henry Dana, his sons Richard Henry, Jr., and Edmund T., Edmund T. Dana and John Greenough. The reactions of Richard Henry Dana and Greenough were characteristic, Dana declaring that the coat of paint over the king was Allston's "*shroud*" and being so overcome that he hid behind the painting for several minutes, and Greenough rushing forward and saying that his expectations had been more than equaled. Greenough and Richard Henry Dana, Jr., subsequently wrote detailed descriptions of its condition at that time.

The chief changes Allston was in the process of making were calculated to give the composition an effect of solemnity rather than the dramatic action of his sketches and his verbal description. Chiefly he was enlarging the principal figures, necessitated by the altered perspective, increasing their height half a head, and repainting the drapery to correspond to them. The right hand of the king was new, on a larger scale, but not glazed and finished. The right hand and shoulder of Daniel, the figure of the queen above the waist, and the heads of the Chaldeans were unfinished. Chalk marks had been made on the head and left foot of Daniel, the left foot of the king, the face of the queen, and the figures of three of the Chaldeans. The drapery of the principal Chaldean had been outlined in oil. The architecture was in the earlier style, but the capitals in the front had been changed from their appearance in the sketches and from the back columns, and part of the pillars at the left had been chalked, one of them so as to cover the curtain hanging over it and the candlestick. Fresh paint indicated that the last repainting was of the head of the chief Chaldean, depicting him with full face, looking slightly to the left. Most conspicuously, a coat of brown paint covered the entire figure of the king, presumably in preparation for enlarging it. He had cleaned his palette and put the color from it on a plate and the brushes, fourteen of them, in water.

The next day Franklin Dexter and Warren Dutton, as the persons whom Allston most relied on for their judgment of his work and for his relations with the public and the subscribers to the painting, were called in. Dexter said his expectations were fully equaled, adding that it would have been difficult to surpass them. Though oppressed by its unfinished state and the confusion arising from the change of plan and almost in despair that unity could be preserved in it, he pronounced it a great picture, whose figures had haunted him ever since he saw them, and declared there was nothing in art superior to some parts of it. Of one part he said that he had seen nothing in Titian to equal it in color and of the group of women that he had never seen its equal except in Rubens's *Descent from the Cross,* in comparison with which it was better in drawing and not inferior in color. A few days later he reported he had dreamed of it and had it before him in nearly all his waking hours. He was more confident than Dutton about it and thought if the king were brought out it ought to be exhibited. In comparison, he said, John Martin's painting of the subject was merely architectural. At that time he brought the Tripartite Agreement to Richard Henry Dana, Jr.,'s office. Attempts were then made by Greenough and Dexter to clean the painting with water and to remove the paint from the king with turpentine but were abandoned for fear of injuring the glazing underneath the figure, and it was decided to consult the subscribers before proceeding farther. When, two weeks later, Morse saw it he called it a "grand work" which grew on him, said all the lines and chalk marks should be preserved to show Allston's intentions, and agreed with Dutton and Dexter that it should remain as it was until its inclusion in the estate was established, after which the paint on the king should be removed, the hand of Daniel covered with drapery, and the figures of the Chaldeans put in order, all in tempera so as to be removable. The decision was finally made to have it cleaned and varnished by the painter and restorer Darius Chase, and when, in December, the subscribers saw it they were so well pleased and Ticknor, Dexter, Jonathan Mason, and Harding in such a state of admiration that Chase was asked to restore the king. No painting was done and the only losses incurred in the varnishing were the chalk marks on Daniel's heel, the king's foot, and the pillar, which would have been shown entirely.[13] It was exhibited by the subscribers at the Corinthian Gallery in Boston in the summer of 1844, accompanied by an explanatory pamphlet, and from 1845 to 1876 at the Boston Athenaeum.[14] In 1846 the painter Thomas T. Spear developed a sketch of it into a large version which he exhibited in several cities and which was at one point taken for the original.

An unidentified visitor also described the painting before it was restored, on the day he saw it. It had been, he said, the desire of his life to see Allston's "'great picture,'" as it was called, he "felt a solemn awe" stealing over his soul as if Allston's spirit stood near, and a "hallowed presence seemed to pervade the room." There was, he declared, "an overwhelming power in every part," and he proceeded to describe the king, queen, Daniel, spectators, and accessory details. He attributed its unfinished state to Allston's growing mind and imagination, said that only those who looked at it "hastily and without feeling, without knowledge of human nature, and without appreciation" of the art that "can make the canvas seem to breathe" would fail to be satisfied and that one who read the fifth chapter of Daniel would be at once impressed by its "religious power." Citing Sir Joshua Reynolds's saying it took him three weeks to discover the beauty of the frescoes in the Vatican, he concluded that it was "a precious relic, the dearer for lacking the finishing strokes," the "noble production of so lofty and pure a mind," on which the last trace of Allston's pencil rested.[15]

The author of this description may have been Robert Weir, who was taken to see the painting by Richard Henry Dana, Jr., on 25 September 1843. Weir, he recorded, stood "motionless & silent before it for full a quarter of an hour," took an "intense" interest in it, and said that though it was in "confusion" because of the changed perspective and "chaotic," it was "beautiful in its parts, & grand in its design."[16] He wrote a poem about that time, "Washington Allston," printed in the *New York Evening Post*, in which he lamented Allston's death and referred to several of his paintings, including "Some prophet, stern and old," meaning probably both *Jeremiah Dictating His Prophecy of the Destruction of Jerusalem to Baruch the Scribe* and *Belshazzar's Feast*, and *The Sibyl*, *Beatrice*, and *Rosalie*.

Several reasons for the long time Allston spent on *Belshazzar's Feast* and his failure to complete it, other than technical ones and his need to produce smaller ones for income, were offered over the years. Stuart predicted to Channing that it would never be completed because of the rapid growth of Allston's mind—the work of this month or year was felt to be imperfect the next; in 1824 he asked Charles Fraser to get him to give it up.[17] William Ware, however, believed that the new ideas that were constantly changing Allston's purpose would have been successfully incorporated had he lived. Its "great charm" he thought, was, in parts of it, its color, Allston's "grand, distinguishing characteristic," and he included it among the examples he gave that Allston found the sources for his forms "in states of the human mind, rather than in any aspects of outward nature." But he felt that it was of a class of subjects to which "his genius was not suited," being large and containing a multitude of figures. He pointed out that the necessity of great physical strength in climbing ladders and using large brushes was particularly trying, adding that finishing touches would customarily have been done by students of a school, which Allston did not have. The suggestion that he employ such assistants was, in fact, made to Allston more than once, but he refused to do so. The painting also belonged, Ware noted, in the category of the sublime rather than the beautiful, the former being depicted by Allston almost but not quite as successfully as the latter. He found only two specific faults: the want of expression in the faces and the treatment of the small column in the front, though not those of the temple. On the whole, however, he gave it prominent place in the broad picture he drew of Allston as having a "general cultivation of mind," and the "highest intellectual culture," who was versatile and in most of whose works there was a largeness of conception, and who had a devotion to art without regard for money or popularity and a conscientiousness that accounted for his relatively slight productivity. In concluding his discussion of it he declared that "art has seldom, in its whole history, produced a mind of more brilliance or compass."[18]

A later generation blamed Allston's failure to finish *Belshazzar's Feast* on his isolation in America from artists and art centers, which was also held accountable for his slight productivity in his late years. It made a great impression on Henry James, who saw it probably in the early 1860s and who regarded it as a symbol of an artist destroyed by American culture. He called Allston "the beautiful colourist . . . withering in a cruel air" and the painting a "great strange canvas, so interrupted but so impressive," with portions "which shone out like passages of melody, of musical inspiration, in some troubled symphony or sonata," but whose "lesson" seemed to be that it was "the mask of some impenetrable inward strain," and which was in essence both "the fact of Italy, of the earlier old Italy" and "the fact of a Cambridgeport also earlier." He concluded in an analysis of the "quiet painter's nostalgia," which had to have been "so much finer than one's own," that thinking of "what, in his divine *Wanderjahre,* he had seen, and to see, that period ended, what he did see . . . acted, creatively in one's mind, in respect to the former."[19] James's contemporaries William Wetmore Story and James Russell Lowell, who also had extended European residences, said much the same thing.

Belshazzar's Feast was, in fact, both a subject uncongenial to Allston's imagination and a work he attempted to finish in America, where his distinctive genius was operative most freely and fully. Both facts mitigated against its completion. Story, James, and Lowell, however, were writers, not artists, and concentrated, like Nathaniel Hawthorne, who referred to the painting in his story "The Artist of the Beautiful," on the fact that the whole was not finished rather than on the parts which were. Many artists, especially younger ones like Benjamin Champney, William Page, Joseph Alexander Ames, and George Fuller, were struck with and influenced by the coloring. Even Ware said it was complete in that aspect, and the writer and lecturer Edwin Percy Whipple, noted for his aesthetic sensibility, spoke of the "mystical beauty" of its parts, with their "marvelous color," and declared it gave him a "new idea of painting."[20] The art critic James Jackson Jarves perhaps made the most judicious estimate of it when, two decades after Allston's death, he called it "the greatest, best composed, and most difficult painting yet attempted by an American artist."[21]

1. Dana, 1:177-78. 2. Walter Channing. 3. RHD p. 9, Addition. 4. Rutledge, "Dunlap Notes," p. 390. 5. Dana, 1:181. 6. Mabel Munson Swan, *The Athenaeum Gallery, 1827-1873: The Boston Athenaeum as an Early Patron of Art* (Boston: Boston Athenaeum, 1940), pp. 14, 16, 48, 50. 7. *A Sketch of Chester Harding: Drawn by His Own Hand,* ed. Margaret E. White (Boston, 1890), p. 143. 8. Flagg, p. 124. 9. *Poem Delivered before the Connecticut Alpha of the Phi Beta Kappa Society, September 13 1825* Boston, 1826); Julius H. Ward, *The Life and Letters of James Gates Percival* (Boston, 1866), p. 236. 10. RHD to Gulian C. Verplanck, 22 Oct. 1839, New-York Historical Society. 11. RHD, p. 7, Addition. 12. Dana, 1:78, 189, 191. 13. Ibid., 1:177-81, 191, 129, 226. 14. Swan, pp. 58-59. 15. Flagg, pp. 340, 344. 16. Dana 1:219. 17. Fraser to Robert W. Gibbes, 3 Aug. 1843 (Dana Papers). 18. Ware, *Lectures,* pp. 7, 18, 116-17. 19. *William Wetmore Story and His Friends* (Boston: Houghton Mifflin, 1903), 1:297-98, 307-309. 20. To Anna Cora (Ogden) Mowatt, 28 May 1844 (Dana Papers). 21. *The Art Idea, Part Second of Confessions of an Inquirer* (Boston, 1864), p. 205.

49. From Washington Irving Birmingham,[1] May 21st. 1817.

My dear Allston: Your letter of the 9th. inst and likewise the parcel containing the pictures came safely to hand and should have been acknowledged sooner, but I have been much discomposed since last I wrote to you, by intelligence of the death of my mother.[2] Her extreme age made such an event constantly probable, but I had hoped to have seen her once more before she died, and was anxious to return home soon on that account. That hope is now at an end,—and with it my immediate wish to return, so that I think it probable I shall linger some time longer in Europe.

I have been much struck with your conception of the Warning of Belchazzar. It is grand & poetical, affording scope for all the beauties & glories of the pencil, and if it is but executed in the spirit in which it is conceived, I am confident will ensure you both profit and renown. As to its future fate however, <leave that to> never let that occupy you[r] mind—unless it be to stimulate you to exertion. As to sending it to America, I would only observe, that unless I got very advantageous offers for my paintings I would rather do so—as it is infinitely preferable to stand foremost as one of the founders of a school of painting in an immense, & growing country like America, in fact to be an object of national pride and affection, than to fall into the ranks in the crowded galleries of Europe; or perhaps be regarded with an eye of national prejudice, as the production of an American pencil is likely to be in England. I will not pretend at this moment to discuss the merits of your design for the proposed painting; I do not feel in the vein; but if at a more cheerful moment any idea suggests itself, that I may think worth communicating, I will write to you—

I cannot express to you how much I have been pleased with the two designs for Knickerbocker—The characters are admirably discriminated, the humour rich, but chaste, and the <whole effect perfectly> expressions peculiarly natural and appropriate. I scarcely know which figure in your picture to prefer; the Constable is evidently drawn *Con Amore,* and derives additional spirit from standing in high relief opposed to the ineffable phlegm of old Wouter. Still however the leering exultation of the fortunate party is given to the very life, and is evident from top to toe—the bend of the knee, the play of the elbows, the swaying of the body are all eloquent; and are finely contrasted with the attitude and look of little Schoonhoven; By the way, I must say the last figure has tickled me as much as any in the picture—But each has its peculiar merits, and is the *best* in its turn. The Sketch by Leslie is beautiful; <He has> The dutch girl is managed with great sweetness & naiveté—the expression of her chin and mouth shews that she is not likely to break her lovers heart. The devoted lear of the lovers eye and the phlegmatic character of the lower part of his countenance form a whimsical combination. The very cat is an important figure in the group & touched off with proper expression. A delicate humour pervades the whole; the composition is graceful and there is a rural air about it that is peculiarly pleasing. I dwell on these little sketches, because they give me quite a new train of ideas in respect to my work: and I only wish I had it now to write, as I am sure I should conceive the scenes in a much purer style; having these pic[tures] [*MS torn*] before me as corrections of that *grossierté* into which the sent[iment of?] [*MS torn*] a work of humour is apt to run. At any rate it is an exquisite gratification to find that any thing I have written can present such pleasing images to imaginations like yours & Leslie's; and I shall regard the work with more complacency, as having in a manner, formed a link of association between our minds.

The law suit was [a]n entirely imaginary incident, without any personal allusion. <I believ> though by a whimsical coincidence there was a Barent Bleecker at Albany[3] who had been comptroller; and his family at first suspected an intention to asperse his official character. The suspicion however was but transient, and is forgotten; so that the picture will awaken no hostility.

I had no idea, when I began this letter that I should have filled the sheet; but words beget words; I shall write to you again before long and will then endeavour to direct my attention to topics more immediately interesting to you. In the mean while give my most friendly remembrances to Leslie & believe me truly Yours.

Washington Irving

ADDRESSED: For / Washington Allston Esqr / Buckingham place / Fitzroy Square / London.
SOURCE: Washington Irving: *Letters,* 1:475-77.

1. Irving's sister Sarah lived in Birmingham, where he often visited. 2. Sarah (Sanders) Irving (1738-1817) died on 9 April (Williams, 1:379). 3. Barent Bleecker (b. 9 June 1760) was a prominent businessman and financier in Albany but never comptroller of the state of New York. The protests against Irving's treatment of Barent Bleecker in his *History of New York,* illustrated in WA's *Wouter von Twiller's Decision in the Case of Wandle Schooven and Barent Bleeker,* were probably made by his brother and sister and their families (Irving, *Letters* 1:479n.).

PARIS 1817

Allston visited Paris for the second time for six weeks in October and November 1817, in the company of Leslie and William Collins, traveling by way of Brighton and Dieppe. They made studies in the Louvre, visited the houses of the principal artists, and had an interview with François Gérard. Of the modern painters, they were most pleased with Pierre N. Guérin. Allston made a copy of Veronese's *Marriage at Cana* (1817) and may have purchased paintings from old masters for Harrison Gray Otis of Boston. In the company of Gulian C. Verplanck, who was also in Paris at that time, he visited the Comedie Française, where he saw Houdon's statue of Voltaire. He stood silent before it for some minutes, Leslie remembered and then exclaimed, "A living statue!"[1]

Allston's visit to Paris at this time stimulated him to greater and more rapid productivity during the several months after his return to England. More significantly, the Venetian paintings he saw in the Louvre gave new impetus to his conception of color. His practice now developed into a combination of underpainting and glazing to produce warm, rich tones that, instead of local or positive color, contained all colors, as it were, floating in suspension. It was first most recognizable in *Uriel in the Sun, Jacob's Dream,* and *Elijah in the Desert* (1817-18) and came to distinguish most of his later works. It was about this time, too, that he abandoned his practice of making elaborate studies of the whole composition and studies of details for large, dramatic works, thus allowing for greater rapidity of composition in such paintings as *Uriel in the Sun* and *Elijah in the Desert.*

Allston described his feelings on returning from Paris to London at this time as being those of the greatest enthusiasm. In a passage that appears only in Flagg he is quoted as having said, "Ah, I was then in health, young, enthusiastic in my art, in a measure independent as to my pecuniary affairs, and I painted solely from the impulse within. I felt that I could do the work of a Titan or a Hercules. But from the moment I felt the pressure of want, and began to look upon my pictures as something I must finish in order to get so much money, from that moment I worked to a disadvantage, and the spirit of the artist died away from me. I never did anything well in my art under the pressure of poverty. I must be free, and feel no motive but such as my subject itself will supply, to work to my own satisfaction and do justice to my art and to my own mind. I painted my pictures of 'Uriel' and 'Elijah in the Desert' in eight weeks, of which I gave five to the 'Uriel' and three to the 'Elijah.'"[2] It seems likely that this passage represents the substance though not the exact words of what Allston said, probably in conversation, possibly to the author of the article "Washington Allston," in the *United States Democratic Review* for October 1843. It was printed by Flagg immediately after the passage in that article giving Allston's description of how he painted *Uriel in the Sun,* within the same quotation marks. It is probable, however, that both these passages came from another, unidentified source used by Flagg.

1. Leslie, pp. 28, 204, 206; Dunlap, 1:325. 2. Flagg, p. 129.

50. To James McMurtrie London

[ca. October or November 1817][1]

I am now engaged on "Jacob's Dream,"[2] a subject I have long had in contemplation. It has been often painted before, but I have treated it in a very different way from any picture I have ever seen; for, instead of two or three angels I have introduced a vast multitude: and instead of a ladder, or narrow steps, I have endeavoured to give the idea of unmeasurable flights of steps, with platform above platform, rising and extending into space immeasurable. Whether this conception will please the matter of fact critics I doubt; nay I am certain that men without imagination will call it stuff! But if I succeed at all, it will be with those whom it will be an honour to please. The picture is of the same size with the landscape I sent out.[3]

[Dunlap said that in this letter WA acknowledged receipt of the first installment of the payment for *The Dead Man Restored*.[4] It was probably also from this letter that Dunlap quoted Allston as saying of Leslie's copy of Guido's head of Christ for McMurtrie, "this copy is a very good one and would embellish any collection."]

SOURCE: Dunlap, 2:180, 244.

1. Probably this letter was written after WA's visit to Paris in September and October 1817. Dunlap quotes from it after his reference to that visit. 2. From Gen. 28:12. It was inspired by a painting of the same subject in the Dulwich Gallery then ascribed to Rembrandt, now thought to be by Arendt (Aert) de Gelder. WA admired it very much and wrote a poem about it. Raphael and Salvator Rosa also painted the subject. For the stairs he was indebted to West's *The Ascension* and possibly John Flaxman's *Celestial Steps*, from Dante's *Paradise*. It was exhibited at the RA in 1819, at which time the *Examiner* for 24 May and Hazlitt in the *Edinburgh Review* for October, who compared it with the Rembrandt, did not judge it very highly, the first objecting to the lack of movement on the part of the angel and Hazlitt finding the setting too much like an architectural design of Vitruvius or Palladio. Others were more favorable. Haydon, in *Annals of the Fine Arts* thought it was the "grandest picture" in the exhibition, predicted that the exhibition would be remembered as that in which it had been shown, and characterized WA's power as lying "in the abstract poetical part of the art, and not in the expression of human passions." The critic in the *New Monthly Magazine and Universal Repository* recognized the influence of Raphael in the angels but declared them "perfectly original" and said there was a "sublimity" in WA's conception of the subject which placed it "among the foremost of the first class of sacred compositions in our time"; the artist himself, he said, "possesses the classical mind of a poet, with the skill of a painter and the manners of a gentleman, and is universally beloved by his brother artists." The *Literary Gazette* for 8 May called it equal to the foremost productions of the season and on 12 June 1819 thought it too direct a copy from Annibale Carracci but pronounced its merits to outweigh its deficiences and the composition "altogether to belong to genius." In that issue WA's poem on Rembrandt's painting appeared, and in the issue of 19 June, a poem by "Trissino" entitled "Jacob's Dream," consisting of four stanzas describing the scene. WA owned the issues from 8 May to 19 June 1819. More than any other of his paintings this one kept his memory alive in England after he left. It was exhibited at the BI in 1825 and in Bristol in 1838. At an undetermined date an engraving of it was made. 3. *Jacob's Dream* is 62 by 94 inches; *Diana and Her Nymphs* is 66½ by 97¾ inches. 4. Walter Channing said that WA told him he had only six pence when the postman Bridgen brought the bill of exchange for this installment, for $1,000. "Reminiscences of Washington Allston," *Christian World*, 22 July 1843.

51. To Francis Bayard Winthrop (Copy)[1] London
Debr. 27, 1817

Dear Sir: I some time since received a letter from you of rather an old date, which a variety of circumstances have prevented my replying to so soon as I wished. I lament the delay.—You express in it great chagrin at having purchased a Landscape[2] of mine, through the advice of Mr. Sullivan[3] about seven years ago. Had you written me on the subject previously to my leaving America, or at any time since while the picture remained in your possession, I would without hesitation have repurchased of you at the original price of five hundred dollars.[4] Though this is not the usual custom of artists, yet it is what I would willingly have done. But you did not write me until last year, and after you had sold it for two hundred dollars.—Allow me incidentally to observe here that the variation in the prices of pictures, whether on private or public sale, is by no means a sure criterion of their merit. There is a picture of Claude,[5] in a great collection here that was originally offered to various Connoissieurs for eight hundred guineas, and refused. The proprietor at last was obliged to part with it for five hundred; the fortunate purchaser soon after sold it for four thousand. I could mention an opposite instance. It was but a few months since that a fine historical picture by Opie was purchased for less than the original cost of the frame. These fluctuations are incident alike to the living and old painters; and are but too common. If a picture then will sell at one time for twice as much as it will sell for at another, the result of a sale cannot be referred to in order to ascertain its intrinsic value. Pictures as often bring more than they are worth, as less; so that a sale cannot with certainty determine their degree of me[rit]. Indeed I think the merit of a picture can be determined only by the united general opinion of real critics.

But to return to the picture which is the subject of this letter. It was the fruit of more than two months labour. If it be thought I have overrated my production, those at least who know me can attribute it but to one cause alone—namely, an error of my judgement (to which artists as well as others are certainly liable:) for those who know me well know that I am above affixing to any work of mine a higher price than I conscienciously think just. However bad the picture might appear in the eyes of others, I certainly did not think it discreditable to me; for if I had thought it bad I would not have sold it. And if there are painters who proportion their prices *to as much as they think the[y] can get,* I hold them unworthy of their profession. Thoug[h] I have occasionally sold my pictures even for what I deemed to be scarcely half their value—in some cases because they were for particular friends, and in others from the pressure of the moment; yet I have never in any one instance demanded a guinea more than seemed to the best of my judgement the just value of my labour. Both as a man of integrity and as a professor of a liberal art, I have always considered myself as "before my conscience" when I have valued my productions. If the price therefore of the picture in question be too high it must be placed solely to an error of my judgement.

But setting the merits of the picture entirely out of the question it would have been (with me) quite sufficient that the picture did not please you; upon that ground alone I would have taken it back had you written to me on the subject when you received it.—Money alone is not [the] whole reward of an artist: it is but secondary to the satisfaction arising from the consciousness of giving pleasure to those who possess or see his works: and I would never deliberately accept the former where I knew it was unaccompanied by the latter. No; were I to paint a picture, by commission, for any nobleman here, and he should dislike it when finished (even though I thought it the happiest effort of my pencil) I would instantly release him from his engagement. Indeed, so far am I from wishing any person to retain a work of mine which he disapproved, that I consider it a misfortune that any circumstances should have given birth to the case.—I am by no means offended that you do not like the picture. Every one has an undoubted right to his opinion; and I hope I am very far from wishing to control the sentiments of any one respecting my own works. I only lament that you did not give me a timely opportunity to remove the incumbrance.

I have made the foregoing remarks with no other view than mere justice to my integrity as a man. They are not intended to refer in any way either to the merits or demerits of the picture—indeed it would not become an artist to speak on these points of his own works; but they are intended simply to shew that in fixing the price I was not actuated by the love of gain, or any other unworthy motive. When an artist values his productions he is necessarily obliged to depend on his own judgement; the result of which he then submits to the public; and it is their province to determine whether or not he rates his work according to its real merit. For the judgement of no artist concerning his own works ever does, or ever ought to regulate the public judgement respecting them. I therefore (as every artist ought to do) remain entirely neutral as to the degree of merit or demerit of the picture; expressing no opinion conerning it; and leaving those points for the decision of others. And since I find that it is the opinion of yourself and friends that the price at which I sold the Landscape was above its merit—in order to remove from myself any imputation of unfairness, I am perfectly willing to comply with your wishes—namely, to send you "a small picture."[6]—I have nothing small by me at present but sketches. Had I a small finished picture that I thought worth sending it should accompany this; but, as I have not, I will paint one for you.[7] My present engagements are of such a nature that they will not allow me to promise it in less than a year from this time. If it is my power to do it sooner it shall be done.—Before I conclude, I repeat, and wish it to be distinctly understood, that I have neither the intention nor the wish to prove anything respecting the merits of the picture. Indeed were I even so disposed, I should be wholly unable to form any opinion [of] it on account of the length of time since I have seen it, and the imperfect recollection I have of it. But I have no wish of the kind; my object being simply to state that I acted consciencously according to the best of my judgement. * <And> For I know that artists <are as liable to err, (as well as others)> as well as other men oftentimes (tho) honestly err in appreciating their own works <I am perfectly willing to abide the judgement given by your friends> & it is certainly possible I also may have erred <I therefore> It is <I have only to add> that whatever <I do shall be done with the most> per

It is my wish in all things to be just and where I may not myself be the proper judge, I willingly <admit> submit [to] the decision of others.

I have only to add that whatever I do shall be done with the most perfect good will.

*That judgment must not & ought not weigh a straw with the public;

ADDRESSED: To Mr. Winthrop SOURCE: Manuscript.

1. Apparently WA sent Winthrop a revised version of this letter, incorporating the changes made in this version, and so called this a copy. 2. *Alpine Landscape* which Winthrop bought in 1810. In 1816 he exhibited it for sale at the American Academy of Fine Arts and sold it that year. 3. William Sullivan (1774-1839), Boston lawyer, politician, and writer. He owned WA's *Falstaff Enlisting His Ragged Regiment.* 4. This was the amount WA customarily received for paintings approximately 36 or 48 by 24 or 36 inches. 5. Claude of Lorraine or Claude Gelée. 6. Presumably WA is quoting from Winthrop's letter. 7. WA did not paint a picture for Winthrop but gave him about 1822 or later his sketch of *The Angel Releasing St. Peter from Prison.* RHD said that Winthrop refused to send the study to the exhibition of WA's paintings, presumably that of 1839, but that WA replied to his remonstrating about the matter by saying, "O, Sir—I can't contend with such men." In recording the incident RHD wrote, "It is painful to me to write down the name of this hard, mean & vulgar man. A. should have treated his very first letter with contempt. & there left him" (p. 28). Winthrop was the only purchaser of a painting by WA with whom he had a serious disagreement about the price, though he often complained that that which he put on one in the beginning was too low for the amount of time he spent on it before it was finished. For small paintings like Winthrop's he sometimes got $600. For large ones, from those measuring 18 to 30 by 30 inches to those measuring 48 by 100 inches, he apparently usually got $1,000, though Beaumont and the marquis of Stafford paid less than that. He sometimes was willing to take less money because of pressing financial needs; Henry Pickering and the BA, on more than one occasion, paid less. He probably let Elias Vanderhorst have three small paintings for only two hundred guineas because of their relationship. By far the largest sum he received was the $3,500 for the immense *Dead Man Restored.* His prices increased somewhat with the years, however. Mrs. Anna Jameson said his patrons cited the high prices they had paid as a matter of exultation, and Edmund S. Quincy said that though he always received what he asked, often before the work was finished, "no one commanded such prices," which were "too high" for a public man like his father to pay; Stuart, he added, asked "only" $150 for a Kit-Cat portrait and $100 for a bust, implying that WA asked more (Jameson, "Washington Allston," *Athenaeum*, 6 Jan. 1844, p. 15; Quincy to Samuel Gardner Drake, 3 Dec. 1872, Wellesley College Library). William Ware implied the same when he said WA "had a proper respect for the prices which his works would bring; he was to live by his art; and he demanded the full sum which he thought they were worth, as a matter of just self-respect," adding that he made no demand until he had satisfied himself with the work in question (p. 8).

52. From Alexander Robertson American Academy of the Fine Arts
New York[1] / 20th January 1818

Sir: I have the honor to inform you that you have been elected an Honorary Member of this Academy and have the pleasure of forwarding a Diploma of the same.

In selecting you as one of its Honorary members this Academy duly appreciates the distinguished rank to which your talents have so eminently raised you in the art, and feel proud to enroll you among those of its Honorary Associates,—

Accept, Sir, the assurance of my personal regard and the high consideration with which I have the honor to be

Your obedient servant / A Robertson / Secretary

Washington Allston Esqr / London

SOURCE: Manuscript.

1. The American Academy of Fine Arts, first called the New York Academy of the Fine Arts, was established in 1802 and dissolved in 1840. WA was an honorary member from 1825 until 1828. He exhibited there in 1816, 1817, and 1822. It was succeeded by the Apollo Association, where he exhibited in 1840 and 1841. The Apollo Association soon became the American Art-Union, which in 1850 exhibited fifty sets of *O & S* (Mary Bartlett Cowdrey, *American Academy of Fine Arts and American Art-Union: Introduction, 1816-1852* [New York, 1953], Collections of the New-York Historical Society, 76, pp. 9, 60).

53. To Washington Irving London, March 13, 1818.

My dear Irving: I received yours of the 5th, and have the pleasure to inform you that the drawing is finished, and now in the hands of the engraver; to whom I gave it (since you were so good as to rely on my judgment) as soon as it was finished. I gave up the subject which Leslie mentioned,[1] and chose another with which I am much better pleased, namely, a Schepen doing *duty* to a Burgomaster's joke.[2]

Leslie agrees with me in thinking it superior to the lawsuit. Indeed, so far as I can judge of my own work, it is one of my happiest comic efforts, if not the best. It contains six figures. I think no one could fail to see that the Burgomaster is bringing forth a joke; for the action is so contrived as to leave no doubt of it. The Schepen who sits opposite to him, is laughing with all his might and main; while the rest of the company, who have nothing to gain by a laugh, are impenetrably, and most Dutchly, grave. But I think I had better not describe it. Descriptions of pictures are generally flat. Besides, their impression is always better, at least truer, when they come upon us without preparation. So the less said the better.

The plate after Leslie's is finished, and I think you will be very much pleased with it. It makes a very beautiful print; is extremely well engraved, but what particularly pleases me in it, is the close rendering of the characters, which is the most important part in subjects of this kind. If the engraver preserves mine as well,

I shall be amply satisfied. I hope the time the engraver demands for graving my drawing will not inconveniently affect your plans. His engagements, he says, are so pressing, just at this time, that he could not possibly promise it sooner than four months hence.

The price, also, is considerably higher than for Leslie's,[3] being from thirty-five to forty guineas. If he can do it for thirty-five, he says, he will; but he will not limit himself to less than forty, nor be bound to five and thirty.

The reason he gives for demanding so much more is the greater number of the figures and the quantity of detail. I was a little at a stand when I heard this; but knowing no other engraver of his abilities that works so cheap, I concluded it must be done by him even at this rate. Do let me know by return of post if you approve of what I have done.

Since my return from Paris I have painted two pictures, in order to have something in the present exhibition at the British Gallery: the subjects the angel Uriel in the sun,[4] and Elijah in the wilderness.[5] Uriel was immediately purchased (at the price I asked, one hundred and fifty guineas)[6] by the Marquis of Stafford,[7] and the Directors of the British Institution, moreover, presented me a *donation* of a hundred and fifty pounds, "as a mark of their *approbation* of the talent evinced, &c."[8] The manner in which this was done was highly complimentary; and I can only say that it was full as gratifying as it was unexpected. As both these pictures together cost me but ten weeks, I do not regret having deducted that time from the Belshazzar, to whom I have since returned with redoubled vigor.

I am almost sorry I did not exhibit Jacob's dream. If I had dreamt of this success, I certainly would have sent it there.

I hope your affairs are being settled to your mind,[9] and that we shall see you here soon.

Yours affectionately, / Washington Allston.

Ogilvie[10] has returned full of health and spirits from his success in Scotland. He has overcome his formidable enemy laudanum, and looks like another being. Leslie begs to be remembered.

SOURCE: Pierre M. Irving, 1:397-99.

1. Leslie had suggested a design of Peter Stuyvesant rebuking a cobbler from Irving's *History*, book 7, chap. 1. He later made a sketch of the subject and exhibited it (Irving, *Letters* 1:607).

2. *A Schepen Doing Duty to a Burgomaster's Joke* (1818), from Irving's *History*, book 3, chap. 2. It appeared, engraved by William Finden, as the frontispiece in volume 1 of the two-volume edition published by Moses Thomas in Philadelphia in 1819.

3. The price for the engraving of Leslie's design was twenty-five guineas (Pierre M. Irving, 1:398).

4. *Uriel in the Sun*, from *Paradise Lost* 3.623-29. West also painted the subject. Allston's immediate inspiration, he said, as reported by the *Morning Herald* for 2 February and the *Examiner* for 9 February 1818, was an otherwise unidentified poem entitled "Visit to the Sun—A Vision," which referred to Uriel as him "That once entranced th' immortal Milton saw." It is his major representation of the angelic nature which he so deeply revered and of his works on a heroic scale the most successful, combining the

tone of mystery with that of reverie. Of all his works it is one of the most beautiful. He may have been to some extent influenced by James Barry's *Progress of Human Culture and Knowledge*. His new technique in coloring was noted by Leslie, who wrote Irving that it had "a very rich and glowing tone," that he had "avoided all *positive* colors," which would have made the figure "too material," that there was neither red, blue, nor yellow in it yet it possessed "harmony equal to the best pictures of Paul Veronese" (p. 205). The golden tone was repeated in several subsequent paintings. It was painted in six weeks and exhibited at the BI in 1818, listed first in the catalog, at which time it was extensively reviewed. Haydon, in *Annals of the Fine Arts*, though finding a weakness in the drawing of the figure, called it an honor to the British school, justifying the exhibition to be called the best in years, and criticized the RA for giving preferential hanging for the work of academicians. The *Examiner* for 9 February said it was "already engraved on our hearts," the *Times* for 2 February commended it as one of the finest pieces in the exhibition, and the *Morning Herald* for the same date compared it in severity of design to the Roman school but also deplored the drawing of the figure. John Keats, writing to his brothers, said he could not stand it, though he thought it was by Leslie. Walter Channing recorded that Allston told him he "first surrounded him [Uriel], and the rock of adamant on which he sat, with the prismatic colors, in the order in which the ray of light is decomposed by the prism," then "laid them in with the strongest colors which represent them . . . next with transparent color, blended them so intimately together that he reproduced the original ray" and quoted Allston as saying, "So dazzling bright was it . . . that it made your eyes twinkle as you look at it." The author of the article on WA in the *United States Democratic Review* for October 1843 incorporated in it this account of how *Uriel in the Sun* was painted but with several variations in phraseology and entirely within quotation marks as being WA's own words throughout. Flagg, who printed this version, probably got both it and the passage in which WA described his feelings on returning to London from Paris in November 1817 from the same, unidentified source. Possibly the undated large chalk *The Sibyl* was intended as a companion piece to *Uriel in the Sun*. 5. *Elijah in the Desert*, from 1 Kings 17:16. Rubens also painted the subject. It was done in three weeks, the shortest time taken for any of his major works. The barren language was in drastic, allegorical contrast to his other landscapes with their verdure. He experimented with mixing his colors with skimmed milk, then varnishing, retouching with oil, and glazing, calling the result successful, though he never repeated the technique. It was exhibited at the BI in 1818 but received relatively little notice. He thought it one of the very best of its kind and hated to part with it when it was sold (Walter Channing). 6. There is considerable discrepancy in the accounts of what WA received for this painting. Walter Channing said the sum paid was $250. Elizabeth Peabody said it was six hundred guineas, though WA had asked half that amount. A few days after WA's death a story was printed in the Boston *Atlas* to the effect that he was in such despair financially at the time that he shut himself in his painting room and prayed for a loaf of bread, at which point the marquis of Stafford appeared at the door, having come to procure it at any price, and bought it; the incident was said to have made WA a devout man. The entire article was contradicted by several of his friends (Peabody, "Religious Character of Washington Allston," *New York Tribune*, 10 Aug. 1843; "Anecdotes of Allston," *Atlas*, 19 July 1843). According to Sweetser, Stafford called and asked where it was to be found and when WA declined to state the price, saying he had often done so but no one had been willing to pay it, asked if £400 would be enough, whereupon WA said that the sum was more than he ever asked but took it.
7. Granville Leveson-Gower, Lord Granville, was the second marquis of Stafford. 8. WA is quoting loosely from the minutes of the Committee of the Directors of the BI for promoting the Fine Arts (Extract from the Minutes, Dana Papers). 9. The Irving firm in Liverpool declared bankruptcy in January 1818 (Williams 1:166). 10. James Ogilvie (1760-1820), scholar and orator, spent several years in America earlier. Of an unstable disposition, he took laudanum for a time and was said to have committed suicide.

54. To the Secretary of the American Academy of Fine Arts

[Alexander Robertson] London, 4th May, 1818.

Dear Sir: I have the honour to acknowledge the receipt of your letter, together with a Diploma from the American Academy of Fine Arts, in New York—who have been pleased to elect me an Honorary Member of their body.—For so distinguished an honour, and thus conferred by an Academy in my own country, I beg you to express to them my best thanks, and to assure them that I shall ever consider this mark of their approbation as one of the most gratifying circumstances of my life.

The establishment of your Institution has been hailed by our professional brethren <of> on this side of the Atlantic with a degree of interest worthy the professors of a Liberal Art. As an artist, I need not say how heartily *I* too have hailed it; but, as an American, more deeply interested in all that may add to the reputation of my native land, I cannot but congratulate my countrymen on the auspicious opening of so [blank space] a fountain of national [blank space]

I remain, dear sir,

Your / Washington Allston

SOURCE: Manuscript. A copy in another hand is in The New-York Historical Society, with the words "fair" and "greatness" in the blank spaces and a different conclusion: "With best wishes, and a confident hope of your success under the able direction of your worthy and accomplished President,[1] I remain, dear sir, Your obliged & obednt servant."

1. Trumbull was president of the academy from 1817 to 1836 (Cowdrey, pp. 20, 58).

55. From George Howland Beaumont Grosvenor Square,[1]
June 29, 1818.

My Dear Sir: I am very sorry I was from home when you called this morning, and it is with concern I hear of your intention to return to America immediately. I am far from the exclusive wish of limiting the arts to this or that country, for I am convinced the more they are spread the greater degree of emulation will be excited, and the more all the benefits they are capable of giving to mankind will be of course extended, and they themselves will be brought to a greater degree of perfection. But I am convinced you are quitting this country at a moment when the extent of your talents begins to be felt, and when the encouragement you are likely to receive will bring them to perfection, and you would then return to your native country fully qualified to improve and direct the exertions which I am happy to hear are now apparent in America.

However, whatever you may resolve upon, depend upon this, that you will be attended by the best wishes of both myself and Lady Beaumont that your endeavors will be crowned with all the successes they so amply deserve. I am, my dear Sir, with much regard,

Sincerely yours, / George Beaumont.

SOURCE: Flagg, pp. 137-38.

1. Beaumont's residence in London.

56. To Washington Irving London, July 24, 1818.

My dear Irving: You are so accustomed to my apologies for epistolary delinquency that they must be to you like old stories; so I had better say nothing about it. Leslie, I believe, has already written you on the subject of the plate. I called on the engraver soon after the receipt of your letter, and was more grieved than surprised that it was not already finished; for I know the press of his engagements, and remembered the difficulty he had in fixing on the time of its completion, when I first put it into his hands. I would have strained a point to scold about it, if I had thought that would have mended the matter. But as it would not, I could only urge the importance of its speedy termination in the strongest way, and leave the rest to the engraver, who then promised to finish it as soon as it was in his power, and he has since engaged to produce a proof in the course of the next week. He begged that I would not insist on seeing the plate, as he never liked to show his works in an unfinished state. As that is also the case with myself, I did not urge it. But I have no doubt, from the ability he has shown in other works, that it will be well done. If it is equal to that he did from Leslie's drawing, I shall be more than satisfied. As soon as I see a proof I will write you.

Now that you are your own master again, your muse, I suppose, has already paid you a visit. Pray do not turn your back upon her, for I have it on the testimony of thousands that she has not a greater favorite than yourself in all Parnassus. Do tell me what you are doing, or mean to do. Your imagination has been so long fallow that I anticipate a most luxuriant harvest when you again cultivate it.[1]

Leslie tells me he has informed you of the sale of Jacob's Dream. I do not remember if you have seen it. The manner in which Lord Egremont bought it was particularly gratifying—to say nothing of the price, which is no trifle to me at present.[2] But Leslie having told you all about it, I will not repeat it. Indeed, by the account he gives me of his letter to you, he seems to have puffed me off in grand style. Well, you know I don't bribe him to do it. And "if they will buckle praise upon my back," why, I can't help it

Leslie has just finished a very beautiful little picture of Anne Page inviting Master Slender into the house.[3] Anne is exquisite; soft and feminine, yet arch and playful, she is all she should be. Slender, also, is very happy; he is a good parody on Milton's "linked sweetness long drawn out."[4] Falstaff and Shallow are seen through a window in the background. The whole scene is very picturesque, and beautifully painted. 'Tis his best picture. You must not think this praise the "return in kind." I give it because I really admire the picture, and I have not the smallest doubt that he will do great things when he is once freed from the necessity of painting portraits.

Believe me affectionately yours, / W. Allston.

I suppose Leslie has told you that the price of printing your plates would be five pounds a thousand[5]—and that on French paper, which is the best; this includes paper. As I shall leave my lodgings in a short time, pray direct me to "the care of Samuel Williams, Esq., No. 13 Finsbury Square." Lord Egremont has invited me to his seat at Petworth, and I shall go down there next week.[6] I have taken my passage in the Galen from this port.[7] Shall not I see you here before I go? She sails about the tenth of August.[8]

SOURCE: Pierre M. Irving, 1:401-403.

1. Irving's *Sketch Book*, his first book since his *History*, was published in 1819-20. 2. Sir George O'Brien Wyndham, Lord Egremont. He purchased *Jacob's Dream* after the success of WA's *Uriel in the Sun*. He wanted it for his London house, but when the room there was found too small had it taken to his large Petworth House on his country estate. It did not arrive until 1819, after its exhibition. The price he paid for it is not known. 3. Leslie's *Slender, Shallow, and Ann Page* was from Shakespeare's *The Merry Wives of Windsor* 1.1.255ff. 4. "Lap me soft in *Lydian* Aires, / Married to immortal verse / Such as the meeting soul may pierce / In notes, with many a winding bout / Of lincked sweetness long drawn out" (Milton, "L'Allegro," lines 136-40). 5. Irving told Leslie to arrange for two thousand copies of printings from both plates (Irving, *Letters* 1:538). 6. RHD, Jr., recollected WA's relating when nearly sixty years of age that on this visit he was looking at a portrait by Van Dyck when Egremont came up and asked his opinion of it. When he said that had he not known otherwise he would have supposed it to be by Reynolds, Egremont asked if he thought Van Dyck inferior to Reynolds; he replied that he did, and Egremont agreed but added, "I hardly dare to say so" (Flagg, p. 354). 7. All WA's friends, notably Beaumont, Egremont, Irving, Leslie, and Wordsworth, deplored his leaving England, urged him to stay, and predicted that he would soon achieve the greatest success there, many assuring him that he would succeed West as president of the RA. Besides the homesickness he said prompted him, he was probably influenced by the failure of his funds, inability to find adequate patronage in England, and the news that through the mismanagement and dishonesty of his agent in South Carolina his patrimony was exhausted. 8. The *Galen* apparently cleared the Isle of Wight on 31 August, taking forty-two days to reach Boston (*Boston Daily Advertiser*, 13 Oct. 1818).

57. From Samuel Taylor Coleridge [1818, before mid-August]

My dear Allston: The Bearer of this is a particular friend of mine, a German Gentleman,[1] of excellent good taste in painting, and himself a Possessor of a very curious collection of the old Netherland Masters. As he was sitting in our parlor talking with me, he kept his eye fixed on your picture[2] (which is now framed & hung up) and at last said "I beg your pardon, but you have a valuable picture of some Venetian Master!"—I answered—Titian, do you think? No, said he—tho' he has the coloring of several of his early works, but the outline is too soft for him.—he was *crisp* to a defect. It is more like a picture of Paul Veronese.—He could scarcely believe me when I told him, it was your's, tho' imitated from an old picture.

He is exceedingly desirous to see the Jacob's Dream—You will find him a man worth knowing, both in head & heart.

When shall we see you?

S.T. Coleridge

Tuesday

SOURCE: Manuscript. Printed in Flagg, p. 127.

1. Probably Karl Aders, a German collector living in London, who with his wife was closely associated with Coleridge. 2. From *Adoration of the Magi* by Titian.

58. To Charles Robert Leslie

On board ship.
23 August [1818]

Dear Leslie: I am at last on board, & after all about as well as I could expect. I send these few lines by the Pilot to let you know that I am safe on my voyage,[1] and to trouble you with one little commission more, which is, to pay to Mrs. Rehoy,[2] at N 87 Great Portland Street, six shillings; for it runs in my mind that my wife had of her four or five toothbrushes, and some writing paper, which have never been paid for. This is but a trifling debt; but still it is a *debt*. I think I also owe Mr. Hitchen,[3] the shoemaker over the way, two shillings for an errand. Will you pay him? This is all in the money way.—But there is one thing I had forgotten to say to you, which is, to beg that you *will not* take in any letters that may be sent to me *directed to Buckingham Place*.[4] I have cautioned Mr. & Mrs. Bridgen and Harriet[5] on this point; and they have *promised not to take in any*. I gave them my reasons for it, and they will inform you. There is no correspondent *whatever* that I wish to hear from who will direct there for me. And those I do expect to hear from I have already requested to direct for me to Finsbury Square; and this I did to those *out of* town as well as in London so that I cannot possibly miss by it any letter I should care for; and by this <[undecipherable word]> rejection of the letters directed to Buckingham Place I shall probably save myself a great deal of annoyance. Mr. Visger has had my address "to the care of Mr. Williams &c" for some time, as I told him his letters would not reach me by any other way; and he has already written to me lately through Mr. Williams and he will not <address> write to me again through any other channel. By this you will see that I am not likely to lose any letters I care for. And, indeed, if I even should, I had much rather lose them then run the risk of the annoyance I apprehend. Mr. & Mrs. Bridgen have promised <to take to> to say, <when> should any be brought to their house, that I have left <the country> London"; and if asked where I am gone, *not to say where*; so that the postmen will of course take such letters back to the post office where they will be opened and sent them back to the writers. I forgot to tell Mr. Brock and Betsey[6] of this. Will you caution them also on this subject? The general post letters are what I most particularly would avoid. There are letters of this unpleasant kind I have had from Bristol and other places. <[Four and a quarter lines of undecipherable words]> This will prevent any more coming.

I know, my good fellow, you will excuse this, for you know what I have already suffered.

Pray let Coleridge & Mr. & Mrs. Gillman know that I <am> have left London as soon as you get this—and Mr. Morgan also. One line will do. My love to them all. Remember me to Mrs. Bridgen and the rest of the family.

And now, god bless you, and grant that we may soon meet on the other side of the water. Truly your friend

W. Allston.

N.B. I have written two long letters to Mr. Day & to Wallis. <You will give them both to Mr. Day with the books.> I think you had better <put> tie the letter to Wallis on the <envelope> book directed to him, and then cover the letter with the paper in which <it is> the book is now wrapt. Let the letter be fastened so that it won't fall when the cover is taken off. Mr. Day will take charge of it. He need not know what it is—I shall enclose these letters in another cover, addressed to you.

In About two or three weeks you will remember the commission about Mr. Gray [?] X. M.[7] He live[s] N 18 Clipstone Street. The evening [sentence unfinished]

Tell Mr. Bridgen <dir> never to take out any letters <directed> to me from the Dead-letter box. If any should be there <stay [two undecipherable words]> remain, for I don't want them.

ADDRESSED: C.R. Leslie Esqre. / N. 8 Buckingham Place, / Fitzroy Square, / London.
SOURCE: Manuscript.

1. The voyage, however, proved to be a stormy one. During part of the bad weather, according to Sweetser, WA remained on deck imperturbably conversing with the captain as to whether two-thirds of the ship's keel was not thrown clear of the sea at one time. En route he painted the watercolor *Galen*, or *Storm at Sea* and made the drawing *Polyphemus Immediately after His Eye Was Put Out, Groping about his Cavern for the Companions of Ulysses* from Homer, *The Odyssey* 9.415-23), a subject also treated by Tibaldi. 2. Not further identified. Apparently she was a shopkeeper. 3. Not further identified. 4. Leslie thought WA's departure from England at this time was occasioned by his being importuned by beggars. His charities were well known. Leslie cited one case in which he gave a woman some of his wife's clothes, only to see her begging afterward in her rags, and said he had received distressing letters from some whom he had aided. 5. Probably the Bridgens' daughter, whom Leslie described as "very pretty" and a "very great recommendation" for their quarters (pp. 179-80). 6. Probably John B. Brock, a merchant at 11 Warnford-Court, Throgmorton Street, not far from the general post office in 1818. During the few preceding years he was in business with two others at 9 Piccadilly nearby (*Post-Office London Directory*, 1818; *Kent's Original London Directory*, 1812-16). Betsey was probably a member of his household. Presumably they took care of WA's mail addressed to the general post. 7. Probably William G. Gray, organ builder, on New Road, MaryleBone (*Kent's*

Original London Directory for 1819 and adjacent years), the section of the city in which Clipstone Street was located. The initials "X.M." have not been explained.

59. To William Collins On board Ship. 23 August [1818]

Dear Collins: I cannot let the Pilot return on shore without sending you a line to say that I am at last (& I thank God) safe on my voyage; & in as good spirits as the parting with so many good friends, & the land I love next to my own, will allow. Dear England, may you be ever happy & prosperous! Say all to Sir George & Lady Beaumont that your knowledge of the deep sense I have of their kindness would suggest. My respectful compliments to Mr. Wordsworth & family,[1] & to Mr. Southey.[2]

By the Bye, it was on my mind the last evening we were together, but it soon slipped my memory, to say a word or two on the subjects of Coleridge & family,[3] which we had been speaking of a few evenings before. It occurred to me that as all his friends, Sir G. &c, are probably acquainted with his domestic affairs, it would answer no purpose to say any thing about it; for it might only irritate some of the parties, without effecting any good. And I think that all concerning Mrs. C. had better not be mentioned to any one there or elsewhere.—I am decided that it ought not to be.[4] On the pecuniary part of the circumstances there is no occasion to be silent where the mentioning it would serve C. But the domestic differences had better be suppressed on many accounts. The mentioning them would not serve C. in any way so as to counterbalance the ill effect that might arise from the irritation it must occasion in the other parties. About family quarrels the least said by others the better for the parties. C. never speaks of his himself, & I know he would deeply regret that in any way they should be talked of.

Do let me hear from you when you return to London, & be particular in all that's going on in the Art. You cannot be too minute. My address is simply Boston, United States. I have no time for more, else I would certainly send a line to Sir G. It was fully my intention to have written [to write] him before I sailed; but the endless preparations for a sea voyage must be my apology for the omission. I must write however from America.

Now farewell, dear C. & that God may ever bless you & yours is the sincere wish of your friend

W. Allston.

P.S. Pray do not give my address to any one, should it be asked. I have given it *to all that I wish to hear from;* & I wish not to hear from any others. If Sir George or any persons like him should honour me by inquiring it, you will of course give it.

N.B. What I mean by the pecuniary part of the circumstances is, the annuity, the life insurance of his daughter, his occasional remittances, & the present provision of his two sons. If these are mentioned I think it would be well without comment as they cannot need it.

ADDRESSED: [In care of Beaumont] ANNOTATED: No 1. *Copy* [the first of three letters from WA to Collins copied by RHD]. SOURCE: Copy by RHD.

1. Wordsworth's wife was the former Mary Hutchinson (1770-1859), by whom he had five children: John, Dorothy, Thomas, Catharine, and William. Only Dorothy (1804-47) and William (1810-83) were living at this time. His sister Dorothy lived with them. 2. Robert Southey.
3. Coleridge married Sara Fricker (1770-1845), by whom he had three children. The Coleridges were notoriously incompatible and lived apart after 1806. WA always referred in public to their separation as an amicable one because, he said, it pained Coleridge to be defended at his wife's expense, but privately he reported that according to Mrs. James Gillman Mrs. Coleridge was, her sister when dying said, irascible, implacable, and impossible to live with. 4. After this sentence RHD wrote: "[N.B. This last clause interlined in the original.]."

60. From James McMurtrie Philadelphia October 18. 1818.

Dear Sir: I have just heard of your arrival at Boston. May we look for you in this city soon? I confidently expect that you will pass some time with us. There is still a balance due you from your picture in my hands. Shall I remit it immediately to you or await your coming on—be pleased to direct me.

very truly Yours / J McMurtrie

W. Allston Esqe.

(over)

charges

freight large picture	$24.26	
Duty	150.	
prts [?]	1. –	
freight landscape & carry to Philad	65. –	
Charges at Liverpol on large picture—£8.4.7	36.57	
	276.83	
Remitted		
Hemphills[1] bill £200 a 14½ adv.	1022.20	
J.B. Raub[2][?]—100—7 pl. [?] adv.	448.88	
J.S. Waln[3]—300—5 adv.	1400.00	
Amt recd for picture—$3500.00		
Int. for bal. whilst in hand	25.00	
		3525.00
Bal. due W. Allston—		$ 377.09

There is an int. a/c with the Academy of fine [Arts] about which I wrote long since, & have not recd yr. instructions. I stipulated for int. on the whole purchase money until paid. It is for you to decide whether to exact it or not. The Academy it is true is poor—but the agreement was absolute.

ADDRESSED: Washg Allston Esqr / Boston. SOURCE: Manuscript.

1. Unidentified. Probably an agent in England. 2. Unidentified. 3. Jacob S. Waln was a Philadelphia merchant (*Philadelphia City Directory* for 1816 and later years).

61. To Henry Pickering Hartford Place, Boston,[1]
1818 Oct. 31

Sir: I am quite ashamed to have so long delayed replying to your very obliging letter. But indeed my time has been so constantly occupied by visiting, and receiving visits from my numerous friends here, <that I> and my feelings so variously excited, that I have not felt myself sufficiently collected to put my thoughts in any order on paper.

I beg you will receive this as my apology, and at the same time <to> accept my best acknowledgement for the honour done me both in the purport and expressions of your letter. With respect to the subjects proposed I should be glad to have some conversation with you, if you will favour me with a call when you next come to Boston.

I remain, Sir, with great respect, your obligd humble Servt,

Washington Allston

ADDRESSED: Henry Pickering Esqre. / Salem—. SOURCE: Manuscript.

1. The *Galen* reached Boston on 12 October 1818. At first WA stayed with his brother William at this address. (*Boston Daily Advertiser,* 13 Oct. 1818; *Boston City Directory* for 1818).

62. From James McMurtrie Philadelphia Novemr. 4. 1818.

Dear Sir: I wrote to you about two weeks ago & directed my letter to Boston. From my not hearing from you I conclude that you have not recd it. I therein stated the account of the money recd by me for yr. picture of the "Dead Man raised." & the remittances I made in the Balance still due you and in my hands being *about* 377 Dollars. Shall I remit you this Sum immediately or await your coming on to Philada? I sincerely hope you will make us a visit and remain some time here. At all events let me hear from you and believe me to be with the greatest regard

Yours very truly / J McMurtrie

Washington Allston esqe.

ADDRESSED: Washg Allston Esqre / Care of I.P. Davis[1] / Boston. SOURCE: Manuscript.

1. Isaac P. Davis.

63. From William Collins London November 4th 1818

Dear Allston: From my very heart's core do I congratulate you upon your election as an Associate of the Royal Academy, a circumstance as honorable to that Body as to yourself—and of which I received the gratifying intelligence yesterday. I immediately sent for Leslie, who came over out of breath and the news I had to communicate to him has I believe kept him to a certain degree in the same state ever since—had you been here—*but you will come*.

And now to the fulfillment of your commission, to send all the news I can, to which end I shall give you a succession of such events as may serve to remind you of the ties you have in this country. The letter you sent me at Sir George Beaumont's came during dinner and I of course made Sir George and her ladyship acquainted with that part of it relating to themselves and if I have any knowledge of the human heart what the two said of you was direct from that spot. May all the success we that day wished you attend your steps.

With the scenery of the North I am charmed—and, considering the time necessarily occupied in travelling, I have not been altogether idle—your hints about Coleridge I did not fail attending to. With his wife I am pleased and his elegant daughter Sarah I have made a painting of. She is a most interesting creature, about fifteen years of age—and the parties we occasionally formed with these good people, Southey and Hartley I shall not soon forget. From Keswick[1] I went with Chantrey[2] to Scotland, and had this part of the world nothing but Edinburgh well might she boast. After spending ten days at Edinburgh I returned to Sir George, and with himself and Lady Beaumont visited Ullswater and Ambleside, where we stayed some days with Wordsworth—with whom I am very much delighted—and in some of our rambles, when he could have no motive but that of gratifying his own love of truth, he left me perfectly persuaded, that among all your friends and admirers you have not a more disinterested one than himself. The kind regards I am desired by Wordsworth, his wife, Southey, and Hartley to send to you are testimonies of a Friendship by no means common and therefore will have their true weight with you.

My very excellent friend Leslie was of course faithfully at his post for nearly two months—a more competent Major Domo I would not desire. Frank[3] has not yet returned from Northamptonshire, Willes[4] is in France, Stark[5] has just returned from Norwich, and I am attempting a mountain sc[ene] [page torn] upon [a] large scale, (the commission I was abo[ut to] [page torn] undertake when I last saw you. My uncle[6] has accepted a Chaplaincy at Cape Coast Castle, five degrees north of the line, which although a lucrative appointment, yet from the nature of the climate, one of considerable risk, of course. We are in great agitation about him.

Having now, at the least possible expense of stile, told you so much, I have only to assure you of the warm wishes and hopes of all your friends, and (as you already know) how much I am, my dear Allston, yours ever,

W Collins

My mother[7] has been unwell, but is now recovered. She desires her best regards. I shall expect a letter from you and I beg to remind you that this is a sample of the quantity of blank paper I am desirous of. Come *home* and take your *seat* at the Lectures, have you no *Esprit de Corps?*

I presented your poems[8] to Lady Beaumont, who had never seen them, and I had the very high gratification to hear them spoken of in terms of considerable approbation, not only by her Ladyship but by Southey and Wordsworth. Southey said, that whatever defects some of them might have, he had no hesitation in saying, they could not have proceeded from any but a poetic mind—in which sentiment he was most cordially supported by Wordsworth, who was present at this time. Fare thee well, God bless you!

How did you find your Mother, your relatives and friends? have you numerous commissions? Write soon—Sir George Beaumont & Wordsworth purpose writing to you.

ADDRESSED: Washington Allston Esqre A.R.A. / Boston / America. SOURCE: Manuscript. Printed in part in Flagg, pp. 140-42.

1. Keswick, the capital of the Lake District, was the home of Southey after 1803 and was constantly visited by the Beaumonts, Coleridge, and Wordsworth. 2. Sir Francis Leggett Chantrey (1782-1841), English sculptor. 3. Francis Collins was younger brother of William Collins, with whom he lived all his life. He was a picture cleaner who had been trained by their father, also a picture cleaner. More than one person testified to his store of curious information about art and artists (W. Wilkie Collins, *The Life of William Collins*, Esq. [London, 1848], 1:4, 181-82; 2:29-36). 4. William Willes (d. 1851), Irish landscape and subject painter, lived for several years in London and Reading. 5. James Stark (1794-1859), English landscape painter from Norwich. 6. Otherwise unidentified. 7. Collins's mother (d. 1833) was Scottish, born in the neighborhood of Edinburgh (Collins, 1:4, 37). 8. Presumably *SS*.

64. To James McMurtrie Boston Novbr 7th 1818.

My dear Sir: The enclosed,[1] which was written more than three weeks ago, I have been prevented finishing before this by such incessant engagements and excitements as have left me not one collected hour in which I could calmly sit down to write. I therefore beg you to excuse the delay, and take my *wish* to have been more punctual for the performance. The same cause has operated in my not before acknowledging your favour of the 18th October; for which I entreat the same indulgence. As I purpose to remain here during the winter, I must beg you to remit the balance due me, of which you speak, to <me in> this place: directing for me to the care of Timothy Williams Esquire,[2] Boston. With respect to the interest <over the purchase money> due from the Pennsylvania Academy, I beg you to state to them, that the delay of the payment of the purchase money not having occasioned me any inconvenience, I with pleasure relinquish it. I am sufficiently rewarded both by the honour they have done me in the purchase of the Picture, and by the sum paid.

The success I have lately met with in England left me with but one finished picture to bring with me—Elijah in the Wilderness—& which had I remained a few weeks longer I had the prospect of also transferring to another proprietor.

I have brought, however, several others, *on the stocks*;[3] some of which are considerably advanced; particularly "Belshazzer's feast, or the hand-writing on the wall:" sixteen feet by twelve in size; which I believe is by several feet larger than the "Raising of the Dead Man."[4] I purpose finishing it here. All the laborious part is over; but there still remains about six or eight months more work to do on it. As I get on with it and other smaller works, which I may probably proceed with at the same time, I will take the liberty occasionally to drop you a line.—In the spring, or summer I may not unlikely pay you a visit. I have a great desire to see your City, and the state of the Arts there.—Though I have not the pleasure of a personal acquaintance with Mr. Sully, I yet so well know him, through his friends, and the friendly services he, in conjunction with yourself, has rendered me, that I must in a particular manner beg you to present him my respects.

I left Leslie well. He intends embarking for America in the Spring.[5] He has lately finished a beautiful little picture of Anne Page inviting Master Slender in, from the Merry Wives of Windsor. It is finely composed & [page torn] I thought it his happie[st] [page torn]

I remain, dear Sir / Sincerely Yours / Washington Allston

ADDRESSED: James McMurtrie Esqre. / Philadelphia. SOURCE: Manuscript. Miscellaneous Manuscripts Collection, LC. Printed in Flagg, pp. 143-44.

1. This letter does not seem to have been preserved. 2. Timothy Williams (1765-1846) was a Boston merchant and the brother of Samuel and Charles Williams. He graduated from Harvard in 1784. He owned WA's *Coast Scene on the Mediterranean* and portrait of Samuel Williams and was a subscriber to the Tripartite Agreement. 3. Besides *Belshazzar's Feast* and studies for it, he brought *Italian Landscape*, or *Italian Scenery; The Sisters; Marriage at Cana;* the five portraits of Jews; *Elijah in the Desert; Christ Healing the Sick*, the sketch of *The Angel Releasing St. Peter from Prison* and the studies for it; *Study from Life*, the portraits of West, his mother, Samuel Williams (ca. 1817), and Mrs. King; the second portrait of himself; *Head of a Woman in Profile;* possibly *Beatrice;* and probably other sketches and unfinished works. 4. *The Dead Man Restored* is 156 by 120 inches. 5. Leslie did not go to America until 1833.

65. From Charles Robert Leslie London November 7th 1818

My dear friend: You will doubtless receive by this opportunity various informations of your election. You had ten votes out of fifteen. Need I say that all your friends most cordially rejoice at it. I carried the pleasing intelligence out to Highgate the day I heard it & while I was there Mr. Gillman received a note from Phillips[1] the R.A., informing them of it as a circumstance that he knew would give them the greatest pleasure. By the bye Collins thinks that your picture of Jacob's dream ought now to be exhibited at the Academy & as he has no doubt you will concur in the same opinion he intends proposing to Phillips to ask Lord Egremont's permission. He told me last night he had seen Sir George, who had just arrived in town, & who heartily partakes of the general pleasure on your account. Sir G. intends writing to you.

I have just returned from a very delightful tour of three weeks through Devonshire. I went as far as Plymouth & visited Plumpton (Sir Joshua's[2] native village). The weather was fine & the scenery the richest I have seen in England. I staid a fortnight with Mr. & Mrs. Dunlop[3] at Dawlish near Exeter, & at the seaside. Mrs. D. is not so well as could be wished, she caught cold while at Dawlish & still feels the effects of it. I am sorry to say poor Mr. Morgan has been very ill; he is getting a little better. I have not been able to visit him since my return to town. Coleridge is as well as he usually is. Mrs. Gillman is better than usual. When Collins was in Cumberland he made a sketch of Coleridge's daughter, a very interesting girl of fifteen, & it is by far the best portrait he ever painted. The *sentiment* (for in speaking of it I may safely use that hackneyed word) is exquisite. I took it to shew Coleridge as one of my own to see if he would discover the likeness which he did; a proof that it must be very strong as he has not seen her for many years & had not the most distant idea that it was intended for her. Coleridge is going to lecture again on philosophy & Shakespeare.[4] Ogilvie is lecturing at the Surrey Institution.[5] Payne has written a tragedy[6] which has been received at Drury Lane & is to be speedily produced. The story is that of Junius Brutus. Kean[7] plays Brutus. Irving is still in town & I believe intends remaining here. He is occasionally *manufacturing*.[8] I have not seen Collard since his return, though I have called on him several times. Lonsdale has not yet returned. Willes has gone to Paris—I called on Mr. West as soon as I heard of your election, but did not see him; his health is pretty good. If Morse is in Boston tell him I have received his letter of the 8th Septr & will answer it immediately. I suppose the Doctor[9] is married by this time, if so give him my love & sincere congratulations upon the occasion. We are in hourly expectation of the news of your arrival. The Bridgens are all well & all send their love to you.

I hope your new title will encourage you to dash on boldly with Belshazzer. Success & every blessing attend you! I have no expectation now of going to America this Autumn, & when the Spring arrives I shall wish to see the Exhibition at Somerset House, so that it is probable I may not get away till about the time of year you did.

Yours with the greatest affection, / Chas. R. Leslie

P.S. As you are entitled to two tickets for the private view of the next Exhibition Collins says if you send a note requesting Mr. Howard to give them to me I may enjoy the benefit of them.

ADDRESSED: Washington Allston Esqr A.R.A. / Boston / Masstts. SOURCE: Manuscript, Houghton.

1. Thomas Phillips (1770-1845), English portrait painter. 2. Sir Joshua Reynolds. 3. James Dunlop, a wealthy American tobacco importer living in England, patron of art and author of a history of American painters (Leslie, pp. 213, 101, 293, 297). 4. At the end of 1818 Coleridge made notes for a set of fourteen lectures on the "History of Philosophy" and another set on "Six selected plays of Shakespeare" to be delivered at the "Crown and Anchor" in the Strand in London (Lucy E. Watson, *Coleridge at Highgate* [London, Longmans, Green, 1925], p. 78). 5. The Surrey Institution on the Surrey side of the Thames was established in 1807 with provision for public lectures and other intellectual pursuits. It was dissolved in 1820 (Thomas Allen, *The History and Antiquities of London, Westminster, Southwark, and Parts Adjacent* [London, 1839], 4:532-33). 6. Payne's historical tragedy in five acts, *Brutus, or the Fall of Tarquin,* opened at the Drury Lane Theatre in London on 3 December 1818. It was a great success, being acted fifty-two times and passing through six editions. 7. Edmund Kean (1787-1853), English actor. 8. Irving was writing *The Sketch Book* (Williams, 1:166-70). 9. Possibly William Maxwell.

66. From Henry Howard Royal Academy November 18. 1818—

Dear Sir: I am gratified in having to acquaint you that on the 2d Inst in a General Assembly of the Academicians, you were elected an Associate of the Royal Academy.

The existing Regulations require an Associate to sign the Instrument of Institution in the presence of the Council when his Diploma is delivered to him; & neglecting to take up his Diploma within one year from his election, he is considered as declining to become a member of the Academy, unless such an apology be made as shall be deemed sufficient by the Council.

Have the goodness to acquaint me, as soon as convenient, when we may expect the pleasure of seeing you again in England, & if you wish for any further information on the subject I shall be happy to give it you, being,

Dear Sir, / Yours very truly / Hy Howard. Sec R.A.

To / Mr Washington Allston.

ADDRESSED: Washington Allston Esq. / Boston. SOURCE: Manuscript.

67. From James McMurtrie Philada Decr 12th 1818.

Dear Sir: Yours of 2d[1] int was yesterday handed to me. I am greatly mortified that circumstances have unluckily occurred which have prevented my remitting the balance in my hands of $377. I hold a mortgage & judgmt bonds for a considerable sum on which the int. is due for some time and it may [be] the end of next week before I receive the money & I possibly may receive it *this day.*—Within a week therefore you shall receive the remittance and if you can forgive the delay that has unfortunately taken place you add to the obligations I lie under to you. In my next I will inform you of what is doing in the fine Arts.

Sincerely Yours / James McMurtrie

W. Allston Esqe

ADDRESSED: Washington Allston Esqre / Boston. SOURCE: Manuscript.

1. In this letter, which does not seem to have been preserved, WA evidently reported that he had not received the balance due him for *The Dead Man Restored.*

68. To James McMurtrie Boston 24 Decr 1818

My Dear Sir: This will be handed you by my particular friend Mr. W.S. Rogers,[1] of the Navy, whom I beg leave to introduce to your acquaintance.—Mr. Rogers has kindly offered to see to the shipment for Charleston, S. Carolina,[2] of my picture, namely the large Landscape of Swiss scenery, with figures representing Diana on the Chace, which I sent out from London, to your care about two years ago, and which is now, I understand, at Mr. Sully's room; I have therefore given him a letter to Mr. Sully for that purpose.

Will you gratify Mr. R. by shewing him your little picture (by me) of the Mother and Child?

Your letter of the 12th of this month has been received communicating your intention of shortly remitting to me the Balance mentioned in it. If it should not be already remitted, and it perfectly suits your convenience I would thank you to hand it to Mr. Rogers.

Stuart has painted an admirable portrait of Trumbull,[3] who has had great success here with his picture having got, in three weeks, 17 hundred dollars by it's exhibition.[4]

I remain dear sir / Yours sincerely / Washington Allston

James McMurtrie Esq.
Philadelphia

SOURCE: Copy.

1. William S. Rogers (1797-1864), of Boston. He was appointed purser in the U.S. Navy on 26 February 1813 and resigned on 17 February 1834 (Callahan, 1:472). In 1835-36 and 1839 he was a member of the Massachusetts legislature. He was a subscriber to the Tripartite Agreement.

2. Morse had offered to exhibit WA's *Diana and Her Nymphs* in Charleston, S.C., where he went in January 1819.

3. The portrait was painted in December 1818 in Boston (Park, 2:767).

4. Trumbull's *The Declaration of Independence, Philadelphia, 4 July 1776,* was painted for the rotunda of the Capitol at Washington. An enlarged replica was exhibited in Faneuil Hall in Boston, from the receipts of which Trumbull received $1,701.56 (Trumbull, pp. 319-20).

69. To Henry Pickering Boston, 29th Decbr 1818.

Dear Sir: I am exceedingly sorry that you should have had the trouble of calling on me so many times without success, and regret that you did not leave your address in Town, that I might have known where to wait on you; which I should not have failed to have done as soon as I had been apprised of your call.

Your letter of the 26th inst. has only served to confirm the high opinion I had previously entertained of your character; but I lament that your extreme delicacy should have refined itself into the belief that there was any thing improper in your first letter; for I considered it not only honourable to yourself, but in every way highly flattering to me; and it was my wish, in my reply, to have expressed this opinion, and to have shewn that I felt both gratified and honoured by the commission it tendered. My motive for defering any discussion on the subjects proposed was because I could explain my sentiments respecting them much better in a few minutes conversation than within the compass of even a long letter. I preferred a personal conference for another reason—namely, that at the same time I made known my objections to the subjects I might learn from you what others you would be willing to have substituted. My objection was not founded in their having been *proposed* to me rather than left to my own choice, but to the subjects* themselves, as being of a peculiar kind in which I cannot feel interested, and on which my powers of invention would consequently be unproductive. Indeed, so far am I from wishing to be the sole chooser, I am <often> always obliged to any one that honours with a commission to help me also to a subject: All that I wish in such a case is to have a negative voice. I beg you therefore to be assured, that though I not feel sufficiently interested in the subjects already proposed to do them justice, I shall be most happy to undertake any others which you may suggest, provided they may be such as are congenial to my imagination, and within my ability. And I have no doubt that in a personal interview of half an hour every arrangement might be made to our mutual satisfaction. For though you have done me the honour, by your last letter, to leave the subjects to my own discretion, it would be a satisfaction to me to learn, from a short conversation, what are the *kinds* of subjects most agreeable to you, that, should I avail myself of the liberty, I might still consult your taste in the selection.—Will you then do me the favour to say when you will be in Town, and where, and at what hour I may have the pleasure of calling on you?

If the pictures are to be figures, with subordinate landscape background, size 3½ feet by 2½ odd inches, the price will be five hundred dollars; if landscapes, with wholly subordinate figures, size from 3 by two, or <to> 4 & ½ by 3 feet, also five hundred.

Should you wish landscapes, I think 4 & ½ by 3 feet not too large for ou[r] modern rooms. A landscape of half the si[ze] [w]ould not require less time in the ex[ecu]tion [page torn].

I have only to add that, if the price be agreeable to you, and any arrangement made as to the subjects, I should be most happy to undertake your commission, and would immediately set about one of them.

I remain, dear Sir, with sincere respect

your obednt servt / Washington Allston

* It may be well for me to notice here that I objected *not* to Landscapes, (of which I am very fond) but to all *classical and allegorical*[1] subjects & figures; and to all subjects where either the figures or the landscapes are not *undecidedly subordinate*.

ADDRESSED: Henry Pickering Esqre. / Salem—. SOURCE: Manuscript.

1. WA objected to the allegorical works of West, Fuseli, and others and, according to Sweetser, said on one occasion that if one was to paint a tub or a candlestick he should do so and not paint an allegorical representation.

70. To Samuel Finley Breese Morse[1] Boston, January 27, 1819

My dear Sir: Before this reaches you, you will probably receive the landscape,[2] which you were so good as to undertake the disposal of in Charleston, or at least to give house-room to there; I mean the landscape I painted in Italy, and which has been for a year or two past in Mr. Sully's room, in Philadelphia. The price I have set on it is two hundred and fifty guineas; not a farthing less. If it is worth any thing, I think it worth three hundred; but I am content to get two hundred and fifty. At any rate, however, I beg you to observe that I would on no account sell it for more than three hundred, even it it should be offered. The price is two hundred and fifty; ask that, and with that I shall be content. I have directed the case containing the picture to be addressed to you, to the care of Mr. Hugh Paterson, who was formerly my agent; and I must beg the favor of you to pay the freight and other charges that may be incident to the landing of it, as I have no longer any account with Mr. Paterson, which I will repay you when we meet; or you may deduct the sum from the sale, if it should be so fortunate as to meet with a purchaser. I shall make no apology for giving this trouble, since I know you would not consider it other than a pleasure to render me a service.

Now the business part of my letter is over, I suppose you will expect something like news concerning the art. Sargent[3] is going on with his second picture of the "Landing of our Forefathers," and I think will make it better than that of the "Entrance into Jerusalem." He is a worthy and liberal man, and I hope he may meet with that praise for it which his love of the art, under so many unexciting, not to say discouraging circumstances, may fairly entitle him to; and under which his perseverance is no small proof that he cultivates it solely for itself. Mr. Stuart has lately painted a fine head of Commodore Perry.[4] Fisher[5] left this for Charleston some time since, and I suppose is now there. Leslie, from whom I lately had a letter, does not contemplate returning to America before the next autumn. John Payne has written a tragedy on the subject of "Junius Brutus," which is now acting with great applause at the Drury Lane. Kean plays the principal part in it. This is all the news I have to tell about others. Now concerning myself: I yesterday received an official communication from Mr. Howard, the secretary of the Royal Academy, informing me that on the 2d of November last I was elected an associate of that body. I had received intelligence of it about three weeks ago, both from Leslie and Collins. I must own this is very pleasing to me, and I am sure it will be very gratifying to you; I am the more pleased too with the distinction, inasmuch as I never would nor did solicit a vote from any academician. And this is a proof that the report of candidates being expected to canvass, or in other words to beg votes, is without foundation. I wish you could see Collins's letter. I suppose you know he was made an associate before you left England. He says I must come back. But that I have thoughts of—at least for many good years, if it should please God to grant me them.

Something like encouragement seems to appear in our horizon; and if we have talents we owe something to our country when she is disposed to foster them. One of the gentlemen concerned told me two days ago that he was appointed one of a committee for engaging me to paint a picture for the hospital here.[6] As yet I have had no formal notice of it; but do not doubt that the communication will soon be made. This, however, is between ourselves. I expect, in your answer to this, a full and particular account of all that you are doing. You cannot be too minute. Remember me most cordially to your wife.[7] And pray present my respects to Mrs. Heyward,[8] Mrs. and Miss Rutledge,[9] and Colonel Drayton[10] and his lady.[11] Remember me also to White, Racot,[12] Frazer,[13] and Cogdell.[14] Believe me sincerely your friend,

Washington Allston.

SOURCE: Prime, pp. 116-17.

1. Morse was in Charleston, S.C., having arrived on 27 January 1819, encouraged to go by John Ashe Alston as well as his uncle Dr. James Finley. He spent the winters of 1818, 1818-19, 1819-20, and 1820-21 painting portraits (Prime, p. 108). 2. *Diana and Her Nymphs*. Morse probably planned to show it in his exhibition room on Market Street in Charleston (Carleton Maybee, *The American Leonardo: A Life of Samuel F.B. Morse* [New York: Knopf, 1943], p. 76). 3. Henry Sargent. His *Landing of the Pilgrims* was hung in Pilgrim Hall, Plymouth, Mass. His *Christ Entering into Jerusalem*, from John 12:12-13, was a success at its exhibition and was sold for $3,000 (Dunlap, 2:63). 4. Oliver Hazard Perry (1785-1819) was in command of the American fleet at Lake Erie in the War of 1812 and thus by courtesy was called commodore. His portrait was commissioned from Stuart by the General Assembly of Rhode Island, his native state, in 1818 (Park, 2:389-90). 5. Alvan Fisher (1792-1863), portrait and genre painter, who spent most of his life in Dedham, Mass. In Charleston a few days later he was praised in the press (Anna Wells Rutledge, *Artists in the Life of Charleston*, Transactions of the American Philosophical Society, n.s. 39, pt. 2 [Philadelphia: American Philosophical Society, 1949], p. 131). 6. WA had evidently heard of a proposal for this commission, for the Massachusetts General Hospital, by the time he wrote Leslie on 4 December 1818. 7. Lucretia Pickering (Walker) Morse (1799-

1825). 8. Presumably Hannah (Shubrick) Heyward. Morse painted her portrait in Charleston (Prime, p. 121). 9. Presumably Mary (Shubrick) Evelyn Rutledge (1753-1837), a sister of Hannah (Shubrick) Heyward, and her step-daughter Sarah Rutledge (1753-1837). Mary married, the second time for both parties, Edward Rutledge (1749-1800), signer of the Declaration of Independence and governor of South Carolina. Sarah was his only child by his first marriage, to Henrietta Middleton; she never married. She was the author of *The Carolina House-Wife, or House and Home,* which was first published in 1851 and went through several editions. (Mabel L. Weber, "Dr. John Rutledge and His Descendants," SCHGM [1930]:23-25.) 10. Morse painted his portrait in Charleston (Prime, p. 121). 11. Drayton's second wife was the former Maria Miles Heyward (1784-1862), daughter of Hannah (Shubrick) Heyward (James B.Heyward, "The Heyward Family of South Carolina," *SCHGM* 59 [1958]: 155). 12. Presumably Prime's misreading of the manuscript for Bacot. Several members of the Bacot family held prominent positions in Charleston in the late eighteenth and early nineteenth centuries. Thomas William Bacot was cashier of the South Carolina Bank and Henry H. Bacot and Peter Bacot were attorneys (*Charleston City Directory* for 1790, 1809, 1813, and adjacent years). 13. Prime's misreading of the manuscript for Fraser. 14. John Stevens Cogdell.

71. From Samuel Finley Breese Morse

Charleston, S.C.,
February 4, 1819.

Washington Allston, Esq.

My Dear Sir: Excuse my neglect in not having written you before this, according to my promise before I left Boston.[1] I can only plead an apology (what I know will gratify you), a *multiplicity* of *business*. I am painting from morning till night, and have continual applications; I have added to my list, *this season* only, to the amount of three thousand dollars; that is, since I left you. Among them are three full-lengths to be finished at the North,[2] I hope in Boston, where I shall once more enjoy the advantages of your criticisms. I am exerting my utmost to improve; every picture I try to make my best; and in the evening I draw two hours from the antique, as I did in London, for I ought to inform you that I fortunately found a fine *Venus de Medicis* without a blemish, imported from Paris some time since by a gentleman of this city, who wished to dispose of it; and also a *young Apollo,* which was so broken that he gave it to me, saying that it was useless. I have, however, after a great deal of trouble, put it together entirely, and these two figures, with some fragments, hands, feet, etc., make a very good academy. Mr. Fraser, Mr. Cogdell, Mr. Fisher, of Boston, and myself, meet here of an evening to improve ourselves. I feel as much enthusiasm as ever in my art, and love it more than ever. A few years, at the rate I am now going on, will place me independent of public patronage; thus much for myself, for you told me in one of your letters from London that I must be more of an egotist, or you should be less of one in your letters to me, which I should greatly regret. And now permit me, my dear sir, to congratulate you on your election to the Royal Academy. I know you will believe me when I say I jumped for joy when I heard it: though it cannot add to your merit, yet it will extend the knowledge of it, especially in our own country, where we are still influenced by foreign opinion, and more justly perhaps in regard to taste in the fine arts than in any other thing.

I have been using a compound, or rather mixture, in flesh, on which I wish your opinion. Yellow-ochre has heretofore been the best yellow that I could use, but it always appeared to me to want *brilliancy; chrome*-yellow, on the contrary, is too bright, or *eggy;* but these two I have mixed *half-and-half,* and find it excellent flesh-yellow. I find this mixture also excellent in the shadows of white drapery, and in reflected lights, when properly tempered with blue and red. A very strong tint of this yellow, laid on boldly in a shadow, gives a clearness and liquidness to it which no other yellow that I have used can give; and gives a warmth and glow to the picture, without being hot. I should like to know the result of your experiment with it.

How does your great picture progress?[3] I hope to see it, when I return, entirely finished. Have you got a good room? How are your Boston friends disposed toward you now? Are they still desirous of keeping you with them, and of giving you something to paint for them? Do write me, dear sir, all about yourself, as you used to wish me to do of myself. I long to see you, and talk over every thing. Do write me, dear sir, soon. You know what a gratification it will be to one who is proud in calling himself your pupil. May God bless you, dear sir, and believe me your affectionate pupil.

S.F.B. Morse

SOURCE: Prime, pp. 117-19.

1. Morse was in Boston probably late in December 1818 (Prime, pp. 107-108). 2. The only known painting that seems to fit this description is the one Morse did of Sarah Alston, but eventually he took nine portraits to be finished in the north (Prime, pp. 110-12). 3. *Belshazzar's Feast.*

72. From Charles Robert Leslie London February 6th 1819

My dear friend: / I received some time ago, yours of 4th December[1] which I must beg your pardon for not answering sooner. I had before received the pleasant intelligence of your safe arrival & cordial reception by your friends. The dangers of your voyage must if possible have given you a keener relish for the endearments of home.[2]

Five commissions for small pictures? bravo! I hope this will last, & I shall hear by the next opportunity that the Hospital have engaged you to paint "Belshazzer" for them.

The British Gallery is now open, but Lord Egremont who is out of town did not send your picture there. As you are now an Associate, all your friends presume you would wish it to be at the Academy, particularly now that Lord E. has not sent it to the Gallery. Phillips mentioned it to me & said he would undertake to ask Lord E.

They have placed my "Anne Page" very well at the Gallery, & it has already been highly spoken of by some of the papers, I have great hopes of selling it.

Newton[3] has sent there a very beautiful picture of Falstaff in the buck-basket,[4] which was mistaken by one of the editors for Stephanoff's[5] & highly praised.

The Exhibition is rich in small pictures. There is a beautiful little sunny gem by Wilkie[6] of "china menders" at a cottage door. Two very clever sketches by John Chalon,[7] of Parisian scenes in which the present french character is admirably hit. A beautiful one by Alfred Chalon,[8] of Moliere[9] reading one of his plays to his housekeeper, a very fine group of fighting horsemen by Cooper,[10] a falling figure foreshortened against a blue sky by Etty[11] which in purity & force of colour resembles Paul Veronese, a Jew's head as a matter of course by Jackson,[12] & though I mention it last, yet very far from *least,* a magnificent picture of the fall of Babylon by Martin, which I think even surpasses his Joshua.[13] I need say no more. It attracts universal admiration; & Sir John Leicester[14] has been to see him on the strength of it. I hope it will benefit his purse. I am at present painting a picture on commission for Mr. Dunlop for 100 Guineas. The subject is from the 112th number of the Spectator, Sir Roger de Coverley & the Spectator going to Church, surrounded by Sir R's tenants.[15] The back ground is from a sketch I made of Mamhead Church in Devonshire. It will contain about 14 principal figures, the largest of which will be 16 inches high, the canvas between four & five feet long, & between three & four high. With the sketch & as far as I have proceeded with the picture I am far better pleased than with anything I ever attempted before. Collins has very nearly completed a most excellent picture for Sir J. Leicester. It is a grander scene than he ever painted before, made up from his Cumberland Sketches & is the most interesting picture of English mountainous scenery I ever saw. He has introduced a group of figures in his best style & over the whole picture he has thrown his greatest luxurience of colour & execution. Thus much for the arts. Your friends here are far as I know all well excepting poor Mr Morgan who was afflicted last Autumn with a severe paralytic stroke. I saw him a fortnight ago & I am sorry to say he did not seem much better than when I visited him last. It has totally incapacitated him for business. His mind does not seem to be impaired but he forgets & mistakes words which makes it difficult at all times to understand him. He knows me & always enquires after you by your name & by what he says shews that he has the most perfect recollection of you.

Coleridge has been delivering most admirable lectures on Philosophy & Shakespeare to thin audiences,[16] I have not been lately at Highgate but I see Mr & Mrs Gillman every week at the lecture room. They talk a great deal about you & in the most affectionate manner. (Mrs Bridgen & all the family are well, they were very much gratified by your letter. They all send a great deal of love to you & want you back here very much. They often tell me they shall never get such another lodger.) I saw Irving today. I wish when you had leisure you would write to him; he will probably remain some time in London.[17] By the bye if you have not already done it, pray write to Collins. You know he sometimes annoys himself causelessly. He talks a great deal about you & is constantly calculating upon all the chances that may bring you here again. As for myself I will not engage you to any regular correspondence. Write to me as often as you feel inclined & delay it as long as you like, being assured of one thing that your letters whenever they do come will be most dearly acceptable to me who must be ever while I have life, yours truly,

C.R. Leslie

P.S. If Morse is in Boston tell him I have delayed answering his letter until I can send his prints & am only waiting until I get the money from Mr. Bromfield.[18]

ADDRESSED: W. Allston Esqre / Boston / Masstts. SOURCE: Manuscript, Houghton. Printed in part in Flagg, pp. 146-48.

1. This letter does not seem to have been preserved. In it WA apparently reported that he had received commissions from the Massachusetts General Hospital and from other sources for five small paintings: certainly that from Pickering and probably for *Landscape, Evening (Classical Landscape)* (1821) which may have been commissioned by Dutton; *Beatrice,* which may have been commissioned by the merchant Theodore Lyman; the smaller *Italian Shepherd Boy* (1819), which may have been commissioned by the merchant John Borland; and *Landscape: Time, after Sunset* (ca. 1819) which may have been commissioned by the merchant Charles R. Codman. They were the third and fifth, probably the sixth, and the ninth paintings in the list he sent Collins on 18 May 1821. The first, second, and fourth do not seem to have been commissioned. Two of the other three were larger and the third of somewhat later date. 2. Leslie refers to the stormy voyage to America of the *Galen.* 3. Gilbert Stuart Newton. 4. From Shakespeare's *The Merry Wives of Windsor* 3.3. 5. Francis Philip Stephanoff (1790-1860), English history and genre painter. 6. Sir David Wilkie (1785-1841), Scottish painter noted for his scenes of humble life. WA dined with him on at least two occasions at Beaumont's. 7. John James Chalon (1778-1854), English portrait and subject painter. 8. Alfred Edward Chalon (1780-1860), English landscape and genre painter. 9. Jean Baptiste Poquelin, known as Molière (1622-73), French comic dramatist. 10. Abraham Cooper (1787-1869), English painter of horses and battle scenes. 11. William Etty (1787-1849), English painter. 12. John Jackson (1778-1831), English portrait painter. 13. John Martin's *Joshua Commanding the Sun to Stand Still upon Gibeon* was a popular success. 14. John Fleming Leicester, 1st baron de Tabley (1762-1827), noted as a patron of art. 15. *The Spectator,* no. 112, bore the date 9 July 1711. 16. In November 1818-March 1819. 17. Irving went to Paris in August 1819, where he stayed for several months (Williams, 1:194-203). 18. Presumably an agent for the banking firm of Samuel Williams. Irving also dealt with him (*Washington Irving and the House of Murray,* ed. Ben Harris McClary [Knoxville: Univ. of Tennessee Press, 1969], pp. 36, 170, 75).

73. From Lyman Spalding

New-York Historical Society. New-York Institution,[1] 10th Feby 1819

Sir: I have the honour to inform you, that at a Meeting of the New-York Historical Society, held on the ninth day of Feby. inst you were elected an Honorary Member of that Institution.

By Order of the Society, / L. Spalding, Corresponding Secretary.

Washing Alston, Esq. / of Boston.

SOURCE: Manuscript. Only the dates, signature, and address are handwritten, the rest being a printed form.

1. From 1816 to 1832 the New-York Historical Society had its headquarters, together with several other organizations, in a building behind City Hall, designated on this account as the New-York Institution (*Collections of the New-York Historical Society*, 2d ser, 1 [New York, 1841], pp. 464, 467).

74. To Gulian Crommelin Verplanck

Boston,
12 March, 1819.

My dear Sir: I have so long delayed replying to your kind letter,[1] that unless I had a much better opinion of your generosity, than of my ingenuity for framing a suitable apology, I should be tempted to delay it still longer—like some spendthrifts, who have accounts to settle without the means put them off from day to day, [with] the delusive hope that Time, or Chance, will in some way or other (they know not how) bring them out clear. As I rely, however, solely on your good nature, I see no other way of profiting of it than by fairly acknowledging, that I am one of those unfortunate wights who always think they can do better tomorrow, or the next week, what they ought to do today; for in truth I have every week since the receipt of your letter been *intending certainly* to answer it the week following. I remember when at College to have gained some credit by a theme on Procrastination.[2] If the praise was then just so great has been my experience of the evil of it since, no doubt some of my friends, without overstraining their partiality, might *now* conclude me equal to a "Prize Essay" on the subject. If you are not a procrastinator, you can hardly sympathize with me; but whether you be one or not, confidently relying on your kindness, I trust that you will forgive the delay which has occasioned this confession; especially when I assure you that your letter gave me unfeigned pleasure, as coming from one for whose head and heart I have the sincerest esteem, and respect.

Pray accept my thanks for your book.[3] I like it exceedingly, and know not how I could better express my pleasure in the perusal than by saying, that it appeared to me just what it ought to be; concise, yet eloquent. The character of Penn[4] I knew but little of, of Roger Williams nothing more than as the principal founder of the town of Providence; but Berkley[5] has long since been a favourite with me, and I was pleased to find his character so happily touched by your pencil; it seems to have been sketched "con amore." He is one of the very few philosophers whom we can love as well as admire; for, as you well observe, even his most eccentric flights, are marked by a moral splendour. In the character of Las Casas[6] also I think you have been eminently successful. Would not his adventures with a little embelishment furnish a good subject for a tale?—Perhaps you will be gratified to learn that your book is also liked by others; Mr. Quincy[7] in particular spoke of it to me in high terms. The North American[8] has a review on it, which I understand is very favourable, but I have not yet read it. Now that your pen is resumed I hope you will not soon lay it aside. We want some good books on national subjects and you have shewn yourself equal to the task of supplying them[9]. . . . I must not close this without some account of what I am doing—At present I am engaged on two small pictures,[10] which will be finished in a few days. After these I shall proceed with some, on commission, somewhat larger,[11] and probably by June I shall be enabled to go on with the large picture I began in England of Belshazzer's impious feast; which I hope to make profitable by exhibition. After that, if it please God, I am commissioned & shall paint a large picture for the Hospital[12] in this town, the subject not yet determined, but it will be from Scripture—So you see my friends here are disposed to give me a substantial welcome—I had a letter from Leslie lately; and am sorry to find that he does not intend returning to America before this time next year—Have you heard from Irving? I hope before the summer passes to see you in New York—What are the artists there quarrelling about[13]—, certainly not to advance the art or even themselves—

I remain sincerely yours, / Wa——Allston

SOURCE: Manuscript copy. Printed in part in Flagg, pp. 148-49. All the copies of Allston's letters to Verplanck are in the same hand, which is not Verplanck's.

1. This letter does not seem to have been preserved. Apparently it accompanied a copy of Verplanck's *Anniversary Discourse* for the New-York Historical Society, which he presented to WA. 2. "Procrastination is the thief of Time" (1799). WA's reference to this composition suggests that he may have been thinking at this time of elaborating it, as he did within the next few years in *Monaldi*. 3. Verplanck's *An Anniversary Discourse Delivered before the New-York Historical Society, December 7, 1818* (New York, 1818). In it Verplanck referred to the four men WA mentions in this letter. 4. William Penn (1644-1718). 5. George Berkeley (1685-1753), Irish philosopher. 6. Bartholomé de Las Casas (1474-1566), bishop of Chiapa, was a Spanish missionary to the Indians in the Spanish colonies in America. 7. Josiah Quincy. 8. The *North American Review,* founded in 1815 in Boston. It was the chief literary American periodical of the time, with a succession of writers as editors, and had as contributors some of the leading writers of the day. It printed reviews of exhibitions of WA's paintings regularly and of his writings, as well as many articles containing references to him. The review of Verplanck's book, written by John Davis, appeared in the March 1819 issue (8:414-45).
9. Verplanck's most recent compositions were the political satires he wrote for the *New York American*, published in 1819 as *The State Triumvirate: A Political Tale*, and *The Epistles of Brevet-Major Pindar Puff.* 10. Presumably *Edwin* (1819), from James Beattie's *The Minstrel,* which was the first painting WA did after his return to America, and *Moonlit Landscape (Moonlight)* (1819), which was the second. *Edwin* was exhibited at the PAFA in 1826 as *The Minstrel*. Shortly afterward it was owned by Nathaniel Amory (Rutledge, "Dunlap Notes," p. 38). No description of it seems to exist, but probably it bore some resemblance to WA's two versions of *Italian Shepherd Boy* (1819, ca. 1819), since Beattie's Edwin is a shepherd with a pipe wandering through natural scenes. In any case, the choice of the subject is significant, being the character of a young poet-musician of a contemplative disposition whose genius is developed through his contact with nature. Though WA did not return to such a subject in his painting, he did so in his writing. *Monaldi,* which was apparently begun about this time, depicts a young painter comparable to Edwin who is modeled on WA himself, and also the foil character of a poet who fails to learn from nature. The poem "The Angel and the Nightingale," which was probably written a few years later and which also has autobiographical overtones, depicts the artist, allegorized as the nightingale, as a musician living in and learning from nature. The fact that WA's second painting was *Moonlit*

Landscape (Moonlight) is also significant. Like Edwin it represents, for all its Italian character but precisely because it is an evocation by his memory of Italy, the paintings more typical of his American than his European years, both works thus being produced immediately after his return. In this connection the transformation of the English shepherd in *Edwin* into an Italian one in the two paintings related to it is noteworthy. 11. Presumably WA refers to the commissions by Mary (Channing) Gibbs for *Jeremiah Dictating the Prophecy of the Destruction of Jerusalem to the Scribe Baruch* (1820), Thomas H. Perkins for *Saul and the Witch of Endor* (ca. 1820), and David Sears for *Miriam the Prophetess* (1821), which were the seventh, eighth, and tenth in the list of paintings he sent Collins on 18 May 1821, as well as that for the Massachusetts General Hospital. The fifth and sixth in the list were small. 12. *The Stoning of St. Stephen*, from Acts 7:58-60. The subject was also painted by West. Though the painting was to be for a hospital, WA thought he should not take a subject relating to disease (RHD, p. 181). He was to receive $5,000 for it but the project never came to completion. 13. A long-standing dispute between the dictatorial Trumbull and the younger artists, led by Morse, in the American Academy of Fine Arts resulted finally in the establishment of the NAD.

75. To James McMurtrie Boston, 17th March, 1819.

My dear Sir: On the 24th of December last, in a letter of introduction which was to have been handed to you by my friend W.S. Rogers, of the Navy, I requested, if then convenient, that you would hand the balance due me to him. Mr. R. who was then going to Washington, has since returned here; and he informs me, that on account of your living some distance from Philadelphia,[1] and his business not permitting him to go out to you he had not had the pleasure of seeing you. He therefore on leaving Philadelphia put the letter into the post office; but knows not if it has reached you.—I shall not regret this delay if it has been an accommodation to you: but I trust that it is now in your power to remit to me; for I would not even now write to you on the subject were I not absolutey obliged to do it <[undecipherable rest of line and half of the next line]> to relieve myself from immediate and pressing pecuniary embarrassments; the balance due me from the Academy being my only resource for though I have several commissions for pictures, yet none of them being finished, it may be even two months before I shall realize any thing <for> from them; & in the mean time other demands will succeed those made at present upon me. I shall therefore feel greatly relieved and obliged if you will favour me with an answer <with the> agreeably to my wishes by the end of the ensuing week.

I remain, dear sir, / Sincerely yours / Washington Allston

SOURCE: Manuscript.

1. McMurtrie moved out of the city on account of his health.

76. From William Wordsworth [21 or 22 March 1819][1]

Transcribed by Mrs Wordsworth for Mr Alston, in gratitude for the pleasure she received from the sight of his pictures, in particular, The Jacob's Dream.[2]

Wm Wordsworth

N.B. The author knows not how far he was indebted to Mr Alston for part of the 3d stanza. The multiplication of ridges in a mountainous country, as Mr Alston has probably observed, are from two causes *sunny* or *watery* haze or vapour; the former is here meant. When does Mr Alston return to England.

SOURCE: *The Letters of William and Dorothy Wordsworth*, ed. Ernest de Selincourt, 2d ed., vol. 3 (Oxford: Clarendon Press, 1970), pp. 504-505.

1. This note was brought to WA by Ticknor, who visited the Wordsworths on 21 and 22 March 1819 (*Life, Letters, and Journals of George Ticknor* [Boston, 1876], 1:287-88). 2. This accompanied a copy made by Mrs. Wordsworth, of Wordsworth's poem, "Composed during a sunset of transcendent Beauty, in the summer of 1817." Lines 41-49 had been revised from the original version, presumably after Wordsworth visited WA's studio in December 1817 and saw *Jacob's Dream*. The revised version was incorporated in the text as it was published in 1820:

And if there be whom broken ties
Afflict, or injuries assail,
Yon hazy ridges to their eyes
Present a glorious scale,
Climbing suffused with sunny air,
To stop—no record hath told where!
And tempting Fancy to ascend,
And with immortal Spirits blend!
—Wings at my shoulders seem to play.

77. From Gulian Crommelin Verplanck [ca. 22 March 1819][1]

Dear Sir: The above[2] has just been handed me to forward to you and lest you should think so empty an honour not worth the postage which it will cost you I take the liberty to fill up the sheet. We had elected Col. Trumbull one of the Vice presidents in compliment to his talents as an historical painter and I therefore thought it proper that you should share in the honours, such as they are, of the Institution. You suggest Las Casas's history to me as furnishing the groundwork of a tale. I hardly think that he could be made the hero; he might however be introduced with great effect, as indeed Marmontel has already employed him in the Incas.[3] Permit me in my turn to recommend him to you. What do you think of (as the subject of a small picture) Las Casas reproaching Ferdinand[4] with the personal guilt of the crimes of his soldiers in New Spain, and the monarch conscience-struck & trembling before him? The scene might be either in the midst of the court which would give room for great variety of expression or you may presume it to have taken place at a private audience which will give you a scene like that of Nathan & David,[5] a subject by the way which I do not remember ever to have seen managed with much ability. I would not trust to invention for the countenance & person of Las Casas but would embody him with the form of Fenelon[6] such as we have him in the better portraits & engravings <of him>.

I have a literary plan which I shall execute as soon as I find opportunity &

materials. It is a sketch of the literary history of this country—containing notices of the various original works printed here, views of controversies religious & political; biographical & critical sketches of distinguished literary men from Cotton Mather & Gov. Winthrop to Barlow & Dwight[7] with perhaps views of the state of eloquence at the bar & in the pulpit, of the public taste & education. The plan is yet very crude & I do not know whether it will be a memoir to be read before one of our societies or an independent work. If I can get the materials I have no doubt that I can make a most entertaining book, whatever its real value may be.[8]

If there is a printed catalogue of the Ebeling library,[9] now at Cambridge I will thank you to produce it for me from one of your Cambridge friends.

I am sorry to hear that Leslie still lingers in England. I should like to send him & Collins a copy of my Historical discourse—but I do not know their address. I much fear that Irving will loiter about London for a long time & waste the most useful part of his life out of his proper sphere. I perceive by your frontispiece to the new edition of Knickerbocker[10] that you have become an accomplice of his in calumniating the fathers of this state of whose fame I consider myself the champion. The new edition, I learn, is curtailed and corrected but has no new matter.[11]

I am / Yours truly / G.C. Verplanck

P.S. If you can procure the Ebeling catalogue, be so good as to send it to me by mail, marking the number of printed sheets on it, as magazines are sent.

ADDRESSED: Washington Allston Esq. / Boston. ANNOTATED: *Verplanck / answered / 2d.* SOURCE: Manuscript. Printed in part in Flagg, pp. 149-51).

1. The date of the postmark on the letter, from New York. 2. The letter from the secretary of the New-York Historical Society to WA on 10 February, at the bottom of which Verplanck's letter was written. He was a member of the society and responsible for its having elected WA to honorary membership (Robert W. July, *The Essential New Yorker, Gulian Crommelin Verplanck* [Durham, N.C.: Duke Univ. Press, 1951] p. 117). 3. Jean François Marmontel (1723-99), French writer. His *Les Incas* (1778) attributed the cruelties of the Spanish invaders in America in the fifteenth century to religious fanaticism. 4. Ferdinand V (1452-1516), of Castile and Leon, who sponsored the colonization of the Americas by Spain. 5. The prophet Nathan confronted David with his sin with Bathsheba, his contrivance to have Uriah killed, and his taking Bathsheba to wife, as recorded in 2 Sam. 12:1-14. 6. François de Salignac de la Mothe Fénelon (1651-1715), French theologian and writer. 7. John Winthrop (1588-1649), first governor of Massachusetts; Joel Barlow; and Timothy Dwight (1752-1817), clergyman, author, and educator. 8. Verplanck did not carry out this project. 9. Christoph Daniel Ebeling (1741-1817), German professor of history at Hamburg University, assembled a collection of several hundred books relative to the early history of America. In 1818 it was purchased by Israel Thorndike for $6,500 and presented to Harvard. The only known printed catalog is *Americanische Bibliothek* (Leipzig, 1777). A manuscript catalog, "Bibliotheca Americana quinquaginta annorum indefessa opera collecta," was compiled in 1809-10 (now at Houghton Library).
10. WA's *A Schepen Doing Duty to a Burgomaster's Joke* in the third edition of Irving's *History.* 11. The third edition had fewer sweeping revisions than the second (1812) but continued changes in almost every chapter, chiefly deletions, which were most numerous in book 3, describing the reign of Wouter Van Twiller.

78. From James McMurtrie [26 March 1819]

Dear Sir: On the 1s day of apl I shall without fail remit you the balance in my hands. At which time I shall fully explain the many unfortunate circumstances which have occurred to render me I fear very culpable in your eyes—till then I entreat you to suspend any harsh opinion you may form against me. I will at this time only say, that you have run no risk whatever of losing a dollar, as I had made such arrangements as totally precluded the possibility of it.

With great regard / I am Dear Sir / Your friend [undecipherable word] /

J McMurtrie
Phil 26 Mar 1819

W. Allston Esqe

ADDRESSED: *Washgn* Allston Esqr / Boston. SOURCE: Manuscript.

79. To Henry Howard Boston, Massachusetts N. America
April 2d 1819

Dear Sir: I have the honour to acknowledge your Letter of 18th of November last, announcing my election as an Associate of the Royal Academy; and I beg you to express to the Members of that Body the high sense I entertain of the honour conferred on me, and to accept yourself my best thanks for the obliging manner in which you have been pleased to communicate it.

The distance which separates me from England, and my engagements here, I hope will be considered by the Council as sufficient apology for my not complying wih the conditions mentioned in your letter.

If my peculiar situation can excuse me from "signing the Instrument of Institution in the presence of the Council," I shall esteem it an additional favour to that for which I am already obliged to the Academy.

I am, dear Sir, / with great respect, / Your obednt servt / Washington Allston.
To / Henry Howard Esqre. Sec R.A.

ADDRESSED: Henry Howard Esqre. R.A. / Secretary of the / Royal Academy, / Somerset House, / London. SOURCE: Manuscript.

80. To the Secretary of the New-York Historical Society [Lyman Spalding] [2 April 1819][1] [Draft]

I have the honour to acknowledge the receipt of your letter of 10 Feby announcing my election as an honry member of the N.Y. histori Soci. <It with a high sense of the distinction which has been confrd on me, that I accept acceptance of the honour> I beg you to express to the Society <my acceptance of the appointment> the high sense of yr distinction which they have conferred.

(To be given to Mr. Morse[2] *this evening*, as soon as he comes in.)

ADDRESSED: S.F.B. Morse Esqre. / [Marlboro'] Hotel.[3] SOURCE: Manuscript, Morse Papers, LC.

1. The letter from Spalding to WA of 10 February is annotated by him "*answered / 2d,*" apparently referring to it. Since WA replied to Henry Howard on 2 April accepting his election as an Associate of the RA, it seems probable that he acknowledged the two honors at the same time. 2. In 1819 Morse spent the early summer and the fall in Charlestown, Mass., with his parents (Morse, 1:225). 3. The Marlboro' Hotel in Boston was on Marlboro' Street at this time (*Boston City Directory,* 1822, 1823).

81. To William Collins Boston 16 April 1819

Dear Collins: I send you a thousand thanks for your kind letter.[1] It should have been answered before; but you who so well know my procrastinating spirit will easily forgive the delay; especially when I assure you, that I have written you at least twenty letters *in my head* whilst I have been smoking my usual evening segar. The only <reason why> way I can account for not putting them upon paper is, that they invariably ended in a reverie on past times, which carrying me back to London, placed us opposite to each other by the fireside, with your good Mother & Frank & Leslie between; where we have generally had so much to talk about, that when I at last thought of leaving you in order to write, the wavering hand of my watch would silently point to the hour of bed.

I need not say how highly gratified I was at my election. Indeed I was most agreeably surprised; for, though I am generally sanguine, yet in this instance I had not suffered myself to calculate on success: It was therefore doubly welcome. To my countrymen here, who value highly all foreign honours, it seems to have given almost as much pleasure as if it had been bestowed on the country: it must therefore be no small aid to my professional interests. But were it wholly useless, I should yet ever value it, as connecting me on more friendly terms with so many men of genius. If you know the members <of> to whose good opinion I am indebted for my election, I beg you will present them my acknowledgements.

I am pleased to find there is nothing like a french taste in Boston. A portrait by Gerard[2] has lately been sent here & still hangs in quiet on its walls, without any raptures to disturb it.

There are few painters here, & none of eminence, excepting Stuart, who certainly paints an admirable portrait. There are some clever ones however, I hear in Philadelphia. Fisher, who was lately here, is a very promising young man, & I think would make a great landscape painter if he would study in England.[3]

Your account of our friends at Keswick was read, as you may well suppose, with no small interest. I longed to have been with you. And if it is lawful to be proud of praise from the wise & good, I may well be so of the esteem of such as Sir George & Lady Beaumont, Wordsworth & Southey.—Perhaps it may be gratifying to Mr. Wordsworth to know that he has great many warm admirers on this side of the

Atlantic. In spite of the sneers of the Edinburgh Review,[4] which, with the Quarterly,[5] is reprinted and as much read here as in England, there is still taste enough amongst us to appreciate his merits. I was also pleased to find the same independence with respect to Coleridge & Southey; who are both read here & admired.

You tell me "to come back." Alas, I fear it cannot be soon if ever. Mr. Howard in his letter to me "wishes to know when I shall return to England."[6] I do not think there is any probability of my returning for many years, if ever. The engagements I have already entered into here will employ me for several years; & I have others in prospect that will probably follow them which will occupy me as many more. Yet, should it be my lot never to revisit England, I still hope to preserve my claim as one of the British School, by occasionally sending my pictures to London for Exhibition; a claim I should be most unwilling to forego—my first studies having been commenced at the Royal Academy & the greater part of my professional life passed in England & among English artists. At any rate, I may have the satisfaction of founding an English School here. I may well stickle for it when I think of the other Schools in Europe. If I ever write on the subject, I shall let them know here how much the Art owes to Sir Joshua.—By the bye, could you procure me a copy (from Sir G. Beaumont) of the inscription for a monument to Sir Joshua, written by Wordsworth?[7] Tell Chantry that I made my report, & shewed his letter to the Committee of Directors for the Statue of Washington in this Town,[8] & they were highly gratified to learn that he had <accepted> engaged to execute it.—The Academy of New York *talk* of forming a gallery of the works of some Old Masters; & the works of the principal living Artists in England, *when they shall have funds for the purpose;* which I hope the State will grant.—I did not forget to celebrate your & Mr. William Ward's[9] birthday on board Ship—& Stark's[10] after I landed. The captain, whose father-in-law is a wine merchant, lugg'd out some choice old Madeira on the occasion. I shall never forget that last evening we spent together. God bless you & yours. Remember me affectionately to your excellent Mother & brother—& to Leslie & Collard, to whom I shall write very soon. I beg also to be particularly remembered to Mr. James Ward,[11] & to Mr. Thompson.[12] who treated me when I last saw him with a cordiality I shall not soon forget. Above all present my best regards to Sir George & Lady Beaumont. Adieu, dear Collins, believe me ever your friend.

Washington Allston.

ANNOTATED: No 2. [The second of three letters from WA to Collins copied by RHD].
SOURCE: Manuscript copy by RHD.

1. Of 4 November 1819. 2. François, Baron Gérard (1770-1837), French portrait painter. WA, Leslie, and Collins met him in Paris in 1817. 3. In 1825 Alvan Fisher visited Europe, going to England, France, Switzerland, and Italy. 4. The *Edinburgh Review* (1802-1929), founded and edited until 1829 by Sir Francis Jeffrey, was notorious for its disapproval of the Lake school of poets; the review in it of Wordsworth's *Excursion* in 1814 was particularly harsh. 5. The *Quarterly Review* (1809-1967), edited by William Gifford from its beginning to 1824, was critical

of the works of the rising generation of authors, notably of Keats's *Endymion* in 1818. 6. A paraphrase of Howard's words. 7. Wordsworth's inscription for the monument to Sir Joshua Reynolds "Written at the Request of Sir George Beaumont, Bart., and in his Name, for an Urn, Placed by him at the Termination of a Newly-Planted Avenue, in the Same Grounds [at Coleorton Hall]" was composed in 1808 and printed, together with other inscriptions for spots in the grounds of Coleorton, in the two-volume edition of his poems of 1815. In it, speaking for Beaumont, he said he had been "From youth a zealous follower of the Art / That he professed" and paid tribute to him both as a painter and a friend. 8. Chantrey was commissioned by the Washington Monument Association, of which John Lowell (1769-1840) was chairman, to execute a statue of Washington for the State House in Boston. The first negotiations were made and a design agreed upon through WA and West, and in February 1819 the commission was given through Samuel Williams. It was set up in 1827 (William T. Whitley, *Gilbert Stuart* [Cambridge: Harvard Univ. Press, 1932], pp. 161, 202-204). 9. William Ward (1766-1826), English engraver, appointed mezzotint engraver to the prince regent and the Duke of York. 10. James Stark (1794-1859), English landscape painter. His birthday was 19 November. 11. James Ward (1769-1859), English painter and engraver, appointed mezzotint engraver to the Prince of Wales. He was a brother of William Ward. 12. John Thompson (1785-1866), English wood engraver.

82. To Gulian Crommelin Verplanck

Boston,
19 April, 1819.

My dear Sir: Enclosed is my reply to the Secretary of the New York Historical Society, in which I have endeavoured to express my acceptance of the honour they have conferred on me in suitable terms of acknowledgement. I have left it open in order to submit it to your judgement.[1] If you think it will do, pray seal it, and do me the favour to send it to the Secretary; if not, I must beg you to inform me, by return of Post, how it should be expressed, and I will immediately re-write it.

One of my friends lately from New York tells me, that he saw a very flattering notice of me in a newspaper just come out there, called the "American";[2] and from the mention of Belshazzer in it, I conclude <it> the article came from you; for which I must beg you to accept my thanks. If you are a writer in that paper I <wish> should like to become a subscriber; for this reason—because, as I know you would not contribute to a dull work, it might be worth reading. Let me know who is the agent here for the Paper.

I had a letter from Leslie a few days since. He writes in high spirits. A little picture, which he painted before I left England, of Anne Page inviting Master Slender in to dinner, was then exhibiting in the British Gallery, & I find by the papers, has been much admired. He is now employed on another, of Sir Roger de Coverly his servants, & the Spectator going to Church, for which he is to have a hundred guineas. He says nothing of his return, so that I conclude he will be likely to remain another year. Irving is still in London, and *not* idle.—I have not yet seen the new edition of Knickerbocker, with plates. I am sorry you should <think> view my design for it in the light of a calumny. Indeed I was so averse to giving pain in the slightest degree or in any way, that my chief motive in the selection of the

"Schepen doing duty to an Alderman's joke," as a subject, was because <it was> I thought it one at which no individual *could* take offence; it being connected with no name, and representing a class of sycophants common to all ages and countries. In fact, it appears to me *so general* that I <am surprised that it> cannot now imagine how it can be viewed as a national satire. Perhaps you do not know that I also have some Dutch blood in me. My maternal grandfather was a Vander Horst.[3] Pray therefore acquit me both of the act & intention of ridiculing the people of New York. If I know myself at all, had I the misfortune to inflict pain on another, I should myself feel it doubly in the recoil.

In about a fortnight I shall have completed two pictures; one from Spenser,[4] the other a Landscape.[5]—I hear that Newton has gained a good deal of credit by a picture of Falstaff in the Buck-basket, now exhibiting in the British Gallery. Has Mr. Trumbull begun his second picture?[6]—My late pupil Mr. Morse is making *thousands* in Charleston, as a portrait painter. He is a very excellent young man, and I have no doubt will make a figure. He is to paint the President[7] when he arrives there, for the City Hall.

I have made enquiries after the Ebling Catalogue; but it is not yet printed. As soon as it is I will send you one. We have nothing new in the literary way here. I shall probably project some employment of the kind for myself duirng the long evenings of the next winter. I have lately read "Discipline"[8] on your recommendation, and admired it exceedingly.

Yours sincerely / Washington Allston

This will go by my sister-in-law, Miss Channing,[9] a sister of Mrs. Russel,[10] whom I believe you know. You will find her a woman of excellent sense. She is accompanied by my Mother-in-Law,[11] who with one of the best of hearts, possesses a dryness of humor that is very rare.

ADDRESSED: Gulian C. Verplanck Esqre. / New-York / Favd by / Miss Channing.
SOURCE: Manuscript, New-York Historical Society.

1. In this letter WA also responded to several passages in Verplanck's letter of 22 March.
2. The *New York American*, a semiweekly and daily newspaper, was begun on 3 March 1819. The article to which WA refers, entitled "Literature and the Arts," appeared in the issue for 3 April 1819. In it Verplanck expressed happiness to learn that WA had returned to America and hoped that he would never follow the example of Copley and West in becoming a permanent foreign resident; he reported that he was engaged in painting several historical works and landscapes for Bostonians and had received the hospital commission. On the basis of seeing a sketch of *Belshazzar's Feast* in London, he predicted that it would vie with Venetian painting in color.
3. John Vanderhorst (Groves, p. 34). 4. *The Flight of Florimel* (1819), from Spenser's *The Faërie Queene* 3.1.14-18, which depicts the maiden escaping from her pursuers as witnessed by Prince Arthur and Sir Guyon. It is WA's most Titianesque and probably most successful work derived from literature, with a softness and golden tone distinguishing it from his earlier landscapes. It is also distinguished for its movement, not typical of his painting in general, which is nevertheless more poetic than dramatic. 5. Presumably *Landscape: Time after Sunset*.
6. Trumbull painted *The Surrender of Lord Cornwallis at Yorktown, 19 October 1781* for the

Capitol in Washington in 1797. WA refers to the large replica, which was finished in 1820 (Trumbull, p. 147). 7. James Monroe (1758-1831) was president of the United States from 1817-1825. 8. *Discipline,* a novel by the Scotswoman Mary (Balfour) Brunton was first published in 1814 in Edinburgh and went through several editions. Probably WA read the edition published in Boston in 1815. He was fond of fiction. One friend thought it was because stories abound in pictures ("Washington Allston," p. 432). RHD, Jr., recollected his discussing Edward G.E. Bulwer-Lytton's *Eugene Aram* (1832), and he apparently read novels of Charles Dickens. 9. Mary Channing (1787-1834), who married Robert Rogers in 1821 (John Dean and Dean Dudley, comps., "Descendants of Gov. Bradstreet," *NEGHR* 8 [1854]: 319; *Columbian Centinel* (Boston), 2 June 1821). 10. Lucy (Channing) Russell (1787-1834), who married William Washington Russell of New York in 1813 (Dean and Dudley, p. 319; Thomas W. Baldwin, comp., *Vital Records of Cambridge, Massachusetts, to the Year 1850* [Boston: n.p. 1914], 1:501). 11. Lucy (Ellery) Channing (1752-1834), who married William Channing in 1773 (Dean and Dudley, p. 318).

83. From James McMurtrie [19 April 1819]

Dear Sir: On the 15st & 16[1] int I remitted you in Bk. U.S. notes (dfts were not to be had) $380. which I trust are duly recd. A very great weight has been thus taken from my mind, altho' I still feel that I have treated you very badly. The only consolation I have is, as I before mentioned to you, that in no event would you have lost the money. By reference to my letter m[a]iling the last remittance I made you to England you will find that I anticipated the receipt from the Academy in purchasing Mr. Waln's bill. Had the payment been made on that day I shd most probably have bot. a bill for the *exact* balance as the amt. I lately stood indebted to you was of no moment to me at that period. It was not an easy matter to get a bill for 80 to 90£ and I delayed it untill a considerable change took place in my circumstances. I became ill & was confined to my house and *bed* for 3 to 4 months—was obliged in consequence of my indisposition to abandon a lucrative business in which I was engaged, and retire into the country. From that period without great difficulty I could scarcely raise the sum I owed you. Within a short time I have made sale of a considerable estate belonging to my wife and I am just beginning to feel myself tolerably easy. Should this explanation prove satisfactory to you my Dear Sir, you will make me very happy by saying so. I feel myself under a very particular obligation to you, and had hopes of cherishing a friendship with you that shd have lasted for life. Should you visit us this Spring which I most sincerely hope will be the case, you will confer a great favor on Mrs. McM. and myself by spending some time with us in the country. We live within 2½ miles of the city, and I have a horse and chair constantly at your service. Were it possible I would go on to Boston purposely to see you, but I think it very probable you will be here in the course of the summer.

I was greatly pleased to hear of your success in England, and almost sorry to hear that you had left it. Leslie does not even *talk* any more of coming out. I fear from some cause or other (of whom I am totally ignorant) he is offended with me. I wrote to him about a year since, requesting he wd paint a picture for my friend Mr.

J.S. Waln of this city value 50 G.—he has not written to me since and refused painting the picture without assigning a reason. Mr. Waln's friend Mr. Large[2] tendered the amt. of the painting as Mr. W. was a stranger. I am greatly distressed at this & only mention it to you in hopes you may know something of Mr. L.'s reasons for his refusal. The subject was left entirely to his own choice.

In the expectation of hearing shortly from you

I remain Dear Sir / Yours very sincerely / *J McMurtrie*

W. Allston Eq. Phila 19. Ap. 1819.

There are two Gentlemen now in Boston who were lately in this City from whom I wished some information relative to Italy—a Mr. Bowdoin[3] & a Mr. Truman.[4] I was unlucky in not seeing either of them. If my health does not improve, I have serious thoughts of going to the so. of Europe for a few yrs and I wanted to know what sum a small family might subsist comfortably and genteelly at Florence or in Switzerland. If you can without trouble get me this information you wd particularly oblige me. My children are boys[5] and their education is what I have most at heart. My means are small, and my habits are not the most economical. Living in this country is extremely high and but few comforts for the money expended. You have lived long in Italy, and if you will spend an idle hour in writing to you [me] the result of yr. own observations together with any information you may gather from those who have resided in Italy as *married* men you will greatly oblige me. *JMcM*

ADDRESSED: Washingt Allston Esqr / Boston. ANNOTATED: *Answered April 23 1819*. SOURCE: Manuscript.

1. These letters do not seem to have been preserved. 2. Probably John Large, Philadelphia merchant, who had both a business and a residential address. James Large had the same business address but no residence listed (*Philadelphia City Directory* for 1819 and adjacent years). 3. Probably James Bowdoin (1794-1833), a Boston lawyer, who served as a member of the state legislator and was active in several philanthropic organizations. He suffered from poor health, left the city for a milder climate in 1832, and died in Havana (James C. Merrill, "Memoir of James Bowdoin," *Collections of the MHS*, 3d ser., 9 [1846]: 224-25). 4. Probably John F. Truman, who was for a short period a partner in the firm of John F. Truman and William P. Shelton, blockmakers, and later operated a tavern in Boston. Nathaniel Truman was also a blockmaker at this time (*Boston City Directory* for 1819 and adjacent years). 5. James McMurtrie, Jr., portrait painter and art collector, who exhibited in Philadelphia between 1843 and 1864, and William B. McMurtrie, portrait and landscape painter, who exhibited in Philadelphia between 1837 and 1844.

84. To James McMurtrie Boston, 26th April, 1819.

My dear Sir: I have the pleasure to acknowledge the receipt of your letters of the 15th & 16th inst. covering the corresponding halves of United States Bank Bills to the amount of Three hundred and eighty Dollars, being the balance (and three dollars over) due me from the Pennsylvania Academy. I should have replied to them sooner, but was prevented by absense from Town. On my return I had the pleasure to receive your favour of the 19th giving an account of the causes which occasioned the delay of the remittance; which explanation I beg to assure you is quite satisfactory. I trust therefore you will make yourself perfectly easy on the subject: my only regret is to hear that you have had any embarrassments to contend with in your affairs; and I sincerely rejoice to learn from you that they have now taken a more favourable turn.

Agreeably to your wishes, I made enquiries of Mr. Truman respecting the expenses of living in Italy; and he says that a family may live very comfortably in Pisa (15 miles from Leghorn) for twenty five hundred dollars per annum; in Florence for less. Mr. T. has not been in Italy, I believe, since 1816. Probably the expenses may be now somewhat increased, in consequence of the present number of English residents. But the English now I understand live far less profusely abroad than formerly; indeed, many go abroad to nurse their fortunes. It is so long since I left Italy (<ten> eleven years) that my own experiences would be now no guide; everything there <since> in that time having been very materially changed; besides, being a single man, my mode of living would suggest nothing in estimating the expenses of a family. I do not remember the precise sum it cost me in Rome, but I believe it was <no more> somewhat near £300 sterling per annum: though many that I knew, who were better managers, lived equally well for a third less.—I will make enquiries also of Mr. Bowdoin, and send you what further information he may give me.—I sincerely regret to learn that your health is so impaired, and hope that its speedy reestablishment may render your visit to Italy rather a matter of pleasure than for health.

I am inclined to think that you are mistaken in supposing that Leslie has taken offence towards you. There was nothing when I left England that would lead me to suppose so. I remember well the commission from Mr. Waln, and my present impression is that he was then pleased with the commission. Perhaps his engagements at the time might have prevented him from entering upon any new one. I dare say he will explain it to the satisfaction of all parties.

I beg you to accept my thanks for your kind invitation; but I fear it will not be in my power to leave Boston for a year at least, on account of my engagements. The Committee of the Hospital here have engaged me to paint a large picture for that institution. But I must first finish the Belshazzer (which will occupy me at least six months) before I can begin it; and I cannot proceed with that until I have <fulfilled> completed some small pictures which I am engaged on, by commission.

My friend and pupil Morse is meeting with great success in Charleston. He is engaged to paint the President for the City Hall.—I once more trust, my dear sir, that this will make you perfectly easy on the subject of the delayed remittance—and I remain

Sincerely yours, Washington Allston

ADDRESSED: James McMurtrie Esqre. / Philadelphia. / Pennsylvania. SOURCE: Manuscript, New-York Historical Society.

85. From Charles Robert Leslie London May 15th 1819

My dear Sir: If I had not lately heard of you by the way of Philadelphia I should be very uneasy at your long silence. I conclude you must have written & the letters have miscarried. In my sister's[1] last letter she tells me Sully has heard that you have taken a painting room[2] for three years & that the Hospital at Boston are going to have your large picture of Belshazzer. I hope this last may be true. I enclose you some notices of the exhibition from the *Examiner*. Your picture of "Jacob's dream" looks beautifully; it is in an excellent situation at the end of the inner room, opposite the door in the centre. It is on a line with the eye. Collins varnished it with the permission of Lord Egremont. It is very greatly admired & all your friends wish you could see it there. My "Sir Roger de Coverley" is the most successful picture I have painted. They have given it a centre on the side of the same room, where you may recollect Hilton's[3] picture of "Una" hung. It was painted for Mr. Dunlop & I have had enquiries of the price from Lord Liverpool, Lord Landsdowne, Mr. Long & several others.[4] It has gained me an introduction to Sir Geo. Beaumont, with whom I dined a day or two ago. Sir Geo. & Lady Beaumont talked a great deal in your praise & seemed to regret very much that you had left this country. Sir Geo intends writing to you. They are going to make a tour through Switzerland very soon. The success of Sir Rogers makes me hope I shall be enabled to live without painting portraits.

To return to the exhibition. Wilkie's "Penny Wedding" is I think the best picture he has painted, for colour & effect & equal to any of his others in character & expression. It is painted for the Prince Regent[5] as a companion to his "Blind-man's-Buff." Callcott's[6] "Rotterdam" is a most admirable picture. I like him better than Turner[7] this year. He has given what is not usual with him a very beautiful sky, & has left out those heavy, leathery clouds he used to be so fond of. Turner has painted Richmond Hill[8], & I think has not done justice to the scene. In aiming at Splendour of effect he seems to me to be meretricious both in this & a picture of an orange-ship striking on a bar. There are however in them both very wonderful things & what no one but Turner can do. Collins has in the exhibition a most exquisite picture of a sea coast. By the bye I am afraid if he does not soon get a letter from you he will feel very much hurt. He says the Academy expect an acknowledgement of the receipt of your diploma. Poor old Mr. West has been very ill, & is now a little better. He was unable to attend the dinner at the Academy this year, which I believe is the first time he has missed. I have not seen or heard of Coleridge or the Gillmans for a long time. Collins & I intend paying them a visit in about a week.

Martin & I talk of going to Scotland about July or August to see the Highlands, we calculate on being gone six weeks. Irving is still in London, & his brother Peter[9] is now with him. Washington is at present in high spirits, he has just sent off the third number of his work to America.[10] You will probably see Mr. Ticknor[11] on his arrival who will give some account of Irving. The two Irvings, Newton & myself are together almost every evening. We visit a good deal at Dr. Bollman's[12] who is a most amiable man & has two very delightful daughters. They give very pleasant parties. You will be surprised to hear that I have become a quadrille dancer. I have not seen Collard very lately; he is so immersed in business that I can scarcely ever get at him. I met with Cook[13] the painter the other day, he talked a great deal about you & said he intended to have called on me to know when I had heard from you. He desired me to remember him to you very particularly whenever I wrote. Brockedon[14] called on me just now & desired the same thing, as indeed do all your acquaintances that I meet. Haydon & Carey[15] have had a violent quarrel. Carey was attacked in the "Annals of Art" & he has returned the salute in an octavo volume identifying Haydon with the "Annals" & exposing the whole system of puffing by which Haydon has done himself so much harm.[16] There is some hopes that the attack will do him good. He has not answered it, & there is a probability that he will lay aside the pen for the pencil. Hilton has painted a very beautiful picture of "Jupiter & Europa" for Sir John Leicester, by far his best, and at [the] [page torn] election was made an R.A.[17]

I have not been able to visit poor Morgan for some time but intend soon to do it.

If Morse is in Boston tell him I would have written to him long ago in answer to his last letter but I wished when I did write to be able to send the prints &c he ordered. The reason I have not been able to send them is that I have not received the money to pay for them from Mr. Bromfield on whom Morse gave me an order. Mr. Bromfield's clerk told me when I called on him that they had no funds of Morse's in their hands but they expected to receive some by the first opportunity & as soon as they did they would let me know, but I have not heard from them since.—I will however write to Morse very soon whether I send the prints or not.

I am dear Sir Yours most truly / Chas R. Leslie

ADDRESSED: W. Allston Esqr A.R.A. / Boston / Masstts. SOURCE: Manuscript, Houghton. Printed in part in Flagg, pp. 152-53.

1. Eliza Leslie (1787-1858), portrait and figure painter and writer. 2. According to Sweetser, a large barn on the estate of John Prince, near the northwest corner of High and Pearl streets. 3. William Hilton (1786-1839), English history and portrait painter. 4. Charles Cecil Cope, 3d earl of Liverpool (1784-1851); Henry Petty-Fitz, 3d marquis of Lansdowne (1780-1863); and William Long, history, genre, and portrait painter, working in London 1821-55. 5. George Augustus Frederick (1762-1830), prince regent, 1811-20; King George IV, 1820-30. 6. Augustus Wall Callcott (1779-1844), English landscape painter. 7. Joseph Mallard William Turner (1775-1851), English painter noted for his use of color. 8. Richmond, on the outskirts of London, is on a hill. 9. Peter Irving (1772-1838) was at this time head of the family firm in Liverpool (Williams, 1:380, and passim). 10. The third number of *The Sketch Book* contained "A Royal Poet," "The Country Church," "The Window and Her Son," and "The Boar's Head Tavern, Eastcheap. A Shakesperean Research." It was printed, like other numbers, in America. 11. George Ticknor. 12. Justus Erich Bollman (1769-1821), German physician. A native of Hanover, he led a peripatetic life. He helped rescue Lafayette from an Austrian prison in 1794, engaged in speculation on both sides of the Atlantic, took part in Aaron Burr's conspiracy, stayed for a time at the home of the physician and politician George Logan in Philadelphia, and in 1809 contributed to *The Portfolio*. Later he lived with his daughters in London (Irving, *Letters*

1:605n.). 13. Richard Cook (1784-1857), English painter and illustrator. 14. William Brockedon (1787-1854), English painter, author, and inventor. WA owned a copy of his *Illustrations of the Passes of the Alps, by which Italy Communicates with France, Switzerland, and Germany,* 2 vols. (London, 1828), inscribed "To W. Allston from the author" and signed by WA. 15. William Paulet Carey (1759-1839), English painter, engraver, and art critic. WA owned copies of two books by him: *Description and Analytical Review of Death on the Pale Horse, Painted by Benjamin West, P.R.A. with desultory references to the works of some ancient masters and living British artists, etc.* (London, 1817) and *Critical Description of the Procession of Chaucer's Pilgrims to Canterbury, Painted by Thomas Stothard,* 2d ed. (London, 1818). 16. Haydon, who was notoriously jealous, attacked Carey in *Annals of the Fine Arts* for an article he wrote praising West's *Death on a Pale Horse,* alleging that West had flattered and tutored him to do so, with the intention of denigrating Haydon. Carey replied with a lengthy book entitled *Desultory Exposition of an Anti-British System of Incendiary Publication* (1819), which was an attack on Haydon, the *Annals,* and its editor James Elmes. Elmes replied to it that Carey was one of the greatest pests in English art circles. The controversy hastened the end of the *Annals* (Eric George, *The Life and Death of Benjamin Robert Haydon, Historical Painter, 1786-1846* [Oxford: Clarendon Press, 1967], pp. 122-23). 17. Royal Academician, or associate member of the RA.

86. From James McMurtrie Phila May 16 1819.

My Dear Sir: I was made very happy by the receipt of your esteemed favor of [space blank][1] Mr. Sully has nearly completed a Gallery for the exhibition of pictures, and it occurred to me that it might be mutually beneficial to both you & him could you furnish occasionally one of your works. The Gallery Mr. S. has constructed is situated in Chesnut St. nearly opposite the State house, which is the most central part of the city. It is lighted by a sky-light. The room is about 20 by 40 feet. You mentioned in one [of] the first letters I had the pleasure of receiving from you on yr. arrival at Boston, that you brot. with you yr. picture of "Elijah in the Wilderness." If it still is in yr. possession and you feel inclined to send it on one half of the proceeds of the exhibition will be to your Credit. Shd you send on yr. large picture of "Belshazzer's feast," you will receive *two thirds* of the proceeds of its exhibition. As the mutual friend of yourself & Mr. Sully I have affixed the amt. you and he [are] justly entitled to, and Mr. Sully most cheerfully acquiescing and feel[ing] himself greatly indebted to you. I know of no situation in which we cd. see your works to more advantage as no insignificant trash of ancient or modern artists will at all interfere with yours. The room is nearly finished, and I feel assured I can be of some little service to Mr. S. when he opens it. There is a considerable desire felt in this City to see more of your works and I know of no other means by which the public can be gratified. Shd you desire it, any arrangement you may make, can be kept entirely confidential but for my own part I think it perfectly honorable. Any communication you are pleased to make on this subject shall be immediately attended to by

Dear Sir / Yours very truly, / *J McMurtrie*

Our exhibition this year is very indifferent—a miniature by Chalon,[2] of London of Mr. Large is one of the best pictures—a head of the same gent. by Leslie, rather feeble, but beautifully drawn—a half length of Napoleon by Perard,[3] in the pure Chinese taste, flat and insipid. Can you suggest any means by which our academy can be made of service to the cause of the Arts? At present it is of very little. I very much wish it wd have suited your views to have established yourself in this city. Are you not too far north for your *health.* I am very sorry you cannot make us a visit this summer.

ADDRESSED: Washgn. Allston Esquire / Boston. SOURCE: Manuscript.

1. WA's letter of 7 November 1818. 2. Alfred E. Chalon. 3. Probably a misreading of the manuscript for "Gerard." François Gérard exhibited the portrait described.

87. From Gulian Crommelin Verplanck

New York May 18th 1819

My dear Allston: I have been intending for this last fortnight to answer your kind letter[1]—but I fear that you have communicated to me some portion of your spirit of procrastination. You were right in your conjecture of my being the writer of the paragraph alluding to your Belshazzar—but I have no concern with the paper in which it appeared further than that one of the persons most interested in it is a relation of mine[2] and that I can occasionally make use of the paper for the service of my friends. It is at present too much devoted to local politics to be at all interesting or even intelligible to you, so that I would not advise you to subscribe. I send you the article in question—together with another paper containing a witty but malicious attack on our poor little Academy.[3] The exhibition however is better than our maligners have anticipated as you may judge of from the catalogue which I send you.

I think the effect of this annual exhibition is very visible in the works of our artists; and in a city of this size a little enquiry always enables us to find some good pictures of old masters or great foreign artists, which, while they add to the interest of the collection do something towards forming the public taste. It is to be sure, our "day of small things" but still, according to the wise man "not to be despised."[4]

I was glad to hear from you that Irving was not idle and I have since been enabled to judge for myself how he has been employed. It is a sort of a secret and if you are not in it I must not betray confidence.[5] As profit is now essential to Irving I must bespeak of your *North American* friends the privilege of using their pages in such a way as his friends here may think advisable to promote the circulation and reputation of his productions. Do not however make this public at present.

By the way I sent you some weeks ago a short article for the North American, A review of a Dutch book on our history.[6] The contribution was of no great value except as being out of the common way and containing some curious facts. I have not heard whether it was received.

I see little of Col. Trumbull—but you knew his misfortunes. His terrible wife repels all society from his house[7] and he lives in a sort of stately misery. He is personally I think a respectable man. I do not know whether he has begun his large pictures for congress. The small pictures have long been finished[8]—I am told that in that very important point of likeness, on which so much of the interest and value of these paintings depend, they are incomparably superior to his large picture—So that his engravings will be more valuable in the way of historical memorials than perhaps the public anticipates.

I hope that you have not altogether abandoned your plan of visiting us. Perhaps a little excursion up our river might be of use to the artist as well as amusing to yourself (a distinction which I suspect I borrowed from Mr. Puff[9] in the critic).

Your Boston friends have been labouring here and at Baltimore for our conversion—I hope without success.[10] I am not very sectarian in my feelings—perhaps not enough so, to be considered a very staunch churchman; but I confess that it is altogether inconceivable to me, how men should with good faith and devotions (which I will not deny them) refine and interpret away the most clearly revealed truth of our religion while they allow all the force of its external evidence.

My friend the Rev. Mr. Jarvis[11] will shortly be settled in a new Episcopal Church in Boston. He will be a great acquisition to that Church—Not exactly eloquent, but of great learning, good sense and good taste and both in manner and feeling rather sincere than fervent. His literary attainments are highly respectable. He delivers our next Anniversary Historical discourse. This was in some sort my appointment, and I think my choice will do me credit.

Yours truly / G.C. Verplanck

P.S. If anything in the way of criticism on our artists, which I may think would interest you, should appear in the papers I will send them to you. The *Advocate*[12] has generally something on the subject, and pretty well done, though in a censorious spirit.

ADDRESSED: Washington Allston Esq / Boston. SOURCE: Manuscript. Printed in part in Flagg, pp. 153-54.

1. Of 19 April 1819. 2. One of the three founders of the *New York American* was Johnston Verplanck, a cousin of Gulian C. Verplanck (Brigham, 1:607). 3. The paper and the article have not been identified. 4. "For who hath despised the day of small things?" (Zech. 4:10). 5. Presumably Verplanck refers to Irving's work on *The Sketch Book*. 6. Verplanck's review of N.C. Lambrechtsen's *A History of the New Netherlands* (1818) appeared in the *North American Review* 9 (Jan. 1819). 7. Sarah Hope (Harvey) Trumbull (1774-1824), became a dipsomaniac (Trumbull, pp. 350-65) 8. Trumbull's first paintings of episodes from the American Revolution were done between 1785 and 1816 in miniature so as to be engraved. In 1817 he was commissioned to paint four, 12 x 12 feet each, for the rotunda of the Capitol, which were done between 1817 and 1824 (Trumbull, pp. 88, 257-60, 309-14). 9. Pindar Puff was the alleged author of Verplanck's *The State Triumphant*. 10. A Unitarian church was organized in Baltimore in 1817, and in 1819, at the ordination of Jared Sparks as the first minister, Channing preached a sermon that was the first full declaration of the Unitarian position in the United States

(George Willis Cooke, *Unitarianism in America* [Boston: American Unitarian Assoc., 1902], p. 111). 11. Samuel Farmar Jarvis (1786-1857). He went to Boston from New York in 1819 to become rector of St. Paul's Episcopal Church, which was consecreated in 1820 (Archives of the Episcopal Diocese of Massachusetts, Boston). 12. The *National Advocate* (1813-26) was a daily newspaper in New York. Its editor from 1817 until its end was Mordecai Manuel Noah, who was also a playwright.

88. From George Howland Beaumont Grosvenor Square, May 29, 1819.

My Dear Sir: I feel myself culpable for having so long neglected to thank you for your book of beautiful poems, and expressing my sincere regret at your leaving England. Coleridge, you know, has observed, that every great and original poet must create the taste by which he is to be relished, as far as he is great and original. This is certainly applicable to painters also, and is necessarily the work of time. This state of probation you had passed, and your value would soon have been well appreciated; it was therefore an additional grief to your friends at losing you, that you should leave them at a moment when they delighted themselves at the thought of seeing your labors requited.

Your picture[1] at the Exhibition looks admirably, and I have heard the Royal Academy much regret your absence, and had intended to elect you a member of their body, and indeed would have done so notwithstanding your absence, could they have received assurance that you meant to return. You will be concerned to hear our valuable and venerable friend Mr. West was so ill it was not in his power to preside at the annual dinner. I saw him day before yesterday, and although I hope he was better he was still very feeble and unable to stand. I believe I have frequently expressed to you my high opinion of his merit, and when we consider the state of art in this country, particularly the time in which he has with such laudable exertion persevered, the greatest praise is due to his labors. Indeed, if we consider the disadvantages of his situation when he first turned his mind to art, we must admit that such a progress, under such circumstances, is not to be found elsewhere in the annals of painting. Without anything to direct his tastes but a few paints, the religion of his parents inimical to his pursuits, I believe about the age of twenty he left America for Italy,[2] and by his astonishing perseverance in about four or five years he produced not only the picture I have,[3] but many others of pure classical merit. Whenever we lose him the arts will experience a severe and almost irreparable loss.

Our friend Wordsworth has just published his "Peter Bell,"[4] which has brought all the minor wits about his ears, and although he seems insensible to the hum and venom of these gnats, I own I wish he would reserve these small poems, which afford such scope for ridicule and misrepresentation to injure and traduce him, for future publication, whatever their merits and beauties may be, and every man of feeling will allow them to be great, and come forward with his great works. Yet I have no doubt time will do him ample justice, and although the good his works must effect sooner or later is indisputable, yet I am unwilling the present generation should pass away without receiving the full advantages of his instructions, or he himself pass through life without his due share of fame, and his family lose the profits of his honorable labors. I send you, by the kindness of your friend Mr. Leslie, a copy of "Peter Bell." I must add that Mr. Leslie has obtained great credit by his picture of "The Spectator" at Sir Roger de Coverley's; for character and expression it stands very high indeed. Mr. Collins has introduced me to him, and I find him a most interesting young man, and I hear he is as deserving as he appears to be.

Your "Jacob's Dream" looks poetically beautiful, and is highly approved of. Our friend Collins has also excelled himself in a coast scene. Lady Beaumont unites with me in best wishes, and cannot help uniting with them a hope of your speedy return to England. We are to set off this week on a tour to Switzerland, and if health is granted to us we expect great pleasure.

I hope you found your mother well.

Ever truly yours, / G. Beaumont.

SOURCE: Flagg, pp. 154-56.

1. *Jacob's Dream*. 2. West, whose family was Quaker, went to Italy in 1760, at the age of twenty-two. 3. Probably *Cicero Discovering the Tomb of Archimedes*, presented to Beaumont by West in June 1796. Between 1802 and 1804 he acquired another painting by West, *Pylades and Orestes*, which he presented to the National Gallery in 1826 (Helmut von Erffa and Allen Staley, *The Paintings of Benjamin West* [New Haven: Yale Univ. Press, 1986], pp. 176, 260). 4. The poem, composed in 1798, provoked much ridicule and elicited several parodies.

89. To William Collins

Boston, Mass: America
June 1st 1819.

Dear Collins: An opportunity now offering direct for London, I am unwilling to let it pass without sending you a few lines, though I have but little to add to my last letter, of April, which I suppose you have long since received. Indeed, unless I make up the letter *all about* myself, I know not how I can say much on this side of the water that will interest you; and that, you know, my *modesty* should forbid. But self, like scandal, will frequently get the better of modesty, for want of other topics. So I must e'en talk of myself, a task I shall be the more reconciled to if it should incite you to a similar breach of good breeding: which, by the bye, I am almost democrat enough to think is too often called in to cover the want of interest towards those to whom it is "exercised." Yet I may safely speak thus of good breeding, if the proper distinction be made between it and politeness: one being artificial, and growing out of the manners of a particular class, or age; the other, the offspring of good sense and benevolence, common to all classes and ages, wherever those qualities are united.—But where am I driving to?—You'll expect from this *Portico*[1] preface that I am going to be very magnificent. No such thing. I have not even the bare-sided body of a Greek Temple to add to it.—Here's heresy in architecture! But say nothing about it; a man has a right to any opinion, however absurd, provided he does not publish it.

I told you at the fag end of the letter already mentioned of the commission I have to paint a large picture for the Hospital in this Town. The choice of the subject is left to me, and I am to receive five thousand dollars for it, with the privilege of exhibiting it for my own benefit in three of our principal cities. By the bye I beg you not to mention the price or these particulars. I have not yet determined on the subject; but I think it will probably be St. Stephen before the Council,[2] of which I made a sketch when in England, but not being completed, I did not shew it there. My friends think the exhibition may produce from 6 to 8000 dollars. If so it will be a substantial affair. It is my intention however to complete the Belshazzer before I commence the picture for the hospital. I suppose I should have nearly finished it by this time had not the lank ribs of my purse called aloud for present supply: which I have fain been obliged to accord it, by painting some small pictures, two of which are done,[3] and two more will be finished in about a fortnight.[4] After them I shall resume Belshazzer, in spite of six tempting commissions;[5] but I shall put them, like choice flowers, in the Hortus siccus[6] of my memory, occasionally to refresh my spirits.—I have a glorious painting-room, twenty feet high; 22 wide & 56 long.[7] Elbow room enough!—Though my thickening engagements <have> seem likely to employ me here for many years, and as I observed in my last, so as to render my return to England uncertain, yet I cannot bear to give up the hope of one day, even tho' distant, seeing my friends in England again. God grant, my dear Collins, that we may meet both in this world and the next.—There is nothing you can say about yourself that will not be interesting to me; therefore do not be afraid of being too minute: tell me about all you have done & are doing. My affectionate regards to your Mother and brother. Pray remember me particularly to Mr. Carey, and all my friends. May God ever bless you

Your friend Washington Allston

[In the margin] Pray let me know if Mr. Howard has received my answer to his letter. I waited a long time in vain for an opportunity to London, and was at last obliged to send it by the way of Liverpool. Tell Leslie & Collard I will write them both by a vessel for Liverpool that will sail in a few days. Best respects to Sir G. & Lady Beaumont also to Willes. Remember me to the Seguirs.[8]

ADDRESSED: William Collins Esqr. A.R.A. / N 11 New Cavendish Street / Grantland Place / London / Ship / London Packet. SOURCE: Manuscript, Boston Public Library.

1. Presumably a pun, alluding to the literary periodical *The Portico* (1816-18), published by the Delphian Club of Baltimore, noted for its chauvinism and criticism of foreign authors.
2. From Acts 7:2-53. Subsequently he changed the subject to the stoning of St. Stephen.

3. *Edwin* and *Moonlit Landscape (Moonlight).* 4. *The Flight of Florimel* and presumably *Landscape: Time after Sunset.* 5. WA refers almost certainly to those from Pickering, the Massachusetts General Hospital, and the others referred to in his letter to Verplanck of 12 March 1819, presumably at least three in number. A sixth may have been for *Beatrice.* 6. A dry garden, a herbarium. 7. The barn on the estate of John Prince, who was a college classmate of WA. 8. The brothers John (1785-1856) and William Seguir (1771-1843) were English topographical painters, in business as restorers of paintings, and superintendents, at different times of the BI.

90. From Charles Robert Leslie London, August 6, 1819

My dear Sir: I received a short time ago yours of the 20th June[1] by the Triton which gave me great pleasure. I had been delighted some time before by the intelligence of your commission from the Hospital contained in your letter to Collins.[2] In my last I gave you some account of the Exhibition—Your picture[3] looked as well as you could have wished. It was varnished by Collins & was in an excellent situation. At the close of the Exhibition I saw it safe home to Lord Egremont's. He has hung up your other picture[4] in the large room, the first you enter up stairs. I am sorry I have not by me any criticism on Jacob's dream but the one in the Examiner, which is not a good one.[5] I regret also that I have no critique on my own to send you.[6] The Marquis of Lansdowne has commissioned me to make a coy of "Sir Roger" for him.

I am at present painting a picture of a party spending a day in the woods which is a very common thing with the people of the middling class in the summer.[7] They go out in a "*shay cart*" as they call it, take their provender with them, & chuse some retired spot where they dine & drink their tea & come home in the evening. It affords an opportunity of painting a domestic group with rural accompanyments. I lately spent a fortnight at Epping forest (where I have been painting another picture of Mrs. Brown)[8] & in my rambles I lighted on some parties of the kind I have described which suggested it for a subject.

I intended to have visited Scotland this summer but found it would take more time & money than I can afford. I have an invitation from Mr. Dillwyn's son who[9] lives in South Wales to spend some time with him there, which I think I shall accept. You will have seen ere this the two first numbers of Irving's "Sketch-Book."[10] We have heard but little of the reception of the first no. but that little is highly gratifying to himself & friends. He is in consequence in very good spirits about it. I wish you would write to him. He is likely to remain in London for some time.[11] His brother Peter is now with him.

The Irvings, Newton, Willes & myself frequently visit at Dr. Bollman's whose family is one of the more delightful I have known. The Doctor is a very amiable man & his daughters are excellent girls, highly accomplished & have about them (which is generally the case with pleasant people) a most agreeable circle of friends.

Mr. & Mrs. Dunlop are gone to Ramsgate.[12] I have not seen Coleridge or the Morgans lately, but hope to visit them soon. I have heard that you were making some designs from Walter Scott's novels.[13] They afford excellent material though the picturesque scenes with which they abound are almost too highly finished by the author to leave anything for the painter to do but merely follow him, which is some disadvantage.

I send you by this opportunity the trees by Lewis & a little print he has made from my sketch of "Chinkford Church"[14] which I believe you did not see. If I had not been particularly lazy you should have had my phiz & Frank Collins' which we must defer 'till next time. Collins sends you some prints in the same case & will also write to you. All your friends that I am acquainted with speak of you most affectionately whenever I see [them] & desire me to remember them whenever I write which I now do in a bunch.

Poor old Mr. West has been very feeble for some time. I called on him to remember you to him, as you desired, & he appeared much pleased to hear of your welfare. He said the Academy had never done a more proper thing than electing you a member.

God bless you says / C.R. Leslie

ADDRESSED: W. Allston Esqr A.R.A. / Boston / Masstts. SOURCE: Manuscript. Printed in part in Flagg, pp. 157-58.

1. This letter does not seem to have been preserved. Apparently it contained the news of his commission from the Massachusetts General Hospital and requested several prints, a poem on Belshazzar's Feast, the catalog of the RA exhibition, and some colors. 2. That of 1 June 1819. 3. *Jacob's Dream.* 4. Presumably *Contemplation.* 5. The review in the *Examiner,* on 24 May, criticized the lack of movement in the angels' wings. 6. He sent one on his *Sir Roger,* however, from the *New Monthly Magazine* for June, which also contained a review of *Jacob's Dream.* 7. *Londoners Gypsying.* 8. Mrs. James Brown. 9. William Dillwyn, who lived at Swansea, for whom Leslie painted a picture of the Dillwyn family in 1839 (Leslie, p. 358) and probably John Dillwyn, his younger son. 10. The second number contained "English Writers in America," "Rural Life in England," "The Broken Heart," and "The Art of Book-Making." 11. Irving remained in London until the summer of 1820 (Williams, 1:194). 12. A seaside resort and seaport near Dover. 13. There is no conclusive evidence that WA was illustrating scenes from Scott's novels this early. 14. Frederick Christian Lewis (1779-1856), engraver and landscape painter. Chingford is a village at the edge of Epping Forest.

91. To Henry Pickering

Boston, 10th August, 1819.

My dear Sir: I have the pleasure to acknowledge, and to thank you for, your very kind letter, enclosing a check on the Suffolk Bank, for Three hundred & forty Dollars, which has been duly presented & paid.

It is with perfect sincerity that I assure you I cannot join in the censure which your modesty is disposed to bestow on your own judgement. I did not consider your choice as determined by a comparison between the "Florimel" and the "Moonlight";[1] which are so wholly distinct in character as in fact to preclude it. I was both aware of, and highly gratified by, your approbation of the Florimel. As works of art I confess I should myself be at a loss to decide which of the two possesses the most technical skill: So that the preference given to either must arise from the nature of the subject. They both gave me equal pleasure in the painting; but the Florimel, being the largest, and having nearly double the work in it, I ought to consider the more important of the two. As to the effect produced on those who have seen them (and the visitors at my Room since wednesday[2] have been numerous) it has been full as various as I expected; some prefering one, and some the other, though they all paid me the compliment to praise both.

Allow me to add, that your visit was in every respect highly gratifying to me, and to assure you, that the picture you have taken[3] could not have a destination that would afford me more pleasure.

I am, dear Sir, / with sincere respect / Your obdnt servt. / Washington Allston
The Picture shall be packed & delivered to Mr. Dogget[4] tomorrow. The box was not finished until today.

ADDRESSED: Henry Pickering Esqre. / Salem, / Massachusetts. SOURCE: Manuscript.

1. *Moonlit Landscape (Moonlight).* It is an Italian landscape, as indicated by its details and by Pickering's poems about it and has a general similarity to *Coast Scene on the Mediterranean,* including the family group in the foreground. It may also have been influenced by a poem. When it was exhibited at the BA in 1829 the entry for it in the catalog incorporated the following unidentified lines: "Hail to thy cold and clouded beam, / Pale Pilgrim of the troubled sky; / Hail! though the mists that o'er thee stream / Lend to thy brow its sullen dye." 2. Apparently on that day, which was 4 August, WA had a private showing of works in his studio. A detailed description of *The Flight of Florimel* appeared in the *Boston Daily Advertiser* for the 12th, incorporating the lines from *The Faërie Queene* and saying that WA had illustrated them "with the fine fancy and vivacity" of their author. 3. Pickering chose *Moonlit Landscape (Moonlight).* He wrote three poems about it: "Reflections on viewing the beautiful Moonlight by the Same Artist" [as that of *Jeremiah*], published in *The Ruins of Paestum and Other Compositions in Verse* (Salem, 1822); "Moonlight, an Italian Scene"; and "On a Picture by Allston: painted for the author," the last two published in *Poems by an American* (Boston, 1830). 4. John Doggett. The painting may still have been with him in 1829; it was listed in the catalog for the BA exhibition of that year in his name.

92. To Henry Sargent [20 August 1819][1]

My dear sir: Will you do me the favour to send, by the bearer, Northcote's Life of Sir Joshua Reynolds,[2] which you were so good as to offer me the loan of some days ago?

You see I am here still—<but> I do not think I shall be able to get to Newport before Monday.[3]

Yrs sincerely / Wa. Allston

Friday 20th.

ADDRESSED: Col. H. Sargent / Franklin Place.[4] ANNOTATED: "hot air" and drawings of a vent. SOURCE: Manuscript.

1. It seems likely that this letter was written at this date. WA was apparently familiar with Sargent and his painting by January 1819. The book he asked to borrow was presumably the second edition of Northcote's work, published in 1819. The first time the twentieth fell on a Friday after his return to America in 1818 was 20 August 1819; the next time was on 20 November 1820. 2. This is the title of the second edition of Northcote's *Memoirs of Sir Joshua Reynolds, . . . Comprising Original Anecdotes, Many Distinguished Persons, his Contemporaries, and a Brief Analysis of his Discourses* . . . (London, 1813), which was revised and enlarged, in two volumes, published by Henry Colburn in London. It seems likely that WA was led by reading it to renew his interest in Reynolds, to judge from the number of references to him in letters and conversation during the next several years. 3. WA had several relatives and friends in Newport but his reason for going there at this time is not known. 4. Sargent lived at 10 Franklin Place in Boston for many years (*Boston City Directory* for 1807 and later).

93. From James McMurtrie Philada 12 Oct. 1819.

My Dear Sir: I was yesterday made very happy by the receipt of yours of [space blank][1] int. That procrastinating disposition which you condemn in yourself is one which I unfortunately possess in the highest degree and it has led me to the neglect of many much loved and valued friends. Your reason for declining exhibiting your picture is conclusive—indeed I never calculated on a *Sale* after exhibition, and from the bad success of Mr. Sully's gallery I am inclined to think I was too sanguine in my expectations of your success.

I have for a long time had a desire to be engaged in some work which would forward the Arts in this country and being at this moment compleatly a man of leisure, but with an active turn of mind, and I may say an enthusiast with regard to the fine arts, it has occurred to me that a series of national prints drawn chiefly from occurrencies which took place during our Revolutionary War engraved by Artists of the first celebrity in Europe, from works of American Artists, might answer a twofold purpose—that of forwarding the Arts in this country and handsomely remunerating those concerned in the undertaking. I would beg leave to suggest for your consideration—that yourself, Mr. Leslie & Mr. Sully shall supply the pictures. I would undertake the entire management of the concern, such as causing the engravings to be made, publishing &c &c advancing all the necessary funds—the Artists to be paid for their pictures out of the proceeds of the work and the balance of profits on the speculation to be equally divided between the parties. Mr. Sully likes the plan well—and is as confident as myself of the result. The engraving must be executed in the highest stile of excellence, by Fittler,[2] Ramibach [*sic*][3] or others of the English school in the line manner. Size of the plates 14 by 10 inches or not exceeding 16 by 11 or 12—the work to come out in numbers with 2 plates in each with a vignette, and a suitable title page (letter press description of the action of the picture of course) so that the work can remain in its book form, or the prints to be framed at the option of the purchaser. I am fully persuaded such a work would not only prove creditable to all concerned, but eventually very profitable. If you think favorably of the scheme let me hear from you as early as convenient,[4] and state what will be the probable expence of each picture (I mean the painting) with the average size. Too large they must not be as the expence attending them to England would be great. No subscriptions are to be sought for untill the first number is out, and the whole matter to be kept as private as [possible] [page torn]

I am Dear Sr / Very truly Yrs / *J McMurtrie*

W. Allston Esqr

ADDRESSED: Washington Allston Esqre / Boston. SOURCE: Manuscript.

1. 30 October 1819. 2. James Fittler (1758-1835), English engraver. 3. Abraham Raimbach (1776-1843), English engraver and miniaturist. 4. Apparently nothing came of this project.

94. To Henry Pickering Cambridge,[1] 28 Ocber 1819.

My dear Sir: It was not that I have been insensible to the value of your good opinion that I did not sooner reply to your very obliging letter; but that I have been under the spell of an unfortunate Spirit of procrastination (which perhaps I ought to be ashamed of) that seldom leaves me at liberty to do what I most wish at the proper time. But, trusting you will allow for what may be considered my misfortune, I beg you to be assured that I have seldom received praise so gratifying in itself, or so delicately bestowed, and for which I could more sincerely express my grateful acknowledgements.

The Sonnet[2] I have read with a double pleasure, as an expression of your friendly feeling for myself, and on account of its own simplicity and beauty; and I am happy to add, that some of my friends, who are distinguished for a cultivated taste, are equally sensible to its poetical merit.

I had not before seen the extract in the Salem Gazette.[3]

Believe me, dear Sir, / with sincere respect & esteem

Your obdnt servt / Washington Allston

Should you be passing through Cambridge, and would favour me with a call, I should be happy to show you a Picture I have lately finished—Dante's Beatrice.[4] You will find me either at Mr. Edmund T. Dana's, or at my Painting-room, in the house formerly occupied by Professor McKeen[5]—a brick house on the Common.[6]

ADDRESSED: Henry Pickering Esqre, / Salem— / Massachusetts. SOURCE: Manuscript.

1. WA spent the latter part of the summer of 1819 in Cambridge. 2. Pickering's sonnet "To Washington Allston" was published in *The Ruins of Paestum*. 3. The extract was probably that which appeared in the issue of the *Salem Gazette* for 29 September 1819, taken from the *Literary Gazette*, describing in detail a painting recently sent to England by a mercantile house in Genoa, painted by A. Carloni of Milan, which depicted Queen Caroline, the estranged wife of George IV, entering Jerusalem during her travels on the continent in the company of her Italian courier

Bartolomeo Pergami and others. 4. Presumably this was a second painting of the subject, since WA did not suggest in any of his references to it that it was a reworking of the one done in England, as he might have been expected to say at least to Leslie, who had seen that one. That which was done in 1819 resembles both WA's portrait of Ann Channing and *The Valentine*. A copy of it "from recollection" by Thomas T. Spear was exhibited at the BA in 1842. 5. Joseph McKean was Boylston Professor of Rhetoric and Oratory at Harvard from 1809 to 1818. 6. WA was apparently using this room for all but *Belshazzar's Feast,* which presumably was in Prince's barn.

95. To James McMurtrie Boston, 30 Octbr, 1819.

My dear Sir: I am quite ashamed to have so long delayed replying to your favour of August last.[1] It was both my wish and intention to have answered it immediately, but being from home when I got it, and a good deal engaged at the time, I defered so doing until my return; since which constant occupation, together with that procrastinating spirit for which more than once I have before solicited your indulgence, have from time to time prevented the performance of what would really have been a pleasure to me. I must therefore entreat you to forgive what would otherwise be an almost unpardonable remissness; and to let my having had the *will to have done as I ought* extenuate my omission of the act.

So far from having taken any exception at the contents of the letter alluded to in your last, I felt myself in a particular manner obliged for the friendly interest you manifested in it for my professional success; and it was my intention so to have expressed myself in reply, and should have done had I answered it when I ought. But while I still beg you to believe me sensible to the friendly motive which advised my sending on the picture of "Elijah in the Wilderness" for exhibition, I cannot avail myself of the advice. My reason is this. From all my experience in England both in my own case, and in that of other artists there, I have always found that <a publick> every successive exhibition of a picture lessens its chance of selling. Those who would perhaps buy a picture from an artist's room, while it is fresh in their minds and unseen but by a few, are apt to look on it with indifference, or at least with diminished interest, when it becomes the gaze of the multitude. It is owing to this that Turner, Collins, and other artists of the first rank in England, still retain some of their best works though painted five or six year[s] ago. The Elijah I consider one of my best efforts, and I confess that its not having met with a sale here has been a disappointment. Although not publickly <exposed> shewn in the form of an Exhibition, it was yet so exposed on private view as to give it all the publicity of an exhibition. Whether its not selling might be ascrib[ed] [page torn] to that or not I cannot tell; but I <would not> do not think it advisable to risk a similar mode of shewing it.

Pray present my respects to Mr. Sully, and beg him to accept my thanks for his obliging offer respecting his exhibition. As soon as I accomplish any thing of sufficient importance to describe to you, I will send you some account of it.—Want of funds has in some degree retarded me; but I have got a going again, and shall soon proceed with Belshazzer.—Have you any news in the way of the arts?

I remain, dear sir, with sincere regard yrs truly / Washington Allston

ADDRESSED: James McMurtrie Esqre. / Philadelphia / Pennsylvania. SOURCE: Manuscript, Chicago Historical Society. Printed in part in Flagg, pp. 158-59.

1. This letter does not seem to have been preserved. In it McMurtrie apparently apologized for the contents of his letter of 16 May 1819 to which he had received no reply.

96. To William Wordsworth

Boston, Massachusetts,
Novbr 15, 1819.

Dear sir: Thinking it may be gratifying to you to know that there are some on this side of the Atlantic who have taste enough to judge for themselves, and the ambition to be thought capable of relishing your writings, I venture to send you some numbers of one of our Literary Journals. Your great Work, the "Excursion", not having yet been republished here,[1] could not, according to the plan of the N.A. Review, form the subject of a distinct article, as I understand was the wish of the Editors.[2] But that has not prevented them incidentally expressing their reverence of your genius whenever an opportunity allowed it—as you will find in the Review[3] of "Hazlitt's Lectures."[4]

You will find the Journal, like other miscelllanies, of unequal merit. Some of the best articles are marked, and at the end of each, and in the Table of Contents, the names of the writers are annexed: the rest are written by other persons. The two principal writers in these numbers, Mr. Channing[5] & Mr. Dana, were the late Editors, and it is regretted are no longer connected with the Work.—As I suppose an American Journal is not often seen in England, perhaps it may please Mr. Southey to see it. There is nothing of mine in it; for, even had I the ability, my professional labours leave me too little leisure for writing. Pray present my best respects to Mr. Southey and to Mrs. Wordsworth & Miss Hutchinson;[6] and tell Mrs. W. as I cannot make my acknowledgements for her present (the Poem brought by Mr. Ticknor) in terms suitable to its value, I must beg her to accept simply my thanks; yet I cannot forbear adding, that to have <thought> been deemed worthy of suggesting, by any effort of my pencil, even one thought of such a Poem, by such a Poet, is indeed an honour as difficult to be forgotten as to be suitably acknowledged.

Should Sir George Beaumont be with you, pray say, that I intend writing him soon; and add my grateful respects both to him & Lady Beaumont. I am unable to reply to your question of, "when I expect to return". I hope one day to see dear England again; but *when* is more than I now know. Even if my visit is but for a summer, I should make the voyage without any effort on the part of inclination.

Believe me, dear sir, / with the highest respect, / yrs sincerely /

Washington Allston

ADDRESSED: William Wordsworth Esqure / Keswick,[7] / Cumberland. SOURCE: Manuscript, The Wordsworth Trust, Dove Cottage, Grasmere.

1. *The Excursion,* published in England in 1814, was not published separately in America. It first appeared there in the first collected edition of Wordsworth's works, *The Poetical Works of William Wordsworth* (Boston, 1843). 2. The "editors" of the *North American Review* to whom WA refers were Edward T. Channing, who was editor from its beginning until October 1819, and RHD, who was his chief assistant for the same period. RHD expected to be chosen to succeed Channing as editor and when he was not, apparently because of objections to his championing of the English romantic poets, he severed his connection with the magazine. Edward Everett was the next editor, from 1820 to 1823 (Frank Luther Mott, *A History of American Magazines, 1741-50* [Cambridge: Belknap Press of Harvard Univ. Press, 1970], p. 226). 3. RHD reviewed Hazlitt's book in the *North American Review* 7 (Mar. 1819): 276-322. He quoted from "The Excursion" and devoted several pages to a description of Wordsworth, expressing opinions no doubt also held by WA. Wordsworth, he said, had "a mind perfectly original, with an imagination full of forms of beauty and grandeur, and with powers of description unsurpassed by any poet of this age" and such an air of "plain truth" that his readers did not feel taken out of the world into the realm of the imagination. "He has formed," he added, "another creation, but it is one within ourselves," giving "a moral sense . . . to all things," though he said it was but "a small class of society that can see or feel" these relations. Of Wordsworth's language, which he called "truly poetical," he declared that "No poet since Milton seems so thoroughly imbued with old English." In conclusion, he said that Coleridge's criticism of Wordsworth in *Biographia Literaria* had "more good taste and philosophy in it" than any written on any writer in modern times. 4. *Lectures on the English Poets* (1818), by William Hazlitt. Appendix 3 was entitled "On Mr. Wordsworth's Poem 'The Excursion.'" 5. Edward Tyrrell Channing (1790-1856), editor and educator, was a brother-in-law of WA's by his first marriage. 6. Sarah Hutchinson (1775-1835) was a sister of Wordsworth's wife. 7. Wordsworth lived at Grasmere when WA first knew him and moved in 1813 to Rydal Mount, both villages near Keswick.

97. To Charles Robert Leslie

Boston, Massachusetts,
Novbr 15, 1819.

Dear Leslie: Being, as you know, one of the *prudent,* whose maxim is "business before pleasure," I shall begin with the business part of my letter. By Captn Tracy,[1] of the London Packet, you will receive a packet for Mr. Wordsworth,[2] which I will thank you to forward to him in the way that will be least expensive. His Booksellers, Messrs. Longman, Hurst, Rees & Orm,[3] will either <do> send it, or put you in the way of doing it. Whichever way, however it may be sent, I wish you would have the goodness to pay for the carriage of it, as I do not wish it to be of any expense to Mr. Wordsworth; and, as I shall have occasion to remit some money to England in the Spring for articles that I may want, I will then reimburse you.

Your letter by the London Packet, together with the Prints, <have been> has been received.[4] Tell Frank Collins I feel greatly obliged to him for hunting up the admirable print of Leivens Lazarus[5] which I value more than I should twenty of Lebrun's[6] battles, fine as they are. Pray say to him, that when he has collected for me to the <value> amount of ten pounds, I wish him to stop, untill I shall be a little more in cash, when I will write to request him to proceed. Thank him also for the present of his brothers print of the sea coast; I am glad to have such a remembrance of the picture and accept yourself my thanks for the print of your Church. I like it exceedingly.—The critiques on your Sir Roger and my Jacob from the New Monthly Magazine[7] were republished here before I got the magazine you sent. I <they> find, as I supposed, they were written by Mr. Carey; indeed I thought they must have been by him, as there is not one of the London picture-criticks who could have done them half so well. Pray present him my best thanks for it. He has described your picture so well that I could almost copy it from the description. I heartily congratulate you on its success, and hope that it may prove a trusty pioneer for you to fame and fortune. The last however is only dreamt of by *young* painters; a dream which becomes dimmer and dimmer as we advance in life. But no matter: the Art itself has so much intrinsic pleasure for its votaries, that we ought to be satisfied if to that is added but enough of <the> Mammon to make the ends of the year meet. Indeed I often think with Collins that if a painter who really loved his Art, had <also> together with fame, as much wealth as he wished, he would be too happy in this world ever to be in a suitable state of mind to leave it. I hope notwithstanding that Collins is getting money so as to lay up something at the end of each year; for a little more than we *have*, I trust, would do neither of us any harm; but every thing is for the best, so we do our duty to Heaven. Tell him I think and talk a great deal about him (as I also do about you) talk to those whom he has never seen; but *who feeling* an interest in all I love and esteem, require not the aid of sight to admit him and you among the number of their friends. How mysterious, when we <think of> ponder on it, is this communication by words; and how real, and distinct an image do they create in our minds of objects far removed, even of those long buried in the grave, over which centuries have passed. Indeed so familiar is the image of Sir Joshua to me, his manners, habits, modes of thinking and even of speaking, created by the description of him, that I feel almost persuaded at times I had actually been acquainted with him. What a world is that of thought! and what a world does he possess whose thoughts are only of the beautiful, the pure, and holy! How fearful then is his, <whose> where the vindictive, the base and sensual make the sum. "As the tree falleth, so it shall lie."[8] Terrific must be the immortality of wicked minds.—I write without order whatever comes uppermost, and consequently have left myself too little room to tell you all I wished. I <have> am now considerably advanced <of> a picture, figures larger than life, Jeremiah[9] & which I shall describe to you in my next; it will be finished in a month. I should not have undertaken it, but that I was obliged to leave Boston, just as I was going to proceed with Belshazzer, on account of an epidemic that prevailed near my painting-room, and made it dangerous to remain there. I therefore have spent the latter part of the summer in Cambridge, where I began this picture, & as I shall have a handsome commission for it, do not so much regret it. I have painted one also from Spenser & of a head of Beatrice; both just sold.[10] The picture of Jeremiah I think, for its materials, one of the grandest compositions I have made. After this is completed I shall proceed with Belshazzer <and> then the Hospital picture, and no more small pictures.—Morse has spent the summer here and has just finished a large whole length portrait of a beautiful girl wandering amidst the ruins of a Gothic Abbey.[11] 'Tis, by a great deal, the best thing he has done, and has gained him great reputation here. 'Tis well drawn, composed & coloured; and would make a figure even at Somerset House. I always thought he had a great deal in him, if he would only bring it out by application. Circumstances made him industrious, and being continued, his industry has grown into a habit. He leaves town this week for Washingon, where he is to paint a whole length of the President for the City Hall of Charleston. My affectionate remembrance to Collins Mrs. C. & Frank. To Collard, Lonsdale, Coleridge Mr. & Mrs. Gilman and the Morgans.

God bless you. Yours ever / W. Allston

[In the margins] I have written to Mr. Howard, the secretary of the Royal Academy, enclosing to him a paper he sent me for my signature; and have requested him to deliver my Diploma to you;[12] which I will thank you to have put into a deal box, and to deliver to Captain Tracy to bring out to me when he returns. Mr. Williams will give you Capn Tracy's address. I shall write to Collins soon, though he still owes me a letter. I would write now if I were not unusually pressed with business that must be attended to immediately. Remember me to Mrs. Bridgen & the family also to Mr. Williams—Charles Williams[13] is in good health—and is gone for a few days to New York. My regards to Newton. Tell me all about the Artists. What is Willes doing? Give my best and most affectionate regards to Irving, and tell him I will write him by the next opportunity. His Sketch Book is greatly admired here. I like all the articles. Pray remember me to Mr. Delafield.[14] Two of my commissions you forgot—the prize Poem on Belshazzer's feast, sold by Hatchard or Rigeway,[15] and the Somerset house last catalogue. Pray remember them. Do not forget to give my best regards to Mr. Cooke[16] and tell him how much pleased I was by his enquiries. Also to Martin Willes Lewis & Brockedon, and above all to pay my respects to Mr. West; to whom I have written a note enclosed to Mr. Howard.

ADDRESSED: Charles R. Leslie Esqre. / N 8 Buckingham Place, / Fitzroy Square, / London / Ship / London Packet. SOURCE: Manuscript. Printed in part in Flagg, pp. 159-60.

1. Charles Tracy was a captain in the Boston-London packet service for many years, with a residence in Boston (*Boston City Directory* for 1816 and later). He was captain of the *Galen* when WA was a passenger on it in the fall of 1818. 2. It contained the issues of magazines referred to in WA's letter to Wordsworth of this date. 3. Thomas Norton Longman (1771-1842) was the head of the family publishing house in London at this time, whose partners were Thomas Hurst, Owen Rees, Cosmos Orme, and later Thomas Brown. He was a publisher of Wordsworth and other prominent nineteenth-century English writers. 4. That of 6 August 1819. 5. Jan Livensz (1607-74), Dutch painter and engraver. In his lecture "Composition" WA described his painting *The Raising of Lazarus* as an example of the smallest possible number of parts which subjects of a "grave or elevated kind" could have, "Variety" in them diminishing in the degree in which they approached the sublime (*LA*, p. 146). 6. Charles Le Brun (1619-90), French painter. He was famous for his series of paintings from the life of Alexander the Great. 7. London periodical (1814-84), with varying subtitles, which had a series of men of letters as editors. 8. "In the

place where the tree falleth, there it shall lie" (Eccles. 11:3). RHD, Jr., recollected that WA often spoke of Coleridge's quoting these words in once talking about future punishment. 9. *Jeremiah Dictating His Prophecy of the Destruction of Jerusalem to the Scribe Baruch,* from Jer. 36:4-7. It was the most ambitious painting WA completed during his final residence in America and one of the last three completed paintings with biblical subjects, the other two being done that year and the next. More clearly than any other it reflects the influence of Michelangelo. He made several studies for it, including a clay model of the head of Jeremiah and a complete study. A servant in the Dana family, Lewis Gray, served as the model for Jeremiah. It was bought by Mary (Channing) Gibbs, Channing's mother-in-law, for $1,000 for the drawing room of her Beacon Hill house. It was first exhibited in WA's rooms early in November and publicly at the hall upstairs in the Boylston Market House from 29 August through November, with an admission price of twenty-five cents, at which time it was highly praised in the press. A long article appeared in the *Salem Gazette* for 25 August under the title "American Painters." After introducing the question of whether or not America was ever destined to arrive at distinction in the fine arts comparable to that of the Greek republics, the author characterized WA as "one on whom the mantle of Raphael had fallen" and predicted his work would not only confer immortality on him but "forever resound to the honour" of the country, and then described in detail and praised *Jeremiah.* On the same date the *Boston Daily Advertiser* carried an article entitled "Mr. Allston's Picture," which said it had just been completed, having taken four months' work, compared the figure of Jeremiah to Michelangelo's Moses, called that of Baruch "one of the most truly Raphaellic designs that has been painted since his day," and concluded that those who had not visited Europe could obtain an idea of the great masters from it and that the question "Who reads an American book or looks at an American painting" could now be answered in the second part. A month later, on 28 September, the same paper printed an extract from a letter, signed P., to a friend at that time in the country who signed himself N. The author said he had never before felt so distinctly the approach of "heavenly power" as when looking at the painting, described the eyes of Jeremiah in particular, and expressed gratitude that WA had sent him away a "more thoughtful and religious man." The realistic jar in the foreground, however, which RHD called "this mere mechanical excellence," received more attention, for its "relief," to WA's vexation; he said he would paint it out and put something else there if he could and apparently cited Reynold's characterization of the Dutch and Flemish schools as being "mechanical" in Discourse 6 and *A Journey to Flanders and Holland* (RHD, p. 10 and Addition). It was exhibited again in the same hall in 1822 and at the BA in 1827. Afterward Mrs. Gibbs sent WA another $1,000, having been offered $2,000 for it by an English visitor. Three poems were written about it: Pickering's "Jeremiah: A vision," published in *The Ruins of Paestum*; Sarah H. Jacob's "Suggested by Allston's Picture of Jeremiah and Baruch in the Prison," published in *The Rhode-Island Book* (Providence, 1841); and one by James Russell Lowell. 10. *The Flight of Florimel* was bought by Loammi Baldwin. *Beatrice* was bought apparently by Theodore Lyman, who also owned WA's *Diana Bathing.* 11. Morse painted a full-length small portrait of Sarah Alston in an elaborate setting of Gothic ruins, as commissioned by her father, John Ashe Alston, who stipulated its size and a "superb" landscape and agreed that it be finished when Morse returned north and that he pay two hundred dollars for it. It was highly praised in the press in both Charleston, S.C., and in Boston, where it was exhibited for a few days in November. Morse also painted a full-sized half-portrait of Sarah in Charleston for her father (Prime, pp. 110-11; Mabee, p. 76; *Boston Daily Advertiser* 6, 12 Nov. 1819). 12. WA refers to a second letter to Howard, not that of 4 April 1819; it does not seem to have been preserved. 13. Charles Williams was a brother of Samuel and Timothy Williams. He was associated with the firm of Welles and Williams in London and Paris. In Paris he was often a companion of Irving's (Irving, *Letters* 1:562-63, 575-76, 608-609, 612-22, 691; *Journals and Notebooks* 2:90, 3:221 and passim). 14. John Delafield (1786-1853) was an American banker in London. After suffering considerable financial loss, he returned to America in 1819 (Irving, *Letters* 1:582). 15. Possibly "Belshazzer's Feast," by historian and clergyman Thomas Smart Hughes, which won the Seatonian Prize at Emmanuel College, Cambridge, and was said to have inspired John Martin's painting of the subject. John Hatchard (1769-1849) was a London publisher and bookseller to several members of the royal family. Rigeway has not been identified. 16. George F. Cook.

98. From Charles Robert Leslie London March 3rd 1820

My dear Sir: I have delayed answering your letter of Novr 15th till Capt Tracey's departure that I might have the more to tell you. I beg pardon for having omitted with my usual forgetfulness your two commissions of the poem and catalogue which I now send you by Captn T. with your Diploma, book of Laws[1] &c. I did not receive the packet for Mr. Wordsworth till within these few days. I have sent it to Messrs Longmans' with a request for them to forward it as you desired. I shall call to-day & pay the eighteen shillings to Middleton[2] & take his receipt.

(I was two months last summer in S. Wales and on my way there I spent a day with *Mr. Visger's* family in *Bristol*. I found them in Portland Square living just as I recollected them six years ago, excepting that they are now all in good health. Mrs. Visger is fatter, Harman is leaner, & his hair nearly white, their son grown into a tall slender young man and their daughters a very fine & well behaved family of lasses.[3] Helen is very much improved in appearance & now takes the lead as eldest sister, Theodosia is a pretty girl somewhat resembling poor Louisa, Henrietta is the plainest, & little Maria retains all that delicate beauty which distinguished her when a child; I could not help regretting that she was grown too tall to be kissed & petted. Eliza has been married two years to Saml Lunell, she has no children. They are still desperately in love with each other, & I believe since I saw them have gone on a tour to Italy. I saw Geo. Lunell but not his wife; she was out of town. Geo. has a son has lost one child & expects to have another soon.) Mr. Visger is very highly pleased with your "*Hermia & Helena*"[4] & not the less so for a strong likeness they have discovered in the front face to Eliza. It hangs at the end of his drawing room opposite the fire place.

I spent an hour or two with *Mr. King* who was delighted to hear of you & of your success. You will be sorry to hear of poor Bird's death.[5] I think it is probable I shall revisit Wales next year and if so shall again touch at Bristol.

I went in consequence of a very pressing invitation from Mr. Lewis Dillwyn[6] (eldest son of old Mr. D at Walthamstow[7]) & spent two months very pleasantly at his house. Mr. L. Dillwyn married a welch lady & as both himself & wife possess considerable propety there, he is a man of some consequence in the county of Glamorgan.[8] I painted three portraits there & had applications for several others which the time I had limited myself to would not permit me to undertake. I made some sketches of the scenery, which is very beautiful & of the costume of the people which is quite peculiar. Since my return I have painted a copy of "Sir Roger" for Lord Lansdowne & am now engaged on a picture of a citizen and his family "*gypsying*" (as it is called), or spending a day in the woods in the manner of gypsys. It contains eight figures & I hope to complete it for Somerset House.[9]

Collins has been elected an Academician together with Cooper.[10] He has painted another very exquisite picture of a coast scene & last year made some beautiful sketches of Devonshire scenery. He, Frank & his mother are all well & desire to be particularly remembered to you. *Martin* has painted a picture of *Macbeth and Banquo* meeting the witches on the blasted heath, it is as usual tremendously grand. He is now employed on your subject of "*Belshazzer,*" making it an architectural composition with small figures, the writing on the wall to be about *a mile long.*

Willes has very much improved; he made his debut this year at the Gallery with his picture of "Danger," from Collins's poem.[11] It looks extremely well there. He will exhibit a large landscape at the Academy, which I think will do him great credit.

My sister sent me some time ago a paragraph from a newspaper containing an extremely well-written description of your picture of "*Florimel.*"[12] It brought it completely before my eyes. I am sure such a subject treated in your way must make a very exquisite picture.

The Gallery was closed a fortnight at the death of the King.[13] It is now open & except in the landscape department I think it one of the best exhibitions I have seen. Newton has there a beautiful little picture of an old man reading some dull book to a young girl without perceiving that she is fast asleep. The corner of a love letter emerging from her boddice speaks for itself. It was purchased almost immediately by a Mr. Chamberlain[14] a perfect stranger to Newton. Wilkie's picture of the interior of a Highland whiskey still is very fine. The master of the place an old fellow of herculean make & somewhat coruplent with his kilt & bonnet, & a brace of pistols in his belt, is criticising a glass of the spirit, which he holds between him & the light, half closing one of his keen eyes & smacking his lips with the air of a perfect connoisseur, it is I think one of Wilkie's happiest efforts.

Young Landseer's[15] picture of the two dogs scratching a man out of the snow is the most interesting animal picture I ever saw. One is licking the hand of the man (who appears to be dead or almost so) as if to assure him that help is near while the other is barking or howling for assistance; and in the distance are seen the monks of St. Bernard making their way toward the sound. Cooper has some exquisite little battle pictures. Collins has nothing there this year. The little picture I sent of "*Contemplation*" is a female figure with a moonlight effect which I began for Juliet[16] but not thinking when it was finished that it expressed her character I gave it another name.

Captain Tracy has given us a gleam of hope that we may see you in the course of the summer though only for a short time. The months of May, June, & July are in my opinion worth all the rest of the year in London, & there is every season some additional exhibition of pictures open. There will this season be at least five principal private galleries open. *Haydon's picture*[17] is completed and will be exhibited at Bullock's rooms in Piccadilly.[18] The weather you know is always delightful at that time of the year. I am sure if you can accomplish it that a visit if only for the season to London will do you great good & that you will paint the quicker & better for it.

I hope I need not say what delight it would be sure to give numbers of your friends besides myself. There is one thing at all events I think you might do & that is if it is quite impossible for you to come yourself, at least *send us a picture* which I should think you might borrow from some of your purchasers, for the next exhibition. The voyages are now performed with so much certainty that there can be little risk either in your borrowing or the owner's lending one for that purpose. You are now sure of a good situation at the Academy & I think it will facilitate your being made an R.A. Let it be something striking & the larger the better. I hope you will come & bring it with you. If you should be obliged to return again before the exhibition you may depend on my taking every care of it or in case of my absence which is not likely to occur, Collins I am sure will attend to it.

Collins, Lonsdale, &c are all well & all desire to be remembered to you. *Irving* has published four numbers of the *Sketch book,*[19] with every chance of success as soon as it becomes known, which you know cannot happen all at once, here. There have been two most favorable notices of it with long extracts in "Blackwood's" & the "New London Magazine."[20] He is at present in Birmingham on a visit to his sister.[21]

Perkins & Fairman[22] the Bank note engravers have astonished the artists here by their mode of producing fac similes of plates. It is to be feared the Bank will not employ them though as far as I can learn it is acknowledged by all who have seen it to be by far the best method of putting a stop to those *legal murders* that have so long disgraced the Old Baily.[23]

Brockedon has invented a mode of drawing very fine wire by which he is likely to make more money than by his pencil.

I think your patience must by this time be pretty well exhausted by all this chit chat which I have run into in the hope that you may pick out of it something to interest or amuse. Be it as it may, all I ask is ample payment in my own coin & so farewell my dear sir till next time

till when / Yours as ever, / C.R. Leslie

ADDRESSED: W. Allston Esq A.R.A. / Boston / Masstts. SOURCE: Manuscript, Houghton. Printed in part in Flagg, pp. 162-64.

1. *Abstract of the Constitution and Laws of the Royal Academy of Arts in London* (London, 1815). 2. John Middleton was a colorman for artists in St. Martin's Lane in London for many years, at this time in business with his son (*Post-Office London Directory* for 1818). WA probably ordered colors from him in his letter to Leslie of 20 June 1819, not preserved. 3. Otherwise than in this letter unidentified, as are Samuel and George Lunnell. 4. From Shakespeare's *A Midsummer-Night's Dream* 3.2.ii, 198-216. It was exhibited at the BI in 1818, at which time it

received mixed reviews. The *Morning Herald* disapproved of the subject matter, but the *Examiner* for 9 February praised it for having sedateness and elegance. 5. Edward Bird (1772-1819), English painter who lived in Bristol. 6. Otherwise unidentified. 7. A village on the outskirts of Epping Forest. 8. In southern Wales. 9. It was exhibited at the RA in 1820. 10. Abraham Cooper. 11. William Collins (1721-59), English poet. 12. Probably Leslie refers to his sister Eliza and to the description of *The Flight of Florimel,* which first appeared in the *Boston Daily Advertiser.* 13. George III died on 16 September 1820. 14. Unidentified. 15. Edwin Henry Landseer (1802-73), English painter, especially of animals. 16. Possibly the character of that name in Shakespeare's *Romeo and Juliet.* 17. *Christ's Entry into Jerusalem,* from John 12:12-13. 18. The Egyptian Hall, also called Bullock's Museum, possibly from the print dealer Bullock (Balston, p. 101). 19. The third number of *The Sketch Book* contained "A Royal Poet," "The Country Church," "The Widow and Her Son," and "The Boar's Head Tavern, Eastcheap: A Shakesperian Research"; the fourth contained "The Mutability of Literature: A Colloquy in Westminster Abbey," "Rural Funerals," "The Inn Kitchen," and "The Spectre Bridegroom." 20. The *New Monthly Magazine.* Neither review has been located. 21. Sarah Sanders (Irving) Van Wart (1780-1849?), whose husband, Henry Van Wart, was in business in Birmingham (Williams, 1:380, passim). 22. Jacob Perkins (1766-1849) and Gideon Fairman (1774-1827) were American engravers of bank notes, at this time working in London. 23. The Old Bailey is the principal criminal court of London. The allusion is probably to crimes committed in connection with counterfeit bills.

99. From Charles Robert Leslie London March 14th 1820

Dear Sir: I enclose you Middleton's receipt for the remaining 18 Shillings which I paid him. They had omitted to enter the 1 £. 5. as paid & it was lucky you had the receipt by you.

You will be sorry to hear of poor old Mr. West's death which occurred last Friday[1] after a long & painful illness.

Hoping to see you with Capt. Tracey on his return

I remain dear Sir / Yours faithfully / C.R. Leslie

P.S. In case you should get this first & be surprised at its brevity it may be well to say that I have written another letter by the same opportunity—

ADDRESSED: W. Allston esqr. SOURCE: Manuscript.

1. West died on 11 March 1820.

100. To Henry Pickering Boston, 18th May, 1820.

My dear Sir: Whilst I beg you to accept my sincerest thanks for your very kind and flattering Letter, I regret to say, that the plan which I had proposed and begun before I left England, together with engagements subsequently entered into here, wholly put it out of my power to avail myself of your liberal offer. I brought with me from

England a large picture rather more than half-finished, which it was my wish to have completed for exhibition immediately after my arrival; but the unexpected delay in the remittance of some money owing to me in Pennsylvania leaving me without the means to proceed with, I was obliged to defer it, and to undertake from necessity smaller works for immediate support to which I have since, for the same reason, devoted my time during the last year; the amount of my remittance, when it came at last having been anticipated by unavoidable expenses. The experience I had in Europe determined me against painting many small pictures, as I found the highest prices I could obtain for them bore no proportion to the time they cost. My only hope then of making my Art profitable beyond a mere and precarious support seemed to be by devoting myself principally to large works, and exhibiting them. This indeed was both Mr. West's opinion and advice; and the success of his picture at the Hospital in Philadelphia[1] encouraged me to hope that the exhibition of large pictures would be as profitable to me in this country, as in England; and for this purpose I began the picture before alluded to, which is sixteen feet by twelve, the subject Belshazzer's Feast; on which I purpose to proceed as soon as I shall have completed a picture now in hand (on commission),[2] which I shall probably be able to do in about six weeks, it being already considerably advanced. After the completion of Belshazzer, I could no longer delay fulfilling my engagement with the Hospital: and if I allow six months for the first, and eighteen months for the Hospital picture, two years <it> will be as short a time as I can reasonably calculate on for the completion of both.

I trust you will excuse this apparent egotism, <which> when I assure you I have been induced to enter into these particulars only out of respect to you; as I might seem insensible to your kindness, were I to decline so uncommon and liberal <one> a proposal as the one you have made me, without assigning a reason. Believe me, my dear Sir, I shall ever entertain a grateful remembrance of this liberality. And I will still hope that at some future time I shall have the satisfaction of seeing some of my Efforts honoured by a place on your walls. These are no empty words of compliment; for I should indeed esteem an honour to have them possessed by one, to whom they will afford so much pleasure.

You have probably learnt of the sale of the Witch of Endor[3] by the Newspapers. It was sold on saturday soon after you were at my Room.—When you come to town and will favour me with a call I shall be most happy to see you. I remain, dear sir, with a true sense of the honour done me, Your obliged servant

Wa. Allston

ADDRESSED: Henry Pickering Esqre. / Salem—. SOURCE: Manuscript.

1. West's copy of his *Christ Healing the Sick* is in the Pennsylvania Hospital, Philadelphia.

2. Probably *Jeremiah*. 3. *Saul and the Witch of Endor*, from 1 Sam. 28:8-25, was painted for the Boston merchant and philanthropist Thomas H. Perkins, who accompanied WA to America from England in 1818. The subject was painted also by Salvator Rosa and West. In the figure of the witch WA was indebted to the Sibyls of Michelangelo and in that of the principal soldier again, as

in *The Dead Man Restored*, to the *Borghese Warrior.* Among his studies for it was one of a foot of the witch. RHD thought that Saul was not ghostly enough, with which opinion WA agreed, and that the "throw" of the figure partook somewhat of the stage, an opinion on which WA seemed to have a doubt "whether it was not so." He often expressed the intention to paint the work over again on a larger scale, saying that it was one of his favorites and that he could improve it and would make Samuel "another thing" (RHD, p. 10). It was probably least well received of all his paintings. An amusing account of the irrelevant remarks made by some of the visitors to the exhibition on 8 May was given by one of the sympathetic ones present, who reported that WA "seemed a little chagrinned, by his nibbling at the ends of his finger nails" (Tim to Sam, 20 May 1820 [Houghton]). The *Boston Daily Advertiser* for 16 May 1820, announcing the sale, reported, however, that friends viewed it with delight in his studio and regretted that there was no place in Boston where it might be seen by the public. It was exhibited at the PAFA in 1822, 1826, 1831, and 1843. An engraving of it was distributed by the New England Art Union in 1851.

101. To Charles Robert Leslie Boston, 31 May, 1820.

Dear Leslie: Judge Jackson,[1] a friend of mine here, having requested me to procure for him the Prints, named below, I shall feel myself particularly obliged if you will take upon yourself the trouble of the Commission: Enclosed you will find a (first) Bill of Exchange (dated 26 May 1820) from Mr. Timo. Williams, of this place, on his brother, Mr. Saml. Williams, London, for the sum of thirty Pounds Sterling; which, as I have calculated, will be sufficient to pay for them, and to defray all charges of packing &c. Should this sum, however, happen to fall short, you will remit one, or more, as may be necessary; but if it overruns, I will thank you to add what other print, or prints, you may think fit. As this is in Frank Collins's line perhaps he will take the trouble off your hands.

(For the list see next page)

By Wilkie.
<The Rent Day,>[2]
Blind Fiddler.—
<Village Politicians.>
<Distraining for Rent.>
Cut Finger.
Blindman's Buff. & any other that may be published.

By Allan.[3]
The Circassian Slaves.
Press Gang.

By Stothard.[4]
The Canterbury Pilgrims.

By yourself.
Ann Page & Master Slender
& Sir Roger de Coverly, if that is engraved.

You must consider this merely as a letter of *business*, which I <have been> am obliged to despatch in a hurry. But I mean to write you another should Captn. Tracy delay sailing another day. Should he not, but sail as he *proposes* tomorrow, you must excuse my defering the answer to your letter[5] 'till the next opportunity for though I have had some days notice of the time Cap. T. would sail, I have yet been so incessantly engaged, that it has been quite out of my power to write. It was my intention also to have written by this time to Collins. So tell him he must for the present take the will for the deed, with my most hearty congratulations <of> on his being made an R.A.[6] [Approximately three lines, including the signature, have been cut out of the manuscript at this point, where a new paragraph began.] My love to C[7] Frank, [words cut out] and all who enquire after me.

SOURCE: Manuscript.

1. Charles Jackson (1775-1855), Boston lawyer, was a judge on the supreme judicial court of Massachusetts from 1813 to 1823. 2. The cancelations were presumably made by someone other than WA, probably Leslie, to indicate the prints he was unable to supply at first. 3. Sir William Allan (1782-1850), Scottish painter. 4. Thomas Stothard (1755-1834), English subject painter. His best-known painting was *Procession of the Canterbury Pilgrims*, which William Carey described in his *Critical Description* of it, of which WA owned a copy. 5. That of 3 March 1820. 6. At this point in the manuscript, in another hand: "(Allston's name in this and some other letters was cut out as an autograph.)" 7. Probably "Collins."

102. To Henry Pickering

Boston,
Thursday, 17th August, 1820.

My dear Sir: I have just completed a Picture,[1] which I should be most happy to shew you. It will be seen by my friends from next tuesday to the end of the ensuing week. But thinking it would be more agreeable to you to see it without such a *crowd* as you found at my room in your last visit, I send you these few lines, to say, that it would give me particular pleasure, if you could make it convenient to favour me with a call on the saturday preceding—that is, the day after tomorrow—when I shall be at my room, from one o'clock until four—without company, excepting, perhaps, Mr. E. Dana.

I have not heard any thing relative to the sale of Mr. West's pictures,[2] or I should have informed you, agreeably to the wish expressed in your last favour.

I am, dear Sir, with sincere respects, Yrs / Wa. Allston

ADDRESSED: Henry Pickering Esqr. / Salem, / Massachusetts. SOURCE: Manuscript.

1. Presumably *Jeremiah*. 2. On 20 March 1820, a few weeks after West's death, his collection of prints, drawings, and paintings by other artists was sold, producing £6,999 in actual bids. The *Columbian Centinel* for 30 August reported the amount as £1,375 or $59,385. His own paintings were not sold until May 1829 (Robert C. Alberts, *Benjamin West. A Biography* [Boston: Houghton Mifflin, 1978], pp. 337, 391).

103. From James McMurtrie Philada Decr 5th. 1820.

Dear Sir: I have just finished two letters to Mr. Sully & Mr. Leslie and I feel so much inclined to say a word or two to you that I cannot resist my inclination. I am pretty certain that you have had no intention of casting me off by your long silence and I of all men have least right to complain on that score being the worst correspondent ever man had. But at all events I have so few friends of that turn of mind on certain subjects which I am so enthusiastically fond of that I cannot afford to lose the smallest of the number least of all one on whom I set the highest value. I have so long suffered my mind to dwell on subjects connected with the fine arts, and being for a long time a man of leisure, the subject has taken such entire possession of me "J'ai un espèce de rage pour les beaux arts"[1] There is they say a pleasure in all madness, and I can answer for the one I am afflicted with, and am by no means desiring of a cure. I have lately seen an account of your last picture of "Jeremiah." Do you not intend we shall see it in Phila? If you do, I entreat you will allow me to use my best endeavours to promote your views in this quarter. Sully is in Baltimore & I do not know any one who cd serve you better, or I shd not recommend myself. At a guess I should say, that any thing you would esteem attractive enough for exhibition wd nett you from $800 to $1000 & perhaps more. If your large picture of "Balshazzers feast" shd ever come on, I think I cd ensure you thrice that amt. There is a room in a house opposite the State house in which Granet's "Chapel" was lately shewn which can at any time be had. It will accommodate a picture of double the size of the chapel picture. This picture was a very popular one, and certainly excellent of *its kind,* its receipts were something above $1500 as I understand. I would beg leave my Dear Sir to call your attention to the plan of occasionally exhibiting a large picture. If you succeed (and you have every reason to expect success) you are much more amply recompensed at *the moment* than you would be by selling the picture, and you would thus in a few years accumulate a noble stock. Rembt Peale's[2] "Court of Death" netted him $1000 in 4 wks in Balt. and he values it at 10.000 dr. This country is completely open to you without a competitor—for Sully cannot afford to paint extensive subjects, nor has his studies been much directed that way and there is no other individual that I know of, that can attempt it with any prospect of success but yourself. Mr. P's "Court of Death" is in my humble opinion an abortion. If you cd put aside that exquisite composition of "Christ healing" as a *failure,* it is past sufferance that such a picture as the "Court of Death" shd be spoken of as it has been in the public prints. Mr. P's principal figure *Death* is a good looking man of about 40 years of age, without one symbol usually given to bespeak the *King of terrors,* and it is absolutely necessary that it should be underwritten, *this is Death.* I told him it wd never do, refine upon it as he would. I asked him if he was about representing Diana, for instance, whether he wd omit the emblem of the chase, crescent &c. He says certainly he wd, and has a world of fine reasoning to shew that all that has hitherto been done in that way as very absurd. You will perceive he is about attempting a *new walk* in the art, of which

I hope his next specimen (the canvass for which is already stretched) may prove more attractive than the one I have just mentioned. Do not however understand me as speaking disrespectfully of Mr. P's talent. Even in the "Court of Death" there is much to praise, taking into view the disadvantages he laboured under, and as a portrait painter Mr. P. is very reputable & has *$150* for them. As a man he is very amiable.

Leslie is painting a picture of "May day in the days of Queen Elizabeth."[3] He will doubtless make a very interesting picture of it. I had no thought when I began this letter of spinning it out to this length. It is a subject however that I do not easily tire on. But I by no means exact one of equal length in return, or indeed one of *any length,* unless time and inclination may serve you. Should you favor me with a line be very sparing of any apologizing for not writing &c. I know all you wd say & admit it fully & hold myself your debtor into the bargain if you will shew me how I can serve you. By the way I lately purchased (or rather made an exchange for) a picture by Hilton of London in—Candle light—a slight sketch, but I think very clever—4 ft. by 2.6. It makes a good centre, between your beautiful picture of the "Mother & Child" and a fine head of the "Virgin at Prayers" by Sasso Ferrati.[4] I hope the day will not be far distant when my means will authorize my requesting some noble subject from your pencil to accomplish which I am resolved to resist all temptations for the present. Some little matters such as prints, etchings of small account I cannot let pass me.

I must now my Dear Sir draw to a close, with the assurance that I feel that regard for you as a man & a professor of that art, to which I am indebted for some of the happiest moments of life, that any interruption of that friendship which I trust still exists between us, would cause real sorrow to one who has great pleasure subscribing himself

Your sincere friend & admirer / J McMurtrie

SOURCE: Manuscript.

1. "I have a sort of madness for the fine arts." 2. Rembrandt Peale (1778-1860), portrait and history painter. He was introduced to WA in London by West when he was there in 1802 and 1803, engaged in exhibiting a skeleton of a mammoth or mastedon for his father and studying painting with West. They must also have met sometime during 1824-26, when he was in Boston studying lithography. In later years, in 1859, he and Morse exchanged memories of "the ethereal Allston" and agreed that in coloring he was the "American Titian" (Prime, 598). WA owned copies of his *Notes on Italy. Written During a Tour in the Years 1829 and 1830* (Philadelphia, 1831) and *Graphics; a Manual of Drawing and Writing for the Use of Schools and Families* (New York, 1835). His most celebrated painting, the large *Court of Death,* was exhibited in many cities for several years. 3. *May Day Revels in the Time of Queen Elizabeth.* 4. Giovanni Battista Salvi (Sassoferrato) (1609-85), Italian painter.

104. To Henry Pickering Boston, 25 Decbr, 1820

My dear Sir: I know not how I can thank you in suitable terms for the high, yet delicate, compliment with which you have honoured me in your eloquent and elegant Verses.[1] Had the efforts of my pencil called forth no other praise, I ought to consider them amply compensated in this. But I should do injustice to many of my friends did I not also gratefully acknowledge theirs.

To know that he has succeeded in giving pleasure to the refined and cultivated is the highest reward that a painter can receive; for, until this is done, however great may be the delight he feels in the pursuit of his art, he can never feel assured that he has not over-rated his powers. Such a reward is made doubly welcome to me now by the just hope which it inspires, that my future efforts, if they have any merit, will meet with those, even on this side the Atlantic, to whom they will be neither unintelligible nor uninteresting.

I am, dear sir, / With sincere respect & esteem, / Yrs / W. Allston

ADDRESSED: Henry Pickering Esqre. / Salem, / Massachusetts. SOURCE: Manuscript.

1. Besides the poems on WA's *Moonlit Landscape (Moonlight)* and "To Washington Allston," Pickering wrote two other poems containing references to WA: "American Painting" and "Painting." The first named WA, along with other American painters, and the second referred to *The Angel Releasing St. Peter from Prison, The Dead Man Restored, Jeremiah, Elijah in the Desert, Jacob's Dream, Uriel in the Sun,* and *Belshazzar's Feast.* Probably at this time he sent the second, if not both.

105. To William Collins Boston, America, 18th May, 1821.

Dear Collins:- As it would be an agreeable novelty for me to begin a letter *without an apology,* I shall endeavour to forget how long I have owed you one; for, though among the worst of your correspondents, I am still willing to believe that you remember me with kindness. How I should have neglected writing to you for so long would be a mystery even to myself, were I not unhappily too conscious of the habit of substituting thinking for writing—and what is worse remaining satisfied with the substitute. My thoughts are often with you, and I have many pleasing dreams of what you and other of my friends in London are doing. But, I confess, as pleasant as this has been both to my imagination and indolence, I begin now to long for something less visionary; and as I have no right to expect anything more substantial unless I make the effort to ask for it, I must at least have recourse to writing. "Oh that I had the wings of a bird,"[1] that I might at will light amongst you, and see, and hear, all that has been done, and is doing. Sommerset House I suppose is now in its glory, and you shining away there <amid> amongst the stars of the first magnitude; Turner,[2] like the Great Bear,[3] turning the lesser lights around him into utter darkness—and Wilkie, like a Chaldean Magician,[4] conjuring sentiment out of pots and kettles—Callcot merrily floating down the stream of time for the land of posterity, & Leslie winning the hearts of the ladies by his spells of grace and beauty; while Sir

Thomas, and Owen,[5] and Phillips are liberally bestowing beauty, and sense, and expression on all who will pay for them. I would willingly give twenty guineas for one day's sight of the Exhibition. Now and then I see the Literary Gazette and the Examiner, and I need not tell you <of> what a treat to me are their imperfect accounts of what is doing in the Art. I devour them with as much avidity as a man afflicted with scurvy, after a long voyage, devours the common grass. But it will yet I hope be one day in my power to see London again with my own eyes. But of *that* day I can have no digested thought for the present. I have work enough cut out to employ [me] [page torn] for some years; so I must content myself as well as I can with what you and Leslie and [the] [page torn] newspapers will tell me. Besides my professional engagements, I have now another tie, which you may not perhaps have heard of—I am going to be married! *when* I cannot exactly say, but probably within a year.[6] The happy day is only delayed until I finish Belshazzer, which <will probably> may be within six months. You will be surprised perhaps that it has not been finished long ago. That it has not been has been, I assure you a great disappointment to me. But poverty, that heirloom of the Art, has been the only cause. And yet I have been constantly employed, ever since I have been here, and have sold my pictures as soon as finished. But the fact is, that I brought little or, almost, no money with me when I returned: and to <be> commence with a large picture that would at least occupy me for a year was what I could not do without a well-filled purse; so I e'en set about filling it: and as you know there has always been a hole in mine, through which some of its contents would often insensibly slip, you may well suppose the amassing so *large* a fund was no easy job. My finances however enabled me [to] [page torn] recommence Belshazzer last September, on w[hich w]ith [page torn] one short interval I have been employed ever since, and shall undertake nothing else until it is completed.—The first three months after my return here was spent in visiting my friends, but since then I have not been a week idle. Some might think I might have done more, but you, who are not accustomed to whistle off your pictures like those of the Lucca Giordano school,[7] will perhaps think the number sufficient for two years. The first I painted was Beattie's Minstrel, then a moonlight—a sunsett[8]—the flight of Florimel from Spenser—Dante's Beatrice, a single figure[9]—Jeremiah dictating to Baruch the scribe, larger than life—Saul and the Witch of Endor—another landscape, after sunsett with cattle[10]—and Miriam the Prophetess singing her song of triumph, large as life.[11]—Now that I have talked <gossip> so much about myself, you cannot do less than tell me all that you have been doing.—My paper now only allows me [to] add my affectionate regards to your Mother and Brother; of which I most cordially beg you to accept a large portion for yourself. I shall write to Leslie tomorrow. God bless you, dear Collins.

Your friend W Allston.

[In the margin] I enclose you some verses I wrote on Kean,[12] who <has> is now here, and has been making, as he ought to do, a mighty stir; so great indeed, that they call it the Kean fever.[13]—Pray present my best respects to Sir George & Lady Beaumont.

ADDRESSED: William Collins Esqre. R.A. / N 11 New Cavendish Street, / Portland Place, / London / Ship— / London Packet. ANNOTATED: No 3 [the third of three letters from WA to Collins copied by RHD]. SOURCE: Manuscript copy by RHD.

1. "And I said, Oh that I had wings like a bird!" (Ps. 55:6). 2. WA thought him the greatest painter since the days of Claude (Leslie, p. 177). Some of his own seascapes and landscapes are comparable to some of Turner's. 3. Ursa Major. 4. The use of the word *Chaldean* in the sense of magician was established in the book of Daniel in the Old Testament, from which *Belshazzar's Feast* was taken. The Chaldeans are among the spectators in the painting. 5. Samuel Owen (1769?-1857), English watercolor painter. 6. WA did not marry Martha Dana until 1830. 7. Luca Giordano (1632-1705), Italian painter, who acquired the nickname Luca Fa-presto (Luke Work-fast) because of the rapidity with which he produced paintings. 8. Presumably *Landscape, Evening (Classical Evening)*. It is the most richly colored of his later landscapes. 9. Presumably the smaller of the two versions of *Italian Shepherd Boy*. Both were based on early drawings, presumably done in Rome, and depict the figure holding a flute. They are possibly related to *Edwin* in the conception of the poet as a shepherd. *Sketch of a Shepherd Boy* was probably done about this time; on the reverse is *Eastern Female Figure*. 10. Presumably *Landscape: Time after Sunset*. In defining human, or poetic, truth in his lecture, "Art," WA described a similar landscape, though with a reclining figure instead of one on horseback, asking what could be "the effect of the purple haze of a summer sunset on the cows and sheep" and the poet "stretched on the same bank with the ruminating cattle" feeling the same kinship (*LA*, p. 84). 11. *Miriam the Prophetess*, from Exod. 15:21. It was the last large painting, 72 by 48 inches, and the last treatment of a biblical subject WA completed. It was commissioned by David Sears, a Boston merchant and art patron, whose wife's name was Miriam. According to Sweetser, he paid $1,000 for it. When it was exhibited at the BA in 1827 the entry in the catalog incorporated a reference to the biblical passage and the lines "Sound the loud timbrel o'er Egypt's dark sea, / Jehovah has triumphed, his people are free" from Thomas Moore's "Sound the loud timbrel," lines 1-2. WA's chalk *Half-Length Study of a Young Woman* (ca. 1821) is probably of Mrs. Sears. 12. WA's poem "On Kean's Hamlet" pays tribute to Shakespeare in the opening lines as one who "standest 'mid the bards of old, / Like Chimborazo, when the setting sun / Has left his hundred mountains dark and dun, / Sole object visible, the imperial One," whose "visionary forms" he saw "as in some necromatic glass," "Like breathing things of every living class, / Goblin and Hero, Villian, Fool, and Sage," so that not even Michelangelo or Raphael could represent "the meanest part / Of all thy vast creation." He thought that not even an actor could do so until he saw John Kemble as Coriolanus and George F. Cooke as Shylock and finally Kean as Hamlet, a "being strange, that only in the brain / Perchance has lived, yet still so rarely knit / In all its parts,—it's wisdom to its wit, / And doubt to faith, loathing to love, so fit,— / It seems like one that lived, and lives again!" In Kean he saw what he had seen "Oft in a day-dream, when my youth was green,— / The Dane himself," and said of him that "He seems to move as in a world ideal," that "Or Kean or Hamlet,—what I see is real!" (*LA*, pp. 367-69). 13. Kean appeared in Boston in *Hamlet* on 19 February 1821. His season lasted from 12 February to 7 March, during which time he also played in *Richard III*, *Othello*, *The Merchant of Venice*, *Macbeth*, *King Lear*, and *The Iron Chest*, by George Colman *(Boston Daily Advertiser)*. WA probably saw him first in London, where he made his first appearance at the Drury Lane Theatre on 26 January 1814, playing *Hamlet* among other roles.

106. To Charles Robert Leslie Boston, 20th May, 1821.

Dear Leslie: So many things must have been done in the Art since you last wrote,[1] that I begin to feel not a little impatient for some account of them; but as I have so longed owed you a letter, I have no right to expect one from you till I pay my debt: so I must e'en, lazy as I am, write to you. Of you and Newton I occasionally hear from such of our countrymen as have met you in London; but they seldom give any distinct account of what either of you are doing; of which, however, the Newspapers sometimes speak, after *their manner,* with more conceit of their own judgment, than distinctness in their <descript> criticisms. The last account which I have seen of you in the latter, was of your "Gypsying Party;" which was almost a year back. I am pleased to find that Newton's last picture, the Importunate Author, from Moliere,[2] was so generally admired. I can have little notion of the picture, it being in a branch of Art he has engaged in since I left London; but from the variety of notices, & all favourable, which I have seen of it, I conclude it must have been generally liked by the Artists, from whom the Newspaper Critics, especially when they agree in praising, <glean [?]> always take their tone.—I hope when you write, to hear that you are engaged on some great Historical Work. And yet I have no reason, <for> except the wish that you might do justice to your genius, for such a hope, as I am aware that such works could not be undertaken without more of the "dirtry trash," alias money, than I believe you have the good fortune to command. If however you can lay up sufficient from the profits of such small pictures as you have lately done and got so much reputation for, I cannot help thinking it a duty which you owe to yourself, and to Posterity, to devote occasionally some portion of your life to the highest department of Art. When you have, as I trust you will not long be without, such sufficient means to carry you through, I do not think even in point of interest <it will> that your time will be thrown away should you devote a year or two to some one great work; for independent of the fame, which I would be willing to insure you, you might perhaps find it <more> profitable by a separate *exhibition* on your own account, than would even a dozen smaller pictures, such as you might paint at the same time. <With your masterly [?] knowledge of the figure, your taste [?] in and [word undecipherable] and [word undecipherable] in expression I should be greatly mistaken if you wouldn't find any rival [?] in England but> By the Bye, have you seen a criticism on <his> Haydon's Entrance of our Saviour into Jerusalem in an article on the state of the Arts in England, in a late Number of the Edinburgh Review?[3] The praise it gives I think just: but cannot say the same of all the censure; one point however in the letter seems well founded—the want of those subtle niceties and inflections in the outlines which make so great a part of the charm in some of the old masters; it was what I always felt the want of in nearly all the pictures of modern date. With respect to the rest of the Review, it is little better than <unnecessary> gross libel on the English School. The speculations of the writer seem to be those of a man who, in hunting after originality, runs down a common thought, till it falls to pieces, then putting it again together, and by sticking on the head where the tail was, is astonished to find what an extraordinary animal he has been chasing. It is a dangerous thing for a writer to think of his own cleverness when he is engaged in the cause of truth; the interest of the cause is too apt to become subordinate to the eclat of the pleader's wit.

But it is time that I say something of myself. Various circumstances have prevented me recommencing with Belshazzer till last September; since which I have, with one interruption, been constantly at work on it. On seeing it at a greater distance, in my present room, I found that I had got my point of distance too near, and the point of sight too high.[4] It was a sore task to change the perspective in so large a picture; but I had the courage to do it; and, by lowering the latter, and increasing the former, I find the effect improved a hundred fold. I have spared no labour to get every thing that came within the laws of perspective correct: even the very bannisters in the gallery are put in by rule. Now it is over, I do not regret the toil, for it has given me a deeper knowledge of perspective than I ever had before; for I could not do that, and many things in the picture which are seen from below, without pretty hard fagging at the "Jesuit."[5] I have besides made several changes in the composition which are for the better; such as introducing two enormous flights of steps, beyond the table, leading up to the inner appartment. These steps are supposed to extend wholly across the hall; and the first landing place is crowded with figures, which being just discernible in the darkness that will shroud that part of the composition, I think will have a powerful effect on the imagination. I suppose them to be principally Jews, exulting in the overthrow of the Idols, and their own restoration, as prophesied by Jeremiah, Isaiah and others,[6] which I think their actions sufficiently explain. The Gallery too is also crowded; the figures there foreshortended as they would appear seen from below—I have written Collins by this opportunity, and given him a list of what I have done since I have been here. Believe me affectionately your friend

Wa. Allston.

[In the margins] Together with this you will receive a letter for Mr. Dutton,[7] who wishes you to paint a picture for him. You will see by his letter that he leaves the subject to you. Mr. D. is a very particular friend of mine, and he has a *real passion* for the Art. His taste also, considering the few good pictures he has seen, is refined and just. You could paint for no one who would more value your works. I could not name a man who takes more pleasure in pictures; so I hope you may find it convenient to gratify him.—I have a piece of news for you—no less than that I am engaged to be married. The finishing Belshazzer is all I wait for to be once more a happy husband.—Remember me most affectionately to Mr. Coleridge and Mr. & Mrs. Gilman. Tell them I can *never* forget them: also to the Morgans, and to Newton & the Messrs. Williams, & to Collard & Lonsdale. When you see Ward & Thompson pray present them my respects. I wish it because they were particularly cordial when I last saw them. And do not forget me to Willes, Martin, The Lewises[8] Brockedon, and Mr. Carey, & Mrs. Bridgen & family; and to Haydon.

If you have never read Brown's[9] novels I recommend you to read them. They are works of great Genius: Wieland & Arthur Mervyn particularly are terrific. I never read them till last winter. He is the brother of your friend Mr. J. Brown.[10] When you sent out the Prints for Judge Jackson, you mentioned Bird's Chevy Chase. If you have not already bought it, I with you would not, for it is badly engraved. I hope you will be able to send out the remainder by the return of Capt. Tracy. Among the pictures mentioned in Collins' letter I <think> consider Jeremiah and Miriam the Prophetess the best I have done here; the last is perhaps the best I ever painted; in the background of which is seen the shore of the red sea and <the> on it the wreck of Pharao's army.

ADDRESSED: Charles R. Leslie [Esqre.] [page torn] / N 8 Buckingham [Place] [page torn] / Fitzroy Squ[are] [page torn] / London / Ship / London Packet. SOURCE: Manuscript. Printed in part in Flagg, pp. 165-67. The copy made by RHD is annotated "No 3," the third letter he copied of the three from WA to Collins.

1. Apparently when Leslie wrote on 14 March 1820. 2. From the ballet comedy *Les Facheux* 3.3. 3. The article was a review in the *Edinburgh Magazine* for August 1820 of Joseph Farrington's *Memoirs of the Life of Sir Joshua Reynolds* (1819), which disparaged English art in general, naming West, Fuseli, and Haydon, calling Haydon a young man of promise whose *Christ's Entry into Jerusalem* was merely a sketch for a great picture. 4. WA was led to change the perspective in *Belshazzar's Feast* after Stuart's criticism. 5. Andrea Pozzo (1642-1709), Italian painter and architect, was a member of the Jesuit order. His *Perspectiva Pictorum et Architectorum . . . Prospettiva des Pittori e Architetti* was first published in 1693-1700. It first appeared in English as *Rules and Examples of Perspective, Proper for Painters and Architects, etc. In English and Latin. Engraved, & tr. John James* (London, 1707), to which WA probably refers. 6. Jer. 30-33; Isa. 40-55. Prophecies of the destruction of pagan nations and the restoration of the Jewish state are also contained in most of the other Old Testament prophetical books. 7. Warren Dutton. There seems to be no record of Leslie's painting a picture for him. 8. Frederick C. Lewis and presumably his two brothers, George Robert (1782-1871), a landscape and portrait painter, and Charles (1786-1836), a bookbinder. 9. Charles Brockden Brown (1771-1819), American novelist in the Gothic tradition. His *Wieland* was published in 1778 and *Arthur Mervyn* in 1799. 10. James Brown. A native of Philadelphia, he was for many years a merchant there (*Philadelphia City Directory* for 1785-1810; David Lee Clark, *Charles Brockdon Brown: Pioneer Voice of America* [Durham: Duke Univ. Press, 1952], pp. 15, 126, 155-57, 181, 194). After moving to England he lived at Snaresbrook, a suburb of London near Epping Forest. He was very attentive to Leslie and Morse shortly after they came to London, and Leslie dined with him and his wife on more than one occasion and apparently painted a picture of her and her dog (Leslie, p. 184). He was still living in 1833 (Dunlap, 2:242).

107. To Henry Pickering Boston, 3 July, 1821.

My dear Sir, If you can make it convenient to favour me with a visit on thursday next at one o'clock, I shall be happy to shew you the picture of Miriam, it being now finished. I wish I had something *more* to make it worth the journey; but as you expressed a wish to see Miriam again, I thought you would be pleased to know when I had completed it.

With sincere respect, / Yrs / W. Allston

ADDRESSED: Henry Pickering Esqre. / Salem—. SOURCE: Manuscript.

108. To Henry Pickering Boston, 13 July, 1821.

My dear Sir: Feeling as I do most truly grateful for your very kind letter, and the high opinion with which you have honoured my last and former efforts, it becomes still more painful to me to make any reply not accordant with your wishes. Indeed I should hardly know how to do it did not former experience of your candour, as well as kindness, lead me, in the present instance, to hope for your indulgence.

Though I have finished many pictures which I did not wish to paint at the *precise time* when they were done, I have yet never undertaken one *subject which I did not feel;* and it has ever seemed to me impossible that I could *otherwise* produce a picture worthy any one's possession. I know not whether my own feelings mix more with my works than those of other Artists do with theirs, but I am well convinced that my hand would be powerless were I to attempt a subject foreign to them. The feelings with which I painted the *Group*[1] you allude to have long since passed away from me; and as a work of art I cannot now approve of it; to copy it therefore, with its present imperfections, would be painful; and to amend it, without any sympathy or pleasure in the subject, would, I more than fear, be impossible.

This is a simple statement of what I conceive to be a painter's mind; it may not be true of other artists, but I feel it to be so of myself. Shall I therefore hope for your indulgence? and that you will allow me, when the completion of Belshazzer shall have put it in my power, to substitute *some other subject*.

I hardly need repeat, for I trust you do justice to my sincerity, that it will give me unfeigned pleasure to know that you are the professor of another effort of my pencil: and allow me to add, that knowing as I do the high esteem with which you honour my productions, and the gratification they afford you, I could not have a stronger inducement to execute whatever I may attempt for you according to the *best* of my ability.

Believe me, dear Sir, / Yours / W. Allston

At some future time I shall be most happy to furnish you with the *catalogue*.[2]

ADDRESSED: Henry Pickering Esqre. / Salem. SOURCE: Manuscript.

1. Possibly WA refers to *The Dead Man Restored*. His regret at having introduced the figures of the mother and daughter and his dissatisfaction with all the figures except the dead man seem to suggest it. It was his principal "group" painting to this time and the most celebrated.
2. Possibly WA refers to the catalog of thirty-two pages prepared by James Christie of the items in West's collection of works of art sold in 1820 (Alberts, p. 387).

109. From Charles Robert Leslie London August 30th 1821

My dear Sir: I received your letter of May 20th some time ago & ought to have answered it earlier. I was not standing on ceremony before I received it, for my friends here would witness for me that I have *talked* of writing to you constantly for the last six months. Have at you then—without more words.

(I had heard, some time before I received your confirmation of it the report of your intended marriage & also the lady's name which by the bye you do not mention. I am exceedingly anxious to hear more about her. Why did you not give me a description of her in your letter? From her having such a brother as I have often heard you describe Mr. E. Dana to be, & from the husband she is to have, I cannot but infer the lady to be very superlative. I hope however you will give me a particular description of her in your next.)

I am sure the alterations you have made in your "Belshazzer" must have improved it. A low point of sight is certainly essential to a large picture which must necessarily be hung above the eye of the spectator; the reverse is very injurious to the effect of Raphael's Cartoons.[1] I wish very much some of your late pictures could find their way here. The Academy I believe are a little disappointed that you have sent them nothing since your election. Could not some of those you have sold be borrowed for the purpose? There would be scarcely any risk in it. You are remembered here with the greatest admiration by everybody acquainted with art & your particular friends are all anxious that you should keep such recollections alive. For myself I feel every day more & more what I have lost in you & feed myself with the hope that you will one day return to England. I have little prospect at present of going to America.

You naturally wish to rouse me to do something in the style of art you are fondest of. But I believe I must for the present, be content with a humbler sphere. My inclinations lead me to subjects of familiar life & manners & what I have done in that way has been more successful than anything else. My last picture was "May-Day in the reign of Queen Elizabeth," which is in some respects an antiquarian picture as I took pains to adhere as closely as possible to the costume & manners of the time. It contains more figures than any thing I have painted. I have sold it for two hundred guineas. I have been lately studying the Dutch School a good deal & find my fondness for those admirable matter-of-fact painters increase in proportion to my acquaintance with them. The two Mr. Hopes have united their galleries in one & it now presents the finest collection of Dutch & Flemish masters I ever saw.[2]

The exhibition this year was considered a very good one though there was nothing of any importance in the historic class, excepting Allan's "Death of Archbishop Sharpe."[3] This picture like all of his, was full of powerful & natural expression. What struck me as its principal fault was a family likeness in some of the heads as if he had used the same model too frequently. Wilkie had two small pictures. The one I liked the best was an interior of a cottage in which there was a young man writing a letter to his sweetheart who was coming in unexpectedly behind him & blinding his eyes with her hands. He called it "Guess my name." The expression was excellent & the light & shadow quite magical but the color of the flesh was very yellow & leathery, a fault he has got into in his late pictures. His other picture I did not like so well. It consisted of a group of figures the principal of which was a baker with a roast shoulder of mutton on a tray on his head, listening to a young girl who was seated on a stile reading a newspaper. It appeared that in aiming to get light in the picture he had run into the error that Sir Geo. Beaumont complains is so common to the English school, of mistaking *whiteness* for *brightness*. Mulready[4] had a picture of a boy who had been sent on an errand & had stopped by the way to play marbles having set down a young child & a pound of candles in the sun. A servant girl had detected & was just about to give him a thrashing. Parts of it were very fine but as a whole I did not like it so well as his last picture. Lawrence quite surpassed himself this year. He sent the whole length of Mr. West which he has painted for the New York Academy.[5] The head of it I think the finest thing he ever painted. He had also a very fine whole length of the Marquis of Londonderry, a beautiful picture of Lady Louisa Lambton & another of Mrs. Henry Baring & her children.[6] Collins had three very fine pictures. One, a beautiful thing of children fishing with a mountainous background. By the bye he was very much delighted at receiving your letter which I suppose he has answered by this time. He is now in the north of Devonshire. Newton's picture of the importunate Author was very successful. The story was most happily told and with great delicacy of humor. An author, (not a poor threadbare one but a man of fashion by his dress) had got hold of a young nobleman by the arm & was reading with great appearance of self satisfaction a huge manuscript, while the gallant was secretly looking at his watch as if he had some appointment which he was anxious to keep & was yet too polite to interrupt the poet. The dresses were of the time of Louis 14th & the scene on a terrace in an old-fashioned French garden. He sold it to Mr. Hope & has painted a duplicate of it for the Earle of Carlisle[7] & is to make another copy for Mr. Murray,[8] the bookseller. Newton has another picture which I think will surpass it. It is a quarrel between fashionable lovers. They are returning miniatures teasing [?] [page torn] while the lady's maid is standing behind the chair of her mistress looking at them. It is in the same costume as the other & the effect of color [is very] beautiful. W. Irving has returned to London & is preparing another book for the press.[9] His "Sketch book" has made him one of the most popular authors of the day. When in Paris he became very intimate with Moore with whom he was very much pleased.[10] Coleridge & the Gillmans were very glad to hear that I had got a letter from you. They talk about you very much whenever I see them which I am sorry to say is not very often.

Haydon has been exhibiting a small picture (for him) of Our Saviour in the Garden, which is the worst thing he has painted. He is going on with the "Raising of Lazarus." West's great picture of the Duke of Wellington[11] is now exhibiting but I fear it [page torn] -ful. The allegory is so very complicated that nobody can [page torn] it. There are some fine bits of colour in it but the [page torn] is very gaudy. The figures are terribly [page torn] even the *animals* are unnatural. Mr. West's sons[12] have built a magnificent gallery in Newman Street & are exhibiting there the principal large pictures of their father. Martin's picture of your subject (Belshazzer) made more noise among the *mass of people* than any picture that has been exhibited since I have been here. The artists however & connoisseurs did not like it much. It was first exhibited at the gallery & drew such crowds that they kept it open a fortnight longer than usual solely on account of that picture. The directors gave him 200 guineas as a premium & the picture was bought for *eight hundred* by a speculator who immediately opened an exhibition of it himself & has made a great deal of money by it. Brockedon is married & has gone to the Continent. Willes is fixed in your old painting room 22 Charlotte Street. I sometimes see Mrs. Morgan & Miss Brent. Mrs. M. is the principal governess in the National School, Baldwin gardens.[13] She complains very much of the fatigue of it. I have not seen Collard for some time. He has got another child, a little girl. Newton, Irving, Willes, Martin &c all desire me to remember them affectionately to you when I write. Mrs. Bridgen's family all beg to be remembered, not omitting Betsy who often tells me I am not half as good as Mr. Allston, indeed she despairs of ever seeing so *nice* a man again. Farewell, my dear sir, & may heaven bless & prosper you in all your undertakings is the sincere wish of,

Yours affectionately, / C.R. Leslie

ADDRESSED: W. Allston Esqr / Boston / Masstts. SOURCE: Manuscript, Houghton. Printed in part in Flagg, pp. 167-71.

1. Ten designs made by Raphael for tapestries for the Sistine Chapel. 2. The art collectors Henry Philip Hope (d. 1839), whose particular interest was Dutch and Flemish painting and whose collection was in Arklow House, Connaught Place, and his brother Thomas Hope (1770?-1831), whose speciality was ancient sculptures and vases and whose house was in Dorchester Street. 3. William Sharp (1618-87), Scottish divine, was murdered by his enemies in the conflict between church and state. 4. William Mulready (1786-1863), English genre and landscape painter. 5. The NAD. 6. Charles William Stewart (afterward Vane), 3d marquis of Londonderry (1778-1854); Lady Louisa Elizabeth Grey (1797-1841), wife of John George Lambton, 1st earl of Durham; Mrs. Henry Baring, wife of the younger brother of Alexander Baring, Baron Ashburton, at that time head of Baring Brothers, the family banking house. 7. George Howard, 6th earl of Carlisle (1773-1848). 8. John Murray (1778-1843), head of the publishing house of that name founded by his father. 9. *Bracebridge Hall; or The Humorists* (1822). 10. Thomas Moore (1779-1852), Irish poet. At this time he gave Irving the idea for the composition of *Bracebridge Hall* and for "Buckthorne" in *Tales of a Traveller* (Williams, 1:202). 11. Arthur Wellesley, 1st duke of Wellington (1769-1852). 12. Raphael Lamar West (1766-1850) and Benjamin West, Jr. "West's New Gallery" was an addition to the house at 14 Newman Street where West lived from 1774 until his death (Alberts, pp. 524, 387, 388, 39-92, 116). 13. Not further identified.

110. To Charles Robert Leslie Boston, 7th Sepbr. 1821.

Dear Leslie. With this you will receive the second number of the "Idle Man,"[1] which I sent by Mr. Welles,[2] and concerning which I then wrote you fully.[3] All I have now to add on the subject is, that should any Bookseller agree to republish them in London, you will request him to designate some bookseller, or agent (his correspondent) in *Liverpool,* to whom the manuscripts from this country may be <[word undecipherable]> transmitted. Mr. Dana wishes this arrangement made, on account of the infrequency of opportunities direct to London from this port, whereas, to Liverpool they regularly occur every month.—A second number was forwarded to you from New York: but I send you another in case of that failing.—I hope soon to hear from you on this subject, and *all too* about *yourself,* which last I hope you will make a long story, as indeed you ought.

I congratulate you with all my heart on the success of your "May-day."[4] The story that we have here is that you sold it for three hundred guineas, and Mr. Sully,[5] who is now in Boston, says it is true. I have seen some account of it in the newspapers; the Examiner's[6] however is the only English one I have met with. I could have wished to have seen a description from a more discriminating critic. I shall not forgive you if you do not give me the "whole history" of it. <[three lines undecipherable]> Tell me all that the artists have said of it—and others out of art, whose opinion is of value. After your exit, let the next that enters for my entertainment be Collins, and Newton, and Ward's Great Picture,[7] and Martin and Willes: You must have by this time a vast deal to tell me about them all.— By the bye, I saw an account of Martin's Belshazzer[8] in Blackwood's Magazine,[9] which I read with great delight, and the more so when it was added to the description that he had not only received 200 guineas premium from the British Institution, but sold it afterwards for 800.[10] I suppose he would not paint *fans* now unless the sticks were made of gold.—It is delightful to hear of such success of those who really deserve it, and especially when they happen to be those whom we also esteem as men. Tell Martin I would have got up before sun rise,[11] and walked twenty miles to have seen his picture: which is saying a great deal for me, who have seen the sun rise about as often as Falstaff saw his knees, and who had almost rather stand an hour on my head than walk a mile.

As I have given either you or Collins, when I wrote by Captn. Tracy, as full an account of what [I] have done, I shall not say any more on the subject at present, except that I am still hard at work on Belshazzer and [page torn] shall so continue until it is completed. [Rest of page cut out.][12]

[In the margins] The Gentleman who will hand you this is Dr. Joshua Hayward, brother to Dr. Hayward[13] whom you lately knew England. His brother I understand has given him a letter of introduction to you; otherwise I should have done it. He is an excellent young man—rather diffident—but of cultivated mind. He has a passion for painting and wished to be a painter; but his friends dissuaded him from it. He goes to attend the Hospitals in London. Remember me to all my friends & you know whom without my specifying them. Mr. Sully sends you his warmest regards, and desires me to say that there is nothing in his power to do for you in Philadelphia which would not give him pleasure.[14] He is a right worthy man and I am as much pleased with him as I expected to be, from the account of his friends. Tell Collins he owes me a letter. [Page torn] N.B. Will you be particular in choosing such as will keep their points—half of those which Mr. Brown[15] sent me are quite useless, spreading like fingers.

ADDRESSED: [page cut out] [Charles] R. Leslie Esqre. / Buckingham Place, / Fitzroy Square. / London. / [page torn] ard. SOURCE: Manuscript. Printed in part in Flagg, pp. 171-72.

1. RHD's periodical the *Idle Man* (1821-22) consisted of six numbers of fiction, poetry, and essays. He edited it and wrote most of the fiction. No. 2 (1821) contained WA's "The Hypochondriac." Evidently WA had sent Leslie no. 1 several months earlier. It contained his poem "Written in Spring." 2. Benjamin Welles. 3. This letter does not seem to have been preserved. It was written probably in June or July, after WA's last letter to Leslie on 20 May. No. 1 of *The Idle Man* was deposited for copyright on 18 May and reviewed for the first time on 23 June. 4. It was exhibited at the RA and engraved by James Henry Watt. 5. Sully came to Boston in July to copy Granet's *Choir of the Capuchin Monastery.* Henry Sargent gave him four months in which to do it, WA five, and Stuart six. When he did it in three WA thought it must be a sketch only, but acknowledged it was a carefully finished copy. (Dunlap, 2:140, 165). 6. The review appeared on 20 May 1821. 7. James Ward's *Landscape with Cattle*. It was acquired by the National Gallery for £1500 at the suggestion of West. 8. Martin said that the subject of Belshazzar's feast was suggested to him by WA's intention to paint it, that they disagreed about the composition, but that WA finally approved his plan. 9. *Blackwood's Edinburgh Magazine*, a monthly periodical founded in 1817 by William Blackwood, who was the editor from a few months after it began until his death in 1834. Martin's painting was praised in the issue for March 1821 at the time of its exhibition at the BI. 10. WA had obviously not received Leslie's letter of 30 August, in which he reported the popularity of the painting. 11. Though he occasionally referred to sunrise in his poems and was impressed by one he saw at Lake Maggiore, WA was noted for his late rising in the morning. Others, besides his brother William and Jarvis earlier, commented on it. According to Sweetser, Martin's reply to his message was that it came from a "bad walker and a worse riser," and once when Sarah Clarke told him she was painting a sunrise and rose early to see it, he asked, "How *does* it look?" (pp. 122, 138). 12. In this portion of his letter WA asked Leslie to procure from Thomas Brown "pencils &c." Leslie cut it out to save the trouble of copying it (RHD, p. 9, Addition). He also ordered from Brown, presumably at the same time, several colors. 13. George Haywood (1791-1863), Boston surgeon. From 1826 he was professor of surgery and clinical surgery at the Harvard Medical School and from 1835 to 1849 was attached to Massachusetts General Hospital in Boston (John Ward Dean, "History of the Register of Deaths," *NEGHR* 18 [1864]: 91; S.K. Lothrop, "Memoir of Nathaniel Bowditch, Esq.," *Proceedings of the MHS*, 1st ser., 1860-62, 5 [1862]: 506). 14. Leslie lived in Philadelphia during his youth, from 1800 to 1811. 15. Thomas Brown, Sr.

111. To Thomas Sully

Thursday Evening Oct 4 [1821]

My dear Sir: If you are not better engaged, I should be most happy to see you, to chat an hour or two, at Juliens.[1] I say this because I am engaged at ½ past *nine*. I have made several attempts to see you. But we seem to have been at cross purposes.

Yrs sincerely / W. Allston

ADDRESSED: T. Sully Esqre. / at Mrs. Fessenden's[2] / next the Atheneum.[3] ANNOTATED: Allston. Boston / No 13 / This note of Washington Allston, the American Titian, to Mr. Sully the portrait painter, was given me by the latter in 1830 / Robert Gilmor. SOURCE: Manuscript, Wellesley College Library.

1. Julien's was a restaurant on Milk Street in Bŏston for many years (*Boston City Directory* for 1800 and later). 2. Abigail Fessenden, a widow, who had a boardinghouse on Tremont Street in Boston from 1813 to 1823. An Abigail M. Fessenden had a boarding house during the same years at various locations in the city (*Boston City Directory* for 1813-23). 3. The BA was located at this time in the Rufus Amory house on Tremont Street (Jane S. Knowles, "Changing Images of the Boston Athenaeum," in *Change and Continuity. A Pictorial History of the Athenaeum* [Boston, 1976], p. 6; Swan, p. 3).

112. To Charles Robert Leslie Boston, 13 Novbr. 1821.

Dear Leslie: I send you many thanks for your letter of August 30th but have not time just now to send you such an answer as it deserves. I will write again, however, soon. At present I can do no more than let you know that I am alive and well.—

You will receive with this, by Captn. Tracy, the Third Number of the "Idle Man." The preceding Numbers, I suppose you have long since got, together with my letters concerning them; wherefore I shall say nothing more now on the subject. (I am looking every day for an answer to them.) I take the liberty also to send, to your care, a packet for Sir Walter Scott, which I must beg the favour of you to forward to him. If he is not in London,[1] you can easily get it to him by leaving it at *his* Bookseller, if, as <which> I suppose, he has one there. If not, by any other means you can. I will make no apology for saddling you with this commission, knowing how much you delight in serving your friends. The Packet to Sir Walter is from my friend Mr. D. <and> containing the three Numbers of his work. It is accompanied by a letter—but without his name—only signed "the Author." He has <purposely> omitted his name from delicacy—which I think very proper, to shew that he does not mean to obtrude him upon Sir W's acquaintance.—I wish you not to make known the contents of the packet to any one—and not to say from whom it comes.

I am rejoiced to hear that Irving is coming out with "another work."[2] By your calling it so, I conclude it is something distinct from the "Sketch Book"—I hope a Novel, or Romance. Every one here is impatient for something more from him. Remember me affectionately to him and Collins & Collard and Coleridge, the Gilmans & Morgans, remember me too to Newton, Mrs. Bridgen & family & all who ask after me.—I think Collins owes me two letters.—I have not a moment more—so I must stop, begging you not to consider this as a letter—but to look for one before a long time.

Yours affectionately / W. Allston.

I wrote you last by Mr. B. Welles—you say nothing in your letter about the remainder of Judge Jackson's Prints. I suppose those you were waiting for are not yet out of the Engravers hands. Do not omit to send your Anne Page.

ADDRESSED: [Half the torn page off] Leslie Esqre. [Buc] kingham Place / [Fitz-] roy Square / London. SOURCE: Manuscript.

1. Scott spent most of his life at Abbotsford, his estate in Scotland, but often made visits to London. He was there from March to May 1815, in early 1820, when he saw both Irving and Leslie, and in 1821 (*The Life of Sir Walter Scott* [Edinburgh, 1902-1903], 5:33-47, 6:182-99, 271-79; Leslie, p. 42). There seems to be no evidence that he and WA ever met. The chief publishing houses with which he was associated were Ballantyne and Company and Constable and Company of Edinburgh, but he also had dealings with Murray and Longman and Company of London.
2. *Bracebridge Hall*, published on 21 May 1822 in New York, on 23 May in London (Willams, 1:439).

113. From Francis Bayard Winthrop New York Novr 17th 1821

Dear Sir: As we are not generally disposed to take it kindly of our friends when they remind us of engagements made and promises broken, I fear this letter will not prove acceptable to you. Perhaps it ought not to be written at all; and an engagement which might be considered in some degree *extorted*, should hardly be looked upon in the light of a promise. Still as it was made in good faith, as it arose out of peculiar circumstances, and was evidently formed on kind and generous feelings, there seems some reason, nay even propriety in relying upon it, and that it could never be other than the intention of the maker to fulfill it. You will see that I refer to an enagagement of yours to present me with a small picture of your execution, arising out of various circumstances connected with the purchase of a picture I once made from you, and about which several letters passed between us.[1] You will also probably recollect the correspondence so far as that I thought (whether well or ill founded) that I had some claim upon you, and that you admitted it in so much, as to make the engagement alluded to. This was repeated after your return to Boston. I know well what your engagements have been since that time. I do not therefore write with the intention of upbraiding you with want of good faith. Nor do I intend to appeal to your honor or generosity. The first would be unfair and unkind, the last unnecessary. I trust I have nothing to do but to remind you of what probably owing to more important and pressing avocations you may have forgotten, and what I cannot but yet believe you intend to perform. Excuse the liberty I have taken and allow me to subscribe

Yr friend & Obdt Servt / Francis B. Winthrop

W. Allston Esqr

ADDRESSED: Washington Allston Esqr / Historical Painter / Boston post pd. SOURCE: Manuscript.

1. There seems to be no record of this correspondence.

114. To Francis Bayard Winthrop Boston, 23rd Novbr. 1821.

Dear Sir: I have received your letter of the [space blank][1] and though I think some expressions in it might well have been spared, yet from the general tenor of it, and particularly the conclusion, I am led to believe that it was not your intention to offend; I have therefore read it without any unfriendly feelings, and am willing to take it in good part.

Why I made the *"Engagement"* [in] my first letter to you, from London, has already [been] explained. I made it voluntarily: and having made it, I considered it as sacred—and as what it was my religious intention to perform whenever my necessities would allow me. Although made so many years since, I have not, as you suppose, forgotten it; I feel it now, and have ever felt it to be as binding and sacred as then; nor was I capable, even for a moment, of entertaining a wish to elude it: on the contrary, it has been one of the sorest mortifications I could have experienced to have been thus compelled by pecuniary embarrassments so often to postpone its fulfilment.

In this, as in all other cases, the shortest and best way is to state the plain truth.—When I returned to America my finances were at so low an ebb, that, repugnant as it was to my inclination, I was constrained to lay aside, and suspend the finishing of, a large Picture I had begun and brought with me from England—to give up this Picture on which rested my only hope of in some degree retrieving the competence I had sacrificed in the acquisition of my Art—and to devote myself without delay to such smaller works as would provide for my immediate support. This was my only course for avoiding the misery of <being> involving myself in debt. And I had hoped, and calculated, that one year devoted to these would supply me with funds sufficient not only for the finishing of Belshazzer (the large picture) but for the fulfilment of my engagement with you. On the strength of this hope I wrote you from this place, expressing my expectation to that effect. Had my calculation turned out correct, I should long before this have finished both Belshazzer and your picture. But so far from this was the event, that at the end of the year, [word undecipherable] I found myself, <at the> in spite of economy, wholly unable to effect more than the mere paying my expenses and keeping clear of debt. I have never found the sale of one picture more than sufficient to support me during the time afterward occupied by the next; nay, it has often been inadequate even for that.—Thus have I been uniformly foiled in almost all my plans for years past—finding myself at the end of each but little better than at the beginning.—

A year ago last September I recommenced Belshazzer, and by this autumn it would have been completed had not an exhausted purse again obliged me to give it up for six months. I have now a third time resumed it; and though the fruits of those six months are already diminished to less than an hundred and fifty dollars, I trust it is also the *last* time; for I have made up my mind rather to borrow money (which I must soon do) than thus fritter away my time for a bare daily subsistence. I can produce nothing approaching to excellence large or small without labour; my pictures therefore for the most part cost a length of time very disproportioned to the prices I have charged for them. But I cannot paint for mere profit, or leave a picture when I know that I can still improve it.[2] Could I have done so I might have been rich before this.

<It is> I am far from <my intention> intending by any of these remarks to attach blame to any one; I could not with justice do it. And it is far, very far from my intention to cast even a shadow of blame on the inhabitants of this Town; on the contrary I shall always remember and acknowledge their kind and ever ready patronage with the warmest gratitude.[3]—The fault, if any, lies with myself, in my not having charged more for my pictures. But I was led into this error by the apprehension that if I charged European prices I should find no purchasers.—I have *now,* however, good reason for believing that this apprehension was unfounded; and that I shall hereafter find a ready sale for my works at double their present prices.

This statement of facts will shew you, sir, how little it has been in my power to follow my inclinations, and consequently how little able I have been to fulfill my engagement with you.*

I have now only to add that your picture is *begun*—and that I mean to proceed with it at the same time (that is by intervals) with Belshazzer; and hope to complete both in the course of the ensuing summer.—I had begun another picture for you several months ago, but not being quite satisfied with the composition, I gave that up. With the composition [of] [page torn] the present one I am pleased.[4]—Your obdnt. Serv[t] [last letter and signature torn out]

*I must, however, in candour blame myself for not having made them (these facts) known to you before; for being a stranger to you, I had no right to suppose that you could know the motives which governed me.

ADDRESSED, in RHD's hand: To Fra. B. Winthrop / From Wa. Allston SOURCE: Manuscript.

1. 17 November 1821. 2. WA was well known for this principle. The consequence was that he often took longer than expected to complete a work, which ultimately cost him more than he had estimated. 3. WA was one of the best patronized artists in America of his or any day. Of the forty-seven in the exhibition of his paintings in 1839 only one was owned by him and it was done in college. Mrs. Jameson obseved that if his "genuis languished" in America it was not for want of patronage or praise, adding, "Whenever a picture left his easel there were many to compete for it" ("Washington Allston," p. 15). 4. Nothing further is known of these paintings.

115. To Richard Henry Dana

Boston,
Tuesday, 23 April 1822.

My dear Sir: I enclose you a letter I received, by Cap. Tracy, from Leslie.[1] You will be pleased to find his previous silence so well accounted for—and still more that Coleridge entertains so high an opinion of your book.—I know Colburn,[2] the bookseller he mentions, very well by *reputation*—and have frequently heard him spoken of, as L. says, as a liberal & enterprising man. I know also that he holds the next rank to Murray—and would be more likely to make a book sell than any other bookseller after him—I cannot help hoping that Coleridge's written recommendation, (which it seems was handed him with the work) will go a great way in inducing him to engage in it. Should he do so, he has good means of making it known; being the proprietor, <was> as well as publisher, of the Literary Gazette,[3] and publisher of the New Monthly Magazine.—I would thank you to take care of the letter—as I wish to have it again.

Yrs sincerely / W. Allston

ADDRESSED: Richard H. Dana Esqre. / Cambridge. SOURCE: Manuscript.

1. This letter does not seem to have been preserved. 2. Henry Colburn (d. 1855), London publisher. 3. The *Literary Gazette* (1817-62), a weekly publication, which was edited by William Jerdan and had a series of literary contributors.

116. To Richard Henry Dana Boston, 30th April, 1822.

My dear Sir: I enclose you a letter which I have just received from Leslie.[1] From Colburn's proposal, it appears to me that he wishes *first*, by publishing in *extracts*, to feel the pulse of <which the public [word undecipherable] that> the public before he ventures on the publication of your work entire. And I also think, from the *reservation* which he makes, that a favourable reception of the former will induce him to undertake the latter. You should not feel discouraged by this partial <offer> proposal; for Captain Tracy, in a conversation this evening about Irving, and the reported price of his new work,[2] told me that <My> when he offered the Sketch Book, notwithstanding the recommendation of Scott, Murray hesitated a long time before he would undertake it. I know the London Booksellers well—nearly as well as if I had dealt with them all my life—for I have known those by whom they were best known; They are proverbially timid; <and with> nor do I wonder at it when literary success has so much of the lottery in it.—<Colburn how> Considering Colburn as influenced by the caution of his calling, I think his offer of ten guineas a sheet a very liberal one; for I remember that Coleridge once told me, the highest price he ever got as a writer of the "Monthly Review,"[3] when that work took the lead of its kind, was but three guineas a sheet.—<In all events,> On the whole, I think the proposal, tho' not what might be wished, worth considering. The Magazine alluded to in the letter is the *New Monthly*, which, you know, has an extensive circulation in this country. And the republication of any articles of your Work in that will of course give it an eclat here with many who would not otherwise venture to form an opinion of it; <The Work> and no doubt very materially increase its circulation.

I last night again read the "Son,"[4] in the Second Number; and I may say to you (though with much better reason) what an artist once said to me, after looking at one of my pictures: "Now, sir, you may go to sleep; for you have done that which will <do> make your way free." My picture did not merit this; but it seems to have been bestowed on me <[undecipherable word]> as one of those fairy gifts, which I was to hold in trust till I should meet with one who deserved it. I could wish then that you would take no thought about the success of your book; but let it work its way: and, its *way it will have*.

Yours sincerely, / W. Allston.

I did not mention the "Son" because I think it better than your *last*,[5] or the *third* Number, or "Domestic Life,"[6] which I do not;) but because I examined it *critically* as a *literary performance*.—Setting aside its pathos (which indeed is to take away its soul) it still presents, in its style, (to continue the figure) one of the most beautiful bodies to be found in the creation of any modern writer. For, fine as the thoughts are, I could find nothing to *forgive*, for their sake, in the expression; in other words, they both seemed to unite, like soul and body, making a living whole, and beautiful as living.—

"It is better to give than to receive," is the only aphorism recorded of our Saviour.[7] Let the pleasure then which you give to others be a consolation to you in your afflictions;[8] I should say rather, the good you do—for no one, I should think, could read the Tale I have been speaking of without being, or, at least, wishing to become, a better man.

ADDRESSED: Richard H. Dana Esqre. / Cambridge. SOURCE: Manuscript.

1. That of 20 March, which does not seem to have been preserved. 2. Colburn offered Irving one thousand guineas for *Bracebridge Hall*, but he placed it with Murray for the same amount (Williams, 1:206-207; *Washington Irving and the House of Murray*, p. 42). 3. The *Monthly Review* (1749-1845), a London periodical, founded by the bookseller Ralph Griffiths and conducted from 1803 to 1825 by his son George Edward Griffiths. Coleridge contributed only one piece to it, "A Letter to the Editor," in the issue for November 1800, regarding the unfavorable review of his translation of Schiller's *Wallenstein* in it. He or WA may have been thinking of the *Monthly Magazine* (1796-1843), a London periodical founded by Sir Richard Phillips, to which Coleridge contributed three poems and two prose pieces in September, October, and November 1796 and January 1797 (Thomas J. Wise, *A Bibliography of the Writings of Samuel Taylor Coleridge* [London: Printed for The Bibliographical Society by R. Clay & Sons, Ltd., 1913], pp. 267, 205-207). 4. "The Son" was written by RHD. 5. "Thomas Thornton," a piece of fiction by RHD, comprised vol. 1 [no. 5] of the *Idle Man* (1821-22). 6. "Domestic Life," an essay by RHD, appeared in no. 1 of the *Idle Man* (1821). 7. "Ye ought . . . to remember the words of the Lord Jesus, how he said, It is more blessed to give than to receive" (Acts 20:35).
8. RHD's wife, Ruth Charlotte (Smith) Dana, died on 10 February 1822 (RHD, Jr., *An Autobiographical Sketch (1815-1842)* [Hamden, Conn.: Shoestring Press, 1953], p. 99).

117. To Charles Robert Leslie

Boston,
8th May, 1822. Massachusetts.

Dear Leslie: I have only time now to acknowledge the receipt of your two last letters, one by Cap. Tracy, and another later, of the 20th March, by the way of New-york. When Cap. Tracy returns I shall write something more *like* a *letter*. In the meantime you must give me credit for the intention and accept my thanks for your print of Sir Roger, which I think admirable. The principal group is, I think, the best; Sir Roger's character seems to be exactly hit—and the widow and her <son> children are just the kind of objects to call forth the good Knight's kindness of nature; next is the Old Maid; then the old man and his daughter—though I don't know whether I do not prefer to the former the little old woman, a little beyond him—perhaps because <as> she seems more <than> completely than the rest to belong to the last century. I am pleased also with the landscape, the church & effect; in short I am delighted with the whole.—

I must thank you also in behalf of my friend, Mr. Dana, for your kind attention to my request. He feels the more obliged as he knows how little time an artist has to spare. Again I must thank you <also> on my own account, for in serving my friend you have served me.—In the enclosed Mr. Dana has replied to Mr. Colburn's proposal, and as he has said all that is necessary upon the subject, I shall only add, that he will be *perfectly satisfied with whatever you do*. You will not therefore wait for any further communication, but do the best you can with his book without scruple; remembering that his main object is to have it *reprinted in London*[1]—if not in so profitable a way as he could wish—at least, in some way or other: as its republication *there*, in any form, will materially promote its circulation here.

I congratulate you with all my [heart] [page torn] on your election into the Academy.[2] As to my becoming an R.A.[3] I fear, as you say, that it is hopeless so long as I continue on this side of the water; and, though I still hope to revisit England, it is <very still> very uncertain when. Sometime next year, however, if possible, I will paint a picture expressly for Somerset House; as I would not be thought to be unmindful of an Institution in which I feel so strong an interest.—By the bye, I cannot help thinking the Law that excludes <me [?]> foreigners, or artists residing in a foreign country, from the honour of membership, a very narrow one. No other Academy has such a law. The Art belongs to no country.—I hope the day will come when that law will be expunged; for I see not any good purpose it can effect.—But don't think I feel sore under it. I assure you I do not.—

Tell Willes, I am greatly obliged to him for his entertaining letter, which I will answer by Cap. Tracy. Why has not Collins written me? he owes me, I think, two letters. But I am so bad a correspondent myself that I will not find fault. Remember me affectionately to him, Mrs. C. & Frank.—I would give a great deal to see Etty's Cleopatra.[4] You and Willes have quite made my eyes *water* with your descriptions of its splendour. I remember his former works well. They generally struck me as "fallings short" of the mark; but I nevertheless used to think [tha]t [page torn] his mark was a good one: he appeared [to] [page torn] be in the right road—though he travelled slowly. Ah, the Old masters, after all, are the only Masters to make a great Artist—I mean an original one. For I have rarely known an artist who neglected them that did not imitate his contemporaries; and often too while he was deluding himself with the thought that he was <had> confining his study to nature. When I think thus of the Old Masters, tis only of their language—not their thoughts. I would not have the latter derived from any source but nature.[5]—Tell Charles Williams that I am extremely obliged to him for paying the Colourman's bill, & that I will repay it to Cap. Tracy, as he desires; also that I will answer his letter by Tracy.—I believe I must have made some mistake in the list of colours that I sent you. I wanted Middleton's *dark purple* Lake—not the crimson, which is sent me.—I can get no purple lake here, and am in great need of it—Will you send me, by first private opportunity, or should an opportunity offer to this place, by a public one, six ounces of *Middleton's purple* Lake. N.B. mind, *Middleton's*; also the same quantity of *Brown's*[6] Lac Lake, for which Cap. Tracy will reimburse you when he returns to London.

Remember me to Mrs. Bridgen & family.

Remember me to Collard and L[onsd]ale [page torn], Newton, Martin, and all others whom you know I esteem; and in a parti[cular] [?] [page torn] manner to Irving—and Coleridge, the Gilman's and Morgans—Wh[en you] [page torn] write again do not forget to send me a copy of what Coleridge said [about the "I] [page torn] dle Man."

Yours sincerely W. Allston.

[In the margin] We have just heard of the arrival of Irving's "Bracebridge Hall." I promise myself infinite pleasure from it. The public here are all agog for it. Irving well deserves all his popularity. If I find a subject in it for a picture, I will make a drawing and send it him.

Without intending to write more than a few lines I have filled my paper. Yet I have not said all I wish to, as I write in a hurry. I shall make no apology for saddling you with postage from Liverpool; for artists are *always rich!*—in being *above* money.

ADDRESSED: Charles R. Leslie Esqre. A.R.A. / N 8 Buckingham Place, / Fitzroy Square, / London. SOURCE: Manuscript. Printed in part in Flagg, pp. 172-73.

1. The *Idle Man* was not published in England. 2. Leslie was elected an Associate of the RA in November 1821 (Leslie, p. 44). 3. Royal Academician was the highest rank the RA bestowed on artists, contingent on their living in England. In 1821 WA was seriously considered for this rank to fill the place vacated by the death of Lawrence. Collins and Henry Thompson urged that he be elected and his name placed third on the first ballot, but he was eliminated from the second. 4. The exhibition of Etty's *Cleopatra* at the RA in 1821 made a great impression.
5. This sentence and the three preceding sentences express some of WA's fundamental theories of art, first, apparently, put in writing here, stated more fully in his letter of advice for Thomas Cole written to Henry Pickering in 1827, his conversations with Henry Greenough, and finally in his lectures on art. 6. Thomas Brown, Sr.

118. To Charles Robert Leslie Boston, 23d July, 1822.

Dear Leslie: The bearer of this, Mr. Jonathan Mason, is a young gentleman of this town whom I beg leave to introduce to your acquaintance. He goes to England for the purpose of studying our Art; and any assistance you may render him in the way of advice in his studies I shall consider as a favour done me. Mr. Mason's manners are so modest and pleasing, and his disposition so amiable, that I feel assured you cannot know him without feeling disposed to serve him also for his own sake. I have advised him to apply himself to drawing from plaster immediately on being settled, in order to bid becoming a student of the R. Academy as soon as possible: Yet not to confine himself to the crayon, but occasionally to paint, that he might acquire betimes some skill in handling the pencil. He has already made several copies from Stuart, which I think do him credit, considering the short time he has been studying; indeed they <may> are much better than could have been expected from one who has had so few advantages; and certainly [?] [word smudged] give considerable promise. But there is another thing very much in his favour, and very important—he unites to a strong passion for the Art a very studious habit.—You will find Mr. Mason a very agreeable acquisition to your society.—

My letter by Captain Tracy* I suppose you have long since got. I do not recollect whether it was long or short, or much what it was about, so that I cannot tell whether I told you any thing concerning myself. I hope I did, however, as I do not find that I have any thing particular to say on that head now; for when I tell you I am still fagging at Belshazzer I believe I shall have told you all. I hope to finish in three months more. That done, I must think of painting something to send to the Royal Academy—yet it is not likely that I shall be able to finish any thing in time for the next exhibition.

Morse is settled in New Haven[1]—and is now engaged on a picture of the Hall of the House of Representatives, at Washington[2]—to contain portraits of the principal members. It must be somewhat advanced I should suppose by this time, it having been begun last Autumn.—I wrote you <ab the> I believe [upper right portion of page torn off] before he sailed [words missing] containing Mr. Col[burn's] [words missing] the "Idle Man;" and I conc[lude] [word or words missing] arrangements with him are [words missing] made Mr. Dana also wrote you [words missing] the same subject. Mr. D. has just [word missing] another Number; it is a tale som[ewhat] longer than the last[3]—and I think [word missing] superiour, being more continuous, a[nd] having more unity, besides partaking [of] a higher character. For my part, I think it very great: it is certainly quite origina[l.]—He will send it out as soon as he can get [it] in proper order—having some few corrections to make first. I do not know (as I have not heard him say) whether he will send it in manuscript, or in printed sheets—if the former, he will have to transcribe it—which will take some time—At any rate, he means to send it, whatever its form, before it is published here.—By the bye, I omitted to tell you that the "Lines written in Spring" in the first number of the Idle Man, and the "Hypochondriac" in the second, are mine.[4] The *cap* to the latter is also mine, not having been able to find a quotation in any book to suit me. If you refer to <them> it, you will find our worthy landlord's name at the bottom of it.[5] Being a *Man of Letters,* and rather erratic in his literary <career> pursuits, I did not know to whom I could better ascribe stray verses.—Tell Irving I am delighted with his "Bracebridge Hall"—that is, the first volume, for I have not yet seen the second. Every individual of the family is as well drawn as <they> could be, and I felt as if I had been reading of real people. "The Stout Gentleman" is exquisite. I felt every drop of rain in it, and could smell even the stable yard: but I was sorry he introduced any thing like a double entendre—I allude to the landlady's visit to the stout Gentleman's chamber. Perhaps he did not mean any thing more than a kiss to have been given.—But some readers would not be satisfied with a kiss.—Remember me to him affectionately. I liked also the "Student of Salamanca." The procession of the Inquisitors with their victims to the stake is terrific. Nothing could be finer than the description of the prisoners and the effect of the whole scene on the multitude; they meet the eye with a horrible breadth.—Remember me to all my friends—Yours sincerely

W. Allston.

* By the way, I am not sure that I wrote you by Cap. Tracy—but if I did not, it was because I had written about a week previous to his sailing.[6] I remember, however, that I sent a letter from Mr. Dana[7] by him.

ADDRESSED: Charles R. Leslie Esqre. A.R.A. / N 8 Buckingham Place, / Fitzroy Square, / London. / Jno. Mason Esqre. SOURCE: Manuscript. Printed in part in Flagg, pp. 173-74.

1. Morse and his family moved to New Haven, where his parents lived, in the spring of 1821, but during the next few years he visited several cities to paint (Morse, 1:237ff.) 2. Morse's *Congress Hall,* or *The Old House of Representatives,* was finished in 1822. WA called it "a magnificent picture" and suggested only a few minor improvements (Prime, p. 128). 3. "Thomas Thornton" was the longest piece of fiction RHD wrote. 4. WA must have known Wordsworth's poem "Lines Written in Early Spring." He probably knew of Boswell's series of essays *The Hypochondriack* and Reynolds's portrait of him in that role; in "The Hypochondriac" he cited Boswell's *Life of Johnson,* and in "Eccentricity" he paraphrased a passage from it. 5. The lines of verse preceding the piece "The Hypochondriac" were attributed to "Bridgen" and a footnote read "A feigned name.—*Editor.*" The verse described a man who "would not taste, but swallowed life at once," since he "did wot not / What most he craved" and "scarce had reached his prime ere he had bolted . . . / Full fourscore years," with the result that he had indigestion (*LA,* p. 181). The name of the narrator himself, Harman, may be an allusion to Harman Visger. The entire piece, with its names of Dr. Joblin, Mr. Cumberback, Timoleon Bub, and Rainbow, is a satire, the most extended use WA made of this mode of expression in writing. 6. WA's letter immediately preceding that of 13 November 1821, sent by Tracy, was dated 7 September 1821. 7. RHD probably wrote concerning *The Idle Man.*

119. To Charles Robert Leslie Boston, 7th Feby 1823

Dear Leslie: I received sometime since a case containing Wilkie's Blind-man's buff, the Rabbit on the wall, and Allan's Circasians, together with several smaller prints from your designs from Knickerbocker & the Sketch Book.[1] There was no note, or letter accompanying them; but I concluded that they were from you, and for Judge Jackson; so I accordingly delivered them to him—all excepting one of the duplicates from my design of Wouter Van Twiller, which I supposed you intended for me. In the case were also the Lakes I requested you to send; for which I beg you to accept my thanks. As there is no bill, however, of these, I must beg you to let me know the amount, and I will remit it by Cap. Tracy.

It being a good rule to put business before, I shall proceed with that <and put> now I am on it, and leave what else I have to say last.—Mr Dogget, a very respectable and worthy man of this town, is desirous of publishing a set of prints from the Five Presidents—Washington, Adams, Jefferson, Madison & Munro—lately painted expressly for him by Stuart.[2] As they are amongst Stuarts best works, and in a manner (from their subjects) of national interest, it is Mr Doggets wish to have them engraved in the best possible manner and only by the first Artists [rest of line and three-quarters of the next undecipherable] He accordingly applied to me for advice to this end.—Not I am so little acquainted with the Engravers in London that I am quite at a loss whom to recommend. Neither can I answer certain other questions; as to the probable cost of the plates, & printing—what time <they> would be <in hand> required to complete them—whether they would be likely to sell in England—and which of the two, the line and stippled manner, would be the best. But all these might easily be answered by an artist on the spot. I therefore took the liberty to say that I would make the necessary inquiries of you. Will you therefore oblige me so far as to give me the information wanted; also to say what engraver would be most likely to do the pictures justice; and which *manner—stippled or line*—would probably render the *likeness* best—which, you know, in subjects of this kind is *all-important*. Stuart thinks the *line* would be preferred, if the engraver unites fidelity <and> with fine execution; so think I & it would besides give the greater number of impressions. If there be not such a one, however, the other must of course be adopted.—There are only two artists that work in the latter that I recollect—Meyer[3] & Scriven.[4] But I do not remember the works of either sufficiently to say which of the two is best. My impression however of Meyer is that he does not give a very accurate likeness. I was not quite satisfied with his engraving of Lawrence's head of Mr West—I mean the large one—the *little one* in likeness was <very> certainly bad.[5] But this between ourselves as I would not give pain. Of Scriven's merit in this particular I cannot speak from any thing that I recollect.—There may perhaps be better stipple-engravers than either—If there are I wish you to mention them.

Lest I make any omission of this information required, I will here transcribe Mr Dogget's memorandum.

Mem. "The size of the Portraits <are> is 40 by 32 inches each.—The engraved part of the plates to be 15 by 12 inches, with 1¼ margin top and sides, and two inches at the bottom for Name &c.

Should like to know the probable number of prints the plates will strike—both line and stippled, and the cost of engraving them in the *best* <man> *style,* by *first-rate Artists.*—The expense of Printing and Paper. the size of paper to be 26 by 22 inches.—The time that <it> would be required to complete the work.—Whether the Prints would be likely to sell in England. And whether <on exhibition> the Pictures themselves would be likely to produce any profit <by> if exhibited there. N.B. The whole of <the> each picture to be engraved—hands, back-ground and all. "And whether, in order to insure uniformity of execution, it would not be best to employ but *one* artist to engrave the whole."

You must not suppose from this <information of particulars> that *you* are to be troubled with the pictures; or that you are expected to have *any thing* to do with making arrangements with the Engravers. The pictures will be consigned to some Merchant in London who will make the bargain and do all else that may be necessary. All that Mr Dogget would think of requesting of you is simply such information, or advice, as it may be in your power to procure and give him as to the above particulars. Mr Dogget is well known to Mr. Mason, who knows him to be a very worthy and unobtrusive man.—I hope that what I have here ventured to ask for him will not put you to much inconvenience. It appeared to me that the information might easily be obtained; I therefore make no scruple in asking it; though, if it were not, I yet know that I might safely appeal to your disposition to oblige.

You see by the little art I shew in condensing what a poor man of business I should make. When I began I thought I should leave at least a page for other matters. But I will make it up soon by another letter without a word of business.—I was exceedingly pleased with your designs from Knickerbocker & the Sketchbook. They and Sir Roger shew what a stride you have made in chiaro'scuro & other matters. The best I think is Rip Van Winkle mounting the hill with the ghostly Dutchman. Rip's nether jaw hangs most ominously, and his dog has a true eye for a ghost. Tis equal to the story, which is saying a great deal. The next best is Icabod Crane & Catrina, which is exquisite—then Van Corlear's leave taking—But they are all good. I was also pleased with the engraving of my Wouter. The characters are all well preserved; but the composition is hurt by the reduction; Yet that could not have been avoided and it looks better reduced than I thought it would But why did the engraver omit the A.R.A. after my name?[6] If it be not too late I should like to have it added.

[In the margin of page 1:] At odd times I have made a number of compositions—but I have laid them all aside until I finish Bel. The best amongst them is Macbeth & Banquo meeting the Witches on the Heath[7]—one of my happiest, I think. The next is Minna and Brenda, on the seashore from the "Pirate."[8] Tell Willes I am quite ashamed to have delayed answering his letter so long—but have not forgotten it, and hope to make amends soon.—I have not heard from you since I set you the fifth number and first of the 2d vol. of the Idle Man. Has Mr. Colburn done any thing with them yet? or will he do any thing? Mr. Dana would [be] glad to hear what is likely to [be] done. Will you let me know, if you can, in your next letter? I think the last Tale must strike all who like to be deeply moved. Remember me affectionately to Collins & Frank—also to Collard & Lonsdale—Mr. Coleridge, my friends at Highgate & the Morgans—and always to Mrs. Bridgen and family. Do not forget me either to Martin and Haydon Mr Mason & Newton.

[In the margin] I have made so many changes in Belshazzer that it is yet unfinished But since they are all for the better I do not regret the time bestowed on it—especially as I find it at last drawing to a close—I hope to complete it by the end of May.—Till then I shall say nothing about it. Morse I hear has just finished a picture of Congress Hall—and is daily expected here to exhibit it.[9]

Yours sincerely W. Allston.

ADDRESSED: Charles R. Leslie Esqre A.R.A. / N 8 Buckingham Place / Fitzroy Squa[re] [page cut] / London. Ship / London / S Candler [?]. SOURCE: Manuscript. Printed in part in Flagg, pp. 174-75.

1. Murray brought out editions of Irving's *History* and *The Sketch Book* in 1824, with engravings of Gilbert S. Newton's portrait of Irving, WA's *Wouter von Twiller's Decision,* and nine designs by Leslie: for the *History, A Dutch Courtship,* Peter Stuyvesant rebuking the cobbler, and William Kraft introducing his new mode of punishment for beggars from book 4, chap. 5, and Antony Van Corlear setting off for the wars from book 6, chap. 6; for *The Sketch Book,* James I of Scotland from "A Royal Poet," Rip van Winkle, Philip of Pokanoket on his night watch, and Ichabod Crane giving a singing lesson to Katrina Van Tassel from "The Legend of Sleepy Hollow." The engravings were by Charles Rolls, John Romney, William Finden, and A.W. Warren. 2. This portrait of John Adams by Stuart was painted about 1815, a replica of his 1798 portrait. The others were apparently painted later. They remained in Doggett's possession for many years. In 1846 a bill was introduced in Congress to purchase them for the White House and they were kept in the Library of Congress until a fire in 1851 destroyed those of Adams, Washington, and Jefferson. Those of Madison and Monroe were auctioned in 1857 (Park, 1:90-91). Apparently they were not engraved. 3. Henry Meyer (1782?-1847), English portrait painter and engraver, chiefly of portraits. 4. Edward Scriven (1775-1841), English engraver, chiefly of portraits. 5. Two heads of West by Lawrence were engraved by Meyer: the first, 152 by 121 inches, done in 1811, and the second, 76 by 62 inches, unfinished (Kenneth Garlick, *Sir Thomas Lawrence* [London, 1854], p. 62). 6. After he became an associate of the RA, WA signed several paintings with these initials after his name: *Jeremiah, Landscape, Evening (Classical Landscape), A Tuscan Girl,* and *Lorenzo and Jessica.* 7. (Before 1823), from *Macbeth* 1.3. The scene was also painted by Fuseli, West, and John Martin. Though no painting from *Macbeth* by WA seems to have survived, Walter Channing reported several years later that one which he called "Macbeth" was "nearly finished" and was engaged for $1,500 (to Morse, 20 Feb. 1835, Morse Papers, LC). 8. (Before 1823); Minna and Brenda were the daughters of Magnus Trail, who lived on one of the Shetland Islands in Scott's novel *The Pirate* (1822). It was perhaps begun as early as 1819. 9. Morse arrived in Boston on 11 February. His painting was exhibited from 22 February until mid-April (Mabee, p. 87; *Columbian Centinel* [Boston], 22 Feb., 12 Apr. 1823).

120. To Henry Pickering Boston, 14th March, 1823.

My dear Sir: I must entreat your indulgence for having so long delayed to thank you for your obliging letter and the volume of Poems.[1] It was my intention to have written you a fortnight ago; but I have been so incessantly occupied that one thing and another have successively prevented me. I trust, however, that you know me too well to impute the delay to any want of respect.

Amongst the larger Poems, I think, the best is the first, which gives the title to your volume. It shews throughout a classical and elegant mind, deeply imbued with the love of what is grand and beautiful. It opens in a natural and dignified manner, and carries the mind on by spirited (though easy) transitions from the present to the past—from the actual to the probable, and finally concludes, as it should—both morally and poetically—with the triumph of Nature. Nothing could <be> more emphatically illustrate this triumph than the *eternal* "Rose of Paestum." It is a fine poetical stroke; though not happier than the "Roman Eagle;" his "pluming his wings a thousand years" is a sublime thought—as is also his fall from the "lofy eyry," "through impotence of age:" but a grander still is that of the "Ruins" being the "Mausoleum of a *dead* city." Of the smaller Poems, which I have not seen before, I like best the "Apollo Belvedere," "I wish I were in Heaven," & the "Mourner of the forest," and "I thought it slept." The last is very touching. But I must not forget "Tockwallendon—" which is extremely beautiful and spirited: no one, I should suppose, could read it without emotion. I could see every struggle almost as if it had been painted. Nor can I conclude without offering my humble tribute of praise to the high moral tone that pervades the whole volume.

I have again read with increased pleasure the two Poems[2] you have done me the honour to found on my pictures. And again I thank you: it would indeed be affectation to deprecate praise so delicately bestowed.

I remain, dear Sir, / with every sentiment of respect / and esteem,
Yours sincerely, / W. Allston.

ADDRESSED: Henry Pickering Esqre / Salem. ANNOTATED: by Pickering: "certain Poems—Alas!" SOURCE: Manuscript.

1. Pickering's *The Ruins of Paestum and Other Compositions in Verse.* 2. "Jeremiah: A Vision" and "Reflections on Viewing the Beautiful Moonlight Picture."

121. To Charles Robert Leslie Boston, 25th March, 1823.

Dear Leslie, Will you allow me to make you acquainted with my friend Mr. Baldwin?[1] Mr. B. is a brother-in-law of Mr. Williams,[2] who might render an introduction from me superfluous; but I wish to introduce him, because he is one of my earliest and most valued friends, and because too I can say that of him which Mr. W., as his brother, might think it not proper in him to add.

I need not tell you that Mr. Baldwin is a gentleman, both in mind and manners—for that you will soon discover of yourself: but I may be allowed to add, what his own modesty would make him the last to betray—that he is also a man of genius. He might have been an Architect, or a Painter, had not a certain *bias* in his brains turned the current of his mind to another course. But if our country has lost a painter by it, she has gained what she more needed, and will do her equal honour—a great Engineer. Yet neither the gentleman, nor the engineer (as highly as you may estimate them) will ever appear needful to recommend him after you shall have known his solid worth as a man.

I have commissioned my Friend to get as much *talk* out of you as he can—all about the Artists and their works—that he may bring home a good budget for my relief. You are, I believe, a little in arrears to me as to news of this kind—that is, if you can owe without value received; <which, however> and, <that> if you do not, it is not my fault, for I would send you news in abundance if I had it.

Morse's picture of the House of Representatives is now exhibiting here. It is really a very beautiful thing. The perspective is quite scientific, and finely managed; as are also the figures, which are very naturally and well disposed. The time is about twilight, when they are lighting the great chandelier.—I always thought Morse had a great deal in him; but he has brought out more in this picture than I ever anticipated. The architecture is exquisitely coloured, and painted with great richness and power. The figures too, with one or two subordinate exceptions, are well drawn and composed. I think it would make no small figure in Somerset House. It should make him an associate if he were there.

Remember me to all my friends, / and believe me ever / sincerely yours, /

W. Allston.

I think it would be a mutual gratification to Mr. Coleridge and Mr. Baldwin if you would make them acquainted in one of your walks to Highgate. Mr. Williams will introduce him to Irving,[3] or I would particularly request it to you.

ADDRESSED: Charles R. Leslie Esqre A.R.A. / N 8 Buckingham Place, / Fitzroy Square, / London. / L. Baldwin Esqre. SOURCE: Manuscript.

1. Loammi Baldwin. 2. Samuel Williams. 3. Irving saw Baldwin almost daily in Paris between 14 September 1823 and 11 January 1824 (*Journals and Notebooks*, vol. 4, ed. Wayne R. Kime and Andrew B. Myers [Boston: Twayne Publishers, 1984], pp. 220-21, 228, 230, 249-50, 253-54, 257, 259-60, 263-64, 267, 270).

122. To Samuel Finley Breese Morse

Boston,
15th April, 1823.

My dear Sir: I beg you to accept my best thanks for your letter,[1] and for your kind attention to <the> my commission. <which> I am sorry however that, circumstanced as I am, it is wholly out of my power to enter at present into the engagement you recommend.[2] The situation of the proposed house &c are every way what I could wish, and I should not hesitate did I feel *certain* of being able to fulfil the engagement. But indeed the future is, for one so *slack in purse* as I am, very uncertain ground to build on; and though I may allow myself to build air castles on it, I should not feel as if I were acting either prudently or honestly to tempt another to erect any thing more substantial for me on so precarious a foundation. In short, though I still adhere to my plan (such as talked over with you) and apprehend no cause of change, it is yet so dependent on contingencies that I can <actual> not rationally do any thing more now than arm me with patience, or indulge myself in wishes. I have been obliged to leave Belshazzer ever since you were here,[3] in order to raise the means wherewith to proceed with it. I hope, however, to resume it in about ten days and thence to continue on it to the end without another interruption. This unwelcome delay will of course protract its completion far beyond the time I had calculated; and it was on that calculation I had formed the hope <of reaching> going to Newhaven in the Autumn. It is true I *may* still finish Belshazzer in time for this; but I cannot be *certain* of it *now*—especially as I was never in my life right in guessing at the *day of finish,* in my labours. So <th> my safest course at present seems to be to defer <all thought> the engaging a house until I shall feel that I am least within a *month* of completing the work that is to supply me with the means of living in it.[4] You will therefore have the goodness to make this known to Dr. Ives,[5] that I may be no impediment to his engaging with the other gentlemen whom you mentioned. At the same time I must beg you to make my best acknowledgements to him <from> for his kindness and liberality—as also to Professor Silliman,[6] whom I most sincerely thank for the friendly interest he has taken in my behalf.—As soon as I shall feel myself on *sure ground* I will lose no time in letting you know. Meanwhile I shall work hard to reach the terra firma—so long to me a terra incognita.—another word—For fear that I have not been sufficiently explicit, I must add, that I would have you on *no account* either engage a house <now> or give any *encouragement* to any ones building one with the view of my taking it—as in case of unforseen circumstances causing me to occasion disappointment it would give me more pain than I am willing to risk, and such as I should not easily get over.

I am sorry to find that you are so low-spirited.[7] You should not give way to discouraging thoughts so soon; for your Picture can hardly be said as yet to have had a <full> fair trial. If its exhibition here has not been profitable to your purse, it has yet gained you a full harvest of praise. I believe all amongst the higher classes have been to see it, and, as far as I can learn, there is but one opinion concerning it—that it does you great honour. I have heard many praise it highly, and *not* a *single* voice against it. It is especially admired by the best judges—such as Mr. Dutton, Mr. Codman,[8] Dana,[9] and others whose opinions go a great way in the circles where they move. Indeed it is so popular amongst these that I cannot account for its lac[[k] of profit except in the circumstance that the lower classes must have been [w]anting [page torn] in curiosity; and as they make the mass of the town, if it does not attract them, the receipts must of course be small. But <because the

tradesmen> I do not think it likely that the same result will happen in the other great towns—New-York, Philadelphia, Baltimore & Charleston.[10] The common people there, if I mistake not, are more accustomed to visit places of public amusement; and those that are in the habit of attending them, I should suppose, would find entertainment in this Picture. Besides, its course is but *just begun*. Be of good heart then—I have no doubt of your success.—I have applied for several weeks past to various of my friends to write about it but without success until today, when Dr. Channing undertook it. <It is> He has written a very handsome notice,[11] giving the picture high praise, and speaking of it in a way that I think will <prepare the public> procure it a good reception in the other Cities it will take in its tour through the States. But he has not said more than it deserves—So live upon praise for the present, and depend on it a little patience will bring you more solid food ere long. Dr. C's piece will appear in a day or two in the Daily Advertiser[12] or Centinel.[13] When it does I will send it you.—My respects to your Father & Mother and to Mrs. Morse and believe me ever yours sincerely

W. Allston.

[In the margins] I wrote to Leslie the other day, and, among other things which I said of your picture, I told him it ought to make you an Associate if you were in London.—When you carry it to New-York, I will write to Mr. Verplanck, who is a particular friend of mine, to give it a good word in the Newspapers. <[Two and a half lines undecipherable]> I sent a message by Dogget's man on Saturday to Mr. Pratt[14] to invite him to my room before he left town—but he did not come—probably he did not get the message.

SOURCE: Manuscript, Morse Papers, LC.

1. Morse presumably wrote WA from New Haven, where he went from Boston. He spent the winter of 1822-23 there (Prime, pp. 125-26). 2. WA had decided to move to New Haven after he married, which he planned to do in the summer of 1823, his principal inducement, he told Morse, being Morse's society. Morse consulted James Abraham Hillhouse, New Haven poet, and others about a possible house there, and Hillhouse suggested one formerly occupied by Morse, which had a painting room, and thought $200 not an exorbitant rent for the house and grounds. It was in a neighborhood near him and the Yale professor Benjamin Silliman, both of whom, he said, would be particularly pleased to have WA in that part of town (Morse to Elizabeth Ann [Breese] Morse, 19 February 1823; Hillhouse to Morse, 23 Sept. 1824, Morse Papers, LC). The plans for the move were not carried out, WA's marriage being postponed and *Belshazzar's Feast*, which was presumably the painting whose sale he said would have made it possible, never being completed. 3. Morse left Boston sometime during the last three weeks of March (Mabee, p. 89). 4. Presumably *Belshazzar's Feast*. 5. Eli Ives (1778-1861), New Haven physician. He was influential in the establishment of the Yale Medical School. 6. Benjamin Silliman (1779-1864), the most prominent man of science in America during the first half of the nineteenth century. For many years he was professor of chemistry and natural history at Yale and was instrumental in the establishment of the Yale Medical School. He was also partly responsible for the foundation of the Trumbull Gallery of art at Yale; his wife was a daughter of Trumbull.
7. Morse was disappointed in the exhibition of his *Congress Hall* in Boston, where it was not financially successful. The receipts for the first day were $40.55 and did not improve (Prime, p.

123). 8. Probably Charles Russell Codman, Boston merchant, whose granite store on Kilby Street was the largest in the city (*Boston City Directory*, 1816-56; Samuel Cutler, "Necrology of the New-England Historic, Geneological Society," *NEGHM* 30 (1876): 245. He owned WA's *Landscape: Time after Sunset*. 9. Probably Edmund T. Dana. 10. *Congress Hall* was exhibited for about seven weeks in New York, closing on 16 July 1823. The receipts were less than those in Boston and plans for exhibitions elsewhere were dropped (Mabee, pp. 89-91). 11. Channing's notice of *Congress Hall*, under the heading "Mr. Morse's Picture," appeared in the *Boston Daily Advertiser* for 19 April 1823, signed "B," praising the work highly. 12. The *Boston Daily Advertiser* (1813-1925) was the leading Boston newspaper of the day and became nationally famous. 13. The *Columbian Centinel* (1790-1840), Boston semiweekly newspaper. 14. Henry Cheever Pratt (1790-1840), painter of portraits, miniatures, landscapes, and panoramas. He was a protégé of Morse's and located in Washington at this time. He was negotiating in Boston to obtain a frame, presumably from Doggett, for Morse's *Congress Hall* and reported to him that WA had said that a baize one, such as he apparently ordered, would not do and a gilt one was preferable and advised him to stay in Boston until the following week (Pratt to Morse, 5 Apr. 1823, Morse Papers, LC). By 1829 he had a studio of his own in Boston.

123. From Samuel Taylor Coleridge

Highgate,
13th June, 1823.

My Friend,—It was more than a gratification, it was a great comfort, to all of us, to see, sit, walk, and converse with two such dear and dearly respected friends of yours, as Mr. and Mrs.[1] Channing.

Mr. Channing I could not be said not to have known in part before. It is enough to add, that the reality differed from my previous conception of it only by being more amiable, more discriminating, and more free from prejudices, than my experience had permitted me to anticipate. His affection for the good as the good, and his earnestness for the true as the true—with that harmonious subordination of the latter to the former, without encroachment on the absolute worth of either—present in him a character which in my heart's heart I believe to be the very rarest in earth. If you will excuse a play on words in speaking of such a man, I will say that Mr. Channing is a philosopher in both the possible renderings of the word. He has the love of wisdom and the wisdom of love.

I was unfortunately absent the first evening. Had they been prevented from repeating their visit, I should have been vexed indeed, and yet not as much vexed as I now know I should have had reason to be. I feel convinced that the few differences in opinion between Mr. Channing and myself, not only are, but would by him be found, to be apparent, not real—the same truth seen in different relations. Perhaps I have been more absorbed in the depth of the mystery of the spiritual life, he more engrossed by the loveliness of its manifestations.

. . .

I will not speak of Haydon's Colossal Picture of Lazarus[2]—for one of the very few disagreements in matters of Taste between you & me was an appreciation of his Genius.

. . .

P.S. Sir George & Lady B. always enquire after you—and at least half an hour's talk follows of you and your works. He spoke on Tuesday of Haydon's Lazarus as almost worthy of Michael Angelo—I told him frankly & with perfect sincerity, that I had never heard that said without thinking it a great exaggeration, one only instance excepted—& that was, your Dead Man revived by touching the Bones of the Prophet. I did not see Haydon's till the morning after when I went with Lady B. I strove to divert my mind of every prejudice, but could not do away or recover from my first impression. But it was very commonplace—theatrical conception—the true Ghost stalk & Ghost stare.

SOURCES: First three paragraphs: William H. Channing, ed., *Memoir of William Ellery Channing, with Extracts from his Correspondence and Manuscripts* (London, 1848), 2:221-22; final paragraph and postscript: RHD, pp. 25-26.

1. Ruth (Gibbs) Channing. 2. *The Resurrection of Lazarus*, from John 11:43-44.

124. To Henry Pickering Boston, 19th June, 1823.

My dear Sir: I am extremely sorry that the proposal you made me should have caused you any uneasiness. And I hope you were not led to feel so from my not having replied to your Note; I only delayed the answer because I was incessantly engaged, and in consequence of your requesting that I would reply to it at my leisure. It was very natural that you should wish to possess a picture[1] which had given you so much pleasure: And I was only sorry that the peculiar circumstances, under which I became its possessor prevented my gratifying your wishes; which I should otherwise have been most happy to have done. The picture was purchased for me, at a time when I had not the means to bid for it myself, by one of my most valued friends, and under such circumstances, that I could not with any propriety dispose of it—indeed without appearing to undervalue the kindness which had made it mine. Had it come into my possession in the ordinary way, I would part with it to you with pleasure.

If you allow me, I will defer my answer to the remaining part of your letter, concerning "a head of the Saviour"[2] untill I shall have had the pleasure of seeing you, which I hope will be soon, as I have nearly completed the "head" which I mentioned to you.[3] As soon as this is done I will let you know. In the mean time I remain, with sincere respect and esteem, Yours

W. Allston.

ADDRESSED: Henry Pickering Esqre / Salem, Massachusetts. SOURCE: Manuscript.

1. Unidentified. Probably it was given to WA in England during his second residence there, possibly by Beaumont if not another wealthy patron such as Egremont. 2. WA did not paint the likeness of Christ after he abandoned *Christ Healing the Sick*, for reasons that he gave

McMurtrie and others. 3. Probably in the painting referred to in WA's letter to Pickering of 8 July 1823.

125. To Henry Pickering Boston, 8th July, 1823.

My dear Sir: I have the pleasure to inform you that the Picture,[1] of which I proposed to give you the refusal, is at length completed; and I shall be happy to shew it to you if you will favour me with a visit, at my painting-room, between one and two o'clock, on thursday. If thursday should not be a convenient day for you, I shall expect you, at the same hour, the next day.

As it is possible that either the subject of the picture, or the price, may not suit you, I must beg that you will feel yourself at perfect liberty to decline it,[2] and that you will not hesitate so to do from any motives of delicacy. I mention the price because, as it is one of my most elaborate works, and has cost me a great deal of time, I feel myself obliged to charge accordingly.

I remain, with sincere esteem / & respect, Yours / W. Allston

ADDRESSED: Henry Pickering Esqre / Salem, / Massachusetts. SOURCE: Manuscript.

1. Possibly *Macbeth and Banquo Meeting the Witches on the Heath* or *Minna and Brenda on the Seashore* or the head of a single figure in one of those compositions. Though in his letter to Leslie of 7 February 1823 he said they were among several compositions he had laid aside until he had finished *Belshazzar's Feast*, he called them the "best" of the lot. The first especially, which he called one of his "happiest," might have been considered one of his "most elaborate" and was apparently one of his largest, if the *Landscape: Macbeth* (?) is a study for it. Both were unlike both the landscape which Pickering bought in preference to the literary *Flight of Florimel* and the religious subjects which he seemed to favor. 2. Pickering apparently did not purchase it.

126. From Charles Robert Leslie London July 18th 1823

My dear Sir: I sit down to perform a promise I made some months ago, of writing you a long letter of all sorts of news.

To begin then with myself. I know that to the surprise of all my friends I have at length left Buckingham place; and I verily believe some of them would have scarcely been more astonished a few months ago, if one of the bricks had eloped from Mrs. Bridgen's wall. The truth is I should have moved long ago had it not been for the great kindness of the Bridgens, who made me as comfortable as it was possible to be in such an intolerable neighborhood.[1] I am now most pleasantly situated at No. 90 Charlotte Street, Fitzroy Square, a few doors from Percy Chapel,[2] which you may recollect as being nearly opposite your old painting room. I have had a window heightened at the top which gives me a very good light, & makes it the best painting room I ever had. My sister has been now long enough with me to understand *all my ways*, she constantly arranges & keeps every thing in order, so that for the present I am as comfortable as I can be. I did not get my "Autolycus"[3] finished for Somerset house & have laid it entirely aside for some time. I have lately been employed entirely on small portraits, alias *pot-boilers*. One of these was posthumous & from a grandchild of Lord Egremont's.[4] I succeeded to his Lordship's satisfaction, for when I told him my price was 25 guineas, he immediately wrote me a cheque for 50. I am to paint him a picture from Don Quixote of Sancho in the apartment of the Dutchess, in which I shall probably introduce a portrait of one of his lordship's daughters.

By the bye I remember your telling me of one of them you nearly fell in love with when you were at Petworth, pray which was it? Lord Egremont talks a great deal about you & I am sure he would be very glad to see you here again. Phillips says your Jacob's Dream is hung in an excellent light at Petworth & looks very grand. The exhibition at Somerset House is considered rather below par this year. Wilkie is almost the only artist of eminence who is equal to himself. His small whole length portrait of the Duke of York[5] is one of the finest things he ever painted. The Duke is in a blue military surtout over a red coat; sitting at a table reading a dispatch. His face is lighted by a reflection from the paper. At his back is a window with a muslin blind through which the picture is lighted, & under the table at which he sits is an immense black dog. The materials (you will perceive) are of the commonest kind; yet disposed with so much art and painted with such exquisite truth, that it is the most interesting picture in the exhibition. Lawrence is inferior to himself this year. He has made Lady Jersey[6] (a very unusual thing for him) look like a vulgar trollope. Phillips's whole length of the Duke of York in his coronation robes, is finely managed, but the head & indeed the whole portrait is very inferior to Wilkie's. I must go back to Wilkie again whose other picture I had like to have forgotten. The subject is a parish beadle putting some vagrants, (an Italian musician, his wife & boy, dancng bear, &c) in the watch house for having made a row at a fair. The subject is an unpleasant one, & the cause for which the poor creatures (foreigners too) are locked up, is not apparent; so that it becomes an act of sheer oppression on the part of the beadle. It is however full of beautiful painting. The italian woman's head & a monkey are perhaps as perfect specimens of imitation as could be produced from the whole range of art. The picture however generally considered [is] too powerful in light & shadow for an out of door scene under any circumstances. Fuseli expressed his surprise to Wilkie to see him painting in the "Carravaggio style"[7] as he called it. Sir Geo Beaumont who you know is a great enemy to the "*white school*" is delighted with this picture & the Duke of York & hails them as indications of a reform in art. Howard's "Solar System" is a beautifully imagined picture, & would delight you, excepting perhaps in the color. A figure of Apollo forms the focus of light in the centre, and around him are revolving personifications of the planets receiving light as they pass in small vases. Mercury, Venus, Mars, Jupiter & Saturn are represented by the deities of those names & the Earth which is the nearest figure by a beautiful female in a green mantle with towers on her head. Her waist is gracefully encircled by the arm of a smaller female in white drapery, half shaded with a crescent on her forehead &

receiving light from the sun in a silver vase. Jupiter, Saturn & the Georgium Sidus[8] are dimly seen in the darker parts of the circle, surrounded by their satellites. The only drawback to this picture is the color, which though not disagreeable is far from being as poetical as the conception.

Turner in all his last pictures seems to have entirely lost sight of the "modesty of nature."[9] The colouring of his Bay of Baia in the present exhibition would have been less objectionable perhaps in Howard's Solar System; but as applied to a real scene; although splendid & harmonious, it is nevertheless a lie from beginning to end. Some people who have been in Italy say it is like the atmosphere there. But if that is the case Claude, Poussin[10] & Wilson[11] must have been very bad painters. Calcott is not so good as usual. Constable's[12] Salisbury Cathedral is one of his best pictures.

You are much wanted in the exhibition. The number of historical & poetical pictures is lamentably small, & of that small number very few are good for any thing. Haydon is in the King's bench.[13] It is said he owes *ten thousand pounds* and of that a considerable sum is for wine. Sir Geo. Beaumont's picture of Macbeth which happened to be lent to Haydon for exhibition was seized with his other pictures and it is doubtful whether or not Sir George will get it without buying it over again. He (Sir G.B.) has lately made a present of all his pictures to the nation as the beginning of a public gallery & it is rumored that Government are going to purchase the collection of Mr. Angerstein, who is lately dead, to add to it.[14]

Sir George & Lady Beaumont often talk of you with great regard. He told me he wrote to you some time ago but is afraid you never got the letter as you did not answer it. I am sure it would gratify him very much to hear from you & to know what you are doing. Coleridge & the Gillman's are also very anxious to hear from you. They were very much delighted with Mr. & Mrs. Channing. For my own part I was so perfectly acquainted with Mr. Channing by report before I saw him that I felt quite like meeting an old acquaintance. The little I saw of him so fully answered to all I had heard; indeed he exceeded my expectations (& as you well know his portrait was drawn for me by a most affectionate hand) that I very greatly regretted I had not a longer time to profit by & enjoy his society. He gave me a sermon of his own the last time I saw him, which I have since read with great admiration. Coleridge was speaking very highly of this sermon a few days ago at Sir George's who regretted that he had not known of Mr. Channing's being in London.

Irving is still in Germany.[15] Willes is in Ireland. I saw Lonsdale a few days ago who is fatter than ever. Collard I have not seen for some time. Newton is quite well. By the bye I forgot to mention his picture of Don Quixote in his study as among the best in Somerset House.

August 18th

This letter was written as you will perceive a month ago but I have nothing to add excepting that

I am yours ever / C.R. Leslie

ADDRESSED: Washington Allston Esqr / Boston / Masstts. SOURCE: Manuscript, Houghton. Printed in Flagg, pp. 175-78.

1. John Neal described it about this time as "a dirty and obscure part of the town" though worth seeing because of the many artists who had lived there (*Observations on American Art: Selections from the Writings of John Neal [1793-1876]*, ed. Harold Edward Dickson [State College: Pennsylvania State College, 1943f?], p. 54). 2. Percy Chapel stood on the western side of Charlotte Street, near Oxford Street, from 1785 to 1867. Its first incumbent, Rev. Anthony Stephen Matthew, encouraged John Flaxman throughout his boyhood (Arthur Mee, *London North of the Thames* [London, 1972], p. 77). 3. Autolycus is a roguish character in Shakespeare's *The Winter's Tale*. 4. Not otherwise identified. 5. Frederick, duke of York and Albany (1763-1827), George III's second son. 6. Sarah Sophia Fane Villiars (1785-1867), wife of George Villiers, 5th earl of Jersey. 7. Michelangelo Amerighi da Caravaggio (1569-1609), Italian painter, noted for his strong contrasts of light and shadow. 8. Uranus. 9. "with this special observance, that you o'erstep not the modesty o' nature" (*Hamlet* 3.2). 10. Nicolas Poussin. 11. Richard Wilson (1714-82), English landscape painter, who spent several years in Italy. 12. John Constable (1776-1837), landscape painter. 13. Haydon was incarcerated in the King's Bench Prison from April to July 1823 for debts and again in 1827 and 1830 for the same reason (George, pp. 148-50, 186-87, 201-204). 14. John Julius Angerstein. 15. Irving was in Germany from July 1832 to August 1823 (Williams, 1:221, 255).

127. To Charles Robert Leslie

Boston, 28th July, 1823.

Dear Leslie: This will be handed to you by my friend Mr. Harding,[1] whom I have more than ordinary pleasure in introducing to your acquaintance, from the interest that I feel assured you will take in him when you come to know him. The object of his visit to Europe is to study the works of the great Masters in our Art; and from what he had already done, and is promised by the character of his mind, I have every reason to anticipate for him no common success. With most men it might have been deemed a misfortune to have been <been born [?]> deprived of those early advantages, which were denied to Mr. Harding's youth; but nature has been too liberal to him to make others feel, whatever his own modesty might cause himself to regret, that he stands in need of them: for Nature has made him not only a painter, but a gentleman—and you know her too well not to know that she always does her work better than schools of any kind.

For Mr. Harding's *history* I must refer you to himself; and I wish you to know it because I think it will increase your respect for him. I am no gossip of *marvels*, and I do not introduce him as such; for I should only injure him by classing him with those ephemeral wonders, whom the idlesness or ignorance of the public are so fond of every now and then enduing with the power of doing better without study than others can with it—in other words, of making something out of nothing: but I would make him known to you as a man of genius—that is, with an ardent aspiration for excellence, with the will & industry to toil for it, and with capacity to attain it.

[Top part of page cut out]

Will you introduce Mr. Harding to Irving and Collins, and Collard; I would give him a letter to each but that I think your introduction of him would procure him as kind a reception. He would be glad also to be known to Newton and Willes & Lonsdale.

[signature cut out]

You will excuse this mutilated page—as you know I am no dandy in letters.

SOURCE: Manuscript.

1. Chester Harding.

128. To Henry Pickering Boston, 15 Oct. 1823.

My dear Sir: I beg you to accept my best thanks for your very generous present: But I know not in what terms to make you a suitable acknowledgement for the kindness which prompted it. You already know my opinion of the Picture, and how much I admire it; I can only add, that its value is more than doubled to me now, in being a token of your esteem.

With sincere respect and / esteem, believe me, dear Sir,

Yours most obliged, / W. Allston.

ADDRESSED: Henry Pickering Esqre / Salem. ANNOTATED by Pickering: I gave Mr. Al. a picture which was reputed to be a *Jordaens*[1]—size about 3 feet long by 2 high. SOURCE: Manuscript

1. Jacob Joardaens (1593-1678), Flemish painter. The picture has not been identified. Pickering subsequently gave the BA a painting by Carlo Cignani and sold three others by old masters to it (Swan, p. 127).

129. To Henry Pickering Boston, 16th March, 1824.

My dear Sir: So many of my letters have begun with apologies, that I feel almost ashamed to add another; and yet I feel that one is due to you for having so long delayed acknowledging your last favour. The truth is, that my professional and other engagements leave me little time to dispose of as I wish; and I was unwilling to write you until I could command sufficient freedom of mind, as well as leisure, to devote to your volume[1] that undivided attention with which Poetry should always be read. I cannot but confess, however, that something of the delay might be placed on the account of a constitutional infirmity, from which I have suffered much on many other occasions—I mean procrastination; and for your indulgence on this score I must trust to your usual kindness.

I feel happy that I am able now to thank you for your Book, and for the kind letter which accompanied it.—As a whole, I think the present volume superior to its predecessor; it has fewer faults, and more beauties; the style too is more condensed, and the versification more harmonious. In point of versification the greatest inequalities are, perhaps, in the principal Poem;[2] with those exceptions, it flows with sweetness, and bears the reader along, from place to place, by natural and agreeable transitions. The part of <it> this Poem which struck me most was the introduction of St. Paul; the idea of the statue of Mars quaking before him[3] is very poetical, and well-marks, though by a *single touch,* the great moral revolution of time: indeed the various characters with which you have peopled the scene, as well as the learned allusions to classic fable, all serve without effort, as Sir Joshua would say,[4] to carry the mind back into antiquity.—As we are apt to have preferences when we read a book whose contents are of different kinds, I should say, that the Poem which pleased me least is the "Ocean Travellers"; those which I like best are the "Invocation to Health," "Mutual Love," "the Wedded Pair," and "Daphne." The picture of Hygeia in the "Invocation" is very beautiful—most happily personifying the "ineffable joy" that "tingles in the veins." "Mutual Love" is both poetical and *true.* No one (I should think) who has only *imagined* love can truly understand the passage which begins with—"Yet if a thought should wander &c"; 'tis only a *real* lover can feel its full force—and *only he* who has felt love in its elevating purity it speaks a <[*word undecipherable*]>, *high truth.* "The Wedded Pair—" seeing the brightness and the calm of Heaven reflected in themselves, and the happy allusion to our first Parents, at the conclusion, also pleased me. I do not know, however, whether I should not, upon the whole, give the preference to "Daphne." There is a fond melancholy about it which will be understood by all who have ever lost a beloved object. The "tamerind and the orange tree" over her grave—her "favourite myrtle"—and the "perfumed gales," all address the affections in the only way they love to be moved for the departed—through soothing images of the imagination.

Begging you once more to excuse this late acknowledgement of your favour, I remain, dear Sir,

with sincere esteem and respect, Yrs / W. Allston.

Addressed: Henry Pickering Esqre / Salem, / Massachusetts. Annotated by Pickering: 2d vol. of poems—I am now surprised at my folly in troubling people with such trash. 1836 H.P. Source: Manuscript.

1. *Athens; and Other Poems* (Salem, 1824). 2. "Athens." 3. Acts 17:22-32 records St. Paul's address on Mars hill in Athens. 4. In Discourse 5, speaking of Nicholas Poussin, Reynolds said that his favorite subjects were "Ancient Fables" and said twice that in the successful depiction of such subject "the mind is thrown back into antiquity" not only by the subjects but the execution.

130. To Gulian Crommelin Verplanck Boston, 2 July 1824—

Gulian C Verplanck Esqr / New York

My dear Sir: I was about to begin this with a[n] apology for having so long delayed replying to your kind letter,[1] but I will not for two reasons; because I have begun so many letters with apologies that I am quite ashamed to make another, and because I think I shall fare much better if I trust for my excuse to your kind indulgence—I need hardly tell you, late as it is, how much pleasure you have given me by your "Discourse."[2] The view you take of the Fine Arts, as connected with the glory and improvement of our Country appears to me both just and important. And I cannot but hope that your strictures on our Architecture will have a beneficial effect; at least they ought to produce it—and if read by all future *committes* whom our good people may appoint to over-rule the designs of regular Architects, they may possibly influence some sensible brick-layer, or baker amongst them, and check his presumption, to the great saving of his time and the publick expense. I do not know a surer way of teaching our country men wisdom than by shewing its economy. If they can be made to feel that money is really wasted on such piles as they are wont to incumber the ground with, they will perhaps be less liberal of their advice; and then we may expect some improvement. The finest speculations on taste in the abstract will do little good when so many claim the liberty of having a taste of their own. Amongst all our good qualities—and I am patriotic enough to think that our countrymen have as great a share of them as any people on earth—it must be confessed that modesty as to matters where they have no means of information is not a very prominent one. On what they *do* understand they are as modest as other folks. But, malgrè the inconveniences of this disposition to assume, a good natured man, perhaps, may see in it only the spray of that spirit of enterprise which has prompted them to dash through every known and unknown sea—to the fame, as well as to the solid advantage, of our country. But the deviations even of this good spirit must be checked in many things before we can become a refined nation. As the present subject, I think you have applied the most efficient corrective; I mean where you appeal to our sanity—the contempt of foreigners goes farther even than considerations of economy. A book abused in England, or a building ridiculed by an Englishman, however irritating, does actually open our eyes to their[3] defects. If we were proud such attacks would only confirm us in what is bad. But we are a vain people—the most malleable of all things—of course, all the better for hard thumps. But we are not all vain, or all ignorant and there are very many I doubt not on whom the refined and speculative parts of your Discourse so eloquently set forth, will not be lost—The artists ought to thank you for the dignity, with which you have invested their art. And I for one, not only do so for that, and for your kind and flattering compliment to myself,[4] but for the honourable mention of *my* Sir Joshua.[5] I call him mine, for I feel as if I had a property in his mind; quoad the *painter,* he has laid the foundation of my own, most of my speculations are built on it, and it is mine by right of settlement.—But I hardly know where I am rambling. Mr. Dana[6] was much pleased your kind remembrance of him, and would I dare say send you a message did he know of my writing. If you see Mr. Cooper,[7] pray remember me to him. I was delighted with the Pilot,[8] tis a great performance. Believe me, dear Sir, with sincerest esteem, yours

W. Allston—

ANNOTATED by RHD: "Revealed Religion," referring to another work by Verplanck. SOURCE: Manuscript copy.

1. This letter does not seem to have been preserved. 2. *An Address Delivered at the Opening of the Tenth Exhibition of the American Academy of Fine Arts*. In it Verplanck called for more independence from European tradition on the part of American artists and architects. 3. Brackets around "their" and "it" written above in another hand. 4. In his address Verplanck called WA "our distinguished countryman . . . a poet and a painter" and said he had often applied to WA the eulogy given by a modern Latinist to a great artist of his own times: "Arte clarus, literis ornatus, moribus pulchrior" ("Shining in art, splendid in letters, beautiful in manners"). This passage occurs in a footnote to his discussion of portrait painting, in which Verplanck said that it was its function "in the hour of affliction and bereavement, to use the words of a living poet . . . not that poetry for which we turn to books, but that which lives in the memory, because it utters the voice of nature, and seems but to respond to the workings of our own thoughts, and to speak the secrets of our own breasts." In this sentence he was probably referring to words of WA. He followed it by quoting a poem by WA in which that sentiment was expressed, written after the death of a loved one, presumably his wife, in reference to the representation of the deceased in painting. The poem was followed by Verplanck's statement that it was an "exalted and sacred office" which art discharged when it could thus "administer to the charities of domestic life." In a subsequent note he included WA among other American painters who had not only successfully studied but had pursued their profession in Europe. 5. Verplanck quoted several times in his *Address* from Reynolds's discourses and called him a Platonic philosopher as well as a painter, whose writings were to be ranked even above his paintings. 6. RHD. Unless otherwise noted, "Mr. Dana" apparently refers to RHD in letters by and to WA. 7. James Fenimore Cooper. 8. Cooper's novel *The Pilot* (1823).

131. To Charles Robert Leslie Boston, 29th Sep. 1824.

Dear Leslie: This will be handed to you by Mr. Pendleton,[1] of Philadelphia, whom I beg leave to introduce to you, at the request of Mr. Dogget, whom I have had occasion to mention to you, in a former letter, as a very worthy man, and as the proprietor of Stuart's Portraits of the five Presidents. I am not personally acquainted with Mr. Pendleton, but I understand that he is well known to Mr. Sully and Mr. Peale,[2] and is spoken of by Mr. Dogget as a very worthy and respectable man. One of his objects in visiting Europe is the disposal of the Pictures above-mentioned; but whether by exhibition or sale I know not. Should you have it in your power to aid him in this by your advice, I know that it will give you pleasure to do so, both for my sake, in behalf of Mr. Dogget, whom I sincerely wish to serve, and for his own, as one of your former townsmen.

I send you many thanks for your last long letter,[3] which I mean soon to answer by one full as long—but I will not promise that you will find it as entertaining as I have found yours. In the mean time accept my hearty congratulations for your success (how much would I not give to see your Sancho) and believe me, without an atom of change, your sincere friend,

W. Allston.

I intend soon to write to Sir George Beaumont & Coleridge & Mrs. Gilman—to whom, with other kind friends, pray remember me most cordially. Remember me also to Irving[4] & Newton and Harding. <and> Tell Harding I shall write him soon—and tell Newton I admire his Don Quixote[5] extremely.—What is Collins doing? do not forget [rest of letter missing].

SOURCE: Manuscript.

1. John B. Pendleton (1798-1866), pioneer in commercial lithography in the United States. From 1825 to 1830 he and his brother William S. Pendleton had a lithographic firm in Boston.
2. Rembrandt Peale. His painting *The Court of Death* was exhibited at his request by Pendleton in several cities for more than a year and it was apparently at Pendleton's suggestion that he went in 1826 to Boston to study lithography. 3. That of 18 July 1823. 4. Irving returned to London from Paris in May (Williams 1:258). 5. Presumably WA refers to a print of Newton's painting *Don Quixote in His Study,* which was exhibited at the RA in 1824.

132. To Henry Pickering Boston, 11 Jany. 1825,

My dear Sir: I send you my thanks for the honour you intend my little Volume,[1] and beg you to be assured that I with great pleasure submit it to your disposal.

I am better pleased in leaving the selection of the Pieces to you, than I should be in making it myself; and for two reasons: first—because I have a just confidence in the delicacy and refinement of your taste—and secondly—because my own might, perhaps, be in a good measure biased by associations connected with their composition—things wholly extrinsic and with which the Reader can have no concern.

My Picture,[2] as you have heard, is not very far from completion—but *how near* I know not. At present it is at a stand, owing to my indisposition. I had the misfortune, while here some weeks since, to break a blood-vessel in the trachea, and am still confined to the house (with the exception of a short walk daily, by means of exercise) in consequence.[3] The bleeding was only for a few days, but my Physician[4] thinks it unsafe for me to return quite yet to my painting-room.

I remain, dear Sir, with / sincere respect & esteem, / Yours / W. Allston.

I had just written the above when your very kind of favour of the 10th inst. was brought to me; and most heartily do I thank you for the generous interest you are pleased to take in my welfare. My indisposition is, as you have conjectured, entirely accidental, and in no wise (<as> my Physician informs me) connected with my constitution, whch is any thing but pulmonary. The voyage you suggest was at first thought of by some of my friends; but they now think it unnecessary. Indeed I should apprehend more from the fatigue of it at this season, than from remaining here. My strength, if I may judge from my present feelings, is quite restored; and I have no doubt that a little more care than I have been accustomed to bestow on myself, with a partial remission of my labours, [wi]ll [page torn] effectually secure me from [any re]lapse [page torn]. Nay, I have reason to thin[k] [page torn] [t]hat the course of medicine, or rather [the?], [page torn] abstinence, which I have undergone in consequence of my late attack, will eventually add strength to my constitution. Even now I feel, or fancy that I do, in better health than before. Even now I feel, or fancy that I do, in better health than before. If I am so, I hope, by the aid of that prudence which I now know how to value, and the blessing of Providence, soon to proceed with my Picture, so as to bring it out in the spring.

—Again for your kind and friendly letter I beg you to accept my warmest acknowledgements. Be assured, my dear Sir, that I do most highly and unfeignedly value the esteem with which you honoured me.

ADDRESSED: Henry Pickering Esqre / Salem, Masstts. SOURCE: Manuscript.

1. *SS*. Apparently Pickering had plans for having some of the poems in it reprinted, but nothing further is known about the matter. 2. *Belshazzar's Feast*. 3. Morse, who learned about the incident from Alvan Fisher, wrote his parents that WA was very ill, "taken with bleeding at the lungs" (12 Mar. 1825, Morse Papers, LC). After WA returned to America in 1818 he suffered attacks of illness of various kinds, increasingly complaining of them, at this time, in December 1825, July 1826, November 1828, December 1831, February 1832, December 1833, February 1834, March and April 1835, June, August, and October 1836, December 1837, probably the beginning of 1838, and February and August 1839. 4. Possibly Dr. Edward J. Reynolds (*Boston City Directory* for 1820-1849/50). RHD, Jr., spoke of him at the time of WA's death as his "physician & friend" (1:187). Subsequent references to his physician until 1839, by which time Dr. George Shattuck acted in this capacity, may be to him.

133. To Alden Partridge Boston, 24 Feby 1825.

Sir: I had the honour to write to you two days ago, viz 22 inst. enclosing you, by my Sister, Mrs. Alston's[1] request, a United States Boston Branch-Bank Bill of Fifty Dollars, being, together with the present enclosed Two dollar Bill of the Boston Bank, the whole of the balance remaining of the sum (as stated by the above mentioned letter) transmitted to me in November last, for my Nephew Joseph's[2] expenses of voyage then contemplated. In the letter above referred to, which you will have received ere this, I have stated the sums expended, and have requested some information concerning my Nephew's affairs; but as your answer to that letter is probably already on its way hither, I will not trouble you by a repetition. Be pleased to favour me with a line in answer to this by next post.

I remain, Sir, very respectfully, / Your obedient servant / Washington Allston

ADDRESSED: Captain Partridge, / Principal of the / Military Academy, / Norwich, / Vermont. SOURCE: Manuscript, Boston Public Library.

1. Mary (Allston) Young Alston. 2. Joseph Alston was the son of Mary (Allston) Young Alston and William Algernon Alston (Groves, pp. 33, 56).

134. From James Longacre [April after 16[1] or May 1825]

W. Allston Esq / Boston—Dr Sir In answer to an enquiry whether I could have the use of his Exhibition Room,[2] during the Month of June next. Mr. Doggett says no—but that the New England Room[3] is now clearing out for the purpose of exhibiting your Picture.[4] Will you have the goodness to inform me whether you intend to occupy it *immediately* & for how long:—it is not of much importance whether I precede or follow you:—but if you are not quite prepared, I should be glad to have it during the Month of June. I am happy to learn from Mr. Morse that the alarm respecting your health is passd.

I am truly / JL

SOURCE: Manuscript copy, William L. Clements Library, University of Michigan, Ann Arbor.

1. This letter was written after 16 April, when Longacre wrote Doggett inquiring about obtaining his Exhibition room for a few weeks (manuscript copy, William L. Clements Library, University of Michigan, Ann Arbor). 2. The room in John Doggett's looking-glass warehouse for the exhibition of pictures which he called "Doggett's Repository." Possibly Longacre wanted to exhibit four prints of the Declaration of Independence, about which he wrote Ethan Allen Greenwood of the New England Museum on 12 March as having been shipped to him the preceding November (manuscript copy, William L. Clements Library, University of Michigan, Ann Arbor). 3. The exhibition room in Greenwood's Museum. 4. *Belshazzar's Feast.*

135. To Charles Robert Leslie Boston, June 6th, 1825.

Dear Leslie: Mr. & Mrs. Dutton,[1] whom I now beg leave to introduce to you, are among my most valued friends. Their object in visiting England is to see and enjoy all that has attraction for cultivated minds; and I have *the more* pleasure in making them known to *you*, as few have gone from our side of the water so capable of deriving pleasure from our Art; for which indeed they have a true and unaffected love.

I need add no more than that I feel assured, that when you shall have become acquainted with my friends, it will give you real pleasure to shew them such attention as you may have in your power.

For all about myself[2] I must refer you to Mr. Dutton, until I shall be more at leisure to put my long-threatened long letter on paper. In the mean time believe me

faithfully yours, / W. Allston.

I am delighted with your portrait of Sir Walter Scott[3]—and want nothing after *that face* to convince me that he is the great "Unknown."[4]

ADDRESSED: Charles R. Leslie Esqre A.R.A. / Lisson Grove, / London / Warren Dutton Esqre / & Lady. SOURCE: Manuscript.

1. Dutton's wife was the former Elizabeth Cutts Lowell (1783-1864). Her portrait was painted about 1810 by Stuart, who also painted portraits of her sister and son (Park, 1:299-300). 2. At this period WA was chiefly engaged on *Belshazzar's Feast,* but his activity was curtailed by ill health. 3. WA refers to the engraving of Leslie's portrait of Scott, painted in 1824. 4. Scott became known by this epithet because he published the Waverley novels anonymously.

136. To William Wordsworth Boston, 6th June, 1825.

Dear Sir: I take the liberty of introducing to you Mr. & Mrs. Dutton, two among my most valued friends, not doubting that you will find in their society something of that pleasure which it has been my happiness to derive from it ever since I quitted your kind and hospitable country. As their visit is not to gratify a mere idle curiosity, but is from an unaffected admiration of what is good and great, I feel assured that in making my friends known [to] you I shall do you as well as them a pleasure.

I take this opportunity to thank you for your kind attentions to my friends, Dr. & Mrs. Channing; whose visit to you is still remembered by them as one of [the] most gratifying events of their tour.[1]

Will you present my respects to Mrs. Wordsworth and Miss Hutchinson.

I remain, dear Sir, / with the highest respect, / Your obdnt servt / W. Allston.

Should you see my excellent friends, Sir George and Lady Beaumont, pray say to them, that I still retain a grateful remembrance of their many kindnesses.

SOURCE: Manuscript, The Wordsworth Trust, Dove Cottage, Grasmere.

1. The Channings visited Wordsworth at Rydal Mount in mid-July 1822. Channing wrote an account of this occasion, saying that Wordsworth walked with him back to Grasmere, where he was staying, talking and reciting poetry, and that both talked so eagerly as to interrupt one another (*Memoir of William Ellery Channing* 2:220-21). Wordsworth's sister Dorothy said he was "very much interested" in Channing and thought "highly" of him. He sent Wordsworth a complimentary message in 1829 and in 1835 wrote him, enclosing a sermon by himself on the evils of war, that his poetry had been a "pure and quickening influence" on his mind and heart, "a familiar friend" and "a fountain of spiritual life," making him a "wiser and better man" (*The Letters of William and Dorothy Wordsworth,* 2d ed., vol. 4, ed. Alan G. Hill, [1978], pp. 606-607).

137. To John Stevens Cogdell Boston, 21st Dec. 1825.

Dear Cogdell: It was my intention to have replied to your very kind letter from New-York much sooner. The uncertainty where you might be on your journey making an immediate answer impracticable, first induced me to defer it until you should have reached home; but various circumstances have since protracted the delay so much beyond that time that I must ask your indulgence.—For the friendly sentiments with which you honour me I beg you to accept my hearty thanks: allow me at the same time to add, that I most sincerely reciprocate them. It gave me no small gratification to learn that my poor attentions were so kindly received. I had often regretted, while you were here, that the urgency of my professional labours left me so few opportunities of contributing to your entertainment; I trusted, however, that you did me the justice to believe it would have given me unfeigned pleasure to have done more, had more been in my power. Your kind letter shews me that I judged right.

I should have liked to have talked whole days with you about the Art, and to have hunted up together every picture in the Town and neighborhood; but of that pleasure, as well as many others, I was constrained not to think, being then (as I still am) Belshazzer's *slave*—as much so indeed as the Genie was to Aladdin's lamp;[1] I wish I could add, with equal power to perform my master's behests; but the painter's magic, as long experience has taught me, is no "hey, presto" work!—indeed it *is work*[2]—that is labour—though of the brain, yet labour—which makes it, as the world might think, no magic at all. This truth <might> would, perhaps, have been received by me with an ill grace some twenty years ago—if <received> at all by a youthful brain full of magnificent projects. I thought then, and I suppose like most young artists, that I had only to dream dreams, and the hand would immediately embody them: and so it did, after a fashion—that is, it put something on canvas, which, by the help of another dream, I made out to resemble the first. But a man who follows up making dreams like him who follow[s] up any other [intellectual][3] <truth[?]> manufacture, soon comes to have a larger apprehension of his business: he also sees clearer, as well as farther, every day: what was before simple becomes complex—what seemed one, a thing of many parts—all having relation, one to another, and each to the whole; what was apparently plain and easy, intricate and subtile; in short, the changes stop not till he seems, as it were, to see quite another thing, and with other eyes. But does not his power increase with his knowledge? Certainly. Yet his labour at the same time accumulates; since his knowledge only informs him that he has more to do. Thus must it be with every artist, if he is not content to repeat himself. If he have a true love of excellence, and the pursuit of it be his real object, he will find it (I should think) impossible to huddle over defects for the sake of sparing himself labour. And if his aim be excellence, though every day makes it more distinct, yet every day also shews its attainment to be more arduous. A sanguine youth <might> may here ask "who then would be a painter?" That same youth, if he have the courage to grow old in his art, might hereafter answer. "Himself;" for he would then have learnt, that to overcome a difficulty is to create a pleasure. To advance is a law of the mind; and (so its object be innocent) every obstacle removed clears away a step nearer happiness. To labour then is both natural and desirable; and wise, since a wise

Providence has so ordained it. What artist then s[hould] [page torn] complain of labour? Not I for one. As it [page torn] the pleasure in my art, I certainly do n [page torn] the moral value of labour too well to complain of it. And yet this one picture, on which I am now employed, has caused me many and many an anxious day. And why?—Because on this alone depends so *much* <[two or more words undecipherable] with than art yet> besides fame; for on this alone has for so many years depended the long-hoped for meeting with a good Mother, and so many other dear relatives. But do not think I am repining, deeply anxious as I have felt, and still feel. I may grieve, but not repine. It becomes neither a man of sense, nor a christian to repine at what he cannot help. I have been long schooled to patience and submission. I endeavour to practice them as christian duties. I am doing my *best*—and this sustains me; and, with Heaven's blessing, I look forward to a happy conclusion.

Your account of Mr. West's Picture,[4] as well as I recollect it, seems to me very just; and I perfectly agree with you in your criticism on the figure of the Saviour. Yet Mr. West <cannot [three-quarters of a line undecipherable]> has only added one more to the uniform failures of all his predecessors. It is indeed, as you have truly said, "a face no mortal has ever, or ever can pourtray." And it is one which I have long since resolved never to attempt.—I sincerely thank you for the kind feelings manifested in the concluding remarks of your letter. What I have to say on the subject I must defer till I have the pleasure of seeing you in Charleston, which I still hope for this winter—though it will be much later in the season than I had calculated; for Belshazzer, though near a close, is still unfinished in spite of all my efforts.—We have had some very severe weather here—the thermometer 4 degrees below zero; the cold and an unusual succession of dark weather here impeded me a good deal. Believe me, with sincere respect and esteem truly yours

Wa. Allston

[In the margin] Pray present my best respects to Mrs. Cogdell,[5] and remember me most cordially to White and Fraser. I suppose my Mother is now at St Thomas's with my sister Mrs. Wigfall.[6] Should you see her, give my love to her and tell her I am well. I wrote her not very long since.[7]—Since you left Boston I have had a very severe attack <of a> similar to the complaint, I told you I had in England. I am now, however, quite well.

ADDRESSED: John S. Cogdell Esqre / Charleston, / South Carolina. SOURCE: Manuscript. Printed in part in Flagg, pp. 221-23, dated 1828.

1. In a supplemental tale in Richard F. Burton's edition *The Thousand and One Nights*, or *The Arabian Nights' Entertainments*, Aladdin obtains a magic lamp and ring, with which he commands two genies who gratify all his wishes. WA may have had his attention particularly drawn to this work by Irving. At an undetermined date he composed a poem, of which nine stanzas survive, about one Abdulla of Bagdad, son of "Ben Hassan, the Proud," who fought valorously on "the banks of the Nile" and ran his sword down the crocodile's jaws "like the <dauntless Ichneumon> Ibex of Egypt," but was disconsolate until love came to him. The names of the characters,

common as they are, are similar to those in Irving's play *Abu Hassan* (1823), adapted from the opera by Maria von Weber and Franz Karl Heimers based on the tale of Abu-al-Hassan, son of a wealthy merchant of Bagdad, in the supplemental tale in Burton's edition called "The Sleeper and the Waker." A few years earlier, during the period when he and WA were associated in London, Irving was interested in adapting certain Arabian tales for Murray, probably from the same work, but nothing came of the matter (Irving, *Letters* 2:16, 102). In his undated satire on architecture in Boston WA also referred to characters in the *Arabian Nights,* though he apparently made them up. 2. The emphasis on continual work on the part of the artist was made by WA throughout his life. Monaldi is characterized as having "perseverance," one of the "practical adjuncts" of genius and the "one mode of making endurable the perpetual craving of any master-passion—the continually laboring to satisfy it," and "never felt that he had been toiling, even when the dawn, as it often happened, broke in upon his labors" (*Monaldi,* p. 25). 3. WA's brackets. 4. West's *Christ Healing the Sick,* which Cogdell apparently saw in Philadelphia. 5. Cogdell's wife was the former Maria Gilchrist of Charleston, S.C. 6. Eliza Moore (Flagg) Wigfall (Webber, "Moore of St. Thomas' Parish," p. 167), WA's half-sister. 7. None of WA's letters to his mother mentioned in his letters to Cogdell seem to have been preserved.

138. To Henry Alexander Scammell Dearborn Boston, March 22d, 1826.

Gen. H.S. Dearborn, / Dear Sir: Understanding that a vacancy has occurred in the Customs, I beg leave to ask your good offices in behalf of my brother, Wm. M. Allston.[1] In a former application, which your friendly sentiments induced me to make some years since, I observed, that for my brother's integrity I would fully vouch: while I repeat this assurance as to his personal character, permit me to add, that I am well assured by others, and more competent judges than myself, that his knowledge and habits of business also qualify him for a faithful discharge of the duties required in the office alluded to.

I need hardly say that Genl. Dearborn's favourable attention to this request would be most gratefully acknowledged, and not less by myself than my brother.

With sincere respect, / Your obedt. servt. / Washington Allston

SOURCE: Manuscript, Gratz Collection, Historical Society of Pennsylvania.

1. Dearborn was collector of the customhouse in Boston from 1812 to 1829. There seems to be no record that William M. Allston received an appointment to a position there.

139. From Horatio Greenough Rome May 9th 1826

My Dear Sir: I had in my letter to Mr. Edmund[1] given a hasty outline of my plans and my progress in order that I might have the benefit of both your remarks for I feared I should not have time to write you—but a circumstance has delayed the departure of my friend, and I seize the interim to express myself more fully—I shall tell my opinions and open my heart to you sir with confidence and with pleasure—sure—that what is true will please you & that where I mistake you will correct me—

When I first came to Rome I was engrossed with the *means* of our art. Happening to fall in with men whose chief merit is in *execution* and hearing nothing but their opinions on art I was led for a few weeks to think more of the mechanical than the truly intellectual part of the art & though I had a strong notion that *something more* than mere drawing and composition was necessary yet my motion was vague. I applied myself with eagerness to my work however—soon mastered all that seemed so wonderful in execution and obtained some notion of form—But the acquaintance of Thorwaldsen[2] made the greatest change in my views—By a *few words* which he said in expressing his opinion on my work—he learned me to think for myself in my art—This I have done—of course imperfectly yet industriously and faithfully. My object now is to obtain in *execution*—a truth of eye and hand & a command over my material which will enable me to model the figure in all its ages from infancy to decrepitude—under any circumstances naked—draped—etc at rest, in action—By means of this power I hope to embody my *composition* of which I wish to make myself completely a master from the mere management of line as in Architecture & single statues up to the true poetry of telling a story with truth and grace. I hope also to pay much attention to *character* a beauty in a work of art perhaps the most gratifying of all to the intellect & which has been always most neglected—in fact none but the very first minds have seized it or discovered its principles.

I would not convey an idea that I think the above powers are to be acquired separately—I have made it a point to study them all together. The only separate studies I follow are those of parts—as the extremities for instance and of drapery which I carry on at my leisure hours.

I have become fond of *portrait*. I have found it a difficult but a very interesting study—to seize the character of an individual—& then there is always so much beautiful & characteristic detail in a face that much of execution & form may be learned from modelling it—

The Italians generally have a *narrow* idea of art—They look merely at execution—there are one or two very honourable exceptions however in my art and there are in yours Camuccini[3] and Benvenuti who are thoroughly *studied* in the *academical* departments but in whose work, except a pleasing management of line, I never saw one jot of what is dear to me in a picture—The English again though they rather *neglect* all that the Italians aim at produce delightful works. Their principal sculptor—Mr. Gibson[4] was a pupil and is a disciple of Canova[5] an artist of whom I think less every day—He was clever. But he was superficial & sensual in his style—& a most barefaced misrepresenter of Nature—He I am convinced will fall *very low very shortly*—It is astonishing to me that an artist ever attempts to imitate another in what *characterises* his style as *individual*. After all the sad examples before our eyes—yet still desirous of doing something *like* what is established in reputation they *ape* instead of truly *imitating*. They *study* the *Greeks* for examples *altogether* instead of studying as the Greeks *did*.[6]

The Germans[7] are in my opinion a most respectable band of artists. Though their second rate men not *comprehending* fully the principles on which their superiours study the old masters fall into *manner*—yet it is not a manner of ignorant knack or facility. It is laborious & has much that is valuab[le in] [*page torn*] it. But their first men are wonderful—A laborious investiga[tion] [*page torn*] of Nature and industrious study of the means of art is with them made to bear in telling the most beautiful poetical stories & in rendering the most delicate & deep sentiment. I shall be much disappointed if they do not found a school of pure & solid art—Something as a Scotch proverb says "that the wind will not pass under"—

I have already finished a figure which occupied me several months and some busts.[8] Whenever I see a fine cast from Nature I purchase it and from these parts I model at my leisure—I find that I see the Antique with a different eye after it—The figure at which I am at present employed is a David—"Thou comest to me with a spear and shield etc."[9] I am getting every day more and more in love with the subject as a study of form and character. I hope hereafter to attempt composition in groups and bas relief—Should I be able I think of remaining here several years more—for to leave Rome not master of my art and that too without any hopes of employment at home would be blasting all I am sure—We have all been delighted here with the news of the sale of your picture[10]—The English all think of having you yet in London—they think you will certainly return—There are several artists here who were here with you—the Rippenhousens[11]—Thorwaldsen—Alvarez[12]—etc—

Should I please myself in my David—I think of sending a drawing of it to Boston—These have been here—Mr Fisher[13] & Mr McLellan[14] of New York—a young painter who has a good notion of colour—. Mr Weir[15] of NY is my present companion—we live together. He is studying historical painting—With every wish for your happiness

Sir am Yours—Horatio Greenough

ADDRESSED: Mr Washington Alston Esqr / *Boston Mass.* SOURCE: Greenough, *Letters*, pp. 7-9.

1. Edmund T. Dana. 2. Albert Bertel Thorvaldsen (1770-1844), Danish sculptor, spent most of his life in Rome. 3. Vincenzo Camuccini (1771-1844), the leading Italian painter of the neoclassical school, lived in Rome. 4. John Gibson (1790-1866), English sculptor, spent most of his life in Rome. 5. Antonio Canova (1757-1822), Italian sculptor, was the founder of the neoclassical school of sculpture. Greenough was probably influenced by WA in his repudiation of this school and his emphasis on the intellectual content of a work of art. 6. In the last few paragraphs Greenough was echoing sentiments often expressed by WA. 7. Presumably Greenough refers to the German painters in Rome who had admired and been influenced by WA during his stay there. 8. Greenough's figure was that of the dead Abel, from Gen. 4:8, and one of his busts was a self-portrait. 9. 1 Sam. 17:45. The statue was not finished, Greenough's

work being interrupted by illness. 10. *The Dead Man Restored.* 11. The brothers Franz (1786-1831) and Johann (1789-1860), Riepenhausen, German engravers and painters, lived in Rome from 1807 until their deaths. 12. Don José Alverez de Pereira y Cubero (1768-1827), Spanish sculptor. He settled in Rome in 1804. 13. Alvan Fisher. 14. Probably Thomas McCleland, or McClelland, who was painting in New York in the 1820s. 15. Robert Walter Weir. (1803-89), New York painter and teacher of drawing, was in Italy studying painting from 1824 to 1827.

140. To John Stevens Cogdell Boston, July 1st 1826.

Dear Cogdell: I suppose you know that I am not famed for being a very frequent correspondent. I must acknowledge that I am not. Perhaps, however, were the number of letters known which I write in the course of a year, I might not be thought quite so sad a one. That I write many letters then supposes many correspondents; which is indeed the case—<for the> in Europe as well as here. When this is considered, together with the little leisures which my arduous profession leaves me, I feel very sure that you will allow much for me.

When I wrote the passage, which you quote from my letter, in your last, I sincerely entertained the hope it expressed; but it was grounded on the contingency of my possessing the health & ability requisite to complete the work on which <have raised so [?]> many other of my hopes have been raised. And I have failed from the want of both. In addition to other calamities, I was taken from my labour two months at one time by a severe attack of the Influenza. Indeed it is no exaggeration when I say, that I have lost, by illness and bad weather, more than four months since October. You tell me very kindly to keep up my spirits. I thank you. It has been no easy matter to do so, I assure you. Were nothing at stake—at least were the stake any other than it is—I should count these interruptions and delays as nothing; for I may say, from experience, that I am patient of toil and obstacle; but when the thought crosses me of how much is depending on my present labour—I have need indeed of all my philosophy to keep in heart. Affliction and various misfortunes have long since taught me the duty of resignation. I may say that I have been inured to disappointments; not that I do not keenly feel them; but that I have learned to submit to them; and it is well for my present work that I have been, requiring as it does not only all my faculties, but their free exercise. I cannot say, however, (though *proof against* absolute despondency) that I have always been able to sustain that entire self-possession so essential to their freedom. I could not always drive from me the benumbing anxious thought; it would come in the midst of my work; and there *have been* times when it has <seemed to> fallen upon me like the *gigantic hand* in the Castle of Otranto,[1] as if stretched forth from my picture, and about to crush me through the floor. This may seem strong; but—if you have ever felt "the sinking of the heart" when in the midst of a work, on the success of which you *all* depended, and that success too depending on a thorough self-possession, you will not think it too strong. This may in part account for my *doing*, and *undoing* and *doing again,* what in <a> happier moments <frame> I might have done at once.—But this is to me a reluctant subject, and I will spare you as well as myself. And it is better that I say no more about my picture until I can have the pleasure of telling you that it is finished.—This, however, I may allow myself to say now, that I have never been so well satisfied with <it> my labours as within the last three months. My health is so much improved that I work eight and nine hours a day.

My friend Mr. Amory[2] has informed me that you had remitted to him, while he was in Philadelphia, the amount of your subscription;[3] for which I beg you to accept my thanks. I shall not however appropriate it to my own use until Belshazzer is ready for delivery to the Subscribers. In the mean time Mr. Amory, who is so kind as to act as Bel's Treasurer, has placed it to your account, and consider it on *interest,* for which he will account to you on the completion of the picture, when I receive the principal.

I have been much gratified by your remark on my Picture of the "Dead Man &c" at Philadelphia; and thank you heartily for the praise bestowed, which is high enough, I am sure, to have satisfied me had my pretensions been much greater. My recollection of the picture is now so indistinct that I should not venture, were I so inclined, to contravert the few objections you have made. It is most probable, were I to see it again, I should agree with you in all, with one exception; and I have no doubt I could point out many faults which your partiality has overlooked. The exception alluded to is <that> to the remark, <that> of the heads of the two Feretrori[4] being too small. Whatever of *style* the character of the design may possess is owing, I think, to this <principle> proportion. It is grounded on a sound principle, extracted from the study of the Antique and the Old Masters, particularly the latter. Michael Angelo owes much of his grandeur to this principle. He has pushed it indeed much farther than I should dare to follow it. I have been much struck however with the justness of your objection to the introduction of the Wife of the Reviving Man; it is so just, that were I to compose the subject again, I should omit her. The incident [her fainting][5] is *dramatic,* and, as such, does not harmonize with the miracle, which is *epic.*—Pray present my best respects to Mrs. Cogdell, and believe me most

Sincerely yours W. Allston.

[In the margin] Should you see my Mother, give my love to her, and say that I am well. I wrote to her a few weeks since. There has been a very handsome notice of Morse's "La Fayette" in the New-York papers.[6]

ADDRESSED: John S. Cogdell Eqre / Charleston, / South Carolina. ANNOTATED by Cogdell: recd 19 July 1826. / Answered—. SOURCE: Manuscript. Printed in Flagg, pp. 208-209)

1. In chapter 5 of Horace Walpole's *The Castle of Otranto* (1764), Bianca sees on the banister of the great stairs a hand in armor of the giant supposed to inhabit the gallery chamber. According to

a prophecy, the castle and lordship of Otranto was to pass from the usurper Manfred to the rightful owner when he should be grown too large to inhabit it. In the "Introductory Discourse" of his lectures on art WA referred to "the Giant of Otranto" to illustrate the way in which the sublime seemed almost to burst imagination (*LA*, p. 68). 2. Nathaniel Amory (1777-1842). He was engaged in business in New Orleans for many years with the firm of Nott and Callender. Later he lived in Watertown, Mass., served from 1827 to 1829 as navy agent at Pensacola, Fla., and passed his last years in Newport, R.I. ("Memoirs of the Family of Amory," *NEGHR* 10 [1856]: 64). He owned at one time WA's self-portrait (1805) and his *Edwin* and was the largest subscriber to the Tripartite Agreement. His daughter Jane R. married John E. Allston, a nephew of WA's (*Rhode Island Republican*, 26 Aug. 1840). 3. Cogdell held two shares in the Tripartite Agreement. 4. WA refers to the two keepers of the tomb at the top of the painting in the background. 5. WA's brackets. 6. Morse painted a full-length portrait of Lafayette during his visit to America in 1824-25 for the city of New York, it was completed early in 1826. The newspaper notice has not been located.

141. From Charles Robert Leslie

London July 28th 1826

My dear Sir: It is, as you know, a very long time since I have written to you, and it is also, as you *do not* know, a very long time since I have every day thought of doing it; but my intention that when I did write it should be a *very long* letter is partly the cause why I have been so *very long* only thinking of it. You have written to me often in the mean time—but you use me very ill:—for, when my expectation to hear a great deal about you, is raised by the sight of your hand writing on the outside of a letter.—the inside,—which as Tony Lumpkin remarks "generally contains the cream of the correspondence"[1] proves to be only a brief account of somebody who has asked you for a letter to me, & not one word of yourself. Mind I don't object to your introducing as many of your friends as you please, to me,—but why cannot the letters you give them carry double & bring me a little more of you then just your name at the end. I feel it somewhat hard that all conversation with you (of whom I think constantly in a way I must not tell you, it is so much above my thoughts of the generality of people) should be entirely at an end when there are such things as pens, ink & paper in the world. I have the vanity to believe you think as often of me as I do of you:—it is then I fear only laziness on both sides that we talk so little across the water. Now as I intend this letter to be a model for you to imitate, I shall begin with what is very apt to be uppermost in the mind of every one I believe but you, namely, self. You have heard that I have got a wife, & perhaps it may not be news to you that I have also a son. He was born on the 14th of May and is a tolerably fine child.[2] I have had however a thousand anxieties already on his account, & I have sometimes thought them all paid for by a simple smile from the little rogue. I live now in that manner that always best suited my inclination;—a secluded life in a large city where I can have all the pleasures of retirement and yet be in the midst of the world. I can have society or not just as I please, and I find with that of my wife & child & a few books I want little else. She is as fond of retirement as I am, and finds amusement enough in attending to her little pet & her household affairs. If my health is granted to me & that of my wife & child I have not another earthly wish, unless it is that I could have you & one or two more I could name with me, & indeed I am unwilling to give up the hope that this may yet be. It is at present much more the fashion for the rich people to employ the living artist than it was when you were in London, whether it will last or not I cannot say; but I do think if you were with us you would not want encouragement.

There was at the B. Gallery an exhibition last summer of the best works of living artists borrowed from the different private collections & I assure you we made a very respectable show. Your Jacob's dream was among them & looked very grand. I gave it a coat of varnish which it much wanted. This year the King[3] has lent them the whole of his collection of the old masters. They are principally Dutch pictures & very fine they are. How I wish I could have but one lounge through these rooms with you. The national Gallery of which Mr. Angerstein's collection formed the nucleus & which is now open to the public at his house[4] has been increased by a donation from Sir George Beaumont of most of his pictures. Among others he has given three very fine small Claudes, a perfect portrait of a man by Rembrandt, a noble landscape by Rubens, the finest Canaletti[5] I ever saw & two very fine Poussins. The Government have also added the "Bacchus & Ariadne" by Titian, a bachanalian subject by Poussin & little Madonna & infant by Coreggio, but for the latter they gave too high a price. This exhibition is open all the year round much on the plan of the Louvre, and as there are always some old pictures in the painting School at the Academy, an artist living in London may have immediate success to fine pictures any day in the year which was not the case when you were with us. I am at present engaged on two pictures. One is for the Duke of Bedford.[6] The subject is Lady Jane Grey persuaded by her friends to accept the crown.[7] The other is a small one from Shakespeare's Henry 8th. Queen Catherine listening to one of her maids, who is playing the lute to her.[8] This is the picture I intend to present to the Academy for my diploma & must be completed by October next. By the bye you are entitled to two tickets every year for the private view at the academy previous to the opening of the exhibition. Now it is a pity they should be lost. If you will send over a written order addressed to Mr. Howard the Secretary they can be given to any of your friends here you please; & if there is nobody else you wish to oblige with them you may make them over to your humble servant who can always dispose of such things. I have not seen Mr. Saml Williams for some time, but intend calling on him to day, being obliged to go into the city. He has borne his reverse of fortune extremely well,[9] owing to the great kindness he has met with I believe from most of his countrymen with whom he was connected, & certainly no man better deserved it at their hands. Washington Irving is now in Spain where he is occupied with some literary project.[10] I had a letter from him not long since from Madrid.[11] He wrote in good health & spirits. I have just written to our friend Morse giving what information I could on the subject of Academies.[12] He seems to be a great man among them at New York. Give my best respects to your friend Mr. R. Dana.

Since my marriage I have reread with greater interest than ever his remarks on the influence a woman has with a man of any sensibility—& I feel personally obliged to him for writing so beautifully & truly on the subject.[13] Please also to give my sincere regards to Mr. Wm. Channing & his lady. He is a man I feel almost sorry that I ever saw, since I could not see more of him, *but* I ought not to say so for a glimpse of such a man is calculated to do one good for the rest of one's life. Yours ever

CR Leslie

ADDRESSED: Washington Allston Esqr A.R.A. / Boston / Masstts. SOURCE: Manuscript, Houghton.

1. Lumpkin, a low character who gives himself the airs of a gentleman in Oliver Goldsmith's *She Stoops to Conquer* (1773), says, "the inside of a letter is always the cream of the correspondence" (4.1). 2. Robert Charles Leslie became a painter (Leslie, pp. 265, 353). 3. George III, king of England, 1760-1820. 4. The National Gallery of Art was located in Angerstein's house at 100 Pall Mall until 1834. 5. Antonio Canale Canaletto (1697-1768), Venetian painter. 6. John Russell (1792-1878), 6th duke of Bedford. 7. Lady Jane Grey Dudley (1537-54) yielded to the entreaties of her father, father-in-law, and husband to agree to the settlement by Edward VI of the crown on her in a conspiracy which brought about her death. 8. *The Famous History of the Life of King Henry the Eighth* 3.1.1-14. 9. In 1825 he stopped payment on obligations amounting to £400,000, causing uneasiness in London financial circles (Irving, *Letters* 2:145-47). 10. Irving went to Spain in February 1826, having been given an appointment in the American Legation there for the purpose of translating Don Martin Fernández de Navarrete's *Colección de los viages y descubrimientos, que hicieron por mar los españoles desde fines del siglio XV,* consisting of abstracts from the journals of Columbus and several related documents, published in 1825 (Williams, 1:297-378). He remained until 1829. 11. Written on 21 April 1826 (*Letters* 2:195-97). 12. Morse probably asked Leslie's help in preparing his address *Academies of Art,* delivered at the NAD in 1827. 13. In "Domestic Life," which appeared in the *Idle Man* 1 (1821), RHD elaborated on his thesis that "in the ordinary affair of life, a woman has a greater influence over those near her than a man."

142. To ? Boston, Sister Street, 1 Novbr 1826

Dear Sir: I am very sorry that my professional engagements[1] are at present of so urgent a nature as to prevent my accepting your obliging invitation to dinner; it would otherwise give me great pleasure to wait on you; but as I cannot do this without the loss of a day, which I could ill spare just at this time, I trust you will have the goodness to excuse me, and to allow me to avail myself of your proposal to favour me with a call. My Lodgings are at Mrs. Smith's,[2] at the corner of Sister Street;[3] where I shall be hapy to see you, at eleven o'clock, on Friday morning, or on any other day, about that hour, which you may name as more convenient to you.

From what I have seen of Mr. Andrews,[4] I am much pleased with his manners, and from the specimens he has shewn me, I think very favourably of his talents—But, as I hope to have the pleasure of seeing you, I had better defer replying to your letter till then. I remain

very respectfully, Yrs / W. Allston.

SOURCE: Manuscript, Houghton.

1. By 9 November WA had been engaged by the proprietor of the *Albany*, a steamboat under construction in Philadelphia, predicted to be "the most splendid ever built," to paint a historical picture in a gallery on board, for which Morse, Vanderlyn, and Sully were engaged for other historical pictures and the principal landscape painters also engaged (Morse 1:288-89). WA did not contribute a painting but the other artists did. 2. Catherine Smith, widow of Artemus Smith, lived on the corner of Sister and Williams streets (*Boston City Directory* for 1825-36). 3. According to Sweetser, when WA lived at this address he got his meals at the famous restaurant of Rouillard at the corner of Milk and Congress Streets. 4. Joseph Andrews (ca. 1805-73), wood and line engraver, worked in Boston except for several trips to Europe.

143. To Charles Robert Leslie Boston, 9 Novbr 1826.

Dear Leslie: I write you again, and yet not with the intention of fulfilling my long-made promise of a *long letter.* But I know you will readily forgive the delay when you shall hereafter learn [written over "hear"] its cause. I have had many things to depress, and to indispose me for writing about myself. And though nothing is more common, yet, as I could never see the benefit, either to ourselves, or friends, of talking about our misfortunes, so I make it a rule to spare both parties by holding my tongue till I can use it to a more useful, or pleasurable purpose. I trust, however, that the difficulties under which I have so long laboured will soon be at an end, and leave me in a condition to play the part of *Hero* to a letter, with more <assurance> pleasure to you, and without pain to myself.—But all this between *ourselves* except and, I will add, Collins—to whom I wish you to assign it as the true cause of my not writing to him, telling him at the same time that I will make him ample amends when my bright day comes.

My purpose in writing to you now is to ask your good offices in behalf of a most valued friend: one who has been to me a *friend in need;* and to whom I could render no service that would <[two words undecipherable] gratified> make me less a moral debtor. Kindness when disinterested can never be repaid; and such has his been to me.

This preface might perhaps seem to announce a more important service than the one I would here render Mr. Amory; but I could not forbear saying what I have—or indeed adding, *malgrè* the occasion, that he is one of the few men who <that> would find it impossible to make you feel "gratitude as a burthen."[1] But to the point. Mr. Amory has shipped, by the Plato, for Liverpool, three Pictures, which will be sent to Messrs Baring and Bates,[2] London, for sale. Now the favour I have to ask of you is to go and look at them, and, *if they please you,* to make favourable mention of them to such gentlemen, should you know any, as you may think likely to become purchasers. In making this request Mr. Amory <joins me in saying that> would not for the world wish [written over "have"] you to utter a syllable in their favour unless you *liked* the pictures; nor would I propose it on any other condition. All we ask is your *unbiased* opinion, and good word, if *favourable* and if the opportunity occur, to speak it. This bring premised, (as the Lawyers say) I may now give my opinion; but I give it without even the wish that it should affect yours, however confidently I speak. The Claude is genuine: I have no doubt of it whatever. No other man ever painted such an atmosphere as is there. Of the Salvator Rosa—I have too little acquaintance with Salvator's hand to say whether it is by him or not. But, if it is not by him <I do not think> it must be an *original* by some other master; it does not look like a copy. But, by whomever it may be, I think is a very fine picture. And so it seems to have been thought by others, having been sold many years since in Paris for two thousand dollars, and at a time when the English were not there, and of course money more scarce. It went thence to Switzerland. The Backhuysen,[3] so far as am acquainted with the master, appears to be genuine. And this too, if not a Backhuysen, I would venture to say is no copy.—These pictures before they came into Mr. Amory's possession belonged to Mrs. Amory's Uncle,[4] who lived many years in France and I believe died there.—You no doubt well remember Mr. & Mrs. A in London.[5] They well remember [you] [page torn]

And now accept my congratulation on the birth of your son and *heir.* I hope [page torn] he will inherit (if your modesty will al[low] [page torn] me to say it) both your virtues and genius. At any rate, he may the former, as he will have the advantage of his father's example; and should that only fall to his lot, better that than only the latter—for goodness before greatness every wise man must wish in those he loves.

I enclose a letter to Mr. Howard, requesting him to transfer to you one of the Tickets, to which you say I am entitled as an Associate; the other I have asked him to give to Collins. Though it is but a trifle, yet I know that Collins will accept it as a mark of my continued regard, which I can assure him has not abated an atom in spite of time and distance.—I have not seen Dr. Channing for a fortnight as [?] he has been in the country, or he would like I know to be remembered to you, of whom he speaks in a way that I know must please you. I need not tell you how much pleasure your continued success has given me. Go on and prosper, and may God bless you and yours.

Ever & truly yrs / W. Allston.

[In the margins] I feel as if I know your wife,[6] though I never saw her—so make my respects to her. Remember me particularly to Mr. G. & C. Williams—and to all who ask after me; to Mr. Coleridge and friends at Highgate and to Sir Geo. & Lady Beaumont, & to Collard. Mr. Macready[7] is now playing here to overflowing houses, and is much admired. I am very much pleased with his manners. He seems modest and is a gentleman.

ADDRESSED: Charles R. Leslie Esqre R.A. Lisson Grove, / London. SOURCE: Manuscript. Printed in Flagg, pp. 211-13.

1. "Gratitude is a burden upon our imperfect nature" (P.D. Stanhope, Lord Chesterfield, *Letters to his Son*, 7 Nov. 1765). The epigram also appears in Denis Diderot's *Encycopedie*. 2. John

Baring, 3d son of the financier Sir Thomas Baring, and Joshua Bates (1788-1864) became partners in the banking house of Baring and Bates in London in 1826 on the failure of Samuel Williams. They had much of the American business there. 3. Ludolf Backhuysen (1631-1708), Dutch painter. 4. Mary (Preble) Amory was the wife of Nathaniel Amory. According to Sweetser, WA gave her his self-portrait of 1805. Her uncle, brother of her father Ebenezer Preble, was Henry Preble (1770-1825), who lived abroad for many years. Before 1794 he was in Paris, where he became a commission merchant, subsequently was the first U.S. commercial agent to Turkey, and from 1818 to 1821 was U.S. consul in Palermo. He had returned to America by 1822 (Capt. George Henry Preble, "The Preble Family," *NEGHR* 24 [1870]: 253-56; Capt. George Henry Preble, comp., "Brigadier General Jedidiah Preble, 1707-1784," *NEGHR* 22 [1868]: 419). Another brother was Commodore Edward Preble. 5. The Amorys were in London at least in the fall of 1811 and early in 1812. 6. Harriet (Stone) Leslie, who married Leslie on 11 April 1825 (Irving, *Letters* 2:754). 7. William Charles Macready (1793-1873), English actor, whom WA probably saw first in London, where he made his first appearance on 16 September 1816. He visited America in 1826 and appeared at the Boston Theatre on 1-4, 6-11, 13-15 November 1826 in *Virginius, or The Liberation of Rome; Macbeth; Damon & Pythyas; William Tell, or The Hero of Switzerland; Hamlet;* and *Coriolanus*. The peformances were so poplar that speculation with tickets caused them to be sold at public auction (*Boston Daily Advertiser*).

144. To George Ticknor Sister Street, 25 May, 1827.

My dear Sir: I have been wishing for an opportunity to express my acknowledgements for an obligation for which I find I have been long unconsciously indebted to you.[1] The generous, and more especially the delicate, manner in which it was confered made an impression at the time that I felt would endure through life: and I have loved to recur to it, as to a bright spot in a memory but too often clouded of late years. I hardly need add that the remembrance of an act so truly kind will lose nothing of its interest now that I know whence it came. I feel that the pleasure of gratitude is doubled in knowing that I owe it to one among the few persons to whom, had it been left to me to choose, I should have most wished to have been obliged.

With unfeigned respect and esteem, / ever gratefully yours, / W. Allston.

ADDRESSED: Professor Ticknor, / Common Street.[2] SOURCE: Manuscript, Dartmouth College Library.

1. Ticknor apparently gave WA money in addition to his subscription to the Tripartite Agreement and contribution in 1835 to the sum raised by some of his friends to pay his debts. 2. Ticknor lived on Common Street from 1823 until his death. He bought his house there in 1829 (*Boston City Directory* for 1823-71; *Life, Letters and Journals of George Ticknor* 1:387).

145. To John Stevens Cogdell Boston, 21 June, 1827.

Dear Cogdell: I have just heard of your arrival in New York, and I send you these few lines to bid you welcome by anticipation to Boston, for, now that you are so near, I cannot doubt that you intend to favour us with a visit.[1] As I am so much in arrears to you in letters, if my apologies were in proportion I fear I should have little room for anything else were I to attempt them now; so, as I hope soon to have the pleasure of seeing you, I shall defer them till then. In the mean time, to take something from my apparent remissness, I must tell you that I sent you (in a letter to my mother) some time since a message respecting your Bust of Dr. Holbrook;[2] which I desired her to tell you I thought did you great credit. I may now add that I consider it, for a first attempt, a very remarkable peformance, and one which gives assurance of future excellence. With some practice and a little hard fagging [you know my doctrine—that nothing is to be done without it][3] I think you will be able safely to sign yourself *Sculptor.* What particularly pleased me in the bust was the *strong marked* character; which satisfied me, though I have never seen the living original, that it must be an excellent likeness. Next to that was the truth of the several quantities—a particular in which most beginners are mainly deficient. As to the faults, they are such as proceed from inexperience, & which time of course will soon enable you to correct. <And I [two words undecipherable]> "I pede fausto."[4]

I suppose you have heard of our Exhibition here.[5] As I am so large a contributor, I suppose I must be careful in speaking of it to except my own works. This, however, I need not be scrupulous about in writing to you, who I know would never suspect me of self-praise. The exhibition then, has surprised every body, myself among them. I assure you that I have seen worse <exhibitions> in London. And what has also been an agreeable matter of wonder <has it> is the astonishing success it has <[word undecipherable] met> had with <from> the public. Day after day, and week after week, it has been thronged to a most delightful degree of annoyance—delightful at least to the astonished artists, to whom it might well have been "jam, jam," but never "satis."—I have seen no account of the Exhibition at New-York. I hope it has been as successful a one. The receipts here have been upwards of 3 thousand dollars. I saw however a very handsome notice of my friend Morse's Address.[6] Pray tell him to send me a copy of it by you.

It gave me great pleasure to hear that the little differences between yourself and Fraser are so happily at an end. Th[ose] [page torn] who love the Arts should of all men be friends. It has been a great source of gratulation to me that some of my nearest friends are Artists. Does Fraser, or our friend White, think of making a northern tour this summer? It would give me great pleasure to meet you all together here.—Mr. Amory (who by the bye is not more of a Scribe than I am) desires his best regards to you. He has a sincere esteem for you. Pray present my best respects to Mrs. Cogdell, who I suppose is with you. Hoping soon to shake hands, believe me

sincerely your friend, / W. Allston

[In the margin] Accept my thanks for the dog.[7] I like it much. It has a great deal of character.

ADDRESSED: John S. Cogdell Esqre / New-York / <[Several undecipherable words] the Post

Office New-York>. Source: Manuscript. Printed, except for the last paragraph and marginal note, in Flagg, pp. 213-14.

1. There seems to be no evidence that Cogdell did so. 2. John Edwards Holbrook (1794-1871), Charleston physician and zoologist, whose early years were spent in Massachusetts; later he went there regularly in the summer. Cogdell presented a cast of the bust, his first, to the BA on 27 February 1827, partly in gratitude for the privileges he enjoyed there in October 1825 ("An All Accomplished Man," *Charleston News and Courier,* 14 July 1901). It was exhibited at the BA in 1841 and several subsequent years. 3. WA's brackets. 4. "The happy step." 5. The first annual exhibition of works of art in the BA Gallery opened in May 1827, at which time three hundred and seventeen paintings and miniatures were shown, including works of old masters from various collections in the city. WA was represented by twelve paintings. 6. On the occasion celebrating the first anniversary of the founding of the NAD, Morse delivered an address tracing the history of academies and institutions for the encouragement of the fine arts. It was published, at the request of the academy, as *Academies of Art: A Discourse, delivered on Thursday, May 3, 1827, in the chapel of Columbia College, before the National Academy of Design, on its first anniversary* (New York, 1827). The *New-York Evening Post* carried a long article about it on 4 May, to which WA may be referring, commending the absence of pretension and display in it and in the delivery. After the prizes were distributed Morse made a short second address in which, expressing sentiments often expressed by WA, he warned the students of painting in the audience not to expect a life of "ease" or "opulence" but rather one of "continued obstacles and discouragements," which could be borne only by "an intense and unextinguishable love of the art." The printed address was severely criticized in the *North American Review* for July, which charged that the academy was presumptuous in assuming the adjective "National." In reply Morse wrote a letter to the *New York Journal of Commerce,* which was printed as *Fine Arts: A Reply to article X, no. LVIII in the North American Review . . .* (New York, 1828). 7. Probably a sketch.

The Boston Athenaeum Exhibitions

Allston's works were more often exhibited at the Boston Athenaeum than at any other place. Established as a library and reading room in 1807, it soon acquired several works of art and in 1827 opened a gallery for the annual exhibition of works in its own and in private collections. Before that time many of them were shown informally. The exhibition of 1827 contained twelve of Allston's paintings, the largest number of his works shown at one time except at the 1839 exhibition in Harding's Gallery. The following were listed in the catalog, together with their owners: *A View [Coast Scene] on the Mediterranean* (Williams), *Florimel [The Flight of Florimel]* (Baldwin), *Rising of a [Thunder]storm at Sea. Pilot Boat Going Off* (Mason), *Miriam (The Prophetess)* (Sears), *Saul and the Witch of Endor* (Perkins), *Landscape, after Sunset [Landscape: Time, after Sunset]* (Codman), *Landscape [Landscape, Evening (Classical Landscape)]* (Dutton), *Beatrice* (Lyman), *Jeremiah Dictating His Prophecy to Baruch the Scribe* (Gibbs), *Katherine, Petruchio, Grumio and the Tailor* (Mrs. George W. Sturgis, wife of the merchant), and *Falstaff and His Recruits at Justice Shallow's [Falstaff Enlisting His Ragged Regiment]* (Sullivan).

The exhibition was highly praised in the *North American Review*, though comparatively little space was devoted to Allston's works, the writer explaining, "We have no room to speak of Allston as we wish." He mentioned several, however: *Jeremiah,* which brought back "the great age of painting," the prophet being a design worthy of Michelangelo, though having a rigid strength too reminiscent of great bodily labor, and the scribe "as beautiful as the imagination of Titian"; *Miriam* and *Saul and the Witch of Endor* as being admirable; and *Beatrice,* "the loveliest creation of his mind." But he called the landscapes "very peculiar," full of fine feeling, poetical imagination and nice observation" but "too much labored" and without "as much of the ease and careless gracefulness of nature, as they have of her brilliant lights, tender glooms, and beautiful forms." He took occasion to regret that *Elijah in the Desert,* "one of the best landscapes that was ever painted," had been allowed to leave the country.[1] A book of poems was published about the works exhibited, *Poetical Illustrations of the Athenaeum Gallery of Paintings,* by William George Crosby (Boston, 1827), which contained four poems about paintings by Allston: "Saul and the Witch of Endor," "Rising of a Thunderstorm at Sea: Pilot Boat Going Off," "Landscape after Sunset," and "The Prophetess."

It was significant, however, that none of these paintings was done after 1821. The reviewer of the Athenaeum exhibition of 1829 in the *North American Review* noted that only *Moonlit Landscape (Moonlight)* was shown at that time and that it was an old painting and asked, "How is it, that he alone, of all our artists the most distinguished, and the most valued, has not produced anything for either of the three exhibitions we have had?" He concluded that there had been many in the 1827 exhibition and that they had been highly esteemed, but pointed out that they had been sent by owners who had long possessed them and that from that time "we have seen nothing, and heard of nothing, which has come from his easel." He would not, he added, "grate harshly on the delicacy of a refined and sensitive mind" but explained, "our admiration of his genius, and our almost irrepressible desire to see more of his productions, lead us to suggest to him the propriety of showing that he is not insensible to the universal homage which his works receive from a discerning public. We think, too, that a man of his celebrity, has become, in some degree, public property; at least he should not treat with neglect, year after year, the anxious expectations of a community that ask only for *something* from his pencil, however slight a production of his genius, which they are already prepared to admire" and concluded that he did not believe Allston was indifferent but regretted only that "any feeling, or any course of events, should have deprived us for so long a time of the pleasure we are sure of enjoying" when looking at one of his pictures.[2] He did not mention the five paintings exhibited at the Athenaeum in 1828, all done earlier, nor *Belshazzar's Feast,* which was abandoned about this time.

The same criticism was voiced regarding the three paintings by Allston exhibited in 1830. In his review of that exhibition in the *North American Review* the editor and diplomat Alexander Hill Everett devoted several pages to a discussion of Allston's work in general, declaring him of all living native artists the one to whose future works the country looked "with reason for the most brilliant exhibitions of talent, and the most valuable accessions" to American public and private collections. He praised those in the exhibition, especially the landscapes, wished that *The Valentine, Miriam,* and *Jeremiah* had also been there, but discussed at some length the fact that relatively few had been produced in the preceding several years. He accounted for it by saying that Allston was "inspired by that exclusive and passionate love for his profession, which is the sure characteristic of a real genius for it, and by a lofty and generous disinterestedness, which has prevented him from consecrating his pencil to its lower and more lucrative departments" but expressed the opinion that though the only thing to complain of in him was that "he is not satisfied himself with the degree of merit, which would satisfy every one else, and employs in correcting, maturing, and repainting a single piece, not always perhaps with any real accession of effect, the time and labor which would have been sufficient for completing a dozen." This "extreme fastidiousness," he conceded, had probably enabled Allston to realize his aims at an earlier period but "the time has now arrived," he thought, when he "might throw it off with advantage, and allow himself a greater rapidity of execution." He hoped that *Belshazzar's Feast* might be finished within the year and that a series of equally meritorious works more rapidly produced might follow.[3]

After the nine paintings listed by Allston in his letter of 18 May 1821 to William Collins as having been done since his return to America in October 1818 his productivity declined markedly. From that time to his death he finished apparently no more than sixteen or seventeen, all the known ones small: possibly one in 1823, one or two about 1828, two in 1831, two in 1832, two in 1835, one in 1837, one before 1839, one in 1839, one about 1840, and two at an undetermined date, probably the 1830s. Eleven others were only partially painted or only sketched, about half of them larger, and still others probably of this period were left in an even more fragmentary state.

Allston nevertheless continued to be exhibited at the Athenaeum each year from 1828 to his death, with the exception of 1839, when the special exhibition was held at Harding's. His paintings shown in 1828 were two versions of *Head of a Jew* (BA), *The Valentine* (Ticknor), *Isaac of York* (BA), *The Robbers [Robbers Fighting with Each Other for the Spoils over a Murdered Traveller]* (Charles Lowell), and *A Landscape [Landscape with a Lake]* (Mason); in 1829, *Moonlight [Moonlit Landscape (Moonlight)]* (Doggett); in 1830, *Landscape with Figures [Italian Landscape]* (G12 ?) (E. Weeks), *Mother and Child* (BA), and *Landscape [Italian Landscape]* (G62) (Eliot); in 1831, *Italian Landscape* (G62) (Eliot), *Miriam the Prophetess* (Sears), *Saul and the Witch of Endor* (Perkins), *The Valentine* (Ticknor), *A View [Coast Scene] on the Mediterranean* (Williams), *Mother and Child* (BA), *Landscape [Landscape, Evening (Classical Landscape)]* (Dutton), *A Spanish Girl in Reverie* (E. [probably the merchant Elijah] Clark), *A Roman Lady Reading* (Edmund Dwight), and *Head of St. Peter* for *The Angel Releasing St. Peter from Prison* (Isaac P. Davis); in 1832, *Storm [Rising of a Thunderstorm at Sea]* (Mrs. Mason), *Landscape: Diana on a Chase* (Baldwin), *A Tuscan Girl* (Sears), and *Lorenzo and Jessica (Jackson);* in 1833 and 1834, *Isaac of York* (BA), and *The Young Troubadour* (John Bryant, Jr.); in 1835, *Samuel Williams* (Williams), *Isaac of York* (BA), and *The Young Troubadour* (the merchant John Bryant, Jr.); in 1836, *Isaac of York* (BA); in 1837, *Italian Landscape [Alpine Landscape]* (Dwight), *Benjamin West* (BA), and *Isaac of York* (BA); in 1838, *Isaac of York* (BA) and *Benjamin West* (BA); in 1842, *Isaac of York* (BA), *Head of a Polish Jew* (BA), and *Landscape, Alpine Scenery* [Diana and Her *Nymphs*] (Davis); in 1843, *A Tuscan Girl* (Sears), *Saul and the Witch of Endor* (Perkins), *Landscape, Alpine Scenery* (Davis), *Isaac of York* (BA), and *Benjamin West* (BA). He withdrew from the exhibitions after the Athenaeum sold his *Mother and Child* in 1837 for $100 plus the Flemish painter Peter Boel's *Fruit and Flower Piece,* owned by the British collector John Watkins Brett, though the paintings by him owned by the Athenaeum and a few others in private hands continued to be shown until his death. Afterward he was represented almost annually until 1873, the most important exhibitions of his work being those of 1847, 1850, 1870, and 1881.

Possibly the ten paintings in the 1831 exhibition, more than in any other except the first, reflect the renewed interest in Allston's work occasioned by his preoccupation beginning about this time with ideal female figures. In his review of the exhibition Franklin Dexter singled out two of these figures and described *A Tuscan Girl,* which was exhibited the next year, for his entire discussion. He considered *The Spanish Girl in Reverie* one of Allston's "very best paintings, both as to composition and execution," and "in atmospheric effect" believed it had never been surpassed. *A Roman Lady Reading,* which he called *Roman Lady Reading Tasso,* he described as a "gem," the "most highly and beautifully finished" of his heads, having such "a charm of expression and of perfect reality" that it might in time become a greater favorite than *The Spanish Girl in Reverie.* "Such pictures," he concluded, "soon become to us something more than mere forms of inanimate beauty," the "mind of the artist" having "endowed them with a portion of his own existence."[4] For two, Allston wrote accompanying poems, "The Spanish Maid" and "The Tuscan Girl," which were printed in the review.

These three paintings, together with the unfinished *Girl in Persian Costume* (ca. 1832), *Rosalie* (1835), *Evening Hymn,* and the unfinished *Una in a Wood* (ca.

1830s), the last having a subject also painted by West, form a group of paintings which Allston did after his return to America in 1818 that are of particular importance. They depict a young girl in a dreamlike attitude, distinguished from the earlier *The Valentine, Study from Life,* and *Beatrice* by having a landscape background, which is also seen in the two versions of *Italian Shepherd Boy* and was probably also in *Edwin,* and by being full-length figures. To this group the earlier *Contemplation* is related and to it belong *The Bride* (1840), *Young Troubadour* (1832), and, though without landscape, *Amy Robsart* (1840), as well as the pair of figures in *Lorenzo and Jessica* and in *Lover Playing a Lute* (ca. 1830s). Altogether these paintings comprise about a third of all Allston did.

The Spanish Girl in Reverie in particular, notable for the title calling attention to the figure's attitude, owes something to Coleridge's play "Remorse," originally "Osorio," which Allston saw at its opening in London. The painting is in effect an illustration for the setting of the third scene of the fourth act of the play, in which Alhadra is alone among mountains by moonlight and soliloquizes about what she sees around her. In Allston's poem "The Spanish Maid" the scene is also mountainous, with particular reference to the Sierra Morena range in southern Spain, and Inez's lover, like Alhadra's husband, is named Isidore and is a warrior, in the play specifically and in the poem by implication a Moor battling Christians.

Most of the figures in these paintings are depicted beside a fountain or body of water or playing a musical instrument or listening to music. In effect these images came to supplant those of Allston's landscapes, which he painted, at least to completion, less often. These paintings are, in fact, his most distinctive, unlike any paintings in America or Europe at the time, and were often recognized as such. In them the influence of Raphael seems to have deepened, as that of Michelangelo—most seen in his monumental historical works, which he had given up painting by now or left unfinished—lessened. In several the technique is also new. In *A Tuscan Girl, Evening Hymn,* and *Rosalie,* as well as *Lorenzo and Jessica,* glazing takes the place of impasto, the glazes are deeper, the lights more luminous, and the shadows more filled with color. He may have been referring to the technique when he said of *Evening Hymn* to Richard Henry Dana, "I feel now, sir, as if I were beginning to understand my art." Dana thought it "the most exquisite thing he has done."[5]

It it is perhaps significant that of these figures only *A Roman Lady Reading,* which in some respects reflects the influence of Michelangelo, Titian, and Sebastiano del Piombo, is a matron, the others being young girls. The only other matrons Allston painted, except for a few groups in landscapes, were the earlier depictions of a mother and child, *Family Group,* and *Mother with Child in Her Lap.* Richard Henry Dana took objection to *A Roman Lady Reading,* which he thought the "most unideal" head he ever saw, adding that Allston seemed to agree with him.[6]

It is also significant that the figure in *A Roman Lady Reading* resembles those in the portrait of Allston's wife and *The Valentine* and that *The Spanish Girl in Reverie, A Tuscan Girl, Evening Hymn, Rosalie,* and the earlier *Beatrice* are notably alike in the rightward and adverted gaze and the features. It would seem that this whole group of paintings was inspired by his wife.

Sweetser thought the "attribute of repose" of Allston's ideal female heads, filling them "with the spirit of contemplation and peace," was "the highest triumph" of what

Lord Napier of Merchiston called "the incomparable pencil of Allston."[7] Probably he meant Sir William Francis Patrick Napier, British soldier, and military historian, and artist, who retired from the Royal Irish Artillery in 1819 and devoted himself to painting and sculpture until 1823, when he began his famous *History of the War in the Peninsula*. During these years Napier lived in London, took instruction from the painter George Jones, who was a student with Allston at the Royal Academy, and was made an honorary member of that institution. Presumably, however, he was referring only to those paintings by Allston which he could have seen in England, particularly *The Angel Releasing St. Peter from Prison, A Mother Watching Her Sleeping Child, Jacob's Dream, Uriel in the Sun, The Sisters, Contemplation,* and *Beatrice,* and possibly the lost *Diana Bathing, Hebe, Silence, Clytie, Hermia and Helena,* and *The Repose in Egypt.* It is possible, in fact, that some of the lost paintings of single female figures done by Allston in England anticipated those he did later in America.

As Allston composed poems for four of these paintings of female figures—"The Spanish Maid," "The Tuscan Girl," "Rosalie," and "The Betrothed," and "The Young Troubadour" as well—it may be said that another poem by him is an accompaniment to the etire group. In "The Angel and the Nightingale" the nightingale is another self-portrait, like Monaldi and like Edwin, though this time in female guise. She is a dreamer, a child of nature, and both a listener to and a producer of music.

Throughout Allston's years in Boston the Athenaeum exhibited works by many of the old masters to whom he referred in his letters and also in his lectures on art, including the Carracci, Claude, Correggio, Raphael, Rembrandt, Reynolds, Rosa, Rubens, Titian, Tintoretto, and several of the Dutch. In 1839 and 1841, casts of Michelangelo's statues for the Medici tombs were presented by Thomas H. Perkins. The private collections exhibited included those by several of Allston's patrons: Nathan Appleton, Charles R. Codman, Isaac P. Davis, Samuel A. Eliot, and Perkins; and by others from outside the city, most notably Antonio Sarti, J.W. Brett, and William Hayward. No doubt Allston renewed his acquaintance with some of these artists by seeing some of their works there, as, for instance, in his citation in his lecture "Art" of a pig in a sty painted by the Englishman George Morland as an example of pleasure to be obtained from humble subjects. Pigs, which appeared in many paintings by Morland, were the subject of several by him in exhibition at the Athenaeum in 1827 and 1837.

In the late 1820's, partly no doubt because of his participation in these exhibitions, Allston began to receive attention also beyond Boston and for more than his painting. The New England writer Samuel Lorenzo Knapp, who lived there during that time, included a description of him among his *Sketches of Public Characters* (1830), saying that Allston had returned from Europe "with a mind enriched by travel and observation, without any diminution of his character or simplicity of his manners," that he consorted with few, having "truly an independent mind," but that he never lacked patronage," naming, however, only three of his larger works.

1. *North American Review* 25 (July 1827): 27-30. 2. Ibid. 29 (July 1829): 258-64. 3. Ibid. 21 (Oct. 1830): 309-37. 4. *Ibid.* 37 (Oct. 1831): 507-10. 5. RHD to Gulian C. Verplanck, 28 Feb. 1835 (Longfellow Historic Site). 6. P. 40. 7. P. 180.

146. To Charles Robert Leslie Boston, 12 August, 1827

Dear Leslie: This will be handed you by Mr. John Greenough, with whom (if he is not already known to you) I beg to make you acquainted. I had enclosed to him a letter of introduction to you before he left Halifax, but, it being doubtful whether it would reach him before he sailed thence, the packet was forwarded by way of New York, with the hope of its meeting him on his arrival in London: this packet I have since learnt was lost in the wreck of the Panthea.[1] And though I understand that Mr. Greenough has already become known to you, I would still add a line or two in his behalf—I need not say as a young artist of talent, which I doubt not you already know him to be—but as a young friend in whom I take a particular interest. I feel assured that for the kind offices, or any friendly advice, which I might ask for him, either as a man or an artist, there will never be wanting a grateful return. And I ask them the more freely of you, as I well know that your disposition to do good is not less than your sense of the paramount importance of a friendly adviser to every young man who has to contend with the difficulties of <you> so ardurous a profession as ours—and one but too often made hopeless by the more formidable temptations of such a town as London.

Of Mr. Greenough's general talent I have a high opinion, and should he profit (as I doubt not he will) of the great advantages for study which London affords, I think I may be justified in anticipating for him, in due time, an eminent rank as an artist. He has had the advantage of a liberal education, and you will find him one of cultivated mind, and of good taste in letters—which, though it does not <always> qualify a man <one> to judge of pictures, much less to paint, must still be a matter of no small moment to a young artist, in as much as refinement in things even remotely connected with it will render him less liable to contract vulgar or narrow views of the Art. He that has elevated views <of> on one subject which he has cultivated is not likely to <move [?]> form mean ones on any other to which he may give his mind. In the truth of this I know you will agree with me, as also in the opinion <of> that no artist of *real* eminence can be found of a vulgar taste even on subjects wholly foreign to his art.

In a former letter—written, I think last Autumn—I enclosed one to Mr. Howard,[2] Secretary to the Royal Academy, requesting him to consider my *Tickets* in future as at the disposal of yourself and Collins. I sent a message at the same time to Collins, stating why I had so long delayed writing him, and also to you why I had not before this redeemed my promise about a long piece of auto-biography. <to yourself> I beg you both to take my *apparent* remissness kindly. It is indeed any thing but real; for you are often in my thoughts—and I need hardly add, that I know how to value such visitors.

Ever truly yours, / W. Allston.

ADDRESSED: Charles R. Leslie Esqre R.A. / Lisson Grove, / Mr. Greenough / London.
SOURCE: Manuscript. Printed in part in Flagg, pp. 214-15.

1. A vessel of the Red Star Lines, Liverpool (William Armstrong Fairburn, *Merchant Sail*

[Center Covell, Me.: Fairburn Marine Educational Foundation, 1945], 2:1299). 2. This letter does not seem to have been preserved.

147. To John Greenough Boston, 12 August, 1827.

My dear Sir: Enclosed you will find a second letter of introduction to Mr. Leslie. I suppose your father[1] has informed you that I had written another, which was lost in the Panthea. <[undecipherable word]> The first was enclosed in a letter to yourself of two closely-written sheets; which I had hoped would shew that I had no disposition to forget you. As you know that I am not celebrated for the frequency of my epistles, you may well suppose that the miscarriage of such an *effort* was learnt with no little regret; but I regretted it the more, as it contained some things which I thought might be of use to you, and which I flattered myself you would value, as coming from one not <often> in the habit of <offering> obtruding his advice. As I took no copy of the letter I should find it difficult now to recall its contents, had I even time to do it, but as I lack this as well as I fear the power, I must defer the attempt to a season of more leisure, which I *trust* will one day come, for I have not known *such a thing* for—I don't know when.

I sent you at the same time a message from Mr. Dana, who requested you to accept the Flaxman,[2] as a present. He sometimes talks of writing to you; but you must not think him unmindful of you though you should never hear from him; for he seldom writes—so seldom indeed that the only way in which I could keep up our correspondence when in England was by *answering* many letters which he never wrote. He often talks about you, and feels kindly toward you; do not therefore interpret his silence otherwise.

I am glad to hear, through Horatio, that you are devoting your time to *drawing*.[3] No reputation, however high during the artist'[s] [page torn] life, will survive him without it—except he be a first-rate colourist, like Sir Joshua. But great as Sir Joshua was—and you know my admiration of him—I still think he would have been ten times greater had he <only> known how to draw,[4] for he had both character and expression, and only lacked the higher invention, because he wanted the *means* of embodying his conception. His capacity for inventing shewed itself <indeed> in his back-ground and his chiaro-scuro, and it would have been equally rich, I have no doubt, in form had he been equally master of that. I am persuaded that *any one* may learn to draw accurately, if he will only be patient, and *fag* for it.[5] To draw *finely*—that is, with grace and beauty—is another thing! this requires genius. But no one can know if he has this genius, until he has *first fagged* to acquire accuracy—I would willingly fill this paper, but I am myself too much fagged with my day's labour. So I must bid you good night.

I shall be glad to hear from you as [page torn] as you feel inclined to write; and I hope that will be often <and I> Tell me all about your studies and progress: the more minute the better; for I think it hardly necessary to tell you that I take an unfeigned interest in your success. May God bless, and prosper you.

Sincerely yours, / W. Allston.

ADDRESSED: John Greenough Esqre / [in another hand] N 214 Strand .— / London
SOURCE: Manuscript.

1. David Greenough (1774-1836), a builder and real-estate dealer in Boston (Greenough, *Letters*, p. 45fn.). 2. Presumably a volume of drawings by John Flaxman. 3. WA repeatedly recommended drawing for artists. Elizabeth Peabody quoted him as saying "Drawing is the first thing, drawing is the second thing, drawing is the third thing" (p. 3). 4. RHD, Jr., recollected WA's saying that Reynolds lacked Van Dyke's correctness in drawing. Reynolds nevertheless emphasized the importance of drawing several times in his discourses. 5. Reynolds also believed that drawing could be learned, in Discourse 2 urging his listeners to "preserve in this custom," assuring them that "this facility is not unobtainable" but was acquired "by an infinite number of acts" and "continual application," and saying in conclusion, "the port-crayon ought to be for ever in your hands."

148. To Henry Pickering

Boston, 23 Novbr 1827.

My Dear Sir: To be of service to young Artists of merit has at all times been to me a pleasant duty: I need hardly say then that in serving any friend of yours I shall find a real pleasure. I therefore most cordially comply with your request. As the limits of a letter, however, will not allow me to offer more than a few general hints, I beg that what I have to say may be considered merely *as such*, and that some allowance be made for the want of connexion. The narrowness of my limits must be my apology for any abrupt transitions.[1]

As you have not mentioned for what part of Europe your Friend[2] means to embark, I suppose you have left it for me to advise on this point. If so, I would recommend his going first to England; where I would have him remain at least half the time he proposes to pass abroad. The present English School comprises a great body of excellent Artists, and many eminent in every branch. At the head of your Friend's department he will find Turner, who, "take him all in all," has no superiour of any age.[3] Turner's "Liber studiorum"[4] would be a most useful work for him to possess. I venture to say this without having seen it—but coming from *him*, I know what it must be. There are many other admirable Landscape-painters whom I could also name; but your friend will hear of them before he has been long in London. I advise this disproportionate stay in England, because I think it important that the *first bias* he receives should be a good one, inasmuch as on this not a little of the future tone of his mind will depend. This bias (in Art as well as in manners) is taken from the *living*—whether we choose it or no; and to impart a true and refined one, together with sound practical principles, I know no modern school of Landscape equally capable with the English; in my judgement it has no living rival; many of them having attained to high excellence, and all knowing—even those who cannot reach it—in what it consists.

On quitting England, a short time may be spent in France, two or three months in Switzerland, and the remainder of the time in Italy. It is hardly necessary to lay out any plan for your Friend when he visits these countries, as he will be enabled to form one more suited to his peculiar wants, by the advice of Artists recently returned from the Continent, whom he will meet in London.

Disjecta membra. You say that your Friend is "a passionate admirer of Nature."[5] Let him never lose his love of her. This may, perhaps, seem to him impossible. But there are Artists, as well as Connoisseurs, who, as Sir Joshua Reynolds says, "have quitted nature without acquiring art."[6] To avoid this, the young artist should study pictures and nature together: he will find them mutually reflect light on each other. In studying the works of other men we are in effect appropriating to ourselves their experience; in this way we may be said to multiply our eyes,[7] and to see a thousand things that might otherwise elude us; in studying nature, we are enabled to separate in Art the true from the factitious: thus we become learned in both. In no other way can a sound critic be formed, much less a sound artist.*[8]

As every Artist must begin by taking many things "on trust,"[9] it is of the last importance that he does not misplace his admiration; for it is not so easy to *unlearn,* as to learn.[10] Hence I would advise the student to select his models from among the highest. In imitating these the difficulty will no doubt be greater than if he followed those who seem nearer to himself: but high attempts have this double advantage, that they make us better acquainted with what we *can not,* as well as what we *can* do.[11] Nor is the former <latter> an unimportant piece of knowledge—if we have but the courage to meet it; it is profitable in more than one sense—since the very process by which we attain to it strengthens our powers in having tasked them to the utmost.*†[11] If many men fail from attempting too much, there are some also who owe their want of success to having attempted too little: for I believe it to be no less difficult for a great mind to excel in trifles, than for a narrow mind to produce a great work.—I would therefore recommend it to your Friend to place at the head of his list Claude, Titian, the two Poussins, Salvator Rosa and Francesco Mola,[12] together with Turner, and the best of the modern Artists, whom I cannot be supposed as meaning to exclude after what I have already said of the English School. I would have him study them all,[13] and master their principles;[14] examine their masses of light, shadow, or colour—observe what are the shapes of these, and how they recall and balance each other; and by what lines, whether of light, shadow, or colour, the eye travels through the picture.[15]

Amongst the painters I have mentioned (with the exception of the two Poussins) no two <of their> styles will be found to have the least resemblance. Yet they are not more unlike than Nature often is at different times to herself.[16] It is for the sake of this difference that I recommend them; as the exclusive study of any one of them,[17] though by the brightest intellect, would never make <another achievement [?]> even a tenth rate Titian or Claude, much less an *original* painter. Every original work becomes so from the infusion (if I may so speak) of the mind of the

Artist;[18] and of this the *fresh materials of nature alone* are susceptible. The works of man cannot be endued with a second life—that is, with the mind of another; they are to another as air already breathed.[19] It is this imparted life which we call genius: we know not how communicated, or what it is; but the spirit within us discerns[20] it in an instant, whether in a picture or a poem, and we pity, love, admire or give the reins <up> to the mind, to travel where it listeth through the nameless regions of reverie.

It is not unusual for young artists to be startled at the depth of tone and powerful chiaro'scuro of the Old Masters,[21] and to think them exaggerated, if not unnatural. But the Old Masters are not only true, but, in their best works, express the highest truth—such as Nature reveals only to a gifted few. Their effects may be called the poetical moods of nature—occurring rarely, and only *known to occur* to poetical minds. I believe Sir Joshua Reynolds had the same thought somewhere, though he has expressed it better.[22]

I think it is Young who says that "An undevout Astronomer is mad":[23] this may well also apply to the Painter. It has been my happiness to know many Artists who were no less estimable for their mortal and religious characters, than distinguished for their genius. I hope your young Friend may be added to their number. He has chosen a profession in itself innocent, and if properly pursued—that is, for its own sake,[24] in a high degree elevating. Indeed it seems as if no one could *truly* love Nature without loving its Divine Author; who in all his works—even in the terrible, <when> if right <interpreted> understood, no less than in the beautiful[25]—speaks only in the language of love.

I feel assured that to you I need not apologize for these concluding remarks. When we hear of a young man of genius it is natural to wish him a happiness proportioned to his endowments.

I remain, dear / Sir, with the highest esteem and respect, /

sincerely yours / W. Allston.

I am very much pleased with the engraving of your "Moonlight."[26]
To Henry Pickering Esqre.

*Reynolds †Sir Joshua Reynolds of whom, as you perceive, I make free use.

SOURCE: Manuscript.

1. This letter constitutes the fullest expression of WA's artistic philosophy apart from his lectures on art and contains the most specific examples of his indebtedness to Reynolds's Discourses.
2. Thomas Cole. He did not go to Europe until 1829, when he was enabled to do so by the art patron Robert Gilmor, Jr. At that time he followed in general the advice of WA. He went first to England, where he met some of the painters whom WA recommended as well as other friends of his but did not stay as long as suggested, and then to Italy, where he stayed longer than suggested, avoiding Switzerland because of the political unrest on the continent (Louis L. Noble, *The Course of Empire, Voyage of Life, and Other Pictures of Thomas Cole, N.A. with Selections from his Letters and Miscellaneous Writings: Illustrative of his Life, Character, and Genius* [New York, 1853], pp. 109-25). He visited Switzerland in 1841, on his second trip to Europe. 3. "He was

a man, take him for all in all, / I shall not look upon his like again" (*Hamlet* 1.2.186-87). 4. Turner's *Liber Studiorium,* published in twenty numbers from 1807 to 1819, illustrated all classes of landscape composition by seventy-one engravings in imitation of drawings in chiaroscuro. 5. Cole's father was induced to come to America from England largely because of his son's curiosity about American scenery. Cole was not only a landscape painter and introduced many details from nature in his allegorical works, but a writer about nature in his journal, short pieces of fiction, poems, and essays, all emphasizing its wild or uncultivated state (Noble, passim; "Lecture on American Scenery Delivered before the Catskill Lyceum, April 1st, 1841," *Northern Light* 1 [1841]: 25-26). Bryant's Sonnet "To Cole, the Painter Departing for Europe" (1828) urged him to keep his "earlier, wilder image bright" amid the more cultivated European scenes. 6. In his note 49 to Charles Albert Fresnoy's *The Art of Painting,* Reynolds wrote, "The only opinions of which no use can be made, are those of half-learned connoisseurs, who have quitted nature and have not acquired art" and in Discourse 12 referred to "those artists who have quitted the service of nature" and put themselves under the service of a "capricious fantastical mistress." 7. WA echoed this sentence in the conclusion of his lecture "Composition," where he called the work of artists of the past, insofar as they were true, an "extension of Nature," in whom "we may be said to possess a multiplied life" (*LA,* pp. 163, 164). 8. In the preceding three sentences WA was in agreement with Reynolds's pronouncements in several discourses. In Discourse 2 he described the third period of a young artist's study as that in which he examines works of art by the "standard of nature . . . corrects what is erroneous, supplies what is scanty, and adds, by his own observation, what the industry of his predecessors may have yet left wanting to perfection"; in Discourse 3 he said that the ancient sculptors, being "indefatigable in the school of nature, would "suggest many observations which would probably escape you, if your study were confined to nature alone"; and in note 56 to Fresnoy he wrote that the rules of art, being formed on the works of those who had "studied nature most successfully," would enlarge the artist's views and teach him to look for and see "what otherwise would have escaped his attention." 9. In Note 8 to Fresnoy Reynolds wrote that a degree of mechanical practice had to precede theory, that "something . . . must be done on trust . . . before the theory of art can be *felt.*" 10. In Discourse 1 Reynolds said one advantage the RA would have which no other nation had would be that "We shall have nothing to unlearn." 11. In Discourse 5 Reynolds urged his listeners to pursue "the higher excellencies" in other artists, trying "what you can, and what you cannot not do"; and in Discourse 12 he said that even if a student was led "to undertake matters above his strength," his discovery thereby of his own deficiencies was "a very considerate acquisition." 12. Pietro Francesco Mola (1612-68), Italian painter. 13. Both WA and Reynolds emphasized the value of the artist's studying the works of all other artists. In his poem "The Two Painters" WA praised Raphael as having learned from "every school" and in his lecture "Form" declared, "There is no school from which something may not be learned" (*LA,* p. 138). In Discourse 6 Reynolds said that the artist would find something "in every school" worth imitating. 14. The preceding two phrases seem to be an echo of Reynolds's saying in Discourse 6 that it was the "principles" of great artists that were to be studied and that the "Sagacious imitator" would study "how the masses of light are disposed, how the effect is produced, how artfully some parts are lost in the ground and others boldly relieved, and how all these are mutually altered and interchanged according to the reason and scheme of the work" and would admire not only the harmony of its coloring but examine "by what artifice one color is a foil to its neighbour." 15. WA echoed these words in his lecture "Art," where he noted the relationship of the color and light in Adrian Ostade's *The Slaughtering of a Pig* as "we travel through the picture"; and in his lecture "Composition," where he discussed line as "the course or medium through which the eye is led from one part of the picture to another" and said that in harmony of parts "the quantities, whether by color, light, or shadow," must be "so disposed as to balance each other" (*LA,* pp. 89-90, 149, 154). 16. Both WA and Reynolds emphasized the variety in nature, WA in his lectures and aphorisms and Reynolds in Discourses 3 and 12. 17. In his lecture "Composition" WA said that the greatest geniuses had the widest range of admiration for others because it was often "from the *differences* which these very excellences in others, as the exciting cause, awaken in themselves" (*LA*, p. 155). In Discourse 2 Reynolds warned against "a bigoted admiration of a single master" and in Discourse 6 said that a "true idea of the perfection of the art" could not be formed by studying a single artist. 18. Both WA and Reynolds emphasized the importance of the mind of the artist in the production of a work of art. In his lecture "Art" WA defined "Human or Poetic Truth" as "that which may be said to exist exclusively in and for the mind," and described Monaldi as endowed with "the most important part, the mind of a painter" (*LA*, p. 80; *Monaldi*, p. 24). In Discourse 8 Reynolds said that whoever wanted to enlarge the boundaries of his art had to go beyond what was in books or the work of his predecessors to "a knowledge of those precepts in the mind"; in Discourse 11, that the general effect of a composition was "to take possession of the mind"; and in Discourse 12, that "the greatest business of study is, to form a *mind*." 19. WA incorporated this sentence and the preceding one almost verbatim in his lecture "Composition," where he wrote: "Every original work becomes such from the infusion, so to speak, of the mind of the Author; and of this the fresh materials of nature alone seem susceptible. The imitated works of man cannot be endued with a second life, that is, with a second mind: they are to the imitator as air already breathed." A few sentences further on he referred to his discussion in "Art" of the principle that "every original work of art is of necessity impressed with the mind of its author" (*LA*, p. 163). In Discourse 6 Reynolds deplored any attempt to copy "the exact peculiar color and complexion of another man's mind" rather than using the "right" or "true" mode of imitation. 20. WA conceived of man as being essentially distinguished, especially in contrast to nature, by having an "inward" life and an "inner" voice. In the "Introductory Discourse" of his lectures on art he said, "there can be but one rule by which to determine the proper rank of any object of pursuit, and that is by its nearer or more remote relation to our inward nature."; in his lecture "Art" defined originality as that found by the artist "by and within himself" and "Human or Poetic Truth" as "a *reality* within us" and "inward life"; and in *Monaldi* declared that it is the "inward voice" awakened in the spectator by a work of art that is "the only true voice of fame" (*LA*, pp. 79, 94; *Monaldi*, p. 21). In the advice which he gave the young artist recorded by Henry Greenough, he said: "Be industrious and trust to your own genius; *listen to the voice within you*, and sooner or later she will make herself understood, not only to you, but she will enable you to translate her language to the world, and this it is which forms *the only real merit of any work of art*" and read aloud his "Sonnet. Art," with its lines saying that Michelangelo in creating his "forms unseen of man, unknown to Earth" embodied an "invisible Idea" and knew "E'en by his inward sense, its form was true" (Flag, pp. 198-99). 21. WA often used the term "old masters" in referring to the great artists of the past. It was the key word in the advice he gave the young artist recorded by Henry Greenough: "I have frequently been told by friends of yours, sir, that they were *afraid* you were running after the old masters. Now if that frightens them, I *would make every hair on their heads stand on end!* for you may depend upon it that you cannot go to better instructors for your art. From them you will learn the language of your art, and (will learn) to see nature as they say it. You will understand, of course, that I am not recommending you to *imitate*, but to *study* them. . . . The *old* masters are *our* masters, and there is hardly an excellence in our art which they have not individually developed" (Flagg, p. 197). Perhaps the most noteworthy characterization he made of these artists was in the advice he sent the painter Daniel Huntington in 1839 to follow the example of the "old masters" for more than their painting, urging him "not to be satisfied with being *one thing*" and noting that they "did every thing. They were sculptors, and architects, as well as painters. Nay, they were poets and philosophers, as Michael Angelo and Leonardo da Vinci. They painted also, all sorts of pictures, and succeeded in all" (Jedidiah Vincent Huntington, "The Allston Exhibition," *Knickerbocker Magazine* 45 [Aug. 1839]: 173). 22. Both WA and Reynolds used the terms "poetry" and "poetical" in describing the fusion of the natural scene and human feeling which produced great art, and both said that the correspondence between the two was captured but fleetingly. WA may have been thinking particularly of Reynolds's Discourse 14, in which he referred to the "heroic" or "higher" style in painting as "This poetry of our art" and said that the Dutch and Flemish style of landscape was "unfit for poetical subjects" and that the painter who was ambitious for "style in landscape" had to "catch his inspiration from those who have cultivated with success the poetry, as it may be called, of the art; and they are few indeed." As examples of "the poetical style in landscapes" he cited two paintings with which WA was surely acquainted: Rosa's *Jacob's Dream* and Sebastian Bourdon's *Return of the Art from Captivity,* the second of which Bourdon bequeathed to Beaumont. WA's own chief descriptions of this style are in his lectures "Art" and "Composition" and the description of Monaldi's painting of the sacrifice of Noah. 23. Edward Young (1683-1765), English poet. The quotation is from *The Complaint; or Night Thoughts* 9.773. Astronomical allusions appear in several of WA's writings. In "The Sylphs of the Seasons" the poet's journey takes him "o'er the Milkyway" and in the "Introductory Discourse" of his lectures on art he contrasted the physical eye, which could travel for millions of miles, with the eye of the mind, which might "swifter than light, follow out the journey, from star to star" (*SS*, p. 12; *LA*, p. 94). He owned copies of Elija Hinsdale Burritt's *Atlas, Designed to Illustrate the Geography of the Heavens,* 3d ed. (Hartford, 1836), and John Pringle Nichol's *Views of the Architecture of the Heavens in a Series of Letters to a Lady at Cashie,* 2d ed. New York, 1842). 24. Three of WA's aphorisms, including the one from Fuseli, stated the importance of loving art for its own sake, and he made the point on many other occasions: in *Monaldi,* the poems "The Two Painters," "The Young Troubadour," and "The Angel and the Nightingale," and in his conversations with Henry Greenough. Reynolds expressed the same sentiment in several Discourses, particularly Discourse 14, devoted to Thomas Gainesborough, whom he characterized above all else as an artist who loved his art. 25. In the "Introductory Discourse" of his lectures on art WA said the sublime included "to a *certain degree*" the "reverse" of beauty and found it manifest most notably in the "terrible," exemplified by the ocean in a storm, Vesuvius in eruption, and Mont Blanc, as well as "the angelic" (*LA*, pp. 67, 64, 58, 61). 26. The engraving of *Moonlit Landscape (Moonlight),* by George B. Ellis, appeared in the literary annual *Atlantic Souvenir* for 1828, together with Pickering's poem "Moonlight, an Italian Scene."

149. To John Rubens Smith Boston, December 1, 1827.

Dear Sir: I have examined your "Compendium of Picturesque Anatomy,"[1] and it is with pleasure that I give to it my sincere approbation: as a work much needed, and of immediate and practical utility to all Students of the several branches of the Fine Arts, for whose benefit it is intended. With this opinion of it, I perform but an act of duty, in recommending it to the patronage of the public—most cordially wishing you the success you deserve.

I remain, sincerely, / Yours, / Washington Allston.

SOURCE: John Rubens Smith, *A Compendium of Picturesque Anatomy, Adapted to the Arts of Designing, Painting, Sculpture and Engraving* . . . (Boston, 1827), p. [1].

1. It consisted of eight unnumbered pages and four plates, the first of three projected numbers but the only one published. Stuart also wrote a recommendation of it, dated 4 December 1827, though he spoke only of Smith's plan and views generally and apparently had not seen the published work.

150. To Josiah Quincy Friday Morning. [Dec. 1827]

Dear Sir: It is so long since I saw the Picture concerning which you inquire that I cannot recall it with sufficient distinctness to give a particular account of it; I remember only the general impression which it left on me—that it was one of Copley's best pictures.[1]

Will you permit me, as one taking more than a common interest in the fame of this great Artist, to add that I should rejoice to see a work so honourable to his name become an heirloom to his native City.

With great respect, / Your obednt servt/ W. Allston.

Honble. Josiah Quincy, Major

ADDRESSED: Honble. Josiah Qunicy, / Mayor, / Hamilton Place.[2] SOURCE: Manuscript, Boston Public Library.

1. John Singleton Copley (1738-1815), portrait and history painter, who settled in London in 1775. WA could have met him there but there seems to be no evidence that he did so. Probably the painting was his full-length portrait of John Adams, painted in London in 1783. It was brought to America in 1817 but found too large for Adams's house in Quincy and taken into keeping by Ward Nicholas Boylston of Roxbury, a relative. Boylston died in January 1828 and it went by his will to University Hall at Harvard, of which he was a great benefactor. In that year it was exhibited at the BA by Mrs. Boylston (Jules David Prown, *John Singleton Copley: In England 1774-1815* [Cambridge: Harvard Univ. Press, 1966], p. 300; Martha Babcock Amory, *The Domestic and Artistic Life of John Singleton Copley, R.A.* [Boston, 1882], p. 87. Probably WA saw it in London. 2. Quincy lived at 1 Hamilton Place from 1835 to 1837 *(Boston City Directory).*

151. To Samuel Finley Breese Morse Boston, 24 Jany. 1828.

My dear Sir: This will be handed you by my young friend, Mr. Horatio Greenough,[1] with whom I wish to make you acquainted. Mr. Greenough is a graduate of our College, and is but lately returned from Italy, where he has passed two years as a student of our sister Art, Sculpture. When I say that he is an Artist of genius, and one for whose character as a man I have a sincere and high esteem, I feel assured that no more needed be added to secure him every friendly attention which you may have it in your power to shew him.

Believe me ever sincerely yours, / W. Allston.

Mr. J.R. Smith informs me that he has sent, for sale, some copies of his "Picturesque Anatomy" to his son[2] in New-York. You will see by my *certificate* how well I think of the work; and I think you will agree with me that every Artist in the country ought to possess it. If you can promote its sale I know you will—both from your love of the Art, and for the pleasure of helping one not *over-rich*—like many of the craft—Lee[?],[3] Meisse,[4] & others "too numerous to mention."

ADDRESSED: S.F.B. Morse Esqre. / President of the National / Academy of Design,[5] / New York. / Horatio Greenough Esqre. SOURCE: Manuscript, Historical Society of Pennsylvania.

1. Greenough was on his way from Boston to Washington and *passed* through New York (Wright, p. 50). 2. Probably John Rowson Smith (1810-64), painter of panoramas. 3. Possibly Samuel M. Lee (d. 1841), scene, landscape, and portrait painter. He was working in Cincinnati in 1826. 4. Probably Gabriel Miesse (1807-?) engraver. Born in Reading, Pa., he settled in Greenville, Ohio, in 1827. Besides engraving he practiced "sympathetic healing" and dabbled in real estate and politics. 5. The NAD was founded in New York in 1826 in opposition to the more traditional American Academy of Fine Arts, with Morse as its first president; he held this office until 1842. WA was an honorary member from 1827 until his death and exhibited there in 1826, 1832, 1841, and 1843. At the time of his death Morse announced the event to the academy on 12 July 1843, delivering a short tribute, and Memorial Resolutions were adopted, including the appointment of a committee to ask Verplanck prepare and deliver before the academy a eulogy and one to procure a bust of WA for the academy (*New-York Evening Post,* 14 July 1843). The two committees, however, did not carry out their commissions.

152. To Gulian Crommelin Verplanck Boston, 31 Jan. 1828.

Honble Gulian C Verplanck— / Member of Congress,—Washington City—

My dear Sir: I have been so long and so deeply in arrears to you as a correspondent that I feel it a hopeless task to attempt to discharge the debt. I would therefore rather trust in your generosity to forgive it altogether, than incur the mortification of offering you, by way of composition, any penny-in-the pound excuses. But, though I own myself insolvent—as respects pen ink & paper, I will not say the same of my thoughts—indeed, I could not with truth; for I have thought much & often of you—of the many high qualities which render your friendship a possession to be prized—& not ungratefully of the persevering kindness with which you have so long over looked my remissness. Perhaps, if I had not believed that you gave me credit for such thoughts & feelings, I should have proved a better correspondent. It is at least certain that if Mr. Dana had not mentioned to you the high opinion which I expressed of your "Evidences of Revealed Religion,"[1] I should have long since written you on *that* subject; but knowing that he did, I deferred, & deferred till—you know the *result*—to you a thing to forgive—to me a cause of self-reproach that has endured to this hour; which I would now in some degree lessen by telling you, in person, that I read your book with more than pleasure—I trust, with spiritual profit; many of your arguments appeared to me new, & the whole I thought cogent & eloquent; as to the Dedication,[2] I would wish I had better deserved it—at any rate, I am grateful for its kindness—

Your kindness is indeed unremitting, for I have again to thank you for your letter of the 9th inst enclosing the "Report of the Debates"[3]—Will you do me the favour to present my best acknowledgements to Major Hamilton[4] for the very kind & flattering notice with which he was pleased to honour me in his eloquent speech in Congress. I felt it the more sensibly from the grateful recollection which I have of the many friendly attentions I used, when a boy, to receive from his family, himself then a bright & playful child—Tell him—though I cannot express my gratitude as eloquently as the cause of it was set forth, that it is nevertheless most warmly & sincerely felt. You will probably soon meet in Washington with a young Sculptor & friend of mine, Mr. Horatio Greenough, who has a letter to you from Mr Dana.[5] He was educated at our college, & has passed two years in Italy, which, from ill health, he was obliged to leave in the commencement of a career of no common promise. It is his intention however to return thither, when his purse will let him, & I think I hazard nothing in saying that, before many years, I shall look for his station among the *very first* in his art. He has genius, learning, & modesty. The last, I would fain believe, is always the natural shadow of the first—At least it follows *his* genius like one [of] the quiet backgrounds of Vandyke.[6] He is besides a gentleman—not merely in manners, but in that better quality which does not meet the eye. Indeed I esteem his character as a man no less than I admire his genius as an artist. I feel sure you will be pleased with him—His main object in visiting Washington is to model a bust of the President.[7] His likenesses are very striking,[8] as he works with as much facility as a painter—indeed, more, as he suffers the original to walk about while he is working which a painter could not do—I hope he will find many others to model, as I know that his purse is not over-heavy—Lest others, however, should mistake Mr. G for a mere sculptor of busts, I may here observe that he is not confined to portraits, but has studied and is qualified to shine in, the highest branch of his art—the inventive; an evidence of which we have in his *dead Abel,*[9] an original, full-sized statue, which he brought home from Italy—a figure of great beauty & truth, & such a *first-work* as I have never before seen.

Believe me ever truly yours, / W Allston

[Rest of page cut off]

SOURCE: Manuscript copy. Printed in Flagg, pp. 215-16.

1. *Essays on the Nature and Uses of the Various Evidences of Revealed Religion* (New York, 1824). WA owned a copy. 2. The dedication read: "To Washington Allston; as a slight mark of respect, for his talents, works, and character, these essays are inscribed by the author." 3. On 2, 8, and 9 January 1828, at the outset of the heated presidential campaign of Andrew Jackson, a native of South Carolina, James Hamilton of that state introduced in the House a bill to provide a picture of the Battle of New Orleans by WA, another South Carolinian, for one of the remaining vacant panels of the rotunda of the Capitol. In the debate over it Charles J. Ingersoll moved to strike out WA's name, substituting the phrase "some suitable artist"; Trumbull, who had painted the first four panels, WA, Sully, and Morse were highly criticized, their "mangled bodies strewing the bloody field," as Trumbull put it (p. 316); and Hamilton said WA had restored the Augustan Age of painting (20th Cong., 1st sess., in the House). The bill was rephrased in the light of Ingersoll's suggestion, but it and the amendments failed to pass. The commission would have been unacceptable to WA in any case because of his objection to painting battle scenes and to Andrew Jackson. After his death it was reported, erroneously, that he sent a disrespectful reply to Hamilton ("Anecdotes of Allston"). 4. James Hamilton (1780-1857), Charleston, S.C., lawyer and politician. From 1822 to 1829 he was a member of the House of Representatives. He became a

major in the War of 1812. 5. In it RHD recommended Greenough for a government commission (Wright, p. 50). 6. Sir Anthony Van Dyck. 7. John Quincy Adams. 8. Greenough had modeled the preceding fall busts of Josiah Quincy, Washington, and possibly Andrews Norton (Wright, pp. 48, 49). 9. From Gen. 4:8.

153. To John Stevens Cogdell Boston, 21 March, 1828.

Dear Cogdell: I received your letter of the 8th inst. at a late hour last evening, and proceed to answer it without delay; though I fear that on the point on which you are so desirous of having my opinion, I cannot reply with that decision which long experience has enabled me to exercise on questions relating to my own branch of the Art. It is certainly true, as you observe, that more expression is given to the eye by carving the retina. And yet it is not practiced by the Moderns, any more than by the Ancients, except in Portraits. In this branch it was sometimes practiced by the Greeks, especially those who flourished under the Caesars; of this I remember an instance, in the head of the Emperor Lucius Verus.[1] But *why* it should be confined to portraits I confess *I* can see no good reason. <and> Yet the Sculptors <be> *might* be able to assign a very satisfactory one. Indeed, on reflexion, I cannot but think that they *are* governed in it by some sound principle—as otherwise the practice would not have been so universal; for I cannot call to mind an example to the contrary in any ancient or modern statue, not professedly a portrait. I state this candidly, lest <I might considered presumptuous from> my own inability to account for it should seem to incline me to justify a departure from it. But, though the question may be said to lie out of my peculiar province, and is consequently one on which I should speak with diffidence, there is yet a *general* [maxim][2] *principle*, applicable to all arts, or rather, I should say, essential to their successful cultivation, concerning which I feel no such distrust; namely, that if the peculiar process, or mode, by which we propose to <ach [?]> produce a desired effect, be the *suggestion* of a *strong impulse*, it is better to risk it, than to follow the prescription of any authority however high. It is only (if I may be allowed the phrase) by thus *acting out themselves* that men of genius originate new modes of excellence, and widen the sphere of intellect. The very difficulties which an untried course presents are but so many additional stimulants to invention—which often grows, like the fabled Salamander, after six years unsuccessful heating of the furnace, out of the fire of the seventh. When our own rule fails, it is *then* time enough to adopt that of others; we <may> shall adopt it then with more advantage, from the conviction that ours was insufficient. But I should be slow to give up any strong impulse <in the formation of any> in any thing relating to the art, until it had *proved* its own insufficiency. I would first give it fair play, and convince myself before I deferred to the judgement of others. Many an artist has drawn the world after him by resolutely following the path which they had predicted would lead to nothing, or worse than nothing. Two painters, and one of them no less a man than Tintoret,[3] advised Ludovico Caracci[4] to <quit> give up painting for some other employment more suited to his abilities; but Ludovico knew what was in him; he persevered, and became the founder of the great Bolognese School.

[Page torn] [Since (?)] I have expressed myself with sufficient [frank (?)]ness, [page torn] you will perceive that the resi [page torn] these remarks is intended to confirm you in the mode you have chosen to treat your subject—that is, to express the retina. If you do it to satisfy yourself, I think I may venture to say that you will be more likely to please others, than if you followed mere authority without conviction.—<It> When it is finished, let me know, without reserve, what you think of it yourself.—I am glad to find that you persevere, and congratulate you on your success in General Moultrie's head.[5]—By the way, J.R. Smith has lately published a very valuable work on what he calls "Picturesque Anatomy," exhibiting the skeleton through the muscles. It is copied from the work of an old Spanish painter;[6] and though the outlines are in bad taste (which is the fault of the original) it is <of> the best treatise for an artist I have seen. I will send you a copy by the first opportunity by water.—As to myself, I am at present well. But I have been far otherwise, having had by the blessing of Providence, a narrow escape from death. So near that the Dr. said had he been fifteen minutes later I should have died. I was poisoned by eating partridge. God bless you. Your sincere friend Wa. Allston.

[In the margins] Major Wilson[7] whom I saw this evening, informs me that my Mother when he left Carolina was well and in Georgetown. I wrote to her a few days ago. Pray present my best regards to Mrs. Cogdell, and remember me to White & Fraser.

ADDRESSED: John S. Cogdell Esqre. / Charleston, / South Carolina. SOURCE: Manuscript. Printed in Flagg, pp. 230-34.

1. A bust of Lucius Aurelius Verus, Roman emperor sharing power with Marcus Aurelius Antoninus from 161 to 169, is in the Capitoline Museum, Rome. 2. WA's brackets. 3. Jacopo Robusti Tintoretto. 4. Ludovico Carracci (1555-1619), Italian painter of the Bolognese school. 5. William Moultrie (1730-1805), revolutionary major general. Cogdell presented a cast of the bust, his second, to the BA in 1828 ("An All Accomplished Man"). It was exhibited there in 1841 and several succeeding years. 6. Crisóstomo Alejandrino José Martinez y Sorlí (1628-94). In his preface Smith said that Martinez published in 1660 two plates, the first of a large projected work never completed, from which his own plates were "compiled, enlarged, and shaded, with such additions to some figures as an alteration of the Groups required." 7. John Wilson, apparently a surveyor and possibly the same John Wilson who, in 1811, married Eliza Gibbes, the daughter of WA's half-sister Elizabeth (Allston) Gibbes (Mary Pringle Fenhager, "Descendants of Judge Robert Pringle," *SCHGM* 62 [1961]: 163; Groves, p. 33). His rank of major has not been identified.

154. To John Greenough Boston, 31 July, 1828.

My dear Sir: This will be handed you by Mr. Long,[1] whom I beg to introduce to you. Mr. Long's object in visiting London is to study our Art; for which he has just quitted the Law, to which he was bred. He is an alumnus of our College, and you will find him a man of cultivated mind, as well as of gentlemanly manners.

I feel assured that I am doing you both a mutual pleasure in this introduction.

I write in great haste as I have but a few moments—otherwise I should write you a long letter, in reply to your two last. But the first moment of leisure you shall have one. In the meantime, believe me,

with undiminished regard, / sincerely yours, / W. Allston.

ADDRESSED: John Greenough Esqre. / London. / Saml Long Esqre. SOURCE: Manuscript.

1. Samuel Pierce Long (1798-1879), landscape painter, of Portsmouth, N.H., and Boston. He graduated from Harvard in 1819 and for a short time practiced law. Later he took up art, spent several years studying and painting in England, and became a writer and lecturer on art as well as a painter (HA).

155. To John Stevens Cogdell Boston, 3 August, 1828.

Dear Cogdell: It was my wish to have written to you long ago, but many things have prevented me; amongst others, not the least has been low spirits, for I have had much to depress me. For this last reason, I doubt not, you will readily, and, as you always do, kindly excuse the delay. It has been in this, as in many other instances, no slight aggravation of my depression that it unfitted me for answering those calls of friendship & duty which I most anxiously desired to fulfill. But I never like to speak of my low spirits, and always avoid it, unless the occasion makes it necessary. Such an occasion seems to me the present; and I mention it, that you might know <the> why I have so long delayed telling you how much I like your last work—the Bust of General Moultrie. Though I expected considerable improvement on your first effort, I found it very much to exceed my expectation; and most heartily do I congratulate you on your success. I can feel no doubt as to the strength of the likeness, though I knew not the old Patriot; I feel assured of it, from the strong individual character it possesses; speaking to the spectator in the language of a *peculiar* mind. In this you have effected the chief purpose of the Sculptor's art—without which, the most expert management of the material, or the most elaborate finish, is but the triumph of the *craftsman.* Character, character, in your Art, as well as in mine, is that which shews the *Artist;* since it is the fruit of the intellect, not of the hand and eye—which we may often see trained to a high degree of skill, with but small aid from the head. Hogarth[1] used to complain bitterly of the Engravers whom he occasionally employed to assist him—some of them his superiors in the mechanical part, though not to be named with him in mind. "Hang your beautiful lines!" he would say; "give me my *character*, if you do it with a hob nail."[2] I think it is hardly necessary for me to say "Go on"; for you ought *now* to feel confidence in yourself. If you have it not, I hope my sincere testimony will impart some. For, <however> as confidence in a weak mind must always, from increasing its weakness, end either in vanity or despair, so in a strong one will the want of it render its very strength abortive, And I doubt if as many men have not failed from distrusting, as from overrating, their powers. Let me therefore urge you to rely on the strength which you have shewn you possess, as on one of the essentials of success.

You have probably heard of our poor friend Stuart's death.[3] He had been breaking above a year past, and he seemed to have been aware for some months before that he could not survive long. The Arts as well as his country have suffered a loss in him that will not soon be supplied. The infirmities under which he laboured even during the last ten years of his life, though they kept him poor, did not, however, <prevent him his> as his late works witness, extend to his mind. His mind was indeed vigorous to the last, and his bereaved family have this consolation—that he has left nothing in his Art, old and infirm as he was, to take from his great name. 'Tis, alas, the only consolation he had it in his power to leave them; for they are quite destitute. But they have not been without sympathy from the people of Boston, who have got up an Exhibition of such of his works as could be collected, for their benefit;[4] in addition to which they have opened a subscription for the purchase of his head of Washington, at two thousand dollars,[5] for the Athenaeum. If your Annual Exhibition[6] were profitable (which I think I understood you to say it was not) I would propose your <adding something to> granting them the benefit of a week or two during your next season.—I wrote a short notice of Mr. Stuart, which was published in the Boston Daily Advertiser, of the 22d of July.[7] If it has not been copied in your Papers, you will probably meet with it at some of the News-paper offices.

If you see my Mother, give my love to her, and say that I am well. I shall write to her in a few days. Will you shew her the Notice of Stuart, if you can get a copy?—Tell White that I was quite charmed with his son:[8] he is <a> modest, gentlemanly & intelligent; and I did not like him the less for the strong likeness he bears to my old friend—I never saw a father so completely *ground young* again in a Son.—Mr. Amory has been appointed Naval Agent at Pensacola,[9] where he has been for some months. My best regards to Mrs. Cogdell. God bless you.

Ever your friend W. Allston

ADDRESSED: John S. Cogdell Esqre / Charleston, / South Carolina. SOURCE: Manuscript. Printed, except for the last paragraph, in Flagg, pp. 219-21.

1. William Hogarth (1697-1764), English painter and engraver. WA was influenced by Hogarth in his early years, particularly in his satiric pieces. At a later period he was asked on one occasion if he thought it was true that "the curve line, is the line of beauty," presumably in reference to the serpentine curve and the words "The Line of Beauty" which Hogarth drew on the palette in his

self-portrait with his dog and which he explicated in *The Analysis of Beauty*. In reply Allston was quoted as saying, "I cannot think that any such partial theory can be true. Every line is beautiful in its place. No subject has been so inadequately written upon as beauty. Nothing that I have ever read on the subject, but is worthless" ("Color Book," p. 55). He owned *The Works of William Hogarth*, ed. John T. Trusler, 2 vols. (London, 1827). According to Flagg, he used to say there was no face so deficient in beauty that he could not see in it something beautiful and that so also he could discover something divine in every human soul. 2. The source of the quotation has not been identified. Hogarth emphasized the importance of character in his *Analysis of Beauty*, chap. 6, and in his painting *The Bench* aimed to show the difference between character, caricature, and the *outré*, giving an illustration of character only; in the second version he added the passage from *Analysis of Beauty* at the bottom of the engraved plate. 3. Stuart died on 9 July 1828. He suffered a stroke early in 1825, from which he never recovered (Charles Merrill Mount, *Gilbert Stuart: A Biography* [New York, 1964], p. 322). 4. An exhibition of 216 portraits by Stuart for the benefit of his family was held in the BA during most of August 1828, from which the proceeds were estimated to exceed $1,000. WA was a member of the committee in charge (Swan, pp. 62-73). 5. This proposal, for Stuart's unfinished portrait of Washington, known as the "Athenaeum portrait," did not materialize, but a subscription to purchase it and the companion portrait of Martha Washington for the BA was completed to the sum of $1,300 in May 1831. WA was a member of the committee in charge of preparing frames for them (Swan, pp. 80-82). 6. The exhibition of the South Carolina Academy of Arts. It was founded in Charleston in January 1821, with Cogdell as secretary and Morse, John B. White, and Fraser among the directors. It was dissolved in 1830 because of lack of support (Prime, pp. 121-22; Rutledge, *Artists in the Life of Charleston*, pp. 138-40). WA was made an honorary member on 28 May 1821 (Certificate, endorsed by WA "South Carolina Academy"). 7. In this notice, entitled "The Late Mr. Stuart," dated 17 July, and unsigned, WA praised Stuart's portraits, particularly his portrait of John Adams for depicting the "image of some dilapidated castle" but calling forth "the living tenant . . . still ennobling the ruin, and upholding it," called him "in its widest sense, a *philosopher* in his Art," and concluded by admiring his lack of jealousy and kindness to younger artists. 8. Edward Brickell White (1806-82), architect and civil engineer. He graduated from the U.S. Military Academy and was active in the organization of the Palmetto Battalion. Fond of painting from boyhood, he designed the membership certificate of the Washington Light Infantry of Charleston ("Journal of John Blake White," 43:109, 117; "Records from the Blake and White Bibles," annotated by Mabel L. Webber, *SCHGM* 31 [1935]: 115). 9. Amory was appointed naval agent at Pensacola on 31 October 1827 and served until 11 July 1829. He applied for the position again in April 1841 but no action was taken.

156. From Horatio Greenough

Carrara[1]—
October 10th, [16, 17]—1828

My Dear Sir—I will seize this moment of leisure (being on the eve of going to Florence for a few days) to give you some idea of my present situation and prospects. I was induced by several considerations to spend a few months here before settling at Florence or Rome—The marble for my busts was to be had here for about ¼ what it would cost in either of those cities—The preparatory labour was less expensive—A boaster[2] gets from 12 to 15$ in Rome, here he's contented with 6 or 7—So that in case spots veins or other blemishes appear, as the work advances, it can be recommenced at a much greater advantage. My personal expences here are about ½ what they would be at Florence even. So that were it not for their magnificent academy, galleries, and the chance of finding some commissions at Florence I could find it in my heart to remain all winter here, for the climate is fine and the country beautiful. The object of my trip to Florence ('tis only a day's ride) is to ascertain whether the statues for the Theatre[3] can be had of the size required—After all the enquiries I have made I doubt it—if they can be found twill be at Florence for Trentanove[4] whom I saw at Leghorn thought there were none of that size & character in Rome. While there I shall have opportunity of availing myself to the experience of some of the first artists and I shall write Mr. Brimmer[5] a particular account of my proceedings—You will oblige me by communicating this to him—So much Sir for Business—

The Florentine yearly exhibition[6] is now open and I shall visit that city so dear to my imagination with double interest—I enjoy Sir highly even the anticipation of sitting in that noble square with the capi d'opera of the cinque cento around and before me[7]—smoking a cigar which I brought from Boston—Ultimus Romanorum[8] the sole remaining one of a hundred of Mr Callender's[9] best "Flints"—It is thought the pictures will be uncommonly fine this year at the exhibition—I will keep this sheet open untill I have seen them—some slight account of them might interest you. I have seen several sculptors, old acquaintances at Rome—Nothing new has appeared as yet among them—Mr. Lough[10] was expected from London—I have it directly from persons capable of judging and who have known him that he is a remarkable man—full of enthusiasm and spirit—ignorant as yet of drawing but an able modeller and gifted with a power of composing—Thorwaldsen is expected here—his Christ is nearly finished in the marble by one of the Carrarese sculptors—he will retouch it here himself—He has since I was in Rome modelled the figure of Poniatowski for the Equestrian statue, a Releiquoi for the tomb of Pius VII,[11] and several smaller works. Gibson is where he was—Wyatt[12] is growing in reputation—From Severn[13] I have not heard though I wrote him immediately on my arrival in Leghorn.

Florence—16. Oct. I will not try to tell you my feelings at finding myself again in this city which seems and always seemed to me the most inspiring place in the world[14]—I went on Sunday to the crowded exhibition—The Academy is I suppose the finest establishment of the kind—I passed through a gallery containing casts of all the finest sculpture in Europe and entered the Exhibition hall—In painting I found almost nothing to like—admiration out of the question—The right path once lost—the talent of Italy has led Italy astray—so that in spite of all this princely encouragement, their works bear no comparison with the first struggles of the cinque cento neither for Expression nor colour nor drawing, rightly so called. The downright proof of the badness of their system is that they do *nothing* well in portrait, in landscape, in history they are the same and so like one another that it's evident that some one vice of art has crushed or is crushing in them every feeling of individual mind. Nature (with the mass) is to them what virtue is to the mass of men a very fine thing to talk about of a good sun shiny day—They believe that they see her come nightly and daily into their hall of the nudo, throw off her clothes—take any character the professor pleases—nay they find her so excessively true that they must dilute a little the *reality* of her character to bring it into the circle of the bello—This they do not in the form only but in composition in colour in chiaro scuro and thus they turn out works cousins german of the opera, the ballet—and all the family of belle cose of their country and age.

Now it seems to me that the early works of Lionardo of Raph—and Michel Angelo[15] point out as directly the road to excellence as one could wish. I look upon the Gallery and the Palazzo Pitti[16] as two great instructors—One learns to think there Sir—And when that's said I believe all is said.

17th—After What I have said of the young men of Italy generally twould be wrong not to do justice to Bartolini[17] whose works I see with an eye alltogether different from that of 3 years since when I visited him for the first time. I was much struck with the figure of a boy treading grapes which I saw at Carrara which was full of nature. I have visited him since and have found his study and his conversation equally instructive—Let me give you a short account of the man—He is by birth a Florentine[18] who has studied by himself with this maxim as I had it from himself Che'la Natura a bellezza e benedetto e quello che le van un' po' vicino.[19]. He was at Paris where [he] bore away the palm from the Frenchmen themselves in drawing with the point.[20] Under Napoleon he was professor of the Academy of Carrara and executed many magnificent works for the Emperor—He fell with his patron and was thrown on English patronage and bust making for his bread[21]—As a composer he's behind Thorwaldsen for he wants his fertile mind and his poetic imagination but in carrying out his conceptions and making every thing he represents keep its place though singly [?] studied he's perhaps before any of them—for he works the marble like a Greek[22]—And now I would say one word on that subject—I have examined the works of Mich Ang of the Greeks of Canova and Thorwaldsen and the result has been that I have determined to master this part of the art for I'm now sure that no workman can do more than boast, (and finish the ornamental parts) of a work of excellence as it should be done. That the Greeks did so is proved by the smaller number of works from the same hand. That Mich Ang did it is safe for no man in his day could help him—the art of taking points[23] was not known—Canova without his exquisite chiselling would have been nobody. Tis rather his surface than his sentiment or science which has charmed this age. Thorwaldsen getting commissions late could only think in clay—he trusted to the exactness of modern method to render him in marble what he entrusted to it [in] clay—He has found more than one man of real merit in the art (as a modeller too) who has been capable of feeling what he wanted and of doin[g] *[page torn]* but not always—The Christ—which I think the finest wo[rk] ou[r] *[page torn]* art has given the world since the golden times of Leo[24] is executing by men unworthy of it (sub rosa some future artist will see the marble in Copenhagen and ask did this figure ever bring tears of admiration into an artist's eyes? Yet in truth it has)—Let any man ask me where the beauty, the glory of the Venus and Apollo[25] lie—I say in answer that I'll not define it but I'll say that it lies within the thickness of [a] dollar in every part of their bodies and I will engage by reducing it that much in one part and increasing it in another to make them ordinary figures—

I requested Bartolini as I was coming to Florence to spend the winter to be my adviser and instructor in drawing and modelling—(being of the opinion of Raffaelo who did not form himself under one sole artist but learned drawing of one perspective of another—colour of a third—travelling over his beautiful country as a bee hums through a garden—now settling upon Titian and now rising to MA)[26]—Bartolini told me it would be a pleasure to him to have me near him offered me an apartment frankly in his own elegant studio.[27] Encouraging me by many flattering things which I might repeat were we smoking together Sir as I have perhaps done before sufficiently to make me suspected vain—I shall profit by his politeness and generosity—the coming winter—

With regard to the casts of the ear from life—I have ransacked the collections of that kind in vain as yet, and I have searched among the models with as little success—I shall be obliged to examine among my acquaintance and as soon as possible I will send them to you—Ultramarine is made here but by one individual who supplies Benvenuti and it is so much dearer than that of Rome that I'm sure I shall be doing as you would wish in sending you but a small quantity of the 2nd quality and waiting untill an opportunity offers of procuring the first from Rome—There it is 16 dollars the ounce here it is 30—

I am in excellent health and spirits quite pleased with the appearance of my marble work thus far and in hopes that something will turn up that will call me to the execution of a figure—Pray Sir don't forget to send me such a picture as you spoke of—I have many acquaintance among the first conversaziones of artists and dillettanti[28] and long to shew them how nobly *we American apples swim.*

I remain Sir with all / affection Yours / and the Master's[29] / Hor. Greenough
I send you ¼ of an ounce of Ultramarine at 16 dollars the ounce.

ADDRESSED: Washington Allston Esq. / Boston—Mass. SOURCE: Greenough, *Letters*, pp. 17-21.

1. Greenough arrived in Carrara, the chief town near the largest marble quarries of Italy, from America about September 1828 (Wright, p. 57). 2. A man who boasts, or roughly hews, the sculptor's model in marble. 3. Probably the Tremont Theater in Boston, which was opened in 1827. The façade contained two niches for statuary, which were added not long before 1843 (Samuel Adams Drake, *Old Landmarks and Historic Personages of Boston* [Boston: Little, Brown, 1906], pp. 291-93). 4. Raimon Trentanove (1792-1832), Italian sculptor, who enjoyed considerable popularity among Americans at this time. 5. Presumably George Watson Brimmer (d. 1838), Boston merchant turned architect and designer and connoisseur of painting. He designed the Tremont Theater (William Reed Deane, "Watson Genealogy," *NEGHR* 18 [1864]: 366; Rose T. Briggs, *Plymouth Rock: Its History and Its Significance* [Plymouth, 1956], p. 8). 6. The annual exhibition of the Academy of Fine Arts in Florence. 7. The Piazza SS. Annunziata, near the Academy, with buildings designed by Brunelleschi, medallions by della

Robbia, and equestrian statue of the Grand Duke Ferdinand I by Giambologna. 8. "The last of the Romans." The term was applied to several Romans—including Marcus Junius Brutus, Caius Cassius Longinus, and Stilicho—and to several later persons as well, notably Congreve and Horace Walpole. 9. Probably Richard B. Callender, Boston dealer in West Indian goods (*Boston City Directory* for 1827). 10. John Graham Lough (1806-76), English sculptor of humble origin. 11. Thorvaldsen executed statues of Christ and his disciples for the Frue Kirke in Copenhagen; a bronze statue of the Polish prince Józef Poniatowski for Warsaw, and a mausoleum for Pius VII in the Clementine Chapel of St. Peter's (Eugene Plon, *Thorvaldsen: His Life and Works,* trans. I.M. Luyster [Boston, 1873], pp. 77-81, 89-95, 146, 219-22, 254-55). He confined his work largely to modeling, allowing his students and assistants to put the models into marble. 12. James Richard Wyatt (1795-1850), English sculptor, went to Rome in 1822 at the encouragement of Canova. 13. Joseph Severn. 14. Greenough visited Florence briefly during his first sojourn in Italy (Wright, p. 39). 15. Greenough was following WA in admiring these artists and, in the preceding paragraph, the "cinque cento" in general. 16. The Galleria degli Uffizi and the Galleria Palatino in the Palazzo Pitti in Florence. 17. Lorenzo Bartolini (1777-1850), the leading Tuscan sculptor of the early naturalistic movement. 18. Bartolini was born in Savignano, near Bologna (Mario Tinti, *Lorenzo Bartolini* [Rome: Reale accademia d'Italia, 1936], 1.26). 19. "That nature is beauty and blessed is he who goes a little near her." 20. Bartolini was in Paris from 1799 to 1808, at first studying in the atelier of the painter Jacques Louis David (Tinti, 1:41-55). "Drawing with the point" means drawing with an etching needle or chisel. 21. Bartolini was appointed director of the School of Sculpture at the Academy of Fine Arts in Carrara in 1807. At this time most of the works which he executed were busts and statues of the Bonaparte family, and his English patrons included Mary Berry and William George Spencer, 6th duke of Devonshire (Tinti, 1:53, 58, 59, 63, 65, 74). 22. Most nineteenth-century sculptors did little more than model in clay, delegating the marble work to assistants. 23. This process consisted of marking points on the marble block corresponding to points of various depths on the model and drilling to these depths in preparation for the rough cutting of the marble (Richard Westmacott, *Handbook of Sculpture* [Edinburgh, 1864], pp. 368-69). 24. Pope Leo X, Giovanni dei Medici (1475-1521), is noted for his patronage of Raphael, his continuation of the construction of St. Peter's, and his literary circle. 25. Presumably the *Venus dei Medici* and the *Apollo Belvedere.* 26. Raphael studied with Perugino in Perugia and with Pinturicchio in Siena, and in Florence became acquainted with such different talents as those of Botticelli, Ghirlandaio, Filippino Lippi, Leonardo, and Michelangelo. 27. Presumably that in Borgo San Frediano, which Bartolini had constructed about this time (Tinti, 1:83). 28. Bartolini, who belonged to the group of artists, writers, and intellectuals in Florence largely responsible for the Tuscan *risorgimento,* had presumably introduced Greenough to other members of this group, notable among them the historian Gino Capponi, the poet Giuseppe Giusti, and the Swiss littérateur Jean Pierre Viesseux (Wright, p. 23). 29. Edmund T. Dana was called "the master" by Greenough and other young associates on account of his "serene wisdom and fine perception in art and letters" (*Letters of Horatio Greenough to his Brother, Henry Greenough,* ed. Frances Boott Greenough [Boston, 1887], p. 67).

157. To John Stevens Cogdell

Boston, 18 Novbr 1828.

Dear Cogdell: I am not a little mortified to have to begin another letter with an apology; but when I think how long it is since I received the first of your three unanswered letters, I feel that one is again due to you. When the first reached me I was very unwell, nor did I soon regard my health sufficiently to give it that attention which the subject required, it being one on which I could not write in a few words. Then I had an unusual number of letters to reply to, previously received from other correspondents, who have increased in number within the last year—several of them <quite> new ones—a circumstance that, while it precluded postponement, at the same time rendered suitable answers (especially from one ungifted, like me, as an epistolary scribe) the more difficult. And when I also mention the state of exhaustion in which the indispensable labours of the day generally leave me by night (the only time I can spare for writing) I feel assured that you will readily allow for, and excuse, the delay.—I might indeed have replied to your second letter in a few lines—and I extremely regret that I did not; but I do assure you (as *simple* as it may seem) that it did not occur to me that I could answer the second without at the same time replying to the first. *This* occured to me only a few days since; and it is upon the strength of this *illumination* [!][1] that I now write, having only time to reply to the former—with the assurance, however, that I will write you on the subject of your first letter as soon as I am able.

In the first place, then, allow me to congratulate you on the honour conferred on you by the City Council:[2] I read the account of it with sincere pleasure. Such a testimony to the merits of your Work, coming too from those who were personally acquainted with the living original, you have just cause to value.

With respect to my "Letter," I assent with pleasure (since you think it may be of use to you) to the publication of *such passages as relate to your Bust.*[3] As to what *relates to myself*', you <wh> will of course *suppress the whole of that.* My *"low spirits"* &c *are not for the public eye*—indeed the mention of them at any time is always as I have said, reluctantly, nay, painfully made; for the troubles that cause them are not imaginary—nothing hypochondriacal—but real and substantial. Whenever I allude to depression, <tis not from> I speak of something very different from what is called the *blues;* which is a thing I am not subject to—if the blues mean a nervous affection. I am not constitutionally melancholy; on the contrary, my natural temperament is cheerful and elastic; in youth it was buoyant and sanguine beyond that of most of my acquaintance. But affliction and misfortunes do make sad changes in men; and I have known much of both: 'Tis from their pressure that I sometimes give way—not from the *blues.* But though I may sometimes suffer, do not suppose that I ever allow myself to murmur. I do not—not even in thought. We may be depressed, and yet patient. And patience I know to be a christian duty, under all circumstances: nor is it without its reward, even in this life, since it seldom fails in the end to bring comfort.

I suppose you have long since learnt that the News-paper report concerning my Picture,[4] which you alluded to in your letter, is wholly without foundation. There was not a word of truth in it. The Proprietors *could not,* if they would, make a present of it to the Atheneum, or to any institution *without the consent of every holder of a share.* Nor on speculation—which I trust will prove a good one. The property in the Picture is secured to every Subscriber, according to the amount advanced by him on the shares, by a *Legal Instrument;* which is in the keeping of

Warren Dutton Esqre, one of the three Trustees (all non-subscribers) who will deliver the picture, when finished, to the Subscribers. Your two shares are acknowledged as paid, and are secured to you in this instrument.—I wish the Newspapers would let me alone. They might have done me a serious injury by this report, if it had not been so soon contradicted. Should there appear any more reports, I beg you not to heed them; for you may depend on my giving you immediate notice of it, whenever the Picture is completed.—I was sincerely grieved to hear of your misfortune, in the heavy loss you have sustained by the New York Bank.[5] Tis a hard case to have so much at a blow swept from the fruits of your talents and industry.—My complaint—which I alluded to in the beginning of this letter—was of a dyspeptic nature. I had a head-ach, with little intermission, for almost three weeks—at times, especially towards night, raging. I am now, however, by dint of medicine and dieting, again well. Should you see my Mother, give my love to her, and tell her that am *now* quite well.

Do not forget my best regards to Mrs. Cogdell. Your sincere friend

W. Allston,

[In the margin] I dined the other day at Col. Wainwright's,[6] where I had the pleasure of meeting your friends Mr. & Mrs. Bay.[7] I should have known Mrs. Bay instantly though I have not seen her since she was a child. She has the same bright face which she had when little Mary W. I had a good deal of talk with Mr. Bay, and was very much pleased with him.

ADDRESSED: John S. Cogdell Esqre. / Charleston, / South Carolina. SOURCE: Manuscript.

1. WA's brackets. 2. Apparently a recognition of Cogdell's success in his bust of General Moultrie. 3. On 19 December 1828 a letter from Cogdell to the U.S. House of Representatives presenting a cast of his bust of Moultrie was laid before the House. Apparently it did not contain a quotation from WA, but William Drayton, through whom it was conveyed, said he understood that "the taste and skill displayed in its execution, had received the commendation" of WA, known, respected, and admired in Europe, whose approval was "no mean testimony of the excellence of any production, appertaining to the fine arts" (*Charleston Courier,* 29 Dec. 1828). 4. The article has not been located. 5. Cogdell had been persuaded by a director of a New York bank to sell his stocks in Charleston and spend the proceeds there, with which investment he planned to go to Europe. In the spring of 1828, however, he received a statement of the bank's failure from the man, whom he never heard from again (Dunlap, 2:219). 6. Robert Dewar Wainright (d. 1841). A native of South Carolina, he was a classmate of WA's at Harvard during his first two years there. Jarvis remembered him as being fashionably dressed, like WA, and "remarkably handsome" and "of a haughty and assured bearing." He entered the marines and became a second lieutenant in 1807, first lieutenant in 1809, captain in 1812, lieutenant-colonel in 1814, brevet major in 1827, and brevet lieutenant-colonel in 1827 (Callahan, 1:700).
7. Possibly one of the sons of Judge Elihu H. Bay of Charleston and his wife. Cogdell executed his bust. His son, William, who died in 1812, was a friend of John B. White. At this period John Bay (1785-1845) was a merchant, serving in 1835-36 at the custom-house, and Andrew Bay was an attorney ("The Private Register of the Rev. Paul Trapper," *SCHGM* 58 [1957]: 259; *Charleston City Directory* for 1809-40/41). Mary W. Bay is otherwise unidentified.

158. To Samuel Finley Breese Morse Boston 30 March 1829.

My dear Sir: This is not a letter, but a string of requests, to which, as I am very much engaged just now, I shall be obliged to confine myself. 1st, Mr. Willis,[1] to whom you entrusted a packet for me, from Italy, told me, that in his hurry on leaving New York he forgot it. He says, however, that it is quite safe, as he left it in the care of Mr. Willard, the Bar-keeper of the City Hotel.[2] Will you do me the favour to forward it by the first safe private <opportunity> conveyance that offers? It contains a quarter of an ounce of Ultramarine, of which I am now very much in want. 2d. An artist from Virginia,[3] who is now my pupil, informs me that several years since he bought at a toy-shop, nearly opposite the City Hotel, some admirable Dutch (Holland) hogs-hair tools. If there are any <th> to be had there now, will you send me a half dozen of them, about the size of your finger, some a little less. 3d. If you know Brown's (the colourman in London) method of preparing his absorbant grounds for canvass, will you send me the receipe? 4th. I have never seen the letter from Leslie, <givin [?]> which speaks of your picture of the Hall of Congress.[4] It was republished in some of our News-papers here, but I could not meet with it. Will you send it me? I do not mean the letter, but what was published from it. Better send the Newspaper. 5th. Do tell me something about your professional *goings-on*. I hope to hear they are succcessful. Whether your Congress Hall has been purchased in England[5] &c. The pupil I alluded to I think will make a great Artist. He draws from plaster with uncommon spirit and precision. He is otherwise a man of talent, and of cultivated mind. I knew him some years since in Cambridge, where he was fitted for College. He was just prepared to enter, when the news of his father's failure in business obliged him to return home.

Ever your sincere friend, / W. Allston.

Will you direct the Packet to me at Mrs. *Catherine* Smith's, (there being two Mrs. Smiths in the neighbourhood) *corner* of Sister Street.

ADDRESSED: Samuel F.B. Morse Esqre. / President of the National / Academy of Design, / New-York. ANNOTATED by Morse: Washington Allston / answd—Ap. 13. SOURCE: Manuscript, Morse Papers, LC.

1. Nathaniel Parker Willis (1807-67), author and editor. In boyhood and after his graduation from Yale in 1827, until moving to New York in 1831, he lived in Boston. There he belonged to a supper club formed about 1827, of which WA was a member, together with Chester Harding, the attorneys Rufus Dawes and Edward G. Loring, Horace Mann, Samuel G. Howe, Charles Sumner, the merchants James K. Mills and J. T. Reed, and a few others (Henry A. Beers, *Nathaniel Parker Willis* [Boston, 1885], p. 92). After WA's death he paid tribute to him in two articles in the *New Mirror*, the successor to the *New-York Mirror*, of which he was coeditor (2 [29 July 1843]: 271; [14 Oct. 1843]: 17), the second accompanied by an engraving of the drawing of WA made by David C. Johnston. 2. The City Hotel was located at 123 Broadway (*New York City Directory* for 1829.) 3. Unidentified. 4. The published letter has not been located. 5. Morse's *Congress Hall* was eventually purchased in America by an Englishman who took it to England, where it remained for many years in storage and a price for it advanced by a London firm. It was brought to New York in 1847 (Prime, pp. 124-25).

159. From Horatio Greenough Florence—April 18th 1829.

My Dear Sir: An Accident reminded me last evening how long it had been since I had written to you—I was in a coffee house near the bridge of the Trinity with young Cooper[1] when an English gentleman to whom I had been hastily introduced the evening before entered and seating himself near us commenced a conversation—The topic was the high degree of civilization common among the peasants of Tuscany and he spoke of his own countrymen pretty freely I assure you—At a pause in the conversation he asked me suddenly if I knew Mr Alston—Yes very well—Do you indeed how is he?—We were in Rome a long time together and we have enjoyed a great deal in each other's company. I asked his name—twas Wallis! Was not that droll? I had often heard this gentleman's name but it never had occurred to me that it might be the same you had mentioned as the England-hater—He has been long settled in Florence—has a fine large palace in S. Gaetano,[2] and is still painting and educating his son. He invited me forthwith to call on him and promised me the sight of a large picture which he has lately finished. Before I close this I shall probably be able to tell you something more of him.

Mr Cooper who has passed the winter here and will remain for some months to come always asks with much interest after you[3] and Mr Dana when I receive a letter. I have found in him a man who understands perfectly what my aim is and who seems to have gradually become thoroughly interested in my success. Mason[4] has probably mentioned to you the group[5] which I am doing for him. He has since it has been advanced been highly pleased with it—This little work has brought me some visitors among others Lord Normanby[6] a man of much taste and great elegance of manners etc who seemed quite pleased with what I had done. I believe I am beginning to find again the thread which fell from my hands in Rome so suddenly and so fearfully[7] but it sometimes seems to me that art is a true Will o' the Wisp. The grand aim of my studies since my return to Italy has been the formation of a *method* both in drawing and modelling which shall enable me to pay in the future my whole attention to form and expression without continual interruption and mortification from doing that first which should be done last—The grand defect of all self taught artists. I am the more resolute on this point because I see it effected every day by the most ordinary minds in every department of the art. Mr Cooper thinks I ought now to try to get some commission from Government which will enable me to take a stand as an American sculptor—I shall certainly be most happy whenever my country gives me an opportunity of shewing how strongly I feel the glorious character of her institutions—by embodying in my art the great principles on which she has founded them—but I have in the mean time no fear—I am sure that if I do myself justice in the works which go from my hand from time to time that tis impossible I can fail of meeting with a fair proportion of encouragement.

I have lately received a letter from Mr. Brimmer[8] in which he asks the expence of having copies made from the old masters here—I mentioned to him the prices stating at the same time my opinion that any copies made by the "craft" of Florence or Rome would in point of colour be no better perhaps worse (for they would mislead young artists) than prints while in drawing etc they would hardly equal—I said thus much because I felt it my duty. You will agree with me in thinking it impossible that the youthful painters can study or the dillettanti stare with much profit at such caricatures of Titian & Paul as come from the dead palettes of the Italians of today.

I was in the study of Benvenuti the other day while he was at work. He was making a cartoon for the dome of the Medicean chapel which is to be painted in fresco by him[9]—The figure on which he was employed was that of Cain rushing *out* of the picture from the body of his brother while the deity above appears calling upon him—The style is French—though there is much knowledge and fine drawing.

I found my way the other day into a chamber in the gallery which seemed to me worth all I had yet seen, twas filled with Venetians—Titian—Paul Bassan[10] Giorgione[11] etc—What brilliancy is there! what music of colour—what grandeur of masses! I know not how it is but tis only when I see a picture of one of those men that I forget my own art and long to be a painter—How is it that the present school who seem to feel breadth and simplicity in form should be so insensible to the beauty of the same qualities in light and shade? The truth is they are ruined by the study of statues—They get all their first impressions in the plaster gallery—

I sent you 3 months since some Ultramarine fearing that you might [have] calculated on me [to] [*page torn*] neglect procuring it elsewhere. Tis not to be had here on so favourable terms [as] [*page torn*] at Rome—which is the reason why I sent you so little and sent Mr Fis[her] [*page torn*] none—Will you mention this to Mr F? Whenever I have an opportunity of employing a friend who understands the matter I shall provide for you both—A little new year's book has arrived here in which is an engraving from Mr F——'s prairie on fire.[12] Mr Cooper said twas the best—the only good illustration he had seen from his books.

You will have seen before this some of my busts[13]—I sigh while I write it—I pray you to remember the difficulties I have had in my way my long frequent interruptions—my sickness—But why should I ask? I know you will be but too disposed to think favourably of them—Believe me I am sensible of many of their defects and though I can *do* no better now yet I can I think see my way clear to much better things—I have great courage and great hunger after glory. I would fain be one of the small band of American "Old Masters." I beg you will remember me to Mr R Dana and to the Master—I am Dear Sir Yrs Affec'y

H Greenough

P.S. Mr Wallis and Mr Cooper desire to be remembered kindly to you—*I do hope* that you remember the picture which you thought it possible you might send me—[14]

ADDRESSED: To / Washington Allston Esqr / Boston. Mass. SOURCE: Greenough, *Letters*, pp. 28-30.

1. The Ponte Santa Trinità crosses the Arno River. Presumably Greenough was with William Yeardly Cooper (1809-31), son of James Fenimore Cooper's brother William, who was traveling with the J.F. Cooper family (*The Letters and Journals of James Fenimore Cooper*, ed. James Franklin Beard, [Cambridge: Belknap Press of Harvard Univ. Press I (1960), 153). 2. Piazza San Gaetano, now Piazza degli Antinori. 3. James Fenimore Cooper spent the winter of 1828-29 in Florence. Shortly after this letter he and Greenough had another exchange of comments on WA which were not so flattering on Cooper's part. Apparently WA had advised Greenough, probably during his recent visit to America and mentioned in a letter from Greenough to Cooper of November or early December 1830, to pursue his art either in Boston or London. "I conceive the advice of Allston to be as bad as possible. Your theater is America, not Boston, which is a dot—your patron the *Government,*" Cooper wrote Grenough on 30 December, from Rome, with something of his prejudice against New England, continuing with his similar prejudice against England: "Why did not Mr Alston study in London himself. He is unknown to the English as an artist, whatever a few friends may think, and the state of England is far worse now than when he left it" (*Letters and Journals* 1:399). 4. Jonathan Mason. 5. *The Chanting Cherubs,* commissioned from Greenough by Cooper, from a detail of two putti in Raphael's *Madonna del Baldacchino* in the Pitti Palace. It was finished in 1830 (Wright, pp. 67-69). 6. Constantine Henry Phipps (1797-1863), created first marquis of Normanby in 1838, at this time was attached to the British Embassy in Florence. 7. Greenough became seriously ill, beginning with an attack of malaria, in Rome in the summer of 1827 and consequently returned to America early the next year (Wright, pp. 46-48). 8. Presumably G.W. Brimmer. 9. The Capella dei Principi, added to the church of San Lorenzo as a mausoleum for the Medici family, has in the dome frescoes of scenes from the Old and New Testament by Benvenuti. 10. Jacopo da Ponte Bassano (1510-92), Venetian painter. Greenough was following WA in admiring the coloring of the Venetian painters of the Renaissace. 11. Giorgio Barbarelli, called Giorgone (1477-1510), Italian painter of the Venetian school. 12. The literary annual *The Token* (1827-42) for 1829 contains an engraving by Elisha Gallaudet of Alvan Fisher's painting *The Prairie on Fire,* illustrating the sentence in chapter 23 of Cooper's *The Prairie* (1827) in which Leatherstocking proposes to fight the prairie fire with a fire of his own. 13. Those of Josiah Quincy, J.Q. Adams, and John Adams were apparently sent to Boston early in 1829 (Wright, pp. 59-60). 14. WA did not send one of his pictures to Greenough at any time.

160. To [John] K[napp](?) [July 1829]

Dear K.: Your vignette[1] is *at last* finished. Will you call for it this evening at Bradstreets,[2] about eight o'clock?

Yours ever / W. Allston

Tuesday, 7 July. 1829.[3]

SOURCE: Manuscript, Baldwin Family Papers, Manuscripts and Archives, Yale University Library.

1. Unidentified. 2. J.P. Bradstreet was the operator of a restaurant in Boston on the corner of Atkinson and Milk Streets from 1827 to 1829 (*Boston City Directory*). 3. The year is in another hand; 7 July was a Tuesday in 1829.

161. To Loammi Baldwin July 29 1829

Dear Baldwin: In the first place, welcome back.[1]—I have *a little picture,* just purchased by the Atheneum,[2] which I should like to show to Mrs. Baldwin[3] and yourself, before it leaves my room. It will be sent to the Atheneum on Friday afternoon. Can you then favour me with a visit between 12 and one o'clock tomorrow, or at the same hour on Friday,:—or, if more convenient to you, any time before six tomorrow afternoon? It would gratify me much to have you see it at my room on account of the better light there than it will have at the Atheneum. I consider it one of my best pictures.

Ever faithfully yrs, / W. Allston

Wednesday, 29 July. / Sister Street

SOURCE: Typescript, Henry Wadsworth Longfellow Dana, "Notebook, 1818-1830"; Longfellow National Historic Site.

1. Baldwin had returned to his home in Charlestown, Mass., a few weeks earlier from Norfolk, Va., where he was designer and builder of dry docks at the navy yard. He was back in Norfolk by December (Baldwin Papers, William L. Clements Library, University of Michigan).
2. *Mother and Child.* A miniature copy in watercolor was made by Hugh Bridport, exhibited at the PAFA in 1827 and at the BA in 1828 as for sale. The painting was purchased by the BA in July 1829 for $500 (receipt signed by WA [BA]). It was exhibited there in 1830 and at the NAD in 1841. RHD described the child to Verplanck as "as beautiful a little piece of original sin as you ever saw" and the whole painting as "one of the most exquisite little cabinet pictures ever seen" (22 May 1829, NYHS; 2 July 1829, Longfellow National Historic Site). It was engraved by Seth Cheney probably about 1832, of whose engravings it was considered the best, and published in *The Token* for 1837. In 1837 the BA exchanged it for Peter Boel's *Fruit and Flower Piece.* 3. Baldwin's second wife, Catherine (Williams) Beckford, a sister of Samuel, Charles, and Timothy and widow of Captain Thomas Beckford (George L. Vose, *A Sketch of the Life and Works of Loammi Baldwin Civil Engineer* [Boston, 1885], p. 25).

162. From Horatio Greenough Florence Sept'r. 19, [20] 1829

My Dear Sir: This is saturday evening and allowing for the difference of longitude you will be about to take your seat in the Cam Hourly—Would that I were in the saddle trotting the uneven Brooklyn road[1] to meet you there at the masters, for since Mr Cooper left Florence,[2] I have scarse had a moment's talk (in my mother tongue) except such as enters one ear and goes out at the other. I have begun several letters to you out of pure longing to get vent—But have not finshed any—I know not why—I believe I'm losing that gift of the G[3] which used to carry me without effort through 5 or 6 pages. I've set down now however in good earnest and I trust in the interest of the moment for excitement and material—For tomorrow morning the annual Exhibition of the Academy opens and there are several works of peculiar pretension to be seen—Our Friend Mr Wallis has 17 historical landskapes there one of which has already been sold to an English nobleman who saw the rooms while the hangmen were at work—Mr Peale[4] exhibits the Washington and a portrait of myself—of the other pictures I will speak afterward—

A Monument to Dante is now erecting in S Croce[5] by the side of that of M. Ang. It is the production of Ricci[6] who presides over the Sculptural department of the Academy. The ashes of the banished bard you are aware are at Ravenna and sticklers for delicate propriety have insisted on the absurdity of erecting any other than an honorary monument. Gov't however probably from an unwillingness to do things by halves, have ordered a regular Sepulchral one—thus opening to the sculptor those convenient stores of common place and convention—the Sarcophagus, the emblematic mourners and the figure of the poet. The work is soon described. Dante sits aloft, half naked—while the figures of Italy and Poesy weep over the Sarcophagus below. To my imagination there is an inconsistency in representing the living figure of a person on the *tomb* raised to his memory. The prostrate figures of Donatello and the earlier sculptors are hard and they are uniform, but they are true to the thought which they are intended to convey and their uniformity rather helps than hinders their effect.[7] The critics are displaying their acumen by tracing resemblances between the Italy and Poesy of Mr Ricci and similar figures of Canova and other sculptors—for my part I should give them more credit could they point out one essential *difference* between any two members of the stupid family, from its first appearance to the present moment.

I confess that I see the works of the sculptors of the age with a different eye from that which I brought home when I left Italy before. Being more familiarized with the mechanical part of the art and with those expedients (not to say tricks) which are become common property in it, I look for thought, for imagination, for feeling—and believe me I am seldom much excited by any *fresh* marbles—Thorwaldsen has my respect always sometimes my admiration—But Flaxman poor Flaxman![8] I hold to be a first rate man—He has given us on a few sheets of paper more to be grateful for than all the brass and marble which art has appropriated at such immense cost for many a year. Were F's outlines from the poets his only works I could account for the neglect of his countrymen—I could excuse the British Gov't for heaping commissions on Westmacott[9] and others even where Flaxman competed for them. But the first artists here still speak with enthusiasm of the colossal group of Saturn and Ops[10]—They tell me that the form was twin to the composition and the detail of the naked was worthy of the time of Pericles. This group was detained at Leghorn by the breaking out of the French war[11] and came into the hands of Bartolini, who had a few years since the satisfaction of restoring it to the original proprietor—The fact is, I believe, from what I have seen with my own eyes of the British nobility and gentry, that they have no real feeling or love of art as a mass—I may be mistaken—

I believe I have spoken to you before of Bartolini—He is my present instructor and friend and had it not been for the facilities which he has afforded me in regard to study, workmen etc, I had long since spent my last dollar—Though I do not go all his lengths in certain opinions on art, yet I do think them the very ones calculated to make him the best of instructors—Nature is his idol and to imitate her exactly his whole desire—To accomplish this end he has formed the most exact mechanical process—He has made the deepest researches into the nature of his materials of any master of the day—He is the P Perugino[12] of modern Sculptors and counts more able men among his pupils than Canova or Thorwaldsen—"Where there is a beautiful model" said he to me when I was introduced to him—"there is Rome"—When I mentioned to him my intention of making a statue—Have you found your model? No Sir—"Look for one. Don't think at your age of beau idealizing and squeezing 4 ugly men into one handsome one—I see by your busts that you are capable of what you intend. If you find a model you will do yourself honour in your statue. Otherwise you will never content yourself." Bartolini's story is romantic—Let me give you an outline of it—Poor in his boyhood of course—few in Italy in these days enter the arena of art with stuffed pockets. At 6 yrs old behold him singing ballads in the Granduke's square[13]—at 7 in an Alabaster shop—where he determined to go to Volterra—the fountain head of the trade where hundreds manage by means of it to—starve—Defrauded by his master at Volterra, he enters the private study by night—traces the prints which had taken his fancy and decamps to Florence and begins to work in the old shop—and to look about him—Is fancied by a French officer who takes him barefooted and with peeping knees into his train, dresses him gives him wages and sets out for France—At Genoa forced to quit his master who is ordered into active service—but persists in going to Paris, takes letters of introduction—Stopped at the Frontier of the Var for want of passport and held in durance vile—Recognized by a friend the ab'e men'd officer and set at liberty—goes to Marseilles—to Lyons—is hoaxed of his cash by another old acquaintance—Drags on to Paris half starved. Presents his letters—they were addressed to a person of importance and were his whole hope. Great man didn't know the gent who had thus honoured him was surprised nevertheless would think of him—might call another day. Began to Study at the School of F. Arts—Half starved—called many times on the great man but was put off from day to day—Carried the prize at the Academy—great glee—went to receive the honourary reward presented with a *bronze* medal. Being very hungry—was enraged—Jerked the medal into the Seine—Worked away the best he could—Walked the street after some time and recognized his friend the officer in a splendid coach—Off. had been promoted—B was so thin and ragged that off didn't recognize him ran up and shouted, was known and taken in by the off. clad, put in a way to study with comfort. Off. leaves Paris—consigns him to a new benefactor begins to make a noise with his works and to have pupils to talk very loud and long against the School of David—Daughter and Sister of his host both in love with him—Turned out of doors—never mind!—works away—Dispute with David[14] in presence of many artists—as to the merits of Raph and Poussin—asks David which he would prefer an eighth of a Raph or of a Poussin. David put in a great rage—Gets commissions—Makes the acquaintance of Denon[15]—employed by Govt—Well situated—Desirous of forming a school—gets permission to go to Carrara as Director of the Imp Works for 3 years. Forms a school and brings forward many promising boys—Executes many works of importance. Downfall of Buonap—Cry raised against the *too liberal* Bartolini by the Mob of Carrara—escapes like a dog and repairs to Leghorn with intention of going to the U States—Repairs to Mr App[16] who had before advised the step—discouraged—Mr McCall[17] comes to Leghorn comm. to find artists to adorn the Capitol—Goes to Carrara and takes a dozen dunderheads whose ignorance and presumption has ruined that building[18]—B. comes to Florence and settles—The English pour in upon Italy—Commissions—busts statues—Vases—bas-reliefs—Monuments up to this hour.

Sunday Sept 20—I made one this morning of a crowd which thronged the Acad door waiting untill the Grand Duke[19] had satisfied his curiosity—a task which he accomplished in 2½ hours—Well Sir! There's not much to talk about after all—A large pict. by Bezzuoli[20] of the Entry of Charles V into Florence—An Ajax saving himself from the tempest and blaspheming against the gods[21]—and a Mary Queen of Scotts listening to the Italian music of David R.[22] form the whole of the remarkable matter—in this exhibition. Bezzuoli has taken a stride in this picture—one too which has gratified many impatient *subjects* of the Benvenuti and Cammuccini dynasty—The pict. is composed with sentiment rather than Science—drawn with a great love and a great Study of Nature—very well coloured—there is throughout a feeling for the picturesque which quality alone would make it a novelty as coming from an Italian of today—The scene is a broad street just inside the gate which forms the greater part of the back ground—A body [of] deputed magistrates with some of the chief citizens of Florence fill the right hand of the canvass and present a fine dramatic bit—in the various feelings produced among them by the tone [of] usurpation taken by Ch—as soon as he found himself within the Walls. The left space is occupied by the crowd and by the characters of the church etc which made part of the ceremony—I said it was well coloured—Let us understand that *well* is only of the first degree of comparison—There is a picture in the Philadelphia Academy[23] which would in [a] trice turn his pearl to lead his brown to earth were it [to] be hung by the side of him—Much merit is due to Bezzuoli—he loves the art and has painted this picture for 1000$ which of course has scarsely covered his expences to say the utmost—The Ajax was the last work of young Sabatelli[24]—whose late death has put us all in mourning—He was so young—yet had such a union of natural and acquired powers that all Italy looked to him as one who would give a new impulse to the art. He had not his equal in drawing or in colour perhaps in the country—in learning as an artist he was behind none—He was as remarkable for his amiable and modest conduct among the artists as for his superiority over them—He was tall and powerful in body—fond of athletic exercises and feats of strength—He fell like Raphael a victim to imprudencies which have robbed the world of many great minds.[25]—The picture of Mary was by Cavalleri[26] a portrait painter much in vogue with the English—It was an attempt to imitate that effect of chiaro Scuro and colour for which some of the Eng. are remarkable. It excited the attention of all the Italians the admiration of many—Twas something new for them—They cannot believe that The old masters coloured differently from themselves—they attribute the tone of Titian to time—Such is the slavery of education—I know many very clever It[alians]—3 or 4 who want but a beck from a hand which they venerate to become fine painters—I doubt if destiny will accord it them in this age in this country—On the whole this was clever imitative work—I don't understand why the artist adopted along with the excellencies of his prototypes that slovenly manner of drawing hands and feet and hiding them as much as possible—perhaps he thought it belonged to the *secret*. Many have spoken to me quite *patronizingly* of Mr Peale's Washington—and I have gnashed my teeth to think I had not one sample of what we are proud of that I might hold it up and say—See! what rank does the man whom you thus acknowledge worthy of your praise hold with us?

And now Sir I shall give you in as few words as possible a bird's eye view of my state and hopes—I have in progress the bust of Mrs Gilmore[27] and the Cherubs of Mr Cooper both in marble. When these are done I shall have finished all orders—For the bust of Mrs G I have rec'd 100$ and shall when tis dispatched see 50 more. For the cherubs I have rec'd 50$ and shall when they are done see 150 more a sum which will do little more than cover the expences if so much. Cooper however does not suspect this—He intends exhibiting the work for my benefit at N York—In the meanwhile I have closed my accounts with my banker and find myself 200$ in pocket—of this 108 will be exhausted by board and lodging for the coming year—Yet Sir do I intend nay I have already made preparatory expences to the execution of a model of a Statue[28]—If I am not to risk something for the art now while my blood is warm and my hopes are high and I have the health and the courage to abide the consequencies when shall I do it—Any thing rather than floundering in lazy hopes! In the mean while should not something unusual take place 1 year, perhaps less will have turned my pocket wrong side out—the Demon Want will seize it and drag me on ship board—There the fiend's power ends—for a short voyage will bring me again into the light of eyes—within sound of voices—and touch of hands of which I often dream and for which in my *fits* my heart yearns as if it would break—Yours truly HG

P.S. I have rec'd a letter from Mr Cooper dated Sept 15 Sorrento the following extract will describe his situation and employments. "I think we shall stay here untill Dec. I am getting fat and I hardly think you would find the bust a likeness—This is a delightful spot—sea breezes—sea bath fruits—and we literally overhang the bay the water washing the foot of the cliffs on which our house may be said to be suspended—I work every day and am in the middle chap of the 'Water Witch.'[29] This is doing well for a month you will say—I had however 5 chapters written at St Illario.[30]—I am glad you have undertaken a Washington. Go on boldly with the work—Make the figure as severe and simple as possible—for these qualities contain the essence of the imaginative in such a man. It will suit our ideas of his character and of our own. Aim rather at the *natural* than the classica[l] [*page torn*] take care always to preserve the dignity of the man and of his st[ation]" [*page torn*].[31]

I had intended to try to get 1500$ to execute my f[igure] [*page torn*] in marble—it could be done for that sum and would no doubt get me wherewithal to pay all my debts—but Mr Gore[32] who is just arrived here paints the *state of pockets* in Boston with so sombre a pencil that I am fearful they already repent the money they have before trusted me with—Master Edmund God bless you—PPS I sent you nearly a year since some Ultramarine and ashes—consigned to the care of Mr Morse of NY—but have heard nothing of its arrival—there was also a cast of an ear.

ADDRESSED: To Washington Alston Esqre / Care of / David Greenough Esqre / Boston. Mass. SOURCE: Greenough, *Letters*, pp. 36-42.

1. The Cam Hourly was the stagecoach which ran every hour from Cambridge to Cambridgeport and Lechmere Point, at the north end of Boston. The "Brooklyn road" was the old road to Cambridge from Boston through the town of Brookline (*Historical Map of the Town of Brookline, Massachusetts* [N.p., 1945]). 2. Cooper left Florence for Rome on 31 July (Cooper 1:373). 3. Gift of the gab. 4. Rembrandt Peale was in Florence from July 1829 to April 1830. The *Washington* he exhibited at the Academy of Fine Arts in Florence was his famous composite "Port-Hole" portrait, so-called because of the effect of a frame around the head.
5. The church of Santa Croce in Florence is noted for its tombs of celebrated Italians and its cenotaph to Dante. 6. Stefano Ricci (1767-1837), Italian sculptor, of the neoclassical school, was at this time professor of sculpture at the Academy of Fine Arts in Florence. He is chiefly known for this monument. 7. Examples of such figures are those by Donatello (ca. 1386-1466) in the Baptistery in Florence and his contemporaries Desiderio da Settignano and Bernardo Rossellino in Santa Croce there and Giovanni Crivelli in the church of Santa Maria in Aracoeli in Rome. 8. Greenough must have known of WA's admiration of Flaxman. 9. Richard Westmacott (1775-1856), English sculptor, who studied under Canova in Rome and early achieved considerable fame, had by this time executed many statues of public figures for St. Paul's and Westminster Abbey in London and for public sites in several other cities. 10. No figures of these subjects (a mythical king of Italy and his wife) by Flaxman seem to be known. Probably the allusion is to his reconstruction, during his stay in Rome, of the *Torso di Belvedere*, which consisted of a male and a female figure. This work, however, was rather generally criticized, and he eventually destroyed it (Allan Cunningham, *The Lives of the Most Eminent British Painters and Sculptors* [New York, 1854], 3:262). 11. Presumably the war declared by France on England and Holland in 1793. 12. Pietro di Cristoforo Vannucci, called Perugino (ca. 1445-1523?), Umbrian painter. 13. The Piazza Signoria in Florence was also called the Piazza Granduca. Bartolini moved with his family from Savignano to Florence when he was six (Tinti, 1:27). Greenough's account of Bartolini's activities in the remainder of the entry for 9 September is generally correct but at variance with or unclear about the facts in certain details as given by Tinti. 14. Jacques Louis David (1748-1825), leading French painter of the neoclassical school, against which Bartolini rebelled. 15. Dominique Vivant Denon (1747-1845), chief art adviser to Louis XV and to Napoleon and director general of the Museums of Paris.
16. Thomas Appleton (1763-1840) of Boston was U.S. consul in Leghorn from 1798 until his death (Isaac Appleton, *Memorial of Samuel Appleton, of Ipswich, Massachusetts* [Boston, 1850],

p. 36). Presumably Bartolini consulted him in 1814, and Appleton probably discouraged him because the War of 1812 had made the completion of the Capitol uncertain. There was, moreover, some dissatisfation with the two Italian sculptors already employed (Charles E. Fairman, *Art and Artists of the Capitol of the United States of America* [Washington; U.S. Printing Office, 1927], pp. 5, 21, 25). 17. Richard McCall was U.S. consul at Barcelona from 1816 to 1825 and acting consul, or navy agent, of the United States there earlier. In August 1815 he was asked to help Giovanni Andrei, one of the Italian sculptors employed in Washington, get to Italy to have the columns for the Capitol and White House executed and also to engage three other sculptors to work on the Capitol. Apparently McCall went to Leghorn to expedite matters (Greenough, *Letters*, p. 44 n. 21). 18. Greenough's account is somewhat inaccurate. Andrei and two other Italians who returned with him to Washington in 1816 were all from Carrara, but two were decorative sculptors only, of creditable performance. Most of the statuary in the Capitol, chiefly the four reliefs in the rotunda, was done by three Italians from other cities, all of whom came to the United States independently (Charles E. Fairman, "Art of the Italian Artists in the United States Capitol," *Congressional Record*, 1930, 62, pt. 3:2630-34). 19. Leopold II (1797-1870), Austrian grand duke, ruled Tuscany from 1824 to 1859. 20. Giuseppe Bezzuoli (1784-1855), Florentine painter. The painting is of Charles VIII, king of France, who entered Florence on 17 November 1494 on his way to take over the kingdom of Naples. 21. The Locrian or Lesser Ajax, who was shipwrecked on his way home from Troy. 22. Mary Stuart, queen of Scots (1542-87), employed as her secretary the Piedmontese musician David Rizzio. 23. WA's *The Dead Man Restored*. 24. Francesco Sabatelli (1803-29), Florentine painter. 25. According to Vasari, Raphael died of a fever contracted when returning from a visit to his mistress. Later authorities agree that his death was hastened by overwork, not only painting but excavating Roman ruins (Giorgio Vasari, *Lives of Seventy of the Most Eminent Painters, Sculptors, and Architects*, ed. E.H. Blashfield, E.W. Blashfield, and A.A. Hopkins [New York, 1897], pt. 3, pp. 121-22). 26. Ferdinando Cavalleri (1794-1865), Italian painter, professor at the Academy of St. Luke in Rome. 27. Sarah Reeve Ladson Gilmor (1790-1866), wife of Robert Gilmor, Jr. (Wright, pp. 55-56, 76). 28. Of Washington. 29. Cooper's novel *The Water-Witch* (1831). 30. The Coopers lived in a villa of this name in Florence, just outside the Porto Romano, from the first of May until the end of July 1830 (Cooper, 1:346). 31. Greenough's quotation is not entirely accurate (Cooper, 1:389- 90). 32. John Christopher Gore (ca. 1806-60), Boston landscape painter, was in Florence as an art student from 1829 to 1832.

163. To Samuel Finley Breese Morse Boston, 28 Oct. 1829.

My dear Sir: I take the chance of this reaching you before you sail,[1] to request you, in case Brockedon is able to return the Twenty Pounds *without inconvenience*, (for I would on no account *otherwise* have him do it) to purchase for me *one ounce* of Ultramarine with a part <with it> the money.[2] This will cost about five guineas; I would not have it exceed this sum by more than half a guinea. The remainder of the money you will hand, agreeably to my request, to Mr. John Greenough.[3] N.B. Do not get the Ultramarine at Brown's. Though all his other colours are excellent, his ultramarine has always been bad. Perhaps Leslie will do me the favour to get it for me. *Field's*[4] I think is the best, what he calls the "*bright*." As your time will be much occupied as well as limited, it may not be very convenient for you to find a safe conveyance for it; I must therefore beg you to ask the favour of Mr. Long to forward it by the *first* safe *private* opportunity, directed to the care of his Brother-in-

Law, Mr. Charles Tappan,[5] Boston. I must trouble you also with another commission; which is, in case you should meet John Howard Payne, to make a tracing, on *french* tracing-paper, from my drawing of "Danger,"[6] which is in his Album; and you can enclose it to me in a letter. I should like to paint a picture from it.

My last request is, that, when you do not know what to do with an odd hour, you would write me some account of the pictures and other objects of art that shall have interested you. *Any thing* about the Art you know will be always most acceptable.

Now, may God, without whom we should desire nothing (for He only knows what is good for us) ever bless and prosper you.

Ever your sincere friend, / Wa. Allston.

P.S. On second thoughts, as I am in *great need* of Ultramarine, I would have you give six guineas for it, if it cannot be had for less. The french tracing-paper (which you will find very useful) you will find at Newman's, Leicester Square.[7]

ADDRESSED: Samuel F.B. Morse Esque. / President of the National Academy of Design / New-York. SOURCE: Manuscript, Morse Papers, LC.

1. Morse sailed from New York to London on 8 November 1829, visited England and the Continent, and returned in October 1832 (Prime, p. 173). 2. In the exhibition at the BI in 1818, at which WA's *Uriel in the Sun* received the first award, Brockeden's *Christ Raising the Widow's Son at Nain* received the second. The next day, Brockeden recalled, WA called on him and "with his peculiar delicacy" said that he (Brockeden) had received less and himself more than was deserved, that he knew Brockeden's picture had been very expensive to him, and offered to lend him some of his own award. Brockeden took only a small part of the sum offered (Flagg, p. 130). 3. Morse gave WA's request to Leslie, who carried it out. 4. George Field.
5. Charles Tappan (1784-1875), Boston merchant. In his early years he lived in Portsmouth, N.H. From 1816 to 1834 he was in the dry-goods business in Boston ("The Tappan [or Toppan] Genealogy," communicated by Herbert Tappan, *NEGHR* 34 [1820]: 55; George Henry Preble, "Three Historic Flags and Three September Victims," *NEGHR* 28 [1874]: 31-32; "The New Hampshire Gazette," communicated by Frank W. Mille, *NEGHR* 26 [1872]: 132). 6. WA's ink drawing *Danger* (ca. 1811-18) is an illustration for William Collins's "Ode to Fear," lines 10-15. It is signed "W. Allston," and below the signature he wrote those lines from the poem, ascribing them to "Collins." In it he was probably inspired by Fuseli's *Prometheus Rescued by Hercules*. 7. John Newman, "stationer, etc.," operated a shop at 7 Castle Street in London (*Post Office London Directory* for 1829).

164. From Horatio Greenough

Florence, Nov'r 17th 1829.

My Dear Sir: As I pass, from time to time, one of those hills which lie so frequent across the road I am travelling, my first wish after my curiosity has been slaked, is always to communicate to you what I have seen and what I think, confident that your wishes for my advancement will prompt you [to] correct my errors to which my inexperience and the nature of the company in which I travel, make me liable. I have I believe arrived at that point in execution without the attainment of which I think no one can give the object of art his whole mind—I copy what I see before me with tolerable readiness and accuracy—whatever the object be whether the naked drapery—hair or even animals and vegetables tis soon rendered by a hand schooled to obey an eye practiced in scanning geometrically its outline and dissecting its variety of surface from light and shade—This security of method I owe to the study of drawing[1]—Twas drawing that taught me the necessity of a scrupulous outline—twas drawing that taught me that the planes[2] of a form are shaded in proportion to their obliquity to the source of light. The foundation of my system of modelling lies in this fact—For fear my language may be obscure I'll try to explain. We will suppose[3] a square mass of modelling earth of which we see only one side which is opposite the source of light. With a flat spattel we cut down the earth on each side at an angle of 45° we have[4] the two sides as being inclined to the source of light become partially shaded—now it's clear that if these planes were followed by others less and less oblique to the source of light we should at length get the side of a cylinder thus.[5] Performing a similar operation at the top and bottom at the angles etc we should at length get a semisphere and we should in the course of the work have produced every variety of tint to be found in the naked for the naked is composed we know entirely of plane convex and sometimes though rare by concave surfaces. To carry any method of execution however simple in its principles to a high degree of finish—requires much time and a delicate eye and hand—which we know require years of practice to obtain them—Here modelling has repaid again what drawing had lent her for with this system I plant my shadows and conduct half tints after having settled my outline with the greatest security—so much so that I find the pen a very agreeable instrument to draw with—

Sublimity—Majesty—beauty truth—seem to me the only true elements of my art either in conception—composition or form—Perhaps I might have said truth supposing it to contain beauty—but truth is not always beauty—therefore I have mentioned both yet I still contend that beauty is always truth nor can I admit as genuine in form a single plane or curve not belonging to the organization nor can I pardon except in colossal works or others where a certain effect is the legitimate object of the work any omission of the parts above mentioned a point in which Canova sinned terribly against my theory who provided the chief muscles were in their place thought of nothing but making sweet gradations of shadows—To take up the thread I dropped—truth is not always beauty and though I can bring myself to allow it's sometimes necessary to make a work merely true—I consider such a work the lowest in the order of works of sculpture—Still I prefer it to the half way attempt to reconcile and mix a grand whole with mean detail—Still truth I think necessary in a work but tis possible truth I mean not reality—I love reality dearly and when I want to enjoy it I go to the market place—the church the wharf and I get at a glimpse more of it than is to be found in all the works of Chantrey. Nor can I help thinking as I see the peasant standing or moving how feeble my art is in imitation and how improper an object reality is for a medium so abstract so refined so poetical as sculpture—I think therefore that instead of attempting to convey trivial detail we should seek to ennoble our works by putting into them all that we can conceive to move the mind—all that's dear in beauty all that's moving in passion all that's grand in thought. I would not go so far as M Ang whose drapery is often unlike any kind of cloth in its planes and foldings—For the eye is disgusted at the impossible—Such is my notion of my art—I am sensible how necessary repeated efforts are [to] enable me to embody them. I know that would require very different commissions from those which fall daily into my hands at present[6] and which though they feed my body starve my soul by keeping me constantly busy on trifles.

Cooper is the noblest patron I have yet found—has the broadest ideas on the subject of art and wishes me well personally I've reason to think. We talk much of you when we are together—He is a true American and is therefore proud of you. I rec'd a letter from him last Sunday in which he insists on my coming to Rome to spend a few weeks with him there—I feel such a longing to get a sight of old friends and old sights there that I may be tempted to go—I have tried the receipt you gave me for a palette and I hope one day to arrive at proficiency enough in painting to paint a portrait for my amusement now and then—but let me protest that of all the subjects which I have ever attempted to understand colour is the most subtle—unaccountable incomprehensible—by long examination I think I have found that comparatively few *pictures* are *coloured*—Even of those of name—Some are drawn in a chiaroscuro with paint somewhat approximating in its general tint to flesh. Others are painted in downright light and shade with a little tinge of colour glazed into them—Almost all seem to have had a conventional palette which is too partially or generally reasoned to embrace the variety of nature or render her delicate distinctions—Titian, Titian is my man and some of the Dutchmen too please me quite as much—There's a picture in the Flemish room by Giordeans[7] of Venus on a car with Love by her side and several marine deities about her which is one of the most luxurious bursts of light and colour that ever feasted eye—Such a union of brilliance warmth and harmony as really I think surpasses every thing Italian I have seen—I fear from the silence with which my work has been rec'd in Boston that they [think] I am not their man[8]—In the mean while unless they send me work or I should find it here—(not probable for travelling Jonathan is very philosophical) I shall in the course of 8 months get aground—Nothing not even my love of my art shall tempt me to stay here one moment at the risk of incumbering my personal friends here—I have been looked on since I have been here by the respectable artists as a man whose game is tolerably sure and pride will send me straight to Leghorn when I find *soundings* growing shallow. There is a roof in Boston which covers 12 heads[9] on which I had hopes to pour oil of comfort—if I fail I know they'll pour it on mine—if I didn't think this I should be truly miserable—In the meanwhile my group advances—my bust of Mrs Gilmore is finished—I'm pressing on from the boy to the man—Not one solid blow struck for a name—at an age when M. Angelo—had nearly finished his colossal David[10]—The grandest piece of the naked that the Christian world has seen done—I knock under. God bless you Sir—Love to Mr Richard—and the Master

Hor Greenough

I hope when I go to Rome to be able to send you some more Ultramarine.

ADDRESSED: To / Washington Allston Esqre / Care of David Greenough Esqre / Boston. Mass. SOURCE: Greenough, *Letters*, pp. 45-48.

1. Greenough must certainly have known of WA's emphasis on the importance of drawing to artists. 2. Greenough wrote "plain" throughout this letter. 3. Here Greenough drew a square. 4. Here Greenough drew a rectangle with shaded ends labeled *a* and *a*. 5. Here Greenough drew a rectangle shaded so as to represent a cylinder. 6. Greenough was exaggerating. The only commission he is known to have received in the fall of 1829 was for the bust of Cornelius Bradford, a friend of Cooper's who was visiting in Florence (Wright, p. 82). 7. Jakob Jordeans. 8. Greenough's busts of John Adams, J.Q. Adams, and presumably Josiah Quincy reached Boston about 1 July 1829, but that of John Adams was not set up, in the First Church in Quincy, until October and those of J.Q. Adams and Quincy not publicly shown until the following spring, at the BA, at which time they were praised though there was some objection to their being undraped (Wright, p. 49). 9. Greenough's parents and all his brothers and sisters except John were living at this time at 7 Chestnut Street, Boston (Wright, p. 22). The children were Henry, Alfred, Louisa (1809-92), Laura (1815-51), Ellen (1814-93), Charlotte (1815-59), and Richard Saltonstall (1819-1904) (Hamilton Perkins Greenough, *Some Descendants of Captain William Greenough of Boston, Massachusetts* . . . [Santa Barbara, Calif. n.p., 1969], pp. 41-42). The other three "heads" were possibly servants. 10. Michelangelo executed this work during the period from his twenty-sixth to his twenty-ninth year. At this time it was still standing before the entrance to the Palazzo Vecchio, for which place it had been ordered.

165. From Charles Robert Leslie 41 Portman Place Edgeware Road

London, Feby 17th 1830

My dear Sir: I don't know whose fault it is that our correspondence has suffered so long an interruption. But I am willing to take any share of the blame you will lay on me provided [you] will be quick in bestowing it, & indeed the dread of it is not very great knowing as I do how gently you deal with all who deserve blame.

Our friend Morse during the short visit he paid to London on his way to Italy[1] was unable to execute a little commission for you & desired me to attend to it. On receiving the 20 £ from Brockedon and telling him that you wished me to purchase an oz of Ultramarine with part of it, he insisted on sending you some of which he brought a large quantity from Italy. I have handed 14 £ to Greenough & have six more remaining till I hear from you what I am to do with it.[2] In the hope of provoking a retaliation in kind from you I have a mind to give you a full account of myself. Here I am, then, with a wife & three children (one boy and two girls)[3] living in a house but 2 doors from one that was inhabited by my father & mother 30 years ago, when I was an urchin. I take my boy, Robert, who is my eldest, a walking by the Paddington Canal, which [where] my father took me when about his age to see the men digging. One of my sisters came from America in the same ship with Morse & is living with us.[4]

I am now painting a picture from the Merry Wives of Windsor in which I have introduced nearly all the characters.[5] I imagine them to be assembled after dinner at Mr. Page's house who you remember had invited them in to make up the quarrel between Falstaff & Shallow, over a venison pasty. Falstaff will be flirting with the two ladies & Slender seated sheepishly by Anne Page. Mr. Page is offering the latter some ale from his best silver goblet by way of making him feel at home. Behind Falstaff are Pistol, Nym, & Bardolph laying their heads together & perhaps plotting some new roguery. Beyond them are Sir Hugh Evans & Shallow. The dinner is just removed & on a side table are the "pippins & cheese"[6] of which Sir Hugh makes mention in the play. I hope to get this picture ready for the exhibition[7] & if so I shall have been quicker with it than anything I have painted. I believe I have lost at least half my life in making alterations in my pictures, most of which were perhaps mere changes & additions without being improvements. My wife & children are powerful persuaders to a more rapid course of proceeding.

You will be surprised to hear that although I have had constant employment for the last 14 years I am as poor as when you were here. I am not more extravagant & my expenses are only the necessary ones of my family. I believe however I can paint better & quicker than I ever could & I have a prospect of doing something by publishing prints of my pictures. I now feel as if I was really in earnest & all my past life but a dream. I sigh in vain over time lost in all sorts of trifling & make sturdy resolutions to go on vigorously & as I hope in the right path for the future. When I recur to our former intimacy I feel sure it is to you I owe my first relish for all the best qualities in art. Many of your maxims that I was not capable of comprehending when I heard them, now come home to me with the fullest conviction of their truth. I wish you were here & I cannot but think you will come; I think also you would now be appreciated & patronized. I can hear but little of you from Americans who come here. They all describe you as living very retired. They agree in the account that you have painted many small pictures & that you have sold them all advantageously, but that your large Belshazzer is still unfinished. I have no doubt you have painted twenty fine pictures on the canvas of that one. What a pity they could not be seperated. I dare say you might finish it as well in 3 days as in 3 years if you would have the resolution. I wish you would & then come immediately to England.

With the exception of Mr. West & Sir Thos Lawrence I believe you were not much acquainted with the principal artists here. You would now be & I am sure you would enjoy their society as much as I do.

I need say nothing of the death of Sir Thomas Lawrence[8] of which I dare say full accounts have reached the American newspapers. His loss is much felt in the immediate circle of his friends who well knew the great kindness of his heart. I remember well his passing by on horseback just as you were stepping into the coach to leave London. The farewell you took of each other was forever—ours I trust is not.

Whenever you can come you will find all your friends who may be left unchanged I assure you. I do not think there is a man on earth for whom Coleridge has a higher regard than he has for you. Lord Egremont speaks frequently of you. He says he thinks there is more of the spirit of Raffaelle in your Jacob's dream than in any picture he knows of painted since his time.

Pray remember me kindly to Mr. Channing who I now hear with great pleasure enjoys perfect health. I have his essays on Buonaparte & on Milton[9] both of which I read with the greatest pleasure & admiration of his talents & of his heart.

My wife who feels as if she knew you begs me to offer her best respects to you,

& I am, dear sir, yours ever / C.R. Leslie

P.S.—I ought to tell you that the Anne Page in my picture is painted from Mr. West's grand daughter whom you must remember as a beautiful child of 13 or 14. She is now married to a Mr. Margary & is still very handsome.[10]

ADDRESSED: Washington Allston Esqr A.R.A. / Boston [crossed out, in another hand: Cambridgeport]. Mstts SOURCE: Manuscript, Houghton. Printed in Flagg, pp. 224-27.

1. Morse was in London en route to Italy from 4 to 22 December 1829 (Prime, pp. 173, 177).
2. RHD appended to his copy of this letter the comment that WA was at this time "suffering deep distress of mind for want of money, and paralyzed in his art by it" but nevertheless had the money left from this transaction given to John Greenough, who was extremely poor (Flagg, p. 225).
3. Robert, Harriet Jane (b. 1 Feb. 1828), and Caroline Anna (b. 19 Oct. 1829) (Leslie, pp. 278, 283). 4. Anna Leslie. 5. *The Dinner at Mr. Page's House*, from Act 1, SC. 2. 6. Act 1, Sc. 2, l. 12. 7. It was exhibited at the RA in 1831. 8. Lawrence died on 7 January 1830. 9. *Analysis of the Character of Napoleon Bonaparte, Suggested by the Publication of Scott's Life of Napoleon* (1828) and *Remarks on the Character and Writings of John Milton* (1828). 10. Maria West (1804-51), only child of West's son Raphael, married Thomas George Margary. Leslie described to Dunlap the occasion on which he and WA were waiting to see West in his painting-room when she suddenly entered and hastily left, West thereupon calling her "*a little Psyche*". Leslie thought the glimpse "almost seemed like the momentary visit of an angel to earth" (Alberts, p. 381; Dunlap, 2:148).

166. To Gulian Crommelin Verplanck

Cambridge-Port,[1] Mass.
1 March 1830

Honble Gulian C. Verplanck / Member of Congress[2] / Washington

My dear Sir: I did not get your letter of 17th[3] ultimo until the night before last (Saturday) and I shall endeavor, agreeably to your wishes, to answer it in as business-like manner; though, I fear, I have but little of that laconic spirit, so essential to it, which I used so much to admire in our excellent friend, S Williams, of Finsbury Square. Without more flourish then, you could not desire to be thanked more heartily than I thank you for this additional instance of the friendship with which you honour me. These are not words of courtesy, but of grateful truth, and yet

I fear there are certain formidable, and to my present [?] apprehension, insurmountable obstacles to my profiting by your kindness. The subjects from which I am to chuse, you say, are limited to American History. The most prominent of these, indeed the only ones that occur to me, are in our military and naval achievements. Herein lies my difficulty—I will not say that I doubt, I *know*, that I have not any talent for battle-pieces; and, perhaps, because they have always appeared to me, from their very nature, incapable of being justly represented: for to say nothing of the ominous prelude of silent emotion, when you take away the <due> excessive movement, the dash of arms, the deadly roll of the drum, the blast of the trumpet—forcing almost a heart into the coward—the rush of cavalry, the thunder of artillery, and the still more fearful din of the human thunder, giving a terrific life to the whole,—and all this must be taken from the painter—what is there left for his canvas. It seems to me (at least in comparison with the living whole) little more than a caput mortuum. All these things & indeed much more can be made present to the imagination by words. In this the Poet & Historian have the advantage of the painter. I know not where, even among the great names of my art, to look for any thing like the *living Mass* of one of Cooper's battles,[4] there are besides many circumstances connected with these subjects—such as monotony of colour, of costume, of form, together with a smallness of parts (even fatal to breadth and grandeur) that make them—at least with *me*—wholly untranslateable in the painter's language—The monotony of colour alone would paralyse *my* hand such being my opinion, you will easily believe that I would have no hope of succeeding in subjects of this nature. Indeed I know from past experience that I *must* fail where the subject is not of itself, that is, in relation to the powers of my art—essentially exciting—In a pecuniary view, it has been, perhaps, my misfortune to have inherited a patrimoney; since it has lasted only just long enough to allow my mind to take its own source till its habit of thought had become rigid, too fixed to be changed when change was desirable—To be more intelligible—having in the commencement for the greater part of my subsequent life only the pleasure of its pursuit to consult, I of course engaged in nothing which had not that for its end—the realizing my conceptions being my chief reward; for though the pecuniary profit was always an acceptable contingency, it was never at that time an exciting cause, so far from it, that I have in some instances undertaken works for less than I knew they would cost. As an *artist,* I cannot, in spite of many troubles, regret this freedom of action, since I feel assured that I owe it to whatever professional skill I may possess. But of late years, since the source of this liberty has been dried up, and the cold current of necessity has sprung up in its stead, I have sometimes *as a man*, almost felt the profession to have been a misfortune. For necessity I find has no inspiration: she has not with me even the forcing power. Willingly, often most willingly, would I have been driven by her, But it seems that at my age it cannot be; my imagination has become too fixed in its own peculiar orbit to be moved by any thing extrinsic—In other words, it seems to me almost morally impossible to compose, much less to finish a picture where the subject does not afford pleasurable excitement—I think you know me too well to doubt my patriotism because I cannot be inspired to paint an American battle. I yield in love of country to no man; no one has ever gloried more in the success of her arms, or more sincerely honoured the Gallant Spirits whose victories have given her a name among the nations—But they need not my pencil to make their deeds known to posterity. Could I embody them as they deserve—or even make others feel what *I* felt, as the fame of them came to me across the water, while I was in kind, hospitable old England (for such, even while a foe to my country, such she ever was to me)—could I send that heroic breeze from our gallant native land to *their* hearts—there would be no lack of inspiration. I would invest them with the *grandeur* of my art, or touch them not. But the power is not mine. I know you will not doubt the sincerity of this conviction, but you will better estimate the strength of it when I add, that at no time could the commission you propose be more acceptable to me in a pecuniary view than at present.

But may there not be some eligible subject in our civil history? For myself, I can think of none that would make a picture, of none at least that belongs to *high art*. But such a subject might possibly have occurred to you. If so, and I find it one from which I can make such a picture as you would have me paint, both for my own credit and that of the nation, be assured I will most gladly undertake it. I am persuaded however that you will agree with me in this that no consideration of interest should induce me to accept any commission from Government that will not tax my powers to their utmost—My *best* indeed may be all unworthy but less than that my country shall not have.

In the meantime, that is, till a practicable subject is found, I must beg you to suspend, if such is in progress "the order for a picture." You will readily appreciate the motive of this request, namely to avoid the censure which the good natured world are ever too disposed to bestow on all those who seem wanting to their own interests. I know the world too well not to foresee that it would do me essential injury were it known that I declined such a commission. They would not *understand* the impracticability I have stated, were they even made acquainted with it—Neither would they believe how grievous to me was the necessity of declining it—There is another class of subjects, however, in which, if I were permitted to chuse from it, I should find exciting matter enough, and more than enough, for my imperfect skill—that is from Scripture. But I fear this is a forlorn hope. Yet why should it be? This is a christian land. And the Scriptures belong to no country but to man. The facts they record come home to all men, to the high and low, the wise and simple. But I must not enlarge on this topic to *you*. Should the Government allow me to select a subject from them I need not say with what delight I should accept the commission. With such a source of inspiration and the glory of painting for my country if there be any thing in me, it must come out—Would it might be so!—But let us suppose it. Well, supposing such a commission given, there's a subject, already composed *in petto* which I have long intended to paint as soon as I am at liberty:—the three Mary's at the tomb of our Saviour[5]—the angel sitting on a stone before the mouth of the sepulchre. I consider this one of my happiest conceptions. The terrible beauty of the angel—his preternatural brightness—the varied emotions of wonder, awe and bewilderment, of the three women—the streak of distant day-break, lifting the city of Jerusalem out of the darkness—and the deep-toned spell of the chiaro'scuro, mingling as it were the night with the day—I see now before me. I wish I could see them on the walls at Washington!—Now as to the price, should such a dream—I will not call it hope—be realized, it would be eight thousand dollars which I believe was the price given to Col. Trumbull for each of his pictures[6]—I should not *refuse* ten should Uncle Sam take the generous fit upon him to offer it—but eight is my price for that particular composition, which would consist of four figures seven feet high—the picture itself (an upright) twelve or thirteen high and ten or twelve wide—Were I to undertake a larger composition from another subject, and of the dimensions of Col. T's, which, I think are eighteen by twelve,[7] the price would then be ten or twelve thousand—I fear this last sum would frighten some of your grave Members—My conscience, however would be quite safe in making the demand, were it even more. And I think I have already given the world sufficient proof that I am not mercenary.—Pray do not let any part of this letter get into print—I beg you will not think, from any thing I have said, that I intend any disrespect to the painters of battles, or that I would underestimate such pictures. I meant only to express my own peculiar notions of them, as pictureable subjects *quoad myself.* There are many of deserved reputation, which show great skill in their authors; and among those of modern date, it would be unjust not to mention, as holding the very first rank, Mr. West's Wolf,[8] and the deaths of Warren and Montgomery,[9] and the Sortie, by Col. Trumbull. Truly you might say; our good friend's laconic mantle has not fallen on the writer of this epistle; I believe if I *could* write shorter letters, I should be a better correspondent, But I have not the secret—

Ever most truly yours / Wa Allston—

I am now a resident of Cambridge-Port—village you may remember between Boston and Cambridge—

[Rest of page cut off.]

SOURCE: Manuscript copy. Printed, except for the postscript, in Flagg, pp. 230-34.

1. About this time WA moved to Cambridgeport, a village about a mile from the center of Cambridge near the Charles River, to a small brick house, built on land previously owned by Martha R. Dana, whom he soon married (J.K. Easterby, ed., *The South Carolina Rice Plantation as Revealed in the Letters of Robert F.W. Allston* [Chicago, Univ. of Chicago Press, 1945], p. 82; H.W.L. Dana, "Allston at Harvard: 1796 to 1800," p. 35). In 1838 and 1847 a street in the southern part was laid out and named Allston Street in his honor. Most of the recollections recorded of him during the later years of his life were of him there. 2. Verplanck was a member of the House of Representatives from 1825 to 1833. 3. In February 1830 Verplanck, as chairman of the Committee on Public Buildings, hoped to sponsor in the general congressional bill for buildings

and other items a painting from American history by WA and on the seventeenth of that month wrote him to that effect. His letter does not seem to have been preserved, but he summarized its contents in a letter of the same date to RHD (Flagg, p. 229). The bill was crowded out at that congressional session. In 1834 the project was revived. In February of that year Jarvis introduced a resolution to appoint a joint committee to consider having the four vacant panels in the rotunda filled, but it was not brought to discussion until 15 December, at which time it precipitated heated debate. To Tristram Burges's doubt that there were four American artists competent to do the work, Henry D. Wise replied that America was rich in the fine arts as well as in historical events and called WA "the finest painter," Sully the finest portrait painter, and Greenough the finest sculptor in the world. Aaron Ward said he was proud to know there were so many Americans fully competent, naming WA among a dozen. The bill was nevertheless defeated (23rd Cong., 2d sess., in the House). 4. Cooper described battle scenes in several novels, including four of the Leatherstocking Tales: *The Last of the Mohicans, The Prairie, The Pathfinder,* and *The Deerslayer.* 5. In the accounts of Matthew, Mark, and Luke there were two Marys at the tomb: Mary Magdalene and, according to Matthew, "the other Mary"; according to Mark and Luke, "Mary the mother of James." But Mark and Luke name a third woman: Salome according to Mark, and Joanna according to Luke. In the "Introductory Discourse" of his lectures on art WA referred to "the two Marys" (*LA*, p. 62). Two of his drawings depict the angel and three Marys. West also painted the scene. 6. Trumbull received $8,000 for each of his four paintings for the Capitol: *The Declaration of Independence, Philadelphia, 4 July 1776; The Surrender of General Burgoyne at Saratoga, New York, 16 October 1777; The Surrender of Lord Cornwallis at Yorktown, 19 October 1781;* and *General Washington Resigning His Commission, Annapolis, Maryland, 23 December 1783* (Trumbull, p. 259). 7. These were the dimensions finally agreed upon, though Trumbull originally proposed they be six by nine feet (p. 258). 8. West's *The Death of Wolfe.* 9. Trumbull's *The Death of General Warren at the Battle of Bunker's Hill, 17 June 1775* and *The Death of General Montgomery in the Attack on Quebec, 31 December 1775.*

167. From Gulian Crommelin in Verplanck

Washington,
March 9, 1830.

My Dear Sir: Your letter[1] only convinces me the more that we must, if we can, have one specimen of "high art" on the wall of the Capitol. By American history mere revolutionary history is not meant. To Scripture I fear we cannot go in the present state of public opinion and taste. But does our ante-revolutionary history present no subject? The "Landing of the Pilgrims," a threadbare subject in some respects, has never been viewed with a poet's and painter's eye. What think you of that, or of any similar subject in our early history? Your townsman, Dr. Holmes, has recently published a very useful, though not important, book of "Annals."[2] A hasty glance over the first volume of this would perhaps suggest some idea. If not, I still fall back upon the "Pilgrims." I have read your letter to Colonel Drayton, who fully agrees with me in honoring your feeling upon this subject, and still wishes to call upon your services in embellishing our national annals. Emulating our friend Williams,[3] not from choice, but from the wish not to lose the mail, I will not turn over the leaf.

Yours truly, G.C. Verplanck

SOURCE: Flagg, p. 235.

1. Of 1 March 1830. 2. Abiel Holmes (1763-1837), Boston clergyman and historian. His *The Annals of America, from the Discovery by Columbus in 1492 to the Year 1826* was published in 1829. It was a second edition of his *American Annals; or a Chronological History of America from its Discovery of MCCCCXCII to MDCCCVI* published in 1805. 3. Probably Edwin Williams (1797-1854), journalist and author. He lived from an early age in New York, where he was active in several associations, including the New-York Historical Society.

168. To Gulian Crommelin Verplanck Cambridge Port, Mass. 26 March 1830[1]

Honble Gulian C. Verplanck / Member of Congress / Washington

My dear Sir: Your two letters of the 9th & 12th,[2] as the business phrase is, duly came to hand. As you full well know that I cannot be insensible to such persevering kindness I will not trouble you with a reputation of thanks, but proceed to answer them in as business like a way, as I can. To the first subject you propose, the Landing of the Pilgrims (not unpicturesque) I have a personal objection. It has already been painted by an old friend of mine, Col. Sargent, a high minded, honorourable man, to whom I would on no account give pain; which I could not avoid doing were I to encroach on what, at the expense of several years labour, he has a fair right to consider as his ground. I do not like rivalry in any shape; and my [word omitted] on the same *subject would* seem like it.—Indeed it would give me no pleasure to beat any one. Nor do I consider this business of "beating" as having any natural connexion with excellence of any kind—which, to be such must be intrinsic, and independent of comparison. Nature never made two minds alike; and if the artist, whether poet or painter, has any of the *mens divinior,*[3] with the power of embodying it, his production *must* have a distinctive excellence, which not a hundred bad or good ones by another can either increase or diminish. This is not the doctrine of the *Reviewing age* but I believe it to be true nevertheless. Moreover, I doubt if competition was ever yet the *cause* of a great work. It is the love of excellence in the abstract, and for itself, that alone can produce excellence. I believe that Raffaelle loved Michel Angelo because he thought him his superiour—for that excellence which he could not himself reach. There may indeed be clever imitations, got up under mere ignoble impulses, a kind of *second hand originality,* as Edmund Dana calls them <making each other—and> that might pass for it; nay, the world is full of them—mocking each other—and some times mocking at, and how bitterly!—But here I am wandering off, like Tangent in the play,[4] I hardly know where—After this excursion I will not trouble you with my objections to the other subject, the "leave taking of Washington,"[5] lest I have no room for one of my own choosing, which I should be glad to have you approve, namely, The first interview of Columbus with Ferdinand and Isabella,[6] at court, after the discovery of America, accompanied by natives &c—exhibited in evidence of his success—As you have read Irving's book[7] it is unnecessary for me to describe the scene—Here

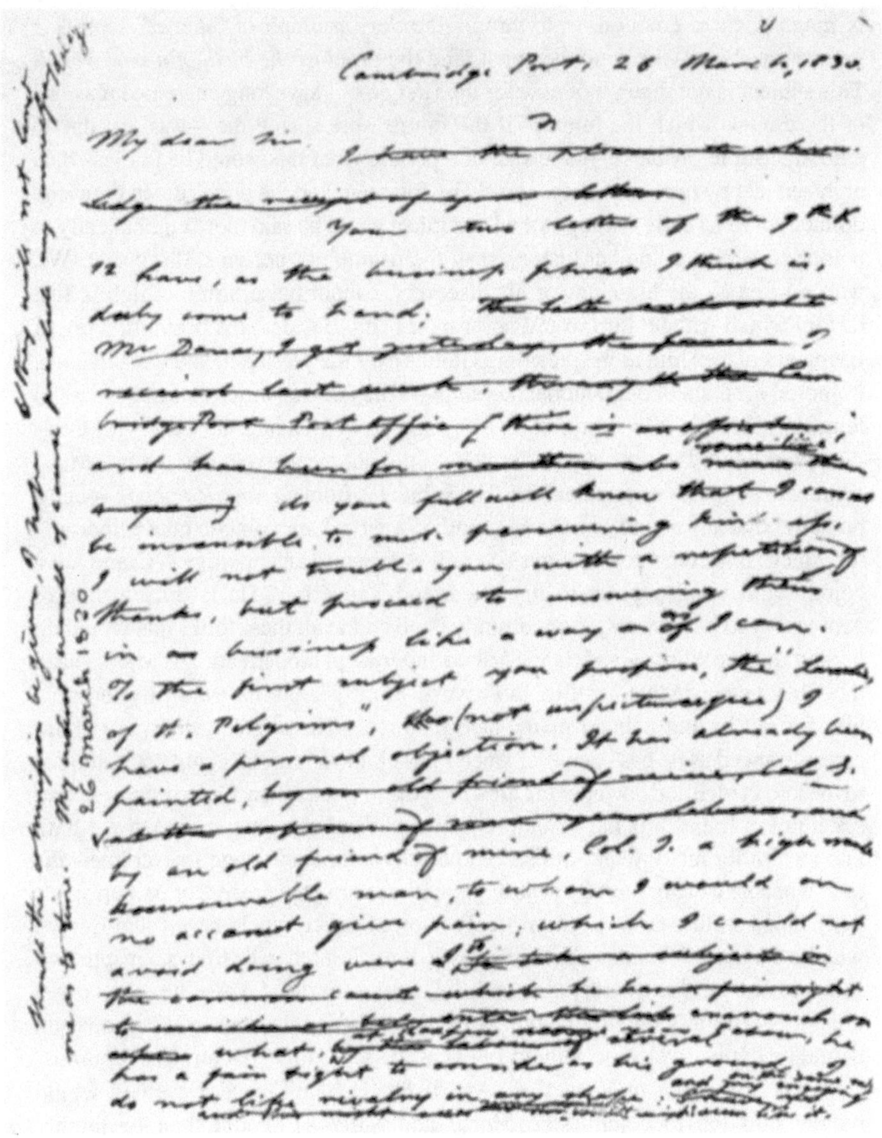

Cambridge Port, 26 March, 1830.

My dear Sir

Your two letters of the 9th & 12 have, as the business phrase I think is, duly come to hand; As you full well know that I cannot be insensible to such favouring kindness, I will not trouble you with a repetition of thanks, but proceed to answering them in as business like a way as I can. To the first subject you propose, the "Landing of the Pilgrims", (not unpicturesque) I have a personal objection. It has already been painted, by an old friend of mine, Col. T. a high minded honourable man, to whom I would on no account give pain; which I could not avoid doing were I to … what, … he has a fair right to consider as his ground. I do not like rivalry in any shape;

26 March 1830

Draft of a letter to Gulian Crommelin Verplanck (No. 168) from Cambridge Port, dated 26 March, 1830. Manuscript in Massachusetts Historical Society, Boston.

is magnificence, emotion, everything—the very triumph of "matter" to task a painter's powers—the announcement, and the proof of *the birth of a new world.* This subject is not thought of now for the first time. I have long cherished it as one of the dreams which the future—if the future were spared me—was one day to embody. But to business.—The size of a picture from this would be not less than eighteen feet by twelve, perhaps twenty by fourteen; and the price fifteen thousand dollars. As to its class, I know not what subject could be said more emphatically to belong to America and her history, than the triumph of her great discoverer. We, who now enjoy the blessings of his discovery, cannot place him too high in that history which without him would never have been. Besides, the beautiful work of Irving has placed him as the presiding Genius over the yet, fresh, and we will hope, immortal fountain of our national literature—The fame of which Columbus was so long defrauded is now restored to him, and it will endure, at least with every American heart. Pray excuse my heroics—I did not mean to get into them—May I venture to suggest one popular hint. The subject is from an *American book*—and a book too that any country might be proud of—Now I am going to take a liberty—for which, however, I feel assured you will not require any apology—Could not a commission be also given to my old friend Vanderlyn? He is truly a man of genius—who has powers, if opportunity is given to call them forth, that would do honour to his country. His Ariadne *has no superior* in modern art. His Marius also, though not equal to that, is still a noble work. Some persons have unjustly censured him for not having painted many such pictures—The wonder with me is how, circumstanced as he has been ever since I have known him, he could have attained to the knowledge and power in the art which those works shew him to possess; for, I say it not in friendship, but in simple justice—Vanderlyn *is a great Artist.* I have known him for many years, in France and Italy intimately—and I never knew the time when he had not literally to struggle with poverty; the process of procuring his daily bread stifling powers that, if freely allowed to act, would have filled Europe with his name.—I fear that, like the subject of my last letter, he finds no inspiration in necessity. Let his country now call his genius forth—I know he will do her honour—With this opinion of him, I need hardly say that my own commission would be doubly welcome, should I hear at the same time that an *equal* commission was also given to Vanderlyn. And if Uncle Sam's generous mood would incline him too to commission Morse and Sully—I should then be threbly delighted—Morse I consider as a child of my own, and you know what I think of him—The quickening atmosphere which he is now breathing in Europe will open some original and powerful seeds which I long ago saw in him. I am much mistaken if he has not *that in him* which will one day surprise. And Sully has historical powers (already proved in his "Crossing the Delaware,")[8] of no common order. Pray direct to me to Cambridge Port. There *is* a post office here, and has been for some time. I was much gratified to learn the interest which Col. Drayton does me the honour to take in my behalf—I knew him some years since in London and I have met with few persons with whom I have been so much pleased on so short an acquaintance—Pray present him my respects and thanks—Should *the* commission be given, I hope they will not limit me as to *time*, as I have several engagements that must be previously fulfilled. My interest would of course preclude any unnecessary delay.

Faithfully yours—Wa Allston

SOURCE: Manuscript copy. Printed in Flagg, pp. 235-38.

1. "6" has been written over "9" in another hand, the date of the draft of this letter being 26 March. This draft is the only draft of a letter by WA of which the final version seems to exist. In all essentials the two are identical, but the draft contains minor revisions in almost every line. Typical of them are "is" for "must be," "impulses" for "motive," "originality" for "*original* excellence," "Besides" for "A word more," "placed" for "stationed," "unjustly denounced" for "wondered," "known him free from pecuniary embarrassment" for "knew the time when he had not literally to struggle with poverty," "procuring" for "providing," "saw him some years since" for "knew a little of him when" (Manuscript copy). 2. This letter does not seem to have been preserved. In it Verplanck apparently urged WA to accept the commission to paint two of the panels in the rotunda of the Capitol and suggested as a subject Washington's taking leave of his troops at the end of the Revolution. 3. "A mind of diviner cast." 4. Unidentified. 5. Presumably a quotation from Verplanck's letter of 12 March. 6. A painting of Isabella ascribed to WA was listed in a sales catalog of 1858 from the collection of Franklin Dexter, and Jarvis referred to a work by WA depicting Columbus on his return from the Western world, but nothing further about either seems to be known (RHD, p. 16). 7. *A History of the Life and Voyages of Christopher Columbus* (1828), a translation of Don Martin Fernández de Navarette's *Colección de los viages y descubrimientos, que hicieron por mar los españoles desde fines del siglo XV.* 8. *Washington at the Passage of the Delaware.*

169. To George Ticknor Cambridge Port, 31 March, 1830

My dear Sir: I find, by the Newspapers, that Congress have voted a Statue to Washington, to be placed in the Rotunda, over his tomb.[1] *Here* is a fine opening for Horatio Greenough, if he only had some friend at the seat of Government to put in a claim for him. I have been looking about <for> to see if such an one could be found, and it has occurred to me to solicit your good offices to that effect, knowing no one who would take more pleasure in doing a kindness to a deserving man of genius. I have thought too that a line from you to Mr. Webster might be of essential service to him.

Greenough's claim would rest on two *very substantial* grounds: 1, that he is *fully competent to the task;* 2, that he is an *American Artist*. In the question of a great National work, the latter indeed ought never to be admitted as any ground at all, except (as in the present case) where it is appended to the former.

You well know that I consider Greenough as one destined—and that too at *no distant day*—to take his station among the *very first* Sculptors of the age. But you have so often heard my opinion of his genius, that [it] is needless to repeat it now. I will only add, that, should this Country give him this commission, *I feel a perfect assurance* that he will produce a work *worthy of the Great Subject*. Besides, it is a work that he would execute con amore; for it so happens that a Statue of Washington has long been a favourite project with him. He took with him to Italy a cast from Hudon's bust,[2] together with a copy by himself, to which he had added some useful hints, from the study of Stuart's Head. And in a letter to me a few months back (which I have unfortunately mislaid) he was so enthusiastic on the subject that he talked of forthwith "setting up the irons" for modelling it on a large scale.[3] But this project has no doubt been abandoned, from the want of means—which seem from his *last* letter (17 Novb 1829) to have been brought to a very low ebb with him; for he says, "Unless some work is sent me, or I should find it here (which is not probable) I shall in the course of eight months get aground."

I am sure you will agree with me, when you read the following additional extract from the same letter, that it would be a cause of deep regret to every one interested in the fate of Genius, that so fair an opportunity, not merely of *employing*, but of *making*, a great Artist should be lost. "Nothing," he says, "not even the love of my Art, shall tempt me to stay here one moment at the risk of encumbering my personal friends here. I have been looked on since I have been here by the respectable artists as a man whose game is tolerably sure—and pride will send me straight to Leghorn when I find *soundings* growing shallow."

I know you will not require any apology for this letter—therefore I make none. Believe me, dear Sir, / with the truest respect and esteem, yrs sincerely

Wa. Allston.

ADDRESSED: Professor Ticknor, / Common Street, / Boston. SOURCE: Manuscript, Dartmouth College Library.

1. Congressional resolutions to have Washington's remains brought from Mount Vernon to the Capitol and a monument erected over them were made periodically from his death in 1799 to 1832, without success as far as the removal was concerned and not until the latter date with pursuant action respecting the monument. On 22 February 1830 a statue was proposed, probably partly in consequence of the erection of Chantrey's statue in Boston. An account of the resolution appeared in the *Boston Daily Advertiser* for 1 March 1830. On 2 April 1830 RHD wrote Verplanck recommending that Greenough be commissioned for it. He thought he would every way do credit, adding that he said so on the authority of WA, whom he had talked to on the subject a few nights earlier and who "expressed himself most fully & unhesitatingly." When RHD asked WA to write Verplanck, however, he said that he would do so had he not written already about two brother painters, referring to his recommendation of Morse and Sully for paintings in the rotunda, and felt it would be pressing his wishes and opinions on Verplanck but that RHD was at liberty to use his name to anyone (New-York Historical Society). 2. Jean Antoine Houdon (1741-1828), French sculptor, executed a bust as well as a standing figure of Washington from life. The bust was considered the definitive study. 3. Greenough's letter of 19[20] September 1829.

170. From Gulian Crommelin Verplanck House of Representatives, May 29, 1830.

My Dear Sir: We (that is our Committee) had determined to try the taste and liberality of Congress by recommending an appropriation for a picture from you on your terms and choice, restricting you only to American History, in which Columbus would, of course, be included; but, unfortunately, for the present our bill for the improvement of the public buildings has been crowded out by the press of other business, and must lie over till next winter.

Though our proposed alterations in the buildings are important both to comfort and taste, there was nothing pressing in the bill now passing, and I only regret the delay on your account. Next winter we shall have the opportunity of taking up the bill early, and I hope with better success.[1] But the extent to which Congress will go in these matters depends much on accidental circumstances.

SOURCE: Flagg, p. 239.

1. The project was not revived until 1834.

171. To John Stevens Cogdell Cambridge Port, Massachusetts, 8 June, 1830.

Dear Cogdell: My patriarchal courtship is at length ended; I am now a happy Benedict[1]—and I know not what I could do better than to bestow on you some of the spirits which the occasion inspires. I was married on Tuesday last at Cambridge,[2] which we left immediately after the ceremony, for our present habitation and home. It is a snug, commodious little mansion, prettily situated in a retired part of this village, and commanding a pleasant view of the adjacent country, taking in a part of the river, and a picturesque little pine wood which used to be the favourite haunt of my younger days, to which I used to saunter after College hours, and dream sometimes of poetry, and sometimes of my Art. These youthful associations have an indefinable charm peculiarly pleasing to me at this time; they seem to bring together the earlier and later portions of my life, mingling them as it were into one, and imparting to the present some of that *eloquent* quiet of the past which my nature has always most loved. You may well suppose that such a home, with the woman of my choice, must have no ordinary value in my eyes, after the restless, wandering Arab life which I have led for the last ten years. Though circumstances have thrown me upon the world for so large a portion of my life, and obliged me to mix so long in its gay and busy scenes, it has seldom if ever afforded me any real enjoyment. Not that my disposition is solitary; on the contrary, it is inherently social; for the truest enjoyment I have ever known has been in that which has been reflected back to me from those I love—<in my [?]> only to be found in the domestic circle, and among a few personal friends. Nothing like this can the world give—nothing but a poor substitute of idle ceremony and heartless shew; what are called its pleasures are none to me; nor can they be deemed such even by a man of the world till they stimulate the mind into an artificial state; that passing off, they are pleasures no longer, but vanish like enebriating illustions, while their places are filled with weariness or disgust. But the sober pleasures of home, taking their source in virtues consonant to our moral nature, have no other condition for their fruition and permanence but equal virtue in the receiver as in the giver. If they fail then of being realized, it is because <of> we are unworthy of them.—I will not attempt to describe my wife to you; I will only say, that in the excellence of her disposition, cultivated intellect, sound religious principles, and practical piety, I have a prospect of as much happiness as any one may look for in this world.

I wrote my Mother on the 28th May, four days previous to my marriage, and announcing its approach. She tells me, in her last letter, by Mrs. Amory (who is now here after a two months journey by land) that you "scolded much about my long silence." I am sure however that you did so very gently, for I know that you are too kind-hearted to scold in earnest, especially after the frankness with which I expressed myself to you, when you were last in Boston, on the subject of letter-writing. But I do not mean to excuse myself for so very long a silence; on the contrary, I acknowledge that it was much longer than it ought to have been; and certainly much longer than I either wished or intended. Perhaps, however, were I to give you the whole history of the interval between this and my last letter, you might not so much wonder at it, bearing in mind at the same time all I have formerly said on this subject as it affects myself. You would among the palliatives of this diary find many sheets of letters to others, which I have been obliged to write, whether I would or not, and at times too of perplexity and trouble, with an exhausted mind and wearied body. But I need not enter into such a history to induce *you* to excuse it; I know the kindness of your nature too well not to feel assured that you do already excuse it. I would however say a word here in relation to the future; that you might be just not only to me but to yourself. When I signed myself your *friend* (never a matter of *form* with me) I did so in sincerity, and from a just appreciation of your many estimable qualities. Do not therefore ever measure my regard by the frequency of my letters. I am sure you will not think a just criterion when I tell you, that with some of my oldest and most intimate friends I do not exchange letters other than once in two or three years. Among these are some for whom I could not well entertain a higher value than I do; and they, I have every reason to believe, have an equal value for me. Yet they never complain that I do not write oftener; they are willing to take me as I am; and never for a moment doubt my friendship, however long the interval between our letters.

I sent you, as I mentioned in the letter to my Mother, through some of your correspondents (Mr. Parker[3] & Mr. Smith[4]) several messages, respecting your "Modestia,"[5] saying how much I was pleased with it. I may now more particularly say, that I think it superior in execution to your preceding works—as it ought to be.

You have well expressed the character, or rather, I should say, embodied the sentiment. There is nothing assumed or theatrical in it, but it is natural and delicate, and does great credit to your invention. There is a remark, however, that I will make which may be of use to you in future subjects of this class, viz: the bridge of the nose is too thin, and the chin too large, for beauty, according to the Antique—at least, secondo il mio gusto.[6] The folds of the drapery are also too small—what the Artists call "cut up." But when I say that upon the whole I prefer the old General, you must not think that I am disparaging this last work. I mention it as merely as exemplifying what I observed in a former letter—that elegance of execution is no match for force of character. The Modestia is certainly the superiour in execution; but it is the personification of an abstraction, and therefore but indirectly, & by an effort of the mind, <address> appealing to our sympathies; whereas the other, as the image of an actual living being, comes home to us at once, and produces its effect (as in nature) before we know why.—I desired my Mother to tell you that I did all I could to obtain subscriptions for your bust of Bishop Dehon,[7] but unfortunately without success. The fact is, that little interest is felt in the Bishop here; and I suppose in consequence of his having lived so many years in other places before he died.—I had got about half through this letter when I was called down stairs to see Mr. F Kinloch, who handed me a letter of introduction from you. I knew his father[8] well—a most estimable man, for whose memory I have the highest respect. I need not say that it will give me sincere pleasure to be of service to him.

Believe me ever your sincere friend / Wa. Allston.

[In the margin] I am grateful to you in the commission which Mr. Kinloch informs me you have received to execute a bust of Mr. Elliott.[9] I thought you would have it to do when I saw his death in the Paper,[10] and that a bust of him was to be made. Present my best regards to Mrs. Cogdell, and Give my love to my Mother and brother Henry, and tell them all about my marriage.

ADDRESSED: John S. Cogdell Esqre. / Charleston, / South Carolina. SOURCE: Manuscript. Printed in part in Flagg, pp. 239-41.

1. A long-time bachelor who has married, from the character with that experience in Shakespeare's *Much Ado about Nothing*. 2. 1 June, in RHD's house (H.W.L. Dana, "Allston in Cambridgeport, 1830 to 1841," *Cambridge Historical Society Publications* 29 [1943]: following p. 16). 3. Probably George Philips Parker of Boston, who married Anna Moore, WA's first cousin (Webber, "Moore of St. Thomas' Parish," p. 168). 4. Possibly William Smith, brother of RHD's wife, whose father had that name. He was a resident of Providence and was often visited by his Dana nephews and nieces (Dana, 1:30, 67, 109-10). 5. It was described as "A fancy bust of Modesty." Apparently Cogdell sent it to Boston, possibly for exhibition at the BA, but there seems to be no record of its being shown there. A cast was apparently shown at the PAFA for several years from 1829. It was at one time owned by Miss Annie Robinson of Charleston ("An All-Accomplished Man"). 6. "According to my taste." 7. Theodore Dehon (1776-1817), a native of Boston, was the second bishop of South Carolina, from 1812 to his death ("The Abiel Abbot Journals," ed. John Hammond Moore, *SCHGM* 68 [1967]: 72). 8. Francis Kinloch (1798-1840), a native of South Carolina, was apparently on his way to Europe. He was in Paris by

October 1831 and the next year went to Florence, where he spent most of the rest of his life. He studied to be an artist but apparently produced little. His father was Cleland Kinloch (b. 1770s) of South Carolina. He was educated at Eton and traveled on the Continent in his early years. He owned Weehaw Plantation near Georgetown and later built the large estate of Acton near Statesburg (Wright, "Francis Kinloch: A South Carolina Artist," *South Carolina Historical Magazine* 61 [1960]: 99-100). 9. Stephen Elliott (1771-1830), South Carolina botanist, banker, statesman, and editor. 10. Elliott died on 28 March 1830. The notice in the Boston papers has not been located.

172. To Loammi Baldwin Cambridge Port, 9 July, 1830.

Dear Baldwin: In case I should not see you today, I will leave for you the following mintues relating to my Painting-Room.[1] Length of the Room fifty feet, breadth thirty three, height twenty- that is from the floor to the ceiling. The window the same as in Mr. Paris's[2] plan. The walls to be *furred* out[3]—(I believe that is the term) in order to make it air-tight. There should also be a cellar of sufficient depth to keep out dampness from below, and a double floor. If you can set down the number and sizes of the different timbers required, I would be obliged to you, provided it does not put you to much trouble.—These I believe are the particulars necessary to enable the carpenters to form a correct estimate of the expense.[4] Should any others, however, occur to you, will you have the goodness to add them.

I wish, if possible, to break ground within ten days.

Ever faithfully yrs / W. Allston.

ADDRESSED: Loammi Baldwin Esqre. / Navy Yard,[5] / Charlestown. SOURCE: Manuscript, William L. Clements Library, University of Michigan.

1. It was designed by WA and built on the north side of Auburn Street about fifty feet west of Magazine Street in the rear of the Baptist church, in the midst of a garden. It had one door, flanked by pillasters and pediments and painted green, and one large window on the northern side running the height of the building to let in the northern light. The other sides were eventually covered with vines. The inside was painted Spanish brown, Sully recorded (Dunlap, 2:140), which heightened the color of the paintings. To the left of the large window was a fireplace, and along the northern wall were cabinets and small closets where WA kept his painting materials and smaller pictures, the doors and walls of which he covered with inscriptions expressive of his artistic and generally philosophic sentiments. The eastern end was occupied by *Belshazzar's Feast,* and on the other walls hung the other paintings and outlines on which he was working (H.W.L. Dana, "Allston in Cambridgeport, 1830 to 1841," pp. 36-37; a picture of it is reproduced following p. 48). According to Sweetser, "the children of the neighborhood had many a ghostly theory about this lone studio of New England" (p. 133). The most detailed description of its interior was that written several years later in his journal by the sculptor Henry Dexter, who came to Boston in the fall of 1836. On 22 August 1838 he called on WA, who after a delay in answering his knock led him from the hall into "a large room, so large that it looked almost empty, though it contained here and there boxes, canvases turned towards the wall, easels, and in one corner a great number of casts of heads, feet, knees, hands—*all* fragments from the antique,—with several figures originally whole, but now much broken." The casts included one of the *Borghese Warrior.* A closet contained a foot of colossal size and two small figures of his own modeling, to be copied in one of his paintings,

probably *Saul and the Witch of Endor* if not *Jeremiah* (John Albee, *Henry Dexter, Sculptor: A Memorial* [privately printed, 1898], pp. 57-59). About the same time, Chester Harding wrote a description of the room, emphasizing its apparent disorderliness. One of the casts was presumably that of an antique head of Thalia, the Greek muse of comedy and lyric poetry, which Leslie said he "made very much his model of female loveliness" (to RHD, 13 Mar. 1844, Dana Papers). Probably it is the bust which appears in David C. Johnston's portrait of him in his studio. He kept a fire throughout the year and once wrote six lines of verse on a pair of old bellows, addressing them as "Where'er I roam, whatever fires I see, / My heart, untravelled, still returns to thee / My own dear bellows!" (Flagg, p. 367). For the two years preceding its construction, presumably after the sale of John Prince's barn, the address of his studio was, in 1828, Market Hall, which was probably the upper part of the so-called City Market at the foot of Brattle Street, for a time occupied as a gallery of fine arts (Drake, p. 130); and, in 1829, his residence on Sister Street. 2. Alexander Parris. At this time he was associated with Loammi Baldwin as consulting engineer in building the dry dock at the Charlestown navy yard. 3. To fur, meaning to fix strips of wood in order to bring them to a level or to the required surface. 4. Enos Litchfield, a Boston housewright (*Boston City Directory* for 1820-38), was employed to make an estimate for the room. He recollected as an example of WA's generosity that, learning of the agent's refusal to pay him, WA gave him ten dollars six or eight years later. 5. At this time Baldwin was superintending the construction of the dry dock at the navy yard in Charlestown.

173. To Charles Robert Leslie

Cambridgeport,
Dec. 14, 1830.

Dear Leslie: This will be handed to you by Mr. Cheney,[1] whom I have particular pleasure in making known to you. Mr. C. is a native of Connecticut, and I believe from the place with Mr. Danforth,[2] who has done himself so much credit by his engraving from your portrait of Sir Walter Scott.[3]

Though the specimens which Mr. Cheney will show you of his engraving will no doubt afford the best evidence of his genius,[4] I cannot deny myself the pleasure of adding my opinion. To me he appears to possess all the essential qualities of a first-rate engraver; and that such he will become, with a little more experience and the many advantages for study which London affords, I entertain not the smallest doubt. His prominent quality, one that I am sure you will agree with me is of the highest order, is his delicate *tact* for expression and character. This, we both know, is as rare among engravers as with painters; but Mr. Cheney adds to this a clearness and grace of line that already entitle him to a decided rank.

As a disinterested lover of the art, I rejoice that he is now in a school so well fitted for the development of his powers;[5] but for this I would regret his leaving America, as I had hoped at no distant day to put them (if agreeable to him) in requisition for myself. As it is, however, I shall not give up the hope of one day or other availing myself of his graver.

After what I have said, it would be quite superfluous to ask your friendly offices in his behalf. I would only add that they would be very gratefully received.

By the time this reaches you or probably soon after, you will receive an answer to your last.[6] In the mean time I beg you to accept my thanks for it, and to believe me ever sincerely yours,

Wa. Allston.

Charles R. Leslie, Esq., R.A. / Mr. Cheney, London.

SOURCE: Ednah Dow Cheney, *Memoir of John Cheney, Engraver* (Boston, 1889), pp. 16-17.

1. John Cheney. This letter was probably not delivered, since Cheney met Leslie otherwise. Cheney was reported to have loved reading it over in his old age. While in London he was closely associated with Leslie, four of whose paintings he engraved (Cheney, *Memoir of John Cheney, Engraver,* pp. 16-17; S.R. Koehler, comp., *Catologue of the Engraved and Lithographed Work of John Cheney and Seth Wells Cheney* [Boston, 1891], pp. 36, 38-39, 45, 61). 2. Moseley Isaac Danforth (1800-62), engraver and painter, was born in Hartford, Conn. He lived in New York in his early and late years and lived in London from 1827 to 1837. 3. Besides the portrait of Scott, Danforth engraved Leslie's *The Sentry Box,* which was perhaps his best-known engraving. 4. Cheney had produced by this time a dozen engravings and several lithographs, most of which had appeared in gift books (Koehler, *passim*). 5. The RA. 6. Leslie's letter of 17 February 1830.

174. To William Algernon Alston Cambridge Port, 4 Jany. 1831.

My dear Sir: I am sorry to say, in reply to your Note, that Mr. Ball's[1] Picture[2] is not yet finished. And I must ask the favour of you (should you write to him) to make my apology, and to assure him that I have not been unmindful of my engagement, but that the delay has been unavoidable. I beg him to believe that nothing could have been farther from my thoughts than any intentional neglect of him. It was my expectation—as it was certainly my interest—to have completed it ere this; but circumstances over which I had no control have prevented me. I regret that I did not, on accepting the commission, leave the time of its completion more indefinite than I did. This is what I have usually done, and indeed what my mode of working has always obliged me to do; the difficulty of satisfying myself rendering it always uncertain how long a time any picture, large or small, will cost me. Besides, I seldom confine myself to one picture, but carry on often three or four at the same time;[3] and this not so much from choice as from necessity. For instance—sometimes I get what the Artists call, "stuck," that is, I come to a part with which I cannot please myself, and which becomes worse and worse the more I work on it; my only remedy then is to lay it aside, <from time> and return to it after a time with a *fresh eye,* when I am generally able to *hit* at once what I might else have laboured for in vain.[4] In the meantime, as I have neither leisure nor inclination to be idle, I proceed with some other picture till I either finish that, or am "brought up" by it in a similar way. This is my usual manner of painting; and I think I may in some degree ascribe to it whatever advances I may have made in my Art; inasmuch as I have often found these *difficulties,* by stimulating my invention, to eventuate in *felicities,* which I might not otherwise have reached. Then, again, I never suffer a picture to go out of my hands until it is as good as *I* can make it; and, to make it *such,* I must work *con amore,* in other words, I must be pleased with my work. <before> This method, I am aware, is not the most profitable in a pecuniary sense; but I know it to be so in reputation; I have besides a satisfaction in the consciousness that no one possesses any picture of mine of which I have not honestly done my best at the time it was painted.

Pray inform Mr Ball that his Picture is more than two thirds advanced, and that I shall do my best to complete it as soon as it is in my power.

I have spun out this epistle longer than I intended—pray excuse it—I could not well have made it shorter.

My love to Mother and Mary and your children.[5]

I remain sincerely yours, / Wa. Allston.

If it is not too much trouble to you, would it not be as well to send a copy of this letter to Mr. Ball? Or would it do to enclose this to him?

ADDRESSED: Boston.[6] ANNOTATED by Alston: *Cambridge Port. 4 Jany 1831. / Washington Allston* / Rec'd 5 Jany. / Ansd. SOURCE: Manuscript, Etting Collection, Historical Society of Pennsylvania.

1. Hugh Swinton Ball. 2. *Spalatro's Vision of the Bloody Hand,* from Ann Radcliffe's *The Italian,* vol. 2, chap. 9, depicts the monk Schedoni and the assassin Spalatro on their way to murder Elena. WA made a sketch of it about 1829 and, among others, pencilled drawings of the head of Spalatro and of Schedoni holding the lamp (ca. 1830) George W. Flagg said that while working on it he would, as he often did, start back from the canvas and assume the attitude of the character he was painting (Henry T. Tuckerman, *Book of the Artists* [New York, 1867], p. 406). It was exhibited in Boston and at the NAD before being sent to Ball in Charleston, S.C. In the summer of 1835 he proposed to Asher B. Durand that he make an engraving of it, but he apparently did not (Durand to John William Casilear, 14 June 1835, Asher B. Durand Papers, Rare Books and Manuscripts Division, The New York Public Library, Astor, Lenox and Tilden Foundations). Several years later it was engraved by the Englishman W.J. Linton for the frontispiece in Clara Clement Waters, *Handbook of Legendary and Mythological Art* (1871). 3. The other paintings WA was working on at this time were probably *The Spanish Girl in Reverie, A Roman Lady Reading, A Tuscan Girl,* and *Lover Playing a Lute.* 4. In the lecture "Art" WA cited Titian's habitual use of this procedure (*LA,* p. 107). 5. William Algernon and Mary (Allston Young) Alston had nine children who lived to maturity: Joseph, William, John Ashe, Josephine, Mary Ashe, Theodosius, Charlotte Marion and Anna Louise (twins), and Edmund (E.D. Allston, p. 387). 6. Alston was presumably visiting Boston for a short period.

175. To John Knapp Cambridgeport, February 23, 1831.

Dear Knapp: As we suppose you have by this time finished preparing for the press, the journal of your voyage to the Island of Formosa or Natchitoches[1] (the public are divided as to which, though they have no doubt you have been to one or the other place), Mrs. A. and myself would be happy to have your opinion on a haunch of Yankee venison at five o'clock on Friday.

N.B.—Mr. Hastings[2] and Mr. E.T. Dana, who will be present, are also very curious (at least I venture to think so) to hear your opinion; especially as to how it compares with the foreign venison which you have doubtless met with in your travels. A bed is provided for you in which you may rest after the labors incident to so important a decision.

Ever faithfully yours, / W. Allston.

SOURCE: Flagg, pp. 243-44.

1. Formosa, an island off the coast of China, and Natchitoches, a town in the parish of the same name in Louisiana, were apparently introduced by Knapp during some evening's comical conversation at WA's. Flagg calls the letter "characteristic," indicating the "informal, and yet epicurean, nature of these occasions." 2. Edmund T. Hastings was a Boston merchant in the sale of West Indian goods and sperm oil in 1834-36. After 1838 his business seems to have been taken over by Edmund T. Hastings, Jr. (*Boston City Directory* for 1834-52).

176. To George Ticknor Cambridge Port, 6 March, 1831.

My dear Sir: As I am quite ignorant of the detail of a Sculptor's expenses, I am unable to return more than a *conjectural* answer to your question, "What would be the probable cost of the Statue," proposed by Mr. Greenough.[1] In London the cost of a block of Carrara Marble, for a statue of the size of life, is (according to my *impression*—for <which> the correctness of which, however, I will not vouch) about three hundred guineas. Now, allowing for the difference in the charges of transportation &c. the same block would not, I should suppose, be had in Florence for less than five or six hundred dollars; and when to this is added the charges of workmen for *boasting out* the marble, that is, hewing it from the solid block to within two or more inches of the outline—a labour seldom or never performed by the Sculptor himself—and for the *setting up* (by a kind of iron skeleton) the clay model, not to mention the living models; it appears to me that a thousand dollars would hardly cover the expenses. It seems then, if I am correct in this, that fifteen hundred would leave too small a profit, and two thousand certainly not too much.

I beg this may be considered only as my *guess*—and the lowest guess. Mr. G himself might perhaps put it lower. If a larger sum however could well be raised, I have no scruple in saying, that I think Mr. Greenough will well merit it.

Accept my thanks for sending me the enclosed, which I have read with great pleasure.

Pray present my best respects to Mrs Ticknor,[2] and believe me, dear sir,

every faithfully / yrs truly obliged, / Wa. Allston.

ADDRESSED: To / Professor Ticknor, / To be left at Mr Hasting's / Store. SOURCE: Manuscript, Dartmouth College Library.

1. Presumably Ticknor was inquiring about the cost of a statue such as Horatio Greenough proposed late in 1830 to erect of Washington in front of the Capitol in Washington (Wright, p.

83). 2. Ticknor's wife was the former Anna Eliot (b. 1800) ("Brief Memoirs and Notices of Prince's Subscribers," *NEGHR* 23 [1869]: 338).

177. To James McMurtrie Cambridge-Port, Massachusetts, 27th May, 1831.

My dear Sir: I have just received your letter of the 19th inst. and agreeably to your request, I sit down to reply to it without delay. I regret however that it is not in my power to give you much available information on the subject of your inquiries. I have never seen Mr. Haydon's picture (the Entrance into Jerusalem) since it was completed; it <being> having been in a very unfinished state when I left England. It was not finished, I think, until about two years after my return home. So far as it was advanced, I thought very highly of it, as a picture worthy the Author, whom I then considered, and I still do, as ranking among the very first of living artists. Indeed I know no living artist, whom, all things considered, I could name as his superior. When I saw it[1] the principal figure, the Saviour, was not painted. Of the finished picture perhaps you may get some notion by consulting the British Periodicals at the time of its exhibition. As to the price at which it may now be had, I cannot offer even a guess: nor can I inform you who is its present proprietor. It was taken by execution, together with several other pictures, upon Mr. Haydon's insolvency some years ago, and sold at auction—for what I know not—I only remember <that> it was said they were most shamefully sacrificed for little more than the cost of their frames.[2] The Judgement of Solomon, I have understood, was a few years since offered to an American Gentleman for five hundred guineas—or, at least, it was signified to him that it might be had for that sum; a sum, in my opinion, far below its value. If I remember right, Haydon told me not long before I left England, that he had had an offer of two thousand pounds for the Entrance into Jerusalem—at that time, as I have before observed unfinished. I mention this to show the estimation in which this picture was then held, not as affording a clue to its present price—which has no doubt varied with the changes it has undergone as to owners & since the unfortunate Artist's misfortune to which I have alluded. This is all the information I am able to give. I think it probable, however, that Mr. Leslie might be able to supply whatever else you may need.

I have but a few weeks since been established in my new Painting-Room, which I have built in this place. Belshazzer has been rolled up, and reposing in a packing-case for more than three years, in consequence of my former large room in Boston passing into the hands of a new owner,[3] who has converted it into a livery stable; since which I have been compelled to work in a small chamber, where I have been employed altogether on small pictures. Belshazzer will still remain for some time to come in his case—some embarrassing debts and my immediate necessities being the cause. I must be free in mind before I continue to finish it. I trust, however, that <it> the time will not be very long. Your Room which you mention must be a noble one. I wish there was such a one in each of our large cities. It is a great diserderatum <for> with me, as I mean hereafter, that is, when I once more become *free,* and should Providence grant me life, to continue myself chiefly to large works.—I suppose you know that I have become a Benedick. I have been married about a year and this village is now my home. It is but two miles from Boston, where [I ca]n [page torn] be at any time, by means of an Hourly Stage, in twenty minutes. I am in better health, and certainly in better spirits than I have been in these ten years.

Believe me, my dear Sir, with undiminished regard, / sincerely yours,

Washington Allston.

Pray give my best regards to Sully, and tell him that I should have been happy to have had one of my Boston Pictures in your Academy's Exhibition, but, belonging to other people, I had no control over them.

ADDRESSED: James McMurtrie Esqre. / Philadelphia, / Pennsylvania. SOURCE: Manuscript. Printed in Flagg, pp. 249-50.

1. WA visited Haydon's studio in London in company with Beaumont to see the progress on the painting. 2. After Haydon was released from prison for his debts in July 1823, in which event his property was seized and advertised for sale, his *Christ's Entry into Jerusalem* was sold for £240. In September 1831 it was purchased by the engraver Cephas Childs and Henry Inman to form the nucleus of the Gallery of Painting in Philadelphia (Clarke Olney, *Benjamin Robert Haydon, Historical Painter* [Athens, Ga., Univ. of Georgia Press, 1952], pp. 113, 153). Two years later it was in the possession of McMurtrie (Dunlap, *Diary of William Dunlap, 1776-1839* [New York: New-York Historical Society, 1931], 3:720). 3. L.M. Sargent sold the building in December 1828.

178. To John Stevens Cogdell

Cambridge Port, Massttts
25th July, 1831

Dear Cogdell: I mentioned in my last letter to my Mother of the 4th inst. that a subject for your chisel had then just occurred to me, which I did not name to her, thinking you would be more gratified to have it <[undeciperable word]> directly from myself. The subject is Hagar and Ishmael, when the latter is about (apparently) to expire from thirst, in the desert. The moment I have supposed is just before the appearance of the Angel, when she is taking the last look of her son, previous to the passage where she says, "let me not see the death of the child." Gen. xxi. 16 v. I think a very beautiful, as well as touching, Group may be made of this: The head of the child resting on the lap of the Mother, who is kneeling and slightly bending over him; with the *head only,* not the body; as the more erect position of the body, contrasting with the inclination of the head, would correspond with the mixed emotion, or rather conflicting thoughts, within—the agony in the thought of seeing him die, and the thought <wish> of lessening it by the cruel alternative of leaving him.

I will mention another subject which also occurs to me as not unsuitable to sculpture: Hermia and Helena, from Shakespeare's Mid-summer Night's Dream; in whom the singleness and unity of friendship is beautifully illustrated. They are described as animated by one soul, in their affections, employments, and amusements; working together <from> on one sampler—likened to twin cherries, growing on one stalk &c.[1] Perhaps you will find some passage in the play that would suggest the action. I certainly should not recommend that of the sampler, which must be, to say the least, but an awkward thing to represent in sculpture. I painted this subject when in England, and not thinking it essential to adhere to the *letter,* instead of the sampler, I made them reading together from the same book. I endeavoured to give the *spirit;* which is all I would recommend to you in naming the subject. With the book, I think they might make a beautiful group in sculpture.

I hope you will excuse my wife's not replying to your letter. Nothing could have been farther from her than intending you any disrespect; but she had certain feminine objections to entering into a correspondence with a gentleman which she felt were not to be overcome. I am sure therefore you will excuse it. The inquiries in your letter I had answered in the postscript of a letter to my Mother so long ago as last December: in which I expressed my regret in being unable to think of any subject for you, and referr <ing> ed you to the Catalogues of the Royal Academy and other London Exhibitions, as most likely to furnish you with one. My Mother was however, at that time, at Waccama; but this I did not then know.

Will you tell my Mother that my Nephew George[2] arrived here a few days since. He is a fine manly little fellow. It will gratify his Grandmother to know that Mrs. A. and myself are quite delighted with him. Indeed I know not how any one could know him with[out] loving him. He carries with him in his delicate and modest manners the <pledge> assurance of having been well brought up; and I find him more intelligent and mature in mind than I should have expected in one of his age. So far as I can now judge, he has every quality to make a fine artist.

I suppose you have learnt, through the Newspapers, that we have had an exhibition here of a group in marble, called the "Chanting Cherubs,"[3] by Mr. Greenough, of Boston, who is now in Florence. It is one of the most beautiful groups in Modern Art. Judging of it, not as the work of a young man, but as one of matured powers, I think it places the author, if not among the first, certainly above the second-rate sculptors of the day. But when I consider his youth, or rather his limited experience, I have no scruple in predicting his elevation to a pedestal among the very first. In addition to a brilliant, versatile genius, Greenough possesses the advantage of a thorough liberal education.[4] He was educated at our College, and was not idle when there, making himself ere he left a good classical scholar. In general requirements also I believe there are few young men in our country who surpass him.

George speaks highly of your bust of Dr. Elliot; he says it is considered the happiest of your works. I hope you will be tempted by one of the subjects I have proposed, to shew what you can do in a work of imagination.—If you do not already possess them, I would recommend your sending to England for the compositions of Flaxman, the sculptor, from Dante & the Greek Poets. They are all in outline, and are worthy of the best age of Art. I have three vols of them.[5] They ought to be in the library of every artist, whether sculptor or painter.

Believe me ever faithfully your friend, Washington Allston.

[In the margins] I am now in my new Painting-Room, which I believe has not its superiour in Europe. At present I am finishing a picture for Mr. Ball of Carolina. Pray present my best respects to Mrs. Cogdell. Mrs. A. wishes me to add hers, and also to yourself. The whole of Flaxman's works may be had, I think, for twenty pounds. They were sold when I was in England by Longman Hurst & co. Pater Noster Row; but they may be had doubtless from other eminent booksellers in London.

ADDRESSED: John S. Cogdell Esqre. / Charleston, / South Carolina. SOURCE: Manuscript. Printed in part in Flagg, pp. 250-53.

1. *Hermia and Helena,* from *A Midsummer-Night's Dream* 3.2., 205, 209, 211, 212. Helena refers to her and Hermia's working on "one sampler," being "Like to a double cherry," "Two lovely berries moulded on one stem," and "two seeming bodies, but one heart." The painting was exhibited at the RA in 1818, at which time it received mixed reviews. The *Morning Herald* for 2 February did not like the choice of subject, but the *Examiner* praised its sedateness and elegance. 2. George W. Flagg. 3. Greenough's *Chanting Cherubs* was exhibited in Boston from 8 April to 1 June 1831. It was reviewed in several newspapers. RHD wrote a poem about it as well as a prose description, which appeared in the *Boston Daily Advertiser* for 22 April (Wright, pp. 71-72; Greenough, *Letters,* pp. 79-80). WA walked in from Cambridge to see it before it was advertised and sent word to Greenough, probably through his brother Alfred, that he had expected much but that his anticipation had been surpassed. He had no idea Greenough could do anything like this, though he expected something very fine, their mother wrote Henry Greenough in Florence. To others present he pointed out certain anatomical details in the knees of the figures which testified to "an intelligent use of the living model" (Wright, pp. 71-72; Greenough, *Letters,* pp. 79-80; *Letters of Horatio Greenough to His Brother, Henry Greenough,* p. 70). 4. In his lecture "Form" WA wrote that every aid should be sought by an artist "which may in any way contribute to the due development of the mental powers; and no one will doubt the efficiency here of a good general education" and that "no species of knowledge can ever be *oppressive* to real genius" (*LA*, p. 136). 5. WA owned copies of Flaxman's *Composition from the Tragedies of Aeschuylus, Engraved by Thomas Piroli* (London, 1793) and of his compositions from Dante and from other Greek poets. His *Compositions from the Divine Poem of Dante Aligheri, containing Hell, Purgatory and Paradise* (1807), *The Odyssey of Homer* (1805), *The Iliad of Homer* (1805), and *Compositions from the Works, Days and Theogeny of Hesiod, Engraved by William Blake* (1817) were published by Longman and his associates of London.

179. From Franklin Dexter [14 September 1831]

I have heard several envy Mrs. Davis[1] the St. Peter[2]—it looks grandly.
I hear that you have sold La Toscana[3]—è vero?

SOURCE: RHD, pp. 23, Addition 28.

1. Susan (Jackson) Davis (1785-1882), wife of Isaac P. Davis (George T. Davis, "Biographical Sketch of Isaac P. Davis," *Proceedings of the MHS, 1st ser. [1819-70], 11:95).* 2. *Study for the Head of St. Peter* in *The Angel Releasing St. Peter from Prison.* A few years later, pressed for money, WA sold it to Elizabeth (Davis) Bliss, wife of the lawyer Alexander Bliss, for $100, with the provision that he might buy it back for the same sum (RHD, p. 23). As a widow she became in 1838 the second wife of George Bancroft, who was listed as the owner in the exhibition of WA's paintings at Harding's Gallery in 1839. 3. *A Tuscan Girl* had been bought by David Sears by the time it was exhibited at the BA in 1832.

180. To Jonathan Mason Newport,[1] R.I. 20th. Oct. 1831.

My dear Sir: I beg you to accept my sincere thanks for your kind letter. I agree with you that the exhibition of Schedoni at Miss Scollay's[2] should be stopped, not only for the reason you give—the probability of <in> the picture's being injured by the numbers who visit it—but on account of the great inconvenience which such a crowd must necessarily occasion to Mrs.[3] and Miss Scollay, making their house a thoroughfare. Will you mention this to Miss Scollay, and say, that *I think the exhibition ought to be closed.*[4] No one, I think, can be offended when these reasons are assigned, and especially when it is added (as I with it might) <that> how much I am gratified by the approbation the picture has received.[5] Moreover, the picture is no longer mine, having been paid for it by Mr. Ball's agent, Mr R. Rogers,[6] before I left Boston; so that I have indeed *no right* to expose it to injury.

So far I perfectly agree with you; and, though I gratefully appreciate the kindness of your motive, I cannot, for several reasons, assent to your proposal as to exhibiting the picture for my benefit;[7] since an application for this purpose could not be made to Mr. Ball without entering into unpleasant explanations, and leading him to think that he had not given enough for it—which would distress me beyond measure, especially as not the slightest blame can, or ought to, be imputed to him in this business. Mr. Ball never limited me either in the price or subject, but simply applied to me for a picture, leaving both to be determined by myself. This was about two years ago. I had then Schedoni roughly sketched on the canvas, which I mentioned to him among other subjects: he chose Schedoni, and I *then* named the price of it. Had I foreseen the time and labour it would cost, I should certainly have named a different price; but I thought it *at the time* sufficient; and Mr. B. without the slightest demur, accéded to it. Now, whether the picture is worth more or not, the engagement <entered into> on the part of Mr. Ball was entered into in the most gentlemanly and honourable manner; I therefore consider myself doubly bound to rest satisfied. And I say to you now *frankly that I am satisfied.*—Whether I lose or gain, I always make it a point of conscience never to repine at any contract which I have once made. Then the terms of *this* particular contract being exclusively of my own proposing, I could not with a shadow of justice complain; <of it> and I would not *for any consideration* appear *even indirectly* dissatisfied with it. It is therefore my *express request* that none of my friends apply to Mr. B for an exhibition of the picture in my behalf. Nay, I should be more mortified than I can express by such an application. Besides, *you know well* that money (as much as I need it) has never been my prominent object. It was said of Paul Veronese, when he painted for Convents, that he was sometimes paid half in money and half in masses. In like manner, I am sometimes contented to be paid part in money and part in praise.

I cannot conclude without again thanking you for the kindness of your letter. Will you present my respects and best thanks to Mrs. & Miss Scollay. I expect to be in Boston about the end of next week. I am sorry to hear that your Father[8] still continues so ill. Perhaps this spell of fine weather may do much for him.

Your sincere and obliged friend, / Wa. Allston.

ADDRESSED: Jonathan Mason junr. Esqre. / Boston, / Massachusetts. SOURCE: Manuscript, Washington Allston Collection (no. 7471), Manuscript Division, Special Collections Department, University of Virginia Library.

1. WA apparently went to Newport not long after finishing *Spalatro's Vision of the Bloody Hand*. 2. Catherine Scollay. *Spalatro's Vision of the Bloody Hand* was first exhibited at the house of her and her mother, who then were living on Bowdoin Street (RHD, p. 11; *Boston City Directory* for 1823-47/9). 3. Mrs. Catherine Scollay, widow of William Scollay, a secretary of insurance (*Boston City Directory* for 1806-48/9). 4. According to RHD, it was exhibited at Joy's Buildings, in Congress Street, presumably after being shown at Miss Scollay's, under the "taking title of 'The Bloody Hand,'" with that phrase appearing "in a lantern like shaped thing of red light" (p. 11). It was sent to New York at the end of January or beginning of February 1832 (*Boston Daily Advertiser*, 25 Jan. 1832). 5. According to RHD, "the people wo'dnt 'bleed'" and attendance was poor when the painting was exhibited at Joy's Buildings. There were favorable comments, however. A little girl who saw it then was reported to have said, shutting the blind in the room, "I want to shut out that light in the picture" ("Washington Allston," p. 433). The author of an article entitled "Spalatro's Vision" in the *Boston Daily Advertiser* for 25 January 1832, describing himself as "one who has not only seen but studied the best works of ancient and modern art" and "almost a prejudiced admirer of the old masters" though conceding he might be "otherwise unqualified to pronounce judgment," praised the color, beauty of design, and technical skill, gave a detailed description, and pronounced it "a grand moral conception" showing the operation of guilt on both the ignorant and the intellectual. It was exhibited a second time in Charleston, S.C. in 1842, together with other paintings, in the Apprentices' Library Society, at which time Charles Fraser wrote in his review that he did not think it a "pretty picture," as it had been called, described the violent emotions it depicted, but said no picture painted in America had "concentrated, in a greater degree the delight and admiration of the intellect" ("Exhibition of Pictures," *Magnolia* 1 [1842]: 171-72). 6. Robert Rogers, Boston merchant. 7. RHD said that the exhibition at Miss Scollay's was gratuitous and that that at Joy's Building "yielded but a trifle" (p. 11, Addition). 8. Jonathan Mason, Sr. (1756-1831), lawyer and statesman. He died on 1 November.

181. From Horatio Greenough

Paris—Oct'r 1831.

To Washington Alston Esqre—

My Dear Sir: The intention I have had for several months of making this journey and the preparation for it must be my excuse for not having written you in the interim[1]—Since my arrival here I have had leisure in abundance, still I was unwilling to write untill I had given a glance at the treasures of Art for which Paris is noted—

I came to Genova in the Columbus steamer and after looking again at my favourite Vandykes[2] and the street of Palaces,[3] took the Diligence to Turin, where in 2 days I succeeded in finding nothing whatever in the shape of Art, if I except their *barocco* brick palaces, which are rather paltry to an eye that comes from farther south—I passed the Alps at Mont Cenis; don't think that I'm going to inflict a description—One may as well be silent about them unless one could employ their own language of waterfall and avalanche and thunder—I will only say that as I walked among the higher hills with each of the four seasons in sight, under a quick succession of shadow and sun light it seemed as if God had spoken his last word to this world and all was hurrying back to Chaos—The ocean's self never produced on my imagination any thing like the effect of those first born of creation—Perhaps it was the reaction that made me so dead to all that there may be of beauty between Chamberi[4] and Paris—at all events I thought I had seldom passed through a more uninteresting country—On arriving in Paris I was again forcibly struck—by the size of the city—its magnificence and luxurious gayness—(for there is less of what I call elegance here than in Italy) its vast pleasure grounds—its numerous bridges and their beautiful and scientific construction—I confess I was prejudiced against Paris—who would not be that had been (as I) in the habit of reading every morning a few pages of Alfieri's autobiography—where this fine city is qualified as a *fetida cloaca* etc etc at every other paragraph[5]—I was eager to see the statues of the great Frenchmen on the Pont de Louis XVI[6]—I remembered the insulting tone assumed in speaking of Italian sculpture in the chamber of Deputies, at the period of their creation—I find in these figures no cause for exultation on the part of this school—Let them be confronted with the statues of Arnolfo and Brunelleschi by Pampaloni[7] and I believe the whole world artists or not will find them inferiour—You remember the Colossi of Monte Cavallo[8]—and the intelligence with which their skeletons are so moved that the eye recognizes the human form at the greatest distance—Well these artists have done just the reverse—Their figures are so upright—so cloaked and scarfed and robed—so clumsily supported and so loaded with accessories that from the Pont Royal[9] they have little more meaning than the blocks from which they have been carved—As you come near to them it's true you see figures well proportioned—sculptured with more or less of spirit—and one or two of them have dignity and expression—Still as collossi for their situation they must be considered as failures—

I have found a great deal to delight me at the Louvre. Paolo was surely one of the greatest fellows that ever breathed—It's useless to tell me that the figures are heterogeneous etc etc, in short to criticise the magician of Venice by rules drawn from Raphael—He that has eyes to see and can feel, will love Paolo too well to dissect him in that cool manner. He held his broad mirror up and a world is there with gleams of exquisite feeling and truth that would seem out of the reach of art—

things Sir not dreamt of in the philosophy of the Roman School[10]—He reminds me of Shakespeare—he must be felt—I would give more for one impression than for 3 unanswerable arguments on a question of art for words are clumsy things after all. I have been less disgusted at the modern french pictures than I had anticipated—perhaps I'm grown callous—As a frenchman addressing himself to frenchmen I think we must allow David great cleverness at least. The french-greek physiog of his ideal figures is nauseous—I felt however that the cold, grey ground-glass atmosphere atmosphere in his pictures prevented my allowing them their full merit—One feels the want of a great coat and a cigar in looking at them—I didn't know Poussin until now—He felt the Italians to the core as well as the greek—Le Sieur[11] rather disappointed me—still even he shews that the modern vices are acquired not inherent—I think Le Brun[12] gains nothing in colour. I liked him better in the prints—Art seems at a pretty low ebb here just now. The number of clever men employed in twiddle-twaddle, caricature, indecent pictures etc is quite surprising—The statue gallery has been shorn of its beams since you were here. Tis but so so after Italy—The Parisians strike me agreeably as to physique—You see a finer animal health generally than in Italy—but the physiog' is inferiour—One is struck by female faces at every step but the eye is seldom won; there's a want of that harmony of lines which so often pleases in an Italian head of even the 2nd or 3rd order—In manner they seem to me to have more of *facon*[13] than the Italians but less politeness—they are quicker but not so intelligent—honester perhaps but still more selfish and that's droll—I have on the whole been so well pleased with Paris that I propose residing here a few months at some future period, before returning to America—

Since I have been here I have remodelled Mr Cooper's bust[14]—I have also modelled a bust of a young N Yorker who is here[15]—one of the Princess Belgoioso of Milan[16] a very pretty and a very clever woman—and have commenced one of Gen'l Lafayette.[17] Mr. Morse[18] who sits here by my side (having just finished his cigar) thinks it the strongness likeness I've made—I hope to send you a lithographic print of it before long[19]—

In the many conversations we had on Art when I was last in America though you expressed much pleasure at the efforts that were making in Architecture among us, yet I remember you fully agreed with me that broader principles of art and a more intelligent imitation were necessary to the formation of a pure and masculine style of building—This remembrance of your sympathy induces me to communicate to you a few thoughts of this art, as I have had opportunity to observe it, my impressions with regard to its present state among us and what it strikes me may be done to improve it—I will give you briefly my opinion of what I have seen and in suggesting any thing I beg to have it understood that I do it with my hat in my hand,—with a deep sense of the merit of those who have modelled our later buildings and a wish that it may be reciprocated by a frank expression of the views taken of my art of its capabilities among us and the hopes of its advancement.[20]

Architecture seems to me to have been enthralled ever since a claim to *universal* and *indiscriminate* admiration has been established for the Greek school—I shall join you of course in excepting the Gothic which by throwing out the greek canons and recurring to nature to express a new sentiment got a new style, at once grand and pathetic as a whole and harmoniously rich in detail—The Gothic embodied the poetry of religion and triumphed over matter to deify spirit—The Green adored matter and instead of sending towers high into the blue as twere to seek a heaven or to shew it when found it kept every member of its temples where the eye might taste their beauty and so proportioned and posed that it should be not only safe but strong—The Gothic by a mysterious combination of lines seems to lift the spirit from earth and shew her her home—The Greek woos the eye and lulls us into content below while its horizontal lines seem to measure the steps the mind may take beyond which all is dark. The uses for which the Greek temple were made were one—the form was unity itself—its parts harmonized with the whole—[21]

The attempts in Italy to graft the christian sentiment on the greek stock—to expand the Pantheon[22] to hold the Hebrew God, to recombine the greek elements into a new form for a new worship seem to me to have produced but a bastard result—No one is readier than myself to admit how much there is for the heart as well as for the imagination and the eye in the Italian church—I love their vast hushed interiour, their mild air and their mellow light—Their historic and poetic shadowings of art which seem as the incense rises and the chant peals, to take life and join in the worship—But these churches—this worship are the product of times in which a corrupt priesthood had engrossed government religion arts, sciences and even society and each of these institutions was promoted or sacrificed as the interests of that priesthood required—Our religion not only does not ask these sacrifices but forbids them—Our church is but an oratory a lecture room—We do not make it too large to be filled by one human voice—it possesses but two important features—the pulpit whence issues the word of God to man—The organ loft whence earth answers to heaven—Here is great simplicity of worship yet do I think these elements capable of very grand combinations—

In America we have since we began to look for art in buildings, made several attempts more or less successful, to place our Architecture on a footing with that of other nations—We have built combinations, Italian in intention at least if not in feeling—but they seem not to have satisfied any one—We have made pointed windows and clustered columns, but the small proportion of our means devoted to this end, have not allowed us either the vastness or the rich detail of the gothic—so that our happiest efforts in this way are as far from their models as in a horseshed from the temple of Venus—In our despair we have recurred to ancient Greece the mother of art—We have warmed at the praises bestowed on her buildings and have resolved to take to ourselves by a *coup de main* both the style and the praise—We have done with her tamples what modern Europe has so often tried with every department of her literature and with no better success. The Dram's Personae may indeed be reduced to the classic 3 or 4, the chorus may be introduced and the lyric entre actes divided into strophe and antistrophe but a pale and insipid imitation is the only fruit—These spirits in the vasty deep of past epochs *will not come when we do call for them*[23]—The parthenon in Philadelphia,[24] shoved in between the common buildings of a street—shorn of its lateral colonnades and pierced every where for light reminds us of a noble captive stripped alike of arms and ornaments and set at work with the other drudges of his conqueror. If his grand air be not quite gone, if some vestige of his former comeliness or some badge of office be still visible about him they only serve to render his present degradation more apparent—

In a letter which I wrote to the committee of the Bunker Hill monument,[25] I endeavoured to shew that by taking a member—a dependent part and making of it a monument, are inconsequent and unmeaning whole would result—for if that member be fitted for its situation all those features which connect it with the surrounding parts become absurd when it stands alone—T'is a limb without a body,[26] a sentence without a verb, a tune broken off in the middle—As a column was in Greece organized to pose upon the earth and to support an entablature; so was the whole fabric constructed with an eye to its exposure and the worship for which it was intended—if well adapted to that exposure and that worship how shall it be fitted for a climate and a service so different?

Let us turn now to Nature the only true school of art—Has she ever been the slave of any one idea of beauty or of grandeur? Her sublimity is manifest alike in the sailing eagle, the bounding lion and the rolling whale—Her beauty asks no sacrifice of the existence or even of the comfort of its wearer—There's scarse a member which may not be found enlarged or annihilated by turns in the animal creation, as the wants of the creature demand. She always organizes the frame for its exposure and its work yet always leaves it beautiful—We propose then that she be imitated in this important respect more compleatly than has been done, we would recommend the use of the combinations we have inherited from preceding schools whenever they will serve our turn and harmonize with the plan of our work—Nor do we mean merely that the object for which a building is constructed shall be nowise sacrificed to an abstract idea of form—we would that the shell of each fabric be as it were, moulded on the wants and conveniences desired—Such has been the case with naval architecture—and he who has seen a ship at sea will confess that in that work man has approached nearest his maker—Our fleets alone can shew that the world is not retrograde—

In a bank for instance where the business transacted requires light we propose to get it not by stealth as if we were ashamed of it, but as openly as tis given by the creator to our own brain and that without fear of consequences—Where the business done within so much connected with what is abroad as in a Bank we propose to render ingress and egress as convenient as possible to numbers, and so on with every want that those employed in such buildings may have experienc'd—

And we shall receive all condemnation of such art as we would the complaint that the greyhound is too light for beauty, the horse too heavy—that horns are monstrous, or the necks of grazing cattle too long for proportion—We can at least shew that he who condemns us condemns with us the principles of creation—nor shall we be mortified at not having pleased men whom God himself has not been fastidious to satisfy—It is true that this style of art asks for much in feeling of which we have but the germ but why should we be discouraged—In our political institutions we have dared to be new—Can we not shew that art too has a reason as well as government? and that no model of past times when science was less and superstition reigned has a perspective right to cramp our convenience or to repress our invention?

That no one individual can accomplish the task we have thus planned is clear at a glance—It requires all the knowledge among us—all the light which can be thrown on the requisites of a building by those who are to occupy it, all the science of our engineers and mathematicians to find the most direct route to their attainment, all the feeling and the imitation of our architects and painters to give a harmonious connection to the parts thus assembled—that these different bodies of men are equal to it is shewn by what they have already achieved in their various departments, for as we are [we] have no reason to decline a comparison with the present nations of Europe as far as *taste* in Architecture is concerned—

As for what painting and Sculpture are to do among us it seems to me that they will depend entirely on our love for our institutions—If we continue to stand tip-toe along the Atlantic shore endeavouring to catch the last word from Europe nothing great will surely be done—But if we will turn our eyes inward a little, calculate results and embody principles then art becomes important and we shall have it for we seldom long feel the want of any thing in America.

I see by some of the papers that some well intentioned persons have been shocked by the nudity of my cherub-boys[27]—I had thought the country beyond that—There is a nudity which is not impure—there is an impurity which pierces the most cumbrous costume—Let my group be compared with hundreds of prints which are to be seen in the English french and American annuals and which are put into the hands of our sisters and wives and I leave it to any conscientious man to say whether I have gone to the full length of the letter with which modern delicacy has measured the range of art—With love to Master Edmund and Richard and respectful compliments to Mrs Alston I remain Dear sir Yours truly—

Horatio Greenough—

SOURCE: Greenough, *Letters*, pp. 80-92.

1. Greenough went to Paris at this time principally to obtain a cast of Houdon's bust of Washington to use in his execution of his *Washington* for the rotunda of the Capitol. He was there from 6 September until about 30 November 1831 (Wright, pp. 91, 93). 2. Anthony Van Dyck spent five years in Italy, during which time he painted a series of portraits of Genoese nobility.
3. The Strada Nuovo, now Garibaldi, was celebrated for its thirteen palaces, all but two built by

Galeazzo Alessi, a pupil of Michelangelo. 4. Chambry. 5. Count Vittorio Alfieri (1749-1803), Italian dramatist, heartily disliked France and the French. He called Paris a *fetènte cloáca* ("stinking sewer") in his *Vita di Vittorio Alfieri da Asti Scritto dor esso* (1800), pt. 1, ep. 3, chap. 5. 6. This bridge, now the Pont de la Concorde, over the Seine was built between 1787 and 1790. Several years later twelve statues were erected on it, each by a different sculptor, representing various French warriors and statesmen. 7. The statues of Arnolfo di Cambio (ca. 1232-1312), Italian sculptor and architect, and of Filippo Brunelleschi (1377-1446), Italian architect, by Luigi Pampaloni (1791-1847), the chief nineteenth-century Tuscan sculptor after Bartolini, occupy niches in the Palazzo dei Canonici in the Piazza del Duomo in Florence. 8. *The Dioscuri* (*Castor and Pollux*), two colossal statues of young men in the act of taming horses, on each side of the obelisk in the Piazza di Monte Cavallo on the top of the Quirinal Hill, are Roman copies of Greek originals of the 5th or 4th century B.C. 9. The second bridge up the Seine from the Pont de la Louis XVI, built in 1685. 10. This sentence contains paraphrases of *Hamlet* 3.2.23 and 1.5.166. 11. Eustache Le Sieur (1616-55), French painter. 12. Charles Le Brun. 13. "Affection." 14. Greenough first modeled Cooper's bust and commenced the marble in 1826 but remodeled it at this time because Cooper, who was in Paris, had gained so much weight. It was put in marble in 1832-33. (Greenough, pp. 24, 41). 15. Albert Brisbane (1809-90), social philosopher and Fourierite. 16. Princess Christina Belgiojoso-Trivulzio (1808-71) was a disciple of Mazzini and an ardent supporter of the Italian revolutionary movement (H. Ramsen Whitehouse, *A Revolutionary Princess: Christina Belgiojoso-Trivulzio* [London: T. F. Uniwin) 1906)]. 17. Marie Joseph Paul Yves Roth Gilbert de Motier, marquis de Lafayette (1757-1834), French soldier and statesman, bearing the rank of general. He was a great friend of Cooper. 18. Morse arrived in Paris from Germany shortly after Greenough, and the two took rooms at 25, rue de Surènne (Wright, pp. 90-91). 19. No such print seems to have been made. The bust was put in marble probably in 1833 and 1834 and an engraving made in 1834. 20. The next few paragraphs of this letter contain the earliest expressions of Greenough's theory of architecture, which became the first functional theory of it to be expressed by an American, set forth most fully in his essay "American Architecture" in the *United States Magazine and Democratic Review* 13 [1834]: 206-10. 21. Greenough was following WA in his comparison in this paragraph of the Gothic and the Greek styles. 22. The Pantheon in Rome, the second building of which was dedicated to the seven planetary deities, was consecrated as a Christian church in 609, dedicated to St. Mary of the Martyrs. The name signifies "most holy place" but is often interpreted as "dedicated to all the gods." 23. *King Henry IV, Part I* 3.1. 53-55. 24. The Second Bank of the United States in Philadelphia, erected between 1818 and 1824, was designed by William Strickland to resemble the Parthenon. Presumably Greenough saw it in 1828. 25. Probably in March 1825 Greenough wrote a letter to the committee of the Bunker Hill Monument Association in Boston, accompanied by a model, in submission of a design in competition for the monument to be erected on the site of the Battle of Bunker Hill in Charlestown, Mass. The competition was announced in January to end 1 April, and a premium of $100 was offered. A plan and a perspective drawing of a 220-foot column was specifically called for, but Greenough proposed an obelisk, with a base to be ornamented by four groups of sculptures or possibly field pieces. In that letter he presented the same argument against considering a column as monument that he did in this letter. WA was on the judging Board of Artists, which agreed in April to award the premium to him and he was asked to submit an estimate for an obelisk, but there was disagreement among other members of the association and the award was not made. Shortly afterward, in May, Greenough went to Italy. The monument finally erected, not finished until 1842, was an obelisk but from another design (Greenough, *Letters*, pp. 3-6; Wright, pp. 33-36). In connection with the plans for the monument WA's classmate Samuel Swett wrote a history of the battle. WA owned a copy: *History of Bunker Hill Battle, With a Plan.* With Notes, and Likenesses of the principal officers, 3d ed. (Boston, 1827). 26. WA had said that a monumental column would remind him of a peripatetic candlestick, adding that a man's leg, "though a very handsome support for his body, when cut off, becomes abhorrent." (Swett, p. 63). 27. During the third week of the Boston exhibition of *The Chanting Cherubs*, the figures were outfitted with dimity aprons. Correspondents in the *Boston Courier* for 9 and 11 May, and *New York Evening Post* for 17 and 24 May, and *Niles' Weekly Register* for 18 June 1831 protested vigorously, and the aprons were subsequently removed (Wright, p. 72).

182. From Franklin Dexter Decr 27th 1831.

Dear Sir: I have had a conversation with Mr. Bartlett[1] on the subject of your note—he accedes to your proposition to receive a part of the proceeds of your pictures as sold by you. From his conversation I judge that if $500 or $600 can be paid in that manner in a reasonable time, the assignees will think they have used due diligence, & will wait your convenience for the balance. I am very sorry to hear you have been ill; if I had known it I should certainly have been to see you & have brought you something to help pass away the time. If you have quite done with Lawrence,[2] I wish you would send him in by Mr. Hastings or to me or else [?]—and if there is in the Athenaeum any novelty in your way I will send it to you.

Yrs very truly / Franklin Dexter

ADDRESSED: Washington Allston Esqr / Cambridge Port / Mass. SOURCE: Manuscript.

1. Possibly Dr. Thomas Bartlett (1767-1856), a physician, who exhibited copies of a work by Correggio and by Rubens and a portrait of Columbus by an unknown artist at the BA in 1829. He carried on for many years a dry-goods business in Boston, from which he retired about 1831 ("Marriages and Deaths," *NEGHR*, II [1857]: 183). Two of WA's college mates were also named Bartlett: William, to whom he apparently referred in his letter to Knapp of 23 October 1800, and Abner, who graduated in 1799. One of his miscellaneous notes carried the name of E[lmer?] Bartlett, who sold picture frames (Dana Papers). 2. Possibly the BA's copy of David E. Williams, *Life and Correspondence of Sir Thomas Lawrence*, 2 vols. (London, 1831).

183. From Gulian Crommelin Verplanck Washington, Feb 21st 1832

My Dear Sir: Knowing the pleasure it must give you to be informed that you have rendered an important service to a friend I enclose you a paper containing our little debate about employing Vanderlyn[1]—& I can assure you that the testimony to his merit which you enabled me to give was what decided the question. The picture would otherwise have been left to be a job for somebody or other according to accident or interest. Vanderlyn understands that limited only to Stuart's head, he has *carte blanche* to give us a magnificent picture. He will visit Boston to copy the engraved head. In the meantime the debate alone is a happy thing for him of which I trust he will take advantage.

We have also given your friend Greenough an order for a pedestrian marble statue of Washington,[2] limiting him only to the Houdon face & leaving him free as to everything else. We have an excellent committee on this subject[3] & I hope to see our Rotunda adorned by your pencil & others worthy to associate with you, under these auspices.

Yours in haste / G.C. Verplanck

ADDRESSED: Washington Allston Esq / Cambridge Port / Mass. SOURCE: Manuscript. Printed in Flagg, p. 253.

1. Vanderlyn was commissioned by the House of Representatives early in 1832 to paint a full-length portrait of Washington, the head to be based on that by Stuart, to hang in the House Chamber to match that of Lafayette there. The paper to which Verplanck refers, recording the debate in the House regarding the commission, has not been located. 2. On 16 February 1832 Congress passed a resolution to commission Horatio Greenough to execute a statue of Washington for the rotunda of the Capitol, with the stipulation only that the head be a copy of that by Houdon. Apparently WA wrote a letter to Verplanck recommending him, which does not seem to have been preserved. On 7 April 1832 RHD wrote Verplanck that it did WA good to know that his letter had, through Verplanck, "been turned to so great benefit to a brother artist" (New-York Historical Society). The statue was executed between 1833 and 1840 (Wright, pp. 123, 134, 142). 3. The members of the Committee on Public Buildings consisted of Verplanck, Jarvis, and H.A.S. Dearborn.

184. To John Stevens Cogdell

Cambridge-Port,
27 Feby, 1832.

Dear Cogdell: It gives me great pleasure that I can bestow sincere praise on your Group of Hagar and Ishmael. It is decidedly your best work, and much exceeds what I had expected: it really does you great honour. And, though it <have> has a good many faults, they are by no means of a *kind* to outweigh its merits. The attitudes of both Mother and Child are well conceived, and they group well together. *Perhaps,* however, the group might have been improved had the Boy's body been a little farther off, and his head resting where it is: I think it would have presented a better profile view. But its chief merit lies in the general conception and the expression; which are certainly the principal points in a work of Art. *It has indeed great power of expression.* The helpless extremity of the Son is very touching, and <the> his physical suffering is affectingly contrasted with that of his Mother. She seems to have just said, "let me not see him die,"[1] and to be taking a *last look:* the deep, silent, maternal agony of that *look* is of *no common order.* The calmness of her action too is finely conceived; it is the effort of one who strives *not* to look into the fearful future; who stands on the brink of an abyss into which she *must fall,* but *will not look.* This is indeed *great.*

Now (as I suppose you would wish me to do) I will point out the faults. But you must not be frightened at the list, since they are only the faults of inexperience. The principal defect is in the disposition of the drapery, the lines of which are too often repeated, and too abrupt; that is, the folds are too small, and cut up, instead of being large, varied and flowing. The horizontal lines also across the Mother's body have an ill effect, and disturb the action of the limbs, which should always, in Sculpture, be indicated, however faintly, by some slight correspondence in the folds that drape them. 2. The next is in the Costume. The *puffs* on the arms, and the folds on the breast are *modern*. The sleeves should have been plain; so the drapery on the chest. 3. The right shoulder of the Boy is out of its place; it could not be so far projected without dislocation, or breaking the clavicle. 4. The protrusion of his tongue is not in good taste, for though this may be *physically true* of one dying of thirst, it is one of those unpleasant truths which should be avoided in Art. Then you should have given him more beauty—I mean of face. 5. The Mothers leg is a little too short. Of the defect in her *raised* arm I say nothing, it having been injured, as you mentioned, in the casting.

These faults, however, as I have already observed, are the faults of inexperience, and such as more practice and the study of good models would very easily enable you to avoid. I would recommend your procuring Prints from the Antique Bas-reliefs of Greece and Rome; the "Admiranda Romanorum" of Santo Bartoli;[2] and Hope's Grecian Costume.[3] The first perhaps could not be had except from Italy; the last you will get from England. These would be of great use to you as to costume[4] as well as for other things: a weeks study of them would let you into the whole mystery of Sculpture drapery.

Now after this praise, will you allow me, my friend, to say a few words of a *prudential nature?* Do not let it tempt you to give up a *certainty* for an *uncertainty*. I say this because my Nephew informs me that when he left Carolina you talked, as he had heard, of going to Italy,[5] to make the Art your profession: if so, you of course must give up your office at the Custom-House,[6] which, if I understand aright, is *now* your principal means of support.—You remember that some years ago you applied to me for my opinion on this subject: <the truth [?]> and that I made no reply, and for *this reason* (which I supposed from your subsequent letters you understood)—because I shrunk from the responsibility. But I *ought not* to have shrunk from it; my conscience soon told me so; and I had made up [my] mind to give it without reserve; and should long since have given it had I not concluded, from your continued silence on the subject, that you had given up the intention. I will, however, no longer delay this discharge of my duty. And I do it now the more readily, as after the high praise I have bestowed on your last work, you cannot impute it to any doubt of your talents. What I am about to say, however, I do not give in the shape of advice; for I as much dislike giving advice as asking it: and I never ask it in my personal concerns, except in some extreme case, where I find it impossible to decide for myself; and such have very rarely occured. I shall merely express my *opinions* on the subject; leaving you to weigh them as you think fit, and to decide for yourself.

If by making the Art your profession you are to *depend* <upo> on it as the *means* of *support* for yourself and family, I cannot but think that you look to a very *precarious* source. What may be the prospects of employment from private individuals you can judge as well as I, and I no better than you, for *I* can have no definite knowledge as to it unless I were myself a sculptor. It has often, however, been doubted by Greenough's friends here, notwithstanding the high and general estimation in which he is held, as well for his private character, as for his talents, whether he will be able to support himself in Boston from private employment alone. And if Boston cannot afford him sufficient, I know not in what other city of the Union he can expect it. His resource, they think, must be at Washington, in works for the Government, or in Europe. Indeed it seems to be the opinion of most persons that I have heard speak on the subject, that employment from the General Government is the only hope for a Sculptor who is *to live by his profession* in our Country. And whether it is that people have been but little accustomed to it, or from some other cause, so far as I have observed, the interest taken in sculpture is by no means so general as that taken in pictures. Then the prices which a Sculptor must charge, even to defray his expenses, are such as very few in our Country are either able or willing to give for works of Art. So that I do not see much prospect even of a bare support, unless he is content to confine himself to Busts, that is, portraits. But, even supposing there were sufficient demand for Sculpture, are you prepared to *coin your brain for bread*—at all times, and under all circumstances; of depression, of illness, and the numberless harrassments of unavoidable debt? to produce an original work of the imagination—requiring of all human efforts a pleasurable state of the mind—with a *dunning letter* staring you in the face? With an honest heart, yearning to give every one his due, and an empty purse, *I know, from bitter experience,* that the fairest visions of the imagination vanish like dreams, never to be recalled, before the daylight reality of such a visitor. Poverty is no doubt a stimulus to general industry, and to many kinds of mental effort; but *not* to the *imagination:* for the industry of the imagination *must be* abortive—is a nonentity, if it have not *peace* as its immediate condition. Pictures that would *otherwise* have brought me hundreds, not to say thousands, have crumbled into nothing under its pressure, and been thrown aside as nothing worth.—I say these things not querulously (for I have an utter dislike to all complaining, and never allow myself in it) but that you might know *what it is to be an Artist by profession,* with no other income than the product of the brain—which, to be at all available, must at least be at peace. And I give them in their naked reality *solely* from a *conscientious regard* for your *peace and happiness as a man.* The love I bear my Art you well know; no one could love it more; and I have given proof of it in the sacrafice I have made to it of my fortune. And yet, with all this love, which I *still* bear it, I thus speak of it as a profession: *because I must speak truth.* But, understand me. When I speak of it thus as a profession, it is when that profession *is associated with poverty. With a competence, however small,* so it be sufficient to secure me from debt, from demands which I cannot satisfy when due—*then* of all professions it is that which I would still chuse. But *debt is slavery.* And *his* mind must be *free* who aspires to any thing great in the Art. If you had a competence—then I should say, as I once said before your unfortunate loss of property, follow your inclinations.—But your case is still a happy one, tho' the Art is not your profession; for it may still be your *employment:* and *it is the employment,* after all, in which its pleasure consists: *this I firmly believe.* Your office allows you I suppose the half of each day to yourself, and secures to you the means of devoting a moiety of the year to the pursuit of the Art, in the *way you like best,* and *independent of the world.* Ah, that word *independent* has a charm which *I* well know how to value, from having known its reverse. But I still have *hope,* and I look to the repossession of it yet.

You observe in one of your letters that, "the columns of the Evening Gazette[7] are open to me." In this you are mistaken. I never wrote a line for that Paper; I do not even know the name of its Editor;[8] nor have I seen the paper for some years. The only Editor that I am acquainted with is the Editor of the Boston Daily Advertiser (now joined with the Patriot);[9] in which was published my obituary notice of poor Stuart. That piece, with one other, written soon after my return from England,[10] are all that I have written for the Newspapers. I do not mention the two or three pieces in verse, as those were published by my friends.[11] I never write for the Newspapers on any subject. I have been often solicited to write notices on various works of art that have come before the public; but these requests I have uniformly declined. Nor can I write now, for it is several years since that, for certain *imperative reasons,* I came to the resolution <that> never to write either notice or criticism for Newspaper, Magazine, or Review, on any work <of> by a living Artist; and this resolution I have repeatedly expressed in public. Perhaps, however, some of my friends may write a notice of your Group. But I can render you better service in conversation, which, you may be assured, I shall not fail to do.—When the weather becomes a little milder I shall send the Group to the Atheneum, as I think it the best place in which it could be presented to the public. At present I do not think it would be advisable to send it.—Mrs. Allston admires it exceedingly; indeed *all* my friends here that have seen it admire it. One lady observed that Hagar seemed actually to look *pale* with wo. [*sic*] My Nephew George is the only person from Boston who has yet seen it. I have few visitors from Boston in the winter, or indeed at any time; with the exception of four or five of my personal friends, scarcely a dozen in the year;[12] so that I have been obliged on finishing a picture, to send it into Town to be seen. Few people care to come two miles to see a picture.

In your letter preceding the last there was a passage, toward the conclusion, which gave me more pain than, I am sure, you would willingly have inflicted; and I should have felt it most deeply had I not ascribed it to inadvertence, and to your not having considered the full import of certain expressions. I am *certain* you would not have written them if you had reflected a moment on the construction they might bear. The passage is this. Speaking of Belshazzer, you say, "Your Picture *ought to have been delivered years ago*—and that hundreds near me think so, though they do not say it, lest they should wound me." And you advise me "to *think* of this matter *with seriousness.*" Now, my friend, I do in my heart *acquit you of all intention of giving me pain;* for you immediately add, "that it is not in your heart to wound me." I fully believe this. But let me ask you one question. Do you *believe* that *it has been in my power to finish Belshazzer?* Your words, *"ought to have been delivered years ago,"* certainly imply the *affirmative; consequently* that its being still unfinished is *because* I *would not* finish it, <though> when I *might, if I had* so *chosen.* If this were the case, I could not be *(what* I *know myself to be)* an honourable man; for I have repeatedly declared it to be my *earnest desire* and *intention* to finish it *as soon as it was in my power.* Then you advise me to *think of it seriously.* Does not this also imply that I have *intentionally neglected* it? Certainly it seems to: for *how else* could I *need* to be *reminded* of so *important* a *Contract;* that could not have been put aside in the memory, except intentionally. It was *this* which hurt me, that any one should think that I *could,* yet *would not* fulfil a solemn contract; that I had *neglected* the performance of it *when in my power,* and *needed to be reminded of my duty.* But *this,* as I have before said, *I am sure you never could have meant.* No, Cogdell—I say it not in *pride,* but in the *simple consciousness of integrity*—I am one of the last men in the world to whom such moral delinquency can be justly imputed. And (though I sincerely believe that *you* do not require such assurance) I here assure you, on the *word of a gentleman,* and, what is more, of an *honest man,* that *it has <u>not</u> been in my power to finish Belshazzer;* and that it still remains in its case *from absolute necessity.* Ever since I entered into the contract with my Subscribers it has been my *paramount object* to *fulfil it;* all my efforts in subsequent works have had *that* for their *ultimate end;* to extricate myself from embarrassments* which (as repeated experi<ments>ience had taught me) rendered it morally impossible for me to do justice either to myself or my subscribers. I have had *no other* view in any thing I have done. And my *personal history,* <would have> were it known, would bear me out in this *to the letter.* But no one has a right to inquire into my private troubles. I trust my *word* is sufficient. I will only add that, that though the efforts alluded to have not effected their end so soon as I had allowed myself to *anticiapate,* they have yet released me from some of my sorest difficulties. In plainer words, I am getting out of debt. Some heavy and *importunate* debts, however, still remain; and these I am daily labouring to discharge as I have the others; that done, I shall be *free.* And it is my fixed resolution not to touch Belshazzer till I am so. Should I attempt it now, it would be to no purpose—except, perhaps, to ruin it. If *labour* could have done it, the *mental* as well as *manual* labour already bestowed on it were sufficient to have completed five such pictures. *I alone know what I can, and cannot do.* 'Tis only with a *free* mind that I can *do justice* to my engagement.

With respect to remarks on me by the World, I shall endeavor to bear them with what philosophy I can muster. I have lived long enough to know that, let a man act as conscientously as he will, he will not escape censure. But my private affairs are no concern of theirs. I am not a pensioner on the public. Do not then trouble yourself to "defend" me. All that I would have any one say in my behalf (if indeed any thing) is, that in a life of more than fifty years I *have never wronged* any *man out of a dollar, and that I do not intend to do it now.* I hold myself amenable only to my Subscribers; and none of them, *to my knowledge*, have complained. Should any one of them, however, think himself aggrieved, feel impatient, or be, from *any cause*, dissatisfied with the delay—I would most cheerfully, and without an unpleasant feeling, release him from his engagement; and if [there] be [page torn] one who has advanced on his share, I will repay it, with the in[ter]est [page torn] as soon as in my power, from the proceeds of my present la[bo]urs [page torn]. I speak in sincerity when I say, that I would most willingly do this, and without a particle of resentment. Nay, I should even take it as a kindness, if there be any so disposed, that he, or they, would consent to this course; since it would be to me a great relief, for I have never ceased to regret that I ever allowed myself to receive any advance on the picture. It has always, *from the first*, been my intention, on delivering the picture, say pay the interest on every advancement. No one has ever yet lost a quarter of a dollar by me, and, if my life and health are spared, no one ever shall.

In conclusion—I again repeat, that I do in my heart acquit you of the slightest intention of hurting my feelings; and I should not have adverted to the subject, had I not felt it due to myself, in order to prevent future misapprehension, to state thus distinctly the imperative necessity that has controled me in relation to the picture, and the just and conscientous ground on which I act.

This long-winded epistle was begun more than a week ago, but I have been prevented finishing it so soon as I wished. We have had a long and most severe winter here, and a sick house—domestics and all. Mrs. A. has still a bad cough, which she has had more than four months. I too have been under the Doctor: but I am tolerably well now.—Poor White's misfortune[13] has grieved me. He is a kind warm-hearted man, whom his early friends here never speak of but with interest. If he is in Charleston, give my affectionate regards to him. Should you see my Mother, give my love to her and tell her that I intend to write to her in a few days. George is getting on as well as could be wished in Boston. Pray, tell his Grandmother that he comes out very often to see us. He is one of the finest boys I have ever known: every one loves him. Mrs. Allston unites with me in best regards to Mrs. Cogdell and yourself.

I remain, sincerely your friend, / W. Allston.

*Here is a sample. It was but four days after the receipt of your letter, to which I am now replying, that I received a letter from a *collecting* attorney, requiring payment of a debt of more than seven hundred dollars—and all the money I had was five dollars and a quarter.—Over my Wife's property I have no control, that being in the care of Trustees.[14] And her income seldom exceeds four hundred dollars.

[On the address sheet: only two sheets] ADDRESSED: John S. Cogdell Esqre. / Charleston, / South Carolina. SOURCE: Manuscript. Printed in Flagg, pp. 254-61.

1. "Let me not see the death of the child" (Gen. 21:16). 2. Pietro Santo Bartoli (ca. 1635-1700), Italian painter and engraver. His *Admiranda Romanarum antiquatatum ac Veteris sculpturae vestigia anaglyphtico opere elaborata, ex marmorlis exemplaribus, quae Romae*

adhuc extant (Rome, 1693) contained eighty-one plates representing masterpieces of Roman civilization. WA owned a copy. 3. "Grecian Costume" was the title of the section on that subject in volume 1 of the two-volume *Costume of the Ancients* (1809), by Thomas Hope. It contained brief descriptions and a large number of plates. 4. WA reportedly owned a copy of a work listed as *I Costumi Religiosi Civiti, e Militari Antichi Egiziani, Etruschi, Greci, & Romani*, not otherwise identified. 5. Cogdell and his wife went to Italy in 1845 and stayed a few months, at which time they met Horatio Greenough and other American artists in Rome and Florence (Cogdell to Hiram Powers, 5 Nov. 1843, 30 Apr., 15 Sept. 1845, Powers Papers, Florence). 6. From 1821 to 1832 Cogdell held the position of naval officer of the port of Charleston, S.C. 7. This Boston newspaper (1814-1906) had varying titles. From 1821 to 1850 it was the *Evening Gazette*. 8. The editor at this time was the Boston journalist William Warland Clapp, Sr. 9. The editor of the *Boston Daily Advertiser* from 1814, when he bought it, to 1854, when he retired from its active control, was Nathan Hale. In January 1832 it united with the *Boston Patriot* (1809-36) and from then until June 1836 the paper was called the *Boston Advertiser & Patriot*. 10. WA's notice of Stuart's portraits of the first five presidents of the United States written for the *Boston Daily Advertiser*. It has not been located. 11. Presumably WA refers to "The Spanish Maid" and "The Tuscan Girl," which appeared in the *North American Review* for October 1831, and to his poem printed in Verplanck's *Address* at the NAD in 1824. 12. In later years, however, WA was visited increasingly by both Americans and Europeans in the city. Walter Channing called him "in an important sense a public man," and Edmund S. Quincy said that he was "easily found and almost every stranger of distinction was taken to see him or invited to meet him" (Quincy to Drake). 13. Mrs. Allston's father, Judge Francis Dana, inherited a fortune from his father Richard Dana, which was invested largely in land. Most of it was lost by his son Francis in speculation (Dana, 1:26). 14. Unidentified.

185. To Robert Rogers [of Boston]

Cambridge Port,
8th March, 1832

My dear Sir: I should have replied to your obliging letter sooner but that a long and important letter of business prevented. It was not, however, on my own business, or I <sh>would have postponed it.

I am *exceedingly gratified* to learn that Mr. Ball[1] is so much pleased with his Picture; and I beg you to express to him my warmest acknowledgements for his generous intention of allowing it to be again exhibited in Charleston for my benefit.[2] His further liberal offer of another Exhibition for me in New York I must however respectfully decline: I feel that to accept it would be to trespass on his kindness. I am *more than satisfied* with the additional exhibition at Charleston. *There*, so far as respects my *pecuniary* advantage, I would have it terminate. But, as I consider Spalato's Vision one of my best pictures, it would afford me much pleasure to have it seen in New-York; and I agree with Mr. Ball in thinking the National Academy of Design the best place to which he could send it.[3]

I forgot to ask you to send the *printed extract* from Mr. Radcliff[4] to Mr. Ball.[5]

But I suppose you have sent it. If you have not, will you do me the favour to transmit it to him; as it be of use in the Charleston Exhibition.

Mrs. Allston unites with me in best regards to yourself and all at Home.

Sincerely yours, / Wa. Allston.

P.S. I will thank you to request Mr. Ball, in hanging the Picture, to place it so that the window which lights it shall be at the *back* of the Monk; that being the light in which I painted it <and> it makes a difference to its disadvantage when seen by a light coming from the opposite direction.

ADDRESSED: Robert Rogers Esqre. / Pinckney Street[6] / Boston. ANNOTATED by Rogers: Cambridge 8 March 1832 / Washington Allston; Rec'd 10 March / Ansd. SOURCE: Manuscript, Manuscripts and Archives, Yale University Library.

1. Rogers's wife and Ball's wife were first cousins (Dean and Dudley, p. 319). 2. *Spalatro's Vision of the Bloody Hand* was exhibited, for WA's benefit, in Charleston, S.C., in March 1832 in King Street at the admission price of fifty cents, twenty-five cents for children (Rutledge, *Artists in the Life of Charleston*, p. 136). 3. It was exhibited at the NAD in 1832. 4. Unidentified. The Radcliffe family was a prominent one in Charleston. The planter Thomas Radcliffe had a celebrated mansion house in the city whose furniture was auctioned in 1821. A few years later a John Radcliffe was residing at 116 Meeting Street (*Charleston Courier*, 13 July 1821; *Charleston City Directory* for 1824). 5. Apparently this extract was distributed at the exhibition of the painting in Boston. Presumably it was the "Communication," signed "Z," which appeared in the *Charleston Mercury* for 1 March 1832. The author referred to it as one of the "splendid conceptions of a master mind" and urged that those who glowed with enthusiasm at such works go to "look on the majestic form" of Schedoni and the "ghastly horror-stricken countenance" of Spalatro. 6. In 1832 Rogers lived at 45 Pinckney Street. In earlier years he lived at number 18 (*Boston City Directory* for 1825 and later).

186. To the Trustees of the Boston Athenaeum[1] [May 1832]

To the Trustees of the Athenaeum.

Gentlemen: An original Group in plaster, the subject Hagar & Ishmael, has been sent to me by a friend in Charleston, John S. Cogdell Esqre. who is the author. May I ask the favour of you to permit me to deposit it for a short time in the room appropriated to Casts,[2] in the Athenaeum.

Very respectfully, / your obdt servt / Washington Allston

Cambridge Port, / May, 1832.

ADDRESSED: To / The Trustees of the Athenaeum / Boston. SOURCE: Manuscript, BA.

1. The trustees in 1832 were Ticknor, Nathaniel Bowditch, George Hayward, Franklin Dexter, Charles P. Curtis, Isaac P. Davis, Edward Wigglesworth, Samuel A. Eliot, and William Hickling Prescott. 2. This room housed the BA's collection of sculpture as well as casts prior to the formation of the Sculpture Gallery in 1839 and was frequently used by artists to study anatomy and drawing (Swan, pp. 134-40).

187. From Gulian Crommelin Verplanck Fishkill Landing[1]
July 25th 1832

My Dear Sir: I send you a New York literary paper containing Mr. Livingston's official letter to your friend Greenough on the subject of his statue of Washington.[2] You must allow that our Committee on Public Buildings at Washington (that is to say your friends Jarvis, your neighbour Gen. Dearborn & myself—for the others cared little about the matter) if we have not done much or as much as we wished—have done well what we have done in employing your friend Vanderlyn & Greenough & on liberal terms.

I was two or three days in New York last week on my return from Washington & found it in a melancholy state. The chief ravages of the Cholera are as yet confined to the most worthless & vicious part of our population yet there are many exceptions which spread alarm & the stagnation of business brings great distress upon the industrious poor. The characteristic habits of those whom the disease has mainly preyed upon however gives me great hopes that it will not spread its devastation unduly throughout our country. It is still a terrible calamity.

Irving[3] was with us at Washington & looks wanderfully well—indeed quite unaltered since I saw him in England in 1817 though changed to those who recollect only his sallow & thin American face. He is now wandering about among his friends in the state & I hope soon to see him again.

Remember me to our friend Mr Dana believe me truly yours,

G.C. Verplanck

ADDRESSED: Washington Allston Esq / Cambridge Port / Mass. SOURCE: Manuscript.

1. The location, in New York State, of the Verplanck family estate. 2. Edward Livingston (1764-1836), as secretary of state, notified Greenough of his commission by Congress to execute a statue of Washington for the rotunda of the Capitol in a letter written on 28 February 1832. It was printed in several periodicals, including the *New-York Mirror* for 21 July 1832, to which Verplanck refers. 3. Irving was in Washington on his return from England, from June to September, staying with Louis McLane (Williams, 2:35, 37).

188. To John Vanderlyn Cambridge Port / Tuesday 6 Novr. 1832

My dear Sir: I have just received your letter[1] and regret to hear that you are indisposed. I have barely time to add (as this goes by private conveyance) that I hope to have the pleasure of seeing you on *Thursday.* I name that date, as tomorrow Mrs. Allston has an engagement in Cambridge.

If you come out on the *two* o'clock stage, we shall have some time to talk on the arts etc. before dinner. We dine at half past 3.

Your faithful friend / Wa. Allston

SOURCE: Typescript, New-York Historical Society.

1. This letter does not seem to have been preserved. Vanderlyn spent part of the fall of 1832 in Boston to make a copy of Stuart's portrait of Washington in the BA in preparation for the portrait of him which he had been commissioned to paint for the House of Representatives. On 4 August Jarvis wrote Vanderlyn that WA, whom he had seen the day before, was pleased to hear of the commission and thought Vanderlyn might procure portraits to paint in Boston, for which he should ask not less than $200 each (Averill, pp. 144-45, 274).

189. To William Ellery Channing

Cambridge Port,
25 Feb. 1833.

My dear Sir: I beg you to accept my best thanks for your kind Loan; which was made doubly acceptable by the very kind manner in which it was offered.[1]

I hope you will excuse my not replying to your Note on saturday. It was brought to me at my Painting-Room, when I was on a *critical part* of a picture, which could not have been left there for half an hour without risk.

Pray present my best regards to Mrs. Channing and Miss Gibbs,[2] whose kindness in giving shelter to my little wandering Troubadour[3] I gratefully appreciate.

With sincere respect, / your obliged friend, / Wa. Allston

ADDRESSED: Revd. Dr. W.E. Channing. / Mount Vernon,[4] / Boston. SOURCE: Manuscript, Autograph Collection, Rhode Island Historical Society.

1. Nothing further seems to be known about this loan. Channing was for many years concerned about WA's financial difficulties and was one of those originating the contribution in 1835 by some of his friends to pay his debts. 2. Sarah Gibbs. 3. *Young Troubadour,* which WA had a difficult time selling. Henry Greenough, who praised "the relief and true modelling" of the figure, said it had in the background a marble boy holding a vase on a garden wall, which was "relieved, not only by light and shade, but by opposition of the colors in the sky" (Flagg, p. 193). Elizabeth Peabody also referred to "the stone Cupid of the Troubadour's Ravine" (p. 40). One of his drawings for it depicted a boy seated on a wall holding a jar. It was exhibited at the BA in 1835 and at Harding's Gallery in 1839. WA wrote a poem, "The Young Troubadour," to accompany it which describes the troubadour playing his guitar and singing beside "A broken fountain, called of yore / The Lover's Fount, where, bending o'er, / A marble Cupid once did pour / The sweetest drops that ever fell," and still seemed to do so though the stream from the fountain had ceased to flow (*LA*, p. 340). Extracts from it were printed in the catalogs of both exhibitions in which the painting appeared. The poem, and by implication the painting, reflects WA's acquaintance with Tasso's *Jerusalem Delivered.* He borrowed a copy of Tasso's works from the Harvard library when he was a student and owned two copies of *Jerusalem Delivered.* His interest in Tasso about this time is attested by Franklin Dexter's reference to *A Roman Lady Reading* as depicting the figure reading that author. In WA's poem the troubadour comes to the House of Este in Italy, together with its crusaders from Palestine, for the festivities at the wedding of Count Julian and Isabel of Sinigal (Sinigaglia, in the Marches), whose favorite page he is. Dissatisfied with his songs about the Count's martial deeds and tournament victories, he sings at last happily about the bride, "his Lady fair." Tasso was intimately associated with the Este family throughout his life. *Jerusalem Delivered,* laid at the time of the First Crusade, was largely written while he was in the service of Duke Alfonso II of Ferrara, whose feats in tournaments are cited, whose sister Leonara he was said to have loved, and at whose wedding, to a Gonzaga of Mantua, he behaved so irrationally that

Alfonso had him committed to a madhouse. He was released at the solicitation of the duke of Mantua, whose mother was Isabella d'Este Gonzago, marchioness of Mantua, a cousin of Alfonso's, one of the most brilliant women of the time. As members of the Guelf party, the Este family were involved in the Guelf and Ghibelline wars, which virtually ruined the city of Sinigaglia, as Dante said. WA's painting *Girl in Persian Costume (A Troubadour)* is related to *Young Troubadour,* as the alternative title given it at the exhibition at the BA in 1857 acknowledged. A figure posed beside water playing a stringed instrument is common to both paintings. The most conspicuous difference between them is the Persian costume of the female figure, WA's only known reference to Persia. It is possibly further testimony to his acquaintance with Tasso's *Jerusalem Delivered,* in which the female knight Clorinda comes from that country. A third painting, *Lover Playing a Lute,* is related to *Young Troubadour* in the pose of the male figure and the fountain in the background. 4. Channing lived at 49 Mount Vernon Street from 1833 to 1836, at no. 61 from 1837 until his death *(Boston City Directory).*

190. To William Dunlap

Cambridge Port Massachusetts
April 6th 1833

William Dunlap Esqre

Dear Sir: The following answer to your first letter[1] was written some days previous to the rect of your last. I owe you many apologies for having so long delayed it, and, with the assurance that not the slightest disrespect was felt or intended I must beg you to pardon it.

Dear Sir: Though I have not the pleasure of your personal acquaintance, your character has long been known to me through several of our mutual friends; I need not add that I could not have this knowledge without feeling towards you the most sincere respect. I will therefore reply to your letter with the frankness of a Friend, assuring myself that you will give this a friendly reception.

I had some years since an application similar to yours from a gentleman of your City, and my first intention was respectfully to decline it; but I suffered myself to be guided by the advice of a friend and consented to supply dates, and some other—but *what* particulars I cannot now recollect. I had partly however sent my answer to this effect when I regretted that I did not adhere to my first purpose; and when the work for which the Biography was required was afterwards given up[2] I then made up my mind to decline all future applications of a like nature.

In common with all Artists I am always gratified when I hear that my works are well received by the Public and especially when they are approved by my brother Artists. Farther than this I have no wish; on the contrary I have such an invincible repugnance to every thing like personal notoriety that I should at once (respectfully) decline the honour you intend me could I do it without subjecting you or myself to unpleasant misapprehension. For the omission of my name in a Work professing to treat of *all* American Artists, would if unexplained very naturally subject *you* to the suspicion of personal hostility towards the individual omitted; and *if explained* would inevitably draw upon *me* another kind (and no enviable kind) of notoriety. I know human nature indeed too well not to be aware that my exposition of my motive, for declining what has become nowadays so common a compliment, would be met by many sneers. I should hear not a little of my fastidiousness or affectation. Under these circumstances and with the real desire to gratify you, I will therefore furnish you with the dates and such facts as I may state without "egotism."

When I tell you that I have had many troubles, I trust you will pardon the lateness of this reply.

With sincere respect Yours / Washington Allston

P.S. To your second letter allow me to say briefly that I will with pleasure reply to the questions proposed in it as soon as the state of my Wife's health will allow me to do so. She has been for some time ill, and still continues so, confined to a dark room, with a distressing inflammation in one of her eyes. I will not delay it however longer than I can help. Of Copley's connexions here I have no personal knowledge. If I can gather through my friends (some of whom I believed are acquainted with them) any information respecting him, I will transmit it as collected. Concerning Mr West, besides his kind reception of me, I do not think I can add any thing to what is already known to the public. Should any new particulars occur to me, I will note them down: the same also of Stuart. Of Bembridge[3] I know only that he left many portraits in South Carolina, but I have no recollection of their merits. I have no knowledge of Ramage.[4]

Will you do me the favour to present my best regards to Mr Morse, with my thanks for his present of colours by Mr Mason.

Perhaps it may gratify you to know that in a conversation I had some years since in London with Charles Lamb, the Author of Elia,[5] he spoke highly of your "Life of Cooke."[6]

SOURCE: Dunlap, *Diary* 4:672-73.

1. Dunlap wrote WA on 18 November 1832 and 30 March 1833 asking for aid in writing his *History of the Rise and Progress of the Arts of Design in the United States* (*Diary* 3:627, 669). WA owned a copy of this work, presented by the author. 2. Unidentified. 3. Henry Benbridge (1743-1812), American painter, a native of Philadelphia. He studied in Rome and painted for many years in Virginia and the Carolinas. He painted a portrait of WA's mother (Nord, pp. 10-11). Dunlap incorporated WA's information about him, with due credit, in his *History*. 4. John Ramage (1748-1802), portrait painter. A native of Ireland, he moved to Halifax, Nova Scotia, and was active in Boston before the Revolution and in New York from 1777 to 1794. 5. The essays in the first series of Lamb's autobiographical *Essays of Elia* appeared in the *London Magazine* between 1820 and 1823 and were published in a separate volume in the latter year. The second series was published in 1833. 6. *Memoirs of George Fred Cooke, Esq., Late of the Theatre Royal, Convent Garden* (1813).

191. To Thomas Sully Cambridge Port, Masstts.
8 April, 1833.

My dear Sully: I received your letter of March 23d only a few days since, and sincerely thank you for your kindness in wishing to make me acquainted with Mr.

& Miss Kemble.[1] I thank you for it as another instance, added to the many which you have already given me, of your friendship.

Were I in other circumstances, I need not say how much pleasure the acquaintance of persons so accomplished would afford me; but, situated as I am, I am constrained to forego it: In truth, the "res angustae domi"[2] leave me no choice in such matters; for I have neither the time to visit, nor the means to entertain them at home.

I write to you thus frankly that, in case *a letter should be asked for,* you would do me the favour to decline it. And, should it be found necessary to assign a reason, I have no objection to the *true one* being given; for mine is an honest poverty, and I am not ashamed of it.

Your letter on Haydon's Picture, which I saw extracted from the National Gazette,[3] does you honour, both as an Artist and a man. The "Entrance into Jerusalem" is indeed a magnificent work of art. Where the excellence is of so high an order, and the beauties so numerous, I should think myself but poorly employed were I disposed to dwell on its faults. Had it a hundred more faults I could overlook them all for the sake of its merits. 'Tis a glorious picture. If Mr. McMurtrie <were> (to whom I beg to be particularly remembered) should write to Haydon, pray ask him to let Haydon know how much I admire it.

Pray have you ever painted a picture from the water colour sketch of yours which I so admired? I mean the Mother and Child.[4] If you have not, and intend it, will you allow me to advise your copying the <water colour> sketch as *closely as possible* as to the *colour.* I think you will be surprised to find how *transparent* and *silvery* an *exact* imitation of it in oil <would> will be. I am certain that Turner—<and> perhaps also Calcot—owe not a little of their richness of tone to the circumstance of their having commenced as painters in Water Colour. The *foil* of the white paper to which their eyes were accustomed was the secret. To imitate this in oil requires not merely a high *key note,* but a powerful empasto and great clearness of tint.—Should you make the experiment, let me caution you against *improving* <yo> on the sketch; if you do, I venture to predict that your labour will be lost. Try to hit the precise tone, especially in the shadows.

My wife has been for some time quite ill, confined to a dark room, with a violent inflammation in one of her eyes; she is getting better I hope, though still unable to bear the light. She unites with me in best regards to Mrs. S.[5] and yourself.

Your sincere friend, / Wa. Allston.

I have had the pleasure to become acquainted with your friend Mr. Audubon,[6] with whom I am greatly delighted. He is besides being a man of genius a modest one. Pray direct me in future at *Cambridge Port.* Some of my correspondents' letters bring with them the marks of *old age,* in consequence of their being directed to Boston. I have just answered one from New York received only five or six days since, that is six weeks old.

ADDRESSED: Thomas Sully Esqre. / Philadelphia, / Pennsylvania. SOURCE: Manuscript, Boston Public Library. Printed in part in Flagg, p. 268.

1. Charles (1775-1854) and his daughter Frances ("Fanny") (1809-93) Kemble, members of the celebrated family of English actors and actresses. They appeared at the Tremont Theatre in Boston from 16 April to 17 May 1833, playing the leading roles in *Fazio, or The Italian Wife; The Stranger, or Misanthrope and Repentance;* Sheridan's *The School for Scandal; Romeo and Juliet; Much Ado about Nothing;* Otway's *Venice Preserved; The Provoked Husband; The Gamester; The Hunchback; The Merchant of Venice; Macbeth;* and *The Grecian Daughter.* They had appeared in Philadelphia in October and November 1832, at which time Sully painted two portraits of Charles and eight of Fanny (Biddle and Fielding, pp. 195-97). They returned to Boston from 4 to 23 September in *The Stranger; Dead Shot; The Provoked Husband; The Hunchback; Perfection; Isabella, or The Fatal Marriage; The Chimney Piece; Much Ado about Nothing; The Wonder; Charles II; The Jealous Wife; King John; The Inconstant; Fazio; Francis the First; The Merchant of Venice; Katherine and Petruchio; Macbeth; Love, Law, and Physic; Hamlet; Petticoat Government; The Wife, or a Tale of Mantua* (*Boston Daily Advertiser*). WA apparently saw them during this year, for he talked of Fanny during Bronson Alcott's visit to him three years later (*The Journals of Bronson Alcott,* ed. Odell Shepard Boston: Little, Brown, 1938), p. 53). 2. "Narrow circumstances at home" (Juvenal, *Satires* 3.164). 3. The extract from the Philadelphia *National Gazette and Literary Register* appeared in the *Boston Daily Advertiser* for 14 February. It concluded with the declaration that, despite the faults of Haydon's picture, "students and artists of this country may congratulate themselves on having within their reach, two works of surpassing merit"—it and WA's *Dead Man Restored.* It was exhibited at Harding's Gallery in Boston for several weeks, until March 1833. RHD, Jr., recollected that his father said when WA saw it then he was so delighted that he would not speak of its defects. 4. Sully produced several compositions entitled *Mother and Child.* Possibly WA refers to the study he made for a Mr. Stevens in 1826-27 (Biddle and Fielding, p. 372). 5. Sarah (Annis) Sully of Annapolis, Md., who was first married to Sully's brother Lawrence. 6. John James Audubon (1785?-1851), painter and writer about North American birds. Sully, who knew him in Philadelphia, gave him a letter of introduction to WA.

192. From William Drayton, Daniel Elliott Huger, and Benjamin F. Pepoon

Charleston, April 9, 1833.

Dear Sir: The enclosed statement concerns the circumstances under which our national flag was unfurled by the American Ambassador at Mexico.[1] It is intended that they should furnish material for a national painting; the object is to spread before the eyes of our countrymen, and particularly of the rising generation, the unseen but highly moral protection afforded by a great, because united, people. Though it is difficult for the mind to calculate the value of the Union,[2] yet the hand of a master may successfully exhibit, at a single glance, that national protection, which, like the pressure of the atmosphere, though omnipotent and powerful, is neither seen nor felt. The sectional excitement at present existing among the States obliterating national feelings, these must be revived; the arts are powerful in their operation, and lasting in their effects. We must have national paintings, national songs, national celebrations to excite and perpetuate national enthusiasm. The flag of every country is its emblem. It should command respect abroad, adoration at home. The man who loves and reveres not his country's flag is prepared to violate her laws, and destroy her Constitution. It is our object to have the Star Spangled

Banner portrayed in the act of overawing, in a foreign land, an infuriated and lawless soldiery; and of protecting from revolutionary violence the objects of political hatred. To have this scene engraved is also our object. That the flag of our country may wave in every house, in every cottage, even in every log-house beyond the mountains. That our children may learn before they can read, to love and reverence the emblem of our country's power, and may realize that it is their guardian and protector, not only on their native soil, but in a land of strangers.

It is particularly wished that the painting and engraving should be finished at the shortest time consistent with their proper execution. You will therefore confer a favor by informing us whether you can undertake to carry our wishes into effect within that time, and on what terms. If you can also engage to have the painting engraved you will oblige us, at an early day, with your views upon the subject.

Respectfully, your obedient servants, / William Drayton, / D.E. Huger, Benjamin F. Pepoon, / *Committee.*

SOURCE: Flagg, pp. 265-66.

1. This statement does not seem to have been preserved. The first American ambassador to Mexico, Joel Roberts Poinsett (1779-1851), unfurled the American flag at his residence in Mexico City shortly after his arrival there about 25 May 1825 while being threatened by an armed mob. At the time, the president of Mexico and other officials were courting the favor of England, and Poinsett met with considerable opposition throughout his term of office (J. Fred Rippy, *Joel R. Poinsett: Versatile American* [Durham, N.C.: Duke Univ. Press, 1935], p. 108). 2. The writers of this letter and most of WA's other friends were supporters of the Union during the decades before the Civil War.

193. To Edward Everett Cambridge Port, Tuesday, 23 April, 1833.

My dear Sir: I shall be happy to receive your proposed visit[1] at one o'clock on Friday. Should either this day, or hour, be inconvenient, I must beg you to name any other more agreeable to you.

I remain, dear Sir, / with the highest respect, / Yrs / Wa. Allston

ADDRESSED: Honble Edward Everett M.C.[2] / Charlestown, / Masstts. SOURCE: Manuscript.

1. It was made to deliver the letter to WA from Drayton, Huger, and Pepoon of 9 April.
2. Member of Congress. Everett was in the House of Representatives from 1825 to 1835.

194. To Jonathan Mason Cambridge Port, 26 April, 1833.

My dear Sir: Will you do me the favour to come and see me. I want *exceedingly* to see you, if only for half an hour. I would not put you to this trouble, but would myself call on you (though I can but ill spare a day) were I *certain* of finding you at home. But as I am not certain of this, <and cannot> I therefore beg the favour of a call from you.

Will you oblige me by requesting Miss Gibbs[1] to send for my nephew, George's, *frame,* which is at my room. I have no means of sending it into Town; and she offered to send for it. The frame is for <the> his picture of the "Ghost story,"[2] which is to go to the Atheneum Exhibition. The picture Miss G. took into Town in her Carriage, last week.

Yrs sincerely / Wa. Allston.

ADDRESSED: Jonathan Mason Esqre. / Mount Vernon,[3] / Boston. SOURCE: Manuscript, Washington Allston Collection (no. 7471), Manuscripts Division, Special Collections Department, University of Virginia Library.

1. Sarah Gibbs. 2. Flagg's *Ghost Story* was exhibited at the BA in 1833. 3. Mason lived at 45 Mount Vernon Street in 1833 and 1834, at number 74 from 1837 to 1846-47 (*Boston City Directory*).

195. To William Drayton, Daniel Elliott Huger, and Benjamin F. Pepoon

[1 May 1833]
[Draft]

Gentlemen: Your letter was handed me a few days since by the Honorable E. Everett. It has caused me both gratification & regret. To be thus remembered by gentlemen of my native State awakens many pleasing sensations within me, mingled with sorrow for the sad occasion which has induced you to honor me with the proposed commission. Strong as my attachment is to the State of my birth & childhood, I entirely sympathize in your feelings of pride & patriotism towards our common country; & I see, also, as you must, that the safety & dignity of each individual State depend upon the Union of all.

There is no act of my life which would give me <so much> such heart-felt satisfaction as that of having done something toward strengthening the patriotism of my countrymen, & arousing once more in them the feeling that we are one people.

I am, however, compelled, Gentlemen, to forego this, & to decline the commission with which you have honoured me. I have imperative engagements upon me that must be fulfilled; before I <[rest of line undecipherable]> and I could not, without absolute injustice, enter upon <any great> a work so important as that proposed by you, till those are completed for which I have for some time stood pledged. While I deeply regret that it is out of my power to comply with your wishes, <& am [word undecipherable]> I doubt not that there are others at liberty, who can carry your wishes into effect, & while they accomplish something for the Union, will add fame to the <honour of> fame of our country in the fine arts.

With great respect, Gentl / Yr obdt <& much honored> servt / Washington Allston.

To—

In sending the enclosed you will permit me to say <that> it is my <wish> request that it <should> be not <laid before the public> published: not because I shrink from any <responsibility> odium which the declaration of my opinion respecting the present state of our country might bring upon me; but from an aversion, which I have ever had of unnecessarily appearing before the public.

Though my lot in life has been cast in other lands, I have never forgotten that of my birth. I cannot therefore but attach a peculiar value to any mark of <kindness> regard from that portion of my country; and I beg to repeat to you individually that I do most sincerely appreciate it in the present instance. And allow me, Sir, also to say, that <it has added> it adds not a little to my gratification <that I am> to find myself indebted for this valued distinction to one,[1] among others, whose personal acquaintance, though short and long past, still remains a pleasant freshness in my memory.

SOURCE: Manuscript copy by RHD, except for the last two paragraphs; last two paragraphs: manuscript. Printed, without the cancelations, in Flagg, pp. 266-68.

1. Presumably Drayton.

196. To Edward Everett Cambridge Port, 1 May, 1833.

My dear Sir: I return you the enclosed letter, with my thanks for your kind attention in sending it for my perusal.

There was much that I wished to say when I had the pleasure of seeing you the other day,[1] but which the fear of trespassing on your time, together with the painful embarrassment occasioned by my inability to accept a commission in all respects so flattering to me, prevented my expressing. The amount of it, however, was to express to you the deep and grateful <[undecipherable word]> sense I had of the honour done me in the proposed commission—more especially as coming from my native State—and the real distress that I at the same time felt at being compelled, by the circumstances named to you, to decline it.

I have the highest respect for the Gentlemen of the Committee, who are well known to me by report—Col. Drayton personally; and I admire and honour them, and those they represent, for the noble and patriotic object of their communication.

With the highest respect, Yrs / Wa. Allston.

ADDRESSED: Honble Edward Everett, M. C. / Charlestown, / Massachusetts.
SOURCE: Manuscript.

1. In his letter to RHD of 30 August 1843 Everett described this visit, saying WA received him with courtesy but excused himself from accepting the commission offered him both because he felt it his duty to devote himself exclusively to *Belshazzar's Feast* and because the battle piece proposed was in a branch of painting which he had not cultivated and did not feel prepared to

undertake. Everett was apparently answering a question asked him by RHD regarding the story in the article in the Boston *Atlas* "Anecdotes of Allston," which had appeared a few weeks earlier, in which it was erroneously stated that James Hamilton, who a few years after the South Carolina proposal recommended WA for a commission to paint panels in the rotunda of the Capitol, was involved in proposing this one and that WA had refused it "with earnestness and emphasis." Speaking in that way, Everett said, was not WA's habit. There was nothing in the proposal to affect him disagreeably and it seemed scarcely possible that he, "the mildest and gentlest of men, could have received it in any other than a mild and gentle manner." "No man," he added, "regarded Mr. Allston with warmer admiration than myself; no one out of his family circle more tenderly cherishes his memory" (Flagg, pp. 263-64).

197. To Jonathan Mason Cambridge Port, 8 May. 1833.

My dear Sir: With this you will receive the case containing "Isaac of York."[1]

Will you allow me to suggest that the case be not opened until you are ready to hang the picture—to avoid the dust. I only, however, *suggest* this. You must do as you think best.

I send you the measure of the *frame*, according to which Mr Dogget is making <that> the one you have ordered. From the *outer edges* of the moulding 3 feet 8 inches high, & 3 feet 2 inches wide. Having this measure, you can easily determine on & retain a *place* for the picture.

If you could borrow a frame that fits it, till Mr Dogget's is ready, would it not be as well to hang it soon? I should prefer it, if a frame of any kind that is gilt could be borrowed for the purpose. But this also I leave to you.

Yours sincerely, / Wa. Allston.

ADDRESSED: Jonathan Mason Esqre / Atheneum Gallery, / near / Atkinson Street.[2]
SOURCE: Manuscript, Manuscripts Division, Special Collections Department, University of Virginia Library.

1. It was painted in a very short time, according to RHD (p. 17). WA said that he hit on the title, which was taken from the name of Isaac of York, the father of Rebecca in Scott's novel *Ivanhoe* (1819), after it was done. Mason was acting as agent between him and the BA, which purchased it on 3 May 1833. WA wrote a receipt for $300 received for it from Mason on account of the BA, at the bottom of which he added, "A Portrait of Isaac of York—vide Ivanhoe." The receipt is endorsed, presumably by Mason, as his having been paid the sum by the treasurer of the BA on 20 May (BA). It was exhibited there that year. In 1840 the Fine Arts Committee of the BA asked for WA's consent to have it engraved by Henry Dutton Morse (RHD, p. 17), but no engraving seems to have been made. 2. The BA moved in July 1822 from its Tremont Street quarters to a house on Pearl Street, where it remained until 1850 (Knowles, p. 7). Atkinson Street no longer exists.

198. To William Dunlap [ca. 20 May 1833][1]

To go back as far as I can—I remember that I used to draw before I left Carolina, at six years of age, (by the way no *uncommon* thing,) and still earlier, that my favourite amusement, much akin to it, was making little landscapes about the roots of an old tree in the country—meagre enough, no doubt; the only particulars of which I can call to mind, were a cottage built of sticks, shaded by little trees, which were composed of the small suckers, (I think so called,) resembling miniature trees, which I gathered in the woods. Another employment was the converting the forked stalks of the wild ferns into little men and women, by winding about them different coloured yarn. These were sometimes presented with pitchers made of the pomegranate flower. These childish fancies were the straws by which, perhaps, an observer might then have guessed which way the current was setting for after life. And yet, after all, this love of imitation may be common to childhood. General imitation certainly is: but whether adherence to particular kinds may not indicate a permanent propensity, I leave to those who have studied the subject more than I have, to decide.[2]

But even these delights would sometimes give way to a stronger love for the wild and the marvelous. I delighted in being terrified by the tales of witches and hags, which the negroes used to tell me; and I well remember with how much pleasure I recalled these feelings on my return to Carolina;[3] especially on revisiting a gigantic wild grape-vine in the woods, which had been the favourite swing for one of these witches.

Source: Dunlap, 2:152-15.

1. WA wrote seven letters to Dunlap in 1833 and 1834, in addition to that of 6 April 1833, which Dunlap received on 9 April: those received on 23 May, 1 July, 15 July, 21 October, 8 November 1834, 21 February, and 18 August 1834 (*Diary* 3:672, 684, 718, 722, 752, 756, 775, 816). The contents of all these letters and the dates of those for which dates are not given by Dunlap are assigned on the basis of the facts that they seem to constitute units of information which arguably number seven and that those for which dates are given by Dunlap were received from four to six days after they were written. Besides those of 18 November 1832 and 30 March 1833, Dunlap wrote letters to WA on 26 May, 18 July, 9 November 1833, 16 July, and 23 August 1834 in reply to those he received and one on 28 September 1834, apparently not in reply to one from WA (*Diary* 3:685, 722, 757, 804, 817, 825). None seems to have been preserved. 2. Dunlap here inserted a paragraph of his own and introduced the next quotation from WA with "Allston continued." 3. In 1800-1801.

199. To William Dunlap [ca. 28 June 1833][1]

I concluded my last with the amusement of my childhood: my next step will be to my boyhood. My chief pleasure now was in drawing from prints—of all kinds of figures, landscape and animals. But I soon began to make pictures of my own; at what age, however, I cannot say. The earliest compositions that I remember were the storming of Count Roderick's castle, from a poor (though to me delightful) romance of that day,[2] and the siege of Toulon;[3] the first in India ink, the other in water colours. I cannot recall the year in which they were done. To these succeeded many others that have likewise passed into oblivion. Though I never had any regular instructor in the art, (a circumstance I would here observe both idle and absurd to boast of,) I had much incidental instruction; which I have always through life been glad to receive from every one in advance of myself. And, I may add, there is no such thing as a self-taught artist in the ignorant acceptation of the word;[4] for the greatest genius that ever lived must be indebted to others, if not by direct teaching, yet indirectly through their works. I had, in my school days, some of this latter kind of instruction from a very worthy and amiable man, a Mr. King[5] of Newport, who made quadrants and compasses, and occasionally painted portraits. I believe he was originally bred a painter, but obliged, from the rare calls upon his pencil, to call in the aid of another craft. I used at first to make frequent excuses for visiting his shop to look at his pictures, but finding that he always received me kindly, I went at last without any, or rather with the avowed purpose of making him a visit. Sometimes I would take with me a drawing, and was sure to get a kind word of encouragement. It was a pleasant thing to me, some twenty years after this,[6] to remind the old man of these little kindnesses.[7]

I became acquainted with Malbone[8] but a short time before he quitted Newport, a circumstance which I remember then regretting exceedingly, for I looked up to him with great admiration. Our not meeting earlier was owing, I suppose, to his going to another school, and being some years older than myself. I recollect borrowing some of his pictures on oiled paper to copy. Our intimacy, however, did not begin till I entered college, when I found him established at Boston. He had then (for the interval was of several years) reached the maturity of his powers, and was deservedly ranked the first miniature painter in the country. Malbone's merits as an artist are too well known to need setting forth by me: I shall therefore say but a few words on that head. He had the happy talent, among his many excellencies, of elevating the character without impairing the likeness: this was remarkable in his male heads; and no woman ever lost any beauty from his hand; nay, the fair would often become still fairer under his pencil. To this he added a grace of execution all his own. My admiration of Malbone induced me at this time (in my freshman year at College) to try my hand at miniature, but it was without success. I could *make no hand of it;* all my attempts in that line being so far inferior to what I could *then* do in oil, that I became disgusted with my abortive efforts, and gave it up. One of these miniatures, or rather attempts at miniature, was shown me several years after, and I pronounced it *"without promise,"*[9] (this anecdote has found its way into Blackwood's Magazine)[10] not knowing it to be my work. I may add, I would have said the same had I known it. I may observe, however, (for I know not why I should not be as just to myself as to another person,) that I should not have expressed a similar opinion respecting its contemporaries in oil; for a landscape with figures on horseback, painted about this time, was afterwards exhibited at Somerset house.[11]

My leisure hours at college were chiefly devoted to the pencil, to the composition equally of figures and landscapes; I do not remember that I preferred one to the other; my only guide in the choice was the inclination of the moment. There was an old landscape[12] at the house of a friend in Cambridge (whether Italian or Spanish I know not) that gave me my first hints of colour in that branch; it was of a rich and deep tone, though not by the hands of a master; the work, perhaps, of a moderate artist, but of one who lived in a *good age,* when he could not help catching something of the good that was abroad. In the colouring of figures, the pictures of Pine[13] in the Columbian museum, in Boston, were my first masters. Pine had certainly, as far as I can recollect, considerable merit in colour. But I had a higher master in the head of Cardinal Bentivoglio,[14] from Vandyke, in the college library, which I obtained permission to copy one winter vacation. This copy from Vandyke, was by Smybert,[15] an English painter, who came to this country with Dean, afterwards Bishop, Berkeley.[16] At that time, it seemed to me perfection; but when I saw the original[17] some years afterwards, I found I had to alter my notions of perfection. However, I am grateful to Smybert for the instruction he gave me—his work rather. Deliver me from kicking down even the weakest step of an early ladder.

SOURCE: Dunlap, 2:154-56.

1. The date of this letter is based on the next several quotations from WA's recollections in Dunlap, which are chiefly about Newport; WA's reference to it as the next after his "last" letter; and Dunlap's introduction to it thus: "Allston, in another letter to the same correspondent, says."
2. *Count Roderick's Castle; or, Gothic Times, a Tale,* 2 vols. (Philadelphia, 1795). Sully said WA told him this was his first original design (Rutledge, "Dunlap Notes," p. 154). 3. On 11 February 1744 a naval battle took place near the French port of Toulon between a British fleet and the combined Spanish and French forces, in which the British lost. Channing remembered that in WA's painting the assailants were depicted with their backs turned (Peabody, *Reminiscences of Reverend William Ellery Channing, D.D.* Boston: Roberts Brothers, 1880, p. 331). Sully said WA told him that battle pieces were his "early delight" (Rutledge, "Dunlap Notes," p. 156). 4. In his lecture "Composition" WA wrote that abundant examples of "self-taught painters" existed only "in our aborigines" (*LA*, p. 159). 5. Samuel King (1748-1819), portrait painter and maker of nautical instruments. He gave instruction in painting to WA and also to Malbone, the miniaturist Ann Hall, and Charles B. King. 6. Apparently WA saw King after his return to America in 1808. 7. Edward G. Malbone. 8. Here Dunlap inserted a sentence referring to WA and Malbone, who also met in Newport, and introduced the next quotation with the words, "On this subject Mr. Alston, in a letter to a friend, has said." 9. According to Jarvis, the portrait was of John Harris, which about 1809 he persuaded Harris's mother to lend him for the purpose of soliciting WA's opinion of the artist, whom he alleged to be a youth of sixteen or seventeen from a prosperous family who aspired to be a painter. WA said the painting was so bad that the young man should abandon such an aspiration and was so affected by learning that the work was his own that he resolved never to discourage anyone who thought he had artistic ability. 10. In "American Writers: No. III" in *Blackwood's Edinburgh Magazine* 16 (1824): 561-62, John Neal recounted the story, saying the person who asked WA's opinion pretended it was the work of a young friend, that WA pronounced it "a wretched affair" and advised the alleged artist to give up painting, and that the painting bore WA's name and the date of seven years earlier, which it did not and which date fell during the time he was first abroad. 11. Presumably *Landscape with Banditti* (*Landscape with a Bridge and a File of Horsemen*). 12. Unidentified. 13. Robert Edge Pine (1730-88), a native of London, who came to America in 1784 and painted a number of portraits of

persons prominent in the American Revolution. At his death his paintings were disposed of by lottery, a considerable number going to the Columbian Museum in Boston. 14. Guido Bentivoglio (1579-1644), Italian cardinal, statesman, and historian. 15. John Smibert (1688-1751), copyist and portrait painter, who spent three years in Italy, came to America in 1728 and settled in Boston in 1730. 16. Berkeley was dean of Dromore and Derry and bishop of Cloyne. He spent from 1728 to 1731 in America, hoping to establish a college in the Bermudas. 17. In the Pitti Palace in Florence.

200. To William Dunlap [ca. 12 July 1833][1]

On quitting college, I returned to Charleston, where I had the pleasure to meet Malbone, and another friend and artist, Charles Fraser, who, by the by, now paints an admirable miniature. My picture manufactory still went on in Charleston until I embarked for London. Up to this time my favorite subjects, with an occasional comic intermission, were banditti.—I well remember one of these, where I thought I had happily succeeded in cutting a throat! The subject of this precious performance was, robbers fighting with each other for the spoils, over the body of a murdered traveller.[2] And clever ruffians I thought them. I did not get rid of this banditti mania until I had been over a year in England. It seems that a fondness for subjects of violence is common with young artists. One might suppose that the youthful mind would delight in scenes of an opposite character. Perhaps the reason of the contrary may be found in this: that the natural condition of youth being one incessant excitement, from the continuous influx of novelty—for all about us must *at one time be new*—it must needs have something fierce, terrible, or unusual to force it above its wonted tone. But the time must come to every man who lives beyond the middle age, when "there is nothing new under the sun."[3] His novelties then are the *rifacimenti*[4] of his former life. The gentler emotions are then as early friends who revisit him in dreams, and who, recalling the past, give a grace and beauty, nay, a rapture even, to what in the hey-day of youth had seemed to him spiritless and flat. And how beautiful is this law of nature—perfuming, as it were, our very graves with the unheeded flowers of childhood.

One of my favourite haunts when a child in Carolina, was a forest spring where I used to catch minnows, and I dare say, with all the callousness of a fisherman; at this moment I can see that spring, and the pleasure conjuror Memory[5] has brought again these little creatures before me; but how unlike to what they were! They seem to me like the spirits of the woods, which a flash from their little diamond eyes lights up afresh in all their gorgeous garniture of leaves and flowers. But where am I going?

[The answer will be][6] Not out of your path. The painter and the poet are alike, "of imagination all compact!"[7] You are both.[8]

There was an early friend, long since dead, whom I have omitted to mention, and I cannot but wonder at the omission, since he is one whose memory is still most dear to me. The name of this gentleman was Bowman; he was a native of Scotland, but had been long settled in Carolina. I believe I was indebted for the uncommon interest he was pleased to take in me to some of my college verses,[9] and to a head of St. Peter (when he hears the cock crow)[10] which I had painted about that time. Be this as it may, his partiality was not of an every-day kind; for when I was about to embark for Europe, he proposed to allow me—nay, almost insisted on my accepting—a hundred pounds a year during my stay abroad. This generous offer, however, I declined, for having at that time a small income sufficient for my immediate wants, it would have been sordid to have accepted it. He then proposed to ship for me a few tierces of rice! That too I declined. Yet he would not let me go without a present; so I was obliged to limit it to Hume's History of England,[11] and a novel by Dr. Moore,[12] whom he personally knew, and to whom he gave me a letter of introduction; the letter however was never delivered, as the Doctor died within a few days of my arrival in London. Such an instance of generosity speaks for itself. But the kindness of manner that accompanied it can only be known to me who saw it. I can see the very expression now. Mr. Bowman was an excellent scholar, and one of the most agreeable talkers I have known. Malbone, Frazer, and myself were frequent guests at his table, and delightful parties we always found there. With youth, health, the kindest friends, and ever before me buoyant hope, what a time to look back on! I cannot but think that the life of an artist, whether painter or poet, depends much on a happy youth; I do not mean as to outward circumstances, but as to his inward being: in my own case, at least, I feel the dependence; for I seldom step into the ideal world but I find myself going back to the age of first impressions.[13] The germs of our best thoughts are certainly often to be found there; sometimes, indeed, (though rarely) we find them in full flower; and when so, how beautiful seem to us these flowers through an atmosphere of thirty years! 'Tis in this way that poets and painters keep their minds young. How else could an old man make the page or the canvas palpitate with the hopes, and fears, and joys, the impetuous, impassioned, emotions of youthful lovers, or reckless heroes? There is a period of life when the ocean of time seems to force upon the mind a barrier against itself, forming, as it were, a permanent beach, on which the advancing years successfully break, only to be carried back by a returning current to that furthest deep whence they first flowed.[14] Upon this beach the *poetry of life* may be said to have its birth; where the *real* ends and the *ideal* begins.

SOURCE: Dunlap, 2:156-58.

1. The date of this letter is based on the next several quotations from WA in Dunlap, which consist of his recollections of his visit to South Carolina in 1800-1801 and Dunlap's receipt of the third letter from him on 15 July. 2. *Robbers Fighting with Each Other for the Spoils over a Murdered Traveller.* 3. "There is no new thing under the sun" (Eccles. 1:9). 4. "Remarking." 5. In "The Calycanthus" WA called his memory of his boyhood "A little Conjurer" (*LA*, p. 328). 6. The words in brackets are Dunlap's and the next two sentences may also be his. 7. "The lunatic, the lover, and the poet, / Are of imagination all compact" (Shakespeare, *A Midsummer-Night's Dream* 5.1.7, 8). 8. Here Dunlap inserted a paragraph about WA's visit

to South Carolina in 1800-1801 and introduced the next quotation with the words, "In one of his letters to his friend, on the subject of his early life and prospects, he says." 9. Probably "First Love," "The Complaint," and "Will the Maniac." 10. Recorded in Matt. 27:74; Mark 14:68, 72; and Luke 22:60. 11. David Hume's *History of Great Britain* was published in 1754-61. 12. John Moore (1729-76), Scottish physician and writer, was the author of the novel *Zeluco* (1789). 13. WA expressed this sentiment in several poems: "Written in Spring," "The Angel and the Nightingale," "To My Sister," "The Calycanthus," "The Magic Slippers," and "To the Author of 'The Diary of an Ennuyée.'" 14. WA employed this image in his lecture "Art" in describing the mood evoked by Reynolds's *Puck* (*LA*, p. 98).

201. To John Stevens Cogdell Cambridge Port, Masstts
9th Oct. 1833.

Dear Cogdell: I have just received your letter of 19 September, by the Brig Chickasaw, and I hasten to send you a few lines in reply, as I suppose, being of a kind of business nature, you may naturally wish to have an acknowledgement of its receipt as early as possible. It will give me great pleasure to render you all the assistance in my power as to its object. The owner of Sir Walter Scott's portrait is Professor Ticknor;[1] to whom I shall address the letter you have enclosed in the one to me.[2] I shall also deliver it in person, and shew the copy of the letter from Messrs King, Poinsett, Grimke[3] &c requesting you to model a bust of Sir Walter.[4] And as soon as I have Mr Ticknor's answer you shall hear from me again. Mr. T. will no doubt also reply to your letter without delay, as he is a man of great urbanity.

I have been thinking of writing to you for several days past, to thank you—as I ought long since to have done—for your bust of Mr Elliot*[5] I beg you now to accept my best thanks for it. It is a work that does you great honour; in execution it is much superiour to your preceding models, and, I should think from its strongly marked character, it must be an excellent likeness. I sent you lately, in a letter to my Mother, a message concerning it, together with my thanks; that it has been much admired by those I have heard speak of it—and those good judges.—What do you say to my presenting it to the Atheneum.[6] I mean in *my* name. You must not think that I do not value it, by my making this propo<sition>al. I make it, because I think it will be of more advantage to you *there* than in my room—where few people will see it. A work of Art always *tells* better (to use a cant, but expressive, word) in a public Institution than in a private house.—This proposal here brings to mind a plan you sometime since mentioned respecting your *Marble* bust of Washington,[7] when completed: that you wished it presented to the Atheneum in *my* name. When you consider that a *marble bust* is a thing of *no trifling value*, would it not come with a better grace from the artist himself? I think it would, and be better received; and so think two of my friends on whose judgement I rely. If *you* think otherwise, however, I will with pleasure do as you wish.

In your Note to me, which came in the box with Mr Elliot's bust, you speak of a letter you had written to me concerning the disposal of Hagar and Ishmael.[8] I have never received that letter. And I dare say its miscarriage was owing to its not having my *proper address:* for I observe that some of your letters are addressed to me, "Boston, or near Boston." I was slightly known a few years ago to one of the clerks in the Boston Post Office; but whether he is still there or not I know not, not having seen him since I left Boston, which is now going on four years. Now no other person there would know where I live, or <if knowing> would probably take the trouble to find out whereabouts "near" Boston to *re-direct* it—which they would have to do before the letter could reach me. Your last letter, which I am now answering, I find is also directed to "Boston." And it is by mere *accident* that it has reached me. It did not come by mail, but was left yesterday morning in the Cambridge Port post office, by a gentleman (I have not learnt whom) who took it out of the Boston office, probably some acquaintance of mine.—I must beg you therefore always to direct to me thus: "Cambridge Port, Massachusetts." N.B. I would here note that Cambridge & Cambridge *Port* are two different places: there is a Post Office at both. I mention this because they are often confounded. It was not long since that I found a letter in that of the former that had been lying there *five months*.

I must beg you also when you have any box, or other like package, to send by water, <that is> to direct them to the care of Mr. Parker,[9] or some other *person in Boston,* who is concerned with shipping, who will see it through the Custom house, store it &c—things that I am wholly unacquainted with; nor have I any friend there whom I can ask to see to it for me. Besides, I live two miles from Boston.—

I am sorry to hear of Mrs. Cogdell's ill health. Mrs. A. joins me in best regards to her and yourself. I wrote to my Mother on the 16th of September. My love to her. Remember me to White. I intend to write him in a few days—whether *before,* or after a *dreadful long* letter that *I have* to write, I don't know. I have seen a good report of the health of your City.[10] May Heaven continue it.

Your sincere friend, / Wa. Allston.

I have had a pleasant visit from Fraser.[11] He brought with him several landscapes that do him honour.

*The Bust, I suppose you know, was exhibited in the Atheneum Gallery; it was well placed, on a table, in the center of the room.

[In the margin] N.B. There are two *lls* in my name. I do not think Miss Gibbs would be willing to let Jeremiah go to Charleston:[12] she declined lending it a second time to the Atheneum.

ADDRESSED: John S. Cogdell Esqre. / Charleston, / South Carolina. ANNOTATED by Cogdell: answered / 28 Octr / 1833. SOURCE: Printed in Flagg, pp. 269-70.

1. The portrait of Scott owned by Ticknor was commissioned by him from Leslie. 2. Cogdell's letter to Ticknor was addressed by WA "Professor Ticknor Boston—." On the address sheet

he wrote, "Mr. Cogdell not recollecting your name, requests me to direct this. W.A." The sheet was endorsed, presumably by Ticknor, "Care of——— / Washington Alston Esq. / Charleston 20 Sept 1853 / Jno. S. Cogdell" (Dartmouth College Library). 3. Presumably Mitchell King (1782-1862), Scottish-born Charleston lawyer and cultural leader ("The Confederate Diary of William John Grayson," ed. Elmer L. Puryear, *SCHGM* 63 [1962]: 225-26); Joel R. Poinsett; and Thomas Smith Grimké (1786-1834), Charleston educator and reformer. 4. No further details about this commission seem to be known. 5. Cogdell entered a cast of his bust of Elliott, his fifth, for exhibition and a possible prize competition in modeling at the BA in February 1833 and wote WA asking him to "exercise an authority" over it after the exhibition was over ("An All-Accomplished Man"). 6. There seems to be no record of this presentation. 7. Cogdell's bust of Washington, his sixth, was shipped to Boston for exhibition at the BA early in 1833 ("An All-Accomplished Man"). 8. The eventual disposal of this painting is not known. 9. William Parker was a shipping broker in Boston, with an address at the custom house in 1833 and 1834 (*Boston City Directory* for 1833-1850/51). 10. Probably WA refers to a notice in the *Boston Daily Advertiser* for 3 October 1833 entitled "Health of the City" reporting a diminishing number of deaths from an epidemic of cholera in New Orleans which he mistook for a report on Charleston, S.C., since it followed a notice from Charleston regarding the loss of rice crops there because of recent high tides. 11. According to Sweetser, Fraser and Robert Charles Winthrop visited WA shortly after he finished *Lorenzo and Jessica,* from *The Merchant of Venice* 5.1.54-69. He inscribed on the back: "Jessica and Lorenzo. 'How sweet the moonlight sleeps upon this bank!' *Merchant of Venice,* Act V, Scene I" together with his name and the date. He repeated to them lines which he had composed on the scene. According to RHD, it was purchased by Patrick T. Jackson for $400 (p. 40). 12. The painting was apparently not exhibited in Charleston.

202. To William Dunlap [15 October 1833][1]

Mr. West, to whom I was soon introduced, received me with the greatest kindness. I shall never forget his benevolent smile when he took me by the hand: it is still fresh in my memory, linked with the last of like kind which accompanied the last shake of his hand, when I took a final leave of him in 1818. His gallery was open to me at all times, and his advice always ready and kindly given. He was a man overflowing with the milk of human kindness. If he had enemies, I doubt if he owed them to any other cause than his rare virtue; which, alas for human nature! is too often deemed cause sufficient.[2]

Of Sir Joshua Reynolds, whose lectures I imported and read before I went to Europe,[3] I have always had a very high opinion. There is a fascination about his pictures which makes it almost ungrateful to think of their defects. They never produced in me any thing like *hesitation,* from the first moment I saw them. His taste was exquisite. Had he been a learned designer, his Infant Hercules,[4] and his Puck, or Robin Goodfellow,[5] show what he might have done in history. I scarcely know, in the whole compass of art, two purer examples of poetic invention.[6] Had it been my happiness to have known him, I would by all means possible to me, have endeavored to ingratiate myself with him.[7]

It is very remarkable, that the three men whose works may be said to have laid the foundation for a new era in art, or, at least, to have revived a good one, should, though contemporaries, have had little or no intercourse with each other; I mean Sir Joshua, Wilson,[8] and Gainsborough:[9] they were scarcely acquainted, and never companions; yet they seem to have emerged, as by consent, with the same power and purpose, from an age of lead.

The following characteristic anecdote of Wilson was told me by Mr. West. Before the Royal Academy was formed, the Society of Painters,[10] (as I think they were then called) held their annual exhibition in Spring Gardens.[11] On a certain year Mr. West and Mr. Wilson happened to be appointed joint *hangers*. It was a memorable year for the crudeness of the performances; in consequence, I suppose, of the unusual number of new adventurers. When the pictures were all up, Wilson, with an expressive grin, began to rub his eyes, as if to clear them of something painful. "I'll tell you what, West," said he, after a while, "this will never do, we shall lose the little credit we have; the public can never stand such a shower of chalk and brick-bats." "Well, what's to be done? We can't reject any pictures now." "Since that's the case, then, we must mend their manners." "What do you mean?" "You shall see," said Wilson, after a pause—"what Indian ink and Spanish liquorice can do." He accordingly despatched the porter to the colour-man and druggist these *reformers;* and, dissolving them in water, actually washed nearly half the pictures in the exhibition with this original glaze. "There," said he, " 'tis as good as asphaltum; with this advantage, that if the artists don't like it they can wash it off when they get the pictures home." And Mr. West acknowledged that "they were all the better for it."[12]

I arrived in London about the middle of June, 1801, near the close of the annual exhibition. The next year, 1802, was the first of my adventuring before the public, when I exhibited three pictures at Somerset House. The principal one, a French Soldier telling a story, (a comic attempt)—a Rocky Coast, (half-length) with Banditti;[13] and a Landscape, with Horsemen, which I had painted at College, as before alluded to. I received two applications for the French Soldier; which I sold to Mr. Wilson,[14] of the European Museum; for whom I afterwards painted a companion to it, also comic—The Poet's Ordinary, where the lean fare was enriched by an incidental arrest.

Malbone returned to America after a short stay—I believe five months—on account of his engagements in Charleston.—I little thought when we parted, that it was for the last time: he died before my return.

Amongst the artists we called upon was Fuseli, to whom we introduced ourselves as Americans. He received us with great courtesy, and invited us into his painting room. Upon my regretting that we had arrived too late to see his Milton Gallery, (it had closed but a few months before) he inquired if I was an artist? I answered, "Not yet; but that I had come to London with the hope of becoming one." He then asked, "In which branch of the art?" I replied, "History." "Then," said he, "you have come *a great way* to starve, sir. There," he added, "is the Milton Gallery," pointing to some rolls of canvas, that reached from the floor nearly to the ceiling. There were three or four, however, belonging to the series still on their stretching frames, which he showed us, and he seemed gratified that we were pleased. But he would not suffer us to like every thing; for when I stopped before one, and expressed the pleasure I felt, (and it was sincere) he said abruptly, "No, sir, you don't like that—you can't like it—'tis bad." As he found, from my quoting Milton, that I was not unacquainted, at least with the subjects of his gallery, he good-naturedly presented me with one of his catalogues. I do not remember the strain in which I talked to Fuseli, but if at all in accordance with the enthusiasm that I felt, I think he could not have been displeased with our visit. I then thought Fuseli the greatest painter living. I am still his admirer, but in a more qualified degree.[15]

Battoni was at that time "in full flower," dividing the empire of art with Mengs.[16] He received Mr. West very graciously in his painting room, and after some questions respecting his country, concerning which he seemed to have had no very distinct notion,—said, "And so, young man, you have come—how far is it?" "Three thousand miles." "Ay, three thousand miles from the woods of America to become a painter! You are very fortunate in coming to Rome at this time, for now you shall see Battoni paint." He thereupon proceeded with his work then in hand, a picture of the Madonna; occasionally exclaiming, as he stept back, to see the effect, "e viva Battoni!"[17]

To Mr. West's character as a man, I will add the following affecting testimony of his wife,[18] a few years before her death. Speaking of him to a lady, a particular friend of mind, she said, "Ah, he is a *good man;* he never had a vice." Mrs. West was then suffering under a paralysis, and could hardly articulate. Such testimony, from one who had been for more than half a century his most intimate companion, is worth more than a volume of eulogy.

I became acquainted with Stuart after my return from Italy, and saw much of him both before, and since my last visit to Europe. Of the character of our intercourse you can form an opinion from these few lines, extracted from an obituary notice of him I wrote (published in the Boston Daily Advertiser, a few days after his decease); his uniform kindness, and the unbroken friendship with which he honoured the writer of this, will never be forgotten. To this I may add, that I learned much from him in my art.[19]

. . . I had a delightful visit from Morse. Its only fault was being too short. The same from my old friend Fraser.[20]

SOURCE: Dunlap, 2:158-61, 187; 1:51, 221, 93; Flagg, p. 40.

1. This letter probably consists of the first quotations about WA's years in London, which come next after his recollections of Bowman, beginning with the reference to West and continuing at least through the reference which Dunlap dated 15 October 1833 (1:221). Dunlap received it on 21 October (*Diary* 3:752). 2. Here Dunlap inserted a paragraph of comment on WA's exclamation and introduced the next quotation with the words, "Of other artists established in London, when Allston visited that city, he speaks thus." 3. WA owned *Works of Sir Joshua Reynolds*, 3d ed., 3 vols. (London, 1801). The collection included, besides Reynolds's fifteen discourses, his

A Journey to Flanders and Holland in the Year MDCCLXXXI; his three letters to *The Tatler;* C.A. du Fresnoy's *The Art of Painting,* trans. William Mason; and Reynold's *Notes on du Fresnoy.* WA must have enjoyed *A Journey to Flanders and Holland,* especially after his visit to these countries in 1803. He might have borrowed a copy of Reynolds's works from the college library when he was a student but it did not acquire one until 1810. 4. Probably the famous *Hercules Strangling the Serpent in His Cradle.* Reynolds also painted an *Infant Hercules.* 5. From *A Midsummer-Night's Dream.* 6. In his lecture "Art" WA cited Reynolds's *Puck* as an example of ideal or poetic invention or truth (p. 98). 7. This sentence comes from Flagg (p. 40), in the context of quotations about Fuseli from WA's letter to Dunlap of 15 October 1833, and was probably omitted by Dunlap. Flagg apparently had access to some of the original texts of WA's letters to Dunlap; he quoted a passage obviously omitted by Dunlap in the letter of ca. 18 February 1834. 8. Richard Wilson. 9. Thomas Gainsborough (1727-88), English portrait and landscape painter. 10. The Society of Painters in Oil and Water Colors was founded in 1804 and had its first exhibition in April 1805. In 1821 it dropped the word "oil" from its name, proposing to admit watercolors only (Whitley, *Art in England, 1800-1820,* 1:318-19). 11. Originally a royal garden, afterward a pleasure resort in Charing Cross, where a large room was used for the exhibition of pictures. 12. Here Dunlap began a new paragraph of quotation, with the words "In one of his letters he has said." 13. *A Seacoast with Banditti.* 14. John Wilson, a native of South Carolina, who founded the European Museum in London in 1789. 15. This and the preceding six paragraphs constitute the series of quotations printed from what was apparently WA's letter to Dunlap of 15 October. Four other quotations, one certainly and an other probably, which was written last, from this letter were printed elsewhere in Dunlap's *History.* Apparently Flagg had access to another part of this letter. In his version of WA's first visit to Fuseli WA said he meant to be an artist "if industry will make me one"; Fuseli replied, "If . . . I have any skill in physiognomy . . . you have more than industry on your side"; WA added, "I have a certain patrimony"; and Fuseli commented, "Ah . . . that makes a difference" (Flagg, p. 39). Subsequently speaking of this interview to an artist friend WA was asked why he did not cultivate a man whom he so much admired and replied that he could not stand Fuseli's profanity. 16. Anton Raphael Mengs (1728-79), German painter. 17. This paragraph, quoted in one of Dunlap's chapters on West, may have occurred in or near the first paragraph in this letter, giving an account of an anecdote about Richard Wilson told him by West. Dunlap introduced it with the words, "Of the latter [Batoni] . . . we have been favoured with the following from Mr. Allston." 18. Elizabeth (Shewell) West (d. 1817), daughter of a Philadelphia merchant. The two sentences about her, quoted in one of Dunlap's chapters on West, may have occurred after anecdotes of West, one certainly and the other probably in this letter. 19. Following this paragraph, quoted in one of Dunlap's chapters on Stuart as from a letter of WA's dated 15 October 1833, Dunlap quoted WA's article on Stuart in its entirety. 20. These two sentences, introduced with the words "Mr. Allston says," occur immediately after Dunlap's quotation from WA's letter of ca. 16 August 1834, but apparently were part of this letter. Morse had intended to go to Boston to exhibit his *Louvre* in the summer of 1833 (Morse to Henry C. Pratt, 26 Mar. 1833, MHS) but finally went shortly before 17 September of that year, on which date he told Dunlap that WA was preparing another letter for him (presumably that of 15 Oct. 1833) and, because of debts and poverty, could not take up *Belshazzar's Feast* for finishing; he was, he said, "painting several small pictures," which he thought would place him beside Raphael in rank. Among them was *Gabriel Setting the Watch at the Gates of Paradise* (1833), from *Paradise Lost* 4.781-83. He eventually destroyed it. The substance of Morse's report of the visit was given by Dunlap in the paragraph in which he quoted Morse as having exclaimed on returning that he went to WA as to the sun (*Diary,* 3:914; *History* 2:187).

203. To John Stevens Cogdell

Cambridge Port, Masstts
25 Oct. 1833.

Dear Cogdell: I wrote you on the 9th inst. in answer to yours of the 27th Sepbr which enclosed a letter to the owner of Sir Walter Scott's picture, with your request concerning it. I have called on Professor Ticknor, to whom the picture belongs, delivered your letter to him, and shewed him the copy of the letter of request to *you*, respecting the bust of Sir Walter, from Messrs King, Poinsett &c, agreeably to my promise. But Mr. Ticknor declines sending the picture to Charleston; which he did, however, in the most delicate and gentlemanly manner. His reasons for declining you will learn from himself, as he told me he should reply immediately to your letter. I exceedingly regret that the circumstances are such as to occasion you disappointment.

I thank you for your kindness to my Mother; of which she made grateful mention in her reply to my last letter. I beg you also to accept my thanks for your kind invitation to me. But you are little aware what an *impossible* thing you propose when you speak of my passing the winter in Charleston. *I am not master of my time,* nor indeed of any thing else, nor shall I be until I have discharged all my obligations. It is always a painful thing to me to speak of my personal concerns; indeed I never even allude to them if I can avoid it. So I will spare both you and myself the unpleasant subject. All I can therefore say is, that I regret I have not the power to accept your friendly offer.

In my last I forgot to ask what you wish to have done with Hagar and Ishmael, as you mentioned, in a Note that accompanied Mr. Elliot's Bust, that you had written me on the subject, <w but> which letter I have never received. The Group is still at the Atheneum, in the same room with the Venus, the Diana and the Antinuous.[1] It is perfectly safe there, and can remain there as long as you wish.—I was glad to hear that White had got a comfortable place in the Custom House.[2] His friend Dana[3] and myself were greatly disappointed in not finding a sale for his Picture.[4] We both hoped to have sold it tolerably well, for it was very much liked; but unfortunately people seemed more disposed to praise than to buy; no one inquired the price. This has been an unlucky year for most of the Artists. We were about to get up a raffle for it, when we found even that avenue closed to us; for it seems that the St. Legislature had passed a law last winter against lotteries of all kinds, specifying even raffles.[5]—I wrote you <at> in my last about Mr. Elliot's bust, how much I was pleased with it &c. We have had an exhibition of the Scotch Statues, in sand-stone, of Tom O'Shanter[6] &c. They are certainly very clever,—and prove the author's genius—Tom and the Landlady are, however, the best.

Pray give my love to my Mother—I have received her kind answer to mine, and will write her before long. And present my best regards to Mrs. Cogdell. Your sincere friend,

Wa. Allston.

ADDRESSED: John S. Cogdell Esqre. / Charleston, / South Carolina. SOURCE: Manuscript. Printed in part in Flagg, p. 270.

1. In 1822 Augustus Thorndike presented the BA casts of eleven full-length ancient statues, which included those of the *Venus dei Medici*, the *Capitoline Venus*, the *Diana of Versailles* or *the Hind*, and the *Capitoline Antinuous*. WA and the sculptor and architect Solomon Willard suggested the height of the column to support the bust of the *Apollo Belvedere* which was presented to the BA in 1825 by Pickering (Swan, pp. ix, 134, 136, 137). 2. John B. White served as a coastwise inspector of customs from December 1832 through 1857. 3. Edmund T. Dana. 4. White's painting *The Grave Robbers*. It was exhibited at the BA in 1833 as for sale. 5. In March the Massachusetts legislature passed a bill providing for penalties from $100 to $2,000 to be exacted for selling lottery tickets, from three to twelve months incarceration for repeated offenses, and from $100 to $2,000 for allowing premises to be used for such sale, and offered a reward of $50 for information leading to conviction in such cases (*Boston Daily Advertiser*, 26 Feb., 12 Mar. 1833). 6. An exhibition of three statues by the Scottish-born James Thom (1799-1850) was held at Harding's Gallery in September and October, closing on 26 October 1833: *Tam O'Shanter, Souter Johnny,* and *The Landlord and Landlady (Boston Daily Advertiser,* 8, 26 Oct. 1833). In Robert Burns's poem "Tam O'Shanter" Tam and his crony Souter Johnny pass the early part of the evening on Tam's way home from market drinking with the landlord and his wife in an inn.

204. To William Dunlap [4 November 1833][1]

It was, a few years ago, with many criticizing people (not critics, except those can be called so *who make their own ignorance the measure of excellence*) to laugh at Fuseli. But Fuseli, even when most extravagant, was not a man to be laughed at; for his very extravagancies (even when we felt them as such) had *that* in them which carried us along with them. All he asked of the spectator was but a *particle* of *imagination,* and his wildest freaks would then defy the reason. Only a true genius can do this. But he was far from being always extravagant: he was often sublime, and has left no equal in the *visionary*; his spectres and witches were born and died with him. As a critic on the art, I know no one so *inspiring*. Having, as you know, no gallery of the old masters to visit here, I often refresh my memory of them with some of his articles in Pilkington's Dictionary;[2] and he brings them before me in a way that no other man's *words* could: he even gives me a distinct apprehension of the style and colour of some whose works I have never seen. I often read one or two of his articles before I go into my painting room; they form indeed almost a regular course at breakfast.

Before I leave Fuseli I must tell you a whimsical anecdote, which I had from Stuart. He was one day at Raphael Smith's,[3] the engraver, when Fuseli, to whom Stuart was then unknown, came in; who having some private business, was taken into another room. "I know that you are a great physiognomist,[4] Mr. Fuseli," said Smith. "Well, what if I am?" "Pray did you observe the gentleman I was talking with just now?" "I saw the man." "What then?" "Why I wish to know if you think he can paint." "Umph!—I don't know but he might—*he has a coot leg.*"[5] Poor Stuart! that same leg—which I well remember to have been a finely formed one, became the subject of a characteristic joke with him but a few weeks before he died. I asked "how he was?" He was then very much emaciated. "Ah!" said he, "you can judge;" and he drew up his pantaloons. "You see how much I am out of drawing."[6]

Now I have got into anecdote, I will relate another, though not at all relevant to this communication, of Sir Wm. Beechy. A young artist one day brought a picture, for the benefit of Sir William's criticism. "Very well, C.," said Beechy;—"very well indeed. You have improved, C. But C. why did you make the coat and the back-ground of the same colour?" "For harmony, sir." "Oh, no! C. that's not harmony, that's monotony." I have often thought this anecdote would have *told* for the latter in Lord Byron's perverse controversy with Mr. Bowles.[7]

I will add another, as little to my purpose, of Fuseli, after he became keeper to the Royal Academy.[8] "Well, Sam," said Fuseli to Strouzer,[9] the academy porter, "what do you think of this picture?" "Law! Mr. Fuseli, I don't know any thing of pictures." "But you know a horse, Sam; you have been in the Guards, you can tell if that is like a horse?" "Yes, sir," "Well?" "Why it seems to me, then, Mr. Fuseli, that—that five men could ride on him." "Then you think his back too long." "A bit, sir."[10]

Titian, Tintoret, and Paul Veronese, absolutely enchanted me, for they took away all sense of subject. When I stood before the Peter Martyr, the Miracle of the Slave, and the marriage of Cana,[11] I thought of nothing but of the *gorgeous concert of colours,* or rather of the indefinite forms (I cannot call them sensations) of pleasure with which they filled the imagination. It was the poetry of colour which I felt; procreative in its nature, giving birth to a thousand things which the eye cannot see, and distinct from their cause. I did not, however stop to analyze my feelings—perhaps at that time I could not have done it. I was content with my pleasure without seeking the cause. But I now understand it, and *think* I understand *why* so many great colourists, especially Tintoret and Paul Veronese gave so little heed to the ostensible *stories* of their compositions. In some of them, the Marriage of Cana for instance, there is not the slightest clue given by which the spectator can guess at the subject. They addressed themselves not to the senses merely, as some have supposed, but rather through them to that region (if I may so speak) of the imagination which is supposed to be under the exclusive dominion of music, and which, by similar excitement, they caused to teem with visions that "lap the soul in Elysium."[12] In other words, they leave the subject to be made by the spectator, provided he possesses the imaginative faculty—otherwise they will have little more meaning to him than a calico counterpane.[13]

I am by nature, as it respects the arts, a *wide liker.*[14] I cannot honestly turn up my nose at even a piece of still life, since, if well done, it gives me pleasure. This remark will account for otherwise strange transitions. I will mention here a picture of a totally different kind, which then took great hold of me, by Lodovico Carracci. I do not remember the title, but the subject was the body of the virgin borne for interment by four apostles.[15] The figures are colossal; the tone dark, and of tremendous depth of colour. It seemed as I looked at it as if the ground shook under their tread, and the air were darkened by their grief.[16]

I may here notice a false notion which is current among artists, in the interpretation they put on the axiom that "something should always be left to the imagination," viz: that some parts of a picture should be left *unfinished*. The very statement betrays its unsoundness: for that which is unfinished must necessarily be *imperfect;* so that according to this rule *imperfection* is made essential to *perfection*. The error lies in the phrase, "left to the imagination," and it has filled modern art with random flourishes of no meaning. If the axiom be intended to prevent the impertinent obtrusion of subordinate objects, (the fault certainly of a mean practice) I may observe that the remedy is no remedy, but rather a less fault substituted for a greater. Works of a high order, aspiring to the poetical, cannot make good their pretensions, unless they *do affect* the imagination; and *this* should be the test—that they set to work, not to finish what is less incomplete, but to awaken images *congenial* to the compositions, but not *in* them expressed; an effect that never was yet realized by misrepresenting any thing. If the objects introduced into a picture *keep their several places* as well in the deepest shadow as in light, the general effect will suffer nothing by their truth; but to give the *whole* truth in the midnight as well as in the daylight, belongs to a master.[17]

I am glad to hear of the safe arrival of my friend Leslie and his family.[18] He is a valuable acquisition to our country, for he is a good man as well as a great artist. Leslie, Irving, and Sir Thomas Lawrence were the last persons I shook hands with on leaving London. Irving and Leslie had accompanied me to the stage-office, and Sir Thomas, who was passing by on his morning ride, kindly stopped to offer me his good wishes. It is pleasant to have the last interview with those whom we wish to remember associated with kind feelings. I regret that the *res angusti domi* prevent my being one at the *dinner of welcome* which you propose giving to Leslie. Pray say for me that I bid him welcome from my heart; no one values him more, for no one better knows his value.

SOURCE: Dunlap, 2:161-64, 245.

1. Probably the quotation in WA's letter to Dunlap beginning with the second series of recollections of Fuseli, followed by those of his visit to Paris, and concluding with the remark about the error of saying a picture should be left unfinished come from the letter containing the reference to Leslie's arrival in America, which Dunlap dated 4 November 1833 (2:245); he received it on 8 November (*Diary* 3:756). He introduced it with the words, "On another occasion, and in another letter, Mr. Allston gives the following opinion of Fuseli." 2. Matthew Pilkington, *A Dictionary of Painters, from the Revival of Art to the Present Period,* ed. Henry Fuseli (London, 1805, possibly earlier, and 1810). For a time, at any rate, WA was using Morse's copy (Morse to his parents, 21 March 1821, Morse Papers, LC). 3. John Raphael Smith (1752-1812), the father of John Rubens Smith. 4. Fuseli was a close friend of the German physiognomist Johann Kasper Lavater and translated his *Aphorisms*. Probably WA was led to some extent by Fuseli to an interest in physiognomy. In one of his aphorisms WA declared phrenologists to be right in placing the organ of self-love in the back of the head, since thereby a vain man saw everyone he approached

obscured by his own shadow, and in the "Introductory Discourse" of his lectures on art he suggested that every man was to a certain extent a physiognomist in being led by instinct to feel instantaneous sympathies and antipathies toward strangers (*LA*, pp. 24, 169). 5. Presumably meaning like the leg of the bird of that name. One of Stuart's legs was noticeably leaner than the other (Mount, p. 30). 6. This was reportedly the only reference Stuart ever made to his leg (Mount, p. 30). 7. Byron engaged in a controversy for several years with the clergyman and poet William Lisle Bowles (1762-1850) regarding Bowles's harsh criticism of Pope's poetry and moral character in his edition of Pope in 1806. It went of for several years, from Byron's *English Bards and Scotch Reviewers* (1809) to Bowles's *Two Letters to the Right Honourable Lord Byron* (1821) and afterward (Jacob Johan Van Renner, *Bowles, Byron and the Pope-Controversy* [New York: Haskill House, 1966]. Hazlitt criticized Byron's position in *Lectures on the English Poets*, which WA knew. 8. Fuseli was made keeper of the RA in 1804. 9. Otherwise unidentified. 10. Here Dunlap inserted a paragraph about WA's visit to Paris in 1803 and introduced the next quotation with the words, "Mr. Allston, in the letter before mentioned, thus expresses his feelings on visiting this splendid accumulation of plunder." 11. Titian's *St. Peter Martyr*, Tintoretto's *Miracle of the Slave*, and Veronese's *Marriage at Cana*. 12. "Lap me soft in Lydian Aires" (Milton, "L'Allegro," line 36). 13. Here Dunlap inserted a paragraph commenting on WA's distinction between color and story and introduced the next quotation with the words, "In pursuing the subject, Allston says." 14. In his lecture "Composition," WA said "the greatest geniuses, as presenting a wider field for excitement, are generally found to be the widest likers" (*LA*, p. 155) and defended paintings of still life. 15. *Interment of the Virgin*. 16. Here Dunlap inserted a paragraph about Carracci and introduced the next quotation with the words "The painter-poet goes on thus." 17. This paragraph concludes the series of quotations of WA's recollections of his visit to Paris in 1803 from what was apparently WA's letter to Dunlap of 4 November 1833. The next paragraph, certainly from this letter, which was probably written last, was printed in Dunlap's account of Leslie. 18. Dunlap wrote WA of the arrival of Leslie and his family in America on 23 October 1833 (*Diary* 3:752) and of the proposal of the NAD to give him a dinner. Leslie declined but spent his last evening in America with the members by invitation (*Diary* 3:752; *History* 2:245).

205. To Charles Robert Leslie Cambridge Port, Massachusetts, 6th November, 1833.

Dear Leslie: As I suppose you well know—increase of years has failed to impress me with a better sense than I formerly had of the charms of Letter-writing—and I do not mean to write a letter now. But I cannot deny myself the gratification of sending you a line, to congratulate you on your safe arrival,[1] and to welcome you among us. <I [undecipherable word]> I have no friend to whom I can more heartily <bid> say, *right welcome*.

Pray present my best regards to your Wife and Children;[2] whom I am predisposed to like on your account, and whom I have no doubt I shall like when I see them on their own. My Wife, who better knows you by *your letters*, than yours can me by *mine*, <an> joins me in this.—I regret that a visit now to New-York is to me among the minor impossibilities; for gold I have none, and all the silver I have is *on my head*.

Faithfully yours, / Wa. Allston.

As I know not where this may find you, I shall direct it to the care of our friend Morse.

ADDRESSED: Charles R. Leslie Esqre. R.A. / Care of S.F.B. Morse Esqre / President of the National / Academy of Design, / New-York. The original address has been canceled and "West Point / N.Y." written in in another hand. SOURCE: Manuscript. Printed in Flagg, pp. 270-71.

1. Leslie and his family came to America at this time in order for him to take a position as teacher of drawing at the United States Military Academy at West Point. Dissatisfied, he returned to England in April 1834 (Leslie, pp. 80, 83, 85). 2. Leslie had at this time five children: Robert Charles, Harriet Jane, Caroline Anna, Bradford (b. 18 Aug. 1831), and Mary (b. 18 June 1833) (Leslie, pp. 265, 278, 283, 292, 293).

206. From Horatio Greenough Florence. Dec 8th 1833.

Dear Mr Alston: I had hoped to have been nearer you by this but have concluded that it would be wrong to risk a long journey before my model is compleated.[1] I have heard of you often—but not so often or quite so directly as I could have wished. Has not your picture from the Italian been engraved?[2] I should like much to see the composition—I learned with pleasure that you had declined a picture for South Carolina on account of your engagements—My poor brother Harry after struggling against the influence of this climate has at length returned home—I know it will not be necessary to ask of you before hand the favour of your counsel and assistance for him in prosecuting the study of painting—but I think I can tell you in a few words what you might not see at once—that he wants encouragement—not excitement for his fibre won't bear it, but gentle and soothing encouragement. To expect much of him seems to palsy him, to be pleased with what he has effected frightens him less—He is good and pure of heart to an uncommon degree. I can't squeeze out of my correspondents any satisfactory news of Mr Dana—I trust Harry will give me [a] treat in that way—The number of artists has much increased in America within a few years—I begin to hope that we shall be numerous enough soon to keep each other warm—I firmly believe that—our claims to respect and encouragement are more fairly viewed in the U States than elsewhere and I do not say this rashly—In France they come nearest us but it savours of nationality perhaps more than of the love of poetry. In Italy the mass with the finest susceptibilities are too ignorant too corrupted to comprehend or feel as they should—The English tone of Art seems to me a sickly exotic—I can't speak of their real connoisseurs because I never have fallen in with them except they were artists—but I have known a greater number of educated refined English who did not care a pin for Art than of every other nation put together. I have just seen the first number of a National Portrait Gallery[3]—in which is one of Harding's portraits—right well engraved—It has comforted me much—The portrait is of Carroll[4] and is excellent. I shewed it at the coffee house last evening and it surprised the Italians.

This book reminds me that Mr Dunlap wrote me he was also concerned in a work relating to art and Artists in America[5] and he said he meant to speak of me—asked the time and place of my birth and accounts of what turned my attention to Sculpture. Now I have just begun to work and to make my attempts a matter of public print further than the news of the day seems to me to risk blowing up of a bladder for those who are to follow to jump on—He says he has obtained much valuable information respecting art in [the] U S from you—I am delighted that a pen is at work in putting down what you have seen and known of this—It will be invaluable—But I hope I do not ask too much when I request you when you write him to say in a few words the substance of what I feel on this point. If as a beginner in the regular practice of Sculpture I have a local and temporary importance (which may be) he may easily say in a note of 30 lines all I ever did. My pride more than any modesty is concerned in this. I have made a model of 2½ feet of the Statue of Washington. I have made him seated—looking straight forward—with a sheathed sword in his left hand and with his right pointing to heaven. He is dressed in a large mantle whose hem is embroidered with stars. He sits on a massive chair ornamented with fruits flowers and Naval and Military trophies—the large spaces on the back of which are filled by bas reliefs representing virtues personified. The hind posts of the chair are surmounted on each side by an Eagle—I shall try to have the sketch pass through Boston on its way to Washington that you may give me your opinion.[6] I beg you will pity me as a sojourner in the land of strangers—I am a poor land-bird at sea—I am tired—but there is as yet no lighting place—I can't turn waterfowl—My notions of men and things are just what they were when I sail'd. A few years and I shall I trust sit by you and smoke and look out a window at the trees and sky of Cambridge—It will seem but a moment then—these months and years of absence—I hear nothing of John[7]—His heart must be made of stern stuff. I only hope he will be true to himself since he seems to forget us—Naturally his impulses were generous and kind—but he was unfortunate—Begging you will present my respectful remembrance to Mrs Alston—to the Misses Dana[8] and to our Poet[9] who is become every bodies' Poet at last that you will tell the Master that I pine to laugh and cry with him. I remain—Yours truly—

Horatio Greenough

ADDRESSED: Washington Alston Esqre / Boston. Mass. SOURCE: Greenough, *Letters*, pp. 169-71.

1. Greenough considered taking the suggestion of Cooper in the summer of 1832 that he accompany him to America, partly to examine the site proposed for the statue of Washington, but declined it because he had not yet had firm confirmation of his commission (Wright, p. 121; Greenough, *Letters*, pp. 145-46). 2. Possibly Greenough refers to *Italian Landscape* (G62), which was not engraved. The only other engraving of a painting by WA about this time was of *Beatrice* in 1834. 3. The *National Portrait Gallery of Distinguished Americans*, ed. James Herring and James B. Longacre (1834), was issued under the superintendence of the American Academy of Fine Arts. 4. Charles Carroll (1737-1806), signer of the Declaration of Indepen-

dence, member of the Continental Congress, and U.S. senator. The engraving appeared in the *National Portrait Gallery* 1:3. 5. Dunlap's *A History of the Rise and Progress of the Arts of Design in the United States*. 6. It did not go through Boston and WA never saw it. 7. John Greenough, then living in London. 8. Elizabeth Ellery Dana and Sarah Ann Dana. 9. RHD, whose *Poems and Prose Writings* was published in 1833.

207. To John Stevens Cogdell Cambridge Port, Masstts
18 Decbr. 1833.

Dear Cogdell: Your letter of the 2d of November has reached me safe. By its date I find that you could not then have got my last letter of October 25th; in which I expressed to you my thanks for your kind invitation, while I stated the *impossibility* of my availing myself of it; but, as you must have received that letter within a few days after you last wrote, it is not necessary to repeat its contents. You must allow me, however, to correct one mistake under which you labour. I have never at any time stood in need of any "inducement" to visit my Mother; that I have not long ago seen her <was> is simply because it was not in my power.

I regret that I have not yet been able to execute your commission respecting the tracing of Sir Walter Scott's portrait. Among other hindrances was the state of my health. I have been much out of order for several weeks, and for the last week confined to my chamber. I write now from a sick room. The Doctr's visits, however, have ceased; he tells me I have no farther need of him, and that I am doing very well. I find my strength returned, in spite of blister and gruel, and expect to be out and at work again in a few days: as soon as I am, and can venture as far as Boston, I will make the tracing of Sir Walter, which shall be forwarded to you as soon as done. As it cannot well be transmitted in a letter without danger of being spoiled, I shall put it into a tin case, and request the favour of Mr. Ticknor to ship it for me by the first vessel to Charleston.

In the meantime will you permit me to make a few remarks on your proposed undertaking. You have, in the first place, to enter the lists with Chantrey; who, whatever may be thought of his Washington, has never failed in his portraits when modelled after the *life*. Where he has had the advantage of a living original, he has always been eminently successful. It was indeed the opinion of Mr. West, that in this particular branch of the Art (*portrait*) he has not been surpassed since the time of the Greeks: this also is the general opinion in England. In the next place, his bust of Scott[1] has been most especially celebrated for its fidelity; <and as well> in our own country, as well as in Europe, for all here who <have> ever saw Sir Walter say the likeness could not be better. In fact, from all I have <speak> heard said of it, and from all accounts of it which I have read, there seems to be but one opinion—namely, that the likeness is perfect. Under how great a disadvantage then must any new competition labour against a work of reputation so general and so fixed.—If in yours <model> you imitate Chantrey's Bust, your work will be considered a *copy*;

and (as you well know) no copy of a work of Art ever gains the copyist any credit worth having. If you do not follow Chantrey, you must of course *deviate* from him, and you have only the traced outlines from a picture as your guide; with the peculiar disadvantage of never having seen the living man. Is the deviation, then, thus forced by necessity upon you, likely to be in your favour? I think in the nature of things it is not. And if *your* bust prove not a better likeness, whatever may be its merits in other respects, it must fail of success. It must be acknowledged *better*, or it will not be valued. Now *this acknowledgement* is to be made by a Public already satisfied, and prepossessed in favour of its rival. I cannot think that any Sculptor,—however great his genius, could with such disadvantages, such formidable odds against him, stand any chance of success. Should he succeed at all, it must be by mere accident; for the chances against him are as a thousand to one.—If your object were simply the gratification of the Friends who requested you to model the bust, the case might be different, as *they*, knowing all these circumstances, would doubtless make every allowance. But your view is farther; you express a hope of reputation by this effort elsewhere, in "England or Scotland." For the reasons above, I fear your hope will not be realized. The Public rarely, if ever, in any country make allowance, either with or without knowledge of circumstances. When <they> it does <the> allowance comes in shape of such *qualified* approbation as to amount to little indeed.

I have made these remarks conscientiously, and in kindness, and offer them from a sense of duty, on the supposition that they might not have occurred to you. On the subject, however, I offer no advice; I only submit the objections for your consideration, that you may take counsel with yourself, and act as you shall think best.

Pray present my best regards to Mrs. Cogdell. I have begun a letter to my Mother, which I shall finish tomorrow; I have only a few lines to add.

Your sincere friend, / Wa. Allston.

The tracing will probably be made, and on its way, before this reaches you. In making it I will attend to all the particulars you have suggested. Mrs. A. joins me in regards to Mrs. C. & yourself.

ADDRESSED: John S. Cogdell Esqre. / Charleston, / South Carolina. ANNOTATED by Cogdell: answered by Vessel / 2 Jany 1834. SOURCE: Manuscript.

1. WA refers to the bust of Scott executed by Chantrey in 1820.

208. To Jonathan Mason Cambridge Port, 27 Decbr 1833.

Dear Sir: I have just had a pressing demand made on me by my Coal Merchant, and another smaller one equally urgent, both together amounting to about a hundred and fifty dollars, which I wish to settle immediately, <and> but which I have no means of doing until Mr. Phillips's[1] picture[2] is finished. You know that I am now at work on this picture; but you also know that it is impossible for me to name precisely the day when it will be completed; all I *can* say is, that I shall not touch another picture, but devote my time exclusively to this, until it is finished.

In this my strait, would your brother, Mr. Powell Mason,[3] who acts for Mr. Phillipps, be willing to advance me this sum (150 dollars) out of what will be due me on the picture's completion? I ask this not as a right (for I have none) but as a favour. Should he not feel authorized to make the advance, or otherwise object, I beg it may not be *pressed*. Also I beg to assure you, that I shall have *no ill feeling* on the subject, should he think it proper to refuse it.

Will you favour me with an answer to this as soon as you conveniently can.— And will you be so good as to get for me at Dix's[4] a small phial of japanner's gold size, and a phial of the *dark* drying-oil, to make magilp with; and find a place for them in your pocket the next time you favour me with a visit. I would not trouble you with this last commission, if I had not forgotten the name of Dix's partner, who stands *first* in the firm—so that I cannot write to them for these articles, as I otherwise <should> would. They will charge them to me.

Yours sincerely, / Wa. Allston.

Should any one now offer me three hundred dollars for the Troubadour,[5] I would sell it for that sum. I have, however, given up all hope of selling it; so that I cannot be disappointed, if it does not sell at this price.

Mr. E.T. Dana has been very ill, but <has> is now getting better. He is however still too ill to see company.

ADDRESSED: Jonathan Mason Esqre. / Mount Vernon, / Boston. SOURCE: Manuscript, Manuscripts Division, Special Collections Department, University of Virginia Library. Printed in part in Flagg, p. 271.

1. Jonathan Phillips (1778-1860), Boston merchant and philanthropist. He opened a store for the sale of hardware about 1801 and operated it until 1826, for several of those years with his brother. He served in the state legislature and senate, was the first president of the Perkins Institute, and often participated in conversations at Channing's home ("Marriages and Deaths," *NEGHR* 14 [1860]: 371; Charles K. Dillaway, "Education, Past and Present," Justin Winsor, "Libraries in Boston", and George Ripley, "Philosophic Thought in Boston," in Winsor, 4:267, 272, 288, 301; "Quarterly Meeting," *Proceedings of the MHS*, 1st ser., 1 [1791-1835] [1879]: 173-74).

2. Presumably the chalk *The Angel Pouring Out the Vial of Wrath over Jerusalem* (ca. 1840), from Rev. 16:17. West also painted the subject. RHD thought it was this painting (p. 16, Addition). According to Jarvis, WA said that the idea came to him during a severe illness in 1829 and that he intended it for a man who had paid him in advance, leaving the selection to him. At that time he began a sketch and modeled the figure of the angel. He was dissatisfied with the first design, however, and obliterated it. On 9 July 1840 he began it again but laid it aside the day after the outline was completed, "in despair," he said, unable to satisfy himself, though his labour on it altogether had been enough to finish a dozen paintings. He was disturbed that "Unkind observations" had been made that he had not treated the man well, estimated that the money he had received would not have covered his expenses while working on it, said that when he afterward painted another for the man it was accepted, and commented that the conclusion of the matter was to his great relief, since "that debt will not trouble me any more." RHD recorded more than once

the labor which WA bestowed on this work and the distress which his failure to complete it caused him, saying that no one could know the "misery of mind this whole affair cost him," until at last "a judicious few" told him it must be laid aside, since he could never finish it while "in such a mental condition." At one point he found the canvas too small and transferred it to a larger one. It is possible that the wrathful nature of the subject, comparable but imagistically unlike that of *Jeremiah,* proved uncongenial to him. The original price set by WA, according to RHD, was $1,000, of which $500 was paid in advance. While it was being painted RHD said to WA that he supposed it would be better worth $1,500 than $1,000, and WA replied, "That it will." WA "would rather starve," RHD added, "than that this should go to Mr. Phillips" (Note on the back of the painting; RHD to William P. Mason, 2 Sept. 1839, Miscellaneous Bound, MHS; RHD, p. 16, Addition; Channing to Jonathan Mason, 24 July 1834, Dana Papers). It seems likely that *Heliodorus Driven from the Temple* (1830s), from 2 Macc. 3:24-27, another unfinished painting of WA's begun about the same time as *The Angel Pouring out the Vial of Wrath over Jerusalem,* is related to that painting. The central figures in both are supenatural agents and are similar in bodily posture and in elevation above an earthly scene. The subjects of both are also similar, in that each depicts a violent visitation of divine judgment on sinful men. It was not a subject congenial to WA, only prophesied in *Jeremiah* and in the unfinished *Belshazzar's Feast.* 3. William Powell Mason (1791-1867), Boston lawyer, brother of Jonathan Mason ("Necrology of the New-England Historic, Genealogical Society," prepared by Dorus Clarke, *NEGHR* 28 [1874]: 96). He owned WA's *Landscape with a Lake.* 4. Apollos Morris and Elbridge Dix operated a paint store in Boston for a short time (*Boston City Directory* for 1833-35). 5. *Young Troubadour.*

209. To Jonathan Mason [11 February 1834]

I am so much *pushed* that I have come to the conclusion to lower the price of the Troubador, [to $280][1]— if that can't be obtained—to $250[2] [but is resolved to keep it if that cannot be obtained. He tells Mr. M. not to delay the offer of the lowest sum, $250, for a day, if the first can't be obtained.] I would not, however, have it longer than one day, as I am so sadly pressed.

SOURCE: RHD, p. 17, 17 Addition.

1. The words in brackets in this letter are RHD's. 2. RHD thought it "exquisite" but that no one had "taste enough" to buy it. By the end of February 1833 it was in the possession of Sarah Gibbs in Newport. WA at last "parted with it," RHD said, for $70 or $80, presumably to John Bryant, Jr. (P. 17 and Addition).

210. To William Dunlap [ca. 18 February 1834][1]

[T]he impressions left by the sublime scenery of Switzerland, are still fresh to this day. A new world had been opened to me—nor have I met with any thing like it since. The scenery of the Appenines is quite of a different character. By the by, I was particularly struck in this journey with the truth of Turner's Swiss scenes—the poetic truth—which none before or since have given; with the exception of my friend Brokedon's magnificent work,[2] on the passes of the Alps. I passed at night and saw the sun rise on the Lake Maggiore. Such a sunrise! The giant Alps seemed literally to rise from their purple beds, and putting on their crowns of gold, to send up a hallelujah almost audible.[3]

It is needless to say how I was affected by Raffaele, the greatest master of the affections in our art. In beauty he has often been surpassed, but in grace—the native grace of character—in the expression of intellect, and above all, sanctity, he has no equal. What particularly struck me in his works was, the *genuine* life (if I may so call it) that seemed, without impairing the distinctive character, to pervade them all; for even his humblest figures have a *something* either in look, air, or gesture, akin to the *venustas*[4] of his own nature, as if like living beings under the influence of a master-spirit, they had partaken, in spite of themselves, a portion of the charm which swayed them. This power of infusing one's *own life,* as it were, into that which is feigned, appears to me the sole prerogative of genius. In a work of art, this is what a man may well call *his own*; for it cannot be borrowed or imitated. Of Michael Angelo, I know not how to speak in adequate terms of reverence. With all his faults (but who is without them) even Raffaele bows before him. As I stood beneath his colossal prophets and sybils, still more colossal in spirit—I felt as if in the presence of messengers from the other world, with the destiny of man in their breath, in repose even terrible. I cannot agree with Sir Joshua that the "Vision of Ezekiel," of Raffaele, or the Moses of Parmegiano,[5] have any thing in common with Michael Angelo.[6] Their admiration of Michael Angelo may have elevated their forms into a more dignified and majestic race; but still left them *men,* whose feet had never trod other than this earth. The supernatural was beyond the reach of both. But no one would mistake the prophets of Michael Angelo for inhabitants of our world; yet they are true to the imagination, as the beings about us are to the senses. I am not undervaluing these great artists, when I deny them a kindred genius with Michael Angelo; they had both a genius of their own, and high qualities which nature had denied the other.[7]

I would recommend modelling to all young painters as one of the best means of acquiring an accurate knowledge of the joints; I have occasionally practiced it ever since.[8]

I have had occasion in former letters more than once to mention the name of another most valued friend, of which I would gladly say more, did not I feel that it is not for me to do justice to his extraordinary powers. I would observe, however, that to no other man whom I have known, do I owe so much *intellectually,* as to Mr. Coleridge, with whom I became acquainted in Rome, and who has honoured me with his friendship for more than five and twenty years. He used to call Rome the *silent* city; but I never could think of it as such, while with him; for, meet him when, or where I would, the fountain of his mind was never dry, but like the far-reaching aqueducts that once supplied this mistress of the world, its living stream seemed specially to flow for every classic ruin over which we wandered. And when I recall some of our walks under the pines of the Villa Borghese, I am almost tempted to dream that I had once listened to Plato, in the groves of the Academy. It was there he taught me this golden rule: *never to judge of any work of art by its defects;* a rule as wise as benevolent; and one that while it has spared me much pain, has widened my sphere of pleasure.[9]

My first work after returning to London—with the exception of two small pictures,[10] (if they can be called exceptions, which were carried on at the same time with the larger one) was the "Dead man revived by Elisha's bones," which is now in Philadelphia. My progress in this picture was interrupted by a dangerous illness, which after some months of great suffering, compelled me to remove to Clifton, near Bristol. My recovery, for which I was endebted under providence, to one of the best friends, and most skilfull of the faculty, was slow and painful, leaving me still an invalid when I returned to London—and indeed as my medical friend predicted, in some degree so to this day. The "Dead man," was first exhibited at the British Institution, common called the British Gallery—an institution patronized by the principal nobility and gentry—the Prince Regent[11] then president: it there obtained the first prize of two hundred guineas. As I returned to London, chiefly to finish this picture, that done, I went back to Bristol where I painted and left a number of pictures; among these were half-length portraits of my friend Mr. Coleridge,[12] and my medical friend Mr. King[13] of Clifton. I have painted but few portraits, and these I think are my best. So far as I can judge of my own production the likeness of Coleridge is a true one, but it is Coleridge in repose; and, though not unstirred by the perpetual ground-swell of his ever-working intellect, and shadowing forth something of the deep philosopher, it is not Coleridge in his highest mood, the poetic state, when the divine afflatus of the poet possessed him. When in that state, no face that I ever saw was like his; it seemed almost spirit made visible without a shadow of the physical upon it. Could I then have fixed it upon canvas! but it was beyond the reach of my art. He was the greatest man I have ever known, and one of the best; as his nephew, Henry Nelson,[14] truly said, "a thousand times more sinned against than sinning"![15]

My second journey to London was followed by a calamity of which I cannot speak—the death of my wife—leaving me nothing but my art—which then seemed to me as nothing. But of my domestic concerns I shall avoid speaking, as I do not consider them proper subjects for *living* biography.[16]

Next to my own country I love England,[17] the land of my ancestors. I should indeed be ungrateful if I did not love a country from which I have never received other than kindness: in which, even during the late war, I was never made to feel that I was a foreigner. By the English artists, among whom I number some of my most valued friends, I was uniformly treated with openness and liberality. Out of the art too I found many fast and generous friends.—And here—though I record a compliment to myself, I cannot deny myself the satisfaction of repeating the kind words of Lord Egremont, a few weeks before I left England. "I hear you are going to America," he said. "I am sorry for it.—Well, if you do not meet with the encouragement which you deserve, in your own country, we shall all be very glad to see you back again." This munificent nobleman had done me the honour to introduce himself to me, and is the possessor of one of my best pictures, "Jacob's Dream."

I have ventured to allow myself this piece of egotism, for the sake of my countrymen, who, I hope, will never let any deserving British artist, who should come among us, feel that he is not welcome. England has never made any distinction between our artists and her own—never may America. In reference to Lord E.'s kind speech, I must stop here to say, that I have received from my countrymen the kindest treatment and the most liberal encouragement—far indeed from what I ever expected, for which I cannot be too grateful.[18]

Among the many persons from whom I received attentions, during my residence in London, I must not omit Col. Trumbull,[19] who always treated me with the utmost courtesy. Among my English friends it is no disparagement to any to place at their head Sir George Beaumont. It is pleasant to think of my obligations to such a man—*a gentleman in his very nature*. Gentle, brilliant, generous—I was going to attempt his character, but I will not; it was so peculiar and finely textured, that I know but one man who could draw it, and that's Coleridge, who knew him well—to know whom was to honour.[20]

A home-sickness which (in spite of some of the best and kindest friends, and every encouragement that I could wish as an artist) I could not overcome, brought me back to my own country in 1818. We made Boston Harbour on a clear evening in October. It was an evening to remember! The wind fell and left our ship almost stationary on a long low swell, as smoothe as glass and undulating under one of our gorgeous autumnal skies like a prairie of amber. The moon looked down upon us like a living thing, as if to bid us welcome, and the fanciful thought is still in my memory that she broke her image on the water to make partners for a dance of fire-flies—and they *did* dance, if I ever saw dancing. Another thought recurs: that I had returned to a mighty empire—that I was in the very waters, which the gallant Constitution[21] had first broken, whose building I saw when at college, and whose "slaughter-breaking [breathing] brass," to use a quotation from worthy Cotton Mather's magnalia, *but now* 'grew hot and spoke' *her name* among the nations!"[22] This patriotic feeling is not a thing for which any credit is claimed, it would only have been discreditable to have been without it.

SOURCES: Dunlap, 2:165-68, 182-83; Flagg, p. 104.

1. The date of this letter is based on the next several quotations from WA's recollections in Dunlap after the letter of 4 November 1833, the first of which appears in the first paragraph of a new chapter in Dunlap; the quotations relate to his experiences after Paris: his trip through Switzerland, stay in Italy, second stay in England, and return to America in 1818, which altogether form a unit and would thus seem to constitute the substance of the letter which Dunlap received on 21 February 1834. It is preceded by references to the paintings WA did in Paris and to his route from there to Italy and introduced with the words, "The traveller in one of his letters, says."

2. *Illustrations of the Passes of the Alps, by which Italy Communicates with France, Switzerland, and Germany*, 2 vols. (London, 1828). WA owned a copy. 3. Here Dunlap inserted a paragraph about WA's acquaintances in Rome and introduced the next quotation with the words,

"Of the effects produced by the great masters of the by-gone days of Italy, on such a mind as Allston's, some idea may be formed from the following effusion of his pen." 4. *Venustá*: beauty. 5. Girolamo Francesco Maria Mazzuoli or Mazzola (1504-40), Italian painter, called Il Parmigiano. 6. In Discourse 15 Reynolds called Raphael's *Vision of Ezekiel* one of his "inventions" from Michelangelo, one of "many rays, which discover manifestly the centre from which they emanated," and said Parmigiano's young mind was "impregnated with the sublimity of Michael Angelo" though he could not draw correctly, but that in his depiction of Moses breaking the tablets he overcame his first defects in "correctness of drawing" and "grandeur of the conception," presumably there following in Michelangelo's tradition. 7. Here Dunlap referred to WA's modeling in clay in Rome and introduced the next quotation with the words, "He has said of this study, in after life." 8. Here Dunlap referred to Coleridge and introduced the next quotation with the words, "In one of his letters, after mentioning a friend, he proceeds." 9. Here Dunlap inserted a paragraph about WA's return to America in 1809, recounted Robert Weir's story about his being called in Rome "the American Titian," spoke of hs return to England in 1811, and introduced the next quotation with the words, "The first labour in which Mr. Allston engaged on his return to England, was his great picture of the 'Dead Man revived by touching Elisha's bones.' He says to his correspondent." 10. *Diana Bathing* and *Dido and Anna*. 11. George Augustus Frederick. 12. WA's second portrait of Coleridge, perhaps the finest of all his portraits, was significantly different from his first. The Gothic arches, lancet window, and niche containing a statue in the background represent Coleridge's fondness for the Gothic tradition, and the averted gaze and book in his hand suggests the interior nature of his thought and imagination, as the first portrait, with its front view and no background does not. Coleridge was ambiguously impressed by it. Writing to John J. Morgan on 16 August 1814 he reported that the portraits of him and King were in nearly the same state of composition, that WA was highly gratified with his and promised that it would be even better than King's, which Coleridge described as "the most looking-glassish, ipissimous, living flesh & blood thing I ever beheld," but that he was no judge. He could not believe, he said, that they could be equal because King's was "so very far finer a face." He was not "*mortified*, tho' I own I should better like it to be otherwise, that my face is not a manly or representable Face," continuing, "Whatever is impressive, is part fugitive, part *existent* only in the imaginations of persons impressed strongly by my conversation—The face *itself* is a FEEBLE, unmanly face," a fact he had never perceived "so intuitively" as in comparing the two portraits, and concluding, "The exceeding Weakness, Strengthlessness in my face, was ever painful to me—not as my own face—but as *a* face (*Collected Letters*, vol. 6 [1971], pp. 1029-30). WA described Coleridge in much the same terms to Bronson Alcott in 1835, saying that during times of thought and when absorbed in meditation "the outward man . . . seemed to be a corpse. The eyes were inverted, as it were, and turned inward; the under lip fell, and the general expression of the countenance was that of idiocy, so entirely was the soul withdrawn from the external world and the animal functions. But the appearance of a friend, a stranger, a human being, seemed to awake him from this exterior sleep; the eyes radiated supernatural splendor, the mouth was full of meaning, and the whole countenance was, perhaps, more purely angelic than that of any modern living man. He gave us the idea of a seraph more fully than had been given in others" (*The Journals of Bronson Alcott*, p. 54). 13. WA's portrait of King depicts him holding a book in one hand and a watercolor brush in the other, with reference to his literary and his artistic pursuits.
14. Henry Nelson Coleridge (1798-1843) was the son of Coleridge's brother James. He married Coleridge's daughter Sara and as the literary editor of his estate edited three volumes as well as *Table-Talk*. 15. *King Lear* 3.3.59. From "So far as I can judge" to the end of this paragraph the quotation is from Flagg (p. 104), who quoted immediately before it the passage printed in Dunlap about WA's portraits of Coleridge and King and who apparently had access to the original letter. Possibly Dunlap did not include it because Coleridge was still living. 16. Here Dunlap inserted a paragraph on the right of the world to know everything concerning one who has become

conspicuous in it. 17. Here Dunlap inserted "says Allston." 18. Here Dunlap inserted a paragraph commenting on the relationship of WA and Egremont. 19. As adjutant-general to General Horatio Gates in the Revolution Trumbull held the rank of colonel. 20. Dunlap introduced the next quotation with the words, "After thus expressing himself respecting his English friends, Mr. Allston continues." 21. The 44-gun U.S. frigate, famous for its exploits in the War of 1812, popularly called "Old Ironsides." Authorized by Congress in 1794, it was built in the navy yard at Charlestown, Mass., and launched in 1797, while WA was at Harvard. 22. "The slaughter-breathing brass grew hot and spoke / In flames of lightning, and in clouds of smoke" (*Magnalia Christi Americana; or The Ecclesiastical History of New England; from its first planting, in the year 1620, unto the year of Our Lord 1698* (London, 1702) vol. 1, bk. 2). The quotation is from two lines of poetry describing the attack of Sir William Phips on Quebec.

211. To John Stevens Cogdell

Cambridge Port, Masstts.
27 Feby. 1834.

Dear Cogdell: I have the pleasure to inform you that the Tracing of Sir Walter's Portrait is at last completed. I exceedingly regret that it has been so long delayed; but the delay was unavoidable. A succession of colds, together with an attack of rheumatism, which followed me out of my sick room, must be my apology. Last week, when I went to make the tracing, was the first time I have been in Town for three months. I traced the head with the utmost care, and, as the paper was large enough to admit it, a part of the body; the detail of the latter, however, and the neckcloth I could not give, they being too dark to be distinctly seen, the neck-cloth black. I have carefully packed it in a tin case, sealed &c. and left it with Mr. Ticknor, who has kindly undertaken to see it shipped by the first safe opportunity to Charleston.

I am sorry to find by your last that what I said in my letter of December should have given you any uneasiness. I was not at all offended, as you seem to have imagined. I only supposed, from your using the word "inducement," that you were under a mistake, and I simply meant to correct it. I never take offence where I have not reason to think offence is intended; and I *could not possibly* suppose that you intended any. So I beg you will think no more of it.

I cannot agree with you in your remarks on Chantry's Bust of Scott,[1] if *that* you speak of is the same with the one I have seen. The Bust I saw—and to which I alluded in my letter of Decbr. as being so universally approved, and pronounced perfect in likeness by those who had seen Scott—is, to me, full of character, and shews the hand of a master in every part. It may be, however, that we speak of two different busts.—I am not expressing here any exclusive liking; for I like both the Picture and the Bust. A Picture and a Bust may well differ from each other, and yet be both like the living original: as all who have known Scott say of both in the present instance. Each art addresses the eye in [a] way of its own.

I hope White got my letter that was so long forthcoming. I wrote him in Decbr. before I quitted my sick room. Give my best regards to him, and tell him that Mr.

Dana[2] has been very ill ever since I wrote; he was taken ill two or three days after; but he is now recovering, though still confined to his chamber.—When you see her, pray give my love to my Mother. Mrs. Allston joins me in best regards to Mrs. Cogdell and yourself.

Sincerely your friend, / Wa. Allston.

ADDRESSED: John S. Cogdell Esqre. / Charleston, / South Carolina. SOURCE: Manuscript.

1. Chantrey executed a second bust of Scott in 1828, which was less successful than the first. Apparently Cogdell referred to the second. The first was widely acclaimed, molded and pirated by the thousands, and described by Scott's biographer J.G. Lockhart as the only one which preserved the expression most remembered by those in his domestic circle. 2. Edmund T. Dana.

212. From Leonard Jarvis Washington 15 May 1834

Dear Allston: I received a note from the Secretary of State[1] yesterday requesting me to call & examine a drawing which he had received from Mr. Greenough of the contemplated Statue of Washington.[2] I have done so and have given my opinion respecting the design. I also suggested to Mr. McLane the expediency of sending you a copy of the drawing for your opinion but this it seems he is precluded from doing by the request of Mr. Greenough that no copy should be allowed to be taken. He wishes however very much to have the benefit of your Science taste and judgment & is willing to defray the expense of your journey to Washington & back if you can afford the time & are willing to come. I thought you might perhaps be pleased with the excursion, that it might [be] of service to your health and that a temporary relaxation from your usual pursuits might enable you to resume them with increased satisfaction. I therefore favoured the project & have now in pursuance of the wishes of the Secretary the pleasure to forward to you a letter from him and to express my hope that the invitation may be gratifying to you and that you will not consider me to have been too officious. Vanderlyn is here engaged upon his picture of Washington with which I think you will be pleased. I want to have some conversation with you respecting some national paintings for the pannels of the Rotunda of the capitol. Do come if you can! Every man here can do as he pleases. You can at your will become acquainted with the lions or let it alone. I am very solicitous for your opinion about the statue for I doubt whether Greenough has not made a mistake in his conception of what it ought to be & as the project was of my own creation & as the selection of the artist was also at my suggestion which was occasioned by your commendation I feel deeply interested that the design as much as the execution should give general satisfaction.

I remain as ever / Dear Allston / Yr old & faithful frd / Leod Jarvis

W. Allston Esqr.

Let me hear from you aye or no upon receipt of this & if you determine to come let it be done speedily.

SOURCE: MANUSCRIPT.

1. Louis McLane (1786-1857) was secretary of state from 29 May 1833 to 30 June 1834. Greenough's letter was addressed to his predecessor, Edward Livingston, who was secretary of state from 1831 to 29 May 1833. 2. Greenough's letter to Livingston of 28 January 1834, explaining his design for his statue. It was received on 14 May (Greenough, *Letters*, pp. 173-75). Jarvis was asked to read it as chairman of the congressional Committee on Public Buildings.

213. To John Vanderlyn Cambridgeport, Masstts
27 May, 1834

My dear Sir: The President having expressed the wish to consult me on the subject of Mr. Greenough's Design for the statue of Washington, & the state of my health together with my engagements—but more especially my health—putting it wholly out of my power to visit Washington, I have taken the liberty to mention you, as an artist every way qualified to be advised with on the subject. I hope you will not object to this.

My regard for Mr. Greenough as a friend, & the high opinion I have of his genius as an artist, render me solicitous that in this important public work he should give satisfaction; & I feel assured that—in referring to you as an adviser on this occasion, I could not have placed his interest in abler & more liberal hands.—Mr. Greenough, I am certain, were he present, would be thankful for your advice. In rendering him this service you will also oblige me, his friend.

Jarvis says, he thinks I would be pleased with your Washington. I have not the least doubt of it; nor do I doubt that you will make a picture worthy the subject. I hope you will give to it a strong *impasto,* as it is to be seen at a distance. I suppose you know as well as I do, that colours, to *tell* through a large medium of air, should not only be strong in tone, but also of a strong body.

Wishing you complete success, & that *solid* reward which your genius has so long deserved,

I remain / your sincere friend, / Washington Allston

To John Vanderlyn, Esq. / Washington.

ANNOTATED: Copy of letter from Allston to Vanderlyn, lent to me to copy, by Robt. Gosman, of Rondout, New York. SOURCE: Manuscript copy by RHD.

214. From Leonard Jarvis Washington 6 June 1834

Dear Allston: I am grieved that the state of your health is such as to render a journey to Washington dangerous, & I regret that we cannot have the advantage of your opinion respecting the statue.[1] I have more faith in your taste & that of Dana than I have in [that] [page torn] of all the rest of my acquaintance. You have it by nature & you have not vitiated but improved it by cultivation.

Greenough's design does not satisfy me. He has undertaken to *idealise* Washington and to make an emblematic statue. It is not *our* Washington that he has represented. He has evidently taken the idea of his statue from that of Jupiter (Stator?).[2] He represents Washington seated with his right arm raised & the hand pointing towards heaven. The left hand resting upon the thigh grasps an antique sword or rather supports it. The left leg is thrown forward, the right is raised upon a step. A robe is thrown round the lower limbs & the loins & the corner appears over the shoulder but the body or rather the paps the chest & the neck & the arms are bare. The parts are well balanced and as a work of art the design is worthy of praise. But I object to the absence of drapery on the upper part of the figure and I should have been better pleased if the arm had some more easy & natural action. I dislike anything theatric & the more perfect the repose that could have been given to this design the better I should have been pleased with it. The position of the figure is otherwise good & the drapery (where there is drapery) is well arranged. Perhaps I am too bold in thus presuming to give my opinion & hope you may not feel inclined to apply the Latin saying to me.[3]

I have seen the Medora and agree with you entirely that it is a beautiful work of art.[4] If Greenough should be equally successful in his Washington we shall have good reason to be satisfied.

Have you ever seen the Washington of Canova?[5] There is a drawing of it in the description of the works of that indefatigable & unequal artist. I consider it as an entire failure. He has converted Washington into a Roman soldier.

I have said to Mr. McLane everything you could desire. He is so desirous to have the advantage of your opinion that as you would not come here he would have sent the design to you if I had given any encouragement; but I thought you might be annoyed with the necessity of giving your opinion in writing and accordingly I did not favour the suggestion.

Don't feel that you are obliged to answer this letter but if you have any inclination to do so I shall be gratified in hearing from you. Our intimacy my good friend is of long standing and I need no memorials to sustain in all their early freshness & vigour the warm feelings of attachment which I imbibed in our youthful days.

I remain very faithfully / Yr friend / Leod Jarvis

ANNOTATED BY WA: *answered 19 June 1834*. SOURCE: Manuscript.

1. WA replied to Jarvis's letter of 15 May in a letter saying that his health would not permit him to go to Washington. It does not seem to have been preserved. 2. In the pose of his statue Greenough was influenced by that of the statue of Zeus by the Greek sculptor Phidias for the temple of the god in Olympia. *Stator,* meaning protector, is one of the surnames of Jupiter, the Roman name for Zeus. 3. Presumably a reference to Lucretius, *On the Nature of the Universe*

2.1041-42: "Judicio perpende: et si tibi vera indentur, / Dede manus: aut ei falsum est, adcingere contra" ("Examine with judgment each opinion: if it seems true, / yield to it; or if false gird up your loins against it"). 4. Greenough's *Medora,* a recumbent statue of the dead Medora from Byron's poem of that title, was executed in 1832-33 for Robert Gilmor, Jr. It was exhibited in Boston from 24 October to 31 December 1833 (Wright, pp. 85-88). WA evidently praised it in his answer to Jarvis's letter of 15 May. 5. Canova's statue of Washington depicted him seated, in the dress of a Roman soldier, holding in one hand a pen and in the other a tablet of laws. It was executed for the North Carolina State House in Raleigh between 1815 and 1821 (Frances Davis Whittemore, *George Washington in Sculpture* [Boston: Marshall Jones Co., 1933], pp. 34-35, plate 7).

215. To Leonard Jarvis Cambridge Port 19 June 1834

Dear Jarvis: I have received yours of the 6 inst., and thank you for your considerate kindness in leaving me to reply to it or not, as I like. This is indeed a kindness to one who has about as much sympathy with letters (when *he* has to write them) as a mad dog with water. On this occasion, however, it is my duty to write.

You have described the design of the statue so minutely that I think I can form as accurate an opinion of it as if I had the drawing before me. I agree with you in every particular of your criticism; and so does E.T.D. and R.H.D. to whom I shewed your description. We were all three struck, as you were, with the inappropriateness of the *raised arm.* We were also of the same mind respecting the *idealizing* of Washington. Now, how to unidealize, without changing the present design—hic labor. It can, I think however be done; but it must be done by the Artist himself, nay, it should not be done by any other person; and I am the last man who would dictate to a brother Artist—neither my principles nor disposition would allow me to do it—especially to one of Greenough's genius. All that can be done—or at least that I am willing to do—is to throw out suggestions, leaving the adoption, or modification, of them entirely to him. This appears to me not only the most delicate but indeed the only efficient course, for no man of genius ever worked successfully from the mere dictation of another. He must coincide with, and enter into the <change> spirit of the change proposed, or his work will not be of a piece. Should Greenough so enter into it—and there is no reason to suppose that, weighing the objections to his present design, he will not—[1]I have the most thorough confidence in his success.

As the opinion of the world, that is, of the competent judges in it—seems to be pretty nearly balanced on the subject of Costume—as many preferring the ancient as the modern—I shall offer no advice on this point, and for two reasons; first, because I would not take upon myself the *responsibility* of *deciding for another* artist on a subject where good judges disagree, and secondly, because Mr. Greenough has already decided for himself. I will however (standing neutral on this question) make a general remark or two on both that may be of use in either case; the subject being the Statue of *any* distinguished person of or <a highborn> near our own time. Supposing the ancient to be adopted, all minutiae and pecularities belonging to a particular age or country, in other words, whatever tends to remove the subject from his own age to another, should, I think be avoided; to adopt a distinction of Sir Joshua Reynolds,[2] it should be clothed with *drapery,* and not in an antique dress. The Greek and Roman helmet, cuirass &c, also, from the peculiar manner in which it is folded, the Roman toga, belong to what is here meant by dress. If the modern be adopted, though it must, *as modern,* be of necessity identified with our own age, it should still be of so general a character as not to fix the mind upon the *fashion* of any particular time in it. Under the head of *fashion* I would class wigs, bag-wigs, queus, frizzed hair, flapped waistcoats bag-sleeves &c.

How far the Ancient costume may be adopted without impairing the individuality of the subject, is more than I can say; that can only be shewn by the skill of the sculptor. As to the other question, how the *prescribed* and scanty form of a <the> modern dress can be managed with grandeur—that also must be left to <the> his skill. The general objection of artists to the modern dress is its meagreness, as not admitting of those masses so essential to <grandeur> a grand effect. In general this is true; but there are some exceptions; for instance, the military cloak—which, without violat <ion> ing of its character (I use this word technically) may be used for all the purposes of *drapery,* admitting of equal breadth and mass with the ancient mantle. But the costume in the statue of a great modern seems to me essentially secondary. The *character* of the *man* is, and should be the principal. If this be true, it necessarily limits the artist in his conception. Whatever ideas he may have of grandeur or majesty, if they do not belong to his original, they can have no propriety in his statue. He depends on his subject for all the grandeur that is admissible.—But if his subject should happen to be of mean appearance? There is then but one alternative—to make the best of a mean person—or not to attempt it; for a noble figure would not represent that person, but his proxy.—In the present case, however, the artist has no such difficulty to contend with, for his original (I mean Washington) was not only great in mind, but of a noble countenance and majestic stature. Perhaps in all history a grander subject for a portrait statue could not be found: for what attitude could be too dignified, what air too grand for Washington? Dignity and majesty were his personal attributes.—With a slight modification, I do not see but that the present attitude which Gr has chosen might be retained with propriety. Bating the *raised arm,* it seems to me (as you have described it) a dignified one.

My notion of the statue of a great Modern who has actually lived is, in a few words, this. It should not bring the person before us as an *active agent,* but simply as the *man* whose deeds and virtues have passed into history, and who is already known to us *by* his deeds and virtues. To this effect, the most *perfect repose* seems to me essential. In Washington especially no conscious action should break it—whose name alone fills the mind with his history. If any man can be said to respose in the fulness of his glory, it is he; for nothing in his great mission has been left imperfect; all has been done, and is in the *past*. We need alone the *man* as a visible object of our love and veneration.

Should this notion be approved and adopted by G there needs but a slight alteration, as I have already observed, so far as concerns the attitude, to realize it; and that is [the alteration][3] to give rest to the uplifted hand and arm, I mean, to bring the hand down, so as to rest on some part of his person, or on the chair. I know not that <any> the hand which holds the sword need be altered; but I doubt the propriety of the antique sword. A *scroll* would answer for the composition quite as well, besides being more appropriate.—Here I beg it to be distinctly <to have it> understood that I *abstain*, for the reasons given, from any decision respecting the costume. If, however, the present be retained, I am clear that the breast and arms should be draped; which might well be done by a close tunic with sleeves.

If you have not already done so, I beg you shew to Mr. McLane that part of my first letter relating to Medora. And, since he is pleased to attach some value to my opinion, I wish you <would> also say to him, that[t] notwithstanding the objections to the present design, I have *no distrust whatever in* Mr. G.'s ability to produce a statue that will do honour to the Country. The classic atmosphere in which he has so long lived has, perhaps, and very naturally, biased his judgement in this instance; but that he *can* conceive equally well in another way I have no doubt; and that, when he shall have distinctly understood what is desired, he will so modify his design as to give satisfaction I have the most intire confidence.—I know G. well, and if I know what genius is, he possesses as much of it as any sculptor living. His natural powers are of no common order, and he has cultivated them by a severe course of study. He is no tyro, nor random flourisher, but a well-grounded scholar in his art. To this I shall only add, that <on such an occasion> I have been conscientious in every word I have written. On such an occasion I would not give my best friend one tittle more of praise than he deserved.

You say that, as a work of art, the "Design" is worthy of praise &c. I should have been disappointed if you had not found it so <otherwise>—still more if you had not liked the Medora.—I particularly request that this letter may not be suffered to get into the Newspapers.

I have no objection that a copy of this letter be sent to Mr. G: but it must be sent *intire* and verbatim—and provided that he be informed that is done with my consent.

SOURCE: Manuscript. The pages are numbered by WA 1-5. Printed in Flagg, pp. 272-76.

1. Greenough did not substantially change the design. 2. In Discourse 7 Reynolds said that, though at first it seemed very reasonable that a statue "should be dressed in the fashion of the times, in the dress which he himself wore," after a time the dress is "only an amusement for the antiquarian" and should be disregarded by the artist in favor of "the naked form" and "the disposition of drapery." He approved of the current fashion to clothe modern figures in ancient dresses chiefly because of "the simplicity of them, consisting of little more than one single piece

of drapery, without those whimsical capricious forms by which all other dresses are embarrassed." 3. WA's brackets.

216. To William Dunlap [ca. 16 August 1834][1]

[M]y friends wrote me that I should have been made an academician some years ago had I been in London, on the occurrence of a certain vacancy; but by the original laws of the academy (for which the present members are not accountable) no one is eligible as an academician who is not a resident of the United Kingdom. This law is peculiar to the English academy, and I cannot but think it a narrow one.[2]

I will mention only a few of the principal [paintings] which I painted during my first visit to England, viz: "The Dead Man restored to life by the bones of Elisha." The "Angel liberating St. Peter from Prison." This picture was painted for Sir George Beaumont, (the figures larger than life) and is now in a church at Ashby de la Zouch. "Jacob's Dream," in the possession of the Earl of Egremont. There are many figures in this picture, which I have always considered one of my happiest efforts. "Elijah in the Desert." This I brought to America, but it has gone back, having been purchased here by Mr. Labouchere, M. P.[3] The "Angel Uriel in the Sun," in possession of the Marquis of Stafford. This is a colossal fore-shortened figure, that, if standing *upright* would be fourteen feet high, but being fore-shortened, occupies a space but of nine feet. The directors of the British Gallery presented me with a hundred and fifty guineas, as a token of their approbation of Uriel. Since my return to America, I have painted a number of pictures, but chiefly small ones. These pictures being pretty well known here, I shall mention only a few of the larger ones, viz: "Jeremiah dictating his prophecy to Baruch, the scribe;" the figures as large as life. "Saul and the Witch of Endor," and "Spalatro's vision of the bloody hand." This last is a small picture, but I mention it because it is perhaps more extensively known, and because, too, I consider it one of my best. The others which I have omitted are landscapes, and, with three or four exceptions, small figures. Although my large picture (Belshazzar's Feast) is still unfinished, yet I ought perhaps to say something about it, as many inquiries have been made respecting my progress in it, and the probable time of its being completed. In assigning this reason for speaking of it in this place, I do not mean to admit any *right* in the public to be made acquainted with it; for so far, it is wholly a matter between the subscribers and myself. Still I am not disposed to withhold all information from a very natural curiosity. On some accounts I cannot but feel gratified with the general interest that has been manifested in relation to it. All, however, that I can now say, is, that so soon as it is in my power to apply myself without interruption to the completion of the picture, I shall do it with the utmost alacrity; and that when circumstances will admit of this, it will not take a long time to finish it. If the subscribers to it have been anxious for its completion, many and many-fold greater has been my desire to see it done: and great indeed would be the relief to my mind. I could long ago have finished this and other pictures as large, had my mind been free: for indeed I have *already* bestowed upon it as much mental and manual labour as, under state of mind, would have completed several such pictures. But to go into the subject of all the obstacles, and the hindrances upon my spirit, would hardly be consistent with delicacy and self-respect. Nor could I be far enough understood if I should do it, to answer by it any essential purpose. Those feelings which are most intimately blended with one's nature, and which most powerfully and continuously influence us, are the very feelings which it is most difficult to give any distinct apprehension of to another. For this reason then, as well as for the others assigned by me, I will be silent respecting them. I may add, however, in conclusion, that I have the prospect of a time, not very far distant, when I expect to be in a condition to complete this picture; an event which is not possible for any one to desire more than myself.[4]

I am pretty sure that Mather Brown was a native of Boston. I have heard that he was the son of a celebrated clock-maker[5]—the maker of the "old south"[6] clock in Boston, which is said to be an uncommon piece of mechanism. Leslie must be mistaken as to my having any anecdotes of Mather Brown. If I ever had any, they have entirely escaped from my mind: I have not the slightest recollection of one, except (if it may be called an anecdote,) my meeting him once at Mr. West's in a *cap-a-pie suit of brown,* even to stockings, wig and complexion. He must, I think have held a respectable rank as an artist, as I remember that he lived in either Cavendish[7] or Manchester-square. But for myself, I have not sufficient recollection of his pictures, to express any opinion on the subject.

. . .

My nephew, G. Flagg, was with me a few weeks since. He has met with a most munificent patron[8]—munificent for any country. Not a quid prop quo patron, as I suppose you know. That boy, if I mistake not, will do great things one of these days. A great thing in his favor is, that his heart is as good as his head.

. . .

I saw some pictures in the Athenaeum (Boston) last year, by a young man of your city—Mount[9]—which showed great power of expression. He has, too, showed great power of expression. He has, too, a firm, decided pencil, and seems to have a good notion of the figure. If he would study Ostade[10] and Jan Steen,[11] especially the latter, and master their colour and chiaro scuro, there is nothing, as I see, to prevent his becoming a great artist in the line he has chosen.

. . .

I rejoice to hear your report of Morse's advance in his art.[12] *I* know what *is in him,* perhaps, better than any one else. If he will only bring out all that is *there,* he will show powers that many now do not dream of.

SOURCE: Dunlap, 2:183-87; 1:228-29; 2:450, 452, 318.

1. The date of this letter is based on Dunlap's reference to the passages about Brown, Flagg, and Mount as being in the letter he received from WA on 19 August 1834 (*Diary* 4:816). 2. This

paragraph may have been included in WA's letter to Dunlap of ca. 18 February, but it sounds rather like an afterthought of his recollections of his years in England. It is separated from Dunlap's final quotation there about WA's arrival in Boston harbor in October 1818 by a paragraph about the return of an American from Europe and his encountering mockery of patriotism and is introduced after WA's election to the RA in 1818 is noted, with the words, "On this subject, he has said in a letter of recent date." At the conclusion of these quotations Dunlap devoted two pages to quotations from letters of WA to McMurtrie (17 Nov. 1818 and 27 May 1831), both referring to *Belshazzar's Feast,* interspersed with a paragraph about that painting, and introduced the next quotation with the following words, suggesting they were written at a later date than the quotations from foregoing letters, "In a letter to a friend, Mr. Allston had said that it was not his wish to give a catalogue of all his pictures. He was afterward prevailed upon to give the following brief notice of a part of his works. 3. Henry Labouchere, Baron Taunton (1798-1869), English politician. He visited the United States and Canada, in company with several other Englishmen, from April 1826 to June 1827. He paid $1,000 for the painting, which he saw at the house of Isaac P. Davis. RHD thought WA was willing to let it go at one time for $750 in his financial distress (*RHD*, p. 9).
4. The next four paragraphs occur in Dunlap's account of Brown, Flagg, Mount, and Morse, the last from a letter from WA "of late date (1834)." 5. Mather Brown (1761-1831), portrait painter, was born in Boston. In 1781 he went to London, where he became a pupil of West and enjoyed great popularity for several years but was eventually recognized as having mediocre ability (Alberts, pp. 148-49). Leslie visited him in his late years and described him as unkempt and living in disorderly surroundings (Whitley, *Artists and their Friends in England, 1700-1799* [New York: The Media Society, 1928], 2:98). His father was Gawen Brown, an Englishman who was a clockmaker, who came to America in the early eighteenth century and settled in Boston. His mother was a great-granddaughter of Cotton Mather (Frederick A. Coburn, "Mather Brown," *Art in America* 11 [1923]: 253). 6. The third building of the Old South Society, the Old South Meeting House, built in 1729. 7. In 1784 Brown moved into the house at 20 Cavendish Square, which was furnished elaborately. He kept a servant in livery and apparently dressed expensively and eccentrically. Unable to afford the rent, he gave it up in 1810 (Coburn, pp. 254, 257). 8. Luman Reed (1787-1836), New York merchant and art patron. 9. William Sidney Mount (1807-68), a portrait and genre painter, spent most of his life in New York. He exhibited paintings at the BA for the first time in 1833: *Interior of a Barn* and *Boys Out of School.*
10. Adrian Ostade (1610-85), Dutch painter. In his lecture "Art" WA named him among a variety of other painters to exemplify "Natural Invention," or the combination of known forms, in contrast to "Ideal Invention," or the embodiment of the unknown but possible. To illustrate his point he compared at length Ostade's *Slaughtering of a Pig* with Raphael's *Death of Ananias* as having in common the operation of the imagination or mind of the artist, even though in "the homely Ostade" through the humblest of materials. In particular he analyzed the light and color in Ostade's painting as directed by his *"mind,"* which had the power to overcome any objections possibly raised by the subject matter alone (*LA*, pp. 87-93). 11. Jan Havicksz Steen (1626-79), Dutch painter. In his lecture "Art" WA included him among the artists he named as exemplifying "Natural Invention." 12. Probably this reference is to information contained in Dunlap's letter to WA of 16 July 1834. Dunlap called on Morse on 3 July 1834, apparently for the first time since his visit of 17 September 1833. He also visited Morse on 7 and 11 November and 3 December 1834, but these are the only times he recorded (*Diary* 3:800, 834, 835, 843).

217. To Charles Bowen Cambridge Port, 7 Nov. 1834.

Dear Sir: I have received your letter of the 5th inst. asking my consent to Mr. Cheney's[1] engraving (for the Token[2] of 1836) my Picture of "Beatrice," now in possession [of] Samuel A. Eliot[3] Esqre; and I have the pleasure to say, in reply, that I cheerfully comply with your request—the more so as Mr. Cheney is to be the Engraver.

I have a high opinion of Mr. Cheney's talents, and feel assured that he will do ample justice to the picture.

I remain respectfully, / Yrs / Wa. Allston.

To Charles Bowen Esqre. / Boston

ADDRESSED: Charles Bowen Esqre. / Boston. SOURCE: Manuscript.

1. John Cheney. He engraved WA's *Beatrice* shortly before November 1834 (Cheney, *Memoirs of Seth W. Cheney, Artist* [Boston, 1881], p. 14). 2. Bowen was the publisher of *The Token* in 1834 and for several succeeding years. The founder and for several years publisher of *The Token* was Samuel Griswold Goodrich. WA owned and signed a copy of *A Pictorial Geography of the World*, 3d ed., 2 vols. (Boston, 1840). 3. Samuel Atkins Eliot (1798-1862), statesman and man of letters. He was one of the subscribers to the Tripartite Agreement.

218. From Samuel Finley Breese Morse Boston

Decr 6th 1834.—

W. Allston, Esqr

My Dear Sir: I have seen two or three of your warm friends,[1] and the loan of Five hundred dollars, I think will be obtained precisely as you wish. So my dear Sir, make yourself easy, and I beg of you not to let your pecuniary difficulties again enter your thoughts. You have works nearly finished[2] which will free you from all your obligations to those whom you owe. You need fear no impertinent, or over curious inquiries, or impatient *friends*, for the gentlemen who are interested for you in the present loan, are not of that character, but have too much nobleness of heart, and sympathy with the mind of a man of genius to wound by any low suspicions of your integrity, or ability to perform all you intend.—May God bless you, my dear Sir, and give you health and spirits.—I leave in the Morning for New York.

Truly your friend and Servt. / Saml F.B. Morse

ADDRESSED: Washington Allston, Esqr. / Cambridge Port. SOURCE: Manuscript.

1. Unidentified. 2. Possibly including *The Evening Hymn; Landscape, American Scenery: Time, Afternoon, with a Southwest Haze* (1835); *Rosalie* (1835); *Family Group; The Death of King John* (ca. 1835); and *Macbeth and Banquo*.

219. From Leonard Jarvis Washington 27 January 1835

Dear Allston: A proposition is before the Senate to purchase for the decoration of the President's house a collection of pictures which were exhibited in this City last year & which had previously, I believe, gone the rounds of our principal cities.[1] You undoubtedly saw or heard of them when in Boston & I want to have you afford me the benefit of your judgment respecting them. I know what I am asking & that you will wish me & my request to Jericho so you will perceive that I am sinning with my eyes open. But there is not a single individual in either house who is competent to pronounce upon the originality or the value of these paintings and you are abundantly able to enlighten us upon both subjects. I enclose you a catalogue & will give you my promise that your opinion shall be kept secret if you desire it & shall only serve for my own guidance.

I have been looking over not overlooking Dunlap's book and find that Mr. Cooper arrogates to himself the credit of having procured for Greenough the order for the Statue of Washington.[2] The presumption of some men is excessive. Mr. Cooper had no more influence in bringing forward Greenough's name or in procuring his employment than the Archibiship of Canterbury. I never heard his name mentioned in relation to this subject. Your friend Verplanck & myself brought forward the proposition in consequence of the high praise you had bestowed upon Greenough & I am very sure if I had not known your opinion I would not have ventured to insist as I did upon the employment of Greenough. It is thanks to you & to you alone that the thanks of your brother artist is due.

I wish I could have seen the notice of you before it was published. I think Dana and I could have added to its interest and could have done you more justice. It annoys me to hear the industry of a man estimated by the rules of works. The high mob which is not a fig but a sham the low mob do not seem to be aware that the best parts of the arts which a painting or poetry requires no light but that of genius and no tablet or canvas but that wonderful instrument the brain and I am inclined to think that the noblest imaginings of the artist have never been embodied from the impossibility of language and of colours to convey the brilliant though perhaps indistinct visions which are floating in the minds of those who are gifted with the higher power of genius.

There is a young man[3] here from the West who is deserving of encouragement for he is one to whom nature has been bountiful. He is self taught & has since his arrival in this city modelled a bust of the President[4] which is decidedly the best likeness I have seen. Indeed it is the only attempt either of the sculptor or painter where the likeness & the character of the president have been preserved without being caricatured. The artist is a modest young man whom you would be pleased with but poor fellow he has [word undecipherable] work to do for not satisfied with modelling in clay. He has undertaken to form living cherubs or imps as the case may be an occupation more pleasant than profitable.[5]

Give Ned a shake by the hand for me & believe me ever most faithfully

Yr friend / Leod Jarvis

Washington Allston Esq

Source: Manuscript.

1. Not further identified. 2. Dunlap said that after the success of *The Chanting Cherubs* Cooper conceived the hope of influencing the government to employ Greenough to execute a statue of Washington for the Capitol and wrote the president and McLane to that effect, thereby influencing the commission to be given (2:419-20). 3. Hiram Powers (1805-73), sculptor. Born in Vermont, he grew up in Cincinnati. From 1834 to 1837 he was in Washington, D.C. In 1837 he went to Florence, where he remained until his death. 4. Andrew Jackson (1767-1854) was president of the United States from 1829 to 1837. Powers executed a number of busts in Washington. 5. In Cincinnati before he turned to sculpture Powers worked in wax works for a museum and devised clockwork mechanisms for a variety of figures, including those of Satan and several monsters.

220. To William Wordsworth

Cambridge Port, Masstts
5 March, 1835.

My dear Sir: Will you allow me to introduce to you my young countryman, Mr. Barnard[1]—a gentleman of education and talent—who visits Europe for the double purpose of pleasure and improvement. As a man of right feeling, having a just veneration for the Land of his Ancestors, Mr. Barnard is naturally desirous of paying his respects to one who has done so much to sustain its moral and intellectual greatness: and it adds to my pleasure in making him known to you, that he is also an ardent admirer of your writings.

I trust I need not say to you, that neither time nor distance have erased from my memory the many kindnesses of my English Friends. The words, "dear England," if not on my lips, are often in my heart: nay, I love her the more *now* for the peril that has threatened her of late.[2]—But in my trust in Providence rests my hope for her.

Pray present my respectful compliments to Mrs. Wordsworth and Miss Hutchenson.

I remain, dear Sir, / with the highest respect, / Yrs / Washington Allston

Addressed: William Wordsworth Esqre. / Keswick, / Cumberland, / England / Henry Barnard Esq. Source: Manuscript, The Wordsworth Trust, Dove Cottage, Grasmere.

1. Henry Barnard (1811-1900), educationist, with Horace Mann having the distinction of being largely responsible for sponsoring popular education in the United States in the nineteenth century. He was in Europe in 1835-36, during which time he visited Wordsworth and other prominent Englishmen and several Swiss educators. 2. WA refers to the involvement of the British Legion in Spain in 1835 and years following in support of the efforts of Maria Christina, the regent, to secure the throne in opposition to Don Carlos, brother of Ferdinand VII.

221. From Horatio Greenough

Florence, March 7th 1835.

My Dear Mr Alston: I remember that when with you once at Cambridge, I asked your opinion on some doubtful point relating to Art and that you said, an answer to my question would cost you at least 3 cigars—[1]Sure I am that it would require that number to fit me to describe to you my gratification in reading the verses you wrote on my groupe, which lately reached me in a letter from my brother Harry.[2] I believe my Dear Sir that gratified vanity was not the foremost or strongest of my pleasures—for your verses were as far from being addressed to minds of the many as my composition was from being adapted to their tastes.

They say there's no love without hope—This I don't believe, but I do believe that a correspondence requires 2 people to make it—I say it from experience and by way of apology to you for my long silence which has not been occasioned by any change in my tastes or character—but simply from the discouragement of your silence—I called a spirit from the vasty deep—He would not come when I did call to him[3]—But though like the clownish wooer I have said nothing, like him I've thought the more. I am happy in an excuse for addressing you again. I throw aside all fear of being irksome to you and I proceed to give you my news. And first of all let me tell you that John G——[4] with whom I have established a regular correspondence is comfortable and likely to be still more so—He is at Islington in a very decent house has one or two respectable persons lodging with him and seems to drive quite a promising business in portrait though in a small way—I am so happy that he has had the character to go through with it! It wrings tears out of me that I can't put him in a way to gratify a little his ambition which you know is strong in him. After 3 years of married life he speaks with much affection of his wife and I think therefore that it's a good match. At the same time that he writes cheerfully and even jocularly he shows clearly that he has grown thoughtful and cautious—I always felt that John had a vast deal of good in his nature though circumstances and his temperament combined against him—We shall see—I hope he will yet be a happy man—

I can as regards myself only talk to you of my statue which is my life—I have hopes of casting it next autumn[5]—I propose exhibiting the cast in the Rotunda and giving Government the choice of taking or refusing the work as they may think fit.[6] I have as authorized by the Vote in Congress made the work after my own heart—Had they ordered this or that costume or action I might have been blamed for disregard of orders—They can now only question my taste and skill and as I give them their entire freedom as regards the marble I think they cannot complain. As a bargain I am not eager for it—though the price is a fair one, as far as I can judge from my expences hitherto[7]—and as for the honour of filling that spot I want to be sure or at least have hopes that it is to be an honour and not a disgrace before I strike a blow in stone.

I received a letter from Mr Everett a few weeks since in which he tells me he fears my plan will never do in our country—He takes a view of the matter directly contradictory to that he has hithertoo taken and at this moment when the work may be said to be done[8]—I question neither his sincerity nor the friendliness of his motives but I draw from his various and inconsistent advice the strongest arguments in favor of an artist's thinking for himself and acting resolutely from his own convictions—I beg you will show this letter to no one. I would not harm Mr E even in his reputation as a connoisseur for the world—I have made up my mind to look for the approbation of a few—I rest my hopes of comfort during my life upon ground which has little relation with the success of my work with the world—Was it not always so? Yes and it will always be so—Do not imagine that I think I have join[ed] [*page torn*] the glorious company of men in advance of their age—I do not—[But of?] [*page torn*] this I am convinced that he who looks to what is abstractly right [in?] [*page torn*] any employment or occupation whatever must give up what Alfieri calls glorietta[9]—and the attempt is as fatal to him as the greatest success—Mr Mason has been here the greater part of this winter. He is as you have no doubt heard married—to [a] young and sprightly widow with all the qualities to make a good wife as the world goes[10]—He is in person and appearance as young as I left him 10 years ago—I have made about 15 busts this winter[11]—I have had a statue rough hewn which I wish to finish but have not time—Love prisoner—to wisdom—his feet are chained and the bird of Minerva[12] sits by on the stone where his chain is fastened. I have tried to represent that twisting impatience which a boy manifests at restraint in his form and an expression of treachery and mischief in his face. I have been grieved to hear of Mr Dana's illness—I hope he is recovered entirely—I heard a strange story of the recovery from many years' melancholy of the brother of Dr Foster—[13]—is this true?—I hear nothing of poor Newton[14]—I propose to model at Washington the bas reliefs of my pedestal while my model is exhibiting[15]—I find it quite out of the question to attempt it here. I can't get the portraits—and the events represented I know too superficially to trust myself—I hope then My Dear Sir to see you in less than a year from this date—Among the thousand tender and happy anticipations which are linked to that hope—the thought of looking once more on your face and on the master's is among the strongest—I beg to be remembered to the master and his brother—to the ladies of the family—and am Dear Sir—

Yours / H Greenough

P.S. Your nephew is here[16]—just arrived—he looks enough like you to give me great pleasure in seeing him. He will remain until spring and then to England—He is studying or to study rather at the gallery—

ADDRESSED: Washington Alston Esqr. / Boston Mass— SOURCE: Greenough, *Letters*, pp. 185-88.

1. WA's fondness for cigars was well known. He customarily deposited the stumps on the fireplace mantel while contemplating his painting and said that next to his religion smoking was his greatest satisfaction. 2. Allston's poem "On Greenough's Group of the Angel and Child" appeared in the *Boston Daily Advertiser*, 30 December 1834. 3. "I can call spirits from the vastly deep. . . . But will they come when you do call for them" (*King Henry IV, Part 1*, 3:1.53, 55). 4. John Greenough. Islington is a district in London. He married Maria Underwood of London on 20 February 1832 (H.P. Greenough, p. 41). 5. The model was cast in plaster early in 1836 (Wright, p. 109). 6. His proposal was not accepted. 7. The original sum appropriated was $20,000, but the expenses to Greenough and to the government ultimately far exceeded it (Wright, pp. 119, 141). 8. In his letter to Greenough of 15 December 1834, Edward Everett reported that the drawing of the statue which Greenough had sent Livingston had been objected to

because of the action of the right hand and the nudity. He also expressed the opinion that it was "too dangerous to address a work of art to a degree of refinement, which does not exist, among those who are to behold it," and concluded by saying that he wanted Greenough to make a popular as well as a good statue. This advice was inconsistent with his letter of 29 July 1832, in which he said he was "much pleased" with Greenough's idea for the design of the statue and urged him to read accounts of Phidias's statue of Zeus (Collection of David Richardson, Washington, D.C.). 9. "Small glory." The source of the quotation has not been identified. 10. In 1834 Mason married Isabella Cowpland, daughter of an English merchant living in Florence (HA). 11. Among them were those of William Cullen Bryant, Capt. Alexander Claxton, Mr. and Mrs. David Sears, Col. and Mrs. Joseph M. White, and presumably William Griffin and a "Mme. Para" (Wright, p. 102). 12. Goddess of Wisdom. 13. John Foster, Cambridge physician (Lucius R. Paige, *History of Cambridge, Massachusetts, 1630-1877* [Boston, 1877], p. 547), graduated from Harvard in 1802. His brother was Thomas Foster, who from boyhood had a nervous disease and at last became a recluse. After going into seclusion for several years he was well until the death of his brother John deranged him again (Sophia Peabody to Elizabeth P. Peabody, 23 June 1831, Henry W. and Albert A. Berg Collection, The New York Public Library, Astor, Lenox and Tilden Foundations). 14. Gilbert S. Newton suffered from attacks of mental disorder and died insane. 15. When Greenough examined the site for the statue in 1836 he found the size of the rotunda called for more ornamentation of the chair than he intended and decided to redesign it and leave the pedestal plain (Wright, p. 131). 16. George W. Flagg.

222. To John Stevens Cogdell

Cambridge Port, Masstts—
9th March, 1835.

Dear Cogdell: I have been long intending to thank you, by letter, for your kind present of the "Drawings of <the> Cork."[1]—I was about to begin an apology for not acknowledging it sooner;* but I have made so many apologies, on the score of letter-writing, during <for> half a century, that I think I may well be excused making any more for the rest of my life. Be assured, however, that, though so late in its acknowledgement, I have not been the less sensible either to the beaut <ies> y of these remarkable Drawings, or to the kindness of the <ir> donor. I had no difficulty in recognizing amongst them the hands of several of the Old Masters, <particularly by> especially Raffaelle, Correggio and Titian. Of one or two indeed I doubted for a moment whether to ascribe them to Rubens, or to some high Venetian colourist; but a little reflexion convinced me that these also were in too pure a gusto[2] for the Flemish School: so I set them down as Tintoretto. The beautiful Drawing[3] which you presented to Mrs. Allston (who begs me to express her thanks for the gift) there can be no doubt is from the delicate hand of Carlo Dolce.[4] Several of them, however, still remain unexamined in their cases; for, as they are too good to be enjoyed alone, I never open them but when the pleasure can be shared by some particular friend. The most remarkable peculiarity of these Drawings, and that which particularly struck me, is this; that they not only satisfy you with their own beauties, but they set the mind to work, in conjuring up visions of its own—a true test of genius in Art. <As> There are indeed some other Drawings of <the> Cork—as, for instance, those of the Hollands and Cogniac

Schools—[5]which <have more> seem to have a similar quality; but it is only the property of repeating *themselves*—or rather of *doubling* their own images to the eyes of the spectator. But no such vulgar effect can in any degree be possible of these ideal Drawings; the associate forms they suggest are essentially poetical—not a reproduction, a mere alter et idem[6]—but from a progeny; the <[undecipherable line]> probable taking birth from the actual and <from> the probable <[undecipherable word]> the possible. In a word, I know <not how better to describe their effect> not to what more analogous I can liken their effect than to those natural visions at day-break, which the Sun reveals to the Earth, when he opens the lids of a thousand sleeping flowers—that look up to him in return—blushing to find themselves so happy and beautiful.

I am glad to hear (through a letter from White to Mr. Dana) that you have been so successful in your bust of Scott. W. speaks highly of it. It gave me also great pleasure to learn, by the Newspapers, that White has so well succeeded in his picture of the "Triumph of the American Flag in Mexico."[7]—As I suppose you intend to present a <copy> cast of your bust of Scott to the Athenaeum,[8] will you allow me to suggest that it will be best received by that Institution if presented in your own name. I have not any objection to presenting it in mine, if such is your wish; but I can assure you that my doing so will not be of the slightest advantage to you. On the contrary I think it will look more respectful coming from you. A work <from> presented by the Artist himself comes with a better grace, and is more likely to be valued, than if it came through another person.

I sent my Mother a little Poem—which I have dedicated to her—on the Calicanthus,[9] commonly called in Carolina the Shrub: it was the favourite flower of my childhood.† I wrote to her little more than two months ago, that is, on the 26 of December, the day after Christmas. It was in that letter that I enclosed the Poem. The Calicanthus is an exotic here; and that which occasioned these verses was the first I had seen since I was a child. I recognized it by its odour on the instant. My Mother will give you a copy of the Poem if you wish it. But I have requested her not to let it get into any Newspaper or Magazine, as I intend publishing it myself whenever sufficient materials for another potential volume shall have accumulated on my hands.[10] Will you give my love to my Mother, and tell her that both my wife and self, after a succession of heavy colds, are at present tolerably well. Mrs. A. joins me in best regards to Mrs. Cogdell & yourself. Your sincere friend,

Wa. Allston.

*In justice to myself, however, I ought not to omit to mention that I sent you a message of thanks long since, through my mother, in a letter to her from my wife.
†Mrs. A. wrote to her also about a fortnight before.

ADDRESSED: John S. Cogdell Esqre. / Charleston, / South Carolina. SOURCE: Manuscript. Printed in part in Flagg, pp. 285-86.

1. Apparently a group of drawings in cork or chalk of old masters done by Cogdell. 2. "Taste." 3. Unidentified. 4. Carlo, or Carlino, Dolce (1616-86), Italian painter, noted for his delicate style and sacred subjects. 5. Unidentified. Possibly a reference to Dutch and a group of regional French artists. 6. "Another and the same." 7. *The Unfurling of the United States Flag at Mexico,* apparently painted for the city of Charleston, S.C., by commission when WA refused to do so in 1833. It was highly praised in the *Charleston Courier* several times from 20 November 1834 to 12 November 1835, the *Charleston Mercury* for 6 December 1834, and the *Southern Patriot* for 8, 13, and 24 December 1834 (Rutledge, *Artists in the Life of Charleston,* p. 242). No reviews in Boston papers have been located. 8. Cogdell presented a cast of it to the BA, according to one account in 1833. Another cast, dated 1834, was acquired by the Charleston Library Society ("An All-Accomplished Man"). 9. "The Calycanthus. Inscribed to my Mother," with the footnote "Written on seeing this favorite flower of my childhood after an interval of many years." In it he represented the flower as a conjurer, inducing in him a dream which time could not destroy of a happy childhood, unmindful of art, passed beneath a "fervid sun," where the pomegranate, pine, and live oak with its mosses grew, particularly of summer evenings ended by his mother's prayer at his bed when he went to sleep (*LA*, pp. 328-30). 10. WA did not publish another volume of his poems. Four others, besides "America to Great Britain," "Written in Spring," the poem in Verplanck's *Address* of 1824, "The Spanish Maid," and "The Tuscan Girl," appeared in separate publications during his lifetime: "On Greenough's Group of the Angel and Child," "Rosalie," "Sonnet on the Statue of an Angel, by Bienaimé, in the possession of J.S. Copley Green, Esq.," and "Sonnet: On the Late S.T. Coleridge." All except that quoted by Verplanck were reprinted, with minor alterations in punctuation and capitalization, in *LA*.

223. To William Dunlap

Mem. wrote to Mr. Dunlap, March 20, 1835.[1]

At present I will only point out one [error]—the only important one—which is contained in the last paragraph but one,[2] which contains but only two grains of truth; namely, that I smoked and sat up late; the rest, that is, what is supposed to have been connected with these habits, is not true. You must not think that I am here wincing at the mention of my faults. I know that I have faults enough and to spare, and what is more, I have long learned to bear the mention of them. But the fault imputed to me by *inference,* in this paragraph, is really not mine. The passage which I allude to as giving a false impression of me is this: "that the time he threw away in smoking his cigar, and delighting his friends with conversation and delightful stories,[3] should have been employed in keeping up by a succession of efforts the name he had obtained."

Now, the inference drawn from this is, that I was an idler, wasting my time in company continuously. I cannot take that to myself. I was then, and am still, a very different man. Next to what is vicious, there is no character more offensive to me, or one that I would most strenuously avoid realizing in my own person, than a company-loving idler. So far from wasting time in company, my friends both in England and here have often complained that I did not go into it enough. I would not be an excuser of late hours. My late hours were spent not in company, but in solitary study: in reading, often in sketching, or in other studies connected with my art.

As to general company, it always was and is to this day irksome to me. And though I take great pleasure in the society of my friends, my visits among them have always been rare, and from choice. Nay, it is the very rareness of these visits that sometimes makes them so pleasant—bringing out what is most pleasant in myself. Strangers who have seen me with my friends, and observed the zest with which I enjoyed conversation, have probably been misled by it, and set me down as one who must needs prefer it to labor. You, indeed, have judged me truly when you say such "minds are never idle." Without assuming the compliment implied, I may say that mine is so constituted that I could not be idle for six months and continue sane. Either that or my hands are always at work.

But much as I love the interchange of mind with the literary and intellectual, still more do I love my art. I have never found the labor in it irksome, though often plied in misery and *abortive*: for when I have been most wretched, and consequently working to no purpose, it has still been to me an unchangeable friend. Although it is not natural for any man to *desire* the exposure of his faults, yet I am not one who would *gainsay* what is true, though it be against me.

SOURCE: Flagg, pp. 277-99.

1. Flagg said that he found this portion of the "rough" of this letter in the copy of his *History* Dunlap presented to WA, which contained this preliminary note. The date may be incorrect, since WA wrote Cogdell on 16 May that he intended writing Dunlap about the errors in Dunlap's account of him when he had the time. 2. In the next to the last paragraph of his account of WA, Dunlap referred to his relatively slight production after leaving London and of reports of his smoking and conversing with friends and offered the explanation that "the robust and untiring man" could make no allowance for "the man of more delicate frame, and for the lassitude and disease which follow in some men the extraordinary exertion of mind and body" but thought there was no "excuse of late hours at night even with temperance, and the waste of heaven's light by appropriating the day to sleep" (2:138). 3. WA omitted Dunlap's phrase "of which he was a most prolific inventor and unrivalled *teller*" after "delightful stories."

224. To George Cheyne Shattuck

Cambridge Port,
23 March, 1835.

Dear Sir: I accept with great pleasure your invitation to dinner on Wednesday: but regret that my engagements for the evening will prevent me availing myself of your kind offer respecting attending Professor Silliman's Lecture.[1]

With great respect, / Yrs most obliged, / Wa. Allston.

SOURCE: Manuscript.

1. During six weeks in March and April 1835 Benjamin Silliman gave a series of lectures in Boston on geology, apparently with some reference to religion, at which time he was widely entertained. On 24 March, a Tuesday, he dined at Shattuck's but apparently did not give a lecture.

On that occasion the other guests were WA, Charles Lowell, Nathaniel Bowditch, Jr., Nehemiah Adams, and the geologist Charles T. Jackson. In his account of that dinner Silliman referred to his meeting WA "many years ago," presumably in 1823, in New Haven, when WA was "a bright young man with black hair, now an old man with snowy locks" (George P. Fisher, *Life of Benjamin Silliman, N.D. LL.D.* [New York, 1866], 1:354). Probably this was the dinner to which WA referred. On 26 March Silliman dined at Lieutenant-Governor Thomas Lindall Winthrop's and afterward gave a lecture. The other guests on that occasion were WA, Edward Everett, the historian Jared Sparks, the writer Alden Bradford, Judge James Savage, a Mr. Williams from Northampton, Judge John Davis, the theologian Dr. Samuel Harris, and two sons of Winthrop. Silliman does not seem to have dined out anywhere in Boston on Wednesday 25 March. WA hardly ever made mistakes in dates but may have done so here.

225. To John Stevens Cogdell Cambridge Port, Masstts
16 May 1835.

Dear Cogdell: I wrote you last on the 10th[1] of March. A day or two after I received a note from Mr. Ticknor, mentioning the arrival of your Bust of Scott. On the same day I wrote to my Mother, and rquested her to inform you of its arrival, and to say that I would go <into> to see it as soon as the nature of my labours would allow me a day for that purpose. I did not get into Boston so soon as I wished, or expected. It is now, however, a considerable time since I have seen the Bust; and I have been every week since intending to write to you about it, but have every week been prevented by letters remaining on my hands to be answered. Mr. Ticknor, I understand, has already written to you on the subject, and I suppose has given his opinion as well as that of others upon it. You have of course been expecting my opinion also: and I will give it with frankness. I will say then, in the first place, that I found it far more successful than I had allowed myself to anticipate from the great disadvantages under which it was modelled. A Gentleman who knew Scott personally thought the upper part of the face and head remarkably like him; but observed, that he did not think the mouth and chin like Sir Walter. Of this, as respects Scott himself, I am no judge, since I never saw him; but, as it respects Leslie's Picture, I think the criticism is just. Being in the same room (Mr. Ticknor's Library) I had an opportunity of comparing them. On doing so, I found all from the bottom of the nose upwards strikingly like the picture; but the mouth and chin of the picture are certainly of a different *character* from yours.—As I take it for granted that you are above wishing to be flattered, and also that you *expect the truth from me,* I have here given my opinion candidly. As a work of Art, however, I think it does you great credit—nay, I should say, honour. In execution it is superiour to your bust of Mr. Elliot; and you may remember how highly I thought of that. And now I beg you to accept my thanks for it.—At my request, Mr. Ticknor has sent the Bust to the Atheneum,[2] where, as I think it will be more for your advantage, I shall deposit it for the present. I shall request the Committee of the Gallery also to place it in the forth-coming Exhibition—which opens, I believe, some time in June; a month later this year than usual.

Pray give my love to my Mother, and tell her that my wife intends writing to her in a few days. We are tolerably well *for us*—excepting that she has a cold—which [page torn] few are exempt from in this cold and backward spring. She unites with me in best regards to Mrs. Cogdell and yourself.—I do not fill my sheet as usual, for I have still four more letters to write, and one of them a very long one.

Your sincere friend, / Wa. Allston.

Mr. Dunlap has been led into an error by some person who could not have known me (except by *hearsay*) in the account given of me in the last paragraph but one in his biography of me. Two small items in it only are true—the rest have *no foundation*. My evenings were spent, not in the way *supposed*, but in solitary study, among my books and sketches. There is no character, not in itself vicious, that I despise more than a gossipping idler. Besides the "pencil" is "in my hand,"[3] *daily*, and, excepting the sabbath, or when precluded by business, has been so for years.—I shall request Mr. Dunlap to correct this in his second edition.[4]—Do not let this which I now write get into the *Newspapers*. I am not *blaming* Mr. Dunlap, who has been most liberal to me of praise, and who meant to be impartial, and who no doubt thought the account received correct. Besides, I have a sincere esteem for him, and would on no account hurt his feelings by any *indirect* correction of it. I intend, when I have time, writing to him on the subject.[5] In the mean time I would not have this false impression remain with my friends at a distance.

ADDRESSED: John S. Cogdell Esqre. / Charleston, / South Carolina. SOURCE: Manuscript. Printed in part in Flagg, pp. 286-87.

1. WA's letter was dated 9 March 1835. 2. It was exhibited at the BA in the first sculpture exhibition in 1839 and also in 1841. 3. Dunlap wrote that he regretted that much of WA's time had been spent "without the pencil in hand." 4. There was no second edition. 5. Presumably WA refers to the letter dated in Flagg 20 March 1835.

226. To George Ticknor Cambridge Port, 21 May, 1835.

My dear Sir: Will you do me the favour (if it be not an incumbrance to you) to take charge of this packet for Mr. Wordsworth?[1] It contains Richard Dana's volume of Poems and prose writings.[2] I do not send it at Mr. Dana's instance; it comes solely from me.

I beg you to say to Mr. W. that I would not task him for an opinion on the volume; I neither ask, nor expect it: for I dislike this indirect mode of begging praise, either for one's self, or for a friend: I send it because I think the work creditable to our Literature.

My best wishes for the health and happiness of Mrs. Ticknor & yourself attend you. Behind you will leave in me one who will ever gratefully remember your many kindnesses.

On <the> a blank leaf of Mr. Dana's book I have taken the liberty to pin a copy of my own verses, on Greenough's Group of the Angel and Child[3]—in the humble print of a Newspaper. Will you explain who Greenough is.

I remain, dear Sir, with sincere respect, your obliged friend & servant
Washington Allston

ADDRESSED: To / Professor Ticknor / Tremont House,[4] / Boston. SOURCE: Manuscript, The Wordsworth Trust, Dove Cottage, Grasmere.

1. Ticknor and his wife embarked for Europe in early June 1835 and remained until June 1838. He and Wordsworth visited each other at Rydal Mount and Ambleside on 1, 2, and 3 September 1835 (*Life, Letters, and Journals of George Ticknor* 1:401, 432-34; 2:183). They also saw each other on the Continent in 1837 and at Rydal Mount in 1838 (*Letters of William and Dorothy Wordsworth*, vol. 6, ed. Alan G. Hill [1982], pp. 88, 395, 418, 430, 583). 2. Published in 1833, revised and enlarged in 1850. A reviewer of it in *Blackwood's Magazine* thought it showed the influence of Wordsworth as well as Crabbe and Coleridge. 3. Horatio Greenough executed a marble group of an angel leading a child in 1832-33, which was called variously *Ascension of an Infant Spirit, The Ascension of a Child Conducted by an Infant Angel*, and *Journey to Heaven* and was exhibited in Boston from 4 November 1834 to 24 February 1835 (Wright, pp. 98-99). WA's poem appeared in the *Boston Daily Advertiser* for 30 December 1834. In it he said that as he stood before the sculpture he felt "that deep mystery,—for aye unknown, / The living presence of Another's mind" and that in the angel the sculptor had had the power "to draw / The veil of sense, and see the immortal race, / The Forms spiritual that know not place" (*LA*, pp. 363-65). 4. Tremont House was the most famous and popular hotel in Boston at the time.

227. To John Knapp

Cambridge Port, 6th June, 1835.

Dear Knapp: It will give me great pleasure to serve Miss Hayward[1]—both for her own sake and for yours. The only pictures which belong to me, that I can lend, are the two heads of my remaining Jews.[2] If these will be of any use to Miss Hayward, one or both are at her service.

Faithfully Yrs / Wa. Allston.

ADDRESSED: John Knapp Esqre. / Court Street, / Boston. SOURCE: Manuscript, Boston Public Library.

1. Possibly Miss C. Hayward, who may have been the daughter of Joshua H. Hayward. In 1843 she owned and exhibited at the BA his *Portrait of a Child* and the portrait of a lady by Stuart, probably Mrs. Hayward, which Hayward had exhibited in 1828. The purpose for which the paintings by WA were solicited is not known. 2. Presumably these were *Head of a Jew* (G45) and *Sketch of a Polish Jew. Head of a Jew* (G44) was bought by the BA on December 10, 1829, for $100 (receipt signed by WA, from Thomas W. Ward, treasurer, and Joseph Coolidge and Franklin Dexter, the committee acting for the Athenaeum, BA), and *Isaac of York* in 1833.

228. To Walter Channing Cambridge Port. 2 July. 1835.

Dear Doctor: Mr. Dwight's Landscape[1] is finished, and I shall be happy to shew it to you and such of your friends as may wish to see it, tomorrow afternoon. Pray come in the afternoon, as the light is better at that time; but not later than half past four.

Yours ever, / Wa. Allston

Dr. Walter Channing—

SOURCE: Manuscript.

1. Edmund Dwight (1780-1849), Boston merchant and philanthropist. WA painted for him *Landscape, American Scenery: Time, Afternoon: with a Southwest Haze,* his only located painting of an American scene and his last completed landscape. Dwight paid $500 in advance for it, with the understanding that if he was not pleased he was under no obligation to take it. WA expected more finally on account of the labor and time spent but no more seems to have been paid (Franklin Dexter to RHD, 25 July 1835; RHD to Dexter, 16, 27, 30 July 1835, Dana Papers). Dwight also owned WA's *Alpine Landscape,* after Francis B. Winthrop, and *A Roman Lady Reading.* In 1828 Gilbert Stuart painted a portrait of WA for him.

229. To John Adams Albro Cambridge Port, / Thursday Evening. [2 July 1835][1]

My dear Sir: I have a picture,[2] just finished, which I shall be happy to shew you, if you will favour me with a visit tomorrow, at half past one o'clock. I mention *this time,* as (excepting from half past one to ½ past two) I shall be engaged all <the rest of> the day. Should your own engagements, however, prevent your coming at that hour, I shall be happy to see you on Saturday, at any time from ½ past one to five o'clock.

With sincere respect & regard, / Yrs / Wa. Allston.

ADDRESSED: Revnd Mr. Albro, / Cambridge. SOURCE: Manuscript, Boston Public Library.

1. Apparently this was the date, a Thursday, on which this letter was written. WA's letter to Walter Channing saying he had just finished *Landscape, American Scenery* for Edmund Dwight and inviting him and his friends to see it the next day was written on this date. In his letter to Anna Leslie of 28 July 1835 he said he would show her a painting, presumably this one, which he had lately finished. 2. *Landscape, American Scenery.*

230. To Anna Leslie [28 July 1835]

Dear Miss Leslie: I regret very much missing the pleasure of seeing you when I was in Town. I had been, with Mr. Dexter, at Col. Perkins's,[1] and seen your copy of your brother's Picture,[2] before I called at your Lodgings. Mr. D. will do me the favour to hand you this, will repeat to you my remarks upon it. With two three slight corrections, I think it must be pronounced by all a most faithful and excellent copy. For myself, I think it does you great honour.

Mr. Dexter has promised to introduce you some day this week to my Painting-Room; where I shall be most happy to see you, though, with the exception of a small picture lately finished,[3] I have but little to shew.

Very respectfully / Yours, / Wa. Allston.

Cambridge Port, / Tuesday, 28 July, / 1835.

ADDRESSED: Miss Anna Leslie, / at Mrs. Stocker's[4] / 4 Tremont Place. SOURCE: Manuscript, Miscellaneous Papers (Washington Allston), Rare Books and Manuscripts Division, The New York Public Library, Astor, Lenox and Tilden Foundations.

1. Thomas Handasyd Perkins. 2. Unidentified. Anna Leslie's copies of Leslie's *Lady Jane Grey* and *Catherine and Petruchio* were exhibited at the BA in 1833 as for sale. 3. Presumably *Landscape, American Scenery.* It is 18 by 25½ inches. 4. Mrs. Sarah Stocker, who moved frequently, lived at this address in 1830 and 1831, on West Cedar Street from 1834 to 1836 (*Boston City Directory*).

231. To William Dunlap *Cambridgeport, October 1st, 1835.*

Sir: In my last of March, I observed that I had noticed in your kind and most friendly account of me, in the "History of American Art," a few trifling mistakes, and two or three *"supposed facts,"* which I would note down (as you requested me to do should I find any) with my remarks, and send you as soon as I had some respite from letter-writing. I must, however, postpone these remarks and write on another subject, for reasons that follow:

On taking up the first volume of your work, I was led to turn first to the life of Stuart. I had been previously told by a friend that some exaggerated praise had there been ascribed to me—though what it was he could not recollect; but I was hardly prepared for what I found in the last paragraph of page two hundred and fourteen, and in the first of the next page, volume one,[1] where I am represented as having spoken of a portrait by Stuart, as superiour to the combined efforts of Titian, Rubens, Vandyke, Rembrandt and Reynolds. Surely such extravagant praise as this must make me appear, if not a flatterer of the living at the expense of the dead, as one at least who talks at random. *But neither the opinion nor the words here reported, were mine.* I could not in conscience have so expressed myself of any work of art of the last two centuries—if, indeed, of any picture whatever. I hardly need add that I read such a report of my conversation with surprise. I must here say, however, that I read it also without any unpleasant feeling toward the reporter, for whom I have a sincere regard. Nor do I notice it now in an unfriendly spirit, being quite satisfied that it could have originated only in an inaccurate memory. I consider it merely is [as] a *misrecollection,* to which I could not possibly attach any ill motive; and as such I would now rectify it. I have often had occasion to remark that nothing is rarer than correct reports of conversation—especially after any lapse of time. Not one man in a thousand, with the best intentions, ever reports a conversation, even a single sentence, as he heard it.

I have a distinct recollection of what I said of the picture in question—a portrait of Mr. Gibbs.[2] It was this: "that I thought it *equal* to any head of Vandyke I had seen and *superiour* to any *portrait* by Rubens." This is all that I could have said, for it is all that I think of it: and surely this is high praise. Of the other picture alluded to, but not named—I suppose the portrait of Mr. Phillips[3]—I could not have said more; for, though an admirable portrait, it is by no means equal to that of Mr. Gibbs, which, so far as I have seen, is the best that Stuart ever painted.

It may not be amiss here to state the grounds of the above opinion: it will show, at least, that I had, as I supposed, some reasons for what I said, and for the particular mention of Rubens and Vandyke. I compared Stuart in this instance with Vandyke, because they seemed to me to have looked at Nature with the same eyes; and though he had less in common with Rubens, I compared him also with the latter because of their resemblance in *this instance* in colour. I am reminded of both these great painters when I see Mr. Gibbs's head; to my eye it has all Vandyke's taste, purity and truth; and with equal brilliancy, more of the last quality than any portrait I ever saw by Rubens. Lest I still be misunderstood, I would here observe, that I speak of Rubens's *portraits*—whose want of truth, in spite of their splendour, I have more than once had occasion to notice when I had seen them in the neighborhood of Titian. But with Rubens altogether, as an artist, I have never compared Stuart, high as I rate him.

I am not disposed to abate a tittle of what I said of Stuart while living, now that he is gone. I still speak of him as I did then—as an artist of great genius—and I shall ever respect his memory, as of one who has left in his fame an inheritance of honour to his country. But I should not be ministering to his *true* fame, were I to give currency to any exaggerated estimate of his powers; there are hundreds of quite as good judges on matters of art as myself, who must, and would detect it: and everyone knows what the *ebb* is to a *forced flow of praise***** Believe me, though we have never met, heartily your friend,

Washington Allston.

****I suppose you know that I have had a visit from Mr. *****[4] and Mr. Durand:[5] I need not add, that I was exceedingly pleased with them both. Durand brought with him his engraving of Vanderlyn's Ariadne: it is an exquisite performance. I had also a delightful visit from my friend Verplanck—who spoke in high terms of your work on American art: and his praise is worth having.***[6]

SOURCE: *New York Mirror*, 24 October 1835.

1. In these two passages, in one of his chapters on Stuart, Dunlap wrote that after Sully had said he never saw a Rembrandt, Rubens, Vandyke, or Titian equal to Stuart's portrait of George Gibbs and asked WA's opinion, WA replied, "I say, that all combined could not have equalled it" and that

John Neagle said WA spoke of it "not only as the best American portrait, but said that 'Vandyke, Reynolds, and Rubens, combined, could not have produced so admirable a work.'" 2. George Gibbs (1735-1803), Newport merchant. He was a brother-in-law of Channing and father of Sarah Gibbs. 3. William Phillips (1750-1827), Boston merchant and philanthropist. 4. Luman Reed. On 26 May 1835 Thomas Cole sent Reed letters recommending him and Asher B. Durand to WA and a letter to Franklin Dexter asking Dexter's aid in getting them to see paintings by WA. When Reed went to Boston later that summer with Durand he asked WA to paint a picture, apparently to be engraved by John William Casilear. WA promised to do so when his present engagements, notably *Belshazzar's Feast,* were completed, but never did. Casilear said WA's declining to paint such a picture at that time was one of the "few disappointments that I have borne with less philosophy" (Durand to Casilear, 14 June 1835; Casilear to Durand, 17 June 1835, Asher B. Durand Papers. Rare Books and Manuscripts Division. The New York Public Library, Astor, Lenox and Tilden Foundations). Apparently nothing came of the project. 5. Asher Brown Durand. He was in Boston with Reed in June 1835 to paint several portraits. At that time he paid WA three visits, and found him "the most interesting object"; he called him "our Country's Greatest Painter" and discussed with him the possibility of engraving *Spalatro's Vision of the Bloody Hand.* He did not agree to WA's proposal that he do so, though he said that had it come earlier when he was less busy it would have given him "the highest satisfaction" and that if he could obtain assistance in the subordinate parts he would undertake it for the sake of "doing some thing for so distinguished an artist." No engraving was made. While in Boston he had a visit from WA which he dreaded as an "ordeal" because of having to show some of his own work, including his engraving of Vanderlyn's *Ariadne* (Durand to Casilear; to Reed, 16 June 1835 [New York State Library, Albany]). In a letter to Durand the next year Isaac P. Davis wrote, "Allston begs to be kindly remembered to you—& speaks of you with great affection (12 June 1836, Asher B. Durand Papers, Rare Books and Manuscripts Division, The New York Public Library, Astor, Lenox and Tilden Foundations). 6. Dunlap commented in a paragraph printed following the letter that the words of WA did not appear in his work as a "deliberate criticism of a judge." He considered, he said, WA's exclamation to Sully but "a mere momentary burst of enthusiasm when standing before this admirable portrait, which he had not for some time seen," and he congratulated "that portion of the publick who are interested in and for the fine arts, that any circumstance has drawn from Mr. Alston the very valuable opinions" contained in his letter.

232. To William Wordsworth

Cambridge Port, Masstts America,
14 April, 1836.

Dear Sir: The kind reception which you have always given to my friends encourages me again to address you in behalf of a young countryman, the reverend Mr. Salisbury,[1] who, in common with most cultivated Americans on visiting England, is desirous of paying his respects to you.

I have not the pleasure of a personal acquaintance with Mr. Salisbury, though his connexions, who are among our first families,[2] are well known to me; but I beg leave to introduce him to you, as a young gentleman who is particularly recommended to myself by one of my most valued friends.

Your last volume of Poems[3] has just been republished here, but I have not yet seen it.

I remain, dear Sir, / with the highest respect / and admiration, yrs.
Washington Allston.

SOURCE: Manuscript, The Wordsworth Trust, Dove Cottage, Grasmere.

1. Edmund Elbridge Salisbury (1814-1901), orientalist and professor of Sanskrit and Arabic for many years at Yale. After graduating from Yale in 1832 he spent a year in the Theological Seminary in New Haven, though he did not enter the ministry (*Obituary Records of Graduates of Yale University* [New Haven, 1910], p. 10). He was in Europe from 1836 to 1841 studying oriental languages. 2. Salisbury's father, Josiah, came from a noted English family and his mother, Abby Breese, was of Huguenot descent. Josiah was a classmate of WA's at Harvard and a member of Channing's church until 1815, when he left it for the Old South Church, in which he was eventually elected deacon (HA). 3. *Yarrow Revisited, and Other Poems* (1835) was published in Boston by James Munroe and Company in 1835. Another issue was published the same year in New York by R. Bartlett and S. Raynor.

233. From Leonard Jarvis [20 June (?) 1836][1]

Dear Allston: Whether you accept or not the committee considered themselves bound to offer you one half of the pannels. "Old Johnny Q,"[2] as I have heard him call himself, would have offered you all four. I will see you as soon as wind & weather will permit. It is not my intention to endeavour to bias your judgment by any urgency on my part but I should be grieved to be in the smallest degree instrumental in inducing you to undertake what at a future day might occasion an unpleasant feeling. I will only say that your refusal would be a severe disappointment to many & that to remove any objections you may have the committee would almost grant you "cart blanche".

Very faithfully / Yr old friend / Leod Jarvis / Monday morning. Roxbury. Washington Allston esq.

SOURCE: Manuscript.

1. Probably this letter was written on 20 June, which was a Monday, before Jarvis had received WA's letter of the 24th. 2. John Quincy Adams.

234. To Leonard Jarvis Cambridge Port, Mass., 24 June, 1836

Dear Jarvis: I have just received your letter of the 18th inst. informing me of the passage of a Bill by Congress for supplying the vacant pannels in the Rotunda with pictures by American Artists.[1] For your friendly intention in my behalf I beg you to accept my best thanks; but I regret to say, that under present circumstances it is not in my power to profit by them. I had anticipated this contingincy, and had long since deliberately made up my mind on the subject. I *am not a free man,* nor shall I probably become one in less than three years; for after the completion of Belshazzer (*which I expect to resume in a few weeks*) I have several other pictures engaged,[2] which I am bound in honour to finish before I undertake any new work. An *expected* picture at an uncertain time is an incubus to my imagination; I have therefore under this feeling, declined five proposed commissions within the last eighteen months.[3] Could you know but the twentieth part of what I have suffered from the (*compelled*) delay of Belshazzer, you would readily believe that my peace of mind requires me to withstand the *present* temptation—for temptation it certainly is: but he is safe who knows when he is tempted, seeing the end in the beginning. Were I free from my imperative engagements nothing would delight me more than to fill one of the pannels of the Rotunda. It has often been a pleasant dream to me; but I am not my own master, and must dismiss all such dreams.

I would not recall, much less repeat, the many injurious speeches that have been made about me for not finishing this picture, though it was a private affair with which the public had nothing to do. Even some who professed to be friendly could not forbear a hard word. I do not however believe there was any ill nature in this; but words, if unjust, may be hard without ill nature. I never quitted Belshazzer at any time but when compelled to do so, by debts contracted while engaged on it, and which I could discharge only by painting small pictures; many of which from being *forced* work, cost me treble the labour and time they otherwise would have done, and consequently left but a pittance of profit—nay, some hardly enough to cover their expenses, and of course without the means of returning to the larger work. You know that I have been unremitting in my labours. For years the sabbath was the only time that I have been absent (except on business) from my painting room, and I never sit there with my arms folded. That I have not brought more to pass was because I was like a bee trying to make honey in a coalhole. But—thanks to some noble-hearted friends[4]—those dark days are now past. They have taken me out of the squirrel cage; my foot no longer falls in the same place, but every step I take carries me onward. By the assistance of these friends, my mind is now at ease; but it would not long continue so were I to accept the commission which your friendship has so kindly laboured to procure me. If in a private affair the public would reproach me for not performing an impossibility, they can hardly be expected to be more considerate when every man in the country might claim to be a party. "Will he never finish that picture for government?" might be asked from Castine[5] to St. Louis. No money could buy off the fiends that such words would conjure up. I am now an old man, and am besides too infirm of body to bear these things as some might; they would soon wear away the little flesh I have. A regard for my peace therefore will compel me to decline the government commission should it be offered me.

But I must wind up this long epistle by again expressing my grateful thanks for your kindness, which I trust you know I most sincerely feel, though for the reasons assigned, I cannot avail myself of it as you had hoped. That it might not be thought (from ignorance of my motives) that I had carelessly "thrown fortune from me," I wish you to show this letter, in *confidence,* to Mr. Preston.[6] I have written freely to you as an old friend, what I could not have written to him, and it will save me the awkwardness of a more formal exposition of the reasons for declining the honour which the Committee[7] would confer on me. Pray present my respects to Mr. Preston.

I am sorry that I cannot comply with the request contained in your Postscript.[8] I will give you my reasons (which I think you will consider satisfactory) when I have the pleasure of seeing you, which I hope will be on your return home.[9]

Give my best regards to Greenough[10] & tell him that I shall be right glad to see him.

Your old and faithful friend, / Wa. Allston

SOURCE: Manuscript copy by RHD. Printed in Flagg, pp. 287-89.

1. This letter does not seem to have been preserved. In it Jarvis informed WA that on that date a joint resolution of the Senate and the House of Representatives to appoint a committee to contract with four American artists to execute four historical paintings of subjects relating to American history to fill the vacant panels in the rotunda of the Capitol was reported by Jarvis from the Committee on Public Buildings. It was passed, with two disapprovals, on 23 June 1836. In the debate the names of WA, Sully, Vanderlyn, Rembrandt Peale, Henry Inman, John Gadsby Chapman, and Morse were mentioned. J.Q. Adams moved that WA at once be engaged for two of the paintings. It was also agreed that Vanderlyn, Weir, Inman, and Chapman be written to by the two chairmen for sketches and designs to be considered (25th Cong., 1st sess., Joint Resolution [Washington, 1836]). 2. They included certainly the painting for Jonathan Phillips, which he did not finish, and probably *Evening Hymn* for Dutton and *Rosalie* for the banker and politician Nathan Appleton. Possibly he was still working on *The Death of King John* and *Macbeth and Banquo*, both of which Walter Channing reported two and a half years earlier were "nearly finished," each engaged for $1,500 (to Morse, 20 Feb. 1835, Morse Papers, LC), neither of which was completed. 3. Their nature is not known. 4. Presumably WA refers to the sum of $3,250 in loans and gifts raised in 1835 by RHD, who acted as the treasurer, Dutton, Ticknor, Walter Channing, W.E. Channing, Dexter, the merchant Samuel Cabot, and two others to pay WA's debts, leaving $1,000, which was kept by RHD, to be used for WA's later needs. On 25 February 1835 RHD settled $2,000 of what WA owed and by 13 July had received an additional $680. At this point the question arose whether or not the $500 paid by Dwight for *Landscape: American Scenery* should be added to WA's debits, if Dwight refused to accept it (RHD to Dexter, 16, 27, 30 July 1835 [Dana Papers]; Walter Channing to Morse, 20 Feb. 1835). 5. Probably WA refers to Castine, Me. There was also a Castine in Ohio. 6. William Campbell Preston (1794-1860), South Carolina lawyer and politician. From 1817 to 1820 he was in Europe, met Irving in Liverpool in the summer of 1817, heard of WA then and may have met him in London (*The Reminiscences of William C. Preston*, ed. Minnie Clare Yarborough [Columbia, S.C., 1933], p. 36). He was a member of the Senate from 1833 to 1842. 7. The joint committee consisted of Preston, Garret Dorset Wall, Silas Wright, Jr., from the Senate, and Jarvis, Adams, John McKeon, Henry Johnson, and Benjamin Chew Howard from the House. 8. Probably Jarvis's letter of [20?] June. 9. Jarvis lived in Roxbury, a suburb of Boston. 10. Horatio Greenough was in Washington at this time to examine the rotunda of the Capitol as the site of his statue of Washington. He was in Boston from July to September 1836 (Wright, pp. 100-13).

235. From Gulian Crommelin Verplanck, Leonard Jarvis, and John Quincy Adams

Washington, July 4, 1836.

Dear Sir: The Joint Committee of the two Houses of Congress, appointed for the purpose of contracting with one or more competent artists for pictures to fill the vacant panels of the Rotunda of the Capitol at Washington, have directed us to inform you of their wish for two of the productions of your pencil.

The only restriction in the choice of the subjects would be that they must be approved by the Committee and that they must serve to illustrate some events, civil or military, of sufficient importance to be the subject of a national picture, in the history of the discovery, or settlement of the colonies which now constitute the United States of America, of the separation of the colonies from the Mother Country, or of the United States prior to the adoption of the Federal Constitution.

You would be left free with regard to the time when the pictures should be finished; the compensation will be liberal, and the payments made in proportions to suit your convenience.

Permit us to assure you of the personal gratification we derive from being the organs of this communication, and to express the earnest hope that neither your inclination nor engagements will prevent your acceptance of the commission.

We remain, very sincerely, / Your obedient servants, / G.C. Verplanck L. Jarvis, / J.Q. Adams, / *The Committee.*

SOURCE: Flagg, p. 290.

236. To Daniel Bates Woods

Cambridge Port, Mass.
6 July, 1836.

Dear Sir: It would give me great pleasure to give you the information you require if you will favour me with a call. I could not make myself intelligible by letter, without writing at considerable length; which my engagements will not allow me to do. And, to say the *truth,* I have a great aversion to letter-writing.

When I recommended the Engravers[1] whom I named, it was not that they should supply you with designs, but to execute the designs of others. The Engraver never *originates* on copper, he is a *translator.*

I shall be happy to see you any day most agreeable to you between one & two o'clock, that is, at noon. I do not name the evening, as that may be inconvenient to you: my dinner hour being now after seven. <As> Noon is the only time during the day that I can receive visitors without inconvenience.

I remain, with respect / yr obt st. / Wa. Allston.

I have no middle name.

ADDRESSED: Mr. Daniel B. Woods, / Theological Seminary, / Andover, / Massachusetts.
SOURCE: Manuscript, Gratz Collection, Historical Society of Pennsylvania.

1. Probably John and Seth Wells Cheney.

237. To Horatio Greenough[1] Cambridge Port 25 July 1836.

My dear Sir: Will you and your brother Henry do me the favour to dine with me next Friday at four o'clock? And will you be so good as to hand the enclosed Note to Mr. Mason who I believe lives in your neighborhood.[2] Should any thing however prevent your coming I will thank you not to deliver it—as I have asked him to meet you—and shall in that case hope to have the pleasure of seeing you with him at another time.

Will you favour me with an early answer by Post.

Yrs faithfully / Wa. Allston.

Mr. Dana will also meet you on Friday.

ADDRESSED: Horatio Greenough Esqre. / Care of David Greenough Esq. / Boston.
SOURCE: Manuscript, David Richardson, Washington, D.C.

1. Greenough arrived in Boston from Washington about the middle of July and remained until 27 or 28 September. His father died on 27 July (Wright, pp. 110, 111, 113). 2. The David Greenoughs lived at 7 Chestnut Street and Mason at 74 Mount Vernon Street, close together on Beacon Hill (*Boston City Directory* for 1836).

238. To Elizabeth Palmer Peabody Cambridge Port, 25 July, 1836.

My dear Miss Peabody: I exceedingly regret that it will not be in my power to call on your Sister Sophia, as I can very ill spare a day at this time. But I shall be happy to see her if she will favour *me* with a visit any day most agreeable to her at noon, that is, *between twelve* and *one o'clock*. I am thus particular in nameing the *hour*—that being the only part of the day when I can receive visitors without inconvenience. I am obliged to deny myself to every one in the afternoon, as an interruption at that time, when I am winding up the labours of the day, might be (as it more than once has been) fatal to my work.

I remain, with sincere respect,

Yrs / Wa. Allston.

so kind as to present me a copy.[1]

SOURCE: Manuscript, Miscellaneous Manuscripts Collection, LC.

1. This phrase seems to have no relationship to this letter and presumably was written in another connection.

239. To Leonard Jarvis [August, before the 15th, 1836].

[M]uch as I wish to serve Morse as a friend whom I highly value, I would not say a word in his favour, had I any doubt of his competency; but I can *conscientiously* say that I do believe him competent to the task.[1]

SOURCE: WA to Morse, 15 August 1836.

1. Painting one of the panels in the rotunda of the Capitol.

240. To Samuel Finley Breese Morse Cambridge Port, Mass: 15 August, 1836.

My dear Sir: I am a good deal troubled by a pain in one of my eyes, from over-use of them; so that I do not intend to write what is called a *letter.* But I send you these few lines, to let you know that I have not been unmindful of you on the subject of your two last letters. I saw Mr. Jarvis soon after I received your first letter—which, thinking it would come well in aid of what I had to say for you, I shewed him. I then spoke of you as you would wish, and as I honestly think you deserve. He was not here when I got the second letter. But I have lately written to him about you—and the letter, though not long, will, I think, carry some weight with it. Among other things, I observed, "that much as I wish to serve Morse as a friend whom I highly value, I would not say a word in his favour, had I any doubt of his competency; but I can *conscientiously* say that I do believe him competent to the task." This is plain language, and I think more to the purpose than would be a whole sheet of flourishes; and Jarvis, who has known me for forty years, knows that I would not have said it <for in serving [?]> to serve my own brother, if he did not deserve it. Keep a good heart, my friend, at all events. God bless you.

Yours affectionately, / Wa. Allston.

I shall no doubt see Mr. J. again when he returns to Boston.

ADDRESSED: Samuel F.B. Morse Esqre / President of the National / Academy of Design, / New-York. SOURCE: Manuscript, Morse Papers, LC.

241. To John Stevens Cogdell Cambridge Port, Masstts 18 Oct. 1836.

Dear Cogdell: I have the pleasure to acknowledge the receipt of your kind letter, by Mr. Gilman.[1] And I thank you for not noticing my long silence. This is as it should be; for it shews that you are willing to *take me as I am;* which all friends should do <towards> as to one another in this imperfect world.

I have just recovered from a severe attack of my old complaint, and, though convalescent, was very feeble when Mr. Gilman called on me, which was about a fortnight since: my strength is now, however, nearly the same as usual. My wife as well as myself has had but an ailing summer; she has suffered much from Erysipilas; but is now, thank Heaven, free from all complaints.

Your project of visiting Italy I hope may be realized. I shall rejoice to hear that you are able to accomplish it; for, as I observed to Mr. Gilman, I believe it would add ten years to your life; not only by the advantage which a change of climate would be to your bodily health, but by the renovation which that delightful country, with its thousand monuments of human genius, would produce in your spirit. You will no doubt when there become more than a mere traveller and spectator. Surrounded, as you will be, by the finest works of Art, I dare say that you will not be in Rome a month before you are hard at work, up to your eyes in clay. With the excitements that must there meet <y> one at every step, *you,* I am sure, will not be content with simply *looking*. You will find yourself growing younger in body, and more elastic in mind, and I should not be surprised if the consequence <be should be> prove a development of powers of which you are now unconscious. The lives of Claude and the french sculptor Falconnet[2]* show that genius may take a start at any period of life. Claude did not touch a pencil till he was forty: and, as Sir Joshua Reynolds well said, we are more likely to have another Raffaelle than another Claude.[3] Up to the same age Falconet was a common labourer (what is called a *boaster out* of marble) in a sculptor's Studio. He could then neither read nor write, and was withal one of the multitude. But the genius which nature had given him suddenly, but secretely, became "a presence" to his mind; and he began to develope by stealth in his scanty portions of leisure; nor was he suspected of genius till it came before the public in full growth. But he did not stop here. The rank to which his Art had raised him made him feel the want of education; which the same energetic industry soon also enabled him to supply; so that he not only learned to read and write his own language in a manner becoming a gentleman, but finally mastered both the latin and greek. I mention this not as a parallel case to yours, for you have not only had the advantage of an early liberal education, but are already advanced in the Art. I have only cited it to shew, that where genius exists it is never too late (while the other faculties remain) to bring it forth. Of the existence of this you have already given proof; And I have now only to wish that you may be placed in circumstances where it may have free scope and come to maturity. To this end and I suppose you will agree with me—<the [-]> ease of mind, especially as regards pecuniary matters, is essential. As the love of gain never yet made a <real> true Artist, <but> while it has marred many, so do I believe that no genius <was ever> *fully* developed under the pressure [of] want. I call that want which involves obligations that we are unable to discharge; which to an honorable mind, is (next to the consciousness of vice) one of the ills of life the most difficult to bear up against.

I will furnish you with letters, when you are ready to depart, with great pleasure, to some <of> who are among my most valued friends in Rome, Florence and London (I have no correspondent in France) each of them eminent artists; whom you will find also excellent men. Shall I introduce you to them as an Artist, or as one who cultivates the art for his amusement?

I was glad to see a complimentary notice of a recent picture by our friend White, in an extract from a Charleston paper.[4] The subject of it was a scene in

Marion's[5] camp. White seems to have taken a new lease of life from the spirit that animates him. Heaven prosper him, for he is a man of right heart. I was much pleased with his Mexican picture, in which Mr. Poinsett behaved so gallantly. I thought it a great advance on his "Grave Robbers." The part that I liked the least was the mountains in the background, in which he failed no doubt from want of practice in mountain scenery. But Mr. Dana, as well as myself, thought the figures managed with great spirit, and the story well told.

Pray give my love to my Mother. I suppose she has before this got my letter. I wrote her little more than a fortnight since: the second of this month. Mrs. Allston joins me in best regards to Mrs. Cogdell and yourself. I remain your sincere friend,

Wa. Allston.

*The colossal bronze statue at St. Petersburg of Peter the great is the work of Falconet.

[In the margin] The Government Commission for the Rotunda *has been offered me;* but I <have> had made up my mind not to accept any new commission until my present engagements are fulfilled. N.B. *This between ourselves.*

ADDRESSED: John S. Cogdell Esqre. / Charleston, / South Carolina. ANNOTATED by Cogdell: Answered 4 Mar. 1837. SOURCE: Manuscript. Printed in part in Flagg, pp. 291-93.

1. Samuel Gilman (1791-1858), clergyman and author. He was a teacher in Boston and a tutor at Harvard for several years until 1819. From then until his death he was minister of the Second Independent Church in Charleston, S.C. 2. Etienne Maurice Falconet (1716-91), French sculptor. In his lecture "Art" WA referred to him as an example in "some of the greatest artists" of the late development of the inventive powers (*LA*, p. 96). He owned *Oeuvres d' E.F.* [*sic*] *Falconet, Statuaire contenant plusieurs écrits relatifs auz beaux-arts, dont quelques—un dont dejà paru, mais fantifs; d'autres sont nouveaux*, 6 vols. (Lausanne, 1781). 3. The source of this statement by Reynolds has not been located. 4. *The Camp of Marion* was noticed in the *Charleston Courier* for 10 September 1836 as being from the "graceful pencil of our meritorious artist and fellow-townsman." The extract has not been located. 5. Francis Marion (1732?-95) was a general in the American Revolution. WA's father served under him.

242. To Hamilton Fish

Cambridge Port, Masstts.
9th Novbr. 1836.

Sir: I exceedingly regret that it was not in my power to see you when you called on me yesterday;[1] but my engagement at the time was of such a nature that I could not have seen any one. I was much distressed that it so happened, and would in consequence have proposed to meet you at twelve o'clock in *Boston,* but that too was equally out of my power. I beg you therefore to be assured that no disrespect was intended.

My Domestic having informed me that you spoke of business, permit me to say, that I shall be happy to receive any communication with which you may favour me on the subject.

I am, sir, very respectfully, / Your obdt servt. / Washington Allston

SOURCE: Manuscript.

1. Fish's reason for wanting to see WA is not known.

243. From Horatio Greenough [22 November 1836]

. . .[1] He[2] lives at Islington comfortably, and has in Newman Street one of the best studios I have seen—He has a numerous acquaintance. . . . [*page cut off*] What shall I say of the world of English Art: The sight of much in so short a time has bewildered me and you must excuse any incoherence in what I may say. As a school I think the English below the French—single men have pie[r]ced the thrall that holds the mass, but these are inferior to the 2nd rate men of Paris. When I look at the works of Hogarth of Wilson and Gainsborough I marvel at the supremacy of Reynolds, unless the pen he considered his sceptre instead of the pencil—I cannot allow the frowsy and beplastered portraits I see here with his name, though at a distance they look like works of the old masters, to be comparable as works of art to Stuart's or Copley's portraits. Hogarth seems to me to be their greatest man—Wilkie's best are stinted are eked out in comparison with him—He is the Fielding[3] of the English school—English in his subjects—in his style he is the natural rich product of the soil and worth all the hot house luxuries of the imitators. You will perhaps be surprised when I tell you that modern (late) buildings of [*page torn*] city are reflections of Paris—Instead of the Palladian magnificence of W[hite]hall [*page torn*] and other old palaces, they content themselves with the external portico, the new fangled Pompeian ornaments, and paint stucco & plate glass complete the 9 days' wonder[4]—I like Chantry's portraits both the busts and the full lengths better than any other modern ones I have seen—I cannot think him an inventor—his imitators of whom are 4 5ths of the English sculptors are poor enough—I would say someth[ing] [*page torn*] of the beautiful water colour pictures but have not space—I beg you to be remembered to Mr Dana and his brother and to Mrs Alston and am Dear Sir with affectionate respect

Yours / Horatio Greenough

London Nov 22 1836 / to Washington Allston[5]

ADDRESSED: Washington Alston esqr / Care of Mr Alfred Greenough / Boston. Mass. / 24th Nov. ANNOTATED: Forwarded by Your ob't Servant / Alfred Greenough / 40 India Whf / Boston 4 Jan 1837. SOURCE: Greenough, *Letters*, pp. 207-208.

1. Most of the first page of the manuscript of this letter has been cut off, leaving at the bottom of the recto only two lines and, directly above them, the words "you in person"; the verso of this manuscript page contains only the last three lines ("What . . . I think the"). 2. John

Greenough. 3. Henry Fielding (1707-54), English novelist and dramatist, crowded his works with details of life in his day, which he often satirized. 4. The Palace of Whitehall was destroyed by fire in 1691, and only its Banqueting Hall, designed by Inigo Jones and built in 1622, was restored. It is this buiding to which Greenough refers. Ornamental designs similar to those on buildings in Pompeii enjoyed a great vogue for many years after the discovery of that city in 1748. 5. These two lines are in another hand. Greenough was in London on his way back to Florence from America for about two weeks, the last in November 1836 (Wright, pp. 113, 195).

244. To Lydia Howard (Huntley) Sigourney

Cambridge Port, Masstts 2 Dec. 1836.

Madam: Your letter, of the 14th of November, has just just reached me—and that by accident—in consequence of your mistake, in directing to Cambridge, instead of *Cambridge Port*—in which latter place I reside. I mention this, as I would not be thought negligent on such an occasion, and especially towards one so highly distinguished for her character and talents. For the compliment implied in your request[1] I beg you to accept my thanks, and to be assured that I am not insensible to the honour done me by the manner in which it was made. But I regret to say, in reply, that the number of my professional and other engagements put it quite out of my power to comply with it. I must, however, add, that, were I free to do so, it would afford me real pleasure to employ my pen (humbly though it would be) for any work devoted to so good a cause.

With respect to the request of the Publisher, I am constrained also to say, that I am unable to comply. To speak frankly, it is some time since I have made up my mind never again to consent to the engraving of any picture of mine for an Annual. For this resolution I have several reasons; but the principal one is, that the *very small scale*, on which the plates for an Annual are necessarily engraved, renders it extremely difficult, if not impossible, for the best engraver to do justice to a picture—or indeed to himself. I have known no good picture that has not suffered in this diminutive translation. As I had come to this resolution long before the receipt of your letter the Publisher in whose behalf you have applied cannot, of course, take any exception <that I> at my declining his proposal.

I am, Madam, / with great respect, / Your obt Servt. / Washington Allston

ADDRESSED: Mrs. L.H. Sigourney / Hartford / Connecticut. [The original address has been cancelled and "Care George Griffin Esq / No 20 Beach Street / Hudson Park" written in in another hand.] SOURCE: Manuscript, Connecticut Historical Society.

1. Mrs. Sigourney had presumably asked WA for the contribution of a painting to be engraved in the literary annual *Religious Souvenir*, of which she was editor in 1836. Most of the artists whom she solicited declined, giving the same reason as WA (Gordon S. Haight, *Mrs. Sigourney: The Sweet Singer of Hartford* [New Haven, Conn.: Yale Univ. Press, 1930], p. 39).

245. To Samuel Finley Breese Morse Cambridge Port, Mass.
2 Jany. 1837.

My dear Sir: I saw Mr. Jarvis on his way to Washington, and I am happy to tell you that I found him, as I expected, well disposed towards you.[1] He said that he would do all he can for you. He has been ill all the summer, which was the reason that he did not meet Mr. Preston here, as he had, I believe, originally intended.

Besides this piece of information, which you ought to have had before this, there is another subject in which <y> I wish to interest you, and which I have no doubt will; that is, the destitute condition of poor Stuart's widow.[2] You may not know that her sole dependence now is on the talents of her daughter Jane,[3] but I am well informed that she has no other source to look for a maintenance. And though the poor Girl is indefatigable, the avails of her industry, as you may suppose, must be but a mere trifle in such a place as Newport.[4] It is true that the living is cheaper there than in most places, but little as they may require, yet even that is wanting. They are no less exposed to suffering than if they lived in a more populous and dearer city. And this, I have been told by persons from Newport, was a fact of bitter experience to them during the last winter. They were in actual want, and would have known it in its extremity, but for the humanity of some of their neighbours. Now this should not be in a country like ours. In after times it will appear incredible that the immediate <descendants> family (not the remote posterity) of one of the first artists that America has produced, whose very name she is now proud to wear upon her young escutcheon—that the wife and children[5] of such a man should, within ten years of his death, be found struggling for a bare subsistence—must appear incredible. But I need not make an oration <of> on the subject. You, I am sure, would not need one. Nor can I think that any other man of feeling to say nothing of patriotism, would require more than a plain statement of the fact. Now to the point. Is it not possible to do something for this unfortunate family in the way of subscription?[6] If it be confined even to the Artists (though I hope it will not) something might be done—at least to help them through this inclement season. Will you set such a subscription on foot? It is my intention to do so in Boston. I cannot but believe that every artist will readily open his purse according to his ability. Mine is at present low enough, but I shall squeeze hard to get something out of it.—I would make one observation: that it is not necessary to make a show of the sums subscribed by each individual (unless they chuse it) as there may be some <who give might be> well disposed to give, yet, having but little to spare, who might withhold it from false shame, if <their names> the amount should be made to stand opposite their names. It is no new thing that pride even in this small way should stifle charity.—I must add, that none of the family in whose behalf I write know any thing about it.

*[I am at a loss to guess what has become of the colours that Mr. Rover[7] was to send me. I am in great want of the Flake White. You remember that I requested them to be sent to the care of Mr. Pendelton. <but> Have they been sent? My Nephew[8]

informs me that Pendleton, as he believes, has left Boston; at any rate he has removed from his store in Washington Street.[9] Now if Mr. P. has left the city, and the Colours have been <fo sent with his former address> sent to Boston, to his care, they must be now on a wild goose chase. Do let me know something about them, as I am sadly in need of them; and send me at the same time Mr. Rover's address, that I may know how to get a letter to him. In case the colours should not yet have been forwarded, I will thank you to request Mr. Rover to direct to the care of Mr. Edmund T. Hastings, 22 <Commercial> Merchants Row Boston;[10] and also that he will inform me, by Mail <how I am to> in what way I am to transmit the money for them.][11]—By the way, would not Mr. Verplanck be a good person to consult with about the subscription for Mrs. Stuart?—I have filled my paper without knowing it.

Yours affectionately, Wa. Allston.

*I have just received the colours.

[In the margin] N.B. Jany 3. I have luckily *just received* Mr. Rover's Colours. They were brought out by the omnibus from Boston—but by whom sent I know not—whether by Mr. Pendleton or some other person; though I think it must be by Mr. P. as I find with the box of colours Mr. Rover's letter to him, containing his bill. Now I wish to pay this bill, but where, shall I find Mr. Pendleton? There is on the letter to him only the general address of "Boston." Will you get his specific address from Mr. Rover, and send it to me, so that I shall know where to find him.

Source: Manuscript, Morse Papers, LC.

1. That is, to have Morse commissioned to paint one of the panels in the rotunda of the Capitol. 2. Stuart's wife was the former Elizabeth Coates, daughter of a physician of Reading, England (Whitley, *Gilbert Stuart,* p. 51). 3. Jane Stuart (1812-88), portrait painter, chiefly, remembered for her copies of her father's works. She had her own room in Boston and after moving to Newport in 1831 returned there occasionally to work, having a studio in the 1850s. She appears to have lived in New York in 1833. 4. Mrs. Stuart, her daughters Jane, Anne, Emma, and a fourth moved to Newport in 1831 (Whitley, *Gilbert Stuart,* p. 220). 5. Stuart had six children who lived to adulthood: Charles (ca. 1781-1813), landscape painter, another son, and four daughters (Mount, pp. 297, 304). 6. No subscription seems to have been made. 7. Henry Rover was an artist's colorman in New York from 1822/29 to 1838/39 (*New York City Directory*). 8. George W. Flagg. 9. Pendleton's address in Boston from 1828 to 1837 was at different locations on Washington Street (*Boston City Directory*). 10. Hastings was located at 22 Merchant's Row in 1827 and 1828. From 1834 to 1836 his address was 37 Commercial Street (*Boston City Directory*). 11. WA's brackets.

246. To Robert Cassie Waterston

Cambridge Port,
23 Jany. 1837.

Dear Sir: I beg you to accept my thanks for Ion.[1] I was very much pleased with the extracts from it which I saw in the Edinburgh Review,[2] and expect to be still more so with the work itself.

I hope we shall soon see you—that is, *after this week,* during which I shall probably be engaged every evening.

Believe me, with sincere regard, yrs / Wa. Allston

ADDRESSED: Robert C. Waterston Esqre / Boston. SOURCE: Manuscript.

1. Sergeant Talfourd, *Ion; a Tragedy: To which are added A Few Sonnets,* 2d ed. (London, 1836). It was printed for private circulation. 2. A review of *Ion* appeared in the *Edinburgh Review* 63 (Apr. 1836): 143-56, which contained several quotations from the title poem.

247. To Leonard Jarvis Cambridge Port, Masstts 3 Feby 1837.

Dear Jarvis: You will see by the enclosed[1] that I have declined the proposed Commission, from your Committee, for one of the National Pictures. After the maturest deliberation, I find this to be the only course by which I can hope to secure my peace of mind. I am not insensible to the kindness of the Committee in the latitude which they allow me as to time: it is in the highest degree (I will not say flattering, for I hate that unenglish word—but) gratifying to me; indeed I feel myself so much honoured by it that, but for the remembrance of what I have suffered for the last ten years, I might be tempted to accept the commission under such a condition. But the *past* is too fresh in my mind to allow me to hazard my peace by entering into any engagement of so public a nature, however remote the time when I may be expected to fulfil it. That *any thing at any time should be expected of me by the public is what I would avoid.* Now the acceptance of the proposed Commission, even under this liberal condition, must of necessity have this consequence: and I feel too well that my shattered nerves are quite unequal to the contemplation even of a distant and contingent public obligation. The thought of leaving an *unfulfilled engagement* to reproach my memory would haunt me in every illness. I hope therefore, if I have not expressed myself with sufficient clearness, that you will make it *distinctly understood,* that I have *declined* the proferred commission as well for the *future* as for the *present.*

I know you will excuse this particularity in an old man, and a nervous one—made so by a series of trials of which the public little dream. I wish to have it in my power, in case of need, to say (especially to the Newspapers) that I am under no engagement of any sort. You will be the less surprised at this minuteness, when I tell you that I saw it announced a few weeks ago, in an extract from the New-York Mirror,[2] that I had *already* "*accepted* the commission for one of the pictures." I have reason to think that this mistake was made with the best intentions—being couched in very complimentary terms—but it was nevertheless very annoying—and the more so as I could not notice it without anticipating my reply to your Committee—which would certainly have been disrespectful. I suppose the report originated in this way: I was told sometime last fall, <that> by a friend who resides in New-York,[3] that it was generally known there that two of the national pictures had been offered me. Upon which I requested him to say, that I *would never* under any circumstances accept more than one; and that I had formed this resolution (as is well known to my friends here) so long ago as when Mr. Verplanck was in Congress. I made this request of my friend with reference to the Artists; that they might know the kind of feeling which I had towards them; not that I wished to be commended for a "good" feeling, but <because that report what> to claim for myself what I considered <it> a *proper* one. From this they no doubt concluded that, as I would not accept the two pictures, I *must therefore* have accepted one! This (conversation) took place sometime before I saw you last, on your way to Washington, and you well know that I had not then definitely made up my mind on the subject, but left <that> it for the last moment, as I wished to give it the fullest consideration.

I have now only to say, that I trust to your friendship for assuring all the Gentlemen of the Committee of my unfeigned gratitude for their kindness. The good opinion which they are pleased to entertain of me is an honour which I shall never forget.

Mrs. A. sends you her kind regards, as does also Ned. Believe me, my old friend, I was truly rejoiced to lern that you have taken a new lease of health. I read something—though I have now forgotten what—from your Doctor[4] two or three years ago, and I remember that it impressed me as coming from a man who knew what he was about. I always thought you had a tough constitution, but at our time of life a few additional rivets don't come amiss to the toughest.

Ever affectionately yours, / Washington Allston.

If you think it adviseable, you are at liberty to communicate as much of the contents of this private letter as you may think proper to the Gentlemen of the Committee.
To the Hon. Leonard Jarvis.

ADDRESSED: Honble Leonard Jarvis, / Member of Congress,[5] / Washington, / District of Columbia. SOURCE: Manuscript. Printed in George Davis Chase, "Some Washington Allston Correspondence," *New England Quarterly* 15 (1943): 629-31.

1. This letter does not seem to have been preserved. 2. The *New-York Mirror* (1823-57) was a weekly periodical devoted to literature, art, and society. The issue for 10 December 1836 carried an article entitled "Washington Allston," which, after stating that he had finished several small paintings "of the first class" within the last two years, that *The Death of King John* was on his easel, and that he had declined receiving any more orders until *Belshazzar's Feast* was finished, went on to say that it was reported "on good authority" that two of the four commissions for paintings for the rotunda had been offered him "but he has accepted only one, and that on condition that he may be allowed his own time for commencing it, with the positive assurance, on his part, that he will not think of it, until the long dormant paintings shall be completed." It added that the subject was left to his choice, with the only restriction that it be an event of American history, and concluded, "Truth and taste will guide the selection; and aid, with learning, genius and skill, in the execution of whatever this eminent artist undertakes." In an earlier article, appearing on 10 September 1836, the *Mirror* said it had heard no more of "The National Pictures" but that the members of the committee in charge of them would meet in Boston again and "Washington

Allston will be near them." 3. Morse. 4. Unidentified. 5. Jarvis was a member of the House of Representatives from 1829 to 1837.

248. To Leonard Jarvis Cambridge Port, Massts 13 Feby. 1837.

Dear Jarvis: I wrote you on the third of this month (february) two letters, one private, enclosing another to you as Chairman of the Committee on the subject of the National Paintings for the Capitol. As I forgot to ask you to *acknowledge their receipt,* I write now to request you to let me know if they have reached you. One line, stating that they have been received will be enough. The *possibility* of the miscarriage of the Mail, in a snow-storm &c, at this season is my <requ> reason for making the request; which I will thank you to comply with immediately on the receipt of this; so that, in case the letters *have* miscarried, I might have time to transmit to you duplicates* before the close of the present Session. It is more especially important that I should be informed of their fate, as I have, in them, declined the proferred Commission from the Committee.

I was quite ashamed of the paper on which the above named letters were written, when I came to notice it the next morning; but it was the best I had in the house, and I could not procure better without some delay.

I did not think to have written more than ten lines when I I began this. <and> I believe my "horror" of letter-writing has one of its sources in my inability to write a short one.

I hope you continue to thrive under your medical discipline.

Ever Affectionately Yrs, / Wa. Allston.

*From the rough copies, which I have preserved.

ADDRESSED: Honble Leonard Jarvis, / Member of Congress, / Washington, / District of Columbia. SOURCE: Manuscript. Printed in George Davis Chase, "Some Washington Allston Correspondence," *New England Quarterly* 15 (1943): 631-32.

249. To Samuel Finley Breese Morse Cambridge Port, Massts 25 Feb. 1837.

My dear Sir: I have received your letter in reply to my last, and thank you for the efforts which you have so kindly made, at my suggestion, in behalf of poor Stuart's Widow: on which subject I shall say more at another time, my object now being to say a few words concerning myself.

I find to my utter surprise a paragraph going the rounds of the Newspapers, stating that I had accepted the Commission, offered by the Committee of Congress, for one of the pictures which they have ordered for the Capitol; and moreover, that I had accepted it under certain conditions—namely of executing it at my own time &c. This statement it seems appeared more than a month ago* in the New York Mirror; from which it has been copied into the papers here.[1] <And> It has worried me more than you can imagine; and the more so that I could not notice it at the time without *anticipating my answer to the Committee*—which I did not send until the *third of this Month* [February].[2] I had delayed my answer until this time, as I observed in my letter to Mr. Jarvis, "in order that I might give the subject the fullest consideration." Now that <my> the answer is at last sent, it is proper that I correct the mistake. I will therefore thank you to have the following paragraphs, which are *enclosed in brackets,* inserted in the New-York Mirror.[3] First, however, assuring the Editor,[4] that I have no ill feeling whatever towards the writer of the paragraph alluded to; indeed I could not reasonably entertain any such feeling (however the mistake might have <[undecipherable word]> troubled me) since it was certainly couched in very complimentary terms. <I should never doubted that it written> and was evidently written with a very friendly motive—or rather, I should say, in a very friendly spirit.—You need make no other preface to the following than this: "Extract of a letter from Washington Allston to a Friend in New-York." I do not wish you even to say who that friend is; that being quite unnecessary.

[There having appeared <more than a month since> nearly two months ago† an article in the New-York Mirror, stating that I had accepted a Commission for one of the National Pictures, voted by Congress. I must request the favour of you to have the following statement inserted in that journal.

When the article alluded to appeared in the Mirror, I had not made up my mind on the subject farther than this—that I would not, under any circumstances, accept more than a commission for one Picture, should I conclude in the affirmative; and this resolution <that> I had formed <[three or fur undecipherable words]> (as is well known to my friends here) so long ago as when Mr. Verplanck was in Congress: that *I did not send my answer on the subject to the Committee until the third of this month [February];* and that in that answer *I have altogether declined the proferred Commission:* <and> further, that I did not rectify the article at the time it first appeared, *because I could not have done so without anticipating my answer to the Committee*—which would have been, to say the least, not respectful: finally, that I had delayed the answer until the time above-mentioned in order to give the subject the fullest consideration. My reasons for the result being wholly of a private nature, I shall not speak of them here.—I trust it is hardly necessary for me to add, that I duly appreciate the honour which I have thus been obliged to decline. I shall ever gratefully remember it; nor shall I soon forget the peculiar favour with which the Committee have honoured me on this occasion.][5]

I cannot imagine how the story should have taken the shape in which it appeared in the Mirror. Could it have grown out of what I requested you to say concerning my resolution (so long ago formed) on no account to accept more than one of the offered pictures? If so, it seems to me strange logic, that because I had resolved not to accept *two,* that people should *conclude* I *must therefore have accepted one!* When I made this request of you, it was with reference to the Artists; that they might know the kind of feeling which I had towards them: not that I wished to be commended for a "good" feeling, but to claim for myself what I considered a *proper* one. This was all that I wished you to make known in New York; here it had been long made known by myself.—Do not suppose that I think the report came from you. I know it could not: as what passed between us concerning the future was altogether contingent and hypothetical, and expressed merely my *wishes*, not *my intentions*, for the latter I did not know myself, as they would depend on future circumstances; and, besides, they took no definite shape, as I was merely building castles with you in private conversation. But now that I have sent my answer to the Committee, I have done with castle-building on public ground. In this matter my resolution is fixed; it is the only way in which I can hope to secure my peace. So there's an end on 't.

The above was written (as you will have seen by a Note on the first page) <above> more than a fortnight ago. [I have since learned the disposition of the "Pictures."][6] I had hoped to have found your name amongst the commissioned Artists; but I was grieved to find that all my efforts in your behalf have proved fruitless. I know what your disappointment must have been at this result, and most sincerely do I sympathize with you. That my efforts were both sincere and conscientious I hope will be some consolation to you. But let not this disappointment cast you down, my friend; You have it still in your power to let the world know what you can do. Dismiss it then from your mind, and determine to paint all the better for it. God bless you. Your affectionate friend,

Washington Allston.

*now more than two months.

†I make this alteration in consequence of the delay of this letter since it was written.

[In the margins] N.B. This letter was written on [the 23rd] [page obscured by mounting tape] of Feby but left without date, as I wished before I sent it, to learn if my answer to the Committee had been received at Washington. I did not ascertain this until three days ago. Accordingly I have dated from *today.* Should any private conveyance offer, pray remember to send me some Ohio Brown. My wife desires her best regards to you. The Postmaster at Cambridge handed me two dollars, at your request. Pray for what purpose?

SOURCE: Manuscript, Morse Papers, LC. Two paragraphs printed in Morse, 1:32.

1. Copies of the article in Boston newspapers have not been located. 2. WA's brackets. 3. The two paragraphs appeared in the *New-York Mirror* for 18 March 1837, followed by "Remarks" by the editors stating that WA had declined the offer for two pictures for reasons they considered "highly admirable," since he wished that other artists might also have an opportunity to be chosen, and that they regretted that any circumstance should prevent the country from possessing at the capital a work by a living painter who was the first in this and "probably in any other country." 4. George Pope Morris (1803-64) became editor in 1824, joined in 1828 by others. 5. WA's brackets. 6. The commissions for the paintings for the rotunda were given to John Gadsby Chapman for *The Baptism of Pocahontas*, Weir for *The Embarkation of the Pilgrims*, Vanderlyn for *The Landing of Columbus*, and Henry Inman. Inman was first refused and

Morse was reconsidered, but J.Q. Adams persuaded Inman to accept. When he died in 1846, before completing his painting, an effort was made to have the commission given to Morse, but it went to William H. Powell, who painted *The Discovery of the Mississippi River by DeSoto* (Fairman, pp. 78, 106, 114-21).

250. To James McMurtrie Cambridge Port, Masstts
2 March 1837.

My dear Sir: I am more ashamed than I can express to have so long delayed replying to your kind letter.[1] But I have had a good deal of late to trouble me—besides, many letters to write—that *must* have been written, *willy* or *nilly.* This I hope you will accept as my apology; and I trust you will so receive it, when I assure you, that though it is twenty years since we have met, not even that interval of time has abated a jot of my regard, or dimmed the impression of your former kindness.

I am happy to agree with you *entirely in all* you propose respecting a Print from the Mother and Child.[2] I have seen some of Cousins'[3] Engravings (or, I suppose I should say, mezzotints, for I believe some Artists make this distinction) and feel satisfied that he will make a fine print from the Picture. The whole of your plan seems to me so judicious, that I should be at a loss to suggest any improvement. The size proposed appears to me the proper one; it should neither be larger nor smaller. I have but one request to make in regard to it—that is, that you will have my name attached to it at full length—i.e. Washington Allston. I ask this, because I remember to have been a good deal annoyed once in London on seeing the initial of my Christian name, "W." changed in an Exhibition catalogue to "Wm."

I am glad to learn that you have any business that will take you to Italy.[4] It is a country which every man who loves the Arts should see, if possible. I dream of it continually. I might almost say, that I am in some part or other of it (in imagination) once a month. I was last night in the Chapel of St. Lorenzo, at Florence, standing before the <tomb> monument of Lorenzo Medici;[5] and, though but in a waking dream so powerfully did I feel the presence of those sublime personifications of Michael Angelo, that I almost began to think of <the> his Morning and Evening as of real beings. I know not how the Greeks may have been affected by their Dryads and river Gods, but the every-day flesh and blood that I see are not more real to my senses, than the Ideal Forms of Michael Angelo seem to my imagination.—The *power* of our Art (and I feel sure that when there you will agree with me) cannot be known out of Italy. It is there only where you will find the existence of invisible Truth proved palpably. At least, I cannot well conceive how any imaginative man can return from Rome and Florence, without having felt that there are other Truths besides such as are begotten thro the senses. And then, perhaps, he may wonder why he catches elsewhere such rare glimpses of the Ideal world he has left. I do not believe in the influence of climate; <in this matter;> for I am unwilling to admit <the> a material agency in this matter. Why we have so little of this ideal revelation *now*, is, perhaps, explained in the matter-of-fact character of the present age.[6] Men are too busy with the palpable useful to open their minds to those higher influences which in other times were considered as the natural cravings of an immortal spirit.—But I am getting out of the latitude of a letter.

Remember me most cordially to my valued friend, Sully, and believe me, dear Sir,

Your sincere friend, / Washington Allston.

ADDRESSED: James McMurtrie Esqre / Philadelphia, / Pennsylvania. SOURCE: Manuscript, Dreer Collection, Painters & Engravers, Historical Society of Pennsylvania.

1. This letter does not seem to have been preserved. 2. Presumably *A Mother Watching her Sleeping Child*. 3. Samuel Cousins (1801-87), English mezzotint engraver. Nothing further about an engraving by him of WA's painting seems to be known. 4. McMurtrie apparently went to Italy for his health. 5. The tomb of Lorenzo de' Medici (1449-92) is in the New Sacristy of the Church of San Lorenzo in Florence. Over it are Michelangelo's statues of *Aurora* and *Crepuscolo*. 6. This sentence and several sentences preceding it are a variation of Monaldi's words, "'Tis now the fashion to talk of Michael Angelo's extravagance, of his want of truth, and *what not*—as if truth were only in what we have *seen!* This matter-of-fact philosophy has infected the age" (*Monaldi*, p. 84).

251. To Catherine Scollay

[3 May 1837 (?)][1]

My dear Miss Scollay: I will endeavour to call on you either on Saturday or next Tuesday, about one o'clock—a little before if I can. It will give me sincere pleasure to be of service to you.

With sincere / respect & esteem, yrs / Wa. Allston

Cambridge Port. / Wednesday, 3 May.

ADDRESSED: Miss C. Scollay, / Bowdoin Street, / Boston. SOURCE: Manuscript, Miscellaneous Papers (Washington Allston), Rare Books and Manuscripts Division, The New York Public Library, Astor, Lenox and Tilden Foundations.

1. The last known letter of WA's from Boston was 28 October 1829 and the first from Cambridgeport 1 March 1830. The only years in which 3 May fell on a Wednesday from then until WA's death were 1837 and 1843. It seems more likely that he was in touch with Miss Scollay at the earlier date, closer to the time that *Spalatro's Vision of the Bloody Hand* was exhibited at the home of her and her mother.

252. To Solyman Brown

Cambridge Port, Masstts
12 June, 1837.

Dear Sir: I have just received your favour of the 6th inst; and, while I beg the Society[1] to accept my sincere thanks for the further honour they have done me, by the flattering proposal in your letter, I feel myself constrained to decline it. To speak frankly, I have a strong repugnance to becoming a mere nominal Member of so important a Literary Society as yours; and, as I have already stated in my former letter, I am so circumstanced that I am quite sure I never can be more to it than a blank appendage. I can only therefore reassure them—which I do most sincerely—of my best wishes for their success.

I remain, dear Sir, / very respectfully, / your obdt st / Wa. Allston.
Solyman Brown Esqre.

SOURCE: Manuscript, Special Collections, Van Pelt Library, University of Pennsylvania.

1. Unidentified.

253. To Anna Brownell (Murphy) Jameson

Cambridge Port,
20 Oct. 1837.

Dear Madam: Will you permit me to ask your acceptance of the Enclosed.[1] It is an attempt to express what I felt on reading your first Work—"The Diary of an Ennuyée"[2]—at least, the first of your writing that I had seen.

Allow me to add—for the sincerity of the sentiments they contain—that the Verses were written while your name (now so justly distinguished) was yet unknown to me. This was in 1834.[3] It was not long, however, before I had the satisfaction of learning to whom I was indebted for so much pleasure; when I obtained your address, in order to transmit to London this expression of my gratitude—for such, with *me* at least, is the feeling left by a good book, or a good picture; but in this I have been disappointed, by the want of a suitable private conveyance; and, as I could not bring myself to oblige a Lady *to pay even sixpence for a compliment,* I was unwilling to commit it to the Post Office. Nor am I less grateful than the Public—is, or ought to be—for your exquisite subsequent works, more especially for your Analysis of Shakespeare's Female Characters.[4]

Believe me, dear madam, that my pleasure in the meeting of today[5] was as sincere as it was unexpected.

With unfeigned admiration / and respect, I remain / Your obt. St.
Washington Allston.

P.S. On looking over the Verses after a long interval, an indistinct impression comes upon me, that for "play-mates of the Soul," in the sixth stanza, I am indebted to *Somebody.*[6] To whom I know not. Perhaps not. If I am, your better memory will no doubt restore the thought to the true author, in which case pray do me the favour to supply the inverted commas. W.A.[7]

ADDRESSED: To / Mrs. Jameson, / Tremont House. SOURCE: Manuscript, Houghton.

1. His poem "To the Author of 'The Diary of an Ennuyée,' One of the Truest and Most Beautiful Books Ever Written on Italy." C.C. Felton delivered it to her (Review of WA's *Lectures on Art, and Poems,* in *North American Review* 55 [1850]: 154). It was one of the most beautiful and touching of WA's poems and the most moving of his recollections of Italy besides his paintings. In it he said

the book awakened him, as from a sleep of years, not the memory but "the breathing, bounding, *present* youth," "that vision clime, / Which, having seen, no eye the second time / May ever see in its own glorious truth;— / As if it *were not,* in this world of strife, / Save to the first deep consciousness of life." . . . "E'en in Thy freshness do I see thee rise, / Bright, peerless Italy, thy gorgeous skies, / Thy lines of harmony, thy nameless hues,— / As 't were by passing Angels sportive dropped / From flowers of Paradise, but newly cropped, / Still bathed and glittering with celestial dews!" He felt "the Tuscan Zephrys" brush him "As if their touch another sense had given" and implored them, "O, now, as once, pure playmates of the soul! / Bear me, as then, where the white billows roll / Of yon ethereal ocean, poised above." In conclusion he entreated the author: "O, thus to me be thou still ministrant, / Still of the universal Love descant / That all things crave,—thus visible in thee, / The type and register of what man was / Before sin thralled him, substituting laws / That fain from suffering would his spirit free; / Nay, more, be hope,—the soul's sure prophecy / Of lost, regained, primeval harmony"(*LA*, pp. 377-79). 2. *The Diary of an Ennuyée* (1826), Mrs. Jameson's first book, was an account in the person of a fictitious character of her trip to Italy, accompanied by a young boy for whom she was governess, in 1825. She gave it, under the title *A Lady's Diary,* to a bookseller on the condition of receiving a guitar if he made any profits, which condition was fulfilled. He sold it to Henry Colburn, who changed the title and published it. WA read it, possibly in the edition published in Boston in 1833, the first in America after the reprinting of the London edition the year it first appeared. It next appeared, with her *Visits and Sketches at Home and Abroad,* printed in New York in 1834. 3. A copy by WA bears the date "June 1834" (Houghton). RHD, Jr., said he added the last stanza after meeting Mrs. Jameson (to his brother Edmund T. Dana, 23 November 1837, Dana Papers). In it he addressed her as "fair Sibyl," said he might not learn "how to say farewell," would part from her "but not forgetting we have met," and wished that "that sweet sadness thou so well dost feign / To thee be ever feigned,—be but the strain / To which the happy soul doth often set / Her happiest moods; for joy and sadness dwell / As neighbors in the heart" (*LA*, pp. 379-80). 4. *Characteristics of Women* (1832). 5. WA met Mrs. Jameson at the home of Mrs. William Minot, wife of a Boston merchant. She was staying at the Tremont House but having meals at Mrs. Minot's and after she expressed great admiration for his pictures and a desire to meet him, Mrs. Minot arranged a dinner, which consisted of WA, Channing, the writer Hannah Farnham (Sawyer) Lee, Jared Sparks, Josiah Quincy, Mr. Minot, their daughter Mary, and herself. The hour was set at six to suit WA, who wanted all the daylight for painting. They did not separate until nearly eleven. "The conversation," she wrote her friend Mrs. Robert Hallowell Gardiner, wife of the well-known agriculturalist, who was a collegemate of WA's, "was intellectual, but very animated, and full of variety, Mrs. J. of course giving the tone but never engrossing attention" (17 Dec. 1837, Dana Papers). 6. The suggested indebtedness has not been identified. 7. Ralph Waldo Emerson read WA's poem on 20 September 1837, possibly through the agency of C.C. Felton, who visited him about that time and through whom WA sent the copy to Mrs. Jameson a few weeks later. Emerson thought that it was "very good & entirely self-taught, original—not conventional" and conveyed an "admonition," but that it failed in celebrating Italy "not as it is, but as it is imagined" and declared, "the man is not yet married to nature who sighs ever for some foreign land" (*The Journals and Notebooks of Ralph Waldo Emerson,*, vol. 5, ed. Merton M. Sealts, Jr. [Cambridge: Harvard Univ. Press, 1965], p. 377). He incorporated part of the entry and referred to the poem as written by an "eminent painter" in the opening sentences of "Self-Reliance" (1841).

254. To William Wordsworth Cambridge Port, Mass: Oct. 27 1837.

Dear Sir: I have asked the honour of your notice for so many of my countrymen, that I should fear to become importunate, by adding another to the list, did I not believe that in the kindness of your nature you will not so consider it. And I should be sorry to think otherwise on this occasion, as the gentleman whom I now beg leave to introduce to you is one whom I could wish you to know, as well for his own sake, as for the just reverence in which he holds your character.

Mr. Sumner[1] is much respected by the Legal Public as the able editor of our best Law Journal, "The American Jurist;"[2] nor is he less esteemed in private for his personal merits; and, for his Literary taste—I know no one among your many ardent admirers on this side the water who better appreciates the Beauty and Wisdom which your Genius has embodied in such enduring forms.

Be pleased to present my respects to Mrs. Wordsworth and Miss Hutchinson.

I cannot send a line to England without imploring a blessing, in my heart, on the Land of my Fathers. England knows not how many here love and honour her.

Believe me, dear Sir, / with the highest respect, yrs, / Washington Allston.

SOURCE: Manuscript, The Wordsworth Trust, Dove Cottage, Grasmere.

1. Charles Sumner. He was in Europe from December 1837 to May 1840. On 8 September he described his recent visit to Wordsworth, who, he said, "spoke in the kindest terms of Mr. Washington Allston, and inquired earnestly after his health and circumstances," regarded him as "the first artist of the age," to whom he was attached by a two-fold relation—"first as his own friend, and then as the affectionate friend of Coleridge," and asked Sumner to convey to him his "warm regards, and those of Mrs. Wordsworth and all his family." Early the next year Sumner visited Collins, who asked about and wanted to be remembered to WA, and heard Southey's opinion that some of WA's poems were "among the finest products of modern times" (Edward L. Pierce, *Memoir and Letters of Charles Sumner* [Boston, 1878], 1:355; 2:70). 2. *The American Jurist and Law Magazine* (1829-46) was edited by Sumner, Luther S. Cushing, and George S. Hillard from 1836 to 1843 (Mott, p. 451).

255. From Anna Brownell (Murphy) Jameson Nov 22 1837

My dear Sir: Praise in such rich words composed—in such glowing form as those which you have arrayed there, what *can* I say? except that I am more grateful and gratified than I can tell you.[1]

I wish I could talk to you of some of your pictures which I saw yesterday.[2] I am easily pleased (thank heaven for it) because excitable by Beauty under all aspects and forms—but scarcely ever *satisfied,* for how seldom are the understanding, the feelings—the taste, appealed to & gratified at once? To offer praise to you seems presumption, but may I not say that in the union of the finest principles of colouring with the intellectual expression and lofty poetic feeling & grandeur of design, with the high & what I must call conscientious, finish of the subordinate parts, you do *satisfy* me more than any living artist I know. Eastlake[3] comes nearest you, among our English painters. I wish you could see some of his pictures & how I wish he could see your Rosalie[4] or your Jeremiah or the Persian Lady—[5]

I please myself with the thoughts of seeing you and listening to you on Friday![6] I hope there will be nobody but Mr. Dana[7]—for I have sympathies with him & in the presence of strange people I never venture a question still less a criticism—I am dear Sir with the highest respect & admiration truly yours

Anna Jameson

SOURCE: Typescript by H.W.L. Dana, Longfellow National Historic Site.

1. Mrs. Jameson had apparently just received WA's letter of 20 October and the poem he sent with it. Possibly she had gone out of Boston during the intervening month. RHD, Jr., said she arrived about 16 November and was leaving on the 23d. On 23 November he said WA had sent her the poem and referred to a passage in the letter, with the implication that he had done so a few days earlier (RHD, Jr., to his brother Edmund T. Dana, 23 Nov. 1837, Dana Papers). RHD, Jr., had met her by that time. 2. Presumably, in addition to the three she refers to in this letter, some of the others she saw in the homes of their owners: *Miriam the Prophetess, A Roman Lady Reading, Jeremiah, Beatrice, Lorenzo and Jessica, Evening Hymn,* and *Saul and the Witch of Ensor* (Jameson, "Washington Allston," *Athenaeum,* 16 Jan. 1844, pp. 40-41). 3. Sir Charles Eastlake (1793-1865), English history painter. 4. Mrs. Jameson saw *Rosalie* in the dining room of Nathan Appleton and was so impressed that she could not take her eyes away though she did not know who the artist was. She called it *Rosalie Listening to Music,* probably on account of WA's poem "Rosalie," describing the title character thus engaged, which she probably read at Appleton's. When she asked WA afterward which came first, the painting or the poem, he replied that as well as he could recollect the conception was simultaneous (Jameson, p. 40). 5. *Girl in Persian Costume*. Mrs. Jameson was the first person recorded as seeing this painting, presumably in the home of John Bryant, Jr., and as seeing, in WA's studio, *The Sisters;* the chalk *Ship in a Squall;* the unfinished *Fairies on the Seashore, Disappearing at Sunrise,* from Shakespeare's *A Midsummer-Night's Dream* 2.1.85-86 or possibly *The Tempest* 1.2.375-76; and the outline *Titania's Court,* from *A Midsummer-Night's Dream* 2.2.1-26. She was warned not to speak of *Belshazzar's Feast*. He declined showing her *The Death of King John* and told her, "You must not judge of my industry by the number of pictures I have painted but by the number I have destroyed" (Jameson, p. 39). 6. RHD, Jr., said she was to take tea with WA on 24 November, which was a Saturday, at which time he was to "happen in" (to his brother Edmund T. Dana, 23 Nov. 1837). Apparently she visited him for the first time on that date rather than the 23d, as her letter seems to suggest. Edmund S. Quincy took her on what he implied was her first visit, on which occasion he showed them several sketches and paintings, and the interview, Quincy said, was "most interesting" (to Drake). Apparently she extended her stay in Boston beyond 24 November. She made presumably at least one other visit, on which occasion she returned at nearly three in the morning, "with the feeling of one 'who had been magnetized,'" and wrote her mother soon after she left the city that she "saw much of him" while there (*Anna Jameson: Letters and Friendships,* ed. Mrs. Stewart Erskin [London: T.F. Unwin, 1915], p. 160). She made these visits the basis of an article on WA in *Athenaeum,* 6, 16, Jan. 1844, though she dated them 1838. 7. RHD, Jr.

256. To Cornelius Conway Felton (?)[1] [1837, after 20 October (?)]

Mrs. Jameson must not suppose that I declined showing her "King John"[2] in its unfinished state, because I had any *secrets* in my practice, which, she is no doubt aware, is the case with some artists. On the contrary, I hold it as a duty freely to communicate all that I know to every artist who thinks it worth the asking. To the younger artists especially, who come to me for advice, I am in the habit of showing my pictures in their various stages, in order to illustrate the principles on which I proceed. The reason I assigned for not showing what I was immediately engaged on, that it *threw cold water* upon me, was the true one. I must beg her not to say that I have written anything on my art, for it *troubles* me to have the public *expect* anything of me. I feel as if they were looking over my shoulder. I may not live to complete what I have begun, and it is better that they should not have it in their power to reproach my memory for any disappointment they might choose to feign or feel.

SOURCE: Jameson, "Washington Allston," pp. 39-40.

1. The addressee and the date of this passage, presumably from a letter, are assigned on the basis of a series of facts about the relationship of WA, Felton, and Mrs. Jameson in consequence of her visit to WA on 20 October 1837. The passage occurs in a footnote to her article on WA in the *Athenaeum* at the point where she reported that on her visit WA declined showing her *The Death of King John* and *Belshazzar's Feast*, and is introduced with her words, "He afterwards, with the sensitive delicacy which belonged to his character, apologized for his refusal in words which I transcribe." She then quoted the passage in question. Apparently it came from a letter which she had received and from which earlier in her article she quoted references to WA, saying that it came from "one of his friends" and that what his own views of fame were "we shall presently see in his words," referring no doubt to the quotation from him in the subsequent footnote. It seems probable that the author of the letter to Mrs. Jameson was Felton. He delivered WA's poem about her book to her personally and no doubt they exchanged views on WA in conversation as the writer of the letter implied he and she did. The letter, moreover, contains several of the same judgments and even some of the same words which occur in Felton's tributes to WA in reviews of his works and works which mentioned him. The writer of the letter had often, he said, rebelled against such "unthinking judgments" as those taking WA to task for apparent delay and idleness, since they did not comprehend "the largeness and the fineness of his views of fame." "We must take genius as it is," he declared, "that mysterious organization, which, however lawless it may seem to others, is yet a law to itself," and said that "the intellectual and spiritual part" of his nature was "beautiful," blended with his "genius as an artist." He reminded Mrs. Jameson that she "once said, that we had no right to him—that you envied us the possession of such a man" and admonished her, "Oh, envy us not! rob us not of the little we have which can call off our American mind from the absorbing and hot pursuit of vulgar wealth and the love of perishing things, to those calm contemplations, which embody in immortal forms the beautiful and the true." The letter to her was probably written after her return to England in 1838. WA's letter to Felton [?] was probably written soon after her visit to him. 2. *The Death of King John*, from Shakespeare's *The Life and Death of King John* 5.7.44-58, unfinished. The subject was an extremely unusual one in painting. It was possibly influenced by Reynolds's *Death of Cardinal Beaufort*, itself derived from Nicolas Poussin's *Death of Germanicus*, which was owned by Egremont.

257. To John Stevens Cogdell Cambridge Port, Mass.
15th Decbr 1837.

Dear Cogdell: I wrote to my Mother in October—as well as I can recollect, on the 27th—when I begged her to thank you for the kind letter which you wrote me at her request, to inform me of my poor Brother's death;[1] I then also requested her to say, that I would answer your letter <when> as soon as I had cleared off some long arrears in the letter way to other correspondents. I have had of late an unusual number to reply to, from various quarters, from Europe as well as our own country. I have now however despatched the greater part; so that I feel somewhat more at liberty to follow my inclinations, and again to thank you for <my> your kindness with my pen.

The melancholy intelligence respecting my poor Brother was rendered still more affecting by my having to communicate it to my brother Henry, whom I had not seen for many years, and who arrived on the evening of the day on which I received your letter. The misfortunes of <as well> one of his amiable and gentle disposition, while they saddened our recollection, have still the more endeared to us his memory. What a strange power has the mind. I can look back over an interval of more than forty years and see him as he was when a baby in the nurse's arms. And more mysterious still when I can connect the countenance of the nervous, laughing child with the mild, yet graver face of his middle age, <and> feeling too that they are one and the same. How <strongly> clearly does this speak to us of the imperishable identity of the Soul through all physical mutations; for it is the soul, and not the outward form, which we thus recall and recognize, unimpaired by time.

I have already, in the letter alluded to, thanked my dear good Mother for her kind prescription; which I shall certainly try, if I am again attacked in the way I described to her; and I don't doubt I shall find relief from it. But temporary relief is all that I can expect from any medicine, as my medical friend in England[2] long ago assured me. My complaint had even then become chronic, and he told me that I must compound for being an invalid all my life—The truth of which has but too well been verified. My complaint is an unusual one, and was originally very dangerous, so much so <[two undecipherable words]> that the friend I speak of (a celebrated Surgeon at Clifton) had great doubt if I should live through it. You may judge what it must have been when I tell you, that for three months together I could not sleep without laudanum, and know not what it was to be free from pain for half an hour—All this was brought on by too severe application while I was painting the "Dead Man restored," when I sometimes, during the long, summer days, went twelve hours between breakfast and dinner. Before that I had the appetite and digestion of an ostrich; but they both soon gave way at such indiscreet neglect; then the intestines began to rebell, and finally to establish a fortress of annoyance which no medicine can now subdue. But I am quite content that it should be so; my blessings have been more than I deserve; and for my present portion of health I am still most thankful.

You ask if I could not "slip away from Cambridge, and make a visit to Charleston this winter?" Ah, if you knew what I have gone through, you would not think this so easy. No—this is not an easy matter to one who is still under the pressure of engagements that have so long embittered his life—to say nothing of the utter want of means. I am not yet my own master.—But I will not talk more about myself; adding only, that in the conscientious discharge of my duty to the best of my ability, I now, as hitherto, <ever> find my best consolation for all disappointments; nay, it is my best ground also for hope, and will, I trust, carry me successfully through all my trials.

I am glad to find that you have resumed the pencil. Not that I would have you abandon the chisel, but because it is better to have two <sources> kinds of agreeable employment, than one.—It has struck me that your Group of Hagar and Ishmael, transferred to the canvas, would make a fine picture. If you think so, allow me to offer a few hints as to the colour; which should be strong, but simple—say, red and blue; the tunic red, and a blue mantle. I do not recollect if the boy has a tunic. If he has, I would have that white and let the foreground be of strong reddish earth, with grey stones; the scene a rocky desert, rather flat, with mountains seen over a plain, at a great distance; and the horizon low, marked by a strip of light under a *murky* sky.—Believe me ever your sincere friend

W. Allston.

[In the margins] If you think with me as to the <color> choice of colour for Hagar and Ishmael, I would recommend for the tunic Venetian red for the light and Indian red and black for the shadows; which you may glaze, if you wish to enrich it, with lake & asphaltum. Never use vermillion in draperies; it is a flat colour.—You will have a visit from my Nephew George, whom I am sure you will like. I wrote by him to my Mother. He left us about two hours since for Carolina, by the way of New-York. You will receive this by mail: it will probably reach you about the time he arrives. You may remember my criticism on Ishmael's tongue: It should not be seen: in a *picture* I am sure it would be offensive. Let his mouth be half open.—Be sure you retain the expression of the Mother; it was very fine.

ADDRESSED: John S. Cogdell Esqre / Charleston, / South Carolina. ANNOTATED by Cogdell: answd 11 June 1838. SOURCE: Manuscript. Printed in part in Flagg, pp. 293-95.

1. Ebenezer Flagg died on 6 September 1837 (Nord, p. 23). 2. John King.

258. To Andrew Beaumont [1837?][1]

It seems hardly necessary to say any thing in this place of an artist whose merit is so well known and of whom his country is so justly proud; yet I cannot forbear expressing my admiration of these splendid efforts of his pencil.[2] Had Mr. Stuart never painted any thing else, these alone would be sufficient to make his fame with posterity. No one (as I believe will be admitted by every competent judge) has ever surpassed him in fixing the very soul upon canvass; but, in the present instance, he has done more; he has invested the individual nature with the ideal of art. In a word, he has here shown himself a profound master; and should we ever have a New-England school of painting, these pictures will be studied so long as that shall last.

SOURCE: *Boston Commercial Gazette*, 2 May 1839.[3]

1. In his letter to William Hayward of 28 May 1839 WA said that he wrote Beaumont, into whose possession Stuart's portraits of the first five presidents had come, "Within a year or two past," in answer to Beaumont's request for the substance of what he had earlier written in his newspaper article about them. Precisely when Beaumont was dealing with them is not known, but WA's dating supports the assumption that it was about the time he finished his term in Congress.
2. Stuart's portraits of the first five presidents. 3. The occasion for the printing of this passage from WA was the exhibition of the Stuart portraits in Boston from 1 May 1839 for fourteen days prior to their being sent to England. It was introduced by the explanation, "Washington Allston, struck with the life and soul of these paintings, wrote for the 'Boston Daily Advertiser' the following voluntary." The canceled "volunteered" in WA's letter to Hayward further suggests that the passage was from the letter to Beaumont.

259. To Elizabeth Ellery Dana Cambridge Port Thursday Eveny.
[*ca.* winter, 1838][1]

Dear Sister Betsey: As I suppose you have no peticler objection to be paid in kind, I send you, in return for your love, an equal quantity of the same—a prime article, and no sham. To say that nothing hant no matter with me would not be true—so I wont say it. But I hant very bad, as I goes to my Room every day, and works as usual. <I have> The matter with me is that I have another wizit from the Tic Dolly Roo—which has playged me considerable—But less today. The Doctur has seen me this afternoon, and subscribed some pills, that I hopes will help me—especially as my Tic is not near so regglar as the tic of the Old South clock[2] at no time.

You see then by this petickler account that I hant no need of being nursed more than my good Wife can nurse me. But I shall be very happy to see you for all that—for, sick or well, it does my hart good to see my dear sister Betsey: So we hope you will cum out <if> when the wether isn't too cold.

Is it true that Charlut[3] is going to open a singing school at Natick?[4] Or that Ned[5] is engaged to dance on the tite rope at the Lion Theatre?[6] I dont believe this last news is correct, as somebody said he saw him driving the Salem Stage, nocking down rite and left all about him.

Did Sarah[7] take the air yesterday, seeing that there was enuf of it for every boddy in an out—hope she is better, than wen she wisited the rural meads of Cambridge Port. My love to her, and all on em in Chesnut Street.[8] Wife jynes in love.

Yrs affectionately, W. A[lston] [rest of page cut off]

Their [?] if you ha / send to Mr Hastings / will come out to / return him something / only to look at and / and wish him to [right half the page cut off]

ADDRESSED: [Miss E.] E. Dana, / [Che]snut Street, / Boston. SOURCE: Manuscript.

1. The date of this letter is based on WA's letter to Cogdell of 21 October 1838, in which he said he had a painful attack of tic douloureux "some time" before writing his mother on 31 September and on the fact that it was apparently written during cold weather. 2. The Old South Meeting House in Boston. 3. Ruth Charlotte Dana. Though she was a singer herself, there is no record that she had a singing school. 4. A small town about fifteen miles from Boston. 5. Edmund T. Dana, son of Richard Henry Dana, Jr. 6. The Lion Theatre on Washington Street in Boston opened on 11 January 1836 for dramatic and equestrian performances. In 1839 it was converted into a lecture and concert hall and named the Meleodon (William W. Clapp, "The Drama in Boston," in Winsor, 4:371). 7. Sarah Ann Dana. 8. RHD's two sisters and two daughters lived with him and his wife at 43 Chestnut Street in Boston from 1843 on (*Boston City Directory*).

260. From Horatio Greenough Florence, Feby. 18th 1838.

My Dear Mr Alston: Since I left you now more than a year since I have scarce had time to collect my thoughts sufficiently to write—I addressed you a few lines from London because I thought you would be happy to hear a rather pleasanter account of my brother than others which I presumed had reached you. I am sorry to say that the poor fellow has since been again in trouble owing to the simple fact that his expences are considerable & his means very small—I fear that he will never get sufficiently free from embarrassment in that country to be able to *begin* properly—and at his age—what can I expect? I often shudder at what may be his fate, for his impulses are as strong as ever and his experience seems only to prick skin deep—

I heard of your health lately from Mr Brimmer[1] who remained here a few days on his way to Rome and who amused me not a little by crumbs that had fallen from Stewart's table and remarks of his own—I heard of you also from Mr Powers[2] who is now fairly settled here and is doing himself great honour in his busts. Since my return here I have besides the work upon my colossus finished a group for Mr Sears[3] and a full length portrait for Col Thomson[4] which represents one of his boys playing at battledoor—My intention was to have made the companion figure representing the brother standing ready to receive the shuttlecock—I have also made the model of a Venus for Mr Lowell[5] and have had of course a dreadful battle with the figure—this being the first female figure entirely naked which I have attempted except in sketches and drawings—or in bas relief—I have attempted to combine symmetry with expression and beauty with innocence taking the more poetic sense of the character and considering the mother of Beauty and the patroness of the graces as simply such—In making this study I have had occasion to examine Nature pretty widely & to scrutinize the received models of antiquity very closely—I submit a few remarks on the Venus dei Medici to your judgement beginning by confessing that if but one statue of a female could be saved—I should say let it be this—The head is scarce worth speaking about, though very beautiful as I presume it has been forcibly married to this trunk, and belonged originally to a smaller figure—I find the length from the *nates* to the heel very great—too great by far—long limbs not being characteristic of the sex but rather the reverse—I find the pubis superficial—bas relief like, and as a consequence the muscles of the inside of the thigh going to a false insertion considerably *outside* the real one—I find the thighs and legs though exquisite less I will not say marked but emphasized than even younger figures in real life—I cannot believe this roundness and smoothness to be other than architectural or mechanical when so far carried & must believe that the science laid out in commencing so rare an ensemble was forgotten or laid aside and the ultimate touches addressed to the eye sensually—I use the word sensually as denoting that finish which appeals to our love of what is smooth even and graduated—The ancles (inner) have an emphasis which cannot be found in a female whose bones are otherwise delicately formed—the feet beautiful as they are seem a little geometric in some of their outlines—want the compound [?] waves and the play of half tint given by the actual bone and muscle—I have finished my model and am about to cast it—I am so interested in the study of this class of figure that I think of remodelling it while my ideas are awake on the subject to try a few experiments—

I am in treaty for a statue of Abdiel a figure which you may remember suggesting to me many years since[6]—I almost dread it I confess—for I fear that the accessories which will be necessary to indicate his nature as an angel may have a fantastic look—but the angel character embodied in a form worthy the words of Milton and alive with kindling and just indignation were a flight above the Apollo—Alas! I feel, believe me Sir, how far I am from being worthy to speak of these great works but I have always thought it best aim at what we dream of in our warmest aspirations rather than to measure our strength and mark out our course by the rules of logic—I am come now to the determination that I will hereafter make fewer works and spend more time in preparing them—The run which has been made upon me and which I have been not always at liberty to check owing to my situation has not been favorable to the creation of ideal forms—I find the imagination, at least mine—will not bear fruit by plowing manuring & sowing—I can work in that way but the work seems to me to want color flavor odour—I must let the sun shine and the rain fall only on the ground whence I would see a real flower of the heart & of the soul spring—I must now express my wonder how you who are in the midst of a people who are the most exacting in the world in their expectations of performance how you have been able to build a wall between your vine and their thirst and give them only old wine when they would have hurraed at new cider![7]

. . . [*page cut off*] Mr Powers has finished Mr Webster's[8] bust in marble, and really I think it one of the very finest portraits I have ever seen—He is now about a head of Judge Marshall[9]—Col Baldwin's bust is nearly compleated.

. . . [*page cut off*] by command myself—I have recently finished the preparatory studies for my large groupe[10]—Washington goes forward bravely & I am in hopes of putting him up in July 1840—[11]

Ho Greenough[12]

SOURCE: Greenough, *Letters*, pp. 228-30.

1. George W. Brimmer. 2. Powers arrived in Florence in the fall of 1837 and spent the rest of his life there. 3. David Sears (1787-1871) was traveling in Europe with his family at this time (Robert C. Winthrop, "Memoir of the Hon. David Sears, A.M.," *Proceedings of the MHS*, 2d ser., 2 [1886]: 405-29). The group on which Greenough was engaged, called *Forest Children*, was of the two Sears children, Grace and Knyvet Winthrop (Wright, p. 102). 4. Col. James Thomson, a New Yorker for many years a resident in Florence (Greenough, *Letters*, p. 193). 5. John Lowell (1769-1840), Boston lawyer and writer. 6. The seraph who alone among the hosts of heaven withstood the invitation of Satan for them to revolt in *Paradise Lost* 5.800-904. 7. The next manuscript page has been cut off, leaving only the last three lines on the recto ("Mr. Powers . . . compleated") and on the verso ("by command . . . July 1840"). 8. Daniel Webster (1782-1852) was at this time a member of the Senate. 9. John Marshall (1755-1835) became chief justice of the Supreme Court in 1801. 10. In 1837 Greenough was commissioned by Congress to execute a group for one of the blockings on the steps of the east front of the Capitol. It consisted of a pioneer woman clasping a child to her bosom, a pioneer man towering from behind, and an Indian who was being restrained by the man from an attack on the woman and child (Wright, pp. 159-61). 11. It was erected on 1 December 1841 (Wright, p. 142). 12. The signature is in another hand.

261. To John Stevens Cogdell

Cambridge Port, Massttts
21 Oct. 1838.

Dear Cogdell: It was my intention to have answered your kind letter, of the 14 September, before this, but I have been prevented in various ways. I wrote to my Mother on the 31st of Sep. and was just about to conclude it, when yours was brought to me from the Post Office. Believe me, my friend, <that I> that I thank you from my heart for all your kindness to my dear Mother—and no less for the past than for this last instance of your friendly disposition. Nor is she unmindful of <them> it, as she speaks of you always with the greatest affection, calling you sometimes her son Cogdell. It is needless to tell you how sincerely I rejoice at the intelligence of your letter concerning the pension to my Mother.[1] Added to her small income, it will, I trust, make her declining years more comfortable than they have been of late.—I have much doubt whether any claim on account of my Father's[2] services will be allowed, as they were those of a Partisan Officer, in Marion's regiment. I may be mistaken, but I have always understood that the partisan officers served gratuitously; in which case the Government may deny <its> the legality of a claim. Old Judge Watys,[3] who was his brother officer, used to call him the "young Captain" and always spoke of him as a gallant officer.—I have often lamented that there is no portrait of my Father. I think it the duty of <every> all Parents to have their portraits painted, for the sake of their children.

The portrait which I painted of my Mother before my second visit to Europe is to me invaluable. It was then considered an excellent likeness—and <so> such too I think it. I never seized a more characteristic expression—that of a strong mind and ardent feelings. My friend Coleridge, who saw it in England, admired the character, as belonging to no common woman—in <the> which I think he judged truly.

Your account of the sickness[4] in Charleston was truly deplorable, and following so soon the disastrous conflagration,[5] must indeed have added to the gloom of the city. "Man is born to sorrow as the sparks fly upwards."[6] It was but a little after I got your letter that the papers reported a considerable abatement of the disease, but later accounts, I find, contradict this, and speak of its increase.[7] I trust, however, that before this reaches you the cold weather will have stopped its progress. And I hope too that this will find Mrs. Cogdell quite recovered.—Though I thought that my Mother was doubly protected from the "Strangers' Fever,"[8] <both> by a southern constitution and her advanced age, it was a great relief to me to be *assured* of it, as I was when your letter informed me that she was well.—As for myself, I have had a most painful visitation in the Tic doloreu; of which I have given a particular account in my letter to my Mother. But it had left me some time before I wrote to her, and I have, thank heaven, had no return of it since. At present I am pretty well, bating one of my annual sore throats—which, however, is about taking its departure also.

You tell me that you had commenced Hagar and Ishmael, but had been obliged to lay it aside on account [of] the sickness and hot weather. I hope that the more cheering days of the coming winter will enable you to resume it. If you preserve the expression of your modelled group, <it will> you will not fail of making a picture of deep interest. There are few subjects so limited in composition so naturally adapted to awaken general sympathy; but it is one in which, from the very circumstance of its simplicity, every thing depends on the expression. I use this last word in its ordinary sense, as relating solely to the figures—their air, attitude and faces. This you already have in the modelled figures. And this would be enough if transferred to canvass. But there is another kind of expression which I hope you will endeavour to add—that of the elements; to make them, as it were, in sympathy with the human emotion.[9] <This> In this consists no small portion of the poetry of our Art; and this is expressed in the character—that is, the forms, tone of colour, in short, the general effect—of the scenery. I remember one of Rembrandt's finest pictures owing its whole sublimity to the back-ground alone. Rembrandt, as you know, had no excellence in form, though no one ever surpassed him in expression, even in its widest sense, for <the> he was a poet in all else. The picture I allude to is Jacob's Dream; which consisted of only three figures, Jacob and two angels; the figure of Jacob, about six inches in length, <and> asleep on the ground, and nothing better than a drowsy dutchman; but the angels, which were only two inches in height, and of course too small to indicate more than the general air, were, from the skill with which he expressed that air in the remote distance, more like angels than any thing I have ever seen on canvass. And they owed this to the back-ground, the midnight sky—the fathomless darkness—I might almost say, the permeable pitch, in which they moved, while the two hardly visible lines of light, which formed the <night> ladder, seemed to sway with the night breeze. Nothing could be more simple than few materials, yet did he contrive to make out of them one of the sublimest pictures I know.—Will you give my love to my Mother. She must have got my letter more than ten days ago.—Mrs. Allston unites with me in best regards to Mrs. Cogdell and yourself. Believe me, dear Cogdell,

ever your sincere friend, / Wa. Allston.

[In the margin] Remember me affectionately to White and Fraser. Cole, of New York, whom I believe you know, had a very beautiful landscape in the last Atheneum Exhibition, called A Dream of Arcadia. You have heard of Power?[10] a young sculptor, from Cincinati, who is patronized I understand by a brother of Col. Preston;[11] he is going to do great things in his art, if I mistake not. He is now in Florence. I saw him here before his departure, and felt assured of his success. He is no common man.

ADDRESSED: John S. Cogdell Esqre. / Charleston, / South Carolina. ANNOTATED by Cogdell: replied to on Feby 1840. SOURCE: Manuscript. Printed in part in Flagg, pp. 295-97.

1. Presumably Cogdell wrote regarding a possible pension for Rachel as the widow of Flagg. No record of such an application or of one for her as the widow of Allston seems to exist.
2. William Allston, Jr. WA was correct about his father's receiving no payment for his military service. The state of South Carolina did, however, twice issue to his estate sums owing him for providing supplies to the militia under his command: £4.14.61/2 plus 6.7 interest on 21 January 1785, and £42.6.81/2 plus £2.10.2 interest on 7 July 1785 (Stub Entries to Indents issued in Payment of Claims against South Carolina Growing out of the Revolution, no. 73, Lib. N, p. 261; no. 434, Lib. U, p. 63, South Carolina State Archives). 3. Thomas Waites (1760-1828) of South Carolina was active in the Revolution from his sixteenth year. In 1780 he was made a captain in Marion's Brigade. After the war he became a lawyer, was appointed judge of the Court of Common Pleas in 1787, and from 1811 until his death was chancellor of the Court of Equity (H.D. Bull, comp., "The Waites Family of South Carolina," *SCHGM* 45 [1944]: 17-18). 4. The epidemic of yellow fever which visited the city in August, September, and October 1838.
5. On 27 April 1838 a fire broke out on King Street in Charleston and burned until the following day, destroying a large part of the commercial district, an estimated 600 to 1,200 buildings in a third of mile. The loss was estimated as being above three million dollars and contributions for the rebuilding came from outside the state, including many from Boston. Accounts from newspapers in Charleston and in other cities and from letters of Charlestonians were carried in the Boston newspapers (*Boston Daily Advertiser,* 5, 8, 10, 12, 24 May; 7, 18, 23 June). 6. "Yet man is born unto trouble, as the sparks fly upward" (Job 5:7). 7. On 4 October the *Boston Daily Advertiser,* quoting from the Charleston *Courier* for 26 September, reported that the deaths in the city had decreased from sixty-eight to thirty-eight in the last two reports of the Board of Health. On 11 October, quoting from the same source for 3 October and from the *New York Evening Star* it reported an "alarming increase" in the deaths during the preceding week. On 30 October it reported that the epidemic, which had caused many to leave the city, had almost entirely subsided and they might safely return. 8. Yellow fever. 9. Several of the phrases in this and the next sentence regarding the "poetical" relationship of the natural scene and human emotions occur in

WA's lecture "Art" and in *Monaldi (LA*, p. 84; *Monaldi*, p. 29). 10. Hiram Powers. 11. John Smith Preston (1809-81), orator and soldier, who was a collector of paintings and statuary. His attention was called to Powers by his brother William C. Preston.

262. To Chester Harding

Cambridgeport, Mass.,
25 December, 1838

Dear Harding: Your letter from Cincinnati[1] brought me an unexpected pleasure (though some perhaps might not think so, from this tardy acknowledgement; but not *you*, who too well know that I am anything but a punctual correspondent), and I sincerely thank you for it. Independent of the satisfaction of being kindly remembered, it was a pleasure to me to hear of the success of one whom I so highly esteem. I regret, however, that this *sublime* place supplies too little subject-matter for a letter to enable me to make a proper return; and my visits to Boston are so rare that I can glean next to nothing from that quarter. I might indeed talk of myself; but that is a subject on which I seldom care to say much at any time. All I shall say on it at present is, that I have been, as usual, hard at work; to what effect, I hope you will see on your return. You know that I am never idle; and, if I bring but little to pass, it is because my notions of excellence are sometimes beyond my reach.[2] I may add to this *indefiniteness,* that I expect to resume "Belshazzar" in the spring.

You say that you think more of your art when you are away from home. This is natural, and must needs be so with one who has so large a family to care for. But I do not think it a subject of self-reproach that it is so; but there would be a just one, if you suffered even the love of art to supplant the duties you owe to them—I do not mean by the neglecting to provide for them, which would be unpardonable; but by taking the place of those personal attentions, those nameless kindnesses, that go to make up so large a portion of domestic happiness. I have often thought of your conduct with regard to your family, and always with increased respect. You have a good wife and good children;[3] a fact that bears the strongest evidence of your right bearing as a husband and a father. Neither do I think that your attentions to them, liberal as I know them to be, have ever caused you to neglect your pencil. Your numerous pictures ought to set your heart to rest on that score. Upon the whole, I cannot but consider your lot a desirable one. Much as I love my art (and I believe no one ever rightly loved it more), I still hold it subordinate to my affections. But there is time for the exercise of both, except, perhaps, where grinding poverty allows no remission of labor. But, even then, no man who continues true to his social nature is ever without some redeeming moment, when he is at liberty to interchange kindnesses; and it is seldom that any one is ever wholly deprived of such moments excepting by his own fault. . . . Present my compliments to Miss Harding,[4] who, I understand, is with you; and believe me, dear Harding,

Ever your faithful friend, / Washington Allston

SOURCE: *A Sketch of Chester Harding. Drawn by His Own Hand*, pp. 144-45.

1. Harding was in the West on several occasions. 2. Probably WA was referring to some if not all the four unfinished paintings Mrs. Jameson saw in his studio the year before. Two are very similar: *Titania's Court* and *Fairies on the Seashore, Disappearing at Sunrise*. Both seem to have been derived from Raphael's *Parnassus* and both exhibit similarities to the work of the English painter Francis Danby, who worked in Bristol. *Titania's Court* was also close to Domenichino's *Hunt of Parnassus*. Flagg remembered seeing and hearing WA describe it in 1836, as he often did, with animation. An adaptation of it by Robert Weir appeared as the frontispiece in Verplanck's edition of Shakespeare (1844-47). Both these paintings are in marked contrast to *The Death of King John*, the other painting from Shakespeare which Mrs. Jameson saw, and to most of WA's earlier treatments of Shakespearean scenes in being poetic rather than dramatic, with their female figures and dreamlike atmosphere. His recent *Lorenzo and Jessica* anticipated them in its atmosphere and in the greater expanse of the figure of Jessica, in contrast to the early *Casket Scene* from the same play. The fourth unfinished painting which Mrs. Jameson saw and to which he may have referred was *Ship in a Squall*, the most dreamlike of all his landscapes and seascapes, the ship having a ghostly, almost hallucinatory appearance. Superficially unlike as they seem, all these paintings except *The Death of King John* are related in their subjectivity to the series of ideal female figures and heads which WA completed in the 1830s. 3. Harding's wife was the former Caroline Woodruff of Caledonia, N.Y. (d. 1845). One daughter was Margaret Eliot Harding White (1823-1903), who prepared her father's autobiography for publication and assisted in the publication of two other works. Two sons fought for the Union and two for the Confederacy in the Civil War. Harding spent his last years with his children in St. Louis (Harding, pp. 30, 147, 22, 32, 171). 4. Probably a sister of Harding.

263. To George Cheyne Shattuck [9 February 1839]

Dear Sir: You were so kind the other day as to propose taking me into Town, to see Mr. Clavinger,[1] and that we should afterwards return and dine with you. I hope to be well enough to attend you on thursday; but I would not give you the trouble to come for me, as it will be quite convenient for me to go into Town in the *one* o'clock stage, so as to meet you at your house by half past one, or a quarter before two. I name this hour because the state of my *system* will not allow me to leave home earlier.

I find myself very much benefited by your advice, and, though not yet freed from my complaint, yet so sensibly improving, that I have good reason to hope for an effectual recovery.

I remain, dear Sir, with the highest respect,

yrs most obliged, / Wa. Allston.

Cambridge Port, / Feby. 9th / 1839.

SOURCE: Manuscript, Shattuck Papers, MHS.

1. Shobel Vail Clevenger (1812-43), Ohio-born sculptor, spent several years in eastern cities modeling busts. In 1840 he went to Florence, where he died.

264. To William Ellery Channing [31 March 1839]

It being some years since I had seen this portrait[1] (being rolled up with other sketches) I was very much struck with the truth of the likeness, & I found it too a better picture than I had before supposed it. There is an anxiety in the expression, wh' I can well allow for, as it was painted but a short time before our departure for England—I believe during the time even of our preparation for the voyage: the expression, however, is to me not unpleasing—rather otherwise, as a visible register of her feelings at that time of trial to herself & children.

SOURCE: RHD, pp. 38, 38 Addition.

1. WA's portrait of Lucy (Ellery) Channing. Elizabeth Peabody said that it was reported to have been painted in one day and that it bore a resemblance to her son W.E. Channing not discernible so clearly in life (*Remarks on Allston's Paintings* [Boston, 1839], p. 12).

265. To Henry Wadsworth Longfellow Cambridge Port, 29 April, 1839.

My dear Sir: I beg you to accept my best thanks for your present of Cigars. I have tried one of them, which proved to be very good. They have quite an *amiable* complexion, and I have no doubt I shall find them redolent of Parnassus. I hope you will come soon, and help me try their poetical qualities.

I remain, dear Sir, / with sincere regards, yrs / Wa. Allston.

To Professor Longfellow.

ADDRESSED: To / Professor Longfellow, / Cambridge. SOURCE: Manuscript, Houghton.

266. To George Washington Porter Cambridge Port, 15 May, 1839.

Dear Sir: I beg you to accept my thanks for your kindness in offering me the loan of the miniature Portrait of the Revd Mr. Paris,[1] of Salem; which, however I must respectfully decline, as I have no wish to possess a likeness of him.

Very respectfully, yrs, / Wa. Allston

To Mr. G.W. Porter

ADDRESSED: Mr. G.W. Porter, / Either N 23 or 25 Bedford Stt.[2] / Boston. SOURCE: Manuscript, Haverford College Library.

1. Samuel Parris (1653-1719/20), the minister of the First Church of Christ in Salem Village, Mass., from 1689 to 1697, was prominently associated with the witchcraft trials in Salem in 1692. The miniature portrays him as in his twenties or thirties (Endicott Family Papers, MHS). 2. At this time Porter boarded at 23 Bedford Street (*Boston City Directory*).

267. To William Hayward

Cambridge Port,
28 May, 1839.

[Draft]

My dear Sir: I have just received your letter of the 27th inst.[1]—It gives me real pain to refuse any request from one whom I so sincerely regard. But <the rule of conduct which various considerations have long since induced me to lay down for myself in relation to all Collections of Pictures, brought before the public, is one which I cannot depart from without violating a solemn resolution: that [two or three undecipherable words]> is never to <express any written opinion. This resolu As my motive for adopting> But I could not comply with your present request <which> without violating a *solemn resolution,* <which various considerations have obliged me to make,> namely, never to express <any> a written opinion concerning any Collection of pictures brought before the public. My motive for this resolution I believe is well known to my friends, so that my <[undecipherable word]> adherence to it on the present occasion cannot affect yours.

Many years ago, immediately after <they> Stuart's 5 Pres. were painted, I <wrote volunteered> wrote a notice of them for one of the Newspapers. Within a year or two past (I do precisely remember <recollect know, which> the time) I was applied to by Mr. Beaumont, into whose possession they had come, to <repeat the> favour him with the substance of what I then wrote concerning them, as the newspaper article <he added> could not be found. What I had once written I could not well refuse to repeat; I accordingly did repeat <it> in substance as well as I could recollect it. And I <This circumstance repeated it another> did so <freely> without scruple, as I had had no reason to change my opinion of the pictures.

<This circumstance naturally led me to> I mention this circumstance lest hearing of <[undecipherable word] knowing> this fact, it should seem that I granted to another what I decline granting to you. But, setting aside the difference of the <circumstance> cases, I had not then made the above mentioned resolution; it was made not long after Mr. B's application. My two principal motives for coming to this resolution, were 1st <*first,*> not to injure any mans property by unfavourable criticism (which truth might compel me to make) 2d not to make myself directly or indirectly responsible for the originality or merits of any picture offered for sale. If I must speak on any occasion, I must speak the truth, on my conscience. In many cases the qualified commendation which truth might compel would be equivalent <with> to most people to condemnation.

In a conversation which I had with you the other day, I expressed myself with frankness on the subject of my conduct in regard to all pictures on <exhibition> offered for sale. And you may remember my saying that when I could not commend I was silent; but that I always *volunteered* praise where I thought it due. <That I did whi>

Whenever I have seen a fine picture I have always praised it: if it is *very* fine, I never wait to be asked but express my opinion, according to my nature, voluntarily

& warmly. I have done this since I saw you in relation to your Rembrandt The Ship-builder and his Wife.[2] I have spoken of it to various persons as a picture of the first class <of Rembrandts> portraits; adding, that if I were a man of fortune I would not hesitate to purchase it. I spoke also in high praise of the fruit piece & <still> group [?] of Game by Van Aerdt[3] So you see I did not wait to <[undecipherable word]> be *asked*.

<I believe in the conversation alluded to, I also never observed It has been my usual habit on visiting [?] in reply to—>

I feel assured that you will properly appreciate <the> my frankness <when> in this letter, and believe <me> that when I <say that I> express a wish to keep myself entirely free from becoming in any way a party to the disposal of pictures offered to the public, that I do it <as m both in kindness to those who own them, and> not only from a proper regard for what I think is due to <my integrity> myself, as a disinterested individual, but in goodwill & kindness to those who own them.

[On the back of the last page] Various considerations have obliged me to make this resolution, and my general motive for it is <well> I believe well known to many of my friends;

SOURCE: Manuscript.

1. In it Hayward apparently asked WA for a commendation of some or all of the paintings he owned which were included in the BA exhibition of 1839. The catalog contained excerpts from letters written by several New York artists praising his collection: C.F. Agate, Daniel Huntington, Charles Ingham, Henry Inman, G. Oakley, William Page, and Frederick R. Spencer. 2. This painting and the next two mentioned were among those owned by Hayward in the BA exhibition. In June he was reported to have made a trip to New York bringing back some additional pictures for both the BA exhibition and that of WA's works at Harding's Gallery (*Boston Commercial Gazette*, 13 June 1839). The Rembrandt and de Gelder's *Fruit Piece*, which were singled out for praise in the notice, may have been among them. If he brought anything by WA it does not seem possible to identify it, since the only paintings by him in the exhibition at Harding's which were not owned by Bostonians were McMurtrie's *A Mother Watching Her Sleeping Child* in Philadelphia and Gilmor's *Edwin* in Baltimore. 3. Arent (Aert) or Aart de Gelder (1645-1727), Dutch historical and portrait painter. The paintings were listed in the exhibition catalog as *Fruit Piece* and *Group of Ded Hare, Pigeons, etc.*, a companion to it.

268. To Rachel (Moore) Allston Flagg

Cambridgeport,
July 14, 1839.

My Dear Mother: I have been waiting for the arrival of sister Polly before I answered your last letter. . . . I am much disappointed that she could not come on while my exhibition[1] was open, but it closed last Wednesday, the 10th inst. The exhibition was extended a month beyond the time originally intended, and it was felt that it would be trespassing on the liberality of the owners of the pictures to ask a further extension, especially as there must necessarily be a continued risk from fire. It would have been a great gratification to me had one I love so dearly as my sister seen these fruits of so many years' labor. There were forty-five pictures at the opening of the exhibition, to which two were afterward added. There were several others in different parts of the country that could not be obtained. This number was anything but expected by the public; and when they took into account their elaborate finish, many could not help expressing their surprise at my industry.

This was *one,* at least, of the results of which I felt sure; and I feel a satisfaction that I am no longer misjudged in this respect. I am now and ever have been, since I made my art a profession, a hard-working man, and as much so from inclination as from necessity; for the law of my nature impels to employment. I cannot choose but work, sick or well; indeed six months idleness would soon upset me. But these are by no means all my works, as some of the newspapers have imagined; the pictures which I left in Europe, though fewer in number, would make a larger exhibition.

I cannot speak in terms too grateful of the kindness of the people of Boston on this occasion; more especially of my immediate friends, the gentlemen of the committee,[2] who conducted the exhibition. It was originally proposed by *them,* and *they* asked of the proprietors the loan of the pictures; I did not solicit one, nor, indeed, would it have become me to have done so.

I have not yet learned what are the profits, and shall not know, perhaps for days, until all expenses have been paid. The expenses, it is supposed, will fall little short of $900, for besides room-rent, doorkeepers, packing, transportation, etc., there was the insurance. As well as my friends can now guess, the net profits will amount to about $1,500.[3]

You say in your last letter that you hope I will take good care of the money I get from this exhibition. I have for many years been in the habit of economizing with what little I have had, and I could not (even if I felt inclined, which I am far from feeling) be profuse with this, for it will nearly all go immediately to my creditors; I shall reserve only barely enough to live on.

Many people who have seen these pictures think I ought not to be poor; but my pictures are in truth the cause of my poverty; they would not be what they are (at least what the public are pleased to consider them) without the time and labor they have cost me; and the greater part of them have not more than paid their expenses, some not that even. I do not say this, however, repiningly. I have long ago discovered that mine is not a money-getting art, and have been content with it nevertheless. I never could make it a trade; no picture ever went out of my hands that was not, for the time being, as good as I could make it; and the consequence has been fame and poverty. Well, be it so; the fame gratifies those who are dear to me, and the poverty I can bear.

As you wish to see some of the "handsome things" that have been said of me, I will send you in a day or two a few papers,[4] and more by sister Polly. Had it been possible, my dear mother, for you to have seen this Exhibition, it would have given me more pleasure than all the praise I have had. I should then have doubly felt that fame was worth more than money. I believe if I had none who loved me I should care little for fame. I could not say so, however, of my art, for that I must love under all circumstances.

. . . .

That heaven may ever bless you is the constant prayer of

Your affectionate son, / Washington Allston.

SOURCE: Flagg, pp. 300-303.

1. At Chester Harding's Gallery. 2. The members of the committee have not been identified. The prefatory pages of the catalog called them "The friends of Mr. Allston," who "have desired to express in some public manner their high sense of his pre-eminence as an Artist and their esteem and affection for him as a man" and who hoped the proceeds of the exhibition might be presented to him "as a token of those feelings." They thought the collection would not only "richly reward the visitor" but be "of very great value to artists," would "sustain the character of this community for a true & elevated taste," and would testify to the artist "the regard in which he is held by his countrymen." 3. According to all reports the exhibition was well attended. By the first day 488 season tickets and almost 80 single tickets had been sold (*Boston Commercial Gazette*, 29 Apr. 1839). The *Boston Transcript* reported on 8 May that "The interest has continued, nay, increases," that on 4 May the number of visitors exceeded those of any former day, and that despite "dull and rainy days" the gallery had never been without company. 4. Several Boston newspapers reviewed the exhibition, all highly favorably. The *Boston Commercial Gazette* printed articles on 25, 26 April and 6 and 27 May. The "number of pieces," "variety of subjects," "excellence of design and execution," and the fact that the artist was a native American were noted; and in "Allston Exhibition," signed "D.," the author, after commenting that it testified to the "taste of our community" as well as the reputation of the artist, said that on entering one was "not struck by any glare, or contrast of coloring" but by "an air of subdued brilliancy, and quiet repose," commented on several in particular, and looked forward to the completion of *Belshazzar's Feast*, predicting that it would become "the nucleus of a permanent Gallery, and the foundation of an Allston if not of an American school." The *Boston Daily Advertiser* for 26 April carried an article entitled "Allston Gallery," in which the author described his third visit there, the first having been made the day before, in which he said he "stood in the very midst of many works of one mind," felt he was "the companion of what had sprung from the human intellect" and a "beholder of the intellectual and the moral made visible" "instinctively" took his hat off, and questioned "who would not have felt it was a holy place."

The Exhibition of 1839

The exhibition of works by Allston at Chester Harding's Gallery in School Street in 1839 was undertaken by several of his friends not only to make him more widely known but to aid him financially. It contained forty-seven works, the largest number ever exhibited by him at one time during his life. It opened on 25 April and was extended beyond the original scheduled time of a month, first to the eighth and finally to the tenth of July, according to one report because of the great number of "strangers" attending. Single tickets were twenty-five cents and season tickets fifty cents (*Boston Commercial Gazette,* 25 April; *New York Evening Post,* 8 July). The original number of forty-five paintings were listed in the catalogue in the following order, together with the name of their owners or locations: *The Dead Man Restored* (PAFA), *Jeremiah* (Gibbs), *The Triumphal Song of Miriam on the Destruction of Pharaoh and His Host in the Red Sea* (Sears), *The Witch of Endor Raising the Spirit of Samuel before Saul* (Perkins), *The Flight of Florimel* (James F. Baldwin, son of Loammi Baldwin), *Polyphemus* (James F. Baldwin), *Swiss Scenery* [*Diana and Her Nymphs*] (Davis), *A Mother Watching Her Sleeping Child* (McMurtrie), *Edwin* (Gilmor), *Beatrice* (Eliot), *Italian Scenery* [*Italian Landscape* (G62)] (Eliot), *The Valentine* (Ticknor), *Landscape: Italy* [*Alpine Scenery*] (Dwight), *American Scenery: Time, Afternoon, with a South West Haze*) (Dwight), *A Roman Lady* [*Reading*] (Dwight), *Landscape* [*Landscape, Evening* (*Classical Landscape*)] (Dutton), *The Evening Hymn* (Dutton), *Landscape: Time, after Sunset* (Codman), *Isaac of York* (BA), *Sketch of a Polish Jew* (BA), *Portrait of Benjamin West* (BA), *An Italian Shepherd Boy* (Robert C. Hooper), *Portrait of the Artist* (1805) (Amory), *Moonlight* [*Moonlit Landscape* (*Moonlight*)] (Jacob Bigelow), *Landscape* [*Landscape with a Lake*] (Powell Mason), *Head of St. Peter* (George Bancroft), *Coast Scene on the Mediterranean* (Williams), *A Sketch of a Polish Jew* [*Head of a Jew?*] (J.S. Copley Greene), *A Sketch of a Polish Jew* [*Head of a Jew?*] (Thomas Dwight), *Poor Author and Rich Bookseller* (Thomas H. Perkins, Jr.), *Landscape* [*Italian Landscape* (before 1839; R150; destroyed by fire in Schenectady, N.Y. in 1912)], *Rising of a Thunderstorm at Sea* (Samuel D. Parker), *Donna Mencia in the Robber's Cavern* (Drayton), *Portrait of Samuel Williams* (Williams), *Rosalie* (Appleton), *Landscape* [*Alpine Scenery* (R59)], *The Tuscan Girl* (Sears), *Lorenzo and Jessica* (Jackson), *The Sisters* (Francis Alexander), *The Young Troubadour* (Bryant), *Falstaff and His Recruits at Justice Shallow's* [*Falstaff Enlisting His Ragged Regiment*] (Sullivan), *Portrait of Lucy Ellery Channing* (Channing), *Landscape* (G fig. 31; Sumner), *Landscape* (1799; R14; Allston), *Storm at Sea* [*Galen*] (Perkins). The last two landscapes were accompanied by the note "These youthful efforts are exhibited as objects of curiosities." Descriptions of *The Dead Man Restored* and *Donna Mencia* and a note differentiating *The Sisters* from Titian's *Girl Holding Jewel Casket* written by Allston and excerpts from his poems "Rosalie," "The Tuscan Girl," and "The Young Troubadour" were also included.[1] Subsequently *The Spanish Girl in Reverie* and the comic *Catherine and Petruchio* were added.

The exhibition attracted wide attention and was praised by some of the leading Boston men of letters, particularly certain Transcendentalists. Four lengthy reviews were printed: by Elizabeth Peabody, Jedidiah V. Huntington, Oliver Wendell Holmes, and Margaret Fuller. There were evidently plans to publish a collection of the reviews, but they were not carried out.

Miss Peabody's was the first to appear. It was a series of essays with the title "Allston Exhibition: Nos. [I]-IX" in the *Salem Gazette* for 10, 14, 17, 21, 24, 28, 31 May, and 4, 14 June 1839, signed "Philokosmos," all with a dateline of Boston. The first, dated 7 May, was written after she had been attending for a week. The series was reprinted as "Remarks on Paintings by Allston" in her pamphlet with the same title published later that year and as "Exhibition of Allston's Paintings in Boston in 1839" in *Last Evening with Allston*. The prefactory note in the pamphlet said of the series that the "few essays here reprinted, were at first prepared only for the newspaper, with no further object in view, than to make known in a neighboring city—the fact—that there existed this rare opportunity of studying the genius of our first Artist" but were reprinted "at the request of some gentlemen who think that the reverential tone in which they are written, may suggest the needed idea, that what it has cost a great artist, with all his genius, years of study to execute, should be looked at as addressing something deeper than the senses." She apologized that the "necessary hurry of the publication precludes any elaborate revision." The review consisted chiefly of minute descriptions of each painting, but she also occasionally made critical comments. They formed, she thought "a great whole," whereas "Almost all communication of one mind with others is partial," and made one "feel anew how great a thing one human mind is," which could be "a mirror of the whole race, of nature, and of something above nature," and was "a foretaste of that fullness of communication which shall take place among spirits in eternity." She thought *The Dead Man Restored* should be shown alone in a very large room, with a full light on it and the spectator in shadow, so nothing of the senses would interrupt his viewing. Allston, she declared, was the only artist who seemed to her to "*paint* SOUND," as he did in *Miriam*. *Saul and the Witch of Endor,* however, was not, to her, "quite sublime enough." Like other critics, she recognized the group of ideal female figures and a few others as "wholly original," calling them "pictures of sentiment" and saying that *Florimel* was the most interesting. Most of the review was devoted to them. She quoted the poem "Rosalie," which Allston had repeated to her as she viewed it for the first time in his studio; "The Spanish Maid," regretting that the painting *The Spanish Girl in Reverie* was not in the exhibition; and "The Tuscan Girl," and regretted that the poem, "The Young Troubadour," which she had seen but was unpublished, was not in the catalog. She praised Allston's painting of flesh, in which he implied "*depth,*" and the "*solidity* of all his objects." In her description of his self-portrait of 1805 she compared it to his present appearance, noting that now his forehead was "higher and broader, and all the formation about the eyes and eye-brows is expanded. His mouth has added to that look of delicacy, a certain maturity of wisdom. Altogether his present aspect is very much freer—more open—more commanding. He looks perhaps more as he will look when his mortal leaf 'withers on the tree of life,' and his spirit shall entirely determine his aspect." Her notice of *Donna Mencia, Spalatro's Vision,* and the two Falstaff pieces was brief, and she discussed the landscapes last, generalizing that "upon purely natural objects . . . the reaction of the mind of the artist is most clearly displayed," in contrast to the human sentiment in others, making her ask, "must not the mind of man, which is to rise beyond this earth, *be richer in power* than nature is in manifestation?" In *Diana and Her Nymphs* her imagination actually saw more, she declared, than Allston intended, adding that it was "precisely the proof of the highest artist that he suggests more than he expresses." About one of them, *Italian Landscape* (G62), she incorporated a poem by an anonymous author. In her last paragraph she quoted lines from Coleridge's "Dejection" and Emerson's *Nature*.[2]

Huntington, the holder of a medical degree, was subsequently a novelist and editor. He made the journey from New York, where he was then living, to Boston on the last day of the exhibition after hearing that it would not come to New York, carrying a letter to Allston from Morse. His review, written in July and printed in the *Knickerbocker Magazine* for August, was addressed to his brother, Daniel Huntington, a recent pupil of Morse, who on departing for Italy early in the year asked him to write a description, since he himself would be unable to attend. In it he described *The Dead Man Restored*, quoting from Allston's words in the catalog, *Jeremiah*, and *Miriam* in detail. More briefly he referred to the *Head of St. Peter;* the three comic pieces from Shakespeare; *Saul and the Witch of Endor;* the three pictures of Jews; the portraits of West, Lucy E. Channing, and Allston's self-portrait; and the landscapes *Diana and Her Nymphs, Landscape: American Scenery, Coast Scene on the Mediterranean, Moonlit Landscape* (*Moonlight*), and *Landscape, Evening* (*Classical Landscape*), saying all were free from "mannerism" and exhibited "cool, gray, silvery, rosy, and golden tones." For his most extensive discussion he singled out a group he thought the "most characteristic expression" of Allston's genius which he called "pictures of sentiment" and which he divided into two classes: those consisting of *The Spanish Girl in Reverie, Evening Hymn, The Tuscan Girl, Lorenzo and Jessica,* and *The Young Troubadour,* all of which had landscapes, and those consisting of *Rosalie, Beatrice,* and *The Valentine* which did not. He quoted Allston's poems "The Spanish Maid," "Rosalie," and a stanza from "The Tuscan Girl," and described in detail most of the paintings in both classes and *A Mother Watching Her Sleeping Child* in relation to them. He briefly mentioned as forming a class by themselves in their depiction of action *The Sisters, The Flight of Florimel,* and *Donna Mencia.* In conclusion he said he had had a "highly interesting interview" with Allston, "whose personal appearance would strike any one as remarkable and characteristic." He was "above the middle height, slender, with brilliant, prominent eyes, and a high, pale forehead, shaded with silver hair," with an expression in repose "gentle, 'feminine, not effeminate,'" but in conversation "extremely animated." Allston asked him to tell his brother to follow the example of the old masters in being versatile, which Huntington thought Allston himself did, being the only instance among modern painters of "completeness of character in an artist," a sculptor, a philosopher, and a poet, who belonged he said, quoting Morse, "not to the present age, but to that of Michael Angelo and Raphael." He concluded that there were two living artists who worked "in the spirit of the ancients"—Thorvaldsen in sculpture and Allston in painting—a fact, he predicted, the world would acknowledge when Allston was dead.[3] A few years later Daniel, together with the painter Cornelius Ver Bryck, his brother-in-law, spent an evening with Allston.

Oliver Wendell Holmes, whose father, Abiel Holmes, was the first minister of the

Shepard Congregational Church in Cambridge, to which Allston belonged, saw Allston first about the time of the 1839 exhibition. He described the occasion to Flagg shortly before Flagg's life of Allston was published as having been "Some fifty years ago" when a question of public interest in Cambridge brought together a large number of people in a church there. Among them he saw a man "who looked so 'like an angel of light'" that he knew him to be Allston. In the meantime he wrote two or three poems about two of Allston's paintings he apparently saw in the Boston Athenaeum exhibition of 1831: "Illustration of a Picture, 'A Spanish Girl in Reverie,'" "To the Portrait of 'A Gentleman' in the Athenaeum Gallery," and possibly "To the Portrait of 'A Lady' in the Athenaeum Gallery." In the second, which was probably about the *Head of St. Peter,* the "gentleman" is said to have a "thing thou fondly deems't a nose" which is "unsightly," eyes which may pass for blue but "if a man can see, / what more have eyes to do?" and a mouth which is a "fissure in thy face, / By something like a chin"—details which could describe Allston's painting. In the third, which may have been about *The Valentine,* the coloring of the portrait is referred to in the lines "I'm not averse to red and white, / But all things have their place, / I think a profile cut in black / Would suit your style of face!"[4] which could apply to Allston's painting.

In his review of the 1839 exhibition in the *North American Review* Holmes began by saying Allston has the "mind of one who has for many years been following his own serene course, passing from land to land, and from school to school, but always true to himself, and leaving traces of his history from time to time in gentle images and harmonious colors," and referred to his "undisputed claim . . . to the first place in the roll of American artists." He then gave a summary of Allston's life, drawing on Dunlap, and a description of his chief paintings in England—*The Dead Man Restored, The Angel Releasing St. Peter from Prison, Jacob's Dream, Elijah in the Desert,* and *Uriel in the Sun*—and *Jeremiah.* He thought that in them Allston had "aimed to reach the loftiest sublimity" in their conceptions and defended the unfinished state of *Belshazzar's Feast,* contrasting the working of "the highest intellectural power, the creative imagination" to that of "artificers, the layers of brick and mortar, the wood-hewers and water-drawers" who worked on all days alike and had to be "always true to their stipulated hour." He divided Allston's works into two categories: the historical, citing *Miriam,* which he called the "happiest" of all, *Saul and the Witch of Endor,* and *Donna Mencia;* and the depiction of "tranquil female beauty," citing *Beatrice, Rosalie, The Valentine, Evening Hymn, The Spanish Girl in Reverie,* and *Lorenzo and Jessica,* but preferring the full-length works to the heads. The landscapes, he declared, showed the "potential character" of Allston's mind as much as any of his works, and he compared them chiefly to those of Claude. He quoted from "Rosalie" and Coleridge's "Genevieve" to demonstrate similarities between them. In conclusion he compared Allston also to Michelangelo, Titian, and Correggio but found the influence of "his own mind" traceable upon their ideas.[5]

In later years Holmes referred to Allston less sympathetically. In *Ralph Waldo Emerson* (1885) he cited *Belshazzar's Feast* as a work over which Allston had labored "with the hopeless ineffectiveness of Sisyphus" and the backgrounds of the landscapes in the Allston Gallery at the Museum of Fine Arts in Boston as being "slighted as if our midsummer heats had taken away half the artist's life and vigor" and the "sketches, impressions, effects, symphonies, invisibilities, and other apologies for honest work" as suggesting, like the poetry of Emerson, "the possibility that there may be something in our climatic or other condition which tends to scholastic and artistic anaemia and insufficiency," in contrast to the "full-blooded" poetry of Browning and the "flaming canvas" of Henri Regnault. In *A Moral Antipathy* (1885) he mentioned among the works in the Boston Athenaeum Allston's "lovely Italian scenery and dreamy, unimpassioned women" and in the Museum of Fine Arts "Florimel in full flight on her interminable rocking-horse." In *Our Hundred Days in Europe* (1887), however, after referring to the gift of an American for erecting in England memorials to certain English writers he said he felt "more and more the truth of the generous sentiment" with which "America to Great Britain" closed: "We are one!"[6]

Margaret Fuller first met Allston at the Boston Athenaeum before 7 January 1839, when she described him to Emerson as being "as beautiful as the town criers have said, and deserves to be Mr. Dana's Olympus, Lares, and Penates, as he is. He got engaged upon his art, and flamed up into a galaxy of Platonism. Yet what he said was not as beautiful as his smile of genius in saying it." She was so fascinated that she forgot to make herself "interesting" and said she would not dare go and see him. She visited the exhibition once or twice a week, thought the paintings grew "ever more beautiful," and said it had been a "home to her,"[7]

Her review, entitled "A Record of Impressions Produced by the Exhibition of Mr. Allston's Pictures in the Summer of 1839," which she wrote in her journal in July 1839 but which was not printed until July 1840, in the *Dial*, was on the whole favorable but expressive of a faint disappointment. She began saying that she had spent "many hours" there but found at its close that she was "less a gainer" than she had expected. She had seen *Beatrice* and *The Valentine* at the age of sixteen, she said, in 1826, when she noted their "calm and meditative cast . . . that self-possessed elegance, that transparent depth" which she most admired in literature, realized that though living in a "bustling, reasonable community" Allston "had kept his foot upon the ground, yet never lost sight of the rose-clouds of beauty floating above him" and "had not been troubled, but possessed his own soul with the blandest patience," and hoped to find through him "probably the *mot d'enigme* for which we are all looking. How the poetical mind can live and work in peace and good faith! how it may unfold to its due perfection in an unpoetical society!" From time to time she had seen other paintings by him, which had been "sweet silvery music, rising . . . above the din of life." He aimed, she wrote, at "the Ideal," from which "high purpose" he never swerved and so never, unlike artists who painted from nature only, fell into sentimentality or the picturesque, though he sometimes failed to reach it, the only possible complaint which could be made of him being "inadequacy." Though pointing out merits of color and composition, she had several objections to the four paintings on biblical subjects, saying that *The Dead Man Restored* shows "a want of judgment" in the choice of subject and the figures were "without much force"; that *Jeremiah* was "rather imposing than majestic," chiefly because the expression of the prophet made him seem "an ordinary man"; that in *Miriam*, which she wished had been larger, the face was "inadequate," wanting "heroic depth";

and that in *Saul and the Witch of Endor,* the introduction of a ghost on canvas was itself "ludicrous" and Saul was in an attitude of "theatrical as well as degrading dismay." On the whole she decided that "the grand historical style did not afford the scope most proper to Mr. Allston's genius." "The Beautiful" was his "dominion," and his "own ground" was in his landscapes and figures, which a "certain bland delicacy" enfolded as an "atmosphere." The figures she mentioned, almost all in repose as she said, were those in *Beatrice, The Valentine, Evening Hymn, Rosalie, Italian Shepherd Boy, Edwin,* and *Lorenzo and Jessica,* all having an excellence which was "subjective and even feminine," telling "the painter's ideal of character," having "A graceful repose, with a fitness for moderate action. Capacity of emotion, with a habit of reverie," and being characterized by "entire though unconscious self-possession" and "Grace, grace always." Allston had, she thought, "an exquisite sensibility to color, and a great love for drapery," though sometimes directing attention too much to the latter. She cited two figures which illustrated the group: *Italian Shepherd Boy,* in which "the beauty, as Mr. Allston loves it best, has not yet unfolded all its leaves," and *Beatrice,* which she thought was not suggested by Dante, whose Beatrice was "possessed of much higher attributes" and had a "celestial destiny," but instead embodied the artist's "own ideal of a poet's love," having "the golden mean" and being "better suited to a prince than a poet."

As for the landscapes, she looked at them with "such unalloyed delight" that she was tempted to wish Allston had concentrated his powers on this genre. They had, she thought, "A power of sympathy" which gave each "a perfectly individual character" and "merged" the painter in his "theme," affecting the viewer as parts of nature; they contained the "soul" but not the "character" of the painter in what was the "highest art," or "Nature and Soul combined; the former freed from slight crudities or blemishes, the latter from its merely human aspect." In passing she noted the comic pieces, which showed "a gentlemanlike playfulness"; *The Sisters,* which was not in repose nor rich in suggestion, aiming to speak but saying little and not being "beautiful enough to fill the heart with its present moment"; *Donna Mencia,* which was perfectly objective, "telling all its thought at once"; *A Mother Watching Her Sleeping Child,* which though "lovely" had "an air of got up naiveté and delicacy" and seemed "selected, arranged by 'an intellectual effort,'" and did not "flow into the artist's mind like the others"; and the heads of Jews, which were "full of character, though Isaac was too dignified and sad," observing that "gold never rusted the soul of the man that owned that face." She concluded with a reference to *The Bride,* which was not in the exhibition, and the quotation of two sonnets written about it. The first, "To W. Allston, On Seeing His 'Bride,'" signed J., was by Samuel Gray Ward, an occasional poet and critic, from whose prose description of it she also quoted. The second, "To Allston's Picture, 'The Bride,'" signed O., was her own composition.[8]

One of the paintings in the exhibition, *Italian Landscape* (G62), inspired two poems. In "Allston's Italian Landscape" James Freeman Clarke described it as depicting a scene fairer than any in Greece or in Pausilippo or Vallombrosa in Italy, which was a peace not earthly but coming after youth from God and guiding the artist's hand to a "second Eden."[9] He was probably the author of the other, untitled, poem about the same landscape, which was incorporated in Elizabeth Peabody's review, by "an unpublished poet" and which contained several of the same phrases and sentiments.

This was presumably the landscape on which Allston worked during the winter of 1828-29 in Harding's studio and is notable on several accounts. It is the one which most clearly evokes his nostalgia for Italy, the most Claudian of all, comparable to Claude's *Landscape with Hagar and Ishmael* and also to Turner's *Crossing the Brook,* his only known vertical landscape, and anticipatory in its figures of those in two later ones, significant in themselves. The male figure is the first of his lute players, and the profile of the female figure in the center resembles that of Jessica in *Lorenzo and Jessica.* Possibly it was related to the Italian landscape described in his "Color Book." It has a prominent Italian pine and a castle on a hill on the right, closely resembling that in the drawing of the landscape with horsemen which was apparently a study for that painting.

Another painting in the exhibition, shown publically for the first time, received the first of a long succession of admiring notices: *Rosalie.* Richard Henry Dana, who was one of the first to comment on it, thought it the "finest" Allston had painted for many years. His poem of the same name was written earlier the same year and originally consisted of three stanzas, inspired by hearing his niece Charlotte Dana sing his favorite air, "*Se intendo*" from Metastasio's *Semiramide* 1.10.23ff, which, he said, called forth feelings that could not be spoken but only breathed or sung. A fourth stanza was added to adapt the poem to the painting and the others put in quotation marks as being her words.[10] It was first printed under the title "Rosalia," the name of the chief female character in *Monaldi,* in the *American Monthly Magazine* in 1836, prefaced by a description of it as "A gem of his double art, from the poet-painter of our country" and followed by a footnote by the editors saying that they could bear personal testimony to the "exquisite-like beauty" of the painting.[11] Probably the testimony was that of Park Benjamin, an admirer of Allston's, who had edited the *New-England Magazine* in Boston until it merged and he became associated with the *American Monthly Magazine* in New York in that year. Allston was accustomed to recite the poem while showing the painting to his friends.[12]

Another painting shown publically for the first time in the exhibition was *The Sisters,* from Titian's *Girl Holding a Jewel Casket,* probably also influenced by West's *Bacchante,* which was inspired by the same painting. It was sold early that year; a paper label on the back reads: "Cambridgeport, January 29, 1839. Received of Francis Alexander fifteen hundred dollars for the Sisters painted by me." Alexander (1800-81), portrait painter and lithographer, was in Boston from 1825 to 1831, from 1831 to 1833 in Europe, and again in Boston from 1833 to 1853, when he finally went abroad, spending most of the rest of his life in Florence.[13]

The most notable American who became acquainted with the work of Allston about this time was Ralph Waldo Emerson, who referred to him repeatedly in his journals, notebooks, letters, lectures, and printed works from the early 1830s to the end of his active life.[14] With his limited aesthetic sense and notion that American art should be independent of tradition, grand and rugged, he was ambivalent in his judgment, praising Allston for his artistic achievement and character at times but disparaging his European affiliations at others. He often grouped Allston with other American artists and writers, chiefly Bryant, Channing, Cooper, Everett, Horatio

Greenough, and Irving, in his analysis of American genius, using him to represent the American painter as distinct from the American sculptor, poet, writer, and orator. He called them all "feminine," "receptive" rather than "creative," and "imitative," but most of them he said he would choose as professors of "my college."

When Emerson visited the 1839 exhibition he "uttered no heresies" about Allston "but only beautiful things," Elizabeth Peabody wrote Sophia, "dwelling, however, on his highest merits least."[15] On 26 May, presumably after that visit, he wrote in his journal that Allston's pictures were "Elysian; fair, serene, but unreal," adding that "all the American geniuses . . . lack nerve and dagger" and that in his recent lecture at Waltham, he had described the impression it made on him as not being a "positive" one, like that made by Homer, Phidias, Dante, Shakespeare, Michelangelo, Milton, and Raphael, but "an eyeless face. It is an actor without fire. Beautiful drawing there is,—a rare merit;—taste there is; the blandest, selectest forms & circumstance; a highly cultivated mind; a beneficial general atmosphere; but no man." A few weeks later, on 12 June, he commented on Allston's *Lorenzo and Jessica,* which he saw at the home of Sophia Peabody in Salem in 1836 when she copied it, that "there is moonlight but no moon," adding that in the *Jeremiah,* "the receiving Baruch is the successful figure. His best figures read & hear and always his genius seems feminine & not masculine." On 3 July he was at the exhibition again, with Margaret Fuller, Sarah Clarke, Edmund Dwight, Alcott, and Samuel Ward, Jr., at which time he declared that the portraits of the Jews were an "offense," that "they degrade & animalize," and that the head of St. Peter was "not yet human," being "too picturesque, & like a bronzed cast of the Socrates or Venus."[16] He thought that Margaret Fuller in her review was right in saying the subject of *The Dead Man Restored* showed "a want of artist's judgment" and that she dealt with *Jeremiah* "very mercifully" and of her remarks on *Beatrice* commented, "I cannot tell yea or no—but it is a pretty story."[17]

Other Transcendentalists, including Alcott, knew Allston probably about this time. He owned a copy of Jones Very's *Essays and Poems* (Boston, 1839). After Allston's death Cyrus A. Bartol, in *Discourses on the Christian Spirit and Life* (1850), described his work on *Belshazzar's Feast* as an example of the desire for perfection. His kinship with this group, for all his differences from it, was recognized by Ednah Dow Cheney, Seth Cheney's wife, who said that though he did not fully belong to their company, since "the old traditions of the church clung closely round him, and there was an aristocratic flavor in his feelings and manners," pointed out that "still in his thought and philosophy he was very closely in sympathy with them, for his art was entirely ideal, as free from realism as that of any true lover of nature could be."[18]

The exhibition attracted attention in New York also. Richard Henry Dana wrote Bryant in enthusiasm:

> Oh that you could see the glorious show that Allston's paintings make! Now that five-and-forty of them are gathered here together, you can hardly imagine the Power with which they break upon every one when first standing in their midst. Prophet, sorceress, the awakening dead, mountains, sea, woods, quiet nooks, streamlets, sunsets, & last of all—for here we linger last—woman, her *soul*—beauty in her face—more than woman, & yet all woman. Cannot our people be

> roused up to come from East & West & North & South to see this great creation, the like of which may not be seen here again for centuries? Surely Allston stands in this age alone."[19]

The *Boston Evening Post,* announcing on 8 July the closing of the exhibition, predicted that probably never again would be seen "an entire collection of this great modern painter." Thomas R. Hofland wrote an article entitled "The Fine Arts in the United States—with a sketch of their present and past history in Europe," printed in the *Knickerbocker Magazine* for July, which coincided with the exhibition, though not mentioning it; he praised American painters chiefly for their historical painting, named Allston first on his list of them, and said that he "confessedly stands preëminent."[20] The next summer the *New-York Mirror* for 25 July carried a brief notice of Allston in an article entitled "Our Landscape Painters," which was probably based on the exhibition of the preceding year. It said that the fact was not generally known that Allston had painted landscapes, which were "few and small, but full of natural beauty," and, erroneously, that some of them were then being shown at the Boston Athenaeum, which did not include anything by him that year.

One notable group from New York which went to Boston to see the exhibition consisted of the banker and art collector Samuel Ward, his son Samuel, Jr., his daughters Julia and Louisa, and the teacher and librarian Joseph Green Cogswell, who was then their tutor and presumably knew Allston during his association with Harvard in 1813-15 and 1820-23 as well as in Boston at other times and when he was in Europe in 1816-23. Apparently young Ward, a lifeling friend of Longfellow, was induced to go by Longfellow's enthusiastic description in a letter to him of Allston's *The Sisters.* "We shall all come to see Allston's picture and the goodly town," he wrote Longfellow on 25 April. He, his sisters, and Cogswell were there early in June. On his way home Ward thought much of "my living friends," he wrote Longfellow, "and of my new acquaintances, the children of Mr. Allston's genius and of his romantic studio." The senior Ward visited the studio about that time and particularly admired *The Sisters.*[21] He had evidently known Allston and his work earlier and for some two years before his death begged Allston for a picture at his own price. Cogswell said Allston had intended *Amy Robsart* for him, but he died in November 1839 before it was completed.[22] Young Ward long remembered Allston. He referred at the time of Allston's death to his lectures, and of Longfellow's poem "Rain in Summer" (1845) he wrote, "there is a grace, a truth, a spiritual beauty about it, which grows upon the mind as one of Allston's pictures does upon the eyes."[23]

The 1839 exhibition of Allston's works was not only the high point of his career. It was a major event in the history of American art and of American literary and intellectual history as well. It was unlike any earlier exhibition in America in presenting the full range of the work of an eminent artist who was also a poet and who was living nearby. It gave many of those who attended their first serious awareness of painting and produced a body of criticism on the fine arts which was more substantial than hitherto individual and incidental essays and was on the whole appreciative. It also inspired not only essays but poems and fiction which explored the realm of imaginative activity. Above all, it projected the image of an artist successfully existing in a world, in America particularly, essentially alien if not sometimes unsympathetic.

1. *Exhibition of Pictures Painted by Washington Allston at Harding's Gallery, School Street* (Boston, 1839). 2. *Remarks on Paintings by Washington Allston* (Boston, 1839), pp. 2, 5, 6, 11-13, 21, 22. 3. "The Allston Exhibition. A Letter to an American Artist Travelling Aborad," *Knickerbocker Magazine* 50 [Aug. 1839]: 163-74. 4. *The Writings of Oliver Wendell Holmes* (Boston, 1891), 13:399, 414; 12:21. 5. *North American Review* 50 (Apr. 1840): 358-81. 6. Holmes, *Writings,* 11:258; 7:3; 10:205-206. 7. *The Letters of Margaret Fuller,* ed. Robert N. Hudspeth (Ithaca: Cornell Univ., Press, 1983), 2:32, 66, 68, 72. 8. "A Record of Impressions Produced by the Exhibition of Mr. Allston's Pictures in the Summer of 1839," pp. 73-84. 9. *Dial* 1 (Oct. 1840): 174-75. 10. James Grant Wilson, *Bryant and His Friends* (New York, 1886), p. 201; Dana, 1:145; RHD, note on manuscript copy of the poem. 11. *American Monthly Magazine,* n.s. 1 (Jan. 1836): 35-38. 12. Clarke, p. 132. 13. Catherine W. Pierce, "Francis Alexander," *Old-Time New England* 44 (Oct.-Dec. 1953): 29-46. 14. The earliest reference in his journals is the account of his visit in August 1833 to Coleridge, who spoke of his association with Allston in Rome and showed him Allston's painting *The Adoration of the Magi.* He incorporated the account, with revisions, in *English Traits* (1836). In 1835 he mentioned Allston three times, once agreeing with his notion of building a "plain" house with "plain furniture" in a passage he incorporated, with revisions, in his lecture "Art" (1836) and in *The Conduct of Life* (1860). In 1836, possibly more often because of the interest taken in Allston that year by Elizabeth Peabody and Alcott, he mentioned him in seven entries, almost altogether as being ineffectual. In the next two years he was more positive, praising Allston's poem "To the Author of 'The Diary of an Ennuyée,'" agreeing with his statement that "His art must be sufficient to the Artist," and saying "Allston is respectable to me" (*Journals and Miscellaneous Notebooks,* vol. 4, ed. Alfred R. Ferguson [Cambridge: Harvard Univ. Press, 1964], pp. 408-11; 5: 47, 92, 105, 176, 195, 210-11, 215, 226, 233, 377, 388, 425; vol. 7, ed. A.W. Plumstead and Harrison Hayford [Cambridge: Harvard Univ. Press, 1969], pp. 24, 198, 341. *The Early Lectures of Ralph Walso Emerson,* ed. Stephen E. Whicher, Robert E. Spiller, and Wallace E. Williams [Cambridge: Harvard Univ. Press, 1964], 2:48, 480). 15. *Letters of Elizabeth Palmer Peabody, American Renaissance Woman,* ed. Bruce A. Ronda [Middletown, Conn.: Wesleyan Univ. Press, 1984], p. 226. 16. *Journals and Miscellaneous Notebooks* 7:200, 199, 211, 221-23. 17. *The Letters of Ralph Waldo Emerson* 2:275. After 1839 Emerson mentioned Allston less often in his journal but at the time of his death described him in a memorable figure of speech. To Margaret Fuller he wrote, after noting Allston's connection with Italy, that it was "not strange that he should die, but that he should have lived 64 years. I never heard of his being young, or a beginner, and suppose that his first strokes were masterly. He was like one of those boulders which geologists sometimes find a thousand or two miles from the mountain from which they were detached, & science cannot show how they were conveyed. A little sunshine of his own has this man of Beauty made in the American forest." He repeated the image of the boulder in a letter to his brother William and a year later in his journal, saying Allston was, in the words of Sir Thomas Browne, "adamas ex teri rupe," a "boulder of a European ledge; a spur of the Appenines on which Titian, Raphael, Paul Veronese, & Michael Angelo sat—cropping out here in this remote America & unlike anything around it, & not reaching its natural elevation." He continued to refer to Allston in his journals and notebooks through 1865 in an embivalent way, to his "genius & defect," his belonging to

a class of "really superior men" which included Franklin and J. Q. Adams, and his having "two or three rooms in different parts of Boston that he could not be found" so as to be removed from distracting external activity (*Journal and Miscellaneous Notebooks*, vol. 9, ed. Linda Allardt [Cambridge: Harvard Univ. Press, 1976], pp. 208, 322, 334, 354, 415, 426, 447, 506; vol. 14, ed. Susan Sutton Smith and Har Hauf [Cambridge: Harvard Univ. Press, 1978] pp. 22, 52; vol. 15, ed. Linda Allardt and David W. Hill [Cambridge: Harvard Univ. Press, 1982], pp. 21, 108, 402, 420, 439). Revised versions of some of these entries appeared in *Essays. Second Series* (1844) and in *Letters and Social Aims* (1876).
18. *Reminiscences of Ednah Dow Cheney* (Boston: Lee and Shepard, 1902), p. 184. Mrs. Cheney, who was fifteen when she attended the exhibition, was one of Allston's most perspicacious critics. That exhibition, she later wrote, "made an era in the mental life of many of the young men and women of that day." Allston was, she declared, "our greatest ideal artist," marking as such "a new character in American Art," who recognized nature as "the revelation of Spirit" and whose landscapes were as far from material forms as were his angels. For all his attachment to European traditions, she thought he also represented "the fine aroma of American life," owing the "warmth and richness of passion" which made him a great colorist to his southern birth. She nevertheless judged that his was the art of "a limited circle, and not of the greatness of the people" and that though his thoughts were profound and original," his "symbolism and expression are not of today," and she sometimes felt "as if he had the new wine, but not the new bottles." *Monaldi* she characterized as "a romance of the mind, not of real life," a "revelation of the inward workings of the spirit, not a drama of action" (*Gleanings in the Fields of Art* [Boston, 1881], pp. 273, 290-94, 296). Her final estimate was that "perhaps the most remarkable thing" about him was "the effect of his personality on other artists, who all looked up to him as 'one of the immortals'" (*Reminiscences*, p. 131). She also wrote an appreciative article about him as a literary figure, "Allston as a Writer, by a Lover of Art" (*Commonwealth* [Boston], 10 Feb. 1866). 19. Wilson, pp. 201-202. 20. *Knickerbocker Magazine* 14 (July 1839): 50. 21. Julia Ward Howe, *Reminiscences*, 1819-99 (Boston, 1899), pp. 429-30. 22. *Life of Joseph Green Cogswell Sketched in his Letters*, ed. Anna E. Ticknor (Cambridge, 1874), pp. 40, 73, 89. 23. Maude Howe Elliott, *Uncle Sam Ward and His Circle* (New York: Macmillam 1938), pp. 251-52, 315, 402.

269. To William Turrell Andrews [21 August 1839]

To William T. Andrews Esqre.

Sir: I have received your letter, communicating to me the Vote of the Trustees of the Boston Atheneum, requesting me to sit to Mr. Clavinger for my bust.[1]

I feel deeply sensible of the honour done me; and whenever my state of health shall be such as to allow it, I shall be happy to comply with the request.

I need scarcely add, how gratifying a circumstance it is that the work is to be executed by an artist of such genius as my friend, Mr. Clavinger.

Be pleased, Sir, to present to the Trustees my respectful acknowledgement.

Very respectfully, / Your obedient servant / Washington Allston

I hope my illness[2] will be my apology for the delay of this reply.

Cambridge Port, / 21 August, 1839.

SOURCE: Manuscript, BA. Printed, except for the last sentence in the body of the letter, in Swann, p. 154.

1. WA at first declined to have his bust made, saying that while he was pleased to have his work seen, he had no wish to be seen himself. About this time, however, he agreed for George W. Flagg to paint his portrait, being moved, he said, by his mother's asking Flagg to do so since she had learned he was physically unable to visit her and she wished to see him again before her death. Both works were executed in 1839, WA sitting to Clevenger and Flagg at the same time in his studio. The bust particularly, on which Clevenger worked for three weeks in an effort to do his best, showed the effects of WA's illness, and one friend thought it surprising that he had done so well (RHD to Verplanck, 22 Oct. 1839; Prime, p. 470). The painting made him more animated. When the bust was exhibited at the BA in 1840 Margaret Fuller thought both it and Clevenger's bust of Edward Everett "admirable as everyday likenesses" but "deserved a genius of a different order," since Clevenger "gives the man as he is at the moment, but does not show the possibilities of his existence" ("The Athenaeum Exhibition of Painting and Sculpture," *Dial* 1 [Oct. 1840], 262). 2. About February 1839 WA had an attack of illness which radically changed his appearance and rendered him a "bodily broken down man," in the words of RHD, who questioned that he would be able to finish *Belshazzar's Feast*. During his sittings for Clevenger he was in "severe & almost constant pain," which produced "an expression of distress and a rigid state of muscles," making a friend who had not seen him for two or three months say he could not live much longer (RHD to Verplanck, 22 Oct. 1839; Prime, p. 470).

270. To William Ellery Channing [27 August 1839]

I have just received the $500[1]—from Mr. Dexter—which is to my entire satisfaction.

[RHD said that this was the "closing" sentence of this letter, whose preceding contents he summarized as follows: "He speaks about the frame, & his wish not to send the picture into town, as its being kept in Dr C—'s [Channing's] house while shut up would injure it in its fresh state" and added: "I *know* that Mr. A. said this for fear that Dr. C. would be troubled about the low price, or Mr. P. would in some way, but A. never considered it near the value of the picture."]

SOURCE: RHD, p. 38.

1. For *The Bride*, which was apparently the painting Jonathan Phillips finally acquired instead of *The Angel Pouring out the Vial of Wrath over Jerusalem*. In his catalog of WA's works RHD listed as no. 114 "Picture in possession Jona Phillips—Female Head." On 2 September 1839 he wrote William P. Mason that "About a fortnight since" WA had finished "as fine a female head as he has ever painted," that Channing had taken Phillips to see it, who was "greatly pleased" and paid WA $500, the remainder of the sum of $1,000 which WA had originally set for the commission, and that the interview with Phillips had been "perfectly satisfactory" to WA, whose mind was "now relieved from what had long been a burden upon it" (Miscellaneous Bound, MHS). Channing told RHD, Jr., however, that when Phillips's picture was done it was worth at least $1,500, that Phillips's agent in enclosing the $500 asked if they should send $500 more, and that WA declined the additional sum, though telling a friend that if Phillips had sent it without asking he should have accepted it, since the painting was worth the higher sum. It depicted the figure beside a marble fountain on an island. WA's poem "The Betrothed" was presumably a companion to it, with its

description of "the almost bride, Sweet Esther" singing and thinking of her betrothed beside a brook. Samuel G. Ward's poem, "To W. Allston, On Seeing His 'Bride,'" signed "J.," referred to the depiction in it of "a green and gladsome isle, / And flowing water" and "in the midst a marble fountain fair." He called it a "new picture" by WA, which convinced him more than ever "of the depth and value of his genius." At first disappointed by the "want of beauty" in the face, he then "observed the peculiar expression of the eyes, and that of the lids . . . as well as the strange complexion, all heightened by the color of the background, till the impression became very strong." He described it as "the story of the lamp of love, lighted, even burning with full force in a being that cannot yet comprehend it" and said that "the character is domestic, far more than that of the ideal and suffering Rosalie," of which it was reminiscent. Margaret Fuller's poem, "To Allston's Picture, 'The Bride,'" signed "O.," described the countenance of the figure but did not mention the setting (Fuller, "A Record of Impressions Produced by the Exhibition of Mr. Allston's Pictures in the Summer of 1839," pp. 83-84).

271. From Samuel Finley Breese Morse [25 October 1839][1]

I am afraid you will think me remiss in complying with your request by Mr. Hayward,[2] but I have only this moment been able to obtain the album of Mr. Payne, from which I have made a careful tracing of your beautiful design of "Danger,"[3] and will take the earliest opportunity to transmit it to you, with the volumes of Meng's works also.[4] I had hoped to have seen you long ere this, but my many avocations have kept me constantly employed from morning till night.[5] When I say morning, I mean *half-past four* in the morning! I am afraid you will think me a Goth, but really the hours from that time till twelve at noon are the richest I ever enjoy.

You have heard of the Daguerreotype.[6] I have the instruments on the point of completion, and if it be possible I will yet bring them with me to Boston and show you the beautiful results of this brilliant discovery. Art is to be wonderfully enriched by this discovery. How narrow and foolish the idea which some express that it will be the ruin of art, or rather artists, for every one will be his own painter. One effect, I think, will undoubtedly be to banish the sketchy, slovenly daubs that pass for spirited and learned; those works which possess mere general effect without detail, because forsooth detail destroys general effect. Nature, in the results of Daguerre's process, has taken the pencil into her own hands, and she shows that the minutest detail disturbs not the general repose. Artists will learn how to paint, and amateurs, or rather connoisseurs, how to criticise, how to look at Nature, and therefore how to estimate the value of true art. Our studies will now be enriched with sketches from Nature which we can store up during the summer, as the bee gathers her sweets for winter, and we shall thus have rich materials for composition, and an exhaustless store for the imagination to feed upon.

SOURCE: Prime, pp. 404-405.

1. The date is given by RHD, who quoted two sentences from this letter (p. 23). 2. William Hayward. 3. WA does not seem to have produced a painting from the design, as he had

proposed in 1829. 4. The edition which Morse sent, signed by him, was *The Works of Anthony Raphael Mengs,* 3 vols., trans. H. Janson (London, 1796). It included a memoir of Mengs by the Spanish critic I.M. de Azara. Probably WA wanted a copy in connection with writing his lectures on art. In the "Introductory Discourse" he cited Azara, whom he identified as Mengs's biographer, disagreeing with his definition of beauty as "this sublime quality" and declaration that "the grand style is beautiful" (*LA*, p. 65). These precise quotations have not been located, but in his memoir in the 1796 edition of Mengs's works Azara described the genies painted by Mengs in the cabinet for holding papiri in the Vatican as being "of an ideal beauty so sublime, that one never tries to view and admire them," referred to the "beauties of the sublime Laocoon," and in his comparison of painting with music said the object of both was "beauty," though "A sound when it is not grand is only a simple imitation" (1:26, 43, 34). 5. Morse was chiefly occupied at this time with securing a patent for his telegraph, but he was still active in the NAD and such projects as the daguerreotype. 6. Morse early experimented with the photographic process which became known as the daguerreotype but did not perfect it until after he met Louis Daguerre (1789-1851) in Paris in March 1839, the year of Daguerre's final success with it (Prime, pp. 404-405).

272. To Israel Keech Tefft

Cambridge Port, 10 Novbr 1839.
Massachusetts.

Dear Sir: I have the honour to acknowledge the receipt of your Letter, informing me, that the Georgia Historical Society[1] have elected me an Honorary Member of their body. For this flattering distinction I beg you to present to the Society my most respectful acknowledgements.

Owing to your mistake as to my residence, I did not receive your letter until some time after it should have reached me. I beg you therefore to excuse the lateness of this reply. My address is Cambridge *Port,* not Cambridge.

I am, Sir, very respectfully, / Your obedt servt. / Washington Allston.
I.K. Tefft Esqre. Corresponding Secretary of the Georgia Historical Society, / Savannah, Georgia.

SOURCE: Manuscript, Georgia Historical Society.

1. Founded on 24 May 1829.

273. To John Stevens Cogdell

Cambridge Port, Mass.
5 Decbr 1839.

Dear Cogdell: By the Brig Josephine, Captain Charles Smith,[1] you will receive two Boxes (of which the above is the bill of lading)[2] containing each a plaster Cast of my Bust; one for my Mother, and the other for yourself, of which I beg your acceptance, as a small <testimony> token of my regard. The Bust was modelled for the Atheneum, at the request of the Trustees, by Mr. Clevenger, a young artist from Cincinnati, whom I consider <a first rate [two words undecipherable]> as one giving evidence of no common mind. He has been passing several months here, previous to his departure for Italy, where, if I mistake not, he will produce a "*sensation.*" He has every quality to make a great artist; and, what is still better, to *adorn* a great artist; for he is modest, amiable and single-hearted, loving his Art for its own sake, and finding his highest pleasure in its labours. It is delightful to meet with such a man. I know not when I have met, as in him, so beautiful a coincidence of Simplicity and Power: One of the few whom the world would have great difficulty in spoiling; for his love of fame, if I understand him aright, is not the mere thirst of praise, right or wrong, but the purer desire of sympathy; which, if ever realized, is both the best reward, and excitement, of Genius. He is a man, in short, whom, if you knew, I am sure you would like with no ordinary liking.

I suppose you already know, from my letter to my Mother, written about a fortnight ago, that the King of Babylon is at last liberated from his imprisonment, and now holding his Court in my Painting-Room. If you have not seen the letter, I would refer you to it, for the particulars <of the drawing themselves> As the time approached for opening the box in which <it> the picture had lain for so many years, I could hardly suppress some sad misgivings as to what time and confinement had done to it. And you can well imagine my delight on finding it without a crack or stain; only two small places on some subordinate heads being rubbed <off> in the unrolling. But I find I am only repeating what I said in the letter to my Mother. So I will end by saying, that I feel in returning to my labour upon it <that> as if I ha <ve> d returned to my proper element.—By the way, I must caution you *not to heed any thing* which you may see in the *Newspapers* concerning this picture.[3] They have already begun in New-York to fabricate the most fantastic paragraphs about it. The writer in one paper says, that "*he* was present at the unrolling!!" that it is already finished, and would be exhibited in a few days. The paragraph too, purporting to be an extract from the letter of a Boston correspondent, the writer adds, "in my next I shall give you a description of the picture!!!" Now the whole of this is a *sheer fabrication.* The only persons present were four workmen and my Brother-inlaw,[4] who came to assist in the unrolling, and raising it on the Easel—but who *would not look at the picture,* as he said, that he did not wish to see it until it was completed.—About fourteen years ago I remember the Newspapers amused themselves pretty much in <that> the same way.[5] But I made up my mind then to take no public notice of these fabrications—nor shall I *now,* as there would be no end to it. I am determined that the Public shall *not know* any thing about Belshazzer—how long I expect to be still employed upon it, or any thing else. When he is ready to make his *debut,* I shall *myself* announce it.—I have said so much on this subject, that I have no space left for any other, so I must end by subscribing myself your sincere friend

Washington Allston.

[In the margins] You will perceive by the Bust that time has laid his finger on me since you saw me. My friends here think it could not be more like me; as well as I know my own face, so too think I. My best regards to Mrs. Cogdell. And give my love to my Mother and tell her that I heard a few days since of our poor

George—the Doct. says that he is quite calm, and was getting along very well.[6] I do not now admit even my friends into my Room—so nobody *can* know anything about the picture. Remember me affectionately to White and Fraser.

ADDRESSED: John S. Cogdell Esqre. / Charleston, / South Carolina. ANNOTATED by Cogdell: replied to in Feby 1840. SOURCE: Manuscript. Printed, except for the last three sentences and two of the postscripts, in Flagg, pp. 303-305.

1. Charles Smith was a ship captain, with an address from 1826 to 1833 in Boston (*Boston City Directory*). 2. The bill of lading, written in another hand at the top of page 1, is as follows: "Boston December 3d 1839—Received in good order from John Doggett & Co. on board the Brig 'Josephine' One Box marked 'John S. Cogdell Esq—Charleston S.C. *No.* 1'—also One Box marked—'*Mrs. Rachael Flagg*—Charleston S.C. care of John S. Cogdell Esq.—*No.* 2.'" 3. The articles have not been located. 4. Probably RHD. 5. Presumably the articles referred to in WA's letter to Cogdell of 18 November 1828. 6. No explanation for this statement, apparently about George W. Flagg, has been found.

274. To Elizabeth Palmer Peabody [9 December 1839]

My dear Miss Peabody: The Picture[1] you speak of in your Note (which I received this morning) is not mine, but Miss Clark's.[2] I did not indeed formally present it, for as a *picture* I did not consider it worth presenting; but I always intended that she should retain it—not as a work to study, but as a kind of a diagram, or skeleton, of my process, to which she might occasionally refer. Should Miss Clark, however, be still in any doubt as to my intention, I must beg you, in my name, to ask her acceptance of it. She will, of course, now feel at liberty to lend it to your Sister, or to any other of her friends, to copy, or to use in any other manner they please.

Believe me, with sincere respect and regard, Yrs. / Wa. Allston.

Cambridge Port, 9th Decbr 1839.

Now that this Note is written I know not how it is to be got to you, as our means of communication with Boston are always uncertain. I fear it will not reach you as soon as you wished.

ADDRESSED: To / Miss Elizabeth Peabody, / Boston / SOURCE: Manuscript, Houghton.

1. Possibly the landscape which Sarah Clarke exhibited at the BA in 1850 (R165). 2. Sarah Anne Clarke.

275. To Henry Wadsworth Longfellow Cambridge Port, 1 Jany 1840.

My dear Sir: I beg you to accept my thanks for your "Voices of the Night."[1] It was my wish to have acknowledged the receipt of it sooner; but, in truth, I could not sooner command the poetic mood (which I hold to be no less essential to the reader than the writer) in order to do justice to your book. I know not how it is with others, but there are days when some prosaic Demon seems to stand at every avenue of my mind. At such times I dare not approach Poetry, lest she "write me down blockhead."

The desirable mood, however, has at length come upon me, when I could open your volume, without fear of injustice either to Writer or Reader; and my forbearance has been rewarded by no common pleasure.

Among the recent Poems I was most touched by the "Prelude," and the "Footsteps of Angels"; they breathe the true spirit of poesy. Nor was I less pleased with the freshness of some of the earlier pieces. "The sunrise on the Hills" is beautifully *painted*. Among the Translations I was especially taken with the "Ode of Don Jorge Manrique."[2] It is an exquisite Poem; and reads so like an original, I cannot help thinking, that, like Coleridge's translation of Wallenstein,[3] (which Scott preferred to Schiller's) it owes not a little to <the> some subtile infusion from the Translator's own mind. Be that as it may, it is so masterly, that I cannot help wishing for more translations of a like spirit.[4]

I remain, dear Sir, / with sincere regard, yrs / Wa. Allston.

ADDRESSED: To / Professor Longfellow, / Cambridge. SOURCE: Manuscript, Houghton.

1. Published in Boston, 1839. This volume comprised three groups of poems: those recently written and published in the *Knickerbocker Magazine;* a selection from Longfellow's poems published in periodicals during and immedately after his college days; and translations he had contributed to periodicals and had inserted in *Hyperion* (1835). 2. "Coplas de Manrique" was a translation by Longfellow of "Coplas por la muerte de su padre" by the fifteenth-century Spanish poet Jorge Manrique, identified in a footnote. Longfellow first published it, together with seven sonnets translated from the Spanish, in *Coplas de Don Manrique* (1833), again in *Outre-Mer,* and finally in *Voices of the Night.* 3. Coleridge's *The Death of Wallenstein* and *The Piccolomini* (1800) were translations of the two last parts of the trilogy *Wallenstein* (1798-99), by John Christoph Friedrich von Schiller (1759-1805), German dramatist and poet. 4. Longfellow continued to translate, from eleven different languages altogether, all his life. His chief achievement was his translation of Dante's *Divine Comedy.* In his theory of translation he advocated relative freedom.

276. To John Stevens Cogdell

Cambridge Port, Mass.
12th Jany. 1840.

My dear Cogdell: Your letter of 28 Decbr has given me a shock which I had vainly thought I was prepared for; but I found I was not. The advanced age <of> together with the increasing infirmities of my poor Mother had long since warned me that she could not long remain in this world; and I had endeavoured to prepare myself for this inevitable and afflicting event.[1] Yet it came upon me with all the force of an unexpected blow.—She is gone—and I shall never see her more—never till we meet in Heaven; which God grant I may, through his grace, be permitted to do. Her image is ever before me—with all the mother's tenderness—with the same benignant expression as when I last parted from her—as fresh as if it had been but yesterday. And I thank God that such is the impression left in my heart; it is a great comfort to me. But this is but secondary to the inexpressible comfort which I feel in the deep conviction of her present happiness: which her true and ardent piety, her perfect christian resignation (of which I have long been assured from her letters) all confirm beyond the shadow of a misgiving. She is now with her Saviour. There is no consolation for the bereaved like this. Nor indeed can there be *any other* to a believing Christian. In the midst of her troubles—which I know have been many, and hard to bear—this has always crossed me as a cheering thought in her behalf—that my Mother was a Christian; and then I felt sure that, happen what might, she would be supported through it.—I can now think of her as my *blessed* Mother—numbered with the "just made perfect"[2]—where there is no more trouble, no more sorrow. I would not exchange this conviction for all the wealth and honours which the world could offer.—I cannot tell you, Cogdell, how I loved my Mother—she herself <was not aware of all the > never knew all the love I bore her. She was the constant object of my daily prayers. And, though separated for so many years, by most trying and adverse circumstances, she was never a day out of my mind. But, dear, blessed Mother, we shall meet at last, I trust, in another and a better world.

And now, my friend, I know not in what words to thank you for the feeling manner <of> in which you have made your melancholy communication. But your own kind heart will tell you all I would say; not only for this last act of friendship to me, but for all your past devoted kindness to my beloved Parent. God bless you for both. While you mourn with me, even as a brother, you have the consolation of knowing that, to her last breath, she loved you as a son. Whenever you were mentioned—which was almost in every letter for the last years of her life—she always spoke of you with the deepest affection. She seemed never weary of repeating your kindnesses. And I never shall forget them.

I did not feel equal to writing to my brother, Henry Flagg, as you requested, on the day your letter reached me; but, unwilling that the communication should be delayed, I requested my wife to write to him for me; which she immediately did, extracting that passage from your letter concerning his being appointed one of the Executors with yourself. She wrote also, on the same day, to Newport, to inform my brother William, though she omitted mentioning the Executors; thinking that you would probably write to him on the subject.—Remember me affectionately to Mrs. Cogdell and believe / me ever your true and grateful friend

Washington Allston

ADDRESSED: John S. Cogdell Esqre / Charleston, / South Carolina. ANNOTATED by Cogdell: answered 27 Jany 1840. SOURCE: Manuscript. Printed, except for the last paragraph, in Flagg, pp. 305-306.

1. Rachel (Moore) Allston Flagg died 27 December 1839 (Register of St. Thomas and St. Denis Parish, District of Georgetown, S.C.). 2. "But ye are come . . . to the spirits of just men made perfect" (Heb. 12:22-23). In *Monaldi* the narrator says that as Monaldi dies he is "holding communion . . . with the just made perfect" (p. 253).

277. To John Stevens Cogdell

Cambridge Port, Massstts
11 Feby 1840.

My dear Cogdell: I have received your kind letter of the 27th of Jany—for which accept my thanks.

You inform me, that I "have no interest in my Mother's Will."[1] This is no more than I was prepared for; and it has occasioned me not the slightest disappointment. I knew that my Mother always considered that I had already received *my Portion* in what I had inherited from my Father;[2] and in this I always cheerfully acquiesced; so that I did not expect to be included in her Will. And I speak sincerely when I add, that I had not even a wish to receive any part of the little which my Mother had to bequeath. Her last letter, written but a few weeks before her death, was one of the most affectionate she ever wrote me; I thought so at the time, and I shall ever value it as the most precious legacy she could <leave me> have left me.

But you also inform me, that there are some Slaves, left by my Grandmother,[3] which were to descend to my Mother's heirs; and that I, as one of those heirs, would inherit a part of them.—Now, my Friend, I have a request to make of you, which I hope and trust you will not refuse me. It is this—that in the division of these Slaves you will act as my Attorney, and take charge of such a portion of them as may fall to my lot; *it being my settled determination not to sell one of them.* By taking charge of them, however, I do not mean that you should take them into your personal keeping, but only that you would take the entire control of them, and hire them out (as formerly) to such persons as you know will treat them kindly. And this I hope you will be able to do without its occasioning you much trouble.—Now, my friend, tell me if I ask too much in this. I hope you will answer No; and that answer will add one more to the many obligations which I already owe you.—I have written to my brother, Henry C. Flagg [I wrote yesterday][4] to this effect; namely that on *no account* should the portion of the Slaves which may fall to my lot be sold; also that I should immediately write to you, and request of you to act as my Attorney on this occasion, and take them under your charge.

Should you consider this letter not enough, and require the still further authority of a Power of Attorney, I will thank you to let me know the *form* required in Carolina of such an instrument, and it shall be sent to you immediately. Don't say Nay, my friend, to this request.* It will make me easy to know that these old dependents of my family are under the paternal care of <a> one of your humanity and kindness.

Before the receipt of your letter I had concluded to give the Bust, intended for my dear Mother, to my eldest Sister Mrs. Alston, and I was pleased to find that we so coincided as to its destination. She is still in Philadelphia, and I wrote to her last week, when I mentioned that I should request you to care of it for her. I suppose she would like to have it remain with you until she returns to Charleston. In a late letter to me, she spoke in the most grateful terms of your unremitting kindness to our beloved Mother.

My best regards to Mrs. Cogdell, and believe me, ever your sincere friend,
Washington Allston.

To John S. Cogdell Esqre / Charleston, South Caro[lina] [page torn]

*This request has, of course, nothing to do with the Executorship, which you have declined.

ADDRESSED: John S. Cogdell Esqre / Charleston, / South Carolina. SOURCE: Manuscript.

1. In her will Rachael (Moore) Allston Flagg bequeathed to Henry C. Flagg, Jr., all her slaves and real and personal property (Charleston County Probate Court, 48 (1839-1840), p. 63). 2. In his will William Allston, Jr., remembered his wife, Rachel, his children Elizabeth and Benjamin by his first marriage and his children Mary and Washington by his second marriage. He left to Rachel and her heirs and assigns three Negroes and their increase, all the household and kitchen furniture from his Charleston house, his best horse and carriage; to Elizabeth one Negro and her child; to Benjamin, Mary, and their heirs and assigns a young Negro each; to WA and his heirs a plantation, Springfield, according to Sweetser, of three tracts of land; to Elizabeth and Mary all his other land; to Rachel and all her children the rest of his estate to be equally divided by the executors (Groves, pp. 35-38). 3. Elizabeth (Vanderhorst) Moore (1737-90). Her portrait was painted by the Swiss-born Charleston painter Jeremiah Theus (Nord, p. 11). In the will of her husband John Moore she was left three slaves for life, who were to go afterward to their daughters Elizabeth Margaret and Harriett, and all but two of the remaining slaves were left to her, their son John, and their daughters Sarah, Elizabeth Margaret, and Harriett (Webber, "Moore of St. Thomas' Parish," pp. 164-65). Rachel (Moore) Allston presumably inherited some of these slaves from John E. Moore. A few days after WA's death a false story was printed to the effect that his father had left him by will a young female slave named Diana, that at the time he was abroad, that on his return he had emancipated her, and that was she was still living as Mrs. Diana Flagg (*New-York Tribune*, 19 July 1843). The reference had to have been to his stepfather, but Flagg's will made no such bequest, leaving his whole real and personal estate to his wife and all his children who were living then and who should live "to the age of twenty-one or attain the same number of days of marriage" (Charleston County Probate Court, 28 [1800-1807], p. 135). WA, moreover, did not go abroad until after the will was proved. 4. WA's brackets.

278. To John Stevens Cogdell

Cambridge Port, Masstts
7 June, 1840.

My dear Cogdell: From the tenor of your last kind letter (march 18th) informing me that the Estate was not likely to be soon settled, I concluded that you would not expect an immediate answer. Indeed there was <answer that [rest of line undecipherable]> nothing that I had to say in reply except that I thanked you again for your continued kindness, and friendly advice, to make myself easy on the subject.

As to this most extraordinary Law-suit,[1] I abstain from all remark; I cannot think of it without the most painful feelings. All I shall say then about it is this: that I will not, either directly, or indirectly, employ Counsel in my behalf. I will not expand *one cent* in defence. I am too poor to risk any thing—and especially for so paltry a stake! I have consulted a legal friend here, who informs me that, as I live in another State, I am under no obligation to "file an answer to the Bill." Not being personally subject to the jurisdiction of the Courts of South Carolina, I will not therefore incur any expense in defending against the Bill, and *shall not appear in answer,* but leave the Court to decide the question.—I have already had too many troubles during my past life not to wish to avoid every thing that may endanger my peace of mind; and money is the last thing for which I would risk it. No. I will not embitter the few remaining years I have to live by any litigation.

In case the Court should decide in favour of *all* my Mother's children, I have one thing to say, as to the disposal of that part of the inheritance from my Grandmother which may fall to me. I have reflected much on the subject, and I find that the intention which I expressed to you, of retaining the Slaves, would be attended with many serious difficulties, not to say with much probable disadvantage to the Slaves themselves; as, in the case of my death, they might be separated, or fall into the hands of unworthy masters: whereas my sole object in that intention was to make them as happy as their condition of servitude would allow.—You judge me rightly when you suppose that I would not think of separating them. I could not for one moment admit the thought. No—I would not consent to such an inhuman act as that of separating husband from wife, or child from parent, for all the wealth of the State, even if I were myself penniless.—Now as my sole object is to do the best for them I can, I have concluded that I could not do better than to sell them to Mr. Belin.[2] Your account of their origin and intermarriage on his estate, together with his character as a kind and human man, has decided me, that they shall be offered to him, in preference to any other person. And so desirous am I that *he* should be their master, that he shall have them on his own terms. I knew Mr. Belin well, when he was a student at Cambridge, and I had a high esteem for him; I have since understood that he has become a religious man: I could not wish therefore for a better owner for them.

Now, my friend, should any of these Slaves fall to me, would you undertake the disposal of them to Mr. Belin? As to terms, or time of credit, I care not a straw about it. All I wish is to make them happy—which I feel assured they will be if he is their master.

I wish you to know a characteristic act of my noble-minded Sister, Mrs. William A. Alston, of Waccama. While she was in Philadelphia, and before either of us had heard of the intended Law-suit, she wrote to me, saying, that she intended to divide her portion of the Inheritance from our Grandmother between my Brother, William M. Allston, of Newport, and myself. While I thanked her from my heart for this generous intention, I did not hesitate to decline it; for, though poor myself, my Brother is *so much poorer,* besides having a family of children,[3] I felt that I ought [not] [page torn] and could not accept it; I therefore begged that she would give it *all* to William.—She is a noble woman.—I hope my Sister got my letter on this subject, and that she did not leave Philadelphia before it reached her—or, at any rate, that, if she had gone before its arrival there, it was forwarded to her.

The Papers announce that Clevenger is about to proceed to Italy.[4] He is to be accompanied by a young man, G.L. Brown,[5] of Boston, who I think will make a first-rate Landscape painter—I have heard a good deal lately of a Mr. Crawford,[6] from New York, who has been some years in Italy, & is there now; a sculptor.—I have no news to tell you except that my health is better now than last year, when I sat for my bust.—My best regards to Mrs. Cogdell. God bless you.

Ever your sincere friend, / Washington Allston

ADDRESSED: John S. Cogdell Esqre / Charleston, / South Carolina. ANNOTATED by Cogdell: answered 30 Jun [?] 1840. SOURCE: Manuscript.

1. Henry C. Flagg, Jr., and Thomas Wigfall, acting for his wife, Eliza (Moore) Flagg, the two remaining Flagg children of Rachel (Moore) Allston Flagg, proposed to bring suit protesting the inheritance by her Allston children of the slaves she inherited from her father. 2. Alard Henry Belin (1803-71). He received an A.B. from Harvard in 1821 and an A.M. in 1824 and subsequently became a planter in Charleston, S.C. (*Charleston City Directory* for 1835-36). His sister Margaret Elizabeth was the wife of Ebenezer Flagg, WA's half-brother (Belin-Flagg Family Bible, private collection). 3. William M. Allston had five children: Samuel R., Harrill, John E., Jane R. (d. 1876), and Washington (Groves, p. 33). 4. Clevenger went to Florence in October 1840. The newspaper reports have not been located. 5. George Loring Brown (1814-89), landscape, portrait, and miniature painter, lithographer, etcher, and wood engraver. Born in Boston, he worked there from 1834 to 1836 and again in 1838. His copy of a painting by Claude, purchased by the BA, was pronounced by WA the best copy of a Claude he had ever seen, a statement he got WA to put in writing so as to raise sufficient money to enable him to go to Europe to make other copies. From about 1840 to 1859 he lived in Europe, chiefly in Florence and Rome, afterward in New York and Boston. 6. Thomas Crawford.

279. From Anne Gillman Highgate June 7th 1840—

My dear Sir: I was very much gratified to see in your own hand writing, that you continue to call me "your *still* dear friend"[1]—and I beg to thank you for the your [*sic*] beautiful and affecting Sonnet,[2] which while it expresses the feelings of a deeply affectionate Heart, shews that the memory and intellect of the writer remain unscared. Long, long may you live to the honour of our *Sister Country,* though your two dear friends, (now alas! departed), as well as myself, would fain you had never left dear England. How often did we *regret* that you did so—at the moment too when your reputation must so easily have procured for you a moderate but honourable independence. Fame however will follow your name *wherever* your days may be passed.

The death of our invaluable Friend[3] was a heart-grief to us—and our greatest consolation was found in dwelling on the *truths* he so sweetly taught and on the beautiful example he set forth in his daily life. Have you read the first volume of his life by my beloved husband[4]—pray let me know. Also have you seen his will[5] and the Epitaph (written also by Mr. Gillman) and inscribed on a simple marble Tablet in our Church[6] to Mr. Coleridge's memory.

Alas! my dear Sir, I have sustained a yet nearer loss. On the first of last June he[7] breathed his last. He had suffered much for several years, but with entire resignation and cheerfulness, though almost deprived of the use of one side. He had unspeakable comfort in my reading Coleridge to him, as well as the Bible, and we felt that next to God, we were indebted to this dear friend, for the *light* that was gleaming on our latter days. But no separation, not even of death itself, is permanent, where we may venture to ask the Giver of all good to bless our friendship. I have experienced many trials, and heavy afflictions during my sojourn here—but one stage of my pilgrimage is now accomplished, and that which remains, though it must be finished alone, is a short one. May my end be peaceful as theirs! with the same well grounded assurance of acceptance thro' Christ.

You will perhaps be surprised to hear that I am *not* in easy circumstances—though I am at present enabled to continue in the house, having a few pupils confided to my care. About twelve years ago we lost twelve thousand pounds, entirely through the misconduct of a relation; but luckily we did not feel it very much, except for the *act*. My eldest Son,[8] a clergyman, and a young man of *strict integrity,* has a very small Rectory in Kent, and takes a few pupils to prepare for College—he is married to a lady-like sensible young woman.[9] My Youngest Son[10] has bad health, and I must support him.

In a letter I received from a friend, speaking of my beloved husband, he says,—"He was indeed a noble hearted man—generous, straight forward and uncalculating too good indeed for the times and the residence in which his lot was cast."

I have ventured to write all this to you my dear Mr. Alston, assured that my letter will find some interest in your affectionate nature. By the bye I must tell you, that your valued painting[11] is in my drawing room, and that I have bequeathed it, as an *heirloom,* to my eldest Son James. Have you seen the last edition of Mr. Coleridge's poems—in three volumes?[12] They contain several beautiful poems written during his latter years. I fear I must not ask you to write to me, for I have heard, such efforts are not agreeable to you—and I too well understand the feeling. I will only say that it will always be a great pleasure to hear *of* and *from* you, and to know that you are well in health, and as peaceful as in this life, may be fairly hoped.

God in Heaven bless you, my dear Sir! continue, I pray you, for the sake of your two dear departed friends, to think with affection of one who so highly esteems and regards yourself.

Anne Gillman

SOURCE: Manuscript, Houghton.

1. If Mrs. Gillman is quoting from a letter of WA's to her it does not seem to have been preserved. 2. WA's "Sonnet on the Late S.T. Coleridge" (a manuscript copy by Mrs. Allston is in the Department of Rare Books, Cornell University Library.) It was published in *Graham's*

Magazine 22 [Jan. 1843]: 27. It was one of his most memorable poems, not only in its evocation of the personality of Coleridge but in its imagery of the interior life, which he regarded as the supreme mark of human nature. Describing Coleridge's voice as blending "With air of Earth its pure ideal tones" and binding in one "The heart and intellect," he lamented that he should no more

> with thee gaze on that unfathomed deep,
> The Human Soul,—as when, pushed off the shore,
> Thy mystic bark would through the darkness sweep,
> Itself the while so bright! For oft we seemed
> As on some starless sea,—all dark above,
> All dark below,—yet, onward as we drove,
> To plough up light that over round us streamed,

and offered the consolation that Coleridge's "living Truths" were left (*LA*, p. 346). 3. Coleridge. 4. *The Life of Samuel Taylor Coleridge*, vol. 1 (London, 1838). Gillman destroyed the material for volume 2. 5. In his will Coleridge requested that a small gold mourning ring with a lock of his hair be presented to six friends (Watson, p. 126). 6. The tablet with the epitaph, a lengthy one, is in St. Michael's Church in Highgate (Gillman, p. 13). 7. Gillman died on 1 June 1839. 8. James Gillman, Jr. (1808-77), elder son of James and Anne Gillman. He graduated from Oxford and as a clergyman served in Barfreystone in Kent from 1836 to 1847 and subsequently in Lambeth in south London (Gillman, pp. 27, 29, 31, 34). 9. The former Sophia Riley (d. 1862), whose father had residences in London and New South Wales, Australia (Gillman, pp. 27, 34). 10. Henry Anthony Gillman. 11. *The Adoration of the Magi*. 12. *The Poetical Works of S.T. Coleridge*, ed. Henry N. Coleridge, 3 vols. (London, 1834).

280. To the Editor of the North American Review [John Gorham Palfrey]

[June 1840]

To the Editor of the North American Review.

Sir.—In a very complimentary article, in the last Number of the "North American Review," on my late exhibition,[1] it was with much regret that I observed an allusion to an old, but unfounded, report concerning my friend, Mr. Martin, imputing to him some unfair dealing in relation to myself. I had hoped that report, *which I have again and again contradicted,* had long since been set at rest. But since this, it seems, is not the case, I feel it to be a duty which I owe to an honorable man and distinguished artist, to state distinctly, *that Mr. Martin has never borrowed from me either thought or hint in a single instance.* He has too much genius to borrow from any one.

As to the thought of lighting my picture of Belshazzar from the "writing on the wall," (which is the *imagined* ground of unfairness,) I never claimed it as *my* invention; for, as the reviewer has justly remarked, the originality consists in giving to the light a preternatural source; and this is well known to have originated with Correggio, as may be seen in his celebrated *Notte;*[2] besides, it has so often been repeated, under various modifications, as long ago to have become a kind of common property in the art; and such indeed I considered it when, in 1816, I adopted it in another picture,—the Angel liberating St. Peter,—where the prison and the figures are both lighted by a supposed *emanation* from the Angel. But Mr. Martin's fame does not depend on such subordinate accessories as this; in my opinion a more original mind than his was never impressed on canvass. In proof, however, of the slight value I ever attached to the accessory in question, it is many years since I have altogether dispensed with it; and this I did, not because Mr. Martin also had it, but because I found that it would very materially interfere with an important part of my composition; so that *my* Belshazzar is not now lighted from the 'writing on the wall.' In Martin's picture, (which is well known here from the print,) the light so proceeding has an admirable effect, and is happily suited to *his* composition; yet do I consider it but *as a grain of sand* in the production of the powerful impression so universally felt from that extraordinary work; nor have I the least doubt, had he seen fit to light the picture from his gigantic candelabra, or from any other source, that still it would have retained its present poetical grandeur, and still have been worthy of imperial munificence.*

If I know myself, I am the last man to seek competition, which I hold to be unworthy a true artist, who should love his art for its own sake. The very word *rival* grates upon my nature. But in this instance competition is out of the question; for the difference between Mr. Martin's work and mine is not of degree, but of *kind;* and things differing in kind (though admitting preference) cannot be compared. Many persons seem not to be aware of this, or that the same subject may be painted by twenty artists, and yet be treated differently by each, provided the artists have all *minds of their own*. Now between Mr. Martin's Belshazzar and mine, *there is not a single point of resemblance;* nor could there well be, since each was conceived according to the character of our individual minds. Yet does not this characteristic difference preclude a deep sympathy between us. At least, I answer for myself, that he could not wish for more than I have often felt under the spell of his genius.

And here, (since I am now, however unwillingly, before the public,) I may as well say to those who might look for any thing like architectural display in my picture, that they will certainly be disappointed; indeed the small space of background which my composition allows, would not admit of it; but, were it even much larger, I should never dream of contending with Martin in architectural magnificence, in which *he stands alone*.

A word more. Since some allusion also has been made to my studies in England, I trust I may be pardoned if I avail myself of the present opportunity to say, that I owe much of whatever knowledge I may possess of my art to the English school; my connexion with which,—and no less from respect than affection,—I shall ever hold in high value. As a body, the English artists are full of talent; and, were it not that to those omitted it might seem invidious, it would give me pleasure to name many individuals among them who deservedly hold a high rank in the art.

Very respectfully, / Your obedient servant, / Washington Allston.

Cambridge Port, June, 1840.[3]

* It is said that Mr. Martin was honored by a *solid* compliment for this picture, from the Emperor of Russia.[4]

SOURCE: *North American Review* 50 (Oct. 1846): 518-20.

1. That by Holmes in the *North American Review* for April 1840. In it Holmes referred to the letter of John Martin quoted by Dunlap in which Martin said he had undertaken to paint the subject of Belshazzar's feast in consequence of an argument he had with WA and repeated the report that WA had borrowed from Martin the idea of making the principal light in his own painting come from the miraculous letters on the wall but went on to say that that idea was only a modification of one long familiar to poets and painters of the supernatural, giving several examples, among them Correggio's "famous 'Notte.'" 2. "Night." The light in this painting of the Nativity emanates from the figures of the mother and child. 3. The sentence introducing the letter said it was received too late for insertion in the July number of the magazine. 4. WA apparently refers to Martin's dedication in September 1828 of the engraving of his painting *The Deluge* to Nicholas I (1796-1855), emperor of Russia 1825-55, who had presented him with a gold medal and a diamond ring in admiration of an unspecified painting (Thomas Balston, *John Martin, 1789-1854* [London: G. Duckworth, 1947], p. 103).

281. To George Harvey

Cambridge Port, 8 July, 1840.

George Harvey Esqre.

Dear Sir: As it is no less my pleasure than my duty to give praise where it is due, I am unwilling that you should leave Boston[1] without knowing how much I have been gratified by your beautiful Drawings of American Scenery.[2] To me it appears that you have been not only successful in giving the character of our Scenery, but remarkably happy in clothing it with an American atmosphere—which you have expressed with equal truth and variety.

Heartily wishing you the success you deserve, I remain,

dear sir, / With sincere regard, / Yrs / Wa. Allston.

ADDRESSED: George Harvey Esqre / Tremont House, / Boston. SOURCE: Manuscript, South Caroliniana Library, University of South Carolina; draft, Dana Papers.[3]

1. Harvey's home was near Hastings-on-Hudson, N.Y. 2. Harvey commenced a series of watercolors, "Atmospheric Landscapes of North America," and in 1838 went to London with a plan to have forty of them engraved and sold by subscription and to have Irving edit the accompanying text. Only four appeared, without Irving's aid (Irving, *Letters* 4:220-21).
3. The draft, which is thoroughly canceled with a variety of lines, has only a few, minor differences in wording, chiefly "quit" for "leave," "telling you" for "knowing," and "quite" for "not only." It also contains, above the salutation and in a firmer hand and deeper ink, the uncanceled phrase "With the irredeemably wicked, in other words, devils," which appeared, "with" being added before "devils," in the "Introductory Discourse" of WA's lectures on art (*LA*, p. 41).

282. To William Wordsworth Cambridge Port, Masstts
19 July, 1840.

Dear Sir: Will you permit me to introduce to you Mrs. Sigourney, of Connecticut, who is very desirous of the honour of paying her respects to you.[1] I have not the pleasure of a personal acquaintance with Mrs. Sigourney; but when I add, that both her literary reputation and private character as a lady have secured to her the respect of her countrymen, I feel assured that I may promise her a kind reception.

I remain, dear Sir, / with the highest respect, / Yrs / Washington Allston
To William Wordsworth Esqre / Keswick, / Cumberland

ADDRESSED: William Wordsworth Esqre / Keswick, / Cumberland / Mrs. L.H. Sigourney
SOURCE: Manuscript, The Wordsworth Trust, Dove Cottage, Grasmere.

1. Mrs. Sigourney visited Wordsworth in August 1840, soon after she arrived in England. He came promptly to her inn and invited her to tea at Rydal Mount; she described the occasion in her *Pleasant Memories of Pleasant Lands* (1842) (Haight, pp. 52, 55, 64). On 14 November 1836, the same day she wrote WA asking him for a contribution to *The Religious Souvenir,* she wrote Wordsworth with the same request. Apparently he did not reply. The next year she sent him a book, probably a volume of *The Lady's Book,* of which she was an editor (*Letters of William and Dorothy Wordsworth,* 6:483).

283. To William Wordsworth Cambridge Port, Masstts
29 July, 1840.

My dear Sir: This will be handed you by my particular friend, the reved Mr. Adams,[1] whom I beg to introduce to you.

Having so often asked the honour of your notice for my countrymen, I should fear to trespass on your kindness by now adding to the number, did I not believe that it would give you pleasure to see one of my personal friends—than whom no one for whom I have asked this favour is better capable of understanding, and appreciating, your genius.

Will you permit me here to say, that I shall soon have occasion to solicit a similar honour for another friend, Dr. Woods.[2] I should be sorry that either of these my most valued friends should visit England without an opportunity of knowing one whom they have so long admired.

With best wishes for the continued health and happiness of yourself and family, I remain, dear Sir,

With the highest respect, / Yrs / Washington Allston.

ADDRESSED: William Wordsworth Esqre / Keswick, / Cumberland. / Revnd Mr. Adams.
SOURCE: Manuscript, The Wordsworth Trust, Dove Cottage, Grasmere.

1. Nehemiah Adams (1806-78), co-pastor with Abiel Holmes at the Church of the Shepard Congregational Society in Cambridge, Mass., from December 1829 to September 1831 and from then until March 1834 sole pastor. From 1834 until his death he was pastor of the Essex Street, or Union, Congregational Church in Boston. WA owned a copy of his *Remarks on the Unitarian*

Belief, with a letter to a Unitarian Friend on the Lord's Supper (Boston, 1832). 2. Leonard Woods, Jr. (1807-78), Presbyterian clergyman. From 1839 to 1866 he was president of Bowdoin College. He and WA became acquainted shortly after 1832, at which time, as tutor in Andover Theological Seminary, he was in charge of the studies of RHD, Jr., at Andover while he was suspended with others from Harvard for six months for disturbance in chapel. RHD, Jr., was deeply impressed by his scholarship, knowledge of foreign languages, acquaintance with literature, both poetry and fiction, religious faith, and freedom from prejudice, and corresponded with and visited him the next year. He visited RHD in 1841, was at the Harvard commencement with WA in 1842, visited the Danas again in February 1843, at which time he preached a sermon which RHD, Jr., summarized in his journal with admiration, again in May and June 1843, and at subsequent times (Dana, 1:22-25, 55, 90, 128, 131-35, 159, 163, 285, 480, 485, 490).

284. To Charles Sumner Cambridge Port, 6 Oct. 1840.

My dear Sir: I hope I shall have the pleasure of seeing you before you write to our Friend, Greenough, on the subject of our short conversation this morning.[1] I should be grieved if, by any sudden <[undecipherable word]> resolution on his part, our Country should be deprived of a National Monument which will do it so much honour.—I have endeavoured to recall the statement which you made to me; but I find that I cannot bring it to mind with sufficient distinctness to say that I quite understand it; and I fear consequently that I expressed too hasty an opinion on the subject. I therefore beg you to consider my sentiments in relation to it *as not yet expressed*—as, indeed, they ought not to be, until I know more about it than I do at present.

It occurs to me that an arrangement might be made by Greenough, without any compromise of self-respect, that shall be satisfactory to all parties. His friends, at least, cannot but be all anxious that a work so honourable to his Country, and so important to himself, should not, if possible, be abandoned.

I remain, dear Sir, / with sincere regard, / Yrs / Wa. Allston.

To Charles Sumner Esqre.

ADDRESSED: Charles Sumner Esqre. / Boston. SOURCE: Manuscript, Houghton.

1. The government delayed over a period of many years making payments to Horatio Greenough for his group *The Rescue*, for which the fee was to be $21,500. His draft on the treasury for $1,000, the second installment, made in February 1840, was refused because the required consular certificate attesting the progress on the work had not been received, and the letter replying to his request for it took him to task for not having finished his statue of Washington and for requesting that the government pay for the pedestal for it. In his reply to that letter, after accounting for the time consumed in executing the statue and explaining that the American consul at Rome was unable to leave his post for the inspection, he asked to be allowed to give up further work on the group and to be given time to reimburse the government for the $4,000 already received. On 12 July he wrote Sumner, who had visited him in Florence the preceding fall, summarizing the matter and adding a postscript that if an attempt was being made to "poison the public mind" against his work he hoped Sumner would make his explanations to the government known (Greenough, *Letters*, pp. 285-87). Apparently it was this letter which prompted Sumner to discuss Greenough's

situation at this time with WA, to whom Greenough had earlier reported his work on the group. The remaining installments were eventually paid to him except the last, which was paid to his estate. The work was erected, after his death, in 1853 (Wright, pp. 159-62, 165-67, 171).

285. To George Whiting Flagg Cambridge Port, Mass—
29 Oct. 1840.

My dear George: I have received your letter, containing the Draft, for Fifty Dollars, on the Suffolk Bank—which I got cashed at the Bank in this place.

I should like much to see your portrait of John.[1] I had a short visit, a few weeks since, from him and his wife.[2] He told me you had been giving him some lessons in the Art; with which I understand he intends to amuse himself on the plantation. He does well in seeking such employment for his leisure hours—which I suppose will not be very few. It is a good thing for rich men to have any kind of intellectual occupation, provided it be not one of vain speculation, which too often puts out the little light <that> they might have carried to such studies, darkening the mind to the great purpose of life—which is, by the cultivation of their moral nature, to prepare them for a better world.

I have resumed my large Picture, after <being> a suspension of many months, occasioned by the want of funds to go on with it. In order to [do] this I took up a picture which I began several years ago, and finished it about the beginning of the summer.[3] But, though it is one of my best pictures, owing to the hard times, I had to wait from that time till within three weeks before I could dispose of it.

You do <well?> right to think of undertaking a large picture; fix your aim high, and the necessary courage for performance will come with it; whereas, if you fear to meditate great things, the very timidity you feel will *infect* even your humbler efforts. No man knows what he *can* do until he tries; and it is better to fail than not try at all; for <if we have [undecipherable word]> we are sure to profit even by our failures, if we have only firmness enough to look the *degree* of talent they indicate in the *face;* it may give us at least some knowledge of our capacity.—I am glad to hear that you have been studying the naked. You would do well also to make anatomical drawing, either from plaster or prints, your winter evenings amusement. At any rate, in all manner of ways, make yourself master of the figure.—I would write more, but our boy interrupts me, by setting the table for tea.—Your Aunt unites with me in love to yourself and all your family.[4] She desires me to add, that she will write to Mary[5] soon.

God bless you, my dear boy, / Your affectionate Uncle, / Washington Allston.

ADDRESSED: Mr. George W. Flagg, / New-Haven, / Connecticut. SOURCE: Manuscript, Dreer Collection, Painters & Engravers, Historical Society of Pennsylvania.

1. John Ashe Alston, the son of William Algernon and Mary (Allston) Young Alston. One of his children was named for WA. His uncle, a brother of William A. Alston, bore the same name (Groves, pp. 56, 54). 2. Fanny (Fraser) Alston (Groves, p. 56). 3. Presumably *Amy*

Robsart. It represented the commission given WA by John Lowell (1799-1836), the founder of the Lowell Institute, in 1834, who stipulated only that it be the size of WA's "last admirable scene from the Italian," presumably *Italian Landscape* (G62), which is 30¼ by 25¼ inches, the price of which he said was $500. *Amy Robsart* is 30¾ by 25¾ inches. He allowed that WA "should choose his own subject, with a hint merely that a pretty woman might be acceptably introduced into it." He was prompted to order a painting, for which he asked his brother Francis Cabot Lowell to engage with WA, while in Ghent in December 1833, a few weeks after he left Boston for a trip around the world. The sight of paintings by Rubens, Teniers, Van Dyke, Rembrandt, and other old masters in a private collection there left entirely in the shade, he said, everything he had seen in America "excepting always the pictures of Allston." He had met with nothing there, he added, that he would rather own than that landscape of WA's, conceding that he would prefer the works of Raphael, above all the cartoons, and excepting those of Murillo and the Carracci, but declaring there were few productions of other old masters that he liked so well as WA's. The idea of possessing one came, he said, partly from this preference but partly from his willingness "to be of some service to so meritorious an artist," even if he should never live to see it. His words proved premonitory, for he died on his way home in India in March 1836 (Ferris Greenslet, *The Lowells and Their Seven Worlds* [Boston: Houghton Mifflin, 1946], pp. 199, 202, 214). The commission was taken over by his cousin John Amory Lowell. Sumner reported to Horatio Greenough on 30 September 1840 that WA had "recently painted" the picture, but the subject had been decided on and the painting substantially finished by late 1839, intended for Samuel Ward, who died at that time. Samuel Ward, Jr., who said it was a great favorite of his, regretted that it could not be bought from John A. Lowell, who, he said, paid $1,100 for it (Elliott, p. 315). 4. Presumably Flagg's parents, brothers, and sisters. The children were Henry C., III; Mary Allston; William Joseph; Jared Bradley; Rachel Moore; and Edward Octavus Flagg (Nord, p. 93). 5. Presumably Mary Allston Flagg (1814-77), George W. Flagg's sister.

286. To George Roberts Cambridge Port, 15 Jany- 1841.

Dear Sir: Your Letter did not reach me until many days after it was written, in consequence of its being directed to Cambridge, instead of Cambridge Port. You must not therefore attribute this delay to neglect.

For the compliment you pay me in the request to become a contributor to the "Double Notion"[1] I beg you to accept my thanks; my engagements, however, are such as to put a compliance with it quite out of my power.

Your kind offer of sending me your Paper you will allow me to decline, as I make it a rule not to accept any publication to which I do not contribute.

I am, dear Sir, / respectfully yrs / Wa. Allston.

ADDRESSED: George Roberts Esqre / Editor of the Double Notion, / Notion Office, / Boston. SOURCE: Manuscript, Haverford College Library.

1. The *Boston Notion* was a weekly newspaper in Boston published by Roberts from 1839 to 1848, with a suspension between June 1842 and 22 April 1843, probably called the "Double Notion" because of its size. It was one of the popular oversize papers of the day, advertising that it provided "104 square feet of reading matter" (Mott, *A History of American Magazines, 1741-1850*, p. 361). It contained the best articles from the *Boston Daily Times* for the week, which consisted largely of reports of crime and accidents copied from other papers. Twice during the summer it was supplemented by the *Quadruple Notion*, also apparently called the *Quarto Notion*. Among the

contributors to it were Emerson and William Gilmore Simms. Simms ordered a copy of WA's *SS* from Roberts (Willard Grosvenor Bleyer, *Main Currents in the History of American Journalism* [Boston: Houghton Mifflin, 1927], pp. 171-75; Jay Bayless, *Rufus Wilmot Griswold, Poe's Literary Executor* [Nashville: Vanderbilt Univ. Press, 1943], pp. 37-39; *The Letters of William Gilmore Simms* [Columbia: Univ. of South Carolina Press], vol. 6, ed. Marie C. Simms Oliphant and T.C. Duncan Eaves [1982], pp. 30-31; vol. 1, ed. Mary C. Simms Oliphant, Alfred Taylor Odell, and T.C. Duncan Eaves [1952], p. 282).

287. To John Stevens Cogdell Cambridge Port, Masstts
31 Jany 1841.

My dear Cogdell: I have long been wishing to write to you, but, to say the truth, my head has been utterly barren of subject-matter for a letter. I remember one of Cowper's[1] most agreeable letters was merely to tell his correspondent that he had nothing to say; and, though it was literally about nothing, he contrived to make it as brilliant as a soap-bubble, reflecting all the hues of the rainbow. Would that I had his epistolary talent to make this so too, for my object in now taking up the pen is simply to say the same thing. But, as I have not his talent, I can only state the plain matter of fact. There is little occurring in this *sublime* place at any time, least of all at this season, and what does occur is not worth noting.[2] Indeed I am in a manner out of the world here, more especially in the winter, though not quite three miles from Boston. About once or twice a month I have a visitor thence to pass an evening with me; and this is pretty much all that I get <of the> sight of from among the busy throng that is moving around me: but this I always thankfully consider as something between charity and a wind-fall. My own visits to Town are very rare, seldom exceeding a dozen in the course of a year—for a visit there always costs me a day, which I <will> can ill afford.—As I formerly said that I did not intend to give any account of Belshazzer until it was finished, I shall only say now, that I am hard at work on it—and *on nothing else*—I remember once telling my Mother, that no picture ever went out of my hand that was not as good as it was in *my* power to make it, for the time being. Neither shall Belshazzer leave my Room until I have done my best on it.—This is not the way, some artists might warily think, to get rich. I knew that, however, more than twenty years ago; yet have I never swerved from this <the> course; for it is better to be poor in a course which [you] know to be honourable, than to be rich in any other. This, with the love of my Art, has for so many years enabled me to endure poverty without repining.

You inform me in your last letter that you were to be nominated Consul for Leghorn,[3] but you did not say whether, if appointed, you intended to accept the office. Has the appointment been yet made? and if so, have you accepted it? Pray let me know. Should you go to Italy, I will give you a letter to a most excellent friend of mine, who resides in Rome—an English artist (a painter). I would also give you one to Greenough, but it would be useless, as he is expected home (with his statue of Washington) in the Ship of War Ohio—which will probably reach the United

States in April or May.[4] But you shall have one to Clavenger, who is now in Florence.—Should you determine to go to Italy, I have a favour to ask of you; which is to inquire of my old friend J.B. White if he is willing to act, in your place, as my attorney, in relation to my affairs about the Inheritance from my Grandmother. Should he be willing to take your place in this matter, I would thank you to communicate to him all my letters to you on the subject—which will possess him thoroughly with my wishes thereon. I think he will not refuse, for he is a true kind-hearted friend; and, I believe, he knows that I think so, though I do not *cumber* the Post Office with my epistles to him.—Should you, however, conclude to remain in Carolina, I do not wish any thing said to him on the subject.

I have reason to *guess* that the projected Lawsuit will be abandoned, if it is not already. And I guess so, because my Wife had a letter from Henry's Wife,[5] saying that my Brother H. wished to know, "what was to be done with Flora[6] and her child (two of my Grandmother's Slaves that have lived for several years in his family) should they fall to my lot?" He thinks, she adds, they should not be sent to Carolina, and inquires if I wish them sent to me.—Does not this seem as if there was not to be any lawsuit?

Since I am on this subject I might as well express to you my intentions respecting them. Should they fall to my lot, I shall neither send them to Carolina nor have them with me, but consult *their wishes solely* as to their place of residence. They have so long been accustomed to the North, that they may prefer remaining in New-Haven; if so, they certainly shall. At all events, should they fall to my lot, *they* shall not be sold, and, of course, they will not be sent to Carolina.—Respecting the others that <you> may fall to my share, I have already expressed my wishes to you.*—Judge Story[7] I think would be very much gratified at receiving the Bust[8] you mention. He has a son[9] in the Law-School, who is an amateur sculptor. He has made a bust of his father, which I am told, (for I have not seen it) is very clever.—My best regards to Mrs. Cogdell, and believe me, my kindhearted friend, ever affectionately

yrs / Washington Allston.

*that is to be disposed of to Mr. Belin.

ADDRESSED: John S. Cogdell Esqre / Charleston, / South Carolina. SOURCE: Manuscript.

1. William Cowper (1731-1800), English poet, celebrated for his letters. WA refers to Cowper's letter to the Rev. William Unwin of 31 October 1779, beginning, "I wrote my last letter merely to inform you that I had nothing to say." WA goes on to describe, however, not the letter of 31 October, which is devoted to a criticism of Johnson's life by Milton, but to Cowper's preceding letter to Unwin, of 21 September 1779, which discourses with sprightliness on the activity of glazing frames for plants and on his eight pairs of tame pigeons (*The Letters and Prose Writings of William Cowper,* vol. 1, ed. James King and Charles Ryskamp [Oxford: Clarendon Press, 1979], pp. 306, 303-304). 2. This sentence suggests that WA shared to some extent the opinion of those critics who blamed his residence in America, particularly in Cambridgeport, for his declining productivi-

ty in his later years. 3. Cogdell was commissioned U.S. consul at Rome on 7 May 1806 but notified the State Department on 3 June 1806 that he declined. No record seems to exist that he ever applied for or accepted another consular appointment. 4. Horatio Greenough's *Washington* was transported from Italy on the merchant ship *Sea,* which reached Washington on 31 July 1841. He had intended accompanying it and said the hope of seeing Allston and the Danas when he arrived outweighed "all the vexations" he foresaw "in plunging once more among the world of business & politics" (Greenough, *Letters*, p. 28). He did not go, however, because of his conviction that the government's protestation of his drafts for the last installment on his group *The Rescue* was to be explained by hostility to him (Wright, pp. 139-41, 224; Greenough, *Letters,* pp. 525-26. 5. Martha (Whiting) Flagg (1791-1875) of New Haven (Norman Gershom Flagg, *Family Records of the Descendants of Gershom Flagg of Lancaster, Massachusetts* [Quincy, Ill., Cadogan-Hatcher: 1907], p. 123. 6. Flora was one of the slaves named in the will of John Vanderhorst (Webber, "Moore of St. Thomas' Parish," p. 164). 7. Joseph Story. 8. Possibly Cogdell's bust, executed after his death, of Henry William De Saussure (1763-1839), South Carolina lawyer, director of the U.S. Mint, and chancellor of the state. 9. William Wetmore Story.

288. To George Cheyne Shattuck

Cambridge Port,
21 Feb—1841.

My dear Sir: I know not how to thank you for your munificent Present:[1] there seems to be no end to your kindness. If skill and kindness can bring me health, I feel that I ought to be a well man under your hands; and I shall certainly do my best to profit by this your last most agreeable prescription.

How I shall ever be able to make you a suitable return for the many benefits you have conferred, I know not; but of this you may be assured, that not one has ever been lost upon me. The generous delicacy with which your favours have always been accompanied makes it *indeed* a pleasure to be obliged.

I remain, dear Sir, / with the highest respect, / Your obliged Friend,
Washington Allston.

ADDRESSED: Doctr. Shattuck, / Staniford Street,[2] / Boston. SOURCE: Manuscript.

1. Presumably a prescription and the medicine for an ailment of WA's. 2. Shattuck lived on Staniford Street, at the corner of Cambridge Street, from 1813 until his death (*Boston City Directory*).

289. To John Stevens Cogdell

Cambridge Port, Masstts
21 Feby 1841.

My dear Cogdell: Your letter of the 13th inst. reached me yesterday, but too late for an answer to it by return of the Mail; and today being sunday, this letter cannot be mailed until tomorrow. But now that I <have> s <a> it down to reply to you, I am so unlearned in the forms of the Law, that I know not in what terms to signify my compliance with your request. I will therefore (to prevent mistake) copy, from the

Master in Chancery's Paper, what I suppose to be the *gist* of the question, and reply to that.[1] He says, "It is insisted on the part of W.A. Alston and Wife, and of Wm. M. Allston, that their ⅖ be charged on, and deducted from, the distributive share of Henry C. Flagg of the Negroes in Mr. Belin's possession—The ⅕ to which Washington Allston is entitled is held under advisement, waiting his instructions." To this I reply, that, in like manner with my brother Wm M. Allston and W.A. Alston and Wife, I also insist on my ⅕. And I see no reason why I should not.—I suppose this will be considered sufficiently <clear> explicit.—I will send, as you request, a copy of the Master's Paper to my brother William immediately.—

I had the pleasure sometime since of meeting Mr. Legare[2] at a dinner-party in Boston, and regreted much that I had not an opportunity of a longer acquaintance, as I have a high admiration of his talents and learning. I have read some of his Articles in the New-York Review,[3] and I know not which most to admire, his scholarship or his eloquence;[4] he is certainly one of our most accomplished writers. Our cause could not be in abler hands.[5]

I do not think that Henry meant to deceive me in the message which he sent me (through his Wife's letter to my Wife) as to the health of Flora—as it is expressly stated in the Message that she was "*sickly.*" I say this in strict justice, as I truly believe. But I will transcribe the very words of the whole Message from Mrs. Flagg's letter, and you can judge for yourself. She says—"My Husband wishes me to ask you if his brother and you would wish to have Flora and her Child (if at the division of Ben's[6] family they should fall to you) sent to you, or what he should do with them—if they should fall to us we shall keep them—but I do not think it would be right to send them back to Carolina. Flora is sickly but a good servant."—This is *verbatim* and all which Mrs. Flagg wrote to my Wife; and her letter (from which I now copy the message) is dated 20th of August, 1840.—Thinking it time enough to reply when the division was made I sent no answer.*

Our friends Mr. & Mrs. Amory are spending the winter in Boston. I expected them to pass an evening with me last week, but they were prevented by Mr. A. having a bad cold. Mrs. Amory appears to be in excellent health. Two kinder hearts are not to be found on Earth.

God bless you and Yours, / Yrs affectionately, / Washington Allston.

*It occurred to me when I received this Message that it was sent *indirectly* to signify that there would be *no law-suit.* And I think now, as then, that I put the right construction upon it.—It was a grief to me which I cannot express that such a suit ever should have been contemplated. Alas, thought I—but I forebore all remark.

ADDRESSED: John S. Cogdell Esqre / Charleston, / South Carolina. ANNOTATED by Cogdell: answd [?] 2 Mar. 1841. SOURCE: Manuscript.

1. Apparently it was decided in Chancery Court that the slaves left by Rachel (Moore) Allston Flagg should be divided between the Allston and the Flagg heirs, three-fifths to the former and two-fifths to the latter, and the terms of their sale fixed. 2. Hugh Swinton Legaré (1797-1843), South Carolina lawyer and statesman. Ticknor, who was a close friend of his, wrote him on 16 June

1841 of dining with WA, Longfellow, William Hickling Prescott, and George S. Hillard and added, "You ought to have been there," with the apparent indication that he had been in Boston with them not long before (*Life, Letters, and Journals* 2:196). 3. Legaré wrote three articles for the *New York Review:* "Roman Legislation" (5 [July 1839]: 209-334), reviewing five books: "Constitutional History of Greece, and the Democracy of Athens" (6 [July 1840]: 1-85), reviewing two books; and "Demosthenes, the Man, the Statesman, and the Orator" (7 [July 1841]: 1-70), reviewing three books. 4. Legaré was celebrated as an orator. His most spectacular case was that of *Ball and Wife vs. the Executors of Ball,* in which he argued successfully that Mrs. H.S. Ball died later than her husband after the ship's explosion which killed them both, by which decision her estate went to her heirs. The case was reported at length in the press (Linda Rhea, *Hugh Swinton Legaré: A Charleston Intellectual* [Chapel Hill, N.C., 1934], pp. 181-83). WA must have known of and been particularly interested in it because of his connections with both Balls. 5. Legaré was active in the cause of the Union from 1828 until his death. 6. Benjamin Allston (b. 1768), WA's half-brother. He married his cousin Charlotte Anne Allston, by whom he had six children (Groves, p. 33).

290. To John Stevens Cogdell

Cambridge Port, Masstts
8 March 1841.

My dear Cogdell, I suppose ere this you have received my answer to your Letter of the 13th of Feby. I replied to it the day after it reached me; I also sent a copy of such parts of it to my brother William as you requested.

I now write to you on a subject which has occasioned me no little anxiety. You may remember how anxiously I expressed myself, in a former letter to you, <of> on the subject of the sale of *my* portion of the Slaves inherited from my Grandmother; namely, that there should be *no separation of Wife from Husband, or Parent from Child;* also, that it was my earnest request they should be disposed of to a kind Master—at the same time expressing the hope that they would become the property of Mr. Alard Belin, with whom they had so long lived, and who I had every reason to believe would always treat them with humanity. I have the same solicitude on the subject *now.* But it seems, from the present aspect of things, that that part of my wish respecting Mr. Belin, is not likely to be realized—inasmuch as this unhappy Lawsuit having thrown the sale of the Slaves upon the Court of Chancery, Mr. Belin declines taking them on the terms the Court offers. May I not trust, however, that the other part of my wish will be accomplished? That <they may not> the *separation* which I should so much deplore will be still prevented—perhaps I should say, avoided?—Could they not be *so* divided that the same family—say, husband wife and child—be sold to the same person? These are particulars which deeply interest me.—<And> May I then beg of you, my friend, in addition to your many, many kindness[es,] to exert such influence as you may have to *this effect?* Could it not be done, at least so far as *my fifth* of the 1<5>6 now with Mr. Belin is concerned? I feel it to be my Christian duty to entreat that it might, if possible, be done. I care *nothing* about any *pecuniary diminution* which such a disposition of them might occasion. Provided they have a kind good master, the terms would not weigh with me a straw.—<M> The plan I would propose is this. Let such a *connected* portion of them as may amount to one fifth in value, according to the estimate already made by the Court, be considered as *mine; then* let them be sold to *one* good Master—though at a *diminished price*. [Perhaps, if this can be done, Mr. Belin will take them; if so, he shall have them on the terms mentioned in my former letter.][1]

Now, my friend, I know that you fully understand me as a man, and will therefore *believe* me, when I distinctly assure you, that I shall *not consider it any sacrifice*—whatever the pecuniary difference the execution of my plan may involve. I have but *one* object—which is to place these helpless Creatures in <to> the hands of one who will take care of them, as a Christian Master. Not all the money in the State would induce me to separate them, or to put them into the power of a bad man, if it is in *my* power to prevent it. If it should so happen then that it shall prove to be wholly out of my power to avert this <[undecipherable word]> serious calamity, it will be no ordinary grief to me.

There is one wish more which I will venture to express—namely, that none of the 16 now in Mr. Belin's service <will> be sold to any one who will take them out of the State. I hope and trust they will not, and I hope that the person appointed by the Court to make the sale will avoid it.—I do not indeed *know* that my Sister Mrs. Alston and my brother, William, of Newport, agree with me as to this last wish, but I *think* (from what I know of their hearts) they must feel as I do about it: nor can I think they would differ from me on the subject of separating families.

But I need say no more—whatever a man of heart and principle *can* do for <their> the well-being of the Slaves in question, I feel assured that you, my friend, will do.

I know not how, my dear Cogdell, I shall ever be able to make you a return for what you have already done for me and mine; but of this be assured—that you have never served a friend more grateful.

My best regards to Mrs. Cogdell—and believe me, affectionately yrs,

Washington Allston.

*I mean with respect to the Slaves now in the service of Mr. Belin.

ADDRESSED: John S. Cogdell Esqre / Charleston, / South Carolina. ANNOTATED by Cogdell: answd. 20 Mar: 1841. SOURCE: Manuscript.

1. WA's brackets.

291. To David H. Williams Cambridge Port, 12 March, 1841.

D.H. Williams Esqre. / Boston.

Dear Sir: I regret to say, in reply to your Letter, in which you pay me the compliment to ask the assistance of my pen, that my engagements put it quite out of my power to become a contributor to your proposed Annual.[1]

I should have replied sooner to your letter but for the mistake as to my address.

Very respectfully, yrs / Wa. Allston.

ADDRESSED: D.H. Williams Esqre / Boston. SOURCE: Manuscript, Pierpont Morgan Library.

1. At this time Williams was proposing a new annual publication to be conducted by an association of literary men of Cambridge and Boston, for which he solicited contributions from Simms and others as well as WA. Instead, he became the editor, with George S. Hillard, and publisher of *The Token* for 1842, Samuel G. Goodrich having given up control in 1841 (Simms, *Letters* 1:234; 6:30-31).

292. To John Stevens Cogdell Cambridge Port, Mass. 24 March, 1841

[*Confidential.*][1]

My dear Cogdell: Did I not know your unwearied benevolence, I should fear to tire you out on the subject of my late letters; but, as I feel assured that the interest you have taken in this matter is no less from your humanity than to serve your friend, I shall make no apology for these additional lines.—Soon after my last letter to you I sent an abstract of its contents to my brother William, of Newport. And I herewith transcribe the following extract from his reply.

"Your letter, my dear brother, was received in course—after which I lost no time in writing to my Sister (*extracting word for word what you wrote to me on the subject*) who will direct my Nephew, John A. Alston,[2] who is jointly with Mr. Cogdell (I suppose) my attorney in the matter which now seems to distress you so much—and [I][3] notice, as I hope feelingly, your observations respecting the Slaves inherited from our Grandmother. I agree with you that they should not be separated (if possible) having formed family connexions with Mr. Belin's people—nor be sold to be carried out of the State. The price it seems was fixed at $550 by the Court, which directed them to be offered to Mr. Belin, and being more than he was disposed to give—would it <[two words undecipherable]> not be well to sell him *yours* at such a rate as to induce him to take the whole? I only suggest this to you, as by so doing all the Slaves might be benefited *by your intentions,* and Mr. Wigfall[4] and Henry satisfied. As for myself (although you know that I am in a manner penniless and without a profession) I would make any reasonable sacrifice which the case may require. My views are well known to my Sister."

Now, my friend, I will most gladly adopt the course suggested by my brother—that is, let Mr. Belin have *my* Share at such a rate as may induce him to take the whole; indeed, to effect this desired object he should have *my* share on ANY terms. But as Mr. Belin might not, even in this case, like to make an offer from himself, *I* will here propose the terms—namely, $100—for each of the Slaves of my fifth part. And the affair might easily be managed in this way. Let the whole 16 be rated, as the Court have already decided, at $550—each; my fifth part of the proceeds [say, from three * Slaves][5] would then be $1650. Well, instead of paying me this sum for my fifth, let him pay me but $300—And, moreover, let this contract be entirely *private between* you and him. I wish no one to know any thing about it, for it is nobody's business but mine. Also, in respect to the payment, let Mr. Belin name his own term of credit.

I have only to add, that you must not think, in the offer here proposed, I am making too great a sacrifice. No, my friend; and I assure you, on the word of a gentleman and a christian, that were the sum in question ten times greater, I would *gladly* relinquish it to effect the desired object. It has not cost me one moment's hesitation; I consider it in fact *no* sacrifice—for it will give me *peace*—which is a treasure far above gold. And at this time especially do I need peace of mind, in order to do justice to the important work on which I am now engaged.—You will therefore, I trust, consider yourself fully authorized to make the proposed private contract with Mr. Belin.

My best regards to Mrs. Cogdell. God bless you and yours.

Yrs affectionately, / Washington Allston.

*As to the fraction, I give it in.

ADDRESSED: John S. Cogdell Esqre. / Charleston, South Carolina. SOURCE: Manuscript. Printed in Flagg, pp. 308-10.

1. WA's brackets. 2. John Ashe Alston. 3. WA's brackets. 4. Thomas Wigfall (1768-1864) married first Rachel (Moore) Allston Flagg's niece Harriet Moore and second, in 1814, her daughter Eliza Moore Flagg (Webber, "Moore of St. Thomas' Parish," pp. 166-67). Harriet (Moore) Wigfall inherited slaves from her father, John Moore, but they do not seem to have been involved in the lawsuit. 5. WA's brackets.

293. From Franklin Dexter Boston March 27. 1841.

My dear Sir: I spoke to Mrs. D.[1] about the matter. I find she agrees with me, that "for reasons stated" (as our good fathers used to say when they found it inconvenient to state them) the lady[2] could not well be called upon—*between ourselves* she is not now in command of funds as she used to be. I know through Mrs. D. that she said lately that she had not money to spare for any object,—naming a very small sum—this will sound strange to you, but I know the cause, though I cannot speak of it.

If your debt to Brown[3] is troublesome to you I can see it paid. I do not mention the other object, because I do not see any obligation you are under to give for it, except from *your superfluities*—which I wish I could live to see. I do not of course undertake to advise you on that subject—but if you can't get the money for it, your conscience may well be easy about it. There is a great deal of misery in the world that you cannot relieve, and where you cannot do so, you ought not to be troubled by it. I feel quite satisfied myself that you have already done in that case all that the most scrupulous conscience could require.[4]

Pray let me know about the Brown debt, if you feel it as an urgent one.

I want a device for a seal ring—a female figure. I remember some beautiful ones in Flaxman's Hesiod—particularly in a stooping or bending attitude. I cannot get Flaxman here. Will you look at yours & see if you can select me a figure?

I should rather have one of your own devising, if such a thing should occur to you, but that is a thing that cannot be found in the brain just when it is wanted, so I would not have you task yours with it.

Apropos how easily you might make money, if you were willing to do it—why should not you sell sketches for small sums, as well as lawyers give advice in small cases for small fees? Your evenings are worth* a guinea[5] a piece at least to you without working at more than a pleasant rate. Your sketches will be sold sometime or other after your death whether you will or no—would not the money be more convenient now? But I know you won't think so.

Yrs very truly / F. Dexter

*I put it low as you will be interrupted by me sometimes.

W. Allston Esq

ADDRESSED: Washington Allston Esq / Cambridge Port. SOURCE: Manuscript.

1. Probably Mrs. Dexter, the former Catherine Elizabeth Prescott. 2. Possibly Sarah Gibbs. 3. Thomas Brown, Jr. 4. Possibly a reference to WA's giving up his share of his sister Mary's inheritance from their grandmother to their brother William. 5. Dexter first wrote and cancelled "$10."

294. To Robert Wilson Gibbes

Cambridge Port Masstts.
18th April 1841

My dear Sir: I am sorry that I cannot inform you where the little Drawing[1] concerning which you enquire, was made; I suppose, however, it was when I was about sixteen or seventeen. The value you are pleased to attach to it, must, I think, be solely on account of its being one of my early efforts, as, from what I remember, it can have but little intrinsic merit. And I beg you to accept my thanks for this mark of your regard.

I pray you to excuse this late reply; a succession of perplexing demands on my time having led me insensibly to postpone it, until I am quite distressed to find how long your letter has remained unanswered.

Your account of Mr. De Veaux's[2] success gives me pleasure. I had a short visit from him just before he sailed for Europe,[3] and was much pleased with his manners.—

I remain, dear Sir, / With sincere regard, yrs / Washington Allston.
Professor Robert W. Gibbes.

SOURCE: Manuscript copy by Gibbes. ANNOTATED by Gibbes: Copy of a letter from Washington Allston to R.W. Gibbes M.D.

1. Portrait of Rubens (1795-1796). 2. James De Veaux. 3. De Veaux visited WA probably in November 1841. He was in Florence by 24 December of that year (R.W. Gibbes, *A Memoir of James de Veaux, of Charleston, S.C.* [Columbia, S.C., 1846], 5:50).

295. From James McMurtrie Phil May 11. 1841.

My Dear Sir: I met your friend Dr. Channing a few evenings since, and it gave me much pleasure to hear that you were in good health & spirits. I lately recd from London several sets of Burnet's Cartoons[1] (5 only of which are yet published)—and I have taken the liberty of sending you a set together with a proof of the portrait of Bishop White[2] from a picture I possess by Mr. Inman[3] of New York engraved by Wagstaffe[4] of London. Be pleased to accept of these trifles as a small testimony of my continued regard. I have a son[5] who has resolved to take orders as a *painter,* and I have accordingly for the present sent him on to N.Y. under the care of my friend Inman, there to remain at *elementary* work for one year. If he shows blood at the end of that time, I contemplate sending him to Europe—*Germany* or *Italy* or both. I had intended sending him at once to Dusseldorf[6] but I thought it would be better to wait until I saw that he actually had something in him that was worth bringing out. Hitherto he has been drawing from the round figure in *crayons,* but he will now proceed with the *brush* from the Antique in umber & white. Of course I know but little of the true course a youth ought to pursue in this matter but I cannot but think that good *elementary* instruction in every art or science is the first thing to be attended to. I shall expect nothing from him for 4 to 5 years, during that time I will continue to maintain him, if he is frugal & industrious. Afterwards he must work his own way. A young man named Leutze[7] has lately come out as an artist here with great success. He has gone to Dusseldorf there to study drawing—but I fear it is rather late. He composes well & colours finely is rapid in his work, full of genius but careless and unsteady & I shd fear that he cannot go back to the *grammer* of his art. I think you wd like Inman's Bishop. The size of the picture is 40 by 30 inches. It was highly commended in England. Wagstaffe has rendered every part but the likeness admirably—in that there is a little departure from the picture. Still it gives satisfaction. I had it published at my own risk, being desirous of doing honor to one of the best men who ever lived and a relative of my wife. Mr. Sully will probably be in Boston this summer. He has but little to do here. Our exhibition is no great thing. Very few pictures indeed beyond mediocrity and I agree with Stuart Newton who said that *tolerable* pictures were like tolerable eggs. Mr. Darby of Boston[8] has just purchased a very beautiful little marble statue by Steinhauser of Rome[9]—a boy catching crabs. I am sorry it has left the city. Mr. Carey[10] of this city has one by the same hand—a girl holding a shell to her ear listening to the sound—exquisitely beautiful. This is a young German who has studied with Thorwaldsen.

It will give me great pleasure to hear from you my dear Sir, but still more pleasure to see you once more. I am now attending to Mr. West's great picture of "Christ Rejected"[11] which is up in the hall of Independence. Mr. B. West[12] presented to the City one of his father's Windsor's pictures[13] "Paul & Barnabas at Lystra" which is to be placed in my large room in S. St.[14] It will be seen there to great advantage as there is a sky light at the far end. The room is 76 ft. long 31 wide—ceiling 17 ft. for about 50 ft. It then comes up to the sky light giving a height of 25 feet for a depth of 24. I have the command of this room for 4 mos. in the year—June to October—& wish it so employed during that time. I must mention this in case any thing may hereafter strike you. It is used as a dancing room the rest of the year. I think it probable Mr. West will make arrangements for something to come out from England next season. The rent I get is 200 Dr. for the 4 mos.

With great regard / I am Dear Sir / Yours faithfully / J McMurtrie

ADDRESSED: Washington Allston Esqr / Cambridgeport / Boston. ANNOTATED by WA: *Answered* / 15. June / *Mr. McMurtrie* / *May 12, 1841* SOURCE: Manuscript.

1. John Burnet (1784-1868), English painter and engraver. 2. William White (1748-1836), first Protestant Episcopal bishop of the diocese of Pennsylvania, consecrated in 1787. 3. Henry Inman (1801-46), portrait and genre painter. He worked early in New York, from 1832 to 1835 in Philadelphia, and again in New York after 1835. 4. Charles Edward Wagstaffe (b. 1808), English engraver, who worked in Boston about 1840-45. 5. James McMurtrie, Jr. 6. The Academy at Dusseldorf in Germany, founded in 1767, was reorganized in 1819 and for several decades thereafter was the chief center of German art. 7. Emanuel Leutze (1816-68), historical painter. 8. Probably Sidney Darby, Boston merchant in West Indian goods with G.P. Richardson, Jr. (*Boston City Directory* for 1841). 9. Friedrich Wilhelm George Steinhauser (1817-1903), German painter and lithographer. He worked in Rome from 1838 to 1848. 10. Henry C. Carey. 11. It was brought to America in 1820. 12. Benjamin West, Jr. (1772-1848). 13. About 1779 West was commissioned by King George III to decorate the Chapel of Revealed Religion which he proposed to erect at Windsor Castle. Thirty-five pictures from the Old and New Testament were planned, some twenty-eight were finished, and a number of others were composed. The project was canceled in 1806 (Alberts, pp. 158-59, 322). 14. McMurtrie's address in 1841 was 117 Spruce Street (*Philadelphia City Directory*).

296. To James McMurtrie Cambridge Port, Mass. 15 June 1841

My Dear Sir: I received your letter of the 11th of May near three <months> weeks since, but delayed answering it until the arrival of the box of Prints, which has just reached me. For this most acceptable present I beg you to accept my best thanks. They remind me of the spirited Etchings of Piranesi,[1] and give more of the character, expression and general spirit of the Cartoons, than any finished engravings I have seen of them. They are such as I think must have pleased Raffaele, had they been done in his time. Hogarth used to say to the engravers whom he occasionally employed to assist him, "give me my *character,* if you do it with a hob nail," often obliterating weeks of their *fine* work without compunction. I wish I could say that the prints which have been engraved from my pictures had any thing like the truth of these admirable Etchings; but I have been particularly unfortunate, for, (with one exception)[2] neither my character, expression, nor effect is to be found in any of them; that from "Jacob's Dream" gave me an immediate fit of the heart-burn, which did not leave me for a whole day—it was engraved for one of the London Annuals by a person who seemed to have had as little notion of the character of the picture as of the human figure.[3]

I think you are quite right in the opinion that your Son[4] should master the merits of our Art in the outset. If he does not possess himself of them now, whilst he is young, he will find it hard, if not altogether impracticable hereafter when he shall become aware of his deficiencies. Let him think no time misspent which he devotes to the human form; tell him to fag at it until he can draw it with as much ease as he can write; he will then be able to realize his most poetical conceptions—but not till *then.* The great fault in discipline among our young artists is in their beginning to "make pictures" too soon, to make a *whole* before they are acquainted with the *parts.*[5] It is an easy matter to produce a pleasing effect, either or colour or chiaro-scuro, but not quite so easy to guess right as to form; and he can do no more than guess who attempts it without knowledge. There are hundreds of artists in every age who pass a long life in producing striking effects without an atom of truth in a single component part. Above all, let his progress be *with knowledge;* for only this can secure an artist from the impertinence of ignorance—from being either irritated or disheartened by false criticism. In a word, let him love his art for it's own sake—not for the contingent applause—and he will not be satisfied without a thorough mastery of it's principles, as well within minutiae as their leading points.

As to Dusseldorf, where you propose sending your Son, I can express no opinion; indeed I have been so long from Europe that I know not which is now the most eligible school for a young artist. I have reason, however, to think highly of the present German school, from what I have lately seen of some of their works, having been honoured with a very magnificent present from Count Rackzinski[6] of Berlin, consisting of his own valuable work on German art,[7] together with numerous Prints from the productions of various living artists of Germany among the principal of whom are Cornelius,[8] Kaulbach,[9] Schnorr,[10] Benderman,[11] and others whose names I cannot at this moment recall. These specimens certainly place the German School very high—especially in purity of taste.

I am much pleased with the Print from Inman; it is a rich composition. If I may be allowed a critical remark, I should say, that the quantity of *dark* is too great; there is consequently not enough of middle-tint. But this I apprehend is the fault of the

Engraver; I dare say the picture is deficient in these particulars. Were the Engraver here with his plate, he could easily *scrape* down some of the darks so as to remove the objection.

You have probably had from Doctor Channing, or others, some account of my late Exhibition,[12] where I had the gratification of refreshing my affection for your little "Mother and Child," for the loan of which I now send you my thanks. The kindness of my friends, both abroad and at Home, on this occasion is one of those pleasant things to think of in my old age.—You mention having the great picture of kind, good Mr. West now with you. There are heads in that picture equal to Raffaele. Nothing can surpass the High Priest and many others. The penitent Thief has a sublime expression.

I remain dear Sir / with unabated regard yrs / Washington Allston

I have not yet heard of Sully's arrival.[13]

James McMurtrie Esq. / Philadelphia / Pennsylvania

ANNOTATED by McMurtrie: The Etchings referred [to] were a set of Burnet's from the Cartoons. The Print an Engraving from Inman's picture of Bishop White. qu [?] "the one exception" among the engravers from Mr. Allston's own pictures. SOURCE: Copy. Printed in Flagg, pp. 310-12.

1. Giovanni Battista Piranesi (1720-78), Italian engraver of ancient architectural subjects.
2. Presumably WA refers to Seth Cheney's engraving of *Mother and Child*. 3. It was engraved for the *Literary Souvenir* for 1830 by the largely self-taught Edward Goodall (1795-1870), best known for his landscape engravings. 4. Probably James McMurtrie, Jr. WA's advice for him in the rest of this paragraph was much the same as he gave John Greenough about drawing and Pickering for Cole. 5. WA discussed the relation of the whole to parts in his lecture "Composition" (*LA*, pp. 151-54). 6. Athanasias Raczynski. 7. *Histoire de l'art moderne en Allemagne*, 3 vols. (Paris, 1836). Prominent among the new German school of romantic painters were those called the Nazarenes or pre-Raphaelites, as well as other names, who eschewed the antique and the Renaissance and formed a simple style in imitation of the young Raphael, Perugino, and others like them and often treated biblical subjects. The chief ones, besides Cornelius and Schnorr von Karolsfeld, whom WA mentions, were J.F. Overbeck, F.W. Schadow, and J.P. Veit. Several went to Rome a few years after WA was there. Overbeck praised WA's *O&S*. 8. Peter von Cornelius (1784-1867), German painter. His father was director of the Dusseldorf Academy and he was briefly associated with it. He admired WA's *O&S*.
9. Wilhelm von Kaulbach (1805-74), German painter. He studied at Dusseldorf. 10. Julius Schnorr von Karolsfeld (1794-1872), German painter. 11. Eduard Julius Bendemann (1811-89), German history painter. 12. That of 1839. 13. There seems to be no evidence that Sully went to Boston at this time.

297. To Charles Sumner Cambridge Port 1 August, 1841.

My dear Sir: As you are so lately from Italy,[1] perhaps you can give me some information respecting a point about which I am in doubt; namely, what is the precise (or rather, usual) route *from* Sienna to Rome. I wish to know, if, in going from Sienna, you pass over Radicoffani; and whether Viterbo is not between the latter place and Rome. I am about to publish a little Work,[2] written above twenty years ago, and I fear that I have made some slight mistake in the geography of this Route, having placed—<Sienna> in course from Sienna—first Radicoffani, then Viterbo.[3] I do not care for the intermediate places. If you do not recollect their relative positions, and have a Road-Book of Italy, will you have the kindness to send it to Mr. R.H. Dana junr's Office,[4] who will find means to forward it to me.

I remain, dear Sir, / with sincere regard, yrs / Wa. Allston.

Addressed: Charles Sumner Esqre. / Court Street,[5] / Boston. Source: Manuscript, Washington Allston Collection (no. 7471), Manuscripts Division, Special Collections Department, University of Virginia Library.

1. Sumner returned to America from Europe on 3 May 1840 (Pierce, 2:147). 2. *Monaldi.* It went to press shortly after the date of this letter. The prefactory "Note" is dated "August 1841." 3. In *Monaldi,* Maldura and Fialtro travel from Siena to Rome, passing first through Radicofani and then Viterbo, in the accurate geographical sequence (pp. 101-102, 121). 4. RHD, Jr.'s law office was in the Old State House in 1842 and 1843 (*Boston City Directory*). 5. Sumner's law office was at 4 Court Street from 1835 on (*Boston City Directory*).

298. To Rufus Wilmot Griswold

[between May and mid-August 1841][1]

Will Mr. Griswold do Mr. Allston the favour to make the following correction in the "Spanish Maid."?[2]

In the last stanza but one, for

"Yet how he'll love this dream tomorrow . . ."

which makes a false rhyme

(if there can be such a thing where there is *no* rhyme)

read

"Ah, what a day this dream will follow!"[3]

inserting a dash after the preceding line.

Cambridge Port.

P.S. Mr. A. would also thank Mr. G. in republishing the Address to Great Britain, to mention that it was first published in Coleridge's "Sibyline Leaves."[4] <I make> Mr. A. makes this request in consequence of <your> Mr. G. having informed him, of its appearing in several works as of English authorship.

This Ode was written in Boston, in 1810—in the year before <my> Mr. A's second visit to England.

Addressed: Mr. Griswold, / <Tremont Street.>[5] / [in another hand] 1 Franklin Place
Source: Manuscript, Yale University Library.

1. Griswold was in Boston from May to the middle of August 1841, acting as editor for the *Boston Daily Times* and the *Boston Notion,* at which time he negotiated with several poets, including WA, Emerson, Holmes, and Longfellow, for poems and biographical sketches to be included in his anthology *The Poets and Poetry of America.* He was encouraged to solicit something from WA, presumably for one of the issues of the *Boston Notion,* by RHD, who wrote him that "Allston has

some beautiful little things by him. But I do not know that your Magazine would be justified in increasing the list of Extraordinaires. Nor do I know that Allston would consent to furnish anything" and offered to speak to him about the matter if Griswold wished (to Griswold, ca. summer 1841, Dana Papers). 2. Griswold's *The Poets and Poetry of America* (1842) contained "The Spanish Maid," "America to Great Britain," "The Sylphs of the Seasons," "The Tuscan Girl" (titled "The Tuscan Maid"), "Rosalie," and the sonnets on Rembrandt's *Jacob's Dream* and Benjamin West, titled "To Rembrandt" and "To Benjamin West." Other editions contained other poems as well. It carried the dedication "To Washington Allston, the Eldest of the Living Poets of America, and the Most Illustrious of Her Painters, This Work is Dedicated" and contained a biographical sketch. WA owned a copy. 3. The first reading appears in *LA*. That suggested in this letter was given in *The Poets and Poetry of America*. 4. The notation was made. 5. Griswold apparently stayed first in the Revere House on Tremont Street (Bayless, p. 40; *Boston City Directory* for 1841).

299. To William Sharp [23 August 1841]

Mr. Allston presents his compliments, and begs Mr. Sharp to accept his thanks for the loan of Field's Cromatography.[1]—It is a work from which he expects to obtain much valuable information.

Mr. A. was personally acquainted with Mr. Field.

Cambridge Port, / 23 August, 1841.

ADDRESSED: William Sharp Esqre / 17 Tremont Row,[2] / Boston. SOURCE: Manuscript.

1. *Chromatography; or, a Treatise on Colours and Pigments and of their Powers in Painting* (1835), by George Field. Passages adapted from it were copied in WA's "Color Book."
2. Apparently Sharp was at this address only for the year 1840 (*Boston City Directory*).

300. To Henry Wadsworth Longfellow [2 October 1841]

My dear Sir: Will you do us the favour to take tea[1] with us on Monday Evening, at seven o'clock, and meet your friends, Mr. & Mrs. Bryant?[2]

With sincere regard, / Yrs / Wa. Allston.

Cambridge Port, / Saturday, Oct. 2d / 1841.

ADDRESSED: To / Professor Longfellow, / Cambridge. SOURCE: Manuscript, Houghton.

1. The Allstons were accustomed to have tea in the evening, at which toast, cake, and preserves were served. 2. William Cullen Bryant and Francis (Fairchild) Bryant (1797-1865).

301. To Charles Coffin Little Cambridge Port, Oct. 20th 1841.

Dear Sir; I have received two Copies of the *same* Sheet—from pages 217 to 228[1]—but I return only one, as I conclude the *duplicate* must have been sent to me by mistake. The two packets reached me together this morning.

Respectfully yrs, / Wa. Allston.

To Charles C. Little Esqre.

SOURCE: Manuscript, Houghton.

1. Of *Monaldi*.

302. To Richard Henry Dana, Jr. Cambridge Port, 24 Oct. 1841.

Dear Richard: Is it not necessary, by some form of Law, to secure the Copy-right of my Book,[1] in order to prevent its being pirated, should any publisher think it worth while to do so? And is it not usual to insert in a new Book an Advertisement, signifying that this had been done? In the first proof-sheet of my Work (where I suppose it would have appeared, if necessary) I did not find it. I take it for granted, however, that the omission there is *all in order.* But I should like to be certain of it. Will you be so good (should it have been inadvertently omitted) to see Mr. Little on the subject. As I am quite ignorant of these matters, you will excuse my troubling either you or Mr. L. <upon it> on this occasion.

Affectionately yrs, / Wa. Allston.

I have had the last Proof-sheet.

ADDRESSED: Richard H. Dana junr. Esqre. / Boston. SOURCE: Manuscript.

1. The copyright, in WA's name, appeared on the reverse of the title page of *Monaldi*.

303. To Richard Henry Dana, Jr. Cambridge Port, 12 Nov. 1841.

Dear Richard: On looking over my Book,[1] I find several inaccuracies, which I should be much mortified to see repeated in an English edition; one of which I think must have been occasioned by a *mis*transcription, as I could not have written *such English*. Will you do me the favour either to make the corrections in the Copy which you send to Mr. Moxon,[2] or to insert the following Errata in your letter to him. I dare say there are other grammatical *slips* which have escaped me. But if so, they must go until the econd edition!!![3]—Of which, however, I do not allow myself to think.

Errata[4]

Page 10 In the fourth line—omit period after "*mad*"—

Page 21 first line—for "common *to* young men," read <*within*> *in*.

page 29 second line—for "*two have* for his leading critic," read *in having*.

page 83 about the middle of the page—for "*To some*, perhaps this may be jargon," read *Elsewhere*.

Chapter 14th. First line—for "Fialtro *had been returned*," read *had returned home*.

page 217 Last line—for "You may see him *tomorrow*," read in a *few days*. [I think this last correction essential, in order to allow time for Rosalia and her Father (who are supposed to be in Rome) to be apprised of Monaldi's situation, and for their subsequent journey to the neighborhood of Naples.—I wonder how I came to overlook this.—For the same purpose, it will be necessary to][5] insert—Page 219 *at length* after *When,* <at> in the sixth line from the bottom. It should read thus: When *at length* the Physician &c.

I am glad to hear, from your Aunt,[6] that <Edmund> the Dr.[7] Thinks Edmund is better.

My regards to your Wife.[8]

Yrs affectionately, / Wa. Allston.

Would it be worth while to ask Messrs Little & Brown[9] to paste a narrow slip of paper, with these *Errata,* at the end of their copies? I have often seen the Errata so added. The expense, of course, I should expect to be charged to me.[10]

ADDRESSED: Richard H. Dana junr. Esqre. / State Street,[11] / Boston. SOURCE: Manuscript.

1. *Monaldi.* 2. Edward Moxon (1801-58), British poet and publisher. He published the edition of *Monaldi* in England, through arrangements made by RHD, Jr. WA wished Little and Brown to have the advantage of the English market if they had taken steps to secure it, but they had not. They promised to send Moxon proof sheets by 15 October. If he preferred to sell some of their edition instead of printing they offered to send two hundred copies if he requested (RHD, Jr., to Moxon, 2 Oct. 1841, *Proceedings of the MHS,* 2d ser., 6, 1890, 1891 [Boston, 1891], p. 398).
3. There was no second edition, as WA apparently anticipated. 4. The errata were incorporated in the English edition. In his letter to Cogdell of 14 November 1841 WA omitted the correction for page 10 and added two more. In the copy of the English edition which he sent Wordsworth he made still more corrections in the margins, as follows:

p. 3, line 10 up: for "whole. In" read "*whole*: in"
line 8 up: for "that" read "the"
line 6-5 up: for "a master spirit." read "that presiding principle."
p. 11, last line: for "place" read "notice"
line 10: delete "lurid,"
p. 12, line 2: for "them;" read "or consider them subordinate;"
p. 44, line 4: for "you." read "him."
p. 62, lines 8-7 up: for "excellence," read "art,"
p. 83, lines 8-9: delete "The time is come when I must use it no more, or with a meaning still dearer."
p. 106, line 9 up: for "me of" read "me too of"
line 6 up: for "on" read "beneath"
p. 139, line 5 up: for "him," read "he,"
p. 195, line 5 up: for "evil" read "wicked"
p. 246, line 12: for "of" read "from"

(Yale Collection of American Literature, Beinecke Rare Book and Manuscript Library, Yale University). 5. Wa's brackets. 6. Presumably Ruth Charlotte (Smith) Dana (1787-1822), RHD's wife (Dana, vol. 3, "Dana Family"). Edmund T. lived with them. 7. Unidentified.
8. Sarah (Watson) Dana (1814-1907) of Hartford, who married RDH, Jr., on 25 August 1841. WA took an interest in their first child, Sarah, born in July 1842, who at the age of six weeks was "knelt to & saluted" by him (Dana, 1:88). 9. James Brown, Boston publisher. 10. At the bottom of the last page WA's wife wrote: "Richard I forgot to tell you that Mr. Bruce [?] said the *tax bills*

had not been paid. If it will accommodate you I will pay him if you *will let me* have *the money* and the bills. I shall be in perhaps Monday or some day soon, after next week—Yours affectionate Aunt M.R.A.—" 11. The Old State House was at the head of State Street.

304. To John Stevens Cogdell

Cambridge Port, Mass:
14 Novbr 1841.

My dear Cogdell: Before this letter reaches you, you will probably have received a little volume[1] which I have just published, and of which I beg your acceptance: I have sent one also to our friend White. They were shipped yesterday by my Publishers, Messrs Little & Brown, of Boston, to the care of Mr. Samuel Hart,[2] bookseller, in Charleston.

This book (as I have stated, in a prefactory Note)[3] was ready for the press as long ago as 1822: but having been written for the Periodical of a Friend,[4] which was soon after discontinued, it was thrown into my desk, where it has lain until the present time. In the Note I add, that it is now published—not with the pretensions of a Novel, but simply as a Tale.

There are some Errata which I shall subjoin at the end of this letter; and I will thank you to make the corrections accordingly with a pen in your Copy.—My friends have for many years past repeatedly urged me to publish; but, for various reasons—which some perhaps would think *no reason,* or at least insufficient—I had kept the work by me so long, that, in fact, I became quite indifferent whether it ever saw the light or not.

Our excellent friend, White, has I hope received permanent benefit from his journey to the North.[5] His visit was a most agreeable surprise to us. It is a pleasant thing in this mutable world to meet with a friend who retains in his old age the warmth and kindly sympathies of his youth. His old friend, Mr. Dana,[6] felt no less pleasure than myself at the meeting. The meeting of three old men, who have been friends for forty years, is not an every-day occurrence.—We were much pleased with his Wife.[7]—I had another unexpected, as well as most gratifying, visit from my cousin, Dr. Edward Mitchell,[8] whom I had not seen since we were School-boys—forty six years ago. He was then a slender, delicate child,—now a stout robust man; I a young dandy, sporting three silk waistcoats, according to the fashion of the day—now a person that *ought to be* venerable, and am indeed!—so far as snowy locks can make one so. We might well have marvelled at the metamorphoses of Time.—And yet, though I am no longer a dandy, I do not find that all my youthful feelings have passed away. In regard to some of them I cannot <fee> admit that I am a day older.—Should you see Dr. Mitchell, give my regards to him—for he is a worthy, good man; and tell him how much pleased I was with his visit. He was much esteemed by my Mother.

It is but a few days since I left a sick room.[9] I was brought down by a severe inward cold, that threw my whole system out of order. But, thanks to my Physician, through a kind Providence, I am again well, and strong enough to pay continuous court to the King of Babylon.

There is nothing going on here in the shape of news which the Newspapers have not already told. I believe Mr. Legare did not come so far as Boston in his last visit to the North: he was probably recalled to the south sooner than he intended to return, by his appointment to the Office of Attorney General of the Union.[10] His appointment has given entire satisfaction to all here who were aware of his merits—and there are very many who are so. Mrs. Allston unites with me in best regards to Mrs. Cogdell and yourself.

Yours affectionately, / Wa. Allston.

Errata to Monaldi:

Page 21. For "common *to,*" read common *in*

———21. Erase, at line eleventh from the bottom, "*that realizing quality which the world must feel before it will reverence.*"

Page 29. In the second line, for "*to have* for his leading critic," read *in having* for his leading critic.

Page 83. About the middle of the page, for "*To some* this may be jargon," read *Elsewhere* this may be jargon.

Chapter 14. In the first line, for "Fialtro *had been returned,*" read Fialtro *had returned home.*

Page 217. In the last line, for "You may see him *tomorrow,*" read You may see him *in a few days.*

Page 219. In the sixth line from the bottom, after "When" insert *at length.* So that it shall read thus—When at length the Physician &c.

[In the margin] At page 119 also, in the third line, after "rid me," insert *too.*

ADDRESSED: John S. Cogdell Esqre. / Charleston, / South Carolina. SOURCE: Manuscript.

1. *Monaldi.* 2. Samuel Hart, Sr., bought out the establishment of John P. Beile in 1841. He was for many years the agent for William Gilmore Simms, who described him as "an amiable gentleman, and loses no chance for making his establishment what it should be" (*Letters* 1:254). 3. WA here quoted the "Note" almost verbatim. 4. *The Idle Man.* 5. No information about this trip has been located. 6. Edmund T. Dana. 7. Eliza (Allston) White, the daughter of WA's uncle Josias Allston (Groves, pp. 28-29). 8. Edward Mitchell (1788-1855), physician, son of WA's aunt Mary (Moore) Mitchell. He resided for many years at Edisto Island, S.C. (Groves, pp. 27-28; Emma B. Richardson, p. 237; Henry A.M. Smith, "The Baronies of South Carolina," *SCHGM* 14 [1913]: 64). 9. This was the beginning of an illness of several weeks which RHD described as being sufficiently severe for WA's life to be feared, from which he only partially recovered, and after which he was "plainly, with short terms of a better state, a broken-down, failing man," whose "intellect was clear as ever," but who was physically "too much weakened" to work satisfactorily. During the last two or three months of his life more especially he spoke of himself as "old & broken" and when not surrounded by his friends was deeply depressed by the thought that his body was no longer fitted for the service of his mind. His wife said that he would wake so gloomy in the morning that she could not later bear to have it cross her mind (RHD to Verplanck, 14 July 1843; Prime, p. 468). 10. Legaré received the notifica-

tion of his nomination to the position of attorney general by President Tyler toward the end of the summer while he was visiting Ticknor (Rhea, p. 200).

305. To Chester Harding Cambridge Port,
Tuesday, 30 Nov: 1841.

Dear Harding: You have certainly a way with you which there is no resisting. I will give you the sitting you ask,[1] but I am sorry to say, that it will not be in my power this week—nor indeed until the middle of the next—as I am very busy in preparing for removal into our new house.[2] I hope, however, to be at liberty by *Wednesday next week*—when you may expect me, if I am well, and it does not storm. Should the weather be very bad, you will of course not expect me until you hear farther.—Nothing therefore occurring to prevent, I shall be at your Room in School Street by two o'clock on that day.—We will dine, if you please, after you have taken the sitting say, between 4 & 5—which will be as long as you can well see to paint.

Sincerely Yrs, / Wa. Allston.

Chester Harding Esqre.

SOURCE: Manuscript, BA.

1. For a portrait of WA. Harding painted one about 1830 or 1831, which was exhibited at the BA in 1831. It depicted him in his blue coat with brass buttons, with the right arm at an angle and the hand thrust into it, giving it such a martial air that friends afterward called him "Colonel Allston." The second, for which WA did not sit, was painted after his death, according to Sweetser about 1845. It was described as a three-quarters portrait, the figure seated and facing right, with the right hand holding a drawing tool, the left hand on the left knee, the right elbow and forearm resting on a table with a piece of paper on top, drapery in the background at right (Longfellow Historic Site, Museum Catalogue Record). An engraving of the head was made by John Sartain, reproduced in *Campbell's Foreign Semi-Monthly Magazine* (5 [Mar. 1844]: 288), of which he was editor for a short time, as the illustration for a reprint of Mrs. Jameson's article on WA in that issue. 2. It was situated on Auburn Street, a little farther from Magazine Street than his studio, from which it was separated by a garden.

306. To John Stevens Cogdell Cambridge Port,
Masstts 5th Decbr 1841.

My dear Cogdell: I have received your letter of Novb 26th, containing a Copy of the Account of Mr. Laurens,[1] the Master in Equity. In reply to your question, whether I gave *my consent in writing* to my Mother when she sold the Negroes of the life Estate to Dr. Mitchell—I answer, that, *I did.* My Mother asked my consent, as one of the *heirs,* and I gave it without a moment's hesitation, most willingly: and I beg that this letter may be considered as *confirming* it.

I think I acquainted you, in a former letter, of my Noble-hearted Sister, Mrs. W.A. Alston's generous offer of her share of the inheritance from our Grandmother, to be divided between my brother Wm. M. Allston and myself; and I have the impression also that I at the same time informed you, that, in rely to her, I declined receiving any part of it, and begged her to give the *whole* to William. With respect to this matter, I have only to add, that I still *hold the same mind*. And (if this letter is, as I hope, <of> a sufficient authority) I hereby relinquish, in favour of my brother, Wm. M. Allston, all <of> that my sister, Mrs. Wm. A. Alston, may have either given or bequeathed of her Share of our Grandmother's inheritance to me. You will therefore, my friend, if <such> said Share of my beloved Sister's be set apart for my brother and myself, consider it *all as his*, and remit it to him accordingly when it shall have come into your hands.

I had received—as you supposed—before your letter reached me, the intelligence of my Sister's death[2]—her son John's letter was received on the 20th of the last month.—Ah, Cogdell, she was a woman of ten thousand—in mind and heart both. Well—it cannot be a great while before I shall be called to follow her. I have often of late thought of that *inevitable* <undecipherable word> hour, that sooner or later must <be appointed> come for me, as well as for those I have loved and lost. This dear Sister is now, as I believe, with her Saviour—for she was a christian, and died in a christian's hope.— From my heart do I feel for her husband, a noble, high-minded man—every way worthy of such a Wife. I have written to him, and I trust that my letter may not be wholly without comfort to him—at least after the first shock from such a bereavement shall have been mitigated by time.

My dear Cogdell, with my whole heart do I reciprocate your kind wishes in my behalf. Mrs. Allston joins me in best regards to Mrs. Cogdell & yourself.

Yrs affectionately, / Washington Allston.

Remember me to Sully;[3] he is a man I have great regard for.

ADDRESSED: John S. Cogdell Esqre. / Charleston / South Carolina. SOURCE: Manuscript.

1. Edward R. Laurens was master in equity or chancery (*Charleston City Directory* for 1840/41). 2. Mary (Allston) Young Alston died on 10 November 1841 (Mabel L. Webber, copier, "Inscriptions from the Alston burying ground at 'The Oaks' Plantation, Waccamaw," *SCHGM* 12 [1911]: 40). 3. Sully arrived in Charleston with his daughter about 2 November and stayed for several months at the Charleston Hotel (Rutledge, *Artists in the Life of Charleston*, pp. 163, 220).

307. To Charles Sumner Cambridge Port, 12 Dec- 1841.

My dear Sir: It will give me great pleasure to see Lord Morpeth[1] at two o'clock, on Tuesday. I hope he will find it convenient to honour me with his visit on that day.

I am much gratified that my little Story[2] pleased you, and thank you for your kind expressions concerning it.

I remain, dear Sir, / with true regard, yrs / Wa. Allston.

Charles Sumner Esqre.

ADDRESSED: Charles Sumner Esqre. / 4 Court Street, / Boston. SOURCE: Manuscript, Houghton.

1. George William Frederick Howard, Viscount Morpeth. 2. *Monaldi.*

308. To Chester Harding Cambridge Port 13 Dec 184[1][1]

[Draft]

Dear Harding: In order to prevent the misapprehension of an important point of our late conversation, as well as to preclude all future misunderstanding, it may be well to express on paper what I said to the Committee in substance. I have therefore to request that you will do me the favour to communicate this letter to the "Association of Artists,"[2] at their next meeting. The point I allude to is concerning the Athenaeum, and my view as to the subject as follows. That Institution having uniformly treated me with marked liberality, and I on my part having always acknowledged the obligation, I think but due to my character to say, and wish it to be distinctly understood that I could not consistently with what I believe to be a right feeling and with honour, allow myself to be identified with *any* party which shall place itself in opposition to it.

But since the present Association not only disclaims all such intention; but expressly states, on the contrary, that its purpose is simply to form an efficient School for Drawing, and the study of the Human figure—without any ulterior object as a Society—I feel it to be a duty which I owe to my professional Brethern not to decline the office[3] to which they have been pleased to elect me: and whilst I send my acceptance, I beg to assure them that I *most cordially reciprocate their kind feeling.*

The other points which have been discussed between us I leave you to state verbally.

N.B. Before you communicate this letter to the Association, I should like to see the Constitution, I beg you therefore not to present it *formally* until you hear from me after I shall have received that paper.

Sincerely yrs / Wa. Allston.

To Chester Harding Esqr. one of the Committee of the Association of Artists.

SOURCE: Manuscript copy, with the date 1840, Boston Public Library. Another copy is in the MHS. The MHS copy is in another hand, is endorsed by RHD "W. Allston to Chester *Harding*. 1841 Dec 12 & copy," lacks the last paragraph and signature and the phrase "which have been discussed between us," and contains a few minor differences in wording, chiefly "the" for "any," "of" for "in," "I have therefore" for "and also," and "whilst" for "while." It would seem that the MHS copy is of an earlier draft.

1. The year in the manuscript is 1840. 2. The Boston Artists' Association was organized a few days before the date of this letter (*Passages from the Correspondence and Other Papers of Rufus W. Griswold* [Cambridge, 1898], p. 103). In its first exhibition, at Harding's Gallery in 1842 WA was represented by his *Beatrice*. The year after his death a memorial exhibition of a small group of

his paintings was held and his *Polyphemus* was shown in the second exhibition, held in September. In 1845 the association joined the BA, and the next several exhibitions were held there and called "United Exhibition of the Boston Athenaeum and the Boston Artist's Association." Other members included Henry Sargent, Thomas T. Spear, David C. Johnston, Joseph Ames, Francis Alexander, Richard M. Staigg, and Thomas B. Read. 3. WA was elected first president of the Association.

309. To John Stevens Cogdell [31 December 1841]

My dear Cogdell: I duly received your letter of the 15 inst . . with a check on the Merchants Bank in Boston, endorsed by you to my order, for $693.32, being for $698.52, on account of my share of my Grandmother's Estate $5.20 being deducted for premium of exchange: and I send you above my receipt in the form you request.[1]

Your letter, to which this is a reply, reached me last week, on the 23 inst: but I was then unable even to *read* much less to answer it, being on a sick bed; indeed I was so ill that my Wife thought it best to withhold it until I had somewhat recovered my strength. You will therefore excuse this delay. I am still confined to my Chamber, but not to my bed, and find my strength returning so rapidly that I expect to be in my Painting Room, and again at King Bell: by the middle of next week. Tomorrow, if the weather permits, I am to take an airing, by the Dr.'s order. There has been nothing dangerous in this illness; it has only been most debilitating, and chiefly distressing on account of a protracted nausea. But, thank Heaven, all this and every other unpleasant circumstance attending my complaint have passed away, and I begin to feel something like myself again. The Doct. says it is a species of the common Cholera; a complaint not before unknown to me—this being the fourth attack from it within six years.

I feel in sufficient spirits to add to my letter, had I at hand any thing worth writing. But a sick chamber (though but a *quondam* one) is not very [sug]gestive [page torn] of agreeable matter. My Wife joins me in best regards to Mrs. Cogdell and yourself.

Believe me, dear C. ever / affectionately yrs, / Washington Allston.
31 Dec. 1841.

ADDRESSED: John S. Cogdell Esqre. / Charleston, / South Carolina. SOURCE: Manuscript.

1. The top of the first page has been torn away.

310. To Richard Henry Dana, Jr. Cambridge Port, 24 Jany. 1842.

Dear Richard: I have received a Note from the Merchants Insurance Company,[1] informing me that my Policy will expire on the 28 of this month—and I herein enclose sixty dollars for the renewal of the Insurance for the next six months, which I will thank you to effect for me. Would it not be well to renew the Policy a day or two before the present expires, in case any business should call you out of town on the last day?

I grieve to say that I am still too feeble to attend the dinner to be given to Mr. Dickens[2]—and have consequently been forced to decline the invitation of the Board of Managers.

Yrs affectly / Wa. Allston.

ADDRESSED: *Insurance money.* / Richard H. Dana junr Esqre. / State Street, / Boston.
SOURCE: Manuscript.

1. Its office for many years was on State Street. In 1842 its capital was listed as $500,000 (*Boston City Directory*). 2. Charles Dickens (1812-70), the English novelist, visited America in 1842 and was in Boston from 22 January to 10 April. A dinner was given for him on 1 February at the Tremont House, where he stayed. It was attended by many prominent Bostonians, including WA, who sat at the head table. Among others were RHD; RHD, Jr.; Josiah Quincy, who presided; George S. Hillard; George Bancroft; Oliver Wendell Holmes, who sang some of his own verses; the publisher James T. Fields; Felton; Jacob Bigelow; Dexter; the English Consul Thomas C. Grattan; and Mayor Jonathan Chapman. It cost $15 a person, lasted from 5 P.M. to nearly 1 A.M., had a menu of ten courses and numerous wines, and featured thirty toasts and thirty orations. Hillard quoted lines from WA's "America to Great Britain," and Dickens gave a corresponding toast to "America and England: and may they never have any division but the Atlantic between them." Introducing WA, Qunicy referred to him as "he who unites the genius of the poet, the pencil of the painter, and the pen of the novelist, his name shall glow forever upon the eternal canvas." WA, in responding, proposed a toast to "the prophetic raven—who only spoke to posterity when he cried 'Never say die' to Barnaby Rudge." Fields afterward said that he saw Dickens take a pinch of snuff from WA's snuffbox, though WA is nowhere else said to have used snuff (*Report of the Dinner Given to Charles Dickens in Boston, February 1, 1842. Reported by Thomas Gill and William English, reporters of the Evening Post* [Boston, 1842], p. 34; Edwards F. Payne, *Dickens Days in Boston: A Record of Daily Events* [Boston: Houghton Mifflin, 1927], pp. 27, 201, 104, 96). RHD, Jr., recorded that the dinner "went off famously," and Julia (Ward) Howe thought that "Of all the wits who made the feast one to be remembered, Allston shone a bright particular star" (Dana, 1:59); Howe, *Reminiscences*, p. 231). In delivering his toast WA may not have spoken very loudly, however. At a meeting of the Harvard alumni a few months later, on 23 August 1842, he made a short speech, which RHD, Jr., said "few heard" (Dana, 1:55), as reportedly had been true when he read his poem at the Phi Beta Kappa Society meeting in 1810, and Cornelius C. Felton spoke of its being difficult to hear him at this time unless one sat near him. WA owned a copy of the *Report* by Gill and English. Grattan, who was in Boston from 1839 to 1846, paid tribute to WA in his account of his stay there in *Civilized America* (1859).

311. To Henry Wadsworth Longfellow

Cambridge Port,
30 Jany 1842.

My dear Sir: I beg you to accept my thanks for your volume of Poems[1]—which I have read with great pleasure.

Your Preface[2] has a simple beauty, both of thought and expression, which to me is quite touching.—You have certainly bent your "inexorable" hexameters into as graceful forms as the English material will admit;[3] they are, to my ear, easier than Southey's,[4] whose English hexameters have hitherto been considered the best. The gentle and pious strain of the good Bishop makes one love him.

Of the smaller poems I like best your own originals. Among these I read with most pleasure the Wreck of the Hesperus,[5] Endymion, Gods-acre, the Goblet of Life and Maiden-hood: the two last are exceedingly beautiful.

I have been five weeks confined by illness—and am still very infirm. It is a great disappointment to me that I have not yet been able to see Mr. Dickens.[6] I hope, however, to be well enough to call on him before he leaves Boston.

With sincere regard, yrs / Wa. Allston.

ADDRESSED: Professor Longfellow, / to be left at Mr. Owen[7] Book-store, / Cambridge.
SOURCE: Manuscript, Houghton.

1. *Ballads and Other Poems* (1842). WA owned a copy of the second edition. The first edition, of about four hundred copies, was published on 23 December 1841; the second, of five hundred copies, on 25 December 1841. Longfellow described it as "neater, than the first, the paper being smoother" (*Letters* 2:650). 2. In it Longfellow described rural life in Sweden, which he visited in 1835. 3. "The Children of the Lord's Supper," a translation of *Nattvardsbarnen* (First communion) by the Swedish poet and bishop Esaias Tegnér, which was included in *Ballads and Other Poems*, was in trochaic hexameter. 4. Perhaps the most famous poem by Southey in hexameter was "The Vision of Judgment," in which he referred to WA. 5. "The Wreck of the Hesperus" was written on 30 December 1839, immediately after Longfellow had been rereading *SS*. He had intended to write the poem soon after hearing of the event, which occurred on 17 December 1839 (*Life of Henry Wadsworth Longfellow*, ed. Samuel Longfellow [Boston, 1886], 1:338-39). Presumably WA's volume inspired him not only to do so but to use the ballad form, which he had not used before. 6. Three days after the dinner for him, on 4 February, Dickens visited WA's studio. In his letters to his friend John Foster during the next few weeks he referred to WA twice, listing him among the Americans who objected to the current international copyright law because it failed to protect both English and American authors from being pirated outside their country; not one of them, he nevertheless noted, "*dares* to raise his voice and complain" of it. He identified WA as the author of *Monaldi* and described him "a fine specimen of a glorious old genius." It was apparently at this time that WA gave him a copy of *Monaldi* (*The Letters of Charles Dickens*, ed. Madeline House, Graham Storey, and Kathleen Tillotson [Oxford: Clarendon Press, 1974], 3:67, 82, 96). 7. John Owen (1805-82), a college mate of Longfellow's at Bowdoin, studied at the Harvard Divinity School but was prevented from preaching by poor health. From 1834 to 1848 he was in the book business in Cambridge and kept the university bookstore (Nehemiah Cleaveland, *History of Bowdoin College* [Boston, 1882], p. 374; *General Catalogue of Bowdoin College and the Medical School of Maine: A Biographical Record of Alumni and Officers 1794-1950* [Brunswich, Me., 1950], p. 59).

312. To Robert Wilson Gibbes

Cambridge Port. Masstts.
6th Feby. 1842.

My dear Sir: It is with unfeigned regret I find myself obliged to say, in reply to your kind letter,[1] that it is wholly out of my power to comply with your wishes respecting a Picture by me. I trust I need not add how much I should be gratified in employing my pencil for any citizen of my native state—more especially for one who has honoured me with such a mark of regard as the giving my name to one of his children;[2] but by numerous engagements leave me no liberty to follow my inclinations. At present I am engaged on a large work (Belshazzer) which I have had in hand for many years—which will occupy me for a considerable time—and to which many imperative motives concur to confine me exclusively until it is finished. Nor shall I be free even then, since the completion of Belshazzer must be followed by many other pictures already engaged—in fact so many that the day cannot be otherwise than distant before I could reasonably hope to complete them all—if indeed my advanced age, to say nothing of my infirmities, should allow me to do even that. As I would not then needlessly occasion disappointment, I feel myself in a manner compelled by these considerations to decline (at least for the present) any additional commission.

I am but just out of a sick chamber, to which I have been confined for several weeks; but I am regaining my strength though very slowly.

Believe me, dear Sir, that I sincerely thank you for your very friendly expressions, and that I most cordially reciprocate your regard. I am much gratified that you liked my little Tale.[3] Should my friend and nephew Col. Robert Allston be now in Columbia, pray remember me affectionately to him.

With sincere regard / Yrs / Washington Allston.

Dr. Robert W. Gibbes.[4]

SOURCE: Manuscript copy by Gibbes.

1. In this letter Gibbes asked WA to paint a picture for him. 2. Washington Allston Gibbes (b. 1841) (H.S. Holmes, "Robt. Gibbes, Governor of South Carolina, and Some of His Descendants," *SCHGM* 12 [1911]: 86). 3. There is an "x" at this point and at the bottom of the page "x Monaldi" in the hand of RHD. 4. The text of this letter was incorporated in a letter from Gibbes to RHD. Preceding the text Gibbes referred to visiting WA in 1831 and explained WA's addressing him as "Dr." as a memory of his being a professor in the South Carolina College. He said he had asked WA in his letter to paint a picture for him. This letter, he added, and that of 18 April 1841 were the only two letters of WA's that he had.

313. To Athanasius Raczynski

Cambridge Port, Masstts.
6 March, 1842.

Monsieur le Comte: For the gift of your valuable Work on Modern Art,[1] together with the Prints from German Artists, which you have done me the honour to present me, I beg you to accept my best thanks.

Permit me, Sir, to say that I was most agreeably struck with the pure taste which every where pervades your volumes; and, as one who loves his Art, and therefore interested in whatever tends to elevate its character, I sincerely hope that the sound criticisms they contain will be felt and appreciated in other countries besides Germany. And I cannot doubt that such will be the case wherever your Work is known—at least with those who acknowledge in Art a higher End than the mere gratification of the senses.

The Prints which accompany your Books give me a high opinion of the present German School. I was particularly pleased to notice in most of them so pure a taste in *form*, and in all the entire absence of the theatrical and fantastic in *composition;* even where some of the subjects might have tempted the Artists to extravagance, I found nothing to revolt me, as "overstepping the modesty of Nature."[2] Indeed one of the most remarkable instances I have ever met of this rare distinction is in Kaulbach's Combat in the air between the Huns and Romans:[3] though in the highest degree visionary, the *improbable* is yet so tempered by the *true*, that the imagination does not doubt it for a moment. Only a genius of a high order—a master of the Poetic Nature—of the *imaginative possible*[4]—could have produced such a work. I know nothing in modern Art which I would place before it: no dream ever brought with it a deeper faith; and I longed, as I looked on it, to take the hand of the Artist, and express to him my admiration.

It is not my purpose to say which of the Artists appeared to me the best; but I cannot forbear mentioning, as among the first, together with Kaulbach, Cornelius, Benderman, Schadow, Schnorr, and Neyer. *[5] <I would name others besides these who deserve to be classed with them, were it necessary.>

For the kind notice with which you have been pleased to honour me, in your account of American Artists,[6] I beg you, Sir, to accept my respectful acknowledgments.

I have the honour to be, Monsieur Le Comte,
your obliged & obedient servant, / W.A.

A. Monsieur Le Comte A. Rackynski, A Berlin,

Insert above.* To these, were it necessary, I might add several other names not unworthy to be classed with them.

SOURCE: Manuscript.

1. *Histoire de l'art modern en Allemagne*. 2. "with this special observance, that you o'erstep not the modesty of nature" (*Hamlet* 3.2.19-20). 3. Kaulbach's *Battle of the Huns* was painted for Raczynski. 4. In his lecture "Art" WA distinguished between the "*probable*" or "Natural" and the "*possible*" or "*Ideal,*" the latter being governed by the "imagination" (*LA*, pp. 87, 93-95). 5. John Adam Neyer (d. 1746), German artist and lock fashioner. 6. In the section dealing with modern art outside Germany, Raczynski gave an account of WA, calling him the first painter in America, drawing on reminiscences of Baron Rumohr and Dunlap, the catalog of WA's 1839 exhibition, and recent information sent him by Ticknor (3:556).

314. To William Wordsworth

Cambridge Port, Masstts
10 April, 1842.

Dear Sir: Will you permit me to introduce to you my friend and countryman, Mr. Savage.[1] Mr. S. is a Senator of our State Legislature, and is one of our most estimable citizens. In this visit to the land of his ancestors, I would not, as my friend, have him unacquainted with one whose genius is now so identified with our common language as to have added another to the many enduring ties which already bind every fair-minded cultivated American to the home of his fathers.

Should you take any interest in American affairs, I could not refer you to one more able than Mr. Savage for a faithful account of the present political state of our Country.

I am pleased to hear that your health is still unshaken: may it long be continued to you, for the sake of your friends and country, as well as for your own.

I remain, dear Sir, with unabated / regard and the highest respect, / Yrs /
Washington Allston.

To William Wordsworth Esqre.

SOURCE: Manuscript, The Wordsworth Trust, Dove Cottage, Grasmere.

1. James Savage (1784-1875), antiquary, best known for his *Genealogical Dictionary of the First Settlers of New England* (1860-62). He was a college mate of WA's. He was several times a member of the house of the Massachusetts legislature and became a senator in 1840 (George S. Hillard, "Memoir of Hon. James Savage, LL.D.," *Proceedings of the MHS,* 1st ser., 1878, 16 [Boston, 1879]: 129).

315. To Thomas Brown, Jr. May 1, 1842

[Draft]

Dr Sir: Though I have <earlier> not acknowledged your valuable Present of the Box of Colours <earlier> at an earlier <date> period, I beg you believe <that I have not been insensible to [undecipherable word] this mark> that <it> this token of your good will <kindness; which I value assure you the more> was no less gratifying than unexpected <& which> as coming from the son of one[1] whom I had known for so many years, and for whose upright character I had so sincere a respect. & I pray you <therefore> to accept my best thanks, with my hearty good wishes your health and prosperity Be assured sir that I shall <ever> always <value this token of your good will> preserve the remembrance value of it—and more especially as coming from the son of one &[2]

Will you be pleased to send me by the next Steamer (via Liverpool) the following Colours: ground in oil, and put up in large bladders, as usual. <As I use a great deal of colour, being at present engaged on a large picture I prefer bladders As I am> Being at present engaged on a large picture, which requires a great quantity of colour, <as I prefer the> is the reason why I prefer <having> the colours in bladders; reserving the tubes, which you sent me, <I shal> for smaller works.

Ten bladders of Fine English Flake White
Ten do of Naples yellow.

Ten do of Yellow Ochre.
Ten of burnt Umber.
Five of burnt Sienna.
Five of Ivory Black.
Five of Vandyke Brown.
Five of Cappagh Brown (if you have it)
<Five of> also Indian Red.

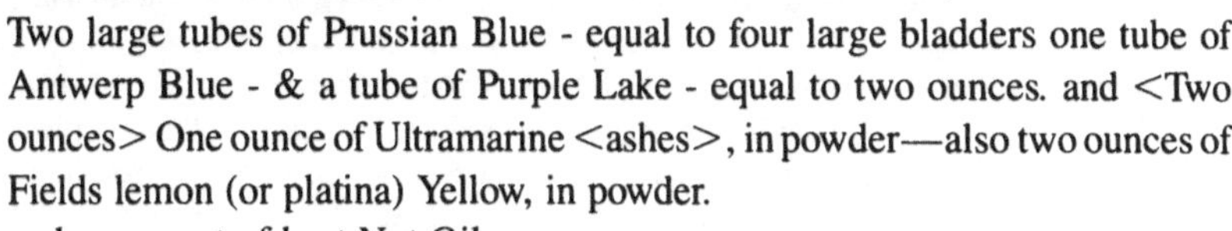

Two large tubes of Prussian Blue - equal to four large bladders one tube of Antwerp Blue - & a tube of Purple Lake - equal to two ounces. and <Two ounces> One ounce of Ultramarine <ashes>, in powder—also two ounces of Fields lemon (or platina) Yellow, in powder.
and one quart of best Nut Oil.

N.B. Mr. A.E. Hoyt,[3] from whom you will soon receive commissions, is a particular friend of mine.

Direct to me, to the care of Edmund T. Hastings Esqre. State Street Boston.[4] In your last address to me you made a mistake as to Mr. Hastings' middle name—<putting M. instead of T.> in I will thank you to be particular—it is T.

P.	Melodizer	Contrast	Ter.	Shadow	drab Deep Shadow
Yellow . . .	Green	Purple . . .	compound of		½ N.
	Orange		Orange & Green	Citron	— Brown
Red	Orange	Green	Purple }	Russet	— ½ N.
	Purple		Orange }		Marone
Blue	Purple	Orange . . .	Orange }	Olive	— Slate
	Green		Purple }		

N.B. The above is reduced from Field[5] and Hay[6]
In the shadow of Yellow the Citron should partake most of the Orange; In that of Red <most> the Russet should incline most to the Purple; In that of Blue the Olive should incline most to the Orange. The Tertiaries stand in the same relation (as contrasts, or supports) to the Secondaries, as the Secondaries to the Primaries; Olive to Orange, Citron to Purple & Russet to Green.[7]

Melodisers

Orange Yellow Green x Green Blue Purple x Purple Red Orange.

[In the margin] I will thank you to <label> put very legibly each colour. I have been ill nearly all the past winter. I should also have had occasion

SOURCE: Manuscript.

1. Thomas Brown, Sr. 2. At several points in this paragraph WA put three "x's," a "2", and a "3", apparently to indicate there were revisions to be followed. 2. Albert Gallatin Hoyt. WA mistook the middle initial. 4. Edmund T. Hastings, Jr., was located in a firm, at first with J.W. Higginson, selling oil and candles at 101 State Street from 1839 to 1852 (*Boston City Directorys*). 5. In *Chromatography,* George Field represented the relationship of these colors in plate 1, fig. 3, "Primary, Secondary, Tertiary colors," and discussed it on pp. 20-21. 6. David Ramsay Hay (1798-1866), Edinburgh decorative artist and writer on art. He was the author of a short book on color which first appeared as *The Laws of Harmonious Colouring Adapted to House Painting* (1828) and went through six editions with slightly varying titles. The third and fourth (1836, 1838) said *Adapted to Interior Decorations, Manufactures, and Other Useful Purposes.* WA referred to one of these editions when he told Henry Greenough that he had recently come across Hay's "Harmony of Colouring for Interior Decorations," which he called "a little unpretending book" that exhibited "many important truths in so plain and practical a shape as to make it a most useful work to any artist" (Flagg, p. 192). He borrowed freely from chap. 2, "On the Analogy Between Colour and Sound," in the diagrams in this letter to Brown. In this chapter Hay illustrated his theory about the combination of colors by reference to notes in music, saying that colors had, in addition to their relation of contrast in opposition, a relation in series, which was "their melody" and that each of the three primary colors was "melodized" by the other two, giving as examples "the yellow is melodised by the orange on the one side, and the green on the other; the blue by the green and purple, and the red by the purple and orange." He referred to Field's diagram in his *Essay on the Analogy and Harmony of Colors,* which juxtaposed the chromatic scale of the colorist to the diatonic series of the musician, but it was his term which WA borrowed. Elsewhere he spoke of "melodizing hues" and "melodizing colors." He identified the secondary colors as orange, purple, and green, which he called "the accidental or contrasting colors" in relation to the primaries, though he said they were composed otherwise than WA said; he identified the tertiaries as olive, citron, and russet, the last two composed as WA said; and he gave as examples of other colors arising out fo the tertiaries "brown, marone, slate" as WA did ([London, 1838], pp. 19-21, 42, 45, 53, 55). 7. This sentence, except for the words in parentheses, is a virtual quotation from Hay, p. 20.

316. To ?

Cambridge Port, 6 May, 1842.

Sir: I am sorry to say, that it is quite out of my power to answer your question, respecting the comparative celebrity of Michael Angelo and Raffaelle for their Cartoons. The Cartoon of Pisa, by Michael Angelo,[1] was equally celebrated, while in being, with the Cartoons by Raffaelle, now at Hampton Court.[2]

Respectfully, / Yr obt st, / Wa. Allston.

SOURCE: Manuscript.

1. Michelangelo's cartoon of the Baptism of Christ, originally at Pisa, is known only by a print. In his lecture "Composition" WA described the figure in it of a warrior, who, suddenly aroused from bathing by the sound of a trumpet, has leaped on the bank and in haste thrust a foot through his garment, the violence of the action being "in unison with the hurry and bustle of the occasion," which was inappropriately imitated by Poussin in the figure of Christ in his treatment of the same subject (*LA*, pp. 159-60). 2. Seven of the originals and three copies of Raphael's cartoons were bought by Charles I of England in 1630 and hung for many years at Hampton Court in a gallery built for them by Christopher Wren. Eventually they were removed to the Victoria and Albert Museum.

317. To Cornelius Conway Felton Cambridge Port, 12 May, 1842

My dear Sir: I have long been wishing to see you, to express myself personally on a subject which you cannot suppose to have been at any moment indifferent to me. But, since it may be still longer before such an opportunity occurs, I now *send* you my thanks—and they come from my heart—for your Review of my Book[1]—so overflowing with kindness—so eloquent, and so hearty, in commendation. Were I a cormorant of praise I could not desire more. Such praise is to be valued, coming from one who is himself an *Artist.*—But, verily, you have imposed on me no slight task—to deserve all you have said to me.

I am glad to hear that your health is restored. I have not seen you since the Dickens' dinner. What a dinner, or rather coena,[2] it was! How bright every face—and all with the *same* light—as if radiant with an effluence from *the Genius* of the banquet.—You remember how feeble I was on the preceding morning. I then doubted if I were not preparing for a relapse; and I went to the Dinner *almost without legs;* but, strange to say, it seemed the next day as if I had as many as a centipede. Perhaps it was owing to my having imbibed the departed strength of a wine glass, whose leg I broke in applauding.

I grieve to think that I shall, probably, never see Dickens again, as I hear that he does not return to Boston. I *took to him* instantly—and felt, though in so large an assemblage, as if I were talking to an old friend. How much more then should I have felt towards him, had we met in a snug circle—such as (I love to think of them) we were wont to meet at our friend, Longfellow's. The impression which Dickens left on me was a very *vane*[3] one—that he was indeed worthy to be the author of his own Books.

Believe me, my dear sir, / with sincere esteem and regard, / Yrs,
Washington Allston.

Professor C.C. Felton

SOURCE: Typescript, MHS.

1. Felton's review of *Monaldi* appeared in the *North American Review,* 54 (Apr. 1842): 397-419. 2. *Cena,* the principal Roman meal, normally taken in the evening. 3. Presumably WA was punning on "vanity," of which Dickens had a great deal, and "vane," referring to Dickens's propensity for treating various social ills in his novels, notably by this time urban crime in *Oliver Twist* and the mismanagement of private schools in *Nicholas Nickleby.* His concern with the international copyright was the most recent example of this varying enthusiasm.

318. To Nathan Hale Cambridge Port, 13 May, 1842.

Dear Sir: I have just seen the first published Number of Mr. Harvey's American Scenery, and I am pleased to find what I had hoped from the Drawings so happily realized in the Engravings.[1]

Yours respectfully, / Washington Allston.

ADDRESSED: Nathan Hale Esqre / Boston. SOURCE: Manuscript, Clifton Waller Barrett Library, University of Virginia.

1. *Harvey's Scenes of the Primitive Forest of America at the Four Seasons of the Year,* the only engravings of Harvey's drawings which were published, was brought out by Hale in 1841.

319. To Samuel Webber Cambridge Port, 19 May, 1842.

My dear Sir: I must trust to your good-nature to pardon this late reply to your letter. The following circumstances will show at least that I had no reluctance to give the required information.

At the time I received your letter the *image* of the little Church,[1] of which you requested a sketch, had entirely faded from my mind—at least in its details; and I was then too feeble to go to Cambridge to refresh my memory, having been very ill nearly all winter. In addition to this, as I could not give you any of the proportions, even with such a sketch as I might make, I <considered> thought it better to wait until I could obtain the regular architectural plan; in orer to [obtain?] which I requested some of my friends to ascertain where it was to be had; when, after much delay, they were informed that it was in the possession of Mr. Hiram Bosworth,[2] a carpenter of Boston, who was the builder. But, though this information was had several weeks since, it brought us no nearer to the object; for Mr. Bosworth was not to [be] found. Feeling therefore not a little mortified at having thus fruitlessly deferred replying to your letter, I concluded to send you even an *imperfect sketch,* rather than wait any longer for what may be obtained from Mr. B. <[three or four words undecipherable]> When I attended church last sunday, I accordingly endeavoured to bring home with me as much of the building as I could carry in my mind; which you will find in this letter.

The architectural plan was not made by me (a thing entirely out of my line) but, from my rough sketch, by a regular architect;[3] so that I am unable to give you a single measurement. I had nothing to do with the interior of the building.

As the accompanying sketch is very imperfect, presenting only a general <notion> figure of the church, I think you had better write to Mr. Bosworth, and empower him to employ some *competent* person to make an accurate copy of the *plan,* together with the measurements, scale &c. If I can learn Mr. B's address, I will send it to you.

Mrs. Allston desires her regards to you & Mrs. W.[4] I remain, dear Sir, with sincere regard, yrs

Wa. Allston.

Dr. Samuel Webber

[drawing of a church]

Front elevation

N.B. There are no windows in front, except the little circular one in the Tower. I do not remember the form of the door.
N.B. There are four windows at the side.

Roof

[drawing of side of church]

Side elevation.

Cornice

[drawing of cornice]

[drawing of the tower]

Side view of the Tower—which is perfectly square.

ADDRESSED: Doct: Samuel Webber, / Charlestown, / Newhampshire. SOURCE: Manuscript, Washington Allston Collection (no. 7471), Manuscripts Division, Special Collections Department, University of Virginia.

1. The Church of the Shepard Congregational Society in Cambridge. It was built in 1830-31, partly from plans furnished by WA. His *Interior of a Church* may have been related to it. It was a wooden building, located at the corner of Mount Auburn and Holyoke streets, in the Greek Revival style. The funds for it being small, it was of the cheapest materials and there was "no opportunity for any thing but simplicity and proportion" (*Letters of Horatio Greenough to his Brother Henry Greenough*, p. 45). The cornerstone was laid on 21 September 1830 and the house dedicated on 23 February 1831. Before it was finished services were held in the Court House. It was demolished in 1915 (Cambridge Historical Commission, *Survey of Architectural History in Cambridge* [Cambridge: Mass. Inst. of Tech. 1973], 4:137; Lucius R. Paige, *History of Cambridge, Massachusetts, 1630-1877* [Boston, 1877], pp. 302-303). Probably Webber wanted a sketch of it for consideration in the rebuilding of the South Parish Meeting House in Charlestown, N.H., which was destroyed by fire in April 1842. It was rebuilt in 1843 but unlike the Cambridge church in the Gothic style (Martha McDanolds Frizzell and others, *Second History of Charlestown, N.H.: The Old Number Four* [Littleton, N.H., 1955], pp. 204, 285). 2. Hiram S. Bosworth worked as a housewright in Boston from 1825 to 1835 and in subsequent years was in the lumber business (*Boston City Directory* for 1825 and later). 3. The church was designed by Henry Greenough (Cambridge Historical Commission, 4:137). 4. Anna Wilson (Green) Webber (Increase N. Tarbox, "Necrology of the New-England Genealogical Society," *NEGHR* 35 [1881]: 289).

320. From James McMurtrie Philada May 20. 1842

Dear Sir: A friend of mine in this city[1] who is making a fine collection of *modern* pictures is desiring of having one from your pencil. He has heard of one you have on hand begun many years since which from description pleases him much. I think it

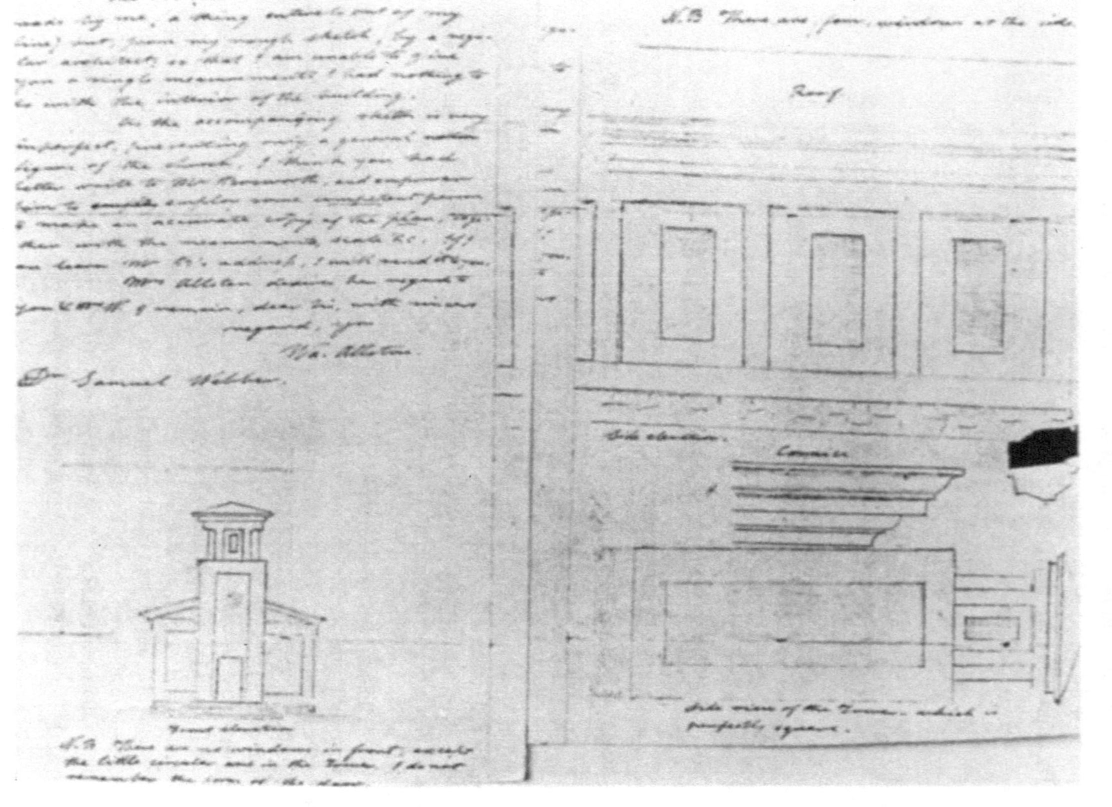

A portion of Allston's letter to Samuel Webber (No. 319), from Cambridge Port, dated 19 May, 1842. Manuscript in Washington Allston Collection, Manuscripts Division, Special Collections Department, University of Virginia.

is somewhat akin to Titian's girl holding up a Casket. I have not the print therefore cannot describe it more particularly. Yours is represented as having several figures & Titian's but one. Will you let me hear from you on the subject. Size of picture, price when finished, in what state of progress it is in progress. He said he shd like to have it as *it is*—unfinished. That I told him I thought you would not consent to.

I recd some time since two drawings by the hand of our old friend Mr. West. One of them "Prometheus Chained to the Rock"[2] is a pen drawing & greatly pleases all our Artists. It has struck me that you wd like to have this drawing and I shd very much covet one of yours in exchange. At a venture I send it to you. If you have any thing in your folio of a like nature (that is on paper either with a pen or in India ink) which you wd set no more value upon that [than] the drawing by Mr. West, you may send it to me by *Harnden's line*[3]—if not, at all events accept Mr. West's in your folio and bide your own time in sending me something of the kind in return. I have a few drawings in my folio which I am anxious to increase in number.

Mr. Sully has returned from his southern cruize pretty successful.[4] But I am sorry to say he arrives at a very dull time in this city. I hope matters are better in Boston—but I fear. My son Jamy gives fair promise of doing well in his profession. Mr. Inman kept him steadily at work at drawing but since his return he has tried his hand at color, from the life, and far exceeded our expectations. I am almost sorry for it for I know he has a long road to travel in severe drawing yet. He has however good sence enough to know this, and is resolved to attain if possible a *hair breadth accuracy* in drawing. I shall send him to Rome in September next and give him means as far as I am able to pursue his studies in a *regular academic manner* for at least 3 years.There is in our exhibition a portrait of yours of old Mr. West[5] which I point out to him as a *Model of truth*. That is the kind of portrait I like. It is made up of *parts*—not a mere generalization—effect & nothing else.[6] It is without comparison the best portrait in our exhibition.

I hope my dear sir you are constantly and profitably engaged and that thro' every instrument we may have another beautiful specimen from your pencil in this City. Col. Drayton, the Academy of fine [arts] and myself are the only possessors of your works in this City.

With great regard I am / Yours—J McMurtrie

W. Allston Esq

ADDRESSED: W. Allston Esqr. SOURCE: Manuscript.

1. Unidentified. 2. For his benefactions to men Prometheus was chained by Zeus to a rock on Mount Caucasus, where an eagle consumed his liver each day and each night it was restored.
3. William F. Harnden operated an express package carrier in Boston (*Boston City Directory* for 1839-1847/48). 4. In Charleston Sully advertised that he would receive commissions and held a lottery for his *Zerlina at Her Toilet*. He showed a copy of Raeburn's portrait of Dugald Stewart beginning in November 1841 and in the spring of 1842 exhibited *The Departure* and *Calliope* at the Apprentices' Library Society, where WA's *Spalatro* was also showing, both of which Fraser praised highly. In 1842 he painted portraits of Mrs. R.F.W. Allston and her great-grandmother

(Rutledge, *Artists in the Life of Charleston*, pp. 163, 220; Fraser, p. 17; Biddle and Fielding, p. 80). 5. It was exhibited at the PAFA in 1842. 6. In the last few sentences McMurtrie echoed some of the sentiments and words in WA's letter to him of 15 June 1841.

321. From John Eagles [24 May 1842]

Mr. Eagles, thinking Mr. Alston would like to see a sketch,[1] however slight, of his beautiful little landscape[2] has begged the favor of Mr. Savage[3] to convey it to Mr. Alston & at the same time the expression of his admiration of Mr. Alston's genius in painting and poetry. We have a lively remembrance of the pleasure of Mr. Alston's society when in Bristol many years ago.

SOURCE: Manuscript, Longfellow National Historic Site.

1. Made by Eagles. 2. *Morning in Italy.* 3. James Savage.

322. To James McMurtrie Cambridge Port, Masstts
23 June 1842

My Dear Sir: I have received your Present, the Sketch of Prometheus by Mr. West, for which I beg you to accept my thanks. But I am sorry to say, that it is not in my power to send you such a Drawing by myself as I could wish; I can only send one or two pencil Sketches[1]—hardly worth your acceptance, except for the good will that accompanies them. I hope, however, to be able, at some future time, to add something better.

Though I have a very considerable number of Sketches,[2] they are, for various reasons, such as I could not well spare; being, for the most part, compositions on large Mill-boards, or on canvasses, for future pictures, with some few that I wish to preserve as memoranda of former works. On paper I have rarely sketched of late years. Perhaps no Artist has been more careless than myself of his sketches; the greater part having been lost, destroyed, given away, or otherwise disposed years ago. I have often of late regretted that I took not better care of them.

The Pencil Sketches referred to, being small, I will enclose within the leaves of a Volume[3] which I published last summer, and of which I ask your acceptance. The Book was first published in Boston, but the copy I send you is from the London edition of it, which I have just received. I shall forward it by Harnden's Express, as soon as I am able to go into Boston—which I hope will be in a few days. At present I am confined to the house by an attack of Erysipelas in my foot. In the meantime you will receive this letter by Mail.

I very much regret that it is not in my power to avail myself of your Friend's wish to possess a picture by me; my engagements being such as to oblige me to decline many commissions, which I should otherwise have been glad to undertake. Besides Belshazzar, on which I am now *exclusively* employed, and shall continue to be until it is completed, I have already engaged Pictures enough to occupy me for many years—perhaps more than I can expect to live.—The Picture you refer to in your letter has been sold several years since. I suppose it is the one which Coleridge named "The Sisters"—and which Sully (it being a favourite with him) may have described to you. One head in it—, as to the *air* and *colour,* but not character or head-dress—was imitated from the picture by Titian called his Daughter, holding up a casket. The other figure, with the rest of the composition, choice of colour etc was mine.

As I have <mentioned> had occasion to mention Belshazzar (which I wish the publick had never heard of—having heard so much concerning it that has no foundation whatever) I would here add a few words on the subject. Perhaps you do not know that this picture has been five times suspended—the last time rolled and boxed up for thirteen years, and each time *solely* because I had not the means to proceed with it—nay, because I had nothing even to live on. You will not be surprised at this, when I tell you, that *no picture* ever went out of my hands, that was not *as good as I could make it, for the time being;* nay, more—that when it did not reach to at least a *certain degree*—my conception, it *never* left my painting-room. This was not the way to become rich; but I had sacrificed a competence in <the> acquiring my Art—and I could not sacrifice my Art for money—even though for ten times what it cost.—Pray do not let any Editors see my letters. However well-disposed—and they have always been so to me—I do not wish to get into the Newspapers. It is not pleasant to have the Public, even though kind, looking over one's shoulder.[4]

I have been very ill nearly all winter; for six weeks confined to my chamber—and for a long time after too feeble to effect much. With the exception, however, of the Erysipilas, which has just now crossed my path, I have pretty much regained my strength.

I am glad to hear that Sully has been so successful in his Southern Excursion. My best regards to him—and pray remember me to Neagle[5]—and tell him I was very much pleased with Mr. Sartain.[6]

Believe me, Dear Sir, with unabated regard

Sincerely Yours / Washington Allston.

James McMurtrie Esq. / Philadelphia / Pennsylvania

SOURCE: Manuscript copy. Printed in Flagg, pp. 317-19.

1. An untitled group and *Silenus and Fauns.* At an undetermined date WA made a pencil drawing *Prometheus,* which was reproduced in *O&S.* It depicted the figure lying chained to a rock in the general pose of the figure in his drawing *Danger.* 2. WA told Elizabeth Peabody a few weeks before his death that he had enough sketches for a hundred years and if he were rich would open a school and sketch and finish only (Peabody, p. 2). 3. *Monaldi.* 4. WA used this expression in talking to Mrs. Jameson. 5. John Neagle. 6. John Sartain (1808-70, engraver and publisher. Born in London, he came to America in 1830 and settled in Philadelphia. His most important publication venture was *Sartain's Union Magazine of Literature and Art* (1849-52).

During his visit to WA at this time they discussed the merits of Stothard, whom Thomas Phillips scorned, and WA commented that he was as good as Raphael (Sartain, *The Reminiscences of a Very Old Man* [New York, 1899], p. 247).

323. To Thomas Willis White Cambridge Port, Masstts.
1 July, 1842.

Dear Sir: I have the pleasure to enclose, for your Miscellany,[1] a Sonnet[2]—which I hope will be acceptable.

It would give me great pleasure to write for the Literary Messenger,[3] were it in my power; but I regret to say, that my professional engagements—which are particularly pressing at the present time—together with the feeble state of my health, would not allow me to engage as a contributor with any reasonable hope of fulfilling my engagement. The only time that I have ever allowed myself for writing is at night—devoting the *day,* as a matter of duty (now become a habit) wholly to my profession. But the labours of the day leave me at present too much exhausted to be followed by literary efforts. I was confined to my chamber for a good part of the last winter—and am far from well now.

I have placed in the hands of your Agent, Mr. T.S. Fields,[4] a copy of my Tale (Monaldi) which he has kindly engaged to forward to you, and of which I beg your acceptance.

I remain, dear sir, / respectfully yours, / Wa. Allston.

T.W. White Esqre.

ADDRESSED: Thomas W. White Esqre. / Richmond, Va. SOURCE: Manuscript.

1. Nothing further seems to be known of this publication. White suffered a stroke of paralysis in September 1842 and it may never have come to realization. 2. WA's "Sonnet: On the Statue of an Angel, by Bienaimé, of Rome, in the Possession of J.S. Copley Greene, Esq." In it the angel is said to have a "celestial face," not to be akin to "aught on earth" but to possess "that supernal purity,—that grace / So eloquent of unimpassioned love! / That, by a simple movement, thus imparts / Its own harmonious peace, the while our hearts / Rise, as by instinct" and the work to be "not material Art,— / But e'en the Sculptor's soul to sense unsealed / O never may he doubt,—its witness so revealed,— / There lives within him an immortal part!" (*LA*, p. 345). It was printed in the *Southern Literary Messenger* 8 (Aug. 1842): 528. Luigi Bienaimé (1795-1878), Italian sculptor, settled in Rome after 1817. John Singleton Copley Greene (1810-72) was a grandson of John Singleton Copley. He owned WA's *Sketch of a Polish Jew.* 3. The *Southern Literary Messenger* (1834-64). White was the founder and, from 1837 to his death, the editor, with aid from others. His most notable editor was Edgar Allan Poe, who also contributed many items to it. WA owned the issue for August 1842, which contained a review of *Monaldi.* 4. Unidentified.

324. From Anne Gillman [2 July 1842]

My dear Sir: I take advantage of a visit of Mr. Prentiss,[1] to send a few lines *even* across the Atlantic, that I may once more thank you for the beautiful Sonnet[2] you so kindly sent me. The thoughts & images truly represent that noble Being. Mr. Carey,[3] to whom I showed it on Sunday was highly pleased and said, "the Sonnet is worthy of the subject"—and you knew his attachment to, & his veneration for Coleridge. I hope you received a letter I sent long ago, to thank you for the valued remembrance. My eldest Son, James, a clergyman, has lately been to Mrs. Wade's,[4] at Bristol, to see your portrait of our departed Friend. He says in a letter to me, "it is a superb painting, and a still more superb likeness, and *powerfully* brought before me, what that great man was in his better days, when under my dear Father's Roof."

Ah! dear Mr. Allston those were indeed happy days—, and I still seem to myself, to *live* only in them. Your friendly image is not unfrequently before me, and I see you seated in our little drawing room, by my beloved husband, and our most valued friend. The former, never, I think recovered this, to us, irreparable loss. Your admirable painting of the White Horses and three figures, is always in the room where I sit, and even much improved by time. I have left it as an Heirloom to James. Coleridge and Mr. Gillman delighted in it.

The visits of those of your young countrymen, whom admirable and affectionate feeling have led hither to see the room he made his study, have given me pleasure—and an opportunity of hearing of yourself, my dear Sir, which will always continue to interest

Your ever affectionate *old* friend / Anne Gillman

July 2d / 1842

ADDRESSED: Mr. Allston / By favor / of. Mr. Prentiss. SOURCE: Manuscript, Houghton.

1. George Lewis Prentiss (1816-1903), clergyman, teacher, and author. He spent two years before his ordination in Europe studying theology and visited Mrs. Gillman in connection with his admiration for Coleridge. 2. WA's "Sonnet on the Late S.T. Coleridge." 3. William P. Carey. 4. Widow of Josiah Wade, who inherited WA's second portrait of Coleridge.

325. To John Stevens Cogdell Cambridge Port, Masstts.
4 July, 1842.

My dear Cogdell: I have received your remittance of Seven hundred & thirty seven Dollars, eighty two Cents (being the balance of my portion of the Inheritance from my Grandmother) by a Check on the Bank of New-York—which has been forwarded for payment.

Washington Allston.

$737.82.

I have deferred answering your first letter of the 14 of June, enclosing a copy of my Account, until I could answer the second (lately received) of the 21 of June, <which you supposed would soon follow [undecipherable word]> the acknowledgement of <the latter> which has been delayed till now in consequence of a lame foot, which prevented my going into Boston, in order to take the necessary steps to get the Check cashed.

Now that this troublesome affair is finally, and so successfully concluded, through your unremitted kind offices—how shall I find words to thank you? But words would but feebly express what I feel. I will leave it then to your own generous heart, which will readily imagine what I would say, could I put into the form of words the deep sense I have, and shall ever retain, of all your kindness. God bless you and yours.

I congratulate you on your present prospect of visiting Italy. And I have no doubt that the new spring it will give both to your mind and constitution will add many years to your life; and that they will be happy ones I venture to predict; for with health and competence (even though it be barely sufficient to secure one from the slavery of debt) what is to prevent a pleasurable flow to time, in the free pursuit of our most innocent[1] Art? Your promised introduction to the Pope,[2] in presenting him the Portrait of Bishop England,[3] I should think must be of great advantage to you. As to the glorious works of Art by which you will be surrounded in Rome—they will breathe a new life into you. Even at this distance of time I live upon them in memory. In that "silent city," as my friend Coleridge used to call it, were some of my happiest dreams; for they were the dreams of Youth, to which even the then gorgeous *present* was but a dark fore-ground to the beautiful and dazzling distance of the *future*. And, though my approaches to that future have uniformly caused it to fade more and more into the common day-light,[4] laying bare to the senses the illusions of the mind, yet I do not regret that I once so dreamed of it; since I have only, as if reversing a telescope, to look back into the Past, even from my present foreground, matter of fact as it is, <and> to see the same delightful, though imaginary distance—dimmer indeed, because diminished—but still the same. The visions of the past are not always lost to us; they may become less defined, but they do not all vanish; and I have still enough of them (thank Heaven) to call up at will, to embellish, as it were with <like> pleasant pictures, the homely walls of the immediate Reality.—No—whatever changes have fallen to my lot, I cannot regret these illusions: my Youth was one—if I may so express it—of *intense life;* and the mere memory of it were sufficient to keep me from repining.

Whenever you are ready to start for Italy, and you send me a line to that effect, your letters for Florence and Rome shall be forth-coming. The letter to Florence will introduce you to Greenough, whom I know you will take to immediately. But I am sorry to find that my friend Severn, an English Artist,[5] for many years resident in Rome, whom I wished to make known to you, has returned to England.[5] I will, however, give you a letter to a young Artist <and> our countryman, Mr. Kellog,[6] now at Rome, with whom, though slightly acquainted, I was exceedingly pleased from the little I saw of him. Mr. Kellog is musical, like yourself, and I dare say you will happily harmonize with each other.

I did not recover from illness last winter as soon as I expected when I wrote to you. I was five weeks confined to my chamber; and even after I was able to go out, it was more than six before I regained sufficient strength to do any efficient work. I am now, however, thanks to a kind Providence, again strong, and able to work with vigour.

It grieves me that I must close this letter with the sad intelligence of our poor friend's death—Mr. Nat. Amory.[7] He died about ten days since, supposed of dropsy in the chest. A nobler hearted, more disinterested friend, no man ever had than I in him. Amongst all the varieties of character, more or less estimable, which I have met with through life, I could not name a better man.

I am glad that Mrs. Cogdell is to accompany you abroad; you will be all the happier. Mrs. A. joins me in best regards to her as well as yourself.

Ever affectionately, your friend, / Washington Allston.

ADDRESSED: John S. Cogdell Esqre. / Charleston, / South Carolina. SOURCE: Manuscript. Printed in part in Flagg, pp. 319-20.

1. WA used this adjective in describing painting in his letter to Pickering for Cole and in "The Two Painters." 2. Gregory XVI (1764-1846), pope, 1831-46. 3. John England (1786-1842), Roman Catholic bishop, born in Ireland, went to Charleston in 1820. WA refers to Cogdell's bust of him. 4. "At length the Man perceives it [the 'vision splendid' of youth] die away, / And fade into the light of common day" (Wordsworth, "Ode: Intimations of Immortality from Recollections of Early Childhood," lines 75-76). 5. Joseph Severn (1793-1879), English portrait and subject painter. WA probably knew him in London. In 1820 he accompanied Keats to Rome, nursing him until his death, and remained until 1841. Horatio Greenough had a long talk with him about WA in London in 1843, at which time he spoke of WA's influence on the German school of painting in Rome (Greenough, *Letters*, p. 349). 6. Miner Kilbourne Kellogg (1814-89), painter of portraits, miniatures, and oriental scenes. He began his art career in Cincinnati in 1840 and studied in Italy from 1841 to 1845. Subsequently he worked in New York and Baltimore. 7. Amory died on 24 June 1842.

326. To Cornelius Conway Felton Monday, July 18. [1842][1]

My dear Sir: I shall be most happy to see you, with Sumner and Dr. Howe[2] this evening—if you will promise to overlook an *unshorn chin*, which I have been forced to leave in its present deplorable state—owing to a rebellious razor that refuses to cut.

Your sincere friend / Wa. Allston

ADDRESSED: Professor Felton, / Cambridge. SOURCE: Manuscript, Houghton.

1. The year is penciled in, in another hand; 18 July fell on a Monday in 1842.

2. Samuel Gridley Howe (1801-76), reformer. He received the degree of M.D. from Harvard in 1824 but spent his life championing various causes for the disabled and oppressed. His most notable achivement was the operation of the Perkins Institution for the Blind in Boston from 1832. His wife, who was Julia (Ward) Howe, daughter of Samuel Ward, remembered long afterward seeing WA in the winter of 1842-43, a few months after this letter was written, on Chestnut Street, presumably going to or from the Danas, and said that he, "with his snowy curls and old-fashioned

attire, looked like an impersonation of winter, his luminous dark eyes suggesting the fire which warms the heart of the cold season. The wonderful beauty of his face, intensified by age, impressed me deeply." They passed without his recognizing her, since he had seen her but once, probably at the 1839 exhibition of his paintings, but she added, "his living image in my mind takes precedence of all the shadowy shapes which his magic placed upon canvas" (*Reminiscences*, p. 43).

327. To John Wheeler Cambridge Port, Masstts
10 July, 1842.

My dear Sir: I thank you for your most interesting letter. I had been for some time prepared for the intelligence of Dr. Marsh's[1] death; nor was the manner of his departure other than I should have looked for:[2] I could well believe of him (could it be asserted of any one) that he had heard in *that* hour, even in the body, the recognition of Him to whom he had consecrated his life—"Well done, good and faithful servant."[3] I know not that I ever met with a person for whom I felt so deep a reverence on so short an acquaintance.[4] But he carried a character in his face not to be mistaken—in which, except in one other instance, I never saw so legibly written *the peace of God.*[5] The moral beauty which was so striking in his expression had an elevation in it, from its connexion with his mind, that I have rarely seen. And how winning the simplicity of his manners: you could not for a moment doubt that they were the necessary growth of a pure heart and no common order of intellect. I rejoice that my great friend, Coleridge, has in him a commentator so every way worthy of his extraordinary powers.[6] They would have loved each other had they ever met.

I regret, with you, that there is no good Portrait of Dr. Marsh. It would certainly be possible for a clever Artist, who had been long and intimately acquainted with him, to paint one from memory; but the intimacy must have been such as to enable the painter to recall the *detail* of his features. For myself, though I shall, perhaps, always retain a distinct impression of his face, it is only in the general effect—or the *whole*—whilst I should be quite at a loss, were I to attempt the particular parts. I think, however, that a tolerable engraving might be made from the Portrait you mention and the Daguerotype together.[7] And, if you are disposed to have it attempted, there is an Engraver in Boston whom I could recommend, and who I think would execute it in a respectable manner. Mr. Pelton,[8] the person referred to, engraved the Print from Hoit's portrait of the late President Harrison[9]—a very accurate transcript of the picture. Mr. Pelton is, besides, at night, my neighbour, though he works in Boston. And perhaps I might be able to give him a hint occasionally as to the general character.

I am particularly gratified by what you say of my Book.[10] My young friend, Edmund T. Dana,[11] will take with him a copy of Monaldi, which I beg you will do me the favour to accept: the copy is <from> of the London edition, which (being printed from a copy I had corrected) is somewhat freer of mistakes than that of Boston.

I remain, dear sir,

with great respect, / sincerely yrs / Washington Allston.

ADDRESSED: To / President Wheeler, / Burlington, / Vermont. SOURCE: Manuscript.

1. James Marsh (1794-1842), philosopher and educator. He was president of the University of Vermont from 1826 to 1833 and professor of philosophy from then until his death. WA knew or owned his translation of essays by Friedrich H. Jacobi, which may have been in manuscript only. 2. During the last weeks of Marsh's life, when he knew he was dying of tuberculosis, he spoke calmly of the fact, and it was reported that "those of his friends who were privileged to sit by him and listen to his heavenly discourse, will never forget the impression left on their minds by those sadly pleasing interviews" (*The Remains of the Rev. James Marsh, D.D., Late President and Professor of Moral and Intellectual Philosophy, in the University of Vermont; with a Memoir of His Life Compiled by Joseph Torrey* [N.p., 1843], p. 131). 3. Matt. 25:23. The sentence is almost the same in Matt. 25:21 and Luke 19:17. 4. Marsh visited WA a "few weeks" before 24 February 1830 and in 1832 asked RHD if WA corresponded with Coleridge and if he had anything of his "Elements of Discourse," and said he would be glad to learn from WA "Something authentic" about Coleridge's character and habits. In February 1841 he spent more than a fortnight in Boston, visiting WA as well as Channing, Ticknor, and Bancroft. He sometimes visited the Danas, whom he possibly met in connection with having his article "Ancient and Modern Poetry" published in the *North American Review* in July 1822, on school holidays or money-raising trips from the University of Vermont (John J. Duffy, *Coleridge's American Disciple: The Selected Correspondence of James Marsh* (Amherst: Univ. of Massachusetts Press, 1973), pp. 110, 142, 256, 3). He took a special interest in WA's nephew Edmund T. Dana when he was a student there and deeply impressed RHD, Jr., on a visit to Burlington in 1836 (Dana, 1:130). 5. ". . . the peace of God, which passeth all understanding" (Philippians 4:7). 6. Marsh edited Coleridge's *Aids to Reflection* in 1829, the first American edition of the work. On 24 February 1838 RHD wrote him to correct his impression that Coleridge had borrowed from Schlegel in his Shakespeare lectures, stating that, on the contrary, Schlegel had expressed views on Shakespeare taken from Coleridge's original lectures, as reported in *Biographia Literaria*, though in subsequent lectures he read from old notes and his auditors thought he was stealing from Schlegel. WA confirmed these facts and told RHD that once while dining at the essayist Basil Montagu's in London the matter was spoken of and Hazlitt said to WA that Coleridge had uttered those opinions "twenty (or many) years ago." WA was, RHD declared, "perfectly clear about it" (Duffy, pp. 215-16). 7. Probably the portrait, by an unknown artist, apparently painted from a daguerreotype, now at the University of Vermont. The daguerreotype does not seem to have been preserved. 8. Oliver Pelton (1798-1882), bank-note and general engraver, who worked principally in Boston. 9. William Henry Harrison (1778- 1841), U.S. president from January until his death on 4 April 1841. 10. Presumably *SS*. 11. WA's nephew.

328. To George Cheyne Shattuck

Cambridge Port,
7 August, 1842.

My dear Sir: I return, by the bearer of this, Dr. Parkman's[1] *Royal Footstool*[2]—and I beg you to express to him my best thanks for his kindness in lending [it] to me. I am quite ashamed to have kept it for so long a time.

I have the pleasure to say, that your skill and kindness again enable me to call myself well.[3]

I remain, dear Sir, ever your obliged & grateful / friend,

Wa. Allston.

Dr. Shattuck, Boston.

ADDRESSED: Doct: Shattuck, / Staniford Street, / Boston. SOURCE: Manuscript.

1. Probably Francis Parkman (1788-1852), Unitarian clergyman. He graduated from Harvard in 1807 and served as pastor of the New North Church in Boston from 1813 to 1849. From then until his death he was vice-president of the Society for the Relief of Aged and Indigent Unitarian Clergymen. RHD, Jr., described him as "A strange, minute, whymsical man, with a good deal of quiet wit," whose anecdotes lost their fun without "his manner, his thin piping voice, his drawl, & the funny twinkle of his eye" (1:520-21). He was the father of the historian Francis Parkman and a brother of the physician George Parkman. 2. Presumably a religious work. The earth is said to be God's footstool in several books of the Bible: Isa. 66:1, Matt. 5:35, Acts 7:49. 3. In December 1841 RHD, Jr., wrote his wife that WA had been "quite poorly" and that Shattuck had ordered him to give up cigars and late hours for the present (31 Dec. 1841, Dana Papers).

329. From Henry Anthony Gillman

The Grove. Highgate.
27th August—1842

My dear Sir: Would you do me the favor to accept of a few plates which have been lithographed from my drawings as a small token of esteem and respect from a junior member of a family, who holds your memory, in the highest esteem. We were all delighted to hear of you, from Mr. Prentiss, who has kindly offered to be the bearer of our letters, and whom we consider to be a young man of great merit, & were very much pleased with. My Brother desires to unite in kindest Remembrances, & believe me my dear Sir to remain

Yours most respectfully / H.A. Gillman

Washington Allston Esq

ADDRESSED: Washington Allston Esq / Cambridge / Boston / by favor of Mr. Prentiss Esq.
SOURCE: Manuscript, Houghton.

330. To John Stevens Cogdell

Cambridge Port, Mass.
26 Sep. 1842.

My dear Cogdell: I have this day received your letter of the 20th inst; and, thinking that you might wish an immediate answer to your question, "whether I had surrendered to my brother William M. Allston my part of my late Sister's portion of the inheritance from our Grandmother, which she had destined for my brother and myself—" I lose no time replying that I had. Soon after the death of my Mother my Sister wrote to me particularly concerning the Inheritance refered to, and expressed her intention to divide her portion of it between my brother and myself. In my answer to this letter, after thanking her for this generous proffer, *I declined accepting any part of it,* and begged her to give *all* she intended for me to William—as he had children and I had none—besides, that I had a profession whilst he was without one. I wrote you also to this effect—so that your impression respecting it is correct.

I am sorry that my brother should have annoyed you by his impatience. I am sure he will be much distressed to find that he has done so; for he is really a kind-hearted fellow,—too much indeed to be insensible to your generous and disinterested offices in the prosecution of our joint affairs. Pray then do not let it trouble you. I cannot think he could have been aware of its impropriety. <It was> I expect him here in a few days; and I have no doubt that he will be grieved when told of it. Your ever-ready disposition to oblige renders you the last man to be "*urged*" to any kindness.

I shall look out for the arrival of the "*Lucas,*"[1] and shall give "Hagar and Ishmael"[2] a hearty welcome. No one would value it more; for I shall value it doubly—for its own merit, and as being the work of a very dear and true friend.

As to strangers meddling with your private concerns, *that* is a penalty which every man at all known to the public must inevitably incur. I not only hear, but am doomed to *read* accounts both of what I have done and am doing as *new to me* as they would be to my antipodes. And nothing is more common than to hear opinions ascribed to me which I never expressed, and could not entertain. Indeed I have had so much of this kind of gossip circulated about me that I have become quite callous to it, giving it no heed—especially as I ascribe [it] rather to idleness, than ill nature. I sometimes say to my friends, that, if I wanted to learn what I was going to do next, I had only to ask the first stranger I should meet.

I am glad to hear that your new quarters please you, as it must have been a trying circumstance the selling your house after so many years residence in it.—I have at last, in my old age, got into a house of my own—built from the proceeds of the sale of land, which but a few years ago rented for no more than 250 dollars. <The> Having the control over the design, the house was constructed not only according to my notions of convenience and comfort, but in some degree to suit my taste. It is somewhat in a different style from our dwelling houses here, and I should not have been surprised if much fault had been found with it by others;[3] but people seem to be generally pleased with it. At any rate, it has one great advantage [page torn] is but fifty feet from my Painting-Room.

Mrs. Allston joins me in best regards to Mrs. Cogdell and yourself.

Ever affectionately yours, / Washington Allston.

ADDRESSED: John S. Cogdell Esqre. / Charleston, / South Carolina. SOURCE: Manuscript. Printed in Flagg, pp. 321-22.

1. The name of a ship. 2. Presumably the painting which Cogdell did of this subject.

3. WA's ideas about domestic architecture were known earlier, Emerson being among those who approved of them.

331. To Thomas Brown, Jr. Cambridge Port, Mass.
11 Oct, 1842.

[Draft]
Dear Sir: It was but a short time since that I had occasion to use the Colours you last sent me—those of 1 July 1842; and I am sorry to say that the White (the colour which I most needed) is so deficient in body that I can make no use of it. It resembles in consistence the Cremlets,* or German White; <and I cannot help thinking it some mistake that your workmen have made mistakenly put up for made some mistake> May <they not> not your workmen have put up by acci[dent] Cremlets instead of Flake White? At any rate this last White, <though labelled> if indeed it be Flake White, as labelled, is entirely different <both> from that which I used to import in your Father's time. I have a little of the latter left, and on comparing <them> the two I find the old White not only a good deal *lower* in *tone,* but possessing *four times the body.* Indeed this new White is so diaphanous that it seemed almost like painting with snow.[1] I had occasion to *paint out* a very light gray and it would not obliterate it after thrice passing over; <not> it will not obliterate even a light tint of vermillion; so that I can put it to no use whatever; and <Thinking the> should be <an wh> quite at a stand had I not fortunately by me a small quantity of the Flake White in <Powder,> which I brought <from London> with me when I <left> returned to this country. This being the case, I will thank you to let me have ten pounds of the *same old* Flake White which you used to <have> send me five or ten years ago, <put up in large bladders, and> ground in oil, put up in large bladders, and ground as *stiff as formerly.* <which the last none of the last colours are>

The Yellow Ochre also I find different from the old, <of which I have a considerable quantity left>. A friend tried some of <it> the new and thought it resembled the French Ochre—of <which> that, however, I know nothing. My objection is that it works *soapy*—that is, it slips about on the canvass. Besides, it seems to want body. I will therefore thank you to send me five large bladders of the *old* yellow Ocher.† <In addition to> this the new Naples Yellow is too much thinned with oil. Indeed I think the general fault of nearly all these new colours is their being ground too thin. Perhaps this last defect may have been occasioned by your workmen being of late <ly most accustomed> to in the habit of preparing <them> colours for Tubes. However that be, I will thank you in the future to direct them to grind all mine stiffer.

Mr. Hoit, an <friend> artist and particular friend of mine, who <goes sails in J[?]> sails in the same steamer <by which this and> and goes to London with this will see you on the subject of this letter and explain to you—if there be need—more particularly what I wish.

I wrote to you several months since concerning the picture[2] (or rather canvass) which is rolled up in your Warehouse and begged you to accept it, if you could put it to any use. I suppose you have long ere this received that letter.

You will oblige me by sending the above named colours as soon as <you> they can conveniently <can> be prepared. And I must beg you to request your Agent at Liverpool *not* to send them, as he did the last, by Harnden's Express, as the expense was <more than> double what it was in the old way—<and> but simply to ship them as directed, namely W. Allston to the Care of Edmund T. Hastings Esqre State Street. Bost.

Will you send me, at the same time, with the Colours, two three quarters and two kitkats—[3] all absorbent, plain cloths (rectangular form) of the usual drab colour.

[In the margins] Postscript *Some years ago I imported <some> ten Pounds of Cremlits White, and after a short trial, threw it all away, on account of <this> the same deficiency‡. And <I> here I would observe that the Cremlits White though higher in tone on the palette than the Flake, <for> its want of body it has not half that brightness of the lower toned Flake on the Canvass.

†likewise ten ditto of Naple[s] Yellow <for this> ground a great deal stiffer; for this
‡I complain of in the present White.

SOURCE: Manuscript.

1. WA used the same comparison in his conversations with Henry Greenough as well as again in writing Brown. 2. *Jason Returning to Demand His Father's Kingdom*. It had been sent from Rome in 1808 to the care of Thomas Brown, Sr. It was sent to Boston by Thomas Brown, Jr., in 1844 (Dana 1:268; RHD, pp. 22, Addition, 42). 3. Canvases for a three-quarter length and a kit-cat size painting.

332. To Charles Robert Leslie Cambridge Port, Masstts.
11 Octbre 1842.

Dear Leslie: This will be handed you by my friend, Mr. Albert G. Hoit, whom I beg to introduce to you as one whom I highly esteem both as a man and an Artist. It is Mr. Hoit's intention to visit France and Italy, as well as England; but his time abroad being necessarily limited, his stay in London will, of course, be short. If you will favour him with such facilities as may be in your power for seeing the various works of Art in London, especially such as are not open to the public, you will much oblige an old friend.

Mr. Hoit having obligingly offered to be the bearer, I take this opportunity to send you a Volume which I published last year.[1] Though so recently printed, it was ready for the press (as you will see by the Note prefixed) just twenty years ago. Not having any copies of the Boston edition by me, I send you one of the London. I send one also to Collins, and one to Mr. Green,[2] the Professor of Anatomy to the Royal Academy. I knew Mr. Green when in London, and I show him this mark of respect as the friend of Coleridge[3] and as one whom I knew Coleridge to have held in high estimation. In an eloquent work of Mr. Green—the Hunterian Oration[4]—which I have lately read I think (but am not certain) that F.R.S.[5] was affixed to his name, in the title page. If so, will you add these letters where I have written it on the blank leaf of my book. I would send copies likewise to Collard and Brockedon but that I fear to burthen Mr. Hoit with a larger packet. I shall, however, request Mr. Moxon, the London publisher, to send them in my name.

I was very ill, so as to be confined to my chamber, the greater part of last winter, and continued very feeble throughout the Spring and Summer; but, thank Heaven, I have now regained sufficient strength to proceed in good heart with my labours. I would tell you more about myself, but that Mr. Hoit, to whom I shall leave it, will be able to say more for me than I could put into a letter.—Do not, however, follow my example when you shall feel inclined to write to me, but tell me *all* about yourself—the more minutely the better—and all about your Wife and Children—to whom, though I have never seen them yet, as part of yourself, I must send my regards. To Collins remember me most affectionately. Though so poor a correspondent, or rather *no* correspondent, I am not therefore forgetful of my friends.—You would hardly believe it, but it is a *melancholy* truth, that I write hundreds of letters to strangers—persons whom I never saw. And why? Because *their* letters *must* be answered, else I have no peace, with a *gentleman's* conscience!—You will think, perhaps, that I fully console myself for this infliction by deducting what I owe to my friends. Be that as it may, I believe they all understand me—and do not measure my regard by the length or frequency of my letters.—Tell Collard and Brokedon also, when you see them, that I still think of both with unabated regard.

I remain, dear Leslie, / Your unaltered friend, / Washington Allston.

ADDRESSED: Charles R. Leslie Esqre. R.A. / London. Mr. A.G. Hoit. SOURCE: Manuscript. Printed in Flagg, pp. 323-24.

1. *Monaldi*. 2. Joseph Henry Green. 3. Green was closely associated with Coleridge, in whose will he was named literary executor. 4. Green was appointed Hunterian orator at King's College, Cambridge, twice. His oration on the first occasion, eloquent but difficult to follow, was *Vital Dynamics: The Hunterian Oration* (1841), in which he attempted to connect science with Coleridge's philosophy. His second was similar: *Mental Dynamics; or Ground Work of a Professional Education* (1847). 5. Fellow of the Royal Society.

333. To James McMurtrie Cambridge Port, Masstts.
23 Oct. 1842.

My dear Sir: About three or four weeks since (it might be longer, as I do not recollect the precise time) I sent you, by Harnden's Express, a Volume which I published last year, enclosing two of my Sketches; one in pencil, a group suggested by a vein in my marble chimney piece; the other a pen and ink sketch of Silenus and Fauns. The latter is rather a favourite composition with me. Will you do me the favour, by a line, to let me know if the Book, with the Sketches, has reached you.

I am sorry that I have nothing more to add—except that I am now in better health than I have known for a year past. I was very ill nearly all last winter, and continued quite feeble throughout the summer; but, thank Heaven, I have regained my strength—and proceed with my labours in good heart.

I saw some years ago, a very beautiful copy in Water Colours, of your "Mother & Child," by Bridport.[1] Can you inform me if Mr. Bridport has still that copy: and if he would sell it—and at what price. And will you also inquire of <if> him on what terms he would make a similar copy in Water colours of my Picture from Gill Blass, now in possession of Col. Drayton, in Philadelphia, should Col. Drayton consent to its being made? The latter copy to be larger than that from the Mother & Child.

I remain, dear Sir, / with sincere regard, yrs / Wa. Allston.

If you are acquainted with Professor Reed,[2] of the University of Philadelphia, I beg to be cordially remembered to him.

ADDRESSED: James McMurtrie Esqre. / Philadelphia, / Pennsylvania. SOURCE: Manuscript, Edward Carey Gardiner Collection, Historical Society of Pennsylvania.

1. Hugh Bridport (1794-ca. 1868), portrait and landscape painter, miniaturist, engraver, lithographer, and architect. Born in London, he came to America about 1816 and settled in Philadelphia, where he and his brother George established a drawing academy at the University of Pennsylvania. 2. Henry Hope Reed.

334. To George Cheyne Shattuck [1 November 1842][1]

Dear Sir: The Apothecary here says that one part of your prescription was so much obliterated that he could not make it out and therefore he felt afraid to attempt to make the Salve.

Will you then be so good as to write another Prescription—which the Bearer will take to Mr. Henchman.[2]

Your obliged friend, / Wa. Allston.

Cambridge Port, / Tuesday Evening. / Nov. 1st

ADDRESSED: Doct. Shattuck, / Staniford Street, / Boston. SOURCE: Manuscript.

1. The date of this letter is assigned on the assumption that the prescription referred to was for erysipilas, from which WA suffered for five weeks beginning early in the autumn of 1842, and that 1 November 1842 fell on a Tuesday. 2. Daniel Henchman was a druggist on Cambridge Street in Boston for many years (*Boston City Directory* for 1816 and later).

335. To Richard Henry Dana Cambridge Port, 6 Novbr 1842.

Dear Sir: I dined yesterday at Mr. Josiah Quincy junr's[1] in company with Mr. J. Quincy Adams, the ex president, who expressed a wish to see a Charge to the Grand Jury, made by your Father[2] in February 1792; and he inquired of me where it was likely to be found: he had applied without success to some Public Office—but what Office I have forgotten. <Martha> I told Mr. Adams that I thought you would be able to say whether such a paper was in <existence> being, and, if so, where it was to be had, and that I would make the inquiry for him. Martha tells me that she thinks you have all <the pa> your Father's papers that remain in the family. If so, and you can find this Charge among them, will you make it known to Mr. Adam's son, Mr. Charles Adams,[3] who, I understand, lives next door (below, I think) to Mr. Jonathan Phillips, Mount Vernon Street.[4] The old gentleman was exceedingly entertaining; his talk shewed nothing of the infirmity of age. We had besides a capital dinner, and a very agreeable time. I should not say nay to such another somewhere.

Wa. Allston

SOURCE: Manuscript.

1. Quincy's father, who was named Josiah, was also called junior, since his father as well as his grandfather was named Josiah. In the fourth generation one of Quincy's sons was named Josiah and in the fifth generation one of his grandsons was named Josiah Phillips. 2. Francis Dana (1743-1811), diplomat and jurist. Dana and several of his fellow judges in Massachusetts upheld the principle of common law in opposition to the popular favor of law administered by equity and the like. He expressed this opinion in a number of charges to the grand jury, notable among them one in 1791, in which he prefaced the consideration of that session's crimes and misdemeanors by "a few cursory observations upon the Constitution of the Commonwealth, which forms the fundamental & unalterable Law of the Land." He declared that "in all Governments, under whatever Forms they are administered, the Legislative, Executive and Judicial Powers are indispensably necessary—that upon the distribution of these Powers depends the portion of Liberty which the subjects or citizens of each enjoy—and that the *Union* of them forms a complete Despotism: whether in One, or Few, or Many." The sentiments which he expressed in this charge "so perfectly coincided" with those of the jury that they requested to have a part of it printed (W.P. Cresson, *Francis Dana: A Puritan Diplomat at the Court of Catherine the Great* [New York: L. MacVeigh for the Dial Press, 1930], pp. 350-51). Possibly this is the charge to which WA referred though the date is not the same, unless it is that of the printed version. Neither the original nor the printed version has been located. He was the father of WA's second wife. 3. Charles Francis Adams (1807-86), diplomat, was at this time a member of the Massachusetts legislature.
4. At this time Adams lived at 57 and Jonathan Phillips at 61 Mount Vernon Street (*Boston City Directory*).

336. From James McMurtrie Phila Nov. 8. 1842.

Dear Sir: The owner of the copy of the Mother & Child will sell it for $100. I saw Col. Drayton a few days since & from what he said I feel sure he will suffer a copy to be made in *Water Colors* of his fine picture. He is as much or more in love with it than when it first came into his possession & wd I am confident do any thing in his power to oblige you. I think it *probable* Mr. Bridport wd do the work for *$200* rather than forego it altogether. This however is a suggestion of my own.

There is a very clever young man here who *composes* well in *outline* somewhat after the manner of Retch[1] (inferior of course but yet *very clever*). I wish to have something from him and I think a scene from "*Monaldi*" wd please me more than one from any other work I can name. Can you name a particular scene which wd not call for too great an exercise of skill? It wd add to the value of the drawing in my eyes, and perhaps stimulate him to extra exertion. Mr. Haviland's son[2] has just returned from Europe. He was much with your old friend Haydon. He is tearing his house to pieces experimenting upon fresco work. He has just painted the Duke of Wellington paying a visit to the field of Waterloo—25 years after the battle—sun setting in glory reapers gathering in the harvest &c a companion to his Napoleon at St. Helena. The latter you may recollect was also a sunset—the sun setting in a deep bank of clouds. He had the Duke's horse in his painting room—the floor & hearth knocked to pieces—just like Haydon. Can you refer me to any engraved likeness of yourself? if in small the better. I have a spare fame over my mantle (a miniature one) & I shd like sometimes to look on your effigy as I am not likely to see the original again. A mere outline *if true* would be sufficient. Neagle has gone to Kentucky to paint Mr. Clay.[3] Sully has nearly finished his large equestrian Washington.[4]

Yours very truly / J McMurtrie

To / Washn Allston Esqre

ADDRESSED: To / Washington Allston Esq / Cambridge Port / Msstts. SOURCE: Manuscript.

1. Friedrich August Moritz Retzsch (1779-1851), German history and portrait painter and etcher. WA owned a copy of his engravings of scenes from Shakespeare. He admired WA's *O&S* (Easterby, p. 155). 2. John Haviland (1792-1852), architect, was born in England, the son of James Haviland, a small squire, and came to Philadelphia in 1816. On his mother's side he was connected with Haydon. 3. Henry Clay (1777-1852), politician and diplomat, retired from the Senate in March 1842 and was at this time living at Ashland, his estate near Lexington, Kentucky. 4. It was executed between September and November 1842 and purchased by subscription by the members of the Union League of Philadelphia. Sully made a study of the same subject in 1841 (Biddle and Fielding, p. 310).

337. To Elizabeth Ellery Dana

Cambridge Port,
Friday Evening, Nov. 11 [1842][1]

Dear Betsey: Martha desires me to say that she would have gone into Town, to see Mrs. Dagget,[2] but, having engaged a person to take up the carpets, she was obliged to stay at home yesterday to see to it—and today (which she had fixed upon for her visit to Boston) she is laid up with a cold and sick-head-ache-the latter occasioned, she thinks, by the former, and that by going too *deeply* (i.e. into the cellar) into the business of yesterday. <[three or four words undecipherable]> Will you mention this <[undecipherable word]> as her apology to Mrs. Dagget. I hope she will be well by tomorrow.

I hope young Richard is by this confirmed in his new diginity of house keeper.[3] Tell him that Dickens has sent him (by Prof. Longfellow) his book on America.*[4] He has sent one also to me.[5]—I dined yesterday with Dr. Howard,[6] together with Edmund[7] and the two Greenoughs.†[8] My love to all your household.

Yrs affectionately, / Wa. Allston.

[In the margins] *It is left with me. †To aid the "flow of soul,"[9] Dr. H. gave us a some [*sic*] Madiera forty years old. How venerable! it almost made the hair on my head rise with admiration. It was like a Lunar rainbow, with a star at each end, and the Man in the Moon reclining on the summit, smoking one of Mr. Gibbens's[10] Trabucos. There's a German simile for you!

ADDRESSED: Miss Elizabeth E. Dana, / 43 Chestnut Street, / Boston. / Favoured by Mr. Gibson.[11] SOURCE: Manuscript.

1. Both Elizabeth Daggett and Horatio Greenough were in Boston on this date. 2. Elizabeth (Watson) Daggett, a sister of the wife of RHD, Jr., was the wife of Oliver E. Daggett, a minister in Hartford. She was in Boston from 6 to 16 November helping the RHD, Jr.'s, get their new house ready for occupancy (Dana, 1:46, 101-103). 3. RHD, Jr., and his wife engaged a house in Boston, at 7 West Cedar Street, on 2 November and were in the process of moving into it from Roxbury (Dana, 1:101). 4. *American Notes for General Circulation* (1842). Dickens also sent copies by Longfellow, who stayed with him in England in October, for RHD, Felton, the publisher George P. Putnam, Bancroft, and Jonathan Chapman, as well as WA (Dickens, *Letters,* 3:351). RHD, Jr., with some of whose judgments at least WA probably agreed, thought it "very amusing" and successful in giving individuals and localities "distinctness & peculiarity" but not when it came to "abstractions or to generalizing, or indeed to any deductions or reflections" of the author, on which occasions the style became "swollen & vaporous." He predicted the book would "make him unpopular without adding to his reputation" and pronounced the man himself "not a gentleman" (1:103). The book, which recounted Dickens's visit to America in 1841-42, was highly critical of the country and the people and aroused a good deal of resentment. 5. Dickens inscribed the copy he sent to WA. In general WA was in agreement with Dickens's criticism of American manners and politics and apparently approved of the review of it in the *Quarterly Review* for March 1842, which he read in April, where America was called a "despot-democracy" (Dana, 1:149). In December 1842 Dickens sent greetings through Felton to WA "and all friends who care for me, and have outlived my book" (*Letters* 3:417). 6. Probably Dr. Nathaniel Howard, who was a druggist in Boston in his early and late years, a physician from 1834 to 1847-48 (*Boston City Directory*). 7. Probably his nephew Edmund T. Dana. 8. Presumably Henry and Horatio Greenough. Horatio was in Boston on his way from Italy to Washington from 23 October or shortly afterward to about 23 November 1843 (Greenough, *Letters,* pp. 319, 321) 9. "There St. John mingles with my friendly bowl / The feast of reason and the flow of soul" (Alexander Pope, "The First Satire of the Second Book of Horace," lines 127-28).
10. Daniel L. Gibbens was a grocer in Boston for many years, from 1840 with his son Samuel H. (*Boston City Directory* for 1807 and later). 11. Probably Charles D. Gibson, Boston merchant, in the flour business with Elijah Bigelow for many years. He and his wife lived a few doors from RHD, Jr., and his family on Cedar Street, with whom they seem to have been well acquainted (*Boston City Directory* for 1839-47/48; Dana, 1:174, 230).

338. From Albert Gallatin Hoyt [14 November 1842]

Samuel Rogers[1] seemed gratified to hear from you, and said it gave him pleasure to show his collection to any friend of yours; and he went with me from basement to attic, pointing out to me every picture and object of *virtù* with all the activity and enthusiasm of the first love of art in a boy. . . . I agreed with you in your high estimate of Stoddard.[2] After seeing Rogers' Titian, "Christ and Mary in the Garden," I perceive now, more than ever, how perfectly you have been imbued with the spirit of the masters of that age, and how little of it there is in the present English school.

[RHD said that this letter was about Hoyt's getting the proper white for WA from Boston. RHD, Jr., said that in this letter Rogers asked Hoyt, "Have you read a wonderful book by a young American, 'Two years before the mast'? It is the best book of the age."]

SOURCES: Flagg, p. 324; RHD, p. 33, Addition; Dana, 1:107.

1. Samuel Rogers (1763-1855), English poet. WA knew him during his second stay in England. His house in London with its collection of pictures, engravings, statuary, and books was a showplace. 2. Probably a misreading of the manuscript for Stothard. Thomas Stothard was, with Flaxman, a decorator of Rogers's house.

339. To John Tomlin Cambridge Port, Masstts 3 Feby 1843.

My dear Sir: I beg you to accept my best thanks for the very kind opinion you are pleased to express of me and my works; which is more particularly gratifying as coming from one of my Countrymen.

I am, dear Sir, / very respectfully, / and sincerely yrs, / Wa. Allston.

John Tomlin Esqre.

ADDRESSED: John Tomlin Esqre. / Jackson, / Tennessee. SOURCE: Manuscript.

340. To Samuel Finley Breese Morse [March between 3 and 24, 1843][1]

[Draft]

My dear Sir: I am in great *professional* <distress> tribulation, being <in> quite at a stand in my labours from want of an essential Colour—<without which I shall be completely at a stand in a week> namely good Flake White. <Now I> The last White which Brown of London sent me, though labelled Flake White, had actually little more body than snow; I can put it to no use whatever it resembles Cremelets White or what is called french, or silver White; both <were colours> of which (after a short trial some years ago now [?] I threw away over 10 lbs as utterly worthless—10 lbs <many years> ago.* I have written <this> to Brown twice† to send me such as his father did formerly, namely the old English Flake White; but have had no answer from him, though 3 steamers have arrived since I wrote. <and I know not when I shall hear from him and and> I am consequently completely at a stand. Now it will be a month or more before another Steamer <is expected>, arrives I must beg you to procure me some in New York which I can use. Will you then do me the favour then to apply to Dechaux[2] (who I understand is the best Colourman in New York) to prepare me, four pounds of English Flake White, ground stiff, and put up in large *bladders* this size. (   ). If he has no english flake, then the best he has; something that has a *good body,* but by no means send me any German or Cremlets, or silver White, which I know, by experience to be too thin in body, however ground, to be fit for anything. And I must beg you <lest the> (to prevent mistake) apply to Decheaux *personally,* and to send the Colour by Harnden's Express. And if Harnden's agent in New York will pay Decheaux I will pay Harnden <agent> or his agent in Boston. And pray let it be as soon as possible.

<I lately received the>

I suppose I am endebted to you for the Report of the Committee in Congress on your Electro Magnetic Telegraph,[3] which I read <as you mu> with great interest. It has settled I think the priority of your Invention beyond question; on which I sincerely congratulate you. And I hope that Cong. will enable me to congratulate you still further on its adoption by them.

*Indeed I have not been able to put the last to any use whatever; & so in a word <I have written Brown> it is good for nothing TB[4] †expressing myself to this effect requested him

SOURCE: Manuscript, Morse Papers, LC.

1. This letter was written after the Senate passed the bill about Morse's telegraph and before WA's letter to him of 24 March. 2. Edward Decheaux was a seller of brushes and other supplies for artists, including paints, in New York for many years (*New York City Directory* for 1830 and later). 3. The bill, authorizing a series of experiments to test the merits of Morse's electromagnetic telegraph, was reported in the *Congressional Globe* for 21 February. It passed the House on 23 February and the Senate on 3 March (Prime, pp. 463, 466). 4. Thomas Brown, Jr.

341. To Samuel Finley Breese Morse

Cambridge Port, Masstts
24 March, 1843.

My dear Sir: As I suppose you have by this time returned to New York[1] I would trouble you again with a few lines on the subject of my last letter. If you have not already seen Decheaux, I must ask the favour of you to call on him as soon after the receipt of this as you conveniently can, and request him to let me have the Colours I wrote for (in the letter above referred to) as soon as possible; for I have been again disappointed as to those which I expected from London. I had a letter from Brown, by one of the Cunard Steamers,[2] informing me that he had shipped the Colours I ordered on board the Alfred Tyler, sailing vessel, which left London on the thirtieth of December. After anxiously awaiting the arrival of this vessel, I have at length learned, from her Agents in Boston, that there is every reason to believe she has been wrecked in some of the late terrible gales.[3] So that I have now not even a *hope* of relief in my artistic strait from England.

All your friends here join me in rejoicing <in you> at the passing of the Act of Congress, appropriating 30 thousand dollars, towards carrying out your Electo-Magnetic-Telegraph. I congratulate you with all my heart. Shakespeare says,

> "There is a tide in the affairs of men,
> That, taken at the flood, leads on to fortune."[4]

You are now fairly launched on what I hope will prove to you another Pactolus.[5] *I pede fausto!*

I am much pleased with Mr. Gray,[6] who brought me some time since a letter from you: he is now painting in Boston. Do you ever see my old friend Verplanck? If so, remember me to him. I still think of him with unabated regard. Mrs. A. sends you hers.

Yours ever affectionately, / Washington Allston.

Pray direct the box of Colours for me, to the care of Edmund T. Hastings Esqre. State Street, Boston.—This has been but a melancholy year to me; I have been ill, with one complaint or another, nearly the whole time—the last disorder the Erysipelas; but this has now nearly disappeared. I hope this letter will meet you as well in health as I take it you are now in spirits.

ADDRESSED: Samuel F.B. Morse Esqre. / President of the National / Academy of Design, / New-York. SOURCE: Manuscript, Morse Papers, LC. Printed in part in Prime, p. 467.

1. From Washington, where he was negotiating for the congressional approval of his electromagnetic telegraph. 2. The Cunard line of steamships, operating between England and America, originated in 1840. 3. Not further identified. 4. *Julius Caesar* 4.3.216-17. The text has "which" instead of "that." 5. A river in ancient Lydia whose sands were a source of wealth after Midas bathed in its source to rid himself of his golden touch. 6. Henry Peters Gray (1819-77), portrait and figure painter, who worked in New York and Boston for several years. He painted a portrait of Rosalia from *Monaldi*, which was exhibited at the NAD in 1842.

342. To Thomas Brown, Jr. — March 25, 1843.

[Draft]

Dear Sir: It is with no <slight> little regret that I have to inform you of the probable loss of the "Alfred Tyler," the vessel in which, according to your letter of the 7 Jany you had shipped my Colours. <Having made inquiries concerning her of the> Her agents, <of that vessel> in Boston her Agents say there <[several words undecipherable, others repetitious]> there is every reason to believe she has been wrecked in some of the late terrible gales: the only intelligence received of her being, that she was spoken with on the 14 of Jany off the Isle of Anglesey.[1] <Having therefore given up all hope of from her, I must beg you request th>

This unfortunate circumstance, together with the previous delay has occasioned me a most serious loss of time. I must beg you therefore, *immediately* on the receipt of this to send me the same Colours—both in *quantity* and *quality,* with those you shipped in the lost vessel. And I particularly request that you will send them by one of the *Liverpool Steamers.* <I can ill afford any> By no means send by a sailing vessel, but by a Steamer, which, <being> besides averaging a much shorter passage, is <attended with> subject to less risk. I can ill afford any further delay; I must have the Colours at *any rate,* whether through Harnden or otherwise. I shall therefore look with *confidence* to receiving them by the first <Liverpool> Steamer for Boston, that sails after you receive this letter. I also wish the Cloths, mentioned in the last order; <I forget> of the same sizes, absorbent ground, plain cloth, rectangular grain. *I never use Ticker*[2] or the lozenge grain.
P.S. You will direct, as usual, (for me) to the care of Edmund T. Hastings. Esqr. State Street, Boston.

SOURCE: Manuscript.

1. An island off the coast of northern Wales. 2. Ticking, a strong, hard linen or cotton from which covers, or ticks, for bed mattresses or pillows are made.

343. From Samuel Finley Breese Morse [4 April 1843][1]

I thank you, my dear sir, for your congratulations in regard to my telegraphic enterprise. I hope I shall not disappoint the expectations of my friends. I shall exert all my energies to show a complete and satisfactory result. When I last wrote you from Washington, I wrote under the apprehension that my bill would not be acted upon, and that I should have another year's perplexing delay, and consequently I wrote in very low spirits. "What has become of Painting?" I think I hear you ask. Ah, my dear sir, when I have diligently and perseveringly wooed the coquettish jade for twenty years, and she then jilts me, what can I do? But I do her injustice, she is not to blame, but her guardian for the time being. I shall not give her up yet in despair, but pursue her even with lightning, and so overtake her at last. I am now absorbed in my arrangements for fulfilling my designs with the Telegraph, in accordance with the act of Congress. I know not that I shall be able to complete my experiment before Congress meet again, but I shall endeavor to show it to them at their next session.

. . .

In the Academy[2] we are preparing our Spring Exhibition. We have one of yours, your sketch of St. Peter in Prison for the large picture for Sir George Beaumont; the sketch you know was in the possession of the late Mr. Winthrop of New Haven. It is in excellent preservation & our artists are all in admiration before it.

SOURCES: First paragraph, Prime, pp. 467-68; second paragraph, RHD, p. 23.

1. The date is given by RHD. 2. The NAD.

344. To John Stevens Cogdell Cambridge Port, Mass.
15 April, 1843.

My dear Cogdell: Though I cannot say that I have any thing worth communicating, I will nevertheless take up my pen—if for nothing more than to let you know that I am still alive; for which, when I think of the number of my contemporaries that have lately fallen around me, I ought to be most grateful to Providence: and I humbly trust I am so. This has been to me a most trying winter. In the first place I had a return of the Erysipelas early in the Autumn, which continued for nearly five months, and at times very painful; nor am I now entirely free from it—though it has taken so mitigated a form that I suffer little, if any, inconvenience from it. In the next place we have had a degree of *persevering* cold weather never exceeded within my recollection. And, lastly, I have been "thrown on my oars," as to my labours, from the want of certain Colours which I could not procure here. I had imported some from my usual Correspondent in London, at the close of the summer; but, when I attempted to use them, I found them so different from <those> the Colours I had been accustomed to, and withall so worthless, that I should have then been completely brought to a stand had I not fortunately had by me a small quantity of the colours of a former importation. By eking out these latter colours, I was enabled still to proceed, <until> and with the *hope* to do so, until I should receive better materials—for which I immediately wrote: The Colours refered to were indeed so bad that I could put them to no use whatever. But here again I was doomed to be disappointed; for my Correspondent, instead of sending the additional and proper, colours I was waiting for, by the regular Steamer, had shipped them in a sailing Vessel, which was *eighty six days* on her voyage.—<[one or two words undecipherable]> So that I was near three months without materials. I have received them, however, at last—about a week since—and am now, thank Heaven, under way again, in better health and good spirits.[1]

But I have talked enough about my own concerns—more than I had at first intended. And now I would learn something of what relates to you. It is not near the time that you proposed to embark for Italy? Pray let me know when you expect to sail, that I might send you the letters of Introduction which I promised. Greenough, as I take it for granted you know, thro' the Newspapers, has long been returned to this country. He is still in Washington, seeing, I suppose, to the erecting of a new building, for the proper exhibition of his statue.[2] I hear he was absolutely startled at the appearance it made in the Rotunda; the shadows falling so perpendicularly as almost to obliterate the features, and otherwise to misrepresent the whole figure. I hope the new building to which it is to be removed, and which will probably be erected under his superintendence, will be such as to do it *justice*—as it is a work, according to the testimony of several competent judges who saw it in Florence,[3] that undoubtedly does him honor.—When he intends returning to Italy I know not. He being out of the question, there are only two persons left for whom I can give letters—Clevenger and Kellog, who are both now in Florence. I am not sufficiently acquainted with Powers to add a letter <for> to him; but Clevenger's <to him lett> introduction to him will serve you quite as well. C's marble bust of me, which he made for the Atheneum, so far surpasses the cast, that, without improving a jot of the likeness, you would hardly know <it> to have been done from it; it is an exquisite work. But the finest bust I ever saw—not excepting any *Antique*—is Powers' marble bust of my friend Col. Baldwin, <also bought for> now in the Atheneum. He is certainly an extraordinary man; and if his statue of Eve[4] be at all equal to it, he has had no equal for some centuries.—As the time draws nigh for your voyage, I suppose your enthusiasm must be pretty near *boiling heat*. Ah, my friend, that is the true country for Art. And it is a proud thing for America that in Art she is now so well represented there. "*I pede fausto,*" and add to it also.—Ever affectionately,

Your friend, / Washington Allston.

[In the margin] Mrs. A. joins me in best regards to yourself and Mrs. Cogdell.

ADDRESSED: John S. Cogdell Esqre. / Charleston, / South Carolina. ANNOTATED by Cogdell: answered 22 April 1843. SOURCE: Manuscript. Printed in part in Flagg, pp. 324-25.

1. WA was engaged principally during the last two years of his life on *Belshazzar's Feast*. At his death his studio contained some thirty other unfinished paintings and sketches. The more complete compositions included *Titania's Court*, two female heads, one of which was done in London, *Una in a Wood, The Death of King John, The Angel Pouring out the Vial of Wrath over Jerusalem*, and two female figures which RHD, Jr., noted, together with what he estimated to be "twenty or thirty sketches" (1:179), some nine other pieces, most notably *The Sibyl*, from the *Aeneid* 6, a subject also painted by West; *Heliodorus Driven from the Temple; Girl in Persian Costume;* and apparently about ten landscapes. The more incomplete included *Lover Playing a Lute, Tavern Scene, Sketch of a Shepherd Boy, Family Group, Mother with Child in Her Lap*, two female figures, and three landscapes. Altogether the Dana Collection, as it came to be called, which included almost everything in WA's studio at the time, numbered nearly three hundred items. The principal unfinished works were exhibited by Mrs. Allston in 1847 and, with others, in 1850 and 1857. 2. Greenough was in Washington, except for a few brief visits to Massachusetts, from November 1842 to the summer of 1843 to arrange for the situation of his *Washington*. No particular newspaper notices have been found. In the rotunda, for which it was designed, the light was too poor for it to be properly seen, and he petitioned Congress and received its approval for the erection of a building outside the Capitol on the eastern grounds, to which the statue was removed late in the summer, after he had returned to Italy. The building put up was a wooden one, intended to be temporary; a permanent one was designed, but no official action was taken on it

(Wright, pp. 145-46, 148-50). 3. It was generally praised there by Americans and English and the Italian press, and two poems were written about it (Wright, pp. 134-35). 4. Powers executed two statues of *Eve Before the Fall*, the first put in marble in 1842, the second in 1850.

345. From Henry Hope Reed [3 May 1843]

[RHD said that in this letter Reed quoted what Wordsworth said in his letter to him of 27 March 1843[1] about Allston's portrait of Coleridge.[2]]

SOURCE: RHD, p. 37.

1. Reed and Wordsworth had exchanged letters earlier referring to WA, in which Wordsworth described their acquaintance and expressed admiration for WA's painting and character (*Wordsworth & Reed* ed. Leslie Nathan Broughton [Ithaca; N.Y.: Oxford Univ. Press, 1933], pp. 39-42, 115). 2. In this letter Wordsworth expressed concern about the disposition of WA's second portrait of Coleridge. It had been bequeathed by Coleridge to Josiah Wade, who died in 1842. Wade's inclination, Wordsworth said, was to send it to America, but he thought it should remain in England and be bequeathed either to the Fitz-William Museum or the college where Wade was educated. Of the portrait he wrote that "it is so admirable a likeness of what that great & good man then was, both as to person, feature, air and character" and that "there is not one in the least to be compared to it" (*Wordsworth & Reed*, p. 95).

346. To Convers Francis

Cambridge Port
16 May 1843

Dear Sir: I return you, *at last*, and with many thanks, your two volumes of Hazlitt,[1] which I forgot to give you when I had the pleasure of seeing you last week, although I had placed them over my mantle-piece for that purpose.

The name of the Historian of Italian Art is Lanzi[2]—not Bottari, as I told you. I wonder how I came to make the mistake, it being not more than three or four years since I read Lanzi; which I obtained, through a friend, from the Atheneum. Bottari is the Editor of a select Collection of Letters, by the most eminent Italian Artists.[3]

With sincere regards, yrs, / Wa. Allston.

[In another hand] To / Rev. Dr. Francis—

SOURCE: Manuscript.

1. Possibly Hazlitt's *Sketches and Essays* (1839) and *Criticisms on Art and Sketches of the Picture Galleries of England* (1843), the most recently published volumes by him. 2. Luigi Antonio Lanzi (1732-1810) was the author of *La Storia Pittorica d'Italia* . . . (1792). Probably WA read the 6-volume translation by Thomas Roscoe, *The History of Painting in Italy* (London, 1828), which the BA owned. The BA also owned a copy of the third edition of the work in Italian (6 vols.; Bassano, 1809). 3. Giovanni Gaetano Bottari (1689-1775) edited *Raccolta di letter sulla pittura, scultura, ed architettura, scritta da' più celebri professori che in dette arti fiorirma dal secolo XV, al XVII*, 7 vols. (1754-73).

347. To Charles Sumner Cambridge Port, 21 May, 1843.

My dear Sir: I wish to have some talk with you on the subject of Crawford's Letter;[1] but, as it will not be in my power to see you in Town, may I ask you to favour me with a visit some evening this week—*after* monday; or, if more convenient to you, some day between *one and two o'clock*?

I am quite charmed with Lord Morpeth's Letter.[2] He is a man to grace an Earldom.[3] I used to think when in England that the better portion of her nobility and gentry made the "cream" of her population.

I am delighted with our friend Longfellow's engagement.[4] He must needs be knee-deep in rose-water.

With sincere regard, yrs / Wa. Allston.

SOURCE: Manuscript, Houghton.

1. On 16 March 1842 [3] Crawford wrote Sumner announcing the completion of his statue *Orpheus and Cerberus*, for which Sumner had raised a subscription and which the BA had bought, and giving instructions about how it should be erected there. He said he had thought of writing WA and asking him to "give a moment's attention" to the placing but decided to leave the matter to Sumner, Longfellow, and Felton. He added, however, that "There is one man above all others in the United States whose judgement I will gladly stand by and that man is Washington Allston" (Lauretta Dimmick, "Thomas Crawford's *Orpheus:* The American *Apollo Belvedere*," *American Art Journal* 19 (1987): 67). He had no doubt heard of WA's response on first seeing an engraving of the statue in late 1840 or early 1841. Longfellow, who was present on that occasion, said WA gave it "warm and cordial admiration," called it "very beautiful," and to the objection by some that it resembled the *Apollo Belvedere* replied, "It no more resembles the Apollo than Orpheus himself resembled Apollo" (Longfellow, 2:284). In his reply to Crawford's letter of 16 March 1843, written a few weeks after WA's death, Sumner said he had shown the letter to WA, who "had always taken a warm interest" in Crawford's success, and in another letter about the statue shortly afterward he again referred to WA's regard for Crawford and said he had counted on WA's advice and influence about placing it (Robert L. Gale, *Thomas Crawford: American Sculptor* [Pittsburgh: Univ. of Pittsburgh Press, 1964], p. 27; Pierce, 2:264-65). 2. Morpeth's letter to Sumner of 2 March 1843, in regard to Sumner's article in the *Boston Daily Advertiser* of 10 January 1843 in which Sumner argued at length that slavery was a national and essentially moral issue rather than a regional one. The article was in answer to one in the same paper, precipitated by Morpeth's declining to write a letter for the antislavery publication *The Liberty Bell* on the grounds of his foreign citizenship, which applied Morpeth's principles to the citizens of Massachusetts as being equally excluded from discussion of the matter. Morpeth expressed appreciation of Sumner's article and gratification that his letter had drawn so much attention (Pierce, 2:229, 238-41). 3. Morpeth was generally well liked. Both RHD, Jr., and Longfellow were favorably impressed by him when he was in Boston. RHD, Jr., said that he had a "homely" face but "excellent" manners, with "no parade, but perfect simplicity; & yet a dignity which would keep off a vulgar or troublesome man," a "careful education," "excellent common sense, & a noble spirit" and that it was "a comfort to fall in with such an one." He told Frances Appleton, who agreed with him, that he preferred Morpeth to Dickens, whose visit occurred a few weeks later, since, though he did not have Dickens's "genius" or "cleverness," was "a well educated, well bred, high minded, agreeable man, with a very good share of intellect." Longfellow described him as "a very simple, cordial man," with red face and white hair, a "very unostentatious, friendly *man,*" a "laughing bachelor" with a "flaming red waistcoat" (Dana, 1:50-51, 59; Longfellow 1:337, 364-65). 4. Longfellow became engaged to Frances Appleton on 10 May 1843, after a

courtship of six years (Longfellow, 2:536). On 19 May RHD, Jr., found WA "very much interested" in the engagement, "liking him & having always admired the beauty of character" of Miss Appleton, and recorded that he burst out saying, "I have a vision" and with raised face and "a mock heroic expression" went on to exclaim, "I see Longfellow up to his knees in golden clouds, with his head knocking against the stars" (1:159).

348. From Franklin Dexter Boston June 3d 1843.

My dear Sir: I am very much pleased and obliged by your expression of so favorable an opinion of my Lear. I suppose you know that the design is Newton; I should have shewed it to you before parting with it, but having promised it to Mrs. Ritchie[1] when it was begun, I dared not let you see it lest I should be discouraged from finishing it.

I have never ceased to regret that I did not discover my love of art before I had been so fixed in life that I was unable to pursue it as a profession. My situation has compelled me to look upon [it] almost as a forbidden pursuit even or a relaxation. For it excites me so much as to render me unfit for the different business that is necessary to my support. For that reason I have limited myself to occasional trials upon the designs of others. I have avoided attempting original compositions, since I found it so absorbing as to disqualify me for the dry & practical matters of the law. This excitement however is not such as would at all have interfered with my happiness, but, on the contrary, would I think very much have promoted it if I could have felt free from other claims. It has been the mistake of my life. Still I have never been willing quite to withdraw my mind from the Art, because I have always thought it possible that a change of circumstances might put it in my power to devote myself to it. That seems now hardly possible, and yet if I were now moderately independent, I should even at this late hour attempt it as a profession. For although I agree with you that the love of money can never make an artist, yet I believe that it must be adopted as a business with that responsibility to the public which one feels in his profession to secure one's best efforts.

It is still possible that a very short time may place me in a situation in which I shall need but a small income from any business in addition to that from my property; if it should occur I could hardly resist the temptation to try to secure that from the Art—and I have regretted that I had not been able without disturbance of my attention to other things, to prepare myself for such an event, when it comes, by a systematic study of Art in my leisure hours. But the course of my life has been so adverse in this particular to my wishes that I almost feel as if it had been kindly ordered that I should not be indulged in them. Still I do not give up the hope of being able to attend more hereafter to the Art as I am less compelled to attend to other things and perhaps I shall find opportunity. This summer (which I shall spend at the Ocean House in Lynn)[2] to make a more deliberate trial of what I can do. If so, I shall ask your assistance where I am in doubt, & your opinion when I have done. I find I prefer figures to landscape, because it is easier to put a soul into the former, & neither are of any worth without it.*

Mrs. Dexter has almost recovered from her lameness, but her general health is feeble. We have good news today from our boy[3] in the East Indies. There is something in every man's lot that seems at times grievous to be borne, but we have many compensations. I shall hope to see you both at your house, and sometime this summer at our lodgings, if you can arrange for a day.

Remember me with best regards to Mrs. Allston.

Yrs very truly / F. Dexter

W. Allston Esq

*I am thinking of a composition from the Tempest Miranda & Ferdinand: "Miranda. I am a fool to weep at what I am glad of."[4]

ADDRESSED: Washington Allston Esq / Cambridgeport / Mass. SOURCE: Manuscript.

1. Probably Mrs. Edward S. Ritchie, whose husband was a hardware merchant in Boston (*Boston City Directory* for 1842). 2. Lynn, Mass., is a seaport, a short distance north of Boston. 3. Otherwise unidentified. 4. Shakespeare's *The Tempest,* 3.2.73-74.

349. To Henry Hope Reed

Cambridge Port, Mass—
13 June, 1843.

My dear Sir: Notwithstanding the lateness of this reply to your Letter, I beg you to believe that I have not been insensible to its kindness; for which I now also pray you to accept my thanks.

The extract from Mr. Wordsworth's letter was as gratifying to me as you had supposed it would be. To be numbered among the friends of the "Great Poet," by himself, is indeed an honour; yet not less do I prize this mark of <his> regard from the *man*. In this incongruous world (but made so by human wilfulness) it is a beautiful thing to see virtue and genius (so often antipodes) dwell together, as in him.

I entirely agree with Mr. Wordsworth as to his proposed disposition of Coleridge's Portrait; for, much as I should value it, as bringing more distinctly before me the image of one whom I deeply loved and reverenced, I cannot but feel that his family and his country have a still higher claim to it. That Mr. Wade's intention respecting it was such as he expressed to Mr. Wordsworth, was intimated to me, through a gentleman of Bristol, several years ago. I have heard nothing, however, on the subject from his heirs; and their long silence since Mr. W.'s death leads me to conclude that Mr. Wordsworth's suggestion has already been acted upon.

In Hazlitt's "Conversations of Northcote" there is a head of the latter which is one of the finest engraved portraits I have seen.[1] I could wish such a Print from my Picture by the same Engraver.[2] I have forgotten his name. So far as I can judge of my own production, the likeness is a true one; but it is Coleridge in repose; and, though not unstirred by the perpetual *ground-swell* of his <ever-act> ever-working intellect, and shadowing forth something of the deep Philosopher, it is not Coleridge in his *highest* mood—the poetic state. When in that state no face that I ever saw was like to his: it seemed almost <intellect> *spirit made visible,* without a shadow of the physical upon it. Could I have *then* fixed it on canvass—but it was beyond the reach of *my* Art.—He was the greatest man I have known, and one of the best—as his Nephew Henry Nelson most truly said, "a thousand times more sinned against than sinning."

Mr. Dana is at present in New Hampshire.[3] My best regards to my friend McMurtrie.—Pray present my respects to Dr. Bethune[4]—from whom I had a very pleasant visit last summer. I beg also to thank him for the Discourse he sent me; which I read with great pleasure—though in one part of it (concerning Michael Angelo) I could not agree with him.[5]

Again I thank you for your Letter.

Sincerely & respectfully yrs / Washington Allston.

To Professor H. Reed.

ADDRESSED: To / Professor Henry Reed, / Philadelphia, / Pennsylvania. SOURCE: Manuscript.

1. William Hazlitt's *Conversations of Northcote* (1830) had as the frontispiece a reproduction of the engraving by Thomas Wright (1792-1849) after the drawing by Abraham Winell. 2. WA's portrait of Coleridge was engraved by Samuel Cousins (1801-87) and published by Moxon in 1854 (Reed to Derwent Coleridge, 17 May, 24 June; 19 Dec. 1853, 27 Mar. 1854, Dreer Collection, Painters & Engravers, Historical Society of Pennsylvania). 3. RHD sometimes visited William Mason in Walpole, N.H. (RHD to Mason, 2 September 1839). 4. George Washington Bethune (1805-62), Dutch Reformed clergyman. At this time he was pastor of the Third Church in Philadelphia. 5. *The Prospects of Art in the United States: An Address before the Artists' Fund Society of Philadelphia, at the Opening of their Exhibition, May 1840* (Philadelphia, 1840). In it Bethune said that "very few, except the learned artist, practiced critic, or observant anatomist, can enter at once into the merits of Michael Angelo," suggested that if "any home-returned tourists" pretended they fell into ecstasies on their first visit to his paintings they talked of excellences which they never saw, and though conceding that he was willing to believe him "the first of Artists" because that rank was given him by the best judges and he might perhaps in time "be educated into an appreciation of his greatness" any such appreciation was until that time "a matter of faith." He preferred Raphael and Domenichino.

350. To George Cheyne Shattuck

Cambridge Port,
Monday, 19 June, 1843.

Dear Sir: Should you be coming out to the Port tomorrow, or the next day, I should be greatly obliged if you would favour me with a visit. I have had a pain in my left side at intervals for a week past, and though not yet become continual, I am not without apprehension that it soon might, if neglected—it having increased much in violence, whenever it returns, within the last three days.[1]

I would go into Town to see you, but that I fear I should want strength to walk from your house to the Omnibus Office, in order to return.

Ever most gratefully yrs, / Wa. Allston

SOURCE: Manuscript, Shattuck Papers, MHS.

1. During the several weeks preceding his death WA's health declined rapidly and he spoke increasingly of the fact. He told one of his sisters-in-law that he was "ready to go," asking only to finish *Belshazzar's Feast,* and John Albro that he was "breaking up."

351. To John Stevens Cogdell Cambridge Port, 29 June, 1843.

My dear Cogdell: I should have replied to your letter, by Mr. Crocker,[1] several days ago but that I have been too much exhausted by the oppressive heat of the weather, besides having a very long and important letter on business (not my own business) due to another correspondent, which required immediate attention.—In answer to your first question—whether I shall be able to meet you in New-York?—I regret to say, that a visit to that City is wholly out of my power; my health is too feeble for such a journey, either by land or water. I have been for some weeks past troubled with a dull pain in my side, which the least fatigue changes into a very acute one: it comes on sometimes in my Painting-room with such violence that I am obliged to suspend my labour until the paroxysm is past—which is generally in about ten minutes. I do not know what would give me more pleasure than to meet you in New-York—but, for this sad reason, it is a pleasure forbidden me.

The <account that you give of the> cutaneous disease in your hand was no doubt, as you supposed, contracted from the *Tools* you had borrowed—especially as their owner was affected in a similar way. It cannot be anything serious; I should not, however, delay consulting a physician, as the neglect of it might occasion you a good deal of future annoyance.—As to the other complaint of which you speak, I can form no opinion. That, of course, you have medical advice for.—You say nothing in this last letter of Mrs. Cogdell's Erysipelas; by which I conclude that she has recovered from it. I hope this is the case, as I know it, by experience, to be very distressing.

You ask if I think your visit to Italy will have the same effect on you now, as I formerly supposed it would. I see no reason for changing my opinion; for, though some ten years have been added to your age, you are by no means beyond the age to feel the influence of a happier and more congenial <change> of employment, and a finer climate: <with every [line undecipherable]> you *will* profit by them, I doubt not, both in body and mind. I have no doubt, were all circumstances propitious to my revisiting Italy, that the change of scene, as well as the climate, would add vigour also to me—could I bear the *voyage*—which I could not, as the

33rd & last Cambridge Port, 29 June, 1843.

My dear Cogdell,

I should have replied to your letter, by Mr Crocker, several days ago but that I have been too much exhausted by the oppressive heat of the weather, besides having a very long and important letter on business (not my own business) due to another corres-pondent, which required immediate atten-tion. — In answer to your first question whether I shall be able to meet you in New-York?— I regret to say, that a visit to that City is wholly out of my power; my health is too feeble for such a journey, either by land or water. I have been for some weeks past troubled with a dull pain in my side, which the least fatigue changes into a very acute one: it comes on sometimes in my Painting-room with such violence that I am obliged to suspend my labour until the paroxysm is past— which is generally in about ten minutes. I do not know what would give me more pleasure than to meet you in New-York — but, for this sad reason, it is a pleasure forbidden me.

The cutaneous disease in your hand was no doubt, as you supposed, contracted from the Tools you had borrowed — especially as their owner was affected in a similar way. It cannot be anything serious; I should not, however,

The last of Allston's extant letters (No. 351), to John Stevens Cogdell from Cambridge Port, dated 29 June, 1843. Manuscript in Massachusetts Historical Society, Boston.

motion of the vessel would soon increase the chronic complaint, which has so long afflicted me, to a degree of torture.

As I have never been in correspondence with Thorwalsden, I could not with any propriety write an introductory letter to him; but I am happy in being able to procure you letters to our Consel, Mr. Green,[2] and to Crawford, the Sculptor, from a friend of mine in Boston,[3] who is an intimate friend of both these gentlemen—either of whom will make you acquainted with Thorwalsden [*sic*], as they are both well known to him. I have no personal knowledge of the persons in Boston of whom you speak.—The letters to Mr. Green and Crawford, from the quarter I refer to, will be worth a dozen from others.

Poor Legare![4] You must no doubt, as well as myself, <I was> have been deeply affected by the news of his sudden death. One of the highest intellects and most noble-hearted statesmen has been lost to his Country. The death of no public man for many, many years has been so universally lamented; even his political opponents seemed to have forgotten their party feelings in the general sorrow. Judge Story pronounces him one of the most learned jurists of his time. And certainly he has not left a more accomplished scholar behind him. He had many, and thorough friends here, in whom his high principle, no less than his <varied> extensive attainments, had won a confidence that connected him with the future welfare and honour of our Country.—But, if he has been taken away from the hope of his friends, and in the midst of his usefulness, it is no slight consolation to them that he was cut off also in the *flower of his integrity.* He has left a great name; but what is far better in his case, *alter et idem,*—a *good* name.

Mrs. Allston joins me in best regards to Mrs. Cogdell and yourself.

Believe [me] ever affectionately yrs, / Washington Allston.

ADDRESSED: John S. Cogdell Esqre. / Charleston, / South Carolina. ANNOTATED by Cogdell: answd 8 July 1843. SOURCE: Manuscript. Printed in part in Flagg, pp. 325-26.

1. Doddridge C. Crocker (1768-1849), Charleston, S.C. merchant. He married Elizabeth Hitchborn of Boston, in that city, in 1790 and had connections in New England for many years ("Inscriptions from the Independent or Congregational [Circular] Church Yard, Charleston, S.C.," prep. Mabel L. Webber, *SCHGM* 29 [1928]: 248; "Marriage and Death Notices from the City Gazette of Charleston, S.C.," contrib. Elizabeth Heywood Jervey, *SCHGM* 51 (1950): 246; "The Abiel Abbot Journals. A Yankee Preacher in Charleston Society, 1818-1827," ed. John Hammond Moore, *SCHGM* 67 [1967]: 55, 57, 60, 72; *Charleston City Directory* for 1802-1806, 1813-24, 1835/6-40/1). 2. George Washington Greene (1811-83), writer and teacher, was U.S. consul in Rome from 1837 to 1845. 3. Probably Sumner. 4. Legaré died on 20 June 1843 at the home of Ticknor in Boston, where he had gone as temporary secretary of state to be present at the unveiling of the Bunker Hill Monument on 17 June (Rhea, pp. 216-18).

352. To William Henry Channing (?) [1843, before 4 July][1]

I know not that I could better describe him [William Ellery Channing] than as *an open, brave, and generous boy.* The characters of boys are, I believe, almost always truly estimated by their companions,—at least morally, though perhaps seldom intellectually; and these are generally assigned to the several classes of the open or the cunning, the generous or the mean, the brave or the cowardly. And I well remember, though he was several months my junior (a matter of some importance among children), that I always looked up to him even in boyhood with respect; nor can I recall a single circumstance that ever weakened that feeling. In our games, he was never known to take any undue advantage, but would give way at once, where there was the least doubt on the point at issue. And though he was but scantily provided with pocket-money, his little chance supplies seemed, in the schoolboy phrase, always to "burn in his pocket;" he could neither keep it there, nor ever expend it wholly on himself. On one occasion, when quite a little boy, he had a present from a relative of a dollar. Such an excess of wealth was never before in his possession; and I can now bring before me the very expression of glee with which he came among us, to disencumber himself of the load. This is the only incident that I can now recall, and this must have been full fifty years ago. He had the same large heart when a boy that animated him to the last. His intellectual endowments are known to the world; but only his early companions, who have survived him, can bear witness to the rare uniformity of his mortal worth; man and boy, he was, in their true sense, high-minded and noble-hearted.

. . .

Though small in stature, his person at that time was rather muscular than slender; I should think it was even athletic, from the manner in which he prolonged the contests with heavier antagonists, in the wrestling matches that were then common among the students. And for animal spirits he was no less remarkable than for his intellectual enthusiasm; amounting occasionally to unrestrained hilarity, but never passing the bounds of propriety. I well remember his *laugh,* which could not have been heartier without being obstreperous.

SOURCE: *Memoir of William Ellery Channing* 1:39, 49-50.

1. William Ellery Channing died on 2 October 1842. It does not seem likely that this letter would have been written during the remainder of that year nor during the five days between WA's letter to Ruth (Gibbs) Channing on 4 July and his death on 9 July 1843. Probably it was written about April or May 1843.

353. To Ruth Gibbs Channing

Cambridge Port, Mass
4th July 1843.

My dear Mrs. Channing: I never could write a letter at the time it ought to be written; & this answer to yours, I fear, forms no exception. In addition, however, to the exhaustion occasioned by the oppressive heat of the weather, I may plead, as some excuse, that I have been troubled of late by a wearing, dull pain in my side, which makes writing more than usually fatiguing to me: Occasionally it becomes very acute, so much so indeed as to force me, while painting, to suspend my labours until the paroxysm is past—

* * * *

With respect to the Portrait[1] I had promised, my necessities compel me to say, that it will be wholly out of my power to undertake it, with any hope of success until I shall have completed Belshazzar. My friends, I have reason to think, are not aware how much depends on this work; which has so long & anxiously occupied me, & which has so often been suspended but *never voluntarily*. But, I trust, you will understand it, when I add (to say nothing of my present embarrassments) that to this source alone can I look for the means of discharging obligations which have weighed upon me for years. Besides there is *that* involved in the undelayed termination of this Picture which is far more important to me than any pecuniary consideration. Until relieved of this burden, I *feel* (& indeed know too well from bitter experience) that no attempt I might make as to the Portrait *could* be successful—It is not with me now as in former days—when the original was painted, when I was young & in health, & with nothing extrinsic to overshadow my Art—

For the last two years a succession of bodily complaints have grievously impeded the progress of the Picture referred to; & the still feeble state of my health warns me that another suspension may be fatal to it forever—But, once freed of this "importunate & heavy load,"[2] I shall be I trust another man, & enabled to bring to this *labor of love*, fresh & unembarrassed, whatever power I possess.

I have made this frank statement, my dear Mrs. Channing, as what I owe both to you & myself; to your kind & generous nature, & to my honour & right feeling, for I know not what would distress me more, than that any *misapprehended* circumstance should lead you to doubt my inclination to fulfill my promise.

SOURCE: Manuscript copy. Printed in Flagg, pp. 327-28. Another copy of all but the first paragraph is in RHD, pp. 39, 39 Addition, with a few differences in punctuation, "that" for "which" and "my own honor" for "my honour."

1. WA's portrait of Channing. An engraving of it appears as the frontispiece in Elizabeth Peabody's *Reminiscences of Rev. Wm. Ellery Channing, D.D.* (Boston, 1880). She said WA condemned it and later did his best to destroy it (p. 342). 2. "Sad was I, ever to paint deprest, / Importunate and heavy Load" (Wordsworth, "Lines Composed at Grasmere, during a walk one Evening, after a stormy day, the Author having just read in a Newspaper that the dissolution of Mr. [Charles James] Fox was hourly expected" [1806], lines 9-10). WA's quoting these lines reflected his increasing occupation with the idea of death and apprehension that he was approaching the end of his own life during the last few weeks before it. That his faith in a life afterward was not altogether as firm as it appeared may also be reflected, since the last two stanzas of Wordsworth's poem, for all their professed comfort, seem to raise some question about it:

A Power is passing from the earth
To breathless Nature's dark abyss;

But when the great and good depart
What is it more than this—

That Man, who is from God sent forth,
Doth yet again to God return?—
Such ebb and flow must ever be,
Then wherefore should we mourn?

Undated Letters

354. From Jacob Bigelow and other members of the committee appointed by the Federal Street Congregational Society for erecting a monument to the memory of Channing.

[1843, after 2 October 1842]

[RHD said this letter was about a design by Washington Allston for a monument[1] to Channing in Mount Auburn Cemetery.[2]]

SOURCE: RHD, p. 36.

1. WA made drawings for the monument, which is about four feet high and eight feet square, which were put into Italian marble by the Boston stonecutter Alpheus Cary. 2. Bigelow was responsible for the foundation of the cemetery in 1831, in an effort to protect the health of the city, which was often endangered by irresponsible burials.

355. To Elizabeth Ellery Dana [After 1 June 1830][1]

Dear Betsey: Will you be so good as to see that the cows dont eat up my wife. Her grass petticoat naturally increases my anxiety when she goes from home.

W.A.

ADDRESSED: Miss E.E. Dana SOURCE: Manuscript.

1. The date of WA's marriage to Martha R. Dana.

356. To Isaac P. Davis [on or after 2 March, 1830][1]

My dear Sir: I accept Mr. Cushing's[2] invitation with great pleasure, and shall hold myself in readiness to attend you, on Saturday at five o'clock.

Yrs sincerely, / Wa. Allston

I.P. Davis Esquire. / Cambridge Port, 2 March.

ADDRESSED: Isaac P. Davis Esqre. / Boston. SOURCE: Manuscript. South Caroliniana Library, University of South Carolina.

1. The last known letter of WA's from Boston was 28 October 1829 and the first from Cambridgeport 1 March 1830. 2. Probably John Perkins Cushing (1787-1862), Boston merchant and philanthropist. He spent nearly thirty years in China as agent for the Perkins mercantile firm. After his return to Boston about 1829 he built a handsome mansion in Summer Street, administered by a staff of Chinese servants, and acquired an estate in Watertown, where he built a celebrated conservatory and where he finally resided. Paintings he owned were exhibited at the BA in 1829 and 1833.

357. To Cornelius Conway Felton [After 19 July 1838][1]

My dear Sir: I shall be very happy to see you and Mrs. Felton,[2] with Miss Higginson,[3] at half past one o'clock.

With sincere regard / Yrs, / Wa. Allston

Friday.

ADDRESSED: To / Professor Felton, / Cambridge. SOURCE: Manuscript, South Caroliniana Library, University of South Carolina.

1. The date of Felton's marriage. 2. Felton's first wife was the former Mary Whitney (d. 1845). 3. Probably either Anna or Louisa Higginson, daughters of Mrs. Stephen Higginson, whose sister-in-law was the widow of WA's brother-in-law Francis D. Channing and lived with her in Cambridge. Thomas Wentworth Higginson was their younger brother (Dana, 1:361, 2:571; Longfellow, 2:117, 217).

358. To Josiah Qunicy [Between 1819 and 1829][1]

Mr. Allston will have the honour to wait on Mr. Quincy on Friday next, agreeably to his obliging invitation.
Decbr 26.

ADDRESSED: To / The Honourable / Josiah Quincy. SOURCE: Manuscript, Manuscripts and Archives, Yale University Library.

1. WA became acquainted with Quincy in 1819, between which date and 1829, when he became president of Harvard, he could have been addressed as "honourable" in his capacity as a national and state legislator and mayor of Boston.

359. To Josiah Quincy [After 1829][1]

Mr. Allston presents his respects, and regrets that it will not be in his power to avail himself of President Quincy's obliging invitation to dinner on Thursday.
Cambridge Port, / Tuesday, Aug. 27th.

SOURCE: Manuscript, Yale Collection of American Literature, Beinecke Rare Book and Manuscript Library, Yale University.

1. Quincy became president of Harvard in 1829.

360. To George Ticknor [After 1823][1]

My dear Sir: I accept your very obliging invitation with great pleasure.

Yours sincerely / W. Allston.

December 31st.

ADDRESSED: Professor Ticknor, / Common Street. SOURCE: Manuscript, Miscellaneous Papers (Washington Allston); Rare Books and Manuscripts Division, the New York Public Library, Astor, Lenox and Tilden Foundations.

1. Ticknor moved to Common Street in 1823.

361. To ? [ca. 1835][1]

. . .

enclosed Letter for my [nephew George W.] Flagg, from his Mother that it might be sen[t] [page cut] be delivered to him.

. . .

I am, Sir, very respectfully,

your obedt servt, / Washington Allston.

SOURCE: Manuscript, Collection of Nathalia Wright.

1. This letter was possibly written to David Greenough asking that the letter to Flagg from his mother be sent to Horatio Greenough for delivery to him. Flagg was in Florence, where he was associated with Horatio, from late February or early March 1835 to the spring of 1836, when he went to England (Greenough, *Letters*, p. 188).

DEATH AND FUNERAL

Allston died in his home on 9 July, 1843 shortly after midnight. Richard Henry Dana described the occasion in detail in letters to Morse and Verplanck several days later. Besides his wife, Elizabeth E., Sarah A., and Charlotte Dana were there at the time, preparatory to going away for the summer. Allston came in from his studio about seven o'clock and was "serene, even cheerful, & playfully affectionate" throughout the evening. After all but Charlotte retired, he talked to her alone, wished he had "some keepsake" for her to take on her trip, put his arm around her and told her she was not only his niece but his child, there being relations nearer than those of blood. He kissed her forehead, lowered his head for her to kiss his cheek, looked upward, and said, "I want you to be perfect." Sitting down, he drew a chair for her near him, took her hand, and explained that he did not feel like talking, but every now and then he spoke in the same strain until they separated for the night. His last words to her were, "God bless you, my child." When he complained of a pain in his chest such as he had felt about three weeks earlier, she advised his taking something for it; he went upstairs and she retired. His wife offered to go down and prepare something but, saying he could do so as well, he went down again, took out his writing materials and put them on a table, sat down, and rested his feet on the hearth and his head on the back of the chair as he sometimes did when taking a nap. When she came in a few minutes later his eyes were still open, but they soon closed.[1]

The morning afterward his body, except for the brain, was examined by Dr. George Shattuck, Jr., and Dr. George Parkman, with Dr. Shattuck, Sr., in attendance. They found no one clear cause for death but a general disorder of several organs, the ossification of two arteries feeding the heart being the chief mark of disease. It was generally noted that his features were relaxed as they had not been for many years, and it was Richard Henry Dana's opinion that the "mental anguish" he had long been under was enough "to deepen disease, & at last to stop the working of the hand," adding, "Had not debt distressed him he might have been living now."[2]

The day after his death the Danas had the sculptor Edward A. Brackett take a mask of his features. Brackett had come to Boston in 1839, modeled a bust of Richard Henry Dana which Allston greatly admired, and long wanted to model one of Allston. From it he made a plaster cast, which Dana thought made Allston look as he did earlier "before disease and distress of mind had so preyed upon him." Robert F.W. Allston preferred it to Clevenger's and ordered a marble copy. It was executed in 1843-44. Brackett wrote a poem about his work, "Lines Suggested on Finishing a Bust of Allston," in which he depicted Allston as gazing

> Upwards unto the living light . . .
> As if thy very soul should seek,
> In that far distant maze,
> Communion with those heavenly forms,
> That, lifting to the sight
> Their golden wings and snowy robes
> Float in a sea of light.[3]

The funeral was held on 10 July at 7:30 P.M., being put at that hour for greater privacy. A service was said at the house by Albro and the church service read at the tomb by Dr. Alexander Vinton of St. Paul's Church. The procession was delayed until eight o'clock and reached the grave site in the churchyard on the Cambridge Common about eight-thirty. Those in attendance, besides the Dana and Channing families, included the Hastings, Quincy, and Willard families; the Gibsons; WA's classmates Knapp, Welles, and Lemuel Shaw; Sarah Gibbs, Waterston, Elizabeth Peabody, Sumner, Judge Story, Felton, Andrews Norton, Henry Dexter, and Benjamin Greene.[4]

A group of Harvard students were also there. Torchlight was used, and in the course of the evening the full moon came from under clouds, making the scene a spectacular one which many there long remembered and which others also took note of. Emerson wrote of the occasion to his brother William, mentioning the moonlight. Sophia (Peabody) Hawthorne, who noted that the first anniversary of her marriage had fallen on the day Allston died, referred to the "lustrous moon" and imagined that "Nature certainly arranged herself in her most heavenly guise, to bid him farewell." Her mother, who had informed her of Allston's death, exclaimed in an inadvertently appropriate figure of speech, "What a light is extinguished!" Margaret Fuller, who was on a trip through Illinois with Sarah and James Freeman Clarke at the time, returned to Chicago on 9 July, on which evening, she recorded, the sunset was "of a splendor and calmness" beyond any they saw and the twilight succeeding it "equally beautiful; soft, pathetic, but just so calm." It seemed to her when she afterward learned that was the day Allston died "as if the glorious pageant was not without connection with that event; at least it inspired similar emotions,—a heavenly gate closing a path adorned with shows well worthy Paradise"[5]

At least eight poems and three extended prose tributes to Allston were written on the occasion of his death. Three of the poems commemmorated the funeral: his nephew William Ellery Channing's "Allston's Funeral," in the *Dial* for October 1843; the Newburyport poet Hannah Flagg Gould's *The Burial of Allston: Dirge Written & Respectfully Inscribed to Mrs. Allston,* published in Boston in 1846; and Elihu Spencer's "Funeral of Allston," in *Graham's Magazine* for January 1852. The last was prefaced by a statement from a New York correspondent of the *Washington National Intelligencer* that it was "one of the most impressive ceremonies ever witnessed." Robert Weir's "Washington Allston" appeared in the *New York Evening Post* in July 1843; "Washington Allston," by Ixion, in the *New-York Tribune* for 13 July 1843; "On the Death of Washington Allston," by Henry T. Tuckerman in the *Boston Courier* in November 1843. According to Sweetser Christopher Pearse Cranch also wrote an obituary poem. Walter Channing's reminiscences, "Washington Allston," appeared in the *Christian World* in July 1843. In his review of Raczynski's *Histoire* in the *North American Review* for October 1843, Felton said his thoughts had been "irresistibly" drawn to the loss suffered in Allston's death and devoted the last several pages to an account of him. He called him "an artist in the truest and highest sense of the word," having "a finished literary education" and being familiar with the best authors in several languages, a writer of both poetry and the prose *Monaldi,* in which the style was "delicate," "melodious," and "picturesque," and a painter whose pictures, particularly *Beatrice, Rosalie,* and *Amy Robsart,* had "all nobleness of soul" and "the purity and elegance of conception" which were so strongly expressed in his writing. He described his character, appearance, manner, and social habits, noting his freedom from personal ambition and professional rivalry, his slender figure, pale countenance, "large hazel eye," waving hair, mild but warm manner, and gentle voice, which had become so weak in late years that it was necessary to sit near to hear what he said, and his nightly conversation, while smoking and drinking wine, of anecdote, criticism, and humor. Altogether, he seemed "a being from another world."[6]

In October 1843 the anonymous article "Washington Allston" in the *United States Democratic Review* also appeared, accompanied by an engraving of Brackett's recent bust of Allston. The author was probably a painter himself, judging from the emphasis put on Allston's practice in painting and specific suggestions about it. Apparently he was drawing on an acquaintance with Allston during later years, since he described not only his "tall, commanding, well-proportioned, and very erect" figure, his "gestures and frequent changes of position," animated expression, manner of opening the door and pouring a glass of wine with "high-bred courtesy," "elegance and polish," taste for fiction, and store of anecdotes, but also the "softened" lines of his face, his "long silver locks," his praise of Hiram Powers, his reading of metaphysical works, his declining health after 1841, and his hardly going out at all for some time before his death. He thus also wrote as though he had a fairly intimate knowledge of Allston's habits. John Greenough was one of several young painters who might have made such observations. He had little to say of Allston's early years, referring briefly to the exhibition of his paintings in 1839, though not as though he had been there, and to only three paintings: *Jeremiah, Spalatro's Vision of the Bloody Hand,* and *The Dead Man Restored.* But he called the last "Resuscitation of the young man on touching the bones of the prophet in the cave" in an unfamiliar way and drew on Walter Channing's account in describing Allston's receiving the first payment for it. He implied that Allston would be ranked chiefly as a historical painter, ignoring the female portraits for which he was increasingly recognized. He was surely writing from personal experience, however, when he declared, "If ever any man was a painter in his appearance that man was Allston," an appearance brought about by "an unwearied study of beauty." He had seen a picture of Fuseli, whom he said he had never seen himself, that reminded him of Allston, though wanting "a certain inward religious expression peculiar" to him. Of all critics, he thought Allston the one safe for a young artist to commit his designs to because of his fidelity yet kindness and sympathy, and he judged the epithet applied to him "Father of American Art" a just one.[7]

Allston was buried in the Dana family vault in the churchyard on the common in Cambridge. There are buried also his father-in-law Judge Francis Dana and most of the judge's immediate family, including his sons Richard Henry and Edmund T.[8]

In the administration of WA's estate Franklin Dexter and RHD, Jr., posted \$30,000 on 9 August 1843. His personal estate was inventoried as \$1,004.75 on 9 January 1844 and \$100.00 was added on 22 May 1844, being four-thirteenth parts in *Belshazzar's Feast,* the particulars being given by a committee consisting of Thomas Dwight, Thomas B. Curtis, and Henry Greenough. There was no real estate. The account was closed on 19 November 1844.[9]

1. Dana to Verplanck, 14 July 1843; Prime, pp. 468-69. 2. Ibid.; Dana, 1:174. 3. Brackett, *Twilight Hours* (1845). 4. Dana, 1:174-75. 5. Emerson, *Letters* 3:187; Lathrop, p. 59; Julian Hawthorne, 1:270; Fuller, *Summer on the Lakes, in 1843* (New York, 1844, p. 51. 6. *North American Review* 57 (Oct. 1843): 369-99. 7. *United States Democratic Review* 13 (Oct. 1843): 431-34. 8. H.W.L. Dana, "The Dana Saga," Cambridge Historical Society Publications, 26 (Cambridge, Mass., 1941), p. 31. 9. Commonwealth of Massachusetts, Middlesex County Probate, East Cambridge, 185:637; 260:278.

OUTLINES & SKETCHES

When the contents of Allston's studio were examined a few days after his death, there were so many unfinished pieces of significance, especially sketches and drawings, besides *Belshazzar's Feast,* that several person suggested an attempt be made to preserve at least some of them. Franklin Dexter proposed to have engravings of them all put in a volume as outlines to be called "Allston's Compositions." Accordingly he and Stephen H. Perkins, who was a nephew of Thomas H. Perkins, made arrangements for the publication of many of them. The resulting work was *Outlines & Sketches by Washington Allston, Engraved by J. and S.W. Cheney,* published in Boston in 1850, copyrighted by Stephen H. Perkins.

The prefatory note was dated 1 January 1850 and was written by Seth Cheney. On the title page was an engraving of a profile of the portrait of Allston by Charles B. King (Arthur Dexter, p. 393). It consisted of eighteen engravings, all from drawings or outlines by him in chalk, ink, pencil, or umber. Only one—*Uriel in the Sun* was of a completed work in its entirety. Four others were of figures from another completed work—*Jacob's Dream.* All the others were of unfinished pieces: *Gabriel Setting the Watch at the Gates of Paradise; The Sibyl; Dido and Anna; Heliodorus; Fairies on the Sea Shore; Titania's Court; Girl in Male Costume* (*Girl in Persian Costume*); *Ship in a Squall; The Prodigal Son,* from Luke 15:13-19; and *Prometheus*. These are the only known versions of *Gabriel Setting the Watch* and *Fairies on the Sea Shore*. In a few copies "Michael" appears instead of "Gabriel." Two were lithographs engraved on stone by John Cheney. Seth Cheney engraved *Heliodorus* and some others entirely. Most were done with a dry point, and some experiments were made in the process "to represent the technical peculiarities of the originals." When it was necessary to reduce the figures in some of the originals, the daguerreotype was used, by which the image was conveyed to the plates and there fixed by tracing the lines through the silver. Some of the originals had been drawn with a double line, and when asked which would be reproduced, Seth said he would give both, explaining, "I will never take it upon me to leave out anything of Allston's."[1]

1. Cheney, *Memoir of Seth W. Cheney, Artist* (Boston, 1881), pp. 99-100.

APPENDICES

Appendix 1
Biographical Notes

These notes include recipients of letters written by Allston, writers of letters to him, certain persons named in the correspondence, and a few not named who made notable observations about him from personal acquaintance or were intimately associated with him.

Albro, John Adams (1799-1866), clergyman. A native of Newport, Rhode Island, he graduated from Andover Theological Seminary. From 1835 to 1865 he was minister of the Church of the Shepard Congregational Society in Cambridge, Massachusetts (Paige, p. 303). When he heard of Allston's death, he said, the news came upon him "like a thunder clap"; he called Allston "a glorious man—a glorious man" and recollected their last interview about two weeks before. Allston had spoken of his failing condition and he had said, "I hope that as your outward man perishes, your inward man is renewed," after which Allston began to speak of his religious feelings and experiences, talking "gloriously, not upon abstractions & dogmas but upon the religion in a man's own soul," dwelling particularly on the doctrine of the Atonement. He performed the service at the house on the day of Allston's burial, expressing in his prayer the hope that Allston's belief in that doctrine would be remembered by the community and his loss blessed. A week later he preached a sermon in which he showed that Allston's piety was active in nature, in spite of his not being involved in public religious affairs, and said that he would never forget the "energy & emotion" with which Allston spoke to him on his last visit of faith in the Atonement (Dana, 1:173, 175, 182). It was printed as *The Blessedness of Those Who Die in the Lord. A Sermon Occasioned by the death of Washington Allston, delivered in the Church of the Shepard Society* (Boston, 1845) and was dedicated to Mrs. Allston.

Allston, Ann (Channing) (1778-1815), Allston's first wife, sister of W.E. and Walter Channing. He painted a miniature and a full-size portrait of her; made two drawings of her head, one in pencil and one in chalk, and a drawing of an ear (ca. 1812-15); and possibly painted her features in *The Angel Releasing St. Peter from Prison*, *Rebecca at the Well*, and *Beatrice*. She may also have inspired *The Valentine*. He wrote more than one poem about her.

Allston, Elizabeth (1766-?). See Gibbes, Elizabeth (Allston)

Allston, Martha Remington (Dana) (1784-1862), Allston's second wife. She was a sister of Richard H. and Edmund T. Dana and a cousin of his first wife (Dana, vol. 3, "The Dana Family").

Alston, Mary (Allston) Young (1778-1841), Allston's sister. She married Thomas Young in 1800 and, after his death, William Algernon Alston in 1806 (Groves, pp. 33, 56). Allston wrote a poem for her: "To my sister. Lines suggested by the recollection of a little bird, carved by the writer, when six years old, out of a green stalk of the Indian corn, as a parting gift to his sister," in which he said that, though a rude toy, the bird, being wrought in childhood by love, illustrated the truth "That all things pure must needs immortal youth / Hold as their heritage, though born of Earth" and declared that the life of its "perennial form" in memory was truer than that he could now with "learned" Art impart (*LA*, pp. 322-23). In later years, after her second marriage, she was described by a nephew as a person who "did not enjoy much rest," "an energetic woman," on whom the care of her household devolved, every morning holding a levee for the Negroes, to whom she gave medicine for their ailments whenever needed and, twice a year, clothing (Allston, p. 85).

Allston, Robert Francis Withers (1801-64), son of Benjamin Allston, Allston's half-brother, and Charlotte Anne Allston, who were second cousins (Groves, p. 33). After graduating from the U.S. Military Academy and serving briefly in the Coast Survey, he devoted his time to the family's rice plantation and became active in politics. When the state militia was formed in December 1832 in connection with the nullification issue, he was made colonel in it and subsequently adjutant-general. He was governor of South Carolina from 1856 to 1858. According to Sweetser, he more than once asked Allston to paint a picture for him but Allston always refused, saying he had to paint for money and presumably was unwilling to charge a relative. He visited Allston at least twice and gave a vivid description of the second visit, in September 1838. At the suggestion of Mrs. Allston he walked to Allston's painting room about one o'clock and found him warming it with a coal fireplace and stove previous to commencing work, having just finished his cigar. Allston brushed a place for Robert's hat, for "every part of the room was covered with dust, as if it had not been swept in 12 months." Allston said he had nothing but sketches to show, showed several heads, which he said he kept for his own study, and at length pulled out "from the apparent rubbish" one of a storm and shipwreck at sea, presumably *Galen*, which was "very spirited," his seas being "always fine." He invited Robert to dine a few days later at four o'clock, explaining that his ordinary dinner hour was seven, since he liked "to work up all the day-light" before dining and then sit up with a friend, if one was present, and a cigar until one or two. Allston had grown much older since Robert last saw him and had lost much flesh, his head being "quite white and venerable," but "his noble countenance" was as "placid, mild, and intelligent as ever" (Easterby, pp. 82-83). In September 1843, after Allston's death, Robert visited Cambridge again, at which time Richard H. Dana, Jr., took him to Allston's studio and described him at length, saying that no one seemed more affected by what he saw, that his feeling was "genuine, of a kind wh. he endeavored to control conceal," and that he "venerated loved" Allston "in a manner rare even among the veneration lovers of that man." He requested that a sketch by Allston be preserved for him at any price and seemed to wish for *Christ Healing the Sick* (1:219-20).

Allston, William, Jr. (?-1781), Allston's father. He married Anne Simmons in 1763 and had five children by her; on 19 January 1775, after her death, he married Rachel Moore and had two children by her (Groves, pp. 27, 32, 33). He was called "Gentleman Billy" to distinguish him from another William Allston (later, Alston), called "King Billy." During the Revolution he was a captain in General Francis Marion's Brigade, which existed from 1780 to 1792, at which time he was said to be from "True-Blue" on Little River in All Saints' Parish. He was reported to be "a firm patriot and good soldier," who might be enumerated among the martyrs to the American cause, since following the Battle of Cowpens he contracted a fever from which he died shortly after returning home (William Dobein James, *A Sketch of the Life of Brig. Gen. Francis Marion and a History of his Brigade From its Rise in June 1780 until December 1782. With Descriptions of Characters and Scenes not heretofore Published* [Charleston, South Carolina, 1821], p. 151). His family believed he was poisoned by a trusted servant. Just before his death the infant Washington was brought to him at his request and he predicted that whoever lived to see him grow up would see a great man.

Alston, William Algernon (1782-1860) a cousin of Allston's and owner of the plantation Rose Hill on Waccamaw Neck in South Carolina. He married as his second wife Allston's sister Mary. One of his nephews described him as appearing to be "a quick easy going man" and, his family being large, the plantation as being "never dull" (Allston, pp. 38-41, 85).

Allston, William Moore (1781-1844), Allston's brother, a posthumous child (Groves, p. 33). In 1790 he attended, with Washington, the school in Newport, Rhode Island, operated by Richard Rogers, and visited England for a short time early in 1801. He was living in Boston at the time Allston returned from Italy in 1808 and for a few years was a merchant there (*Boston Daily Advertiser,* October 1818; *Boston City Directorys* for 1818, 1820). Later he lived in Newport. He married Rogers's daughter Ann. Richard H. Dana thought he owned Allston's study for *Catherine and Petruchio* (RHD, p. 15).

Amory, Mary (Preble) a Newport resident after the death of Nathaniel Amory, her husband. According to Sweetser, Allston gave her his self-portrait (1805).

Amory, Nathaniel (1777-1842), a businessman for many years with the firm of Nott and Callendar. He lived at a large estate in Watertown, Massachusetts, served as naval agent at Pensacola, Florida, from 1827 to 1829, and passed his last years in Newport ("Memoirs of the Family of Amory," *NEHGR,* 10 (1856): 64). He owned Allston's self-portrait and for a while his *Edwin* and was the largest subscriber to the Tripartite Agreement. His daughter Jane R. married John E. Allston, a nephew of Washington Allston (*Rhode Island Republican,* 26 Aug. 1840).

Andrews, William Turrell (1794-1879), a graduate of Harvard in 1812, was a Boston lawyer who held several offices in civic and cultural associations in the city. He was a trustee of the BA for many years (*Memorial Biographies of the New-England Historic Genealogical Society* [Boston: The Society, 1907], 7 (1871-1880), pp. 344-45.

Angerstein, John Julius (d. 1823), was a Russian who came to London as a boy about 1750, became a broker, founded what was later Lloyd's of London, and with the advice of West assembled a valuable collection of paintings. It was sold to the government in 1824 and with others given by Beaumont and the BI formed the nucleas of the National Gallery of Art, founded in that year (Alberts, pp. 328-329).

Avery, John (1739-1806), lived most of his life in Boston but moved about a good deal. He was active in various capacities during the Revolution and served as the first secretary of the state of Massachusetts from 1780 until his death (Clifford K. Shipton, ed., *Sibley's Harvard Graduates, 1756-1760,* 14 ([Boston, 1968]: 384-89).

Baldwin, Loammi (1780-1838), known as the father of civil engineering in America. He was in Europe in 1807 and 1823-24 studying public works. In 1825 he was with Allston on the Board of Artists of the Bunker Hill Monument Association to choose a design for the monument. He was called "Colonel" probably because of his position as engineer in charge of repairing old forts and constructing Fort Strong on Noddle's Island in 1814 as defenses against attacks by British ships. He owned Allston's *The Flight of Florimel, Polyphemus,* and for a while *Diana and Her Nymphs* and was a subscriber to the Tripartite Agreement. Allston painted his portrait.

Ball, Hugh Swinton (1808-38), of Mephaw House near Charleston, South Carolina, where he had a sizable art collection. His wife, Anne Elizabeth Channing, was a first cousin of Allston's first wife. The couple, who had a summer home in Newport, Rhode Island, perished in the explosion of the ship *Pulaski* off the coast of North Carolina (Mabel L. Webber, copier, "Inscriptions from the Churchyard at Strawberry Chapel," *SCHGM* 21 [Jan. 1920]: 163; Park, 1:206-207).

Beaumont, Andrew (1790-1853), a member of the House of Representatives from Pennsylvania from 1833 to 1837.

Beaumont, Sir George Howland (1753-1837), a connoisseur and collector of art, patron of artists, and amateur painter. He was a founder and for many years a director of the British Institution and on familiar terms with the leading artists, writers, and scientific men of his day, particularly with Wordsworth. Coleridge introduced him to Allston sometime before 29 April 1812. Soon afterward the two dined at his house in London, and subsequently Allston was often there, joined by Coleridge, Wordsworth, and others. He did not seem to think very highly of the first painting by Allston which he saw (*The Love Letters of William and Mary Wordsworth,* p. 110), but when he visited Allston's studio in August he was so taken by the study for *The Dead Man Restored* that he commissioned an altar painting, *The Angel Releasing St. Peter from Prison,* for the parish church at Ashby-de-la-Zouch, where he was rebuilding his family's Coleorton Hall. He also acquired in 1816 a landscape by Allston on Coleridge's recommendation, but which one is not known.

Beechey, Sir William (1783-1839), English portrait painter. He was usually kind to young artists but once when Allston showed him one of his portraits commented, "Sir, that is not flesh but mud; it is as much mud as if you had taken it out of the kennel and painted your picture" (Leslie, p. 186). Among Allston's later anecdotes of him recorded by Henry Greenough was of his telling Gainsborough that he had discovered how to paint into glazing and of Gainsborough replying that until then he had thought he was the only man in England who knew the secret.

Bigelow, Jacob (1787-1879), Boston botanist and physician. At one time he owned Allston's *Moonlit Landscape (Moonlight).*

Bowen, Charles, Boston publisher. From 1825 to 1831 he owned and published, with others, the *North American Review.* From 1830 to 1832 he was in business with Frederick T. Gray in the firm of Gray and Bowen, and from 1833 to 1837 by himself (Mott, *A History of American Magazines, 1741-1850,* p. 219; *Boston City Directory*).

Bridgen, Mr. and Mrs. He was a London postmaster (Walter Channing), who died in 1824. He was noted, Leslie said, for having a bad temper and mistreating his wife, though he was devoted to her and remorseful afterward (Prime, p. 91). She took lodgers at 2 Cleveland Street in London, opposite 8 Buckingham Place, where Allston lived for a time, and he, Leslie, and Morse ate at her establishment. For many years she had artists, whom she liked because, she said, "they were so innocent." Allston began two portraits of her but did not complete either one (Neal, *Observations on American Art,* pp. 54, 86).

Brown, James (1800-55), Boston publisher. He formed a partnership with Charles C. Little in 1837, known for a while as Charles C. Little & Company. Later, the name changed to Little Brown, and finally to Little, Brown & Company.

Brown, Solyman (1790-1876), poet, teacher, clergyman, and one of the founders of dentistry as a profession in America. He also exhibited some talent as a sculptor and a painter in oil. He spent most of his life in New York City.

Brown, Thomas, Jr., colorman to artists, called "Young Brown" to distinguish him from his father, Thomas, Sr. He had an establishment at 163 High Holborn in London from 1818 to 1848 (*Post-Office London Directorys*). His gloomy and melancholy disposition was attributed by Royal Academy students to unrequited love (Whitley, *Artists and Their Friends in England, 1700-1799* 1:336).

Brown, Thomas, Sr., colorman to artists. He was in business on Goswell Street in London from the late eighteenth century to 1824. He, his predecessor, and his son Thomas, Jr., between them supplied all the presidents of the Royal Academies with materials, as well as other artists and many Royal Academy students. He was known as "Old Brown" to distinguish him from his son, from whom he also differed in having a genial disposition (*Post-Office London Directorys;* Whitley, *Artists and Their Friends in England, 1700-1799* 1:335-36).

Bryant, William Cullen (1794-1878), poet and editor. A native of Massachusetts, he spent most of his life in New York, where he was associated with the *Evening Post* from 1827 until his death, from 1829 as editor-in-chief. He and Allston met in August 1821 in Cambridge, when he delivered the address at the meeting of the Phi Beta Kappa Society at Harvard. Richard H. Dana remembered the occasion long afterward as being in Trowbridge Hall, at which time he, Edmund T. Dana, Channing, and Willard Phillips were also present (Parke Godwin, *A Biography of William Cullen Bryant with Extracts from His Private Correspondence* [New York, 1883], 2:126]. When Bryant visited Cambridge again in August 1826 he and Allston talked of their mutual friend Gulian C. Verplanck, and when in 1828 it was proposed that the vacant panels in the rotunda of the Capitol be painted, he urged that Allston be commissioned for one of them, "while he is not only alive but in the vigor of his genius," as he put the matter to Verplanck (*Bryant,* 1:109).

He often sent regards to Allston through Dana, asked Dana to introduce Edward A. Brackett to Allston, and negotiated for the distribution by the American Art-Union of fifty sets of Allston's *Outlines & Sketches.* In his *Selections from the American Poets* (1840) he included Allston's "The Sylphs of the Seasons," "The Paint-King," and "Rosalie." In the letter he wrote Richard Henry Dana after Allston's death he compared that occurrence to the experience of the pilgrims in Bunyan's *Pilgrims' Progress,* who in passing over the river to the land beyond seemed hardly to dip their feet in the waters, recalled that artists looked up to Allston's judgment, sure that what they had done well would please him, and said it was a credit to the age that it could discern the worth of such a man. When he met Leigh Hunt in England in 1845 he was "constantly reminded" of Allston by Hunt's "erect attitude and his easy equable manner of talking," though Hunt's voice in comparison with Allston's was "harsh." He thought it "well done" of Richard Henry Dana, Jr., to publish Allston's *Lectures on Art,* commenting, "We wanted another edition of his poems . . . and the lectures were needed by our artists and our judges of art, to teach them how to think on such subjects, how to look at nature and how to compare nature with the representations of her on canvas" (Bryant 1:109, 112, 271, 291; 2:146, 255, 262, 243, 335; 3:131-32). Allston admired Bryant's poetry, saying of "Green River" when he read it over in the summer of 1838, "That man is a true poet, his *heart* is in it. What he gives you comes from his own spirit" (Godwin, 1:364). He owned a copy of Bryant's *Poems* (Cambridge, Mass., 1821). Possibly he wrote at least one letter to Bryant, which has not been preserved; on an otherwise empty sheet of notes by Richard Henry Dana appears "Rough of Letter to Bryant, about Belshazzar." William Ware thought there was much "closely kindred" in the "genius" of Allston and Bryant, observing that "both love, prefer the calm, the thoughtful, the contemplative" and that they depicted "oftener than any other themes, this silence, rest, deep repose of nature" (*Lectures*, p. 171).

Channing, Ruth (Gibbs) (1798-1881). She was a daughter of George Gibbs and Mary Channing, who was a sister of William Ellery Channing's father William. She and W.E. Channing were married in 1814 (George Gibbs, *The Gibbs Family of Rhode Island and Some Related Families* [New York, 1833], p. 16; *Vital Records of Cambridge, Massachusetts, to the Year 1850* [Boston, 1914], 1:129; Dean and Dudley, p. 319).

Channing, Walter (1786-1876), Boston physician and Allston's brother-in-law by his first marriage. After graduating from Harvard in 1808 he decided at first to become an artist. Allston was probably referring to him when he said art had lost one of his acquaintances to medicine. He was a member of the faculty of the Harvard Medical School for nearly forty years. A few weeks after Allston's death, he wrote an account of him, printed in *The Christian World* for 22 July 1843, which was based, he said, on an acquaintance of "between forty and fifty years," during which time, except for their residences abroad, he had "never been long removed from his society." He described Allston's years at Harvard; gave some of his opinions of the sculptors of antiquity; cited his practice of modeling and of study at night; called him one of the "most industrious" men he had ever known; gave examples of his financial difficulties; summarized what he said of his technique; praised his late female portraits and his landscapes; declared him "the most *individual* man" he had ever known; cited examples of his generous judgment of others; and noted his religious sensibility and reading of religious books. A few days before it appeared he read it to Richard H. Dana, Jr., "with great feeling," "several times unable to proceed from emotion," and Dana was reduced to tears twice, telling him it was "beautiful, touching, & calculated to make the public feel deeply & feel truly" about Allston (Dana 1:182). He owned Allston's *Catherine and Petruchio, Grumio and the Tailor,* drawing of a maniac crushing a dove, illustration for Schiller's *Robbers,* a watercolor painted in college, and at one time his illustration for Walpole's *Mysteries of Udolpho*.

Channing, William Ellery (1780-1842), Unitarian clergyman, founder of the Unitarian movement in America, and minister of the Federal Street Church in Boston from 1803 until his death. He was Allston's brother-in-law by his first marriage and one of his closest friends throughout his life. They met in Newport, Rhode Island, where they attended the same school, and were students at Harvard at the same time. During his college years Channing lived with his uncle and aunt, Francis and Elizabeth (Channing) Dana, the parents of Allston's friends Richard H. and Edmund T. Dana, in Cambridge. He often stopped at Allston's room, once received from him an illustration for an assignment in mensuration, consisting of pyramids of figures heaped on one another's shoulders, all caricatures of the professors and tutors, which got an amused reception when presented in class, and in his junior year wrote Allston expressing his indecision about the choice of a profession (*Memoir of William Ellery Channing* 1:50, 72). In later years he pointed out to Elizabeth Peabody some of Allston's early haunts in Newport, recalled that he stayed within doors to paint, said that he was inspired by reverence for Allston from boyhood and that every picture he brought out was an event to him. Though he customarily retired at nine o'clock, he left word to be called whenever Allston came visiting, which was always after ten, and would sit up with him until one or two (Peabody, *Reminiscences of Channing*, pp. 331-32, 25). He often said to Richard Henry Dana that what was done for Allston was done for art and the world for ages to come.

Allston's description of Channing to Leslie was drawn, Leslie said, "by a most affectionate hand" (Leslie to Allston, 18 July 1823). He valued no one's judgment of a work of art, he declared, so much as Channing's. At the news of Channing's death he was deeply affected, saying that though they did not think alike about everything they never spoke of their differences, and exclaiming, "Dr. Channing was a good man! an excellent man! . . . I loved him!" (Peabody, *Reminiscences of Channing*, pp. 449-50). Presumably the major subject on which they differed was religion, Allston being a Trinitarian. He painted Channing's portrait and designed the monument to him in Mount Auburn Cemetery in Cambridge. Channing owned the portrait of his wife painted by Allston. Allston owned a copy of Channing's *Self-Culture* (Boston, 1838).

Channing, William Henry (1810-84), son of Francis Dana Channing, who was a brother of Allston's first wife. He graduated from Harvard in 1829, became a writer and clergyman, and in the 1840s was invited to become pastor of the Unitarian Church in Ranshaw Street in Liverpool (Dean and Dudley, p. 319).

Cheney, John (1801-85), engraver. From 1826 to 1828 and 1834 to 1837 he worked in Boston. He went abroad apparently at the end of 1830, staying in England for two years and subsequently in Paris. He engraved two of Allston's paintings and two of the pieces in his *Outlines & Sketches*.

Cheney, Seth Wells (1810-56), crayon artist and engraver, brother of John Cheney. He engraved one of Allston's paintings and all but two of the pieces in *Outlines & Sketches*. After Allston's death he wrote John that when he thought of "all those great minds, Channing and Allston, living and trusting, all their thought and actions elevated by, and dying at last in some religious faith" he was disposed to despise himself for doubting its truth. He looked back at Allston's works "with the greatest pleasure" and rejoiced that after leaving the works of art in Europe, from which he wrote, he should have them "to fall back upon" (Cheney, *Memoir of Seth W. Cheney, Artist*, pp. 79-81).

Clarke, Sarah Anne (1808-96), landscape and portrait painter. She was a sister of James Freeman Clarke and a close friend of Sophia Peabody and Margaret Fuller (Emerson, *Letters* 3:198, 4:352). In the summer of 1832 she took two of her paintings to Allston, who assured her, she said, "with no hesitation," that she could make landscape painting her profession. In 1838 she felt torn between the advice of Allston and that of Emerson, who told her that her first and highest duty was to her own "instincts" and that Allston was not a "Titanic genius" but "an inarticulate sound." She called Margaret Fuller's review of Allston's 1839 exhibition a "piece of dogmatism" and wrote a letter to Emerson rejecting the objection there to the subject of *The Dead Man Restored*. Her brother James Freeman Clarke at first thought she was the author of the review but also scolded Margaret Fuller for her "audacity" in accusing Allston of "want of force" (Joel Myerson, " 'A True and High Minded Person': Transcendentalist Sarah Clarke," *Southwest Review* 59 [1974]: 164, 169, 171, 172). She owned a copy of *Monaldi* soon after it was published. Many years after Allston's death she wrote an article about him, "Our First Great Painter, and His Works" *Atlantic Monthly* 5 [1865]: 129-40), in which she described his chief landscapes, which were "poetic in the truest sense," and female heads and figures, which displayed "his peculiar genius." She analyzed his coloring and his process of first inlaying his pictures in solid crude color with a medium that hardened like stone and leaving them for months and even years to dry before finishing them with glazing. In particular she referred to "those strange eyes that Allson loved to paint,—eyes which see verities, not objects," looking "not into space, but into spirit."

Cogdell, John Stevens (or Stephano) (1778-1847), sculptor, painter, and lawyer. A native of Charleston, South Carolina he was admitted to the bar at an early age, but during a trip to Europe for his health in 1800 his interest in art was encouraged by the works he saw, particularly in Italy, and on his return he took up painting and drawing as well as the practice of law. He and Allston possibly first met in the spring of 1801 in Charleston. On his second visit to Boston, in October 1825, Allston persuaded him to attempt modeling in clay. The following year, when he again visited the city, he studied anatomy and thereafter executed a number of busts (Dunlap, 2:218, 219). He was the only subscriber to the Tripartite Agreement who was not a resident of Boston. During the last two decades of Allston's life he was his chief correspondent in America. Though acknowledging Allston's encouragement, he was capable of jealousy. "I am sorry the great Alston [*sic*] did not condescend to write one line to the humble Cogdell," he wrote Samuel F.B. Morse on an occasion when Morse apparently conveyed to him some complimentary remarks about him in a letter received from Allston (Sept. 1819, Morse Papers, LC).

Cole, Thomas (1801-48), landscape and allegorical painter. Born in England, he came to America with his family in 1819. Eventually he settled in Catskill, New York, and became the leading member of the Hudson River school of landscape painters. He and Allston first met in 1828, probably in the fall, when Cole made a trip to the White Mountains in New Hampshire. He was probably the young artist to whom Allston gave advice personally, presumably at that time, as recorded by Henry Greenough in his letter to Richard Henry Dana about Allston's method of painting. Allston paid the young artist some compliments, assuring him he was "in the right road" (Flagg, p. 197) and praising the old masters for study, and went on to discuss the importance of drawing to an artist, his own practice in doing so, the necessity of an artist's following his inner voice, and his own love of his art.

Cole visited Allston again in later years, probably about the time he made a trip to Europe in 1841-42. Possibly it was then that Emerson heard he said no one in America could paint a hand like Allston (Emerson, *Journals and Miscellaneous Notebooks* 7:314). At the time of Allston's death he wrote a lengthy evaluation of him in his journal, beginning, "Allston is dead! As a man he was beloved by all who were so fortunate as to be acquainted with him. It was not my lot to have a very great intercourse with him; that which I had has caused me to regret his loss exceedingly." As an artist, he wrote, Allston was "truly distinguished" and his works would never cease to be considered great, his taste was "pure, and elevated far above that of most of his contemporaries," and he "always aimed at the highest beauty, both of execution and sentiment, ever considering the former as the servant of the latter." He singled out *The Dead Man Restored, Miriam,* some of the smaller pictures painted in later years, and the sketches and half-finished pictures seen in his studio as being "among his finest works," "exquisite" and "charming." He also described Allston in person, as being "about the middle size, and when I knew him, spare and almost emaciated," with a countenance "pale, marked with deep lines, and full of mobility," "very prominent" eyes, a "retreating" forehead, his hair "falling on his shoulders in silvery ringlets," his walk "peculiar, a sort of springing gait, as though his spirit could scarcely be kept from rising by its mortal cumbrance." At the end of the century he inscribed a poem, presumably his own, entitled "A Sunset," describing the subject in terms of angels' wings, which was apparently inspired by Allston's death (Noble, pp. 350-52).

Coleridge, Samuel Taylor (1772-1834), English poet and critic. He was the greatest of all the personal influences on Allston's thought and the closest to him of all those in the romantic tradition of which he was a part. They first met in Rome almost immediately after Coleridge arrived, Coleridge establishing himself by 31 December 1805 in the neighborhood of the Piazza di Spagna near Allston, and the two were together almost daily until Coleridge left the city in May 1806. They associated nearly exclusively with artists, visited churches and museums, and took occasional trips into the Campagna. It was at Allston's suggestion that Coleridge spent three weeks with him at Olevano in February and March 1806 to avoid being apprehended when the French army entered Rome. Shortly after he returned to England he said that he had acquired "more insight into the fine arts" during his time in Rome, where he had planned to stay only three days, than he could have in England in twenty years (*Collected Letters* 2:623). Among the works of art they saw together he remembered particularly Michelangelo's *Last Judgment,* Raphael's frescoes in the Farnese Palace, and presumably paintings in the Church of Trinità dei Monti. He greatly admired Allston's *Diana and Her Nymphs,* of which he thought it "not too much to say—quam qui non amat, illum omnes et Mussae et Veneres odere." He said it proved "How exquisitely *picturesque* . . . (in the strictest sense of the word)" was the effect of the mountains and their diversities around Olevano, wrote a detailed description of it in his notebook, and proposed to compose a poem about it to be addressed: "To Alston After the formation of a new acquaintance formed by some weeks or months uninterrupted Communion worthy of all our esteem, affection & perhaps admiration, an intervening Absence—whether we meet again or only write—raises it into friendship, and encourages the modesty of our nature, impelling us to assume the language and express all the feelings, of an established attachment." He quoted Allston, with his penchant for making and remembering pithy phases, as saying that a certain painter "works too much with his pipe in his mouth—looks too much at the particular Thing, instead of overlooking—ubersehen" and that a Negro in America once described a pig he had sold in the words, "He's little, but he damn'd old" (*Notebooks* 2:2759, 2796, 2805, 2909, 2792).

Their next and longest association was during Allston's second stay in England, from 1811 to 1818. Coleridge lived for most of this time in or near London and was in Bristol in October and November 1813 and from April to September 1814, during part of which time Allston was there also. He was engaged in issuing a new edition of *The Friend,* writing essays for the *Courier* (London), publishing some half-dozen volumes, including *Biographia*

Literaria, and lecturing on a variety of literary, political, and social subjects. In London he was an almost daily visitor to Allston's studio, where Leslie and Morse remembered his conversation. When his play *Remorse* opened at the Drury Lane Theater on 23 January 1813 he was accompanied to the performance by Allston, Leslie, Morse, and Charles B. King (Prime, p. 53). Through him Allston met many of the most prominent writers and art patrons in England, and he said, Richard Henry Dana, Jr., recollected, that he could have introduced all the writers in London but did not think them worth Allston's while.

During their association in Bristol he was particularly sensitive about their relationship, complaining of Allston's insistence on being an American and embarrassing him on one occasion by admonishing him to consider the world his country and England his home. He blamed Mrs. Allston, whom he called the "little Hydatid," for encouraging Allston in identifying himself with Americans; he accused her of keeping him from visiting Allston, though Allston could visit him, and wished she were as disagreeable as his wife so that Allston could hate her. When Allston did not write him from London during the early part of 1814 he felt he had "altogether forgot" him. He was nevertheless deeply sympathetic throughout Allston's illness and financial losses at that time and supportive of the exhibition of his paintings in Bristol. Probably it was after Mrs. Allston's death in 1815 that they traveled together to Scotland and spent most of a day at Calne and that Allston stayed for days at a time at Highgate, where Coleridge moved in April 1816 (*Collected Letters,* 3:518, 492).

Coleridge admired Allston's painting during that period, particularly *The Dead Man Restored,* and suggested the title for *The Sisters.* He also admired Allston's poetry and incorporated his poem "America to Great Britain" in his *Sibylline Leaves* (1817), with the note, "this poem, by an American gentleman, a valued and dear friend, I communicate to the reader for its moral, no less than its patriotic Spirit." Allston himself said in a footnote to the poem that it alluded "to the moral union of the two countries" (*LA,* p. 292). In the margin of his own copy Coleridge wrote beside the poem, "By Washington Allston, a painter born to renew the fifteenth century" (Longfellow National Historic Site).

After Allston's return to America Coleridge described him to Leslie as a man of "high & rare Genius . . . whether I contemplate him in the character of a Poet, a Painter, or a philosophic Analyst" (*Collected Letters,* 492; 5:208).

In the account of himself he wrote for Dunlap, Allston described the great impression Coleridge made on him, beginning with their Roman acquaintance. His portraits of Coleridge, gift to him of *The Adoration of the Magi,* and poem about him particularly attest to his feeling. He named the Queen of Fairies in "The Paint-King" Geraldine, which was the name of the bewitched lady in "Christabel"; quoted from "The Rime of the Ancient Mariner" in *Monaldi* and in his lecture "Art" and alluded to a passage in it in his poem "The Angel and the Nightingale"; and in that poem he paraphrased Coleridge's poem, "The Nightingale." His regard for Coleridge's writings is also reflected in the title of his painting *The Sisters* and in both the painting *The Spanish Girl in Reverie* and the poem "The Spanish Maid." Richard Henry Dana, Jr., recollected hearing Allston tell many anecdotes about Coleridge, several of them occurring when they were traveling together in Italy, England, and Scotland and centering on Coleridge's repartee in conversation. When he was in the mood to exercise it, Allston thought, there were no bounds to Coleridge's wit (Leslie, p. 194). He often said, Dana recollected, that Coleridge had been of the greatest advantage to his mind in every way—in his art, poetry, general opinions, and religion.

Allston owned a number of works by Coleridge: *Confessions of an Inquiring Spirit,* ed.

Henry N. Coleridge (London, 1840); *Letters, Conversations and Recollections of S.T. Coleridge,* ed. Thomas Allsop, 2 vols. (New York, 1836); *Poems,* 3d ed. (London, 1803); *Remorse, A Tragedy* (London, 1813); *Specimens of the Table Talk of the Late Samuel Taylor Coleridge,* ed. Henry N. Coleridge, 2 vols. (London, 1817); *Zapolya: A Christmas Tale in Two Parts* (London, 1817); and *Lyrical Ballads with a few other poems,* by Coleridge and Wordsworth (London, 1798).

The area in which Allston and Coleridge were most congenial and most comparable was aesthetic theory. As philosophers both were generally in the Platonic tradition, most notably represented at the time by contemporary German idealism. There were significant differences between them, however, Coleridge being closer to the Germans and Allston more of a Realist. Allston was probably led by Coleridge to develop his thought by their conversations and by Coleridge's writings during the years they were together in England. Coleridge, primarily interested in the nature of poetry, turned his attention to the fine arts after meeting Allston, though only briefly. His aesthetic opinions were expressed chiefly in the years of their association, in *Essay on Taste* (1810), *Essay on Beauty* (1818), *On the Principles of Genial Criticism* (1814), and in a few chapters in *Biographia Literaria.* Allston's philosophy, set forth in his late lectures on art, was essentially an independent one. The more metaphysical parts of them, however, "Preliminary Note—Ideas" and "Introductory Discourse," are comparable in certain particulars to chapter 13 of *Biographia Literaria,* "On the Imagination, or Esemplastic Power." Both regarded art, like most romantics, as a combination of subject and object or "Ideas" (Allston's term) and "Nature" (Coleridge's term), whose "corrective" or "assimilant" (terms used by both) was predetermined or passive until synthesized by a *tertium aliquid* (a term used by both), which Coleridge called the "Primary Imagination" or "living Power," manifested ultimately in the "infinite or I AM," and Allston a "higher Power" or "Living Principle," essentially theistic, pervading all forms of life and enabling the percipient to recognize the product of the synthesis. In his related argument against David Hartley's associationism in chapter 7 he cited Allston's *Dead Man Restored* as an example of an imaginative work that could not thus be properly explained. At this point, however, they differed, Coleridge describing the "Secondary Imagination" as distinct from the "Primary Imagination" only in degree and mode, and Allston's defining "Primary Ideas" as "archetypes of the Universe" and "Secondary Ideas" as a reflex product of the mind.

As romantics, both Allston and Coleridge conceived of nature as a reflection of man's inner state or feelings. It is perhaps significant that Coleridge quoted in one of his lectures during the exhibition of Allston's paintings in Bristol one of his most notable expressions of this concept, the lines "O Lady! we receive but what we give, / And in our life alone does Nature live!" from "Dejection: An Ode."

Both Allston and Coleridge, like other romantics, preferred the Gothic to the classical style. On one occasion in London Coleridge contrasted the two by saying to Allston that Grecian architecture was a "thing" and a Grecian temple could be made of "two brick-bats and a cocked hat" but that the Gothic was an "idea" (Flagg, p. 66). Allston, who gave up classical subjects for the most part after his Roman sojourn, in later years was quoted as explaining that he had abandoned his painting *Jason,* begun at that time, because "The whole sympathy of my mind is with the Gothic and Romantic formes [*sic*]. Even the Greek architecture I have never admired, for what is it? You have the Pediment everlastingly and for the sides of the building a mere parallelogram. It always looks like a barn if you step on one side. For my own part, I prefer the Roman Architecture, which is considered enriched by the arch and the Dome" ("Color Book," pp. 66-67).

Another generally romantic interest which Allston and Coleridge shared was the supernatural. Among the ghost stories for which Allston was noted was one he told Coleridge: while at Harvard a student attempted to convert one of their friends from an adherence to Thomas Paine's rationalism by appearing to him as a ghost, having taken the precaution of removing the ball from the pistol that always lay at the head of his bed. On waking and seeing him, the friend called his appearance a joke, ordered him to vanish, and threatened to shoot him if he did not after three minutes; at the end of that time he pulled the trigger of the pistol and when it did not fire, became convulsed with fright and afterward died. Coleridge told the story on 1 May 1823, as recorded in his *Table Talk,* to illustrate his distinction between false ghost stories and genuine psychic phenomena of dreams.

Both Allston and Coleridge were also interested in the state of madness or the irrational. In an entry in his journal made after his return to England from Rome, Coleridge wrote that a scene depicting Tycho Brahe listening to the "oracular Gabble of the Ideot," the dwarf Seppé or Sep, supposed to have second sight, whom Brahe kept at his feet and fed by hand, would be "an admirable subject for an Allston" (*Notebooks* 2:3110). Shortly before he died Allston conversed with Elizabeth Peabody about the girl possessed by a learned devil whom Coleridge saw in Germany and referred to in chapter 6 of *Biographia Literaria* (Peabody, p. 6).

Still other subjects on which Allston and Coleridge expressed similar views and presumably discussed in conversation were the French Revolution and the character of Napoleon, which both deplored; religion, in which Coleridge turned to Trinitarianism about the time Allston went to England in 1811; and true fame, as contrasted to mere reputation or popularity, which Allston treated in several poems and aphorisms. Coleridge commented on Allston's future fame more than once, on one occasion saying that it would come as a result of his "Love of *Beauty,*" added to his "quiet unenvious spirit, to his lofty feelings concerning his Art, and to [the] religious Purity of his moral character," adding, "His best productions seem to please him principally because he sees and has learnt something which enables him to promise himself—'I shall do better in my next' " (*Collected Letters* 3:352).

Collard, Frederick William (1772-1860), English pianoforte manufacturer. Leslie described him as a man of "excellent sense, though generally so facetious that one feels inclined to laugh at everything he says" and recalled that when Allston was in London there were frequent evening parties with him, James Lonsdale, Samuel F.B. Morse, Charles B. King, and himself at their respective homes (Leslie, pp. 176-77). When Morse was in London in 1829 looking for the house on Tinney Street where the Allstons lived, he encountered Collard in a nearby street, who said he had often visited there (Dunlap, 2:318). After Allston left England, Collard recalled to Leslie the many hours, he spent, both day and night, with Allston in his studio and described him as "one of the most benevolent, intelligent, and interesting men" he had ever known, though he placed him with some "of the highest class, who are subject to let their imaginations outstrip their industry, and the dreams of their intention" preoccupy their time. It was because of this tendency that he lamented Allston's quitting England, where "the furor of emulation, with its consequent spur to industry" was stronger than in America, where he feared the "more limited sphere, the want of rivalry . . . the praise he was likely to receive, and the ease with which he might live" would prevent the full development of his abilities. In the letter he wrote Leslie after Allston's death he characterized him as gentle in disposition, quietly indulging his own imagination, and having simple, retiring habits; he said he could still see him sitting in an easy chair holding a cigar and "luxuriating" in conversation or the projection of some artistic design, and expressed regret that their correspondence had lapsed (Flagg, pp. 138-39, 373).

Collins, William (1788-1847), England landscape and figure painter. He was introduced to Allston by Leslie in 1814 and said that from then until Allston left England he saw more of him than almost any other friend. He discussed religion as well as art with him, had many of his own religious difficulties resolved in their conversation, and recognized his literary as well as artistic abilities. Allston frequently visited him, his mother, and his brother, Frank, showing such "affectionate kindness," Collins said, that he always considered him one of the family. His son W. Wilkie Collins, the novelist, described the impression Allston made by saying that "to a profound and reflective intellect, he united an almost feminine delicacy of taste and tenderness of heart which gave a peculiar charm to his conversation, and an unusual eloquence to his opinions" (*The Life of William Collins,* 1:99, 134-35). In later years Allston spoke of him often, and when *Monaldi* was published sent him a copy. In his letter to Richard Henry Dana written after Allston's death he recollected becoming acquainted with Allston's real character during his visit to Paris in 1817 and described his "sweetness and subdued cheerfulness" under inconveniences, his reverence for sacred things, and "the entire purity and innocence of his conversation" (Flagg, p. 126). He named one of his sons, who became a painter, Charles Allston, for whom Allston was godfather.

Cooper, James Fenimore (1789-1851), novelist. He and Allston probably met in January 1824, when Cooper visited Boston to see his friend Captain William B. Shubrick. A year earlier Richard Henry Dana had written him, encouraged by Allston to do so, apprising him of the discontinuation of the *Idle Man,* of which Cooper had promised to write a review. In his reply Cooper expressed surprise to learn that Allston, a "stranger" to him in all but reputation, had returned from England, though adding that he was in reputation "a stranger to no man in America," asked to be mentioned to him, and said that when in Boston, "I shall certainly *see him,*" whether or not he saw the fabulous sea serpent that Shubrick had promised to show him. On his return to New York he sent "an abundance of good will" to Allston through Shubrick. Two years later at the farewell dinner given him by the Bread and Cheese Club of New York on his departure for Europe, Allston and Irving were elected honorary members on his motion (*The Letters and Journals of James Fenimore Cooper* 1:94-95, 111, 141). He was in Europe from 1826 to 1833, during which time he expressed both criticism of Allston's European affiliations and praise of one of his paintings. Chapter 18 of *The Prairie* (1847) alludes briefly to Allston.

Crawford, Thomas (1813?-57), sculptor. Born of Irish parents, he grew up in New York. In 1835 he settled in Rome, where he lived, except for two visits to America, the rest of his life. Allston apparently saw only one example of his work, an engraving of his *Orpheus and Cerberus,* but admired it very much. A few months before Allston's death Crawford and Charles Sumner, who were close friends, exchanged letters in which the regard of both for Allston and of Allston for Crawford was expressed. The last two times Sumner and Allston saw each other they spoke of him (Pierce, 2:265), and Allston on the last evening of his life praised Crawford's work to his nephew Edmund T. Dana.

Dana, Edmund Trowbridge (1779-1859), Allston's brother-in-law by his second marriage. With his brother Richard Henry Dana he was one of Allston's two closest friends throughout his life, Allston often calling him his "brother" in mentioning him to Leslie (Leslie to Allston, 30 August 1821). They were students together at Harvard, where he and Leonard Jarvis were constant visitors to Allston's room, one or the other often spending the night. After graduating he started on the grand tour of Europe but returned when the family funds failed. From 1801 to 1804 he was in London studying painting, at which time he and Allston were often together ("The Journal of John Blake White" 42 [1941]: 68; 43 [1942]: 35). He painted at least one landscape, a coast scene, in 1827. In 1813 he helped direct the publication of *Sylphs of the Seasons* in Boston and Cambridge (*LA*, p. vi). In the years after returning from England in 1818 and before marrying in 1830, Allston was accustomed to spend Saturday and Sunday in a spare room at his quarters in Trowbridge House in Cambridge (Dana, 1:523-24, 835). About that time Dana was well known for wearing a blue frock (*Letters of Horatio Greenough to his brother, Henry Greenough*, p. 67). At his death he left land to Cambridge for an athenaeum to be used for lectures and a library and left the city land which was named Dana Park. He never married (H.W.L. Dana, "The Dana Saga," pp. 95, 98-99).

Dana, Edmund Trowbridge (1818-69), son of Richard Henry Dana (Dana, vol. 3, "The Dana Family"). As boys, he and his brother Richard Henry Dana, Jr., were accustomed to spend evenings at Trowbridge House in Cambridge listening to the conversation of Allston and their uncle Edmund T. Dana, from whom they heard of many English painters, actors, and statesmen. Edmund, the nephew, graduated from the University of Vermont in 1839 and received the degree of LL.B. from Harvard Law School in 1841. As a young man he was widely popular and noted as a good conversationalist. For several years he was a partner with his brother Richard in law but, accused of taking his work lightly, he resigned and went to Europe in 1848, where he remained until 1856. In 1854 he received the degree of J.U.D. from Heidelberg University. For the rest of his life he was a semi-invalid (*General Catalogue of the University of Vermont* [Burlington: Free Press Assoc., 1901]; Dana, 1:97, 342, 376; 2:719, 776, 832, 835, 3:941, and passim; "Necrology of New-England Colleges, 1868-9," *NEGHR* 24 [1870]: 180) He was the last person, besides members of the household, to see Allston alive, having spent an hour and a quarter with him on the evening of 9 July 1843, a few hours before his death. He described it in "The Last Hours of Washington Allston," *New-York Tribune*, 17 July 1843. It was not one of Allston's well days, he said, and his voice was feeble, but he discoursed typically on a variety of subjects: Thomas Crawford's new works; the merit of American sculpture in general; Clevenger's bust of him; his portrait of West, which he said could be relied on for accuracy in contrast to that by Lawrence, who tended to idealize; West's peering over his "Franklin" half-glasses; and the incompetence of some judges of works of art, declaring, "Art is, indeed, in some sense, an imitation of Nature, but it is not every one who has seen natural objects that is competent to judge of art; besides, how few truly *see* nature." As usual, he asked grace before the evening meal.

Dana, Elizabeth Ellery (1789-1874), sister of Allston's second wife. She lived with Richard Henry Dana and his family, where she was known as "Aunt Betsey" (Dana, vol. 3, "The Dana Family" and passim).

Dana, Richard Henry, Jr. (1857-82), lawyer and author. He was intimately associated with Allston all his life and acted for him in several financial and literary affairs. During his last three and a half years at Harvard and his two and a half years in Harvard Law School he customarily spent an evening each week in Allston's company and from him and his uncles Edmund T. and Francis Channing Dana learned all his "childish notions of Europe" and of famous English artists, poets, actors, and politicians. He read the manuscript of his book *Two Years before the Mast* (1840) to Allston and his father, both of whom expressed interest in it and advised publication. In the last two years of Allston's life he entered in his journal, which he began to keep in 1841 about the time of his marriage, many notations of their meetings, including frequent dinners and tea with all the Danas, and repeatedly described Allston's appearance and manner. No picture, he wrote, was more pleasing to his "heart & fancy" than to see Allston with "the feelings & habits of a gentleman, with a noble nature, a beautiful countenance & graceful person," his countenance marked with "taste & thought," seated at his fire in the evening after a day's work, the smoke from his cigar mingling with gray curls of his hair and rising "to aetherialise the whole," sometimes having dined on roast beef and boiled rice.

He was, with Franklin Dexter, an executor of Allston's estate. In 1850 he edited and wrote the preface of his *Lectures on Art, and Poems*. Nine years after Allston's death he wrote a lengthy description of him occasioned by the destruction by fire of the house he lived in in Cambridgeport for so long. In it he pictured Allston's dining after dark, with candles in silver sticks, white cloth, a few dishes and the never failing decanter of Madeira; wearing a blue coat with gilt buttons, drab pantaloons, brown or buff waistcoast, and white cravat; protracting the meal with anecdote or criticism, the smoke from his cigar afterward arising "like a halo about his curling hair," so that then "the beauty & the dream of life seemed truly to have begun." "Take him for all in all," he concluded, "—I ne'er shall look upon his like again!" and finally quoted from Wordsworth's "Ode: Intimations of Immortality": "But yet I know, Where'er I go, / That there hath passed away a glory from the earth" (Dana, 1:44, 149, 166, 266; 2:835, 500-501). After Mrs. Allston's death the unfinished works in Allston's studio were put under his and Charlotte Dana's care.

Dana, Richard Henry, Sr. (1787-1879), poet and essayist. He was Allston's brother-in-law by his second marriage and with his brother Edmund T. Dana one of his two closest friends throughout his life. After graduating from Harvard he had a brief career in law and politics and then devoted himself to literature. His poetry, first published in *The Buccaneer and Other Poems* (1827), was recognized as being influenced by George Crabbe, Wordsworth, and Coleridge. He was associated with the *North American Review* for several years after its establishment in 1815. In 1839-40 he delivered a series of eight lectures on Shakespeare in Boston, New York, Philadelphia, and other cities. He was noted for his melancholy disposition, said to have originated in the illness he contracted when with his brother Edmund T. he helped a man smitten with the plague in Cambridge in 1817 into a hot bath; at that time the financés of their two sisters died (H.W.L. Dana, "The Dana Saga," pp. 95-97). The title of his periodical the *Idle Man* was thought to reflect his own character, and the phrase became his literary nickname. When he included some of the items in it in his *Poems and Prose Writings* (1833) he singled out "The Hypochondriac" by Allston as one of those compositions whose omission was "like parting with old companions" (p. 147). More than once he came to Allston's aid financially.

After Allston's death he planned to write his biography, for which he made elaborate notes, but he never did. Henry H. Reed thought him eminently fitted to do so, not only having had such an opportunity of knowing him but being "not unlike" Allston in "imaginative cast of character and in the truth and delicacy of his feelings" and "kindred in spirit," free from the "taint of Sociniasm common among the intellectual atmosphere in that part of the country" (*Wordsworth & Reed,* p. 111). His poem "The Death of Washington Allston," first appearing as "Washington Allston" in *Graham's Magazine* for November 1843, accounted for the sad appearance of Beauty by the fact that "The fine-beholding eye, whose constant look / Was turned on thee, is dark; and cold the hand / Gave more than vision took," and offered the consolation, with which Allston would have agreed, that Beauty was of heavenly birth, concluding "There He, who reverent traced Her steps on earth, / Now sees him face to face" (*Poems and Prose Writings* 1:138). He was probably also the author of the sonnet "On Seeing the Drawings of the Angels in Allston's Picture of Jacob's Dream," signed "D." (Dana Papers).

Dana, Ruth Charlotte (1814-1901), daughter of Richard Henry Dana (Dana, vol. 3, "The Dana Family"). She was Allston's favorite niece, whose musical talent particularly endeared her to him. She played the piano and sang. He was inspired by her singing to write the poem "Rosalie" and inscribed the poem "The Parting" to her. On one occasion he told her, perhaps in reference to the love of music which they shared, that if there was any one thing which he was sure he possessed it was a sense of harmony. She was said to have been the model for the kneeling female figure in *Belshazzar's Feast,* and probably Rosalia in *Monaldi* is partly modeled on her. He told her father that he liked talking to her because she always understood his meaning at once. He once said to her, "The big, ardent mind must be doing something, or it pines and dies. It must be filling up the awkward void; storing time with acts and making life substantial" (Flagg, p. 398). She was the last person except his wife to speak with him on the last evening of his life. His first portrait of Coleridge was in her possession until her death. At Mrs. Allston's death the unfinished works in his studio were put under her care and that of Richard Henry Dana, Jr., and in 1876 she arranged for them to go to the Boston Museum of Fine Arts. Jared B. Flagg was much indebted to her for information in his biography of Allston.

Dana, Sarah Ann (1791-1866), sister of Allston's second wife. She lived with the family of Richard Henry Dana (Dana, vol. 3, "The Dana Family" and passim).

Davis, Isaac P. (1771-1855), Boston merchant, brother of Judge John Davis. He had no middle name and used "P." as further identification. He was a friend of many artists, owner of a small art collection, and active in several civic associations in the city (Davis, pp. 93-99). For a short time after his return to America in 1818 Allston received mail in his care. He owned Allston's *Diana and Her Nymphs, Italian Landscape* (G 13) and for a while had in his house *Elijah in the Desert* and *Head of St. Peter.* The *Head of St. Peter,* however, was apparently considered his wife's property.

Dearborn, Henry Alexander Scammell (1751-1829), politician and author. During the War of 1812 he was the senior major-general in the U.S. Army. Among other civic activities he served in 1825, as did Allston, on a committee for the erection of the Bunker Hill Monument. Prompted by the exhibition of *Belshazzar's Feast* after Allston's death he wrote an article describing it in details in which he declared that the exhibition had "established an era in the history of painting," said the work was valuable as affording students an opportunity to trace the successive steps Allston took in its execution, called him "the American Apelles" and compared it to Apelles's damaged *Anadyomne* which no artist could be found capable of repairing, and judged him more indebted to Greek than Italian art ("Allston's Feast of Belshazzar," *Knickerbocker Magazine* 24 [Sept. 1844]: 205-17).

De Veaux, James (1812-44), portrait painter, native of Charleston, South Carolina. In 1829 William H. Gibbes, husband of Allston's half-sister Elizabeth and father of Robert W. Gibbes, forwarded to Allston, whom he called "an artist of very high character," a sketch by De Veaux of Joseph and his brethren, with which Allston expressed satisfaction and in consequence offered advice on his education. William H. Gibbes then asked Allston to teach him, but Allston declined, saying he was not in the habit of taking pupils, and recommended that he go to Harding, then in Washington, or be placed under John Bowman in Charleston. De Veaux spent a few years in Philadelphia, from 1832 to 1838 in Europe, from 1838 to 1841 in South Carolina and Virginia, and from 1841 until his death in Italy. A few months before he died he wrote a friend, "SULLY is our REYNOLDS, and ALLSTON our wonder,—I would not give him for less than Michael Angelo! He is as fine as all the old masters together!" When he heard of Allston's death he wrote in his journal that "the greatest of American painters, has been taken from earth to join his God!" Gibbes dedicated his memoir of De Veaux to Charles Fraser, referring to his native state of South Carolina as "the mother of your distinguished friend, the illustrious ALLSTON" (Gibbes, pp. 8, 55, 185, 37).

Dexter, Franklin (1793-1857), Boston lawyer. He had a lifelong interest in art and some artistic talent of his own, to which Allston was probably referring when he said art had lost one of his friends to law. He was in frequent communication with Allston about his artistic and financial affairs. Thomas Cole called him a "gentleman of excellent taste," who could obtain for visitors an opportunity of seeing Allston's "best pictures" (Cole to Lurman Reed, May 1835 [New York State Library, Albany]). With Richard Henry Dana, Jr., he was one of the administrators of Allston's estate. Dana remembered him at the time carrying, as apparently was his custom, his green Harvard bag under his arm. After visiting Europe in 1847 he came home, he said, with the conviction that Allston was or showed that he could have been "the greatest landscape painter that ever lived" (Dana, 1:179-84, 340). He had a small collection of paintings that included a landscape sketch by Allston and a painting of Isabella of Spain said to be by him and was a subscriber to the Tripartite Agreement.

Drayton, William (1776-1846), lawyer, soldier, and congressman. His early years were spent in Charleston, South Carolina, where he and Allston presumably first met in 1801. They met again in London in 1815. In 1833 he settled in Philadelphia. In the letter he wrote to Richard Henry Dana after Allston's death he said he remembered him for his union of bright intellect, sweetness of temper, and mildness of manner and for his fascinating power of conversation. In the War of 1812 he was first lieutenant-colonel, then colonel, and finally inspector.

Dunlap, William (1766-1839), painter and writer. He studied painting under Benjamin West in London for three years. On returning to America he became a theatrical manager, resorting to painting at intervals and writing plays, biographies, and histories, notably of the theater and the arts in America. Most of his activity was in New York.

Durand, Asher Brown (1796-1886), engraver and painter. He spent most of his life in New York. He and Allston met only once, in the summer of 1835. Possibly it was under Allston's influence that soon afterward he turned entirely to painting, particularly landscapes. Several years after Allston's death he praised his technique in an article he wrote on landscape painting in which he cited with approval Allston's objection to obvious technique and recorded an occasion on which he replied to some friends who were praising a very young artist for the "*freedom*" of his execution, "Ah . . . that is what we are trying all our lives to get rid of," and then brought out of a closet a head he had painted from life at one sitting when a young man, placed it beside a finished work on his easel, and said, "There . . . that is freely painted." "No other comment was required," Durand concluded; "in the one, paint and the brush attracted attention, in the other, neither was visible, nothing but the glow of light and color which told its truth to Nature" ("Letters on Landscape Painting, No. 7," *Crayon,* 2 May 1855, pp. 273-74).

Dutton, Warren (1774-1857), Boston lawyer. Between 1809 and 1821 he served in the Massachusetts legislature. With Allston and others he served on committees of the Bunker Hill Monument Association in 1825 and of the Boston Athenaeum for the exhibition of Stuart's paintings in 1828 ("Record Book of the Suffolk Bar," *Proceedings of the MHS,* 1st ser., 1881, 1882, 19 [1882], 176-78; Whitley, *Gilbert Stuart,* pp. 197, 198, 215). He was, Richard Henry Dana said, one of Allston's "very best friends" (Dana to Gulian C. Verplanck, 28 Feb. 1835). When he and Franklin Dexter were called in after Allston's death for consultation about *Belshazzar's Feast,* Richard Henry Dana, Jr., who did not know him until then, described him as a "tall, intellectual looking man, with such a face & manners as one does not see every day," and Dexter agreed, adding, "Oh, that's he! Over hanging grey brows, & a stern expression,—Looks like a dragon—that's the man" (Dana 1:179-81, 183-84). He owned Allston's *Landscape, Evening* (*Classical Evening*) and *Evening Hymn* and was a subscriber to the Tripartite Agreement.

Eagles, John (1783-1855), Bristol clergyman, painter of poetic and fanciful landscapes, author of *The Sketcher* (1856) describing them, and art critic. In the latter capacity he often aroused animosity, as when John Ruskin objected to his articles in *Blackwood's Edinburgh Magazine*. In 1822 he moved from Bristol to a curacy at Halberton in Devonshire but returned regularly to Bristol (Francis Greenacre, *The Bristol School of Artists* [Bristol: Bristol City Art Gallery, 1974], pp. 243-49; Whitley, *Art in England, 1800-1820,* vol. 2 [1930], p. 300).

Everett, Edward (1794-1865), clergyman, teacher, statesman, and orator. Allston may have met him first in 1818, when he visited London during the two years he spent in Europe preparing himself to teach Greek literature at Harvard.

Felton, Cornelius Conway (1807-62), classical scholar. He taught Latin and Greek at Harvard from 1829 to 1860 and during the last two years of his life was its president. He was noted for the breadth of his intellectual interests, which included art. Two of his four printed appreciations of Allston were in reviews of art history books, the others being reviews of *Monaldi* and *Lectures on Art.* In his review of William Dunlap's *History* in the *North American Review* for July 1835 he said that the works of Allston would "make this a splendid era in our history," that he had a "mind of great compass, and varied culture," literary as well as artistic talent, and an imagination seeming "to dwell forever in a world of ideal beauty,—in the kingdom of forms," contrasted his scenes of "Pity and Terror" with his "mild and gracious images of Romance and Love," and declared that "no American has approached so near the great masters of past ages." He called his works among "the most illustrious examples of the loftiest poetry of art," and noted his "calm intellect," "serene spirit," and the "delicious pieces of poetry, anecdote and criticism" in his letters (41 [1835], 164-65).

Field, George (177?-1854), English chemist, who made several experiments in the application of science to painting. Allston probably met him during his first stay in London, when he was one of the founders of "The British School" there (Whitley, *Art in England, 1800-1820,* 1:46). He visited Allston's studio in 1816 and said that *The Sisters* was painted exactly in accordance with his theory of color. Allston owned a copy of his *Chromatics; or, An Essay on the Analogy and Harmony of Colours* (London, 1817). It was probably to this work that he referred when he told Henry Greenough that had he known that Field's work on the "Harmony of Colors," which he called "a very scientific book," was then in preparation he should like to have compared notes with him (Flagg, p. 172). He also knew Field's longer work, *Chromatography; or, A Treatise on Colours and Pigments, and of their Powers in Painting, &c.* (1835). His "Color Book" contains a list of pigments divided into permanent and impermanent ones taken from it and the introductory note acknowledges the author though not specifying the book (pp. 20-25; Field, tables 4-8, pp. 187-91). He was also in agreement with Field's comments there on certain pigments, notably the praise of ultramarine and vermilion and the judgment that the best white was that which is opaque and reflects light, but apparently he did not take note of Field's caution that asphaltum had a disposition to contract and crack.

Fish, Hamilton (1808-93), New York politician and statesman. He was also active in civic and social affairs, a member of the New-York Historical Society, and prominent in the Episcopal church. He was a friend of Washington Irving and Gulian C. Verplanck and, from early boyhood, of Samuel F.B. Morse.

Flagg, Ebenezer (1795-1837), Allston's half-brother, who lived in Georgetown, South Carolina. He was a member of the Society of the Cincinnati among other organizations, served from 1826 to 1830 in the state senate, graduated from the Medical College of South Carolina in Charleston in 1832, and practiced medicine in All Saints' Parish in South Carolina. Allston supposedly painted his portrait (Nord, pp. 22-23).

Flagg, George Whiting (1816-97), genre and portrait painter, son of Henry C. Flagg, Jr. He was said to have received his first instruction from James Bowman in Charleston, South Carolina, where his family moved from New Haven, Connecticut, in 1824. In the summer of 1831 he went to Boston to learn from Allston, and a year later, when he was sixteen, Allston said he had taught him all that he knew about art (Louise Hall Tharp, *The Peabody Sisters of Salem* [Boston: Little, Brown, 1950], p. 59). During their association, according to Sweetser, he designed *Ghost Story* and *Young Greek* and painted *Jacob and Rachel at the Well,* which prompted Allston to comment, "Now you may consider yourself an artist" (p. 103), and *Contentment,* which he praised. Allston repeatedly prophesized his success and wrote a poem for him intended to show that the elevated mind could find no satisfaction in mere pleasure. Paintings by him were exhibited at the Boston Athenaeum in 1831-33. In the fall of 1834, with the assistance of Luman Reed, he went to Europe, where he studied in London, Paris, and Italy. On his return he worked in Boston and New Haven and about 1843 settled in

New York. He arranged the hanging and varnishing of the pictures in the exhibition of Allston's paintings in 1839 and on that occasion convinced him that the effect of *The Dead Man Restored* would be finer if the mountain peaks were relieved against a plain blue sky instead of the clouds and if the lower group of figures was more strongly painted; Allston at first disagreed but finally said he would paint the picture over and incorporate the two suggestions if he could afford it. In 1839 he painted Allston's portrait.

Flagg, Henry Collins, Jr. (1790-1863), Allston's half-brother. He graduated from Yale in 1811, studied law in New Haven, returned to Charleston, South Carolina, but when the climate there proved unhealthy for his family, settled in New Haven. There, except for the years from about 1824 to 1833, when he was again in Charleston, he spent the rest of his life. He practiced law, except for two years during which he edited the *Connecticut Herald,* until 1842, served for two years as clerk of the county court, five as mayor, and one as a member of the state senate. He was noted for his public addresses, three of which were printed (Franklin L. Dexter, *Biographical Sketches of the Graduates of Yale College with Annals of the College History* [New Haven: Henry Holt, 1911], 5:384-86). Allston painted his portrait. Jared B. Flagg was much indebted to him for information in his biography of Allston.

Flagg, Henry Collins, Sr. (1742-1801), physician. A native of Newport, Rhode Island, the son of a wealthy shipping merchant, he went south with General Nathaniel Greene and became surgeon general of the army in the South during the American Revolution. He was present at the battle of Savannah, Georgia, and was said to have amputated the leg of Count Pulaski shortly before Pulaski's death. He was a member of the Society of the Cincinnati. For several years he practiced in South America before settling in Charleston, South Carolina. He married Allston's widowed mother in 1784 (N.G. Flagg, p. 122). Though he wanted Allston to become a physician he became reconciled to his pursuit of painting.

Flagg, Jared Bradley (1820-99), painter and clergyman, son of Henry C. Flagg, Jr. Although he is not mentioned in Allston's correspondence, the two were closely associated in his early years. At about the age of sixteen he went to stay with Allston, who gave him instruction in painting. In his biography of Allston he drew on his recollections at that time, referring to the "peculiarities" of his "uneventful life," which might be termed "picturesque" and which rendered him an object of interest as well as respect by his neighbors. He was the only author of reminiscences to give details about Allston's days, most others concentrating on his nights. He usually rose, Flagg said, about ten, when he made "an elaborate toilet" and breakfasted on the strongest coffee, a bit of salt fish or ham, an egg, bread and butter, never allowing any one to prepare his breakfast or his bed. After breakfast, he had a cigar and read in some book on art; at about one o'clock he entered his studio, taking a pitcher of drinking water with him. He customarily smoked a cigar and contemplated the picture on his easel before beginning to paint. Making his palette took him not less than half an hour. After painting he would clean his palette, contemplate the painting until dark, return home, and then often go back to see that he had locked the studio. For several years afterward Flagg was prominent as a painter in Hartford, Connecticut. Later he entered the Episcopal ministry. His son Montagu was a well-known genre painter.

Flagg, Rachel (Moore) Allston (1757-1839), Allston's mother. She was descended from French and Dutch families, and two of her Moore ancestors were governors of the Carolina colony. In 1775 she married, as his second wife, William Allston, Jr., by whom she had three children. After his death she married in 1784 in some opposition to her mother, Henry C. Flagg, by whom she had three children. In the interval Lord Cornwallis and his staff occupied her plantation (Webber, "Moore of St. Thomas' Parish," pp. 165-66). When told there was a Washington in the house Cornwallis asked to see him and was shown the infant Washington Allston. In April 1791 George Washington visited the plantation. Allston painted her portrait and wrote a poem for her.

Flaxman, John (1755-1826), English sculptor and draftsman. Allston lived in the house next to him in Fitzroy Square in London. According to Sweetser, he recollected that Flaxman, on being complimented on his designs from Homer and Dante, once showed him a variety of sketches which he had made in the streets and houses of the city. He knew of no better exercise in drawing, Allston said in his conversations with Henry Greenough, than the study of Flaxman's illustrations and would have a young artist copy two or three figures from them every day. He owned copies of three of Flaxman's works.

Francis, Convers (1795-1863), clergyman. He graduated from Harvard in 1815 and received an A.M. degree from the Harvard Divinity School in 1818. From 1819 to 1842 he was pastor of the church in Watertown, Massachusetts, and from 1842 until his death Parkman Professor of Pulpit Eloquence and the Pastoral Care at Harvard. After accompanying the clergyman and German scholar Frederick Henry Hedge to see Allston on one occasion, he wrote to the theologian Theodore Parker that they "had a delightful visit, staying till 11 o'clock," that Allston was "one of the most interesting talkers I ever knew," and that he said of Goethe's art criticisms they "were entirely without value, jejune, meagre or false" (24 May 1839, Longfellow National Historic Site).

Fraser, Charles (1782-1860), Charleston, South Carolina, miniature painter. He practiced law until 1818 and thus was able to support himself as an artist. His early association with Allston encouraged him to paint. The two first met in Charleston early in 1801. In Boston he visited Allston "often" in 1824 and again in 1833 (Alice R. Huger Smith and D.E. Hugh Smith, *Charles Fraser* [Charleston: Garnier, 1924], p. 22). In later years he described Allston's painting as having a "peculiar style of high finish" and paraphrased one of his maxims as being "that as nature is no where found slovenly or negligent, the art that professes to imitate her, should be elaborate in its process, and never fall short of its object from want of care" ("Exhibition of Pictures," p. 172). In the letter he wrote to Richard Henry Dana after Allston's death he characterized him as essentially philosophical in view, having as his constant aim "character," considering art as "the reflex of nature in her moral and intellectual workings," exhibiting a moral elevation in his own character and conversation in keeping with his art, and uniting as few artists did practical excellence with profound science, and said he never left Allston's society without feeling improved (Flagg, p. 377). To Robert W. Gibbes, however, he expressed the opinion that later generations would not have the high opinion of Allston's works that his own did, since he left little more in them than to show what he was capable of doing (3 Aug. 1843, Dana Papers).

Fuseli, Henry (Heinrich Füzzli) (1741-1825), painter and writer, a native of Zurich. After spending a brief time in England and several years in Italy, he settled in England, where he became professor of painting at the Royal Academy. He was noted for his melodramatic subjects, often evoking terror or horror, and his exaggerated treatment of them, and painted many scenes from Milton, Shakespeare, and Homer. Following Reynolds, he greatly admired Michelangelo for his sublimity and grandeur, Raphael for his humanity, and other Italians of their time, including Leonardo and Correggio. He disparaged portrait painting and the delineation of nature in landscape, recognized the importance of the imagination, and pointed out that dreams were an unexplored region in art. Allston first saw works by him in engravings in the Charleston, South Carolina, Library. His most important critical work was his *Lectures on Painting*, consisting of the lecture he delivered at the Royal Academy from 1801 to 1825. Allston apparenly owned or had access to the edition of them in *The Life and Writings of Henry Fuseli*, ed. John Knowles (1831). He quoted from Lecture 12 (1825) in one of his own aphorisms, the only one to which he attributed authorship, transcribing it, with minor inaccuracies, as "No genius work of Art ever was, or ever can be, produced but for its own sake; if the painter does not conceive to please himself, he will not finish to please the world" (*LA*, p. 167). He expressed the same sentiment in two more aphorisms and in others echoed Fuseli's "Aphorisms, chiefly Relative to the Fine Arts," including his condemnation of contemporary opinion, fashion, and pride. Personally Fuseli was noted for his eccentricity, outspoken and given to profanity but socially charming. Allston said that once when called on to judge a painting he had told the owner that it was "a most extraordinary picture" but afterward explained that he had meant it was "a most extraordinary *bad* picture" (Walter Channing).

Gibbes, Elizabeth (Allston) (1766?-), Allston's half-sister. She married William Hassell Gibbes (Groves, p. 33).

Gibbes, Robert Wilson (1809-66), South Carolina physician, author, and scientist, the son of Allston's half-sister Elizabeth (Groves, p. 33). For most of his life he lived in Columbia. He had several scientific collections, planned as the nucleus of a museum, and a notable art collection. He owned Allston's portrait of Rubens, a copy of George P.A. Healy's portrait of Allston after Harding's portrait, a cast of Clevenger's bust of Allston, and a copy of Allston's *Outlines & Sketches*. He visited Allston in 1831, according to a note he made on a copy of Allston's letter to him of 6 February 1842.

Gibbs, Sarah (1784-1866), daughter of George Gibbs and Mary Channing, a cousin of Allston's first wife. She had a monument to her parents placed in St. Mary's Church in Portsmouth, Rhode Island, where they were buried, the design of which Gibbs family tradition ascribed to Allston but which was apparently designed, at least finally, and put in marble by Horatio Greenough. She was in Florence at the end of 1835 and at that time expressed dissatisfaction with Greenough's first design, feeling that "personal private feeling was somewhat too much expressed." It was finished in or slightly later than 1840 and included an inscription by Channing. Probably Greenough talked of the matter with Allston in 1836 when he was in Boston, and Allston may have thus influenced his revised design (Wright, pp. 104, 208; Gibbs, p. 107). During her visit to Italy in 1835 and 1836 Miss Gibbs also arranged to have a marble table made in Rome under Allston's direction (in possession of Newport Historical Society). In addition to her home in Boston, she had the estate "Oakland" near Newport (Gibbs, pp. 16, 106).

Gillman, Anne (Harding) (1789-1860), wife of James Gillman, Sr. She was rather short, had what Leslie called "a very fine face," and impressed all who knew her with her courtesy and her exceptional kindness. She was, her granddaughter said, very devout, "a woman of old-fashioned reticence in speech," who commonly avoided any mention of "bodily ills or purely medical topics." Leslie said she would sit for him whenever he wished and described her as "a very excellent, charming woman," who was one of four English women he had met of whom he could make that judgment. After her husband's death she went to live with her son James, Jr. (Watson, pp. 6, 22, 46; Leslie, p. 199).

Gillman, Henry Anthony (1814-58), younger son of James and Anne Gillman. He evidently had some artistic talent, but little more than passing references in Coleridge's letters and accounts of Coleridge's residence with the Gillmans is known about him. He never married (Gillman, pp. 22, 26).

Green, Joseph Henry (1791-1863), English anatomist and surgeon. He was a professor of anatomy at the Royal Academy from 1825 to 1852, in which capacity he gave six lectures a year on anatomy and its relation to the fine arts. He became acquainted with Allston through Coleridge. Several years later, in December 1829, he paid tribute to Allston in one of his lectures and quoted two of his sonnets as illustrative of some of the principles he was advancing. Morse, then in London, was present and Green prefaced his lecture by saying he was glad to see him there, since he was going to mention an American who was an honor to the Royal Academy (Prime, p. 175; Dunlap, 2:316-17). The fact that he did so, he wrote a friend in America shortly afterward, testified to how "lasting the impression" of their intercourse was, "brief indeed, but unreserved," and went on to say, "who, indeed, who had enjoyed the inestimable privilege of converse with such a man, could ever forget the purity, the depth and simplicity of his mind." He declared that Allston had "studied his art with poetic feeling and philosophic thought," doubted "whether his productive genius or aspiration as an artist" could be "fully appreciated without a knowledge of his poems," and cited his sonnets on Italian painters and works of art as reflecting not only what his own works had realized but the fact that however great his technical skill, his "high aim and excellence were the imagination working in the service of the moral being" (Flagg, pp. 394-95). In the letter he wrote to Richard Henry Dana after Allston's death he emphasized the relationship of Allston and Coleridge, saying that Coleridge never failed when Allston's name was mentioned to express high admiration of his genius as a poet and painter and spoke highly of his character as a man; he added that Allston had similar feelings toward Coleridge and embodied the character of Coleridge in his portrait of him as "the philosopher with the seraph's wings" (Flagg, p. 107).

Greenough, Alfred (1809-51), next to the youngest of the Greenough brothers of Boston (H.P. Greenough, p. 41), after John, Henry, and Horatio. He knew Allston from boyhood. Though interested in art, he never studied it. He attended Harvard from 1823 and 1825, subsequently became a commission merchant in the Mediterranean trade in Boston and was noted for his articles in the *Morning Post* in favor of the Democratic party. During the years Horatio and Henry spent in Italy in the early 1830s he wrote them letters in which Allston often figured, mostly relating him to Horatio's activities but also describing his "bright blue body coat & buff pantaloons" and some of his pictures, including the "perfectly beautiful" *The Spanish Girl* and *A Roman Lady Reading* (*Letters of Horatio Greenough to His Brother Henry Greenough*, pp. ix, 64, 67, 74).

Greenough, Henry (1807-83), architect, occasional painter, and writer (H.P. Greenough, p. 41). He and Allston were closely associated from the time of Greenough's student days at Harvard, from 1823 to 1825, until Allston's death, except for Greenough's years abroad from 1830 to 1833. In the interim he practiced architecture in Boston, during which time Allston helped him get at least one commission. Probably it was at this time that they began to have the conversations he described in the letter he wrote to Richard Henry Dana after Allston's death about his method of painting, which they presumably continued in the late 1830s. At the end of his letter to Dana, Greenough described Allston's character in adulatory terms, alluding briefly to the "perfection of his intellectual and religious nature" and going into detail about "the graceful dignity, the refined elegance, and benignant urbanity of his manners," in which respect he was "the perfect model of a gentleman." He added that "Etiquette of the most approved mode, and conforming to the strictest rules of conventionalisms sat upon him like an easy, familiar garment" and enabled him "to mingle with the noble and refined" but did not oppress "those of the most simple and homely breeding." He noted Allston's freedom from envy, malice, and detraction, accounting for it by the fact that "his mind, by nature benevolent in the highest degree, had been, by religious culture, so chastened and purified" as to elevate him above such feelings. As an artist he characterized Allston as combining the excellence of the old masters without falling into their defects, excelling in drawing and in sculpture as well as painting, and praised him also as a poet. He concluded that if "genuine unaffected modesty is a sure proof of real merit, the name of Allston must some day take a high risk, even above the *Old Masters*" (Flagg, pp. 201-203).

In 1844, after Allston's death, Greenough evidently proposed to write a series of articles about him and completed at least two for the Boston *Morning Post.* Richard Henry Dana urged him to write others in connection with the exhibition of *Belshazzar's Feast* that summer but he apparently did not (Dana to Greenough, 7 Aug. 1844, Longfellow National Historic Site). At Christmas in 1844 Mrs. Allston presented him two studies of hands and heads in profile by Allston, probably done about 1815. He devoted a chapter, "Allston," in his novel *Ernest Carroll* to reminiscences about Allston by two of the characters, one of whom, Carroll, says he owes Allston "all the really valuable knowledge" of his art which he has. Several other remarks by Carroll and one made by another character are paraphrases of statements made about Allston by Horatio and Henry Greenough in letters, to Allston and Richard Henry Dana, respectively. Carroll's description of Allston's use of pigments is a condensation of the description of it in Henry's letter to Dana. Several years later Henry published passages from letters of Allston, accompanied by reproductions of sketches by him of *Belshazzar's Feast, The Angel Releasing St. Peter from Prison, Jeremiah,* and *Dido and Anna,* in "Washington Allston as a Painter, Unpublished Reminiscences of Henry Greenough" (*Scribner's Magazine* 11 [Feb. 1892], 220-29).

Greenough, Horatio (1805-52), the first professional American sculptor. After graduating from Harvard in 1825 he went to Rome to study and eventually settled in Florence, where he lived most of the time until 1851. He met Allston during his junior year in college and during his last two years there was one of a group that spent Saturday nights at the quarters of Edmund T. Dana in Trowbridge Hall in Cambridge listening to him converse and smoking cigars. They were often together during his visits to America from May 1827 to May 1828, in the summer of 1836, and from October 1842 to July 1843. Commenting in a letter to his brother John in London that Allston might secure affluence if he were finished with *Belshazzar's Feast,* he wrote in 1828 that he wished Allston would go back there, adding, "He always seems like an eagle tied to his roost. There is no atmosphere of art." At that time Allston gave him a recipe for a palette, asked him to send him some ultramarine and a cast of an ear from life, promised to send a painting for exhibition in Florence, and suggested to him the subject of Abdiel from *Paradise Lost* for a statue, which he executed several years later. One of his early sketches was of the same scene as Allston's *David Playing before Saul,* and he may have been influenced by works of Allston in his sketches of a shepherd boy and Jacob and Rebecca made in 1828 as proposals for a design for a statue for Robert Gilmor, Jr. He was probably indebted in the pose of his *Washington* and the angel in his monument to George and Mary Gibbs to Allston's *Jeremiah.* He was greatly influenced by Allston in his philosophy of art and architecture, also conceiving of the greatest art as an expression of thought rather than a mere representation of objects, though recognizing the importance of studying nature and the old masters. During his early years abroad he wrote more fully to Allston than to anyone else, and his letters to him constitute the fullest record of his artistic development at that time.

In the account of his life that he sent to Dunlap in 1833 he called Allston a "father" to him, teaching him how to discriminate, think, and feel, saying if he never passed mediocrity he should attribute the fact to his absence from Allston, who made him seem "an emanation of his own soul." "*A note to Allston's life,*" he wrote his brother Henry at the same time, "might tell all of me which is essential." After Allston's death he wrote Richard Henry Dana three letters of recollections and estimates of Allston, couched in highly emotional terms. He had seen Allston a few days before his death and only wished that, like Charlotte Dana, he had heard the "last breathings of his blessed spirit." Though he felt a sense of not having sufficiently appreciated Hugh Legaré while living, heard him "as an angel" and declared that "when far from him he exercised over me a power no other man ever did." He hoped no attempt would be made to tamper with Allston's unfinished works and looked to the "*men* who will be born of *him*" rather than a biography as a fit monument of Allston's career. Wherever he had been, he said, he had found one or two persons who owed to Allston "the birth of their souls." He cited Allston's independent appreciation of the Venetians and Michelangelo and treatment of biblical subjects, his influence on the German artists in Rome, his varied style, and his faithfulness to art in spite of limited patronage and fame, and called him "America's 'first born poet painter.' " In conclusion he declared him "the head the chief—the Adam of American Idealists. He is the first of that noble Spartan band—sure to fall because the host of the Persian are overwhelming, but sure to carry with them to the ground whereon they fall not only the sense but the proof of having acted the noblest part that God grants to a man, that of sacrificing body to mind—expediency to right—fact to truth—now to hereafter" (Wright, pp. 30, 40, 35; Dana, 2:835; *Letters of Horatio Greenough to His Brother Henry Greenough,* p. 29; Greenough, *Letters,* pp. 168, 340-42, 349-50).

Greenough, John (1801-52), (H.P. Greenough, p. 41), landscape painter. Like his brothers, he was acquainted with Allston from his college days. After graduating from Harvard in 1824 he went to London, where he lived, except for a few excursions to Italy, until 1841. On his return he had a studio in Boston for several years. He was given to enthusiasm and indiscretions, was often in need of money, and failed to succeed professionally (Wright, "John Greenough, an American Artist," *Old-Time New England* 50 [Fall, 1949]: 43-52).

Griswold, Rufus Wilmot (1815-57), journalist, anthologist, and author. Three of his anthologies included writings by Allston: *The Poets and Poetry; Readings in American Poetry* (1843), which contained "America to Great Britain" and "Rosalie"; *The Prose Writers of America* (1847), which contained seven extracts from *Monaldi*, his aphorisms that were published by Mrs. Jameson in her article on him, and two brief extracts from his letters to Dunlap. The last volume also contained an introductory sketch, in which he said Allston was entitled to an "enviable and enduring reputation" in literature, characterized his prose as having a "remarkable command of language, great descriptive powers, and rare philosophical as well as imaginative power," and cited *Monaldi* as depicting an artist comparable to Allston in being akin to artists of the past. Referring to Dunlap's allegation of Allston's idleness, he quoted him as saying, "I am famous among my acquaintances ... for industry: I paint every day: and never pass an hour without accomplishing something." He also described dining with Allston a few days before his death, mentioning his thin face, expressive eyes, long hair, soft voice, and "simple and old-fashioned" dress, which consisted of a blue coat with bright buttons, buff vest, and drab pantaloons. It was probably through Griswold's solicitation that Allston's poem "Sonnet: on the Late S.T. Coleridge" was published in *Graham's Magazine*, for which he was assistant editor, with George R. Graham, from May 1842 until October 1843.

Hale, Nathan (1784-1863), Boston journalist. His chief association was with the *Boston Daily Advertiser*. Among his other activities was the printing of a series of New England maps.

Harding, Chester (1792-1866), portrait painter. After several difficult years getting established in various frontier locations, he settled in Boston early in 1823 and soon achieved such popularity that Gilbert Stuart, who was temporarily eclipsed, coined the term the "Harding fever" to describe it. From August of 1823 to September 1826 he was in Europe. He took a letter of introduction to Leslie, probably from Allston, and declared after seeing pictures by old masters in John J. Angerstein's gallery that he "would give more for Mr. Allston's unfinished picture than for a score of such." Soon after his return he told Sophia Peabody that Allston was his "beau ideal of a man and a gentleman and his dearest friend" (Tharp, p. 49). He became, he said, "intimately acquainted" with him. In his autobiography he gave a detailed description of Allston at that time. "His habits," he wrote,

> were peculiar in many respects. He lived alone, dining at six o'clock, and sitting up far into the night. He breakfasted at eleven or twelve. He usually spent three or four evenings, or rather nights, at my house every week; and I greatly enjoyed his conversation, which was of the most polished and refined order, and always instructive. I sometimes called at his studio. It was an old barn, very large, and as cheerless as any anchorite could desire. He never had it swept, and the accumulation of the dust of many years was an inch deep. You could see a track, leading through it to some remote corner of the room, as plainly as in new-fallen snow. He saw few friends in his room; lived almost in solitude, with only his own great thoughts to sustain him.

He also remembered Allston's talent for recounting anecdotes. When he visited Samuel Rogers in London in 1847 and heard him tell a story of a woman buried by mistake appearing to her husband, he wrote his family, "Imagine Allston telling the story, and you will get a pretty good idea of Mr. Rogers's manner." He thought Allston made a mistake in changing the perspective of *Belshazzar's Feast*, which he called "only a monument of wasted genius," and felt he would have taken a high place had he worked in London in the midst of the best works of art and artists (*A Sketch of Chester Harding*, pp. 142-43, 176). Richard Henry Dana, Jr., recollected that on one occasion he said he suggested to Allston he could relieve his financial distress by paining two or three pictures off hand that would sell though not do justice to his power and received a rebuke as if forgery or peculation had been recommended. He painted two portraits of Allston.

Harvey, George (ca. 1800/1801-78), landscape and miniature painter. A native of England, he came to America at the age of twenty and spent several years in the West before establishing himself as an artist. In 1829 he was in Boston. Soon afterward he went to England to study. He returned in 1833 and built a home near Hastings-on-Hudson, New York, not far from Washington Irving's "Sunnyside," which he helped design in 1835 and 1836 and remodel in 1846 and 1847. In later years he went back and forth between America and England, in which country he died (Irving, *Letters* 2:835, 844-46, 880; vol. 4, [1982], pp. 96, 99, 192).

Hawthorne, Nathaniel (1804-64), novelist. Although he is not mentioned in Allston's correspondence, the two knew each other, particularly through Sophia Peabody, whom Hawthorne married in 1842. He attended the 1839 exhibition of Allston's paintings though making no recorded comment about it, but he was much impressed by the unfinished state of *Belshazzar's Feast*. Shortly after Allston's death he commented in his notebook, probably between December 1843 and April 1844, "Allston's picture of Belshazzar's Feast—with reference to the advantages, or otherwise, of having life assured to us, till we could finish important tasts on which we were engaged" (*The American Notebooks*, ed. Claude M. Simpson, vol. 8 of *The Works of Nathaniel Hawthorne*, [Columbus: Ohio State University Press, 1972], p. 242) and in "The Artist of the Beautiful," (1844) wrote, "The painter—as Allston did—leaves half his conception on the canvass, to sadden us with its imperfect beauty, and goes, if it be no irreverence to say so, in the hues of heaven," declaring that an ideal artist had to possess "a force of character hardly compatible with delicacy to picture forth the whole." He introduced Allston in "The Hall of Fantasy" (1843) but removed the reference when the piece appeared in *Mosses from an Old Manse* (1846). Chapter 15 of *The Marble Fawn* (1860) devotes a paragraph to "a poet-painter," clearly Allston.

Hawthorne, Sophia Amelia (Peabody) (1809-71), Elizabeth Peabody's sister and wife of Nathaniel Hawthorne. Though apparently no letters passed between her and Allston, they saw each other frequently after the Peabody family moved from Salem to Boston in 1828. At that time she was in frail health but engaged in drawing, painting, and copying paintings, in all of which activities Allston took great interest. About 1830 she sat for her portrait to Harding, who spoke warmly of Allston and of whose portrait of him she made a copy. By May 1832, when she called Allston, somewhat whimsically, "Tiger of the age," she had completed a landscape of her own, which he came to see. She told him she painted it "in perfect ignorance," at which, she said, he "hummed" and said, "But you have not painted it ignorantly," that it did her great credit, that he had no fault to find with it, and that he was much surprised, since it was superior to what he had expected. On that occasion he vigorously objected to the drawing, coloring, and composition of a French painting she was copying, it being of the French school before the Revolution, though he conceded that as long as she had commenced she might as well go on, since she could learn thereby to handle colors.

He wished that she might copy nature instead and said that she should study from sculpture, casts, and living models. When he agreed to let her copy his own work, Elizabeth asked for his *Lorenzo and Jessica,* his latest work, which she had just seen in his studio. He also suggested that Sophia visit his nephew George W. Flagg and ask that he repeat all he had learned about art from him (Tharp, pp. 49, 344-45, 55-59). In an account of the interview Sophia had with him presumably on this occasion, Elizabeth said he began to talk to her about going to Europe and devoting herself to art, advised her, when she said she was an invalid, to copy only masterpieces, and, on hearing that the owner of *The Spanish Girl in Reverie* (probably Elijah Clark) refused her request to borrow it for copying, expressed indignation and said he would be proud to have her copy any work of his (Julian Hawthorne, *Nathaniel Hawthorne and His Wife* [Boston, 1884], 1:65-66).

From 1832 to 1835 she was out of the city, but when Elizabeth called on Allston about the time of her return he inquired before sitting down "most particularly" about her health, prospects, and employment. Early in 1836 she apparently borrowed Allston's *Flight of Florimel,* of which she made a copy (Peabody, *Letters,* pp. 153, 155; Tharp, p. 346). When Elizabeth called again, apparently a few months later, Allston said he was delighted to hear Sophia had sold her copy of *Lorenzo and Jessica* and had promises of getting $100 a canvas but was disappointed that she had done no original work.

In 1837 she borrowed his copy of Flaxman's "Greek Poets," from which she intended to make copies (Tharp, pp. 107, 115). When Elizabeth visited him in June 1839 she wrote Sophia again of his interest in her, saying he "seemed transported with delight on hearing of your freedom from pain, and was eager to know what you were going to paint." When Elizabeth said Sophia had several things going but did not like to tell of her plans, he commented that she would then be more likely to execute them and that it was a good thing to have several paintings in process at once because that would save time, since she could rest herself by change (Peabody, *Letters,* p. 226). In reply Sophia said Allston's interest in her health was "kind and inspiring" (Rose Hawthorne Lathrop, *Memoirs of Hawthorne* [Boston, 1897], p. 30). When she was disappointed by the engraving of her drawing of the title character in Hawthorne's story "The Gentle Boy" for the special edition published in January 1839, Allston consoled her by saying artists were always at the mercy of ignorant engravers (Tharp, p. 119).

A few weeks after Allston's death, Ellery Channing, the son of Walter Channing, called on her for information about him (*The American Notebooks by Nathaniel Hawthorne,* ed. Randall Stewart [New Haven: Yale Univ. Press, 1932], p. 312).

Haydon, Benjamin Robert (1786-1846), English history and portrait painter. Allston often spent evenings with him in London, together with Morse and Leslie (Leslie, p. 147). According to Sweetser, when he went at Beaumont's request to see Allston's painting *The Angel Releasing St. Peter from Prison* he commended him for abandoning portraiture and commented that next to knowing what one could do was knowing what one could not. As an art critic he favorably reviewed several of his paintings. After Allston's death, however, he characterized him as "a mild, amiable delightful creature—a Poet as well as a Painter," who "smoked cigars, and had all the procrastinating habits of an American," and though "undoubtedly a Man of genius . . . wanted energy of will" (to Theodore Dwight, 14 May 1843, Dwight Papers, MHS).

Hayward, Joshua Henshaw (1797-1856), portrait painter. He became Allston's pupil in 1818. Subsequently he practiced medicine and engaged in the drug business with associates in Boston (*Boston City Directorys* for 1825-56). In his letter to Richard Henry Dana after Allston's death he compared Allston's conversation to the impressions made by beautiful scenery where the outline but not the detail remained. He remembered his freedom from sarcasm as contrasted to the sort of bitter epigram Gilbert Stuart was accustomed to make, his fondness for telling and listening to anecdotes, and his lack of suspicion. He characterized Allston's style as his own despite his study of all schools, having "less vigor than the old masters but "far more sweetness and delicacy," and called him "the Dante" of painters, whose impersonations "breathed more of heaven than earth." He also noted his kindness to young artists, often correcting the drawing of a picture by another; on one occasion, when Hayward asked for advice on the best color for the background of a portrait he painted it himself, saying, "There, I would give it some such color as that" (Flagg, pp. 379, 380).

Hayward, William, New York art collector and a print seller. He specialized in engravings, especially English ones. His collection of old masters was said to have been assembled during a period of ten years of "diligent research, liberal outlay, and extensive travel, both in the United States and in England." It was exhibited in New York in 1837, and in 1839 he brought it to Boston, where, at the Boston Athenaeum, it was put up for sale, either collectively or separately (*New York City Directorys*, 1834/35—1843/44; *Catalogue of the Thirteenth Exhibition of Paintings in the Athenaeum Gallery* [Boston, 1839], preface).

Hazlitt, William (1778-1830), English essayist and critic. He and Allston met in 1803 in Paris, if not earlier in London. In later years he was often in Allston's company in London and often reviewed his paintings, usually favorably. They were not altogether congenial, however. He once asked Allston where he got his models, some of which he thought looked Asiatic and the like of which he had never seen in the streets of London, and Allston replied that he got them from his imagination, whereupon Hazlitt looked at him, Allston said, as if to say, "You are the greatest liar I ever met" (Flagg, p. 123). Allston took issue with his preference for Raphael over the ideal aspect of Michelangelo in his article "Fine Arts" in the *Encyclopaedia Britannica* in 1817 and said, Richard Henry Dana, Jr., recollected, Hazlitt would not have gone far beyond copying, being entirely destitute of imagination, with no idea there could be any faces but portraits and no idea of art beyond its mimetic character. In Allston's recollections in America of his years in London, Hazlitt was nevertheless prominent (Alcott, p. 53).

Howard, George William Frederick, Viscount Morpeth (1802-64), who became the seventh earl of Carlisle in 1848. In 1841-42 he made a tour of the United States and Canada. In Boston from October until the end of December 1841 he was chiefly taken about by Charles Sumner (Longfellow, 2:337, 364). By that time Allston's *Uriel in the Sun* was owned by his sister, the duchess of Sutherland, wife of the marquis of Stafford, by then the first duke of Sutherland, who liked it so well that she wanted to have another painting by Allston, for which Morpeth negotiated. After examining several sketches, he suggested it be *Titania's Court* and Allston assented, asking that Morpeth present his compliments to the duchess and say to her that his pictures were his children and since she had treated one with such kindness and courtesy he would be happy to commit another to her care. The price agreed upon was £5,000, or $25,000, and the condition was made that the work would not be done until

Belshazzar's Feast was finished. According to the custom in England she would have advanced part of the sum, but Allston would not agree to that arrangement.

A few months after Allston's death, Morpeth communicated with Sumner about the possibility of acquiring *Titania's Court, Heliodorus Driven from the Temple,* or *Diana and Her Nymphs,* which Isaac P. Davis wanted to sell for £300. Sumner thought *Diana and Her Nymphs* would be worth more than that in thousands if it were in Allston's later warm manner but, though beautiful, it was in his opinion "cold and dry" (Pierce, 2:276). Apparently nothing came of the negotiations. Several years later Morpeth referred to Allston in a lecture as "a man of real genius, who suffices to prove that the domain of the fine arts, though certainly not hitherto the most congenial to the American soil, may be successfully brought, to use their current phrase, into annexation with it" (*Travels in America; The Poetry of Pope: Two Lectures Delivered to the Leeds Mechanics Institution and Literary Society, December 5th and 6th, 1850* [New York, 1857], p. 12). According to Sweetser, when *Outlines & Sketches* was published William Hickling Prescott sent Morpeth a copy, praising it highly and freely quoting Allston's poetry.

Howard Henry (1769-1847), English portrait and history painter. In his early life he studied in Italy. He was made secretary of the Royal Academy in 1811 and 1833 became professor of painting there.

Hoyt, Albert Gallatin (1809-56), portrait and landscape painter. Born in Sandwich, Massachusetts, he graduated from Dartmouth and in 1839 settled in Boston. He was in Europe from 1842 to 1844.

Huger, Daniel Elliott (1779-1854), Charleston, South Carolina, planter and attorney, known as Judge Huger. In early years he served as secretary of state in South Carolina and as secretary to the governor ("Letters from Col. Lewis Morris to Miss Ann Elliott," contrib. Morris Rutherford, *SCHGM* 40 [1939]: 127; *Charleston City Directorys,* 1801-55).

Irving, Washington (1783-1859), author and diplomat. During the years 1804-06, 1815-32, and 1842-46, he lived in Europe, mostly traveling and serving in diplomatic posts in England and Spain. He and Allston first met in Rome on 27 March 1805 and spent much time together there until Irving left in April. At the time he described Allston in his journal as "a young gentleman of much taste & a good education," whose society was "peculiarly agreeable" (1:262, 268, 270). After Allston's death he wrote an account of their association, particularly then, for *Cyclopaedia of American Literature,* edited by Evert A. Duyckinck and George Duyckinck, in which he spoke in extravagant terms, called Allston "inexpressibly engaging in appearance and manners," described his "light and graceful form, with large blue eyes, and black, silken hair waving and curling round a pale, expressive countenance," everything bespeaking one of "intellect and refinement," being "copious, animated, and highly graphic" in conversation, having not only sensibility but benevolence and "a chaste and gentle humor," altogether captivating him more completely than anyone else on a first acquaintance.

He recalled Allston's excited admiration of Michelangelo's *Moses* and reverence before St. Peter's, and said he was so impressed that he briefly considered, partly because of his own talent in drawing, remaining in Rome and becoming an artist, sharing an apartment with Allston, and taking instruction from him. Allston taught him, he said, how to appreciate works of art by selecting a few to concentrate on, advising him, "You may as well attempt to enjoy every dish in a Lord Mayor's feast" as attempt to attend to every work in a great collection unless he had a year to spend on it. He also remembered him as an "admirable story teller," unsurpassed with ghost stories, and given to acting a story as well as telling it. Allston was, he concluded, "one of the purest, noblest, and most intellectual beings that ever honored me with his friendship." He incorporated two of Allston's letters to him in the account ("Washington Allston," vol. 2, pt. 1 [New York, 1866], pp. 14-16). He was probably thinking of their association in Rome when he once said of Allston, "The pleasure he derives from his own thoughts is so great that he seems to forget that there is any thing to do but think" (Flagg, p. 67).

They met again briefly in Boston when Allston was there from 1808 to 1811. Their longest association, however, was in England during the years 1815-18. Irving, who spent most of these years in Liverpool, was in London for a short time in July 1815, for five or six weeks before 5 April 1816, for about three weeks at the beginning of August 1817, and in July 1818 and the following months, during which time the two were often together (Irving, *Letters* 1:402, 440, 488, 493, 530; Williams 1:169). According to Sweetser, he read to Allston his story "The Legend of Sleepy Hollow," probably in the summer of 1818, and expressed doubt about publishing it, on which occasion Allston encouraged him to do so. The depiction of Leslie and his wife in his story "The Wife" was said to have been based on Allston's first marriage. He admired *Jacob's Dream* greatly and said he knew it so well he could delineate the whole in pencil. Shortly before Allston returned to America he made a special trip from Birmingham, where he was staying with his sister, to Coleridge, presumably at Highgate, to try to dissuade him from going. Not a prolific letter writer, he wrote Leslie about this time not to wait for his replies to Leslie's letters, "as I am if possible more averse to letter-writing even than Alston" (*Letters* 1:608). In 1826, both Irving and Allston were elected honorary members of the Bread and Cheese Club of New York (Williams 1:427, 476).

They met for the last time in Cambridgeport soon after Irving returned to America from England in 1832. About 1835 Allston painted the costume and hands of the portrait of him by John Wesley Jarvis, done in 1808 ("Remarks by the President," *Proceedings of the MHS*, 2d ser., I, 1884-85 [Boston, 1885], 33). In later years Irving told his nephew Pierre M. Irving that Allston was "the most delightful, the most lovable being" he ever knew, one he would like to have had always at his side and to have gone through life with, his nature "so refined, so intellectual, so genial, so pure." A few weeks before his death the mention of Allston's name was reported to have "set his soul all glowing with tender affectionate enthusiasm" (Pierre M. Irving, 1:405; vol. 4 [1864], p. 325).

Jameson, Anna Brownell (Murphy) (1784-1860), British writer. A native of Dublin, she married Robert Jameson, a barrister, in 1825, but they often lived apart. In 1836 she went to Canada, where he had been appointed chancellor of the province of Toronto, but left him to journey through the country and the eastern United States. She planned to write a book on American art but never did so. Soon after her visits to Allston in the fall of 1837 she wrote to her friend Ottilie von Goethe that she would take care that his fame would be known in Germany (*Letters of Anna Brownell Jameson*, ed. H. H. Needler [Oxford: Clarendon Press, 1939], p. 200). After his death she wrote an article about him, "Washington Allston," printed in the *Athenaeum* in January 1844, which was the first substantial account of his life and work up to the time she saw him to appear in an English publication. She gave a summary of his life, drawing on Dunlap, described the paintings by him which she saw in Boston and other cities, and analyzed his personality. She characterized his paintings as having rich color, softness of execution, correct drawing, and both grandeur and grace and noted a predominant violet tint in the flesh and shadows. "No man," she declared, "ever more completely stamped the character of his mind upon his works." She thought, however, that "the ideal powers" had lately overwhelmed his "powers of execution" and that his taste, which was "singularly pure—even to fastidiousness," had gone on refining and his ideal had become more spiritual, his moral sense more elevated, until they seemed to have "overpowered the material of his art—to have paralyzed his hand."

She thought him an "extraordinary man," having "a vehement poetical sensibility," a "nervous temperament," yet a "sort of dreamy indolence," "a touch of the listless and the morbid," and of his person noted the "dignity of his figure" yet "rather careless dress," long hair, and "soft" voice. She also referred to his literary talent, saying he "felt, thought, painted like a poet," and quoted his poem on Rembrandt's *Jacob's Dream,* passages from his letters, and nineteen of his aphorisms around the walls of his studio, "some on fragments of paper stuck up with a wafer or a pin, some on the wall itself," which he told her were to serve as "texts for reflection before he began his day's work." When she heard of his death, she concluded, it was "not with regret or pain, but rather with a start, a shudder, as when a light—which, though distant, is yet present—is suddenly withdrawn," being convinced America had lost her third great man, the other two being Washington and Channing. In her *Companion to the Most Celebrated Private Galleries of Art in London* (1844) she called him "not only the greatest painter America has yet produced, but one of the greatest painters of the age."

Jarvis, Leonard (1781-1854), politician. He lived for many years in Maine, where he held positions as sheriff and collector of customs. After moving to Massachusetts he became a member of Congress and from 1838 to 1841 was a navy agent for the port of Boston. In his recollections of Allston written in 1844 he described their association in college, their meetings in London in the summers of 1815 and 1816, and said that whenever he visited Boston he made it a point to seek him out. On one occasion, when he urged him to show *Belshazzar's Feast,* Allston replied that if it were shown he should never finish it. After Allston's death he told Richard Henry Dana, Jr., that he loved him "as a brother, & so did every one who knew him" and that he had "friends of various descriptions; & people who agreed in nothing else, agreed in their admiration of him" (Dana, 1:224).

King, Charles Bird (1785-1862), portrait painter, a native of Newport, Rhode Island. He and Allston were often together, with Leslie and Morse, in London, when he lived there from 1805 to about 1813. At that time he painted Allston's portrait. Most of his later life was spent in Washington, D.C.

King, John (1766-1846), English landscape painter and surgeon. Originally Nicholas Johann Koenig of Switzerland, he went to England at the end of the eighteenth century, painting in London before going to Bristol in 1799. There and in Clifton he practiced as a surgeon. He was much interested in poetry and was a friend of Southey and Coleridge as well as a patron of local artists (Papers in the City of Bristol Record Office). He and Allston met in 1813, when Allston became his patient. A few years later he acquired, presumably after Elias

Vanderhorst had it and before Allston left England, Allston's *Morning in Italy.* Allston painted his portrait.

Knapp, John (1779-1849), Boston lawyer. For several years he was a representative in the Massachusetts legislature. He was also an occasional poet (HA).

Lamb, Charles (1775-1834), English essayist and critic. Allston sometimes dined with him in London, on one occasion, 30 April 1818, with Henry Crabb Robinson, Benjamin Haydon, John Monkhouse, and two others. At that time Robinson described him as having "a mild manner, a soft voice, and a sentimental air with him,—not at all Yankeeish," but thought that his conversation did not "indicate the talent displayed in his paintings" (*Diary, Reminiscences, and Correspondence of Henry Crabb Robinson,* ed. Thomas Sadler [London, 1869], 25:91-92). Allston was much attached to Lamb, read Thomas Noon Talford's *Letters to Charles Lamb, with a Sketch of His Life* (1837), and, as Richard Henry Dana, Jr., recollected, recounted many anecdotes of him. On one occasion, in the company of Allston, Coleridge, and a few others, Coleridge spoke highly of Dr. Andrew Bell, and Lamb commented that it was because he was so fond of Mrs. Bell, only for Allston to learn after Lamb left that Coleridge had never been heard to speak of her. Allston owned a copy of Lamb's *John Woodvil; a Tragedy, to which are added Fragments of Burton, The Author of the Anatomy of Melancholy* (London, 1802).

Lawrence, Sir Thomas (1769-1830), English portrait painter. During his second stay in England, Allston became well acquainted with him, though he characterized him in later years as too eye-catching. He remembered, as Richard Henry Dana, Jr., recollected, visiting John J. Angerstein's gallery and disagreeing with a young artist who was greatly taken with Lawrence's portrait of Angerstein, while ignoring a superior Van Dyke there. Lawrence's biographer, possibly reflecting his views, identified Allston among American painters by his "broad humor, in the style of Hogarth" (D.E. Williams, 2:6).

Leslie, Anna (1792-after 1860), portrait painter and copyist, sister of Charles Robert Leslie. Born in Philadelphia, she was taken with her family about 1793 to London and returned with them to Philadelphia in 1800. In the 1820s and in 1850 she visited her brother in London. During the 1830s and in 1840 she lived with her sister and brother-in-law, Henry C. Carey, in Philadelphia. About 1844 she established herself in New York, with occasional residences in Philadelphia (Leslie, pp. 2, 13, 66, 302-303, 333, 344; Irving, *Journals and Notebooks* 3:357, 505-506; Irving, *Letters* 2:754).

Leslie, Charles Robert (1794-1859), painter and writer. He was born in London of American parents and except for his early years in America spent most of his life there. Shortly after he returned in December 1811 he met Allston, took rooms with Samuel F. B. Morse, and began to study at the Royal Academy and with Allston. During the next few years he and Allston, together with Morse, were closely associated in and about London, and at the time of Allston's illness in 1813 he stayed with the Allstons briefly at Clifton. He, Allston, and Morse formed a "kind of family," he thought, and during the absence of Allston and Morse in Bristol, he said, he felt as he used to feel when away from his mother and sisters. He considered it "a great honor" to be called Allston's pupil (Prime, p. 73).

Allston directed his attention to the Venetian school of painting, though he was not at first impressed, remembering that when Allston pointed out Titian's *Three Ages* in

Bridgewater House as an exquisite work, he thought he was laughing at him. Allson also acted, he said, as a guide at the most critical period of his life, when he most wanted guidance. After Morse left London, Allston spent every evening with him, at which time he said he would not want to stay in England if Allston left (Leslie, pp. 22, 184). About 1816 he painted Allston's portrait. In 1817 he went with Allston and Collins to Paris.

Shortly after Allston left England, Coleridge wrote him that he would be the more welcome on visits, since "you are all we have of Allston" (*Collected Letters,* 4:927). Subsequently he was Allston's chief correspondent in England. It was mainly through his letters that Allston was kept apprised of current events in art circles in London and probably through Allston's letters to him that Allston's activities in America were known in England. He was widely acquainted with the leading artists, writers, and actors of his day, of whom he left lively accounts in his posthumously published *Autobiographical Recollections.* Allston owned a copy of his *Memoirs of the Life of John Constable, R.A. Composed Chiefly of his Letters* (London, 1843).

Leveson-Gower, George Granville, Lord Granville (1758-1833), **first duke of Sutherland** and second marquis of Stafford. He was a great patron of art and for a time president of the British Institution. His wife was a watercolor painter. Once, Richard Henry Dana, Jr., recollected, when Allston said the old masters diminished those who came after them he assured him that it was not so in his case.

Little, Charles Coffin (1799-1869), Boston publisher. In 1837 he and James Brown formed a partnership.

Longacre, James Barton (1794-1869), engraver and painter of sepia and watercolor portraits. He early established his own business in Philadelphia. In July 1825 he went, with John Neagle, to Boston with letters of introduction to Allston and Gilbert Stuart. On 26 July Isaac P. Davis took him to George Ticknor's to see Leslie's portrait of Scott and also Allston's *The Valentine*, which he later engraved. On 29 July Allston took him to the Massachusetts General Hospital to see Stuart's portrait of William Phillips, and he and Neagle dined with him at Rouillard's restaurant at three o'clock (Whitley, *Gilbert Stuart,* pp. 187-88).

Longfellow, Henry Wadsworth (1807-82), poet and professor. His association with Allston began a year or so after he arrived in Cambridge in 1836 to assume the professorship of modern languages and belles lettres at Harvard. One of his lectures in the summer of 1838 formed the basis of his sketch "The Life of an Artist in Rome," which was published in the *New-York Mirror* for 19 January 1839 and as part of book 3, chapter 5, of his romance *Hyperion,* published that summer. Apparently he drew on what he knew of Allston's stay in Rome, and indeed in his review of the book in the *North American Review*, C.C. Felton compared the artist in the sketch to Allston (50 [Jan. 1840]: 396).

Certainly Longfellow had met Allston by early 1839. In March of that year he saw his painting *The Sisters,* which he called "A beautiful fancy sketch," though he erroneously reported that it had been sold for $500. By that time he had apparently called on the Allstons, for he commented that Mrs. Allston "drops asleep in the evening over her knitting work." The next month he saw other paintings by Allston, presumably at Harding's Gallery, and was especially impressed by the landscapes. In reference to them he quoted to Richard Henry Dana a line or two from Dante's *Purgatorio* and a few days later sent him the entire passage

(28.1-33), in a translation of his own, differing from that which he subsequently published. He exclaimed, "Are not these paintings truly Dantesque in their beauty? The Poet and the Painter seem to have had the same kind of inspiration" and concluded,—"the effect on my mind in reading this and in looking at some of Allston's Landscapes is the same" (*Letters*, pp. 135, 144-45). In December of the same year he was prompted by Park Benjamin's expression, presumably in a letter to him, of "great curiosity and interest" in Allston to read *The Sylphs of the Seasons,* which he said he had often read before but never with so much delight. He wrote a notice of it in his reply, which was printed in the New York *Evening Signal,* of which Benjamin was editor, on 7 January 1840. In it he called Allston's landscapes "magic," described him as living in Cambridgeport as the Sylph of Summer did, uniting "the body's indolence" with "the vigor of the mind," and quoted liberally from the title poem and the poems on paintings by Tibaldi and Rembrandt.

A few months later, on 9 April 1840, he wrote in his journal that he stopped at Allston's painting room on his way to town and described the occasion: "It stands in the Port, an awkward-looking house on the common, with one long window, looking North. Knocked at the green door. All silent, went over to his house. It was past eleven, and a lovely Spring morning. He was still in his chamber; and for aught I know in his bed. He keeps late hours. The parlor window was wide open and the smell of cigars still lingering there, showed how late the evening session had been" (H.W.L. Dana, "Allston in Cambridgeport: 1830 to 1841," p. 44). He called again two days later with C.C. Felton in the evening but Allston was not at home. On several subsequent occasions he called, once with Charles Sumner, and he and Allston dined together, with others, often. Reporting being there on 13 June 1841 with George Ticknor and William Hickling Prescott, he said it was "a very pleasant dinner."

Longfellow disparaged *Monaldi* when it appeared that year, however, as having "a coarse kind of horror in it, adapted to the taste of times when it was written; the times when Monk Lewis and Radcliffe danced the Carmagnole together in grave-yards" (*Letters*, 2:355). The other members of the Five of Clubs group, which he organized soon after coming to Cambridge, were also friends of Allston's: Felton, George S. Hillard, Sumner, and the litterateur Henry Russell Cleveland, who wrote of dining there on 21 August 1838 (to Sumner, 22 Aug. 1838, Longfellow National Historic Site).

At the time of Allston's death there were plans for having a eulogy delivered, which a number of artists invited Longfellow to carry out, but apparently nothing came of them (Elliott, p. 382). For many years afterward he continued to refer to Allston in letters (3:438; vol. 4 [1972], p. 68; vol. 5 [1982], pp. 61, 136, 474, 599; vol. 6 [1982], pp. 440, 791). In 1860, he made the memorandum that "One man may sweeten a whole town. I never pass through Cambridge Port without thinking of Allston. His memory is the quince in the drawer and pefumes the atmosphere" (Richardson, p. 2). Allston owned a copy of his *Poems on Slavery* (Cambridge, 1842), as well as two other volumes by him for which he thanked him in letters.

Lonsdale, James (1777-1839), English portrait painter. He often joined Allston, Morse, Leslie, Frederick W. Collard, and Charles B. King in evening parties in London. Leslie thought his manner much like Collard's (p. 177).

Lowell, Charles (1782-1861), Boston clergyman. Though not mentioned in Allston's correspondence, the two were closely associated from their years as college classmates. After graduating he went to Edinburgh to study philosophy, and, going with other members of his family to the Continent in the latter part of 1804, was in Paris at the same time as Allston. Shortly after his return he was ordained in 1806 as the minister of the new Unitarian West Church in Boston, where he remained until 1851. He shared Allston's fondness for the Lake poets, visited Wordsworth and Southey during his years as a philosophy student, and subsequently corresponded with Southey and with Sir Walter Scott. He owned Allston's *Robbers Fighting with Each Other for the Spoils over a Murdered Traveller, Italian Landscape* (R150), and a drawing of three apples and a branch. According to Edward Everett Hale, the Lowell home, "Elmwood," was not far from Allston's studio in Cambridgeport and Charles Lowell and Allston were "intimate" (Greenslet, pp. 87-88, 94, 117, 121, 132; Leon Howard, *Victorian Knight-Errant: A Study of the Early Literary Career of James Russell Lowell* [Berkeley: Univ. of California Press, 1952], pp. 6, 313; Hale, *James Russell Lowell and His Friends* [Boston, 1899], p. 12).

Lowell, James Russell (1819-91), poet, critic, and diplomat, son of Charles Lowell. Though not mentioned in Allston's correspondence, he knew Allston through his father and throughout his life referred to him familiarly in his writings. He visited the exhibition of Allston's paintings in 1839 more than once and wrote a poem on *Miriam;* it took him scarcely half an hour, written partly on the sheet which he submitted for its publication, and was, he said, an "undecided [sort] of production written too fast to be either very bad or very good." He sent it to the *Boston Daily Advertiser,* but it was never published (*Letters of James Russell Lowell,* ed. Charles Eliot Norton [New York, 1894], 1:37). In his recollections of Cambridge in later years, in both poetry and prose, Allston was prominent. In his poem "An Indian Summer Reverie" (1846) he referred to the fact that "There gentle Allston lived, and wrought, and died, / Transfiguring street and shop with his illumined gaze" and said that he had seen as a boy "That misty hair, that fine Undine-like mien, / Tremulous as down to feelings' faintest call" and besought the Lowell house to "count it to thy fame / That thither many times" he came. His essay "Cambridge Thirty Years Ago" (1854) seems to have grown out of a sketch of Allston begun in 1853 for *Putnam's Monthly Magazine*. In it he said that among the "associations poetic and venerable" in Cambridgeport one of the most prominent was Allston mounting the stagecoach, with his "fastidiously neat" apparel, "*nimbus* of hair," and face "that seemed like pale flame," but giving forth "a single incongruity—a smell of dead tobacco-smoke." He called him "thus far the greatest English painter of historical subjects"; considered "how strong must have been the artistic bias in him, to have made him a painter at all under the circumstances," there being no traditions for art in America at the time, and "how almost miraculous that he should have been a great and original one" and declared that he carried with him to Italy "a nature open on the southern side, and brought it back so steeped in rich Italian sunshine that the east winds (whether physical or intellectual) of Boston and the dusts of Cambridgeport assailed it in vain" (*The Writings of James Russell Lowell* [Boston: Houghton Mifflin], vol. 7 [1894], p. 185; vol. 1 [1893], pp. 72, 73, 75-77).

Of one of Allston's paintings hanging in a ballroom he said it overlooked "with its serene and steadfast eyes the butterfly throng beneath it . . . seeming to gaze from these narrow battlements of time far out into the infinite promise of Eternity," causing one to see "the free, erect, and perfected soul" (Edward Wagenknecht, *James Russell Lowell—Portrait of a Many-Sided Man* [New York: Oxford Univ. Press, 1971], pp. 64, 63). He also referred to Allston in several of his other essays—"Dryden" (1868), "Harvard University" (1886), "Milton" (1872), and "Old English Dramatists." He could be facetious, as when he said of

Elijah in the Desert, comparing it to David Mason's life of Milton, that "a good deal of research at last enables us to guess at the prophet absconded like a conundrum in the landscape where the very ravens could scarce have found him out, except by divine commission." His final reference was, however, sympathetic, as he exclaimed how "scant a pasture" Boston had offered the imagination and mused on the "fate of the great painter who perished slowly of inanition over yonder in Cambridgeport, he who had known Coleridge and Lamb and Wordsworth, and who, if ever any, 'With immortal wine / Should have been bathed and swum in more heart's ease / Than there are waters in the Sestian Seas' " (*Writings,* vol. 4 [1894], p. 63; vol. 12 [1894], p. 14). In 1857 he was listed as the owner of an "Italian Landscape" by Allston exhibited at the Boston Athenaeum, probably that originally in his father's possession.

McMurtrie, James (1784-1854), Philadelphia stockbroker, patron of art, and amateur painter. He and Allston met in London in August 1815 (Prime, p. 91) but apparently never again. (*Philadelphia City Directorys* for 1817 and later)

Malbone, Edward Greene (1777-1807), portrait and miniature painter, a native of Newport, Rhode Island. He and Allston first met there before he left in September 1794 and became friends in Boston in 1796-97. During the summer of 1800 both were in Newport again. Early in 1801 they met in Charleston, South Carolina, and in the summer traveled together to London, where Malbone remained until late October of that year. He painted Allston's portrait in watercolor in miniature on ivory in 1800-01 and a portrait in miniature of Ann Channing about 1800 in Newport (Ruel Pardell Tolman, *The Life and Works of Edward Malbone, 1777-1807* [New York: New York Hist. Soc., 1958], pp. 12, 15, 21, 154). During their time together in London Allston was shocked to find that he had no regard for the old masters and preferred modern painters. One of the books Allston owned was apparently previously owned by Malbone: Carl Friedrich Grosse, *The Dagger* (London, 1795). It is inscribed by Allston on the title page and in another hand "Edw Malbone" on the first page. The back cover contains a caricature drawing, presumably by Allston.

Martin, John (1789-1854), English history and landscape painter noted for his biblical subjects and architectural details. He and Allston were introduced in 1814 by Leslie, who said Allston admired his *Sardak in Search of the Waters of Babylon* and wanted to meet him. When Allston returned to America in 1818 he took with him a copy of Martin's book *Character of Trees in a Series of Seven Plates* (1817), drawn and etched by him. Several years later Martin wrote an account of himself in the *Athenaeum* for 14 June 1834, in which he denied a story that Allston had encouraged him with advice and money in his early years but said that their friendship caused him deeply to regret Allston's departure from England, adding, "I have rarely met a man whose cultivated and refined taste, combined with a mild, yet enthusiastic temper, and honourable mind, more excited my admiration and esteem" (Thomas Balston, *John Martin, 1789-1854* [London: G. Duckworth, 1947], pp. 53, 154).

Mason, Jonathan (1795-1884), portrait and figure painter. A member of the Harvard class of 1815, he never graduated because of a temporary deafness. He was in Europe in 1823, 1829, and in the winter of 1834-35. In Boston he held offices in several civil and mercantile associations ("Necrology of the New-England Genealogical Society," prepared by Increase N. Tarbox, *NEGHR* 27 [1884]; 36); Greenough, *Letters,* pp. 28, 179, 180, 187). Apparently he acted as Allston's agent for several years. He owned Allston's *Rising of a Thunderstorm at*

Sea and a landscape, possibly *Paysage—Site Sauvage,* both of which were also exhibited in his wife's name.

Morgan, John J., English lawyer. He was a longtime friend of Samuel Taylor Coleridge, adviser regarding the publication of his writings, and sometime amanuensis for him. During the years when Allston knew him he was in great financial distress. Allston met him and his wife in London shortly after he arrived in 1811. In the fall of 1813 they moved to London Street, where the Allstons lived, and subsequently the four were closely associated in Bristol. Morgan described Mrs. Allston's relationship to him and his wife as "more than a sister" (Prime, p. 81). In the summer of 1814 Morgan was receiving his mail addressed to Allston's care in Bristol. In August 1815 he suggested to Coleridge's friend William Hood that an edition of Coleridge's works be accompanied by an engraving from either Allston's or Dawe's portrait of him, but nothing came of the matter (Coleridge, *Collected Letters* 3:35, 343-48, 442-43, 520; 4:584, 634).

Morse, Jedidiah (1761-1826), clergyman, stationed at the church in Charlestown, Massachusetts, for over thirty years. He is best remembered as the father of American geography.

Morse, Samuel Finley Breese (1791-1872), artist and inventor, son of Jedidiah Morse. Best known for his invention of the electric telegraph, he was in his early years a history and portrait painter. Apparently he and Allston first met in the spring of 1810, shortly before he graduated from Yale, and he remained one of Allston's closest friends. In 1811 he accompanied the Allstons to England and from then until the summer of 1815, when he returned to America, was intimately associated with them, living near them in London and Bristol, and seeing them almost daily in London. He described the three of them and Leslie as forming "one domestic circle," in which they often talked of their "beloved country" and would "rejoice in her successes, or lament at her reverses" in the War of 1812 and added that "perhaps there were never four human beings, not attached by ties of blood, more fervently endeared to each other" (to Samuel F. Jarvis, 8 Feb. 1815, Morse Family Papers, Manuscripts and Archives, Yale University Library). He expressed his feelings about Allston in a letter to his parents in 1813 in almost idolatrous terms, calling him "that excellent man," saying he did not have "the slightest imperfection," was "amiable, affectionate, learned, possessed of the greatest powers of mind and genius; modest, unassuming, and, above all, a *religious* man," never speaking "a peevish word" or "an inconsiderate sentence," for whom his love "could only compare with that which ought to exist between brothers," and concluding, "I could write a quire of paper in his praise, but all I could say of him would give you but a very imperfect idea of him." He never felt so "low-spirited" as when Allston was ill, he wrote about the same time, often thinking "if he should be taken away at this time, what an irreparable loss it would be, not only to me, but to America, and to the world" and adding "Oh! he is an angel on earth. I cannot love him too much. Excuse my warmth; I never can speak of Mr. Allston but in rapture" (Prime, pp. 59, 84-85). When, after Mrs. Allston's death, Allston lived with him and Leslie, the three often attended the theatre together, sometimes with Washington Irving.

He was the first of Allston's pupils, of which there were few, and the chief one whom Allston acknowledged, saying soon after introducing him to Benjamin West in the fall of 1811 that he should have a quarrel with West unless West should give up all pretensions to him. In London, Morse reported, Allston superintended all he and Leslie were doing, encouraging him when he was perplexed by praising what was good but always telling him what might be bad in his work. He found it sometimes "mortifying" when he had been painting all day and began to be pleased with what he had done to hear Allston say after a long silence, *"Very bad, sir; that is not flesh . . . it is mud, sir; it is painted with brick-dust and clay"* but consoled himself that Allston was "not a *flatterer,* but a *friend,*" and would not only tell him to "*put a few flesh-tints here, a few gray ones there, and to clear up such a part, by such and such colors*" but would take the palette and brushes and show him how (Prime, pp. 245, 42). In turn Allston accepted advice from Morse, as he often did from others. On one occasion, probably in London, as they stood in front of an unfinished painting by Allston in which he was dissatisfied with the color of the drapery, Morse advised him to paint it flesh color to be in keeping with the mass of light in the painting. In response Allston replied, "It is so. It is in nature," and added, "Your theory has saved me many an hour's labour" (Dunlap, 2:318).

In later years he often visited Allston in America. Returning from a visit in the fall of 1833 he said he went "as to the sun to imbibe light" (*Diary of William Dunlap* 3:742; Dunlap, *History* 2:187). When he found, a few years before Allston's death, that he was likely to succeed with his telegraph and make a fortune, he told Channing that he determined to release Allston from all pecuniary obligations so that he could paint freely. He also said to Channing that men should ask what they would do for Raphael should he return and then do that for Allston. When Allston died he announced the fact to the National Academy of Design on 12 July 1843, delivering a short tribute in which he declared that "the artist, the scholar, & the Christian gentleman" were combined in Allston "in a degree never surpassed" and that he had "lost a father & a brother in one" (*New-York Evening American,* 14 July 1843). A few days later Richard Henry Dana wrote him of Allston's failing health in the preceding few years and of his death and asked him to send any letters of Allston's which he might have and an account of their acquaintance, especially of his views of him as an artist.

Shortly afterward at the request of Franklin Dexter, writing for the family, he went to Cambridgeport to consult with them about what to do with *Belshazzar's Feast* (Prime, pp. 468-71). At that time, on being shown a female head among the works in Allston's studio, he commented that Allston had the "true sentiment of delicacy toward the female character," exhibited "great feeling" for him, sought out the brushes with which he had last painted and selected one, which was given him, and spoke of his religious effect on all who knew him (Dana, 1:189-90). In 1865 he bought and presented to the National Academy of Design Leslie's portrait of him together with his brush, saying that he was "more than any other person my master in art" (Prime, p. 708). The next year he bought for $7,000 and presented to Yale his *Jeremiah.* Allston owned a copy of his *Foreign Conspiracy against the Liberties of the United States* (New York, 1835). Though he thought highly of Morse as a painter, there is no evidence that he shared his strict religious views or his chauvinism in politics.

Neagle, John (1796-1865), portrait painter. He spent most of his life in Philadelphia. In July 1825 he and James Longacre visited Allston, bringing letters of introduction to him and to Gilbert Stuart. At that time he dined on three occasions at Allston's house and once with him and Longacre at Rouillard's restaurant. Allston went with him to Stuart's painting room to see Neagle's picture of Stuart, complimented him on it, and regretted that he could not see Stuart's portrait of George Gibbs, the house of Gibbs's daughter Sarah being shut at the time (Whitley, *Gilbert Stuart,* pp. 187-88; Dunlap, 2:377, 1:215). Neagle owned the clay head model which Allston made for *The Dead Man Restored.*

Newton, Gilbert Stuart (1794-1835), painter of portraits and scenes drawn from literary works and humorous and domestic life. He was a nephew of Gilbert Stuart. Born in Nova Scotia, he spent most of his life in England. He met Allston in Paris in 1817 and traveled with him and William Collins to London, where he shortly afterward shared living quarters with Leslie. Leslie and Washington Irving called him "the Childe" because of his affectation (Leslie, pp. 220-61 and passim). Richard Henry Dana, Jr., recollected Allston saying that he dined with him once in Boston in 1832, expecting to hear news of art and artists in London but was dejected that not a single one was praised.

Northcote, James (1746-1831), English history and portrait painter. Noted for his conceit and arrogance, he dsparaged to Allston the painter William Hamilton, according to Sweetser, and more than once in later years expressed disdain of Allston. When, at a dinner party with Coleridge and Lamb shortly after Coleridge met Allston in Rome, Coleridge praised Allston's work, he expressed surprise that Allston was unknown if so good, as Coleridge, imitating his accent, relayed with amusement to Allston on his return to England. After the success of *The Dead Man Restored,* he asked another artist if Allston meant to "coot" him out. On one occasion Allston pleased him by telling him of a favorable comment on a book he had written, presumably his *Memoirs of Sir Joshua Reynolds*. In Allston's recollections in later years he was prominent (Alcott, p. 53).

Norton, Andrews (1786-1853), biblical scholar and man of letters. Although not mentioned in Allston's correspondence the two were well acquainted. They may have met at Harvard, though Norton did not enter until the year Allston graduated. He was prominent in the theological controversies of the time, in which he held the Unitarian position. According to Sweetser, Allston was a "frequent visitor" at "Shady Hill," his estate in Cambridge, and he owned some "minor pictures" by Allston, probably *David Playing before Saul* and *Moses and the Serpent,* which were subsequenly in the possession of his son Charles Eliot Norton (p. 145). Probably he also owned the manuscript of Allston's poem "Ah, where is my Phillida gone?" which went from Charles Eliot Norton's library after his death to Harvard.

Palfrey, John Gorham (1796-1881), clergyman and editor. He bought the *North American Review* in 1835 and was the editor from 1836 to 1842.

Partridge, Alden (1785-1854), military educator. He graduated from the U.S. Military Academy at West Point in 1805, became first lieutenant of engineers in 1806 and captain in 1810 and remained there as a teacher, later becoming acting superintendent. In 1817 he resigned from the army, having been court-martialed on several charges of neglect of duty and sentenced to be cashiered, though the sentence was remitted by the president. Thereafter he established a series of military schools, of which the American Literary, Scientific and Military Academy at Norwich, Vermont, was one. It opened about 1823 and was widely advertised in the South (Callahan, 1:773; "South Carolinians at the Partridge Military Academy, 1826," *SCHGM* 41 [1960]: 11; "The Memoirs of Frederick Adolphus Partridge," ed. Samuel Gaillard Stoney, *SCHGM* 65 [1944]: 146).

Paterson, Hugh, notary public and insurance broker in Charleston, South Carolina (*Charleston City Directory* for 1801-1804).

Payne, John Howard (1791-1832), actor, dramatist, editor, and diplomat. He lived from 1813 to 1832 in Europe, nearly all the time in London. Allston first knew him as well as all his family in Boston, where the father was master in the Berry Street Academy from 1796 to 1807 and where Payne as a precocious star acted briefly in the old Federal Street Theatre in the spring of 1809 (Leslie, p. 190; Gabriel Harrison, *John Howard Payne, Dramatist, Poet, Actor, and Author of Home Sweet Home! His Life and Writings* [Philadelphia, 1875], pp. 13, 39; Charles H. Brainard, *John Howard Payne, A Biographical Sketch of the Author of "Home, Sweet Home" with a Narration of the Removal of his Remains from Tunis to Washington* [Washington, 1875], p. 10). According to Sweetser, in later years he described Allston to Irving as "always a gentleman," who would "talk by the hour" told and acted ghost-stories, had "touches of gentle humor," was "Rather indolent," would lie in bed, smoked cigars, and was a "man of real genius" and a "noble painter" (p. 173). He owned Allston's drawing *Danger.*

Peabody, Elizabeth Palmer (1804-94), Boston educator and author. She was a lifelong admirer of Allston and published more accounts of him during his life than anyone else. The "first revelation" of his "genius" to her, she said, was his *Beatrice,* which she repeatedly visited at the Boston Athenaeum in 1826. She also remembered seeing *Moonlit Landscape (Moonlight)* there and *Rosalie* in his studio, on which latter occasion he recited his poem of the same title (*Last Evening with Allston,* pp. 46, 57-58). After a visit with him about 1835 she reported that he said "a hundred fine things" and spoke at length of Goethe, agreeing with her that the current Goethe-worship was "ridiculous nonsense," saying that he was certain Goethe knew "*nothing at all* about *Art,*" and that his admiration of Jacob Phillip Hackert proved him incapable of understanding art, since Hackert "had not a particle of genius" (*Letters,* pp. 58, 153-54).

On 13 January 1835 she took Bronson Alcott to see him for the first time, on which occasion they reached the house at an early hour after dark and stayed until past midnight, while discussing art, artists, writers, and actors, among them Canova, Coleridge, Wordsworth, Hazlitt, Lamb, James Northcote, Sarah Siddons, Fanny Kemble, Charles Mathews, and Benjamin Disraeli (Alcott, p. 53). The two went again on 22 May 1836, to tea, she because of her article on Allston in the *American Monthly Magazine* that month, which had pleased him; she reported that his praise made her feel as though she was receiving a proposal and so flustered her that she started away without her bonnet, though he and Alcott did not notice, being occupied in disagreeing about Coleridge (Tharp, pp. 106-107). On another occasion when she called on him, on 23 June 1839, she wrote her sister Sophia that he was "in delightful spirits, but soft as a summer evening," that they talked of Sophia, that she gave him a copy of Hawthorne's *Twice-Told Tales* in exchange for a copy of her own which she had evidently previously lent, and that he said he "thirsted for imaginative writing, and all the family had read the book with great delight" (*Letters,* p. 226). When she opened her bookshop in 1839 she took his advice and stocked artists' supplies; through his arrangement she became sole agent in New England for the London colorman Thomas Brown (Tharp, p. 136). He offered to help her further by writing letters to artists in London from whom she might secure material for the publication of Channing's pamphlet *Emancipation,* dealing with the emancipation of slaves in the West Indies, which she published in 1841. She said that he entered her shop only once, at which time she had just heard of Channing's death, and that she saw him only once again, on the occasion of her last evening spent with him (*Reminiscences of Channing,* pp. 42, 449-50; Tharp, pp. 138-39).

Miss Peabody wrote three essays and one letter to a newspaper about Allston. The first,

"Alston the Painter," appeared in the *American Monthly Magazine*, n.s. 1 (May 1836): 435-46, reprinted, with a few revisions, as "Life and Genius of Allston" in her *Remarks on Allston's Paintings* and *Last Evening with Allston*. It was the first comprehensive account of him to be given, drawing for biographical details on Dunlap. In a long introductory section omitted when it was reprinted, she adopted Auguste Comte's division of the times of man into the eras of the infinite, the finite, and that in which the relations of the two were developed and gave as examples of the third era Michelangelo and Allston. In this connection she characterized Allston as having been "endowed by nature and education with every advantage" and having added "a holy life, flowing on the one hand from a deep sensibility to religion" and on the other "a severe and uncompromising self-restraint as to every questionable indulgence." As examples of his development into a more "spiritual philosophy," she cited *Beatrice* and *Rosalie*.

In another section omitted in the reprinting, she took up the subject of *Belshazzar's Feast,* whose unfinished state, she said, was complained of only by "the short-sighted, or one-eyed public," and pointed out that Allston had succeeded while working on it in making "*sunshine* in so many *shady places* of private life," in contrast to the public place it was destined for. As examples of such works she named *The Valentine, Beatrice,* and *Rosalie* as belonging to "a new class of pictures," not to be merely looked at but to be "communed with as living beings," adding that *Lorenzo and Jessica, A Tuscan Girl, A Spanish Girl in Reverie, Young Troubadour, Evening Hymn, Italian Landscape* (G62) *Landscape, Evening (Classical Landscape), Moonlit Landscape (Moonlight),* and *Spalatro's Vision of the Bloody Hand* belonged to this group. In a third passage not reprinted she discussed briefly the "Ethics of Art," quoting Henry N. Coleridge's statement that genius needed "an outward aid" and saying that "in our business-like country" the "national treasury" contributed little "to educate these, its diviner children!"

After the essay was printed in *Remarks on Allston's Paintings,* Allston said he wished "that all those personal remarks in the book" had been omitted, adding, "I have never coveted personal notoriety." He particularly objected to the statement that his had been "a holy life." As he explained, "The word holy is there used while speaking of me in a way in which it should not be used about any one. I am sure I know no individual who deserves it. No man lives a holy life, and least of all myself. If it had been a moral life I would not have objected to it, but [it] was painful to me to see that word used regarding myself. But it was well meant, and I am not offended. With that person I could not be angry if I would." He went on to say, however, "With regard to what is there said of my pictures, I should never argue with any one however I might differ from them. What they see in my pictures they see, and it is not my affair to explain them. Some things [I] agree with, others not; but it does not admit of argument" ("Color Book," pp. 67-69).

Miss Peabody's second essay about Allston, the longest, was her review of the 1839 exhibition, originally appearing in the *Salem Gazette* in May and June 1839 in a series of nine articles. It too was reprinted in her *Remarks on Paintings by Allston* and *Last Evening with Allston.*

Her last essay, "Last Evening with Allston," was first printed in *Emerson's Magazine and Putnam's Monthly* 5 (Oct. 1857): 497-503, and reprinted in *Last Evening with Allston, and Other Papers*. Her visit on that occasion took place about three weeks before his death. She could recall, she said, some of his remarks "nearly in his own words," and she enclosed some of them in quotation marks. He brought out of an old portfolio a dozen little India ink sketches which were studies for pictures made in the preceding century, some of which he had painted and some he purposed to paint, and gave her one, *Old Man Resting Against a Rock,* which he signed and dated.

He told her of the large number of sketches he had and of his desire to found a school as old Italian artists had and sketch and finish only, leaving students to do the rest of the work under his direction. Touching on a variety of subjects, he praised the drawing school of one of the Morses in New York, possibly Alpheus O. Morse, recommended drawing and modeling for a painter, spoke admiringly of Spenser, quoted a stanza of his poem "To the Author of 'Diary of an Ennuyée," described some of his religious experiences, reciting "The Atonement," and cited instances of the interaction of material and spiritual worlds in Hebrew and Christian books, dying saints, and the smiles of children. She also described his corpse before it was put in the coffin looking more healthy than Clevenger's bust of him, gave an account of his last evening with his family, and said that whenever he parted, even from members of his family and for the night only, "it was done with so much sensibility that it would do well for the last time." Finally she described his funeral (pp. 1,18).

A few weeks after his death she wrote a letter to the *New-York Tribune,* entitled "Religious Character of Washington Allston," signed "E," which appeared on 10 August 1843, in reply to the article "Anecdotes of Washington" in the Boston *Atlas* as reprinted in the *Tribune,* in which she corrected the story about the sale of *Uriel in the Sun,* particularly that it caused Allston to become religious. She said that in the "considerable acquaintance" she had had with him his association with Coleridge was "a very common theme of conversation" and consequently she knew something of the "chronology of his spiritual history" and "the character of his religious feeling," neither of which supported the allegations of the article in the *Atlas.* A "profound religious humility," she wrote, was "the keystone of his character, and the foundation of the magnanimity which made him at once the most dignified of gentlemen, and the most gentle and amiable of friends." She concluded by hoping others would send their recollections of him to the Danas and Channings, to be used in published accounts.

Allston owned a copy of her edition of Alcott's *Record of a School: Exemplifying the General Principles of Spiritual Culture* (Boston, 1835).

Peabody, Sophia Amelia *See* Hawthorne, Sophia Amelia (Peabody).

Pepoon, Benjamin F. (d. 1854), Charleston, South Carolina, attorney. He was a forceful supporter of the Union in the decades preceding the Civil War. ("Death Records [1829-1865]," comp. Henry A. DeSaussure, *SCHGM* 49 [1958]: 177; "Poinsett-Campbell Correspondence," ed. Samuel Gaillard Stoney, *SCHGM* 42 [1941]: 153-55; *Charleston City Directorys* for 1816-1837/38).

Perkins, Thomas Handasyd (1764-1854), Boston merchant and philanthropist. He was an officer in the state militia and consequently generally known as colonel. In 1818 he traveled back from Europe with Allston. He owned his *Saul and the Witch of Endor* and *Galen* or *Storm at Sea* and was a subscriber to the Tripartite Agreement.

Pickering, Henry (1781-1838), merchant and writer. Born in Newburgh, New York, he entered the counting room of his cousin Pickering Dodge in Salem, Massachusetts, in 1803. After the failure of the business there he returned to Newburgh, where he supported himself by literary work. Though not a college graduate, he was familiar with Latin, Greek, and French literature. He also collected works of art, edited *The Scientific Journal,* published in

Boston in 1837, and published four volumes of poetry. A miniature of him was painted in London (Harrison Ellery, *The Pickering Genealogy* [Cambridge, 1877], 1:264-65). Allston owned copies of at least three of his volumes: *The Buckwheat Cake, a Poem* (Boston, 1831) and those for which he thanked Pickering in letters. Probably Pickering sent him a copy of the fourth also.

Porter, George Washington (1818-99), clergyman. He was born in Beverley, Massachusetts. In 1839 he was a teacher in Boston. He was ordained in 1846 and subsequently was in charge of parishes in several New England states and New York as well as being the proprietor of a school in Boston. In 1861 he was given the degree of S.T.D. by Hobart College (*Boston City Directory* for 1839; William Dana Orcutt, *Good Old Dorchester: A Narrative History of the Town, 1630-1893* [Cambridge, 1893], pp. 279-81; *History of the Town of Dorchester, Massachusetts* [Boston, 1859], p. 416; "Necrology," *The Church Almanac* [New York, 1900], p. 409; *Church Militant* 2 [Mar. 1899]: 13).

Quincy, Josiah (1772-1864), politician and educator. From 1823 to 1827 he was mayor of Boston and from 1829 to 1845 president of Harvard. His son Edmund S. said that he and his family were intimate friends of Allston from 1819 on and that while they resided in Cambridge Allston always sent for them to come to his studio whenever a picture was finished. Edmund said that he purchased several of Allston's works but they were not retained by the family (Quincy to Drake).

Raczynski, Count Athanasius or Atanazy hrabia (1788-1874), Polish diplomat, art critic, and art collector. He served as representative from Prussia in Denmark, Spain, and Portugal and wrote books on Portuguese and German art (*Der Grosse Brockhaus* [1956]).

Reed, Henry Hope (1808-54), editor and critic. From 1831 until his death he was professor of English literature at the University of Pennsylvania. He was the first American exponent of Wordsworth and edited a number of works by and about him. He and Allston met in the summer of 1842, when, introduced by a friend, he spent several hours in the evening at Allston's house, on which occasion Allston discoursed on Wordsworth, Coleridge, and Lamb, and, hearing his hope of visiting England, said, "with the emphasis of an earnest sincerity," "I want you to see Wordsworth." He did not do so, however, until he made the visit several years later, a few months before he died. In commenting on Allston's death to Wordsworth, he said Allston had been "warmly loved, as well as admired for genius in his art" and in the letter he wrote Richard Henry Dana after Allston's death spoke of his "gentleness and purity," "placid magnanimity" and "moral culture" and quoted from Allston's letter to him of 13 June 1843 (*Wordsworth & Reed*, pp. 82, 111, 112; Flagg, p. 375).

Roberts, George, Boston journalist. The chief newspaper with which he was connected was the penny *Boston Daily Times*, which he and William H. Garfield founded in 1836 and of which he was the proprietor until it ceased publication in 1857. He also ran the *Boston Notion* and *Roberts' Semi-Monthly Magazine for Town and Country* (15 Jan. 1841-1 Jan. 1842), which merged with the *Quarto Notion*. He had a reputation for unreliability. Richard Henry Dana, Jr., who once argued a suit brought against him in England by a London firm, thought "no decent man in Boston" would be seen speaking to him" (Mott, *American Journalism 1690-1960* [New York: Macmillan, 1950] p. 238; Dana, 1:196, 242).

Robertson, Alexander (1772-1841), miniaturist and landscape painter. He was secretary of the American Academy of Fine Arts from 1817 to 1825.

Rogers, Robert (1758-1835), of Newport, Rhode Island. He operated a classical school there from 1786 for several years. He also served several Baptist churches in the city and nearby and was active in the development of the Redwood Library and the administration of Brown University (*Biographical Cyclopedia of Representative Men of Rhode Island* [Providence, 1881], 146). In later years he remembered that on his nightly rounds of the school to see that lights were out he always found Allston reading. Allston painted his portrait.

Rogers, Robert, a Boston merchant. From 1834 to 1836 he was a notary public at the Custom House (Boston Directories, 1821-29). His wife, Mary Channing, was a sister of WA's first wife (Dean and Dudley, p. 319).

Sargent, Henry (1770-1845), portrait and history painter. He spent from 1793 to 1799 abroad in study. Finding the profession of an artist unpromising in America he entered the army. As a member of the state militia he was first a first lieutenant, then captain, and in 1815 aide-de-camp to the governor, with the rank of colonel.

Scollay, Catherine (1783-1863), landscape and figure painter. She exhibited paintings of her own and a few by other artists at the Boston Athenaeum in 1827, 1828, 1830, 1833, 1837, and 1848. A series of six views of Trenton Falls in New Jersey by her were lithographed by John B. Pendleton.

Scott, Sir Walter (1771-1832), Scottish novelist and poet. His writings inspired Allston over a period of several years: in a drawing of Rob Roy, from the novel of that name (1817); *Minna and Brenda by the Seashore, Isaac of York,* and *Amy Robsart.* He burlesqued Scott's "The Fire-King" in "The Paint-King," and his painting *Rosalie* and poem "Rosalie" bore the name of the lady in that poem. In his lecture "Art" he cited Scott's characters as examples of "Ideal Invention" and thus timeless (*LA,* p. 97). The narrator of "The Hypochondriac" in quoting the opinion of the *Edinburgh Review* that metrical romances may be "imported . . . in bales" probably had reference to poems by Scott as well as Byron and others. When the church of the Shepard Congregational Society in Cambridge was being built Allston often took friends to see the site and repeated the lines from *The Lay of the Last Minstrel* about "fair Melrose" (2.1.1-2). He owned copies of Scott's *The Lady of the Lake* (Boston, 1810) and *Marmion* (Philadelphia, 1808).

Sharp, William (ca. 1802-?), pioneer color lithographer, portrait and landscape painter, and drawing teacher. Born in England, he came to America in 1838 or 1839 and settled in Boston.

Shattuck, George Cheyne (1783-1854), leading Boston physician of the day and noted as a philanthropist. Allston designed the monument he placed in 1837 in the Shattuck-Cheever plot in Mount Auburn Cemetery, his wife being a member of the Cheever family. It was put in marble by Alpheus Cary (Eleanor Shattuck to George Shattuck, 4 Apr. 1837, Shattuck Papers, MHS; RHD, p. 36).

Sigourney, Lydia Howard (Huntley) (1791-1865), author. She spent most of her life in Hartford, Connecticut. Her poems and prose writings, generally of moral instruction and predominantly on the theme of death, were highly popular, appearing in books, annuals, and periodicals. Possibly she met Allston on visits to Boston in 1841 and 1842, when she saw Richard Henry Dana, Jr., there, if not before (Dana, 1:55, 108).

Smith, John Rubens (1775-1849), painter and engraver, who was born in London, came to America by 1809. He lived in Boston until 1814 and afterward in New York and Philadelphia, where he established a drawing academy. Though he had the reputation of being an excellent teacher, his quarrelsomeness made him unpopular, on which account he is said to have left Boston. Allston knew him both there and in London and no doubt knew of his animosity toward the National Academy of Design, which did not invite him to become a member.

Southey, Robert (1774-1843), English poet. He was a close friend and by his first marriage a brother-in-law of Coleridge. While in college Allston had the "independence," as Jarvis put it, to like his poetry. They were introduced in London by Coleridge during the first few days of September 1813, at which time Southey said he thought that *The Dead Man Restored* alone would give Allston a reputation higher than any artist of the age (*New Letters of Robert Southey* 2:70, 73). He also praised Allston's poems, declaring them to be among the finest productions of modern times and saying certain ones, despite defects, could have proceeded only from a "poetic mind" (Pierce, 2:70). In *A Vision of Judgment* (1821), he referred to Allston's fame in England and America. Like Coleridge, he was interested in America and, according to Sweetser, once told Allston that if there were not many old books there he could not live there. Allston owned copies of his *Carmen Triumphale, for the Commencement of the Year 1814*, 2d ed. (London, 1821), and *The Expedition of Orsua, and the Crimes of Aguirre* (London, 1821).

Spalding, Lyman (1775-1821), physician and surgeon. He received an M.B. from the Harvard Medical School in 1797, the year after Allston entered college. Soon afterward he established himself in New York, where he was active in several civic organizations.

Story, Joseph (1779-1845), jurist. He became a member of the U.S. Supreme Court in 1811 and professor of law at Harvard in 1829. In his oration "The Scholar, the Jurist, the Artist, and the Philanthropist" Sumner described his leaving the churchyard after Allston's burial: "In vivid words . . . he poured forth his admiration and his grief. Never was such an Artist mourned by such a Jurist" (*The Phi Beta Kappa Address* [Boston, 1846]). Richard Henry Dana, Jr., recorded "the interest he took in preserving the memorials of his fame as an artist and a poet," his grief at Allston's grave, and afterward his being "foremost in every thing that was proposed tending to secure the passing impressions" of Allston's genius and fame among us (*Life and Letters of Joseph Story*, ed. William W. Story [Boston, 1851], 2:321-22).

Story, William Wetmore (1819-95), sculptor, essayist, and poet. After practicing law in Boston for several years, he went in 1847 to Italy to devote himself to sculpture and in 1856 settled in Rome, where he remained the rest of his life. In his review of the Boston Athenaeum exhibition of 1842 in the *Pioneer* (1 [Jan. 1843]), under the pseudonym I.B. Wright, he singled out Allston's *Diana and Her Nymphs*, saying that "Among the many daubs, it shone like a bright star. . . . The pine tree in it lives, and one can almost hear the wind whispering through its leaves" (p. 15). In later years, from his point of view as a European resident, he more than once contrasted the genius and achievement of Allston with the American environment in which his last years were spent. Writing to James Russell Lowell in 1855, he noted his and Lowell's need of a sympathetic audience and declared that Allston "starved spiritually in Cambridgeport; he fed upon himself. There was nothing congenial without, and he turned all his powers inward and drained his memory dry. His works grew thinner and vaguer every day, and in his old age he ruined his great picture," adding that his was a "rich and beautiful" nature, in which "the south ran warm."

Many years later he had sufficiently revised his estimate to write the committee in charge of the Allston Celebration in Boston on 1 November 1880 a lengthy letter, couched in extravagant terms. He called Allston "one of our great men. Pure in his life as a child, modest in his character, and of a delicacy and refinement of imagination in his art that entitles him to take rank with the great masters." Though he was too young and shy to see Allston in his early years, he recalled his conversation during a long evening when taken to see him by Charles Sumner and other conversations which led him into the presence of art "as a high-priest leads the trembling neophyte to the altar." Allston's appearance itself made him remain "the most ideal and poetic person" he ever saw. He concluded by enclosing three sonnets of his own composition, in which he said that Allston and his art were "Hallowed" by "A gentle nobleness, a quiet grace / From some ideal sphere of beauty caught" and that he was "in life's prose . . . half out of place / An exile . . . from higher realms"; and spoke of the "faint perfume" of his "delicate, fine verse" and his "high philosophies of art" (Flagg, pp. 388-89, 392-93). In his poem "George Stillman Hillard. In Memoriam" his reminiscences of Hillard's contemporaries included Allston, in the lines "And once the lambent eyes, the hallowed head, / Of Allston, by an inner dreamlight led" (*Proceedings of the MHS,* 1st ser., 1882, 19 [Boston, 1881-82]: 346-48).

Stuart, Gilbert (1755-1828), portrait painter. He and Allston first met in Boston, soon after Allston returned from England in 1808 and were often associated. In 1825 John Neagle asked him why the two did not get up an academy of arts in Boston, to which he replied that "men of wealth and pretension generally interfered, to the detriment of arts and artists (Dunlap, 1:216). In the same year they were together on the Board of Artists of the Bunker Hill Monument Association to choose a design for the monument. They were frequently contrasted both in painting and in personal manner. In August 1823 the painter Nathaniel Jocelyn made notes, accompanied by drawings, about the palettes of both, which had significant differences. Allston's had three tints of yellow ocher, Chinese vermilion, Antwerp blue, and ivory black, and Stuart's had two tints of ocher, vermilion, and blue as mixed with white and also mixtures of Van Dyke brown and burnt umber, of black and yellow, and of black and vermilion, the latter mixture being for shadows. Allston called Stuart's "a very philosophical" palette and said if he were to practice portrait painting he did not know but he should adopt it. Both palettes were of mahogany, but Stuart's was small (Manuscripts and Archives, Yale University Library). William Ware spoke of the "coarse red and white of a great deal of Stuart's work" in contrast to the color of the Venetians whom Allston followed, and in later years George Inness contrasted the realism of Allston's portrait of West with Stuart's "pink fancy" as well as Lawrence's "piece of bosh" of the same subject. Thomas Gold Appleton, Nathan Appleton's son, told the story that Samuel Lawrence of London said on seeing paintings by them side by side that Stuart had accomplished more perfectly than Allston what he had attempted but that Allston had attempted what Stuart could not have conceived (Ware, p. 67; Inness, "A Painter on Painting," *Harper's New Monthly Magazine* 56 [1868]: 460; Appleton, "Portrait Painting and Gilbert Stuart," *International Review* 10 [1881]: 64-71).

Stuart's barbed wit and habit of punning were noted for being unlike Allston's manner. A revealing instance of the difference between them was Stuart's comment, as Jarvis recorded, on a sea piece painted by Allston shortly after returning to Boston that he did not think anybody could best Allston "in making water." His portrait of Allston, painted a few months before his own death, was unfinished but was considered by Allston's friends the best of all. Richard Henry Dana said of it, "It is a mere head, but such a head, and so like the man."

Sully, Thomas (1783-1872), English-born portrait painter. He came with his family to America in 1792 and lived with them for several years in Charleston, South Carolina, where he was influenced by his schoolmate Charles Fraser to take up art. He was early helped by Gilbert Stuart in Boston and soon established himself in Philadelphia. He and Allston met in Boston several times: in the summer of 1821; in December 1826, at which time, from the eighteenth to the twenty-eighth, he painted *Moonlight Scene* from Allston's *Moonlit Landscape (Moonlight)* (Biddle and Fielding, p. 371); and in June 1831. Probably it was in 1826 that Allston took him, at his request, to see *Elijah in the Desert* at the house of Sarah Gibbs, who invited them also to see Stuart's portrait of her father, (Dunlap, 1:214). He designated Allston as "number one" among painters, though expressing the opinion that he produced nothing after his return from Europe which equaled that produced there (Averill, p. 335), and studied his technique carefully. He recorded that Allston observed that though Stuart condemned vermilion he could not find a substitute but that he himself used "Venetian red," which, "if of good quality and well washed" would answer every purpose if a glazing of madder lake" were added, a superior kind of which was called in Italy *terra rosa*. Allston recommended emphatically, Sully further recorded, "solid tinting in painting flesh, especially for large pictures that are to be seen at a distance." He quoted Allston as saying, "Paint pure, decided tints: if too raw, you may correct them by scumbling—glaze at pleasure" and "never use brown drapery to a dark or yellow complexion; it will look like a snuff-bag," and as recommending "the use of a very slight glazing of asphaltum to a portrait, face and all." He also quoted Allston's advice, "O, do not undertake any thing that cannot be accomplished by your own means" (Dunlap, 2:140, 185).

Sumner, Charles (1811-74), statesman and orator. His acquaintance with Allston probably began soon after he graduated from Harvard in 1830. From 1837 to 1840 he traveled abroad. While in London in 1839 he wrote George S. Hillard, passing on William Collins's inquiry about and wishes to be remembered to Allston. In his letters to Horatio Greenough during the next few years he often gave news of him. In that of 30 September 1840, in reply to Greenough's letter of 12 July, in which Greenough had asked to be remembered to Allston and "his brothers" and looked forward to seeing them again, he said Allston had inquired a great deal about him and would be delighted to see him again, reported that *Belshazzar's Feast* had been unrolled and stretched across the entire end of his studio but was covered with a curtain "as a breakwater of our curiosity," and that his recently completed *Amy Robsart*, was "a beautiful woman," who had "golden hair, and that sweet look of feeling which you find in all Allston's pictures, particularly of women,—*qualem decit esse sororum*," and added that when Greenough came they would go out and have a long evening with him.

The next February he wrote that he and Longfellow had passed an evening with Allston "some weeks" ago, on which occasion when they rose to go he took out his watch and seeing that it was twenty minutes of twelve said, "Do make it even." He hoped Greenough's desire to have Allston come to Italy would materialize, since he declared he would "bud anew" there. In September of the same year he quoted Allston as saying *Monaldi*, then in press, was "about as large as 'The Vicar of Wakefield'" and said he longed to see it, since Allston's "beautiful mind must throw delightful colors" on the subject of the life of an artist in Italy. After Allston's death he endeavored to raise $2,000 for a monument to him. Judge Joseph Story, Franklin Dexter, George S. Hillard, and he were to control the project, and Thomas H. Perkins was to head it, but according to Sweetser, Mrs. Allston opposed it (Greenough, p. 287; Pierce, 2:70, 167, 184, 186, 188, 264; Dana, 1:176). In his oration "The Scholar, the Jurist, the Artist, the Philanthropist," delivered before the Phi Beta Kappa Society of Harvard on 27 August 1846, he took Allston as his example of the artist. He characterized him there as "a good man" as well as "a consecrated artist, an expounder of the principles of art equal to Leonardo da Vinci, Albrecht Durer, Sir Joshua Reynolds, and Henry Fuseli, and a writer of sonnets comparable to those of Michelangelo. Yet Allston's paintings, he said, seemed to suggest "a higher genius than they display; and we are disposed sometimes to praise the master rather than the work." In conclusion he speculated that had Allston lived his "Virgilian sensibility and modesty" would have ordered the destruction of *Belshazzar's Feast,* as Virgil had his manuscripts destroyed, and compared that painting to the one by Titian finished after his death by Jacomo Palma but inquired "where is the Palma to complete *Belshazzar's Feast?*" (*Phi Beta Kappa Address*).

Taylor, John Duncombe, planter, officer, and politician in Antigua. He was baptised on 2 February 1774, elected to the Antiguan Assembly in 1799, and became a member of the Council in 1833 (information from Kevin Reed, Hamilton, Victoria, Australia). He married Mary Cooper Vanderhorst.

Taylor, Mary Cooper (Vanderhorst) daughter of Elias Vanderhorst. She was the wife of John Duncombe Taylor, by whom she had one child, Cordelia Duncombe Taylor (information from Kevin Reed, Hamilton, Victoria, Australia).

Tefft, Israel Keech (1794-1862), Savannah banker. Born in Rhode Island, he was taken to Boston in childhood and in 1816 moved to Savannah, where he spent the remainder of his life. He had great interest in literature and history, numbered among his visitors many prominent Americans and Europeans, and assembled one of the best autograph collections in the United States (*Dictionary of Georgia Biography,* ed. Kenneth Coleman and Charles Stephen Gurr [Athens, 1893], 2:964-65).

Ticknor, George (1791-1871), educator and author. Though he must at least have known of Allston earlier, they met probably for the first time in London in 1815 before 31 May, shortly after he arrived there on his way to Germany for study. At that time he expressed admiration for *Donna Mencia* in the Royal Academy exhibition. Allston wrote a letter of introduction for him to Samuel Taylor Coleridge, which he delivered on 28 January 1819, on his return to England en route home, asking that he be introduced also to Wordsworth and Southey and calling him, Coleridge said, "a man of liberal principles" (*Collected Letters* 3:916). In 1825 they were together on the Board of Artists of the Bunker Hill Management Association to choose a design for the monument. On first entering the library in his house on Common Street, Allston expressed unlimited approval. In 1828 Ticknor corresponded with Henry C. Carey about possibly engraving *The Flight of Florimel,* but he called it not one of Allston's favorites and did not think it would engrave well (Ticknor to Carey, 18 Feb. 1820, Pierpont Morgan Library). In general, however, he admired Allston's painting. *Miriam* he thought a virtual creation of sound. He wrote Richard Henry Dana from Rome in 1837 that there was not a man in Europe who could paint like him. On several occasions he dined with Allston, as on 16 June 1841, when William Hickling Prescott and George S. Hillard were also present (*Life, Letters and Journals of George Ticknor,* 2:76, 196). He owned Allston's *The Valentine* and was a subscriber to the Tripartite Agreement.

Tomlin, John (1806-50), poet and story writer. Most of his life was spent in Jackson, Tennessee, where he had a store and acted as postmaster for several years. He corresponded with several contemporary writers, the most prominent of whom was Poe (Elizabeth C. Phillips, *The Literary Life of John Tomlin* [Ph.D diss., University of Tennessee, 1953]).

Vanderhorst, Elias (1738-1816), brother of Allston's maternal grandmother, Elizabeth Vanderhorst (Webber, "Moore of St. Thomas' Parish," pp. 164-65). He married Mary Raven Cooper in 1763 and 1774 went to England with his family. From 1792 to 1812 he was U.S. consul in Bristol.

Vanderlyn, John (1775-1852), history and portrait painter. He and Allston first met in London in Benjamin West's studio soon after he arrived in July 1803 and in the fall they traveled together to Paris, where Vanderlyn was to procure copies of paintings by old masters and casts of antique scupture for the American Academy of the Fine Arts in New York. They were together again in Rome often, where Vanderlyn spent from November 1805 to December 1807, living part of the time at least a few doors from Allston in the house of Salvator Rosa. At that time he described him as "full of genius & talent & with all that an excellent worthy character" (Averill, p. 68). After Allston's death he wrote an account of him, "Tribute to the Memory of Washington Allston by a Brother Artist," *Charleston Courier,* 15, 16 July 1844, in which he expressed regret that he had been "doomed" to linger out his life in an environment uncongenial to art and that he had had no commission for a public hall or a private collection and referred to his "highly cultivated and poetic mind" and "fair and amiable character." He owned a drawing reportedly by Allston depicting three standing female figures facing a kneeling figure in the attitude of supplication.

Van Schaick, Myndert (1782-1865), New York merchant. (*New York City Directory* for 1817-65/66). He and his wife knew Allston in Bristol in 1813 at which time presumably he commissioned from him his *Rebecca at the Well.* Shortly before returning to America in the fall of 1814 he sent greetings to Allston through Morse (Morse, 1:151). He was a state senator from 1833 to 1836 and held other civic offices in New York (Edgar A. Werner, *Civil List and Contitutional History of the Colony and State of New York* [Albany, 1888], p. 334; "Obituary Notices," *New York Genealogical and Biographical Records* 3 [1827]: 152).

Verplanck, Gulian Crommelin (1786-1870), author and politician. He and Allston met in 1817, probably soon after he went to England in the spring. They saw each other in Paris that fall and presumably again when he was in London, often with Irving, later in the year (Irving, *Letters* 1:476, 512). Allston owned copies of his *Discourses and Addresses on Subjects of American History, Arts, and Literature* (2 vols.; New York, 1833) and *The Right Moral Influence and Use of Liberal Studies* (New York, 1833), as well as two other books by him, for which he thanked him in letters.

Visger, Harman, Bristol merchant, U.S. consul there from 1825 to 1832. His cousin, who was captain of the vessel on which the Allstons and Samuel F.B. Morse sailed to England in 1811, gave them letters of introduction to him. Allston knew him in Bristol in 1813 and 1814. For a short time about May 1814 his address was at Visger's. Early that year Visger corresponded with Morse about buying one of Allston's paintings and said he would prefer a landscape or a comic piece to *Diana Bathing*. He also engaged Allston to paint a large transparency of a gigantic figure shrinking in terror from an imp sitting on his shoulder, but nothing further seems to be known about it. In November 1814 he bought three paintings by him, which may have been the several mentioned by Coleridge, who said he paid £160, rather than the sum he did pay. Shortly after it was exhibited at the British Institution in 1818, he bought his *Hermia and Helena* and for a time owned his *Morning in Italy.*

Wallis, George Augustus (1770-1847), Scottish landscape and history painter, in later years an art dealer, who lived for many years in Italy. Allston knew him in Rome, where Wallis learned the technique of glazing from him, and in London during the years 1814-18. He had a wide reputation for mendacity. After their return to England in 1806, Coleridge wrote Southey that he had lost thirty pounds "in *Customs*" by Wallis's "[ingrati]tude to Allston," apparently referring to some arrangement among the three (*Collected Letters* 3 [1956], 43). Richard Henry Dana, Jr., recollected Allston's telling that on one occasion in Rome Wallis asked him how he obtained the cloud effects which were admired in one of his paintings, and, when he went to Wallis's studio and painted in clouds for him, said in response to Coleridge's feigned admiration that he had already known Allston's method. In his novel *Ernest Carroll,* Henry Greenough, who presumably met him in Italy, pictured Wallis as the elderly English painter Bruce, who reminisces about his association with Allston. Carroll would have known Bruce even before meeting him, he said, from Allston's mimicry of him. Referring rather to the association in Rome of Allston and Coleridge, Bruce-Wallis says he and Allston were "inseparable in Rome . . . they called us Damon and Pythias." Bruce is probably speaking reliably as Wallis, however, when he remembers that at that time Allston was completely absorbed in studying the processes by which the old master colorists produced their effect, says he should never have left England, and refers to a letter he wrote Allston from London after his return to America, saying he had seen a picture by Reynolds "painted by damned dishonest means"—Reynolds being a stickler for the Italian method of coloring—and to an occasion in London when Allston asked after his housekeeper Caterina in Rome and was told that she was dead, though in fact she had been turned off, after being his mistress, without money (pp. 149, 152, 161).

Waterhouse, Benjamin (1754-1846), physician and pioneer vaccinator. He was a native of Newport, Rhode Island, where he was a friend of Henry C. Flagg. As a boy he took up painting briefly and went to London with Gilbert Stuart. Allston knew him as a student when he was professor of the theory and practice of physics at Harvard; in his senior year he took a course from him in natural history. In later years he said that for Allston he had "always had the strong partiality of a friendship partaking of the paternal; for he was under my special care during his college life." During the exhibition of Allston's paintings at Harding's Gallery in 1839, he wrote in his journal on 3 May that he felt he could claim him as "in some sense my *éleve*" and referred to his "justly acquired reputation," though he was sorry to see "laboured eulogiums" on him in newspapers, since his pictures "speak for themselves and need no puffing by little trumpeters." He felt that Allston had "considerately and properly" sent him and his family tickets of admissions as heretofore (H.W.L. Dana, "Washington Allston at Harvard, 1796-1800," p. 15; William Roscoe Thayer, "Extracts from the Journal of Benjamin Waterhouse," Cambridge Historial Society Publications, *Proceedings for the Year 1909*, p. 33). Allston owned a copy of his *An Essay on Junius and His Leters, embracing a sketch of the life and character of William Pitt, earl of Chatham, and Memoirs of certain other* *distinguished individuals; with reflected historical, personal, and political, relating to the affairs of Great Britain and America from 1763 to 1785* (Boston, 1831).

Waterston, Robert Cassie (1814-93), clergyman, writer, and public speaker (J.P. Quincy, "Memoir of the Rev. R.C. Waterston," *Proceedings of the MHS*, 2d ser., 8 [1893]: 292-302). He visited Allston frequently, keeping the dates from 10 April 1835 to 2 June 1840 in a memorandum book (Longfellow National Historic Site). According to Sweetser, about 1838 Allston gave him a sketch made in 1798. A few days before Allston died he paid him a visit, bearing an invitation from Robert Weir to visit him, but Allston declined because of being so busy painting and said that his wrists were so tired every night that they ached. It was Waterston who informed Wordsworth of Allston's death.

Webber, Samuel (1797-1880), physician, son of the Harvard president of the same name. He settled in Charlestown, New Hampshire, in 1823. He was active in educational, financial, and medical groups both there and elsewhere and wrote several poems, an Indian Tale, and a treatise on English grammar ("Necrology of the New-England Genealogical Society," prepared by Increase N. Tarbox, *NEGHR* 34 (1881): 289-90).

Welles, Benjamin (1781-1860), Boston banker. In 1803 he was in England when Allston was there, and the next year they traveled to Italy, where they were together until he left in the spring. In later years he was engaged in banking with his cousin John Welles in a company auxiliary to the banking house of Welles and Company of Paris (HA). He was a subscriber to the Tripartite Agreement. At the news of Allston's death he was so overcome that he could not speak and wept "like a child" (Dana, 1:173).

West, Benjamin (1738-1820), history painter. After spending three years in Italy, he settled in England in 1763, where he soon acquired fame. He became historical painter to the king, second president of the Royal Academy, instructor to and sponsor of a series of young American artists, whom he habitually urged to visit Europe for study, and a collector of paintings by old masters. Breaking with the tradition of portrait painting in America, he was a pioneer in both the neoclassical and the romantic movements. He was a good, but wooden, draftsman, and though not noted for his use of color, he recommended the study of Titian, especially, to achieve sublimity and majesty. By the time Allston went to England his popularity was waning. Allston painted his portrait and wrote a poem about him, "Sonnet to My Venerable Friend, the President of the Royal Academy," praising his youthfulness in age, his freedom from envy and selfishness, and his achievement of true fame. Though he came to revise his original high opinion of West, Allston was closer to him than to any other painter in England throughout his years there and his most successful follower.

Wheeler, John (1796-1862), educator. He graduated from Dartmouth College in 1816 and from Andover Theological Seminary in 1819. From 1833 to 1849 he was president of Dartmouth (Duffy, pp. 8, 9, 59).

White, Thomas Willis (1788-1843), printer and editor. He worked in Boston from 1813 to 1817. His most important enterprise was the founding and editorship of the *Southern Literary Messenger* in Richmond, Virginia.

Williams, David H., Boston bookseller (*Boston City Directory* for 1838-43).

Winthrop, Francis Bayard (1787-1841), merchant. Born in Boston, he moved with his family in his early years to New York and after graduating from Yale in 1804 returned there. From 1823 until his death he lived in New Haven. At one time he was a member of "The Society for Architectural and Rural Improvements" in the city (Franklin L. Dexter, pp. 730-31; Roger G. Osterweis, *Three Centuries of New Haven, 1638-1938* [New Haven: Yale Univ. Press, 1953], pp. 270-71). He owned Allston's *Alpine Landscape* and in 1829 was said, probably erroneously, to have his *Rebecca at the Well* (Bryant, 1:275). He also owned several works by the genre painter John Lewis Krimmel (Dunlap, 2:464).

Woods, Daniel Bates (1809-92) clergyman, son of Leonard Woods, Jr. He graduated from Amherst College in 1832 and from Andover Theological Seminary in 1837 and was ordained in 1839. He spent his life preaching and teaching, in New York State, Virginia, Philadelphia, Ohio, and Missouri (*Andover Theological Seminary General Catalogue, 1808-1908* [Boston: T. Todd, 1909], p. 160).

Wordsworth, William (1770-1850), English poet. Even before meeting Allston, he said, he was led by Coleridge to admire and love him, and it was chiefly because of Coleridge that he placed him in such high regard, his "direct personal knowledge" of him being "very slight," since they met no more than half a dozen times (*The Letters of William and Dorothy Wordsworth,* 3:1185). He nevertheless expressed admiration for Allston's character as well as his paintings and his poetry on many occasions. They apparently first met on 6 May 1812, when he was staying at Sir George Beaumont's house in London and Allston, Dr. Andrew Bell, and the journalist John Taylor came for dinner. Allston, he said, was "elegantly dressed" and seemed to enjoy what was said, though did not talk much. During the next few weeks they were together several times. On 9 May he visited Allston's studio and spent an hour discussing his *Cupid and Psyche,* which deeply impressed him, chiefly by its unusual coloring, but which he thought could have been improved by less contrast between the white of the figures and the gloom of the background, and he suggested "diffusing" instead a "luminousness," which would gradually fade away; Allston agreed, saying he would attempt to follow the suggestion if he repainted the subject. At that time Wordsworth wrote his wife that he had seen no new man that had interested him except Allston and described him as "slim & somewhat lank & delicate in appearance, seeming taller than he is with jet-black hair, and a complection out of which the colour appears to have been taken by a hot & relaxing climate. But his features though small are animated and intelligent." On 17 May he, Allston, Coleridge, and Sir David Wilkie were dinner guests at Beaumont's. The next day he, Coleridge, and John J. Morgan called on Allston, and Allston, Coleridge, and Wilkie dined at Beaumont's, on which occasion he wrote his wife that he liked Allston "much" (*The Love Letters of William and Mary Wordsworth,* pp. 135, 161). He regretted that Allston had not stayed in England, since though "his genius & style of painting were too much above the standard of taste, at that time prevalent, to be duly acknowledge[d] at once, by the Many" he would eventually have obtained general admiration and would have continued to be near the works of the great masters which could but have been beneficial to him (*Wordsworth & Reed,* p. 41). After Allston's return to America Wordsworth sent him a copy of his *Peter Bell.* On hearing of his death he spoke of him as "that admirable artist and amiable Man" (*Wordsworth & Reed,* p. 109). He wrote Richard Henry Dana shortly afterward that in the works of Allston he saw that his "decided power of higher conception, and his skill in dealing with the material" were "far beyond that of any other painter of his time" and that "it was truly as Coleridge used to say, 'coloring, and not color'" (*The Letters of William and Dorothy Wordsworth* 3:1184).

Allston admired his poems, asked for a copy of one, left among his papers a handwritten copy of "The Linnet" (Houghton) and sent him a copy of the English edition of *Monaldi*, inscribed "To William Wordsworth with the respects of the Author. Cambridge Port, Mass., America," with corrections of the text made in the margins. It was subsequently signed by Wordsworth. In the "Introductory Discourse" of his letters on art Allston quoted part of line 67, "shades of the prison-house," from "Ode on Intimations of Immortality from Recollections of Early Childhood" to illustrate his point that the pleasure received from the perception of harmony is limited only temporarily, and in his late years he recollected his associations with Wordsworth and imitated his reciting of his poetry (*LA*, p. 18; Alcott, p. 54). Like him, Allston repeatedly described in his poems the kinship between nature and the mind of man as first and most joyously felt in early years. The name of Lucy in his poem "The Complaint,"conventional as it was in elegies at the time, was that of the maiden made famous by Wordsworth in his five "Lucy poems" of 1799. In his last known letter, written a few days before his death, he quoted from one of Wordsworth's poems.

Wyndham, Sir George O'Brien, third earl of Egremont (1751-1837). He was famous as a patron of art and for his hospitality toward artists, being especially close to Turner and also to Wordsworth. When Allston knew him he was vice-president of the British Institution. His country estate, Petworth House, was a veritable museum, noted for its Van Dykes and Holbeins, and a landscape showplace. He himself expressed preference for Hogarth and Raphael and in later years said *Jacob's Dream* reminded him of Raphael. Leslie said that next to Beaumont he was first to appreciate Allston's merit (Dunlap, 2:246). He owned his *Jacob's Dream, The Repose in Egypt,* and *Contemplation.*

Appendix 2
Artistic Masters

Among the old masters, Allston's chief attachment as an artist was to the painters of the Italian Renaissance, whom he both admired and followed. In technique it was their color that most impressed him, and in content it was their ideality. Sir Joshua Reynolds was of almost equal importance to him, primarily because of his theories of art. The chief other artists of whom he took notice were the Dutch and Flemish, most of whom he thought less than great in their characteristic realism but praiseworthy for their faithful imitation of natural forms.

The Italian Masters

Cagliani, Paolo, known as **Paolo Veronese** (1528-88), Italian painter of the Venetian school. He was the painter next after Titian to whom Allston was most indebted and most often compared for his color. Allston saw paintings by him probably first in West's Gallery in London and certainly in Paris in 1803. The catalog of the exhibition of his paintings in Bristol in 1814 described *Casket Scene from "The Merchant of Venice"* as being "in the manner of Paul Veronese." He copied Veronese's *Marriage at Cana* and in his lecture "Composition" called it "a Venetian Entertainment" and cited it as an example of the utmost length to which variety could be carried in a subject of a "gay and light character" (*LA*, pp. 144-45). Sarah Clarke remembered that he said he liked to "echo" Veronese's colors (p. 13).

Correggio, Antonio Allegri da (1494-1534), Italian painter. Allston was often compared to him, especially in coloring. In his lecture "Composition," he cited the remark of Annibale Carracci on seeing a painting by Correggio for the first time that he thought a style totally opposite might be captivating, thus influencing Guido to realize the suggestion; and named Correggio, among other artists, exemplifying differing economy of line (*LA*, pp. 155, 151). In *Monaldi* the cavalier S——says a vulgar critic may think Monaldi's work unnatural but another kind of critic is required "to understand our rapt Correggio," and Monaldi says Correggio's "magic chiaro-scuro" is missing in Raphael (pp. 29, 80). Allston told Henry Greenough that he mixed spirits of turpentine and Japan gold size for glazing foliage and such parts of his painting as he wished to glaze over several times in one day according to a practice which seemed to be very nearly that said to have been used by Correggio. In his "Color Book," in point 9 of the section "Lights & Shades," he advised a painter to let the shadows of human figures or animals blend imperceptibly into the lights and other shadows instead of making them "hard" and "strong" and concluded, "It is in this that Correggio excels" (p. 11). According to Sweetser, Thomas T. Spear said that about 1840 Allston told him that Correggio was the master on whose works he had modeled his style and extolled Correggio's "mottled" manner; in consequence he explained his own custom of painting with mingled blue, red, and yellow, carefully stippling over the work at the end with the color he wished to be predominant, and repeatedly advised Spear to "paint in the family of the *ishes*," that is, to avoid sharp and pronounced colors and prefer reddish to red, bluish to blue and the like (p. 144).

Leonardo da Vinci (1452-1519). Allston made only a few references to him, but all reflect admiration for his conception of the ideal artist. In "The Two Painters" his shade is appointed by Minos as the judge in the debate between the Colorist or Painter of Body and the Painter of Mind because when on earth he "displayed / The scattered powers of human kind / In thy capacious soul combined" and is asked to "judge as thou wert still in life." In delivering his verdict the shade condemns the Painter of Mind for following "the Schools / Distorted by pedantic rules" instead of Nature and holds up Raphael to be imitated among painters and condemns the Painter of Body for ignoring man's higher nature. He sentences both to paint together for five centuries in the hope that each will mend the fault of the other and they may be returned to earth "Yet there One only Painter be," since "two Half-Painters make but One." (*SS*, pp. 81, 85). In his "Color Book" Allston quoted two passages from Leonardo's *Tratta della Pittura*, one the admonition that an artist should take relaxation from his painting periodically and the other the observation that "Whoever flatters himself that he can retain in his memory all the effects of nature is deceived; for our memory is not sufficiently capacious; therefore be constant in consulting nature, which will supply us with an infinite series of effects as well as forms, endless in their varieties" (pp. 19-20).

Michelangelo Buonarroti (1475-1564). He was the artist who most dominated Allston's imagination and influenced him, whom he ranked above all others for the ability to transcend the physical and temporal. He wrote three poems about him: "Sonnet on a Falling Group in the Last Judgment of Michael Angelo, in the Capella Sistina," saying that his "giant hand" had hurled human forms down through "space interminable"; "Sonnet. Art," in which he was said to have given birth "To forms unseen of man, unknown to Earth" and to have brought to view "The invisible Idea," whose form he knew "by his inward sense" to be true; and "On Michael Angelo," in which he was said to stand alone, having "a supernal light" within him. (*SS*, p. 149; *LA*, pp. 327, 375). The imagery in the second also occurs in his "Sonnet. Thought." In a version of part of the second, written on a drawing for his painting *Christ Healing the Sick* depicting a recumbent and a standing figure, Michelangelo is declared "Link'd to no class abstracted & alone," who "standest aloof, and yet to vulgar eyes / A fragment loosen'd from the common mass," whose "shape" was "uncouth scarce worthy, or for use / Or useless ornament to be replaced."

In his lectures on art he called Michelangelo "the mighty sovereign of the Ideal, than whom no one ever trod so near, yet so securely, the dizzy brink of the Impossible," characterized his "genius" as "essentially *Imaginative*," estimated the influence on him of the *Torso Belvedere* as being akin to the "unembodied creatures in his own mind," named him among other artists exemplifying economy of line, and referred to several specific works: *Lorenzo de' Medici*, which he called "an embodiment of the mind"; the lost *Baptism*, whose details he enumerated; the *Aurora*, which he described at length, saying it was the most striking example of the personification of "Sentiment, of the Abstract" and referring to "the suggestive sorcery of this sublime Statue"; and the prophets and sibyls of the Sistine Chapel as "that gigantic race," giants in mind as well as body, which do not seem like beings to be "affected by the ordinary concerns of life." He recognized faults in Michelangelo, however, saying that they came "from erecting into a model the exaggerated *shadow* of his own practice; from repeating lines and masses that might have impressed us with grandeur but for the utter absence of the informing soul" or "character," as exemplified in many of the figures in the *Last Judgment* (*LA*, pp. 101, 139, 138, 140, 132, 133, 139, 141-42).

In *Monaldi*, as Monaldi and Rosalia stand before a cartoon by Michelangelo Rosalia says that many blame his moroseness for his not touching their heart but that "*something*" in his works lifts one above "our present world," that she never leaves the Sistine Chapel without feeling it impossible to believe anything to his discredit, and that he makes her "think" rather than "feel," the effect being more than "mere sensation"; and Monaldi explains his alleged lack of human sympathy by suggesting his heart was "so sublimated by his imagination that his too refined affections . . . sought a higher sphere," adding that his figures were "neither men nor women—at least like us that walk the earth—but rather of a race which minds of a high order might call up when they think of the inhabitants of the planet Saturn," and defends him against the current talk of his extravagance and want of truth (pp. 82-84). In agreement with Monaldi, one of Allston's aphorisms states that Michelangelo's fame is "a nonentity" in the absence of a congenial surrounding atmosphere (*LA*, p. 173).

Allston also knew and agreed with some of the ideas in Michaelangelo's poetry. In the "Introductory Discourse" of his lectures on art he quoted from it in refuting Winckelmann's charge in *History of Ancient Art* (bk. 4, chap. 2, sec. 14), that though Michelangelo often spoke of lofty beauty in his poems his female and youthful figures were unnatural, saying that his "Bellà and Bellezza" were not intended in a literal sense but "to express abstract Perfection, which he allegorized as the mistress of his mind, to whose exclusive worship his whole life was devoted" (*LA*, p. 65). Both Italian words and variants of them occur repeatedly in Michelangelo's poetry in the Neoplatonic contrast he made between physical and spiritual love, the latter having its source in God, notably in Sonnets 54, 57, 60, and 72. Allston's concept of beauty, as manifest not only physically and morally in the universe but residing in and emanating from a higher realm, set forth most explicitly in this discourse, was also essentially Platonic (*LA*, pp. 101, 140, 160, 132-33, 65).

Raphael Sanzio (1473-1542). He was the greatest influence after Michelangelo on Allston's painting. Allston characterized him above all for the ability to represent human forms and feelings. He wrote a poem about one of his paintings, "Sonnet on the Group of the Three Angels before the Tent of Abraham, by Raffaelle, in the Vatican," in which he described feeling as he viewed it as though "another sense" had descended from heaven "Of Grace, harmonious, boundless, and intense." In "The Two Painters" the judge, who is Leonardo's shade, calls Raphael's ghost "Elysium's fairest boast"; says he learned "from every School," from Leonardo "to smile," from Michelangelo "a nobler Form," and from Fra Bartolomeo the "magic spell" of color; and thinks his "charms" are such as appeal to "those of Mind" (*SS*, pp. 151, 82-83). In his lectures on art Allston described at length Raphael's *Death of Ananias* and alluded to it a second time, called Raphael "refined," and said he perhaps caught more from others than anyone, borrowing from the forms of the antique, Leonardo, Michelangelo, and Fra Bartolomeo, yet having fewer lapses into "manner" than any other artist, as in the figure of St. Catherine in the *Sistine Madonna* and the *Sacrifice at Lystra*. He described Raphael's mind as "an ever-flowing fountain of human sympathies" and declared that "in all that concerns man" he might well be called "a master," who "reigned over the hearts of his fellows" and whose figures left no doubt that they all had mothers, brothers, and kindred. In depicting "the human being in his endless inflections of thought and passion," he thought, there was "little probability he will ever be approached." He named him among other artists exemplifying Natural Invention and differing economy of line (*LA*, pp. 90-93, 139, 155-56, 140, 141, 159-60, 151).

Monaldi is described chiefly as a follower of Raphael. The subject of his early painting of the sacrifice of Noah was painted by Raphael. He is hailed by his contemporaries, who are said to number more than any train of admirers since Raphael's time, as coming in Raphael's "spirit," and is commissioned by the pope to paint a companion painting to one of Raphael's Madonnas. While viewing it Monaldi is introduced to Rosalia by her father and engages with them in a conversation about Raphael and Michelangelo, in which Rosalia says that Raphael must have been "a very amiable man" judging from his works and that the Madonna is her and her father's favorite. Monaldi says that criticism can affect Raphael but little either way, since he "speaks to the heart" and that, though in execution he had faults and was surpassed by nature in beautiful faces, the superior characteristics of Titian and Correggio in color and chiaroscuro would not have added to the "sentient spirit" which he communicated and which made his viewers supply his deficiencies. Until he saw this work, Monaldi declares, he had never known the power of painting. He expresses the opinion that self-reproach must have been no small punishment for some of Raphael's conduct if it was "at all proportioned to his exquisite perception of moral beauty" and refers to his having been "beloved" as well as "admired" by his contemporaries. After Monaldi has left them Rosalia's father says he could almost think they had been talking about Raphael (pp. 30, 25, 79-82, 85).

In conversation Allston expressed much the same opinion of Raphael as he did in his writings. Richard Henry Dana, Jr., recollected that he said Raphael was "in painting what I take Mozart to have been in music. He was the painter of the affections" (Flagg, p. 366).

Allston often compared Michelangelo and Raphael. In his lecture "Form" he said it was chiefly to the Italian school that the student should be directed and above all to these artists, whom he called "the two great sovereigns of the two distinct empires of Truth,—the Actual and the Imaginative," since their highest efforts comprised "certain revelations of Nature which could only have been made by her privileged seers" (*LA*, p. 138).

He told Henry Greenough that Michelangelo's style of drawing was "mannered, peculiar to his individual nature and intellect, while Raphael's was truer to nature and more suitable to form a school of drawing," and Richard Henry Dana, Jr., recollected his saying that Raphael "had not the genius of Angelo, yet he will always have the sympathies of mankind with him. The creatures of Michael Angelo are often superhuman, the results of a glorious imagination; but the creatures of Raphael, beautiful as they are, have always a father and a mother" (Flagg, pp. 198, 366).

He finally ranked Michelangelo above Raphael in his pursuit of the ideal and in his imaginative power. In his own painting he was indebted to Michelangelo's monumental forms and supernatural beings, as in his several depictions of Old Testament stories. But he was closer himself to Raphael, as in the evocation in his most distinctive works of an essentially human, feminine spirit. He adopted poses of figures from Raphael more often than from Michelangelo, and the number of his comments on Raphael is somewhat greater than those on Michelangelo. It is significant that his ideal artist Monaldi is identified with Raphael. His *Uriel in the Sun* with its larger-than-life figure having a warmly sweet expression perhaps best represents the combination of the Michelangelesque and the Raphaelesque elements in his genius.

Reni, Guido (1575-1642), Italian painter. In his lectures on art WA ranked him above Raphael in depicting the purely beautiful and said he surpassed his master Annibale Carracci in achieving a style closer to Caravaggio than Carracci had imagined (*LA*, pp. 31, 155). In

Monaldi Romero, a mosaic worker, makes a miniature copy of a "Magdalen" by him (p. 136).

Tintoretto, Jacopo Robusti (1518-94), Italian painter of the Venetian school. In his lecture "Composition" Allston quoted the inscription on the door of his painting room about the ideal combination of Michelangelo and Titian. He also referred to it in his advice to the young artist recorded by Henry Greenough, in which he also said that Tintoretto was indebted to Michelangelo for the elevation of his forms and to Titian, to whom he was "nearly allied in genius," for introducing him to the "mysteries of nature"; but that, "though irregular, eccentric, and often inferior," he went beyond Titian to "poetical regions" of which Titian never dreamed (*LA*, pp. 156-57). Richard Henry Dana, Jr., recollected Allston's saying the same thing about his coloring.

Rosa, Salvator (1615-73), Italian landscape, history, and portrait painter. In his early years Allston was greatly influenced by him. In his lecture "Composition" he described his line as effective in its diversification, though in contrast to that of Claude, and called Vernet an imitator of him (*LA*, pp. 149, 161).

Titian (ca. 1477-1576), **Tiziano Vecelli** *or* **Vecellio.** He was one of the great influences on Allston after Michelangelo and Raphael and one to whom he was often compared in coloring, most notably by the Germans in Rome, who called him "the American Titian" during his stay there (Dunlap, 2:167). Probably he saw works by Titian first in the collections of West and others in London and certainly admired them in Paris in 1803. He made a copy of a detail from Titian's *Adoration of the Magi,* which was taken by more than one viewer for an original Titian or Veronese, and took the blond figure in *The Sisters* from Titian's *Girl Holding a Jewel Casket.* In his "Color Book" and also in his conversations with Henry Greenough he quoted Titian's phrase about internal light, and he acknowledged following Titian's practice in the use of a neutral mixture in glazing and in intermingling colors on his brush. In his lectures on art he referred to Titian's habit of occasionally turning a work to the wall to forget it until he could see it with fresh eyes, a fact which he got from Marco Boschini's *Descrizione ci tutte le pubbliche pittore della citta Venezia e isole;* said Raphael would have benefited from knowing him; and named him among other artists differing in economy of line. He told Jedidah Vincent Huntington that Titian was not only the best portrait painter but the best landscape painter, or at least inferior only to Claude (Huntington, p. 172). More than once he compared Titian and Tintoretto, saying that the younger learned from the elder but in some instances went beyond his "more cautious spirit" (*LA*, pp. 107, 151, 156-57). Richard Henry Dana, Jr., recollected his characterizing Titian as "poetical" in color, perhaps the only way he was poetical, but that no one could be truer in objects of the senses and that Tintoretto sometimes surpassed him in color (Flagg, p. 866). According to Sweetser, in later years he was given one of G.P.A. Healy's copies of Titian in gratitude for his friendship.

The French Masters

Gelée, Claude, or **Claude Lorrain** (1600-82), French landscape painter, who spent most of his life in Rome. He was the landscape painter whom Allston most admired and to whom in his landscapes he was most often compared. In his lectures on art he referred more than once to Claude's late development, classifying him with some of "the greatest artists" in this respect and accounting for his eventual achievement by his becoming acquainted with the great works of art in Rome. It was the growth of Claude's mind thereafter which he emphasized. "In all that respects the mind," he said, he was "literally a child" before then, and his progress through the rudiments of art seemed to have been "scarcely less slow and painful than that of a child through the horrors of the alphabet," being "the struggle of one who was learning to think." But the rudiments once mastered, "he found himself suddenly possessed, not as yet of thought, but of new forms of language; then came thoughts, pouring from his mind, and filling them as moulds without which they had never, perhaps, had either shape or consciousness." He compared the system of lines in his scenes and those in Salvator Rosa's, characterizing Claude's as having "perfect *unity,*" as if, "circumscribing his scenes by a magic circle, he had imposed his own mood on all who entered it," combined with "the feeling embodied in the complete image of intellectual repose,—fulness and rest," so disposing the mind that the "charmed eye" could then glide into the scene, to stop after passing from one spot to another "instinctively closing, and giving place to the Soul, there to repose and to dream her dreams of romance and love" (*LA*, pp. 96, 157-58, 149-50). In this passage, indeed, Allston was describing the mood and the process by which it was created in his own painting.

Poussin, Gaspar (1613-75), French landscape painter who spent most of his life in Rome. He was the adopted son of Nicolas Poussin.

Poussin, Nicolas (1594-1665), French landscape painter who lived in Rome much of his life. Allston admired him and in his general treatment of landscape was influenced by him. He was pleased to think he saw the same scenery which Nicolas and Gaspar Poussin did at Olevano. In his lectures on art he referred to Nicolas only in passing, however, objecting to his borrowing figures of Michelangelo and Raphael and naming him among other artists as an example of "Natural Invention" and of differing economy of line (*LA*, pp. 159-60, 88, 151).

Reynolds

Reynolds, Sir Joshua (1723-92), the first great English painter and chief expositor in English of theory and practice in the visual arts. Allston became acquainted with his *Discourses,* delivered as president of the Royal Academy from 1768 to 1790, about the time he graduated from college and was influenced by them the rest of his life. He expressed his admiration for and indebtedness to Reynolds many times, most specifically in his letter to Henry Pickering of 23 November 1827 and his conversations with Henry Greenough. It is perhaps significant that he called the first of his lectures on art "Introductory Discourse" and in subsequent lectures referred to it by that term. In his lecture "Form" he called Reynolds's *Discourses* "in many respects admirable" and thought, Sully said, that Reynolds had "more philosophy than Fuseli" (*LA*, p. 122; Rutledge, "Dunlap Notes," p. 36).

As painters, Allston and Reynolds were colorists and idealists, and both took as their chief masters the artists of the Italian Renaissance. Both also set forth theories of art which broke with academic, predominantly neoclassical tradition. The only paintings by Reynolds to which Allston referred were *Puck* and *Hercules Strangling the Serpent in His Cradle,* both of them imaginary conceptions.

The theories of art formulated by both Allston and Reynolds were based on the conception of a work of art as the product of the mind of the artist acting upon the forms of nature and guided by the great works of the past. In disparaging rules, both excepted those based on the study of nature, and in advocating the study of nature recognized the variety and imperfection in individual natural forms, from which it was the function of the artist to abstract the general, ideal form. In advocating also the study of the great artists of the past both stipulated they meant studying their "principles" rather than making slavish copies of their works and distinguished between "borrowing" or the adaptation of "a thought" or an "attitude," which they sanctioned, and "plagiarism" or "imitation" without much modification, both using also the words "transplanting" and "appropriation." In their discussion both cited Raphael's use of an antique bas relief in his *Sacrifice at Listra,* but whereas Reynolds approved it, Allston did not.

Verbal echoes of Reynolds's pronouncements on a variety of other subjects occur in Allston's lectures and other writings. Though both praised the *Apollo Belvedere,* the *Venus dei Medici* and a few other antique statues, in Discourse 8 Reynolds said that their "general characteristic is bordering at least on inanimate insipidity," and in an aphorism describing the variety in nature Allston concluded that "The insipidity of many of the antique Statues may be traced to the false assumption of identity in the corresponding parts" (*LA*, p. 170). With the generally low estimate which both had of Dutch painters, Reynolds proposed in Discourse 6 that had Jan Steen "had the good fortune to have been born in Italy, instead of Holland" he would have been elevated by the study of Italian painters, and in his "Introductory Discourse" Allston said that an artist born in Italy would not go to Holland "to realize his Idea" but that "many a Dutchman has sought in Italy what he could not find in his own country" (*LA*, p. 31).

Both objected to the use of modern dress in statues, in some of the same words. In Discourse 3 Reynolds said that the ancients had "little or nothing to unlearn," since their manners approached the simplicity of nature but that modern artists had to remove the veil with which "the fashion of the times" had covered her; and in Discourse 7, after giving the *Laocoön* and the *Apollo Belvedere* as great examples of the "naked" in Greek sculpture, said that the simplicity of Greek dress made such absence of costume less of a sacrifice than it was in modern times and contrasted the appearance of a European, with his shaven face and artificial hair, and that of a Cherokee Indian, with his painted body, concluding that whichever of the two despised the other for inattention to the fashion of his country was the "barbarian." In his "Introductory Discourse" Allston illustrated the "strange disfigurements of the human form" by supposing a "fashionable" couple to be met on the borders of a new settlement in the American West by an Indian hunter who would be unable to imagine "what kind of animals they were" and in his "Color Book" was quoted as saying the education of a modern artist consists of getting rid of false notions in "an artificial state of Society," so that "The more he learns the more he returns to a state of Simplicity. The Greeks had nothing to unlearn. The human figure was constantly before them in its unclothed beauty, and they were perpetually studying it. Their children were naked always." A version of the description in his "Introductory Discourse" of a savage seeing a fashionable couple follows, and the passage concludes: "The business of an artist, is to educate himself in unlearning, rather than in learning" (*LA*, pp. 22-23; "Color Book," p. 53).

The chief difference between Allston and Reynolds as writers about art was that Reynolds's slight philosophizing was in the vein of eighteenth-century rationalism, whereas Allston's theories were an expression of romantic, Neoplatonic idealism. One of the most specific examples is their differing conceptions of Beauty. Both called it "intellectual," giving as an example the *Torso Belvedere*, but Reynolds, in Discourse 3, which was devoted to the subject, said it was applicable to "general" and "perfect" form in contrast to imperfect individual forms. In his "Introductory Discourse" Allston identified it with Truth and Holiness as phases of "One Intuitive Universal or living Power" and in his lecture "Form" took exception to Reynolds's declaration in Discourse 3, which he quoted with slight variations, that "The *beauty* of the Hercules is one, of the Gladiator another, of the Apollo another; which of course makes so many different Ideas" on the grounds that it assumed beauty to be "the summit of every possible excellence" and that it applied the term to "objects of the same kind rather than those differing in kind" (*LA*, pp. 121-22).

Personally Allston and Reynolds were similar in their reputation for geniality, conversational powers, modesty, encouragement of young artists, and many charities. Both were widely read and exhibited their familiarity with literature and music as well as the arts of painting and sculpture in their writings.

Dutch and Flemish Schools

In general Allston ranked the Dutch and Flemish painters below the Italians, giving his highest praise to Rembrandt and Rubens, though questioning even them in some respects. In his lectures on art he referred to the "wide, nay, almost impassible, interval between the familiar subjects of the lower Dutch and Flemish painters, and the higher intellectual works of the great Italian masters." More particularly he declared that "a coarse mind may feel the beauty in the hard, soulless forms of Van der Werf, yet turn away with apathy from the sanctified loveliness of a Madonna by Raffaele." He conceded, however, that there were "abundant examples" in some Dutch pictures of insignificant objects on the principle that they could give a "pleasure" which the objects themselves did not, a pleasure produced by "the intimate truth." In his citation of the works of Ostade, Steen, and Brouwer as examples of Natural Invention he recognized the genuine if limited achievement of them and others like them. And toward the end of his last lecture "Composition" he gave expression again to his lifelong respect for and willingness to learn from all artists, of whatever school, when he wrote, "Thus have the great schools of Italy, Flanders, and Holland lived and walked after death, till even their ghosts have become familiar to us" (*LA*, pp. 88, 34, 26, 162). His imaginative writings also reflect his opinion of Dutch painting. In "The Two Painters" Alexander the Great calls the colorist's painting of him Dutch, with its revoltingly realistic physical details. The narrator of "The Hypochondriac" wishes to be a Dutch painter, with the somewhat more sympathetic explanation that he would thus be able to render due honor to tobacco. Several of WA's comic pieces were nevertheless in the Dutch tradition. Though the illustrations for the Falstaff scenes and Irving's *History* were dictated by the sources, *A Scene in an Eating House* was independently conceived. Its subject was called Flemish by the *Bristol Gazette*.

Rembrandt Harmenszoon van Rijn or **van Ryn** (1606-69), Dutch painter. Allston's opinion of him was rather ambivalent. He wrote a poem about one of his paintings: "Sonnet on Rembrandt; Occasioned by His Picture of Jacob's Dream," in which he called Rembrandt "thou strangest of all beings strange," whose "visionary scenes,"

> like the rambling of an idiot's speech,
> No image giving of a thing on earth,
> Nor thought significant in Reason's reach,
> Yet in their random shadowings give birth
> To thoughts and things from other worlds that come,
> And fill the soul, and strike the reason dumb. (*SS*, p. 152)

In the "Introductory Discourse" to his lectures on art he referred to "the agony of the wretched Judas" in Rembrandt's "terrible picture" *The Tribute Money* as being an example of the necessity of treating tragic scenes only through "that ideal panoply" of the imagination (*LA*, p. 36), and in *Monaldi* the cavalier S——says that a critic other than one who saw with his eyes only was needed to understand "even—in spite of his abortive forms—the Dutch Rembrandt" (p. 29). Richard Henry Dana, Jr., recollected that Allston called Rembrandt the "Dryden of the art" (Flagg, p. 365).

Rubens, Peter Paul (1577-1640), Flemish painter. Allston admired him very much. He drew his portrait, copied a detail in one of his paintings, and wrote a poem about him: "Sonnet on the Luxembourg Gallery," in which he described Rubens's

> mysterious art,
> The charm that vexes, yet enslaves the heart!
> Thy lawless style, from timid systems free,
> Impetuous rolling like a troubled sea,
> High o'er the rocks of reason's lofty verge
> Impending hangs; yet, ere the foaming surge
> Breaks o'er the bound, the refluent ebb of taste
> Back from the shore impels the wat'ry waste. (*SS*, p. 153)

Part of it, with variant readings, was printed with the title "Rubens" in *Lectures on Art,* beginning, "Thus o'er his art indignant Rubens reared / His mighty head, nor critic armies feared," and saying his "lawless style" was free from "vain pretension" (p. 376).

He complained to Henry Greenough, however, that Rubens's method of painting flesh, as described by George Field, was faulty in having streaks of separate colors, which reminded him of a prize fighter bruised black and blue. "The fact is, sir," he said, "Rubens was a liar, a splendid liar, I grant you, and I would rather lie like Rubens than to tell the truth in the poor, tame manner in which some painters do." It was a false idea of Rubens, he continued, "that white is the poisoner of shadow" and feared that saying of his had led many painters astray. Flagg also recorded a conversation in which he said that in his opinion Rubens "has injured more artists than he has benefited" (Flagg, pp. 185, 409).

Van Dyck, Sir Anthony (1599-1641), Flemish painter. Richard Henry Dana, Jr., recollected Allston saying to Lord Egremont that he was superior to Reynolds in correctness but lesser in genius and on another occasion that when he read of Van Dyck's having received as a present from a prince twenty pounds of ultramarine he envied him more than if hearing that it had been twenty thousand pounds of sterling.

Appendix 3
Writings

Allston engaged in literary composition from an early age to the last years of his life. His earliest known piece was the poem "An Address to the Great Georgiana," sent to Channing in his letter of 14 February 1796 while a schoolboy, and his last compositions were his lectures on art, on which he was still working at the time of his death. During his lifetime two volumes by him were published, one of poetry and one of fiction, and some dozen separate pieces appeared in periodicals. After his death all his writings except *Monaldi* were published as *Lectures on Art, and Poems*. Like his painting, his writing displays considerable versatility, encompassing theory, critical essays, fiction, and aphorisms, couched in satire as well as straight expression. The chief mark of his style which is not exhibited in his public writing or even in his published aphorisms is a certain proverbializing or coining of figures of speech, in which he engaged occasionally in letters but chiefly in conversation.

The Sylphs of the Seasons, with Other Poems

Allston wrote most of the poems in *The Sylphs of the Seasons, with Other Poems* during the years from 1808 to 1811 when he was in Boston. Three had been previously published in periodicals: "First Love. A Ballad," "The Complaint," and "Will the Maniac. A Ballad." In 1810 he composed at least "America to Great Britain," and on 23 August in that year read a poem at the annual meeting of the Phi Beta Kappa Society at Harvard, probably "The Sylphs of the Seasons"; it was reported to have lasted forty-five minutes, to have been received with pleasure but to have been delivered in so low a voice as to be almost inaudible to those seated at a distance. That year Anna Cabot Lowell described him as "a poet as well as a painter" (to Mrs. Anne Grant). Richard Henry Dana said the poems in the volume were written in "moments of rest from his professional pursuits, at odd times, and with great rapidity," and were read and admired by his friends (Review of *The Sylphs of the Seasons, with Other Poems*, *North American Review* 5 [Sept. 1815]: 369). Subsequently he made a few revisions in the title poem, "The Paint-King," and "Eccentricity."

The Sylphs of the Seasons, with Other Poems was published in London by W. Pople in Chancery Lane early in July 1813 (Morse, 1:110) and in September or slightly later that year in Boston and Cambridge by Cummings and Hilliard. Edmund T. Dana and Sidney Willard made the arrangements for the American edition (*LA*, p. vi). It contains sixteen poems, varied in subject matter. The three longest, between 400 and 650 lines, are the title poem, a romantic treatment of nature, probably influenced by Thomson's *The Seasons*; "The Two Painters," a satirical fantasy; and "Eccentricity," a satirical denunciation of contemporary fashion, with its names of Tortoso and Ortuno. There are also a burlesque of Gothic narrative, two love lyrics, six sonnets on artists and works of art, and three "ballads," as they were called in a footnote: "First Love," "The Complaint," and "Will the Maniac," written "at a very early age" and previously published in periodicals. Possibly the title of the second is an echo of Edward Young's *The Complaint; or, Night Thoughts*. In form most are variations of the ballad stanza, two with rhyming couplets, one of them in iambic pentameter, several having an additional line or two, and the title poem having a seven-line stanza. The sonnets are variations of the English variety, with highly irregular rhyme schemes. They are the most successful of the pieces, with their generally striking imagery. He was sensitive to the charge of possible plagiarism. In a note to a line in the title poem he pointed out its similarity to one in a poem by the English James Montgomery, otherwise unidentified, and stated that his was written long before he read Montgomery's. Later he showed the same apprehension regarding a phrase in "To the Author of 'The Diary of an Ennuyée.'"

The volume was praised by many of Allston's friends in England, among them Coleridge, Southey, and the Beaumonts, but apparently received only two contemporary reviews, both some time after it appeared; two more were written after his death. The first, signed "B," appeared in the *Analectic Magazine,* 6 (1815), 151-58, of which Irving had been the editor for two years previously. The author may have been Channing, who signed the same initial to the notice he wrote a few years later of Morse's painting *Congress Hall.* He quoted at length from the title poem and briefly from three others, pointed out the indebtedness of "The Paint-King" to Matthew G. Lewis's *Tales of Wonder,* and pronounced the author, though an amateur and not to be placed beside the "great living English poets," nevertheless "endued with a greater share of brilliant qualities of the poet than any American" unless the Philadelphian William Cliffton. A review by Richard Henry Dana appeared in the *North American Review* for October 1817. He called the volume "clearly original" and many of the subjects new and praised the poems for their appeal to the heart, direct reflection of nature, avoidance of worldly sentiment, and "easy" and "musical" versification; but he ranked them with "the lighter kind of poetry," in contrast to that of Scott, Byron, and Wordsworth. He commented on the satire and wit in "The Paint-King" and "The Two Painters"; quoted at length from the title poem, from "The Two Painters," which he compared to Swift, Matthew Prior, and John Gay, and from "Eccentricity," which he compared to Pope; and alluded to "Myrtilla," "To a Lady Who Spoke Slightingly of Poets," and the sonnets on paintings by Raphael and Michelangelo, which almost reconciled him to the form. He objected to the revisions of some of the manuscripts and characterized the language as not strictly "poetick," not being that of a wide reader of the old English poets. He wished Allston would write fewer "moral" poems in the manner of Cowper and Thomas Campbell and more inspired by his imagination (5:365-89).

A decade after its publication a curious objection to *The Sylphs of the Seasons* was voiced by the eccentric novelist and essayist John Neal, whose criticism was the most adverse Allston ever received, not only as a painter and poet but also as a man. Neal lived in Boston from 1809 to 1815 as a member of a dry-goods firm, moving from there to Baltimore, where he was an editor of the *Portico,* and going to England in 1823, where he remained four years. His most extended reference to Allston was in his novel *Randolph* (1823), begun in 1821. He had certainly read *The Sylphs of the Seasons* but could have seen only a few paintings and probably drew on legends about Allston's personal habits, well established before he went to England in 1818. He characterized him as "an amiable man, of indefatigable labor; and a fine genius, rather than a bold one. He is chaste and fine, but timid. This may be seen as well in his poetry, as in his painting. There is an artificial heat in both. He wants passion; and even true greatness; for there is too little evil in his heart to help him in the generation of Greatness—a spirit that is, always, of a troubled countenance, and appalling expression, even in her repose," who would "toil all night long, in secrecy and loneliness;—and then, lie abed all day; or, till dinner time, with an affectation of carelessness and indolence, that is very amusing." He conceded that Allston's faculties were of "a very uncommon union of the bold and beautiful" but thought there was "a sort of artificial heat in some of his doings, much as if it were latent, elaborated with great care, and much difficulty; not that sort of inward fervor which flashes into spontaneous combustion, whenever it is excited or exasperated" (pp. 17, 18, 29). A year after *Randolph* was published he singled out "The Paint-King" for a long diatribe in the third of his series of articles entitled "American Writers" in *Blackwood's Edinburgh Magazine* in 1824-25. Misspelling his name with one *l* and *Paint* as *Paiut* throughout and making other mistakes in fact, he called Allston a "fine artist" who had written some poetry and, he was "sorry to say, one poem—called the 'Paiut King.'" He conceded there were "two or three fine passages" in it but objected that he did not know whether Allston was making fun of Lewis or imitating him and charged that Allston "ran ashore . . . while trying to steer two courses at once," that he "began the poem in a frolic; worked away, helter-skelter, until he had written something more seriously than he desired—and much better than he wished: when, like many a living author, whom we could name,—without patience or self-denial enough to preserve the idea, till it would come in play—discretion enough to throw it aside altogether; or dexterity enough to interweave it, without spoiling the whole piece—he lugs it in, to the ruin of his original plan." After giving examples of his point from Homer, Cowper, Lewis, Byron, and Thomas Moore, he quoted a line about the mountain Chimborazo from Allston's poem "On Kean's Hamlet," which he had probably been shown by Leslie, and said it was worthy of the whole of "The Paint-King" "forty times over" and also repeated in garbled form the story about Allston's not recognizing his portrait of John Harris. He was somewhat more sympathetic in the fifth article, reporting that Allston had been "given" $10,000 for *Belshazzar's Feast*, "a price unheard of in America," for which he took some credit because of his protest against the neglect of the fine arts in America in his article "North America: Peculiarities, State of the Fine Arts, Paintings" in *Blackwood's Edinburgh Magazine* for August 1824, in which he named Allston among other artists (16:560-61, 133; 17:207).

A few months after Allston's death *The Sylphs of the Seasons* was considered by William Gilmore Simms in his article "The Writings of Washington Allston" in the *Southern Quarterly Review,* in which he also took note of other poems by Allston published in Griswold's *Poets and Poetry of America* and *Monaldi.* Allston was not, he said, a poet "in the high, perhaps the only proper sense of the term . . . not an original thinker in verse,—not a seer," and his poems were rather "those of the accomplished and educated gentleman"; Most of them, he said, might be classed as "fugitive," "the elegant trifles of a well drilled, well ordered mind," which nevertheless were inspired by a muse which was a sister to his "legitimate mistress," "the muse of painting," which itself encouraged his "liaison" with "her of song." He singled out for particular attention "The Sylphs of the Seasons," which he thought the best and whose idea he suggested was borrowed from William Shenstone's "The Judgment of Hercules"; "The Two Painters"; "The Paint-King," which he called "a very happy imitation" of the style of M.G. Lewis; "Rosalie"; "America to Great Britain," which he recognized as an imitation of one of the odes of Thomas Campbell; and "The Tuscan Girl." The last three he quoted in their entirety (8 [Oct. 1843], 381-89).

C.C. Felton also considered the poems in *The Sylphs of the Seasons,* together with whose published in *Lectures on Art,* in his review of that volume in 1850. He thought Allston's poetical style remarkable for the "careful finishing" of every part and for an "exquisite purity of language" comparable to "the fine coloring of his pencil" and judged "The Sylphs of the Seasons," "The Paint-King," and "America to Great Britain" "among the most beautiful poems in American Literature." He quoted in their entirety "Rosalie" and "On

Greenough's Group of the Angel and Child" and several stanzas of "To the Author of 'The Diary of an Ennuyée'" (*North American Review* 71 [1850]: 151-55).

Monaldi

Allston began writing *Monaldi* about 1819 and finished it in 1822, intending it for *The Idle Man,* but that periodical ceased publication in 1822 and he did nothing with the manuscript for nearly twenty years. He then gave it his attention throughout the 1830s, about the time he was turning increasingly to literary composition, with his poems accompanying his paintings, his Doolittle sketches, and his lectures on art.

Monaldi: A Tale was published between 24 October and 12 November 1841 by Charles C. Little and James Brown in Boston, and printed by John D. Freeman and Charles Bolles. The title page carried as a motto the opening lines of one of his poems given the title "A Fragment": "Who knows himself must needs in prophecy / Too oft behold his own most sad reverse." An English edition was published early in December 1841 by Edward Moxon in London. In 1843 a German translation, *Eine Erzälung . . . Aus dem Englischen des amerikeschen Malers Washington Allston übersatzt von Kahldorf* [pseud.], was published in Leipzig by F.A. Brockhaus. The translator was Robert Wesselhoeft, a German physician who came to America in 1840 and practiced medicine in Cambridge for several years, who also translated some of Longfellow's poems. He had finished it by 20 November 1841 (Longfellow, *Letters* 2:338, 357).

Monaldi is essentially an elaboration of Allston's college essay "Procrastination is the Thief of Time." In each narrative the hero is a young Italian painter who is a follower of Raphael and Michelangelo, the young woman with whom he falls in love is named Rosalia, and the setting is for the most part in Rome. Allston's reference to the essay in his letter to Verplanck of 12 March 1819 is evidence that he was remembering it not long before writing the tale. In terms of literary genres *Monaldi* is a Gothic romance, having like many other specimens an Italian setting and exclusively Italian characters, giving prominence to a villain practicing elaborate deceptions, and making use of Catholic institutions for atmospheric effect. It is not typical of that genre, however, in its realistic scenic details and its portrayal of an ideal artist. Allston had projected such a character in his poem "The Two Painters, A Tale" but only by implication. There the shades of the Painter of the Body and the Painter of the Mind are ordered to learn from each other so that they may become one painter. It is perhaps significant that both this poem and *Monaldi* are called "tales." The ideal artist is also pictured in his poem "The Angel and the Nightingale" but in terms of music rather than painting and almost entirely as a servant of nature addressing himself to kindred natures.

The character of Monaldi is to a great extent a self-portrait of the author. Like Allston, he is not wanting in academic learning but not distinguished in it, a lover of nature, and a follower of the Italian painters of the fifteenth century, particularly Raphael but also Michelangelo. Like Allston he is passive and inclined to dreaming, yet diligent in study and work, is not vain, does not crave popularity but values the sympathy of kindred minds, "that purest form of fame," and readily bestows praise on excellence in others. At first opposed in the "critical age" by those ambitious for the reputation of critics who apply only personal dogma and by the multitude armed with authority, he at last achieves recognition (*Monaldi,* pp. 56, 26). It would seem to be more than a coincidence that his name, not a common one, is also that of a character mentioned in passing in "The Bag of Gold" in Samuel Rogers's *Italy,* part 2 (1828). Possibly it was taken up by Rogers during his visit to Italy in 1814-15, during which time he composed some of the poem (P.W. Clayton, *Rogers and His Contemporaries* [London, 1889], 1:297, 299, 316, 331, 341). He and Allston were on familiar terms during Allston's second stay in England, and it is possible that the name Monaldi was mentioned.

Monaldi is, in fact, most distinctively an autobiographical composition. Not only are many of the descriptions of scenes drawn from Allston's recollections of his sojourn in Italy but the names of several artists whom he knew there are introduced, the most notable example being Rosalia Landi and her father, who have the name of the painter Gaspare Landi. Two of the paintings as described are in all particulars two of Allston's own paintings. More figuratively, his disturbed state of mind after the death of his wife in 1815 is reflected in Monaldi's derangement after he thinks Rosalia is in effect lost to him through her alleged infidelity.

Monaldi received several reviews, most of them during the first few months after its appearance. Most expressed interest and to some extent surprise at finding the talents of painting and writing combined in Allston, compared the moral sentiments conveyed in the tale, particularly in the character of Rosalia, and quoted extensively from the text. The first critical attention it received was from Wesselhoeft, in the introduction to his edition. Allston, he said, was "not only a historical painter with the pencil and pallet, but also with the pen" and "one of the best poets in this country," adding, "He is, moreover, a very noble man." He continued his comparison of Allston's talents by declaring, "In the arrangement of the whole, in the distribution of light and shade, in the economy of the piece, there is somewhat pictorial" and suggesting that the whole was "like a great landscape-historical picture, with fore-ground, middle-ground, and back-ground."

Brief notices appeared by unidentified critics in *Monthly Miscellany of Religion and Letters* 3 (Dec. 1841): 49-51; *New York Review* 10 (Jan. 1842): 211-16; *Boston Quarterly Review* 5 (Jan. 1842): 119-21; and *Southern Literary Messenger* 8 (Apr. 1842): 286-89).

Margaret Fuller wrote a review which was published in the *Dial* 2 (Jan. 1842): 395-99. The tale, she thought, cast "some light upon the mind which, more than any other, has represented among us the pure reign of beauty." After comparing it to *Othello,* she quoted the first several pages, which had "graceful lightness of expression and fineness of thought" and said there were many other similar passages, all of which spoke "with the Ariel tone we dream of in the enchanted solitudes to which the pencil of the artist has introduced us" and made the reader feel "the 'real presence' of that inward life revealed to most men, only at rare intervals, but here flowing like a brook hidden amid sighing reeds, with a steady silver sound." She evidently did not own a copy of the book but read the one belonging to Sarah Clarke, which she lent her mother (Fuller, *Letters,* 2:260).

In the same month a review appeared in the *Christian Examiner* 31 (Jan. 1842): 374-81, by the author and editor Sarah Josepha (Buell) Hale, who lived in Boston from 1828 to 1841. She thought many would read it out of curiosity to see how a painter would write but found a harmony of spirit between Allston's paintings and his book, especially in the fact that both had so few characters. She admired the depiction of Rosalia in terms of a beautiful spirit rather than physical beauty, praised the style as having "shunned all modern affectations . . . all mingling half-German jargon with pure English"; thought Allston was "at home" in the descriptions of Italian scenes and the passages on paintings and painters; compared him and

Dickens as contemporary literary "luminaries" though moving in orbits far apart, commended the work for inculcating "a useful, a religious lesson", but doubted that it would be popular.

A review by the clergyman and educator James Henley Thornwell, from Cheraw, South Carolina, in the *Southern Literary Messenger* (Apr. 1842): 286-89, was more knowledgeable than the other short ones. He recollected that in Boston, where he was in the summer of 1839, "No place was so attractive as the gallery" of Allston's paintings and pronounced him "more truly a poet" in the tale than in *The Sylphs of the Seasons*.

The longest and most analytical reviews were those by Felton, Simms, and George Washington Peck. That by Felton appeared in the *North American Review* 54 (Apr. 1842): 397-419. In it he called Allston "the foremost painter of his age," who but for his overshadowing fame as such would be renowned as "one of our most graceful and imaginative poets," alluding to *The Sylphs of the Seasons*. As a painter, he characterized him as free from envy, noted the appreciation of him by art historian Ernest Platner, and predicted that upon his death he would be ranked with the great Italian artists of the past. He thought the tale might have been longer to do better justice to the characters and the varied passions but admired the depiction of the two young men and was enthusiastic about the character of Rosalia. He approved the style, with its "rich and harmonious prose," "nice selection of epithets," "faultless arrangement of the members of the sentences," and "rhythmical cadence" of thought and expression, and praised the descriptions of natural scenes, the expression of moral sentiment, and the maxims of art. In conclusion he quoted lengthy passages.

Simms first reviewed *Monaldi* in the unsigned "Monaldi—by Washington Allston" in the *Magnolia*, n.s., 1 (Dec. 1842): 381-90. Most of it was a summary of the plot, praising particularly the psychological fidelity rather than any use of stock Gothic supernatural devices, but he also recognized Allston's stature as a painter and though saying he had seen few of his paintings and naming only *Donna Mencia*, "the most exquisite," expressed the wish that his Carolina friends who were equal to the task, such as Fraser, would give an account of them. He further noted that Allston was not so well known as "one of the best of American poets" and purposed at a later date to make an analysis of all his writings. He already knew *The Sylphs of the Seasons*, of which he ordered a copy in March 1841. *Monaldi*, he said, was not less a poem because it was written in prose.

The article Simms proposed finally came out after Allston's death, "The Writings of Washington Allston," in the *Southern Quarterly Review* 8 (Oct. 1843): 363-414, which contained criticism of *The Sylphs of the Seasons*, *Monaldi*, and the poems which had been published in Griswold's *The Poets and Poetry of America*. He several times disparaged it as having been hurried and full of errors of sense and grammar (Simms, *Letters*, vol. 5 [1956], p. 325; 1:69-378, 385, 392). Passing briefly over Allston's achievement as a painter, he recognized him as "one of the first, if not the very first, of the painters of the age," chiefly because of his work "in the very highest branches of his art—the dramatic, the historical," noting his "grouping" in particular and saying that he had "achieved the joint triumph of the dramatist and painter" more than any other painter. In the main part of his article he said he had read all the writings of Allston which had appeared in book form, but had reason to think they were much more numerous in view of his "mental activity" and "his free and elaborate command of language," and he hoped that if a collection were prepared use would be made of his correspondence, which he believed would be found to be "not less valuable for its hints on art, than for its beauties of style, and amenities of friendship." In all that related to the ideals of art and the morals of artists, he declared, "this good and great man is complete authority," being "Gentle, benign and thoughtful." He devoted his essay to recounting the main events of Allston's life to 1818, quoting liberally from his letters to Dunlap, for their "poetry" more than their bearing on his painting, and also from Walter Channing's article in the *Christian World,* which had recently appeared. In his consideration of Allston's poetry, he thought it at best accomplished, most valuable for its relationship to his painting. He repeated that *Monaldi* was not less a poem because written in prose and that it was superior to the tradition of such Gothic romances as those of Ann Radcliffe in being free from "vulgar tricks" and turning on events which had been used "time out of mind, by the novelist and dramatist." In summarizing the plot he quoted from it extensively and concluded that its chief merit was not in the story but in the manner in which the materials had been used, "in the felicitous discrimination of character; in the happy language, the appropriate illustrations, and the occasional fancies and reflections," concluding, "Monaldi is a work of art" (8 [Oct. 1843], 381-89).

Simms took notice of Allston as writer as well as painter on several other occasions. In his article "Southern Literature" in the *Magnolia,* n.s., 3 (Feb. 1841): 69-74, he speculated that had Allston's resources been limited to the South his income would scarcely have supplied him with paintbrushes unless, "descending to the lowest department of his profession, he had appealed to the vanity of the individual, by transmitting his complacent visage to posterity." As editor of *The Charleston Book* (1845) he included "Rosalie," "The Tuscan Girl" (giving the title as "The Tuscan Maid"), and an extract from chapter 2 of *Monaldi* and named Allston with Fraser, Sully, and others as Charleston artists (*Letters,* vol. 3 [1984], p. 378; "Our Early Authors," *XIX Century,* vol. 1 [Charleston, S.C., 1869], pp. 278-79). There seems to be no evidence that Simms and Allston ever met, though Simms frequently visited New England cities after 1832, including Hingham, near Boston, in the summer of 1843 (William P. Trent, *William Gilmore Simms* [Boston, 1892], p. 69).

Peck's review, "Monaldi," appeared in the *American Whig Review* 7, n.s. 1 (Apr. 1848): 341-57. He was a Boston author and literary critic, a friend of Richard Henry Dana, Jr., and he made a point of placing Allston in relation to other literary figures. He accounted for the relatively brief notice of the book at the time of its publication by saying it was "one of those exquisite works of art which never make an extensive acquaintance with the world," and only become known "by slow degrees during the lapse of years." After a detailed summary of the plot, he recommended it rather because it was "a delightful old-fashioned tale, full of real observation, philosophy, character, pictures, true affection," understandably neglected by those who read Bulwer-Lytton "for excitement," G.P.R. James "out of habit," and George Sand "for reasons not to be understood," comparable to "a fine old painting" that might hang for years in a row of daubs without attracting attention. He recommended it to readers of Godwin and Scott and ranked it with Johnson's *Rasselas* in "embodying thought." He particularly praised its style, contrasting its restraint and refinement with opposite qualities in Tennyson, Carlyle, and W. Jerrold, implicitly comparing it to that of Addison and Goldsmith, and saying it was not "rigid" but "bends to the story," in the conclusion dying away "with the lofty grandeur of an old Handelian cadence." He thought there was a "beautiful *consentaneousness*" of the style and thought and compared the simply expressed yet profound thought with Mozart's "humorous oracular decisions in music." Allston's own character and life, he declared, was reflected in the book, which carried the reader "through a more noble and refined life, than we could venture to image to ourselves in this dusty road of ordinary existence," making him feel "that the glory and the dream *shall not* pass away; and that, though we have fallen, yet will we not be utterly cast down, for underneath this gloomy, actual day, there is a greener earth and a serener heaven."

The work still attracted attention in the 1850s. The author of a review of Griswold's *The Prose Writers of America* in the *Southern Literary Messenger* for April 1850 (6:434) thought Griswold had "scarcely spoken with sufficient distinctness and emphasis of the extraordinary merit" it had as a work of fiction, declaring, "The wonderful mind which was but dimly and imperfectly exhibited by the pencil was here revealed, not indeed upon a great scale, but with entireness of moral and intellectual effect. Indeed, we may say that it is the only perfect picture that ALLSTON ever painted; for the genius which it displays, though employing 'the instrument of words,' is essentially pictorial in its character and impression." In 1856 the *Crayon* printed other passages from the work, one on Michelangelo and one on Raphael (3 [Aug.]: 255-56; [Oct.]: 297).

Allston's poem "A Fragment" ("O, who hath lived the ills to know") also has a character named Monaldi, who comes from a noble family in Fiorenza (not a place name in Italy but similar to several places named Fiorenzuola), and who is both handsome and virtuous but falls in love with a maiden who is beautiful but "An evil *yet* without a name" and an agent of "Vice" and "The Giant Sin," who has "A trancing, but a poisoned, kiss," and makes of him "a hellish sacrifice!" (*LA*, pp. 371-73) Though Monaldi in Allston's tale comes to a similar end, Rosalia is not responsible for it. The young woman in the poem is conspicuously unlike her and those in Allston's other poems about young women, as well as the characters implied in his female portraits. Apparently Monaldi's experience with her reflects the story of Jason and Medea, to which there is oblique reference in other lines of the poem.

Lectures on Art, and Poems

Allston began writing his lectures on art, Richard Henry Dana, Jr., said, soon after moving to Cambridgeport in 1830, intending to deliver them to "a select audience of artists and literary men of letters in Boston" (*LA*, p. viii). He completed four and left rough drafts of two others. The manuscripts of them all have numerous revisions on almost every page.

In the winter of 1842-43 Allston invited C.C. Felton and Longfellow to his home to hear him read them aloud. Felton vividly described the occasions in his review of Athanasius Raczynski's *Histoire de l'art moderne en Allemagne* in the *North American Review* for October 1843. Allston, he recalled, would first place his lights each in a certain position, set his footstool between his chair and the fire, warm his feet, put his manuscripts in order, and then read, stopping occasionally to answer a question or explain a point, his eyes growing larger and his voice stronger and his countenance taking on an "almost supernatural expression" until he seemed a prophet declaring "a new revelation of the religion of art" (57:398-99). Samuel Ward, Jr., who no doubt got his information from Longfellow, said that both he and Felton pronounced them "magnificent—far beyond Reynolds" (Elliott, p. 381).

In composing such pieces Allston was following the tradition of several English painters of the late eighteenth and early nineteenth centuries who delivered lectures on art at the Royal Academy, notably Reynolds, Fuseli, and Opie. All to some extent expressed opposition to the prescriptive rules of academies. His differed from theirs in their greater philosophical basis and their subjective conception of the creation and appreciation of art, viewing it as both expression and communication rather than as imitation. In his generally idealistic philosophy he followed Coleridge and the German romantics, but in his subjectivity he was ahead of his time, anticipating aesthetic theory which became dominant toward the end of the century. Not only was he the first philosopher of art in America, but his lectures comprise the first art treatise in America or England in the nineteenth century.

The four completed lectures were entitled "Introductory Discourse," "Art," "Form," and "Composition" and were introduced by an essay entitled "Preliminary Note—Ideas." In "Preliminary Note—Ideas" Allston defined an idea as "the highest or most perfect *form* in which any thing, whether of the physical, the intellectual, or the spiritual, may exist to the mind"; he divided ideas into two classes, primary, "the *manifestation* of objective realities," and secondary, "the reflex product . . . of the mental constitution"; and he defined the first as having a "*dual* reality," being manifest in both the senses and the mind, and the second as being exemplified above all in works of the imagination, communicated to others. He devoted "Introductory Discourse," the longest lecture, to a discussion of "*mental pleasures,*" which he predicated as having their source in "One Intuitive Universal Principle or living Power, realized in the ideas of "Beauty, Truth, and Holiness," which together he called *Harmony,* and each of which he defined, concluding with an analysis of the Sublime and a recognition of the true object of Harmony as being "the Infinite Creator." In "Art" he discussed what he called the four characteristics of art as distinguished from nature, namely "Originality," "Human or Poetic Truth," "Invention," and "Unity." In "Form" he limited the subject to the human form, which he conceived of as a correspondence between the "outward" and the "inward," to be represented in art, illustrating the point by reference to Michelangelo and Raphael. In "Composition," which has indications of not being completely finished, he discussed "Unity of Purpose," "Variety of Parts," "Continuity," and "Harmony of Parts," apparently tending toward a conclusion representing art as the highest point in the development of man's nature and powers.

In 1850 the lectures and the "Preliminary Note" were published as *Lectures on Art, and Poems,* edited by Richard Henry Dana, Jr., by the firm of Baker and Scribner in New York. The volume contained also a preface by Dana, briefly giving the facts of Allston's life with particular attention to his religious feelings and his reading, the poems printed in *The Sylphs of the Seasons,* thirty-four additional poems, forty-one aphorisms, two brief prose fragments from a sketch and a sketch book, and "The Hypochondriac." It thus provided an opportunity for an assessment of his total achievement as a poet, and only the omission of *Monaldi* kept it from comprising his complete literary canon. His literary executors had planned to publish a biography, his correspondence, and his writings in two volumes, but when the first two projects were delayed and there were frequent calls for his poems and lectures, it was decided to issue them alone ("Allston's Poems and Lectures on Art," *Sartain's Union Magazine of Literature and Art* 6 [1850]: 434).

Of the thirty-four, ten had been previously printed individually. Allston evidently intended to publish a volume of thirty-one of them, excluding "America to Great Britain," "Written in Spring," and "The Atonement." He copied the thirty-one in a notebook, whose pages he numbered, in what seems to be the general sequence of their composition, probably during the last year or so of his life. This manuscript is followed in *Lectures on Art,* with only a few variations in sequence and titles. In the printed volume the initials "M—E—D—," "R—C—D—," and "S" are substituted for the names "Mary E. Dana" (his niece), "R. Charlotte Dana," and "Mrs. Salter," presumably the wife of the physician Dr. Richard H. Salter, in the titles of "The Marigold," "The Parting," and "The Magic Slippers" in the manuscript, probably to preserve the privacy of these persons. In the manuscript four untitled poems, together with "Song," come at the end of the sequence, in effect emphasizing their unfinished state and suggesting a final venture into an unresolvable realm, as do some of Allston's late sketches. In *Lectures on Art* each of the untitled poems is given the title "Fragment" and they and "Song" are distributed among the last twenty, thus eliminating whatever unity they had as a group. "To the Author of 'The Diary of an Ennuyée,'" which comes between "The Magic Slippers" and "The Parting" in the manuscript, is last in *Lectures on Art,* where it provides not only a more forceful conclusion but also a fitting one, memorializing as it does the interval in Allston's life from which the most prevailing inspiration of both his painting and his writing was derived. He also made a copy of "The Atonement," probably about this time, on two sheets that bear the numbers 57a and 57b, which do not resemble those in the manuscript but which would place them immediately after the sonnet on Coleridge on page 57 there. It seems likely that he never completed this poem to his satisfaction. In the manuscript one line and half of another are cancelled, for which others are substituted, and five other lines are cancelled, for which there are no substitutions. In any case, it was apparently written in its final form after the copy of the thirty-one poems was made. In *Lectures on Art* it is appropriately placed immediately after "Gloria Mundi," the only other poem in the group that treats the same subject.

Apparently Allston submitted one of the thirty-one, "The Night-Mare," to some publication separately, since a draft of that poem bears the notation "sent 9 Feby." The "Memorandum" he wrote on it is particularly significant, being his only known statement about his method of poetic composition and evidence of a greater desire to experiment metrically than he generally exhibited: "My only rule in the execution of this Poem was, to let the thoughts find their own metre; the result is, an unpremeditated variety in the rythm [*sic*]—which has, perhaps, added something to the wildness of the story. W.A."

The poems first collected in *Lectures on Art* are less noteworthy and as a group call for less critical attention than those in *The Sylphs of the Seasons*. They are not so varied in subject and form, though they have somewhat more irregular rhyme schemes and are more didactic, often treating religious doctrines and theories about the nature of man, and have no traces of satire. Six are sonnets, five are accompaniments of paintings by him, and four are about other works of art or artists. The eight-line "Rubens" is a variation of the concluding octet of "Sonnet on the Luxembourg Gallery" in *The Sylphs of the Seasons*. Six are fragments. Of those printed for the first time, however, four are notable, both biographically and artistically: "To My Sister," "The Calycanthus," "To the Author of 'The Diary of an Ennuyée;" and "The Angel and the Nightingale." The last is the longest of all Allston's poems, consisting of seventy-four stanzas in a seven-line variation of the Spenserian stanza. It is an autobiographical fable, depicting in the fortunes of the nightingale, from fame to neglect to final vindication, Allston's early success, relative neglect in America in his middle years, and ultimate achievement of a correspondence of subject and style peculiarly his own. It is placed first in the sequence of the later poems, after the early "America to Great Britain" and "Written in Spring," as if to introduce them, but probably it was written in the middle or late 1830s, around the time of the poems about the ideal young women of his paintings.

Numbers for the aphorisms were added, presumably by Dana. At the top of one of the manuscript pages of them Allston wrote "Parthenian [?] literally, "virginal,"] Axioms," possibly to suggest they were original with him.

Lectures on Art, and Poems received fairly wide attention, being noticed at least nine times in periodicals during the first few months after it was published, all in 1850: in the *Literary World,* 20 April, pp. 398-400, and 6 July, pp. 13-14; *Graham's American Monthly Magazine* 36 (June): 415; *Sartain's Union Magazine of Literature and Art* 6 (June): 434; *American Art-Union Bulletin,* June, pp. 38-41; the *Knickerbocker Magazine* 35 (June), 537-38; the *North American Review* (July); the *American Whig Review* (July); and the *New Englander* 8 (Aug.): 445-52. Most of the reviews were short and largely reportorial. That by Noah Porter, Jr., in the *New Englander* was slightly longer but chiefly devoted to a characterization of Allston as a Christian rather than an artist or a writer. The most substantial ones were written by Felton and Peck. All emphasized the lectures to the virtual exclusion of the rest of the volume.

Felton's review appeared in the *North American Review* 71 (July 1850): 149-68. As he had in his review of Raczynski's *Histoire,* he described Allston's personal characteristics, noting his gentleness and freedom from jealousy, his voice of "singular sweetness," "the purity and felicity of his wit," and his "social nights," and surveyed the range of his poetry before considering the lectures. They were, he declared, "the most important addition to the literature of art which has been made within our memory." He related them to writings by Germans, and by Lanzi, Vasari, Benvenuto Cellini, Flaxman, Reynolds, Charles Bell, and John Ruskin, and concluded that Allston was better qualified to discuss the subject of art than any of his predecessors because of his combination of study of the great works of art of the past and a thorough classical education. He noted the influence of Coleridge's philosophy on Allston but said that it was "so blended with his independent meditations" that it served only "to heighten them by the hues of a spiritual manner of thinking, harmonizing admirably with the poetical light thrown by his own genius over all the objects of thought." After describing them in general as "the essence" of his "entire artistic life," having "their root in his inmost nature" and displaying his "exquisite style" "in its highest perfection," he quoted passages from each of them without comment.

Peck's review appeared in the *American Whig Review,* n.s. 6 (July 1850): 17-32. Though he called the lectures "profound and elaborate . . . rich in new and true thoughts and in apt expressions and beautiful illustrations," he thought their "very closeness" would stand in the way of their "immediate usefulness" and apologized for his essential summary of them, full though it was and relying on liberal quotation. He recognized, however, that the "Introductory Discourse" expressed "something which takes deeper root than the rules" of Hugh Blair and James Beattie and predicted that it would "hereafter be known as the basis and corner-stone to a new philosophy of art." He explained his failure to include the poems in his essay by saying they demanded a separate one, said it would have been pleasant to quote several, particularly "the splendid lyric" "America to Great Britain," and referred the reader to his review of *Monaldi* a few years earlier for "an attempt to do some justice to the rare elegance and refinement of ALLSTON'S prose writing, and to his merit as a profound thinker and critic of art."

Satire

Allston had a strong satiric bent, which would not seem to have comported with the essentially romantic and dramatic nature of his imagination. In his painting it is chiefly to be seen in some of his juvenilia and his illustrations for scenes from Shakespeare and Irving, also done during his early years. It was most often expressed, however, in literary composition, from several pieces written in college to a few late ones and in some of his letters, such as those to his sister-in-law Elizabeth E. Dana and to John Knapp. The objects of his satire were various: melodramatic literature, pretentiousness, national character, dialect, hypochondria, fads in architecture, reform movements. It was never directed at an individual and it was always more genial than sharp.

Of the unpublished compositions left by Allston at his death and not included by Richard Henry Dana, Jr., in *Lectures on Art, and Poems,* only four seem to have been finished, all satiric. One—the poem "An Elegy in Exile," about his classmate Rufus Hosmer—belongs, like his poem "An Address to the Great Georgiana," to his life as a young student. The other three address themselves to issues which were current during his maturity and about which he expressed or implied concern in his letters: architecture and the temperance movement.

"The Doolittle Fragments"

In 1838 three sketches under the title "The Doolittle Fragments," apparently written by Allston, appeared in the *Boston Daily Advertiser* on 14 June, 25 July, and 28 August, as from one Timothy Doolittle; the first two were allegedly written by his great-grandfather Augustus Doolittle. The first sketch records a conversation between Augustus's friend Baron Grimm, presumably a reference to the French author Baron Friedrich Melchior Grimm, and an eighteenth-century abbé who was an author, probably a reference to Charles Irénée Castel, abbé de Saint-Pierre. The Baron consoles the abbé, who complains that his books are not appreciated because of ignorant critics and jealous rivals and that he will achieve fame only after death. The baron offers him a hair-trigger gun with which to kill himself. When told that one of the abbé's books holds that the soul is material, the baron suggests that he set aside a day in which to enjoy his posthumous recognition and use the weapon the next day. The abbé, however, realizing that he may thus enjoy his posthumous fame at any time, rejects the notion of suicide and invites the baron to a dinner the next night, at what the baron calls "the close of your *thousand year day*" (echoing the phrase in 2 Pet. 3:8), which they will finish with champagne and have wine which the baron prefers being "a little older than the fame." The piece repeats to some extent the theme of Allston's painting *The Poor Author and the Rich Bookseller* and echoes his discussion of fame in both his poetry and in *Monaldi,* but the satire is made more intricate by the introduction of references to some of the prominent French philosophes and critics.

The second sketch consists of a series of aphorisms on the subject of dress for ladies and gentlemen, in which colors are suggested which are said to be becoming to the wearers but which are actually calculated to render them disagreeable in appearance.

The third sketch is entitled "A Night Adventure in Wales." It is about twice as long as the other two and purports to be by an English artist, "S——," who describes an evening he spent in "17——" at a small inn in Wales. After he went to bed someone, who he thought was the hostess with intent to murder him, attempted to enter his room, whereupon he threw at the person a heavy wooden saddle which was hanging on the wall, thus knocking him down and sending him fleeing. In the morning he learned that the intruder had been a servant who had gone to get the saddle in order to ride to market early the next day. The narrator's description of the isolated inn, the nocturnal scene, and his first unfavorable impression of the hostess and her little black pig is in the banditti tradition, which influenced several of Allston's early paintings, but the conclusion satirizes that tradition, as in the morning light both hostess and host persuade the artist that the episode is a laughing matter and he happily sketches the two in their kitchen, together with the little black pig. The concluding scene, without its satirical implications, is related to several paintings by Allston: *Falstaff Enlisting His Ragged Regiment, A Scene in an Eating House,* and *Tavern Scene.*

This sketch is based on an experience Allston had during his first stay in England when he spent a night at a country inn on the coast, probably in the vicinity of Bristol. As Leslie recounted it, he had bolted the door of his room and retired when he was awakened twice by feeling a cold hand pass over his face. He called out but got no answer and in the morning found both the door unbolted and the one window slightly open. The occurrence was explained by the hostess, who was in mourning, who told him that her father had recently died and left the inn to her and her brother, that the brother took to drinking and was so often out late at night that she locked the door against him, and that the night before he had come home tipsy, apparently climbed into the upstairs room where Allston was, and finding the bed occupied, unbolted the door and went down the stairs, at the foot of which she found him asleep that morning (To Richard Henry Dana, 7 Sept. 1843, 28 Jan. 1844).

Architecture

Allston had a great interest in architecture throughout his life. One of his earliest recollections was of building a little cottage with sticks, and some of his juvenilia are drawings of houses. Many of his paintings, beginning with *Italian Landscape* (G12), contain architectural forms, the most notable being the Italian landscapes, the portraits of Coleridge and Samuel Williams, *Rebecca at the Well, Belshazzar's Feast, Jeremiah, Lorenzo and Jessica, Evening Hymn, The Death of King John, Helidorus Driven from the Temple,* and *Interior of a Church.* He repeatedly alluded to buildings in his lectures on art. The year he graduated from college he deplored the sameness of American architecture and subsequently agreed with Verplanck and Horatio Greenough in their calls for a new architectural style in America. He drew plans for the church of the Shepard Congregational Society in Cambridge and sketched its facade, designed his last studio and the last house in which he lived, and expressed opinions on domestic architecture of which Emerson approved. Among his drawings is one showing the plan and elevation of a two-story round building with classical columns, the only structure of this shape which he is known to have depicted. He owned a copy of *Ancient Reliques; or Delineations of Monastic, Castellated, and Domestic Architecture,* vol. 1 (London, 1812), and *Rudiments of Ancient Architecture,* 4th ed. enlarged, trans. G.H. Noehden and J. Stoddart (London, 1810); the book is signed by him, and one page of it contains drawings of several figures and the plan of a building.

Only two substantial treatments of the subject of architecture written by him seem to exist, however, and those in the vein of satire. They nevertheless express a serious and significant point of view, which he is otherwise known to have held. They consist of two pages of prose and ten lines of verse. The chief identifiable character in both is Charles Bulfinch, who was the principal architect in Boston from 1787, when he returned from a European tour, until 1817, when he went to Washington as architect of the Capitol. From his return in 1830 until his death in 1844 he lived for the most part in retirement. It seems probable that both pieces by Allston were written during his years in Boston from 1808 to 1811. It would seem unlikely that after his return from England in 1818 he would have given attention to Bulfinch, who was not in the city, or to the Exchange Coffee House, which was destroyed by fire a few weeks later. These were the years in which he composed most of the poems in *The Sylphs of the Seasons,* with their satiric touches.

Both pieces reflect the emergence in Boston during the early years of the nineteenth century of the Greek Revival in architecture, which was spreading rapidly throughout the country. Bulfinch was more representative of the preceding, simpler Federalist style, but he too made use of classical elements. Allston did not distinguish between the two styles and with his prejudice against Greek forms objected to both, though he correctly depicted the competition between architects and builders in the city at this time of its first great growth. He might have been expected to sympathize somewhat more with Bulfinch, who adapted classical patterns to original conceptions so as to effect what could be called a distinctively American style, such as Allston repeatedly called for, whereas the Greek Revivalists often slavishly imitated them, in a manner which Allston deplored in all the arts. He should have found Bulfinch, with his cultivated background, Harvard education, and travel abroad, personally more congenial than the chief architects who followed him, among them Alexander Parris and Solomon Willard, with whom Allston had dealings, who were largely self-taught and were engineers as well. There seems to be no evidence, however, that Bulfinch and Allston had any personal association (Talbot Hamlin, *Greek Revival Architecture in America* [London: Oxford Univ. Press, 1944], pp. 1-118, passim).

The text of the prose piece on architecture follows:

> We are sorry to state that the unhappy difference between the celebrated Architects, Messrs Bulfinch[1] and Barjesus,[2] is not yet settled. Their warfare has been long and bloody; how it will terminate we know not. We hope, however, that should they longer contend <their> they would aim at a little more originality. Their contest bears <two words undecipherable> so great a resemblance to that between The Genie Coggin and the Fairy Alden, in the Arabian Nights Entertainment,[3] that we should have no doubt of its being a direct plagiarism <from that> were we not convinced <that> of its impossibility <of> from their both being unable to read. As this combat has excited considerable attention, a brief account of it may not be uninteresting to our readers. On the fifth of last month they met by agreement on Cambridge Common[4] when Mr. Bulfinch commenced a furious attack on Mr. Barjesus, in the shape of a cottage;[5] Mr. Bar received the shock with great firmness in the character of a light-house.[6] Mr. Bull then changed to a likeness of the state house steps,[7] but Mr. Bar soon foiled him in the beacon-hill column.[8] <Again> Mr. Bull then became a tremendous gothick meeting house;[9] this, however, was insufficient to intimidate the valiant Bar, who instantly assuming the form of a Steeple,[10] completely ran Mr. Bull thro', and as it were spitted his architecture.—The remainder of the battle will be described in our next. [Manuscript: J.R. Lowell Papers, Houghton. Annotated by Lowell: "W. Allston" and "Nehemiah Allston."[11]]

The text of the poem follows:

On the Domes
of the State house & the Exchange Coffeehouse[12]

Oh, wondrous Town, what wondrous ways thou hast.
To show the wondring world thy wondrous *taste*!
Go, starveling Connoissieurs! repair to Rome,
And feast your eyes with Peter's empty dome!
Such flimsy piles great Boston scorns to raise,
She "solid pudding" loves, not "empty praise":
Hence from afar to epicurean eyes
Two mighty emblems of her *taste* arise,
To Phoebus' table offer'd by his Lover—
An *Indian Pudding* this, and that the *Cover.* (Manuscript, Houghton.)

It is not known how Allston's prose satire on Boston architecture got among the papers of James Russell Lowell, which were presented to Harvard in 1903 by Charles Eliot Norton, editor of Lowell's letters. It is possible that it came from the estate of his father, Charles Lowell, who owned paintings and a drawing by Allston. It would seem more likely, however, that it was solicited by James Russell Lowell for one of the periodicals with which he was associated in the early 1840s. The chief one was *The Pioneer: A Literary and Critical Magazine,* which he and Robert Carter published in Boston for three issues, in January, February, and March 1843, and discontinued because of lack of funds. The contributors included Poe, Hawthorne, Whittier, Thomas W. Parsons, Story, John Neal, Jones Very, John S. Dwight, Elizabeth Peabody, and the editors, and Lowell also solicited manuscripts from Longfellow and Emerson, among others. The first issue contained Story's review of the Boston Athenaeum exhibition of 1842, with his praise of Allston's landscape there. The prospectus promised, however, that "satire and personality will be sedulously avoided," and the articles in all the issues were uniformly serious. Lowell was also writing for another periodical at that time, which had a somewhat different aim, the *Boston Miscellany of Literature and Fashion,* published from January 1842 to February 1843, edited by Nathan Hale, Jr., until the end of 1842 and then by Henry T. Tuckerman. Inviting Lowell to be a contributor, Hale suggested he send "some bright, joyous prose" and said it would not be amiss for him to be "funny" (Horace E. Scudder, *James Russell Lowell: A Biography* [Boston: Houghton Mifflin, 1901], 1:354). A few months after the last issue Allston's death occurred, about which Tuckerman wrote a poem. In any case, the most reasonable explanation for Allston's sketch not appearing in print at any time would seem to be that it represented in a disparaging light several prominent Bostonians, with some of whom he himself was having amicable dealings.

As for "On the Domes of the State House & the Exchange Coffeehouse," Allston must have seen it as a piece of trivia, not meriting print. It was apparently printed in a periodical, however. A clipping of it seemingly from a newspaper is preserved in the Dana papers at the Longfellow Historic Site, but without the name or the date of the publication.

1. Charles Bulfinch (1763-1844). The chief facts about him given in the following notes come from Charles L. Place, *Charles Bulfinch, Architect and Citizen* (Boston, DaCapo Press, 1925). 2. The name of a Jew, mentioned in Acts 13:6, where he is called a false prophet.

3. There are no such characters in *The Arabian Nights Entertainment*. Both surnames were fairly common in Boston throughout Allston's last residence there, among them those of several laborers and housewrights. In using them he may have been thinking also of Jacob Coggin, minister of the church in Tewksbury, Mass., who attended Harvard when he did, and was known for his lack of sophistication, being described by RHD, Jr., as "an awkward simple clergyman from the out-of-the-way country town of Tewksbury," who was once introduced by the Rev. Francis Parkman, in a characteristically humorous fashion, as "brother Coggin, the angel of the Church at Tewksbury" (Dana, 2:521). The name also is reminiscent of that of Uriah Cotting (d. 1819), Boston engineer and builder, who was associated with Bulfinch in several enterprises but was active chiefly independently in nearly every one involving the development of the city for business during the first two decades of the century (Harold and James Kirker, *Bulfinch's Boston 1787-1817* [New York Oxford Univ. Press, 1964], pp. 196-99). In any case, they represent the type of architect-builder who became prominent in Boston after Bulfinch. 4. The Common in Cambridge is of no particular architectural interest, but that in Boston was under Bulfinch's direction as both architect and chairman of the board of selectmen; it was made into a park and lined on three sides with row houses designed by him: Park Street (1803-1804), Colonnade Row on Tremont Street (1809-11), and Beacon Street (from about 1800). 5. The domestic residences designed by both the Federalist and Greek Revival architects had much more formality than the "cottage," a house characterized by informality and a relationship to the landscape which was closer to the romantic than the classical tradition and which came into popularity toward the end of Allston's life. Presumably his use of the word here is satiric. 6. Alexander Parris built a number of lighthouses (Walter H. Kilham, *Boston after Bulfinch* [Cambridge: Harvard Univ. Press, 1946], p. 23), structures representing feats of engineering rather than of architecture, which was considered one of the fine arts. 7. The chief achievement of Bulfinch's early period was the Massachusetts State House on State Street (1794-98). Its most distinctive feature, however, was the dome, to which Allston referred in his poem comparing it and the dome of the Exchange Coffee House. The reference to the steps is ironic. 8. Bulfinch designed the Beacon Memorial Column on Beacon Hill (1790); it replaced the beacon erected in 1634, which had been blown down in 1789. The idea of erecting it as a memorial to Boston's part in the Revolution was his.
9. Bulfinch designed the Federal Street Church (1809) in the Gothic style, the first building to be erected in this style in New England and his only use of it. He wished thus to introduce something new, his mother-in-law said, adding that it was "generally approved, and particularly appropriate to the Saintly devotion of the preacher," who was Channing. The Bulfinch family was invited to be present, and a pew was reserved for them at the dedication (*The Life and Letters of Charles Bulfinch*, ed. Ellen Susan Bulfinch [Boston, 1896], pp. 168-69). With his preference for the Gothic WA must have been particularly interested in this building not only because of its architecture but because of Channing's ministry there. 10. Many churches in Boston had steeples, built by Bulfinch and others. One of the most famous was that designed by the English-born Peter Banner, a contemporary of Bulfinch. His original design for the steeple of Park Street Church, his first edifice in Boston, which he built in 1809, called for a final lantern section which would have risen an additional eighteen feet, making the total height 223 feet from the pavement to the final ball. After much discussion, the committee in charge of the construction decided against the greater height and Banner had to reduce it, to his lasting regret (Kilham, p. 15). 11. The name Nehemiah, drawn like that of Barjesus from the Bible, was the name of the prophet and of the book in the Old Testament attributed to him. His chief achievement was the rebuilding of the walls of Jerusalem after the Exile, with great enthusiasm and devotion. Presumably Allston intended using the name as a pseudonym for the author of a series of satiric articles about the architecture of Boston, in this one depicted as virtually newly built by the skill and the dedication of Bulfinch. 12. The Exchange Coffee House, on Congress Street near State Street, was finished in 1807 and destroyed by fire in November 1818. It was the largest hotel in Boston, being

seven stories high and covering an area of twelve thousand square feet, and cost in construction half a million dollars. The architect was Asher Benjamin, better known for his books for builders than for his own buildings, who lived in the city from 1803 until his death in 1845. Bulfinch was often credited with it, though it was clumsy in comparison with his typically graceful designs, probably partly because several years earlier he had proposed such a hotel and because it was almost the only public building in Boston not designed by him where he would, when he was acting head of the government as chairman of the board of selectmen, receive important visitors to the city (Kirker and Kirker, p. 204; Charles A. Cummings, "Architecture in Boston," Winsor, 4:475; Edward Stanwood, "Topography and Landmarks of the Last Hundred Years," Winsor, 4:58, photograph). The dome of the State House is large and that of the Exchange Coffee House was very low. In contrast to both, that of St. Peter's is perforated with small windows, and both the lantern and the ball may be entered. It thus might be called "empty" in relation to the "solid" American ones.

The Temperance Movement

Allston was noted from his student years for having Epicurean tastes and habits. He customarily drank Madeira wine after dinner and smoked cigars at all hours, most notably in the evening and until he retired early in the morning. The two indulgences when carried on together were almost invariably accompanied by conversation among a few friends on a variety of subjects. A few months before his death he called the dinner in Boston in honor of Dickens a *cena* and praised some Madeira which he had been given in poetic terms, quoting lines from Pope which linked the drinking of wine with social talk.

He was no more intemperate, however, than he was abstinent, and his whole pattern of life, like his thought, was generally moderate. He opposed, though by satire rather than directly, the various social reforms which were widespread in his day, especially in New England. Vegetarianism and temperance or abstinence from drinking alcohol were fads which grew rapidly in popularity there during the first half of the nineteenth century. The temperance movement, which spread throughout the country during this time, was encouraged in Boston chiefly through the churches. It seems, however, that Allston associated vegetarianism and temperance specifically with the Transcendentalists, who espoused both. His references to "the Water-drinking and Vegetable Society in Germany" and "the great Van der Wind" in his satire about temperance suggests not only the Germanic origins of American Transcendentalism but the promulgation by its followers of its doctrines in public lectures, writings, private conversational gatherings, and cooperative communities. Alcott was the most extreme and the most conspicuous of the group, but Margaret Fuller, Elizabeth Peabody, Channing's nephew William E. Channing, and others well known to Allston were more or less zealous members.

At an undetermined date but probably in the late 1830s Allston composed a satiric poem, "Convivial Song," which was primarily on total abstainers but also on vegetarians and reformers in general who offered new social theories for old ones. In these years the Transcendental movement in America reached its height. In 1834 Alcott opened a school there, with Elizabeth Peabody as his assistant, in which he set forth unorthodox theories of education which aroused such opposition, widely expressed in newspapers, that he was forced to abandon it a few years later. In 1836 the Transcendental Club was organized in Emerson's home; in 1839 Margaret Fuller began a series of conversations in Elizabeth Peabody's home on some of the social issues of the day; in 1840 the *Dial,* the unofficial organ of the Transcendentalists, was founded; in 1841 Brook Farm was established; and in 1842 Fruitlands was established, both of which communities incidentally proscribed meat and alcohol in diet. The two communities marked, in fact, not only the climax but the virtual end of the whole movement in New England, which Allston almost lived to see.

If Richard Dana, Jr., had a reason for not including "Convivial Song" in *Lectures on Art, and Poems,* it was probably not only that its satire would have presented a marked contrast to the other poems there but that, like Allston's satire on architecture in Boston, it held up for ridicule, however mild, some of his close associates. Actually, however, the dietary restrictions and reforming programs of the Transcendentalists were a less significant contrast between their commitments and his than a difference only implied in his lines: that between the conversations which occupied them and those which customarily took place around his evening table, accompanied by cigars and wine, about art, poetry, beauty, and the great achievements of the past.

Convivial Song:

Lately sung at the great anniversary <meeting> dinner
of the Water-drinking and Vegetable Society in Germany.

Are the fiddles all ready?—Then fiddle away
My merry men all, and welcome <this> the day
With <the grand new march call'd the march of the mind>
  the very magnificent March of the Mind.
Compos'd for the Age by the great <Mister> Van der Wind;
And let every note, like the tongue of a bell,
To every thing old <[undecipherable two words]> sound a funeral knell;
For every thing old is grown musty and fusty,
And ragged, and rotten, and musty and dusty.

Chorus.

Then fill, boys, fill! give the tables a thump,
  And manfully stand, with nor wink nor a blink;
  And up with your bumpers of water, and drink
To the reign of the beautiful Pump!
  Pump, pump, beautiful Pump!

Let one-eyed Reformers, who see but half way
<To the land of perfection [three or four words undecipherable]
  talk their breath all away>
To the land of White Livers declaim the beard gray
<Of> On the light to the world which *they* have let in
By turning out whiskey, and brandy and gin
Who stand on one leg, while they reel on the other,
Each thinking himself not himself but his brother.
We go the whole hog gainst the Spirits of Evil,
And send wine and cider, and beer to the Devil.

Chorus

And soon shall no other than Satan drink tea,
And Belzebub's breakfast of coffee shall be.
As for us, we abjure them; and how many more
Of the like diabolicals, spread the world o'er,
We shall send back to Satan we do not avow—
Perhaps <coat> shoes and stockings—but *mum* of that now.
So <now> here's to our only true brothers, the Fishes,
<Here's> Good health and long life, and our very best wishes.

Chorus

Appendix 4
Reading

Allston was a great reader, from his school days to the end of his life. Richard Henry Dana, Jr., described his reading as engaged in to the last "with the earnestness of youth" and consisting not only of the study of metaphysical works but "a constant recurrence to the great epic and dramatic masters, and occasional reading of the earlier and the living novelists, tales of wild romance and lighter fiction, voyages and travel, biographies and letters" (*LA*, p. vii). The books he borrowed from the college library while a student at Harvard are early testimony to this variety. Several were related to the courses he was taking, including Blair's *Lectures*, Buffon's *Natural History*, Cheselden's *Anatomy*, Hume's *Essays*, Kames's *Elements of Criticism*, Plutarch's *Lives*, and histories of Greece and Rome. Others represented his personal interests: those in literature by Goldsmith, Samuel Johnson, Shakespeare, Spenser, and Tasso, and two volumes of *The Spectator;* six or more on painting and aesthetics, including Walpole's *Anecdotes of Painting in England*, three collections of travels and voyages, a life of Mme de Maintenon, an Italian grammar, and David Ramsay's *History of the Revolution of South Carolina*, in which he must have been particularly interested because of his father's participation in that conflict.

In later years he regularly read magazines of a general literary nature, both English and American, and Boston newspapers. In the late 1830s, after his health declined, his wife was given strict orders not to let him and his brother-in-law Francis Dana leave the house, which they customarily did twice a week to get the semiweekly Boston *Atlas*, since, as Richard Henry Dana, Jr., put it, "she could never conceive of the true value of a newspaper," at whose remonstrances, he added, Allston "scowls & gives a new injunction—equally fruitless" (to his brother Edmund T. Dana, 24 Sept. 1837, Longfellow National Historic Site). He owned a considerable number of books and periodicals and sometimes borrowed books from others and from the Boston Athenaeum. A close relationship existed between what he read and what he painted, many of his paintings having literary sources. His painting and his writing were also closely related, many of his poems being about works of art and artists and several paintings having poems or prose descriptions to accompany them. Some of his closest associates in America and England were writers, most of them among his correspondents, and he often introduced literary allusions in his letters.

The Bible

The Bible was of all literary works the one which most inspired Allston's painting from first to last, with an intermission of twenty years, and which he alluded to and quoted from most extensively in his poetry and prose, as well as in his letters. Of his twenty paintings and drawings of biblical subjects and copies of paintings by Titian and Veronese in that category, sixteen are from the Old Testament, eleven from the New Testament, and one from the Apochrypha. In *Monaldi* the only paintings by Monaldi which are described are of biblical scenes: Noah offering a sacrifice after the subsiding of the flood waters, from Genesis 8:20, and "the King of Hell" with a damned mortal before him, from Revelation 9:11.

In a passage written in a book of sketches of presumably late date Allston called the Bible "the only true philosophy, the sole fountain of light, where the dark questions of the understanding which have so long stood, like chaotic spectres, between the fallen soul and its reason, at once lose their darkness and their terror," and recollected that he had never lighted on "*any truth*" which he "*inwardly felt*," including that in the realm of the philosophy of art, that "did not find its illustration and confirmation in some great doctrine" in it (*LA*, p. 177). He owned a Bible published in New York in 1807 as well as a New Testament in Greek and Latin. He also owned a copy of *Triumphi Christi . . . in eilf blättern* (Munich, 1839), consisting of illustrations from the Bible by the German painter, draftsman, and etcher Joseph von Führich, who was a friend of some of the German artists he knew in Rome.

He repeatedly referred to the Bible in his lectures on art to illustrate his theories. In the "Introductory Discourse," he quoted and paraphrased the description of man's creation in his assertion that both real and ideal ideas were manifested by a higher power; explained the supposed pleasure in evil as the use of a false nomenclature which began with the "first Fratricide"; in his discussion of the sublime, especially as it was related to the Infinite, quoted from the command of God for light, some of Isaiah's words describing his vision of the seraphim, and those describing Elijah's experience on Horeb; gave as examples of the highest manifestation of the sublime the visitations to Abraham, Lot, the two Marys at the sepulcher of Jesus, and, quoting in part, the keepers of the sepulcher; and in his differentiation between the perception of the real and ideal, quoted from Paul's letter to the Corinthians about spiritual discernment. In his description of Raphael's *Death of Ananias* in "Art," he paraphrased Peter's words to Ananias and quoted the words of the mourners for the prophets slain by a lion in the reign of King Jeroboam and in "Form" referred to an elderly person as one who has "entered into the conventional valley of dry bones," alluding to Ezekiel's vision (*LA*, pp. 4, 25, 39, 56, 68, 62, 63, 6, 91, 92, 126).

His poems contain numerous biblical allusions. In "The Sylphs of the Seasons" a conventional reference to Mammon occurs. In "The Two Painters" the colorist exhibits a painting of Daniel in the lion's den which a critic calls unfaithful to the biblical text, where Daniel's legs are said to be unbroken rather than unnatural as the painter represented them. In "Eccentricity" part of the description of Elijah's vision on Horeb is quoted, and Humility is addressed as having been heard at Bethlehem. In "The Paint-King" Geraldine's words are compared to the language of Eve. In "The Angel and the Nightingale" the epigraph is a paraphrase of the statement in Matthew and Luke that to him who has shall be given. In "The Atonement" Paul's words to the Corinthians about the resurrected Jesus and the resurrection of Christian believers are paraphrased. In "Sonnet: Art" Micheangelo's recogniton of the truth of his ideal forms is compared to Elisha's perception of the chariot of fire which took Elijah to heaven. In "On Greenough's Group of the Angel and Child" the passage in Mark about Jesus blessing children is paraphrased. And in "A Word: Man" evil thought is said to have continued since its first manifestation in Abel's death. In *Monaldi* not only does Monaldi paint biblical scenes but in dying paraphrases Paul's words to the Hebrews about the chastisement of those whom God loves and quotes his words to the Philippians about the peace of God; Maldura, described as one to whom the region beyond the external world is, in the words of Matthew, one of "outer darkness," alludes to the wisdom of Solomon and at the end is said to fall from pride before the voice of his conscience as the walls of Jericho before the horn of Joshua; the prior of the convent where Monaldi dies comforts him with one of the beatitudes; and the narrator says that as Monaldi dies he holds communion, in the words of Hebrews, "with the just made perfect."

Classics

The references in Allston's early letters to Greek and Roman authors and personages reflect the classical nature of his schooling and education at Harvard as well as the prevailing neoclassical tradition in arts and letters of that period. He owned, probably acquired then, a copy of Livy's *Historiarum ab Urbe Condita, libri qui supersunt, cum priores ad optimas editiones castigati* (Boston, 1798), on the endpapers of which he drew several faces. In his early years especially he manifested an interest in the classics in both painting and writings. Some thirteen or fourteen paintings and drawings have classical subjects: *Landscape (Aeneas and Achates Come Ashore[?]);* one of the sons in the antique group *Laocoön; Caius Marius in the Dungeon; Cupid Playing with the Helmet of Mars; Diana and Her Nymphs in the Chase; Jason Returning to Demand His Father's Kingdom; Dido and Anna;* the two versions of *Cupid and Psyche; Hebe; Diana Bathing; Polyphemus Immediately after His Eye was Put Out, Groping about His Cavern for the Companions of Ulysses, The Sibyl; Silenus and Fauns; Prometheus;* and *Clytie*. Two *Italian Landscapes* (G12, 31) have buildings with classical facades. Besides two of his juvenile poems, several in *The Sylphs of the Seasons* contain classical references: the title poem refers to the Fates; "The Two Painters, A Tale," to Charon, the Sytx, Minos, Diogenes, Mercury, Homer, Phoebus, Orpheus, Parnassus, the Muses, Socrates, Galen, Elysium, Jove, and the Fates; "Eccentricity," with its epigraph from the *Aeneid* 6.436, to Prometheus and a "Hercules figure"; "The Paint-King," to the "Ovidean art," Pygmalion, Prometheus, and a titan; and "To a Lady Who Spoke Slightingly of Poets," to the Muses. "The Complaint," with the characters of Colin, Lindor, and Daphne, is in the pastoral tradition. Only a few later poems contain such references: in "A Fragment" ("O, who hath lived the ills to know") Monaldi's form is said to be such as would have been deified like Jason's in ancient Greece; "Gloria Mundi" has the conventional phrase as the title; and the author is addressed as a sibyl in "To the Author of 'The Diary of an Ennuyée.'" The subject of the painting by Tibaldi described in his sonnet about it is Aeolus. In his lectures on art he referred to a fashion maker as a "Petronius of the Shears," doubted that the expression *Eureka,* which he attributed to Pythagoras rather than Archimedes, had anything of "self" in it, proposed that the death of Pliny the Elder was caused by his fascination with the sublime in the eruption of Vesuius rather than by mere curiosity, named the characters of Homer as examples of "Ideal Invention," thus being timeless, and cited with apparent approval Horace's recommendation of nine years for the revision of a poem (*LA*, pp. 23, 33, 58, 97, 107). The narrator of "The Hypochondriac" says that epics are out of fashion, that Homer and Virgil are read only to justify schooling in them, that no modern can write a tragedy, and that cigars make him feel that he is in Elysium. In later years, as he described his preference for Gothic rather than classical architecture, he spoke of Pericles and Aspasia and was led in consequence to say that he "never had any sympathy with the classics ("Color Book," p. 64).

Shakespeare

After the Bible, Shakespeare was the major literary influence on Allston's painting and writing. He borrowed a copy of his works from the Harvard Library, saw in the Charleston, South Carolina, Library in 1800-1801 prints from the paintings in John Boydell's Shakespeare Gallery in London, and visited the gallery during his first stay there. He began to draw on Shakespeare's works in his paintings in Italy and a number of them were so inspired from then until the last years of his life: *Falstaff Enlisting His Ragged Regiment, Falstaff Playing the Part of the King, Casket Scene from "The Merchant of Venice," Catherine and Petruchio, Grumio and the Tailor, Hermia and Helena, Macbeth and Banquo Meeting the Witches on the Heath, Lorenzo and Jessica, The Death of King John, Titania's Court,* probably *Fairies on the Seashore Disappearing at Sunrise,* and *Landscape: Macbeth [?].* Four of his drawings were identified by H.W.L. Dana as from *Henry VIII,* 1.1; *The Tempest,* 4.1; *The Winter's Tale,* 1.2.27ff; and *The Merchant of Venice,* 3.1.80-137.

His sonnet "On Kean's Hamlet" is essentially a tribute to Shakespeare. In his lectures on art he referred to and quoted from him more than any other author. He called him "the greatest master of Truth," whose characters had the moral element or "soul" essential to the true "Human Form," and cited a variety of them as examples of his theories: of truth which had to be modified by the imagination to be pleasing by the "Smothered moan of Desdemona" and the "fiendish adjuration of Lady Macbeth"; of "Ideal Invention" by the characters in general, who were thus timeless; of mixed modes even in the principle of harmony by Richard II, with both intellect and courage, but not by "the fiend Iago," whose intellect seemed "animalized"; of the temporary banishment of the ideas of beauty, truth, and goodness by "mockeries of the brain" similar to the "fume-born phantoms" from the witches' cauldron in *Macbeth;* of the invisible world being connected with the "unknown Infinite" by the witches and the ghost in *Hamlet*; and of the sublime and the beautiful sometimes requiring a conjuror to tell them apart by the two Dromios in *The Comedy of Errors.* He quoted from *The Tempest* Prospero's characterizations of Ariel and Ariel's plea to Prospero on behalf of Alonzo and his companions to illustrate his theory that even imaginative characters embody moral ideas and Caliban's imprecations upon Prospero and Miranda to illustrate "Ideal Invention" and from *Hamlet* Hamlet's description to his mother of his father in contrast to his uncle to illustrate physical perfection of form. In "America to Great Britain" he characterized Shakespeare's language as being, like Milton's, "free and bold" (*LA,* pp. 115, 36, 97, 50, 46, 61, 65, 115, 119, 98, 291).

In a plot sequence in *Monaldi* reminiscent of *Othello,* Monaldi believes Maldura's story about Rosalia's infidelity and in consequence makes an abortive attempt to kill her. The narrator of "The Hypochondriac" refers to Boswell's description in the entry of 17 April 1778 of his *Life of Samuel Johnson* of his distress at the thought of going at death into a state of being in which Shakespeare's poetry did not exist and quotes, like King Lear to Cordelia, the proverb about nothing coming of nothing.

He owned a copy of *The Plays of William Shakespeare, accurately printed from the text of Mr. [George] Steevens' last ed., with a selection of the most important notes [by John Nichols]* (8 vols.; London, 1797), each volume of which he inscribed; volume 1 contained Nicholas Rowe's life of Shakespeare). He also owned *Gallery of Shakespeare, or Illustrations of his Dramatic Works, engraved in aqua-fortis from [Friedrick August Moritz] Retzsch, with scenes selected from Shakespeare and explanations by J.W. Lake. Ser. 1. Hamlet* (London, 1828).

Spenser

Edmund Spenser (ca. 1552-99) was the only other Elizabethan writer who appealed to Allston, doubtless because of his fancifulness. He borrowed a copy of *The Faerie Queene* from the Harvard College Library, from which poem he painted *The Flight of Florimel* in early maturity and later *Una in a Wood,* as well as making a number of sketches of Una. Shortly before he died he told Elizabeth Peabody that Spenser was an inexhaustible source of subjects and that he wanted to take many more from him and arranged for her to bring him models for a painting of the scene in *The Faerie Queen* (4.6.21) in which Sir Artegall's sword drops from his hand when he beholds Britomart (Peabody, pp. 3-4).

Milton

John Milton (1608-74), after Shakespeare, made the deepest impression on Allston of any English writer. From *Paradise Lost* he painted *Satan at the Gates of Hell Guarded by Sin and Death* and at later dates *Uriel in the Sun* and *Gabriel Setting the Watch at the Gates of Paradise.* In London during his first stay there he saw the remnants of Henry Fuseli's famous Milton Gallery. He owned a copy of Milton's *Paradise Lost, with a life of the author (by J. Evans). To which is prefixed the celebrated critique by Samuel Johnson* (London, 1799). In his lectures on art he paraphrased *Comus* (line 262), as "lapped in Elysium" in describing mental pleasures in contrast to sensuous ones, calling Milton one who "felt and embodied the subtile mystery in immortal verse" and from *Paradise Lost* (5.117-19) lines spoken by Adam regarding Eve's troublesome dream in illustrating the principle that "in the Mind alone is to be found the true or ultimate Rule"; in discussing the supernatural as the highest manifestation of the sublime, he cited Raphael, Michael, Abdiel, and, quoting from 4.845, Zephron. He described Milton's line as a "surging sweep." In "America to Great Britain" he referred to "the language free and bold," also used by Shakespeare, in which Milton described Satan's fall in book 1 of *Paradise Lost (LA,* pp. 14, 136, 63, 151, 291).

The Eighteenth Century

Allston was acquainted with several eighteenth-century writers, particularly Alexander Pope (1688-1744). He quoted or alluded to works by Pope in his letters from 1803 to 1842 and in several of his other writings. In "The Two Painters" he paraphrased line 308 from "The Epistle to Dr. Arbuthnot" ("Who breaks a butterfly upon a wheel?") and quoted it in a footnote, and in his lecture "Composition," comparing line in painting to versification in poetry, he quoted Pope's description of Dryden's "long, majestic march" in "The First Epistle of the Second Book of Horace" (line 269). He owned *The Works of Alexander Pope, Esq., in four volumes complete With his last corrections Carefully Collated . . . with former edition [sic]; together with notes from the various critics and commentators,* edited by J. Bell (London, 1778).

Other poets of the period whom he read included, in college, the Della Cruscans, as Jarvis remembered, naming Robert Merry in particular; Thomson, who inspired him in both painting and writing; and Churchill, a copy of whose *Poems* (London, 1765) he owned and inscribed "Washington Allston Harvard College, 1799." He also owned copies of Waller's *Poems* (9th ed.; London, 1712), Crabbe's *The Borough: A Poem, in Twenty-four Letters* (New York, 1810) and *Tales of the Hall* (2 vols.; Boston, 1819), and a two-volume edition of the poems of James MacPherson attributed to Ossian. In his lecture "Composition" he not only cited Dryden's style but characterized Crabbe as having an "abrupt gait" and Abraham Cowley a "sauntering walk" (*LA,* p. 151).

His poem "Eccentricity" is perhaps most comparable to many of these poets with its criticism of the age and its treatment of nature. Early in it he invoked the spirit of Cowper, exclaiming that could "poor Cowper" revisit earth "what indignation strange / Would sting thee" to find "courtly" poetic diction in literature, the industrialized cities "by gross mechanic toil / Tricked out to charm with meretricious air, / As though all France and Manchester were there," and worst of all "the altered region of the mind," where "Folly" replaces "wisdom." He used the word *nature* not in the typical romantic sense but in the earlier one to refer to the entire compass of human nature and activity, condemning the artist who instead of adapting nature in his works deferred to the world's hatred of her "naked state," and so became arrogant, attentive to applause and fashion, striving for the novel, extravagant even in dress, immoral, and given to "courtly" rather than plain poetic diction. His criticism was directed not only to painters, poets, wits, and philosophers but to the urban, "refining," "mechanic" and "material" age, and finally to all those who had never heard the voice of conscience; trampled on Scripture, equated body and mind, denied life after death, exalted reason in itself rather than a gift from nature "To guide the soul upon her way to heaven." He urged that they seek "that sweet praise, the tribute of the good, / For wisdom gain'd, through love of truth pursued" and admonished "Presumptuous man" to recognize his dependent state, exclaiming, "Come then, Humility, thou surest guide!" (*SS*, pp. 100, 91, 92, 104, 102, 109, 112, 113, 11, 113).

For all his association and kinship with the chief English romantic poets, Allston disapproved of extremely individualistic departures from the basically rational literary tradition of the preceding period. When he read the extracts from Thomas Carlyle's sketch of Mirabeau in the *French Revolution* printed in the *Westminster Review* for January 1837 he thought, like Richard Henry Dana, the style was an "outrage." He did not see any original ideas in it, Richard Henry Dana, Jr., recollected he said, but "a great deal of original English." Carlyle, he added, "takes a common thought and belabors it with his Babylonish jargon until it appears like something original. The man has made a god of his own intellect, and worships it with perpetual summersets" (Duffy, p. 216; Flagg, p. 361).

Gothic Romances

Gothic romances captivated Allston's imagination as much as did any single writer with the exception of Shakespeare. Though only his two illustrations from Ann Radcliffe and one from LeSage specifically attest in his painting to his taste for such writers, it is reflected in his early fondness for and imitation of Salvator Rosa. He was indebted to others, particularly Matthew G. Lewis, whose "The Cloud King" in *Tales of Wonder* he burlesqued in "The Two Painters," and Horace Walpole. In the "Introductory Discourse" of his lectures on art he characterized the sublime as "filling, distending, stretching every faculty" until it seemed almost like the giant in Walpole's *The Castle of Otranto* "to burst the imagination" (*LA*, p. 68). He read *The Fatal Revenge* (1807) by Charles Maturin and his *The Milesian Chief* (1812), which he thought much better; William Mumford's *The Five Nights of St. Albans* (1829), and novels of Charles Brockden Brown ("Washington Allston," p. 432; Leslie, p. 17). He owned copies of Carl Friedrich Grosse's *The Dagger* (London, 1795) and *Miniature Romances from the German, with Other Protrusions of Light Literature*, translated by Thomas Tracy (Boston, 1841), which included F.H.K. LaMotte Fouqué's *Undine* and an

Italian translation of Coleridge's poem "Love." The reading of the narrator of "The Hypochondriac," which consists of accounts of voyages, travels, shipwrecks, murders, and ghost stories, is related to this genre, as more distantly is the *Peregrinations* of the sixteenth-century Portuguese adventurer Ferdinão Pinto, who is referred to in his "Introductory Discourse" as "the greatest liar" who nevertheless must have loved the truth (*LA*, p. 33).

Appendix 5
Technique in Painting

Allston's letter to Morse of 18 February 1812 contains his first known description, slight as it is, of his technique in painting. He experimented with several techniques throughout his early years. Besides his use of glazing adopted in London during his first stay, the mingling of colors begun after his first visit to Paris, and his method developed in Italy of painting mountains, during his second stay in England he apparently settled on his process of painting heads, at which time he also experimented with painting foliage, with shade in background and with mixture for pigments.

The fullest account of his practices in painting and drawing is that given by Henry Greenough in the letter he wrote Richard Henry Dana after Allston's death, based on conversations which he and Allston had, presumably during the years from 1825 to 1830 and in the late 1830s. The chief deviation from his practices as described there seems to have been that in later years he gave up making preliminary sketches, drawing in chalk first on the canvas, and often delayed the glazing process indefinitely. Greenough's account also contains the fullest testimony, after Allston's letter to Henry Pickering of 27 November 1827, of the influence exerted on him by Reynolds.

In the early stages of their acquaintance, Greenough said, he heard Allston first describe his mode of preparing a palette to paint flesh and then his system of coloring some five or six times in very nearly the same words, which he repeated as nearly as possible, in Allston's phraseology though not exactly in their original order. He said he had practiced the same process in painting a head for the preceding fifteen years, or since about the time of his stay in America from 1808 to 1811, and was perfectly satisfied with it. He began, he said, by drawing it in outline and first applying a dead color of black, white, and Indian red, then mixing yellow, red, and blue, the "three primitive colors," with white, to form his "virgin tints." For shadows he mixed the three to a neutral hue coming close to olive. In mixing the colors he used a brush instead of a knife, thus giving his flesh a "luminous" appearance, he said, or what Titian called the "luce di dentro." That phrase, he added, when he first heard it, probably in 1803 in Paris, opened to him "a world of light." He now applied the tints, from the lowest to the highest, keeping "the mass of light warm," with a "predominance of reds and yellow, rather than blue," and touching up the color, in a process which took half an hour. He particularly emphasized his use of color in the shadows, remarking that unless they were painted "solidly" the head would not be brilliantly colored and that it was a very common error to think that shadows should be painted thin to get transparency, which would be obtained at the expense of "force" (Flagg, pp. 182, 183, 184, 186).[1] He endeavored to finish his impasto in a day. For the glazing he mixed asphaltum, Indian red, ultramarine, a tinge of megilp and Japan gold size to a neutral tint that he called "Titian's dirt" (Flagg, p. 187) and applied it in different proportions over a period of a day or two. This process he compared to that used in watercoloring except that the paint was left moist. He often finally painted into the glazing.

To a certain degree, he said, he observed the same system in painting other substances, even pebbles and rocks. In painting figures he used the same hue for drapery and adjacent figures but different colors and hues for portions in large masses that were in the light, in which case he painted the drapery first with umber and white, then went over it thinly with white so that the under shades showed through, as he said was characteristic of Titian's white. He described his method of painting mountains, which Greenough observed had a tone and color unlike those of any other artist, as in his Alpine scenery and *The Spanish Girl in Reverie*, by saying he used successive layers of colors and detailing the steps he took in the latter painting.

One evening he commenced a conversation with Greenough by saying he had been amused that day by hearing of a young painter who had taken literally Reynold's precept that he should "on the background dispense all the treasures of his palette" and had compounded with his palette knife all the odd tints happening to be there, when what Reynolds had meant was that "the colors of the head or figure should be somewhere repeated, otherwise, it would be a spot in the picture," he commented that Reynolds "was the last man to grind his colors together" (Flagg, p. 189).[2] As an example of his own practice he described the experiment he made in the background of *The Angel Releasing St. Peter from Prison*.

He also expressed his opinion of certain pigments. He thought white lead "most useful" but lamented that manufacturers in an attempt to get greater purity had ruined its body, said he preferred it to Cremlitz white or silver white, adding, "I do not care so much about the extreme whiteness as the opacity" and saying it looked beautifully white "but you might almost as well paint with snow! Brilliancy of color depends more upon the opacity of the lights than the transparency of shadows, because the proportion of shadow to light is small." He called raw and burnt sienna powerful but needing to be used with care, preferred raw sienna and white to Naples yellow for gold light, and said that Prussian blue was useful for glazing but that ultramarine was "of all colors the most unexceptionable." He disagreed with Reynolds about vermilion, which he gave the "*spunk* of lake" by touching in ultramarine and which he added whenever he used lake to give it body. Reynolds, he commented, did not like vermilion but was obliged to come to it at last, and he thought the pictures he painted with it were the only ones which had "stood the test of time" (Flagg, pp. 200-201).

On one occasion Greenough was present when Allston gave several pieces of advice to a young artist, probably Thomas Cole about 1828. He particularly emphasized the importance of drawing, saying, "With regard to preparatory studies, I should warmly recommend your devoting a portion of every day to drawing; for this reason, that if an artist does not acquire a correct design *while young*, he never will. Sir Joshua Reynolds always felt conscious that his powers were very much limited and his works incorrect for want of the *early habit* of drawing. A painter may be blest with every gift of nature, but unless he has acquired the art of design he can never *express himself.* If you would not be tormented by a consciousness of having noble and beautiful conceptions to which you cannot give birth, you must give much of your time to drawing. For this purpose I should recommend a course of study *somewhat different from what is generally pursued*. I would devote my attention principally to outline. It is perhaps well enough to learn how to make a finished drawing, but when you have once done that, your time had better be spent in making drawings of the figures in highly studied outline only." He then described his own practice thus: "[I] make a finished otline always before touching the brush to canvas. I draw the outlines of such figures as I intend to drape, making out the figure as nicely as if it were to be painted naked. I take a large, rough piece of common chalk, which makes a broad mark, and then with my finger or a bit of bread I can rub out a portion and thus get a *little more* or *little less* much better than by using a fine point. When I have arranged the contour of my figure or head I trace the final outline with umber. I would recommend your studying your outline as highly as if it were not to be disturbed, but when you paint use your *brush as freely as if you had no outline to go by.* This is the only way to avoid the hardness of effect which is apt to arise from a close study of the outline. I frequently paint my figures over the outline and let my background encroach upon the contour of the figure again several times in the course of the painting" (Flagg, pp. 197-98).[3] In these remarks Allston echoed Reynolds's words in Discourse 2 that if ability in drawing were not "acquired whilst you are young, there will be no time for it afterward" followed by his quoting Michelangelo as saying it was a pity the Venetian painters did not learn to draw in their youth.

During his conversations with Greenough, Allston often referred to other artists, including Michelangelo, Tintoretto, Rubens Beechey, and Leslie, and the colorist George Field. He also recalled experiences he had had in Paris, Switzerland, Rome, and London, described experiments he had made in *Diana and Her Nymphs, Elijah in the Desert,* and *Italian Landscape,* or *Italian Scenery,* as well as *The Spanish Girl in Reverie* and *The Angel Releasing St. Peter from Prison.*

Allston himself seems to have made notes of several technical matters in painting which were copied into his "Color Book," apparently begun after his return to America in 1818. It contains a table of measurements of the human figure as established by ancient sculptors; sections entitled "To prepare Drying Oil," "Lights & Shades," "Color and Effect," "Allston's method of painting a head," "Method for a landscape"; a list of permanent colors for oil and watercolor painting; and several quotations from him relating to his theory and practice. None of the entries is in his hand. Probably the first twenty-five pages, the substance of which was apparently originally written by him, were copied by Henry Greenough, in whose handwriting they seem to be written; and very likely the remaining pages, which are in another hand, represent notes Greenough made from conversations they had.

The notes in Allston's "Color Book" about his methods are less discursive than his account in his conversations with Greenough but are in general agreement with it. Both call for beginning with a chalk drawing, using successive layers of different colors—with the notation that red and blue each brought out the quality of the other—finishing the first painting in a day, and glazing. In the conversations he was attentive only to mountains in the category of landscape and went into more detail regarding heads. There are several instances of similar phraseology. "Allston's method of painting a head" contains a reference to Titian's "'*Lucida dentro,*' a light within," the advice to begin painting the darker side of a head first and to take the colors "in a bundle" on the brush, and the comment that the colors should be strong, saying, "Be sure to lay a good body of color in the lights. This is difficult to manage, and at first looks heavy, but glazing will refresh it and the effect is a solid sweetness you can never attain if you content yourself with facile distribution of thin color which at first pleases the eye, but does not long satisfy it." In the same section he is quoted as saying, "In painting from nature, you cannot go wrong in following your eye, never reason about it. Let your hand go and it will surely find its way to the right tint, and you will be surprised at the strength of the colors that you use. If you stop to think what color will be right, you will choose one too weak and at a distance it will look like nothing." Respecting drawing he is quoted as preferring chalk to crayon, explaining, "In designing take a large lump of chalk and you will find it obey the hand & the mind more readily than the port crayon. After you have made out the general features then take the chalk or the port crayon to finish & perfect your sketch" (pp. 37-38, 34, 37, 38).

Allston's "Color Book" also contains several instances of his reliance on Reynolds. The table of measurements of the human body as represented in the statues of the ancients is a paraphrase of Reynolds's quotation, in his Note 8 on Fresnoy's *Art of Painting*, from Roger de Piles's note on Fresnoy's verses 145-46. The section "Lights & Shades" has two echoes of Reynolds. In point 9 Allston said that in the shadows of the human figure or animals the feature limb or muscles should not be marked "with hard, strong shadows" but blended into the lights and other shadows surrounding them and commented on that practice by Correggio and in point 11 said that if "grandeur or breadth" is desired, the lights of the object should "mingle with the lights of the sky, or background, and the shadows mass with the shadows. Sir J. Reynolds has shewn in his practice, that this mode in addition to grandeur, gives a graceful softness" (pp. 4-6, 11-12).[4]

Perhaps the most interesting entry in Allston's "Color Book" respecting his own technique is the description of an Italian landscape otherwise unknown, painted in August, probably in the early 1820s. He described it to a visitor, probably Greenough, who interspersed Allston's words with his own. He gave it, Allston said, "an Italian distance," adding, "I have always felt the want of those distances in the scenery of this country. And we have no mountains here, at least I have never seen any thing but round hills. Nothing like the broken, romantic, angular character of the Alps & Pyrenees. Neither have they any mountains in England, Scotland or Wales. Their mountains are but dumplings." The painting had a mountain, a castle, a waterfall in the middle, a river, a road, and an "Italian pine."[5] He first laid on blue-gray and bluish green over the mountain, purple over the water, these tints combined with red and yellow for the middle distance and the water under the hill, the latter two for the road, and patches of green in the foliage in the foreground uniting it with the sky and the center. At this point the visitor commented: "The piece is now in dead color & though spectial [spectral?] in its appearance exhibits the same serene tranquillity of expression that is seen in all the pictures of Allston. It is a soul shining through them, not a superficial smoothness gained by high finishing. His pictures indeed are susceptible of the highest finish; but their expression depends not on it." After a week, on 20 August, he commenced a second stage in his painting, said by the visitor to give "local tint & texture to the objects." With a tint of white and blue he scumbled the under part of the tree's foliage "to give it air and rubbed it in among the foliage every where, painting zephyrs, as he said." The next day he laid on greens where there had been yellow ocher, "using yellow ochre slightly changed [charged?] with blue & for deeper greens more blue," covering the trees and ground except the road and introducing the stones and stumps with these colors. The next time he applied stiff colors, made stiffer by mixing gold size with them, and leaving "depressions & elevations among the leaves & irregular lumps to be taken advantage of in glazing." He now painted the waterfall with blue and black, which looked blue, carried the green a little up into the castle "because a large mass of any color looms up in that way" though it was imperceptible unless one knew it was there, and commented, "Now . . . that castle is perfectly asleep." After allowing the picture to dry for a fortnight, he glazed it with burnt umber and megilp. To finish it he said he would "paint into the wet glaze with body colors & when that was dry glaze again and if still unsatisfied paint again into that, & so on as long as he pleased" (p. 42-52). Possibly Sarah Clarke was referring to this painting when she named one as "the grey 'Mountain Landscape,' a world composed of stern material" (p. 130).

In giving an account of this painting Allston also described another aspect of his method which was not strictly technical. He had never, he said, been able to persuade himself "to do things in the easiest way" nor "to hurry over parts & leave vacant spaces" nor to take advantage of his "long practice to make a picture which required no thought nor trouble," adding, "I can truly say that I never painted a picture which did not cost me the whole of my mind" ("Color Book," pp. 50-57).[6]

Several of Allston's practices as a painter and pieces of advice to young painters were recorded by the author of the article about him in the *United States Democratic Review* for October 1843. In effect all of them tended, like some of the passages in his "Color Book" but in contrast to the general tenor of his conversations with Greenough, to emphasize an individualistic, intuitive element in the creative process as he knew it. He could not remember, the author of the article said, to tell Sophia Peabody what steps he followed in painting *Lorenzo and Jessica* to assist her in making a copy of it. His advice on one occasion was, "Do not be anxious, but put faith in your fingers. When I paint I often do not look at my palette; I take off my colors by a secret sympathy between my hand and the pigments." The author of the article also noted Allston's infrequent walks out of doors, which sometimes brought the comment that had he gone out more often his landscapes would have been better or at least more "real," and in that connection recounted once visiting a woods with him when the scene reminded him of one in his boyhood which he described in detail, saying it seemed that he had visited the spot that day, so vivid was this memory of it. More realistically and with a characteristically vivid figure of speech, he told a student, "Your trees do not look as if the birds could fly through them." Of the profession of painting he was quoted as saying, "It is a calling full of delays and disappointments, and I can never recommend any one to pursue it. It he *must* be a painter, let him come prepared to bear up a mighty burden." It was a description of a profession in which technique at its best was relatively unimportant.

Allston owned several books on artistic technique and on the history of painting and the lives of painters: Carington Bowles's popular *The Artist's Assistant in Drawing, Perspective, Etching,* 6th ed. (Birmingham, 1801); William Enfield's *Young Artist's Assistant; or, Elements of the Fine Arts,* 2d ed. (London, 1822); John Thomas James's *The Italian Schools of Painting, with Observations on the present state of the art,* 2 vols. (London, 1820); Hannah F.S. Lee's *Historical Sketches of the Old Painters* (Boston, 1841); and Giorgio Vasari's *Vite de' piu Eccellenti Pittori scultori e architetti,* 8 vols. (Florence, 1770). Mrs. Lee, whose book first appeared in 1838, lived most of her life in Boston; after Allston's death she wrote a brief notice of him, "Washington Allston," in *Howlitt's Journal* (18 Dec. 1847, pp. 395-96). He also owned Sir Martin Archer Shee's *Elements of Art: A Poem* (London, 1809), on the title page of which he drew the head of a soldier and a face. Probably he knew Shee, who later became president of the Royal Academy.

1. In describing his tints and shadows Allston echoed Reynolds's words in Discourse 8, in which he said the "masses of light" in a painting should be "of a warm mellow color yellow, red, or yellowish white"; in Note 41 to Fresnoy's *Art of Painting,* where he named the same colors and referred to the lack of "mellowness or warmth" in modern painting; and in Note 44, where he deplored the fear of "dark shadows by modern painters, saying that without them a picture would want "solidity and strength." 2. In making the reference to Reynolds Allston was echoing passages from his Notes 42 and 43 to Fresnoy, in which he recounted the anecdote of a young painter applying to Rubens for assistance in painting backgrounds and enunciated the rule that "the same colour which makes the largest mass be diffused and appear to revive in different parts of the picture," since a single color would otherwise "make a spot or blot." 3. Allston was the best and most versatile draftsman of his day and one of the most prolific. About three hundred of

his drawings survive, apparently a small number of those he made. The earliest, mostly caricatures, were in ink. During his Roman sojourn he turned to chalk, which he eventually used most often. Pencil he used infrequently. From the time he was in Switzerland most of his drawings were studies for paintings, a few for portraits and landscapes but most for history paintings. There are drawings for almost all paintings in that category: entire compositions, anatomical parts, and draperies. He also made other drawings of landscapes and anatomical parts, and of portraits, costumes, marine scenes, comic pieces, architectural elements, and mechanical devices. A few are portraits and several are from casts and antique sculpture. The early ones, taken from observed natural and human forms, chiefly in London, Switzerland, and Rome, were followed in later years by the imagined forms of the later paintings. Most were on loose sheets, only a few pages of his surviving sketchbooks being used (ca. 1800-1805, 1812-18, 1830). 4. In Discourse 8 Reynolds described the effect of "melting and losing the shadows in a ground still darker" and said it was found to perfection in the best works of Correggio and Rembrandt; in Discourse 4 said that to give "a general air of grandeur at first view," all little lights and variety of tints should be avoided and that "a breadth of uniform and simple color" would contribute to quietness and simplicity; and in Note 56 he recommended painting "soft and tender" in contrast to the disposition of artists to paint "harder than nature." 5. Apparently Allston made a study for this painting in a small sepia wash drawing, *Landscape with Horsemen,* which has all these elements and in addition a group of horsemen. At an unknown date the drawing was inscribed as having been done while he was in college and presented to Henry C. Flagg, Jr., by William Allston. He has been assigned the date of ca. 1799 probably because it resembles *Landscape with Banditti* of 1798, particularly in the figures of horsemen and the waterfall, which appear in no other painting by Allston, and in the shape of the group of trees at the right. The pine, however, apparently belongs to a later date. Only in *Landscape, Evening (Classical Landscape)* and *Italian Landscape* (G62), both painted long afterward, are there distinctively Italian pines, being those common in the vicinity of Rome especially known as "umbrella pines." 6. In Discourse 4 Reynolds said that the value of every art was "in proportion to the mental labour employed in it, or mental pleasure produced by it," and that "exertion of mind," the only circumstance that truly ennobles an art, was the great distinction between the Roman and the Venetian schools; and in Discourse 11 he declared that to achieve the effect of a whole in a work of art required not only study and practice but "the painter's entire mind."

Appendix 6
Religious Beliefs

Allston's family was affiliated with the Episcopal church in South Carolina, and he was apparently considered nominally religious in his maturity. On hearing of Morse's engagement in 1817, Leslie wrote him, "You and I have seen how very greatly true Christianity conduces to domestic comfort in the instance of Mr. and Mrs. Allston" (Prime, p. 102). He seems to have manifested little deep interest in religion, however, until after his wife's death in February 1815. He told Elizabeth Peabody that the divinity of Christ was "revealed" to him on a foggy night in November, probably in that year, in London, as he was struggling to overcome a sense of self-imprisonment. The thought that came to him then was in verse and he expressed it in his poem "The Atonement" (Peabody, pp. 7, 8). Shortly before leaving England in 1818 he sent copies of Thomas Chalmers's *Discourses on the Christian Religion, Viewed in Connection with Modern Astronomy* to one or two of his friends whose opinions he feared were inclined to deism, hoping that since they were of scientific and literary attainments Chalmer's line of argument might have weight but taking care that his identity as the sender be unknown. (Leslie to RHD, 28 January 1844).

Several years later he was confirmed, on Sunday 8 April 1821, in St. Paul's Episcopal Church in Boston, by the Reverend Alexander Viets Griswold, bishop of the diocese. After moving to Cambridgeport he usually attended the Church of the Shepard Congregational Society in Cambridge, but, according to Sweetser, on saints' day and other ecclesiastical festivals went to St. Paul's. The Danas also attended the Shepard Congregational church, the family occupying pew 20 (Dana, 1:181). Taken to task by the daughter of an Episcopal clergyman in Newport for thus apparently leaving the Episcopal church, he said, hoping to broaden her notions of religion, that he was neither an Episcopalian nor a Congregationalist but endeavored to be a Christian. It was apparently after his religious experience that he discontinued *Christ Healing the Sick*, the only painting besides the early *And Christ Looked at Peter* in which he depicted Christ, and said on more than one occasion that that character was too exalted to be represented by him. In his later years he was described by many, among them Walter Channing, Richard Henry Dana, Jr., Leonard Jarvis, Elizabeth Peabody, and William Ware, as deeply religious, believing firmly in the doctrines of Christianity, and reading not only the Bible but books about it. In Ware's opinion he had "a religious mind," not in a "one-sided, technical sense, but in the universal sense," was comparable to Fra Angelico, Fra Bartolomeo, and the nineteenth-century German religious painter J.F. Overbeck and in Catholic times would have been a monk (*Lectures*, pp. 11, 117). At the very last he declared more specifically than in his lectures on art that the imagination did not create but only saw the spiritual creations of God. Among his last words were those to a young friend urging her to devote herself to religious service (Peabody, pp. 4, 6-10; Walter Channing). In the article "Anecdotes of Allston" in the *Boston Atlas* for 19 July 1843 it was said that the sale of *Uriel in the Sun* had made him a devout man before which he had been skeptical in religion, negligent of religious duties, and given to joking about divine matters, a statement which was vigorously contradicted by Edward J. Reynolds, John Codman, George Hayward, Edmund T. Dana, and Elizabeth Peabody, among others, The next day the *Boston Evening Post* said it was authorized to contradict the story and a relative did so (Dana, 1:186-88).

A number of Allston's friends were clergymen, including, besides Channing, John Albro, Nehemiah Adams, his classmate Joshua Bates, George Washington Bethune, J.S. Buckminster, John Codman, Convers Francis, Charles Lowell, James Marsh, Ware, and Leonard Woods, Jr., as well as the biblical scholar Andrews Norton. Two of his nephews, sons of Henry C. Flagg, Jr., were Episcopal clergymen, and Richard Henry Dana, Jr., who took an active part on the side of the Trinitarians in the schism between them and the Unitarians in the Congregational church in the 1820s and 1830s, was eventually affiliated with the Episcopal church.

He was particularly impressed by the doctrine of the Atonement. Besides the poem of that title, he wrote in a book of sketches a description of it, in which he called it a "mystery" which alone could cleanse man from sin, quoted from another's description of it as being that which "even the angels sought to comprehend and could not," and, quoting further, declared, "Equally deep, too, and unalienable, is my conviction that 'the fruit of sin is misery' " (*LA*, p. 176). Albro said that on his last visit to him Allston talked "particularly & most solemnly" on the Atonement as "the foundation of a Christian's hope," and in his sermon after Allston's funeral, in which he said Allston was "above piety" but "quite philosophical," declared that he would never forget the "energy & emotion" with which he spoke at that time of his faith in that doctrine (Dana, 1:172, 183). Edmund T. Dana, his nephew, also said he spoke of it during their conversation the last evening of his life and called it "the chosen object of his religious contemplation and conversation" ("The Last Hours of Washington Allston," *New-York Tribune*, 10 July 1843). "The Atonement, the Atonement [*sic*] was the very life of his soul," RHD put it to Gulian C. Verplanck (14 July 1843).

Allston's early poems contain only a few conventional allusions to God, heaven, scripture, and the soul, but some eight of his later ones, in addition to "The Atonement," have theological overtones: "The Angel and the Nightingale," "Gloria Mundi," "Sonnet: The French Revolution," "The Tuscan Girl," "Sonnet: Immortality," "The Marigold," "A Fragment" ("Who knows himself must needs in prophecy"), "A Word: Man," and "A Fragment" ("O, who hath lived the ills to know"). The most prominent theme among these poems is the existence of sin on earth, originating from outside both nature and man but operating both on and through man, which though superficially beautiful is contrasted with heaven as the home of the soul; but closely related to it is the theme of a double nature in man, who is both good and evil. These themes are also present in *Monaldi*, where the peaceful external world is contrasted with the "evil spirits" within Maldura and Fialtro, and Monaldi's last painting, produced in his madness, is of "the King of Hell," the same image used to describe the origin and progress of the French Revolution in the sonnet of that name. It is also suggested in his lecture "Form,"in which he said that Man was "a compound being . . . as well as of Mind as of body . . . a responsible being, and therefore a free agent" (*LA*, pp. 129-30).

On the back of a pencil sketch and in a book of sketches, Allston wrote two extended descriptions of human nature as thus conceived. In the first he warned that no man should "trust to the gentleness, the generosity, or seeming goodness of his heart, in the hope that they alone can safely bear him through the temptations of this world. This is a state of probation, and a perilous passage to the true beginning of life, where even the best natures need continually to be reminded of their weakness, and to find their only security in steadily referring all their thoughts, acts, affections, to the ultimate end of their being," and declared that no obstacle was too mighty to the humble who sought to be "sustained only by that holy

Being who is life and power, and who, in his love and mercy, has promised to give to those that ask." In the other passage he wrote that no act of kindness could be canceled by one of unkindness nor a good act undo an ill one, "For good and evil have a moral *life,*" existing for eternity, and continued by asking, "How, then, can a man who has *once* sinned, and who has not of *himself* cleansed his soul, be fit for heaven where no sin can enter?" and then citing the doctrine of the Atonement in answer (*LA*, pp. 175-76).

According to Sweetser, Allston once wrote a long essay on Christianity as supplying an inherent want of human nature. No such essay seems to have been preserved, however, and the several pages of much-revised notes which he left on the general subject of religion are more philosophical than doctrinaire. The most notable page is in the form of a diagram.

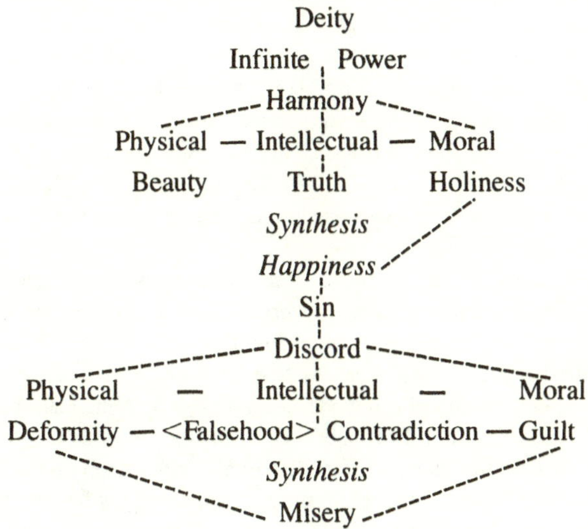

Allston explicated the first half of this diagram in the "Introductory Discourse" of his lectures on art, but he developed the second half, indicating the consequences of sin, only briefly and fragmentarily in notes. There he analyzed right and wrong in the context of the doctrine of the Fall of Adam, argued that freedom was incompatible with wrongdoing, and cited Paul's statement in Acts 14:17 that God "left not himself without witness, in that he did good" to defend his argument that Adam's "holy desires" might have continued had they not been supplanted by others when he "sinned." He defined evil as "that which produces pain" and concluded that "If the Idea of Evil be, as we hold, bred in the mind, it is not relative; it cannot therefore be a mere negation of Good: it is then absolute." In this sentence he was apparently answering and echoing Emerson's declaration in his Harvard Divinity School Address of 1838 that "Good is positive; Evil is merely privative, not absolute; it is like cold, which is the privation of heat. All evil is so much death or nonentity"[2] (*The Complete Works of Ralph Waldo Emerson* [Boston: Houghton Mifflin, 1903-1904) 1:124. It seems probable, indeed, that in these notes Allston was specifically refuting the Transcendentalists' position.

It is significant, however, that in his lectures on art Allston incorporated only the emanations from "Deity" in his diagram, basing his entire "Introductory Discourse" on his concept of God as the origin of beauty, truth, and goodness, the creator of nature, and author of all art. The themes of sin and evil are, moreover, in conspicuous contrast to his paintings in general and the poems accompanying them. Only *Belshazzar's Feast*, *Jeremiah*, *The Angel Pouring Out the Vial of Wrath over Jerusalum*, and *Heliodorus Driven from the Temple* deal with stories of retribution and only one of them was completed. These themes seem to have concerned him in his later years, probably beginning in the 1820s and increasingly at the last, but never proved congenial with either his painting or his philosophy of art, generally optimistic as they were.

Seventeen of his forty-one aphorisms are essentially moral in sentiment: inveighing against a craving for distinction that keeps one from praising excellence in others; the love of gain by a painter; envy in the guise of praise of the subordinate; selfishness or "sensibility kept at home"; "detracting witticism"; absence of the "ennobling sentiment" of reverence and of the restraining principle of benevolence or "self-bias"; overrating oneself; self-love or vanity; lies, of which the worst kind is a half-truth, which breed other lies; falsehood, which in competition with truth results in superfluous speech but which will ultimately be overcome by truth, it being hard for one to "lie all over"; wanting to get the better of anyone or arguing for victory for oneself; making anyone an idol, since the best men have faults; and calling humility the "only true independence," the greatest fool the "proud fool," and all excellence "a variety of truth" (*LA*, pp. 167-73). Throughout "Gloria Mundi," "The Two Painters," "Eccentricity," and "The Angel and the Nightingale" also humility is praised and pride condemned.

Richard Henry Dana, Jr., noted that as he retired from society he inclined to metaphysical studies, "took particular pleasure in works of devout Christian speculation," and read "a due proportion of strictly devotional literature" (*LA*, pp. vi-vii), and Walter Channing said that the "Older English divines" were his "special favorites." He owned a number of religious, moralistic, and philosophical works besides those by Nehemiah Adams, Buckminster, and F.H. Jacobi, most of them published during the last years of his life: Gerard Alexander, D.D., *An Essay on Taste*, 3d ed. (Edinburgh, 1780); Joseph Butler, *The Analogy of Religion Natural and Revealed to the Constitution and Course of Nature, to which are added, two brief dissertations: I. Of personal identity; II. Of the nature of virtue. To which is prefixed a life of the author, by Dr. Kippis, with a preface, giving some account of his character and writings, by Samuel Halifax, D.D.* (New Haven, 1822); the *Christian Spectator* 3:1 (Jan. 1821), 4:11 (Nov. 1, 1822), a periodical published in New Haven, representing orthodox New England theology, all but one volume signed by Allston; Arthur Cleveland Coxe, *Athanasion, with Notes and Corrections, Also Miscellaneous Poems*, 2d ed. (New York, 1842); William Batchelder Greene, *The Doctrine of Life, With some of its Theological Implications* (Boston, 1843); Thomas Smith Grimke, *Reflections on the Character and Objects of All Science and literature and on the relative excellence and value of religious and secular education, and sacred and classical literature in two addresses and an oration with addition and improvements, With an appendix* (New Haven, 1831); William Nicholson, *Introduction to Natural Philosophy*, 2 vols. (Philadelphia, 1795); William Paley, *A View of the Evidences of Christianity* (Hallowell, 1826); and *Taste: A Suggestive Essay by "Discipulus," pseud.* (Boston, 1841). He also owned a copy of William J. Plumer, Jr.'s *Poems* (Boston, 1841), which were, like Pulmer's others, religious in nature.

Appendix 7
Politics

Allston was a patrician by nature, not only in his appearance and manner but in his social and political affiliations and by implication in his painting. In college Edmund T. Dana and Jarvis called him "Count." He belonged to the Federalist party, which Jarvis thought was for no better reason than that which Charles II had for preferring the Church of England to that of Scotland, namely that it was the more "gentlemanly religion." His dislike of Andrew Jackson was well known. A few months before Allston's death Richard Henry Dana, Jr., described him as "less of a Republican than ever," and quoted him as declaring that the manners of gentility, with its "courtesies, deferences, & graces," of which Dana thought him a good example, were passing away and that if things continued "In 30 years there will not be a *gentleman* left in the country," and recollected his saying that few Americans felt the country's faults better or had "less confidence" in its "form of government," though he would defend it against criticism by a foreigner (1:149). During his second residence in England, according to Sweetser, William Collins said that if he were met in the street with a sack of coals on his shoulder Allston would at once be recognized as a gentleman. Many others, among them John Howard Payne, Walter Channing, and James Russell Lowell, applied the term to him. Many years after his death one of his pupils described his painting gallery as being "the only gentleman in the company" (Cheney, *Gleanings in the Fields of Art*, p. 293). He owned the writings of the Boston Federalist Fisher Ames: *Works of Fisher Ames. Compiled by a number of his friends. To which are prefixed notices of his life and character* (Boston, 1809). He had the reputation in college of not being knowledgeable about foreign affairs, replying, Jarvis remembered, to Arthur M. Walter's asking him what he could say about the Treaty of Westphalia that it "was a very pretty treaty" and that he knew "history" instead.

He always took an interest in current affairs, however, his attention to foreign politics stimulated partly no doubt by his years spent abroad, especially in England. Among his earliest compositions were his depiction of the siege of Toulon, caricatures of Napoleon, and comic treatment of the French national convention. In his "Sonnet: The French Revolution" Allston described it as an outgrowth of the tree of evil in the Garden of Eden, whose fruit was plucked and eaten by "The King of Hell," who, "drunk with sin and blood, Earth to her centre shook," and in the "Introductory Discourse" of his lectures on art called it the consummation of every sin since Cain's and pitied the "poor prisoner in the Bastile" (*LA*, pp. 324, 39, 71). Four of his early paintings obliquely reflect his attitude to Napoleon's conquest of Europe: *Jason*, depicting that character confronting the usurper of his kingdom; *Caius Marius in the Dungeon*, the character being eventually released but exiled among the ruins of Carthage, destroyed by Roman armies; *Dido and Anna*, in which Dido is asking Anna to plead with Aeneas not to leave Carthage, while he is having his men strip the forests there to obtain lumber for their ships to proceed to Latium to make war; and *Cupid Playing with the Helmet of Mars*, Cupid being emblematic not only of love but of all peacetime pursuits as opposed to those to which Mars is devoted. His poem "America to Great Britain" reflects his sympathies with England during the politically unsettled early 1800s in Europe and America. In their time together in England during the War of 1812 he, his wife, Morse, and Leslie often discussed American affairs sympathetically. Richard Henry Dana, Jr., noted in connection with his reading that he had "a strong interest" in the politics of both countries, "as to which his principles were highly conservative" (*LA*, p. vii). Not only did he feel for England an affection next after that which he felt for his own country, as he said, but he identified himself with the contemporary English school of art, not the French with its neoclassicism or even the Italians of the past for all his admiration of them. His affiliation with the Episcopal church in his later years was, in effect, one with Anglicanism as well as an acknowledgment of part of his inheritance.

Among his friends were several politicians, notably Jarvis, Verplanck, and Josiah Quincy, a few patrons, including Drayton, brief acquaintances, such as Edward Everett and Hamilton Fish, and other members of the House of Representatives, among them James Hamilton, who supported the attempts to have him given a government commission. In England his chief patrons were Beaumont, the earl of Egremont, and the marquis of Stafford. In the "Introductory Discourse" of his lectures on art he commemorated the English politician John Wilkes as being "one of the ugliest, yet one of the most admired men of his time," who answered the criticism that he squinted too much by saying, "No, Sir, not more than a gentleman ought to squint" (*LA*, p. 26).

His paintings did not directly reflect his political bias, and indeed he repeatedly refused to paint scenes from recent historical events. Of the four dealing implicitly with Napoleon's conquest of Europe, only one, a copy was completed and two were little more than begun. All his painting, nevertheless, rejecting as he did the current vogue of realism in America, was not calculated to appeal to the masses but to the few, as several of his critics pointed out.

Appendix 8
Interest in Drama

Allston was strongly attracted to drama throughout his life. In college he not only took part in plays but was capable of acting the fop at a charity ball of a French dancing master, as Jarvis, who said he was "exceedingly fond" of the theater, remembered. He attended the theater in London and in Boston, knew John Howard Payne personally, and admired the acting of George F. Cooke, Edmund Kean, about whom he wrote a poem, William C. Macready, Charles Mathews, and Fanny and John Kemble. In the "Introductory Discourse" of his lectures on art he referred to Sarah Siddons as "the great Mrs. Siddons" and praised her for her restraint in acting emotional scenes, moving "not a step but in a poetic atmosphere," in contrast to the "painfully accurate" screams of another celebrated actress in the role of Belvidera in Otway's *Venice Preserved* (Alcott, p. 53; *LA*, pp. 36-37). He probably saw Mrs. Siddons play this role in London in 1812, her farewell year (Leslie, p. 175). Leslie recollected going with him, Morse, Irving, and Payne to see her and John and Charles Kemble in Shakespeare's *Henry VIII* (Prime, p. 245). He was critical of Alexander Rae, who took the role of Don Ordonio in Coleridge's *Remorse*, saying he did not have the proper inflections of the voice to make the audience attend to him alone on the stage (Leslie, p. 189). In one of his aphorisms he analyzed the technique of acting, declaring, "He is but half an orator who turns his hearers into spectators. The best gestures (*quoad* the speaker) are those which he cannot help. An unconscious thump of the fist or jerk of the elbow is more to the purpose, (whatever that may be) than the most graceful *cut-and-dried* action" and "an impertinent gesture is more likely to knock down the orator than his opponent" (*LA*, pp. 170-71). Among the books he owned were copies of plays by Shakespeare, Schiller, Coleridge, and Lamb.

Besides his illustrations for plays, he painted an actor in *Man of the Theatre*, possibly a portrait of John Kemble after Lawrence and one of Mrs. Siddons, and many dramatic episodes from poetry and fiction, made sketches of theatrical scenes and often introduced dialog in his poems. Many of his paintings not of specifically dramatic scenes were dramatic in the groupings of the figures, as William Gilmore Simms recognized.

He made several attempts at writing plays, none of which was apparently completed. The earliest which seems to be recorded is the "tragedy" described in his letter to Knapp of 24 August 1803. He may also have been referring to a play of his own in his letter to Irving of 15 April 1817. Among the manuscripts he left is a fragment of a burlesque play entitled "The Suicide," laid in a London rooming house and including dialog between Monsieur Le Chevalier Brigand and a servant.

Two of his literary compositions were dramatized: "The Paint-King" as *The Fairy Romance of the Paint King*, by Charles H. Saunders, in the form of a recitative, presented at the Boston Museum of Fine Arts in 1845, and *Monaldi*, produced as a play in New York in 1872 by Steele Mackaye, whose portrait in the title role was painted by F.B. Carpenter.

He had, moreover, some tendency to being dramatic himself. He was noted in conversation for using gestures and for voice modulations, in telling stories for imitating others, and in painting for sometimes assuming the attitudes of figures which he was depicting.

Appendix 9
Interest in Music

Allston had a great fondness for music all his life. Richard Henry Dana, Jr., recollected his saying that he had been more affected by it than he had ever been by either painting or poetry. He often employed musical terms in referring to paintings. While in college he played the violin and throughout his early years, according to Sweetser, especially after his return from Europe in 1808, had the reputation of being a good dancer, particularly of the popular cotillion. His family remembered his enjoyment of Charlotte Dana's singing. While in Italy he undoubtedly attended the opera, as reflected in *Monaldi.* Several of his paintings, especially in the 1830s, depict a figure with a musical instrument, singing, or listening to music, and *David Playing before Saul* and, later, *Miriam the Prophetess* are depictions of biblical musicians. The repetition of color in his landscapes made them, Sarah Clarke thought, "more musical than pictorial," comparable to odes, anthems, and symphonies (p. 130).

Both "The Parting" and the poem "Song" were written for music, and other poems contain musical references. The title character in "Rosalie" hears the "strain" of her lover as if stealing "in music to her soul"; that in "The Young Troubadour" is a singer; in "The Betrothed" the brook sings a song; and in "The Angel and the Nightingale" song is said to have "magic power" and a description is given of "This all-subduing mystery of Sound, / That with a breath can from our stubborn clay / Set free the Soul, and launch her forth to stray, / With wandering stars, through yon blue depths profound, / Where blessed spirits bask in empyrean day!" (*LA,* pp. 331, 304, 308).

In his lectures on art he cited Mozart, Paganini, and Haydn to illustrate the point that more than the senses must be called into play to appreciate "*mental pleasures*" and described "one of the mightiest ministers of the Imagination—the great Law of Harmony,—which cannot be *touched* without awakening by its vibrations, so to speak, the untold myriads of sleeping forms that lie within its circle, that start up in tribes, and each in accordance with the congenial instrument that summons them to action" (*LA,* pp. 332, 308, 14, 15, 146). In *Monaldi* reference is made to the skill in music "common in Italy"; there are said to be "few cares which do not yield for a time to the influence of fine music"; Rosalia plays on the piano passages from Corelli and twice sings from an opera by Metastasio, for which Monaldi accompanies her on the violin and at which time he discovers and declares his love for her; her father asks her to play his favorite pieces from Pergolesi; she also sings a popular new polka and a polacca; she, her father, and Monaldi attend an opera in which Girolamo Crescentini sings; and a "little Venetian air" is arranged to be the signal to the scheming Fialtro when Monaldi returns to his house to investigate the report of her infidelity (pp. 89, 128, 90-92, 95, 178).

Richard Henry Dana, Jr., recollected his comparing Raphael and Mozart in their appeal to human sympathy. Among the periodicals he owned was *The Euterpeiad, an Album of Music, Poetry and Prose* 1, no. 13 (15 Oct. 1830).

Two of his poems were set to music: "Song" by the English tenor John Braham, who made a tour with his son in America in 1840 and 1841 and sang the composition at his farewell concert in the Melodeon Theatre in Boston on 17 February 1841 ("New Song: The Poetry by Washington Allston," printed program, Dana Papers); and "The Paint-King" by the English entertainer Thomas Comer, who came to America in 1827 and was well known for his Irish impersonations (*The Peerless Geraldine, a Favorite Recitative and Air. As Sung by Mr. G.C. Gormon. At the Boston Museum in the Fairy Romance of the Paint King, Dramatized from Washington Allston's Poem by Charles H. Saunders, the Music Composed by Thomas Comer* [Boston, 1845]). Braham also wrote a musical accompaniment for Hannah F. Gould's poem "The Burial of Allston."

Appendix 10
Influence and Reputation

Allston founded no school of painting and left no followers in the strict sense of the term. He was known and his work was admired and to some extent imitated, however, by several artists who were in Boston during the last decade or so of his life and who are not represented in his correspondence. Several, it is notable, were turned from painting to sculpture on his advice. Most of the painters were most impressed by his color.

Two of the earliest were Henry Kirke Brown (1814-86) and Benjamin Champney (1817-1907). Brown met Allston shortly after going to Boston in the fall of 1834 to study painting with Harding, who introduced them. Allston not only complimented his work but advised him to study sculpture, the consequence being that he took up this art and achieved prominence in it. After practicing it for a few years in Cincinnati, he spent a winter in Boston and went to Italy in 1842. From Rome in 1844 he wrote George Fuller, "study Allston's pictures wherever you find them, for his best are nowhere surpassed" (*George Fuller, His Life and Works,* ed. Josiah B. Millet [Boston, 1886], pp. 18, 19, 72, 73).

Champney also went to Boston in 1834. He remembered following Allston, "with his silvery hair hanging upon his shoulders; a prominent, observant eye, and a kindly, benevolent expression," around the Boston Athenaeum and listening to his comments about pictures, which were "always intelligent, but tempered with constant kindness." He also recalled attending the 1839 exhibition of Allston's paintings, where there was "nothing flippant, but every work rich in color and low in tone," which helped him later to appreciate the great artists of Italy. Probably about 1840 he, in company with his friend the portrait painter Robert Cooke, also studying in Boston, took a landscape and a few other pieces he had painted to Allston for comment. They were received in "the kindest manner," encouraged, and advised, as they had planned, to go to Paris. Champney thought that no modern artist had "shown more feeling for harmonious colour" than Allston, that *Belshazzar's Feast* even in its unfinished state "had parts almost equal to Titian in color," that his portrait of West was particularly expressive, that "The subtle genius of the man shines through all his works, and one feels a reserved power in their all," and that "no American artist has equalled Allston in all the qualities that go to make a great painter" (*Sixty Years' Memories of Art and Artists* [Woburn, Mass., 1900], pp. 8, 13-15, 138).

Henry Dexter (1806-76), after spending several years in Connecticut and Rhode Island, moved to Boston, where he spent most of the rest of his life, in the fall of 1836. He was at that time a painter but partly because of Allston's encouragement turned to sculpture. He wrote a vivid account of their first meeting, which occurred on 22 August 1838. He arrived at Allston's studio at noon, as they had agreed, but when his knock was not answered and he found the keyhole firmly plugged up, he left. He returned about one o'clock, and was about to leave again when a voice called out, "Wait a minute," and Allston received him as cordially as he ever was by his most intimate acquaintance. After locking both doors and withdrawing the key, Allston led him into the painting room, showed him several models he had made for copying in paintings, and offered to lend him a cast of the *Borghese Warrior* to copy. In reply to Dexter's inquiry about his method of preparing absorbent grounds, he said he would with great pleasure send his formula and showed not only a canvas thus prepared with a sketch on it but several other sketches, including *Titania's Court* and *Christ Healing the Sick*. The formula called for boiling a pound of whiting, half an ounce of glue, half a pint of raw linseed oil, and a pint or quart of water together, spreading it on the canvas while hot, and pumicing it down when cold (manuscript sheet, BA). Dexter apparently visited him on several subsequent occasions, and was with him the evening before his death (Albee, pp. 49, 57-59).

William Page (1811-85), the New York painter, may have met Allston as early as 1838, when he went to Boston in the fall to paint a portrait of J.Q. Adams, certainly shortly afterward. Allston admired the initial studies for his painting *Jephthah's Daughter*, begun in the summer of 1840 but never finished, and predicted that it would be "the greatest picture that had ever been conceived on this side of the Atlantic" ("The Arts in the United States," *Art Journal*, n.s. 3 [1851]: 191). After 1843 he lived in Boston. He followed Allston in his primary concern for coloring but was not entirely satisfied by that aspect of Allston's work, saying it lacked depth and was often "foxy" ("The Art of the Use of Color in Imitation in Painting," *Broadway Journal* 1 [29 Mar. 1845]). He too studied the Venetians, particularly Titian, and in his theories about art was also generally Platonic, though his more immediate source was Swedenborgianism. Possibly his interest in landscape painting, which was begun during his Boston years, was partly stimulated by that of Allston (Joshua C. Taylor, *William Page: The American Titian* [Chicago, 1957], pp. 20-21, 258, 97-98, 62, 92, 22-23, 82, and passim).

During the last two or three years of Allston's life three young artists in particular were drawn to his work, admiring his coloring especially, and sought to imitate his method. Thomas Ball (1819-1911) presumably knew him from boyhood in Boston but visited him only once in his studio, in 1842 or 1843. He went to get his opinion on the painting which he had just done of the Holy Family. The studio he described as being big, wooden, and one story high so as to accommodate *Belshazzar's Feast*. A caller could receive no answer by knocking, he learned, but was told by some boys playing nearby to throw some rocks on the roof and Allston would "come out fast enough." It was a "most delightful visit," he recalled. Allston came to the door, "a most ethereal-looking old gentleman, with long, flowing hair as white as snow, clean-shaven face, almost as white as his hair," and when Ball introduced himself as a young artist, invited him in and talked to him "in the most simple and fatherly way about his early Art struggles." He judged the painting favorably but also found faults, which he constructively criticized, commenting that though the hands of two of the figures were too large, the fault was better than if they were too small, as they were sometimes made by Stuart, so much so as to suggest birds, and that the distribution of color was not what it should be. He drew the well-known diagram of the three overlapping circles showing the three primary colors and their compound opposites, which Ball found revealing and valuable, and expressed regret that he could not show *Belshazzar's Feast*, explaining that he did not like to have it seen in a "transition state." Ball went away with the impression that he was "the truest artist and most angelic man" he had ever met (*My Three Score Years and Ten: An Autobiography* [Boston, 1891], pp. 100-101). About 1850, like Henry Kirke Brown and Henry Dexter, Ball turned his attention to sculpture. In 1855 or 1856 he executed a statuette of Allston in Italy, where he spent most of the rest of his life.

Joseph Alexander Ames (1816-72), portrait painter, a native of the Boston suburb of Roxbury, had a studio in the city from 1841 to 1846. About 1840 he painted a portrait of Allston, depicting him in profile, turned to the left.

George Fuller (1822-84), of Deerfield, Massachusetts, came to Boston first in the winter of 1842-43, where he remained, sharing a studio with Ball, until 1850. In the 1870s he established himself in the city permanently. There seems to be no evidence that the two met, but he described Allston as "the greatest of modern painters" (*George Fuller,* p. 73). Ball thought the effect of his admiration at that time for Allston could be traced in all his works. Those of his late years are, in fact, closer to Allston's in their poetic spirit than those of any of his successors.

In the tribute to Fuller written at the time of his death Ball described the influence which Allston had on him, Ames, and himself in the 1840s, saying, "We were then struggling after Allston's color; being fascinated, as were all the young artists of that day, with his unfinished canvass, which had been exhibited not long before. 'Belshazzar's Feast' was our particular study, as that seemed to show his method in all stages of his work." He himself considered it "a perfect mine of color." Of the three he thought Ames was "striving after Allston's method . . . with more success " than Fuller or himself. "We shall never have another Joe Ames or George Fuller," he declared, "till some of our young artists learn to appreciate Allston as highly as they did," though he concluded, "I think I hear a chorus of young voices exclaim, 'What an old fogey!' " (*My Three Score Years and Ten,* pp. 113-14).

About 1840, possibly in connection with the formation of the Boston Artists' Association, in which Allston was involved and of which they, like Ames, were members, two other young artists painted his portrait. David Claypoole Johnston (1797-1865), an actor as well as an engraver, lithographer, and painter, settled in Boston in 1825. His *Washington Allston in His Studio* shows him standing with his palette before his easel, on which is a canvas depicting two female figures in the dress of the day, such as he never painted, with a bust and several other accessory objects at the side and back. He also drew a portrait of Allston in the same pose though seated, with male and female figures on the canvas in what seem to be theatrical costumes and without the accessories in the background. An engraving of it appeared as the frontispiece in the *New Mirror* 2 (14 Oct. 1843). Allston owned copies of *Scraps,* a series of plates each containing a number of comic sketches which Johnston issued over a period of several years, nos. [1], 5, 6, and 9 ([1830], 1832, 1833, 1836).

Richard Murrell Staigg (1817-81) was born in England and came with his family to America in 1831. He worked for a while in Newport, Rhode Island, where, according to Sweetser, he won the encouragement and counsel of Allston for his miniature of Mrs. Nathaniel Amory, and spent the most of the rest of his life in Boston. His portrait of Allston is a miniature watercolor on ivory.

One other portrait of Allston was painted about this time, erroneously attributed to himself, by an unknown hand. It resembled those by Flagg and Harding (E.D. Allston, pp. 14 [ill.], 79-80).

From 1841 to 1846 the painter and poet Thomas Buchanan Read (1822-72), who lived during most of his mature years in Philadelphia, had a studio in Boston. He was encouraged and aided in his painting by Allston, who doubtless took an interest in his writing as well, and later said he received from him valuable suggestions about the use of color (Henry Clay Townsend, *A Memoir of T. Buchanan Read* [Philadelphia, 1800], pp. 8, 15).

In 1847 ten of Allston's paintings and drawings were included in the twentieth annual exhibition of the Boston Athenaeum, and in the same year the American Art-Union in New York had a head of him modeled for a medallion by Peter Paul Duggan. It was engraved by Charles Cushing Wright, and 50 copies in silver and 250 in bronze were distributed. Three years later, in 1850, both Allston's *Lectures on Art, and Poems* and *Outlines & Sketches* were published. At the Boston Athenaeum exhibition that year, possibly in connection with the appearance of those works, 131 of his works were included, a greater number than have ever been assembled.

William Morris Hunt (1824-79), who was chiefly influenced by the contemporary French school of painting, was attracted to Allston's work in the 1850s. He settled in Boston in 1862, founded the Allston Club there in 1866, passed on his knowledge of Allston's methods of painting to his students, and at his death was compared to Allston in his love of his art for its own sake (Gerdts, p. 169).

Through Hunt, with whom he studied in 1859, John LaFarge (1835-1910) also came to admire Allston's paintings. In 1869 he advised the collector and art dealer Samuel Avery to see as many of them in Boston as he could. He himself sought out several in private homes there and praised particularly *Italian Landscape* (G62), *Beatrice*, and *Lorenzo and Jessica*. *The Valentine* he thought less valuable (Gerdts, p. 169).

Meantime the Allston Association was founded in Baltimore, Maryland, in 1859. Its purpose was the "reproduction of the aims and acts of the great artist whose name it bears" (Gerdts, p. 169).

In the 1860s Allston was represented in two of the publications of the New York editor Evert A. Duyckinck: *The National Portrait Gallery* (1862) and the revised edition of *Cyclopaedia of American Literature* (1866), of which his brother George L. Duyckinck was coeditor. Allston's portrait in the first was painted and engraved by the New York painter Alonzo Chappel. Presumably he never saw Allston and drew on the portraits of him by Harding and Johnston, as he did on the work of others for portraits in that work. Like Johnston's, he depicts Allston full length, seated, in his studio, with accessories of a bust, easel, palette, table, and chair, and portfolio, as well as a second portfolio. The direction of the gaze, the hair, and the features, particularly the eyes, closely resemble those in Harding's portrait. In the *Cyclopaedia of American Literature* Allston was represented by "America to Great Britain"; "Winter," from "The Sylphs of the Seasons"; "Rosalie"; "Invention in Art in Ostade and Raphael, from the 'Lectures on Art,'" and Irving's reminiscences of Allston. Evert Duyckinck wrote the biographical sketches in both publications.

In the twentieth century, interest in Allston has been revived among historians and critics rather than artists, a perhaps significant fact. In 1947 an exhibition of his works was held at the Detroit Institute of Arts and the Museum of Fine Arts in Boston, organized by Edgar P. Richardson, who the next year published his study of Allston, the first to provide a catalog of his works and to place him in the context of both American and European art. In 1979, in celebration of the two hundredth anniversary of his birth, an exhibition of the best of his works was held at the Museum of Fine Arts in Boston and the Pennsylvania Academy of Fine Arts in Philadelphia. In connection with this exhibition William H. Gerdts, who helped organize it, wrote his definitive study of Allston, which is both biographical and critical, incorporating a catalog of his works.

Appendix 11
Recipients and Correspondents

Note: Numbers refer to letters, not to pages.

Recipients of Allston's Letters

Albro, John Adams, 229
Alston, William Algernon, 174
American Academy of Fine Arts, Secretary (Alexander Robertson), 54
Andrews, William Turrell, 269
Baldwin, Loammi, 161, 172
Beaumont, Andrew, 258
Boston Athenaeum, Trustees, 186
Bowen, Charles, 217
Brown, Solyman, 252
Brown, Thomas, Jr., 315, 331, 342
Channing, Ruth (Gibbs), 353
Channing, Walter, 228
Channing, William Ellery, 1-5, 189, 264, 270
Channing, William Henry, 352
Cogdell, John Stevens, 137, 140, 145, 153, 155, 157, 171, 178, 184, 201, 203, 207, 211, 222, 225, 241, 257, 261, 273, 276-278, 287, 289, 290, 292, 304, 306, 309, 325, 330, 344, 351
Coleridge, Samuel Taylor, 25, 42
Collins, William, 59, 81, 89, 105
Dana, Elizabeth Ellery, 259, 337, 355
Dana, Richard Henry, Jr., 302, 303, 310
Dana, Richard Henry, Sr., 115, 116, 335
Davis, Isaac P., 356
Dearborn, Henry Alexander Scammell, 138
Drayton, William, et al., 195
Dunlap, William, 190, 198-200, 202, 204, 210, 216, 223, 231
Everett, Edward, 193, 196
Felton, Cornelius Conway, 256, 317, 326, 357
Fish, Hamilton, 242
Flagg, George Whiting, 285
Flagg, Henry Collins, Sr., 6, 8
Flagg, Rachael (Moore) Allston, 9, 268
Francis, Convers, 346
Fraser, Charles, 11
Gibbes, Robert Wilson, 294, 312
Greenough, Horatio, 237
Greenough, John, 146, 154
Griswold, Rufus Wilmot, 298
Hale, Nathan, 318
Harding, Chester, 262, 305, 308
Harvey, George, 281
Hayward, William, 267
Howard, Henry, 79
Huger, Daniel Elliott, et al., 195
Irving, Washington, 47, 48, 53, 56
Jameson, Anna Brownell (Murphy), 253
Jarvis, Leonard, 215, 234, 235, 239, 247, 248
Knapp, John, 10, 12-14, 160 [?], 175, 227
Leslie, Anna, 230
Leslie, Charles Robert, 58, 97, 101, 106, 110, 112, 117-119, 121, 127, 131, 135, 143, 147, 173, 205, 332
Little, Charles Coffin, 301
Longfellow, Henry Wadsworth, 265, 275, 300, 311
McMurtrie, James, 36, 40, 43, 50, 64, 68, 75, 84, 95, 177, 250, 296, 322, 333
Mason, Jonathan, Jr., 180, 197, 202, 209
Morse, Jedidiah, 30, 34
Morse, Samuel Finley Breese, 21, 24, 26, 27, 31, 41, 70, 122, 151, 158, 163, 218, 240, 245, 249, 340, 341
New-York Historical Society, Secretary (Lyman Spalding), 80
North American Review, Editor (John Gorham Palfrey), 280
Partridge, Alden, 133
Paterson, Hugh, 17
Payne, John Howard, 29
Peabody, Elizabeth Palmer, 238, 274
Pepoon, Benjamin F., et al., 195
Pickering, Henry, 61, 69, 91, 94, 100,

102, 104, 107, 108, 120, 124, 125, 128, 129, 132, 148
Porter, George Washington, 266
Quincy, Josiah, 150, 358, 359
Raczynski, Athanasius, 313
Reed, Henry Hope, 349
Roberts, George, 286
Robertson, Alexander. *See* American Academy of Fine Arts, Secretary
Rogers, Robert (of Boston, Mass.), 185
Rogers, Robert (of Newport, R.I.), 7
Sargent, Henry, 92
Scollay, Catherine, 251
Sharp, William, 299
Shattuck, George Cheyne, Sr., 244, 263, 288, 328, 334, 350
Sigourney, Lydia Howard (Huntley), 244
Smith, John Rubens, 149
Spalding, Lyman. *See* New-York Historical Society, Secretary
Sully, Thomas, 111, 190
Sumner, Charles, 284, 297, 307, 347
Taylor, Mary Cooper (Vanderhorst), 32
Tefft, Israel Keech, 272
Ticknor, George, 144, 169, 176, 225, 360
Tomlin, John, 339
Unidentified, 316, 361
Vanderhorst, Elias, 15
Vanderlyn, John, 19, 23, 35, 188, 213
Van Schaick, Myndert, 44
Verplanck, Gulian Crommelin, 74, 82, 130, 152, 166, 168
Waterston, Robert Cassie, 246
Webber, Samuel, 319
Welles, Benjamin, 16
Wheeler, John, 327
White, Thomas Willis, 323
Williams, David H., 291
Winthrop, Francis Bayard, 51, 114
Woods, Daniel Bates, 236
Wordsworth, William, 96, 136, 220, 232, 254, 282, 314

Correspondents

Adams, John Quincy (et al.), 235
American Academy of Fine Arts, Secretary, 52
Beaumont, Sir George Howland, 22, 28, 45, 55, 88
Bigelow, Jacob, et al., 354
Coleridge, Samuel Taylor, 18, 37, 57, 123
Collins, William, 63
Dexter, Franklin, 179, 182, 293, 348
Drayton, William, et al., 192
Eagles, John, 321
Gillman, Anne (Harding), 279, 324
Gillman, Henry Anthony, 329
Greenough, Horatio, 139, 156, 159, 162, 164, 181, 206, 221, 243, 260
Howard, Henry, 66
Hoyt, Albert Gallatin, 338
Huger, Daniel Elliot, et al., 192
Irving, Washington, 49
Jameson, Anna Brownell (Murphy), 255
Jarvis, Leonard, 212, 214, 219, 233, 235 (et al.)
Leslie, Charles Robert, 65, 72, 85, 90, 98, 99, 109, 126, 141, 165
Longacre, James, 134
McMurtrie, James, 39, 46, 60, 62, 67, 78, 83, 86, 93, 103, 295, 320, 336
Morse, Samuel Finley Breese, 38, 71, 217, 271, 343
New-York Historical Society, Secretary, 73
Pepoon, Benjamin F., et al., 192
Reed, Henry Hope, 345
Robertson, Alexander. *See* American Academy of Fine Arts, Secretary
Spalding, Lyman. *See* New-York Historical Society, Secretary
Vanderlyn, John, 20, 33
Verplanck, Gulian Crommelin, 77, 87, 167, 170, 183, 187, 235 (et al.)
Winthrop, Francis Bayard, 113
Wordsworth, William, 76

Appendix 12
Allston Paintings and Drawings Referred to in the Correspondence

This listing gives the date of composition, catalogue number in Gerdts (G), Richardson (R), and/or Bolton (B), and present location or final disposition, when known, of each work. No note is made for those that seem to have been lost or whose dates are unknown. For references to these works in the correspondence, see index entry for Allston, Washington: paintings and drawings by.

Adoration of the Magi, ca. 1804-11, after Titian; G fig. 42; private collection
Agony of Judas, The, 1814; G, p. 81
Alpine Landscape, 1810; G, pp. 92, 115
Amy Robsart, 1840; G fig. 55; Phoenix Art Museum, Phoenix, Ariz.
And Christ Looked at Peter, 1801; G, p. 29
Angel Pouring out the Vial of Wrath over Jerusalem, The, ca. 1840; G fig. 59; Boston Univ.
Angel Releasing St. Peter from Prison, The, 1814-16; G28; MFA. Sketch of, R71; Countess Laslo Szechenyi, New York. Study for head of St. Peter, G27; Eleanor A. Bliss. Studies for, G figs. 30-34, 77; Virginia Steele Scott Foundation, Pasadena, Cal.; Museum of Art, Providence, R.I.; Metropolitan Museum of Art, New York; Fogg; MFA
Apollo Belvedere (drawing of), 1801
Beatrice, ca 1816-19; G53; MFA
Belshazzar's Feast, ca. 1817-43; G fig. 45; Detroit Institute of Arts. Study, 1817; G43; MFA. Studies, 1817-43; G42, 93, 96; Fogg.
Bride, The, 1839; G, p. 143; destroyed in Boston fire, 1862
Buck's Progress, The, 1796; G figs. 69, 70, 71
Caius Marius in the Dungeon or *Marius at Minturnae,* bet. 1801 and 1804; G, p. 29
Caricature Heads, drawings, ca. 1798-99; G fig. 73; Huntington Library, San Marino, Cal.
Casket Scene from "The Merchant of Venice," 1807; G18; BA
Catherine and Petruchio, Grumio and the Tailor, 1809; G, p. 59
Channing, W.E., elevation of cemetery monument to, ca. 1842; B293; Fogg
Christ Healing the Sick, 1813; G29; Worcester Art Museum
Christ Looking at Peter, 1800
Clytie, bet. 1811 and 1818; G, p. 93
Coast Scene on the Mediterranean, 1811; G23; Columbia Museum of Art and Science, Columbia, S.C.
Contemplation, ca. 1817-18; G38; Lord Egremont, Petworth House, Sussex, Eng.
Crowning the Victors at Olympia (copy of James Barry painting), 1801-03; B244; private collection
Cupid and Psyche, 1805-08; G, pp. 54, 76, 93
Cupid Playing with the Helmet of Mars (after Rubens), 1804; G6
Damon and Musidora, bet. 1796 and 1800; G, p. 14
Danger (drawing), ca. 1811-18; G91; Walters Art Gallery, Baltimore

David Playing before Saul, ca. 1805; G9; Carolina Art Association, Gibbes Art Gallery, Charleston, S.C.
Dead Man Restored to Life by Touching the Bones of the Prophet Elisha, The, 1811-14; G25; PAFA
Death of King John, The, 1837; G68; Wadsworth Atheneum, Hartford, Conn.
Diana and Her Nymphs in the Chase, 1805; G11; Fogg
Diana Bathing, 1814; G, pp. 76, 83, 86
Dido and Anna, 1813-15; G26; Lowe Art Museum, Univ. of Miami, Fla.
Donna Mencia in the Robber's Cavern, 1815; G35; MFA
Drawings, miscellaneous, 1796-1843; B1-300; various locations
Eastern Female Figure, ca. 1820; B69A; Fogg
Edwin, 1819; G, p. 132
Elijah in the Desert, 1817-18; G49; MFA
Eruption of Vesuvius (copy of old painting), 1795; G, p. 13
Evening Hymn, 1835; G66; Montclair Art Museum, Montclair, N.J.
Fairies on the Seashore, Disappearing at Sunrise, bef. 1837; G fig. 62; engraving in *O&S*
Falstaff Enlisting His Ragged Regiment, 1803-08; G fig. 18; Wadsworth Atheneum, Hartford, Conn.
Falstaff Playing the Part of the King, 1803-08(?); G, p. 54
Ferns and Leaves (drawing), ca 1804; G77; Fogg
Flight of Florimel, The, 1819; G52; Detroit Institute of Arts
French National Convention as a Rasher of Frogs, The, 1800, R21
French Soldier Telling a Story, A, 1801-02; G, pp. 29, 83
Gabriel Setting the Watch at the Gates of Paradise, 1830-33; G, pp. 152, 240; engraving in *O&S*; drawing of Gabriel for, R141, B85; Fogg
Galen or *Storm at Sea,* 1812; G, p. 114
Garden of the Villa Malta and drawing, bet. 1804 and 1808
Girl in Persian Costume (A Troubadour), ca. 1832; G65; Wadsworth Atheneum, Hartford, Conn.
Half-Length Study of a Young Woman (drawing), ca. 1821; G95; Fogg
Head of a Jew, 1817; G44; MFA
Head of a Jew, 1817; G45; Hirschl and Adler Galleries, New York
Head of a Soldier, 1811-13; B281; Mrs. Allston Dana
Head of a Woman in Profile; R159; Rosamond Dana Wild, Kittery Point, Me.
Hebe, bef. 1814; G, pp. 83, 93
Heliodorus Driven from the Temple, ca. 1830s; G69; Lowe Art Museum, Univ. of Miami, Fla.
Hermia and Helena, 1818; G, p. 94
Interior of a Church; G, p. 163
Isaac of York, 1817; G47; Hirschl and Adler Galleries, New York
Isabella of Spain; R172
Italian Landscape, ca. 1805; G12; Addison Gallery of American Art, Phillips Academy, Andover, Mass.
Italian Landscape, ca. 1805; G13; Baltimore Museum of Art
Italian Landscape, 1810; R57, 59
Italian Landscape, ca. 1828-30; G62; Detroit Institute of Arts

Italian Landscape or *Italian Scenery,* 1814; G31; Toledo Museum of Art

Italian Peasants, ca. 1805-08; B152; Fogg

Italian Shepherd Boy, 1819; G50; Detroit Institute of Arts

Italian Shepherd Boy, ca. 1819; G51; Brooklyn Museum, Brooklyn, N.Y.

Jacob's Dream, 1817; G39; National Trust, Petworth House, Sussex, Eng. Angels in (tracings from canvas), ca. 1818; B41A, B, C, D; Fogg

Jason Returning to Demand His Father's Kingdom, ca. 1807-08; G17; Fogg

Jeremiah Dictating His Prophecy of the Destruction of Jerusalem to Baruch the Scribe, 1820; G58; Yale Univ. Art Gallery. Studies: G56, 57; Studies, 1819, ca. 1820; Sisterhood of St. Mary; Herschl and Adler Art Galleries, New York; Yale Univ. Art Gallery

Judas Iscariot, 1800; G, p. 24

juvenilia, ca. 1790-1800; R, pp. 183-84; G, pp. 16-17, 203-06; various locations

Landscape, 1798; G fig. 3; BA

Landscape, bef. 1839; R150

Landscape, ca. 1820s

Landscape; owned by Beaumont

Landscape; owned by Dexter

Landscape, American Scenery: Time, Afternoon, with a Southwest Haze, 1835; G fig. 56; MFA

Landscape (Aeneas and Achates Come Ashore), ca. 1800; G fig. 7; Fruitlands Museum, Harvard, Mass.

Landscape, Evening (Classical Landscape), 1821; G61; IBM Corp. Armonk, N.Y.

Landscape: Macbeth (?); R187; Fogg

Landscape of American Scenery, 1810; G, p. 47

Landscape Study, ca. 1805; G fig. 16; Hirschl and Adler Galleries, New York

Landscape, Time after Sunset, ca. 1819; G55; Corcoran Gallery of Art, Washington, D.C.

Landscape with a Lake, 1804; G8; MFA

Landscape with Banditti (Landscape with a Bridge and a File of Horsemen), 1798; G fig. 5; Greenville County Museum of Art, Greenville, S.C.

Landscape with Horsemen (drawing), ca. 1799; G72; Carolina Art Association, Gibbes Art Gallery, Charleston, S.C.

Landscape with Rustic Festival, 1798; G2; private collection

Landscape with Trees and a Tempietto, ca. 1804-05; B165; Fogg

Laocoön, Son in (drawing), ca. 1801; G fig. 75; Fogg

Lorenzo and Jessica, 1832; G64; Elizabeth von Wentzel

Lover Playing a Lute, ca. 1830s; G70; Mugar Memorial Library, Boston Univ.

Macbeth and Banquo Meeting the Witches on the Heath, bef. 1823; G, p. 130

Man of the Theatre, ca. 1803; G, p. 30

Marriage at Cana (after Veronese), 1817; G40; Mugar Memorial Library, Boston Univ.

Mensuration (drawing), ca. 1796-1800; G71; Fogg

Merchant of Venice, The, drawing from

Minna and Brenda on the Seashore, bef. 1823; G, p. 130

Miriam the Prophetess, 1821; G fig. 47; William A. Farnsworth Library and Art Museum, Rockland, Me.

Moonlit Landscape (Moonlight), 1819; G54; MFA

Morning in Italy, ca. 1805-08; G14; Shelburne Museum, Shelburne, Vt.
Moses and the Serpent, ca. 1805; G10; Carolina Art Association, Gibbes Art Gallery, Charleston, S.C.
Mother and Child, 1829; G, pp. 90, 139, 163
Mother Watching Her Sleeping Child, A, 1814; G fig. 28
Mother with Child in Her Lap; R192
Mount Pilat, Switzerland (drawing), 1804; G76; Fogg
Old Man Resting against a Rock (drawing), ca. 1799-1800; G73; Fogg
Outlines and Sketches. See *Gabriel Setting the Watch at the Gates of Paradise; Fairies on the Seashore, Disappearing at Sunrise*
Paint King, The (engraving), ca. 1813; R76; plate, Dana Papers
Paysage—Site Sauvage, 1802-03; G, p. 34
Peter When He Heard the Cock Crow, 1800; G, p. 24
Pine Tree (drawing), ca. 1804; G, p. 214; Fogg
Poet's Ordinary, The, 1802-03; G, pp. 29, 83
Polyphemus Immediately after His Eye Was Put Out, Groping about His Cavern for the Companions of Ulysses, 1818; G, p. 114
Poor Author and the Rich Bookseller, The, 1811; G24; MFA
Portraits. *See* listing beginning on p. 000.
Prodigal Son, The, ca. 1812; G, p. 240; B245; Fogg
Prometheus, ca. 1812; G, pp. 239-40; B246 A, B; MFA
Rain at Sea, bef. 1814, G, p. 84
Rebecca at the Well, 1816; G36; Fogg
Repose in Egypt, bef. 1818; G, p. 96
Rising of a Thunderstorm at Sea, 1804; G7; MFA
Robbers Fighting with Each Other for the Spoils over a Murdered Traveler, 1801; G fig. 12. Photograph, Longfellow National Historical Site, Cambridge Mass.
Rob Roy, ca. 1819; B253; Fogg
Rocky Coast with Banditti, A, 1800; G fig. 6; Museum of Early Southern Decorative Arts, Winston Salem, N.C.
Roman Lady Reading, A, ca. 1830; G fig. 51; Newark Museum, Newark, N.J.
Romantic Landscape, ca. 1803; G5; anonymous loan to exhibition of 1979-80, MFA
Rosalie, 1835; G67; Society for the Preservation of New England Antiquities, Boston
Santo Domingo Black Boy, ca. 1796; G, p. 13
Satan at the Gates of Hell Guarded by Sin and Death, 1801; G, p. 24
Saul and the Witch of Endor, ca. 1820; G60; Mead Art Museum, Amherst, Mass. Study of foot, ca. 1820; G59; Lowe Art Museum, Univ. of Miami, Fla.
Scene in an Eating House, A, 1813; G30; Layton Art Collection, Milwaukee Art Center
Schepen Doing Duty to a Burgomaster's Joke, A, 1818; G fig. 38. Engraving in Washington Irving, *Knickerbocker's History of New York*
Sea Coast with Banditti, A, bet. 1801 and 1804; G, p. 29
Ship in a Squall, bef. 1837; G fig. 57; Fogg
Sibyl, The; G fig. 60; Lowe Art Museum, Univ. of Miami, Fla.
Siege of Toulon by Napoleon, 1787-96; G, pp. 13, 203
Silence, bef. 1816; R91
Silenus and Fauns, ca. 1826; B132A, B, C; Fogg

Sisters, The, ca. 1816-17; G37; Fogg
Skeleton with Caricatures (drawing), ca. 1801; G74; Fogg
Sketch, 1798; owned by Waterston
Sketch for Gibbs's marble table, ca. 1835-36
Sketch for Shattuck monument, ca. 1837
Sketch of Shepard Congregational Society Church, 1843
Sketch of three female figures; owned by Vanderlyn
Sketches: Two studies of hands and heads; given to Henry Greenough
Sketch of a Polish Jew, 1817; G46; Corcoran Gallery of Art, Washington, D.C.
Sketch of a Shepherd Boy, ca. 1835; R189; B fig. 338; Fogg
Spalatro's Vision of the Bloody Hand, 1831; G fig. 58. Studies, ca. 1830s; G97-98; Fogg
Spanish Girl in Reverie, The, 1831; G63; Metropolitan Museum of Art, New York
Squinting Fiddler, The, 1800; R20
Stoning of St. Stephen, The (St. Stephen Before the Council), 1818; G, p. 152; reproduced in Flagg, fol. p. 90
Storming of Count Roderick's Castle, The, 1787-96; G, p. 203
Student, The; G fig. 66; BA
Study from Life, 1813-15; G fig. 35; Metropolitan Museum of Art, New York
Sunrise, 1810; R58
Tavern Scene; R186
Tempest, The, drawing from
Three Apples and a Branch, 1796-1800; B172; Huntington Library, San Marino, Cal.
Three Marys and the Angel at the Tomb of Jesus, The, 1814-30; B79A, B80; MHS; Fogg
Tippler, The, 1799; G fig. 8; Amherst College, Amherst, Mass.
Titania's Court, 1837; G fig. 63; Vassar College, Poughkeepsie, N.Y.
Tragic Figure in Chains, 1800; G3; Addison Gallery of American Art, Phillips Academy, Andover, Mass.
Tree in a Landscape, ca. 1801-04; G75; MHS
Tuscan Girl, A, 1831; G fig. 52; Robert Vose
Una in a Wood, ca. 1830; G fig. 53; Lowe Art Museum, Univ. of Miami, Fla.
Uriel in the Sun, 1817; G41; Mugar Memorial Library, Boston Univ.
Valentine, The, 1809-11; G22; private collection
Walking with a Good Stick, ca. 1796-1800
Winter's Tale, The, drawing from
Wouter von Twiller's Decision in the Case of Wandle Schoonhoven and Barent Bleeker, 1817; G fig. 37; engraving in Washington Irving, *Knickerbocker's History of New York*
Young Troubadour, The; G, pp. 141-42; as "Boy Seated on a Wall, Holding a Vase," ca. 1833; B127; Fogg

Portraits

Allston, Ann (Channing), 1809-11; G21; Henry Channing Rivers. Drawings, 1812-15; G87-89; MHS; Fogg
Allston, Washington (self-portrait), 1796-1800; G fig. 2; Fogg
Allston, Washington (self-portrait), 1805; G15; MFA

Auboyneau, Armand, 1800; G, p. 23
Baldwin, Loammi; G, p. 114; Fogg
Bentivoglio, Guido (copy of copy by Smibert of Van Dyck), ca. 1800; G, p. 15
Bridgen, Mrs., bet. 1815 and 1818
Buckminster, Joseph Stevens, bet. 1808 and 1811
Channing, Francis Dana, 1808-09; G19; private collection
Channing, Lucy (Ellery), 1811; G fig. 20; Fine Arts Museums of San Francisco
Channing, William Ellery, 1811; G20; MFA
Coleridge, Samuel Taylor, 1806; G16; Fogg
Coleridge, Samuel Taylor, 1814; G32; National Portrait Gallery, London
Dana, Edmund Trowbridge, ca. 1797; G, p. 16; Longfellow National Historic Site, Cambridge, Mass.
Dana, Edmund Trowbridge, 1809; R54
Flagg, Ebenezer, 1800-1801
Flagg, Henry Collins, Jr., 1809; G, p. 57
Flagg, Rachel (Moore) Allston, 1809; G fig. 19; private collection
Harris, John, 1796; G1; MFA
Kemble(?), John (after Thomas Lawrence), ca. 1801-04; G, p. 30
King, Emmaline (Edgeworth?), 1814; G, p. 86
King, John, 1814; G33; Fine Arts Museum of San Francisco
King, Samuel, 1800(?); G, p. 23
Rogers, Robert, 1800; G fig. 10; Redwood Library and Athenaeum, Newport, R.I.
Rubens (drawing, copy), ca. 1795-96; G, p. 14
Siddons, Sarah (Kemble), bef. 1818; R111
Southey, Robert, 1814; G, p. 86
Spalding, Matthias, 1801; G4; private collection
Sullivan, Lydia (Worcester), Sons of; R173
Taylor, Mary Vanderhorst, 1814; G, p. 86
Waterhouse, Andrew Oliver, 1796-97; G, p. 16
Waterhouse, Hannah (Proud), 1796-97; G fig. 1; private collection. Drawing of, 1798; B fig. 493; Fogg
West, Benjamin, 1814 (head), 1837; G34; BA
Willard, Joseph, 1798; G fig. 4; BA

Portraits of Allston by Other Artists

Ames, Joseph Alexander, G fig. 106; private collection
Ball, Thomas
Brackett, Edward Augustus, G fig. 107; Worcester Art Museum
Chappel, Alonzo, G fig. 50
Clevenger, Shobal Vail, G fig. 104; BA
Duggan, Peter Paul (or Paul Peter)
Flagg, George Whiting, G fig. 67; Kennedy Galleries, New York
French artist in Newport, R.I.
Harding, Chester, G fig. 48; Providence Athenaeum
Healy, George Peter Alexander

Johnston, David Claypoole, G fig. 65; Bowdoin College Museum of Art
King, Charles Bird, engraving in *O&S*
Leslie, Charles Robert, G fig. 102; National Academy of Design, New York
Malbone, Edward Greene, MFA
Paul, Jeremiah, G fig. 11; Mrs. Burnet R. Maybank
Staigg, Richard Morrell, G fig. 105; MFA
Stuart, Gilbert, G fig. 103; Metropolitan Museum of Art, New York
Walker, Frederick
Unknown artist, Brooke Club, New York

Selected Bibliography

Principal Authorities

Bolton, Kenyon C., III. "The Drawings of Washington Allston (A Catalogue Raisonné)". Ph.D. diss., Harvard Univ., 1977.

Flagg, Jared B., *The Life and Letters of Washington Allston.* New York: Charles Scribner's Sons, 1892.

Gerdts, William N., and Theodore E. Stebbins, Jr. "*A Man of Genius*": *The Art of Washington Allston (1779-1843).* Boston: Museum of Fine Arts, 1979.

Richardson, Edgar P., *Washington Allston: A Study of the Romantic Artist in America.* Chicago: Univ. of Chicago Press, 1948.

Sweetser, Moses F. *Allston.* Boston: Houghton, Osgood; Cambridge: Riverside Press, 1879.

Additional Sources

Averill, Louise Hunt. *John Vanderlyn, American Painter (1775-1852).* Ph.D. diss. 1949. Yale Univ.

Biddle, Edward, and Fielding Mantle. *The Life and Works of Thomas Sully.* New York: Kennedy Galleries, 1970.

Channing, Walter. "Reminiscences." *Christian World,* Aug. 5, 1843, p. 105.

Cheney, Ednah Dow. *Gleanings in the Fields of Art.* Boston: Lee and Shepard, 1881.

———. *Memoir of John Cheney, Engraver.* Boston: Lee and Shepard, 1889.

———. *Memoir of Seth W. Cheney, Artist.* Boston: Lee and Shepard, 1881.

———. *Reminiscences of Ednah Dow Cheney.* Boston: Lee and Shepard, 1902.

Clarke, Sarah. "Our First Great American Painter, and His Works." *Atlantic Monthly* 15 (Feb. 1865): 129-40.

Coleridge, Samuel Taylor. *Collected Letters of Samuel Taylor Coleridge.* Ed. Earl Leslie Griggs. Oxford: Clarendon Press, 1956-1971.

———. *The Notebooks of Samuel Taylor Coleridge.* Ed. Kathleen Coburn. New York: Pantheon Books, 1955-1961.

Dana, Richard Henry, Jr. *The Journal of Richard Henry Dana, Jr.* Ed. Robert F. Lucid. 4 vols. Cambridge: Bellnap Press of Harvard Univ. Press, 1968.

Dunlap, William. *Diary of William Dunlap 1776-1839.* New York: New-York Historical Society, 1931.

———. *History of the Rise and Progress of the Arts of Design in the United States.* 2 vols. New York: George P. Scott, 1834.

Emerson, Ralph Waldo. *The Journals and Miscellaneous Notebooks of Ralph Waldo Emerson.* Cambridge: Harvard Univ. Press, 1960-1982.

———. *The Letters of Ralph Waldo Emerson.* Ed. Ralph L. Rusk. New York: Columbia Univ. Press, 1939.

Greenough, Horatio. *Letters of Horatio Greenough, American Sculptor.* Madison: Univ. of Wisconsin Press, 1972.

Groves, Joseph A. *The Alstons and Allstons of North and South Carolina.* Atlanta: Franklin Printing and Publishing, 1901.

Harding, Chester. *A Sketch of Chester Harding Drawn by His Own Hand.* Ed. Margaret E. White. New York: Houghton Mifflin, 1970.

Irving, Pierre M. *The Life and Letters of Washington Irving.* New York: G.P. Putnam, 1862-63.

Irving, Washington. *Journals and Notebooks.* Richard D. Rust, genl. ed. Boston: Twayne, 1969-1986.

———. *Letters.* Ed. Ralph M. Aderman, Herbert L. Kleinfield, and Jennifer S. Banks. Boston: Twayne, 1978-1982.

Johns, Eliza. "Washington Allston's Library." *American Art Journal* 7 (Nov. 1975): 35-40.

Leslie, Charles Robert. *Autobiographical Recollections.* Ed. Tom Taylor. Boston: Ticknor and Fields, 1860.

Longfellow, Henry Wadsworth. *Letters of Henry Wadsworth Longfellow.* Ed. Andrew Hilen. Cambridge: Harvard Univ. Press, 1966-1982.

Morse, Samuel F.B. *Samuel F.B. Morse: His Letters and Journals.* Ed. Edward Lind Morse. Boston: Houghton Mifflin, 1914.

Nord, Barbara K. *The Flagg Family in South Carolina: The Nineteenth Century.* Austin, TX.: Peripatetic Press, 1984.

Park, Lawrence. *Gilbert Stuart.* New York: W.E. Rudge, 1926.

Peabody, Elizabeth Palmer. *Last Evening with Allston, and Other Papers.* Boston: D. Lothrop, 1886.

———. *Letters of Elizabeth Palmer Peabody: An American Renaissance Woman.* Ed. Bruce D. Ronda. Middletown, Conn.: Wesleyan Univ. Press, 1984.

———. *Reminiscences of Rev. William Ellery Channing, D.D.* Boston: Roberts Bros., 1880.

Pierce, Edward. *Memoir and Letters of Charles Sumner.* Boston: Roberts Bros., 1878.

Prime, Samuel Irenaeus. *The Life of Samuel F.B. Morse, LL.D.* New York: D. Appleton, 1875.

Rutledge, Anna Wells. *Artists in the Life of Charleston.* Transactions of the American Philosophical Society, n.s. 39, pt. 2. Philadelphia, 1949.

———. "Dunlap Notes." *Art in America* 39 (Feb. 1951): 38-48.

Swan, Mabel Munson. *The Athenaeum Gallery, 1827-1873: The Boston Athenaeum as an Early Patron of Art.* Boston: Athenaeum, 1940.

Ticknor, George. *Life, Letters, and Journals of George Ticknor.* Boston: James R. Osgood, 1876.

Ware, William. *Lectures on the Work and Genius of Washington Allston.* Boston: Phillips, Samson, 1852.

"Washington Allston." *United States Democratic Review* 13 (Oct. 1843): 431-34.

Whitley, William. *Art in England, 1800-1820.* New York: Macmillan, 1928.

———. *Artists and Their Friends in England, 1700-1799.* New York: Medici Society, 1928.

———. *Gilbert Stuart.* Cambridge: Harvard Univ. Press, 1932.

Williams, Stanley T. *The Life of Washington Irving.* New York: Oxford Univ. Press; London: Humphrey Milford, 1935.

Wordsworth, William. *The Letters of William and Dorothy Wordsworth.* 2d ed. Ed. Ernst de Selincourt. Oxford: Clarendon Press, 1967-.

———. *The Love Letters of William and Mary Wordsworth.* Ed. Beth Darlington. Ithaca, N.Y.: Cornell Univ. Press, 1981.

Wright, Nathalia. *Horatio Greenough: The First American Sculptor.* Philadelphia: Univ. of Pennsylvania Press, 1963.

Index

For references to letters to and from Allston, see by name of recipient or sender in Appendix 11, pages 638-39. Information on Allston's paintings and portraits (dates, catalog numbers, and locations) is shown in Appendix 12, pages 640-46.

Abernethy, John, 63 (#24) n 4
Adams, Charles Francis, 500
Adams, John, 202, 268 n 13
Adams, John Quincy, 95, 253, 268 n 13, 384 n 1, 395-97, 431 n 17, 500, 635; unrecovered letter to, 394
Adams, Louise Catherine (Johnson), 95
Adams, Nehemiah, 375 n 1, 447 (#283), 447 n 1, 626, 628
Addison, Joseph, 612. *See also* Leslie, C.R.: paintings by
Aders, Karl, 120-21
Albany (ship), 233 n 1
Alberti, François, 38
Albro, John Adams, 524, 530, 626
Alcibiades, 28
Alcott, Bronson, 325 n 2, 428, 430 n 14, 570, 572, 609
Alexander, Francis, 427, 473 n 2
Alexander, Gerard, 628
Alfieri, Vittorio, 48, 305, 370
Alfred Tyler (ship), 505-06
Allan, William, 176, 187, 202
All Saints' Parish, S.C., 15 n 1, 531, 548
Allston, Ann (Channing) (first wife): courtship and marriage, 58; in England, 59-60, 63-64 (#24) nn 2, 3, 64 (#25), 65, 72, 73 n 2, 76, 121, 629; described by Coleridge, 539; death, 80 n 1, 83-84, 92 n 6, 97 n 1, 353, 567; portrait of, by Malbone, 566; poems about, by WA, 21, 23, 218 n 4, 315; mentioned, 533, 536, 551. *See also* WA, portraits
Allston, Anne (Simmons), 531
Allston, Benjamin, 37 n 1, 440 n 2, 455, 530; family of, 455
Allston, Charlotte Anne (Allston), 530
Allston, Elizabeth. *See* Gibbes, Elizabeth (Allston)
Allston, Francis, 36 n 1
Allston, John E., 230 n 2, 532
Allston, Martha Remington (Dana) (second wife): marriage, 103, 181, 187, 284 n 1, 291; described by WA, 292, 301; correspondent for WA, 438, 452, 454, 467-68 n 10; on *Belshazzar's Feast,* 103; at WA's death, 523-24, 578; greetings sent from: *see WA letters, passim*; mentioned, 297, 319, 315, 317, 320, 323, 371, 408, 500, 501, 520, 530, 531, 543, 545, 553, 563
Allston, Mary. *See* Alston, Mary (Allston) Young
Allston, Rachel (Moore). *See* Flagg, Rachel (Moore) Allston
Allston, Robert Francis Withers, 523; wife of, 485 n 4
Allston, Washington: advice to young artists, 71, 200, 223, 244-47, 249 n 20, 313-15, 352, 364, 405, 436, 449, 462, 536-37, 546, 556-58, 568, 588, 620-21, 623, 634-35; appearance and manners, 59, 11 n 1, 264 n 6, 375 n 1, 422-23, 468, 491-92 n 2, 531, 534, 538, 544, 552-53, 555, 559, 561-62, 565, 576, 582, 629, 634; astronomy, interest in, 14 n 1, 250 n 23, 625; architecture, interest in, 17-18, 21, 25, 44, 104, 159, 217, 306-07, 430 n 14, 482-83, 495, 495 n 3, 540-41, 553, 605-09, 614; artistic philosophy and conception of artist, 24, 43, 54, 55 n 5, 72, 75, 113, 140 n 10, 168, 183, 186, 198, 199 n 5, 223, 225 n 2, 236, 246-47, 253-57, 258 n 2, 286, 312, 314-15, 343-44, 352, 371-72, 388, 540-43, 586; birth, 15 n 3; charities and generosities, 121, 122 n 4, 220, 276 n 2, 281 n 2, 295 n 4, 441, 459; conversational characteristics, 11 n 1, 63 n 4, 75, 374, 423, 538-39, 542, 544, 546, 550, 555, 559-60, 570, 576, 583, 631; conversation on last evening, 543; death, funeral, estate, obituaries, tributes, 252 n 5, 523-25, 545-46, 560, 564, 568, 572, 576, 581-82, 623; drama and theater, interest in, 18, 20 n 22, 100, 241, 539, 567, 631; drawing, importance placed on, 46, 200, 244, 245 nn 3, 4, 5, 279 n 1, 449, 462, 537, 550, 553, 572, 587, 620; drawings, care-

Allston, Washington (*cont'd*)
lessness with, 468; drawings left at death, 508 n 1, 538, 545, 568, 572; engraving, comments on, 101, 185, 202, 256-57, 269 n 2, 295, 385, 399, 462-63, 492, 557; engravings of works, 97 n 1, 100 n 2, 116-17, 176, 204 n 1, 247, 297 n 2, 347 n 2, 381 n 5, 391, 512-13, 563 (*see also* WA, paintings: *Outlines & Sketches*); feminine nature, idealization of, 7 n 5, 17, 34-35, 47, 50, 240-42, 295, 423-24, 535, 537, 568, 577, 603; financial difficulties, 65, 65 n 3, 111 n 4, 117 n 6, 141, 159, 165-67, 175, 181, 194, 207, 235, 281, 311, 316-17, 321, 324, 340 n 20, 349-50, 365 n 3, 366, 383, 392, 407, 419, 458-59, 487, 518, 535, 539, 544; influence and reputation, 195 n 3, 634-37; lawsuit over mother's estate, 439-40, 440 nn 1-3, 441, 442, 442 n 1, 452-58, 470-71; letters of introduction, 62, 190, 200, 205, 214-15, 218-19, 221-22, 243-44, 251, 256, 295, 368, 381, 388, 403, 447, 477-78, 497-98, 555, 578; letter-writing, aversion to, 12, 25, 31-32, 49, 92, 119, 145, 177, 180, 183, 198, 203, 215, 217-19, 221, 228, 233, 236, 244, 252, 262-63, 292, 345, 371, 385, 387, 396, 414, 498, 560; library, 8 (#4) n 2, 21-22, 30 n 16, 38, 46, 48-49, 58-59, 63 (#23) n 2, 86 n 11, 94 n 1, 103, 111 n 2, 154 nn 14, 15, 177 n 4, 179 n 2, 250 n 23, 253 n 1, 258 n 1, 302, 310 n 25, 321 n 3, 334, 337, 342, 354 n 2, 366 n 3, 389 n 2, 393, 428, 447-48 n 1, 462, 465 (#298) n 2, 474, 475, 488 n 3, 501 n 1, 535-36, 539-40, 548, 550-51, 557, 562-64, 566, 568, 572-74, 576, 579-80, 605, 613-17, 623, 628-29, 631-32, 636 (*see also* reading); patrimony, 36-37 n 1, 51-52, 340 n 15; pupils, 71, 92 n 12, 136, 148, 151, 265, 546, 548-49, 558, 562, 567-68, 572, 629; reading, 149 n 8, 612-18; religious affiliations and beliefs, moral refinement, 72, 80, 117 n 6, 222, 263, 276, 406, 438, 471, 530, 535-36, 542-43, 553, 567-68, 571-72, 625-28, 630; sculpture, interest in and modeling by, 22, 42-43, 45, 66-67, 96 n 2, 170 n 9, 251, 253-54, 256, 294 n 1, 298, 301, 312-14, 360-62, 535, 543, 553 n 1, 572, 634-35 (*see also letters to Cogdell and Greenough, passim*); sea, response to, 39-40, 47; studios and painting rooms, 58, 60 (#21) n 1, 152, 153 n 2, 159, 184, 211, 294, 294 n 1, 295 n 1; studios designed by, 299, 302, 495, 514, 531, 555, 564-65, 634-35; supernatural, interest in, 68, 330, 541, 570; angels, interest in, 42, 82-83 (#35) n 4, 83 (#36), 97 n 1, 116 n 4, 250 n 25, 284. *See also* Alps; classics; England; exhibitions; Harvard College; Italy; schools of painting; Switzerland; U.S. Capitol; WA, paintings and drawings by; WA, portraits by; WA, portraits of; WA, writings of

—art and profession of artist, dedication to, 15, 34; love of art for its own sake, 250 n 24, 374, 420, 451, 476, 537; money of secondary importance to art, 113, 237 n 6, 304, 419, 623

—autobiographical accounts. *See WA letters to Dunlap, passim*; WA, writings of: *Monaldi*; "The Angel and the Nightingale"

—disposition and personal habits: amiability, 11 n 1, 54, 86-87, 546, 567, 579; sociability, 11 n 1, 145, 374, 481, 542; dreams and day-dreaming, 7 (#1) n 5, 24, 47-48, 59, 145, 180, 241, 399, 490, 560-61 (*see also* painting practices); procrastination, 11 n 1, 12, 13 nn 1, 2, 24, 32, 54, 92, 139, 145, 155, 163-65, 180, 557; sensitivity to feelings of others, 7 (#2), 7 n 1, 8 (#4), 8 n 1, 148, 286, 376, 557-58, 567, 576, 634 (*see also* lawsuit); generosity toward competitors, 276 n 2, 286, 288, 535; daily routine, 373-74, 376, 385, 531, 555; late hours, 11 n 1, 59, 190, 191 n 11, 373, 536, 570, 577; fondness for tobacco, 370 n 1, 347, 368, 370 n 1, 373, 416, 502, 531, 542, 549, 553, 564, 565, 570, 644; enjoyment of dining, 111 n 1, 39, 481, 500, 502, 544, 564, 609-10; aversion to cold, 11-12 n 4, 295 n 1, 531

—illnesses: of 1813, 64 (#24) n 2, (#25) and n 3, 65, 69-70, 224, 353, 406, 539, 561-62; of 1825-39, 219, 220, 220 n 3, 221, 224, 228, 255, 262, 264, 311, 317, 348, 350 n 2, 356, 358, 376, 383, 387, 394-95, 406, 408, 412; of 1839, 415, 431, 432 n 1, 442; of 1841-43, 468, 469 n 9, 473-76, 481, 482, 486-87, 490-91, 494, 498-99, 505, 507, 513-14, 517-18, 568. *See also WA–Shattuck correspondence, passim*

—memberships in art and historical associations: American Academy of Fine Arts, 115, 118; Bread and Cheese Club, 542, 560; Georgia Historical Society, 434; National Academy of Design, 252 n 5; New-York Historical Society, 138, 142, 143 n 2, 144, 147; South Carolina Academy of Fine Arts, 258 n 6; unidentified, 400-401. *See also* Royal Academy of Art

—painting practices: habitual retouching, 194-95, 239, 296-97, 419, 451; inability to paint under pressure, 194, 195 n 2, 296, 383; preliminary contemplation of canvas, 549, 561; imitation of pose of subject, 297 n 2; painting indoors and from memory, 25, 536, 623; on getting "stuck," 296, 297 n 2

—painting technique, 619-24; use of coloring and glazing, 39-40, 44, 46, 54, 60, 60 n 3, 66, 73-74, 117 nn 4, 5, 241, 324, 358, 537, 577, 580, 592, 619-24; noted for coloring, 42, 46, 272, 537, 547, 558, 561, 582-83, 634; colors ordered, 171, 199, 261, 265, 267, 274-75, 503-07, 554; palette, 549, 576, 623. *See also* Cagliari, Paolo; Titian; WA, writings: "Color Book"

—political sympathies, 629-30; patriotism, 16-18, 19 n 1, 25, 96-97, 100, 217, 392, 568; preservation of Union, 326 n 2, 327-28, 389, 454, 469, 478, 572. *See also* England; French Revolution; Jackson, Andrew; Napoleon Bonaparte; War of 1812

—prices of paintings, 65-66, 69, 76, 83, 86-88, 90-91, 95, 112-14, 114 nn 4, 7, 117 n 6, 119, 132-33, 141 n 12, 159, 161, 170 n 9, 175, 182 n 11, 194-95, 195 n 2, 204 n 7, 211, 284, 288, 303-04, 329 (#197) n 1, 337 n 11, 350, 350-51 n 2, 351 (#209), 351 n 2, 366 n 3, 377 (#227) n 2, 378 (#228) n 1, 384 n 2, 427, 432 (#270) n 1, 450 n 3, 559, 563, 568; disproportionate to time spent, 114 n 7, 194-95, 284, 297, 351 (#209) n 2, 383, 419

—satire in works and letters, 8-10, 16-19, 20 n 18, 22-23, 30 n 19, 58, 101, 115, 148, 201 n 5, 297-98, 408, 520, 604-11. *See also individual works by title*

Allston, Washington, paintings and drawings by (*see also* WA, portraits by; WA, portraits of):

—*Adoration of the Magi,* 41, 120, 430, 443, 489, 539, 588

—*Agony of Judas, The,* 75

—*Alpine Landscape,* 59, 112-13, 193, 378 (#228) n 1, 582, 620; *See also* BA Exhibitions; Harding's Gallery; *Italian Landscape*

—*Amy Robsart,* 241, 429, 449, 450 n 3, 524, 574

—*And Christ Looked at Peter,* 27, 625

—*Angel Pouring out the Vial of Wrath over Jerusalem, The,* 349-50, 350 n 2, 432 (#270) n 1, 508 n 1, 628

—*Angel Releasing St. Peter from Prison, The,* 66, 70 (#28) n 3, 81, 82 n 5, 90-91, 93, 97, 242, 363, 444-45, 530, 533, 553, 557, 621; sketch of, 114 n 7, 507; head of St. Peter, 240, 424, 545, 620

—*Apollo Belvedere* (drawing of), 30 n 21

—*Beatrice,* 48, 96 n 2, 106, 128, 138 n 1, 160 n 5, 164, 165 n 4, 168, 181, 241-42, 404 n 2, 472 n 2, 524, 530, 570-71, 636; engraving, 347 n 2, 365, 536. *See also* BA Exhibitions; Harding's Gallery

—*Belshazzar's Feast,* 102-06; during 1817-28, 66, 82, 83 n 5, 93, 102-03, 108, 116, 128-29, 136, 140, 147, 151-52, 154-55, 159, 165 n 6, 166, 168, 172, 175, 178, 181, 184, 186-87, 190, 191 n 8, 194-95, 200, 203-04, 207, 219-21, 223-24, 229, 239, 263-64, 280, 294 n 1, 299, 328 (#196) n 1, 340 n 20, 351 (#208) n 2, 363, 381 n 4, 382-83, 395 n 2, 404 n 5, 405 n 1, 414, 420 n 3, 424, 428, 432 (#269) n 2, 444-45, 535, 555-56, 571, 595, 605; during 1839-43, 103-04, 435, 444-45, 451, 469, 476, 486-87, 508 n 1, 518, 545, 558-59, 577, 628; final disposition and criticism, 104-06, 525, 547, 553, 556, 568, 575, 578, 634; WA on delays of, 103, 315-17, 435, 449, 469, 473; Tripartite Agreement to purchase, 102-03, 317, 532-33, 537, 547, 572, 579, 581

—*Bride, The,* 241, 426, 432, 432-33 (#270) n 1

—*Buck's Progress, The,* 22

—*Caius Marius in the Dungeon* or *Marius at Minturnae,* 30 n 19, 55 n 10, 614, 629

—*Caricature Heads* (drawings), 22

—*Casket Scene from "The Merchant of Venice,"* 45, 47, 56 n 11, 74, 76, 415 n 2, 584; drawing, 45

Allston, Washington, paintings and drawings by (*cont'd*)
—*Catherine and Petruchio, Grumio and the Tailor,* 58, 87, 238, 421, 615; study, 58, 532
—Channing, W.E., elevation of cemetery monument to, 536
—*Christ Healing the Sick,* 88 n 1, 89-90, 93, 128 n 3, 178, 210 n 2, 531, 585, 625, 634-35
—*Christ Looking at Peter,* 15 n 4, 23
—*Clytie,* 99 n 6, 614
—*Coast Scene on the Mediterranean,* 55 n 1, 58, 128 n 2, 162 n 1. *See also* BA Exhibitions; Harding's Gallery
—*Contemplation,* 160, 241-42, 583
—*Crowning the Victors at Olympia* (copy of James Barry painting), 30 n 9
—*Cupid and Psyche,* 45-46, 55, 56 n 11, 59, 582, 614
—*Cupid Playing with the Helmet of Mars,* 38, 614, 629
—*Damon and Musidora,* 21
—*Danger* (drawing), 276, 276 n 6, 433, 570
—*David Playing before Saul,* 45, 554, 569, 632
—*Dead Man Restored to Life by Touching the Bones of the Prophet Elisha, The,* 62 n 2, 63-64 (#24) n 2, 65 n 5, 66-68, 69 n 2, 72-73, 75-77, 83, 86, 87 (#39), 87 n 2, 88, 90, 96 n 2, 114 n 7, 128, 176 n 3, 186, 186 n 1, 210, 229, 272, 325 n 3, 353, 363, 406, 525, 533, 537-40, 549, 569; sale of, 66, 83, 86, 87, 87 n 2, 93, 95, 111, 124-25, 127, 130-31, 131 n 1, 141, 144, 149-51, 175, 227; clay model, 72 n 3; WA's criticism of, 68, 186, 186 n 1, 229. *See also* Bristol Exhibition; Harding's Gallery
—*Death of King John, The,* 366, 384 n 2, 395 n 1, 404 n 5, 405, 405 n 1, 415 n 2, 508 n 1, 605
—*Diana and Her Nymphs in the Chase,* 40, 43-44, 56 n 11, 59, 65, 69, 74-75, 83, 90, 94-95, 98, 131, 133, 134 n 2, 533, 538, 545, 559, 576, 614. *See also* BA Exhibitions: Harding's Gallery
—*Diana Bathing,* 62 n 1, 74, 88, 170 n 10, 242, 353, 580, 614
—*Dido and Anna,* 62 n 2, 64 (#25) n 2, 355 n 10, 553, 614, 629; engraving, *O&S,* 527
—*Donna Mencia in the Robber's Cavern,* 92 n 6, 421, 499-500, 578, 598
—drawings, miscellaneous, 624
—*Eastern Female Figure,* 182 n 9
—*Edwin,* 140, 140 n 10, 159, 181, 230 n 2, 241-42, 418 n 2, 421, 532
—*Elijah in the Desert,* 110, 116, 117 n 5, 128, 154, 165, 238, 363, 545, 566, 577, 621
—*Eruption of Vesuvius,* 7, 21
—*Evening Hymn,* 42, 366, 384 n 2, 404 n 2, 571, 605, 632. *See also* BA Exhibitions; Harding's Gallery
—*Fairies on the Seashore, Disappearing at Sunrise,* 404 n 5, 415 n 2, 527, 615
—*Falstaff Enlisting His Ragged Regiment,* 45, 55, 56 n 11, 114 n 3, 238, 591, 605, 615
—*Falstaff Playing the Part of the King,* 45, 55, 56 n 11, 591, 615
—*Ferns and Leaves,* 92 n 5, 241, 366, 508 n 1, 40
—*Flight of Florimel, The,* 148, 148 n 4, 159, 161-62, 168, 172, 181, 238, 421-22, 425, 533, 557-58, 616
—*French National Convention as a Rasher of Frogs, The,* 23, 629
—*French Soldier Telling a Story, A,* 11, 338
—*Gabriel Setting the Watch at the Gates of Paradise,* drawing of Gabriel for, 340 n 20, 527, 616
—*Galen* or *Storm at Sea,* 122 n 1, 531, 572
—*Garden of the Villa Malta* and drawing, (bet. 1804 and 1808), 41
—*Girl in Persian Costume (A Troubadour),* 240, 322 n 3, 404 n 5, 508 n 1, 632; engraving, *O&S,* 527
—*Half-Length Study of a Young Woman* (drawing), 182 n 11
—*Head of a Jew* (G44), 101 n 2, 128, 377. *See also* BA Exhibitions; Harding's Gallery
—*Head of a Jew* (G45), 101 n 2, 128
—*Head of a Soldier,* 41
—*Head of a Woman in Profile,* 128 n 3
—*Hebe,* 74-76, 242, 614
—*Heliodorus Driven from the Temple,* 351 n 2, 508 n 1, 559, 605, 628; engraving *(O&S),* 527
—*Hermia and Helena,* 171, 173-74, 242, 301, 302 n 1, 580, 615
—*Interior of a Church,* 483 n 1, 605
—*Isaac of York,* 329, 329 n 1, 377 (#227)

n 2, 574. *See also* BA Exhibitions; Harding's Gallery
—*Isabella of Spain*, 289 n 6, 546
—*Italian Landscape* (G12), 40, 43-44, 240, 605, 614
—*Italian Landscape* (G13), 40, 43, 545
—*Italian Landscape* (R57, 59), 59. *See also Alpine Landscape*
—*Italian Landscape* (G62), 346, 347 n 2, 450 n 3, 571, 624 n 5, 637. *See also* BA Exhibitions; Harding's Gallery
—*Italian Landscape* or *Italian Scenery* (G31), 74, 76, 96 n 2, 128, 614, 621
—*Italian Peasants*, 44
—*Italian Shepherd Boy* (G50), 138 n 1, 140 n 10, 181, 182 n 9, 241
—*Italian Shepherd Boy* (G51), 140 n 10, 182 n 9, 241
—*Jacob's Dream*, 66, 96 n 2, 110, 111, 116, 119, 120 n 2, 121, 128, 141, 152, 157-58, 160, 168, 212, 231, 242, 354, 363, 500, 545, 583; engraving, 462; engraving, *O&S*, 527; *angels in* (tracings), 527; engraving, 527
—*Jason Returning to Demand His Father's Kingdom*, 44, 56 n 11, 66, 68, 496, 540, 600, 614, 629
—*Jeremiah Dictating His Prophecy of the Destruction of Jerusalem to Baruch the Scribe*, 106, 140, 162 n 3, 168, 170 n 9, 175, 177-78, 181, 185, 238-39, 295 n 1, 336, 351 n 2, 363, 404 n 2, 525, 553-54, 568, 605, 628
—*Judas Iscariot*, 15 n 4, 23
—juvenilia, 21-23. *See also works by title*
—*Landscape* (G fig. 3), 20-21
—*Landscape* (R150), 421, 565
—*Landscape* (ca. 1820s), 622
—*Landscape* (Beaumont), 533
—*Landscape* (Dexter), 546
—*Landscape, American Scenery: Time, Afternoon, with a Southwest Haze*, 44, 366, 378 (#228) and n 1, 378 (#229), 379, 384 n 4, 421
—*Landscape (Aeneas and Achates Come Ashore)*, 21, 614
—*Landscape, Evening (Classical Landscape)*, 138 n 1, 181, 547, 571, 624 n 5. *See also* BA Exhibitions; Harding's Gallery
—*Landscape: Macbeth* (?), 211 n 11, 615
—*Landscape of American Scenery*, 44, 366
—*Landscape Study*, 43
—*Landscape, Time after Sunset*, 44, 138 n 1, 148, 159, 181, 238, 421
—*Landscape with a Lake*, 19, 40, 43-44, 56 n 11, 59, 351 n 2. *See also* BA Exhibitions; Harding's Gallery
—*Landscape with Banditti (Landscape with a Bridge and a File of Horsemen)*, 15 n 4, 21, 30 n 21, 331, 338, 624
—*Landscape with Horsemen*, 624 n 5
—*Landscape with Rustic Festival*, 21
—*Landscape with Trees and a Tempietto*, 46
—*Laocoön, Son in* (drawing), 30 n 19, 614
—*Lorenzo and Jessica*, 47, 337 n 11, 404 n 2, 557, 571, 605, 615, 623, 637. *See also* BA Exhibitions; Harding's Gallery
—*Lover Playing a Lute*, 241, 297 n 3, 322 n 3, 508 n 1, 632
—*Macbeth and Banquo Meeting the Witches on the Heath*, 203, 211, 211 n 1, 366, 384 n 2, 615
—*Man of the Theatre, A*, 30 n 19, 631
—*Marriage at Cana, The*, 110, 128
—*Mensuration* (drawing), 535-36
—*Merchant of Venice, The*, (drawing from), 615
—*Minna and Brenda on the Seashore*, 203, 211, 211 n 1, 574
—*Miriam the Prophetess*, 141, 181, 182 n 11, 185-86, 238-40, 404 n 2, 421, 565, 578, 632
—*Moonlit Landscape (Moonlight)*, 140, 141 n 10, 159, 161, 162, 162 n 1, 181, 247, 533, 570-71, 577. *See also* BA Exhibitions; Harding's Gallery
—*Morning in Italy*, 43, 93, 486, 562, 580
—*Moses and the Serpent*, 45, 569
—*Mother and Child*, 92 n 5, 240, 269, 269 n 2, 536; study, 92 n 5
—*Mother Watching Her Sleeping Child, A*, 91, 94, 96 n 2, 98, 131, 179, 242, 399, 418 n 2, 421, 462, 499-501, 536
—*Mother with Child in Her Lap*, 92 n 5, 261, 503 n 1
—*Mount Pilat, Switzerland* (drawing), 40
—*Old Man Resting against a Rock* (drawing), 22, 572
—*Outlines & Sketches*, 463 n 7, 487 n 1, 501 n 1, 527, 534, 536, 551, 559, 636-37
—*Paint-King, The*, 62 n 2
—*Paysage-Site Sauvage*, 38, 567
—*Pine Tree* (drawing), 622
—*Poet's Ordinary*, 30 n 19, 338

Allston, Washington, paintings and drawings by (*cont'd*)
—*Polyphemus Immediately after His Eye Was Put Out, Groping about His Cavern for the Companions of Ulysses*, 122 n 1, 473 n 2, 532, 614
—*Poor Author and the Rich Bookseller, The*, 58, 421, 604
—*Prodigal Son, The*, 527
—*Prometheus*, 527
—*Rain at Sea*, 76, 76 n 2
—*Rebecca at the Well*, 96, 97 nn 1, 4, 101, 530, 579, 582, 605
—*Repose in Egypt*, 242, 583
—*Rising of a Thunderstorm at Sea*, 29, 38-40, 56 n 11, 59, 566. *See also* BA Exhibitions; Bristol Exhibition; Harding's Gallery
—*Robbers Fighting with Each Other for the Spoils over a Murdered Traveler*, 23, 240, 333, 565
—*Rob Roy*, 574
—*Rocky Coast with Banditti, A*, 15 n 4, 21
—*Roman Lady Reading, A*, 42, 297 n 3, 378 (#228) n 1, 404 n 2, 552. *See also* BA Exhibitions; Harding's Gallery
—*Romantic Landscape*, 30 n 19
—*Rosalie*, 106, 366, 384 n 2, 404, 404 n 4, 433 (#270) n 1, 524, 570-71, 574. *See also* BA Exhibitions; Harding's Gallery
—*St. Peter When He Heard the Cock Crow*, 9, 15 n 4, 23, 334
—*Santo Domingo Black Boy*, 21
—*Satan at the Gates of Hell Guarded by Sin and Death*, 23, 616
—*Saul and the Witch of Endor*, 140, 175, 175-76 n 3, 181, 238, 240, 295 n 1, 363, 404 n 2, 421
—*Scene in an Eating House, A*, 74-76, 605
—*Schepen Doing Duty to a Burgomaster's Joke, A*, 115-16, 119, 143, 147-48, 591
—*Sea Coast with Banditti, A*, 30 n 19, 338
—*Ship in a Squall*, 404 n 5, 415 n 2; engraving, *O&S*, 527
—*Sibyl, The*, 106, 117 n 4, 508 n 1, 614; engraving, *O&S*, 527
—*Siege of Toulon by Napoleon*, 22, 330, 332 n 3, 629
—*Silence*, 88, 89 n 6, 242
—*Silenus and Fauns*, 486, 498-99, 614
—*Sisters, The*, 64 (#25) n 2, 128, 404 n 5, 429, 484-85, 487, 539, 548, 563, 588. *See also* BA Exhibitions; Harding's Gallery
—*Skeleton with Caricatures* (drawing), 31 n 22
—Sketch (1798), 581
—Sketch for Gibbs's marble table, 551
—Sketch for Shattuck monument, 574
—Sketch of Shepard Congregational Society Church, 483
—Sketch, three female figures, 579
—Sketch, two studies of hands and heads, 553
—*Sketch of a Polish Jew*, 101 n 2, 377, 488 n 3. *See also* BA Exhibitions; Harding's Gallery
—*Sketch of a Shepherd Boy*, 182 n 9, 508 n 1
—*Spalatro's Vision of the Bloody Hand*, 296-97, 297 n 2, 303-04, 304 nn 4, 5, 318-19, 363, 381 n 5, 400 n 1, 485 n 4, 525, 571
—*Spanish Girl in Reverie, The*, 297 n 3, 424, 539, 552, 557, 571, 620-21. *See also* BA Exhibitions; Harding's Gallery
—*Squinting Fiddler, The*, 23
—*Stoning of St. Stephen, The, (St. Stephen Before the Council)*, 140-41 n 12, 159
—*Storming of Count Roderick's Castle, The*, 21, 330, 332 n 2
—*Student, The*, 59, 241
—*Study from Life*, 62 n 2, 128, 241
—*Sunrise*, 58
—*Tavern Scene*, 74, 508 n 1, 605
—*Tempest, The* (drawing from), 615
—*Three Apples and a Branch*, 46
—*Three Marys and the Angel at the Tomb of Jesus, The*, 284, 285 n 5
—*Tippler, The*, 22
—*Titania's Court*, 404 n 5, 415 n 2, 508 n 1, 558-59; engraving, *O&S*, 527
—*Tragic Figure in Chains*, 22, 25
—*Trees in a Landscape*, 30 n 19
—*Tuscan Girl, A*, 47, 297 n 3, 302, 571. *See also* BA Exhibitions; Harding's Gallery
—*Una in a Wood*, 240, 508 n 1, 616
—*Uriel in the Sun*, 66, 110, 116-17 n 4, 120, 242, 276, 363, 558, 572, 587, 616, 625; engraving, *O&S*, 527
—*Valentine, The*, 58-59, 165, 424, 530, 563, 571, 579, 637. *See also* BA Exhibitions; Harding's Gallery

—*Walking with a Good Stick,* 22
—*Winter's Tale, The,* (drawing from), 615
—*Wouter von Twiller's Decision in the Case of Wandle Schoonhoven and Barent Bleeker,* 99, 100 n 2, 101, 108-09, 202-03, 204 n 1, 591
—*Young Troubadour, The,* 321, 321 n 3, 350-51, 35 (#209) n 2, 571. *See also* BA Exhibitions, Harding's Gallery
Allston, Washington, portraits by:
—Allston, Ann (Channing), 21-22, 58-59, 63 (#23) n 1, 80 n 4, 82 n 4, 165 n 4, 218 n 4, 241, 530, 536
—*Allston, Washington* (self-portrait) (1796-1800), 21
—*Allston, Washington* (self-portrait) (1805), 44, 128, 230 n 2, 421, 532-33
—Auboyneau, Armand, 23
—Baldwin, Loammi, 533
—Bentivoglio, Guido, 22, 332
—Bridgen, Mrs., 583
—Buckminster, Joseph Stevens, 58
—Channing, Francis Dana, 58-59
—Channing, Lucy (Ellery), 58, 516, 516 n 1
—Channing, William Ellery, 58, 518, 536; engraving, 518 n 1
—Coleridge, Samuel Taylor, (1806), 44, 56 n 11, 539, 545, 567
—Coleridge, Samuel Taylor, 74, 353, 355 n 12, 489, 509, 509 n 2, 512-13, 539, 552, 605
—Dana, Edmund Trowbridge (ca. 1797), 58
—Dana, Edmund Trowbridge (1809), 21
—Flagg, Ebenezer, 23, 549
—Flagg, Henry Collins, Jr., 58, 549
—Flagg, Rachel (Moore) Allston, 58-59, 128, 412, 550.
—Harris, John, 21, 331, 595
—Kemble(?), John, 30 n 19
—King, Emmaline (Edgeworth?), 75, 76 (#32) n 5, 128
—King, John, 74
—King, Samuel, 21
—Rogers, Robert, 21
—Rubens (drawing, copy), 459, 551
—Siddons, Sarah (Kemble), 570, 631
—Southey, Robert, 75
—Spalding, Matthias, 30 n 19
—Sullivan, Lydia (Worcester), Sons of, 42
—Taylor, Mary Vanderhast, 76
—Waterhouse, Andrew Oliver, 21
—Waterhouse, Hannah (Proud), 21; drawing of, 21
—West, Benjamin, 76, 128, 485, 543, 576, 581, 634. *See also* BA Exhibitions; Harding's Gallery
—Willard, Joseph, 21
—Williams, Samuel, 128 n 3, 421, 605
Allston, Washington, portraits of, by other artists: Ames, Joseph Alexander, 635; Ball, Thomas, 635-36; Brackett, Edward Augustus, 524, 534; Chappel, Alonzo, 637; Clevenger, Shobal Vail, 431 (#269) n 1, 434, 508, 551, 572; Duggan, Peter Paul (or Paul Peter), 636; Flagg, George Whiting, 434 n 1, 636; French artist in Newport, R.I., 7 n 1; Harding, Chester, 470, 470 n 1, 551, 556, 636-37; Healy, George Peter Alexander, 551, 588; Johnston, David Claypoole, 636; King, Charles Bird, 527, 561; Leslie, Charles Robert, 563, 568; Malbone, Edward Greene, 566; Paul, Jeremiah, 23; Staigg, Richard Murrell, 473 n 2, 636; Stuart, Gilbert, 378 (#228) n 1, 576-77; Walker, Frederick, 11 n 1; unknown artist, 636
Allston, Washington, writings of:
—"Abdulla, the son of Ben Hassan the proud," 224-25 n 1
—"Address to the Great Georgiana, An," 9-10, 23, 593, 604
—"Ah, where is my Phillida gone?" 23, 569
—"America to Great Britain," 373, 425, 664 n 2, 539, 615, 629
—"Angel and the Nightingale, The," 48, 68, 140 n 10, 242, 250 n 24, 335 n 13, 539, 596, 602, 613, 626, 628, 632
—"Aphorisms," 86 n 4, 249, 250 n 24, 344-45 n 5, 550-51, 555, 561, 586, 590, 601, 603, 628
—"Artist sublime, I own thy powerful spell," 26-27
—"Atonement, The," 572, 601-02, 613, 625-26
—"Betrothed, The," 242, 432-33 (#270) n 1, 632
—"Calycanthus, The," 40, 48, 334, 335 n 13, 372, 550, 602
—"Color Book," 37 n 1, 43, 46, 55 n 7, 60, 258 n 1, 427, 540-41, 548, 571, 585, 588, 590, 614, 621-23
—"Complaint, The," 334, 588, 593, 614
—"Convivial Song," 610-11

Allston, Washington, writings of (*cont'd*)
—"Dead Man Restored to Life by Touching the Bones of the Prophet Elisha, The," 67
—"Doolittle Fragments, The," 37 n 1, 604-05
—"Eccentricity," 201 n 4, 593, 613-14, 617, 728
—"Elegaic Poem," 14 n 1
—"Elegy in Exile, An," 20 n 18, 604
—"Energy of Character," 13, 13 n 1
—"First Love—A Ballad," 334, 593
—Flagg, George Whiting, poem for, 548
—"Fragment, A" ("O, who hath lived"), 45, 596, 600, 614, 626
—"Fragment, A," ("Who knows himself"), 626
—"Gloria Mundi," 602, 614, 626, 628
—"Hypochondriac, The," 14 n 1, 68, 191 n 1, 201, 201 n 4, 545, 574, 591, 601, 614-15, 618
—juvenilia, 23-25 (*see also works by title*)
—"Late Mr. Stuart, The," 257, 258 n 7, 315, 339
—*Lectures on Art, and Poems,* 38, 47, 59, 534, 544, 547, 592-93, 595, 600-604, 610, 612-13, 626, 636-37; "Preliminary Note—Ideas," 540, 601; "Introductory Discourse," 14 n 1, 40-42, 47, 68, 230, 249 n 20, 250 nn 23, 25, 434 n 4, 434 (#271) n 4, 446 (#381) n 3, 540, 583, 586-87, 589-92, 601, 603, 613-18, 627, 629-32; "Art," 39-40, 47, 182 n 10, 242, 248 n 15, 249 n 18, 250 n 22, 297, 335 n 13, 340, 365 nn 10, 11, 389 n 2, 414 n 9, 477 n 4, 539, 574, 585-86, 588-89, 601, 613-15; "Form," 248, 302 n 4, 585-86, 591, 601, 613, 615-16; "Composition," 40, 169 n 5, 132 n 10, 248, 250 n 2, 332 n 4, 335 n 13, 463 n 5, 480 (#316) n 1, 584, 587-89, 591, 601, 616, 632; poems: *See by title*
—"Lorenzo and Jessica," 337 n 11
—"Magic Slippers, The," 68, 335 n 13, 602
—"Mad Lover at the Grave of his Mistress, The," 541
—"Marigold, The," 602, 626
—*Monaldi,* 596-600; autobiographical elements, 38, 41-43, 47-48, 242, 596; and "Procrastination is the Thief of Time," 140 n 2, 596; and "A Fragment (Who knows himself)," 465, 466, 466 n 1, 467, 467 n 2, 596; composition, 696; publication, 463-64, 464 n 2, 468-69, 577; complimentary copies, 471, 486, 488, 492, 497-99, 501, 537, 542, 583, 597; criticism, 431 n 18, 471, 475 n 6, 476 n 3, 481, 524, 545, 547, 555; compared to *Othello,* 597, 615; Monaldi as artist, 39, 59, 86 n 4, 140 n 10, 225 n 2, 249 nn 18, 20, 250 nn 22, 24, 400 n 6, 584-86, 592, 596, 604; Rosalia, 427, 505 n 6, 545, 596; references to Bible, 250 n 22, 438 n 2, 613; references to Coleridge, 539
—"Myrtilla," 48, 594
—"Night-Mare, The," 68, 602
—"On the Domes of the State House & the Exchange Coffeehouse," 607
—"On Greenough's Group of the Angel and Child," 83, 368, 377, 595-96, 613
—"On Kean's Hamlet," 182 n 12, 595, 615, 631
—"On Michael Angelo," 585
—"Notice," 315, 407-08, 417
—"Paint-King, The. A Tale," 62 n 1, 68, 534, 539, 574, 613-14, 632-33
—"Parting, The," 545, 602, 632
—play, three acts of a, 100
—"Procrastination is the Thief of Time," 19 n 3, 24, 139, 140 n 2, 596
—"Rosalie," 48, 242, 404 n 4, 421-24, 427, 534, 545, 555, 570, 574, 595, 599, 632, 637
—"Rubens," 592, 602
—"Scene in an Eating House, A," 74, 591
—"Song," 602, 632
—sonnets: quoted by J.H. Greene, 552; praised by Sumner, 578. "Sonnet. Art," 585, 613; "Sonnet. The French Revolution," 626, 629; "Sonnet. Immortality," 626; "Sonnet. Thought," 585; "Sonnet on a Falling Group in the Last Judgment of Michael Angelo, in the Capella Sistina," 42, 585, 594; "Sonnet on the Group of the three Angels before the Tent of Abraham, by Raffaelle, in the Vatican," 42, 82 n 4, 83 n 4, 586, 594; "Sonnet on the Late S.T. Coleridge," 40, 442, 443-44 n 2, 488-89, 539, 555, 602; "Sonnet on the Luxembourg Gallery," 40, 592, 602; "Sonnet on my Venerable Friend, the President of the Royal Academy," 581; "Sonnet on Rembrandt: Occasioned by his Picture of Jacob's Dream," 59, 111, 111 n 2, 561, 591-92; "Sonnet on Seeing the Picture of AEolus by Pellegrino Tibaldi,

in the Institute at Bologna," 41, 614; "Sonnet on the Statue of an Angel, by Bienaimé, in the Possession of J.S. Copley Greene, Esq.," 83 (#35) n 4, 488 n 2
—"Spanish Maid, The," 240-42, 315, 422-23, 464, 539
—Stuart, Gilbert: description of his portraits of the first five presidents ("Notice"); 315, 407-08, 417
—*Sylphs of the Seasons, The, with Other Poems*, 59, 127, 219, 403 n 1, 451 n 1, 475, 492, 543, 564, 575, 593-96, 598, 602, 606. *See individual poems by titles*
—"Sylphs of the Seasons, The," 40, 59, 68, 250 n 23, 534, 595, 613-14, 637
—"Then for a beam of joy to light," 80 n 4, 218 n 4, 315, 530
—"To the Author of 'The Diary of an Ennuyée,' One of the Truest and Most Beautiful Books Ever Written on Italy," 40, 48, 335 n 13, 401, 401-02 nn 1, 3, 7, 430 n 14, 572, 594, 602, 614
—"To a Lady Who Spoke Slightingly of Poets," 594, 614
—"To the Moon," 34-35
—"To My Sister," 335 n 13, 532, 602
—"Tuscan Girl, The," 47, 240, 242, 315, 421, 423, 595, 599, 626
—"Two Painters, The: A Tale," 75, 248 n 13, 250 n 24, 584-86, 591, 593-96, 613-14, 616-17, 628
—Washington, George, poem in celebration of birthday, 23
—"We are sorry to state that the unhappy difference," 606
—"Will, the Maniac—A Ballad," 25, 593
—"Written in Spring," 191 n 1, 201, 335 n 13, 601-02
—"Word, A: Man," 613, 626
—"Young Troubadour, The," 242, 250 n 24, 321 n 3, 421-22, 632
—"Where'er I roam, whatever fires I see," 295 n 1
Allston, Washington (nephew), 442 n 3
Allston (later Alston), William, 531
Allston, William, Jr. (father), 36 n 1, 389 n 5, 411, 413 n 2, 439, 440 n 1, 531-32, 549, 612
Allston, William Moore (brother): early years, 7 n 4, 36 n 1, 531; in Boston, 125 (#61) n 1, 552; recollections of WA, 15 n 4, 23, 59, 191 n 11; in Newport, 441, 456-57; financial difficulties, 225, 441, 459 n 4; and mother's estate, 438, 441, 454-57, 459 n 4, 471, 494-95, 624 n 5; children, 442 n 3; letter from quoted, 457
Allston Association, 637
Allston Club, 637
Allston Street, 284 n 1
Alps, 40-41, 305, 351, 622
Alston, Fanny (Fraser), 449
Alston, John Ashe (nephew), 449, 457, 471
Alston, John Ashe (uncle), 45, 134 n 1, 170 n 11, 449
Alston, Joseph, 220
Alston, Mary (Allston) Young: WA's poem to, 532; and mother's estate, 440 n 2, 441, 454, 457, 459 n 4, 470-71, 494-95; children, 440 n 2; death, 471; unrecovered letters from, 93, 440; mentioned, 12, 14 n 1, 15, 220, 297 n 5, 418, 439
Alston, Sarah, 170 n 11
Alston, Washington, 449 (#285) n 1
Alston, William Algernon, 449 (#285) n 1, 454, 457, 471, 532; unrecovered letter to, 471
Alvarez de Pereira y Cubero, José, 42, 227
American Academy of Fine Arts: WA exhibited at, 92 n 1, 115 n 1; honorary member of, 115, 118, 141 n 13, 146, 155, 188, 347 n 3, 574, 579
American Art-Union, 115 n 1, 534, 636; *Bulletin*, 603
American Jurist and Law Magazine, 403
American Literary, Scientific and Military Academy, 569
American Monthly Magazine, 427, 570, 571
American Revolution. *See* Allston, William, Jr.; Bunker Hill Monument; United States Capitol; Washington, George
American Whig Review, 599-600, 603
Ames, Fisher, 629
Ames, Joseph Alexander, 107, 473 n 2, 635-36; portrait of WA, 635
Amory, Jane R., 532
Amory, Mary (Preble), 60 n 1, 234, 292, 454, 532, 636
Amory, Nathaniel, 60 n 1, 102, 140 n 10, 229, 233, 236, 257, 454, 491, 532
Analectic Magazine, 67, 594
Andover Theological Seminary, 448 n 2, 530, 581, 582
Andrews, Joseph, 232
Andrews, William Turrell, 432
Angelico, Fra, 625

Angerstein, John Julius, 66, 213, 231, 532, 555, 562
Anglesley, Isle of, 506
Annals of the Fine Arts, 93 n 3, 111 n 2, 117 n 4, 153
Antinuous, Capitoline, 342 n 1
Antinuous Belvedere or *Hermes*, 43
Antwerp, 38-39
Apelles, 546
Apollo, 10, 32, 45, 607
Apollo Association, 115 n 1
Apollo Belvedere, 19, 30 n 20, 39, 43, 82 n 4, 261, 342 n 1, 410, 590
Apollonius Rhodius, 45
Appenines, 351, 430
Appleton, Frances, 510, 510-11 n 4
Appleton, Nathan, 242, 384 n 2, 404 n 4, 576
Appleton, Samuel, 102
Appleton, Thomas, 272
Appleton, Thomas Gould, 576
Apprentices' Library Society, 304 n 6
Arabian Nights' Entertainment, 223, 606
Archimedes, 614
Argonauts. *See* Apollonius Rhodius
Ariadne, 99
Ashby-de-la-Zouch, 61, 363, 533
Aspasia, 614
Athenaeum, 404 n 6, 405 n 1, 555, 560-61
Atlantic Souvenir, 250 n 26
Atlas, 117 n 6, 329 (#196) n 1, 572, 612, 625
Auboyneau, Armand, 23
Audubon, John James, 324
Avery, John, 10, 11, 532
Avery, Samuel, 637
Azara, I.M., 434 (#271) n 4

Backhuysen, Ludolf, 234
Bacot, Mr., 134
Baldwin, Catherine (Williams) Beckford, 269
Baldwin, Loammi, 19, 102-03, 170 n 10, 205-06, 238, 240, 410, 532, 553
Ball, Anne Elizabeth (Channing), 455 n 4, 533
Ball, Hugh Swinton, 296-97, 302-03, 318-19, 455 n 4, 533
Ball, Thomas, 635-36
Baltimore, Md., 208, 637
Bancroft, George, 303 n 2, 474 n 2, 502 n 4
Bancroft, Elizabeth (Davis) Bliss, 303 n 1
Bank of New York, 489
Barbarelli, Giorgio, 267
Barber, Henry, 9
Baretti, M.A., 49
Baring, Mrs. Henry, and children, 188
Baring and Bates Banking House, 233
Barlow, Joel, 78, 143
Barnard, Henry, 368
Barry, James, 30 n 19, 117 n 4
Bartlett, Abner, 311 (#182) n 1
Bartlett, E[lmer?], 311 n 1
Bartlett, Joseph, 11 n 4
Bartlett, Thomas, 311
Bartlett, William, 19, 311 (#182) n 1
Bartol, Cyrus Augustus, 428
Bartoli, Pietro Santo, 313
Bartolini, Lorenzo, 260-61, 270-72
Bartolomeo, Fra, 47, 586, 625
Bassano, Jacopo da Ponte, 56 n 11, 81, 267
Bates, Joshua, 626
Bath, 29 n 16
Batoni, Pompeo, 79, 339
Bay, Mary W., 264
Beattie, James, 33, 181, 603
Beaumont, Andrew, 417, 533
Beaumont, George Howland: patron of WA, 61, 67, 70, 75, 82 n 4, 93, 94 n 3, 97, 363, 557, 583; described by WA, 354; mentioned, 120 n 7, 250 n 22, 532-33, 582-83, 594, 630. *See also Collins–Leslie correspondence, passim*
Beaumont, Margaret (Willes), 61, 93, 98, 118, 123, 126-27, 145-46, 152, 158-59, 166, 210, 213, 222, 234
Beaumont, Rachel (Howland), 70
Bedford, Duke of, 231
Beechey, William, 27, 67, 343, 533, 621
Belgiojoso-Trivulzio, Princess Christine, 306
Belin, Alard Henry, 441, 442 n 2, 454-58
Bell, Andrew, 562, 582
Bell, Charles, 603
Bellinzona, 41
Benbridge, Henry, 99 n 4, 323, 323 n 3
Benderman, Eduard Julius, 462, 477
Benedick (*Much Ado about Nothing*), 291, 300
Benjamin, Park, 427, 609
Benucci, Filippo, 42
Benvenuti, Pietro, 47, 52, 53 n 3, 226, 261, 267, 272; unrecovered letter to, 53 n 4
Berkeley, George, 139, 332
Berlin, 462
Berni, Francisco, 48

Bethune, George Washington, 513, 626
Betsey (Bridgen?), 121-22, 189
Bible: WA's use of in paintings and writings, 67, 140, 223, 612-13: quotation from, in letters, 27, 168, 180, 197, 300, 312, 333, 412, 438, 492, 604, 627; copies owned, 8, 8 (#2) n 2, 613, 443. *See also* WA, paintings and drawings *by title*
Biddle, Nicholas, 42
Bienaimé, Luigi, 83 n 4, 488 n 2
Bigelow, Jacob, 474 n 2, 533
Bird, Edward, 171, 185
Birmingham, Eng., 173, 560
Blackwood's Edinburgh Magazine, 173, 190, 331, 547, 595
Blair, Hugh, 603, 612
Blake, William, 302 n 5
Bleeker, Barent, 109
Blenheim, 63 n 2
Bliss, Elizabeth (Davis), 303 n 1
Blücher, Gebher Leberecht von, 73
Boccaccio, Giovanni, 48
Boel, Peter, 240, 269 n 2
Bolles, Charles, 596
Bollman, Justus Erich, 152, 160
Bologna, 41; School of Painting, 255
Borghese Warrior. See Fighting Gladiator
Borland, John, 138 n 1
Borzacchini, M. Guelfi, 49
Boschini, Marco, 588
Boston: WA in, 124-281, 324, 331-32, 336, 354, 356, 367, 378, 532, 537, 545, 566, 606, 619, 625, 630, 632; WA's visits to, and visitors from, in Cambridgeport, 315, 348, 375, 387, 389, 414-15, 436, 451, 474-75, 481, 490; mentioned, 314, 364, 393, 423, 427, 429, 433, 446, 460-61, 468-69, 473-74, 486, 537, 563
Boston Artists' Association, 472, 472-73 nn 2, 3
Boston Athenaeum: WA exhibited at, 45, 103, 105, 114 n 7, 162 n 1, 170 n 9, 182 n 11, 236, 238-42, 269, 269 n 2, 311, 315, 321 (#188) n 1, (#189) n 3, 322 n 3, 329 (#197) n 1, 424-25, 570, 575, 607, 636-37; WA purchased by, 76, 269, 377; portraits of WA exhibited at, 432 (#269) n 1, 470 n 1; books borrowed from, 301, 509, 612; WA's advice to, 257, 342 n 1, 547; Cogdell exhibited at, 335-36, 341, 372, 375, 508; trustees of, 431, 434; mentioned, 191, 279 n 8, 327, 364, 413, 548, 574, 634. *See also* Boston Artists' Association
Boston Commercial Gazette, 407-08, 420 nn 2, 3, 422
Boston Courier, 33 n 2, 524
Boston Daily Advertiser: WA's contributions to, 37 n 1, 257, 315, 339, 368, 377, 408 n 1, 417, 420 n 3, 604-05; notices of WA paintings, 170 n 2, 176 n 2, 304 n 5, 420 n 3; mentioned, 63 (#23) n 4, 208, 290 n 1, 325 n 2, 337 n 10, 413 nn 5, 7, 555, 565
Boston Daily Times, 464 (#298) n 1, 573
Boston Evening Post, 429, 625
Boston Miscellany of Literature and Fashion, 607
Boston Museum of Fine Arts, 545, 631, 637
Boston Notion, 450, 464 (#298) n 1, 573
Boston Patriot, 315
Boston Quarterly Review, 597
Boston Theatre, 235 n 6
Boston Transcript, 420 n 2
Boswell, James, 201 n 4, 615
Bosworth, Hiram S., 482
Bottarelli, F., 49
Bottari, Giovanni Gaetano, 509
Bourden, Sebastian, 250 n 22
Bowditch, Nathaniel Ingersoll, 319, 375 n 1
Bowdoin, James, 150, 151
Bowen, Charles, 533; unrecovered letter from, 365
Bowles, Carington, 623
Bowles, William Lisle, 343
Bowman, John, 27-28, 333-34, 546, 548
Boydell, John, 614
Boylston Market House. *See* Exhibitions
Brackett, Edward Augustus, 524, 534
Bradford, Alden, 375 n 1
Bradstreet, J.P., 268
Braham, John, 632-33
Bramante, Donato, 42
Brattle, Thomas, 11 n 1
Bread and Cheese Club, 542, 560
Brent, Charlotte, 64, 85, 189
Brett, John Watkins, 240, 242
Bridgen, Mr. and Mrs., 87, 111 n 4, 121-22, 129, 137, 169, 184, 189, 192, 199, 201, 204, 211, 533
Bridgen, Harriet. *See* Bridgen, Mr. and Mrs., passim
Bridport, Hugh, 269, 499, 501
Brighton, 110
Brimmer, George Watson, 259, 266, 409

Bristol, Eng.: WA in, 29 n 16, 36 n 1, 63-64 (#24) nn 2, 3, 64, 65, 65 n 1, 72, 73 n 2, 75-76, 122, 174, 353, 486, 489, 512, 538-39, 547, 562, 567, 579, 605; mentioned, 60, 561. *See also* Bristol Exhibition
Bristol Exhibition of WA, 56 n 11, 66-67, 72-73, 74-76, 85 n 3, 111 n 2, 540, 584
Bristol Gazette, 75, 591
Bristol Mercury, 75
British Institution for Promotion of the Fine Arts: WA exhibited at, 65, 67, 69-70, 92 n 6, 93, 94 n 4, 111, 117 nn 4, 5, 231, 276 n 2, 580; premium from, 75, 116, 363; 82 n 1, 136, 147, 172, 189-90, 353, 532, 563, 583
British School (London), 30 n 21, 146, 548
Brock, John B., 121-22
Brockedon, William, 89, 153, 169, 173, 184, 275, 276 n 2, 351, 498
Brockhaus, F.A., 596
Bromfield, Mr., 138, 153
Brompton, 70
Brouwer, Adrian, 591
Brown, Charles Brockden, 185, 617
Brown, Gawen, 364
Brown, George Loring, 442, 442 n 5
Brown, Henry Kirke, 634-35
Brown, James (of Boston), 467-68, 534, 563, 596
Brown, James (of Snaresbrook), 185; wife of, 160
Brown, John, 21
Brown, Mather, 364
Brown, Solyman, 534
Brown, Thomas, Jr., 458-59, 503-04, 507, 534, 570; unrecovered letter from, 505
Brown, Thomas, Sr., 56 n 11, 191, 199, 265, 275, 478, 497 n 2, 504, 534
Browne, Thomas, 430 n 17
Browning, Robert, 425
Bruce, Mr. (?), 467
Brunelleschi, Filippo, 305
Brunton, Mary (Balfour), 148
Brussels, 38
Bryant, Frances (Fairchild), 465
Bryant, John, Jr., 351 (#209) n 2, 404 n 5
Bryant, William Cullen, 97 n 1, 248 n 5, 371 n 11, 427, 434-35, 465; unrecovered letter to, 535
Buckminster, Joseph Stevens, 58, 626, 628
Buffon, Georges Louis Leclerc, Comte de, 28, 31 n 23, 612
Bulfinch, Charles, 606-09
Bullock's Museum, 173
Bulwer-Lytton, Edward G., 1st baron, 149 n 8, 599
Bunker Hill Monument, 103, 308, 310 n 25, 532, 545, 547, 576, 578
Bunyan, John, 534
Burges, Tristram, 285 n 3
Burnet, John, 460-61
Burr, Aaron, 153 n 12
Burritt, Elija Hinsdale, 250 n 23
Butler, Joseph, 628
Byron, George Gordon, sixth baron, 85, 102, 343, 574, 594

Cabell, Joseph Carrington, 38
Cabot, Samuel, 384 n 4
Caesar, Julius, 28
Cagliari, Paolo (called Veronese), 19, 39, 43, 56 n 11, 57, 81-82, 92 n 3, 110, 117 n 4, 120, 137, 267, 305, 343, 430, 584, 588, 612
Cagliostro, Alessandro di, 48
Callcot, Augustus Wall, 152, 180, 213, 324
Callender, Richard B., 259
Calne, 83, 539
Cambio, Arnolfo di, 305
Cambridge, Mass.: WA in, 7, 10-13, 15, 21, 39, 164, 168, 265, 291, 347, 368, 398, 424, 437, 475, 530, 534, 543-44, 553; mentioned, 320, 569, 573. *See also* Harvard College; Mount Auburn Cemetery; Shepard Congregational Society
Cambridgeport, Mass.: WA in, 107, 281-84, 284 n 1, 286-302, 312, 560, 564-65, 568, 576, 600, 625; last house, 470, 495; mentioned, 451, 452-53 n 2
Campbell, Thomas, 594
Campbell's Foreign Semi-Monthly Magazine, 470 n 1
Camuccini, Vincenzo, 45, 54, 226, 272
Canaletto, Antonio Canale, 231
Canova, Antonio, 42-43, 226, 260, 270-71, 277, 359
Caravaggio, Michelangelo da, 212, 587
Carey, Henry Charles, 461, 562, 578
Carey, William Paulet, 153, 159, 168, 177 n 5, 184, 489
Carlisle, Earl of, 188
Carlos, Don, VII (claimant to throne of Spain), 368 n 2
Carlyle, Thomas, 599, 617
Carolina Coffee House, 29 n 16

Carpenter, Francis Bicknell, 631
Carr, William Howell, 67
Carracci, Annibale, 43, 111, 242, 450 n 3, 584, 587
Carracci, Ludovico, 242, 255, 343, 450 n 3
Carrara, 258-59, 298
Carroll, Charles, 346
Carstens, Asmus, 45
Carter, Robert, 607
Carter, William, 42
Cary, Alpheus, 520, 574
Casilear, John William, 381 n 4
Castel, Charles Irénée, 604
Castelli, Bernardo, 42
Castine, Me., 383
Cavalleri, Ferdinando, 273
Cellini, Benvenuto, 603
Century, 599
Cervantes, Miguel de, 22
Chalmers, Thomas, 625
Chalon, Alfred Edward, 137, 155
Chalon, John James, 137
Chamberlain, Mr., 172
Chambery, 305
Champney, Benjamin, 107, 634
Channing, Ann. *See* Allston, Ann (Channing)
Channing, Edward Tyrrell, 166
Channing, Ellery, 557
Channing, Francis Dana, 58-59, 520 n 3, 536
Channing, Lucy, 148
Channing, Lucy (Ellery), 58, 148
Channing, Mary, 148
Channing, Ruth (Gibbs), 209, 213, 222, 232, 321, 416, 524, 535
Channing, Walter: "Reminiscences of WA," 111 n 4, 117 nn 4, 5, 6, 318 n 12, 524-25, 535, 599; mentioned, 87, 204 n 7, 384 nn 2, 4, 530, 557, 625, 628-29
Channing, William (grandfather-in-law), 58, 535
Channing, William (WA's nephew), 524, 609
Channing, William Ellery: association with WA in boyhood and college, 22, 332 n 3, 516-17, 534-36; admiration of WA's painting, 463, 516; concern about WA's finances, 321, 384 n 4, 568; association with Coleridge, Leslie, and Wordsworth, 209, 213, 222, 222 n 1, 232, 234, 281; WA's admiration of, 516-17, 536; mentioned, 106, 156 n 10, 170 n 9, 208, 402 n 5, 416 (#264) n 1, 427, 460, 530, 551, 561, 570, 593-94, 608. *See also* WA, portraits by
Channing, William Henry, 516-17, 536
Channing family, 524, 572
Chantrey, Francis Leggett, 126, 146, 277, 348-49, 356, 390
Chapman, John Gadsby, 381 n 1, 398 n 6
Chapman, Jonathan, 474 n 2, 502 n 4
Chappel, Alonzo, 637
Charles VIII of England, 272 n 20
Charleston, S.C., 208; WA in, 7 (#1) n 1, 13, 15, 23, 29 n 1, 333, 546, 551, 566; WA exhibited in, 92 n 6, 131, 133 n 1, 134 n 2, 297 n 2, 336, 485 n 4; friends and relatives in, 338, 439, 533, 537, 549-50, 559, 569, 577; Morse in, 135, 148, 151, 170 n 11. *See also WA–Cogdell correspondence, passim*
Charleston, S.C., Library, 551
Charleston Book, 599
Charleston Courier, 388
Charleston Mercury, 319
Charlestown, Mass., 145 n 2, 567, 581
Chase, Darius, 105
Chauvin, Pierre, 78
Cheney, Ednah Dow (Littlehale), 428-29, 431 n 18
Cheney, John, 295, 296 n 1, 365, 366 (#217) n 1, 385, 527, 536
Cheney, Seth Wells, 269 n 2, 385, 428, 527, 536
Chickasaw (ship), 335
Childs, Cephas, 300 n 2
Chimborazo; 182 n 12
Chingford, 161
Christian Examiner, 597-98
Christian Spectator, 628
Christian World. See Channing, Walter: "Reminiscences of WA"
Christie, James, 186 n 2
Churchill, Charles, 22, 616
Cincinnati, O., 413-14, 434
City Hotel (New York), 265
Clapp, William Warland, 318 n 8
Clark, Elijah, 240, 557
Clarke, James Freeman, 426-27, 524, 536-37
Clarke, Sarah Anne, 59, 191 n 11, 428, 436, 524, 536-37, 584, 597, 622, 632
classics: WA's knowledge of and attitude to classical tradition, 159, 307, 311 n 26, 540, 606, 614; references to mythological persons and places in poems, 614. *See also Greek and Latin authors by name*

Claude. *See* Gelée, Claude
Claxton, Alexander, Claxton, 371 n 11
Clay, Henry, 501
Cleveland, Henry Russell, 564
Clevenger, Shobal Veil, 104, 415, 435, 442, 452, 508, 543; bust of WA, 432 (#269) n 1, 434, 508, 551, 572
Cliffton, William, 594
Clifton, 63 (#24) n 2, 64 (#25), 65 n 8, 69, 353, 406, 561-62
Coate, Mr., 70
Codman, Charles Russell, 138 n 1, 207, 238, 242
Codman, John, 12 n 4, 625-26
Cogdell, John Stevens: in Boston, 222-23, 537; WA's criticism of and advice to, 236, 254-57, 263, 264 n 3, 292-93, 300-301, 312-13, 348-49, 375, 407, 412; power of attorney for WA, 439-41, 452-55, 473, 489-90, 494-95; unrecovered letters from, 222, 254, 335-36, 337 n 5, 341, 348, 387, 406, 473, 489, 494, 514; mentioned, 102, 134, 135
Cogdell, Maria (Gilchrist); 224, 229, 236, 255, 257, 264, 293, 302, 317, 336, 341, 349, 357, 372, 514
Coggin, Jacob, 608
Cogniac School of Painting, 371
Cogswell, Joseph Green, 429
Colburn, Henry, 163 n 2, 195-96, 198, 200, 204, 402 n 2
Cole, Thomas, 103, 245-47, 381 n 4, 413, 537-38, 546, 587, 620
Coleridge, Derwent, 52, 123
Coleridge, Hartley, 53, 123, 126
Coleridge, Henry Nelson, 353, 513, 539-40, 570
Coleridge, Samuel Taylor, 538-41; association with WA in Rome, 40-42, 44-45, 75, 430 n 14, 490, 538; in London, 64 (#24) n 2, 65 n 3, 533, 538-39; in Bristol, 63 (#24) n 1, 74-75, 538-39; admiration of WA's paintings and poems, 45-46, 56, 62 n 2, 66, 74-75, 412, 464, 538-40, 594; of WA personally, 53, 68, 281, 403 n 1, 538, 541, 552, 563; at death of WA's wife, 80 n 4, 83-84; esthetic theory of, 75, 157, 540-41; romanticism of, 195-96, 541; politics of, 97 n 8, 541; WA's admiration of, 146, 437, 492, 497-98, 513, 552; recollections of, 539, 562, 570, 572-73; gift of painting to, 443, 539; WA influenced by, in paintings and writings, 44-45, 64 (#25) n 2, 241, 424, 539, 631; ownership of books by, 539-40; unrecovered letter to, 578; mentioned, 354, 443, 552, 566-67, 575, 585, 603. *See also* WA, portraits by; WA, writings of; *WA–Leslie correspondence, passim*
Coleridge, Sara (Fricker), 53, 123, 124 n 3, 126
Coleridge, Sara, 23, 126, 129
Collard, Frederick William, 87, 129, 146, 153, 159, 169, 184, 189, 192, 199, 204, 213, 215, 234, 498, 541-42, 564
Collins, Charles Allston, 542
Collins, Francis, 126, 145-46, 159, 161, 167, 169, 172, 176-77, 181, 198, 204, 542
Collins, Mrs., 127, 145-46, 159, 169, 172, 181, 198, 542
Collins, William (poet), 172, 276 n 6
Collins, William (painter): in Paris, 110, 542, 569; 104, 134, 158, 165, 168, 177, 199 n 3, 239, 403 n 1, 497-98, 542, 577; unrecovered letter from, 126-27. *See also WA–Leslie correspondence, passim*
Collins, William Wilkie, 542
Colman, George, 21
Columbia, S.C., 551
Columbian Centinel, 177 n 2, 208
Columbian Museum, 103, 332
Columbus, Christopher, 286, 288, 289 n 6, 291
Comer, Thomas, 633
Common-Place Book of Romantic Tales, 57
Comte, Augustus, 571
Connecticut, 447
Connecticut Courant, 10 n 1
Constable, John, 213
Constitution, The (ship), 354
Cook, Richard, 153
Cooke, George Frederick, 169, 182 n 12, 323, 631
Cooke, Robert, 634
Coolidge, Joseph, 377 (#227) n 2
Cooper, Abraham, 137, 172
Cooper, James Fenimore, 218, 266-67, 268 (#159) n 3, 269, 273, 278, 282, 306, 367, 427, 542
Cooper, William Yeardly, 266
Cope, Charles Cecil, third earl of Liverpool, 152
Copley, John Singleton, 24, 58, 251, 251 n 1, 323, 390

Corduba, 9
Corelli, Arcangelo, 632
Corinthian Gallery (Boston), 105
Cornelius, Peter von, 462, 477
Cornwallis, Charles, first marquis, 550
Correggio, Antonio Allegri da, 24, 231, 242, 371, 424, 444, 551, 584, 587, 624 n 4
Costumi Religiosi Civiti, e Militari Antichi Egiziani, Etruscani, Greci, & Romani, I, 318 n 4
Cotting, Uriah, 608
Cottle, Joseph, 75
Count Roderick's Castle; or, Gothic Times, a Tale, WA's painting from, 21, 330, 332 n 2
Courier (London), 97 n 8
Cousins, Samuel, 399, 512
Cowley, Abraham, 616
Cowpens, Battle of, 531
Cowper, William, 451, 594, 617
Coxe, Arthur Cleveland, 628
Crabbe, George, 544, 616
Cranch, Christopher Pearse, 524
Crawford, Thomas, 442, 510, 510 n 1, 516, 542-43
Crayon, 600
Cregan, Martin, 87 n 10
Crescentini, Girolamo, 48, 632
Crocker, Doddridge C., 514
Crosby, William George, 238
Cummings and Hilliard Publishers, 593
Cunard Line, 505
Curtis, Charles B., 319
Curtis, Thomas Buckminster, 525
Cushing, Ezekiel Dodge, 62
Cushing, John Perkins, 520
Cushing, Luther Stearns, 403

Daggett, Elizabeth (Watson), 501-02
Daguerre, Louis, 433
Dalmazzoni, Angelo, 46
Dana, Edmund Trowbridge (brother-in-law): early association with WA, 7, 164, 177, 534-35, 544, 629; in London, 29 n 16, 543; called "brother" by WA, 187, 543; artistic sense, 207, 286, 341, 360; and publication on *SS,* 593; called "the Master" by Greenough, 266, 274, 279, 347, 453 n 4, 553; WA's portraits of, 21, 58; mentioned, 104, 298, 350, 356, 367, 467, 525, 605
Dana, Edmund Trowbridge (WA's nephew), 104, 409, 453 n 4, 492, 542, 626
Dana, Elizabeth Ellery, 347, 524, 543, 604
Dana Francis, 318 n 13
Dana, Mary Elizabeth, 602
Dana, Richard, 318 n 13, 500, 525
Dana, Richard Henry, Jr.: biographical sketch of WA, 600, 612, 628; as lawyer for WA, 467-68 n 10, 473-74; and publication of *Monaldi,* 466-67; editor of *LA,* 534, 544, 600-601, 603, 610, 612; description of WA, 544, 625, 629; at WA's death, 104-06, 525, 544-46, 561; recollections of WA, 39, 42-43, 75, 103, 120, 149 n 8, 170 n 8, 245 n 4, 325 n 3, 402 n 3, 569, 580, 587, 592, 617, 632; mentioned, 404 nn 1, 6, 448 n 2, 474 n 2, 494 n 1, 502 n 4, 535, 573-74, 599, 608, 626
Dana, Richard Henry, Sr.: review of *SS,* 593-94; poems on WA, 545; on WA's later poems: 464-65 n 1; on WA's paintings, 104, 269 n 2, 428-29, 432 n 2; on Stuart's portrait of WA, 577; and WA's finances, 281 n 2, 384 n 4; as correspondent of Verplanck, 218, 244, 252-53, 285 n 3, 320, 432 (#270) nn 1, 2, 432 (#269) n 2; account of WA's last illness and death, 469 n 9, 523; as biographer of WA, 544; "Notes on WA," 45, 76 n 5, 114 n 7, 170 n 9, 176 n 3, 241, 269 n 2, 304 nn 5, 7, 329 (#197) n 1, 328-29 (#196) n 1, 337 n 11, 350-51 n 2, 351 (#209) n 2, 503, 532, 535; letters about WA to, 476 n 4, 546, 550, 552, 554, 558, 573, 582, 619; greetings from Greenough by WA, 309, 346-47, 390; WA's esteem for, 58, 166, 195-98, 200-201, 359-60, 376, 389, 425, 617; mentioned, 293 n 2, 325 n 3, 367, 372, 448 n 2, 474 n 2, 513, 525, 530, 532, 534, 536, 543, 547, 563, 578, 626. *See also Idle Man*
Dana, Ruth Charlotte, 48, 408, 427, 523-25, 632
Dana, Ruth Charlotte (Smith), 197, 293 n 4, 467, 554, 601-02
Dana, Sarah, 467 n 8
Dana, Sarah (Watson), 467
Dana, Sarah Ann, 347, 408, 523-25
Dana Collection, 508 n 1
Dana family, 524, 572, 625
Danby, Francis, 415 n 2

Danforth, Moseley Isaac, 295
D'Angerville, Mouffle, 38
Dante Alighieri, 48, 111, 164, 168, 181, 270, 302, 426, 428, 550, 558, 563-64
Darby, Sidney, 461
David, Jacques Louis, 271, 306
Davis, Isaac P., 102, 125, 240, 242, 319, 365 n 3, 381 n 5, 520, 545, 559, 564
Davis, John, 16, 375 n 1, 545
Davis, Susan (Jackson), 302
Dawe, George, 46, 567
Dawes, Rufus, 265 n 1
Dawlish, 129
Day, Alexander, 57 n 4
Dearborn, Henry Alexander Scammell, 312 n 3, 320, 545-46
Decheaux, Edward, 504
Degan, Frederick, 53
Dehon, Theodore, 293
Delafield, John, 169
Delaplaine, Joseph, 91
Della Crusca Academy (Florence), 47
Della Cruscans, school of, 616
Della Pittura Veneziana, 49
Delos, 17
Denon, Dominique Vivant, 272
Derby, Elias Haskins, 33 n 7
Derby, Mrs., 19
Derby, Richard Crowninshield, 33
De Saussure, Henry William, 453 n 8
Descamps, Guillaume, 57, 79
Detroit Institute of Art, 637
De Veaux, James, 460, 460 n 3, 546
Dexter, Catherine Elizabeth (Prescott), 458, 512
Dexter, Franklin: and paintings by WA, 104-05, 240, 289 n 6, 321 (#189) n 13, 319, 378-79, 381 n 4, 432, 527; artistic talent, 511-12, 546; at WA's death, 525, 544, 546, 568, 578; and WA's finances, 384 n 4; son, 512; mentioned, 474 n 2
Dexter, Henry, 294 n 1, 524, 634-35
Dial, 425, 524, 597, 609
Diana of Versailles or *The Hind*, 342
Dickens, Charles, 149 n 8, 474, 474 n 2, 475, 475 n 6, 481, 502, 502 nn 4, 5, 609
Dieppe, 110
Dillaway, Charles Knapp, 46
Dillwyn, John, 160
Dillwyn, Lewis, 171
Dillwyn, William, 160, 171
Dioscuri, 310
Disraeli, Benjamin, 570
Dix, Elbridge, 350
Dobson, Thomas, 20
Doggett, John, 103, 162, 202-03, 208, 218, 221, 240, 329, 436 n 2
Dolce, Carlo (or Carlino), 371
Domenichino, Zampieri, 44, 415 n 2, 513 n 5
Donatello (Donato di Bardi), 270
Drayton, Maria Miles (Heyward), 134
Drayton, William, 91, 92 n 7, 93, 134, 264 n 3, 285, 288-89, 328, 485, 499-500, 546, 630; unrecovered letter to, 92 n 7
Dryden, John, 592, 616
Drury Lane Theatre, 129, 134, 182 n 13, 539
Dudley, Lady Jane Grey, 231
Duff, William, 24
Duggan, Peter Paul (or Paul Peter), 636
Dulwich Gallery, 110
Dunlap, William: source for contemporary accounts of WA, 424, 547, 561, 571, 599; objections to account of WA, 367, 373-74, 376, 379-80, 555; unrecovered letters from, 322, 330 n 1; mentioned, 539, 546-47, 554
Dunlop, James, 129, 137, 152, 161; wife of, 129, 161
Dunmow, 69
Dupaty, Charles, 48
Durand, Asher Brown, 44, 82 n 1, 297 n 2, 380, 381 nn 4, 5, 547
Dürer, Albrecht, 578
Dusseldorf, Academy at, 460, 462
Dutton, Elizabeth Cutts (Lowell), 221-22
Dutton, Warren: appreciation of art, 104-05, 184, 207, 221; WA letter of introduction for, 221-22; mentioned, 102, 138 n 1, 238, 240, 264, 384 n 2, 547
Duyckinck, Evert Augustus, 559, 637
Duyckinck, George L., 559, 637
Dwight, Edmund, 240, 378, 384 n 4, 428
Dwight, John Sullivan, 607
Dwight, Thomas, 525
Dwight, Timothy, 143

Eagles, John, 547
East Indies, 512
Eastlake, Charles, 404
Ebeling, Christoph Daniel, 143, 148
Edgeworth, Maria, 75
Edinburgh Review, 146, 183-84, 393, 574
Egremont, Earl of. *See* Wyndham, George O'Brien

eighteenth-century authors, 616-17
Elgin Marbles, 66
Eliot, Samuel Atkins, 102, 240, 242, 271, 319, 366
Ellery, Lucy, 58, 148
Ellery, William, 57
Elliott, Stephen, 293, 301, 335-36, 203, 375
Ellis, George B., 250 n 26
Elmes, James, 154 n 16
Elysium: 614. *See also* Milton, John
Emerson, Ralph Waldo, 48, 402 n 7, 427-28, 430 nn 14, 16, 17, 524, 536-37, 605; mentioned, 423, 425, 607, 609, 627
Emerson, William, 430 n 17
Emerson's Magazine and Putnam's Monthly, 571
Enfield, William, 623
England: WA's attachment to, 353-54, 368, 403; WA's departure from opposed, 118, 120 n 7, 353, 560, 582. *See also* WA, writings: "America to Great Britain"
England, John, 490
Epping Forest, 160
Etty, William, 137, 198
Euripides, 34
European Museum (London), 30 n 19, 338
Eustaphieve, Akxiei Grigor'ich, 70
Euterpeiad, 632
Evans, J., 616
Evening Gazette, 315
Evening Star, 413 n 7
Everett, Alexander Hill, 239
Everett, Edward, 167 n 2, 327, 327 n 1, 369, 375 n 1, 427, 432 (#269) n 1, 547, 630
Examiner, 62 n 1, 67, 74, 92 n 6, 93, 111, 116 n 2, 117 n 4, 152, 160, 174 n 4, 181, 190, 302
Exeter, 129
Exeter Exchange, 97
Exhibitions of WA's paintings: American Academy of Fine Arts, 115 n 1; Boston Artists' Association, 472-73 n 2; Boston Athenaeum, 238-47; Boylston Market House, 170 n 9; Bristol, 73-76; British Institution for Promotion of the Fine Arts, 65 n 6; National Academy of Design, 252 n 5; Paris Salon, 77; Pennsylvania Academy of Fine Arts, 89 n 5; Royal Academy of Art, 30 n 21. *See also* Charleston, S.C.; Harding's Gallery; Sully, Thomas

Fairman, Gideon, 173
Falconet, Etienne Maurice, 388-89
Farnese Hercules, 40, 47
Federal Street Congregational Society, Church of, 520, 535, 608
Federal Street Theater, 569
Felix Farley's Bristol Journal, 75
Felton, Cornelius Conway: critical notices of WA, 59, 524-25, 547-48, 563-64, 600, 603; mentioned, 401-02 nn 1, 7, 405 n 1, 474 n 2, 502 n 4
Felton, Mary (Whitney), 52
Fenelon, François de Salignac de la Mothe, 142
Ferdinand V of Leon and Castile, 142, 286
Ferdinand VII of Spain, 368 n 2
Fessenden, Abigail, 191
Field, George, 276, 465, 479, 548, 592, 621
Fielding, Henry, 390
Fields, James Thomas, 474 n 2
Fields, T.S., 488
Fighting Gladiator or *Borghese Warrior,* 28, 30-31 n 22, 176 n 3, 294 n 1, 634
Filicho, Antonio, 55
Filicho, Filippo, 55
Finden, William, 100 n 2, 116 n 2, 119, 204 n 1
Fish, Hamilton, 548, 630
Fisher, Alvan, 133, 135, 145, 227, 267
Fittler, James, 163
Flagg, Capt., 29
Flagg, Ebenezer, 12, 23, 406, 442 n 2, 548
Flagg, Eliza Moore, 11, 224, 442 n 1
Flagg, George Whiting: in Boston, 92 n 6, 297 n 2, 301, 313, 315, 317, 327, 364, 392-93, 407, 548-49, 557; and exhibition at Harding's Gallery, 92 n 6, 549; resemblance to WA, 370; portrait of WA, 432 n 1, 636; WA's poem to, 548; unrecovered letter to, 522
Flagg, Henry Collins, Sr., 7, 12, 14-15, 36 n 1, 406, 438-39, 549-50, 580; will of, 440 n 3
Flagg, Henry Collins, Jr., 12, 58, 293, 440 n 1, 452, 454, 457, 548-49, 624, 626
Flagg, Jared Bradley, 415 n 2, 424, 545, 549, 626
Flagg, Martha (Whiting), 452, 522
Flagg, Mary Allston, 449
Flagg, Rachel (Moore) Allston: and paintings by WA, 15, 419-20, 451; and portraits of WA, 432 (#269) n 1, 434; WA's poem to, *see* WA: writings: "The Calycanthus"; greetings from WA sent by Cogdell, 224, 264, 317, 357, 376; by

Flagg, Rachel (Moore) Allston (*cont'd*) H.C. Flagg, Sr., 11; letter of introduction for WA, 36 n 1; death, 437-38; estate, 439, 440 n 1, 441, 470, 494-95; unrecovered letters to, 12, 224, 229, 236, 255, 257, 292-93, 300-301, 335-36, 341, 349, 372, 375, 389, 406, 411-13, 435; mentioned, 15 n 3, 127, 348, 468, 531, 549-50. *See also* WA, portraits
Flaxman: John, 111, 244, 270, 274 n 8, 302, 459, 550, 557, 603
Flora (slave), 452, 454
Florence, Italy: WA in, 41, 45-47, 50, 332, 399; acquaintances in, 388, 413, 452, 490, 508; mentioned, 52, 151, 298, 302 n 3, 427. *See also WA–Greenough correspondence, passim*
Formosa, 297
Foster, Andrew, 19
Foster, John, 370, 475 n 6
Foster, Thomas, 370
Fouqué, Friedrich Heinrich Karl, baron La Motte-Fouqué, 616-17
France, 388. *See also* Paris
Francis, Convers, 550, 626
Franklin, Benjamin, 431 n 17
Fraser, Charles: association with WA in Charleston, 23, 333-34; in Boston, 336, 339, 550; on WA, 304 n 6, 550; mentioned, 106, 134-35, 258 n 6, 436, 546, 577, 598-99
Frederick, Duke of Albany and York, 212
Frederick I of Germany, called Barbarossa, 23
Freeman, John O., 596
French Revolution, 541, 629; WA's sonnet on, 626, 629; WA's painting *The French National Convention as a Rasher of Frogs,* 23, 629
Fresnoy, Charles Alphonse du, 248 nn 6, 8, 9, 622, 623 nn 1, 2, 624 n 5
Fuller, George, 107, 634
Fuller, Margaret. *See* Ossoli, Margaret (Fuller)
Fürnich, Joseph von, 613
Fuseli, Henry: WA's recollections of, 26, 338-39, 340 n 15, 342-43, 551, 616; mentioned, 26, 20 n 19, 31 n 1, 204 n 7, 212, 250 n 24, 276 n 6, 525, 550-51, 578, 589, 616

Gainsborough, Thomas, 250 n 24, 338, 390, 535
Galen (ship), 120-22, 122 n 1, 123-24, 125 n 1, 136, 146, 169 n 1, 572; WA painting of, 122 n 1, 531, 572
Gallery. *See* British Institution for Promotion of the Fine Arts
Gally, John, 23
Gardiner, Robert Hallowell, and wife, 402 n 5
Garfield, William H., 573
Gattel, C.M., 38
Gay, John, 594
Gelder, Arendt (Aert) de, 111 n 27, 418
Gelée, Claude (or Claude Lorrain), 24-25, 112, 182, 213, 231, 234, 242, 246, 388, 424, 442 n 5, 588-89
Genazzano, 43
Geneva, 40
Genoa, 305
George III of England, 172, 231
George IV of England, 30 n 21, 152, 353
Georgetown, S.C., 255, 548
Georgia Historical Society, 434
"Georgiana," 8, 10 n 1
Gérard, François, 110, 145, 155
Gerdts, William H., Jr., 637
Germany, 476
Gibbens, Daniel L., 502
Gibbes, Elizabeth (Allston), 12, 36 n 1, 255 n 7, 440 n 2, 546, 551
Gibbes, Robert Wilson, 546, 550-51; unrecovered letter from, 475
Gibbes, Washington Allston, 476
Gibbes, William Hassell, 36 n 1, 546, 551
Gibbs, George, 42, 380, 535, 551, 568
Gibbs, Mary (Channing), 14 n 11, 170 n 9, 238, 535, 551
Gibbs, Sarah, 321, 327, 336, 351 (#209) n 2, 458, 524, 551, 568, 577
Gibbs, William, 82
Gibson, Charles D., 502
Gibson, John, 226, 259
Gibson family, 524
Gifford, William, 146 n 5
Gillman, Anne (Harding), 94, 94 n 2, 122, 124 n 3, 129, 137, 152, 169, 184, 188, 192, 199, 213, 219, 234, 551-52; unrecovered letter to, 442
Gillman, Henry Anthony, 443, 552
Gillman, James, Sr., 94, 94 n 2, 53 n 5, 122, 128, 137, 152, 169, 184, 188, 192, 199, 204, 213, 234, 443-44, 489, 551-52
Gillman, James, Jr., 443, 489, 494, 552; wife of, 443

Gilman, Samuel, 387
Gilmor, Robert, Jr., 191, 247 n 2, 554
Gilmor, Sarah Reeve (Ladson), 273, 278
Giordano, Luca, 181
Giorgione, 267
Glycon, 47
Godwin, William, 599
Goethe, Johann Wolfgang von, 550, 570
Goldsmith, Oliver, 577, 599, 612
Goodall, Edward, 462
Goodrich, Samuel Griswold, 366 (#217) n 3
Gore, John Christopher, 274
Gosman, Robert, 55, 62, 82
Gosport (ship), 18
Gothic tradition: WA's affiliation with, 41, 68, 307, 540, 608 n 9, 614, 617-18
Gould, Hannah Flagg, 524, 632
Graham's American Monthly Magazine, 443-44 n 2, 524, 545, 555, 603
Granet, François Marius, 62, 63 n 4, 78, 178
Grant, Anne, 60
Grasmere, 167 n 7
Grattan, Thomas C., 474 n 2
Gray, Frederick T., 533
Gray, Henry Peters, 505, 505 n 6
Gray, Lewis, 170 n 9
Gray, William, 122
Gray, William G., 122-23 n 7
Green, Joseph Henry, 497-98, 552
Greene, Benjamin, 524
Greene, George Washington, 516
Greene, John Singleton Copley, 488 n 2
Greene, Nathaniel, 549
Greene, William Batchelder, 628
Greenough, Alfred, 302 n 3, 390, 552
Greenough, David, 244, 274, 279
Greenough, Henry: conversations with WA, 38-40, 60, 74, 82 n 3, 98 n 2, 249 n 21, 250 n 24, 321 n 3, 480 n 6, 533, 537, 548, 550, 584, 587-89, 592, 619-22; *Ernest Carroll,* 39, 553, 580; mentioned, 302 n 3, 368, 482, 502, 525, 552
Greenough, Horatio: association with WA in Cambridge and Boston, 46, 251, 269, 347, 368, 386, 391 n 5, 502, 553-54; praised and recommended by WA, 251, 253, 289-90, 301, 302 n 3, 311, 314, 359, 360 n 4, 362; requests of WA filled in Italy, 261, 267, 274, 279; influence of WA on, 268 n 10, 279 n 1, 306, 410, 554, 605; WA called "father" by, 554; statue of Washington, 289-90, 291 n 1, 298, 311, 320, 357-62, 367, 369, 451, 507-08; *The Rescue,* 448; Bunker Hill Monument design, 308, 310-11 n 26; family of, 278, 279 n 9; mentioned, 244, 285 n 3, 384, 427-28, 450 n 3, 490, 491 n 5, 552, 577. *See also* WA, writings: "On Greenough's Group of the Angel and Child"
Greenough, John, 104, 243, 275, 279, 281 n 2, 347, 369, 390, 409, 525, 554; unrecovered letter to, 244
Greenough, Maria (Underwood), 369
Greenwood, Ethan Allen, 103, 221
Gregory XVI, Pope, 490
Greig, John, 63 n 2
Grey, Louisa Elizabeth, Lady Lambton, 188
Griffin, William, 371 n 11
Grimke, Thomas Smith, 335, 341; book owned by WA, 628
Grimm, Friedrich Melchior, 604
Griswold, Alexander Viets, 625
Griswold, Rufus Wilmot, 464-65, n 1, 465 n 2, 555, 598, 600
Grosse, Carl Friedrich, 566, 616
Gúerin, Paulin-Jean-Baptiste, 42
Gúerin, Pierre Narcisse, 110
Guarini, Giovan Battista, 48
Guattani, Giuseppe Antonio, 42, 44

Hackert, Jakob, 47, 570
Hale, Edward Everett, 565
Hale, Nathan, Jr., 607
Hale, Nathan, Sr., 315, 555
Hale, Sarah Josepha (Buell), 597-98
Halifax, 243
Hall, Margaret (Hunter) (Mrs. Basil), 103
Hamilton, James, 252, 329 (#196) n 1, 569, 630
Hampstead, 29 n 16
Hampton Court, 29 n 16, 63 n 2, 480
Handel, Georg Friedrich, 102
Harding, Catharine (Woodruff), 414
Harding, Chester: portraits of WA, 470, 470 n 1, 551, 556, 636-37; description of WA's studio, 555; letter of introduction for, 214-15; family of, 414, 415 n 3; mentioned, 103, 105, 219, 265 n 1, 346, 427, 546, 556, 634
Harding, Miss, 414
Harding's Gallery: WA exhibited at, 67, 92 n 6, 238-40, 421-31, 432-33 (#270) n 1, 418 n 2, 420 nn 1,2, 549, 556, 565, 580, 634; mentioned, 321 (#189) n 3, 325 n 3, 342 n 6, 444, 463, 536, 563

Harnden's Express, 485-87, 497-98, 504, 506
Harris, John, 21
Harris, Samuel, 375 n 1
Harrison, William Henry, 492
Hart, Samuel, 468
Hartford, Conn., 549, 574
Hartley, David, 540
Harvard College: WA as student at, 7, 8, 10, 11, 11 nn 1, 3, 4, 12 n 4, 13, 13 n 1, 14 n 1, 15 n 6, 20 n 14, 21-24, 68, 264 n 6, 291, 331-33, 356 n 21, 478 n 1, 535-36, 541, 561, 569, 575, 580, 589, 608, 624 n 5, 629, 631-32; books borrowed from library, 20, 22, 23-24, 31 n 1, 33 n 4, 321 n 3, 612, 614-16; WA at later commencements, 448 n 2, 474 n 2, 593; mentioned, 76, 251, 253, 256, 265, 429, 452, 543-44, 547, 550, 552-54, 563, 566, 573, 577
Harvey, George, 481, 556
Hastings, Edmund T., Sr., 298, 311, 393, 409
Hastings, Edmund T., Jr., 298 n 2, 479, 497, 505-06; and family, 524
Hastings-on-Hudson, N.Y., 556
Hatchard, John, 169
Haviland, James, 501
Haviland, John, 501
Haworth, Mr., 44
Haws, Mr., 8
Hawthorne, Nathaniel, 107, 556, 570, 607
Hawthorne, Sophia (Peabody), 386, 428, 436, 524, 536, 555-57, 623
Hay, David Ramsay, 480, 480 nn 6,7
Haydn, Franz Joseph, 632
Haydon, Benjamin Robert, 62 n 1, 87, 93, 94 n 3, 111, 117 n 4, 153, 173, 183-84, 188, 204, 209-10, 213, 299, 300 n 1, 324, 325 n 3, 501, 557, 562
Hayward, C., 377
Hayward, George, 190, 319, 625
Hayward, Joshua Henshaw, 102, 190, 377 (#227) n 1, 558
Hayward, William, 242, 408 n 1, 418 n 2, 433, 558
Hazlitt, William, 38-39, 62 n 1, 67, 73, 111 n 2, 166, 345, 509, 512, 558, 570
Healy, George Peter Alexander, 551, 588
Hedge, Frederick Henry, 550
Hedge, Levi, 12 n 4, 51
Heilson, John J., 97 n 1
Hemphills, 124
Henchman, Daniel, 499
Hercules, 110
Hermes, 43
Hesiod, 302 n 5
Hesperides, 46
Hewlings, Mr. and Mrs., 87
Heyward, Hannah (Shubrick), 134, 135 n 11
Higginson, Anna, 521
Higginson, Louisa, 521
Higginson, Mrs. Stephen, 521 n 3
Higginson, Thomas Wentworth, 521 n 3
Highgate, 94 n 1, 128, 137, 204, 206, 234, 442-43, 539, 560
Hillard, George Stillman, 455 n 4, 564, 576-79
Hillhouse, Abraham, 208 n 2
Hilton, Williams, 152-53, 179
Hitchen, Mr., 121
Hofland, Thomas R., 82 n 3, 429
Hogarth, William, 22, 256-57, 257-58 n 1, 390, 462, 562, 583
Holbein, Hans, 583
Holbrook, John Edwards, 236
Holland School of Painting, 371
Holmes, Abiel, 285, 423, 447 (#283) n 1
Holmes, Oliver Wendell, 424-25, 446 n 1, 474 n 2
Homer, 9, 46, 122 n 1, 302 n 5, 428, 550-51, 614
Hone, Philip, 96, 97 n 5
Hood, William, 567
Hope, Henry Philip, 187-88
Hope, Thomas, 187, 313
Horace, 14, 51, 614
Hosmer, Rufus, 18, 604
Houdon, Jean Antoine, 110, 290, 311
Howard, Benjamin Chew, 384 n 7
Howard, George, sixth earl of Carlisle, 188
Howard, George William Frederick, Viscount Morpeth, 471, 510, 558-59
Howard, Harriet Elizabeth Georgiana, Duchess of Sutherland, 558
Howard, Henry, 129, 134, 146, 159, 169, 212-13, 231, 234, 243, 559; unrecovered letter to, 169, 170 n 2, 243
Howard, Nathaniel, 502
Howe, Julia (Ward), 429, 474 n 2, 491-92 n 2
Howe, Samuel Gridley, 265 n 1, 491
Howitt's Journal, 623
Hoyt, Albert Gallatin, 479, 493, 496-98, 559
Hudson River school of painting, 25, 537

Huger, Daniel Elliott, 559
Hughes, Thomas Smart, 171 n 15
Humboldt, Alexander von, 42
Humboldt, Wilhelm von, 42
Hume, David, 334, 612
Humphrey, Michael, 73 n 3, 76
Hunt, John, 94 n 5
Hunt, Leigh, 94 n 5, 534
Hunt, William Morris, 637
Huntington, Daniel, 249 n 21, 423
Huntington, Jedidiah Vincent, 423, 588
Hutchinson, Sarah, 166, 222, 368, 403

Idle Man, 189-90, 192, 195-201, 204, 231-32, 468, 542, 544, 596
Ingersoll, Charles J., 253 n 3
Inman, Henry, 300 n 2, 384 n 1, 398-99 n 6, 460, 462-63, 485
Inness, George, 576
Irving, Peter, 152, 160
Irving, Pierre, 560
Irving, Sarah Sanders, 174, 560
Irving, Washington: association with WA in Rome, 42, 559-60; in England, 120 n 7, 344, 560, 567, 579, 631; visits WA in Cambridgeport, 560; recollections of WA, 68, 80 n 4, 559-60, 637; *A History of New York*, 99, 100 n 2, 101, 108-09, 115-16, 116 n 2, 119, 143, 147-48, 202-03; *The Sketch Book*, 129, 152, 160, 169, 173, 188, 192, 196, 202-03; *Bracebridge Hall*, 192, 199, 201; *Abu-Hassan*, 224-25 n 1; *A History of the Life and Voyages of Columbus*, 286, 288; mentioned, 117 n 4, 155, 170 n 13, 320, 428, 542, 548, 556, 559-60. *See also WA–Leslie correspondence, passim*
Isabella, Queen of Castile, 286, 289 n 6
Isaiah, 184
Islington, 369, 390
Italy: general influence on WA, 387-88, 514; Italian authors known to WA, 48-49; references to in paintings, 44, 141 n 10, 162 n 1. *See also* WA, writings: *Monaldi;* "To the Author of 'The Diary of an Ennuyée'"; *cities by name*
Ives, Eli, 207
Ixien, 524

Jackson, Andrew, 253 n 3, 367, 629
Jackson, Charles, 176, 185, 192, 202
Jackson, Charles Thomas, 375 n 1
Jackson, John, 137
Jackson, Patrick T., 102, 240, 240, 337 n 11
Jackson, Tenn., 503
Jacob, Sarah H., 170 n 9
Jacobi, Friedrich H., 493 n 1, 628
James, George Payne Rainsford, 599
James, Henry, 106-07
James, John Thomas, 623
Jameson, Anna Brownell (Murphy), 114 n 7, 195 n 3, 402 nn 3, 4, 404 nn 1, 2, 4-6, 405 n 1, 415 n 2, 470 n 1, 487 n 4, 555, 560-61. *See also* WA, writings: "To the Author of 'The Diary of an Ennuyée'"
Jarves, James Jackson, 107
Jarvis, John Wesley, 560
Jarvis, Leonard: recollections of WA, 11 n 1, 14 n 1, 15 n 6, 20-24, 58-59, 68, 80 n 4, 191 n 11, 264 n 5, 332 n 9, 350 n 2, 543, 561, 575, 629; in England with WA, 80, 561; member of Committee on Public Buildings, 312 n 3, 320, 321 (#188) n 1, 358, 387, 392, 397, 630; mentioned, 19, 38, 79, 289 n 6; unrecovered letter to, 359 n 1, 394; unrecovered letter from, 383
Jarvis, Samuel Farmer, 156
Jefferson, Thomas, 16, 202
Jerdan, William, 196 n 3. *See also Literary Gazette*.
Jeremiah, 184
Jerrold, Douglas William, 599
Jersey, Lady, 212
Jesus Christ, 90-91, 92 n 3, 197, 210, 210-11 n 2, 224, 284, 625. *See also* WA, paintings
Joardaens, Jacob, 215, 278
Jocelyn, Nathaniel, 576
Johnson, Henry, 384 n 7
Johnson, Samuel, 599, 612, 616
Johnson, W.T., 87
Johnston, David Claypoole, 265 n 1, 295 n 1, 473 n 2, 636-37; portrait of WA, 636
Johnston, John, 58
Jones, George, 242
Josephine (ship), 434
Joy's Buildings, 304 nn 4, 5
Julien's Restaurant, 191
Justamond, John O., 38
Juvenal, 324

Karolsfield, Julius Schnorr von, 462, 477
Kaufman, Angela, 49
Kaulbach, Wilhelm von, 462, 477

Kean, Edmund, 129, 134. *See also* WA: writings: "On Kean's Hamlet"
Keats, John, 117 n 4
Kellogg, Miner Kilbourne, 490, 508
Kemble, Charles, 323-24, 631
Kemble, Frances, 323-24, 570, 631
Kemble, John, 30 n 19, 182 n 12, 631
Kentucky, 501
Keswick, 126, 145, 166, 447
King, Charles Bird, 539, 541, 564; portrait of WA, 527, 561
King, Emmeline (Edgeworth), 75
King, John, 64 (#24) n 2, 64, 64 n 3, 65, 69, 72, 171, 406, 561-62; WA's portrait of, 74
King, Mitchell, 335, 341
King, Samuel, 21, 58, 331
Kinloch, Cleland, 293
Kinloch, Francis: 293
Knapp, John, 51, 524, 562, 604, 631
Knapp, Samuel Lorenzo, 242
Knickerbocker Magazine, 70, 99, 101, 108, 423, 429, 437 n 1, 603
Knight, Richard Payne, 63 (#23) n 1
Koch, Joseph Anton, 41-42, 44
Krimmel, John Lewis, 582

Labouchere, Henry, 363
La Farge, John, 637
Lafayette, Marquis de, 103, 306
Lake Maggiore, 41, 191 n 11, 351-52
Lamb, Charles, 323, 566, 569-70, 573, 631
Lambrechtsen, Nicholas Cornelis, 155
Lambton, Lady, 188
Landi, Gaspare, 42
Landsdowne, Lord, 152, 160, 171
Landseer, Edwin Henry, 172
Lane, John Bryant, 87
Lanfranco, Giovanni, 43
Lanzi, Luigi Antonio, 509, 603
Laocoön, 30 n 19, 82 n 4, 590
Large, James or John, 150 n 25, 155
Las Casas, Bartholomé, 139, 142
Laurens, Edward R., 470
Lawrence, Samuel, 576
Lawrence, Thomas, 27, 30 n 19, 67, 181, 188, 189, 199 n 3, 202, 212, 280-81, 311, 344, 543, 562, 576, 631
Le Brun, Charles, 67, 167, 306
Lee, Hannah Farnham (Sawyer), 402 n 5, 623
Lee, Nathaniel, 18, 36 n 5
Lee, Samuel M., 251
Legare, Hugh Swinton, 454, 469, 516, 516 n 4, 554
Leghorn: WA in, 54-55; mentioned, 52, 53, 56, 56 n 11, 58, 81, 151, 451
Leicester, John Fleming, 137, 153
Leipzig, 596
Leo X, pope, 260
Leonardo da Vinci, 47, 249 n 21, 260, 551, 578, 584-86
Leopold I, grand duke of Tuscany, 272
Lesage, Alaine-René, 92 n 6, 617
Le Sieur, Eustache, 306
Leslie, Anna, 152, 172, 211, 280
Leslie, Bradford, 345, 498
Leslie, Caroline Anna, 279, 345, 498, 562-63
Leslie, Charles Robert: associations with and recollections of WA in England, 41, 45-46, 63 n 2, 66-67, 80 n 4, 82 nn 1, 4, 92 n 12, 94 n 3, 96 n 2, 117 n 4, 120 n 7, 122 nn 4, 5, 145-47, 533, 539, 541-42, 557, 561-64, 566-67, 569, 625, 629-30; in Paris, 110; requests of WA filled, 167, 169, 171, 174, 176, 192, 195, 198, 202-03, 218, 233-34, 275, 276 n 3, 497; portrait of WA, 563, 568; paintings by, commented on by WA, 65, 91, 93, 95, 295, 375, 378; sketches for *History of New York,* 108-09, 115-16, 119-20 n 1, 203-04; visit to America, 344, 345 n 18, 345-46; mentioned, 86-88, 103, 126, 140, 143, 149, 159, 163, 178, 295 n 1, 299, 542, 621; unrecovered letters to, 136, 160, 189, 243; unrecovered letters from, 196, 244
Leslie, Harriet (Stone), 230, 234, 279-80, 345, 498
Leslie, Harriet Jane, 279-80, 345, 498
Leslie, Lydia (Baker), 279
Leslie, Mary, 345
Leslie, Robert, 279
Leslie, Robert Charles, 230, 234, 279-80, 345, 498, 551-52, 560
Leusden, Jan, 8 (#4) n 2
Leutze, Emanuel, 460
Levenson-Gower, George Granville, 1st duke of Sutherland and 2d marquis of Stafford, 67, 114 n 7, 116, 117 n 6, 363, 558, 563, 630
Lewis, Charles, 184
Lewis, Frederick Christian, 161, 169, 184
Lewis, George Robert, 184
Lewis, Matthew Gregory, 594-95, 617

Linton, W.J., 297 n 2
Lion Theatre, 408
Litchfield, Enos, 295 n 4
Literary Gazette, 111 n 2, 181, 196
Literary Souvenir, 462
Literary World, 603
Little, Charles Coffin, 466-68, 534, 563, 596
Livensz, Jan, 167, 169 n 5
Liverpool: WA in, 59-60, 88; mentioned, 24, 159, 189-90, 199, 233, 478, 497, 506, 536, 560
Liverpool, Lord, 152
Livingston, Edward, 320, 357
Livius, Titus, 614
Lloyd, John, 96
Lockhart, John Gibson, 357 n 1
Logan, George, 153 n 12
London: WA in (1801-03), 15 n 4, 19, 21, 23, 25-29 nn 1, 16, 30 (#11) n 21, 31-36, 37 n 1, 43, 88 n 4, 333-34, 338, 342-43, 534, 548, 575, 579, 581, 584, 588, 615-16, 619, 621, 624 n 3; WA in (1811-18), 46, 60, 60 n 1, 62, 62 n 2, 63 (#23) n 2, 64-65 n 1, 66-67, 69-72, 70-83, 89-97, 99-120, 145, 182 n 13, 227, 235 n 6, 241, 251 n 1, 280-81, 281 n 10, 323, 353-54, 364, 388, 465, 491 n 5, 493 n 6, 497, 534, 538-39, 546-47, 550, 557-58, 560-63, 565, 567, 569, 578, 597, 623, 625, 629-30; mentioned, 390, 401, 409, 460, 554-55
London Courier, 75
Londonderry, Marquis of, 188
London Magazine, 201 n 4, 323 n 5
London Packet, 167
Long, Samuel Pierce, 256, 275
Long, William, 152
Longacre, James, 57, 563, 568
Longfellow, Henry Wadsworth, 429, 455 n 2, 475 n 5, 481, 502, 510, 510 n 1, 510-11 n 4, 563-64, 577, 596, 600, 607
Longman, Hurst, Rees, and Orm, publishers, 167, 171, 302
Lonsdale, James, 87, 129, 169, 173, 184, 199, 204, 213, 215, 541, 564
Loring, Edward G., 265 n 1
Lorrain, Claude. *See* Gelée, Claude
Lough, John Graham, 259
Lowell, Anna Cabot, 59, 593
Lowell, Charles, 46, 59, 240, 375, 607, 626
Lowell, Francis Cabot, 450 n 3
Lowell, James Russell, 107, 170 n 9, 565-66, 575, 607, 629
Lowell, John (1769-1840), 147 n 8, 409
Lowell, John (1799-1836), 450 n 3
Lowell, John Amory, 450 n 3
Lucas (ship), 495
Lucius Verus, 254
Lucretius, 359
Lunnell, Eliza (Visger), 71
Lunnell, George, 71
Lunnell, Samuel, 71
Lydia (ship), 59
Lyman, Theodore, 138 n 1, 170 n 10, 238
Lynn, Mass., 511

McCall, Richard, 272
McCleland (or McClelland), Thomas, 227
McKean, Joseph, 164
Mackaye, Steele, 631
McLane, Louis, 357, 359, 362
McMurtrie, James, Sr.: interest in art, 149-50, 154-55, 163-64, 178-79; mentioned, 324, 461, 513, 566; unrecovered letters to, 38 n 1, 128, 130; unrecovered letters from, 149, 165, 399, 500-501. *See also* WA, paintings: *The Dead Man Restored,* sale of; *Mother Watching Her Sleeping Child*
McMurtrie, James, Jr., 150, 460, 462, 485
McMurtrie, Mrs. James, Sr., 98, 149
McMurtrie, William B., 150
Macomber, Charles, 19
McPherson, James, 616
Macready, William Charles, 234, 235 n 6, 631
Madison, James, 202
Magnolia, 304 n 6, 598-99
Malbone, Edward Greene, 27, 29 n 16, 80 n 4, 331, 333-34, 338; portrait of WA, 566
Mann, Horace, 265 n 1
Manrique, Jorge, 437
Margary, Maria (West), 281, 281 n 10
Margary, Thomas George, 281
Maria Christina, queen of Spain, 368 n 2
Marion, Francis, 389, 389 n 5, 411, 531
Market Hall, 295 n 1
Marlboro' Hotel, 145
Marmontel, Jean François, 142
Marsh, James, 492, 626
Marshall, John, 410
Marsoli, Luigi, 41
Martin, John, 82 n 3, 87, 103, 105, 137, 152, 169, 171 n 15, 172, 184, 189-90, 191 n 11, 199, 204, 204 n 7, 444-45, 566

Martinez y Sorli, Crisóstorno Alejandrino José, 255
Mary Magdalene, 17
Mary Stuart, queen of Scots, 272
Mason, Isabella (Cowpland), 240, 370, 567
Mason, Jonathan, Sr., 304, 304 n 8
Mason, Jonathan, Jr., 103, 105, 200-201, 203-04, 238, 240, 266, 323, 370, 386, 566-67
Mason, William Powell, 350, 351 n 3, 354, 432 (#270) n 1
Massachusetts Centinel, 23
Massachusetts General Hospital, 134, 138 n 1, 141 n 11, 151-52, 159, 160, 160 n 5, 161 n 1, 168, 175, 563
Mather, Cotton, 143, 354
Mathews, Charles, 570, 631
Maturin, Charles Robert, 617
Maxwell, Joseph William, 38, 40, 51, 129
Mazzuoli (or Mazzola), Girolamo Francesco Maria (called Parmigiano), 352
Melodeon Theatre, 632
Melpomene, 34
Mengs, Anthony Raphael, 43, 339, 433
Mercer, John, 38
Merchants' Bank, 473
Merchants' Insurance Co., 473-74
Merchant Tailors' Hall, 73. *See also* Bristol Exhibition
Merry, Robert, 616
Metastasio, Pietro Trapassi, 48, 427, 632
Mexico, 325-26
Meyer, Henry, 202
Michelangelo Buonarroti, 585-86; WA's admiration of, 17, 24, 28-29, 68, 210, 229, 249 n 21, 286, 352, 480, 538, 554, 558-59, 585-86, 588, 621; WA influenced by, 67, 175 n 3, 241, 286; WA compared to, by critics, 66, 170 n 9, 238, 423-24, 428, 430 n 17, 571, 578; references to, in WA's writings, 24, 41, 43, 47, 68, 182 n 12, 584-86, 589, 596, 600-601; poems about, 42, 585, 594, 613; mentioned, 61, 242, 260-61, 278, 399-400, 513, 546, 551
Middleton, John, 171, 174, 199
Miesse, Gabriel, 251
Migliorini, Mr., 52-53
Milan, 41
Miller, J.M., 77-78
Mills, James K., 205
Milton, John, 14 n 1, 23, 26, 68, 82 n 3, 116, 119, 281, 338-39, 343, 410, 428, 551, 554, 566, 616. *See also* WA, paintings
Milton Gallery, 338, 616
Minerva (ship), 12
Minot, Mary, 402 n 5
Minot, William, and Mrs., 402 n 5
Mirabeau, comte de, 617
Mitchell, Edward, 468, 470
Mitchell, Mary (Moore), 469 n 8
Mohammed, 18
Mola, Pietro Francesco, 246
Molière, 137, 183
Monkhouse, John, 562
Monroe, James, 38, 148, 151, 169, 202
Montagu, Basil, 493 n 6
Montanus, Benedictus Arias, 8 (#4) n 2
Mont Blanc, 40-41, 250 n 25
Mont Cenis, 305
Montgomery, James, 594
Monthly Anthology, 33 n 2, 57
Monthly Magazine, 197 n 3
Monthly Miscellany of Religion and Letters, 597
Monthly Review, 196
Mont Pilat, 40
Moore, Anna, 293 n 3
Moore, Elizabeth (Vanderhorst), 439, 440 n 3, 441, 452, 455, 457, 459 n 4, 470-71, 473, 489, 494-95
Moore, Elizabeth Margaret, 440 n 3
Moore, Harriett, 440 n 3, 458 n 4
Moore, John (author of *Zeluco,*) 334
Moore, John (WA's grandfather), 440 n 3
Moore, John Elias, 7 (#1) n 1, 36 n 1, 440 n 3
Moore, Rachel. *See* Flagg, Rachel (Moore) Allston
Moore, Sarah, 440 n 3
Moore, Thomas, 182 n 11, 188
Morgan, John J., 75, 85, 122, 129, 137, 153, 161, 169, 184, 192, 199, 204, 355 n 12, 567, 582
Morgan, Mary, 64, 85, 161, 169, 184, 189, 192, 199, 204, 567
Morland, George, 242
Morning Chronicle, 62 n 1, 67, 73
Morning Herald, 116 n 2, 117 n 4, 302
Morning Post, 97 n 8, 552
Morpeth, Lord, 471, 510, 558-59
Morris, Apollos, 350
Morris, George Pope, 37
Morse, Alpheus, 572

Morse, Elizabeth Ann (Breese), 72, 80, 208
Morse, Henry Dutton, 329 (#197) n 1
Morse, Jedidiah, 208, 567
Morse, Lucretia (Pickering), 134, 208
Morse, Samuel Finley Breese: association with WA in England, 59-60, 70-72, 72 n 3, 79-80 (#34) nn 1, 2, 4, 82 n 4, 93, 523, 539, 541, 557, 562-63, 567-68, 625, 629, 531; praised and recommended by WA, 71-72, 79-80, 148, 169, 207-08, 229, 288, 364, 386-87, 392, 398; as pupil and admirer of WA, 60, 288, 340 n 20; activities in Charleston, 133, 151, 258 n 6; as president of NAD, 141 n 13, 236, 251, 252 n 5, 265, 276, 345-46, 387, 568; in Boston and Cambridgeport, 104, 145 n 2, 169, 204 n 10, 339, 340 n 20, 344 n 2, 366, 394, 395 n 3, 568; in New Haven, 201 n 1, 206-07; messages to WA from Europe, 274, 279, 306, 323, 561, 563, 567-68, 579-80; messages to WA by Leslie, 129, 138, 153, 200, 231; at WA's death, 252 n 5, 523, 568; unrecovered letters to, 135, 423; unrecovered letters from, 423
Moultrie, William, 255-56, 263, 264 n 3, 293
Mount, William Sidney, 364
Mount Auburn Cemetery, 39, 520, 536, 574
Moxon, Edward, 466, 596
Mozart, Wolfgang Amadeus, 587, 599, 632
Mulready, William, 188
Mumford, William, 617
Murillo, Bartolomé Esteban, 450 n 3
Murray, John, 188, 196
Museum of Fine Arts, 424-25

Napoleon Bonaparte, 21-22, 39, 260, 272, 281, 541, 629-30
Napoleonic Wars, 45, 54
Napier, William Francis Patrick, 242
Naples, 47-78
Natchitoches, La., 297
Natick, Mass., 408
National Academy of Design: WA exhibited at, 252 n 6, 269, 297 n 2, 304 n 4, 318, 319 n 3, 434 (#271) n 6, 506-07, 568, 575; WA honorary member, 252 n 6; mentioned, 97 n 1. *See also* Morse, Samuel Finley Breese
National Advocate, 156
National Gallery of Art, 532
National Gazette and Literary Register, 324
National Portrait Gallery of Distinguished Americans, 346
Neagle, John, 68, 287, 381 n 1, 501, 563, 568, 576
Neal, John, 214 n 1, 332, 594-95, 607
Nehemiah, 607
Newburgh, N.Y., 572
New England Art Union, 176 n 3
New Englander, 603
New-England Magazine, 427
New England Museum, 103
New Hampshire, 513
New Haven, Conn., 58, 200, 207, 208 n 2, 452, 548-49, 582, 628
Newman, John, 276
New Mirror, 265 n 1, 636
New Monthly Magazine and Universal Repository, 111 n 1, 161 n 6, 168, 173, 196, 197 n 3
Newport, R.I.: WA in, 7, 7 n 1, 8, 8 (#3) n 3, (#4) nn 1, 9, 10, 10 n 1, 11 n 1, 14-19, 21, 23, 162, 197-98, 303-04, 331, 332 n 1, 531, 535-36, 574; relatives and friends in, 42, 351 (#209) n 2, 392, 438, 457, 530, 532-33, 535-36, 549, 561, 566, 580, 625, 636
Newport Mercury, 10 n 1
Newton, Gilbert Stuart, 103, 137, 148, 370, 460-61, 511, 569. *See also WA–Leslie correspondence, passim*
Newton, Isaac, 14 n 1
New York, N.Y.: WA's departures and arrivals, 54, 59; acquaintances and connections in, 395, 398, 423, 442, 504, 514, 534, 572, 579; mentioned, 460. *See also* National Academy of Design
New York American, 147, 155
New York Evening Post, 106, 524, 534, 568
New York Evening Signal, 564
New-York Historical Society, 138, 142, 143 n 2, 144, 147, 156, 548
New-York Mirror, 265 n 1, 320, 394-95, 395-96 n 1, 396-98, 429, 435, 563
New-York Review, 454, 597
New York Tribune, 117 n 6, 524, 543, 572
Neyer, John Adam, 477
Nichol, John Pringle, 250 n 23
Nicholas I, emperor of Russia, 446
Nicholson, William, 628
Niles' Weekly Register, 311 n 27
Noah, Mordecai Manuel, 157 n 12

Norfolk, Va., 269 n 1
Normanby, Marquis of, 266
North American Review, 139, 140 n 8, 155, 166, 238-39, 424, 444-45, 524, 533, 544, 547, 563, 569, 600, 603
Northcote, James, 27, 162, 569-70
Norton, Andrews, 253, 524, 569, 626
Norton, Charles Eliot, 569, 607
Noyes, Moody, 23
Nugent, Thomas, 38
Nuova Roccolta delle pire belle veduta di Roma, 46

Oakley, Paul, 82 n 1
Odevarre, Joseph Dionysius, 62, 79, 82
Ogilvie, James, 117 n 10, 129
Ohio (ship), 451
Old Masters, 43, 71, 183, 198-99, 229, 247, 249 n 21, 371, 423, 537, 563. *See also individual artists by name*
Old South Meeting House, 364, 408
Olevano, 41, 44, 46, 538, 589
Olympia, 34
Opie, John, 27, 92, 112, 600
Orleans Collection, 81
Ossian, 616
Ossoli, Margaret (Fuller), 48, 425-26, 428, 430 n 17, 432 (#269) n 1, 433 (#270) n 1, 524, 536-37, 597, 609
Ostade, Adrian, 248, 364, 365 n 10, 591
Otis, Harrison Gray, 110
Otway, Thomas, 631
Overbeck, Johann Friedrich, 463 n 7, 625
Owen, John, 475
Owen, Samuel, 181
Oxford, 63 (#24) n 2

Pactolus River, 505
Paganini, Nicolò, 632
Page, William, 107, 635
Paine, Thomas, 22, 541
Paley, William, 628
Palfrey, John Gorham, 569; letter to, 444-45
Palladio, Andrea, 111 n 2
Palma, Giacomo Negretti, 578
Pampaloni, Luigi, 305
Panthea (ship), 243-44
Para, Mme, 371 n 11
Paris: WA in, 38-40, 77-78, 110, 116, 117 n 4, 343-44, 542, 558, 563, 565, 569, 579, 584, 588, 619, 621; WA Exhibition in, 77
Paris Salon, 77
Parker, Anna (Moore); 293 n 3
Parker, George Philips, 292
Parker, Theodore, 550
Parker, William, 336
Parkman, Dr. Francis, 523
Parkman, Rev. Francis, 494, 608
Parkman, George, 494 n 1
Parmigiano, 352
Parnaso e gli Italiani Viventi, 49
Parnassus, 18, 117, 416
Parris, Alexander, 294, 606
Parris, Samuel, 416
Parsons, Thomas W., 607
Partridge, Alden, 569
Paterson, Hugh, 15, 31, 36 n 1, 133, 569
Paterson, John, 31
Paul, Jeremiah, 23
Paul, Judge, 18
Paulino dos Reis, Maximo, 62, 79, 82
Payne, John Howard, 68, 80 n 4, 129, 134, 276, 433, 569-70, 629, 637
Peabody, Elizabeth (Palmer), 524, 607, 609, 625
Peabody, Elizabeth Palmer, 47, 117 n 6, 245 n 2, 321 n 3, 416 (#264) n 1, 422-23, 426-28, 430 n 4, 536, 541, 556-57, 570-72
Peabody, Sophia Amelia. *See* Hawthorne, Sophia Amelia (Peabody)
Peale, Rembrandt, 88 n 4, 178, 179, 179 n 2, 218, 270, 273, 384 n 1
Peale, Rubens, 88, 88 nn 1, 4, 89
Peck, George Washington, 598-600, 603
Pelton, Oliver, 492
Pendleton, John B., 218, 392-93, 574
Penn, William, 139
Pennsylvania Academy of Fine Arts: WA exhibited at, 67, 88, 89 n 5, 92 n 6, 96, 97 n 4, 140 n 10, 176 n 3, 269 n 2, 272, 485, 637; mentioned 155, 460. *See also* WA, paintings: *The Dead Man Restored*, sale of
Pensacola, Fla., 257, 532
Pepoon, Benjamin F., 572
Percival, James Gates, 103
Percy Chapel, 211
Pergolesi, Giovanni Battista, 632
Pericles, 270, 614
Perkins, Jacob, 173
Perkins, James, 102
Perkins, Stephen Higginson, 527
Perkins, Thomas Handasyd, Sr., 102, 141

n 11, 175 n 3, 238, 240, 242, 378, 527, 572, 578
Perkins, Thomas Handasyd, Jr., 102
Perry, Oliver Hazard, 133
Persia, 322 n 3
Peru, 18
Perugino, 271
Pessuti, Giocchino, 42
Peter I of Russia ("The Great"), 389
Petronius, 614
Petty-Fitz, Henry, third marquis of Lansdowne, 152, 160, 171
Petworth, 120, 120 n 6, 212, 583
Phi Beta Kappa Society, 103, 474 n 2, 534, 593
Phidias, 359, 428
Philadelphia, Pennsylvania: WA's friends and relatives in, 308, 439, 441, 499, 562-63, 568, 577. *See also* Pennsylvania Academy of Fine Arts; *WA–McMurtrie correspondence, passim*
Phillips, Jonathan, 349-50, 384 n 2, 432, 432 (#270) n 1, 500
Phillips, Richard, 197 n 3
Phillips, Thomas, 128-29, 136, 181, 212, 488 n 6
Phillips, Willard, 534
Phillips, William, 380, 563
Phipps, Constantine Henry, first marquis of Normanby, 266
Phoebus. *See* Apollo
Pickering, Henry, 114 n 7, 138 n 1, 160 n 5, 170 n 9, 247 n 1, 342 n 1, 572-73, 589, 619
Piles, Roger de, 622
Pilkington, Matthew, 342
Pine, Robert Edge, 22, 332
Pinto, Ferdinão, 618
Piombo, Sebastiano del, 61, 66, 241
Pioneer, 575, 607
Piranesi, Giovanni Battista, 461-62
Piroli, Thomas, 302 n 5
Pisa, 53, 151, 480
Pius VII (pope), 259
Platner, Ernest, 49 n 14, 598
Plato, 352
Plato (ship), 233
Pliny the Elder, 614
Plumer, William J., 628
Plutarch, 31 n 25
Poe, Edgar Allan, 474 n 2, 488 n 3, 579, 607
Poinsett, Joel Roberts, 325, 335, 341, 389
Poniatowski, Jozef, 259
Pope, Alexander, 34, 345 n 7, 502, 594, 609, 616
Pople, W., 593
Poquelin, Jean Baptiste (Molière), 137, 183
Porter, George Washington, 573
Porter, Noah, 603
Port Folio, 70
Portico, 159, 594
Portsmouth, R.I., 551
Poussin, Gaspar, 43, 46, 74, 246, 589
Poussin, Nicolas, 25, 39, 43, 45-46, 74, 213, 231, 246, 271, 306, 405 n 2, 480 (#316) n 1, 589
Powers, Hiram, 367, 409-10, 413, 508, 525
Pozzi, Andrea, 184
Pratt, Henry Cheever, 208, 209 n 14
Preble, Edward, 235 n 5
Preble, Henry, 234
Prentiss, George Lewis, 488, 494
Prescott, William Hickling, 319, 455 n 2, 559, 564, 579
Preston, John Smith, 413
Preston, William Campbell, 383-84, 384 n 6, 392, 413
Prince, John, 153 n 1, 160 n 7, 295 n 1
Prior, Matthew, 594
Protogenes, 46
Providence, R.I., 139
Providence College, 7
Putnam, Aaron Fall, 18-19
Putnam, George Palmer, 502 n 4
Putnam's Monthly Magazine, 565
Pyrenees, 622
Pythagoras, 614

Quadruple or *Quarto Notion*, 573
Quarterly Review, 146, 502
Quincy, Edmund S., 59, 114 n 7, 318 n 12, 404 n 6, 573
Quincy, Josiah, 59, 114 n 7, 139, 253, 268 n 13, 402 n 5, 474 n 2, 500; and family, 524, 573, 630

Raczynski, Athanasius, 462, 477, 524, 573, 600, 603
Radcliffe, Ann (Ward), 21, 68, 296, 297 n 2, 599
Radcliffe, Mr., 318
Radicofani, 463-64
Rae, Alexander, 631
Raimbach, Abraham, 163
Ramage, John, 323

Ramsgate, 161
Raphael Sanzio, 586-87; WA's admiration of, 17, 24, 28-29, 43, 68, 75, 286, 305, 352, 365 n 10, 371, 388, 462-63, 480, 488 n 6, 538, 558, 591, 600-601, 613, 632; WA influenced by, 45, 62 n 2, 82 n 4, 111 n 2, 241, 415 n 2, 588; WA compared to, by critics, 67, 98, 111 n 2, 170 n 9, 340 n 20, 423, 430 n 17, 568, 583; references to, in WA's writings, 24, 43, 68, 182 n 12, 242, 248, 584-86, 589, 596; WA's poems about, 42, 586, 594, 600-601; mentioned, 57, 187, 260-61, 271-72, 428, 551
Raub(?), J.B., 124
Read, Thomas Buchanan, 473 n 2, 636
Reed, Henry Hope, 499, 509 (#354) n 1, 545, 573
Reed, J.T., 265 n 1
Reed, Luman, 364, 380, 381 n 4, 548
Regnault, Henri, 425
Rehoy, Mrs. 121
Reinagle, Hugh, 103
Reinhart, Johan C., 41
Religious Souvenir, 391 n 1
Rembrandt van Rijn, 58, 60 n 3, 61, 101 n 2, 102, 111, 231, 242, 379, 412, 418, 450 n 3, 591, 624 n 4
Reni, Guido, 17, 62, 88, 98, 111, 584, 587-88
Retzsch, Friedrich August Maritz, 501, 615
Reynolds, Edward J., 219, 625
Reynolds, Joshua, 589-91; WA's admiration of, 120 n 6, 146, 168, 244, 379; WA influenced by, 39, 60 (#21) n 3, 146, 163 n 2, 217, 405 n 2, 584, 589-91, 619-22; WA compared to, by critics, 578, 603; *Discourses,* 34, 170 n 9, 216, 245 n 5, 246-47, 248 nn 8, 11, 13, 14, 16, 249 nn 17, 18, 22, 250 n 22, 24, 335 n 14, 337-38, 352, 361, 388, 621-22, 623 n 1, 624 nn 4, 6; references to, in WA's writings, 68, 242; biography of, 162; mentioned, 105, 201 n 4, 390, 546, 550, 580
Rhode Island College, 7
Ricci, Stefano, 270
Richardson, Eben, 8
Richardson, Edgar Preston, 637
Richmond Hill, 152
Riepenhausen, Franz, 42, 227
Riepenhausen, Johann, 42, 227
Rigeway, Mr., 169
Ritchie, Mrs. Edward S., 511
Rizzio, David, 272
Roberts, George, 451 n 1, 573
Robertson, Alexander, 574; letter to, 118; letter from, 115
Roberts' Semi-Monthly Magazine for Town and Country, 573
Robinson, Henry Crabbe, 562
Roderigo Visigoth king, 23
Rogers, Ann, 532
Rogers, Mary (Channing), 148
Rogers, Robert (of Boston), 149 n 9, 303
Rogers, Robert (of Newport), 7 (#1) n 1, 21, 532, 574
Rogers, Samuel, 503, 555, 597
Rogers, William S., 131, 141
Rolls, Charles, 100 n 2, 204 n 1
Romantic tradition, WA's affiliation with, 540-41. *See also* WA: artistic philosophy; WA: supernatural, interest in
Rome: WA in, 38, 41-46, 48, 51-52, 54, 55 nn 6, 10, 56, 75, 79, 151, 182 n 9, 254 n 1, 266, 352-53, 399, 430 n 14, 538-40, 563, 569, 579-80, 621, 624 n 3; WA on his stay in, 46, 388, 490; references to, in WA's writings, 16-17; mentioned, 255-57, 409, 461, 485, 578-79. *See also* WA, paintings: *Evening Hymn; A Roman Lady Reading;* WA, writings: "Procrastination Is the Thief of Time"; "On the Domes of the State House"
Romney, John, 100 n 2, 204 n 1
Rosa, Salvatore, 24, 27, 41, 43, 111, 175, 234, 242, 246, 250 nn 22, 579, 588, 618
Roscoe, Thomas, 509 n 2
Ross, Robert, 84
Rotterdam, 38
Rouillard's Restaurant, 233 n 3, 563, 568
Rover, Henry, 392-93
Rowe, Nicholas, 615
Rowney, T., 60
Roxbury, Mass., 384, 635
Royal Academy of Art: WA student at, 28, 29 n 1, 30 n 21, 62 n 1, 81, 146, 242, 337-38, 342-43; as associate member, 126, 128-30, 134-36, 144-45, 152, 161, 169, 171, 173, 187, 203, 204 n 6, 231, 234, 243; considered for full membership, 120 n 7, 173, 198, 199 n 3, 363; exhibited at, 74, 92 nn 6, 7, 10, 94 n 4, 111 n 2, 117 n 4, 157, 160, 302 n 1, 331, 338, 578; mentioned, 80, 172, 177, 180-81, 200, 208, 301, 338, 497, 534,

550, 552, 559, 562, 581, 589, 600, 623. *See also* Somerset House; *WA–Leslie correspondence, passim*
Royal Exchange, 31
Royal Footstool, 493
Rubens, Peter Paul, 21, 38-49, 105, 117 n 5, 231, 242, 371, 379-80, 450 n 3, 591-92, 621
Rudiments of Ancient Architecture, 49
Rumohr, Karl Friedrich, 42, 46
Ruskin, John, 547, 603
Russell, John, sixth duke of Bedford, 231
Russell, Lucy (Channing), 148
Russell, Thomas, 53
Russell, William Washington, 149 n 10
Rutledge, Mary (Shubrick) Eveleigh, 134
Rutledge, Sarah, 134
Rydal Mount, 116 n 7

Sabatelli, Francesco, 272
St. Francis of Assisi, 48
St. Gotthard Pass, 40
St. Januarius, 48
St. Louis, Mo., 383
St. Luke's Academy, 42
St. Paul's Episcopal Church, 157 n 11, 524, 625
St. Petersburg, Russia, 389
St. Thomas' Parish, S.C., 15, 15 n 3, 224
St. Rosalia, 48
Salem, Mass., 416, 428, 556, 572
Salem Gazette, 164, 170 n 9, 422, 571
Salisbury, Abby (Breese): 382 (#232) n 2
Salisbury, Edward Elbridge, 381
Salisbury, Josiah, 382 (#232) n 2
Salter, Mrs. Richard, 602
Salvi, Giovanni Battista (Sassoferrato), 179
Sand, George, 599
Sargent, Henry, 133, 286, 473 n 2, 574
Sargent, Lucius Manlius, 70, 103, 299
Sartain, John, 470 n 1, 487
Sartain's Union Magazine of Literature and Art, 470 n 1, 603
Sarti, Antonio, 242
Sassoferrato, 179
Saunders, Charles H., 631
Savage, James, 375 n 1, 477, 486
Savannah, Ga., 578
Schadow, Friedrich Wilhelm, 463 n 7, 477
Schick, Gottlieb, 41-42
Schiller, John Christoph Friedrich von, 21, 437
schools of painting, WA on: admiration of Italian, 584-88, 630; distaste for French, 39, 145, 556, 630; identification with English, 146, 183, 245, 445, 630; reservations about Dutch and Flemish, 371, 584, 591; praise of contemporary German, 462, 477, 491 n 5; influence on contemporary German, 554, 588
Scientific Journal, 572-73
Scollay, Catherine, 303-04, 574
Scollay, Mrs. William, 303-04
Scotland, 539, 622
Scott, Walter, 161, 192, 193 n 1, 196, 222, 295, 329 (#197) n 1, 335, 341, 348, 356, 372, 375-76, 437, 563, 574, 594, 599
Scriven, Edward, 202
Sears, David, 102, 141 n 11, 182 n 11, 238, 240, 371 n 11, 409
Sears, Miriam (Sears), 182 n 11, 371 n 11
Sebastiano del Piombo, 66
Seguier, John, 159
Seguier, William, 159
Seneca, M. Anneus, 10 n 6
Severn, Joseph, 259, 490, 491 n 5
Severn, The, (ship), 95
Sewall, Stephen, 11 n 4
Shakespeare, William: WA influenced by, 68, 614-15, 617; references to, in WA's writings, 9, 14 n 1, 182 n 12, 595, 615, 631; references to Benedick, 300; references to Falstaff, 19; editions of, 612, 615; performances seen, 182 n 13, 231, 325 n 1, 631; quoted, 24, 65, 245, 353, 477, 505; mentioned, 306, 308, 428, 544, 550. *See also* WA, paintings
Sharp, William (archbishop), 187
Sharp, William (painter), 574
Shattuck, Eliza Cheever (Davis), 574
Shattuck, George Cheyne, Jr., 524
Shattuck, George Cheyne, Sr., 219 n 1, 408 n 3, 524, 574
Shaw, Lemuel, 524
Shee, Martin Archer, 623
Shenstone, William, 595
Shepard Congregational Society, Church of, 424, 447 (#283) n 1, 482, 530, 574, 605, 625
Shewen, Harriet Cooper (Vanderhorst), 37 n 3
Shewen, Henry Thomas, 37 n 3
Shubrick, William B., 542
Siddons, Sarah (Kemble), 570, 631
Siena, 41, 49-51, 463-64
Signiora P—, 17

Sigourney, Lydia Moward (Huntley), 447, 447 n 1, 574
Silliman, Benjamin, 207, 208 n 2, 374, 374-75 n 1
Simmons, Anne, 531
Simms, William Gilmore, 451 n 1, 595, 598-99, 631
Skipworth, Fulwar, 55
Smibert, John, 22, 58, 332
Smith, Barney, 72
Smith, Catherine, 232, 265
Smith, Charles, 434
Smith, John Raphael, 342
Smith, John Rowson, 251
Smith, John Rubens, 255, 575
Smith, William, 292
Society of the Cincinnati, 548-49
Society of Painters in Oil, 338
Somerset House, 91, 93, 129, 169, 172, 180, 198, 206, 211-13, 331, 338. *See also* Royal Academy of Art
South Carolina: WA's references to, 327-30, 333, 346, 476, 452, 476; mentioned, 407, 546
South Carolina Academy of Arts, 257, 258 n 6
Southern Literary Messenger, 488, 488 n 2, 581, 597-98, 600
Southern Quarterly Review, 595, 598-99
Southey, Robert, 21, 45, 64 (#24) n 2, 75, 123, 126-27, 145-46, 166, 403 n 1, 475, 475 n 4, 576, 578, 580, 594
Spalding, 576; letter to, 144; letter from, 138
Sparks, Jared, 156 n 10, 375 n 1, 402 n 5
Spear, Thomas Truman, 105, 165 n 4, 473 n 2, 584
Spencer, Elihu, 524
Spenser, Edmund, 33, 148, 162 n 2, 181, 572, 612, 615-16. *See also* WA, paintings
Spring Gardens, 67, 338
Staël, Anne Louise Germaine Necker, baronne de Staël-Holstein, 42
Stafford, Marquis of. *See* Levenson-Gower, George Granville
Staigg, Richard Murrell, 473 n 2, 636
Stark, James, 126, 146
Steen, Jan Havicksz, 364, 591
Steinhauser, Friedrich Wilhelm George, 461
Stephanoff, Francis Philip, 137
Stevens, Mr., 325 n 4
Steward, Joseph, 103
Stewart, Charles William, third marquis of Londonderry, 188
Stewart, William A., 97
Stockard von Bernkopf, Joseph Otto, 62, 79, 82
Stocker, Sarah, 379
Storer, James, 63 (#23) n 2
Story, Joseph, 452, 516, 524, 576, 578
Story, William Wetmore, 107, 452, 575-76, 607
Stothard, Thomas, 176, 488 n 6, 503
Strouzer, Mr., 343
Stuart, Daniel, 97 n 8
Stuart, Elizabeth (Coates), 392-93, 396
Stuart, Gilbert: WA's praise of, 27, 131, 133, 145, 202, 218, 257, 339; association with WA, 322-23, 343, 563, 568, 576; and exhibition of paintings by, 257, 257 n 5, 547, 558, 576-77; prices of, 114 n 7; portraits of WA, 378 (#228) n 1, 576-77; and *Belshazzar's Feast,* 102, 106; WA's concern for family of, 392, 393 nn 4, 5; mentioned, 24, 56, 92 n 8, 200, 250 n 1, 290, 311, 321 (#188) n 1, 323, 390, 409, 555, 569, 580. *See also* WA, writings: "The Late Mr. Stuart"; "Notice"
Stuart, Jane, 392
Sturgis, Mrs. George W., 238
Suetonius, 31 n 24
Suffolk Bank, 161, 449
Sullivan, George, 42
Sullivan, Richard, 42
Sullivan, William, 112, 238
Sully, Sarah (Annis), 324
Sully, Thomas: and sale of *The Dead Man Restored,* 83, 89, 95; and exhibition of paintings by WA, 98-99, 131, 133; in Boston, 103, 190, 191, 191 n 5, 294 n 1, 380-81 nn 1, 6, 577; unrecovered letter from, 325; mentioned, 45, 92 nn 6, 7, 128, 152, 154, 163, 165, 178, 218, 233, 253 n 3, 285, 288, 332, 384, 460, 463, 471, 485, 487, 501, 546, 577, 589, 599
Sumner, Charles, 265 n 1, 403, 403 n 1, 450 n 3, 491, 516, 524, 542, 558-59, 564, 575-78
Sumner, William Hyslop, 19
Sun, 75
Surrey Institution, 129
Sutherland, Duchess of, 558
Sutherland, Duke of. *See* Levenson-Gower, George Granville

Sweetser, Moses, cited: 21, 36 n 1, 43, 45, 58, 63 (#24) n 2, 75, 99 n 6, 102, 117 n 6, 122, 133, 153 n 2, 182 n 11, 191 n 11, 233 n 3, 235 n 4, 241, 294 n 1, 337 n 11, 440 n 2, 524, 531-32, 548, 550, 559-60, 569-70, 578, 581, 584, 588, 625, 627, 629, 632, 636
Swett, Samuel, 310 n 25
Swift, Jonathan, 10 n 2, 594
Switzerland: WA in, 40, 44, 351-52, 621, 624 n 3. *See also* Alps; *cities by name*

Talford, Thomas Noon, 562
Talfourd, Sergeant, 394 n 1
Talisman, 97 n 1
Tangent (character in play), 276
Tappan, Charles, 276
Tasso, Torquato, 48, 240, 321-22 n 3, 612
Taste: A Suggestive Essay by "Discipulus," 628
Taylor, John Duncombe, 36, 578
Taylor, Mary Cooper (Vanderhorst), 36, 578
Taylor, Mr., 7
Taylor, Tom, 74
Tefft, Israel Keech, 578
Teniers, David, 450 n 3
Tennyson, Alfred, first baron, 599
Thalia, 295 n 1
Thespis, 10
Theus, James Jeremiah, 440 n 3
Thom, James, 341
Thomas, Moses, 116 n 2
Thompson, Henry, 199 n 3
Thompson, John, 146, 184
Thomson, James, 13 (#8) n 1, 19-21, 23, 593, 616
Thomson, Col. James, 409
Thorndike, Augustus, 342 n 1
Thornwell, James Henley, 598
Thorwaldsen, Bertel, 226-27, 259-60, 271, 423, 461, 516
Tibaldi, Pellegrino, 41, 122 n 1
Ticknor, Ann (Eliot), 298, 377
Ticknor, George, 102-05, 152, 166, 240, 319, 335, 341, 348, 356, 375, 384 n 4, 454-55 n 2, 470 n 10, 516 n 4, 563-64, 578-79
Times (London), 117 n 4
Tintoretto, Jacopo Robusti, 242, 255, 343, 371, 588, 621
Titans, 110
Titian: admired by WA, 39, 41, 246, 343, 371, 379-80, 562, 584, 588, 619; WA influenced by, 39, 41, 44, 148 n 4, 241, 427, 484-85, 487, 612 (*see also* WA, paintings: *The Adoration of the Magi; The Sisters*); WA compared to, by critics, 46, 62 n 2, 105, 238, 424, 430 n 17, 503, 578, 634; WA called "The American Titian," 179 n 2, 191, 355 n 9, 588; referred to in WA's writings, 242, 297 n 4, 587, 621; admired by Greenough, 261, 267, 273, 278; mentioned, 231, 581, 635
Token, 267, 269 n 2, 365, 457 n 1
Tomlin, John, 579
Torlonia, Giovanni, 54
Torso Belvedere, 591
Tracy, Charles, 167, 169, 171-72, 174, 177, 185, 190, 192, 195-202
Tracy, Thomas, 617
Transcendentalists, New England, 422, 428, 609-10. *See also individuals by name*
Traveller, 96
Tremont House, 377, 474 n 2
Tremont Theater, 259, 425 n 1
Trentanove, Raimon, 259
Tripartite Agreement. *See* WA, paintings: *Belshazzar's Feast*
Triton (ship), 160, 199
Trollope, Frances (Milton), 67
Truman, John F., 150-51
Truman, Nathaniel, 150 n 4
Trumbull, John, 27, 30 nn 18, 21, 36, 58, 67, 103-31, 141 n 13, 142, 148, 156, 253 n 3, 284, 354
Trumbull, Sarah Hope (Harvey), 156
Tuckerman, Henry Theodore, 524, 607
Tudor, John Henry, 18, 31
Tudor, William, 57
Turin, 305
Turner, Joseph Mallord, 40, 74, 152, 165, 180, 182 n 2, 213, 245, 324, 351, 427, 583
Tuthill, George Leman, 64 (#24) n 2
Tyler, John, 470 n 10

United States Capitol: proposal for WA to paint for, 252-53, 253-54 n 3, 281-84, 284 nn 1, 3, 285-89, 291, 312, 329 (#196) n 1, 357, 382-85, 389, 394-98, 534
United States Democratic Review, 110, 117 n 4, 304 n 5, 525, 623

United States Military Academy, 569
Unwin, William, 452 n 1

Vanderhorst, Elias: 63-64 (#24) n 2, 114 n 7, 561-62, 578-79
Vanderhorst, Eliza Cooper, 36
Vanderhorst, Elizabeth, 579
Vanderhorst, Harriet Cooper, 37 n 3
Vanderhorst, John, 148
Vanderhorst, Mary Raven (Cooper), 579
Vanderlyn, John, 37 n 1, 38, 43, 96, 233, 288, 311, 320, 357, 380, 384 n 1, 398 n 6, 579; in Boston, 320; unrecovered letter from, 320; mentioned, 321 n 1
Vandermoere, John Josse, 40
Van der Werf, 591
Van Dyck, Anthony, 22, 120 n 6, 245 n 4, 253, 305, 332, 379-80, 450 n 3, 562, 583, 592
Vannucci, Pietro (Perugino), 271
Van Schaick, Myndert, 101, 579; wife of, 96, 579
Van Wart, Sarah Sanders (Irving), 174, 560
Vasari, Giorgio, 49, 603, 623
Vaughan, John, 91
Venice, 47
Venus Capitoline, 342 n 1
Venus dei Medici, 19, 47, 261, 342, 409-10, 590
Ver Bryck, Cornelius, 423
Vermont, University of, 543
Vernet, Claude Joseph, 40, 588
Veronese. *See* Cagliari, Paolo
Verplanck, Gulian Crommelin: in Paris with WA, 110, 579; association with New-York Historical Society, 143 n 2; regard for WA's paintings, 97 n 1, 142, 415 n 2; member of Committee on Public Buildings, 252-53, 290 n 1, 312 n 3, 367, 395-97, 630; tributes to WA, 218 n 4, 252; visit to WA, 380; WA's death reported to, 523; WA's regard for, 208, 217, 252, 505, 534, 605; mentioned, 269 n 1, 393, 548
Verplanck, Johnston, 155
Versailles, 46
Very, Jones, 428, 607
Vesuvius, 7, 47, 250 n 25, 614; WA's paintings of, 7, 21
Victory (ship), 95
Villiars, Sarah Sophia Fane, Lady Jersey, 212
Vinton, Alexander, 524
Virgil, 8, 21, 23, 34, 62 n 1, 578, 614, 629
Visger, Capt., 579
Visger, Harman, 64-65, 73 n 2, 75-76, 121, 171, 201 n 5, 579; family of, 171
Vitruvius, 111 n 2
Viturbo, 43, 463-64
Volozan, Denis, 98
Voltaire, François Marie Arouet de, 40, 110
Volterra, 271
Von Goethe, Ottilie, 560

Waccamaw, S.C., 14 n 2, 15, 36 n 1, 301, 441, 532
Wade, Josiah, 74, 509 (#345) n 2, 512; widow of, 489
Wade Hampton (ship), 11
Wagstaffe, Charles Edward, 460
Wainwright, Robert Dewar, 11 n 3, 264
Waites, Thomas, 411
Wales, 37, 604-05, 622
Walker, Frederick, 11 n 1
Walker, John, 59
Wall, Garret Dorset, 384 n 7
Waller, Edmund, 616
Wallis, Emilie, 53
Wallis, George Augustus, 41, 52-53, 77, 122, 266-67, 269, 580
Wallis, Trajan, 53, 266
Waln, Jacob S., 124, 149-51
Walpole, Horace, 22, 228, 612, 618
Walpole, N. H., 513 n 3
Walter, Arthur Maynard, 30 n 16, 31, 33 n 2, 629
Waltham, Mass., 428
Walthamstow, 171
Ward, Aaron, 285 n 3
Ward, James, 146, 190
Ward, Julia. *See* Howe, Julia (Ward)
Ward, Louisa, 429
Ward, Samuel, Jr., 428-29, 450 n 3
Ward, Samuel, Sr., 429, 450 n 3
Ward, Samuel Gray, 426, 433 (#270) n 1
Ward, Thomas W., 377 (#227) n 2
Ward, William, 146, 184
Ware, William, 59, 106-07, 114 n 7, 535, 576, 625-26
War of 1812, 60, 353, 545-46, 567, 629
Warren, A.W., 100 n 2, 204 n 1
Washington, George, 202, 290, 361-62, 550. *See also* WA, writings: juvenilia
Washington, D.C. *See* United States Capitol
Washington Monument Association, 146
Washington National Intelligencer, 524

Waterhouse, Andrew, 21
Waterhouse, Benjamin, 11, 11 n 3, 19, 21-22, 30 n 19, 580-81
Waterhouse, Hannah (Proud), 21
Waters, Clara Clement, 297 n 2
Waterston, Robert Cassie, 545, 581
Watertown, Mass., 532, 550
Webber, Anna Winslow (Green), 482
Webber, Samuel, 581
Webster, Daniel, 289, 410
Weeks, E., 240
Weir, Robert Walter, 105-06, 228, 398 n 6, 415 n 2, 524, 581
Welles, Benjamin, 18, 31, 31 n 1, 40, 51, 102, 111, 170 n 13, 189, 192, 524, 581; unrecovered letter to, 31 n 1
Welles, John, 55, 581
Welles, Samuel, 55
Wellesley, Arthur, first duke of Wellington, 188, 501
Wellington, Duke of, 188, 501
Wesselhoeft, Robert, 596-97
West, Benjamin, Jr., 188-89, 461
West, Benjamin, Sr.: WA on painting and character of, 26, 39, 90-91, 175, 202, 280, 284, 348; encouragement and praise of WA, 28, 31 n 1, 58, 62 n 1, 66, 161, 323; encouragement of other young artists, 28, 280-81, 364, 546, 567, 579, 581; gallery of, 26, 81, 177, 188-89, 532, 584; WA's poem on, 581; death, 174; WA's recollections of, 337-39, 543; drawings of, 485-86; and Chantrey, 147 n 8, 348; subjects also painted by WA, 42, 45, 66, 82 n 4, 90, 102, 116 n 2, 141 n 12, 175 n 3, 204 n 7, 350 n 2, 427, 485-86, 508 n 1; mentioned, 69, 77, 81, 120 n 7, 461. *See also* WA, portraits; *WA–Leslie correspondence, passim*
West Elizabeth (Shewell), 339
West, Maria, 281, 281 n 10
West, Raphael Lamar, 62 n 1, 188-89, 281 n 10
Westmacott, Richard, 270
Westminster Review, 617
Wheeler, John, 581
Whipple, Edwin Percy, 107
White, Edward Brickell, 257
White, Eliza (Allston), 468
White, John Blake: in London with WA, 27, 29-30 n 16, 36 n 1; and S.C. Academy of Arts, 258 n 6; as possible attorney for WA, 452; visit to WA, 468; unrecovered letter to, 356. *See also WA–Cogdell correspondence, passim*
White, Joseph, and wife, 371 n 11
White, Thomas Willis, 581
White, William, 460
White Mountains, 537
Whittier, John Greenleaf, 607
Wigfall, Eliza Moore (Flagg), 11, 224, 442 n 1
Wigfall, Harriett (Moore), 440 n 3, 458 n 4
Wigfall, Thomas, 442 n 1, 457
Wiggin, Benjamin, 63 (#23) n 4
Wigglesworth, Edward, 319
Wilde, Richard Henry, 49
Wilkes, John, 630
Wilkie, David, 137, 152, 172, 176, 180, 187, 202, 212, 390, 582
Willard, Joseph, 21-22
Willard, Mr., 265
Willard, Sidney, 30 n 16, 38, 524; and family, 524, 593
Willard Solomon, 342 n 1, 606
Willes, William, 126, 129, 159-60, 169, 172, 184, 189-90, 198, 203, 213, 215
Williams, Charles, 169, 184, 199, 234
Williams, David E., 311, 581
Williams, David H., 581
Willams, Edwin, 286
Williams, Mr., 375 n 1
Williams, Roger, 139
Williams, Samuel, 62, 63 n 7, 76 n 4, 91, 95, 120-21, 147 n 8, 169, 176, 184, 205, 231, 234. *See also* WA, portraits
Williams, Timothy, 102-03, 127, 170, 176, 238, 240
Willis, Nathaniel Parker, 265, 265 n 1
Wilson, John, 30 n 19, 338
Wilson, Major John, 255
Wilson, Richard, 213, 338, 390
Winckelman, Johann Joachim, 586
Windsor, 29 n 16, 63 n 2, 461
Winthrop, Francis Bayard, 114 n 7, 378 (#228) n 1, 507, 582
Winthrop, John, 143
Winthrop, Robert Charles, 337 n 11, 375 n 1
Winthrop, Thomas Lindall, and sons of, 375 n 1
Wise, Henry, 285 n 3
Woods, Daniel Bates, 582
Woods, Leonard, Jr., 447-48, 582, 626
Wordsworth, Dorothy (sister of William), 53, 123

Wordsworth, Dorothy (daughter of William), 123
Wordsworth, Mary (Hutchinson), 123, 126, 141, 166, 222, 368, 403, 582
Wordsworth, William: association with and esteem of WA, 126, 582; appreciation of WA paintings, 45-46, 94 n 3, 120 n 7, 141-42, 142 n 1, 509, 509 nn 1, 2, 512, 582-83; appreciation of WA's poetry, 127; association with Beaumont and Coleridge, 53, 97, 533, 582; writings of, 146, 157-58, 166, 167 n 3, 201 n 4; quoted by WA, 490, 518, 583; WA's esteem of, 123, 145-46, 512, 573, 578, 583; copy of *Monaldi* sent to, 467, 483, 583; on WA's death, 581-82; association with Richard Henry Dana, 166-67, 171, 376, 544, 594; mentioned, 566
Wordsworth, William (son of William), 123
Wright, Charles Cushing, 636
Wright, Silas, Jr., 384 n 7
Wright, Thomas, 512
Wyatt, James Richard, 259
Wyer, Edward, 32, 32 n 1
Wyndham, George O'Brien, Earl of Egremont, 119, 120 nn 6, 7, 129, 136, 152, 160, 212, 281, 353-54, 363, 405 n 2, 583, 592

Yale College, 208 nn 2, 5, 6, 549, 567-68, 582
York, Duke of, 212
Young, Edward, 24, 247, 593
Young, John, 66
Young Mary (Allston). *See* Alston, Mary (Allston) Young
Young, Martha (Allston), 13
Young, Thomas, 13, 14 n 1, 530

www.ingramcontent.com/pod-product-compliance
Lightning Source LLC
La Vergne TN
LVHW090755070826
844660LV00022B/998
* 9 7 8 0 8 1 3 1 5 5 4 5 6 *